# TECHNICAL PROGRAM PLANNING COMMITTEE

**JONATHAN S. EPSTEIN**
Idaho National Eng. Labs.
Idaho Falls, ID
*Chair TPPC*

**RANDOLPH W. LLOYD**
Idaho National Eng. Labs.
Idaho Falls, ID
*Vice-Chair TPPC*

**ELIZABETH A. FUCHS**
Sandia National Laboratories
Livermore, CA
*Chair, National Meetings*
*Council*

**ARUN SHUKLA**
University of Rhode Island
Kingston, RI
*Chair, Technical*
*Division Council*

**KRISTIN ZIMMERMAN**
General Motors R&D
Warren, MI
*Chair, Education*

**Y.J. CHAO**
University of South Carolina
Columbia, SC
*Chair, Research*

**HENRY R. BUSBY**
The Ohio State University
Columbus, OH
*Chair, Applications*

**GARY L. CLOUD**
Michigan State University
East Lansing, MI
*Intersociety Liaison*

**KENNETH A. GALIONE**
SEM, Inc.
Bethel, CT
*Managing Director*

**KRISTIN L. MacDONALD**
SEM, Inc.
Bethel, CT
*Assistant Managing Director*

**KATHERINE M. RAMSAY**
SEM, Inc.
Bethel, CT
*Conference Manager*

# EXECUTIVE BOARD

**MARK E. TUTTLE**
University of Washington
Seattle, WA
*President 1995-1996*

**KENNETH A. GALIONE**
SEM, Inc.
Bethel, CT
*Secretary 1995-1996*

**ARUN SHUKLA**
University of South Carolina
Kingston, RI
*Member 1994-1996*

**ELIZABETH A. FUCHS**
Sandia National Laboratories
Livermore, CA
*President-Elect 1995-1996*

**T. DIXON DUDDERAR**
AT&T Bell Laboratories
Murray Hill, NJ
*Past President 1994-1995*

**IGOR EMRI**
University of Ljubljana
Ljubljana, Slovenia
*Member 1995-1997*

**RAVINDER CHONA**
Texas A&M University
College Station, TX
*Vice President 1995-1996*

**GARY L. CLOUD**
Michigan State Univeristy
East Lansing, MI
*Past President 1993-1994*

**JOHN L. SULLIVAN**
Ford Motor Company
Dearborn, MI
*Member 1995-1997*

**ROBERT F. SULLIVAN**
IBM Corporation
San Jose, CA
*Treasurer 1995-1996*

**WALTER G. REUTER**
EG&G Idaho, Inc.
Idaho Falls, ID
*Member 1994-1996*

iii

**ABOUT SEM** - The Society for Experimental Mechanics, Inc. (formerly) the Society for Experimental Stress Analysis (SESA) was founded in 1943 as a non-profit scientific and educational organization. Its objective is to "further the knowledge of stress and strain analysis and related technologies."

The members of SEM encompass a unique network of leaders in experimental mechanics in the United States and abroad. They are active in academia, government and industrial research and development and include scientists, engineers, manufacturers, consultants, users and vendors of plant equipment, services and systems. SEM also maintains close contact with other professional groups throughout the world with cooperative meetings and joint membership options.

## PUBLICATION POLICY

For further information concerning publication policy, contact:

Society for Experimental Mechanics, Inc.
Publication Dept.
7 School Street
Bethel, CT 06801
203-790-6373
203-790-4472 FAX
E-mail: services@sem1.com

Society for Experimental Mechanics, Inc.
ISBN: 0-912053-50-X                    ISSN: 1046-672X

Printed in the United States of America, May 1996

ML

# *Abstract Proceedings of the*

# *1996 VIII International Congress*

# *on Experimental Mechanics and*

## Experimental/Numerical Mechanics in

## Electronic Packaging

**Cosponsored by:**

- Japan Society of Mechanical Engineers (JSME)
- Korean Society of Mechanical Engineers (KSME)
- British Society for Strain Measurement (BSSM)
- European Permanent Committee for Experimental Mechanics (EPCEM)
- Slovene Society for Experimental Mechanics
- International Measurement Confederation (IMEKO-TC 3 and TC 15)
- Italian Society for Stress Analysis (AIAS)
- Strain Society of South Africa
- VDI/VDE GESA
- American Society for Nondestructive Testing, Inc. (ASNT)
- Shock and Vibration Information Analysis Center (SAVIAC)
- International Society for Optical Engineering (SPIE)
- Experimental Mechanics Division of the Committee of Mechanics of the Polish Academy of Sciences

Society for Experimental Mechanics, Inc.
7 School Street
Bethel, Connecticut 06801 USA
(203) 790-6373; FAX (203) 790-4472
E-mail: sem@sem1.com
Home Page: http://www.sem.bethel.ct.us/

ISSN: 1046-672X

ISBN: 0-912053-50-X

## SECTION ONE

## Experimental/Numerical Mechanics
## in Electronic Packaging

**Page No.**

Sessions I through X ...................................................................... 1-88

## SECTION TWO

## VIII International Congress on Experimental Mechanics

Sessions 1 through 62 ................................................................... 1-518

# SECTION ONE

## EXPERIMENTAL/NUMERICAL MECHANICS IN ELECTRONIC PACKAGING

## TABLE OF CONTENTS

**Session I.    Material Characterization I**

Measurement of Interface Strength and Fracture Toughness of Plastic
IC Packages ..................................................................................................... 1
> A.Y. Kuo, Optimal Corporation (USA); T.R. Hsu, San Jose State University (USA);
> L.T. Nguyen and K.L. Chen, National Semiconductor Corporation (USA)

Creep Behavior of Solder Balls in a TBGA Module ....................................... 2
> T.M. Niu and W. Infantolino, IBM Corporation (USA)


**Session II.    Material Characterization II**

Mechanisms of Creep and Failure in Eutectic Solders ............................... 4
> J.W. Morris, Jr. and H.L. Reynolds, University of California, Berkeley (USA)

Measurement of Young's Modulus and Residual Stress in E-Beam Evaporated Aluminum and
Thermally Evaporated Chromium Films Using Blister Method ...................... 5
> H.J. Moon, Y.Y. Earmme, S.S. Park and Y.H. Cho, Korea Advanced Institute of
> Science and Technology (Korea)

Characterization of Silicon Nitride Thin Film by Interferometry and FEA ......... 7
> S.T. Park, M.S. Dadkhah and E. Motamedi, Rockwell Science Center (USA)

Fatigue Life Prediction of Leadless Solder Joints ...................................... 9
> Y.H. Pao, V. Reddy, E. Jih, J. Hu, R.K. McMillan and V. Jairazbhoy, Ford
> Motor Company (USA)

Analysis of Electromigration in Angled Metal Line .................................... 11
> K. Sasagawa, Y. Honma, M. Saka and H. Abé, Tohoku University (Japan)

In-situ Field Emission SEM Creep Testing of 63Sn/37Pb with Emphasis on Colony Boundary
Deformation .................................................................................................. 13
> S.A. Schroeder, W.L. Morris, M.R. Mitchell, Rockwell Science Center (USA);
> and A. Evans, University of California-Santa Barbara (USA)


**Session III.    Stress Analysis**

Effects of Residual Stress and Stress Relaxation on Joint Strength ........................ 15
> T.R. Guess and E.D. Reedy, Jr., Sandia National Laboratories (USA)

Numerical Analysis on Via-hole Filling Process in Multilayered LSI
Interconnection ......................................................................................... 17
      T. Kitamura, R. Ohtani, Y. Hisaki and Y. Umeno, Kyoto University (Japan)

Thermo-mechanical Reliability of a "Sandwich" Substrate with Integrated Passives ................ 19
      R.C. Dunne and S.K. Sitaraman, Georgia Institute ofTechnology (USA)

Estimation of Internal Stress of Epoxy Resin in Curing Process ............................................. 21
      K. Ikegami and T. Ono, Tokyo Institute of Technology (Japan)

Chip-capacitor Cracking Due to Printed Circuit Board Flexure ................................................. 23
      M.K. Chengalva and R.K. Agarwal, Delco Electronics Corporation (USA)


**Session IV.   Package Reliability I**

Improved Solder Joint Reliability by Cu-Alloy42 Composite Lead Frame ................................. 25
      T.G. Chung, H.H. Kim, S.H. Ahn and S.Y. Oh, Samsung Electronics Co. (Korea)

Design Optimization of Thin Plastic IC Packages for Improved Solder Joint Reliability ............. 27
      B. Han and D.V. Caletka, IBM Microelectronics Division (USA)

Improvement in Performance of IC Packages with Thermal Leads ........................................... 29
      P. Mithal, A.R. Syed and R.K. Agarwal, Delco Electronics Corporation (USA)


**Session V.   Package Reliability II**

Thermal Fatigue Reliability Enhancement of Plastic Ball Grid Array (PBGA) Packages ........... 31
      A.R. Syed, Delco Electronics Corporation (USA)

A Parametric Study on the Thermal Fatigue Reliability of Flip Chip Solder Joints
in Electronic Packaging .......................................................................................... 33
      J.Y. Kim and S.B. Lee, Korea Advanced Institute of Science and Technology (Korea)

Accelerated Life Test Development for Combined Stresses .................................................... 35
      K. Upadhyayula and A. Dasgupta, University of Maryland (USA)

Fatigue Life Analysis of Solder Ball Joint in Bare Chip Bonding ............................................. 37
      Y. Tsukada, S. Mizumoto, H. Nishimura, IBM Japan (Japan); M. Sakane
      and M. Ohnami, Ritsumeikan University (Japan)

High Cycle Fatigue Life Assessment of PCB Assembly Using Experimental Modal Analysis .... 39
      A. Kleyner and T. Torri, Delco Electronics Corporation (USA)


**Session VI.   Numerical Modeling Methodology**

How to Use Finite Element Analysis to Predict Solder Joint Fatigue Life ................................. 41
      R. Darveaux, Amkor Electronics (USA)

Thermal Analysis of an Underhood Mounted Power Control Module ............... 43
    R.K. Agarwal and K. Gschwend, Delco Electronics Corporation (USA)

Micro-macro-micro Modeling in Electronic Packaging ............................... 44
    S. Michaelides and S.K. Sitaraman, Georgia Institute of Technology (USA)

A Finite Element Analysis of Stresses Generated in Curing Epoxies ............ 46
    R.S. Chambers, D.B. Adolf, J.E. Martin, T.R. Guess, R.R. Lagasse
    and S.E. Gianoulakis, Sandia National Laboratories (USA)

## Session VII.   Experimental Testing Methodology I

Moiré Interferometry as Applied to Electronic Packaging Product Development ....... 48
    B. Han, Y. Guo and C.K. Lim, IBM Microelectronics Division (USA)

Investigation of Crack Tip Fields Near Copper-solder Interfaces ............... 49
    H. Krishnamoorthy and H.V. Tippur, Auburn University (USA)

Temperature Dependent Mapping and Modeling Verification of Thermomechanical
Deformation in Plastic Packaging Structures Using Moiré Interferometry ............. 51
    X. Dai, C. Kim, R. Willecke, University of Texas at Austin (USA); T.W. Poon,
    SEMATECH (USA); and P.S. Ho, University of Texas at Austin (USA)

Moiré Analysis and Modeling of Area Array Assemblies ........................ 53
    T.I. Ejim, AT&T Bell Laboratories (USA); and J.P. Clech, EPSI Inc. (USA)

Effect of Underfill Encapsulation on Solder Joint Reliability of Plastic Ball Grid Array
Package Assembly ............................................................. 55
    K. Verma, State University of New York at Binghamton (USA); B. Han, IBM
    Microelectronics Division (USA); M. Prakash, State University of New York at
    Binghamton (USA); and D. Caletka, IBM Microelectronics Division (USA)

## Session VIII.  Experimental Testing Methodology II

Thermal Strain Analysis in PBGA Solder Joints Using Hybrid Method ................ 57
    Y. Guo, Motorola (USA); and L. Li, IBM Microelectronics Division (USA)

Finite Element Model Validation Using Temperature Dependent Laser Moiré Interferometry .... 59
    A. Skipor, D. Ommen, D. Jeffery, J. Baird, Motorola (USA); X. Dai and P. Ho,
    The University of Texas at Austin (USA)

Three Dimensional Optical Interferometry/Finite Element Hybrid Analysis of a
PBGA Package ................................................................. 61
    Y.P. Wang, M. Prakash, State University of New York at Binhamton (USA); and
    Y. Guo, IBM Microelectronics Division (USA)

Thermo-mechanical Characterization of Electronic Packaging Materials Using Moiré
Interferometry ............................................................... 64
    E. Stout, N.R. Sottos, University of Illinois at Urbana-Champaign (USA);
    and A.F. Skipor, Motorola (USA)

## Session IX.   Experimental Testing Methodology III

Applied Laser Methods for Deformation Analysis of Electronic Package ................................... 66
    T. Kumazawa, M. Kitano, H. Miura and H. Doi, Hitachi, Ltd. (Japan)

Application of Speckle Pattern Interferometry to Electronic Packaging ........................ 68
    A. Villani, Digital Equipment Corporation (USA); and M. Prakash, State
    University of New York at Binghamton (USA)

Real-time Holographic Interferometry of Power Modules ........................................ 70
    M.S. Dadkhah and A.D.W. McKie, Rockwell Science Center (USA)

In-process Board Warpage Measurement in a Lab Scale Wave Soldering Oven ...................... 72
    M.R. Stiteler, SCRA (USA); I.C. Ume, Georgia Institute of Technology (USA);
    and T. Ejim, Lucent Technologies (USA)

## Session X.   Experimental Testing Methodology IV

On-line Automated Profilometry of Silicon Wafers ................................................... 74
    J.F. Cardenas-Garcia, S. Zheng, J. Hashemi, Texas Tech University (USA);
    and J. Kalejs, A-S-E Americas, Inc. (USA)

Holographic Diffraction Image Velocimetry for the Measurement of Three-dimensional Solid
Deformations ............................................................................................... 75
    J.S. Slepicka and S.S. Cha, University of Illinois at Chicago (USA)

Physics-of-failure Methodology for Thermal Cycling of Solder Joints ........................... 76
    T. Rothman, Intel Corporation (USA); A. Dasgupta and P.T. Tsai, University
    of Maryland (USA)

Measurement of Die Stresses in Chip on Board Packages Using Piezoresistive Sensors ......... 78
    S.T. Lin, R.J. Moral, J.C. Suhling, R.C. Jaeger and R.W. Johnson,
    Auburn University (USA)

## ADDENDUM
*(Papers listed in the Addendum are ones which were submitted after the printer's deadline.
Therefore, these papers could not be listed under the appropriate session titles.)*

Experimental Determination of the Shear Modulus of Compliant Adhesives Using Single
Lap-shear Tests *(Session I)* ................................................................................... 80
    L.L. Roy, D.B. Barker and S. Mallick, University of Maryland (USA)

Processing Mechanics in Microelectronic Devices *(Session IV)* ................................ 82
    J. Zhu, C. Ji and S. Liu, Wayne State University (USA)

Life Prediction Models in Electronic Packaging Using Finite Element Analyses and Design of
Experiments *(Session V)* ................................................................................... 84
    Sidharth and D.B. Barker, University of Maryland (USA)

CAD-Based Thermo-mechanical Analysis Tools for Electronic Packaging *(Session VI)*............ 86
    W.X. Zhou and R.E. Fulton, Georgia Institute of Technology (USA)

Finite Element Model Predictions and Measured Die Surface Stresses in
Delaminated IC Packages *(Session IV)*...................................................................................... 88
    J.N. Sweet, S.N. Burchett, D.W. Peterson and J.A. Emerson, Sandia National
    Laboratories (USA)

# Measurement of Interface Strength and Fracture Toughness of Plastic IC Packages

An-Yu Kuo, Optimal Corporation, San Jose, CA
T.R. Hsu, San Jose State University, San Jose CA
Luu T. Nguyen, K.L. Chen, National Semiconductor Corporation, Santa Clara, CA

As a result of large mismatches in coefficients of thermal expansion between dissimilar materials, delamination (cracking) has been observed frequently in plastic IC packages. In plastic IC packages, cracks usually occur at material interfaces of epoxy molding materials (EMC)/leadframe, EMC/die, die attach/die, and die attach/die attachment pad. Excessive materials delamination may lead to premature and unacceptable failures of the IC packages. Materials interface strength and fracture toughness are important material properties to evaluate plastic package cracking.

In this study, fracture toughness of EMC materials at different moisture and temperature conditions are measured in the laboratory. Future test plans have also been made to measure interface strength and toughness of EMC/leadframe and EMC/die interfaces. The 3-point bending fracture tests are selected for the EMC fracture toughness measurements. The test specimens are 101.6mm X 25.4mm X 6.4 mm in dimensions. Dimensions of the test specimens satisfy the plane strain requirement at the crack tip for the fracture toughness tests. A procedure were adopted to generate stable natural precracks emanating from a machined chevron notch in the fracture test specimens. The 3-point bending test specimens are subjected to the following 16 temperature/ moisture conditions (expressed in relative humidity) in an environmental chamber for up to 3 weeks until the specimens are saturated with moisture :

| 20 °C | 50 °C | 100 °C | 150 °C | 200 °C | 230 °C | 260 °C |
|-------|-------|--------|--------|--------|--------|--------|
| 40% | 40% | 40% | 40% | 40% | 40% | 40% |
| 60% | 60% | 60% | 60% | 60% | | |
| 80% | 80% | 80% | 80% | | | |

Four specimens are used for each of the above 16 test conditions to enhance statistical significance of the test results. After the preconditioning of the specimens, the pull/shear and fracture toughness tests are then conducted in a high temperature chamber attached to loading frame. Since each test is completed within one hour after retrieval of the specimens from the environmental chamber and the moisture loss of the specimens in the high temperature (dry) chamber during this period is calculated to be less than 1.8% of the total moisture content, the moisture loss to the dry test chamber environment is negligible. Four molding compound materials, B8, B17, B21, and B24, commonly used by National Semiconductor Corporation are chosen to mold the test specimens.

Preliminary test results indicate that fracture toughness of the EMCs will remain relatively constant when the temperatures are below the EMC materials' glass transition temperatures. When temperatures are higher than the glass transition temperatures, the EMC fracture toughness drops to substantially lower values. By comparing the fracture toughness results for different EMCs and test results by other researchers, it is discovered that there may exist a master curve for EMCs' fracture toughness if the fracture toughness data are plotted against a normalized temperature, $(T/T_g)$ where $T_g$ is the glass transition of the EMCs.

It is also seen that moisture causes a dramatic decrease in interface strengths but has little effects on EMC's fracture toughness. This can explain why many plastic IC packages had suffered from material interface delamination but not necessary popcorning failures after moisture intrusion. As mentioned above, moisture would reduce the material interface strengths and, thus, cause delamination under hygrothermal loading. However, the fracture toughness of the EMC material would not significantly degrade under moisture exposure. Therefore, the delamination sizes had to be large enough and the resulting hygrothermal stresses had to be high enough to make the stress intensity factor at the crack tip greater than the fracture toughness of the EMC materials.

1

# Creep Behavior of Solder Balls in a TBGA Module

Tyan-Min Niu, William Infantolino
IBM Corporation
1701 North Street, E22/2573
Endicott, NY 13760

In recent years, there has been a great increase in the use of surface mount chip carriers in electronic packaging. One general type of surface mount chip carrier is the ball grid array (BGA) module. This technology uses solder balls to form the connection between the module and circuit card. At the end of the module assembly process, the product must be tested and often goes through a burn-in process. Burn-in is an accelerated test conducted at elevated temperature for some period of time to eliminate early life failures from the product population.

This test requires that some type of probe array contact the solder balls to make electrical contact. These probes apply a continuous load to the solder balls for the duration of the test at an elevated temperature. Depending on the design, this probe may put a variety of normal and side loads on the solder ball which may result in a solder creep concern. Side loads can be particularly damaging because the force applied at the base of the ball results in a moment at the solder ball / module interface which can tend to roll the ball. The combination of force level, temperature and time determines the severity of the creep concern. The subject of this paper is the characterization of solder ball creep at elevated temperature for the tape BGA (TBGA) module.

Individual solder balls were tested using a unique general purpose micromechanical tester [1]. The tester is designed for the study of electronic packaging structures and their material behavior. It can apply a load to the test specimen along up to six degrees of freedom, i.e. three orthogonal translations and three rotations. The displacement resolution of each closed-loop stage is 0.1 micron in translation and 0.001° in rotation. The load cell also consists of six degrees of freedom of the force/moment sensors subjected to 18 N / 1.4 N-m of load capacity with 0.004 N / 1E-4 N-m of resolution. An easy-mouting, small environmental chamber is capable of surrounding the grips to control the testing ambient ranging from -130°C to 650°C. The tests are controlled by a PC using suitable data control and acquisition programs. A high-resolution microscopic RGB camera with a video monitor were provided for enhancing the specimen alignment with the fixture as well as video recording.

The setup of a single solder ball shear creep test is shown in Figure 1. The bottom surface of the TBGA sample was glued to the left side of the fixture. A micro-plow, made from stainless steel, was clamped at the right end in the fixture while the plow head at the left end was just allowed to kiss the side surface of the solder ball before reaching the test temperature, 140°C. The nominal diameter of each solder ball is 0.635 mm and the root/pad diameter is 0.41mm. The test load range was chosen to be from 15 g up to a high fraction of the ball shear strength which was determined from ball shear tests done with the same setup but a different control software. Other loading orientations of the ball creep test, such as normal (compression) and combined shear-normal directions, were also studied to simulate the ball creep during the burn-in process.

Figure 2 shows the evolution of the typical TBGA 10Sn-90Pb ball shear creep versus testing time under loading at the 140°C burn-in temperature. The tertiary creep behavior was found at shear loading higher than 60 g. The ball compressive creep behavior at 125°C can be found in Figure 3. These test results were used to determine the equivalent force limit at the base of the solder ball that did not cause excessive solder ball movement for the time and temperature of the burn-in cycle. These results, along with an evaluation of the force applied by a particular test probe, allows one to determine if excessive solder creep will be a problem with a given burn-in cycle. The user can develop their own solder ball movement criteria based on card level assembly and other concerns. For the particular socket evaluated in this study for TBGA, solder creep was not a concern for the typical burn-in cycle.

The study on the single solder ball structure using the micromechanical tester allows much better defined loading (direction and magnitude) than testing done on an array of solder joints from a conventional tester. It also can help assess product reliability. This is particularly true where grain size effect becomes important as in solder joints.

References:

[1] T.M. Niu, E.J. Burke, W. E. Black and J. R. Case, "6-Axis Submicron Fatigue Tester," EEP-Vol. 2, Proceedings of the Joint ASME/JSME Advances in Electronic Packaging, 1992, pp 937-945.

Figure 1. TBGA ball shear creep test setup

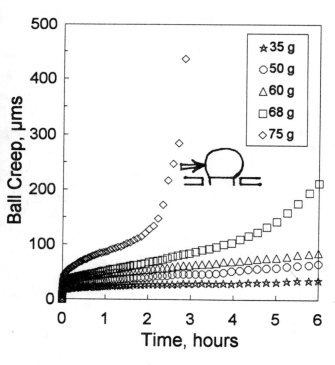

Figure 2. TBGA ball shear creep vs. time

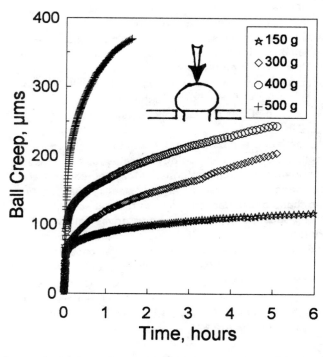

Figure 3. TBGA ball compressive creep vs. time

# Mechanisms of Creep and Failure in Eutectic Solders

J.W. Morris, Jr. and H. L. Reynolds
Department of Materials Science, University of California, Berkeley, and
Center for Advanced Materials, Lawrence Berkeley Laboratory
1 Cyclotron Road, MS 66-200, Berkeley, CA 94720

As the microelectronics industry has matured, quality and reliability have become almost as important as performance in defining advanced technology. The metallic conductors that connect the active elements of a microelectronic device are critical to its reliability. The small size and severe operating environment of these interconnects makes them liable to unusual metallurgical failure modes that must be understood and controlled to guarantee reliable performance. Because of their unique features, these failure modes are scientifically interesting as well as technologically important.

The most threatening cause of failure of solder interconnects in microelectronics is thermal fatigue. Its source is the thermal expansion mismatch between the devices joined by the solder, which causes cyclic strains as the local temperature fluctuates during service. The metallurgical problem is a challenging one since typical solders (particularly including eutectic Sn-Pb, the workhorse of the industry) are two-phase materials that have unstable, as-solidified microstructures, and are used at temperatures very near their melting points. The consequence is that failure occurs through creep fatigue in a microstructurally unstable material, a type of mechanical behavior that was virtually unresearched at the time this work began.

The dominant microstructural mechanism of failure in eutectic solders is a creep-driven catastrophe in which inhomogeneous plastic deformation creates concentrated shear bands within the material. Local recrystallization within these bands causes a microstructural softening that further concentrates the strain and drives failure. The inhomogeneity of the failure mechanism has the consequence that those who attempt to predict solder life in service must account for the changing pattern of plastic deformation and teh changing mechanical properties as the microstructure evolves. On the other hand, understanding the mechanism points the way toward metallurgical modifications to improve the reliability of solder joints.

Recent research has identified three metallurgical paths that can lead to dramatic improvements in the fatigue resistance of eutectic solders. (1) Alloy additions, such as In and Cd additions to eutectic Pb-Sn, could be used to break up the eutectic microstructure and improve fatigue properties. (2) Pro-eutectic or third-phase particles could be used to interrupt shear bands and improve fatigue resistance. (3) Rapid solidification can create a fine-grained, superplastic microstructure in eutectic solders, leading to dramatic improvements in fatigue life.

# Measurement of Young's Modulus and Residual Stress in E-Beam Evaporated Aluminum and Thermally Evaporated Chromium Films Using Blister Method

Ho J. Moon, Youn Y. Earmme, Sang S. Park and Young-H. Cho
Department of Mechanical Engineering
Korea Advanced Institute of Science and Technology
373-1 Kusung-dong Yusung-gu Taejon 305-701 Korea

Recent advances in manufacturing the micromachines, aided by semiconductor integrated circuit technology make possible the advent of the microelectromechanical systems (MEMS), which unifies the micromechanical component and its operation circuit. The MEMS technology is applied to the development of the microcomponents such as accelerometers, pressure sensors, microvalves and gyroscopes. In order to develop the MEMS component it is necessary to measure the material properties such as the Young's modulus, residual stress, etc., since it may be that the properties of the thin (and small) materials are different from those of the bulk material due to the effect of the grain size, dislocation density and structure of the thin film, etc., e.g., as in gold[1].

In this study, the $p^+$-silicon membrane is fabricated on silicon wafer using the process of the anisotropic silicon micromachining, and subsequently the aluminum or chromium thin film is deposited on the $p^+$-silicon membrane(Fig. 1). The size of the specimen is 2.82 mm x 2.82 mm and the thickness of the $p^+$-silicon, aluminum and chromium is 1μm, 0.5 μm and 0.2 μm respectively. The sequence of the manufacturing process is shown in Fig. 2.

The load-deflection (at center) relations in a blister test are obtained from the principle of the minimum potential energy for single layered membrane ($p^+$-silicon) and double layered membranes (Al/$p^+$ or Cr/$p^+$), respectively and they are slightly modified by comparison with the results of the finite element method. These relations contain the Young's modulus and residual stress of the $p^+$ layer or/and the Al (or Cr) layer. By measuring the deflection at center as a function of the load, the Young's modulus and residual stress of the $p^+$-silicon, aluminum and chromium respectively are obtained.; the Young's modulus and residual stress of the $p^+$-silicon membrane are deduced first from the single layer load-deflection (at center) curve(Fig. 3) obtained from the blister test, and subsequently the Young's modulus and residual stress of the aluminum or chromium thin film on the $p^+$-silicon membrane respectively are deduced from the double layer load-deflection(at center) curve(Fig. 4,5).

A blister test apparatus is composed of a holder of specimen, a cylinder, a pressure gauge and a microscope(Fig. 6). The deflection at center is measured using a constant focal length of the microscope.

The Young's modulus of 125.±15. GPa and tensile residual stress of 77.±5.0 MPa respectively are obtained for the $p^+$-silicon film, showing a good agreement with the values of [2]. The Young's modulus of 65.±7.8 GPa and compressive residual stress of 15.±1.0 MPa respectively are obtained for the electron-beam evaporated aluminum film. The Young's modulus is almost the same as that obtained from the tensile test for the bulk material[3] while the residual stress is slightly different from that from an X-ray diffraction test for thin film[4]. The Young's modulus of 310.±37. GPa and tensile residual stress of 55.±3.6 MPa respectively are obtained for the thermally evaporated chromium film. The measured Young's modulus of the chromium film is larger than that of the bulk material or sputtered film[5]. The residual stress of the chromium film shows the large difference from the value of Bromley et al.[6]. This large difference may be attributed to the different fabrication process.

Acknowledgement :

This study was supported by the Agency for Defense Development contract UD940065BDD and KOSEF contract 94-0200-02-02-3.

References :

[1] Nix, W. D., "Mechanical Properties of Thin Films," Metal. Trans., Vol. 20A, pp. 2217-2245, 1989.
[2] Lee, H. J., Han, C. H. and Kim, C. K., "Heavily boron-doped silicon membranes with enhanced mechanical properties for X-ray mask substrate," Appl. Phys. Lett., Vol. 65, pp. 1385-1387, 1994.
[3] Thornton, J. A. and Hoffman, D. W., "Stress-related effects in thin films," Thin Solid Films, Vol.17, pp.5-31, 1989.
[4] Korhonen, M. A. and Paszkiet, C. A., "X-ray determination of residual stresses in the aluminum films deposited on silicon substrate," Scripta Metallurgica, Vol. 23, pp. 1449-1454, 1989.
[5] Petersen, K. E. and Guarnieri, C. R., "Young's modulus measurements of thin films using micromechanics," J. Appl. Phys., Vol. 50, pp. 6761-6766, 1979.
[6] Bromley, E. I., Randall, J. N., Flanders, D. C. and Mountain, R. W., "A technique for the determination of stress in thin films," J. Vac. Sci. Tech. B, Vol. 1, pp 1364-1366, 1983.

Table 1. Young's modulus and residual stress measured from square membrane

| Material | E(GPa) | | $\sigma_r$(MPa) | | $\nu$ |
|---|---|---|---|---|---|
| | Measured | Reference | Measured | Reference | Assumed |
| $p^+$ | 125±15. | 130[2] | +77±5.0 | +93[2] | 0.28[2] |
| Al | 65±7.8 | 63[3] | -15±1.0 | -25±5[4] | 0.31[3] |
| Cr | 310±37. | 180[5] 280[5] | +55±3.6 | +140[6] | 0.30[6] |

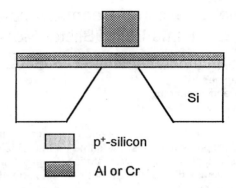

Fig. 1   Double layered square membrane.

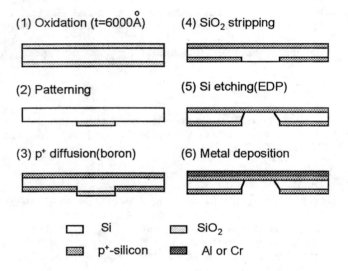

(1) Oxidation (t=6000Å)          (4) SiO₂ stripping

(2) Patterning                   (5) Si etching(EDP)

(3) p⁺ diffusion(boron)          (6) Metal deposition

☐ Si          ▦ SiO₂

▨ p⁺-silicon  ▨ Al or Cr

Fig. 2   Fabrication process for a square membrane.

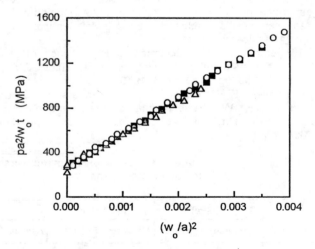

Fig. 3   Load-deflection (at center) curve for p⁺ membrane. (p, pressure, a, half width, $w_o$, deflection at center, t, thickness)

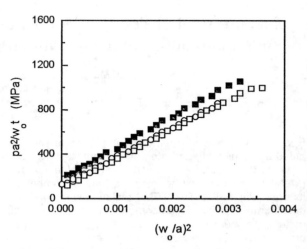

Fig. 4   Load-deflection (at center) curve for Al/p⁺ membrane. Here t is the thickness of the double layer.

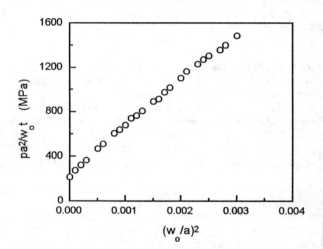

Fig. 5   Load-deflection (at center) curve for Cr/p⁺ membrane. Here t is the thickness of the double layer.

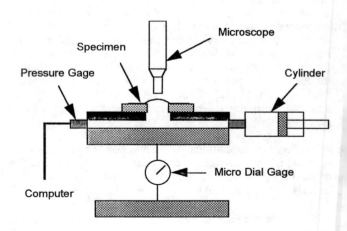

Fig. 6   A blister test apparatus.

# Characterization of Silicon Nitride Thin Film by Interferometry and FEA

Sangtae Park, Mahyar S. Dadkhah, and Ed Motamedi
Rockwell Science Center
1049 Camino Dos Rios
Thousand Oaks, CA 91360

## 1.0 Abstract

The majority of pressure sensors manufactured today are based on deformation of a micromachined membrane under applied pressure [1]. The membrane deformation can be measured directly by interferometry and the data can be used as a tool for pressure sensing. However, an accepted method of pressure sensing is where the membrane deformation is measured electrically by piezoelectric, piezoresistive, or electrostatic phenomena. In addition to the method being used, the performance level of the device is greatly affected by the mechanical properties of the membrane. Presently, silicon nitride is one of the best candidates for the thin film material used as membranes in silicon pressure sensors. In this paper, we will introduce a thin film characterization method that uses interferometry combined with finite element analysis (FEA) to model the diaphragm displacement. Displacements calculated in the FEA are used [2] for direct comparison with the experimental results from interferometry. From this hybrid analysis, we can deduce the correct mechanical properties for the silicon nitride thin film. Even though we are considering the silicon nitride thin film for this paper, the characterization method is applicable to any other thin film materials.

## 1.1 Design and Processing

A square shaped diaphragm 1 mm square and 0.2 μm thick was formed by silicon nitride thin film. It was fabricated on a silicon wafer through bulk micromachining using an anisotropic silicon etchant — tetramethyl ammonium hydroxide (TMAH) [3]. After comparing with other thin films in the semicondutor industry, silicon nitride was chosen for its high yield strength (14 GPa) and Young's modulus (385 GPa) which is suitable for the sensitivity requirement of this application. In addition to its excellent mechanical properties, silicon nitride has superior chemical properties; it is highly selective to silicon (~ $10^3$) in TMAH [4]. Currently, it is one of the best mask materials that can be used for most silicon etchants. The silicon nitride film used in our process was deposited by Low Pressure Chemical Vapor Deposition (LPCVD) at a low, slightly tensile stress level (~ 0.2 GPa) [5]. This helped in lengthening the lifetime of diaphragm during and after the fabrication process.

## 1.2 Interferometry Measurements

To characterize the diaphragm for pressure sensing, the chip was mounted on the front side of a quartz disk that was machined to have gas inlet directed into the diaphragm. The gas inlet consisted of 0.75 mm hole on the quartz disk with a tube attached on the backside of the disk. With nitrogen gas at known pressure applied to the diaphragm, the out-of-plane motion was detected by laser interferometry. The laser interferometry was based on a version of Twyman-Green interferometer [6], which is most widely used for measuring out-of-plane displacements. Since interferometry is highly sensitive, it is very important to minimize vibrations acting on the specimen and the optics. Thus the entire apparatus including the pressure loading frame was mounted on an optical table. A 50 mm diameter collimated laser beam was used for the interferometer. Using a beamsplitter, about 25% of the object beam that was reflected off a mirror and another 25% from the specimen were transmitted to the camera. When the two beams were adjusted to fall on top of each other, differences in the optical path length between the two beams due to the nonuniformity of the specimen translated into an array of light and dark fringe pattern. The fringe patterns were photographed with a 4" × 5" camera using a 50 mm diameter f/4 lens. The camera was located such that 1 mm of the specimen filled 30 mm on the film. An example of these fringe patterns is shown in Fig. 1. Each fringe represents a change in displacement of $\lambda/2$ where $\lambda$=0.632 μm is the wavelength of the laser.

## 1.3 Finite Element Analysis

Finite element analysis was used to model the diaphragm displacement. An elastic two-dimensional analysis was used with geometrical symmetry to simplify the problem to 1/2 of the specimen. The finite element solver ABAQUS with shell elements providing all six degrees of freedom was used to solve the problem. Since displacement is most accurately calculated in the finite element method, this was chosen for direct comparison with the experiment.

## 1.4 Results

The first part of the characterization was done using the laser interferometer to measure the out-of-plane motion of the diaphragm, which directly relates to the pressure applied on the diaphragm. The applied pressure was varied from 0 to $6.90 \times 10^4$ Pa (10 psi), and the maximum displacement detected by interferometry was about 20 μm. The plot of this result is shown in Fig. 2a. To find the linear regime of this device, another set of measurements was made. The diaphragm displaced linearly in the range of 0 to 6 μm, with the applied pressure varying from 0 to $1.38 \times 10^4$ Pa (2 psi). The plot of this result is shown in Fig. 2b. In this experiment, the resolution of this measurement technique was about $1.72 \times 10^3$ Pa (0.25 psi), and the observed dynamic range was about 40. We are working to combine the interferometry data and FEA simulation result to customize a characterization method for extracting mechanical properties of the membrane. These results will be presented.

### References:

[1]  Peterson, K., "Silicon as a mechanical material", *Proc. IEEE,* vol. 70, no. 5, pp 420-457, 1982.

[2]  Zienkiewicz, O.C., *The Finite Element Method,* McGraw-Hill, London; New York, 1977.

[3]  Tabata, O., Asahi, R., Funabashi, H., Shimaoka, K., Sugiyama S., "Anisotropic etching of silicon in TMAH solutions", *Sensors and Actuators A,* 34, pp 51-57, 1992.

[4]  Schnakenberg, U., Benecke, W., Lange, P., "TMAHW etchants for silicon micromachining", *Proc.* 1991 IEEE Workshop on Micro Electro Mechanical Systems, pp 815-818, 1991.

[5]  Sekimoto, M., Yoshihara, H., Ohkubo, T., "Silicon nitride single-layer x-ray mask", *J. Vac. Sci. Technol.,* 21(4), pp 1017-1021, 1982.

[6]  Hecht, E., Zajac, A., *Optics,* Addison-Wesley Publishing Company, pp 322-324, 1979.

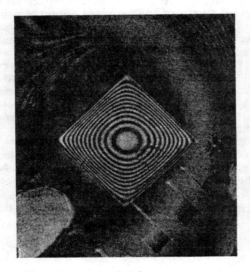
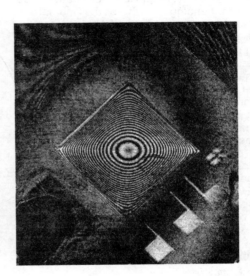

1 psi

2 psi

Fig. 1 Out of plane displacements of diaphragm

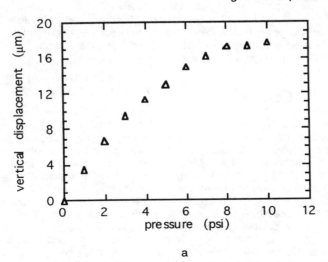
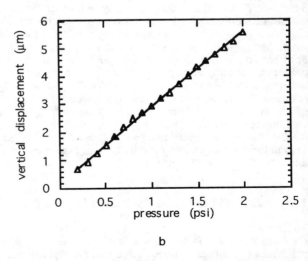

a

b

Fig. 2 a) Pressure Sensor Measurement showing non-linearity;

b) Pressure Sensor Measurement showing linearity

# Fatigue Life Prediction of Leadless Solder Joints

Y.-H. Pao, V. Reddy, E. Jih, J. Hu*, R. K. McMillan* and V. Jairazbhoy*
Research Laboratory
* Automotive Component Division
Ford Motor Company
Dearborn, Michigan 48121-2053

## ABSTRACT

One major reliability issue today's electronic packaging technology is facing is solder interconnect failure due to thermal fatigue [1-5]. In the present study, the thermal cyclic behavior of 62Sn-36Pb-2Ag leadless solder joints (1206 and 2512 LCRs) mounted on PCB test boards are subjected to one-hour temperature cycling between -40°C and 100°C with 5-minute ramp and 25-minute hold time. There are 10 LCRs on each test board with such an arrangement that the LCRs are placed in a 0°/90° manner to minimize the effect of joint orientation.

The time-dependent stress and strain in the solder joint during thermal cycling are predicted with the nonlinear finite element method for different solder stand-off thicknesses. The elastic properties of the board, LCR, copper pad, and solder are considered temperature dependent, and the inelastic behavior of solder is assumed to be governed by the steady state creep. The creep parameters of 62Sn-36Pb-2Ag were previously determined based on the stress relaxation data using an in-house developed bi-material beam specimen. The viscoplastic constitutive equation is implemented in a finite element program ABAQUS to model the test, and the results are used to evaluate the strain range and the effect of the design parameters, such as solder height, solder length, fillet shape, and inner end configuration. Figure 1 shows the stress/strain hysteresis response for three different solder stand-off thicknesses. With the modeling results correlations are established between the design parameters and the fatigue life.

The thermal fatigue results, combined with the FEA predictions, are also used to develop a life prediction model for crack initiation and propagation in the solder joint. It was found that the inner end configuration has a significant effect on the crack initiation life, which can be a major fraction of the total life of the joint (Figure 2). The crack propagation in the solder fillet is assessed with fracture mechanics and compared with that in the solder between LCR and the test board. The current test data are also compared with some existing data in the literature. The failed solder joints are also examined with scanning electron microscopy (SEM) and electron microprobe to identify the dominant failure mode(s) and associated failure mechanisms. More than one failure mode has been observed, and it is apparent that more than one life prediction models to account for cracking at different stages are needed to fully address the reliability of the solder joint. Nevertheless, the current life prediction model (for solder cracking only) not only is useful for designing reliable solder joints, but can be applied to optimize accelerated thermal cycling tests for the solder joint.

References:

[1] Y.-H. Pao, R. Govila, S. Badgley, and E. Jih, 1993, "An Experimental and Finite Element Study of Thermal Fatigue Fracture of PbSn Solder Joints," ASME Trans., J. of Electronic Packaging, Vol. 115, March, pp.1-8.
[2] R. Govila, E. Jih, Y.-H. Pao, C. Larner, and S. Dolot, 1994, "Thermal Fatigue Damage in Solder Joints of Leadless Chip Resistors," ASME Trans., J. of Electronic Packaging, Vol. 116, June, pp. 83-88.
[3] J. Hu, "An Empirical Crack Propagation Model and Its Applications to Solder Joint," Proc. of INTERpack '95, Advances in Electronic Packaging, Vol. 2, pp. 1001-1005.
[4] E. Jih and Y.-H. Pao, 1994, "Evaluation of Critical Design Parameters for Surface Mount Leadless Solder Joints Subjected to Thermal Cycling," ASME WAM, November 6-11, Chicago, IL, AMD-Vol. 187, Volume 2, pp. 213-227.
[5] Y.-H. Pao, E. Jih, and V. Reddy, 1995, "Thermal Reliability Prediction of Automotive Electronic Packaging," SAE International Congress and Exposition, February 27 - March 2, Detroit, MI. 950991.

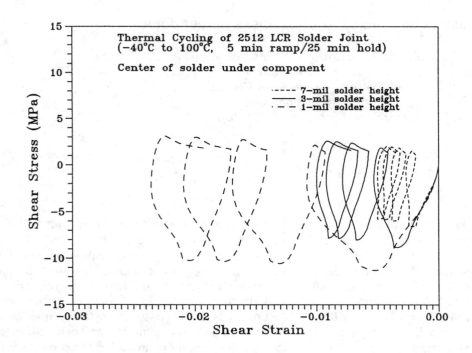

Figure 1: Shear stress/strain hysteresis loops of solder joints with different thicknesses subjected to thermal cycling between -40°C and 100°C for four cycles.

## Thermal Cycling of 2512 and 1206 LCRs

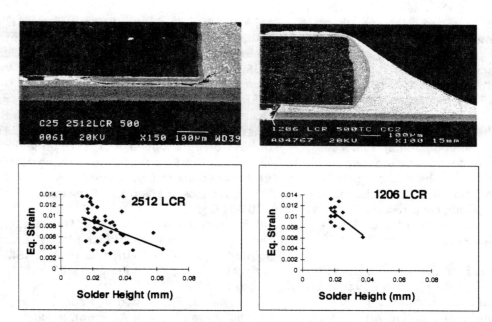

Figure 2: A comparison of 2512 and 1206 LCRs solder joints after 500 thermal cycles showing that a sharper inner end angle would result in an early initiation of crack.

# Analysis of Electromigration in Angled Metal Line

Kazuhiko Sasagawa, Yoshikazu Honma, Masumi Saka and Hiroyuki Abé
Department of Mechanical Engineering,
Tohoku University
Sendai 980-77, Japan

Scaling down of packaged silicon integrated circuits is remarkable. To try more scaling down, however, many problems have to be solved. For example on the metal line which is consisted of thin film, the higher current density due to scaling down causes electromigration which is a phenomenon that metallic atoms are transported by electron wind and that void, i.e. depletion of metallic atoms, and hillock, i.e. accumulation of atoms, are formed in the metal line. As the void is glowing, the macroscopic current density increases and then the excessive Joule heating leads to metal line failure. Electromigration phenomenon is closely related to current density distribution and temperature distribution. The failure mechanism is interesting.

In general there are many corners in metal line pattern. Therefore clarification of the distributions of current density and temperature near the corner is necessary from the viewpoint of the metal line reliability. These distributions near the corner of an angled metal line have been analyzed [1] in the connection with the singularities of the current density and the heat flux at the vertex of the inner corner.

Considering the results obtained from the analysis, the possibility of metal line failure near the corner due to electromigration is expected. However, the mechanism of electromigration failure in the angled metal line has not yet been clarified. Most of studies about electromigration have treated only straight strip shaped metal line, and there has not been a study of electromigration treating the metal line angled in one plane with corner.

In this study the metal lines angled with various angles are treated under subjecting to input current of various densities. The electromigration damage in the angled metal line is investigated by numerical simulation and experiment.

In the numerical simulation, Huntington-Grone's equation [2] which provides the flux of metallic atoms due to electromigration is utilized. It is assumed in the simulation model that the metal line consists of uniform collapsed hexagonal grains and the transportation of metallic atoms occurs only along the grain boundaries. Huntington-Grone's equation is written as [2]

$$J = \frac{ND}{kT} Z^* e\rho j \cos\varphi \qquad (1)$$

where $J$ is the atomic flux, $N$ the atomic density, $k$ Boltzmann's constant, $T$ the absolute temperature, $Z^*$ the effective valence, $e$ the electronic charge, $\rho$ the resistivity, $j$ the current density, $\varphi$ the angle between current flow and grain boundary, and $D$ is the diffusion coefficient which is given by

$$D = D_0 \exp\left(-\frac{Q}{kT}\right) \qquad (2)$$

where $D_0$ is a prefactor and $Q$ is the activation energy.

The metal line supposed in the simulation is shown in Fig. 1. Current density distribution and temperature distribution are analyzed by means of 2 dimensional finite element method, where the heat conduction from metal line to substrate is considered on the temperature analysis in the same way as Ref. [3]. The simulation is carried out for a certain time.

Figure 2 shows the void distributions near the corner, which were obtained from the simulation under the same density of input current (3.45 MA/cm$^2$). In this figure $\beta$ is the half of the angle of inner corner. The formation of void became noticeable with increasing in corner angle even if the input current density was the same. By calculating the void volume near the corner under the all conditions examined it was clarified that the void volume near the corner increases with increasing in the corner angle and/or the input current density.

In the experiment, on the other hand, acceleration tests of electromigration was carried out with high current density and high temperature which were the same conditions as the simulation. After the test the metal line was observed by scanning electron microscope with taking a picture as shown in Fig. 3, and void area was measured by means of image processing the SEM micrograph. The volume of void was inferred based on the measured void area. Consequently the experimental results on the void volume indicated the similar tendency to the simulation results.

The formation of the void near the corner as shown by the numerical simulation and experiment with the characteristic that the void volume increased with increasing in the corner angle and/or the input current density is the result expected from the analysis of the current density distribution and the temperature distribution near the corner [1].

Acknowledgments:

This work was partly supported by The Ministry of Education, Science, Sports and Culture under Grant-in-Aid for Encouragement of Young Scientists 07855013 and Grant-in-Aid for Developmental Scientific Research (B)(2) 05555028.

References:

[1] Sasagawa, K., Saka, M. and Abé, H., "Current Density and Temperature Distribution near the Corner of Angled Metal Line," Mech. Res. Commun., Vol. 22, No. 5, pp. 473-483, 1995.
[2] Huntington, H.B. and Grone, A.R., "Current-Induced Marker Motion in Gold Wires," J. Phys. Chem. Solids, Vol. 20, pp. 76-87, 1961.
[3] Kirchheim, R. and Kaeber, U., "Atomistic and Computer Modeling of Metallization Failure of Integrated Circuits by Electromigration," J. Appl. Phys., Vol. 70, pp. 172-181, 1991.

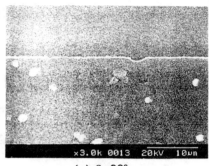

(a) $\beta$ =90°

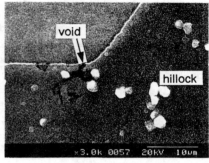

(b) $\beta$ =117°

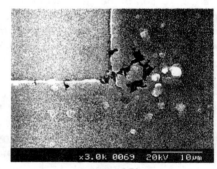

(c) $\beta$ =135°

Fig.3 SEM observation of the corner of angled metal line

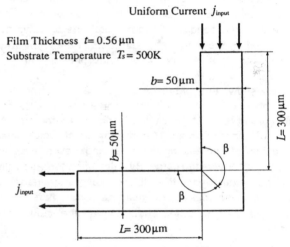

Uniform Current $j_{input}$

Film Thickness $t$= 0.56 μm
Substrate Temperature $T_s$ = 500K

$b$= 50 μm

$b$= 50 μm

$L$= 300 μm

$\beta$

$\beta$

$j_{input}$

$L$= 300 μm

Fig.1 Supposed metal line

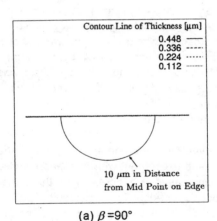

Contour Line of Thickness [μm]
0.448 ——
0.336 -----
0.224 ·····
0.112 ·······

10 μm in Distance
from Mid Point on Edge

(a) $\beta$ =90°

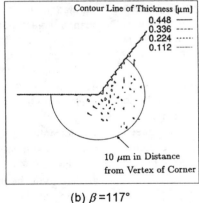

Contour Line of Thickness [μm]
0.448 ——
0.336 -----
0.224 ·····
0.112 ·······

10 μm in Distance
from Vertex of Corner

(b) $\beta$ =117°

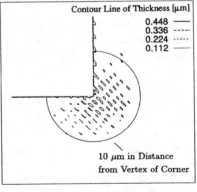

Contour Line of Thickness [μm]
0.448 ——
0.336 -----
0.224 ·····
0.112 ·······

10 μm in Distance
from Vertex of Corner

(c) $\beta$ =135°

Fig.2 Void distribution near the corner obtained by the simulation

# IN-SITU FIELD EMISSION SEM CREEP TESTING OF 63Sn/37Pb WITH EMPHASIS ON COLONY BOUNDARY DEFORMATION

S. A. Schroeder, W. L. Morris, and M. R. Mitchell
Rockwell Science Center
1049 Camino Dos Rios
Thousand Oaks, CA 91360

A. Evans
University of California
Santa Barbara, CA

Initial experiments on solder deformation in the *in-situ* mechanical test facility, built for a field emission SEM that was designed specifically to provide data suitable for mapping of 2-dimensional strain fields will be described. The facility capabilities will be detailed, the key performance specifications determining component selection identified, and the mapping options and the factors affecting accuracy and sensitivity discussed. The computer controlled loading fixture operates either in load or displacement control. Displacement vectors from which the strain field maps are extracted are obtained by a software controlled cross - correlation calculation using pairs of images digitized directly or digital images scanned from micrographs. The strain resolution achievable and information obtainable via 2-dimensional strain field mapping for these various applications will be discussed.

The Sn/Pb study is one of the mechanics of localized shear deformation. *In-situ* tensile, double lap-shear, and thin-walled torsional shear testing modes at room and elevated temperatures will be detailed. Deformation is observed to concentrate on colony boundaries, leading to eventual void and crack coalescence and linkage. Deformation along colony boundaries is not as prevalent under the near-shear conditions of the lap-shear and thin-walled torsional shear testing modes. Grain boundary cavitation has been previously invoked as one possible mechanism for tertiary creep. Further work by Dyson suggests cavitation accounts for differences observed in tertiary creep in tension and torsion. Additional evidence for cavity formation or microcracking along grain boundaries in the eutectic tin-lead system results from the surprisingly large observed anelastic (the time-dependent recoverable strain) effect.

Progressive colony boundary damage will be mapped by obtaining sequential 1024x1024 *in-situ* FE SEM images during loading. Subsequent image analysis through strain field mapping and animation will be used to highlight and quantify the relative deformation. High magnification image sequences are used to observe colony crack tip growth and coalescence mechanisms. Incorporated with calculations of the surrounding stress distribution, a representative, rate-dependent bridging law can be developed from creep induced crack propagation

## References:

[1] James, M. R., Morris, W. L., and Cox, B. N., "High Accuracy Automated Strain-Field Mapper," *Exp. Mech.*, Vol. 30, No. 1, pp. 60-67, 1990.

[2] Schroeder, S. A., and Mitchell, M. R., Eds., *Fatigue of Electronic Materials*, American Society for Testing and Materials, STP 1153, 1994.

Figure 1. Torsional test apparatus used for *in-situ* FESEM creep testing.

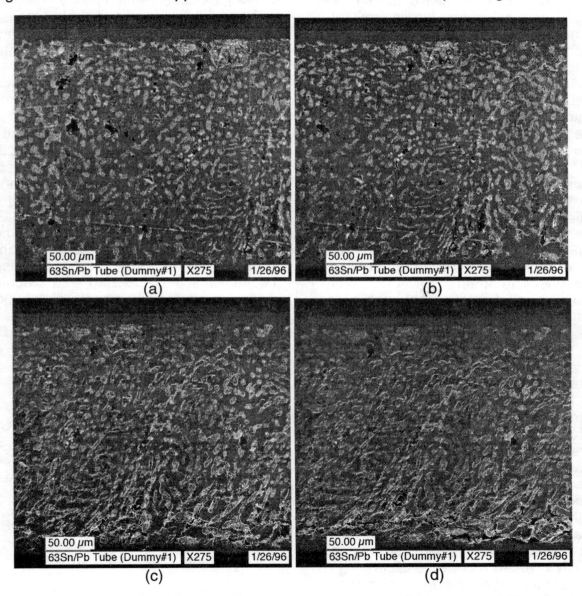

(a)

(b)

(c)

(d)

Figure 2. Secondary SEM image of tubular joint at 0, 4.5, 6.5, and 8.1 MPa shear stress.

# Effects Of Residual Stress And Stress Relaxation On Joint Strength

T. R. Guess and E. D. Reedy, Jr.
MS 0958   Box 5800
Sandia National Laboratories
Albuquerque, NM   87185, USA

A closely coupled experimental/analytical study investigates the utility of a proposed failure criterion, based upon a critical interface corner stress intensity factor, to accurately predict the strength of butt tensile joints. A schematic of the butt joint is shown in Fig. 1; it has two stainless steel rods bonded together with an epoxy adhesive. The proposed fracture criterion [1] suggests that the strength of an adhesively bonded butt tensile joint of one bond thickness can be estimated from strength data for a joint with a different bond thickness by the simple relation

$$s_{t2}^{ult} = s_{t1}^{ult} (h_1/h_2)^{1/3}$$

where $2h_i$ is bond thickness, $s_{ti}^{ult}$ is the nominal butt tensile strength, and subscript $i = 1, 2$ identifies the two joints with differing bond thickness. This relation applies to thin bonds when the adhesive's Poisson's ratio is between 0.3 and 0.4, the adherends are relatively stiff, and small scale yielding conditions hold at the interface corner. This failure analysis is based on the magnitude of the asymptotic stress state at the adhesive/metal interface corner. Fig. 2 shows that there is good agreement between theory and experiment for the case of butt joint specimens cured and tested at room temperature. The epoxy adhesive (Shell Epon 828 epoxy resin with Texaco T403 hardener in a 100/36 weight ratio) is cured at room temperature to minimize residual stress in the bond. Measured joint strength agrees with the predicted bond thickness dependence; joint strength increases by a factor of 2 as bond thickness is reduced from 2.0 to 0.25 mm.

Assuming linear elastic material behavior and residual stress levels that do not change with time, joint strength and the corresponding interface corner stress intensity factor are expected to reflect the effect of both applied load and residual stress. Detailed finite element calculations indicate that when a butt joint is cooled, a small yield zone develops at the interface corner [2]. For the adhesive properties and bond thicknesses used, the yield zone is embedded within the singular interface corner stress field and its length is much less than the bond thickness. In the tested butt joints, fracture always initiated near the interface corner [1, 3]. Accordingly, the stress state in the region of the interface corner is presumed to control the fracture process. In additional sets of butt joint experiments, mechanical stress was introduced by tension loading of specimens and residual stress by testing at temperatures well below the cure temperature. The expected decrease in joint strength with the addition of residual stress was not observed; see Fig. 3. This result calls into question the assumptions of elastic behavior and constant residual stress levels. To check the validity of these assumptions for Epon 828/T403 epoxy adhesive, mechanical properties tests were performed on bulk material to measure its response at various test temperatures. Data included compression modulus, compression yield strength and compression stress relaxation as a function of stress level, strain rate, and temperature and Mode I fracture toughness as a function of temperature. To illustrate material behavior, typical compression stress relaxation responses as a function of test temperatures are shown in Fig. 4 and selected bulk adhesive properties are listed in Table 1.

Considerable stress relaxation can occur in specimens loaded to apparent yield, regardless of the test temperature (see Fig. 4). Substantial stress relaxation occurs in the yielded adhesive at temperatures as low as -60°C. At this test temperature, the Epon 828/T403 epoxy (cured 18 hours at 35°C) is more than 100°C below its glass transition temperature, yet the stress decreases by 30% over a period of 30 minutes. This adhesive displays a highly nonlinear, stress level dependent, viscoelasticity at stress levels approaching the adhesive's apparent yield strength. The adhesive's yield strength displays a relatively large increase over the 20°C to -60°C temperature range (75%), while Young's modulus shows a much smaller increase (9%). There is a moderate increase in Mode I fracture toughness $K_{IC}$ with decreasing temperature. The critical energy release rate $G_{IC}$ is the only property that does not increase steadily with decreasing temperature.

Relaxation of residual stress in the region of the interface corner may explain the apparent insensitivity of the measured butt joint strength to residual stress generated by cooling. The test data indicates that the stresses in the interface corner yield zone, where fracture initiates, will relax if given sufficient time. Residual stress in the tested butt joints is present for hours or days prior to mechanical loading, providing ample time for substantial stress relaxation. Consequently, the interface corner stresses introduced by a subsequent mechanical loading are combined with residual stresses that are much less than those estimated by a linear analysis. Accordingly, the influence of residual stress on butt joint strength can be much less than would be predicted by a linear analysis.

Although this work is focused on butt joints, one might expect similar relaxation phenomena to occur whenever severe geometric and material discontinuities exist (e.g., encapsulated dies in the electronics industry).

**References:**
[1]. E. D. Reedy, Jr., and T. R. Guess, Intl. J. Solids Structures 30, pp 2929-2936, 1993.
[2]. E. D. Reedy, Jr., Intl. J. Solids Structures 30, pp 767-777, 1993.
[3]. E. D. Reedy, Jr. and T. R. Guess, J. Adhesion Sci, Technol, 9, pp 237-251, 1995.

**Acknowledgment:**
This work was performed at Sandia National Laboratories and supported by the U. S. Department of Energy under contract DE-AC04-94AL85000.

**Table 1**. Bulk adhesive properties of Epon 828/T403. Specimens cured at 35°C for 18 hours.

| Test Temperature °C | Young's Modulus (GPa) | Apparent Yield Strength (MPa) | $K_{IC}$ (MPa-m$^{1/2}$) | $G_{IC}$ (J/m$^2$) |
|---|---|---|---|---|
| 20 (RT) | 3.66 | 100 | 0.81 | 157 |
| -20 | 3.86 | 137 | 0.94 | 202 |
| -60 | 4.00 | 175 | 0.96 | 202 |

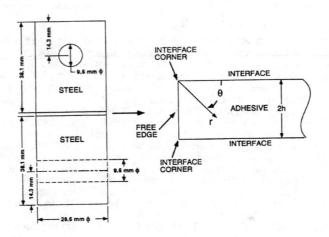

**Fig.1.** Schematic of cylindrical butt joint.

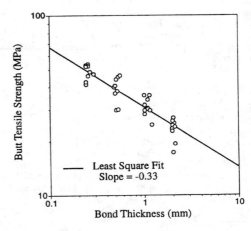

**Fig.2.** Log-log plot of measured butt tensile strength as a function of bond thickness for the condition of minimal residual stress.

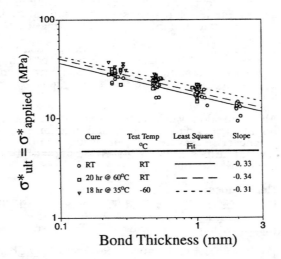

**Fig. 3.** Log-log plot of measured butt tensile strength as a function of bond thickness The characteristic failure stress includes the applied stress but not the residual stress.

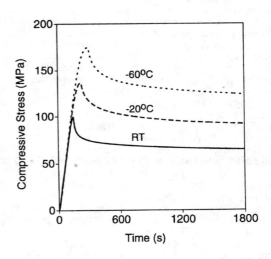

**Fig.4.** Stress relaxation data for an Epon 828/T403 epoxy adhesive cured 18 hours at 35°C and tested at 3 temperatures.

# Numerical Analysis on Via-hole Filling Process in Multilayered LSI Interconnection

Takayuki KITAMURA, Ryuich OHTANI, Yoshimasa HISAKI and Yoshitaka UMENO

Kyoto University
Department of Engineering Physics and Mechanics
Yoshidahonmachi Sakyoku Kyoto, Japan

As recent advances on LSI (large scale integrated circuit) technology requires further reduction of the circuit size, multilayered structure has been intensely investigated. To develop the method for making the interconnection between the layers is one of the key issues in the forming process of the sophisticated structure. Reflow, in which the via-hole is filled with the conductor metal by the surface diffusion at high temperature, is a promising method though the detail of the process has not been elucidated yet. In this study, the process is numerically simulated on the basis of differential equation of surface diffusion.

The motion of atoms due to the surface diffusion is governed by the

$$J_s = \left(\frac{D_s \delta_s}{\Omega k T}\right)\frac{\partial\left(\gamma_s \Omega \kappa\right)}{\partial s} \tag{1}$$

where $J_s$ is the number of atoms per unit time crossing a unit length on the surface, $D_s$ the surface diffusivity, $\delta_s$ the thickness of the diffusion layer, $k$ the Boltzmann constant, $\Omega$ the volume per atom, T the temperature, $\gamma_s$ the surface energy, $\kappa$ the curvature, and $s$ the arc length along the surface. $\kappa$ is given by the sum of principal curvatures. Then, taking into consideration the conservation of matter, the normal velocity of surface relative to neighbors, $v$, is given by

$$v = -\frac{D_s \delta_s \Omega \gamma_s}{kT}\left\{\frac{1}{r}\frac{\partial}{\partial s}\left(r\frac{\partial\kappa}{\partial s}\right)\right\} \tag{2}$$

in an axisymmetric problem. The equation can be normalized as

$$\bar{v} = \frac{1}{\bar{r}}\frac{\partial}{\partial\bar{s}}\left(\bar{r}\frac{\partial\bar{\kappa}}{\partial\bar{s}}\right) \tag{3}$$

using the following non-dimensional transformation.

$$\bar{v} = \frac{vkTr_o^3}{D_s\delta_s\Omega\gamma_s} \tag{4}$$

$$\bar{\kappa} = \kappa r_o \tag{5}$$

$$\bar{s} = \frac{s}{r_o} \tag{6}$$

$$\bar{r} = \frac{r}{r_o} \tag{7}$$

$$\bar{t} = t\frac{D_s\delta_s\Omega\gamma_s}{kTr_o^4} \tag{8}$$

The surface of the conductor metals deposited near a via-hole, which is a circular cylinder as shown in Fig.1, is discretized and the motion of the surface points is calculated under the reflow process solving the differential equation, Eq.(4), by a finite dellevence method. The simulation is conducted for various aspect ratio of cylinder, (depth)/(radius), and various initial thickness of metal on the side wall. It should be careful that the aspect ratio defined here is not the ratio of via-hole but that of the space surrounded by the conductor metal in the hole.

Figure 2 shows examples of the reflow process simulated. In Fig.2(a), the hole is perfectly filled with the conductor metal while a void is formed in the conductor during the process as shown in Fig.2 (b). The condition for the complete filling is examined by

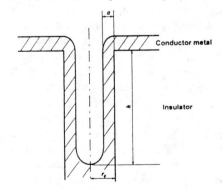

Fig.1 Configuration of via-hole and deposited metal on the cross section of LSI.

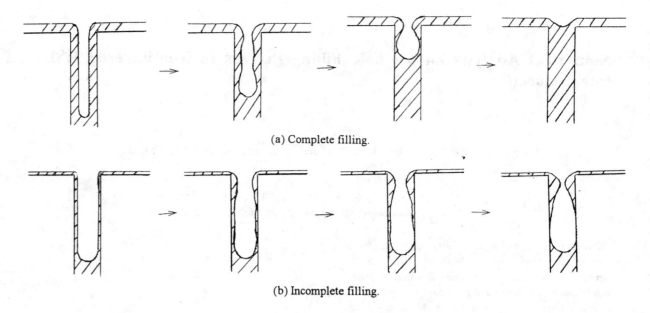

(a) Complete filling.

(b) Incomplete filling.

Fig.2 Via-hole filling process simulated.

the simulation and the result is summarized in Fig.3 The conditions for the perfect filling is strongly dependent on the initial thickness of metal as well as on the aspect ratio of via-hole. It should be noticed that the reflow process is independent of the material and the temperature except the time. In other words, the change in the shape of conductor go through the same process in the same initial thickness the aspect ratio because the surface diffusion is purely governed by the curvature of conductor as represented by Eq.(1).

Figure 4 shows the non-dimentional time for the complete filling. As the non-dimensional time can be converted into the real time by Eq.(8), the time scale is strongly dependent on the temperature and the conductor metal through the diffusion coefficient. For example, the process is shortened by the larger diffusion coefficient when the temperature is high or the conductor is made of metal with the lower melting temperature (e.g. aluminum). The scale shown on the right side in Fig.4 presents the real time in the case of copper at 1173K for a via-hole with the diameter of 1 micron. This implies that the reflow process is effective in the forming process of LSI conductor. Eq.(8) also points out that the time is dependent on the 4th power of hole size, $r_o$. The dependence implies that the reflow process is not effective to the filling of large hole. On the contrary, it becomes more and more useful for the small via-hole, which will be advantageous to the process in future development of LSI.

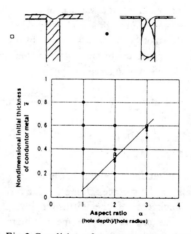

Fig.3 Conditions for the complete filling.

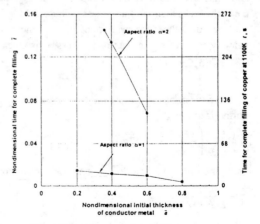

Fig.4 Time for complete filling.

18

# Thermo-Mechanical Reliability of a "Sandwich" Substrate with Integrated Passives

Rajiv C. Dunne
Graduate Research Assistant
and
Suresh K. Sitaraman
Assistant Professor
Computer-Aided Simulation of Packaging Reliability (CASPaR) Laboratory
The George Woodruff School of Mechanical Engineering
and
Packaging Research Center
Georgia Institute of Technology
Atlanta, GA 30332

Voice: 404-894-3405
FAX: 404-894-9342
e-mail: suresh.sitaraman@me.gatech.edu

## Introduction/Scope of Research

A key factor involved in the miniaturization of most electronic products today is the obstacle posed by passive components. The mission of the Packaging Research Center at Georgia Tech is to develop a substrate with integrated passives, which would serve as the building block for a low cost, high performance, ultrathin and lightweight electronic package. This "sandwich" structure (Figure 1), consisting of the capacitor, inductor, resistor and opto-electronic layers in addition to the power, signal and ground layers, aims to provide a 10x improvement in electronic product performance, while simultaneously reducing the cost and size by a similar factor. However, the thermo-mechanical reliability of this multi-layered structure is a major concern, due to the new geometries, materials and fabrication techniques involved. The coefficient of thermal expansion mismatch between the layers makes such a structure susceptible to severe and localized stresses in the narrow boundary regions of the interfaces.

In this research, a parametric study is performed to determine substrate warpage and the resulting stress-strain distribution for various layer thickness, under thermal loading representative of operation/fabrication conditions. Comparisons are made with an approximate thermo-elastic analytical formulation to calculate the interfacial peel and shear stresses, which are important failure indicators for delamination. A sensitivity analysis is also done to determine the effect of (i) temperature-dependent material properties and (ii) treating the dielectric and Copper layers as bilinear elastic-plastic materials. Based on these results, design guidelines are suggested for improved thermo-mechanical response of this " sandwich " substrate under the given thermal loading conditions.

## Research Methodology

A simplified 2D finite-element plane strain model of the "sandwich" structure is considered [1]. The order-of-magnitude difference between the devices involved in the substrate necessitates the classification into a global (the multi-layered substrate) and a local system (interconnect vias, metallization, capacitor arrays, etc.). The proposed substrate consists of a base layer of FR4 (fire-retardant epoxy-glass) laminate and seven dielectric layers (Polyimide or Benzo-cyclo-butene) interspersed with Copper metallizations, and a Copper termination layer on the top. As the first step, it is assumed that all the materials involved are free of flaws with perfect adhesion existing at the interfaces. This model does not include the intricate geometric details of the interconnect vias and the passive components.

A single-step static stress analysis using ABAQUS 5.4 has been done to determine the global stress-strain distributions with T = 150 °C (heating) and T = -65 °C (cooling). A parametric study is done to determine the substrate warpage and investigate the magnitude and location of the peak peel (normal) and shear stresses in the multi-layered structure, with respect to the thickness of the FR4 base layer and the dielectric layer's, as well as the dielectric layer materials (PI-2720 and Cyclotene 3022 ). The interfacial fracture toughness essentially depends on the relative magnitude of this normal versus shearing action arising due to the CTE mismatch between the layers, and it is important to understand this behavior to predict potential delamination sites. A sensitivity analysis is also performed with temperature-dependent material properties, and with the dielectric and Copper layers as bilinear elastic-plastic materials. Incorporation of temperature-dependent material properties suggests drastic variations in the magnitude/location's of the interfacial stresses [2], while the bilinear material behavior predicts localized yielding near the free edge.

For comparison purposes, an approximate thermo-elastic analytical calculation for this multi-layered substrate has also been done [3-7]. Finally, based on the observed stress-strain distribution and substrate warpage under the given loading conditions, design guidelines and improvements are presented to ensure the thermo-mechanical reliability of this new MCM substrate.

## References

[1] Dunne, R. C. and S. Sitaraman, " Thermo-Mechanical Modeling of a Novel MCM-DL Technology ," Proceedings of the 46th Electronic Components and Technology Conference, Orlando, Florida, 1996.

[2] Hsu, T-R, " On Non-Linear Thermo-Mechanical Analysis of IC Packages ," ASME Advances in Electronic Packaging, pp. 325-336, 1992.

[3] Suhir, E., "Interfacial stresses in bimetal thermostats," *ASME Journal of Applied Mechanics*, Vol. 56, pp. 595-600.

[4] Suhir, E., " An Approximate Analysis of Stresses in Multilayered Elastic Thin Films ", ASME Journal of Applied Mechanics, 1987.

[5] Yin, W.-L., "Interfacial thermal stresses in Layered Structures: The Stepped Edge Problem," *ASME Journal of Electronic Packaging*, Vol. 117, pp. 153-158, 1995.

[6] Mirman, B. and I. Mirman, "Thermal Stresses in Axisymmetric Bimaterial Assemblies: Microelectronic applications," *ASME Advances in Electronic Packaging*, pp. 425-435,1992.

[7] Eischen, J. W. and S. W. Reagan, "Elastic-Plastic Analysis of Bimaterial Beams with Strain Hardening-Multiple Yield Sites," *ASME Advances in Electronic Packaging*, pp. 17-23,1993.

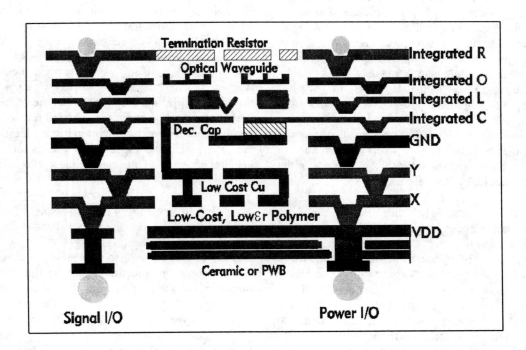

Figure 1. Schematic of the " Sandwich " substrate with Integrated passives

# Estimation of Internal Stress of Epoxy Resin in Curing Process

Kozo IKEGAMI and Tatsuhiro ONO
Tokyo Institute of Technology
Precision and Intelligence Laboratory
Nagatsuta, Midoriku, Yokohama 226, Japan

## INTRODUCTION

Epoxy resin is widely used in plastic packaging as well as in structural application. Internal stress in curing process of the resin influences on the structural function of the resin. Estimation of the internal stress is important for the structural application. There are few papers which treated internal stress of resin considering phase transition [1] [2] [3].

In this paper, the internal stresses of epoxy resin in hardening process and cooling process are analyzed by using viscoelastic models. The models are formulated on the basis of experimental results of the changes in the elastic modulus and the volume in hardening process and cooling process. The internal stress is calculated by using the finite element method. The distribution of the internal stress is examined.

## INTERNAL STRESS IN HARDENING PROCESS

The elastic modulus of the resin in hardening process is measured by the torsional vibration method. The change of the shear modulus in the hardening process is shown in Fig. 1. The temperature history is also illustrated in the figure. With increasing the temperature to cure, the modulus decreases. But, falling temperature after curing, the modulus increases gradually. The volume metric change of the resin is measured by the dilatometer. Figure 2 shows the volumetric change. The resin shrinks in curing process as well as cooling process. This shrinkage is originated by chemical reaction and thermal deformation in curing and cooling processes.

The constitutive reactions of the resin in hardening process is

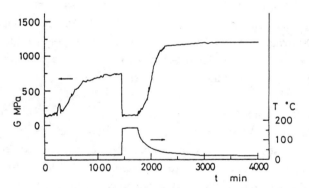

Fig. 1 Shear modulus in hardening process

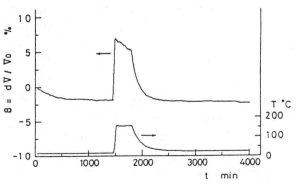

Fig. 2 Shrinkage ratio in hardening process

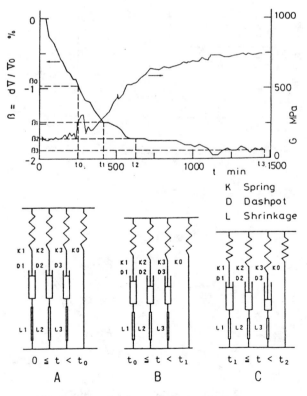

Fig. 3 Viscoelastic model in hardening process

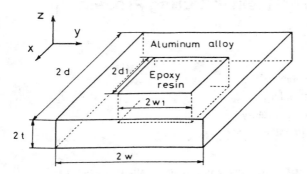

Fig. 4  Specimen for internal stress

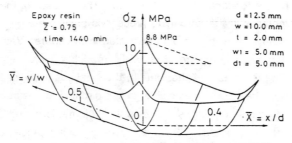

Fig. 5  Internal stress in hardening process

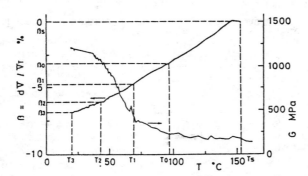

Fig. 6  Shear modulus and shrinkage ratio in cooling process

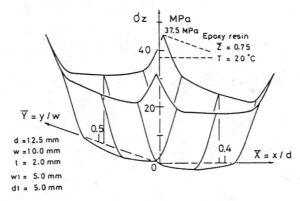

Fig. 7  Internal stress in cooling process

formulated by using viscelastic model with dashpots and springs. The models are given in Fig. 3 with the figure illustrating the change of the material properties. The different models are used for the different time periods divided by three different time intervals.

The resin model for calculating the internal stress is shown in Fig. 4. The model is a resin block which is contained in a molding cavity. The internal stress of the model in hardening process is calculated by the finite element method. The calculated result is shown in Fig. 5. The stress concentrates at the edge of the block.

## INTERNAL STRESS IN COOLING PROCESS

The shear modulus and shrinkage ratio of the resin in cooling process are measured by using plate specimens. Figure 6 is the shear elastic modulus and shrinkage ratio of the resin by the experiments. The shear modulus increases gradually in the initial stage. Then the value increases rapidly and approaches to a certain value. The shrinkage ratio decreases gradually with falling temperature.

The mechanical behavior is formulated by the viscoelastic model shown in Fig. 3. The material constants of the model is assumed to have temperature dependency. The calculated distribution of the internal stress in cooling process is shown in Fig. 7. The resin is heated to 150Åé from 20Åé and held for 300 minutes to cure, and then cooled to room temperature. Comparing Fig. 5 with Fig. 7, the internal stress in cooling process is larger than the internal stress in hardening process.

## CONCLUSIONS

The internal stress in hardening process and cooling process was analyzed by viscoelastic models. The models were formulated on the basis of experimental results on the material constants and shrinkage ratios during hardening process and cooling process. The finite element method was applied to estimate the internal stress. It is found that the internal stress in cooling process is dominant component in the internal stress of the resin.

## REFERENCES

[1] Miyano, Y. et al, J. Japan Society of Mechanical Engineers, Ser. A, Vol. 46, 1980, pp. 779-789

[2] Amijima, T. et al, J. Adhesion Soc. Japan, Vol. 21, 1985, pp. 319-328

[3] Nakamura, A. et al, J. Japan Society of Mechanical Engineers, Ser. A, Vol. 86, 1987, pp. 114-120

# Chip-Capacitor Cracking due to Printed Circuit Board Flexure

Mahesh K. Chengalva and Rakesh K. Agarwal

Delco Electronics Corporation
Subsidiary of Hughes Electronics Corporation
M/S CT-30-B, Corporate Technology Center
Kokomo, Indiana 46904, USA

## ABSTRACT

The capability of chip capacitors to withstand circuit board flexure is studied. Mechanical strain on a circuit board is employed as an indicator of chip capacitor strain capability. Three-point bend tests are conducted to determine strain capability of the chip capacitors. Strains encountered during manufacturing are obtained from loads during an in-circuit electrical test. Experiments are conducted using strain gauges. Finite Element analysis (FEA) is used to obtain the strain field caused by circuit board deformation. Good correlation is obtained between FEA results and those obtained from experiments. Regions of the circuit board showing large deformation for chip-capacitors are identified. The results aid in the proactive debugging of in-circuit test fixtures and in developing acceptable limits for circuit board flexure.

## INTRODUCTION

Chip capacitors are ceramic parts with intermediate layers of conductor metal. Excessive circuit board flexure can cause cracking of chip capacitors and may also result in damage to solder joints. Cracks in chip capacitors may not be visible to even detailed visual inspection, and the capacitor may still be electrically functional. Failure during usage is a possibility.

Mechanical loads on a component mounted on a circuit board are largely determined by local strains on the circuit board. Leaded components have lead compliance to absorb strains on the component body due to circuit board flexure. However, chip capacitors are leadless and strains on them are closely related to circuit board strains. In order to obtain the loading intensity on chip capacitors in the present study, strain gauges have been mounted on the circuit board.

In an in-circuit test (Figure 1), a circuit board assembly is probed with spring loaded nails from the bottom side and supported with push-downs on the top side. Several hundred nails may be required for a complete electrical test. The number of push-downs is usually much smaller. In the present study, the ratio of push-downs to nails is about 1:7. Each nail exerts a maximum force of approximately 0.4 kg. The circuit board bends due to mismatch in the positions of nails and push-downs resulting in a complex strain field. Uneven wear of push-downs further complicates issues in high volume production. Regions of excessive strains may result in cracked chip capacitors. These capacitors escape the in-circuit test and other inspection because of marginal degradation of electrical parameters and cracks that are invisible to the naked eye.

## FINITE ELEMENT ANALYSIS

A linear elastic Finite Element analysis has been carried out using ABAQUS. The circuit board is modeled using approximately 15,000 3-D solid elements. Components on the circuit board have been neglected to reduce the complexity of the model. This assumption yields an upper-bound on strains because components tend to increase the effective stiffness of the board.

The location of nails and push-downs were obtained from the CAD database of the in-circuit tester design in an IGES format and imported into the analysis pre-processor, PATRAN. A mesh was created that ensured a node at each nail and push-down with location error of less than 0.5 mm.

The load case corresponding to a 1.25 mm wear-out on six push-down pins located along an edge of the circuit board is analyzed. This simulates the observed wear on the in-circuit tester.

## EXPERIMENTAL PROCEDURE

Strain gauges were installed near chip capacitors on circuit boards. A total of ten strain gauges were placed on the circuit boards in locations determined as high strain regions by FEA simulations. The number of gauges was constrained because of limited available space in a maze of push-downs, dead-stops and nails through which strain gauge wiring had to be routed to strain amplification and recording apparatus.

Strains measured by these strain gauges were recorded as a function of time during the loading process. Typical loading times were of the order of a few seconds. The transient strain readings are more useful than the 'before and after' measurements because of the dynamic nature of loads during an in-circuit test. It was observed that in certain strain gauges, maximum strains were recorded at an intermediate point instead of at the end of the loading process.

The loading-unloading sequence was repeated thrice. Repeat measurements indicate that differences due to handling prior to loading into the tester cause insignificant changes in the strain readings.

## RESULTS

Finite Element analysis predicted regions of high strain in certain locations on the circuit board, which is consistent with the locations of damaged chip capacitors obtained from experimental investigation. A maximum allowable strain value of 1200 microstrain (or 0.12 % strain) is obtained from experimentation on 0805 chip capacitors.

## CONCLUSIONS

The present study shows that Finite Element analysis in conjunction with experimentation can be employed effectively in the error proofing of in-circuit test fixture design. Locations of push-downs, probes and positive stops can be optimized to ensure minimum flexure of the circuit board, so that strain on chip capacitors does not exceed the critical value.

The purpose of experimentation with strain gauges in this study was not to duplicate the FEA simulation but to enhance it. Strain gauge analysis yields accurate values of strain in a few select locations on the board. FEA, on the other hand, yields approximate strain levels throughout the board. Taken together, the results give a much better understanding of circuit board flexure.

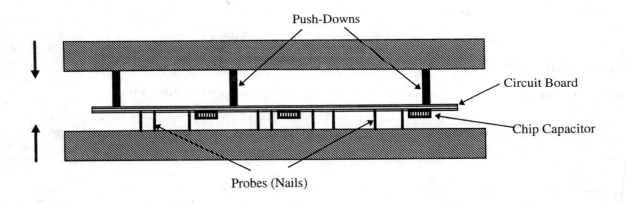

Figure 1.    Schematic of the In-circuit Test Setup.

# Improved Solder Joint Reliability by Cu-Alloy42 Composite Lead Frame

Tae Gyeong Chung, Hyeong Ho Kim, Seung Ho Ahn, Se Yong Oh
Package Development Dept., Semiconductor Business, Samsung Electronics Co.,
San #24, Nongseo-Ri, Kiheung-Eup, Youngin, 449-900, Korea

As the improvement of the integral circuit technology has resulted in the development of electronic packaging technology, the trend of electronic package becomes thinner and denser. At this time, the thin small outline package(TSOP) of 1.0mm thick becomes popular with the small outline package(SOP) of the thickness of 2.7mm. In 1996, 4-Mbit and 16-Mbit DRAMs are dominated for the memory device market. Also, 64-Mbit and 256-Mbit DRAMs are expected to be main memory device within two to four years[1]. As a memory density of integrated circuits increases, the actual chip size of memory devices also increases. For instance, the ratio of the chip-to-package for the first generation of 16-Mbit DRAM was around 70%, but for the same generation of 64-Mbit DRAM was about 80%. Once increasing the chip-to-package ratio, many problems should be solved to get high yield. Those are related to the electronic package reliability issues, such as popcorn cracking and solder joint applications. To jump over the reliability problems, the correct selection of the lead frame is a number one priority. It is well known that copper-alloy lead frame has better solder joint reliability characteristics than alloy-42 lead frame (58% Fe-42%Ni) does. In package reliability issues, however, alloy-42 lead frame is superior to copper-alloy lead frame[2]. In this work, we have been investigated on the package reliability and solder joint reliability for alloy-42 lead frame and composite lead frame. Finite element analysis was used to conduct the experimental results. 28-leaded TSOP(II) type packages, 400 mil package size, with alloy-42 and composite lead frames were used to check the package reliability and solder joint reliability's characteristics.

The composite lead frame shown in Figure 1 has a sandwich structure of alloy-42/copper/alloy-42. The total thickness is 150 $\mu$m for the composite lead frame used in these experiments. However, the thickness of top and bottom alloy-42 layers were fixed after the optimum thickness of that was decided from the finite element analysis. Total 18 numbers of TSOPs were mounted onto both sides of printed circuit board made of FR-4 epoxy resin that etched copper conductors and lead patterns with solder pads. As shown in Figure 2, the memory module used in these experiments consists of 1M x 144 organization with 16-Mbit DRAM packages. The thermal cycling test was carried out to evaluate solder joint reliability from 0 ℃ to 125 ℃. One cycle time was applied for 30 minutes. An optical

microscopy and visual inspections were performed to detect the drawbacks of the package as well as the solder joints. For detail inspections, cross-sectioned of the specimens were observed using the secondary and the backscattered electron microscopy.

The thickness of top and bottom alloy-42 layers in composite lead frame was selected to minimize the stress distribution from the finite element simulation. Figure 3 shows the variations of the Von Mises stress values at the die paddle edge of the TSOP package with respect to the clad thickness. In general, it is known that the stress value at die paddle edge is higher than any other part of packages. This phenomenon is shown at Figure 3. Also, the alloy-42 lead frame causes lower stress, 2.60 kgf/mm$^2$, than the composite lead frame, 3.62 kgf/mm$^2$, or the copper lead frame, 6.45 kgf/mm$^2$ because of the coefficient of thermal expansion(CTE) match between Si chip and alloy-42 lead frame. In the composite lead frame, 30$\mu$m thickness of top and bottom alloy-42 material was revealed the minimum stress value with respect to the different its thicknesses. Therefore, the composite lead frames which have the sandwich structure of alloy-42(30$\mu$m)/copper(90$\mu$m)/alloy-42(30$\mu$m) were used to the assembly of the 28-leaded TSOP packages.

Preconditioning test has been performed to evaluate the package crack for 28-leaded TSOP(II) package with alloy-42 and composite lead frame. It is well known that package cracking occurred when a package with absorbed moisture is exposed to a high temperature, generally maximum temperature of 240 ℃, during the reflow soldering. In addition to the absorbed moisture, there are other factors to affect the package cracking, such as reflow temperature, lead frame design, epoxy molding compound and adhesive materials. The popcorn package cracking was not observed, but the partial delamination between the die paddle and epoxy molding compound, after the preconditioning test.

Table 1 represents the effects of lead frame on the solder joint fatigue life as function of the number of temperature cycling. To investigate the crack propagation of the solder joints, the test samples were regularly checked. The solder joint crack of TSOP with alloy-42 lead frame initiated about 200~300 temperature cycles and propagated about 400~500 temperature cycles. On the contrary, 800 temperature cycles were required to initiate the crack when the composite lead frame was used. This enhancement of the solder joint reliability for using the composite lead frame resulted from that CTE of plastic package is close to that of printed circuit board. Viswanadham et al.[2] predicted that the thermal cycle was improved with the use of copper lead frame instead of alloy-42 lead frame, about 53%. From this, we can suppose the global CTE of TSOP for composite lead frame is higher than that for alloy-42 lead frame, and lower than that for copper lead frame. It is considered, therefore, the use of composite lead frame is superior to the use of alloy-42 lead frame for the solder joint reliability, and this trend is corresponding to our simulation results.

Reference

[1] Electronic News, December 6, 1995
[2] P. Viswanadham, M.Stennett, A.Emerick and R.Huggett, Advances in Electronics Packaging, Vol.12, 1993, pp1127-1132

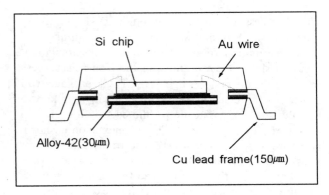

Figure 1    Cross-sectional view of TSOP with composite lead frame.

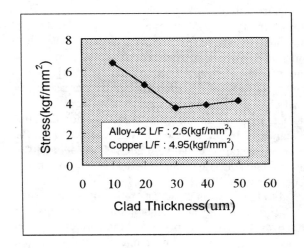

Figure 3. Von-Mises stress represented as a function of clad thickness at the edge of die paddle.

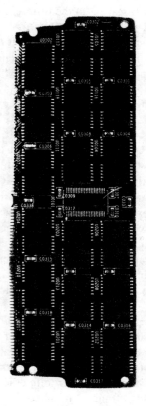

Figure 2    Memory module surface-mounted onto the printed circuit board.

Table 1  Comparison of solder joint crack  in TSOPs with composite and alloy-42 lead frame.

| T/C  L/F | 150 | 200 | 400 | 800 | 1000 |
|---|---|---|---|---|---|
| Alloy-42 | × | △ | ○ | ○ | ○ |
| Composite | × | × | × | △ | △ |

×  :  No Crack

△  :  Crack Initiation

○  :  Crack Initiation and Propagation

# Design Optimization of Thin Plastic IC Packages for Improved Solder Joint Reliability

B. Han and D.V. Caletka
IBM Microelectronics
MS E22, Bldg. 257/3A
1701 North St.
Endicott, NY 13760
Tel: 607-757-1077
E-mail: bhan@vnet.ibm.com

Coefficient of thermal expansion (CTE) mismatch between thin plastic IC packages and printed circuit boards (PCB) is a major cause of solder joint failure when the surface mounted packages are subjected to a cyclic thermomechanical load. This failure mechanism is highly pronounced with the family of packages known as TSOP's ( Thin Small Outline Package ) due to the high silicon to mold compound ratio which results in a relatively low package CTE ( 7 - 11 ppm/°C lengthwise and 7 - 16 ppm/°C widthwise ) [1,2] compared to that of typical PCB's ( 16 - 20 ppm/°C ). Previous work [2,3,4] has primarily focused on given TSOP designs. Reliability effects of discrete silicon - mold compound ratios and die size, along with lead pitch / dimensions, lead material ( Cu vs. A42 ) and package design (die pad vs. Lead on Chip) have been evaluated. Analytical and experimental results have clearly indicated that packages with higher global CTE and increased lead compliance exhibit up to a 5X increase in thermal fatigue life over a worst case design.

Historically, increases in reliability of TSOP joints has been accomplished through soldering process development efforts. Optimization of solder paste application, stencil and solder pad design have yielded significant improvements [5,6]. Current packaging trends would suggest that lead count and package footprint will continue to increase, including those of the TSOP family. It may become necessary to optimize some or all of the design variables which can affect the package CTE and lead compliance in order to achieve current levels of reliability on larger packages. These variables include lead thickness, CTE of mold compound, lead material, package design and chip size. With the possible exception of die size, the package designer has a considerable number of choices to work with.

In this paper, an FEM analysis is conducted to investigate the relative reliability effects of the five design variables above for TSOP I type packages. The method developed by R. Darveaux [3] is employed and compared against an approach based on CTE mismatch and lead compliance [7]. In the latter approach, component CTE is estimated with 3D linear finite element models. The CTE results are compared to Moire Interferometric measurements and used to calculate lead forces. An assumption is made that joint thermal fatigue life is proportional to the forces on the joint and are related through a Coffin-Manson relationship. Figure 1 depicts a typical 3D finite element model used for package CTE calculations. This model is subsequently extended and employed in the full nonlinear analysis of the solder joint strains and relative reliability evaluation.

Initial results indicate that the Lead on Chip package design advantage may be due solely to increased lead compliance as calculated package CTE shows no improvement over that of an identical (chip size) die pad package design. Results clearly show ( Figures 2 and 3 ) that global package CTE can be tailored by varying the mold compound CTE. Typical TSOP I designs are affected more in the lateral (widthwise) direction than the longitudinal direction. Figure 4 presents the relative reliability results based on the package CTE and lead compliance for 3 different lead frame thickness values. The effect of the widthwise package CTE is also estimated and presented.

References:

[1] B.Han and Y. Guo, "Determination of Effective Coefficient of Thermal Expansion of Electronic Packaging Components: A Whole-field Approach", IEEE Transactions on Components, Packaging and Manufacturing Technology - Part A, (accepted for publication), 1996

[2] D.M. Noctor and J.-P. Clech, "Accelerated Testing and Predictive Modeling of the Attachment Reliability of Alloy 42 and Copper Leaded TSOPs", Proc. Nepcon East, 1993, pp. 193-206

[3] R. Darveaux, "Optimizing the Reliability of Thin Small Outline Package (TSOP) Solder Joints", EEP - Vol. 10-2, Advances in Electronic Packaging, ASME 1995, pp. 675-685

[4] J. Lau, S. Golwalkar, D. Rice, S. Erasmus, R. Surratt and P. Boysan, "Experimental and analytical studies of 28-Pin Thin Small Outline Package (TSOP) Solder-Joint Reliability", Proc. ASME WAM, Dec 1-6, 1991

[5] J. Lee and D. Caletka, "TSOP Encapsulation and Reliability Modeling", Proc. ASME IEPC, 1993, pp. 1135-1141

[6] P. Viswanadham, M. Stennett, A. Emerick, and R. Haggett, "Second Level Assembly and Reliability Aspect of Thin Small Outline Package", Proc. ASME IEPC, 1993, pp. 1127-1134

[7] R. W. Kotlowitz, "Comparative Compliance of Representative Lead Designs for Surface-Mounted Components", IEEE Transactions on Components, Hybrids, and Manufacturing Technology, Vol. 12, No. 4, Dec 1989, pp. 431-447

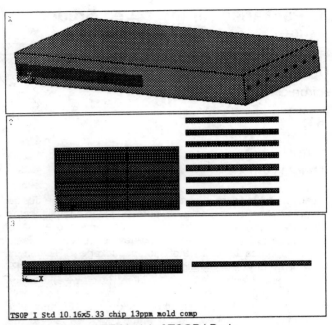

TSOP I Std 10.16x5.33 chip 13ppm mold comp

**Figure 1** - Typical FE Model of TSOP I Body

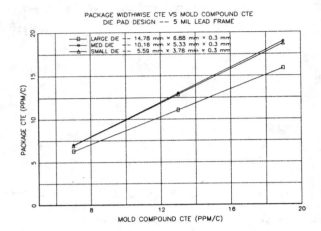

**Figure 3** - Package Widthwise CTE vs Mold Compound CTE

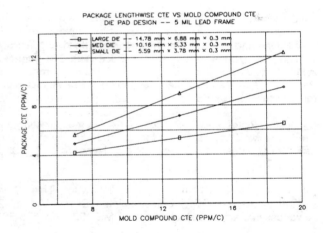

**Figure 2** - Package Lengthwise CTE vs Mold Compound CTE

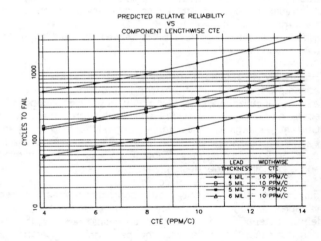

**Figure 4** - Predicted Relative Reliability vs Component Lengthwise CTE

# Improvement in Performance of IC Packages with Thermal Leads

Pankaj Mithal, Ahmer R. Syed and Rakesh Agarwal

Delco Electronics Corporation
A Subsidiary of Hughes Electronics Corporation
M/S CT-30-B, One Corporate Center
Kokomo, Indiana 46904

## ABSTRACT

Effectiveness of thermal-leads in reducing junction temperature of a die in an integrated circuit (IC) package is investigated. Thermal performance of a 160 leaded PQFP with and without thermal-leads is analyzed numerically. Experiments are conducted with a thermal die that has a resistor for power dissipation and a diode built-in the die for direct junction temperature measurement. Junction temperature obtained from FEA and experiments are in excellent agreement. Reduction in die junction temperature is obtained in the range of 0.2 to 0.4 C/W per thermal-lead and maximum power dissipation of 0.8 W in a given application without the use of thermal-leads for the 160 PQFP.

## INTRODUCTION

Thermal-leads are leads that are directly attached to the die paddle. These leads provide much lower thermal resistance to heat dissipated at the IC junctions compared to electrical input or output (I/O) leads because the I/O leads are terminated at a distance from the paddle and electrical interconnection is made between the lead and the junction through a wire bond. Outside the package, thermal-leads look identical to the regular I/O leads. The number of thermal-leads used in a package obviously depend upon a number of factors including its size, power dissipation and particular demands of the application.

Thermal die contains a resistor which can be used to dissipate desired amount of electrical power at the IC junction surface, and it also contains a temperature measuring diode that can be used for monitoring the temperature of the die.

This article describes some recent efforts at Delco Electronics in exploring the influence of thermal-leads to reduce the junction temperature of plastic encapsulated IC packages. Both experimental and numerical techniques are used in the investigation and the package considered in this study is a 160 pin PQFP with a PST5 thermal die.

## EXPERIMENTAL STUDY

The 160 PQFP IC package used in this study had standard 160 PQFP package with a PST 5 thermal die. The overall size of this package was 28mm X 28mm and the size of the thermal die was 7.77mm X 7.77mm. For the purposes of this study two of these packages (four total) were mounted both sides of a six layer FR-4 PCB. The test vehicle used in this study was a recent year model of a typical electronic assembly. The PCB was installed inside the unit in a horizontal position, thus two packages were facing the top cover of the housing and the other two were facing the bottom cover. To simulate the effect of the additional heat load that would be experienced by the package in its intended application, twelve TO220 devices were also installed. In an effort to further simulate the ambient temperature conditions the assembly was placed inside a thermal chamber with a perforated box placed around it to alleviate any forced convection. 31 thermocouples were placed on the internal and external surfaces of the housing including the circuit board, in the air space between the circuit board and the housing, and on the body of IC packages. The data obtained from the thermocouples is recorded using a data logger.

The thermal performance of 160 PQFP with 24, 8 and no thermal-leads was evaluated at the four power dissipation levels, 0.5 W, 1.0 W, 1.5 W and 2.0 W., two ambient temperature levels of 75 °C and 105 °C and three levels of power dissipation by the 12 TO220s, 0. W, 1.25 W and 2.5 W each.

## FINITE ELEMENT ANALYSIS

A 3-D finite element model of the setup used in experimental investigation was constructed. 160 PQFP was modeled with the die. Leads thermally equivalent to I/O and thermal-leads were modeled and geometry was approximated with least compromise in heat transfer mechanism. Effect of die attach layer was accounted for in the thermal resistance through the die using equivalent thermal resistance in series. Circuit board was modeled under the 160 PQFP. The housing was modeled surrounding the circuit board assembly.

Boundary conditions in the model account for radiation, convection and conduction interior and exterior to the housing of the circuit board assembly. Power dissipation was applied to the face of the die that is away from the paddle. Nodal heat sources were prescribed on the housing per the experimental setup. Total power dissipation of the assembly was 31 W including 1 W at the 160 PQFP. Two cases were analyzed. Case 1 had 24 thermal-leads with ambient temperature external to the assembly at 111 °C and natural convection. Case 2 had no thermal lead.

## RESULTS

Less than 3 °C difference between temperatures recorded in experiments and the thermal model used in this investigation at 1 W power dissipation by 160 PQFP and 30 W by TO220's with 105 °C ambient and natural convection around the assembly housing for 24 and no thermal-leads. The following table presents a summary of junction to ambient thermal resistance obtained from experiments.

## CONCLUSION

Thermal-leads can be effectively employed in reducing junction temperature of packaged IC's. A validated thermal model can reliably assess thermal performance of electronic assemblies.

| Package Type | $\Theta ja$ (°C/W) | $\Theta ja + 3\sigma$ (°C/W) | % Improvement |
|---|---|---|---|
| No Thermal-leads | 27.4 | 28.7 | -- |
| 24 Thermal-leads | 16.9 | 19.2 | 33.0 |
| 8 Thermal-leads | 20.7 | 25.2 | 25.0 |

# Thermal Fatigue Reliability Enhancement of Plastic Ball Grid Array (PBGA) Packages

Ahmer R. Syed
Delco Electronics Corporation
700 E. Firmin Drive, MS T100-26
Kokomo, Indiana 46904-9005

The leadless, area array design of Plastic Ball Grid Array (PBGA) package results in improved manufacturing yields and denser packaging. This is especially true for I/O counts greater than 200. However, these design factors also influence the thermal fatigue reliability of the package in the negative sense. Because of the close proximity of the die to the Bismaleimide Triazine (BT) substrate, the effective coefficient of thermal expansion (CTE) of the package in the region of die is much lower than the rest of the package. This results in a greater CTE mismatch between the package and the circuit board in this region. Since solder joints are the only medium providing connection between the package and the board, they have to absorb this thermal mismatch. This ultimately results in thermal fatigue failure of solder joints after repeated temperature cycling. The failure occurs much quicker in PBGA than in leaded fine pitch packages because of the lack of compliant leads.

This paper examines how the thermal fatigue life of solder joints for PBGA packages can be improved by changing some design parameters of the PBGA package. To minimize the resources required for extensive testing, a combined experimental and numerical approach is adopted. A previously published fatigue life prediction model by the author [1] is first validated. This is accomplished by conducting actual tests and finite element analysis simulations on three Plastic Ball Grid Array (PBGA) package configurations. A designed experiment is then used to study the effect of four design parameters. The experiments were numerically conducted and the fatigue lives were predicted using the validated life prediction model.

A mechanistic, damage accumulation based life prediction model previously published by the author [1] is further simplified in [2] for the case of eutectic tin/lead solder as

$$C = N_f \left( Y_{GBS} D_{GBS} + Y_{MC} D_{MC} \right) \qquad (1)$$

where $D_{GBS}$ and $D_{MC}$ are the accumulated creep strains for grain boundary sliding and matrix creep respectively. $Y_{GBS}$ and $Y_{MC}$ are the constants to be determined, $C$ has a value of 1.0, and $N_f$ is the number of cycles to failure. The above life prediction model

assumes that the damage per cycle is constant.

To determine the value of the constants $Y_{GBS}$ and $Y_{MC}$, thermal cycling tests were done on three BGA configurations: standard, perimeter array, and thicker BT substrate BGAs. The standard BGA had a full array of 15 x 15 balls at 1.5 mm pitch with BT substrate thickness of 0.36 mm. For the perimeter array BGA, an array of 7x7 balls were removed from underneath the die resulting in four perimeter arrays with 176 total I/Os. Finally, the thicker substrate BGA had BT substrate thickness of 0.76 mm instead of 0.36 mm. The parts were mounted on circuit boards and temperature cycled using three different profiles as shown in Figure 1. Each part was continuously monitored during temperature cycling and the 15th instant of resistance more than 400 ohms is taken as the time to failure. The failures were also verified by measuring the resistance across the package with an ohm meter.

The tests were also simulated using three-dimension nonlinear finite element analysis approach, as described in [2], to determine the accumulated grain boundary sliding and matrix creep strains. The test and simulation data for only two test conditions were then used to determine the constants $Y_{GBS}$ and $Y_{MC}$ of the life prediction model given by (1). The minimum life, as determined from three-parameter Weibull analysis were used for cycles to failure. The values of constants $Y_{GBS}$ and $Y_{MC}$ so determined are 0.022 and 0.060 respectively. These values were then used to predict the fatigue for the remaining test conditions. The measured and predicted fatigue lives are plotted in Figure 2, showing that the fatigue life is predicted within 10% of measured life for each case.

Once the fatigue life prediction model is validated, an experiment was designed to study the effect design parameters on the fatigue life of solder joints. The four parameters considered are : BT substrate thickness, array configuration, pad size on the package side, and the ball pitch. A full factorial experiment was designed with two levels for each parameter as listed in Table 1. The experiment was conducted numerically using the finite element analysis approach [2]. All analyses were done for a one hour temperature cycle between -40 and 125°C with a dwell of 15 minutes at each extreme. The accumulated grain boundary sliding and matrix creep strains were determined for each combination and were used to predict the fatigue life using (1).

The predicted fatigue lives were statistically analyzed to determine the effects of main factors as well as their interactions. The results of statistical analysis indicated that all factors and their interactions are statistically significant. The improvement in fatigue life, on the average, caused by changing each factor from standard to alternate level is listed in Table 2.

Considering the main effects, the thickness of BT substrate is the strongest factor resulting in 2X improvement in fatigue life on the average when the substrate thickness is varied from 0.36 mm to 0.76 mm. The increased thickness of the substrate causes BT to dominate the effective CTE of the package, bringing it closer to the circuit board CTE. This in turn increases the fatigue life of the solder joints. Even with thicker substrate, the joints underneath the die tend to fail first. Perimeter array package, with no joints under the die, shifts the failure to joints exposed to lower CTE mismatch which improves the life by 35% on the average. Finally, finer pitch balls and larger size pads increase the load bearing area for the same package size, resulting in 38% and 16% improvement, on the average, in fatigue life respectively.

The two factor interaction of substrate thickness and array configuration is more significant than any other two factor interactions, resulting in almost 3X improvement in fatigue life on the average when 0.76 mm substrate with perimeter array is used instead of 0.36 mm substrate and full array. Finally, the three factor interaction of substrate thickness, array configuration, and ball pitch results in 4.25X improvement in fatigue life on the average when alternate levels were used for these factors.

The raw data as well as the predicted optimum value from ECHIP™ indicate that an overall factor of 5.2 improvement in fatigue life can be achieved if BGAs with 0.76 mm thick substrate, perimeter array, 0.635 mm pad, and 1.27 mm ball pitch is used instead of the standard BGAs (0.36 mm substrate, full array, 0.635 mm pad, and 1.5 mm pitch). This can further be improved by 10% if 0.76 mm pad can be used with 1.27 mm ball pitch.

### References

[1] Syed, A. R., "*Creep Crack Growth Prediction of Solder Joints During Temperature Cycling - An Engineering Approach*", ASME Journal of Electronic Packaging, Vol. 117, June 1995, pp. 116 - 122.

[2] Syed, A. R., "Thermal Fatigue Life Enhancement of Plastic Ball Grid Array (PBGA) Packages", to be published in the proceedings of 46th Electronic Components and Technology Conference.

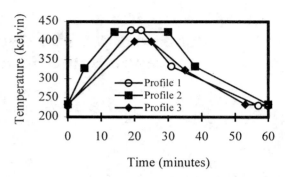

**Figure 1** : Temperature Profiles used for Tests

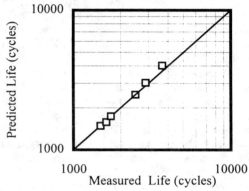

**Figure 2** : Predicted vs. Measured Fatigue Lives

### Table 1: DOE Parameter Settings

| Parameter | Standard | Alternate |
|---|---|---|
| BT Thickness | 0.36 mm | 0.76 mm |
| Pad Size | 0.635 mm | 0.76 mm |
| Array | Full | Perimeter |
| Ball Pitch | 1.5 mm | 1.27 mm |

### Table 2: Predicted Fatigue Life Improvement

| Factor | Life Improvement factor (Alternate/Standard) |
|---|---|
| *Main Effects* | |
| BT Thickness | 2.00 |
| Array | 1.35 |
| Pitch | 1.38 |
| Pad Size | 1.16 |
| *Two Factor Interactions* | |
| BT Thick. and Array | 3.00 |
| BT Thick. and Pitch | 2.92 |
| BT Thick. and Pad Size | 2.47 |
| Pad Size and Array | 1.57 |
| *Three Factor Interactions* | |
| BT Thick., Array, & Pitch | 4.25 |
| BT Thick., Pad, & Array | 3.12 |

# A Parametric Study on the Thermal Fatigue Reliability of Flip Chip Solder Joints in Electronic Packaging

Jin - Young Kim and Soon - Bok Lee

Korea Advanced Institute of Science and Technology
373-1 Kusong dong, Yousung-gu, Taejon 305-701, Korea

The reliable electronic packaging design is an important issue. In a flip chip the electrical signal transfer and mechanical bonding are achieved through solder joints. Since the electronic packaging may undergo operating conditions of thermal cycling, repeated inelastic deformation by thermal coefficient mismatch of adjacent components can cause the fatigue failure of solder joints[1]. In general, a number of parameters control the fatigue life of solder interconnections. These include operating temperatures, frequencies, the temperature hold time, thermal coefficients of expansion of the silicon chip and the substrate, as well as the geometry of the solder bump. In this study, the influence of the temperature cycles are investigated.

To access the reliability, a stress - strain analysis of solder joints is conducted by finite element analysis. The flip chip with 38 by 38 solder balls of 95Pb/5Sn is considered for the analysis. Instead of a 38 by 38 flip chip full model, two dimensional model along the diagonal direction of the chip is used as shown in Fig.1. Since 95Pb/5Sn solder material has low melting temperature and low yield stress, inelastic deformation (creep and plastic) occur in 95Pb/5Sn solder joints in addition to elastic deformation[2]. Also the influence of temperature effects on material properties cannot be neglected. So, inelastic stress-strain curves which represent the plastic and creep deformation behavior under different temperatures are taken into account to simulate the deformation behavior of 95Pb/5Sn solder material more exactly. As a loading condition, trapezoidal-shaped cyclic temperature loadings are considered(Fig.2).

From the FEM analysis it is shown that the maximum peak stress occurs during the temperature down period and this stress is relaxed during the hold time(Fig.3). The distribution of stress components of each solder joint shows a great change during a temperature cycle and it is also shown that a solder joint at the outer edge undergoes the largest variation of the magnitude of stress and strain components(Fig.4). Since large stresses can cause a sudden fracture and usually stress relaxation is accompanied with large inelastic strains(Fig.5), both of them should be minimized to prevent from mechanical failure of solder joints[3]. To examine the inelastic strain effects on the solder bump's life, fatigue experiment was conducted[4]. From the results of this experiment, it is known that there is a power law relationship between the inelastic strain and the fatigue life as following.

$$\frac{da}{dN} = C\left(\Delta \varepsilon_p\right)^n a \, \exp\left(-\frac{Q}{kT}\right) \tag{1}$$

In the present study, from the viewpoint of thermal loading effects on the solder joint failure, the temperature effects on the maximum stress and maximum plastic and creep strain are examined with six parameters. Those are the hold time at the minimum temperature, the hold time at the maximum temperature, the ramp down rate, the ramp up rate, the maximum temperature, and the minimum temperature. The contribution of each parameter to the maximum equivalent stress, the maximum equivalent plastic and creep strain are calculated with Taguchi method[5]. As a result, it is proved that the maximum equivalent stress is dominated by the minimum temperature, while the plastic strain and creep strain are dominated by the maximum temperature. On the other hand, the hold time is proved to have no significant effect in our case. In case of plastic strain, it is also proved that the temperature down rate has a significant effect(Fig. 6,7,8).

Since FEM analysis needs a complex mesh generation and takes a long time for calculation, a simple deformation model has been developed by utilizing the mismatching between thermal expansions of silicon chip and substrate, bending effect on flip chip geometry.

$$\frac{d\gamma}{dt} = \left(\alpha_s - \alpha_c\right)\frac{L}{h}\frac{dT}{dt} - \frac{1}{G_{eff}}\frac{d\tau}{dt} \tag{2}$$

From above equation, it can be imagined that if there is no temperature change the effective stiffness of the chip assembly $G_{eff}$ becomes $d\tau/dt$, so $G_{eff}$ can be determined from the slope of stress strain curve during temperature holding period. The stress - strain behavior calculated from the simple shear deformation model is compared with the results of FEM analysis. From these results, it is shown that the simple model can predict stress-strain behavior reasonably well for solder joints which are near the edge of chip, while the simple model shows a large deviation from the FEM results for solder joints near the center of chip. (Fig.9,10).

Reference

[1] K.C.Norris and A.H.Landzberg,"Reliability of controlled collapsed interconnections," IBM J. Develop. vol. 13,

pp.266, 1969.

[2] S.Knecht and L.R.Fox,"Constitutive relation and creep-fatigue life model for eutectic tin-lead solder," IEEE Trans. Comp. Hybrids. Manuf. Technol.,vol.13, no.2,pp.314,1984.

[3] S.Vayman,"Effect of temperature on isothermal fatigue of solders," IEEE Trans. Comp. Hybrids. Manuf. Technol., vol.13, no.4,pp.909,1990.

[4] S.B.Lee and J.K.Kim,"A mechanistic model for fatiguelife prediction of solder joints for electronic packages,"in press,Int.J of Fatigue,1995.

[5] P.J.Ross, Taguchi techniques for quality engineering, McGraw-Hill company,1988.

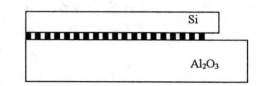

Fig. 1. Two dimensional model

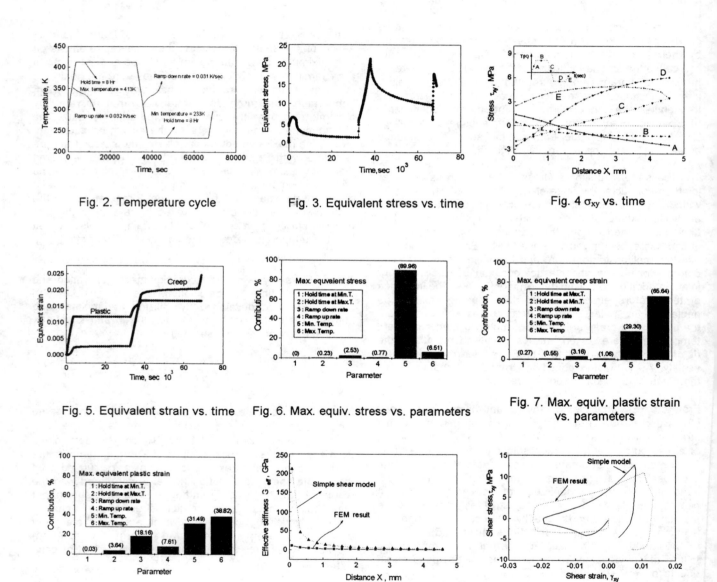

Fig. 2. Temperature cycle

Fig. 3. Equivalent stress vs. time

Fig. 4 $\sigma_{xy}$ vs. time

Fig. 5. Equivalent strain vs. time

Fig. 6. Max. equiv. stress vs. parameters

Fig. 7. Max. equiv. plastic strain vs. parameters

Fig. 8. Max. equiv. plastic strain vs. parameters

Fig. 9. Comparison of effective stiffness between simple model and FEM analysis

Fig. 10. Comparison of stress-strain behavior between simple model and FEM analysis

# Accelerated Life Test Development For Combined Stresses

K.Upadhyayula and A.Dasgupta
CALCE-Electronic Packaging Research Center (EPRC)
University Of Maryland, College Park, MD-20742

Recent advances in technology coupled with the relentless drive to remain competitive in world markets, is motivating industries to focus more on *product effectiveness* and better *reliability assessment techniques*. In order to enhance product reliability, it is necessary to have a thorough understanding of the failure mechanisms [1] that could be activated in typical electronic products. Effective measures can then be taken to prevent the manifestation of these failure mechanisms due to the stresses experienced during the life-cycle operation profile.

The application of accelerated stresses is a cost-effective means for investigating the vulnerability of a product to potential failure mechanisms. The magnitude of the stresses applied are driven by trade-offs between the need for adequate test-time compression and the need to avoid unrealistic failure mechanisms for a given application environment. The use of combined stress environments offers the promise of enhanced test-time compression, but at the cost of a significant increase in the complexity of quantifying the damage mechanisms. A two-phase study in progress at the CALCE-EPRC involves: (a) *Experimentation phase*: conducting qualification tests to achieve test-time compression under accelerated combined stresses. (b) *Simulation phase*: quantifying the damage metrics for the observed failure mechanisms using a Physics-of-Failure (PoF) approach.

This paper presents the first phase (experimental investigation) which involves the application of accelerated combined stress environments to circuit card assemblies (CCAs). Specifically, the interactions and synergy between combinations of thermal cycling and vibration stresses are explored. The focus of the study is primarily on interconnect failure mechanisms, which includes solder joints, leads, PTHs, PWB substrates etc. The CCAs tested are populated with a combination of insertion-mount and surface-mount daisy chained components. The assemblies are subjected to various combinations of thermal cycling and multidirectional random vibrations of a repetitive shock nature. The specimen layout is shown in Figure 1.

The stresses are applied in an accelerated stress test chamber, which is capable of temperature ranges of 150°C to -100°C at a temperature rate of change of 60°C/minute on the product and is also equipped with four pneumatic actuators capable of providing vibration levels upto 90Grms on moderately light and properly fixtured test articles. The circuits are continuously monitored using event detectors which record transient electrical opens throughout the duration of the stress test. The accelerated test profiles used for this study are shown in Figures 2a and 2b. The test matrix used to facilitate the study of the synergy between the thermal and vibration loads on the durability of the interconnects is illustrated in Table 1.

Controlled experiments reveal some interesting failure phenomena as shown in Figure 3. The interconnects for some components are found to be more vulnerable to the repetitive shock (RS) vibration at room temperature than to the combined application of thermal cycling ($\Delta$T) and vibration loading, due to creep-fatigue interactions in solder joints. However interconnects on other components reveal an opposite trend. The former trend is an apparent contradiction of the popular Palmgren-Miner's rule [2] for damage superposition.

The visco-plastic dissipation energy, represented by the area of the cyclic hysteresis loop in a stress-strain diagram, is used as a metric of creep-fatigue damage which accumulates in solder joints in each cycle [3]. The vibration stresses occur at relatively high frequencies (over 30Hz) and the stress amplitudes induced are relatively small compared to the thermal stresses. The high frequency, low-magnitude vibration loads induces primarily elastic-plastic behavior in the solder joints. Thus, the vibration stress excursions can be viewed as many small elastic-plastic hysteresis loops superposed on each large visco-plastic hysteresis loop caused by thermal cycling. The magnitude of the vibration loops can change with the temperature dependent material properties of the solder material and the PWB materials. The resulting change in vibrational damage can lead to complex interaction effects not investigated to date. This calls for a more sophisticated understanding of the synergy of the combined stress environments on the durability of the interconnects. Ongoing research at CALCE is directed towards understanding this complex synergy between the different stresses and quantifying the damage metrics using PoF models.

Acknowledgments:

The authors would like to express their gratitude to United Technologies Hamilton Standard for providing the samples for this study and wish to thank the members of CALCE Electronic Packaging Research Center for their support.

References:

[1] Hu, J.M., Barker, D., Dasgupta, A., Arora, A., "The Role of Failure Mechanism Identification in Accelerated Testing", Journal of the Institute of Environmental Science, pp.39-45, July 1993.

[2] Miner, M.A., "Cumulative Damage in Fatigue", Journal of Applied Mechanics, vol.12, 1945.

[3] Dasgupta, A., Oyan, C., Barker, D., Pecht, M., "Solder Creep-Fatigue Analysis by an Energy-Partitioning Approach", ASME Trans. Electronic Packaging, vol.144, pp.152-160, 1992.

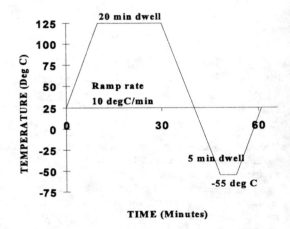

Figure 2a. Thermal Profile used for the test program

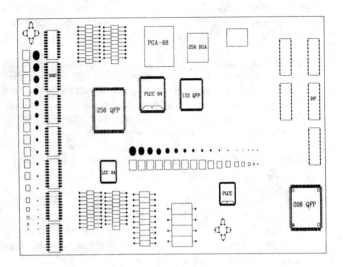

Figure.1 Schematic of the test specimen

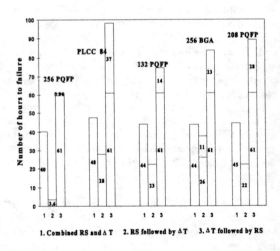

Figure 3. Observed failures under combined loads

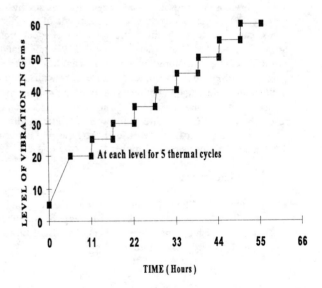

Figure 2b. Vibration Profile used for this study

| Specimen # | n hours | n hours | n hours |
|---|---|---|---|
| 1 (step-stress destruct test) | - | - | - |
| 2 (combined) | ΔT+RS | | |
| 3 (sequential) | | RS | ΔT |
| 4 (sequential) | - | ΔT | RS |

Table 1. Test matrix for the test program

# Fatigue Life Analysis of Solder Ball Joint in Bare Chip Bonding

Yutaka Tsukada, Syogo Mizumoto, Hideo Nishimura
800 Ichimiyake, Yasu-cho, Yasu-gun, Shiga-ken 520-23 Japan
Yasu Laboratory, IBM Japan


Masao Sakane, Masateru Ohnami
1916 Noji-cho, Kusatsu-shi, Shiga-ken, 525 Japan
Department of Mechanical Engineering, Ritsumeikan University

Bare chip bonding of semiconductor chip using solder ball flip chip joint has a superior electircal performance and high productivity. It has been utilized for packaging large computers because of its advantage over other packaging technologies. However, since the life of the flip chip joint is dominated by the CTE mismatch of the chip and carrier, the carrier material has been limited to use low CTE material such as alumina. Encapsulated flip chip joint which has been introduced by the author's group succeeded to use an epoxy base carrier which has a high CTE such as 15-30 ppm/ºC. The life of the joint was extended by several times over the conventional method [1].

Figure 1 shows a cross section of the package. A chip was attached to the carrier which has wiring layers constructed by sequentially built up epoxy dielectrics and copper conductors and a base by an ordinally glass epoxy printed circuit board. This build-up structure enables a large number of signal lines escaped from a chip attach area and also reduces a stress around the joint by a cushion effect. The joint is made of a 5Sn-95Pb lead rich solder (melting point: around 320ºC) provided as a chip bump and a 63Sn-37Pb eutectic solder as a carrier side bump. The eutectic solder bump melts to form the joint with chip bump by reflow process with a temperature around 210ºC which allows to use an epoxy base material for the carrier. The completed joint structure is shown in Figure 2 where the joint height is 130μm, the diameter of chip side terminal is 160μm and the carrier terminal is rectangular by 102×127μm. After forming the joint, a space between the chip and carrier is filled with an epoxy encapsulant so that the stress caused by the CTE mismatch is dispersed within the package.

Thermal cycle test has been made using a chip with a large number of I/O's for logic chip applications. Two kinds of structure, encapsulated and not-encapsulated, were tested with total 5 different temperature ranges. The temperature ranges

in the encapsulated group were 85ºC for cell-A, 100ºC for cell-B and 140ºC for cell-C. The not-encapsulated group had temperature ranges of 40ºC for cell-D, 70ºC for cell-E and 100ºC for cell-F. The chip size for the test is 7.5mm square and 0.6mm in thickness. It has 273 chip bumps which are shorted out each other for a measurement of the joint resistance change. A frequency of the thermal stress is 3 cycles per hour. Failure of the test specimen is defined as a 30 mΩ resistance increase of the joint measured by a DC potential drop method. The joint has obvious cracks by this resistance increase since the initial resistance is about 2-3 mΩ.

The specimens in the not-encapsulated group failed earlier than those in the encapsulated group. The encapsulated group has a significantly longer life. The resistance change of any chip in cell-A did not reach to 30 mΩ, but was arround 10mΩ even beyond 40000 cycles. Ones in Cell-B showed the life over 10000 cycles. This is a significant extention of the joint life if we refer the conventional flip chip bonding on alumina showing the life around 2000 cycles under 100ºC temperature range. By micro cross sectional analysis of the failed joints, quite different appearances of the joint crack were observed in two groups. In encapsulated group, there are many micro hair cracks in the middle of the joint which is a 5Sn-95Pb area as shown in Figure 3(a). A magnified view of the crack is taken from an area indicated by a box in the joint total view. In not-encapsulated group, the joint has a major crack in 63Sn-37Pb area which is in the lower part of the joint as shown in Figure 3(b).

A finite element analysis with elastic-creep condition was made for each group. Figure 4 shows Von Mises strain distributions in the joint when applied 100ºC delta temperature. (a) shows an encapsulated case where the entire strain is very low and slightly concentrated at the 5Sn-95Pb area in the center part. This condition quite agreed with the cross sectional analysis shown in Figure 3. (b) shows a not-encapsulated case. The entire joint is under shear mode. Upper right corner and lower left corner are in tensile and each of opposite side are in compression. The strain in the 5Sn-95Pb area is larger than the 63Sn-37Pb area and the highest point at upper right corner. The 63Sn-37Pb solder has high point in lower left corner but still lower than the point in the 5Sn-95Pb. In the not-encapsulated case, the strain size and the cracked part in the cross sectional analysis did not match. This is considered that the 63Sn-37Pb solder cracks with a lower strain compared with the 5Sn-95Pb solder in the tested temperature range.

A conclusion obtained is that the bare chip bonding by an encapsulated flip chip joint has a significant extension of the joint life and the mode of failure at the end of the life is clarified.

Reference

[1] Y.Tsukada, Y.Mashimoto, T.Nishio and N.Mii, "Reliability and Stress Analysis of Encapsulated Flip Chip Joint on Epoxy Base Printed Circuit Board", Proceedings of ASME/JSME Joint Conference for Advanced in Electronics Packaging-Milpitas CA, Vol.2, pp827-835 (May 1992)

Figures

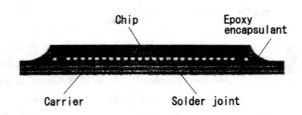

Figure 1  Bare Chip Bonding Cross Section

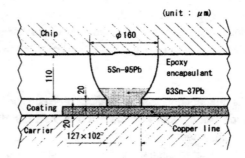

Figure 2  Joint Structure

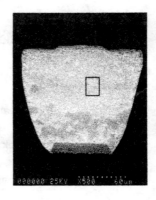

Magnified View

(a)  Encapsulated Joint

(b)  Not-Encapsulated Joint

Figure 3  Failed Joint Cross Section

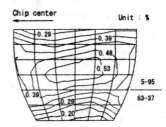

(a)  Encapsulated Joint

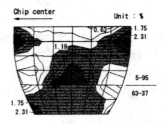

(b)  Not Encapsualted Joint

Figure 4  Strain Distribution

38

# High Cycle Fatigue Life Assessment of PCB Assembly Using Experimental Modal Analysis

Andre Kleyner, Thomas Torri
Delco Electronics Corporation
700 E. Firmin Street, Kokomo, IN 46904

## INTRODUCTION

The article discusses the implementation of modal analysis techniques to predict the fatigue life of an electronic assembly subjected to random vibration by estimating the number of vibration cycles (positive/zero crossings) to failure. This is implemented through a combination of the techniques of experimental modal analysis and real time animation with environmental testing in order to help achieve design objectives.

Cracks in the component's leads or solder joints are known to be one of the primary failure modes in electronic packages when subjected to random vibration in automotive applications. The conventional modal analysis is usually performed using an impact hammer or modal shaker with sinusoidal vibration, or white noise type random vibration as a source of excitation with a measurable force. However, all the above types of input are different from the real life environment and the results cannot always be correlated with the performance of the electronic unit in the field. More so, in the case of a real-life vibration the unit is mounted on a car or tested on electro-dynamic shaker using a mounting bracket; thus the force applied to the test structure is not measurable. All this makes the application of conventional modal analysis difficult for fatigue life prediction. Thus, some type of synthesis between modal testing and environment testing must be utilized.

## THEORETICAL FORMULATION

The maximum allowable printed circuit board (PCB) displacement $Z_m$ where the component can be expected to achieve a fatigue life of over 20 million stress reversals in a random vibration environment, can be estimated using Steinberg's equation [1] based upon $3\sigma$ PCB displacement:

$$Z_m = \frac{0.0282 \times B}{Ch\sqrt{L}} \quad (1)$$

where $Z_m$ is the maximum allowable displacement (mm), $B$ is the length of PCB edge parallel to component (mm), $C$ is the constant for different types of electronic components, $L$ is the length of electronic component (mm), $h$ is thickness of PCB (mm).

Equation (1) is based on the vibration modes of simply supported board and cannot be applied to PCBs with other types of boundary conditions. However, with the knowledge of PCB mode shapes obtained from modal analysis, the parameter B can now be defined as a distance between two nodes of vibration on both sides of the component. This does not always correspond to the longest side of the circuit board. Under normal distribution assumption, the deflection of a PCB subjected to a random vibration can be calculated as [1]:

$$Z_{3\sigma} = \frac{3 \times 249 \times G_{rms}}{f_{res}^2} \quad (2)$$

where $Z_{3\sigma}$ = $3\sigma$ PCB deflection at the measurement point, mm.
$G_{rms}$ = vibration level at the measurement point
$f_{res}$ = first resonant frequency of the board, Hz.

Twenty million stress reversals on $3\sigma$ level of vibration is considered to be sufficient for automotive applications based on a mission life of 100,000 miles. Assuming that the stress is proportional to the board displacement, the number of stress reversals to failure $N_f$ is:

$$N_f = 20 million \times (\frac{Z_m}{Z_{3\sigma}})^b \quad (3)$$

The value of **b** = 4.5 is suggested for surface mounted solder joints and **b** = 6.4 has been suggested for wire leads.

The authors suggest the use of Coefficient of Robustness defined as:

$$R = \frac{Z_m}{Z_{3\sigma}} \times 100\%, \qquad (4)$$

where **R=100%** will correspond to a minimum acceptable level of robustness - in this particular case - 20 million stress reversals in a random vibration environment. The coefficient **R** can be used as a uniform measurement of robustness while comparing products of different sizes, geometry, and mission lives.

## TEST SETUP

The electronic unit is tested under worst case dynamic conditions and $g_{out}/g_{in}$ frequency response functions (FRF) are recorded to be used for modal analysis, where $g_{in}$ is acceleration measured at the shaker head and $g_{out}$ is the measured acceleration at the respective grid point on the circuit board. Modal analysis is then performed using a technique such as Operation Deflection Shapes (ODS).

In addition to that, $G_{rms}$ values are measured at every grid point using a spectrum analyzer. Integration should be done for every Power Spectral Density (PSD) trace at half-power peak level, which will single out the energy pertinent to the particular resonant frequency. Most of the time the first resonant frequency is responsible for the highest PCB deflection, thus **$G_{rms}$** should be measured around the lowest resonant frequency **$f_{res}$** on a PSD plot.

## STEP BY STEP PROCEDURE

The procedure described above can be broken down into the following steps:

1.  The circuit board is placed inside its case, then the unit is properly assembled, mounted on an electro-dynamic shaker, and tested at the representative field level vibration profile. FRFs of $g_{out}/g_{in}$ are recorded for every point of the grid. Modal Analysis is performed using ODS mode.
2.  **$G_{rms}$** half-power values are recorded for every grid point using a spectrum analyzer and **$Z_{3\sigma}$** are calculated using equation (2).

3.  The **$Z_m$** values are obtained at component locations based on equation (1). The value of the parameter **B** is based on the real mode shape and some engineering judgment. For example, in the case on Fig. 1 the smallest value should be chosen from **$B_1$** and **$B_2$**
4.  Based on equation (3), the number of stress reversals to failure is estimated for the worst case package on the PCB.
5.  The product is ranked against previously tested products based on the **R**-value from equation (4) which represents the robustness of the current design based on worst case package-location situation.

## CONCLUSION

A procedure was demonstrated that allows combining modal and environmental testing in order to estimate the fatigue life of electronic components without employing finite element modeling or intensive mathematical calculations. It also helps to create a rating of robustness **R** to rank different products against each other. Products can also be ranked based on their predicted absolute number of cycles to failure. A real life example is presented in the unabridged version of this paper.

## REFERENCE

[1]:    Steinberg Dave S., "Vibration Analysis for Electronic Equipment," 2nd Edition, John Wiley & Sons, New York, N.Y. 1988.

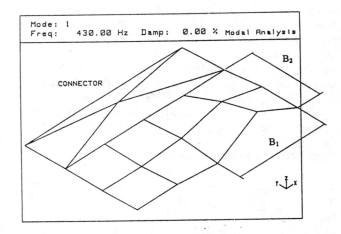

Figure 1. The board's mode shape with two different **$B_1$** and **$B_2$** parameters.

# How to Use Finite Element Analysis to Predict Solder Joint Fatigue Life

Robert Darveaux
Amkor Electronics
1347 N. Alma School Road, Suite 100
Chandler, AZ 85224

A model has been developed to predict solder joint fatigue life for surface mounted components. This model has been correlated to a wide range of thermal cycle test data on CBGA, PBGA, and TSOP assemblies. This paper will focus on aspects of the finite element analysis that affect the fatigue life prediction, such as time and temperature dependent material properties, element size, singularities, boundary conditions, load step size, and interpretation of the results. A detailed procedure will be given so that any skilled analyst should be able to use the model.

The development of the solder joint fatigue model was first presented in Ref [1]. The model utilizes finite element analysis to calculate the viscoplastic strain energy density per cycle during thermal or power cycling. The strain energy density is then used with crack growth data to calculate the number of cycles to initiate a cracks, and the number of cycles to propagate cracks through a joint. The crack growth experiments are described in detail in Ref [2]. The measured crack growth rates were originally correlated with calculated strain energy density using a combination of linear finite element analysis and 1-D non-linear simulations. Later, in Ref [1], the correlations were refined using non-linear finite element analysis. The crack growth correlations from [1] are

$$N_o = 7860 \, \Delta W^{-1.00} \qquad (1)$$

$$\frac{da}{dN} = 4.96\text{E-8} \, \Delta W^{1.13} \qquad (2)$$

where $N_o$ is the number of cycles to crack initiation, $da/dN$ is the crack growth rate in inches per cycle, and $\Delta W$ is the viscoplastic strain energy density per cycle in psi. These correlations were used to predict fatigue life under a wide range of test conditions for PBGA, CBGA, and TSOP assemblies in Refs [1,3]. The package failures in each data set were fit to a 3-Parameter Weibull distribution [4]

$$F_j = 0 \qquad \qquad \text{for } N < N_{ff}$$

$$F_j = 1 - \exp\left[-\left(\frac{N - N_{ff}}{\alpha_w - N_{ff}}\right)^{\beta_w}\right] \text{ for } N > N_{ff} \qquad (3)$$

where $F_j$ is the median rank failed, N is the number of cycles, $N_{ff}$ is the failure free life, $\alpha_w$ is the characteristic life at which 63.2% of the population has failed, and $\beta_w$ is the shape parameter which indicates the amount of scatter in the data.

A plot of the predicted failure free life versus the measured failure free life is shown in Figure 1. It is seen that the model gives good correlation over two orders in magnitude in failure free life. Only two data sets fall outside the +/- 2X bands, and the model was conservative on both of those (measured life was greater than predicted life).

A plot of the predicted characteristic life (63.2% failed) versus the measured characteristic life is shown in Figure 2. Again, there is good correlation to the data. Overall, the model has been shown to provide accurate predictive capability over a wide range of test conditions and package types. A scatter of +/- 2X is typical for metal fatigue, and is certainly comparable to other state-of-the-art solder fatigue predictive tools. If the model is used only to calculate acceleration factors for different temperature excursions of a given assembly, the accuracy will be better than +/- 2X. In other words, relative fatigue life predictions are easier and more accurate to make than absolute life predictions.

The predictive technique works well, but it does have some limitations. It was pointed out in Ref [5] that the finite element analysis results are very sensitive to mesh density. As element size is reduced, the calculated strain energy density increases. This is an artifact of the finite element procedure and is due solely to the singularities at the edges of the joint. Therefore, in the simulations performed to establish the fatigue life correlations above, the minimum element size was maintained at approximately .003" x .001" in all of the models.

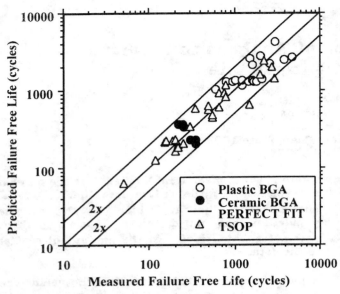

Figure 1. Failure free life correlation.

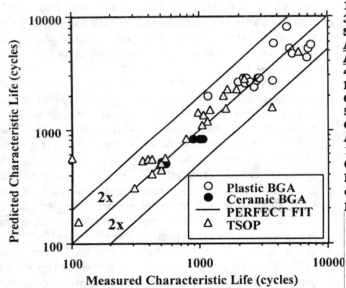

Figure 2. Characteristic life correlation.

This approach of using a consistent minimum element size obviously worked, but it can be improved upon. An alternate technique has been developed where the strain energy density values are averaged across the elements along the solder joint interface where the crack propagates. The strain energy values of each element are normalized by the volume of the element.

$$\Delta W_{ave} = \frac{\sum \Delta W \bullet V}{\sum V} \qquad (4)$$

where $\Delta W_{ave}$ is the average viscoplastic strain energy density per cycle, $\Delta W$ is the viscoplastic strain energy density per cycle of each element, and V is the volume of each element.

The new method was applied to the PBGA test data, and the correlation is shown in Figure 3. This technique provides a good fit to the data, and it is much less sensitive to finite element mesh density. It should be noted that averaging values over the solder joint interface was also done successfully by Sauber and Seyyedi in Ref [6]. However, they chose to use strain range instead of strain energy density.

1] R. Darveaux, K. Banerji, A. Mawer, and G. Dody, "Reliability of Plastic Ball Grid Array Assembly," Ball Grid Array Technology, J. Lau Editor, McGraw-Hill, Inc., New York, 1995.

2] R. Darveaux, "Crack Initiation and Growth in Surface Mount Solder Joints," Proc. ISHM International Symposium on Microelectronics, 1993, pp.86-97.

3] R. Darveaux, "Optimizing the Reliability of Thin Small Outline Package (TSOP) Solder Joints," Advances in Electronic Packaging 1995 - Proc. ASME Interpack '95, pp. 675-685.

4] R. B. Abernethy, The New Weibull Handbook, Publisher: R. B. Abernethy, North Palm Beach, FL, October 1993.

5] R. Darveaux and A. Mawer, "Thermal and Power Cycling Limits of Plastic Ball Grid Array (PBGA) Assemblies," Proc. Surface Mount International, 1995, pp. 315-326.

6] J. Sauber and J. Seyyedi, "Predicting Thermal Fatigue Lifetimes for SMT Solder Joints," Journal of Electronic Packaging, Vol 114, December 1992, pp. 472-476.

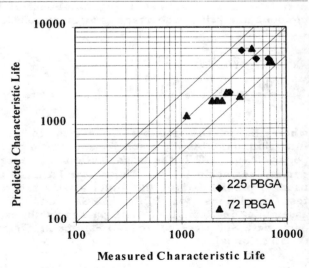

Figure 3. Characteristic life correlation using averaging method.

42

# Thermal Analysis of an Underhood mounted Power Control Module

Rakesh K. Agarwal and Klaus Gschwend

Delco Electronics Corporation
Subsidiary of Hughes Electronics Corporation
M/S CT-30-B, One Corporate Technology Center
Kokomo, Indiana 46904, USA

## ABSTRACT

Thermal performance of an underhood mounted power control module (PCM) is investigated using numerical and experimental techniques. Steady state and transient thermal analyses are conducted using the finite elements method. Excellent agreement is obtained between the temperature profiles obtained from the finite element analysis and experiments. Further, the assessment of steady state and transient temperatures, with application specific power distribution, are in excellent agreement with those observed in the road tests. Thermal performance of the PCM in terms of allowable ambient temperature and air speed combinations is estimated from the model for continuous operation of the PCM in a specific application based on maximum solder joint temperature on a circuit board.

## INTRODUCTION

Electronics in automotive applications continue to increase every year with emphasis on reduced size, weight and often higher functionality per assembly. Advances in electronic packaging and higher integration at the silicon chip are enabling packaging engineers keep up with this challenge. The net impact though is higher power dissipation density. Consequently, thermal management and design for thermal advantage are becoming critical to ensure reliable electronics, especially, in underhood automotive applications.

Today's competitive environment demands `lean-and-mean', timely and cost effective product design for a winning product. Predictive computer modeling in the concept design stage of a product is essential in evaluating design options because of unavailability of hardware being designed. Further, modeling allows true optimization of a design due to short analysis time compared to evolutionary changes based on lessons learnt from prototypes of a product. Finite element methods [2] offer an excellent tool for accomplishing this task. Rapid prototyping techniques may be employed for building hardware required for experimental validation of FE models.

In this paper, thermal modeling of a power control module (PCM), an electronic assembly, is presented. A finite element model of a PCM is constructed. P/Thermal is utilized to obtain temperature distribution from the model. Experiments are conducted to validate results obtained from the model. The validated FE model is used to predict road test thermal performance of the PCM in steady and transient ambient temperature conditions. The FE analysis predictions are compared with temperatures observed in the road tests.

## CONCLUSIONS

Excellent agreement between results obtained from FE model and those observed in field tests show that an experimentally validated thermal model can be effectively employed in assessing thermal performance of electronic assemblies. However, realistic power dissipation estimates are critical in these assessments, especially for electronics that use digital circuits. It is noted that the realistic power estimates are not the simultaneous superposition of worst case power dissipation from each electronic component. To obtain a "lean and mean" design realistic power estimates are critical.

## SUMMARY

A large number of product packaging designs can now be studied for cost effective design alternatives that meet or exceed design requirements, in their concept design phase using up-front analysis. Finite element modeling complemented with validation experiments can serve as a good analysis tool. Rapid prototyping methods can be used to obtain specimen in metal or in plastic that are representative of the intended product for conducting heat transfer experiments to validate a model.

# Micro-Macro-Micro Modeling in Electronic Packaging

Stelios Michaelides
Graduate Research Assistant
and
Suresh K. Sitaraman
Assistant Professor


Manufacturing Research Center
and
Computer-Aided Simulation of Packaging Reliability (CASPaR) Laboratory
The George W. Woodruff School of Mechanical Engineering
Georgia Institute Of Technology
Atlanta, GA 30332-0405


Voice:404-894-3405
FAX: 404-894-9342
e-mail: suresh.sitaraman@me.gatech.edu

## Introduction and Background

Micro-electronic packages continue to become smaller, lighter, faster and cheaper. Flip Chip technology, where the silicon die is directly attached to the substrate, demonstrates many desirable characteristics when compared to other packaging technologies. These characteristics include substrate area reduction, cost reduction, denser integration, improved thermal and electrical performance and higher yields due to the elimination of lead coplanarity problems. At the system level, the flip-chip technology provides advantages such as six sigma solder assembly yields, enhanced performance, elimination of some passive components, and reduction in size, weight and cost. Despite the many advantages that flip-chip technology has to offer, there are also serious obstacles to its widespread use. These disadvantages are related to its reliability performance, especially when used with organic substrate.

In many applications (such as automotive underhood environments) flip chips are required to operate under extreme ambient temperatures. Normal chip operation, as well as severe environmental conditions, result in thermal expansion in the die, the interconnects and in the substrate. The large difference in the values of the CTE between the die and that of most organic substrates results in the presence of thermal stresses inside the die, solder and substrate [1,2]. The thermal stress is manifested as shear strain on the solder bumps and it eventually results in fracture and electrical failure of the component.

Although finite-element technique has been used by a number of researchers to determine the thermal stresses in the solder bumps, most of them have reported that FEM in modeling electronic packages is not straight forward because one needs to work with devices that differ in size by several orders of magnitude [1,3]. Attempting to create and solve a single model of the flip chip would result in problematic computer storage requirements and numerical difficulties. Another difficulty arises from the high homologous operating temperatures that necessitate the use of nonlinear constitutive equations to describe the mechanical behavior of the materials [4,5].

## Research Objectives, Methodology, and Results

The aim of this research is to provide design guidelines that help maximize the fatigue lifetime of flip chips in harsh environments, using a Micro-Macro-Micro model. Control parameters, such as the pad and die dimensions, substrate height, solder location etc., and their appropriate values will be determined based on the results obtained through the Micro-Macro-Micro model.

Ideally, it would be preferable to construct a single finite-element model with sufficient amount of details to represent all of the devices including the solder joint regions to determine the plastic strain distribution. Such a model would be computationally expensive. In the three-step micro-macro-micro model, first a micro-analysis will be done on leads and solder joints to determine equivalent beam elements, then a macro-analysis will be done on the entire assembly where leads and solder joints will be modeled using equivalent elements, and finally a detailed micro-analysis will be done modeling leads and solder joints in detail and applying the boundary conditions obtained through the macro-analysis.

The upper and lower boundaries of the micro-model will be displaced in sufficiently small steps laterally and axially in compression to determine the nonlinear stiffness characteristics of the solder joint structure. The reaction forces (shear and moment for simple shear for the lateral movement and compressive stresses for the axial moment) are determined in the micro-model. The equivalent beam stiffness, in the elastic region, is determined by applying the same displacements and ensuring that the reaction forces match those obtained through the micro-model. In the plastic region, however, the stress-strain curve of the equivalent beam elements is adjusted to maintain similar matching of reaction forces between the micro model and the equivalent beam model. Such an "equivalent" model will reduce the number of elements in the macro model by two orders of magnitude [1]. After micro-modeling, the macro model is created by modeling the larger devices as plate elements and smaller devices as equivalent beam elements. Only one quarter of the geometry needs to be modeled due to symmetry. a series of temperature steps is chosen to simulate the thermal cycle. Warpage prediction is done using the macro model.

The macro-level displacements are used as boundary conditions for the third-step micro-level model of the solder bumps. The micro-model provides detailed strain contours which will be used to optimize the shape of the solder bump. For the characterization of 63/37 Sn/Pb solder behavior, a power-law equation or a Bodner-Partom unified creep-plasticity model may be used [4]. The substrate is modeled as an orthotropic material. For the lifetime estimation a generalized Coffin-Manson equation [2], that relates the total strain (elastic and plastic) to the number of cycles to failure, is used. The Micro-Macro-Micro method, used in the research, is found to be a successful approach for modeling the

mechanical behavior of an electronic package. It is conceptually simple, easy to implement and the computational cost is not prohibitive.

## Bibliography

1. Corbin J.S., "Finite Element Analysis of Solder Ball Connect(SBC) Structural Design Optimization", IBM *J. Research and Development* Vol. 37, No.5, pp.585-596, September 1993.
2. Barker D., Vodzak J., Dasgupta A., Pecht M., "Combined Vibrational And Thermal Solder Joint Fatigue-A Generalized Strain Versus Life Approach", *J. of Electronic Packaging*, Vol.112, pp.129-134, June 1990
3. Shephard, M.S., Sham, T.L., Song, L.Y., Wong, V.S., Garimella, R., Tiersten, H.F., Lwo, B.J., Le Coz, Y.L., Iverson, R. B."Global/Local analyses of multichip modules: automated 3-D model construction and adaptive finite element analysis.", *Advances in Electronic Packaging American Society of Mechanical Engineers*, EEP Vol. 4-1 1993.
4. Skipor A., Botsis J., Harren S., "Constitutive Characterization of 67/37 Sn/Pb Eutectic Solder Using The Bodner-Partom Unified Creep-Plasticity Model", *Advances in Electronic Packaging, ASME 1992.*
5. Busso, E., Kitano, M., Kumazawa, T., "Visco-plastic constitutive model for 60/40 tin-lead solder used in IC package joints.", *Journal of Engineering Materials and Technology*, Transactions of the ASME, Vol. 114 n 3 Jul 1992
6. Lau, J.H., "Thermomechanical Characterization of Flip Chip Solder Bumps For Multichip Module Applications", *IEEE/CHMT Int. Electronics Manufacturing Technology Symposium*, 1992.
7. Lau, J.H., "Thermal Fatigue Life Prediction of Flip Chip Solder Joints By Fracture Mechanics Method", *Engineering Fracture Mechanics*, Vol.45, No. 5., 1993.
8. Verma S., Dasgupta A., Barker D., "A Numerical Study of Fatigue Life of J-Leaded Solder Joints Using The Energy Partitioning Approach", *J. of Electronic Packaging, Transactions of the* ASME, Vol. 115, Dec. 1993.

# A Finite Element Analysis of Stresses Generated in Curing Epoxies

R. S. Chambers, D. B. Adolf, J. E. Martin, T. R. Guess, R. R. Lagasse, and S. E. Gianoulakis
Sandia National Laboratories
P.O. Box 5800
Albuquerque, NM 87185

Analyses are routinely performed to compute stresses in cured polymers employed as electronic encapsulants, printed wiring boards, and composite structures. Finite element codes can predict the stresses which develop due to thermal gradients and mismatches between the thermal expansion coefficients of constituent materials incurred in nonisothermal operations. For crosslinking polymers such as epoxies, however, stresses can evolve during curing due to reaction exotherms, cure shrinkage, and imposed deformation fields. These "initial" stresses have typically been ignored since no complete theory has existed for modeling this behavior. This shortcoming has now been removed by the development of a formalism [1] for calculating the evolution of thermophysical properties and viscoelastic stresses during the cure. The curing model has been implemented in a structural finite element program which in turn has been coupled to a thermal code so that the reaction kinetics, heat transfer, and stress generation can be computed in complex three dimensional geometries. A demonstration of these capabilities is presented.

As a first step in validating the formalism for modeling the chemical kinetics and stress generation in a crosslinking polymer, a complete set of material properties was collected for the diglycidyl ether of bisphenol A cured with diethanolamine (DEA). Using these material properties, a validation test was analyzed and the results were compared to experimental measurements. The validation test consisted of thin-walled aluminum tubes filled with the epoxy and cured in an oven held nominally at 90˚C. Each test involved two tubes. One tube was instrumented with strain gauges to measure the hoop and axial strains at three points around the circumference of the middle of the tube. The second tube was fitted with temperature sensors to measure the surface temperature on the outer wall of the tube and the temperature histories in the epoxy at the center and near the inner wall inside the tube. A schematic of the tube instrumentation is shown in Figure 1. In modeling the curing process, the outer wall temperature history of the aluminum tube was specified to be equal to the temperature measured during the experiment. This was done to depict a reasonable set of thermal boundary conditions representative of the actual oven environment. The kinetic equations and material properties were then used to predict the subsequent exotherm and degree of cure throughout the epoxy. A comparison between the temperature history measured in the center of the tube and the value computed in the finite element analysis is shown in Figure 2. The agreement is excellent with the most uncertainty occurring at early times when the temperature is still changing after the epoxy has been mixed, poured into the tubes, and placed into the oven. Based on the thermal and reaction history predicted by this analysis, the structural finite element code was used to model the evolution of shrinkage and stress generation in the epoxy-filled tube. The corresponding plot comparing measured and predicted hoop strains is provided in Figure 3. Here the out-of-roundness in the aluminum tubes is apparent from the spread in the magnitude of the measured hoop strains taken at points equally spaced around the circumference of the tube. Because the finite element model was constructed as a section sliced from a three dimensional axisymmetric geometry, the asymmetry was not represented in the analysis. The discontinuity in the strain gauge data at about 900 minutes into the test was precipitated by a delamination and fracture of the constrained epoxy. However, up to the time of failure, the general agreement is quite good both in the shape and magnitude of the predicted strain history. Although more validation tests are planned, the preliminary agreement has given confidence that the formalism, numerical implementation, and finite element software development are functioning as expected.

Acknowledgement:

This work was supported by the U. S. Department of Energy under contract DE-AC04-94AL85000.

## References

1. Adolf, D. B. and J. E. Martin, "Calculation of Stresses in Crosslinking Polymers," *J. Comp. Mat.*, Vol. 30, No. 1, 1996.

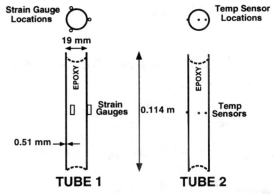

Figure 1.    Tubes and Instrumentation Setup Used in Validation Tests

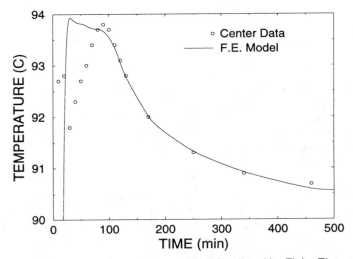

Figure 2.    Center Tube Temperatures Measured and Predicted by Finite Element Analysis

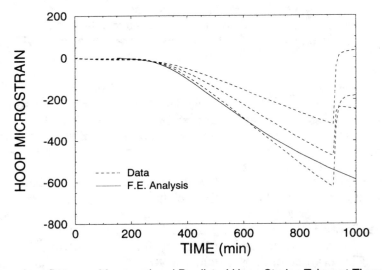

Figure 3.    Comparison Between Measured and Predicted Hoop Strains Taken at Three Points Around
Circumference of Epoxy-Filled Tube During Curing

# Moiré Interferometry as Applied to Electronic Packaging Product Development

B. Han, Y. Guo and C.K. Lim

IBM Microelectronics Division
MS E22, Bldg. 257/3A
1701 North St.
Endicott, NY 13760

Moiré interferometry is a rather new technique but has matured rapidly to emerge as an invaluable engineering tool. Moiré interferometry is characterized by several excellent qualities [1]: (1) real-time technique-the displacement fields can be viewed as loads are applied, (2) in-situ measurement technique-broad range of engineering materials can be tested, including metals, ceramics, solder material, composites, etc., (3) high displacement measurement sensitivity, (4) high spatial resolution-measurements can be made in tiny zones, (5) high signal-to-noise ratio-the fringe patterns have high contrast, excellent visibility, and (6) large dynamic range-the method is compatible with a large range of displacements, strains, and strain gradients. These unique features of moiré interferometry make it an exceptionally attractive tool for deformation studies of a broad range of problems in electronic packaging.

Recently, the applicability of the method was extended to electronic packaging product development [2], where a special grating replication technique was first employed to allow specimen grating replication on an electronic packaging assembly with a complex geometry. Numerous other applications have been followed thereafter. This survey paper reviews recent developments in moiré interferometry as a tool for deformation studies of electronic packaging products and illustrates several selected applications in electronics packaging, more specifically, (1) thermal deformation analyses [3], (2) verification of numerical models [4] and (3) determination of effective coefficient of thermal expansion [5].

REFERENCES:

1. D. Post, B. Han and P. Ifju, *High Sensitivity Moiré: Experimental Analysis for Mechanics and Materials*, Springer-Verlag, 1994.

2. Guo, Y., Lim, C. K., Chen, W. T., and Woychik, C. G., 1993, "Solder Ball Connect (SBC) Assemblies under Thermal Loading: I. Deformation Measurement via Moiré Interferometry, and Its Interpretation," *IBM Journal of Research and Development*, Vol. 37, No. 5, pp. 635-648.

3. B. Han and Y. Guo, "Thermal Deformation Analysis of Various Electronic Packaging Products by Moiré and Microscopic Moiré Interferometry," *Journal of Electronic Packaging, Transaction of the ASME*, Vol. 117, No. 3, pp. 185-191, 1995.

4. B. Han, Y. Guo and C. K. Lim, "Verification of Numerical Models Used in Microelectronics Packaging Design by Interferometric Displacement Measurement Methods," *Journal of Electronic Packaging, Transaction of the ASME*, (submitted for publication), 1995.

5. B. Han and Y. Guo, "Determination of Effective Coefficient of Thermal Expansion of Electronic Packaging Components: A Whole-field Approach, *IEEE Transactions on Components, Packaging and Manufacturing Technology-Part A*, (accepted for publication), 1996.

# Investigation of Crack Tip Fields Near Copper-Solder Interfaces‡

Hariram Krishnamoorthy and Hareesh V. Tippur†
Department of Mechanical Engineering
202 Ross Hall, Auburn University, Alabama 36849-5341

Dissimilar materials with drastically different electrical, mechanical, and thermal properties constitute electronic packages. Often interfacial regions are the sites of failure initiation through cracking. The concepts of interfacial fracture mechanics would be necessary for characterizing interfacial failures encountered in electronic packages. Of many different interfaces which occur in a typical package, the ones between copper and solder are quite common. At the moment, the availability of fracture toughness and crack growth resistance data for this material combination is rather limited. Pratt et al., [1] have reported fracture toughness of copper and eutectic solider joints by using homogeneous fracture mechanics concepts and ASTM standard specimens for mode-I testing. This paper presents preliminary experimental results on deformation fields near interfacial cracks in copper-solder (63/37) bimaterial models using moire interferometry.

The samples were prepared from commercially available strips of copper and solder. The machined strips of the two materials were bonded to each other along an edge under controlled laboratory conditions by heating the copper strip by thermofoils in a specially designed Teflon fixture. The joining surface was treated with RMA flux (Kester 185) prior to soldering. A 4 mm edge crack was introduced into each sample ($a/W = 0.33$, $W = 12.5$ mm, thickness=5 mm). The sample surfaces were finished using sand paper (600 to 2000 grit) in the interfacial region and line gratings (3000 lpi) were printed parallel to the interface in order to map the crack opening displacement contours. The well known photoresist technique is used for printing the lines gratings. The specimens were loaded in three point bending configuration (support distance=82 mm) as shown in Fig.1(a) using a displacement controlled loading device. The location of the loading point $s$ is varied between the experiments in order to study the influence of the sense of the shear stress on the crack tip deformations. The specimen grating was interrogated by two collimated intersecting laser beams for generating the moire fringes. An existing Mach-Zehnder interferometry set-up [2] with a slight modification is used for creating the two intersecting collimated laser beams on the specimen plane. The standing wave and the specimen gratings interfere and form moire fringes. In each experiment, the interference patterns and the applied load data were acquired for approximately 60-100 seconds during which crack tip

deformation fields were imaged from no-load conditions to crack initiation and quasi-static propagation. An example of moire fringes representing contours of constant crack opening displacements ($u_2$ fringes) are shown in Figs.1(b) and (c). These fringe patterns correspond to situations when the applied load was acting at a distance of 5 mm away from the interface on the copper (Fig.1(b)) and the solder (Fig. 1(c)) halves of the bimaterial flexural samples. The differences in the crack tip fringes are evident for these two cases when the sense of the imposed shear acting on the interfacial plane are reversed. Extraction of fracture parameters from the deformation fields is currently underway.

## References:

1. R.E. Pratt, E.I. Stromswold and D.J. Quensnel, 'Mode-I fracture toughness testing of eutectic Sn-Pb solider joints', J. Electronic Materials, Vol.23, No.4, 1994.

2. P. Ganeshan and H.V. Tippur, 'Thermal-Mechanical loading of interface cracks: Crack tip stress measurement and crack initiation', AU/ME/HT Report 95/10, submitted to Experimental Mechanics, 1995.

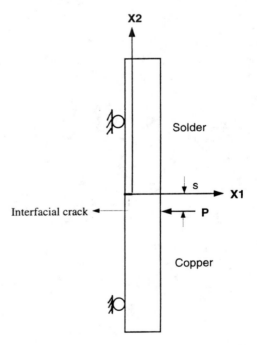

Figure 1(a): Bimaterial specimen and the loading configuration.

---

‡ for presentation at the VIII Intl. Cong. on Experimental Mechanics, Nashville, TN, 1996.
†Graduate Student and Associate Professor, respectively.

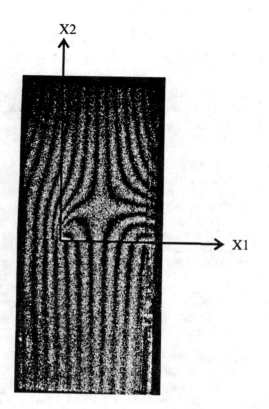

Figure 1(b): Moire fringes for positive shear stress acting on the interfacial plane; load level 390 N.

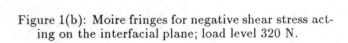

Figure 1(b): Moire fringes for negative shear stress acting on the interfacial plane; load level 320 N.

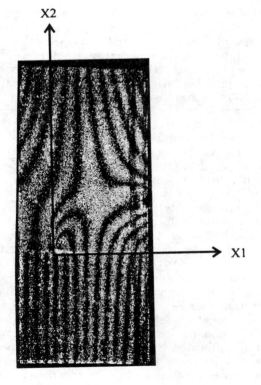

# Temperature Dependent Mapping and Modeling Verification of Thermomechanical Deformation in Plastic Packaging Structures Using Moiré Interferometry

Xiang Dai[a], Connie Kim[a], Ralf Willecke[a], Tze W. Poon[b], Paul S. Ho[a]

[a] Interconnect & Packaging Group, University of Texas, PRC/MER, Mail Code R8650, Austin, TX 78712
[b] SEMATECH, Assembly and Packaging, 2706 Montopolis Dr., Austin, TX 78741

Moiré interferometer is an optical technique to measure whole-field in-plane deformation of a specimen [1]. The inherent sensitivity and spatial resolution of this method make it well suited for a broad range of investigations for thermomechanical behavior of electronic packages. However, moiré interferometry studies of thermal loading on electronics packages are commonly carried out between two fixed temperatures. The information deduced is restricted only to the changes occurring between the reference and room temperatures, with no information provided between those two temperatures. In electronic packages, the materials usually have temperature dependent properties and thus give rise to temperature dependent thermomechanical behavior. Therefore, it is necessary and meaningful to follow the evolution of the overall and local deformation as a function of temperature. Furthermore, experiments are usually carried out without environmental control. As smaller, cheaper, and lighter packages are pursuit in the microelectronics industry, polymeric materials begin to play a more and more important role in boosting the performance and reducing the cost. It is also known that those polymeric materials are sensitive to the environment. The environmental effect, such as moisture induced swelling, and thermomechanical effect can not be separated and studied thoroughly without environmental control. The environmental effect itself, such as moisture uptake, can not be investigated either.

For these reasons, an environmental chamber, where both temperature and atmosphere can be controlled, has been developed for moiré interferometry. With this chamber, one can carry out real-time, in-situ mapping of thermomechanical deformation as a function of temperature in an atmosphere with controlled amount of humidity. It is demonstrated through a study on a glob top encapsulated chip on board (COB) package [2].

The environmental chamber and support carriage were used with a Portable Engineering Moiré Interferometer(PEMI) from IBM to acquire in situ deformation patterns as a function of temperature in a controlled atmosphere. The package was first cut in half to expose a cross-section (Fig. 1). A specimen grating was replicated over the cross-section area from an ULE glass grating mold at 102 °C. The specimen was put into the environmental chamber and was heated to 102 °C in dry nitrogen ambient. The system, including the supporting carriage and PEMI, was tuned to obtain null (u and v) fields over the specimen surface at 102 °C. The moiré patterns of u and v displacement fields (Fig. 2 and Fig. 3) were collected by a CCD camera and recorded in a digital format by a personal computer at 82 °C, 62 °C, 42 °C, and 22 °C upon cooling.

The deformations of the die-encap interface (Fig.4 and Fig. 5) as a function of temperature are evaluated. Thermal strains at certain critical locations are also deduced as a function of temperature. To further evaluate thermal strain concentrations, an area in the encapsulant near the die edge is chosen to be examined. A computer aided image processing was performed to calculate the strain values over the whole area. And the calculated strain values were used to construct the thermal strain contour maps.

The experimental results are compared with the modeling results of a finite element analysis. The overall trend of the modeling results is found to be consistent with that of the experimental results. The quantitative discrepancy may be from the inaccurate material property data and the linear elastic assumption used in the model.

Acknowledgments

This work was supported in part by the Semiconductor Research Corporation under the contract 94-PJ-320 at the University of Texas at Austin.

References:

1. Post, D., Han, B., and Ifju, P., High Sensitivity Moiré, Spring-Verlag, NY, 1994.

2. Robinson, D. L., Papageoge, M., and Naito, C., "A New Epoxy Based Liquid Encapsulant with Performance Comparable to Mold Compounds," The International Journal of Microcircuits and Electronic Packaging, Vol. 17, No. 2, 2nd Quarter 1994, pp. 176-183.

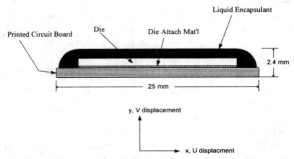

Figure 1 A glob top chip on board package under study.

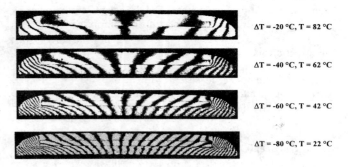

ΔT = -20 °C, T = 82 °C

ΔT = -40 °C, T = 62 °C

ΔT = -60 °C, T = 42 °C

ΔT = -80 °C, T = 22 °C

Figure 2 Horizontal (U) displacement fields under thermal loading conditions (reference temperature = 102 °C).

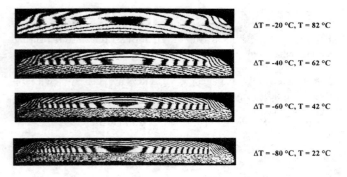

ΔT = -20 °C, T = 82 °C

ΔT = -40 °C, T = 62 °C

ΔT = -60 °C, T = 42 °C

ΔT = -80 °C, T = 22 °C

Figure 3 Vertical (V) displacement fields under thermal loading conditions (reference temperature = 102 °C).

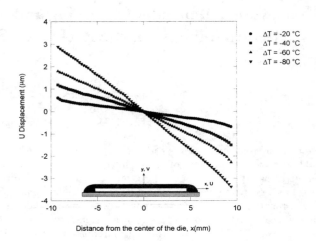

Figure 4 Horizontal displacement of the die-encap interface under thermal loading conditions.

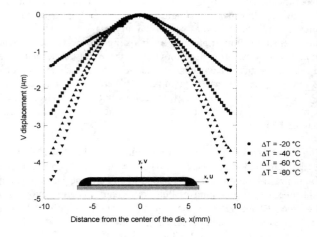

Figure 5 Vertical displacement of the die-encap interface under thermal loading conditions.

# Moiré Analysis and Modeling of Area Array Assemblies

T. I Ejim
Lucent Technologies
Bell Labs Innovations
P. O. Box 900
Princeton, NJ. 08551
and
J-P Clech, EPSI Inc.
P. O. Box 1522
Montclair, NJ. 07042

There are a number of interconnect levels that affect the functionality of a circuit pack. One of those, the second level interconnect, typically uses solder (lead-tin) to connect the electronic component to the printed wiring board (PWB) and therefore allows communication between the components on the board. The reliability of this second level interconnection is known to be very dependent on material properties and design parameters of the component and the printed wiring board. Advances in packaging technology are placing more demands on solder interconnect reliability, with solder joints of leadless PBGA assemblies being more susceptible to early wear-out failures than solder joints of the compliant leaded assemblies. A quick technique for both qualitative and quantitative evaluation of the attachment reliability of second level interconnection is very useful for emerging components. In recent years, the reliability of area-array plastic assemblies has received considerable attention.[1], [2], This paper will discuss the application of moiré interferometry and empirical modeling in evaluating the attachment reliability of the emerging plastic ball grid array (PBGA) electronic packages.

The first part of this paper will describe a design-for-reliability model, Solder Reliability Solutions (SRS 1.0) and reliability predictions made with it. Results show that the design parameters that impact on the PBGA assembly reliability include pad diameter, die size and thickness, laminate thickness and solder joint height.
The Solder Reliability Solutions (SRS 1.0) model includes the following features:
- Bending of parts which is important for the leadless PBGAs where the component flexural compliance, which depends on package contents and construction, provides for significant stress and strain relief in the solder joints.

- Inelastic strain energy is from complete hysteresis loops with different dwell times on the hot and cold sides of the thermal cycling profile.
- The local mismatch stress/strain response is determined from the combined and simultaneous action of solder/board and solder/lead (or component) CTE and modulus mismatch. The analysis uses a tri-layer model which also accounts for local effects of board to lead (or component) CTE and modulus mismatches.
- The fatigue life correlation is done as the joint characteristic lives scaled for the solder crack area versus the calculated cyclic inelastic strain energy.[3]

The second part will show the results of parametric analysis done with moiré interferometric technique and compare them with the SRS 1.0 predictions. Moiré fringes were used to calculate the maximum strain induced on the solder joints for a given thermal load. The calculated strains were normalized to the surface mount pad diameters, component standoff heights and the BT-substrate thickness to get the impact of these parameters on attachment reliability. The results show that the pad size, the solder joint height and the package substrate thickness affect the maximum solder joint strain for a 60°C change in temperature. The results are in agreement with the trend in characteristic life values from life test results

New BGA designs like the enhanced 540 I/O packages with integral heat spreader, the metal BGA (MBGA) and Tape BGA (TBGA) were also evaluated with the moiré interferometry and the results will be presented and also compared with life test results.

References:
1. Theo I. Ejim, Albert Holliday, Frank E. Bader and Steven Gahr, Designed Experiment to determine Attachment Reliability Drivers for PBGA Packages,

Surface Mount International conference proceedings, San Jose, Ca. August 1995, pp385-392.

2. Robert Darveaux, and Andrew Mawer, Thermal and Power Cycling Limits of Plastic Ball Grid Array (PBGA) Assemblies, Surface Mount International conference proceedings, San Jose, Ca. August 1995, pp 315-326.

3. J-P Clech, J. C. Manock, D. M. Noctor and F. E. Bader, AT&T Comprehensive Surface Mount Reliability Model: Validation and Applications, Proceeding of the 1993 Surface Mount International Conference, San Jose, Ca.

# Effect of Underfill Encapsulation on Solder Joint Reliability of Plastic Ball Grid Array Package Assembly

K. Verma[1], B. Han[2], M. Prakash[1] and D. Caletka[2]


Dept. of Mechanical Engineering
State University of New York at Binghamton
Binghamton, NY

IBM Microelectronics Division
IBM Corporation
Endicott, NY

Plastic Ball Grid Array (PBGA) package provides enhanced fatigue reliability of solder ball interconnections compared with Ceramic Ball Grid Array (CBGA) packages because of reduced coefficient of thermal expansion (CTE) mismatch between the package and the printed circuit board (PCB) [1]. Although the reliability is sufficient for most of general consumer products, a higher level of reliability is required for harsher environments such as automotive under-the-hood or military applications [2].

The innovative underfill encapsulation technique has been implemented successfully for a flip chip on an organic substrate package in spite of a large CTE mismatch between the chip and the substrate. In the package, the encapsulation fills a space between the chip and substrate, which results in significant reduction of the fatigue damage of solder joints. Recently, the use of the encapsulation technique was extended to PBGA package assemblies for further enhancement of solder joint reliability [2] but the effect of the encapsulation was not clearly understood.

In this paper, a non-linear 3-D FEM analysis is conducted to examine the effect of the encapsulation on solder joint strains. The assembly examined in the analysis is a 255 I/O PBGA package connected to a FR4/glass PCB by eutectic solder ball arrays, as illustrated in Fig. 1. A 3-D FEM model is built for the assemblies without and with encapsulation using ANSYS V.5.2. As illustrated in Fig. 2, the model contains only one center row of solder balls due to the limitation of memory and computation time. The total permanent strains (effective plastic + creep strain) accumulated during thermal cycles are calculated and the results are used to estimate reliability enhancement provided by the encapsulation. The creep model used in the analysis is based on the constitutive relations suggested by Knecht and Fox [3].

Figure 3 shows a preliminary result from a 2-D analysis, where the normalized maximum permanent strain is plotted along the solder balls. The effect of encapsulation is clear. With the encapsulation, the location of the maximum permanent strain is shifted from the solder joint located at the edge of the chip to the one with the largest distance from the neutral point. The encapsulation increases the stiffness of interconnection layer, and thus reduces the effect of the presence of the silicon chip. The preliminary result also indicates that the magnitude of the maximum permanent strain is reduced approximately by 30% with the encapsulation.

## REFERENCES

1. R. Darveaux, K. Banerji, A. Mawer and G. Dody, *Ball Grid Array Technology*, J. Lau ed., Ch. 13 Reliability of Plastic Ball Grid Array Assembly, McGraw-Hill, NY, 1995.

2. T. R. Lindley, "BGA Solder Joint Reliability Study for Automotive Electronics," *Proceedings of ICEMCM '95*, pp. 126-133, 1995

3. S. Knecht and L. R. Fox, "Constitutive Relation and Creep-Fatigue Life Model for Eutectic Tin-Lead Solder," *IEEE Transactions on Components, Hybrids, and Manufacturing Technology*, Vol. 13, No. 2, pp. 424-433, 1990.

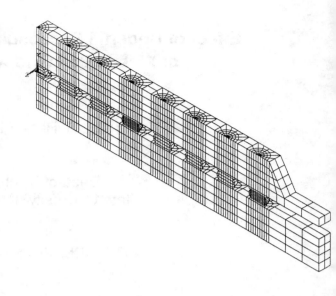

Fig. 2  3-D FEM model

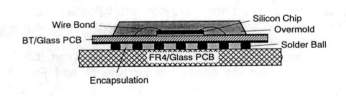

Fig. 1  Schematic diagram of PBGA assembly

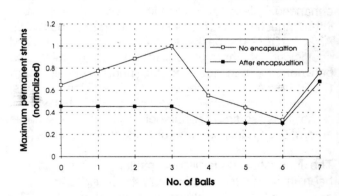

Fig. 3  Normalized maximum permanent strains along the solder balls from a preliminary 2-D analysis, where solder ball #0 is located at the neutral axis.

# THERMAL STRAIN ANALYSIS IN PBGA SOLDER JOINTS USING HYBRID METHOD

Yifan Guo
Motorola Semiconductor Products Sector
2100 E. Elliot Rd. Tempe, AZ 85284
Li Li
IBM Microelectronics Division
1701 North Street, Endicott, NY 13760

The mechanical reliability of the solder joints in the Ball Grid Array (BGA) technology has significant impact on the system reliability of an electronic device and, therefore, is critical in package designs and qualifications. The major concern of solder joint reliability is the solder fatigue during system operation. Since the solder fatigue life is related to the thermal-mechanical strains, the mechanical reliability analysis of the solder joints can be conducted through the analysis of the thermal-mechanical strains.

In recent years, many new analytical and experimental techniques have been developed and applied to electronics industry. Numerical methods, such as finite element method (FEM), have become so powerful due to super computers and advanced software that complicated geometry and material properties can be modeled and simulated. Experimentally, moiré interferometry, a highly sensitive optical method which provides in-situ measurements and full-field display of deformations and strains in the package assemblies and individual solder joints, has evolved into a powerful experimental tool in thermal strain analysis. The hybrid method which combines numerical and experimental methods to achieve high efficiency and accuracy has also been developed and applied in the thermal strain analyses in electronic packaging [1].

Plastic ball grid array (PBGA) package is a package where organic material, such as glass/epoxy laminate is used as the chip carrier (Fig. 1). Because of the influence of the silicon chip, The PBGA module usually has lower effective CTE (Coefficient of Thermal Expansion) than the PCB (Printed Circuit Board). The CTE mismatch in the package induces thermal strain and stress in the solder joints during thermal cycles and causes solder fatigue failures. The thermal strain and stress are closely related to the solder joint geometry and therefore, the fatigue life can be dramatically improved by optimizing the joint geometry.

In practice, the solder joints are formed when the solder balls are attached to the modules and the substrates. The joint geometry varies due to the different attachment processes. For example, in the so called SMD (solder mask defined) attachment process or the NSMD (non solder mask defined) attachment process (Fig.2), the contact area (between the solder and the copper pad) and the fillet shapes are very different, which results in significant difference in local joint geometry. Because the local strain distributions and the maximum strains are closely related to the local geometry of the solder joints, during thermal cycles, same components assembled with different attachment processes showed great difference in solder fatigue life.

Due to the small scale of the local joint structure, it is extremely difficult for an experimental tool to directly measure the accurate strain values. Moiré interferometry can provide accurate relative displacements and average strains in the solder joint and its vicinity by measuring the global deformation of the whole package assembly. However, the local strain distribution in a particular solder joint, which determines the maximum strain, can not be resolved accurately. A local FEM model, which precisely models the local joint geometry with fine meshes, can offer much better resolution in the local strain concentration of the solder joint. Because only the strain concentration factors, rather than the absolute strain values, are calculated in the FEM model, the strain results are mostly sensitive to the joint geometry but relatively insensitive to the solder property when different joint geometry are compared. By combining the accurate average strain measured from the experiments and the strain concentration factor calculated from the local FEM model, much more realistic maximum strain values are obtained.

Figure 3 shows an example of moiré fringe patterns where the relative displacements and average strains are obtained. The actual values, which are listed in the Table 1 as the shear displacement and average shear strain, represent the thermal deformations in the assembly due to a temperature change of $\Delta T=80°C$. The shear displacement values are used for the boundary conditions in the local FEM analysis. The local FEM models (Fig.4) calculate the strain concentration factor for each joint configurations using the relative displacements obtained from the moiré experiments as the displacement boundary conditions. The combined strain values are shown in the Table 1 as the maximum strain which is the average strain multiplied by the strain concentration factor. These maximum strain values were used to estimate the fatigue life of each type of solder joints assembled with different ball attachment processes.

Reference:

[1] Y. Guo and CK Lim, "Hybrid Method for Strain/Stress Analysis in Electronic Packaging Using Moiré Interferometry and FEM," Proceedings of 1994 SEM Spring Conference, June 6, 1994, Baltimore.

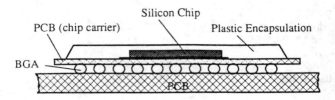

Fig.1 Plastic Ball Grid Array (PBGA) package.

Fig.3 Fringe patterns of U and V displacement fields of a PBGA package under thermal loading of ΔT=80°C.

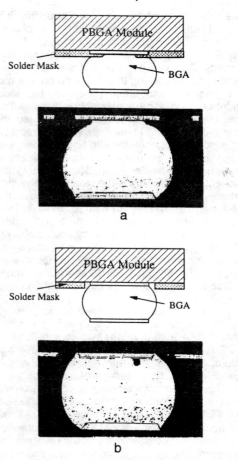

Fig.2 SMD and NSMD attachment of solder balls to PBGA modules. a. SMD, b. NSMD.

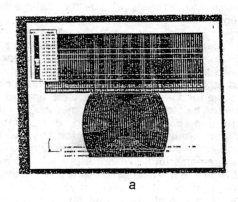

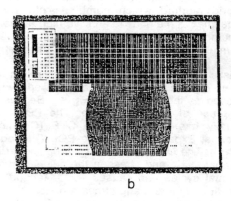

Fig.4 Local FEM models of SMD and NSMD attachment. a. SMD, b. NSMD.

### Table 1. Maximum Strain Values of the SMD and NSMD Packages

| Attachment Process | shear displacement μm | average shear strain (%) | strain concentration factor | Maximum strain (%) |
|---|---|---|---|---|
| Solder Mask Defined (SMD) | 2.7 | 0.45 | 5.8 | 2.61 |
| Non-Solder Mask Defined (NSMD) | 2.2 | 0.37 | 2.8 | 1.04 |

# Finite Element Model Validation Using Temperature Dependent Laser Moiré Interferometry

Andrew Skipor
Motorola
Corporate Manufacturing Research Center
1301 E. Algonquin Rd.
Schaumburg, IL 60196

Denise Ommen, David Jeffery, John Baird
Motorola
Logic & Analog Technologies Group
Chandler, Arizona

Xiang Dai and Paul Ho
The University of Texas at Austin
Austin, Texas

Growth in the use and capability of FEA tools in the last few years has been rapid. Use of these tools could potentially reduce package introduction time by improving material/process design applications with less dependence on experimental work for design development and proof of durability. The success of these modeling efforts is directly dependent upon the quality of the material property data, i.e., understanding nonlinearity in a quantitative sense such as time dependent behavior as found in solder joints, and anisotropy as in printed circuit boards.

To investigate validation of finite element results, that is "measure" the displacement field, the laser moiré interferometry technique was used. Measured values can include time dependent or anisotropic effects. When there is correlation between measured and FEA results, the analysis becomes important as a visualization aid, helping to understand the "physics" of the package structural problem, that is, the underlying material interactions and effects of boundary conditions. Understanding these interactions enables effective design development.

68 lead PLCC and 64 lead TQFP packages were selected as vehicles for experimental evaluation by laser moiré interferometry. These plastic packages represent "typical" yet significantly different package designs. The PLCC is an older design where the die, die flag, and leads represent a very small fraction of the total package volume. On the other hand, for the TQFP which represents a more recent small outline package design, the die, die flag, and leads represent a much larger volume fraction than that of the PLCC package. Since the volume fraction of the package contents in the TQFP is greater then that of the PLCC, appreciable differences should be observed in their deformation resulting from thermal expansion mismatch between components.

Moiré interferometry is an optical technique providing whole-field in-plane contour maps of displacement where each contour (fringe) represents a line of constant displacement [1]. When two gratings are co-planar and the line spacing of one is changed relative to the other, a moiré pattern is observed. The moiré pattern contains the two-dimensional displacement field data, from which the strain field can be obtained by differentiation. In the technique used here, an optically generated virtual grating interacts with the grating applied to the specimen to produce a moiré pattern.

The physical grating was bonded (replicated) to the specimen at two different temperatures, 100°C and 80°C. The temperature at which the grating is applied to the specimen represents the reference condition of the specimen. The specimen with the physical grating is then cooled to room temperature and illuminated by a virtual grating created by the intersection of two laser beams. The moiré data produced in this way has fairly high contrast and visibility. The Portable Engineering Moiré Interferometer (PEMI) system from IBM was used. The displacement resolution is 0.417 microns per fringe. Extensive details of moiré interferometry and the experimental method can be found in [2].

An environmental chamber and support carriage for moiré interferometry was used to acquire in-situ deformation patterns as a function of temperature in a controlled atmosphere. The sample was placed into the environmental chamber and heated up to 100°C in dry nitrogen ambient. The system including the supporting carriage and PEMI was tuned to get null (U and V) fields over the TQFP package at 100°C. The moiré patterns of U and V displacement fields were recorded by computer at 80°C, 60°C, 40°C and 21°C.

The 68 lead PLCC 1/8th symmetry 3D model was meshed with 8-node linear brick elements. The 64 lead TQFP is a 1/8th symmetry 3D model utilizing 8-node linear brick and 6-node linear prism elements. Temperature dependent Young's modulus and coefficient of thermal expansion properties were measured. Specimens for the material property characterization were excised from molded packages fabricated using standard production processing [3].

The PLCC and TQFP models were analyzed with the assumed zero stress state at 175°C. Solutions were obtained for nodal displacements at 100°C, 80°C, and 21°C. Changes in displacement with respect to the 175°C state are dependent on both the direct and interactive effects of the CTE and elastic moduli of the materials within the package.

In-plane displacements were computed from the 175°C zero stress state to the three temperatures in question for the top surface of the plastic packages. The expectation was that FEA and moiré would indicate the structural effect of the die and flag on the plastic package surface. The change in displacement from 100°C to 21°C and 80°C to 21°C from the analysis was compared to the moiré results. In addition, finite element results were generated at 40°C, 60°C, 80°C, and 100°C.

Figure 1 is the moiré pattern on the top surface of the TQFP package at 21°C with a 100°C reference (replication) temperature. The corresponding pattern generated from numerical analysis for the same surface at 21°C with an 80°C reference temperature, is also presented in Figure 1. For both the analytical and experimental result, each fringe represents 0.417 microns of displacement. Figure 2 shows the moiré and finite element displacement field results for the TQFP. Model results were plotted with both the assumed 100°C and 80°C reference temperatures. The experimental results with the 80°C reference temperature appeared to have better agreement with the 100°C model results. It was later determined that the actual temperature inside the oven was less than 100°C but greater than 80°C.

Slight expansion of the top surface of the package was found over the die region, even though the package exhibited overall shrinkage due to cooling, Figure 2. This result is due to the bending of the package as it cools. Warping or bending of the package is in part the result of mismatches in CTE of the die, die attach, flag, and mold compound. In effect, the restrained shrinkage of the top plastic surface is overcome by the warpage of the part producing a net in-plane expansion of the encapsulating plastic in this region over the die.

Close agreement between analytical and moiré experimental results show the analytical tool, based on elastic material behavior, bonded interfaces and temperature dependent material properties is important in understanding the structural interactions within the package.

Acknowledgments:
Support from Motorola APDAC-LATG and CMRC organizations is appreciated. Moiré environmental chamber research was supported in part by the Semiconductor Research Corporation under the contract 94-PJ-320 at the University of Texas at Austin.

References:
[1 ] Dally, J. and Riley, W.F., Experimental Stress Analysis, McGraw-Hill, 1978, p. 380.
[2] Post, D., Han, B., and Ifju, P., High Sensitivity Moiré, Springer-Verlag, New-York, 1994.
[3] Darveaux, R., Norton, L., and Carney, F., "Temperature Dependent Mechanical Behavior of Plastic Packaging Materials," Proc. 45th Electronic Components & Technology Conference , IEEE, 1995, pp. 1054-1058.

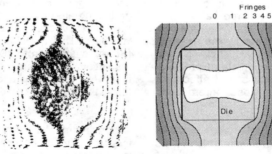

Figure 1   64 lead TQFP moiré (left) and finite element result (right).

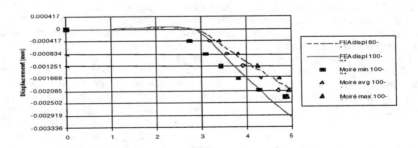

Distance from center of package (mm)

Figure 2   Displacement of the top surface of the TQFP package.

# THREE DIMENSIONAL OPTICAL INTERFEROMETRY/FINITE ELEMENT HYBRID ANALYSIS OF A PBGA PACKAGE

Yu-Po Wang, Mani Prakash
State University of New York, Binghamton, New York

Yifan Guo
IBM Microelectronics, Endicott, New York

**Extended Abstract**

## Introduction

Area array packaging is rapidly gaining acceptance in the packaging industry as a low cost alternative to fine-pitch leaded packages such as QFP's. The common area array surface mount components are ceramic and plastic Ball Grid Arrays (BGA's). Plastic Ball Grid Array (PBGA) package provides better fatigue reliability of the solder ball interconnections because of a relaxed coefficient of thermal expansion (CTE) mismatch between the chip carrier and PCB as compared to a Ceramic Ball Grid Array(CBGA). A PBGA package can be expected to survive long past the expected product lifetime and predicting their reliability accurately is important in the electronic packaging community. More often than not, large three dimensional, computer intensive finite element models are necessary to determine the thermal strain used in the reliability calculations. The accuracy of the results is dependent on the assumptions in the model, material properties and boundary conditions. Thermal strains in the solder ball are evaluated by considering a micro model of the joint.

This paper presents the concept of using three dimensional optical interferometry measurements (u,v and w displacements) as input to a micro model of a solder ball and its vicinity. This hybrid model uses Moire Interferometry for inplane (u and v) measurements and Twyman Green interferometer to measure the out of plane measurements. The measurements are made on a top surface of a BGA package. This method is an extension of two dimensional moire/fem hybrid models developed by the authors[1,2] to include the out of plane component.

## Concept of Hybrid Analysis

The concept of using a hybrid method combining experimental techniques such as moire interferometry and numerical techniques like FEM have been used by researchers[3-5] and is beginning to be applied in the field of electronics packaging[1,2]. As an alternative to traditional macro-micro finite element model, the three dimensional hybrid model uses full field moire and Twyman Green experiments to input boundary conditions to a micro model of critical sections of the structure being analyzed.

In packaging owing to the complexity of the problem involving several materials and interfaces with varying material properties, hybrid method can be shown to be extremely effective. Interferometry techniques can inherently can produce relatively accurate global values for displacement and strains for a composite material and micro FE models are accurate in predicting localized thermal strains in critical locations of the structure being analyzed.

Previous studies have used a pure FEM macro-micro approach, and have obtained the boundary conditions for the local model from the global model. This technique involves complex macro modeling whose accuracy depends on material properties, boundary conditions and mesh sizes used in the model in addition to large computational facilities and time required to solve the model. A hybrid method combining experiments and finite element modeling eliminates the necessity for a macro FEM. Moreover, the modeler can spend his or her time in making a detailed micro model in the vicinity of the solder ball and the inclusion of nonlinear material behavior becomes managable in time and resources.

Results of studies on BGA packages will be presented. The viability of this technique and its applicability to electronic packaging problems will be analyzed. Inference regarding the limitations of this technique will also be presented.

## Moire Interferometry

Moire Interferometry is a whole full-field experimental technique for determining in-plane displacements. This technique has been successfully implemented in the field of electronics packaging[1,2]. A specimen grating having 1200 lines/mm is replicated on the specimen at an elevated temperature. The specimen grating deforms along with the specimen when cooled to room temperature. The deformation of the grating represents the deformation of the specimen due to the thermal loading. The Moire Interferometry setup produces interference of two coherent beams of light to produce a virtual grating. The virtual grating is superimposed on the specimen grating, and the interaction of the two grating produces a fringe pattern which is a contour map of fringe order N. The displacements in the fringe pattern are proportional to the fringe orders N. Fringe patterns of orthogonal displacement fields are recorded to obtain the in-plane displacement fields U and V, corresponding to the x and y directions respectively. The U and V displacements can be obtained from the fringe patterns by the following equations;

$$U = \frac{N_x}{f} \qquad V = \frac{N_y}{f}$$

where Nx and Ny are the fringe orders in the corresponding fringe patterns and f is the frequency of the reference grating. The frequency of the reference grating is f = 2400 lines per mm and the displacement sensitivity is 417 nm per fringe order. Figure 1 shows the optical arrangement to measure inplane measurements in the three dimensional measurement setup.

## Twyman Green Interferometer

Twyman Green interferometry is a technique to determine surface contour with sub-micron sensitivity. A plane wave front formed from a laser is used to illuminate the surface of a plane mirror and the specimen. The mirror surface is used as the reference surface. The fringe pattern is an optical interference between the reflected beams from the specimen surface and the reference surfaces. The sensitivity of this technique is 3100 numbers of fringes per 1 mm displacement. So, the contour interval is 322 nm per fringe order. Figure 2 shows the optical arrangement to measure out of plane displacement in the three dimensional measurement setup.

## References

1. Strain Sensitivity to Geometry and Material Properties in Column Grid Array (CGA) interconnect using Hybrid Analysis, Y.P. Wang, V. Prakash, Y. Guo, *Proc. of ASME International Mechanical Engineering Conference & Exposition, San Francisco*, Nov 13-17, 1995.

2. Hybrid Method for Strain/Stress Analysis in Electronic Packaging Using Moire Interferometry and FEM, Y. Guo & C.K. Lim, *Proceedings of 1994 SEM Spring Conference & Exhibits*, June 1995, pp 321-327.

3. Hybrid Experimental-Numerical Stress Analysis, A.S. Kobayashi, Ch. 17, *Handbook of Experimental Mechanics*, 1987, pp 314-387.

4. A Localized Hybrid Method of Stress Analysis: A combination of Moire Interferometry and FEM, J. Morton, D. Post, B. Han, M.Y. Tsai, *Experimental Mechanics*, 1990, pp 195.

5. New Developments in Localized Hybrid Method of Stress Analysis, J. Morton, M.Y. Tsai, *Experimental Mechanics*, Dec 1991,pp 298-305.

6. Moire Interferometry Study of Plastic Ball Grid Array Packages, V. Prakash, Y. P. Wang, V. Valluri, *Advanced Packaging*, v4, pp 95 (also published in *Proc. of Interpak'95*).

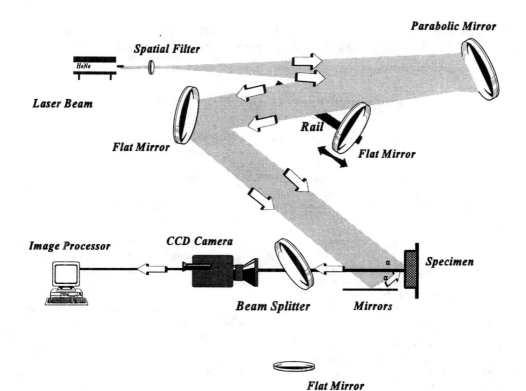

Figure 1: Moire Setup

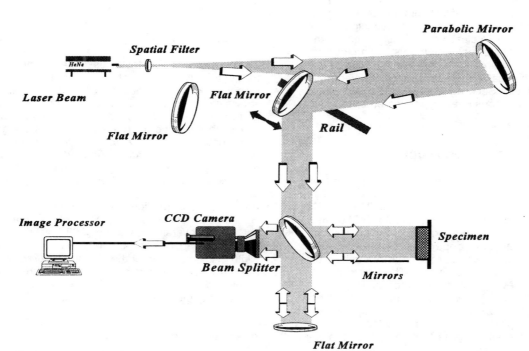

Figure 2:Twyman Green Setup

# Thermo-mechanical Characterization of Electronic Packaging Materials Using Moiré Interferometry

E. Stout, N. R. Sottos
Department of Theoretical and Applied Mechanics
University of Illinois at Urbana-Champaign
Urbana, IL 61801
phone: 217-333-1041, fax:217-244-5707, email: n-sottos@uiuc.edu

Andrew F. Skipor
Motorola Corporate Manufacturing Research Center
Schaumburg, IL 60196
phone: 708-576-0754, fax: 708-576-2111 email: aas002@email.mot.com

## Introduction

Trends towards smaller packages and higher circuit densities have made electronic packaging increasingly complex. High volume assembly techniques require surface mounting of components on printed wire boards (PWB). Understanding the thermal and mechanical response of these various components is critical for optimizing manufacturing processes to yield maximum performance and reliability. Although the finite element method has been widely utilized to predict the thermo-mechanical behavior of different package assemblies, experimental characterization remains essential for measuring properties of components and validating computational predictions.

Moiré interferometry has emerged as one of the leading experimental tools for investigating electronic materials. Moiré interferometry is a high-sensitivity whole-field method to measure in-plane displacements of a strained body. An attractive feature of the moiré technique is its capability to analyze both elastic or inelastic deformations for isotropic and anisotropic materials. The current investigation uses moiré interferometry to characterize the thermo-mechanical response of several electronic packaging materials. Such material data is essential for accurate modeling of component response and prediction of failure.

## Micromechanical Test Apparatus

The thermo-mechanical response of several electronic packaging materials was investigated using a compact, four-beam moiré interferometer (PEMI model 2001-X, IBM Corp). The instrument has a 40 mm circular field of view and creates a virtual reference grating of 2400 lines/mm. A micromechanical test apparatus was developed specifically for use with the compact moiré. A schematic of this test fixture is shown in Fig. 1. The fixture orients the sample for viewing by the interferometer and is capable of applying either bending or tensile loads to the specimens. Proper positioning and alignment of the specimen is accomplished by mounting the loading fixture on a rotation stage which is in turn mounted to a x-y translation stage as shown in Fig. 1. Both the x-y stage and the interferometer are mounted on a pneumatic vibration isolation table. The interferometer cabinet is also equipped with several position/alignment adjustments. Proper alignment of the specimen grating to create a null field is achieved by simultaneous adjustment of the load fixture and the interferometer.

The fixture applies a load to the specimen via a stepper motor attached to a worm gear driven rail table. The action of the tester is controlled using the virtual instrument software package LabView. This program filters the analog signal from the load cell amplifier by averaging 3000 load readings at 12 kHz. This averaged reading is recorded as a function of time to produce load versus displacement curves based on the constant velocity of the rail table. The rail table applies loads by moving at a specified velocity between 50-100 microns per second and then stops once LabView records a load at or above a user determined limit. The S type load cell (Fig. 1) can measure loads in tension or compression up to 50lb. with an accuracy of .015 lb.

## Thermo-mechanical Testing

The micromechanical tester described above was utilized to quantitatively characterize the thermo-mechanical response of several electronic packaging materials. Fig. 2 shows typical u and v displacement fields for a BGA (ball grid array) structure in four point bending. Additionally, the reliability of the micromechanical test apparatus was investigated by testing a well characterized material and using the resulting moiré fringe data to calculate the material properties. Tension and bending calibration specimens were fabricated out of both aluminum (2024) and epoxy. Rectangular bending samples were machined from flat stock to dimensions 127 x 19.0 x 6.35 mm. Rectangular tension specimens were also machined from flat stock to overall dimensions of 63.5 x 9.5 x 3.2 mm with a reduced gage section of length 9.5 mm and 3.2 mm in width. A comparison of the strain measured by the moiré system in both bending and tension with values either measured by conventional mechanical tests or predicted by elasticity theory will be presented.

## Acknowledgment

Support for this work by Motorola Corporate Manufacturing Research Center is greatly appreciated.

64

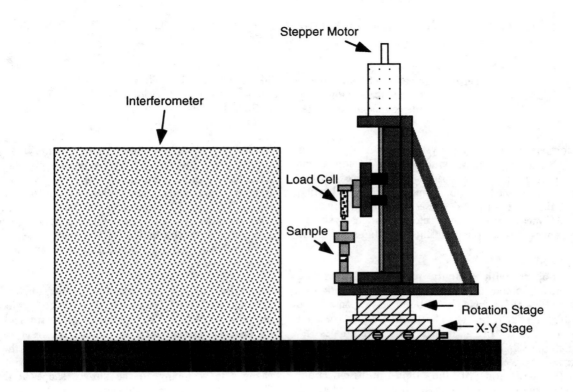

Fig. 1 Schematic of Micromechanical Tester.

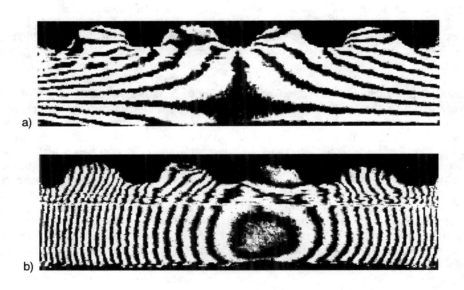

Fig. 2 a) u displacement and b) v displacement fields during four point bending of BGA (Ball Grid Array) structure.

# Applied Laser Methods for Deformation Analysis of Electronic Package

Tetsuo Kumazawa, Makoto Kitano, Hideo Miura and Hiroaki Doi
Mechanical Engineering Research Laboratory, hitachi, Ltd.
502 kantatsu tsuchiura Ibaraki,300, JAPAN

New deformation measuring systems without making contact with the object under study have developed, and can be applied to actual packages. Three optical methods are explained in this paper. We also describe the applications of each of these methods in thermal deformation measurement and deformation analysis of actual packages to demonstrate the usefulness of these methods.

To study objects with highly reflective surfaces, we used an interferometer to obtain Fizeau fringes. In this method, a 10 mW He-Ne laser beam is expanded and paralleled by lenses (Fig. 1). The parallel light passing through a window of a furnace and illuminates an optical flat plate below. Light is repeatedly reflected at the interface between the optical flat and the object surface. By repetition of the light multi-reflection, interference fringes called Fizeau fringes are formed. Deformation of the object results in changes in the interface distance and causes changes in the fringe pattern since the surface of the optical plate always remains flat. Figure 2 shows the deformation when a ceramic package cap is heated from 20℃ to 150℃. The data were calculated from the maximum number of obtained fringes on the diagonal base compared with finite element method calculations. Curved deformation was slightly reduced when the package was jointed to a ceramic board.

A method to measure displacement in small areas within an electronic package and also the light diffusive surface of the objects, i.e., actual packages is based on micro-speckle interferometry. A schematic diagram of the speckle interferometer that has microscopic functions and incorporates two techniques is shown in Fig. 3.
One is speckle photography which produces Young's fringes from a double-exposure photograph ( a specklegram). A beams of light passing to the object shown by broken line in Fig. 3 is used as the optical arrangement for this double exposure photograph. A mirror was used to change the optical pass from a two-beam arrangement (described below) to this speckle photography arrangement.
The second technique used is two-beam illumination interferometry that is in-plane displacement measuring method. The object is illuminated from two different directions of in the same time, as shown by the solid' lines in Fig.3. The speckle pattern image made before the deformation is stored in a frame memory, then interfered to the image after deformation which is stored

in real time in another frame memory. Obtained fringes by interfering are enhanced by an image processor and displayed on a video screen. Magnification when using these techniques is in the range 1.75 to 50 depending on the lens magnification. The sensitivity of the measurement changes in accordance with the incident light angle. The accuracy of the two-beam method is $\pm 0.1 \mu$ m at an incident light angle of 40° .

The third method is intended to measure the thermal deformation of comparatively large objects with diffusive surfaces. The measurement instrument is based on distance measurement by laser. A laser illuminates an object at an incident angle (Fig. 4), and the light is reflected from the object surface. The reflected light spot changes in according to the surface shape of the object. By precisely measuring the position of the reflected light spot, the distance between the light spot position and the object is acquired. All surfaces of the object are scanned by a laser spot. A deformation pattern is obtained by subtracting the initial distance (i.e., to the undeformed surface) from the distance after deformation( i.e., to the deformed surface).
The specifications of the out-plane displacement are : temperature range of 20℃ to 200℃, maximum object size is 220 x 260 mm, maximum measurable displacement is $\pm 3$ mm, and accuracy is $\pm 2 \mu$ m (at 20℃) and $\pm 5 \mu$ m (at 150℃).
Figure 5 shows the deformation of a TCP (Tape Carried Package) in a display panel measured by using the developed apparatus. Plastic substrates were arranged on three sides around a center nematic panel. Driving and controlling TCP packages which consisted of a chip and a tape were mounted on these substrates as well as on the panel glass. The initial shape of the TCP at room temperature (26℃ ) was shown as a grid pattern, where the intersect points of the grids are measured points. Thermal deformation occurred in the z direction (i.e., normal to the panel) on the substrate side when the sample was heated from 26℃ to 86℃. In this figure, the chip shape is represented by a flat surface so that it is easier to understand the deformation. The displacement of TCPs at the center is very small. On the other hand, displacement at the corner edges is large.

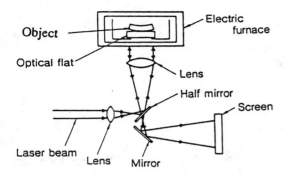

Fig. 1 Schematic diagram of Fizeau Interferometer.

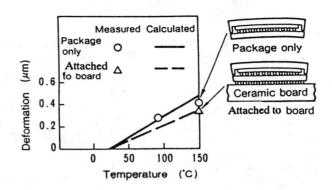

Fig.2 Deformation of package cap : comparison of measured date and calculations

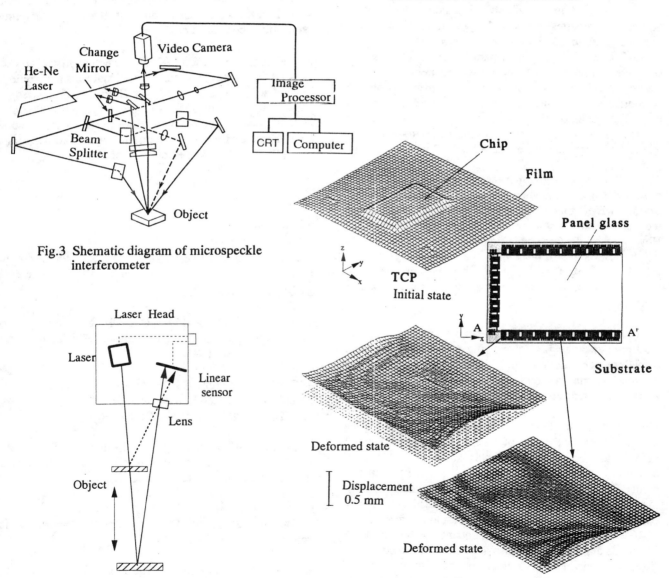

Fig.3 Shematic diagram of microspeckle interferometer

Fig. 4 Principle of distance measurement.

Fig.5 Thermal deformation of TCP mounted on a board ( temperature difference △T = 60 ℃)

# Application of Speckle Pattern Interferometry to Electronic Packaging

Angelo Villani
Digital Equipment Corporation
Hudson, Massachusetts 01749

Mani Prakash
State University of New York, Suny
Binghamton, NY 13902-6000

Most recently, Electron Speckle Pattern Interferometry (ESPI) was considered as alternate to Moire' Interferometry for verification of models in electronic packaging. ESPI has similar capabilities as Moire' Interferometry[1,2,3]: strains can be measured over small areas, it is easy to use, and it does not require a vibration isolation table. In addition, ESPI requires no sample preparation: no cross-sectioning, no grid, and the sample does not have to be perfectly flat. With ESPI, out of plane measurements can be conducted simultaneous to in plane measurements, results are recorded in a computer, various data manipulation can be conducted, and ESPI also has vibration analysis capability [4,5]. The disadvantages of ESPI is that it may not have the same level of accuracy as Moire' Interferometry, and ESPI costs more than twice that of Laser Moire'.

The table top Moire' Interferometry, which has been developed at IBM Endicott, is currently being used by various Computer/Electronic Companies, Universities, is relatively inexpensive, and it is very accurate over very small areas. However, significant sample preparation is needed. Applying the grid is an art, takes time, and the sample's surface must be perfectly flat. Samples must be cross sectioned to study strains and only inplane displacements can be measured.

To determine the accuracy and applicability of ESPI to electronic packaging, the following tests were conducted: displacement controlled 3 and 4 point bend tests, evaluation of strains around a stress concentration point, and evaluation of the expansion coefficient of materials.

Fig.1 illustrates the average x-direction displacement along the highly stressed region of a beam subjected to 3 and 4 Point bend tests. A z-direction displacement of 125µm is applied at the center of the beam. From these displacements, ESPI Interferometry strain was calculated. As illustrated in Table 1, the strain values obtained with simple beam theory and with ANSYS FEM results are in the range of 16% to 32% lower than values obtained with ESPI. Fig.1 illustrates that the average displacement values recorded by ESPI are generally linear with applied displacement and smooth along the beam, as predicted by theory. This experiment was repeated with various materials and similar consistent results were obtained.

ESPI was used to determine the behavior of a stress concentration point on a beam subjected to bend testing. Fig. 2 illustrates the fringe pattern around a stress concentration point. ESPI was also used for crack propagation studies[6]. A ball park figure of the expansion coefficient of a PCB was determined; however, additional testing is required with a more controlled environment.

A preliminary evaluation of ESPI was conducted and results are better than expected. Additional tests are required. If good accuracy is obtained with ESPI when it is used for the evaluation of packages that are subjected to assembly and environmental conditions, ESPI may be considered as an alternate and easier technique which can be used for a broad field of studies of electronic packages.

## References

1. Han, B., "Moire' Interferometry as a Tool for Electronic Packaging Product Development." ASME, InterPack ex'95, March 26-30, 1995.

2. Han, B., Guo, Y., and Lim, C.K., "Moire' Interferometry as a Tool for Engineering Education." ASME, InterPack '95, March 26-30, 1995.

3. Guo, Y. "Experimental Determination of Effective Coefficients of Thermal Expansion in Electronic Packaging" ASME, InterPack '95, March 26-30, 1995.

4. Deaton, J.B., Wagner, J.W., and Rogowski, R.S., "Electronic Speckle Pattern Interferometry on a Microscopic Scale." Journal of Nondestructive Evaluation, Vol. 13, No. 1, 1994.

5. Shubert, W. "SD800 Electronic Speckle Pattern Interferometry." Technical Note. 1995.

6. Chen, C.H., and Hsu, J., "The Determination of Mixed-Mode Stress Intensity Factor by Electronic-Speckle-Pattern Interferometry." National Taiwan University. 1995.

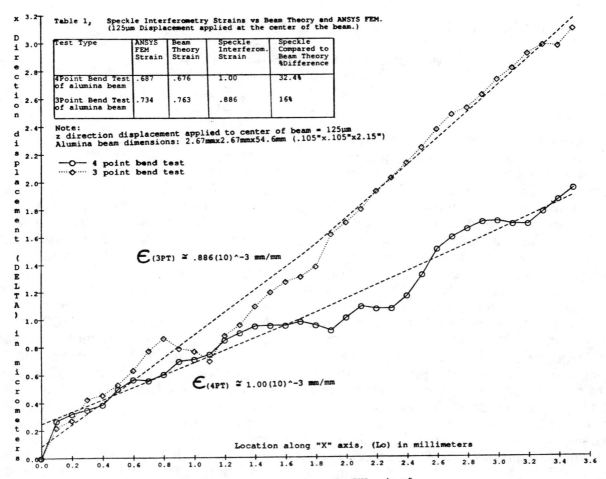

Table 1, Speckle Interferometry Strains vs Beam Theory and ANSYS FEM.
(125μm Displacement applied at the center of the beam.)

| Test Type | ANSYS FEM Strain | Beam Theory Strain | Speckle Interferom. Strain | Speckle Compared to Beam Theory %Difference |
|---|---|---|---|---|
| 4Point Bend Test of alumina beam | .687 | .676 | 1.00 | 32.4% |
| 3Point Bend Test of alumina beam | .734 | .763 | .886 | 16% |

Note:
z direction displacement applied to center of beam = 125μm
Alumina beam dimensions: 2.67mmx2.67mmx54.6mm (.105"x.105"x2.15")

—○— 4 point bend test
····◇···· 3 point bend test

$\varepsilon_{(3PT)} \cong .886(10)^{-3}$ mm/mm

$\varepsilon_{(4PT)} \cong 1.00(10)^{-3}$ mm/mm

x Direction displacement (DELTA) in micrometers

Location along "X" axis, (Lo) in millimeters

Fig. 1, Average measured displacement vs. Location along the "X" axis of
the highly stressed region of a beam subjected to 3 and 4 point bend tests.

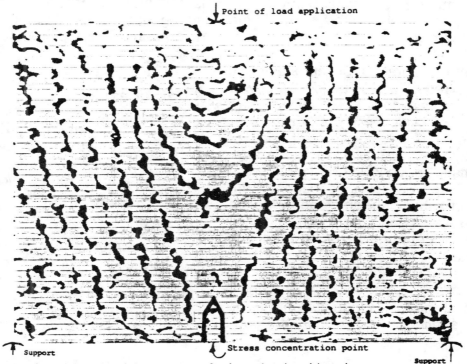

↓ Point of load application

↑ Support ↑ Support
Stress concentration point

Fig. 2.  Y Direction fringe pattern of a beam that is subjected
to 3 point bend tests and containis a stress concentration
point.  The applied beam displacement is 4 mils.

69

# Real-Time Holographic Interferometry of Power Modules

Mahyar S. Dadkhah and Andrew D.W. McKie
Rockwell Science Center
1049 Camino Dos Rios
Thousand Oaks, CA 91360

A real-time holographic interferometry system has been developed that allows out-of-plane displacement fields to be measured with a resolution of ~0.27 μm [1-4]. Typically, prior to mechanical or thermal loading of the specimen, a hologram is recorded of the object in its steady state configuration. Subsequently, any distortion of the object will result in the generation of interference fringes when viewing the object through the hologram. The strain-induced displacement fields resulting from distortion of the sample are captured with a CCD camera system and analyzed on a Macintosh computer. This system provides a real-time image capture rate of up to 33 frames/sec, allowing rapidly varying stress-induced displacements of the specimen to be accurately recorded. Initially, experiments were performed to validate the optical configuration with measurement of the deformation fields produced by mechanical loads on a simple beam, a notched specimen and a circuit board being demonstrated using the real-time holography system.

Assembly and integration of the electronic components required to build a power cycling system was completed, allowing up to 300 A to be cycled through the power module. The holographic interferometry system was then used to map the out-of-plane thermally induced deformations of a 24 A SMC power module during the application of a high current load. When a current of 30 A was first applied to the power module, the temperature of the gate junction instantaneously increased by 8-10°F. Conversely, a similar temperature drop was observed when the current was removed from the power module. When current of 160 A was applied, an instantaneous temperature rise of about 60°F was observed. QuickTime™ movies were generated which illustrate both the instantaneous and long term displacement of the power module as the current is applied. These movies show that within 200 ms of applying the 30 A, the gate surface of the power module undergoes a displacement of 0.27 μm, drops to zero out-of-plane deformation and then increases again as the temperature increases slowly. Also for applied current of 100 and 160 A, the surface of the gate region moved ~ 0.7 μm and 1.0 μm within 300 ms and 500 ms, respectively. When the current is turned off it was observed that very little instantaneous change in the thermal displacement occurred even though the power module was cooling. However, the centroid of the deformation fields shifted to the center of the lead gate. Since the deformation does not drop synchronously with the temperature, it is evident that the solder undergoes creep during the cycle. Figure 1 shows typical holographic fringe patterns of a 24 A power module.

## References:

[1] Rastogi, Pramod K. (Ed), *Holographic Interferometry*, Springer-Verlag, 1994.

[2] Hariharan, P., *Optical Holography*, Cambridge Univ. Press, 1984.

[3] Robinson, D.W. and Reid, G.T (Ed), *Interferogram Analysis*, IOP publishing, 1993.

[4] Steel, W.H., *Interferometry*, Cambridge Univ. Press, 1983.

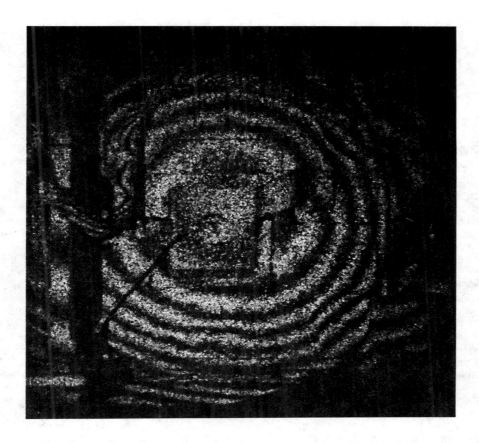

Figure 1.  Typical holographic fringe patterns of a 24 A power module.

# In-Process Board Warpage Measurement in a Lab Scale Wave Soldering Oven

Michael R. Stiteler
SCRA
5300 International Blvd.
Charleston, SC 29418

I. Charles Ume
School of Mechanical Engineering
Georgia Institute of Technology
Atlanta, GA 30332-0405

Theo Ejim
Lucent Technologies
P.O. Box 900
Princeton, NJ 08542

In the modern electronic industry, a dramatic increase in printed wiring board assembly (PWBA) component density has been achieved during the last decade. The use of surface mount packaging, with lead pitches commonly of 12 mils or less, has increased the importance of accurate component placement during manufacturing. Warpage of printed wiring boards (PWBs) during the soldering process can result in component misregistration during placement, while post production warpage can place damaging stress on component solder joints that provide not only an electrical connection between the board and the component, but a mechanical connection as well. Despite the importance of warpage in PWB/PWBA reliability, prior to this research no practical method of measuring in-situ board warpage during soldering was available.

An automated on-line warpage measurement system for PWB/PWBAs has been developed to address this need. The system was originally used to measure warpage while simulating infrared reflow soldering using a shadow moiré technique [1,2]. Recently this same technique was used to measure PWB warpage during wave soldering in a lab-scale wave soldering oven.

As shown in Figure 1, the system consists of an insulating oven and an array of infrared heating elements which preheat the PWB/PWBA; a camera, light source, and reference grating (Ronchi Ruling) used to form and record shadow moiré images; and a translation table which moves a quartz heating element beneath the specimen to simulate the board moving over a solder wave.

To generate shadow moiré images, a reference grating is placed directly above the test specimen. The reference grating (also called a Ronchi Ruling) is typically made of glass onto which parallel, equally spaced opaque lines are etched. A shadow of the reference grating (called the specimen grating) is produced on the surface of the specimen by transmitting a collimated beam of light through the grating. If the test specimen is flat and parallel to the reference grating, no moiré pattern is produced. When the specimen surface is inclined or curved, a moiré pattern is produced consisting of light and dark lines called fringes (see Figure 2). This moiré pattern can be analyzed to determine the out-of-plane displacement (warpage) of the specimen [3]. Using a light incident angle of 45 degrees and a camera viewing angle of 0 degrees, the out of plane warpage between any two adjacent fringes is equal to the line pitch of the reference grating. For example, if a 100 line per inch (lpi) reference grating is used, the out-of-plane displacement between any two adjacent dark fringes (or two adjacent light fringes) is equal to 1/100 inches, or 10 mils.

To provide preheating and cooling control, a thermocouple is attached to the surface of the PWB which provides feedback to a PID controller. The PWB is preheated by the infrared array. Then the high intensity quartz heating element is translated beneath the specimen using the x-translation table shown attached to the right side of the oven in Figure 1 to simulate the wave. Finally, the infrared array and PID controller regulate the natural convection cooling rate of the PWB. Using this fully automated system, wave soldering temperature profiles have been accurately simulated to within 2°C during the heating cycle and within 6°C during the cooling cycle (forced cooling has not yet been incorporated).

Moiré images of three identical PCMCIA panels with thicknesses of 18, 21, and 31 mils are shown in Figure 3. These images were recorded as the wave passed beneath the center of each board. A reference grating of 100 lpi was used to form these images, translating to a 10 mil out of plane displacement between each dark fringe. Defining maximum warpage as the out-of-plane displacement between the highest and lowest points on each board, the maximum warpage is 85, 60, and 35 mils for the 18, 21, and 31 mil boards respectively. Until now, this inverse relationship between board thickness and warpage during wave soldering could not have been demonstrated by actual measurements.

Using this new system, warpage during the entire wave soldering process may now be observed in real time, recorded on videotape, and analyzed. With experience, this previously unavailable information will undoubtedly become increasingly more useful to those in the PWB/PWBA manufacturing industry, as well as to those in the educational community.

References:

[1] Tsang, C., Stiteler, M., and Ume, C., "Real-Time Measurement of Printed Wiring Board Flatness in a Simulated Manufacturing Environment," *INTERpack '95*, Lahaina, Hawaii, March 26-30, 1995.

[2] Stiteler, M. and Ume, C., "System for Real Time Measurement of Thermally Induced PWB/PWA Warpage," ASME 1995 International Mechanical Engineering Congress & Exposition, San Francisco, CA, November 1995.

[3] Kobayashi, A. ed., Handbook on Experimental Mechanics, Prentice Hall, NJ 1987, pp. 282-313.

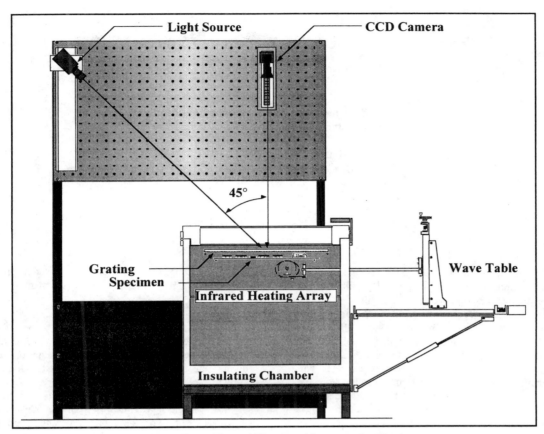

Figure 1. Front View of Warpage Measurement System

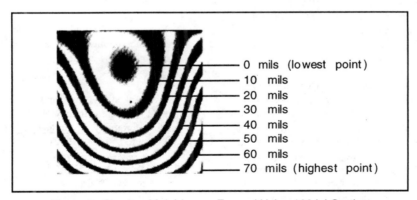

Figure 2. Shadow Moiré Image Formed Using 100 lpi Grating

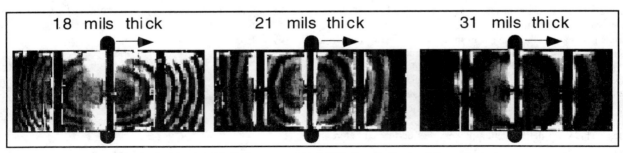

Figure 3. Shadow Moiré Images of PCMCIA Panels During Wave Soldering

# On-Line Automated Profilometry of Silicon Wafers

**J. F. Cardenas-Garcia, S. Zheng and J. Hashemi**
Department of Mechanical Engineering
Texas Tech University
Lubbock, Texas 79409-1021

**J. Kalejs**
A-S-E Americas, Inc.
4 Suburban Park Drive
Billerica, Massachusetts 01821-3980

The purpose of this paper is to show the experimental set-up and results of implementing the on-line automated profilometry of silicon wafers produced by the edge-defined film-fed growth (EFG) technique [1, 2, 3]. An optical profilometer for full-field 3D shape measurement, which can remotely assess object shape was used [4, 5, 6]. The advantage of this experimental approach compared to other optical methods for 3D shape measurement, is that this technique is not only faster but also more accurate. This technique, which like Fast-Fourier Transform (FFT) Profilometry, is based on the principle of phase measurement of the deformed grating pattern which carries the 3D information of the object surface being measured. It can automatically and accurately obtain the phase map of the height information of the object at every pixel from the analysis of a single video image. This approach has advantages over an experimental technique such as moiré contouring, as there is no need to locate the center of fringes, or assign fringe orders, or even needing to make a distinction between concave and convex surfaces.

The experimental set-up includes a projector, a CCD camera and a 486/50 micro-computer with an image processing board. The whole measurement procedure is fully automated and was implemented in an industrial environment on-line. It takes less than 15 seconds to process a 752 x 480 pixel image to get the height map, which was within the constraints of tracking the shape of the evolving silicon wafer surface. With a commercially available accelerating board and suitable software, real-time measurement could be easily accomplished.

The measurement accuracy has been found to be good enough for this industrial application. For example, in calibrating the experimental set-up, the statistical mean error obtained after measuring a semi-cylindrical surface (whose radius is 32.25 ± 0.01 mm) is 0.142%. This value is obtained after evaluating the results for 100,490 points on the surface. The average relative error is -0.05% with 0.045 mm standard deviation. Additional work involved the determination of silicon wafer warp after the EFG produced silicon sheets were cut into approximately 100 mm squares. This warp determination process was performed before and after cutting, showing the stress relaxation produced by the cutting operation in terms of warp measurement.

References:

1. J. C. Lambropoulos, J. W. Hutchinson, R. O. Bell, B. Chalmers and J. P. Kalejs, "Plastic deformation influence on stress generated during silicon sheet growth at high speeds," Journal of Crystal Growth, Vol. 65, pp. 324-330 (1983).

2. P. A. Mataga, J. W. Hutchinson, B. Chalmers, R. O. Bell and J. P. Kalejs, "Effects of transverse temperature field nonuniformity on stress in silicon sheet growth," Journal of Crystal Growth, Vol. 82, pp. 60-64 (1987).

3. Y. Kwon, S. Danyluk, L. Bucciarelli and J. P. Kalejs, "Residual stress measurement in silicon sheet by shadow moiré interferometry," Journal of Crystal Growth, Vol. 82, pp. 221-227 (1987).

4. M. Takeda, H. Ina and S. Kobayashi, "Fourier-transform method of fringe pattern analysis for computer based topography and interferomerty," Journal of the Optical Society of America, Vol. 72, pp. 156-160 (1982).

5. M. Takeda, and K. Mutoh, "Fourier Transform profilometry for automatic measurement of 3-D object shapes," Applied Optics, Vol. 23, pp. 1760-1764 (1983).

6. S. Tang and Y. Y. Hung, "Fast profilometer for the automatic measurement of 3-D object shapes," Applied Optics, Vol. 29, pp. 3012-3018 (1990).

# Holographic Diffraction Image Velocimetry for the Measurement of Three-Dimensional Solid Deformations

James S. Slepicka and Soyoung S. Cha

Dept. of Mechanical Engineering, University of Illinois at Chicago  MC 251

842 W. Taylor St., Chicago, IL 60607

In recent years, various nonintrusive coherent optical techniques have been increasingly employed for the measurement of stresses and deformations incurred by solid objects in many industrial production and testing phases. Some areas of application include on-site evaluation of production and packaging processes for electronic devices, vibration measurement, fracture mechanics, and detection of defects and flaws in finished components. Typically, methods such as laser speckle photography and laser speckle interferometry have been applied where noncontact, high-accuracy, gross-field displacement measurement of intermediate-to-large size objects is required. However, their scope of utilization is limited to only in-plane and out-of-plane displacements, respectively, thus restricting their use to simple or pure planar motions. In addition to requiring specialized equipment, these speckle methods may not be desirable since they can only cover an upper or lower extent of the total dynamic range of object motion. Similarly, conventional holographic interferometric techniques, while capable of multi-dimensional measurements of a wider range of object sizes, require multiple viewing directions and can also suffer from limited dynamic range. In practice then, there exists a gap between the maximum and minimum measurement limit of these techniques.

Here, we present an improved holographic technique termed Holographic Diffraction Image Velocimetry (HDIV) which has the capability of measuring instantaneous three-dimensional (3-D) three-component (3-C) displacement fields from a single observation direction. It exhibits a wide dynamic range and improved accuracy over an extended range of object shapes and sizes. It is based on the dual-reference-beam double-exposure time-sequence capture of 3-D gross-field images on a single holographic plate. Each individually-recorded scene can be independently reconstructed and digitized, allowing convenient comparison between the initial and displaced images. An imaging system consisting of a solid state camera along with image relaying and magnifying optics is used to scan the reconstructed field, section by section. At each section, both in-plane (perpendicular to the optical axis) and out-of-plane velocity components are separately extracted by measuring the displacement of pre-applied surface markers, i.e., paint droplets or solid particles which can be allowed to settle on the object surface. In-plane displacement components are determined by a variable-size transplacing-window cross-correlation (VS-TWCC) technique. This involves the use of a sufficiently narrowed-down aperture to produce initial and displaced image sections with a reasonable depth-of-field from the interrogation window and the search window, respectively. The image sections are then statistically cross-correlated to find the accurate in-plane displacement with accuracy limited by the finite CCD sensor pixel size. If desired, sub-pixel accuracy can be obtained through interpolation of the cross-correlation signal peak. One advantage of this independent-image-frame technique is that there is no displacement sign ambiguity which can arise if autocorrelation of superimposed images is performed. Thus, the direction of the displacement is obtainable owing to the known time sequence of the two exposures.

Once the in-plane motion has been determined, several diffracted images of the displaced field are acquired using a reduced depth of focus (large aperture) at known locations along the optical axis, with the camera laterally fixed at the in-plane displacement location as determined from the previous step. Each diffracted image is then directly compared to the initial image through an image cross-product (CP) operation to determine the out of plane displacement.

Experiments performed with 15 $\mu$m particles deposited on a surface undergoing rotation about the optical and vertical axes have shown out-of-plane resolutions on the order of $0.2\lambda/\theta^2$ where $\theta$ is the effective optical system aperture and $\lambda$ is the illumination wavelength. This corresponds to a typical uncertainty in out-of plane displacements of about 10 $\mu$m for $\theta = 0.1$ rad. Although the HDIV is in a developmental stage, experimental results have shown it to be a promising method for obtaining accurate 3-D 3-C solid deformation information. Measurements based on holographically-recorded local speckle pattern motions are also being investigated. This method, while similar in data acquisition and processing, can have the added advantages of adjustable image-element (speckle) size to increase its dynamic range as well as minimal surface preparation requirements.

# Physics-of-Failure Methodology for Thermal Cycling of Solder Joints

Timothy Rothman
Intel Corporation
Memory Components Division
Folsom, CA 95630

Abhijit Dasgupta
CALCE Electronics Pack. Research Center
University of Maryland
College Park, MD 20742

Pei-Tsung Tsai
CALCE Electronics Pack. Research Center
University of Maryland
College Park, MD 20742

This research presents a case study where existing physics-of-failure (POF) models and Bayesian statistical methods are used in conjunction with test data from accelerated temperature cycling of leadless solder joints, to develop acceleration transform models which can be used to quantify the test-time compression achieved. Combinations of substrate materials and package styles are evaluated, and valuable information is obtained from a relatively small population of test specimens under accelerated stresses, because the critical variables are identified, and their influences on the stress magnitude are quantified. In addition to accelerating the stress levels, the total test time is further minimized by tailoring the stress drivers in each sample such that multiple stress levels can be achieved under a single loading, which eliminates the need for repeating the test at multiple load levels. Such techniques are essential for cost effective and timely development of highly reliable modules under accelerated stresses. This paper presents the details of how the statistical methods are applied and a summary of the acceleration transforms obtained from the test.

Testing to ensure adequate reliability and quality is usually done under accelerated stresses to achieve test time compression. Accelerated tests can be categorized based on their purpose. Qualification tests as defined in this study are performed during product development and are intended to assess the product's ability to conform to nominal design and manufacturing specifications by satisfying long term reliability requirements. Reliability enhancement testing is performed to guide the ruggedness of products when the demonstrated reliability is deemed to be inadequate. Screening provides a means by which an investigator may find fragile or faulty items in a electronic module by means of a test with appropriately accelerated stresses without weakening or causing the failure of sufficiently robust items. In each case, the necessity to quantify the results of the test remains. Using acceleration transforms based on physics-of-failure evaluation of statistical parameters provides the investigator with information other than just pass-fail.

The physics-of-failure approach involves the use of testing procedures which are based on quantitative models of the expected failure mechanisms derived and validated from previous test results. In addition, the physics-of-failure approach provides a method to obtain acceleration transforms and useful trends from limited amount of test data with confidence. This study attempts to apply the physics-of-failure approach to accelerated testing of surface-mount components with leadless solder joints, and proposes a practical procedure for extracting information from a single accelerated test.

Fifteen double-sided, symmetric, multilayered circuit board modules each consisting of different combinations of materials with three different size daisy-chained ceramic leadless chip carriers (LCCs) are chosen for this study. The thermal rate of change is chosen to be 10 °C/min., with a high temperature dwell at 90 °C for 23.5 mins. and a low temperature dwell at -55 °C for 5.5 minutes. The effect of the size of the components, placement of the components, and materials used to manufacture the modules can be evaluated independently [1], and comprehensive acceleration transforms can be created from a single load history because of the multitude of stress levels reached in different solder joints.

The cycles to failure at a given percent probability of failure can be computed from the maximum-likelihood Weibull distribution parameters. However, in order to measure the uncertainty in determining these parameters, a rigorous statistical approach is applied. These distribution parameters are evaluated using a Bayesian approach. [2, 3] The maximum likelihood estimates of the two parameter Weibull distribution provide the maximum-likelihood that when these parameters are used, the failure data will fall as closely as possible to the distribution within a degree of uncertainty. This degree of uncertainty is of paramount importance when attempting to estimate fatigue life.

The two-parameter Weibull cumulative distribution for $t > 0$ is described as:

$$P(t) = 1 - \exp^{-[t/\theta]^B} \qquad 1$$

There are n failures from the population occurring at times $X_1, X_2, X_3...X_n$, and d samples have not failed at the end of the test at time T. The joint probability for n failures and d censored data is proportional to the conditional likelihood, P, of the data on the distribution parameters P(Data|$\theta$, B).

$$P(Data|\theta, B) \propto p(X_1)dx\, p(X_2)dx\, p(X_3)dx... p(X_n)(1 - P(T))^d \qquad 2$$

where p(t) is the Weibull probability density. From Equation (1) this reduces to:

$$P(Data|\theta, B) \propto \frac{B^n}{\theta^{nB}}\left[\prod_{i=1}^{n} X_i\right]^{B-1} \exp\left[-\theta^{B-1}\left[dT + \sum_{i=1}^{n} X_i\right]^B\right] \qquad 3$$

In this study, we assume a flat prior probability density ($\pi_0$) by making no assumptions about the distribution parameters (by assuming $\pi_0$ is not a function of $\theta$ or B). From Bayes' formula, the posterior density ($\pi$) becomes:

$$\pi(\theta, B|Data) \propto P(Data|\theta, B)\pi_o(\theta, B) \qquad 4$$

Combining Equations (3) and (4) and normalizing such that the volume under the three-dimensional density plots is equal to unity gives:

$$\pi(\theta, B | Data) = \frac{\dfrac{B^n}{\theta^{nB}} \left[ \prod_{i=1}^{n} X_i \right]^{B-1} \exp\left[ -\theta^{B-1} \left[ dT + \sum_{i=1}^{n} X_i \right]^{B} \right]}{\int\limits_{\theta=0}^{\infty} \int\limits_{B=0}^{\infty} \dfrac{B^n}{\theta^{nB}} \left[ \prod_{i=1}^{n} X_i \right]^{B-1} \exp\left[ -\theta^{B-1} \left[ dT + \sum_{i=1}^{n} X_i \right]^{B} \right] dB d\theta} \qquad 5$$

The experimental failure data is separated into twelve groups based on a POF model of the shear strain range $\Delta\gamma$, estimated as:

$$\Delta\gamma = \frac{\Delta\alpha\Delta T L_d}{2h} \qquad 6$$

where $\Delta\alpha$ is the differential thermal expansion between the circuit board module and the component, $\Delta T$ is the cyclic temperature swing, $L_d$ is the maximum diagonal distance between solder joints, and h is the solder joint height.

Equation (5) is then applied to each of the twelve data sets to obtain three dimensional contours of the distribution parameters at 5%, 50%, and 95% confidence similar to that shown in Figure 1. Based on the confidence on the calculation of the distribution parameters (or lack thereof), the outliers are systematically eliminated from the database.

The time to failure based on X percent probability of failure is computed using Equation (1).

$$N_f(X\%) = \theta\left[-\ln(1 - X\%)\right]^{1/B} \qquad 7$$

Regression of the distribution parameters versus shear strain range with the outliers eliminated from the data gives $\theta = 31.195\gamma^{-1.0917}$ and $B = 2.0$. Note that $\theta$ varies with $\Delta\gamma$, while B remains independent of $\Delta\gamma$ (although varying slightly). This value of $B = 2.0$ is dramatically different from the value of $B = 4.0$ as reported by Engelmaier, and can greatly effect the time to failure based on percent probability of failure. Substitution of these values of $\theta$ and B into Equation (7) at any desired percent probability of failure provides time to failure as a function of shear strain range. Figure 2 shows curves obtained using this approach at the mean and 5% and 95% probability of failure. Note that this acceleration transform model is based on $\Delta\gamma$, not temperature. The temperature can be back calculated from each strain level using Equation (6).

The Bayesian statistical approach in conjunction with physics of failure methodology provides a systematic method for computing probability distributions, relating the distribution parameters to physical quantities, and determining which data is contaminating the distributions. Failure analysis can then be used to confirm if there is a good reason for eliminating the outliers. The reason outliers appear in this study is the small population size, the data being censored, and the fact that a flat prior distribution is assumed. All three of these effects are interrelated. [1]

The Bayesian approach provides a method to obtain confidence contours on both parameters of the Weibull distribution. The confidence contours also provide a quantitative method to recognize and eliminate outliers. In this study, prior knowledge of the distribution parameters is not assumed. Assuming no prior knowledge of the distribution parameters is a conservative approach, and in cases of relatively small sample size, existing data suggests a less conservative approach. [2]

Ultimately, the goal in any accelerated test, whether that test is performed for the purposes of screening, qualification, or reliability enhancement, is to quantitatively assess the damage, then relate the damage to the operational environment. Application of the physics of failure approach with the aid of Bayesian statistical methods, enables the investigator to obtain crucial acceleration transform information from a potentially noisy data set with confidence. This type of hybrid approach is necessary to develop predictive tools, particularly in the age of technological advancement when the electronics industry is continuously changing.

[1]. Rothman, T. P, *Physics of Failure Methodology for Accelerated Thermal Cycling of LCC Solder Joints*, Masters Thesis: Submitted to the Dept. of Mechanical Engineering University of Maryland, College Park, 1995.
[2]. Box, G., Tiao, C., *Bayesian Interference in Statistical Analysis*, Addison Wesely Publ. Co., Reading Mass., 1973.
[3]. Lindley, D., *Scandinavian Journal of Statistics*, Vol 5., 1, 1978.

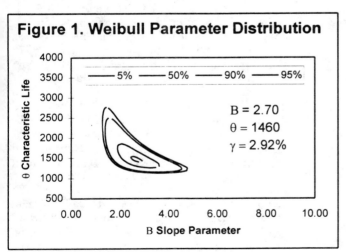

## Figure 1. Weibull Parameter Distribution

B = 2.70
$\theta$ = 1460
$\gamma$ = 2.92%

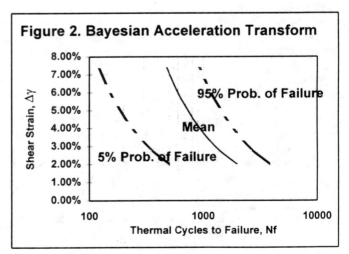

## Figure 2. Bayesian Acceleration Transform

# MEASUREMENT OF DIE STRESSES IN CHIP ON BOARD PACKAGES USING PIEZORESISTIVE SENSORS

S. T. Lin, R. J. Moral, J. C. Suhling, R. C. Jaeger*, R. W. Johnson*
Departments of Mechanical and Electrical* Engineering, and
Alabama Microelectronics Science and Technology Center
Auburn University
Auburn, AL  36849-5341
USA

Stresses in electronic packages can cause premature mechanical failures due to such causes as fracture of the die, severing of connections, die bond failure, solder fatigue, and encapsulant cracking. These stresses often are thermally-induced and result from uneven expansions and contractions of the various assembly materials due to mismatches in the coefficients of thermal expansion (CTE's). Piezoresistive stress sensors (semiconductor strain gages) are a powerful tool for experimental structural analysis of electronic packages [1-8]. Figure 1 illustrates the basic application concepts. The structures of interest are semiconductor (e.g. silicon) chips (die) which are incorporated into electronic packages. The sensors are resistors which are conveniently fabricated into the surface of the die using current microelectronic technology. The sensors are not mounted on the chips. Rather, they are an integral part of the structure (chip) to be analyzed by the way of the fabrication process. The stresses in the chip produce resistance changes in the sensors (due to the piezoresistive effect) which can be easily measured. Therefore, the sensors are capable of providing non-intrusive measurements of the state of stress at points on the surface of a chip, even within encapsulated packages (where they are embedded sensors). If the piezoresistive sensors are calibrated over a wide temperature range, thermally-induced stresses can be measured. Finally, a full-field mapping of the stress distribution over a die's surface can be obtained using specially designed test chips which incorporate an array of sensor rosettes.

In this study, special (100) silicon test chips containing an array of piezoresistive stress sensor rosettes have been applied within several chip on board (COB) electronic packaging configurations. In the COB packages considered in this study, the semiconductor die were directly attached to the printed circuit board (PCB) substrates using a silver-filled epoxy die attach adhesive. Fine gold wires were used to provide the interconnections from the die bond pads to the metal traces on the PCB's. The die were then encapsulated using a "glob-top" epoxy coating. The utilized test chips had planar dimensions of .45 x .45 inches, and were fabricated with optimized measurement and calibration rosettes [4-6]. The response of the sensing elements on the die to stress has been calibrated using several methods including four-point bending [7], wafer level calibration [8], and hydrostatic testing. The initial resistances of all of the sensors on the test die were also recorded using an automated probe station. The characterized test chips were then attached to the PCB and encapsulated. Transient sensor resistances were monitored during encapsulant cure, and the post packaging room temperature resistances of the sensors were recorded. Using the measured resistance changes and the appropriate theoretical equations [1], the stresses in the die due to various aspects of the packaging process have been calculated. Experimental results have been correlated with the predictions of nonlinear three-dimensional finite element simulations of the packaging process. For example, Figure 2 illustrates experimental measurements and finite element predictions of the in-plane shear stresses occurring on the surface of the die after encapsulation cure.

## REFERENCES

1.  Bittle, D. A., Suhling, J. C., Beaty, R. E., Jaeger, R. C. and Johnson, R. W. (1990) "Piezoresistive Stress Sensors for Structural Analysis of Electronic Packages," Journal of Electronic Packaging, Vol. 113(3), pp. 203-215, 1991.

2.  Suhling, J. C., Carey, M. T., Johnson, R. W. and Jaeger, R. C., "Stress Measurement in Microelectronic Packages Subjected to High Temperatures," in the Proceedings of the Symposium on Manufacturing Processes and Materials Challenges in Microelectronic Packaging, AMD Vol. 131, pp. 143-152, ASME 1991 Winter Annual Meeting, Atlanta, GA, December 1-6, 1991.

3.  Kang, Y. L., Suhling, J. C., Johnson, R. W. and Jaeger, R. C., "Silicon and Silicon Carbide Stress Sensors for Application to Electronic Packaging," in the Proceedings of the 1994 SEM Spring Conference on Experimental Mechanics, pp. 311-320, Baltimore, MD, June 6-8, 1994. [50%]

4.  Jaeger, R. C., Suhling, J. C., Carey, M. T. and Johnson, R. W., "Off-Axis Piezoresistive Sensors for Measurement of Stress in Electronic Packaging," IEEE Transactions on Components, Hybrids, and Manufacturing Technology (CHMT-Advanced Packaging), Vol. 16(8), pp. 925-931, 1993.

5.  Jaeger, R. C., Suhling, J. C. and Ramani, R., "Errors Associated with the Design, Calibration of Piezoresistive Stress Sensors in (100) Silicon," IEEE Transactions on Components, Packaging, and Manufacturing Technology - Part B: Advanced Packaging, Vol. 17(1), pp. 97-107, 1994.

6.  Jaeger, R. C., Suhling, J. C. and Anderson, A. A., "A (100) Silicon Stress Test Chip with Optimized Piezoresistive Sensor Rosettes," in the <u>Proceedings of the 44th Electronic Components and Technology Conference (ECTC)</u>, pp. 741-749, Washington, DC, May 1-4. 1994.

7.  Jaeger, R. C., Beaty, R. E., Suhling, J. C., Johnson, R. W. and Butler, R. D., "Evaluation of Piezoresistive Coefficient Variation in Silicon Stress sensors Using a Four-Point Bending Test Fixture," <u>IEEE Transactions on Components, Hybrids, and Manufacturing Technology (CHMT)</u>, Vol. 15(5), pp. 904-914, 1992.

8..  Suhling, J. C., Cordes, R. A., Kang, Y. L. and Jaeger, R. C., "Wafer-Level Calibration of Stress Sensing Test Chips," in the <u>Proceedings of the 44th Electronic Components and Technology Conference (ECTC)</u>, pp. 1058-1070, Washington, DC, May 1-4. 1994.

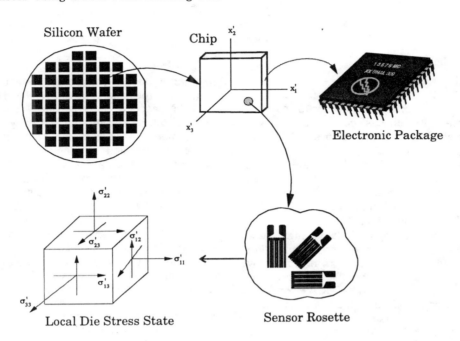

Figure 1 - Piezoresistive Stress Sensor Concept

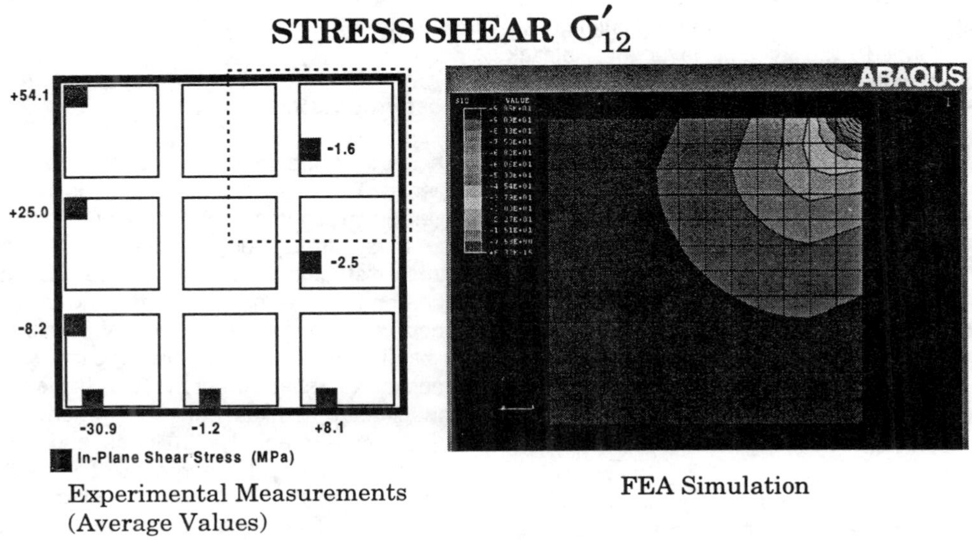

## STRESS SHEAR $\sigma'_{12}$

Experimental Measurements
(Average Values)

FEA Simulation

Figure 2 - Typical Results for a Chip on Board Package
(FEA Results are for Top Right Quadrant)

# Experimental Determination of the Shear Modulus of Compliant Adhesives Using Single Lap-Shear Tests

Loren L. Roy, Donald B. Barker, and Shashank Mallick
CALCE Electronic Packaging Research Center
University of Maryland, College Park, 20742

## Abstract

In some high performance applications of electronics such as Integrated Microwave Assemblies, compliant adhesives serve to attach ceramic circuit card assemblies (CCA's) to aluminum backing plates. The aluminum transfers large amounts of heat created by the electronics on the ceramic circuit card to the environment. Typically, such assemblies can undergo a temperature increase from the zero stress state of 100°C or more. Since ceramic has a coefficient of thermal expansion (CTE) of approximately 6 ppm/°C and the CTE of aluminum is about 23 ppm/°C, large strains and stresses in the ceramic result during normal operation. These strains can result in premature failure or fracture of the ceramic substrate and possibly the solder joints of the chip carriers mounted on the surface of the CCA. Compliant adhesives can absorb some of the strain due to the large CTE mismatch and lower the state of stress in both the ceramic and the solder joints. In order to estimate the stress level in a CCA prior to constructing a prototype, a designer must obtain the mechanical properties of the adhesive.

The present study focuses on the experimental determination of the shear modulus of compliant adhesives. The authors create lap-shear specimens by machining two aluminum plates bonded with a thin layer of Ablestik ECF563, a compliant adhesive. A hydraulic tensile testing machine with modifications loads the specimen while eddy current non-contact transducers mounted on the aluminum measure the shear displacements - the relative motion of the two halves of the lap-shear specimen. A constant strain rate results due to the linear response of the adhesive and the constant displacement rate control of the tensile tester. The shear modulus results from the slope of the stress-strain curve in the linear response region modified using a Finite Element Analysis simulation. The adhesive tested exhibits homogeneous isotropic behavior by assumption.

## Experimental Equipment

Extracting the shear modulus using a single lap-shear test specimen requires a tensile loading apparatus, a device for measuring the relative displacements of the two halves of the specimen and a data acquisition system for recording the data. A hydraulic MTS machine (Materials Testing System) with a range of 0 to 10,000 pounds loads the specimen through a compliance enhancing device used to increase the resolution of the machine. The micro-profiler of the MTS machine provides the constant displacement control of the hydraulic ram. Two eddy current non-contact displacement transducers mounted on the sample with specially fabricated adapters measure the shear displacements. A Data Translations 16 bit data acquisition board with custom software reads and records the signals from the transducers, and the authors use Excel 5.0 to reduce the data and create the curves.

Since the inherent bending mode displacements of a lap-shear specimen in tension are quite large, it is incumbent upon the experimenter to isolate the shear mode displacements. Because of symmetry, any bending of the sample due to the moment created in a lap shear specimen would occur about the centerline of the shear area. The second mode of bending results from violations of symmetry in the sample due to machining process tolerances or slight variations in the adhesive bond. This problem is resolved by mounting one transducer symmetrically on either side of the specimen while averaging the signals. Specially designed aluminum holders adhered on the centerline using a cyanoacrylate adhesive satisfy both of the above requirements simultaneously.

## Post Processing and FEA

Because of the inherent eccentric loading in a lap-shear specimen, a pure state of shear is not possible, and the average stress does not accurately express the variations in the shear stress along the bondline. In general, the shear stress distribution depends on the relative thickness of the adherends and the adhesive and the thickness of the bondline. In the present study, the ratio of the maximum to minimum shear stress in the bondline is about 20 using thin bondline lap-shear theory. To achieve accurate results for the shear modulus, an FEA model of the lap-shear specimen is created with loads and boundary conditions similar to the actual experiment. The relative displacements are found in the center of the shear area from the FEA simulation. The authors calculate the strain in the adhesive by dividing the relative displacement by the thickness of the bondline and the FEA output shear modulus by dividing the average stress by the strain. The ratio between the FEA input and output shear moduli is used to modify the experimental results.

## Results and Discussion

As suggested by ASTM standards, lap shear specimens can be useful in extracting the shear modulus of adhesives providing thick adherends and bondlines are used. Since many adhesives come in sheets, it is not practical to have bondlines thicker than the sheets provided by the manufacturer. Correspondingly, difficulties arise when machining samples using thick adherends as suggested by ASTM since the adhesive bond can likely become compromised by the incurred loads. In the current research, the authors use a thin adhesive layer and thin adherends. The authors obtain the shear modulus accurately by coupling the experimental results with an FEA simulation.

Researchers at CALCE EPRC have previously determined the tensile modulus of Ablestik ECF563 at room temperature assuming a Poisson's of .42. The researchers used a Rheometrics Solid Analyzer (RSA II) as the loading device and data acquisition tool. Assuming that the adhesive exhibits homogeneous isotropic behavior, Hooke's Law yields a result of 108,000 psi for the shear modulus. The present authors have determined a shear modulus of 117,000 psi that is within 8% of the previous work.

## Conclusion

The lap-shear test described is a useful tool in extracting the shear properties of compliant adhesives that come in thin sheets from the manufacturer. The thin adherends make it feasible to machine the samples after being adhered to ensure uniformity of the lot tested. The results are in good agreement with previous work using Hooke's law relationships to convert tensile moduli to shear moduli assuming homogeneous isotropic behavior.

# Processing Mechanics in Microelectronic Devices

Jiansen Zhu, Changrong Ji, and S. Liu
Institute of Manufacturing Research
Mechanical Engineering Department
Wayne State University
Detroit, MI 48202
(313)577-3875 (0)
(313)577-8789(fax)
e-mail: sliu@me1.eng.wayne.edu

Many processes are involved in fabricating a microelectronic device. For instance, a typical IC packaging such as flip-chip, BGA, and standard plastic packages needs to go through die attach, underfill/encapsulation, and surface mounting assembly processes. All these processes induce residual stress and may cause cracking and delamination [1-3]. For a flip-chip assembly, direct chip on organic board becomes possible with the underfill material. Currently, efforts from both industry and academia are focusing on the computer aided engineering (CAE) of various manufacturing processes. However, due to the complexity of electronic packaging in materials and processes, a countable CAE tool needs quality assurance. One of the most important means for this quality assurance is experimental mechanics. Processing mechanics with both modeling and verification as two major components is essential for helping designers optimize structural designs and improve manufacturing quality.

The measurement of the material behavior in terms of both macro mechanics and micromechanics at the elevated temperature are important to determine their constitutive laws and failure quantities and are essential for the finite element modeling of actual packaging assembly. In addition, the determination of thermally induced strains in a microelectronic package is an essential requirement for the assessment of fatigue and failure issues in the device.

Moiré Interferometry measuring is a whole field, real time, and highly precise method. It is especially effective for the non-uniform in-plane deformation measurements and has been used in the research and development for the microelectronic packages. For instance, currently IBM has been promoting the portable moiré device in the past few years [4,5].

In this paper, recent progresses in both modeling and verification are briefly reported. The focus is on the recent moiré interferometry work by IBM portable moiré interferometry on several popular packaging types: BGA, flip-chip, glob top, and TSOP. A vacuum chamber was self-designed and built for a real time measurement. High sensitivity and high temperature gratings are used for some of the packages. Modeling work is focused on the global/local modeling.

Figure 1 shows a schematic of BGA. Figure 2a and 2b show the U and V displacements measured from a constant temperature drop of -56 C. Other results and modeling work will be presented at conference.

References:

[1] S. Liu, J.S. Zhu, J.M. Hu, and Y.-H Pao, ``Investigation of crack propagation in ceramic/adhesive/glass system," IEEE Trans., CHMT, Sept. 1995.
[2] S. Liu, Y.H. Mei, and T.Y. Wu, ``Bimaterial interfacial crack growth as a function of mode-mixity," IEEE Trans., CHMT, 1995.
[3] S. Liu and Y.H. Mei, ``Behaviors of delaminated plastic IC packages subjected to encapsulation cooling, moisture absorption and wave soldering," IEEE Trans. on CHMT, Sept. 1995.
[4] Y.Guo, C.K. Lim, W.T. Chen, and C.G. Woychik, "Solder Ball Connect (SBC) assemblies under thermal loading: I. Deformation measurement via moiré interferometry and its interpretation, IBM J. of Research and Development , Vol.37, No.5, Sept. 1993.
[5] D. Post, B. Han, and P. Ifju, "High Sensitivity Moiré: Experimental Analysis for Mechanics and Materials," Springer-Verlag, NY, 1993.

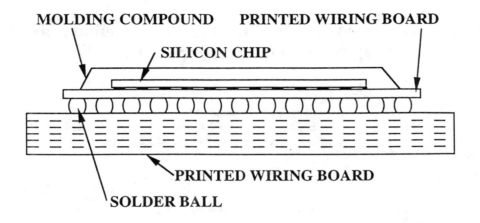

FIGURE 1.  BALL GRID ARRAY PACKAGE

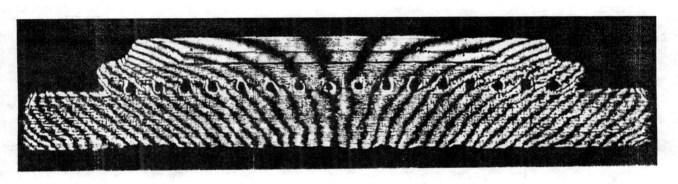

FIGURE 2a.  U-DISPLACEMENT ($\Delta T$= 24°C - 80°C)

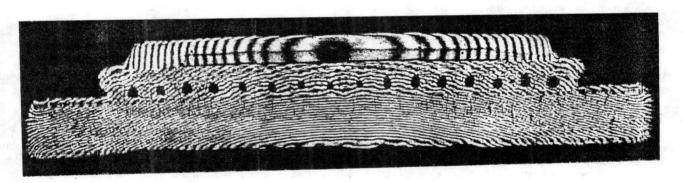

FIGURE 2b.  V-DISPLACEMENT ($\Delta T$= 24°C - 80°C)

# Life Prediction Models in Electronic Packaging using Finite Element Analyses and Design of Experiments

Sidharth and Donald B. Barker
CALCE Electronic Packaging Research Center
University of Maryland, College Park, MD 20742

## ABSTRACT

As the electronic systems become more complex, their reliability assessment becomes a challenging issue. The behavior of these structures is complicated, due to the interaction of the geometries and material properties, so that it becomes extremely difficult to formulate mathematical closed form life prediction models, even with numerous simplifying assumptions. The design for maximum reliability of a structure requires a sensitivity analysis of the various parameters. The Finite Element Analyses (FEA) method is a common numerical technique used to evaluate any design. If a large number of FEA are conducted by arbitrarily varying various parameters, it might be extremely difficult to confidently conclude about the factors affecting the design. Design of Experiments (DOE) approach not only minimises the number of runs required, but also allows conclusions about the various parameters involved with statistical confidence. The advantage of such models is that a designer can use them as simple, quick and easy analyses tools for evaluating the effect of the structures' parameters on its design. However, if this statistical approach is not performed rigorously, it might lead to inaccurate models and conclusions. This paper addresses some key issues involved in the correct use of Full Factorial DOE approach to developing life prediction models from FEA data, and, provides insights to avoid any erroneous practices. The approach is illustrated through an example in vibration fatigue of surface mount assemblies.

## BACKGROUND

The chemical and process industries, and the semiconductor and electronics industries have used Design of Experiments (DOE) techniques in some form to improve process yield, enhance quality of the product, and making both, the product and process, more robust. In manufacturing industries, there is a definite link between the scientific study of industrial processes and the quality and reliability of goods produced. In product design, its use has been made at finding out optimal design configuration using response surface methods.

Its application for design in electronic packaging has been limited. The present paper reviews some of the applications of DOE in design. The present paper concerns itself with full factorial DOE, though most of the statistical principles apply to fractional factorial designs as well. This paper also provides useful insights to those potentially inclined to model data using this technique.

## INTRODUCTION

The goal of all experimenters is to be able to determine the behavior of something unknown and to draw inferences about a larger population based on a few experiments. The experiments are not perfectly repeatable and the effect the various factors are confounded with that of each other, and therefore it becomes difficult to analyze data from any experiment. A designed experiment is a technique to extract maximum conclusive information with minimum effort. If an experiment is repeated, different results are obtained every time and hence the use of statistics is warranted. The role of statistics is to separate the observed differences in the data into those caused by various factors and those due to random fluctuation. The classical method to do this, the Analysis of Variance (ANOVA), conducts statistical tests to find out what influences the experiment and what does not. The use of a commercial statistical analysis software like SAS, SPSS, BBN, BMDP, Echip, Minitab, Statgraphics and NCSS is recommended to avoid delving into unnecessary computational details of ANOVA.

## MODEL

The various models may be classified as : *mathematical* and *statistical*. The difference between the two categories is outlined. DOE models are statistical models.

Experimental design can be useful in sufficient checking of proposed mathematical models, so that any glaring discrepancies can be identified or it may be used to tune existing simple mathematical models to predict the behavior of more complicated systems, but this can only be done if the model and the system show some kind of consistent trends in the behavior with factors but can't match in terms of magnitude.

It is difficult to guess the functional form for any data or phenomenon. The physics of the problem and previously conducted studies may aid in guessing the functional form in a few cases. In the absence of any preferred form, polynomial form may be a typical choice. The motivation for using the polynomial form is explained. The actual behavior of any system may or may not follow a polynomial form. The truth is that any statistical model is an idealization of the behavior of the system, and, is to be thought of as a combination of independent variables in a definite fashion to describe the behavior of the system with some statistical confidence. There is no sanctity attached to the terms in the model. Also, the myth, that some variables are significant, holds only within the domain of the chosen functional form of the model. Different functional forms considered for the same data will yield different set of factors/interactions which are significant.

### Anaysis of Variance (ANOVA)

ANOVA is a method for considering variation among data and attributing that variation to factors controlling the behavior of the experiment. The basic assumption in ANOVA is that the error is normally and independently distributed with a mean 0 and variance $s^2$. Normality ensures that the error follows a normal distribution. The reasons for models deviating from normality are explained, along with ways to deal with it. Two important terms which are repeatedly used in subsequent discussions, namely the F-test and the coefficient of determination, are also defined and their importance explained.

### APPROACH

The total approach for conducting DOE with FEA data is being outlined in the following in detailed steps :

Step 1. Definition of the problem, dependant variable (response variable) and the independent variables (factors)

Step 2. Computation of the total runs required and decision on a full factorial or fractional factorial design

Step 3. Finite Element Analyses runs

Step 4. Use of Analysis of Variance (ANOVA) to identify the significant factors and interactions affecting the response variable and quantifying the same

Step 5. Choice from a subset of models. There will never be "the best" model.

Step 6. Validation of the model by conducting additional Finite Element runs (verification runs) at intermediate values of the levels of factors chosen.

Step 7. Reformulation of the model, using transformation of variables, inclusion of higher order terms and/or higher order interactions, on failure of validation in Step 6.

Step 8. Redesign of the experiment, if required, and repetition of Steps 1 through 7.

Each of the steps are explained in sufficient detail and caveats and nuances which might lead to erroneous models outlined.

### EXAMPLE

The above methodology is applied to a practical problem in electronic packaging, that of quantifying corner lead displacements in a peripheral leaded package mounted on a PWB subject to bending in two directions. The corner lead has been found to be very susceptible to failure in actual operating environments and therefore a model for quantifying the displacements, hence stresses is imperative for these leads.

### CONCLUSION

In this paper, a methology for building a model for life prediction has been outlined and its use demonstrated for a practical problem in electronic packaging, that of computing the out-of-plane displacement of the corner lead in component-lead-board assemblies subject to bending in two directions has been described. The correct approach to using DOE has been outlined in detail and various methods to avoid erroneous practices outlined based on statistical principles.

# CAD-Based Thermo-mechanical Analysis Tools for Electronic Packaging

## Wen X. Zhou and Robert E. Fulton

School of Mechanical Engineering
Georgia Institute of Technology
Atlanta, Georgia 30332-0405

Due to the lack of appropriate mechanical modeling methodology, mechanical reliability analysis of an electronic packaging product is generally performed by mechanical experts only after electrical design. Most of available MCAD systems are used primarily for drafting, layout and parts lists, but only marginally affect the realm of an engineering analysis[1,2]. The mechanical FE model building phase generally requires 80~90% of total analysis time. To respond to the growing needs of mechanical modeling and simulation in electronic design process, a new modeling approach, termed Modularized & Parametric FEM (MP/FEM) methodology, can be utilized to rapidly create a CAD-based mechanical analysis module for a reliable thermo-mechanical analysis.

A quick way of defining the modularization concept is to refer to group technology. Its essential argument is that many electrical components and/or products can be grouped into classes or families of similar shapes. Each single family of topological shapes is called a Modularized Generic Primitive (MGP). Individual members of a family can be distinguished by a few parameters. A new geometric shape can be created by linear transformations of an existing one. The transformations affect only the geometry size, but not the topology of a shape. Each MGP is defined topologically, instead of as a detailed geometric size. The overall relationship among MGPs, components, assembly, and product is represented as a graph tree. This tree is referred to as a Constructive Module Assembly Tree (CMAT). The CMAT is an undirected graph, or a rooted tree, where the root is the electrical product itself. (Figure 1).

The main idea of parametric modeling is to create, or define, a FE model template, instead of a model, by parameters and their forming rules. The template can be used to generate an actual model by populating data of the parameters in the template. The parametric modeling approach has several advantages, which include flexibility, interchangeability, and transportability.

Once a type of component is fully studied, it can be saved in a CAD system for other product in future design. Since the object model in the CAD system preserves the geometry and topology, the same model and its associated mesh information can be reused as long as the physical properties remain the invariant. When the finite element analysis for an object is required, the user may request information stored in the CAD system by inputting a CMAT tree for that object. Hence, the model of an object, once created with the help of a solid modeler, can be stored in a CAD system to be reused for another object that is geometrically and topologically equivalent to this master model. Figure 2 shows the flexibility of a TSOP model with J-lead.

One test case is to create a FE model of a populated board for thermo-mechanical analysis (Figure 3). Compared to conventional modeling techniques, it can reduce modeling time by 100X. The test board contains 2 DCA, 2 TSOP with gull lead, 1 TSOP with J-lead, and 8 passive components. (Figure 4). The component models can be operated as an "icon", which can be translated, or rotated. Thermal, bending, or modal analysis may be performed by simply switching the element type connected to the entire model. Figure 4 shows the stress plot of a thermal analysis.

### Reference:
1. Lau, J. H., "Chip on board technology for multichip modules",Van Nostrand Reinhold
2. Demaria, D., "CAD tool and Design for Manufacturing. Part I" Printed circuit Design. pp10 -14. May 1991

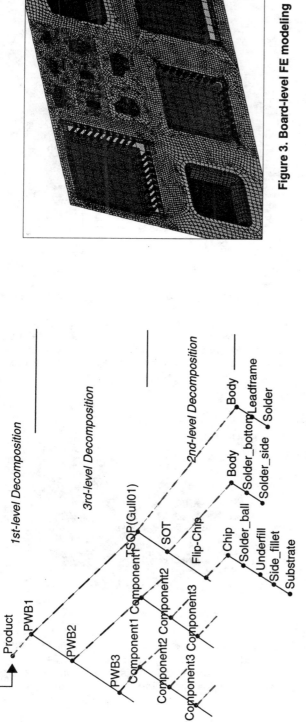

**Figure 1. Graph representation of CMAT.**

Root Node of $G_{CMAT}$

1st-level Decomposition

3rd-level Decomposition

2nd-level Decomposition

Product

PWB1

PWB2

PWB3

Component1 Component1

Component2 Component2

Component3 Component3

TSOP(Gull01)

SOT

Flip-Chip

Chip

Solder_ball

Underfill

Side_fillet

Substrate

Body

Solder_bottom

Solder_side

Body

Leadframe

Solder

**Figure 3. Board-level FE modeling**

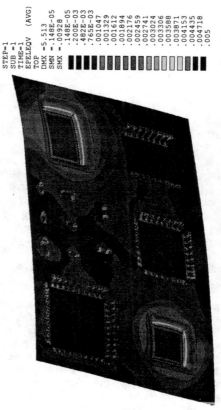

STEP=1
SUB=1
TIME=1
EPELEQV (AVG)
TOP
DMX =5.513
SMN =.148E-05
SMX =.00928

.148E-05
.205E-03
.482E-03
.765E-03
.001047
.001329
.001612
.001894
.002176
.002459
.002741
.003024
.003306
.003588
.003871
.004153
.004435
.004718
.005

**Figure 4. Thermal stress result**

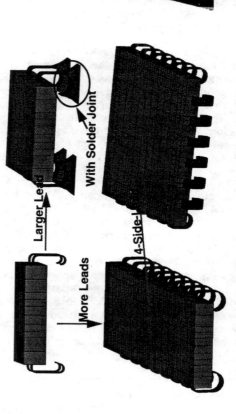

Larger Lead

With Solder Joint

More Leads

4-Side-L

**Figure 2. one-to-many modeling of TSOP with J lead**

87

# Finite Element Model Predictions and Measured Die Surface Stresses in Delaminated IC Packages*

James N. Sweet
Steven N. Burchett
David W. Peterson
John A. Emerson
Sandia National Laboratories
Albuquerque NM 87185-1082

Delamination of plastic encapsulant or polymeric die attach materials in integrated circuit (IC) packages is a major cause of reliability problems in current devices. These delaminations may occur either during the package fabrication or later during solder surface mounting of the package when the package temperature increases to ≈ 225°C for a short time. The delamination may be accompanied by die cracking or damage to the conductors on the IC surface. Even if there is no mechanical damage, the free volume in a delaminated region provides the opportunity for liquid water to collect and possibly do damage to underlying metal conductors.

In order to predict the reliability of a prospective packaging system, it is important to be able to calculate the change in package stresses produced by various types of delaminations. In addition, the ability to make these predictions correctly is a critical test of the finite element model (FEM) used to analyze the package. Package delaminations not only change the coupling of the IC die to adjacent materials, they also result in a change in the state of package bending which plays a major role in determining the stress at the IC surface.

We have developed some FEMs of several plastic package configurations and evaluated the change in die surface stress produced by delaminations at the die attach layer and the die upper surface - encapsulant boundary. Upper surface delaminations can result in significant stress changes but are not as prevalent as lower surface delaminations. Delaminations of the die attach layer or the encapsulant from the die paddle or lead frame can also produce significant increases in die surface stresses in thin packages.

Stress measurements on packaged ICs have been made with the ATC04 Assembly Test Chip, as previously described [1], [2]. In these measurements, the *in-plane* components of the stress tensor are measured at the die surface using piezoresistive stress sensing circuits. The differential stress between two different package states is found from the resistance shift or change produced by the stress. In our experiments, the resistance values are determined at the wafer level prior to assembly and then after assembly or environmental stressing steps. Fig 1 shows a layout of a basic single ATC04 chip. There are 25 addressable stress sensing cells on the die surface, as shown.

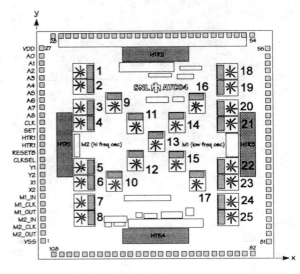

Fig. 1 Layout of the ATC04 chip, showing locations of the 25 piezoresistive stress sensing cells and the numbering scheme for these cells. Each cell has a *rosette* of 4 p-type and 4 n-type implanted resistors and a temperature sensing diode.

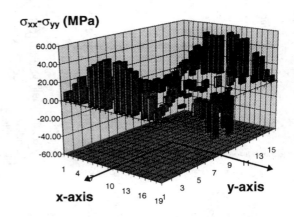

Fig. 2 Measured distribution of the in-plane compressive stress difference, $\sigma_{xx}-\sigma_{yy}$, for a 2x2 ATC04 array die in a square 160 lead PQFP. This stress was measured after molding and post-mold cure.

---

* This work performed at Sandia National Laboratories was supported by the U. S. Department of Energy under contract DE-AC04-94AL85000.

σ$_{xx}$ (MPa)

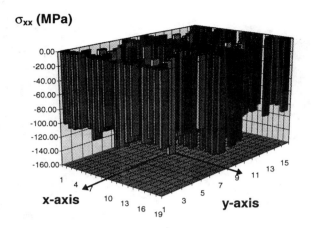

Fig. 3 Measured compressive stress at the die surface for the same part as in Fig. 2. Actually, the chip measures the quantity $\sigma_{xx}$-$\sigma_{zz}$ but $\sigma_{zz}$ is small in magnitude at all sensor locations.

The x-y plane is at the die surface and the z direction is normal to that surface. In this package, a 2x2 array of die was used, producing 100 stress measurements over the die surface.

An example of the measured in-plane compressive stress difference, $\sigma_{xx}$-$\sigma_{yy}$, for a 160 lead plastic quad flat pack is shown in Fig. 2. The distribution of the compressive stress, $\sigma_{xx}$, over the die surface is shown in Fig. 3. The actual quantity measured is approximately $\sigma_{xx}$-$\sigma_{zz}$, but FEM calculations show that the magnitude of $\sigma_{zz}$ is small over the chip region where the sensors are located. A delamination at either die surface will produce a change in the measured stress pattern. In a recent paper on stresses in a small outline J lead package (SOJ), by Miura, Kumazawa, and Nishimura, FEM calculated stresses are shown for various delamination situations [3]. In the case of delamination at the die-die pad or lead frame interface, only a small change in compressive stress is found. In contrast, a delamination at the die upper surface leads to about a decrease in the magnitude of the compressive stress to about 40% of its pre-delamination value. In similar calculations for a liquid encapsulated (*glob-topped*) chip on a ceramic substrate, we find that an FEM calculated upper surface delamination produces a stress magnitude decrease to 50% of the initial value, while a die-attach delamination produces a slight increase in the stress magnitude at the chip surface. The details of how the die top surface stress changes with delamination depend on how the state of package bending is affected by this delamination.

One interesting observation in our initial FEM calculations for glob-top encapsulation is that the in-plane shearing stress, $\sigma_{xy}$, at the die surface does not change much as a result of a top surface delamination but decreases in magnitude significantly after die-attach delamination. Hence, comparison of compressive and shearing stress shifts can

yield a prediction of the location of a suspected package delamination.

In a recent experiment from which the data shown in Fig. 2 were taken, 68 parts were packaged in 160 lead PQFPs. After molding, three of the parts were found to have about 40% of the compressive stress characteristic of the remainder of the group. In contrast, the shearing stress magnitude for these parts was the same as that of the remaining parts. Scanning acoustic microscopy was performed on these parts as well as samples from the rest of the group and the results will be discussed. We shall also discuss FEM calculated results for the 160 lead PQFP.

These recent experiments and calculations show that the combination of FEM stress analysis and stress measurement with the ATC04 Assembly Test Chip can provide detailed information about the thermal stresses produced by transfer molding and the change in these stresses caused by delamination at a die-polymer interface.

**References:**

[1] Sweet, J. N., Peterson, D. W. and Emerson, J. A., "Liquid Encapsulant and Uniaxial Calibration Mechanical Stress Measurement with the ATC04 Assembly Test Chip", *Proc. 44th Electronic Components and Technology Conference*, IEEE, pp. 750-757, 1994.

[2] Sweet, J. N., Peterson, D. W. and Emerson, J. A, Burchett, S. N., "Experimental Measurements and Finite Element Calculations for Liquid Encapsulated ATC04 Assembly Test Chips", *Applications of Experimental Mechanics to Electronic Packaging*, ASME publication AMD-Vol. 214, , pp.61-71, 1995.

[3] Miura, H., Kumazawa, T., Nishimura, A. "Effect of Delamination at the Chip/Encapsulant Interface on Chip Stress and Transistor Characteristics", *Applications of Experimental Mechanics to Electronic Packaging*, ASME publication AMD-Vol. 214, pp.73-78, 1995.

# AUTHOR INDEX

AUTHOR NAME............ PAGE NO.

Abé, H. ...................................11
Adolf, D.B. ...............................46
Agarwal, R.K. ...........................23
Agarwal, R.K. ...........................29
Agarwal, R.K. ...........................43
Ahn, S.H. .................................25
Baird, J. ..................................59
Barker, D.B. .............................80
Barker, D.B. .............................84
Burchett, S.N. ...........................88
Caletka, D.V. ............................55
Caletka, D.V. ............................27
Cardenas-Garcia, J.F. ...............74
Cha, S.S. .................................75
Chambers, R.S. .........................46
Chen, K.L. ..................................1
Chengalva, M.K. ........................23
Cho, Y.H. ...................................5
Chung, T.G. ..............................25
Clech, J.P. ...............................53
Dadkhah, M.S. ............................7
Dadkhah, M.S. ..........................70
Dai, X. .....................................51
Dai, X. .....................................59
Darveaux, R. .............................41
Dasgupta, A. .............................35
Dasgupta, A. .............................76
Doi, H. .....................................66
Dunne, R.C. ..............................19
Earmme, Y.Y. ..............................5
Ejim, T. ....................................72
Ejim, T.I. ..................................53
Emerson, J.A. ...........................88
Evans, A. ..................................13
Fulton, R.E. ..............................86
Gianoulakis, S.E. .......................46
Gschwend, K. .............................43
Guess, T.R. ...............................15
Guess, T.R. ...............................46
Guo, Y. .....................................48
Guo, Y. .....................................57
Guo, Y. .....................................61
Han, B. .....................................27
Han, B. .....................................48
Han, B. .....................................55
Hashemi, J. ...............................74
Hisaki, Y. ..................................17
Ho, P. .......................................59

Ho, P.S. ....................................51
Honma, Y. .................................11
Hsu, T.R. ....................................1
Hu, J. .........................................9
Ikegami, K. ................................21
Infantolino, W. .............................2
Jaeger, R.C. ..............................78
Jairazbhoy, V. ..............................9
Jeffery, D. .................................59
Ji, C. ........................................82
Jih, E. ........................................9
Johnson, R.W. ............................78
Kalejs, J. ..................................74
Kim, C. .....................................51
Kim, H.H. ..................................25
Kim, J.Y. ...................................33
Kitamura, T. ...............................17
Kitano, M. .................................66
Kleyner, A. ................................39
Krishnamoorthy, H. .....................49
Kumazawa, T. ............................66
Kuo, A.Y. ....................................1
Lagasse, R.R. ............................46
Lee, S.B. ..................................33
Li, L. ........................................57
Lim, C.K. ..................................48
Lin, S.T. ...................................78
Liu, S. ......................................82
Mallick, S. ................................80
Martin, J.E. ...............................46
McKie, A.D.W. ...........................70
McMillan, R.K. .............................9
Michaelides, S. ..........................44
Mitchell, M.R. ............................13
Mithal, P. ..................................29
Miura, H. ..................................66
Mizumoto, S. .............................37
Moon, H.J. ..................................5
Moral, R.J. ................................78
Morris, W.L. ..............................13
Morris, Jr., J.W. ............................4
Motamedi, E. ...............................7
Nguyen, L. ...................................1
Nishimura, H. ............................37
Niu, T.M. .....................................2
Oh, S.Y. ....................................25
Ohnami, M. ...............................37
Ohtani, R. .................................17
Ommen, D. ................................59
Ono, T. .....................................21

Pao, Y.H. ................................9
Park, S.S. ................................5
Park, S.T. ................................7
Peterson, D.W. ............................88
Poon, T.W. ................................51
Prakash, M. ...............................55
Prakash, M. ...............................61
Prakash, M. ...............................68
Reddy, V. .................................9
Reedy, Jr., E.D. ..........................15
Reynolds, H.L. ............................4
Rothman, T. ...............................76
Roy, L.L. .................................80
Saka, M. ..................................11
Sakane, M. ................................37
Sasagawa, K. ..............................11
Schroeder, S.A. ...........................13
Sidharth, .................................84
Sitaraman, S.K. ...........................19
Sitaraman, S.K. ...........................44
Skipor, A.F. ..............................59
Skipor, A.F. ..............................64
Slepicka, J.S. ............................75
Sottos, N.R. ..............................64
Stiteler, M.R. ............................72
Stout, E. .................................64
Suhling, J.C. .............................78
Sweet, J.N. ...............................88
Syed, A.R. ................................29
Syed, A.R. ................................31
Tippur, H.V. ..............................49
Torri, T. .................................39
Tsai, P.T. ................................76
Tsukada, Y. ...............................37
Ume, I.C. .................................72
Umeno, Y. .................................17
Upadhyayula, K. ...........................35
Verma, K. .................................55
Villani, A. ...............................68
Wang, Y.P. ................................61
Willecke, R. ..............................51
Zheng, S. .................................74
Zhou, W.X. ................................86
Zhu, J. ...................................82

# VIII INTERNATIONAL CONGRESS ON
# EXPERIMENTAL MECHANICS

## TABLE OF CONTENTS

**Page No.**

**Plenary**

An Approach to Hybrid Method for Stress Analysis Using Photoelastic Image Data ................... 1
    M. Takashi, S. Mawatari, Aoyama Gakuin University (Japan); and Y. Omori,
    University of Washington (USA)


**Session 1.    Photoelasticity I**

Low Birefringence Measurement in Polymers ....................................................... 3
    S.J. Haake, The University of Sheffield (United Kingdom)

Experiences in Using STL-Epoxies for Photoelastic Investigations ........................... 5
    W. Steinchen, B. Kramer and G. Kupfer, University of Kassel (Germany)

Two Dimensional Photoelasticity Analysis by Digital Image Processing ..................... 7
    N. Plouzennec, J.C. Dupré and A. Lagarde, Université de Poitiers (France)

Electronic Techniques in Isodyne Stress Analysis ............................................... 9
    J.T. Pindera, University of Waterloo (Canada); J. Josepson, Institute of Cybernetics,
Estonian Academy of Sciences (Estonia); and D.B. Jovanovic, University of Nis (Yugoslavia)

A Photoelasticity in Thin-walled Bar Theory ....................................................... 11
    M. Sikon, Cracow University of Technology (Poland)

Color Digital Imaging System for White-light Isoclinic Analysis ............................... 13
    D.E.P. Hoy and W. Zhao, Tennessee Technological University (USA)


**Session 2.    Structural Testing I**

Monitoring of the Alamillo Cable-stayed Bridge During Construction ........................ 15
    J.R. Casas and A.C. Aparicio, Technical University of Catalunya (Spain)

Further Improvement in the Manufacture of Sheet Metal Parts ................................. 17
    S. Ali Saeedy, E.J. Obermeyer and S. Abdi Majlessi, Michigan Technological
    University (USA)

Structural Evaluation and Reinforcement Design of a Large Steel Bridge Span ........... 19
    J.L.F. Freire, J.T.P. Castro, Catholic University of Rio de Janeiro (Brazil);
    and R.D. Vieira, CEFET-RJ and Strainlab Stress Analysis (Brazil)

An Investigation of Automobile Handling Characteristics with ADAMS ....................................... 21
    B.K. Cho, S.J. Song, G.H. Ryu and S.W. Cho, Seoul National University (Korea)

Strain Gage Application on Wire Ropes ............................................................................... 23
    R. Steindler, University of Rome "La Sapienza" (Italy)

## Session 4.    Residual Stress - Interferometric Methods

Whole-field Nondestructive Residual Stress Evaluation of the Rails by Twyman/Green
Interferometry ................................................................................................................... 25
    B.S. Wang and F.P. Chiang, State University of New York at Stony Brook (USA)

Residual Stresses Measurement Using a Radial Interferometer - a Preliminary Analysis .......... 27
    A.A. Goncalves, Jr., C. Kanda, J. Boettger, Federal University of Santa Catarina
    (Brazil); and M.R. Rodacoski, Federal Center of Technical Education (Brazil)

Accurate Measurement of Residual Stress in Glass Rod by Photoelastic Experiment ............. 29
    T.H. Baek, Kunsan National University (Korea); J.C. Lee, Myung Ji University
    (Korea); and D.H. Kim, Won Kwang University (Korea)

Residual Stress Interference by Two Micro-vickers Indentation ................................................ 31
    O.S. Lee, Inha University (Korea)

Residual Thermal Strain Measurements Inside Pb/Sn Solder Joints ......................................... 33
    F. Dai, L. Shi, L. Huang and X. Tang, Tsinghua University (P.R. China)

## Session 5.    Thermal Methods
Sponsored by the Thermal Methods Technical Division

Applications of Infrared Thermography of Non-destructive Testing of Materials ....................... 35
    M. Jonasz, M. Jonasz Consultants (Canada)

Thermoelastic Stress Analysis of the Interfacial Conditions in Pin-loaded Lugs ....................... 37
    J.M. Dulieu-Smith and M.C. Fulton, University of Liverpool (United Kingdom)

Reproducibility and Reliability of the Response from Four Independent
SPATE Systems ................................................................................................................. 39
    J.M. Dulieu-Smith, University of Liverpool (United Kingdom); and P. Stanley,
    University of Manchester (United Kingdom)

## Session 6.    Fracture Mechanics I

Preliminary Studies of Three Dimensional Effects on Artificial Cracks at Simulated
Rocket Motor Liners by the Frozen Stress Method .................................................................. 41
    C.W. Smith, E.F. Finlayson, Virginia Polytechnic Institute and State
    University (USA); and C.T. Liu, U.S. Air Force Phillips Laboratory (USA)

Role of Mode-mixity on 3-D Interfacial Crack Tip Stresses ...................................................... 43
    J.K. Sinha and H.V. Tippur, Auburn University (USA)

Experimental Micromechanics Study on Polymer Interface Reinforced with Copolymers .......... 45
    Q. Wang and F.P. Chiang, State University of New York at Stony Brook (USA)

Photoelastic Determination of Stress Intensity Factors for Interfacial Cracks ........................... 46
    C.R. Vilmann and I. Miskioglu, Michigan Technological University (USA)

Stress Singularity Field of a Mixed-mode Three-dimensional Crack by an Embedded
Speckle Photography ............................................................................................................. 48
    K. Machida, Science University of Tokyo (Japan)

A Mechanical Analysis for a Crack Perpendicular to Interface of Bimaterial by
Moiré Interferometry ............................................................................................................. 50
    Y. Kang, Tianjin University (P.R. China); H. Lu, Ryerson Polytechnic
    University (Canada); Y. Jia and Y. Qiu, Tianjin University (P.R. China)

Elastic-plastic Mixed-mode (I/II) Fracture in Aluminum Sheet Alloys ......................................... 52
    F. Zafari, M. Ramulu and A.S. Kobayashi, University of Washington (USA)


Session 7.    Optical Techniques Applied to Sensors

Photoelastic Fiber-optic Accelerometers ................................................................................... 54
    W. Su, MRL Inc. (USA); J.A. Gilbert, M.D. Morrissey and Y. Song, The
    University of Alabama in Huntsville (USA)

Multiaxial Transducer Utilizing Bulk Birefringence Based Sensors ............................................ 56
    J.J. Ditri, A.S. Redner, Strainoptic Technologies, Inc. (USA); and K. Zysk,
    Arnold Air Force Base (USA)

Damage Evaluation of Fatigue Using Laser Speckle Sensor ..................................................... 58
    A. Kato and K. Ito, Chubu University (Japan)

Characterization of Frequency Response of Laser Displacement Meter Using Laser
Interferometry and Davies Bar ............................................................................................... 60
    A. Umeda and K. Ueda, National Research Laboratory of Metrology (Japan)

Morphological Characteristics of Flying Insects ........................................................................ 62
    S. Sudo, K. Tsuyuki, Iwaki Meisei University (Japan); H. Hashimoto, F. Ohta
    and K. Katagiri, Tohoku University (Japan)

Dynamic Strain Measurement Using Diffraction Grating Strain Sensor ..................................... 64
    A. Asundi, The University of Hong Kong (Hong Kong)


Session 8.    Modal Analysis

The Relationship Between the Structure Dynamic and Cutting Process
Model Parameters ................................................................................................................. 66
    S. Dolinsek and J. Kopac, University of Ljubljana (Slovenia)

Vibration Behavior of a Partial-bulkhead Stiffened Cylinder ...................................................... 68
    N.H. Zhu and F.P. Chiang, State University of New York at Stony Brook (USA)

Modal Analysis of Railway Track Components ................................................ 70
  J. Sadeghi and R. Kohoutek, University of Wollongong (Australia)

The Torsional Vibration of a Damped Continuous Bar ................................... 72
  S. Derry, The Orbital Engine Company (Western Australia); S. Drew and
  B. Stone, The University of Western Australia (Western Australia)

Spectral Analysis for Non Stationary Signals from Mechanical Measurements:
Parametric vs Non Parametric Methods ........................................................ 74
  T. D'Alessio, III Università di Roma (Italy)

Investigation of Unsteady Fluid Force Acting on Array of Cylinders in Cross Flow .................... 76
  Z. Yan, H. Tanaka and K. Tanaka, Kyushu Institute of Technology (Japan)


**Session 10.  Structural Testing II**

Finite Element Analysis of Elasto-dynamic Behavior Under Impact Load in
Three-dimensional Model ............................................................................... 78
  G.W. Hwang and K.Z. Cho, Chonnam National University (Korea)

Wave Propagation Past Structural Joints and Other Local Non-uniformities ................ 80
  L.E. Kannal and J.F. Doyle, Purdue University (USA)

Experimental Measurement of Wrinkling in Plane Elastic Sheets ....................... 82
  C.H.M. Jenkins, W.H. Spicher and A. Vedoy, South Dakota School of Mines
  and Technology (USA)

Evaluating Disbonds in Lattice/Skin Structures with Electronic Shearography ............ 84
  A.K. Maji, U.S. Air Force Phillips Laboratory (USA); and D. Satpathi, University
  of New Mexico (USA)

A Study on the Sound and Vibration Property of Korean Bell ............................. 86
  S.H. Kim, Kangwon National University (Korea); J.M. Lee and S.J. Lee,
  Seoul National University (Korea)

Structural Testing of Externally Prestressed Concrete Beams ........................... 88
  A.C. Aparicio, G. Ramos and J.R. Casas, Technical University
  of Catalunya (Spain)


**Session 11.  Impact & Dynamic Response of Composites**

Impact Response of Foamed Composites ...................................................... 90
  D. Liu, Z. Wang and X. Dang, Michigan State University (USA)

The Effects of Hail Damage on the Fatigue Strength of a Graphite/Epoxy
Composite Laminate ...................................................................................... 92
  R.A. Skordahl and M. Mahinfalah, North Dakota State University (USA)

Influence of Notches within Fibre Reinforced Materials under Impact Loads ............ 94
  D.H. Müeller, T. Franz and A. Tenzler, Bremer Institut für
  Konstruktionstechnik, Universität Bremen (Germany)

Experimental Investigation of the Effect of Flexural-torsional Coupling on
Vibrational Characteristics of Angle-ply Laminates ....................................................... 96
    T. Maeda, V. Baburaj and T. Koga, University of Tsukuba (Japan)

A Probabilistic Analysis of Fatigue Cumulative Damage and Fatigue Life Using
Markov Chain Model in CFRP Composites ..................................................................... 98
    J.K. Kim and D. Kim, Hanyang University (Korea)
Net Shape Manufacturing and Its Affects on the Impact Response of Fiber
Reinforced Plastics ....................................................................................................100
    M. Ramulu and D. Arola, University of Washington (USA)


**Session 13.    Long Term Durability and Accelerated Testing of Composites I**
Sponsored by the Composite Materials Technical Division

**Plenary**
Accelerated Durability of Continuous Fiber Polymer Composites ...............................102
    S.E. Groves, S.J. DeTeresa and M.A. Zocher, Lawrence Livermore
    National Laboratory (USA)

Long Term Durability of Polyester Thermoplastics Based on Laboratory and
Automotive Field Studies ............................................................................................103
    A. Golovoy and J.L. Sullivan, Ford Motor Company (USA)

Assessment of Durability and Damage of Adhesives in Pure Shear Using a Bonded
Beam and Dynamic Mechanical Thermal Analysis ....................................................104
    H.F. Brinson, University of Houston (USA); R.A. Dickie and M.A. DeBolt,
    Ford Motor Company (USA)

The Durability of Glass-fiber/Epoxy Composites Evaluated from Single-fiber
Fragmentation Tests and Full-scale Composites Immersed in Water .........................106
    C.R. Schultheisz, C.L. Schutte, W.G. McDonough, K.S. Macturk, M. McAuliffe
    and S. Kondagunta, National Institute of Standards and Technology (USA)

Solvent Sensitivity of High Performance Composites ................................................108
    A.P.C. Furrow, D.A. Dillard, Virginia Polytechnic Institute and State University
    (USA); T.L. St. Clair and J.A. Hinkley, NASA- Langley Research Center (USA)


**Session 14.    High Temperature I**
Jointly sponsored by SEM/JSME

Effect of Oxygen Embrittlement on Crack Growth in a Nickel-based Superalloy .......110
    G. Zhang, Beijing Institute of Aeronautics and Astronautics (P.R. China);
    B.S.J. Kang and L. Wilson, West Virginia University (USA)

Flexural Strength and Fracture Toughness Evaluations of Fine Ceramics at
Elevated Temperature ................................................................................................112
    Y. Ochi, University of Electro-Communications (Japan); K. Haraguchi, Mitsubishi
    Electric Co. Ltd., (Japan); and A. Ishii, University of Electro-Communications (Japan)

Creep-fatigue Test on LMFBR Structure with Weldment in Flowing Sodium at
Thermal Transient Test Facility ...........................................................................................114
    M. Kikuchi and H. Umeda, Power Reactor & Nuclear Fuel Development
    Corporation (Japan)


**Session 15.**    **Optical Measurement Applications**

An Automated System for Tire Topology Measurement Via Laser Scanning ...........................116
    J.L. Turner, D.O. Stalnaker, F.M. Chen and P.B. Wilson,
    Bridgestone/Firestone, Inc. (USA)

Strain Measurement on an Ultra-thin Metallic Glass Ribbon ...............................................118
    H. Lu, Ryerson Polytechnic University (Canada)

Moiré Interferometry at Cryogenic Temperatures for Thermal Deformation of
Superconducting Composites ............................................................................................120
    M. Tu, Y. Xu, P.J. Gielisse and I. Kulisic, Florida Agricultural &
    Mechanical University/FSU (USA)


**Session 16.**    **Applications of Optical Methods in Residual Stress Measurements**
Sponsored by the Residual Stress Technical Division

Automated Measurement of Residual Stresses by Phase-shift Shearography .......................122
    Y.Y. Hung, K.W. Long, J.Q. Wang and J.D. Hovanesian, Oakland University (USA)

Determination of Sub-surface Residual Stress Profiles by a Holographic-hole
Drilling Method .................................................................................................................124
    A. Makino and D.V. Nelson, Stanford University (USA)

Residual Stresses and Holography ....................................................................................126
    S.K. Foss, Deere & Company Technical Center (USA); D.V. Nelson
    and A. Makino, Stanford University (USA)

Interferometric Strain Rosette for Residual Stress Measurements .....................................128
    K. Li, Oakland University (USA)


**Session 17.**    **Fracture Process of Composites**

Cutting Phenomena of Aramid-glass Hybrid FRP with Ultrasonic Vibration ..........................130
    A.K.M. Masud, E. Nakanishi, J. Suzuki and K. Isogimi, Mie University (Japan)

Drilling Induced Failure Mechanisms in Carbon Fiber Composite Materials ..........................132
    Z.M. Khan, Iowa State University (USA); and B. Mills, Liverpool John Moores
    University (United Kingdom)

Crack-fiber Interactions at Interfaces in Brittle Composites ...............................................134
    M.C. Larson, Tulane University (USA)

Effects of the Stress State on the Dynamic Damage Behavior of Particulate
Reinforced Titanium Composites ........................................................................................135
    W. Tong and X. Li, University of Nebraska-Lincoln (USA)

Cracking Process and Delamination Strength of WC-Co Film Sprayed by
High-speed Flame ...................................................................................................137
      K. Nakasa, M. Kato, Hiroshima University (Japan); M. Kamata and
      N. Hara, Hiroshima Prefectural Industry Center (Japan)

Experimental Investigation of the Thermal Fatigue Life of Multilayer Thin
Film Structures ......................................................................................................139
      X. Sun and S. He, Tsinghua University (P.R. China)


**Session 18.    High Temperature II**
Jointly sponsored by SEM/JSME

Slow Crack Growth versus Creep Cavity Coalescence:  Competing Failure Mechanisms
During High-temperature Deformation of Advanced Ceramics ................................141
      M.G. Jenkins and T.L. Stevens, University of Washington (USA)

High Temperature Fatigue Crack Growth Behavior of Y-Base TiAl Intermetallics ....................143
      T. Hansson, Y. Mutoh, S. Kurai, Nagaoka University of Technology (Japan);
      and Y. Mizuhara, Nippon Steel Corp. (Japan)

Tensile Stress-strain Response and Creep Properties of $Si_3N_4$ Ceramics at
Elevated Temperatures ..........................................................................................145
      K. Hatanaka, K. Oshita, Yamaguchi University (Japan); and
      H. Shiota, Gifu University (Japan)


**Session 19.    Photoelastic Coatings - 40th Anniversary I**
Sponsored by the Applied Photoelasticity Technical Subdivision

The History of Photoelastic Coatings at Boeing ....................................................147
      R. Slaminko, The Boeing Co. (USA)

Photoelastic Coating and Strain Gage Analysis of Aluminum-lithium Welded Joints ...............148
      S.C. Gambrell, Jr. and S. Kumar, The University of Alabama (USA)

Industrial Experience in the Use of Full-field Automated Reflection Polariscopy for
Airbus Experimental Stress Analysis ......................................................................150
      E.W. O'Brien and I.J. Jones, British Aerospace Airbus Ltd. (United Kingdom)

Photoelastic Coating in Jet Motor Engine Design ..................................................152
      M. Taroni, Société Nationale d'Etude et de Construction de Moteurs d'Aviation
      (France); and D. Paraskevas, PK-LAB (France)


**Session 20.    Long Term Durability and Accelerated Testing of Composites II**
Sponsored by the Composite Materials Technical Division

Long Term Durability of Polymeric Composites for Application to Supersonic
Commercial Aircraft Development ...........................................................................154
      T.S. Gates, NASA Langley Research Center (USA)

The Role of Interphase in Long-term Performance of a Polymeric Composite
under Fatigue and Creep Loading ................................................................155
        S. Subramanian, Adtech Systems Research (USA); C.T. Liu, U.S. Air Force Phillips
        Laboratory (USA); and K.L. Reifsnider, Virginia Polytechnic Institute and
        State University (USA)

Post Impact Tension/Compression Fatigue of Graphite/PEEK Laminates ................................157
        P. McAuliffe, S.C. Yen and K.T. Teh, Southern Illinois University
        at Carbondale (USA)

Measurement of High-strain-rate Properties of Polymer Composites by Hopkinson
Bar Technique ................................................................................159
        P.K. Dutta and B. Coutermarsh, U.S. Army Cold Regions Research and
        Engineering Laboratory (USA)

Prediction and Measurement of Press-fit Forces and Stresses in Fiber Reinforced
Composite Flywheel Rotors ....................................................................160
        C.E. Bakis, R.P. Emerson and C.W. Gabrys, The Pennsylvania
        State University (USA)

**Session 21.**  **Optical Methods I**
Jointly sponsored by SEM/JSME

Fourier Detection and Analysis of Fringe Patterns ...........................................162
        C.A. Sciammarella, B. Trentadue and F.M. Sciammarella, Illinois Institute
        of Technology (USA)

Continuous Observation of the Whole Process of Deformation by Digital Speckle
Pattern Interferometry ........................................................................164
        S. Toyooka and X. Gong, Saitama University (Japan)

Modal Testing of a Turbopump Liner Using Time-average Panoramic
Holo-interferometry ...........................................................................166
        J.L. Lindner, NASA Marshall Space Flight Center (USA); and
        J.A. Gilbert, The University of Alabama in Huntsville (USA)

A Novel, Optical Nondestructive Deformation Analyzer Based on Electronic
Speckle-pattern Interferometry and a New Plastic Deformation Theory ...........................168
        S. Yoshida, Suprapedi, R. Widiastuti, Marincan, Septriyanti, Julinda,
        A. Faisal and A. Kusnowo, Indonesian Institute of Sciences (Indonesia)

Application of Dynamic Holographic-electronic Speckle Pattern Interferometry to
Study Full-field Dynamic Deformations in Solids ..............................................170
        M.A. Ahmadshahi, S. Krishnaswamy and S. Nemat-Nasser,
        C.E. Niehoff & Co. (USA)

**Session 22.**  **Advances in Experimental Mechanics**
Sponsored by SEM's Republic of China Local Section

A Novel 3-D Computer Vision Technique for Deformation Measurement and
Nondestructive Testing ........................................................................172
        Y.Y. Hung, B.G. Park and L. Lin, Oakland University (USA)

Hybrid Evaluation of Repair Efficiency of Composite Patching ................................................174
    W.C. Wang and C.H. Day, National Tsing Hua University (Taiwan, RO China)

Can the Fracture Toughness be Used for Fracture Assessment of Structures? ........................176
    Y.J. Chao, University of South Carolina (USA)

An Improved Method for Whole-field Automatic Measurement of Principal
Stress Directions ....................................................................................................................178
    T.Y. Chen and C.H. Lin, National Cheng Kung University (Taiwan, RO China)


**Session 23.    Time Dependent Materials I**
Sponsored by the Time Dependent Materials Technical Division

Experimental Evidence and Modeling of the Differing Time Scales of Structural
Recovery and Mechanical Relaxation Observed During Aging of Glassy Polymers ................180
    C.R. Schultheisz, D.M. Colucci and G.B. McKenna, National Institute of
    Standards and Technology (USA)

Nonlinear Polymer Response Under Biaxial Stress States .....................................................182
    H.B. Lu and W.G. Knauss, California Institute of Technology (USA)

Viscoelastic Responses and Physical Aging in Rubber-toughened Epoxy Glasses ................184
    A. Lee, Michigan State University (USA)

Transient Phenomena in Torsional Creep Measurements ........................................................186
    I. Emri, R. Cvelbar, University of Ljubljana (Slovenia); and
    A. Nikonov, Saratov State University (Russia)


**Session 24.    Photoelastic Coatings - 40th Anniversary II**
Sponsored by the Applied Photoelasticity Technical Subdivision

Extension of Zandman Coatings - Isodyne Coatings and Permanent Strain Coatings ..............188
    J.T. Pindera, University of Waterloo (Canada)

A Photoelastic Study of the Effectiveness of Bonded Repairs on Aging Aircraft ......................190
    R.L. Hastie, R. Fredell and J.W. Dally, U.S. Air Force Academy (USA)

Photoelastic Coating - 40 Years Evolution of Measuring Techniques .....................................192
    A.S. Redner, Strainoptic Technologies, Inc. (USA)

Corneal Birefringence Thirty Years Later ...............................................................................194
    J.D. Hovanesian, Oakland University (USA); and
    J.A. Hovanesian, Henry Ford Hospital (USA)

An Investigation of Yield in Normalized Mild Steel Using a Photoelastic Coating ....................195
    I.M. Allison, University of Warwick (United Kingdom)

**Session 25.    Long Term Durability and Accelerated Testing of Composites III**
Sponsored by the Composite Materials Technical Division

Measured Effects of Long-term Exposure to Elevated Temperatures and Loads
on Composite Materials ...................................................................................197
      K.R. Lupkes and M.E. Tuttle, University of Washington (USA)

Measurement of Residual Stress in Laminated Composites ...............................198
      P.G. Ifju, B.C. Kilday, S. Liu and X. Niu, University of Florida (USA)

Application of Carbon Fiber Composite for Bridge Columns ...............................200
      M.G. Abdallah, Hercules Inc. (USA); R.J. Nusimer, Alliant Techsystems (USA);
      F. Seible and R. Burgueno, University of California, San Diego (USA)

Load Transfer Across Seams in a Flexible Composite ........................................202
      C.H.M. Jenkins, R. Skalleberg and S. Wen, South Dakota School of Mines (USA)


**Session 26.    Optical Methods II**
Jointly sponsored by SEM/JSME

Automatic Whole-field Measurement of Photoelastic Fringe Orders Using
Generalized Phase-shift Method ......................................................................204
      E. Umezaki, H. Watanabe, Nippon Institute of Technology (Japan);
      and A. Shimamoto, Saitama Institute of Technology (Japan)

High Speed Shearography for Measuring Transient Deformation and Vibration .......206
      Y.Y. Hung, C.T. Griffen and F. Chen, Oakland University (USA)

Photoelastic Analysis Using a Linearly Polarized RGB White Light ....................208
      J. Gotoh, S. Yoneyama, S. Mawatari and M. Takashi, Aoyama Gakuin
      University (Japan)

Electronic Speckle Pattern Shearing Interferometer Using Two Holographic Grating ......210
      C. Joenathan and L. Buerkle, Rose Hulman Institute of Technology (USA)

Shape Measurement by Grid Projection Method Without Influence of Aberration
of Lenses .......................................................................................................212
      M. Fujigaki and Y. Morimoto, Wakayama University (Japan)


**Session 27.    Testing Aging Infrastructure**
Sponsored by the Structural Testing Technical Division

Fatigue Evaluation of the Holston River Bridge ................................................214
      J.H. Deatherage, D.W. Goodpasture and E.G. Burdette, The University
      of Tennessee-Knoxville(USA)

Evaluation and Repair of the North Avenue Pedestrian Bridge .........................216
      A. Longinow, G.J. Klein, Wiss, Janney, Elstner Associates, Inc. (USA);
      and K.M. Tarhini, Valparaiso University (USA)

Experimental Study of a Segmental Bridge Structure ................................218
    M. Zoghi, The University of Dayton (USA); and T.J. Beach, CON/SPAN
    Bridge Systems (USA)

X-ray Stress Measurements on Large Structures ................................220
    B. Pardue, Technology for Energy Corp. (USA)

The Stiffness Decoupler - A New Approach to Base Isolation of Structures ............221
    K.K. Hu, P.G. Kirmser and S.E. Swartz, Kansas State University (USA)

Monitoring of Structural Integrity Using Experimental Techniques ...................223
    J.L.F. Freire, J.T.P. Castro, Catholic University of Rio de Janeiro (Brazil);
    and R.D. Vieira, CEFET-RJ and Strainlab Stress Analysis (Brazil)

Static and Dynamic Tests of Driven Piles in Loess Soil .............................225
    E.G. Burdette, J.H. Deatherage and D.W. Goodpasture, The University
    of Tennessee-Knoxville (USA)


**Session 28.    Time Dependent Materials II**
Sponsored by the Time Dependent Materials Technical Division

An Apparatus for Measuring a Time-dependent Poisson Ratio ........................226
    T. Skitek, I. Emri, University of Ljubljana (Slovenia); and
    N.W. Tschoegl, California Insitute of Technology (USA)

Experimental Investigation of the Nonlinear Viscoelastic Response and Subsequent
Volume Changes of Two Engineering Polymers in Tension and Compression .............228
    D.M. Colucci, P.A. O'Connell and G.B. McKenna, National Institute of
    Standards and Technology (USA)

To What Extent Can the Numerics Give Support to the Experimental Evaluations .........230
    B. Stok and P. Koc, University of Ljubljana (Slovenia)


**Session 29.    Nondestructive Evaluation of Composites**

Nondestructive Strength Evaluation of Ceramic-Metal Joints by Ultrasonic Technique ...........232
    Y. Arai, E. Tsuchida and M. Yoshino, Saitama University (Japan)

Composite Structure NDE with Laser Doppler Vibrometer ...........................234
    F.P. Sun, F. Lalande and C.A. Rogers, Virginia Polytechnic Institute and
    State University (USA)

Time-averaged Digital Specklegraphy (TADS) for NDE of Crevice Corrosion
and Composite Debond ...........................................................236
    F. Jin and F.P. Chiang, State University of New York at Stony Brook (USA)

Application of Digital Image Correlation to Microfracture Testing of
Particulate-reinforced Titanium Composites ......................................238
    W. Tong and S. Huang, University of Nebraska-Lincoln (USA)

Phase-stepped Deflectometry Applied to Shape Measurement of Bent
Composite Plates ..................................................................................................240
     N. Fournier, M. Grédiac, P.A. Paris and Y. Surrel, École des Mines de
     Saint-Étienne (France)

Discrete Wavelet Analysis of Acoustic Emissions - Identification of CFR
Composite Failure Modes ......................................................................................242
     G. Qi, A. Barhorst and J. Hashemi, Texas Tech University (USA)


**Session 30.    Experimental Mechanics of Wood & Wood-based Composites**
Sponsored by the Wood and Wood-based Composites Technical Subdivision

Instrumentations and Experimental Techniques for Evaluating Long-term
Engineering Performance of Wood-based Composites .........................................244
     R.C. Tang, Auburn University (USA); J.H. Pu, J.M. Huber Corp. (USA);
     and J.N. Lee, Auburn University (USA)

Measurement of Mechanical Properties of Knots in Lumber .................................246
     L. Luo and J.Z. Wang, Michigan Technological University (USA)

Strain Measurement on Wood ...............................................................................248
     J.R. Loferski, Virginia Polytechnic Institute and State University (USA)

A Novel Technique for Measuring Micro- and Macromechanical Properties of
Individual Wood Fibers .........................................................................................249
     S.M. Shaler, L. Mott, University of Maine (USA); and L.H. Groom, USDA
     Forest Service (USA)

Density Determination of a Wood Particle Mat During Consolidation Using
Nuclear Technology ...............................................................................................251
     P.M. Winistorfer, W.W. Moschler, W. Xu and B.L. Bledsoe, The University
     of Tennessee-Knoxville (USA)

Dynamic Model for Analysis of Periodic Circular Wood Cutting Process Stability ....252
     B. Bucar and M. Houska, University of Ljubljana (Slovenia)


**Session 31.    Engineering Education and Training for the Future**

Elastic Transverse Impact on Fixed End Beam .....................................................254
     D. Goldar, Delhi College of Engineering (India)

A Self-teach Laboratory for Multi-DOF Vibration ..................................................256
     T. Barrett-Leonard, N. Scott and B.J. Stone, The University of
     Western Australia (Western Australia)

Cross-roads of Engineering Experimental Mechanics ...........................................258
     J.T. Pindera, University of Waterloo (Canada)

**Session 32.  Moiré and Holographic Interferometry Techniques**

Numerical Phase Shifting Technique for Fringe Pattern Analysis in Real
Time Investigation ....................................................................................260
    F. Brémand, Université de Poitiers (France)

Planar Surface Reconstruction Using Soliton Wavelet and Structured Light ...........................262
    W.F. Ranson, III and D.N. Rocheleau, University of South Carolina (USA)

Investigation of Displacements due to Normal and Tangential Loads on a
Finite Width Bar ....................................................................................264
    M. Ciavarella, G. Demelio, W.M. Sun and B. Trentadue, Politecnico di Bari (Italy)

Optimizing Load Cell Design Using an Experimental/Numerical Method ...............................266
    Z. Guo and B.R. Oakes, SI Technologies, Inc. (USA)

Thermal Deformation Measurement in SMT Assembly by Moiré and Holographic
Interferometry ....................................................................................268
    F. Dai, Tsinghua University (P.R. China); W. Wang, City University of
    Hong Kong (Hong Kong); L. Shi, Tsinghua University (P.R. China);
    K.M. Leung, City University of Hong Kong (Hong Kong); and D. Zou,
    Tsinghua University (P.R. China)

**Session 33.  NDT of Metallic Structures**
Sponsored by the Structural Testing Technical Division

Integration of Microscopic Material Level and Macroscopic NDE of Aged
Steel Structures ....................................................................................270
    D.N. Farhey, A.E. Aktan, A.M. Thakur, R.C. Buchanan and
    N. Jayaraman, University of Cincinnati (USA)

Steel Bridge Rating Using the Falling Weight Deflectometer Technique ...............................272
    H.G. Melhem, S.K. Iyer and K.K. Hu, Kansas State University (USA)

Acoustic Emission Tester for Aircraft Fire Extinguisher Bottles ....................................273
    A.G. Beattie, Sandia National Laboratories (USA)

Whirling of Sun Gear Shaft in Planetary Gear Train Affected by Torque ...............................275
    M. Yoshino, Nagaoka College of Technology (Japan); and
    S. Yanabe, Nagaoka University of Technology (Japan)

**Session 34.  Time Dependent Behavior in Wood & Wood-based Composites**
Sponsored by the Wood and Wood-based Composite Technical Subdivision

Time-dependent Structural Behavior of Wood Composite Panels:  Effect of
Environmental Conditions ....................................................................................277
    R.C. Tang, J.N. Lee, Auburn University (USA); and
    J.H. Pu, J.M. Huber Corp. (USA)

Development of Tension and Compression Creep Models for Wood Using
the Time-temperature Super-position Principle ............................................279
    J.R. Loferski, B.H. Bond, J. Tissauoi and S.M. Holzer, Virginia
    Polytechnic Institute and State University (USA)

Time-dependent Strength of Wood Subjected to Several Loading Conditions .........280
    J.Y. Liu, R.J. Ross and E.L. Schaffer, USDA Forest Service (USA)

Development and Assessment of Soybean-based Adhesive/Wood and
Agrofiber Composites ............................................282
    D.O. Adams, M. Kuo, D. Myers, D. Curry and H. Heemstra, Iowa State
    University of Science and Technology (USA)

**Session 35.    The Business of Experimental Mechanics**
Sponsored by the Education Committee

Issues in Workforce Composition Analysis ............................................284
    D.C. Koech and J.D. Rogers, Sandia National Laboratories (USA)

From Invention to Innovation: Creation of Value Through Intellectual
Property Development ............................................286
    K.B. Zimmerman and T.E. Anderson, General Motors R&D Center (USA)

Environmental Assessment of Vehicles ............................................287
    J.L. Sullivan, Ford Motor Company (USA)

**Session 36.    Aging Aerospace**
Organized by W.G. Reuter, Idaho National Engineering Laboratory (USA)

Technical Challenges in Operating an Aging Commercial and Military Transport
Aircraft Fleet Provide Impetus for New R&D Initiatives ............................................288
    C.E. Harris, NASA Langley Research Center (USA)

Aging Aircraft Life Extension - Composite Repairs of Primary Metallic Structure ........290
    J.B. Cochran, R.P. Bell and H.R. Michael, Lockheed Martin Aeronautical
    Systems Co. (USA)

The Effect of Elevated Temperature Exposure on the Damage Tolerant Properties
of Aluminum Alloys Intended for Elevated Temperature Application ........................292
    A.P. Reynolds, University of South Carolina (USA)

**Session 37.    Transducers and Sensors I**

Dynamic Response of Strain Gages up to 300kHz ............................................294
    K. Ueda and A. Umeda, National Research Laboratory of Metrology (Japan)

Non Contact and Whole Field Strain Analysis with a Laseroptical Strain Sensor ........296
    A. Ettemeyer, Dr. Ettemeyer GmbH & Co. (Germany)

High Temperature Strain Gages with Application of New Organosilicate Adhesives ...............298
    E.J. Nekhendzy, V.A. Kratikov, Y.I. Khodobin, R.A. Tarasov, Polzunov
    Central Boiler and Turbine Institute (Russia); S.P. Wnuk and
    V.P. Wnuk, Hitec Products, Inc. (USA)

An Innovative Method for the Measurement of Post-penetration Residual Velocity .................300
    S.W.R. Lee, The Hong Kong University of Science and Techology (Hong Kong)

## Session 39.    Interface of Composites

Interlaminar Shear Testing of Composites .....................................................302
    S. Chimalakonda and S.R. Short, Northern Illinois University (USA)

Analyses of Double Cantilever Beam Adhesion Test Specimens ............................304
    K.L. DeVries and P.R. Borgmeier, University of Utah (USA)

Deformation and Stress Analyses of Double-lap Adhesive Joints with Laminated
Composite Adherends .......................................................................306
    M.Y. Tsai, Virginia Polytechnic Institute and State University (USA);
    J. Morton, Structural Materials Center, DRA (United Kingdom); and
    D.W. Oplinger, Federal Aviation Administration Technical Center (USA)

Stress Field of Reinforced Matrix with Imperfect Interface Under Residual
Stress and Transverse Loading ..............................................................308
    B.S. Wang, F.P. Chiang and S.Y. Wu, State University of New York
    at Stony Brook (USA)

Drop Weight Testing of Concrete Beams Externally Reinforced with Carbon
Fiber Reinforced Plastic (CFRP) Strips .....................................................310
    D.M. Jerome, Wright Laboratory (USA); and
    C.A. Ross, University of Florida (USA)

## Session 40.    Dynamic Fracture and Impact I
Jointly sponsored by SEM/JSME

A Method of Pulsed Holographic Microscopy to Photograph Fast Propagating
Cracks with Higher Spatial Resolution ......................................................312
    S. Suzuki, Toyohashi University of Technology (Japan)

Measurements of Interlaminar Fracture Toughness in Composite Laminates
Under Impact Loading .......................................................................314
    Y. Yamauchi, M. Nakano and K. Kishida, Osaka University (Japan)

Mechanics of Dynamic Crack Propagation Along Bimaterial Interfaces:
The Intersonic Regime ......................................................................316
    R.P. Singh and A. Shukla, University of Rhode Island (USA)

Grating Interrogation Using Oblique Diffraction for Dynamic Local
Strain Determination ........................................................................318
    V. Valle, M. Cottron and A. Lagarde, Université de Poitiers (France)

**Session 41.     Aging Infrastructure**
Organized by W.G. Reuter, Idaho National Engineering Laboratory (USA)

The Role of Nondestructive Evaluation in our Infrastructure ....................................320
    C.J. Hellier, Hellier Associates, Inc. (USA)

Instrumentation, Testing and Monitoring of the Construction and Service of a
Steel-stringer Bridge ..................................................................................................321
    V.J. Hunt, A. Levi, R. Barrish, K. Grimmelsman, A.E. Aktan and
    A.J. Helmicki, University of Cincinnati Infrastructure Institute (USA)

Bridge-type-specific Management of Steel-stringer Bridges in Ohio .........................323
    M. Lenett, F.N. Catbas, V.J. Hunt, A.E. Aktan, A.J. Helmicki and
    S.J. Shelley, University of Cincinnati Infrastructure Institute (USA)

A Simple Intensity Based Fiber Optic Sensor for Health Monitoring of Structures
Using Displacement Measurements .............................................................................325
    F. Sienkiewicz, A. Shukla and J. Gomez, University of Rhode Island (USA)


**Session 42.     Optical Methods in Experimental Mechanics**
Sponsored by SEM's Republic of China Local Section

Vibration Measurement of Composite Plates Containing a Circular Defect by ESPI .................327
    W.C. Wang, S.Y. Lin and C.H. Hwang, National Tsing Hua University
    (Taiwan, R.O. China)

Vibration Measurement of Composite Plates Containing Defect at Different
Depths by Amplitude Fluctuation ESPI Method ...........................................................329
    W.C. Wang, C.H. Hwang and S.Y. Lin, National Tsing Hua University
    (Taiwan, R.O. China)

The Experimental Analysis of Kinematics and Contact Stresses of Double-dwell Cams ..........331
    M.J. Wang, Ming Hsin Institute of Technology and Commerce
    (Taiwan, R.O. China); W.C. Wang and Y.M. Chen, National Tsing Hua University
    (Tawian, R.O. China)

Analysis of Growing Crack Tip Deformation Using Both In-plane Deformation and
Caustics Obtained from Out-of-plane Displacement ....................................................333
    P.F. Luo, J.S. Wang, Chung Hua Polytechnic Institute (Taiwan, R.O. China);
    Y.J. Chao and M.A. Sutton, University of South Carolina (USA)

The Determination of Fiber-bridging Tractions in Fiber-reinforced Composites .......................335
    C.H. Chen and R.R. Chang, National Taiwan University (Taiwan, R.O. China)

A Tomographic Technique for Determining Contact Stress .........................................337
    M.W. Witte, Chrysler Corporation (USA); J.D. Hovanesian, Oakland University
    (USA); and J.A. Hovanesian, Henry Ford Hospital (USA)

**Session 43.    Technical Committee on Strain Gages II**
Sponsored by the Technical Committee on Strain Gages Technical Division

Stresses in Rigid Pavement due to Environmental Factors ........................................339
    J.J. Von Handorf, S.M. Sargand and G.A. Hazen, Ohio University (USA)

Monitoring Dynamic Response of Pavement by Strain Gages ................................341
    A.A. Sharkins, S.M. Sargand and I.S. Khoury, Ohio University (USA)


**Session 44.    Applications I**

An Experimental Study on Mechanical Behavior of Gilded and Painted Leather
of the XVIII Century ........................................................................................343
    F. Bonetti and P. Cappa, University of Rome "La Sapienza" (Italy)

Performance Evaluation of Endoscopic Optical Systems by Means of Digital
Fourier Analysis ..............................................................................................345
    F.P. Branca, University of Rome "La Sapienza" (Italy); T. D'Alessio, III Rome's
    University (Italy); Z. Del Prete, F. Marinozzi and E. Pichini, University
    of Rome "La Sapienza" (Italy)

A New Device for Evaluation of the Batteries State of Charge ................................347
    P. Cappa, L. Fedele and V. Naso, University of Rome "La Sapienza" (Italy)


**Session 45.    Dynamic Fracture and Impact II**
Jointly sponsored by SEM/JSME

Dynamic Fracture Behavior of Brittle Polymers Under Biaxial Loading ...................349
    K. Arakawa, D. Nagoh and K. Takahashi, Kyushu University (Japan)

Dynamic Fracture of Brittle Materials ................................................................351
    K. Ravi-Chandar and B. Yang, University of Houston (USA)

Proposed Mixed-mode Dynamic Fracture Toughness Testing Method Using a
New Specimen ..................................................................................................352
    H. Wada, A. Hinoshita, Daido Institute of Technology (Japan); C.A. Calder and
    T.C. Kennedy, Oregon State University (USA)

Short Pulse Impact in Graphite Epoxy Composites ............................................354
    H.A. Bruck and J.S. Epstein, Idaho National Engineering Laboratory (USA)

Visualization of Stress Waves in Blasting Processes by a Laser-shadowgraph
Method and Its Applications to Dynamic Fracture Control ....................................356
    Y. Nakamura, Yatsushiro National College of Technology (Japan)


**Session 46.    Other Industry Aging Problems**
Organized by W.G. Reuter, Idaho National Engineering Laboratory (USA)

Aging Petrochemical Plants ..............................................................................358
    R.M. Kay, Exxon Chemical Company (USA)

Containment Strategy for the Safe Disposal of Nuclear Waste ................................360
        W.L. Clarke, Lawrence Livermore National Laboratory (USA); and
        T.W. Doering, Framatome Cogema Fuel (USA)

Fatigue Crack Growth Behavior of Creep Damaged Specimens of Type 304
Stainless Steel ....................................................................................361
        S.B. Lee, B.S. Park and J.Y. Kim, Korea Advanced Institute of
        Science and Technology (Korea)


**Session 47.    Photoelasticity**

Strain Distribution Induced by Implanted Tibial Component with Various Stem
Geometries ........................................................................................363
        A. Salehi and M. Cooper, Smith & Nephew Orthopaedics (USA)

Fuzzy Logic Approach for Analysis of White-light Isochromatic Fringes ...................365
        D.E.P. Hoy and F. Yu, Tennessee Technological University (USA)

Assembly Stresses Effects on Multiple Holes ...........................................367
        N.T. Younis and S.J. Baker, Purdue University at Fort Wayne (USA)

Photoelastic Property of Silicon Single Crystal ..........................................368
        Y. Niitsu and K. Gomi, Tokyo Denki University (Japan)

Examples of Industrial Analysis Using a 3D Fully Automated Photoelasticimeter
(3D-CAPE) - Technical and Economical Aspects.  Link with the Finite
Elements Calculus ...............................................................................370
        D. Paraskevas, PK-LAB (France)


**Session 48.    Applications II**

A Study on Stress-strain Behaviors of Dual Phase Steels Caused by the Change
in Various Microstructural Factors ..........................................................372
        Y.S. Yu, M.J. Choi and T.Y. Oh, Kyung Hee University (Korea)

Vibration Control of a Moving Structure by Neural Network ...........................374
        S.Y. Lee and H.S. Jeong, Kunsan National University (Korea)

Oblique Impact of a Rotating Elastic Solid on a Deformable Surface ...................376
        S.J. Haake, The University of Sheffield (United Kingdom)


**Session 49.    Optical Techniques Applied to Fracture Mechanics**

Application of Caustic Method to Dynamic Phenomena (Characteristics of
Caustics Created in Two Dimensional Cutting) .........................................378
        J. Wang, Virginia Polytechnic Institute and State University (USA);
        J. Suzuki and K. Isogimi, Mie University (Japan)

Stress Intensity Factor for Plates of Discontinuous Cross Section with Corner
Cracks Under Out-of-plane Bending ......................................................380
        E. Matsumoto, H. Fujiwara, A. Saito and K. Kushiki, Kinki University (Japan)

Photoelastic Analysis of Panel-stiffened Plates with Cracks ................................382
    A.D. Nurse, Loughborough University of Technology (United Kingdom);
    R.L. Burguete and E.A. Patterson, The University of Sheffield (United Kingdom)

Digital Sherography for NDT of Reinforced Concrete ...........................................384
    W. Steinchen, L.X. Yang and G. Kupfer, University of Kassel (Germany)

**Session 50.    Structural Applications**

Experimental Investigation on the Dynamic Characteristics of Helical Gears ...........................386
    C.I. Park, Kangnung National University (Korea); and J.M. Lee, Seoul
    National University (Korea)

Piezoelectric Accelerometers Application on Sandwich Glasses ..............................388
    G. Kajon, Experimental Institute of Italian Railways (Italy); L. Monteleone and
    R. Steindler, University of Rome "La Sapienza" (Italy)

Material Damage Research Using FEM Modal Analysis and Experimental Data ......................390
    L. Lin and C. Chen, Central South University of Technology (P.R. China)

Static and Dynamic Testing of Tubular Sections in Bending Collapse:
Experimental Method ................................................................................392
    J.F. Corbeil, J. Arteau and A. Lan, Quebec Occupational Health and
    Safety Research Institute (IRSST) (Canada)

**Session 51.    JSME/SEM Time Dependent Materials I**
Jointly sponsored by SEM/JSME

Time Dependent Plasticity of Refractory Metals Near Room Temperature ......................394
    B. Weiss and R. Stickler, University of Vienna (Austria)

Effect of the Fiber Contents on Creep Behavior of FRTP .........................................396
    S. Somiya, K. Igarashi and N. Iwamoto, Keio University (Japan)

Theoretical and Experimental Studies in the Mechanical Behavior of Solid
Polymer Foams .......................................................................................398
    H. Weber, University of Karlsruhe (Germany)

Transient Behavior from Stable-to-unstable Crack Growth in a Viscoelastic Wide Strip ...........400
    K. Ogawa, Aoyama Gakuin University (Japan); A. Misawa, Kanagawa Institute
    of Technology (Japan); and M. Takashi, Aoyama Gakuin University (Japan)

Effects of Fluid on Polymeric Composites - A Review ............................................402
    Y.J. Weitsman, The University of Tennessee (USA)

**Session 52.    Stress Analysis of Composites**

Development and Characterization of Brittle-matrix Model Composites ......................403
    R.D. Cordes and I.M. Daniel, Northwestern University (USA)

Whole-field Investigation of End-constraint Effects in Off-axis Tests of Composites ...............405
    E. Alloba, F. Pierron, Y. Surrel and A. Vautrin, École des Mines de
    Saint-Étienne (France)

The Effects of Residual Stress on the Physical Aging of a Thermoplastic Composite .............407
    D.R. Veazie, Clark Atlanta University (USA)

Parametric Study on the Sensing Region of a Driven PZT Actuator-sensor ...........................409
    J. Esteban, F. Lalande and C.A. Rogers, Virginia Polytechnic Institute
    and State University (USA)


**Session 53.    Photoelasticity III**

A Photoelastic Study of Contact Between a Cylinder and a Half-plane .......................................411
    R.L. Burguete and E.A. Patterson, The University of Sheffield (United Kingdom)

A Combined Method with Transmitted and Scattered Light for 3-D Photoelastic
Stress Analysis ............................................................................................................................413
    K. Ezaki, A. Ikeda, S. Mawatari and
    M. Takashi, Aoyama Gakuin University (Japan)

Photoelastic Analysis of Polycarbonate Loaded by Spherical Indentator
Using Strain-freezing Method .....................................................................................................415
    A. Shimamoto, Saitama Institute of Technology (Japan);
    E. Umezaki, Nippon Institute of Technology (Japan); and
    S. Takahashi, Kanto Gakuin University (Japan)

A Study on the Development of Stress Optic Law of Photoelastic Experiment
Considering Residual Stress .......................................................................................................417
    J.S. Hawong, Yeungnam University (Korea); J.G. Suh, Kyungdong
    Junior College (Korea); and S.H. Choi, Yeungnam University (Korea)

Analysis and Behavior of Bonded Double Containment Joints ..................................................419
    S.S. Issa and M.H. Zgoul, University of Jordan (Jordan)

Stress Measurement by Infrared Laser Photoelasticity ..............................................................421
    Y. Niitsu and K. Gomi, Tokyo Denki University (Japan)

Development of Multi-channel-type Photoelastic Apparatus and Quantitative
Characterization of Residual Strain Profiles in Mass-produced GaP Wafers ...........................423
    Y. Nishiwaki, M. Fukuzawa and M. Yamada, Kyoto Institute
    of Technology (Japan)


**Session 54.    Fracture Mechanics I**

T* Integral Analysis for Aluminum CT Specimen .......................................................................425
    Y. Omori, University of Washington (USA); H. Okada, Georgia Institute
    of Technology (USA); K. Perry, Jr., J.S. Epstein, Idaho National Engineering
    Laboratory (USA); S.N. Atluri, Georgia Institute of Technology (USA);
    and A.S. Kobayashi, University of Washington (USA)

Interaction Between Corrosion and Fatigue of Aluminum Alloy ...............................................427
      M.L. Du, F.P. Chiang, S.V. Kagwade and C.R. Clayton, State University
      of New York at Stony Brook (USA)

Strength and Fracture Toughness of the Silicon Nitride and Silicon
Nitride/Ag-Cu-Ti Joints ...............................................................................................429
      I. Ferreira, State University of Campinas (UNICAMP) (Brazil)

Deformation of Explosion Clad Plate with a Crack ...................................................431
      I. Oda and K. Shiraishi, Kumamoto University (Japan)

A New High Velocity Micro-particle Impact Technique Applied to Abrasive
Waterjet Cutting Head Design .....................................................................................433
      M. Nanduri, D.G. Taggart and T.J. Kim, University of Rhode Island (USA)


**Session 55.    JSME/SEM Time Dependent Materials II**
Jointly sponsored by SEM/JSME

Time Dependent Behavior of Mode I Delamination in Unidirectionally Reinforced
CF/PEEK Under Cyclic Loading at Elevated Temperature ........................................435
      T. Kitamura, R. Ohtani, Kyoto University (Japan); and
      Y. Uematsu, Osaka University (Japan)

Time Dependent Failure Mechanisms of Fatigued SMC ...........................................437
      B. von Bernstorff, BASF AG (Germany)

Time and Temperature Dependence on Flexural Fatigue Behavior of Unidirectional
CFRP Laminates Using Pitch-based Carbon Fibers ..................................................439
      Y. Miyano, K. Nakamura, M. Nakada, Kanazawa Institute of
      Technology (Japan); and M. Mohri, Nippon Oil Company, Ltd. (Japan)

Time Dependent Phenomena on Using Composite Materials for High
Temperature Aircraft Applications ..............................................................................441
      A. Horoschenkoff, K. Schmidtke, Daimler Benz AG (Germany);
      and M. Reiprich, Daimler-Benz Aerospace Airbus (Germany)

Viscoelastic Analysis of Residual Stress in Injection Molds Owing to
Molding Conditions .....................................................................................................443
      M. Shimbo, Y. Miyano, S. Nagata, Kanazawa Institute of Technology (Japan);
      M. Yamabe and M. Ishijima, Nissan Motor Co. Ltd. (Japan)


**Session 56.    Fracture Mechanics III**

Dynamic Ductile Fracture an Experimental-numerical Analysis ................................445
      J. Lee. M.T. Kokaly and A.S. Kobayashi, University of Washington (USA)

The Dynamic Fracture Toughness Evaluation of Metal Matrix Composites ..............447
      M.K. Park, S.M. Bahk, Myongji University (Korea); and
      S.K. Choi, Keumkang Limited Central Research Institute (Korea)

Inverse Analysis for Embedded Fractures ...............................................449
      W.D. Keat, Clarkson University (USA); and
      M.C. Larson, Tulane University (USA)


**Session 57.    Transducers and Sensors II**

Develop a 3-D Contact Pressure & 2-D Slip Displacement Detecting Sensor .........................450
      S.H. Kim and K.Z. Cho, Chonnam National University (Korea)

A New Strain Gage Method for Measuring the Crack Propagation Toughness
in Non-isothermal Fields ...............................................................455
      R.J. Sanford and G.S. Sayal, University of Maryland (USA)

Application of a New Signal Conditioner on Long-term Strain Gage Measurements ................457
      P. Cappa, Z. Del Prete and
      F. Marinozzi, University of Rome "La Sapienza" (Italy)

Wireless Strain-measurement Using a Prestressed Sensor ......................................459
      L. Nilly, N. Nicoletti and M. Renner, ESSAIM-MIAM-Université de
      Haute Alsace (France)

Vibration Measurement by Digital Speckle Image Processing ...................................461
      N.H. Zhu and F.P. Chiang, State University of New York at Stony Brook (USA)


**Session 58.    Shape, Strain, Roughness Measurement by Means of Optical Techniques**

Measurement of Three Dimensional Shape and Its Surface Strain by Digital Image
Correlation Method .....................................................................463
      T. Mihara, H. Sumitomo, M. Yoshinari and K. Date, Tohoku University (Japan)

Improvement of Optical 3-D Deformation Measurement of Fuzzy Logic Control ...................465
      H. Weber, T. Wolf and B. Gutmann, University of Karlsruhe (Germany)

Optical Surface Roughness Measurement Using Standard Deviations of Two-dimensional
Gaussian Function Approximating Scattered Light Intensity Distribution ......................467
      M. Kurita and Z. Deng, Nagaoka University of Technology (Japan)

Modified Grid Method for Plastic-strain-ratio Measurement in Sheet Metal ....................469
      S.Y. Lin, R. Czarnek and P.K. Chaudhury, Concurrent Technologies
      Corporation (USA)

Ultra-high Sensitivity Moiré Interferometry by the Aid of Electronic-liquid Phase-shifter
and Computer ...........................................................................471
      Z. Luo, H. Zhang, Z. Mu, F. Su, Tianjin University (P.R. China);
      and M. Tu, Florida Agricultural & Mechanical University/FSU (USA)


**Session 59.    Residual Stress - Applications and Modeling**

Contribution of Experimental Mechanics for the Integration of Residual Stress
Problem in Mechanical Design and in Quality Control ........................................473
      J. Lu, University of Technology of Troyes (France)

Evaluation of Stress Corrosion Process by X-ray Diffraction Technique ..................................475
    H. Kato and K. Nakai, Saitama University (Japan)

Modeling the Residual Strains in a Burnished Annular Plate ........................................477
    N. Nicoletti, D. Fendeleur, E. Aubry and M. Renner, ESSAIM-MIAM
    Université de Haute Alsace (France)

Measurement of Residual Stress in SSME AT HPFTP 3rd Impeller Pump
Side Rub Stop .............................................................................................479
    G.R. Swanson, NASA, Marshall Space Flight Center (USA)

The Experimental Investigation on Residual Deformation of Single-shear Sheet
Specimen Using Ultrasonic Technology ...............................................................481
    X. Sun, Tsinghua University (P.R. China); and
    K. Kawashima, Nagoya Institute of Technology (Japan)


Session 60.    Speckle Techniques

Digital Speckle Metrology: Techniques and Applications ..........................................483
    F. Chen, C.T. Griffen and Y.Y. Hung, Oakland University (USA)

Speckle Interferometry with Electron Microscopy and Its Applications .........................486
    Q. Wang and F.P. Chiang, State University of New York at Stony Brook (USA)

The Analysis of Shadow Mask Vibration Mode for CDT Through the Use of ESPI ...............487
    W.H. Kim, S.W. Chang, S.H. Kim and
    D.S. Ryu, Daewoo Electronics Co., Ltd. (Korea)

Three Dimensional Photoelastic Analysis of Cylindrical Pipe Under Internal Pressure Restricted
Radially at One End of the Pipe .......................................................................489
    H. Fujiwara, E. Matsumoto and A. Saito, Kinki University (Japan)

Automated Deformation Measurement with Incorporation of Electronic Speckle
Shearography and Carrier Technique ..................................................................491
    B.S. Wang, State University of New York at Stony Brook (USA);
    and X. Zhang, Shanghai Marine Diesel Engine Research Institute (P.R. China)

Digital Shearing Speckle Correlation Fringe Pattern Formed by Using a
Linear Correlation Calculating Method ...............................................................493
    Y.M. He and B.B. Zhang, Huazhong University of Science and
    Technology (P.R. China)


Session 61.    Time Dependent Materials: Rock, Concrete and Related Materials

Study of the Mechanical Properties of Plain Concrete Under Dynamic Loading ................495
    C. Albertini, E. Cadoni and K. Labibes, European Commission, Joint Research
    Centre, Institute for System, Informatics and Safety (Italy)

Finite Element Modeling of Photoplastic Processes in the Cold Drawing of
Polycarbonate Bars ......................................................................................497
    J.H. Lee and D.J. Choi, University of Alaska Fairbanks (USA)

600ºC Creep Analysis of Metal Material with Moiré Interferometry Method ............................499
    H. Xie, F. Dai, Tsinghua University (P.R. China); P. Dietz and
    A. Schmidt, Technical University of Clausthal (Germany)


**Session 62.    Fracture Mechanics IV**

Determination of the Stress Intensity Factor for Steel Materials and 7075-T6
Aluminum Alloy Using the Reflected Caustic Method ................................................501
    S. Tsukagosi, Kanto Gakuin University (Japan); A. Shimamoto,
    Saitama Institute of Technology (Japan); and S. Takahashi, Kanto
    Gakuin University (Japan)

The Effect of Magnetic Field on the Experimental Determination of $K_I$ by Means of
ACPD Technique ...........................................................................................................503
    J.H. Lee, M. Saka and H. Abé, Tohoku University (Japan)

A New Procedure for the Determination of Stress Intensity Factors from
Thermoelastic Data .......................................................................................................505
    R.A. Kitchin, The University of Sheffield (United Kingdom); A.D. Nurse,
    Loughborough University of Technology (United Kingdom); and
    E.A. Patterson, The University of Sheffield (United Kingdom)

Measurement of Crack Tip Location, Orientation, and Mixed Mode Stress
Intensity Factors Using Near Crack Tip Strain Gages ................................................507
    G.R. Swanson, NASA, Marshall Space Flight Center (USA);
    and L.W. Zachary, Iowa State University (USA)

Crack Initiation and Propagation in Stress Interaction Field ......................................509
    S.H. Song, Korea University (Korea); and J.S. Bae, Korea University
    Graduate School (Korea)

Evaluation of Fracture Strain from Measurements of Aspect Ratio for Ferrite Grains ..............511
    M. Ohashi, National Research Institute of Police Science (Japan)


**ADDENDUM**
*(Papers listed in the Addendum were submitted after the printer's deadline. Therefore, these papers
could not be listed under the appropriate session titles).*

A General Form for Calculating Residual Stresses Detected by Using Holographic
Blind-hole Method .........................................................................................................513
    S.T. Lin, National Taipei Institute of Technology (Taiwan, RO China)
    *(Session 22)*

Residual Stresses in High Pressure Lamps ................................................................515
    B.E. Buescher, Jr., D.A. Anderson, The Idaho National Engineering
    Laboratory (USA); K.E. Perry, NIKE Air Laboratory (USA); C.E. Scott, General Electric
    Lighting Products (USA); R.L. Williamson and J.S. Epstein, The Idaho National
    Engineering Laboratory (USA)
    *(Session 16)*

Reliability of a Single Crystal NiAl Alloy for Turbine Blade Applications ....................................516
    J.A. Salem, R. Noebe, J. Manderscheid, NASA Lewis Research Center (USA);
    and R. Darolia, General Electric Aircraft Engine Co. (USA)
    *(Session 14)*

Thermal Spray Technologies for Infrastructure Repair and Maintenance ..................................518
    C.C. Berndt, State University of New York at Stony Brook (USA); M.L. Allan,
    Brookhaven National Laboratory (USA); H. Herman, J. Brogan, R. Benary,
    R. Zatorski, State University of New York at Stony Brook (USA); and
    M. Leote, Triborough Bridge and Tunnel Authority (USA)
    *(Session 41)*

# An Approach to Hybrid Method for Stress Analysis Using Photoelastic Image Data

Masahisa TAKASHI*, Shizuo MAWATARI* and Yoshika OMORI**

\* Aoyama Gakuin University, College of Sci. and Eng., 6-16-1 Chitosedai, Setagaya, Tokyo 157, Japan
\*\* University of Washington, Dept. of Mech. Eng., Seattle, WA 98195, USA

## I. INTRODUCTION

Analytical methods for stress, strain and displacement in an elastic body are broadly classified into three categories, such as theoretical, numerical and experimental analyses. Although each method has its own merits, it seems, however, difficult to accomplish the purpose of analysis including error estimation under general and complicated mechanical conditions with a certain single method belonging to an individual category.

All methods for elastic analysis could be started from a theoretical approach. It is pointed out in a framework of this approach, however, that a computable expression for analytical solution on important problems in general applications could be hardly obtained. The other two approaches, namely experimental and numerical ones, have to be adopted inevitably to facilitate and accomplish analysis under consideration. Though experimental analysis is undoubtedly forceful , yet, it is generally difficult to apply the methods to practical situations, such as complicated specimen shape and loading conditions, because high level technique and elaboration are usually required to perform accurate measurement.

Numerical analysis has attained spectacular progress with the support of rapid spread and exploitation of the field of computer science and technology. In spite of remarkable development of computational mechanics field, there still exist several substantially difficult problems such as the correct representation of boundary condition disregarding before or after deformation and the generation, propagation of error in numerical computation and so on. Accordingly, it should be pointed out that the establishment of a method for error estimation of result analyzed against true value is not easy only from numerical and/or computational approach.

The authors would like to propose a new hybrid approach for solving the problems mentioned above in this paper. In order to obtain firstly a solution of dominant equation in the mechanical field under consideration, clues to the elimination of difficulties are investigated comparing the fundamental concepts and methods of theoretical, experimental and numerical approaches to elastic analysis each other. Then, we would like to propose a basic concept and algorithm about a new hybrid method which is not only efficient and accurate but can involve error estimation selfcontainedly.

## II. FUNDAMENTAL ASPECTS OF HYBRID ANALYSIS

The analyses of displacement, strain and stress in a framework of elasticity are generally treated as boundary value problems in a mechanical field under consideration.

In this study, the authors will take the subject of developing a new method for hybrid stress analysis as follows;

1) Displacement, strain and stress are all certain functions which satisfy appropriate structural equations and boundary conditions inside a region under consideration and on the corresponding boundary, respectively.
2) The subject of displacement, strain and stress analysis is to construct representative functions with high fidelity in qualitative standpoint and with high accuracy in quantitative viewpoint as possible.

In this circumstance, new conceptions for the form of representation, the space of approximate function and the method for determination of indeterminate coefficients will be considered and reconstructed, referring to those adopted in the current methods. They can be mentioned briefly as follows from the viewpoints of section II-1 to -4.

### II-1 Basic Types of Theoretical Solution

From the standpoint of boundary value problem, the current theoretical solution could be classified in the following three types;

1) Variable Separation Method (e.g. Fourier Method, Expansion with Eigenfunction)
2) Green Function Method (or Singular Eigenfunction Method, Method using integral Equation)
3) Variational Formulation Method (e.g. Energy Method, Variation Method)

### II-2 Techniques for Discrete Analysis

Let us discuss on procedure and technique for a discrete analysis under consideration. Because the solutions expected in the methods mentioned previously are not computable in general, it is necessary to establish the approximate functions as member in a function space of finite dimension. The most important point should be, in this case, placed on selection and/or determination of appropriate base functions and the order of their dimension. Types of discrete analysis is classified as follows;

1) Alternative Method by Finite Difference
2) Finite Partial Sum of an Expansion by Infinite Series
3) Division into Small Domains

### II-3 Method for Determination of Indeterminate Coefficients

When constricting an algorithm for determining indeterminate coefficients involved in the approximate function, the most $\lambda$desirable$\ddagger$ conditions will be clarified from the following three viewpoints.

1) Domain for Approximation
2) Condition for the best approximation
    a) Minimization of Error Norm
    b) Solution of Algebraic Equations
3) Coordinate System of Approximate Function
    a) Laglangian coordinates: coordinates set on the state before deformation.
    b) Eulerian coordinates: coordinates set on the state after deformation.

## II-4 Error Estimation

There are three different methods of error estimation of results analyzed against true solution as follows;

1)   Method Based on Error Estimation Formula
2)   Method with Guaranteed Accurate Computation
3)   Comparison with Measured Data

## III. A NEW CONCEPT FOR HYBRID ANALYSIS

In this study, let us start from the following representation of Navier equation in a domain $G$,

$$\Phi u(x) = \mu \Delta u(x) + (\lambda + \mu)\text{grad div}\, u(x) = -f(x), \text{for all x} \in G \quad (1)$$

where $\lambda$ and $\mu$ are Lame's constants and $f(x)$ is body force on $G$. Thus, using body force $f(x)$ on $G$ and a continuously differentiable vector function $\upsilon(x)$ on $S$, the solution of eq.(1) is written in a form as follows using the representation by Somigliano<sup>1</sup>s equation;

$$u(x) = -\int_{G} \Gamma(x-y)f(y)dy + \int_{S}\left\{\Gamma(x-y)\frac{d\upsilon(y)}{dn} - \left(\frac{d\Gamma(x-y)}{dn_y}\right)^t \upsilon(y)\right\}ds$$
$$(2)$$

where

$$\Gamma(x) = \frac{1}{8\pi(\lambda+2\mu)}\left(\frac{\lambda+3\mu}{|x|}\delta_{jk} + \frac{\lambda+\mu}{|x|}\frac{\partial|x|}{\partial x_j}\frac{\partial|x|}{\partial x_k}, \quad \begin{matrix} j\downarrow & 1,2,3 \\ k\rightarrow & 1,2,3 \end{matrix}\right). \quad (3)$$

The continuously differentiable function $\upsilon(x)$ is determined by boundary conditions. In order to construct the approximate function of eq.(2), we Compare the features in each category of theoretical background for boundary value problem, techniques for discrete analysis, determination of indeterminate coefficients and error estimation. Then, a new basic concept for hybrid stress analysis is arisen taking the following five aspects into consideration.

1) Classification of Domain by Diffeomorphism
    The shape of analytical domain is classified into **equivalent class** using the relationship in **Diffeomorphism**. Precise and accurate experiments would be enough to be performed only for the **representative** in each class. In case of complicated shape of domain for analysis, we can divide it into several simple-shaped subdomains. Thus, the result obtained is easily transformed theoretically into a certain diffeomorphic domain. Accordingly, the propriety of results could be expected, also the varieties of specimen shape and loading conditions can be diminished.
2) Approximation of Boundary by Algebraic Variety

**Parametric representation** of boundary may be constructed from measured data. In order to practice this procedure, deformed boundary is approximated with **a family of piecewise algebraic variety**. Then, it could be possible to construct computable approximate representative function which is compatible both to boundary and internal conditions.

3) Structure Conservative Approximation of Function
    When approximating an original function, it would be ideal and desirable for the approximate function to hold the structure of similar type with the original one and to be represented by linear combination of a base function having a essentially local support. A typical example of the structure is **biharmonic nature** of function. In addition, a function having a essentially local support in the case of several variables function could be a rapidly decreasing base function. Thus, **a biharmonic and rapidly decreasing spline function** is used as a basis in the space of the approximate function.

4) The Best Approximate Function on a Characteristic Set
    It is desirable that an approximate function applicable to various force fields have smaller number of base functions. Here, to determine the **indeterminate coefficients** involved in the best approximate function utilizing experimental data, we consider **a characteristic set**, i.e., a part of boundary or a partial set inside the domain analyzed, on which boundary conditions or its equivalent conditions can be determined and highly accurate data can be obtainable. Thus, difficulties in the computation of singular integral on boundary and noise reduction could be avoided.

5) Morphological Error Estimation
    The accuracy of approximate representative function obtained by the method mentioned above is evaluated by comparing the results with experimental data. The **morphology**, i.e. the characteristic features corresponding to experimental data, is constructed from the approximate representative function and is drawn graphically. Thus, we are able to evaluate the errors between measured and constructed patterns qualitatively, furthermore, to compare the values on points of characteristic sets quantitatively. It should be emphasized that the method proposed here is not only convenient but useful for error estimation under actual situations, even when taking the conventional states of the arts.

## IV. CONCLUDING REMARKS

The fundamental concept of a hybrid method proposed in this study is started from an idea to construct a representative function of approximate analytical solution which can include computable error estimation selfcontainedly. To establish the type of hybrid method for stress, strain and displacement analysis, the authors have developed a theoretical background taking the support from experimental data and numerical treatment into consideration. Since not only the class and method of experiments adopted are not so deviated from the current techniques but also the variety of computational methods is limited to the range of algorithm in mathematical programming, it would not be so hard to apply the hybrid method to various types of analysis in comparison with the individual method of experimental or numerical analysis, in spite of small number of application examples of the method in this stage of time.

# Low Birefringence Measurement In Polymers

S. J. Haake
Department of Mechanical and Process Engineering
The University of Sheffield, Mappin Street, Sheffield, S1 3JD, England.

Many polymer films are filled with particles to either increase the surface roughness or to increase the strength of the film. Occasionally, however, impurities are present in unfilled films and these can cause problems such as tearing. It is possible to use the birefringence in the polymer to try to identify the onset of voiding and tearing. Methods for the determination of low birefringence were studied and a full field automated technique based on phase stepping used to analyse polymers with inclusions.

The study concentrated on the use of image processing methods. Three methods were compared; phase-stepping [1], spectral analysis [2] and half-fringe photoelasticity [3]. In the present study it was estimated that the largest retardation that might be present was approximately 150 nm (about 0.25 fringe in sodium light).

The phase stepping system employed here uses six orientation of the output quarter waveplate and polariser to solve for the four unknowns, $\delta$ the retardation, $\theta$ the isoclinic angle, $i_v$ the initial light intensity and $i_m$ the background light intensity. The half fringe photoelasticity method uses two images, a dark field and a light field image and the spectral analysis method used three light field images at wavelengths of 570, 650 and 730 nm. The latter two methods do not find the isoclinic parameter.

The methods were tested using an unloaded constrained beam containing residual edge stresses (Fig 1.). The apparatus consisted of a circular polariscope with diffuse white light and sodium light sources. The image of the beam was viewed with a Panasonic BP100 monochromatic camera, digitised as 256 grey levels and stored and processed using a Compaq Deskpro XL5100.

Phase stepping has the advantage over other systems that it calculates the isoclinic parameter as well as the retardation. It also has the base intensity $i_m$ as one of its variables, although this is not calculated [1]. Spectral analysis and half fringe photoelasticity do not determine $i_m$ explicitly, however, and must be determined by recording an extra image in a dark field present with a completely unstressed specimen. Since the range of digitised intensities is low when low birefringence is measured, failure to acknowledge $i_m$ causes significant errors in the determination of $\delta$.

Figure 2 shows the fringe order found using the three methods along the vertical line shown in Fig. 1 calculated using $N=\delta/\lambda$ (where $\lambda = 589.3$ nm). The manual data was recorded using the Tardy compensation method and each value on the Fig. 2 is an average of five measurements. It can be seen that the fringe order increases towards a maximum of 0.21 fringes at the edges of the specimen and has a low plateau of approximately 0.06 fringes in the central portion of the beam. The manual data had an average standard deviation of ±0.005 fringes. All three methods predict correctly the shape of the fringe order distribution and also the values at the edge of the specimen. The differences between the methods are most noticable across the flat section in the centre of the beam. Phase stepping is affected least by noise while spectral analysis is affected most with half fringe photoelasticity somewhere in between. Figure 3 shows whole field fringe order across the beam.

It was concluded that phase stepping provided the most reliable data for the analysis of low birefringence and was subsequently used to determine retardations around inclusions in a 1mm thick model of a filled polymer. The matrix was manufactured from a Petrarch silicone elastomer and the inclusions were 1mm diameter glass cylinders with their axes perpendicular to the plane of the film. It was found using a calibration specimen that the retardation rose linearly with the stress applied and that the matrix had a fringe constant of 3.5 MPa mm fringe$^{-1}$.

Specimens with single and double inclusions were subjected to gradually increasing uniaxial loads. Stresses were analysed at the poles of the inclusions and at their equators in a direction perpendicular to the line of load. Initially, the stress at the poles was higher than the nominal stress for low loads (typically 1.4 times). As the load was increased, however, the matrix debonded from the inclusion and the stress at the poles dropped such that it was lower than the nominal stress (typically 0.3 times). The stresses at the equator of the inclusion remained almost constant and equal to the nominal stress.

These factors were used to analyse the stress patterns around inclusions in real a 30 μm thick polymer under uniaxial loading. The naturally occurring inclusion was 5 μm in diameter and the field of view across the polymer was approximately 50 μm. Figure 4 shows fringe order, isoclinic parameter and shear stress pattern across the top of the inclusion as it was loaded. The fringe order clearly drops at the top of the inclusion indicating that voiding around the particle had occurred The isoclinic and shear stress patterns also exhibit distinct peaks which could be used to recognise voiding in polymers.

References:
1. S. J. Haake, Z. F. Wang, E. A. Patterson, "Evaluation of automated full field analysis using phase stepping", Experimental techniques, 17 19-25 (1993).
2. S. J. Haake, E. A. Patterson, "Photoelastic analysis of frozen stressed specimens using spectral contents analysis", Exp. Mech., 32 (3), 266-272 (1992).
3. A. S. Voloshin, C. P. Burger, "Half fringe photo-elasticity - a new approach to whole field analysis", Expt. Mech., 23 304-314 (1983).

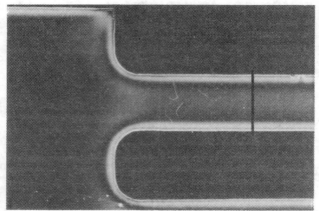

Figure 1. Photograph of an unloaded constrained beam with edge stresses.

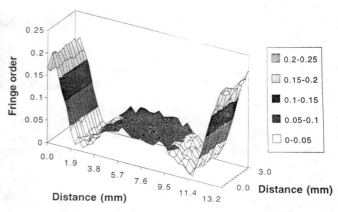

Figure 3. Full field three dimensional view of fringe order across the beam in Fig.1 using phase stepping.

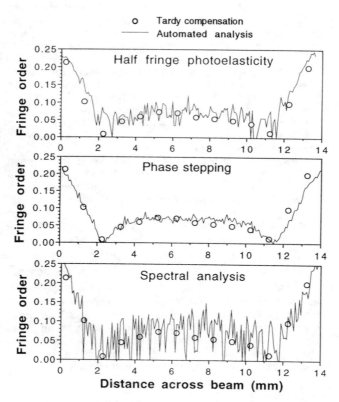

Figure 2. Fringe order (at λ=589.3 nm) versus distance along a vertical line across the beam in Fig. 1 using phase stepping, half fringe photoelasticity and spectral analysis.

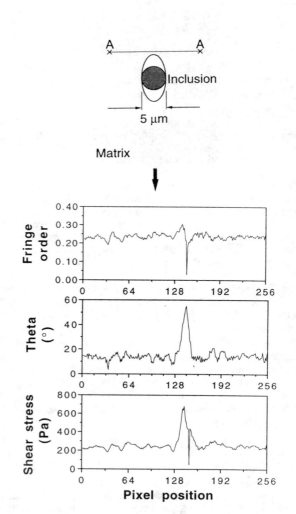

Figure 4. Fringe order, isoclinic parameter and shear stress along line AA across the top of a 5 μm inclusion in a 30 μm thick polymer film (scale: 5 pixels per μm).

4

# Experiences in using STL-Epoxies for Photoelastic Investigations

W. Steinchen, B. Kramer, G. Kupfer
University Gh Kassel
Department of Mechanical Engineering
Laboratory of Photoelasticity, Holography and Shearography (SHS)
Mönchebergstr. 7, 34109 Kassel
Germany

Soon after the introduction of Stereolithography (STL) for rapid prototyping (RP) on the European market in 1988, photoelastic investigations using transparent birefringent STL-resins have been realized in the Lab SHS. The main problem has been to determine the material properties of those new resins, because Ciba-Geigy as the manufacturer of the resins have not received any results so far. A first step towards the application of STL-resins in the field of photo-elasticity had been the determination of the photoelastic constant S (resp. the material fringe value). These investigations were realized both for the preceding acrylates XB 5081-1, XB 5134-1, XB 5143 plus XB 5149 and the new epoxies SL 5170 and SL 5180. These results have been compared with the most commonly used resin for photoelasticity, Araldite B.

STL is a relatively new method of generating three-dimensional components from a liquid STL-resin without relying on traditional tools or molding techniques. It was developed in the US in the late 1970s and early 1980s. It involves a unique combination of polymer chemistry, laser physics, optics, material science, viscous fluid dynamics, computer science and electrical and mechanical engineering.

In building a structure by CAD a computer defines the object layer by layer, which, depending on the drawing style and the STL-resin used, are between 0.05 and 0.7 mm. For each layer, a vector pattern that corresponds to the selected parameters is created from the preset values. The data for the part to be manufactured is used to guide a laser (wavelength about 325 nm) in the x- and y-axes, while a punched metal platform, immersed in a liquid resin, controls the z-axis, building a three-dimensional plastic component layer by layer (Fig. 1) [1], [2].

S was determined by using the well-known photoelastic calibration methods like the tensile test (specimen: a tension test bar), the compressive test (test sample: a diametral loaded circular disk) and the bending test (specimen: a beam supported at both ends subjected by pure bending) [3]. Considering this, a slight dependence on the photoelastic constant S vs. the force F resp. the isochromatic fringe order $\delta$ is obvious (Fig. 2), when evaluating the calibration mesurements i.e. the linear proportionality of the graph F = f($\delta$) for higher fringe orders [4], [5]. This characteristic behaviour has been observed for different methods and materials used to determine the photoelastic constant. One of the reasons for the increase of the photoelastic constant in the range from the 0th to the 1st fringe order are residual stresses within the cured resins. The slight linear increase resp. decrease in the range of more than one fringe order cannot be clarified finally up to now.

At present, alternative investigations using both transmission ellipsometry whose consistency is 1/15.000 and UV- and IR-absorption spectroscopy are realized to clarify the relations between the photoelastic constant and the structure of the STL-resin.

When using transmission ellipsometry the phase angle $\Delta$ instead of the isochromatic fringe order $\delta$ is measured expressing the angle of the phase difference with respect to the light waves created by the birefringence $\Delta n_{1,2} = n_1 - n_2$. The phase angle is linearly connected with the isochromatic fringe order. The results of this investigation show nearly the same behaviour like these gained by a commonly used polariscope (Fig. 3).

Contrary to photoelasticity the transmission ellipsometry measures the residual stresses induced by RP production and allows to eliminate this influence on the photoelastic constant especially in the range of $\delta$ = 0.0 - 0.6 fringe order.

The following increase S vs. F for $\delta > 1$ (cf. Fig. 2) was investigated using UV- and IR-absorption spectroscopy because the deviation of 10 - 15% was observed despite of eliminating the residual stresses. Recording absorption spectra using IR-light with two different planes of polarization (i.e. $0^{\circ}$ and $90^{\circ}$) results in two different absorption spectra of the same sample at the same amount of tension (Fig. 4). The specimen which had an overall thickness of 19 μm consisted of a PE-film (13 μm) coated with a STL-epoxy (6 μm).

For finding a connection between the principal refractive indices $n_1$ and $n_2$ dependent on the force F and finally the photoelastic constant S it must be investigated the appearance of the load dependent dispersion anomaly. $n_1$ and $n_2$ and their difference $\Delta n_{1,2}$ are determined for the relevant absorption bands $k = 2\pi/\lambda$ where $\lambda$ is the corresponding wavelength (Fig. 5). When calculating $S = \lambda F/(A\Delta n_{1,2})$ where A is the cross section of the specimen, the diagram S vs. F is depicted in Fig. 6 which shows an analogous behaviour like in Fig. 2. These results must be substantiated by investigations in series. The photoelastic fringe patterns created in STL-components are as well as by the used resins up to now; a few applications like a connecting rod of a passenger car, a rocker of a lorry etc. are shown in the oral presentation during the symposium.

Acknowledgements:

The authors gratefully acknowledge Ciba-Geigy Research Centre and 3D Systems for manufacturing the STL components and Deutsche Forschungsgemeinschaft (DFG), project No. Ste 248/13.

References:

[1] Jacobs, P.F., et al., „Stereolithography and other RP&M Technologies, from RP to RT", SME Dearborn and ASME press, New York, 1996, p. 392.

[2] Gebhardt, A., „Rapid prototyping", Hanser Verlag, München 1996, p. 322.

[3] Steinchen W., „Fotopolymere der Stereolithographie für spannungsoptische Untersuchungen", Kunststoffe 83, 1993, pp. 385-388.

[4] Steinchen, W., Hirchenhain, A., „Fotopolymere der Stereolithografie als spannungsoptische Werkstoffe - Kalibrierung und Anwendung für ebene und räumliche Untersuchungen", Engineering Research, Bd. 59, 1993, No. 7/8, p. 153 ff.

[5] Steinchen, W., Kramer, B., Kupfer, G., „Photoelasticity cuts Part-Development Costs", Photonics Spectra, May 1994 pp. 157-161.

[6] Holzapfel, W., Riß, U., „Computer-based high resolution transmission ellipsometry", Applied Optics, Vol. 26, No. 1, 1987, pp. 145-153.

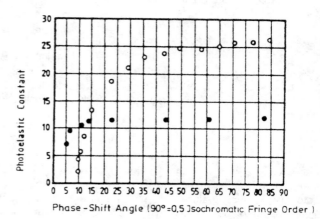

Fig. 3. Photoelastic constant S vs. phase shift angle φ

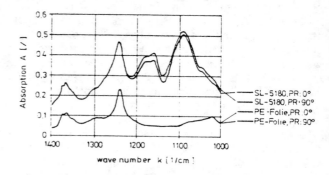

Fig. 4. IR-Absorptionsspektrum (PE-film/SL-5180; ε = 0%; t = 19 μm)

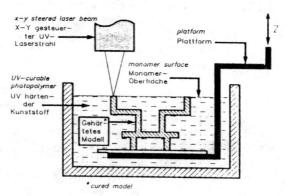

Fig. 1. Schematic view of part being built using stereolithography

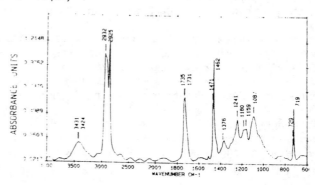

Fig. 5. IR-Absorptionsspektrum SL-5180 (PE-film/SL-5180; ε = 3,33%; t = 19 μm)

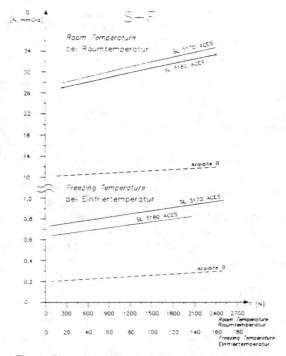

Fig. 2. Photoelastic constant S vs. force F at room and freezing temperature for the recent epoxy resins

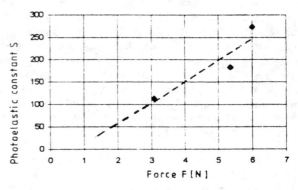

Fig. 6. Photoelastic constant S vs. force F (SL-5180, k = 1087, 68421cm⁻¹)

6

# Two dimensional photoelasticity analysis by digital image processing

Nathalie Plouzennec, Jean-Christophe Dupré and Alexis Lagarde
Université de Poitiers - Laboratoire de Mécanique des Solides
Unité de Recherche Associée au C.N.R.S. (861)
Bd 3 - Téléport 2 - BP179
86960 FUTUROSCOPE CEDEX - FRANCE

Photoelasticity coupled with the frozen stress technique is still one of the most widely used optical method for stress analysis by industrialists. To use this technique, three dimensional stressed specimens are sliced by a mechanical process to obtain two dimensional models. The slices are then analyzed in a polariscope. There are different ways to determine the photoelastic data. They can be measured manually point by point. But it is time consuming and requires skill in the identification and measurement of isoclinic and isochromatic fringe order. By the help of CCD camera and computer, another way is to automate the photoelastic data acquisition and analysis to provide faster results. Amongst the different automated photoelastic fringe analysis recently investigated, there are techniques based on the use of circular polariscope [1], [4]. For good results, the quarter wave plates need to be very accurate and perfectly positioned. Others methods utilize two [3] or three [4] wavelengths. Generally the more wavelengths you have the more images you need, but it has the advantage to give the fringe order automatically. For the numerical treatment, many solutions are available as for example FFT based procedure [2].

This paper presents a new computerized method for the whole field determination of isoclinic and isochromatic parameters in a birefringent model. This method uses a very simple experimental set up (plane polariscope). Few manipulations allow to obtain the four fringe images used to calculate isoclinic and isochromatic parameters. The images are recorded by a CCD camera and stored in a personal computer, then the calculations are done in short time.

The configuration of a plane polariscope is shown in Fig. 1.

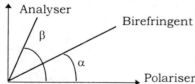

Fig. 1 Schematic of a plane polariscope

The emerging light I is given by the following relationship.

$$I = \frac{I_0}{2}\left[1 + \cos 2(\beta - \alpha)\cos 2\alpha - \sin 2\alpha \sin 2(\beta - \alpha)\cos\varphi\right] \quad (1)$$

where : $\beta$ is the orientation of the analyzer,
$\varphi$ is the isochromatic parameter,
$\alpha$ is the isoclinic angle,
$I_0$ is the light intensity when the model is unloaded.

The isoclinic angle and the isochromatic parameter are calculated using only four configurations of the polariscope. They correspond to : 1) $\beta = 0$ ($I_1$); 2) $\beta = \pi/4$ ($I_2$); 3) $\beta = 0$ and $\alpha \rightarrow \alpha+\pi/4$ ($I_3$); 4) $\beta = \pi/2$ ($I_4$). The intensities $I_1$, $I_2$, $I_3$ and $I_4$ are obtained thanks to equation (1). And $I_0$ is calculated by $I_0 = I_1 + I_4$.

First, a mask corresponding to the location of the specimen in the image is defined, by comparing the light intensity variation between the different configurations of the polariscope. Thus, $\alpha$ and $\varphi$ are only calculated for the points which belong to the specimen.

Then, the isoclinic angle is determined [5]. It can be calculated thanks to equation (2).

$$\tan 2\alpha = \frac{2I_2 - I_0}{2I_0 - 2I_3} \quad (2)$$

$\alpha$ is undetermined when $2I_2-I_0=0$ and $I_0-I_3=0$, which is verified for $\varphi=2k\pi$ (maximum of the isochromatic fringe) or $\alpha=(2k+1)\pi/4$ (maximum of the isoclinic fringe).

Another equation allows to calculate $\alpha$ :

$$\tan 2\alpha = \frac{2I_0 - 2I_1}{2I_2 - I_0} \quad (3)$$

In this case, $\alpha$ is undetermined when $2I_2-I_0=0$ and $I_0-I_1=0$. It is verified for $\varphi=2k\pi$ or $\alpha=k\pi/2$.

So using equation (2) or (3), the only values of the isoclinic parameter $\alpha$ remaining indeterminate are for $\varphi=2k\pi$ corresponding to the location of the maximum isochromatic fringe pattern. The missing points are obtained by a 2D linear interpolation. This process requires that the zones to be interpolated should be as small as possible. The values of $\alpha$ are in the range $]-\pi/4, \pi/4]$.

Anywhere, the value of α is known mode π/2 due to the inverse tangent function. Thus an unwrapping process is suitable to restore the continuity of α on the entire field. The unwrapping algorithm is based on a scanning process starting at one point. A point can only be treated if at least one of its eight adjacent points is already unwrapped. π/2 is added or subtracted while the phase difference between the point and its adjacent points is more than π/3.

When α is anywhere determined, the isostatics plotting can be performed to obtain a better visualization of the principal stress directions. From a starting point M, a vector of a fixed length is drawing with the angle α. At the new point defined by the end of the vector, the process is repeated until the boundary of the object is reached. For the same starting point M, the plotting procedure is made for the other directions (the vector is drawing with the angles α+π/2, α+π and α+3π/2). The same process is begun again for another starting point M', automatically chosen in order to obtain the entire isostatic field.

When it is done, the next step consists in the determination of the isochromatic pattern. It is possible to calculate the isochromatic parameter using :

$$\cos\varphi = \frac{2I_1 + 2I_3 - 3I_0}{I_0} \qquad (4)$$

φ is calculated in each point of the specimen mode π. Its values are in the range [0,π]. It is necessary to unwrap the isochromatic parameter. But the arcosine function does not include discontinuities as the arcsine function. So φ is unwrapped thanks to a global analysis. The area where the function needs to be unwrapped corresponds to the extrema of the function. So the first thing to do is to determine the lines corresponding to the maximal and the minimal values of φ. When it is done, knowing the zero order fringe, the other fringes are automatically identified. Afterwards, the isochromatic parameter can be unwrapped. Knowing the isochromatic parameter in every point of the specimen, the principal stress difference can be calculated.

All the results are given automatically by our program. Throughout the calculations, the experimenter can operate in the treatment if necessary. To illustrate our method, an experimental result is presented for a disk under diametrical compression.

For each configuration of the polariscope, an image is recorded by a CCD camera and stored by a PC. They are represented in Figure 2 a, b, c, d. Afterwards, they are treated thanks to our program. The shape of the disk is defined. Then the isoclinic angle is calculated, unwrapped and the isostatics are plotted (Fig. 2-e). Finally, the unwrapped isochromatic parameter is obtained (Fig. 2-f).

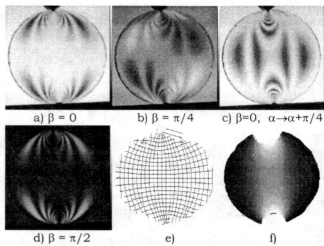

a) β = 0          b) β = π/4          c) β=0, α→α+π/4

d) β = π/2          e)          f)

Fig. 2 disk under diametrical compression
a), b), c), d) four configurations of the polariscope; e) Isostatics; f) Isochromatic parameter.

Few minutes are needed to obtain the results for the entire specimen. For a simulation, the results are calculated with an accuracy smaller than 0.8° for the isoclinic angle and 5° for the isochromatic parameter. For the experiments, the accuracy of the isoclinic angle is not as good because of imprecisions due to variations of intensity, quality of polarizers...

A new whole field photoelastic fringe analysis is presented. This method is based on a simple experimental set up and few manipulations. Only four configurations of a plane polariscope are needed to determine the principal stress directions and the principal stress difference in short time. As this method could be used with oblique incidence, it would allow to separate the principal stresses.

References :

[1] Patterson, E.A., Wang Z.F., "Towards full field automated photoelastic analysis of complex components", Strain, pp. 49-56, May 1991.
[2] Morimoto, Y., Morimoto, Y. Jr., Hayashi, T., "Separation of isochromatics and isoclinics using Fourier transform", Exp. Tech., pp. 13-17, Sept./Oct. 1994.
[3] Umezaki, E., Tamaki, T., Takahashi, S., "Automated stress analysis of photoelastic experiment by use of image processing", Exp. Tech., pp. 22-27, 1989.
[4] Kihara, T., "Automatic whole field measurement of principal stress directions using three wavelengths", Recent advances in experimental mechanics, J.F. Silva Gomes et al. Editors, pp. 95-99, 1994.
[5] Dupré, JC., Brémand, F., Lagarde, A., "Photoelastic data processing through digital image processing : isostatics and isochromatics reconstruction", International conference on Photoelasticity : new instrumentation and data processing technique, London, November 1993.

# Electronic Techniques in Isodyne Stress Analysis

Jerzy T. Pindera

Department of Civil Engineering, University of Waterloo, Waterloo, Ontario, Canada N2L 3G1

Jüri Josepson

Institute of Cybernetics, Estonian Academy of Sciences, Tallinn, Estonia

Dragan B. Jovanović

Faculty of Mechanical Engineering, University of Niš, Niš, Yugoslavia

The direct purpose of the study was to develop electronic techniques for collecting, processing and evaluating information in experimental isodyne stress analysis. The original technique involved recording of the isodyne patterns using chemical photography and a manual evaluation of the normal and shear isodyne functions within the selected measurement planes; the final step was a manual evaluation of the derivatives of isodyne functions which are proportional to the normal and shear stress components, respectively. As it is known, the isodyne functions represent cross-sections through an isodyne field, [7]. This field is directly related to the recorded isodyne fringes which represent lines of equal intensity of normal forces at the surface of a specimen, and could be generalized for a three-dimensional stress state which exists in the planes within the thickness of a specimen. Thus, the recorded isodyne fringes allow determination of normal and shear isodyne functions and of isodyne surfaces spanned above the specimen contour. The major problem of the conventional recording technique is that a manual evaluation of the recorded isodyne fringes is time-consuming.

The procedure developed to date and presented in this paper is a hybrid electronic-manual procedure. It involves electronic recording of the experimental isodyne fields, manual determination of the isodyne orders in the chosen sections within the chosen measurement planes, electronic determination of the indicated and load-induced isodyne functions, and electronic determination of the isodyne surfaces.

It is shown that the new technique satisfies all the theoretical conditions and constraints imposed by the theories of the analytical and optical isodynes, [7]. It is also shown that the developed techniques are more reliable and accurate, and more cost-efficient than the traditional techniques of photomechanics. The final objective was to demonstrate that the isodyne stress analysis allows obtaining reliable data on the actual three-dimensional stresses in a cost-effective manner.

The general objective of the study was to contribute to the accuracy and cost-effectiveness of the experimental isodyne stress analysis. This goal follows the developing paradigm shift in analytical and experimental stress analysis which puts stress on the engineering requirements regarding the reliability and economic aspects of the applied procedures. It was shown [7] that three-dimensional isodyne stress analysis can contribute to three specific requirements of engineering design procedures:

1- testing reliability and accuracy of predictions of analytical and numerical procedures for determination of stresses and strains, [6];
2 -producing reliable data on the actual stress fields in real bodies made of real materials; such data are needed to develop new, more reliable analytical and numerical procedures, [8];

3 - determination - in a form of bench marks - of practical boundaries between the regions in plates where stress state insignificantly deviates from a plane stress state and the regions where the stress state is noticeably three-dimensional, [7, 10].

The electronic techniques under development satisfy a system of conditions and constraint, which represent theoretical foundation of three-dimensional isodyne stress analysis. The major conditions are:

- Creep patterns of polymeric materials must be known, to avoid errors caused by mechanical and optical creep which may be different, [2- 4];
- It must be recognized that the stress states in plates are always three-dimensional when the in-plane stress gradients are not equal to zero, [7]; thus the stresses in regions of notches and crack tips are always strongly three-dimensional and the actual stress concentration factor cannot be represented by a single number, [5, 9];
- It is very practical to base the practical, simplified relations between stresses and light velocity on a more basic phenomenological theory which is non-refuted, [7, 10];

Thus, an optoelectronic system of an isodyne recorder should satisfy particular design conditions:
- Only the information-carrying part of scattered light should be recorded, [7];
- Planes of the specimen surface, of the measurement and of the recording should be parallel, [7];
- Planes of measurement should be adjustable within the thickness of the specimen, [7];
- Loss of intensity of light travelling within measurement planes should be compensated;
- Electronic recording should be possible within the visible and infrared spectral bands;
- Curvature of light beams within the specimen, known as strain gradient effect should be accounted for, [10].

A sample of obtained results is given in Fig. 1. It presents stress state in a square plate loaded by three forces. Plate was loaded in a constant deformation mode to eliminate optical creep, [2, 3, 4]. The isodyne fields used for evaluation of presented normal stress components, acting in direction of the external loads, were recorded in 9 planes parallel to the middle plane of the plate. The stress components were evaluated electronically. Three graphs presented at the left side of the Figure show the distribution of the normal stresses close to the plate surface, at three different distances from the central load. The graph at the lower right corner of the Figure presents distributions across the plate thickness of the difference between the same normal stress components and the thickness stress components. It is evident that at the distance equal to 0.6 plate thicknesses from the upper boundary the normal stress components are at least 25% higher at the plate middle plane than at the plate surface. The assessed increase in the normal stress value is about 30%. Such an information on the actual three-dimensional stress state in real plates demonstrates the ability of isodyne stress analysis to contribute to the above listed three tasks of modern engineering mechanics. In particular, it is shown that: the stresses in notches and at crack tips are always three-dimensional; that common techniques of transmission photoelasticity do not yield reliable results in regions of notches; that some common singular solutions of plane elasticity yield wrong data on stress components regarding their magnitude and even their sign, [11]; that the curvature of a light beam caused by the strain gradient should be considered, as a major factor [10].

It is shown that the first task of the isodyne stress analysis is to determine the isodyne surfaces. This must be done electronically. The results show that it is easy to determine electronically other derived quantities such as the normal and shear force intensities and the normal and shear stress components at arbitrary distance from the plate surface. At the present the major task is to develop a satisfactorily reliable program for the electronic approximation of experimental data, [1].

References:

[1] Fritsch, F. N. and Carlson, R. E., "Monotone piecewise cubic interpolation", SIAM J. NUMER. ANAL., 17 (2), 1980, pp. 238-246.
[2] Pindera, J. T., "Studies of Rheological Photoelastic Properties of Some Polyester Resins.Parts 1, 2 and 3" (in Polish). Engineering Transactions (Rozprawy Inżynierskie), Polish Acad. Sciences, 7, (3, 4) 1959, pp. 361-411, 481-520, 521-540.
[3] Pindera, J. T. and Straka, P., "On Physical Measures of Rheological Responses of Some Materials in Wide Range of Temperature and Spectral Frequencies", Rheologica Acta, 13 (3), 1974, pp.338-351.
[4] Pindera, J. T., " Foundations of Experimental Mechanics - Principles of Modeling, Observation and Measurement". In: J. T. Pindera (Ed) New Physical Trends in Experimental Mechanics, Springer-Verlag, 1981, pp. 199-327.
[5] Pindera, J. T. and Krasnowski, B. R., "Determination of Stress Intensity Factors in Thin and Thick Plates using Isodyne Photoelasticity." In: L.A. Simpson (Ed) Fracture Problems and Solutions in the Energy Industry, Pergamon Press, 1982, pp. 147-156.
[6] Pindera, M.-J., Pindera, J. T. and Ji, X., " Three-dimensional Effects in Beams - Isodyne Assessment of a plane Solution", Experimental Mechanics, 29 (1), 1989, pp. 23-31.
[7] Pindera, J. T. and Pindera, M.-J., Isodyne Stress Analysis, Kluwer Academic Publishers, Dordrecht, 1989.
[8] Pindera, J. T., "Local Effects and Defect Criticality in Homogeneous and Laminated Structures". Trans. ASME, J. Pressure Vessel Tech, 111, 1989, pp.136-150.
[9] Pindera, J. T. and Liu, X., "On the Actual Three-dimensional Stresses in Notches and Cracks", Composites Engineering 1, pp. 281-301.
[10] Pindera, J. T., Hecker, F. W. and Baicheng, W., " Testing theoretical bases of caustic methods in fracture mechanics and stress analysis". Theoretical and Applied Fracture Mechanics, 15, 1991, pp. 11-33.
[11] Sokolnikoff, I. S.," Mathematical Theory of Elasticity," McGraw-Hill, New York, 1956.
[12] Thum, A. and all, "Verformung, Spannung und Kerbvirkung" (Deformation, Stress and Notch effect), VDI-Verlag, Düsseldorf, 1960.

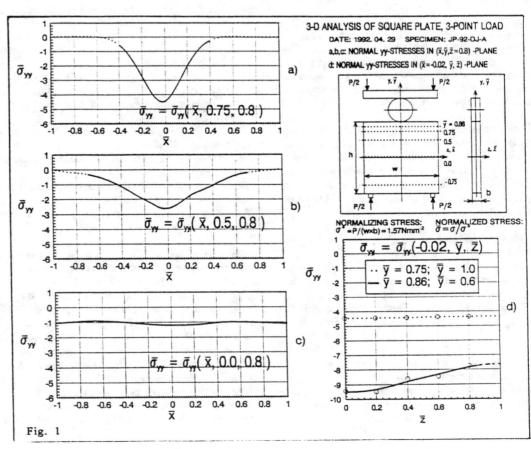

Fig. 1

# A PHOTOELASTICITY IN THIN-WALLED BAR THEORY

Marek Sikoń
Cracow University of Technology
Warszawska 24
31-155 Cracow

Recently theoretical and experimental procedures have been combined to solve the problems in solid mechanics.

A photoelasticity in thin-walled bar theory enable us utilize a optical parameter to obtain mechanical quantities namely: bimoment $B_\omega$, bending-twisting moment $M_\omega$, and cross-section stress state.

This analysis allows us to avoid solving of differential equations used commonly in the analytical computations of the bimoment.

The aim of analysis is to determine relation between the system of outer forces:

$$S(N, Q_y Q_z) , \; M_R(M_x, M_y, M_z) , \; B_\omega , \qquad (1)$$

system of internal forces and optic parameter $\psi$, using the rules of photoelastic measurement [1], [2], [3] and thin-walled bar theory [4], [5].

We define: a global system of coordinates $(x,y,z)$, local curvilinear system $(x,s,n)$ and a system of optically active directions $(1', 2', 3')$, Fig. 1.

At the point of median line "c" of the bars an elementary internal force with the normal stress density $\sigma_x$ is expressed by a component of dielectric permability $\kappa_x$, in the following way:

$$\kappa_x = \kappa_0 + 2C_1\sqrt{\kappa_0}\,\sigma_x . \qquad (2)$$

Optic state is described by superposition of dielectric permabilities:

$$\kappa_x^N + \kappa_x^{M_R} + \kappa_x^{B_\omega} , \qquad (3)$$

caused by elementary internal forces $(dN, dM_R, dB_\omega)$ in bending centre.

We transform a tensor of dielectric permability $T_\kappa$ from a system of optically active directions to a local system [6]:

$$T_\kappa\left(1',2',3'\right) \xrightarrow{\;\vartheta,\alpha\;} T_\kappa\left(x,s,n\right) . \qquad (4)$$

We define a geometry of measurements to satisfy birefringence law by component $\kappa_x$ only.

Introducing assumptions of thin-walled bar theory, Cauchy conditions, Hook's law and the kinematic equilibrium conditions between the system of internal forces:

$$\int_C dN , \; \int_C dM_R , \; \int_C dB_\omega , \qquad (5)$$

and the outer forces (1) in the bending center R Fig.1, and using (2), (3), (4) we write:

$$\frac{\lambda}{2\pi C_\sigma} \frac{d\psi^{(s)}(x,s)}{ds} = \frac{N(x)}{A} + \frac{M_y^S(x)}{J_y} z(s) + \qquad (6)$$

$$- \frac{M_z^S(x)}{J_y} y(s) + \frac{B_\omega(x)}{J_\omega} \omega(s) ,$$

The above relation is used in experiments to analyse a sequence of cross-sections of the bar along the "x" axis by scaterred light photoelasticity. The direction $\mathbf{x}$ of light is chosen in order to be always tangential to the arc coordinate "s" (i.e. $\vartheta=0$, Fig.1).

A photoelasticity of transmitted light, when $\mathbf{x} = 1^{(n)} = n$, $\vartheta=90[\deg]$, Fig.1, satisfies conditions of measurement described in this work at the points $(s=s^*)$ on the boundary of the bar only. In this case we write:

$$\frac{\lambda}{2\pi g C_\sigma} \int_g d\psi^{(n)}(x,s^*) = \cdots , \qquad (7)$$

on the left side of the equation (6). Other points require an additional measurement. The normal $(m_n)$ and oblique-incidence $(m_\vartheta)$ photoelasticity measurements give:

$$\frac{\lambda}{g C_\sigma}\left[ m_n^2 - \left(m_n^2 - m_\vartheta^2 \sin^2 \vartheta\right)\frac{1}{\cos^2 \vartheta}\right]^{1/2} = \cdots , \qquad (8)$$

on the left side of equation (6), Fig.1.

Using the formulations (7) the bimoment function can be written in following way:

$$B_\omega(x) = \Gamma_1^* m^*(x) + \Gamma_2^* , \qquad (9)$$

where:

$\Gamma_1^*, \Gamma_2^*$ are constants expressed by optical and mechanical quantities, $m^*(x)$ is a function of isochromatic order determined experimentaly by a reflection light photoelastic technique Fig.2, at the boundary points of the C-bar, loaded by a force N Fig.3.

Knowing the value of $B_\omega(x)$ we determine bending-twisting moment from the relation:

$$M_\omega(x) = \frac{dm^*}{dx}\Gamma_1^* , \qquad (10)$$

and cross-section stress state:

$$\sigma_\omega(x,s) = \left(\Gamma_1^* m^*(x) + \Gamma_2^*\right)\frac{\omega(s)}{J_\omega} , \qquad (11)$$

$$\tau_\omega(x,s) = \frac{S_\omega(s)}{g J_\omega}\frac{dm^*}{dx}\Gamma_1^* , \qquad (12)$$

$$\sigma_x(x,s) = \frac{N}{A} + \frac{M_y^S}{J_z}z(s) - \frac{M_z^S}{J_y}y(s) + \frac{\Gamma_1^* m^*(x) + \Gamma_2^*}{J_\omega}\omega(s) , \qquad (13)$$

$$\tau(x,s) = -\frac{\Gamma_1^*}{J_\omega}\frac{dm^*}{dx}\int_{-s_0}^{s}\omega(s)ds , \qquad (14)$$

at each point of the C-bar.

References:

[1] Lagarde, A., „Static and Dynamic Photoelasticity and Caustic", Recent Developments, Springer-Verlag, New York, CISM 290, 1987.

[2] Aben, H., „Integrated Photoelasticity", McGraw-Hill, New York, London, 1979.

[3] Stupnicki, J., „Optical research methods in mechanics", in „Technical Mechanics" Polish Academy of Science, PWN, T. X, part IV, 1984, (in Polish).

[4] Życzkowski, M., „Technical Mechanics" Polish Academy of Science, PWN, T.IX, 1988, (in Polish).

[5] Piechnik, S., „Strength of Materials in Civil Engineering Department", Warsaw-Cracow, PWN, 1978, (in Polish).

[6] Sikoń, M., „Transformation of Stress Tensor in Photoelasticity", XVI Symp. Mech.&Machine Design, Warsaw 1993, (in Polish), pp.320-328.

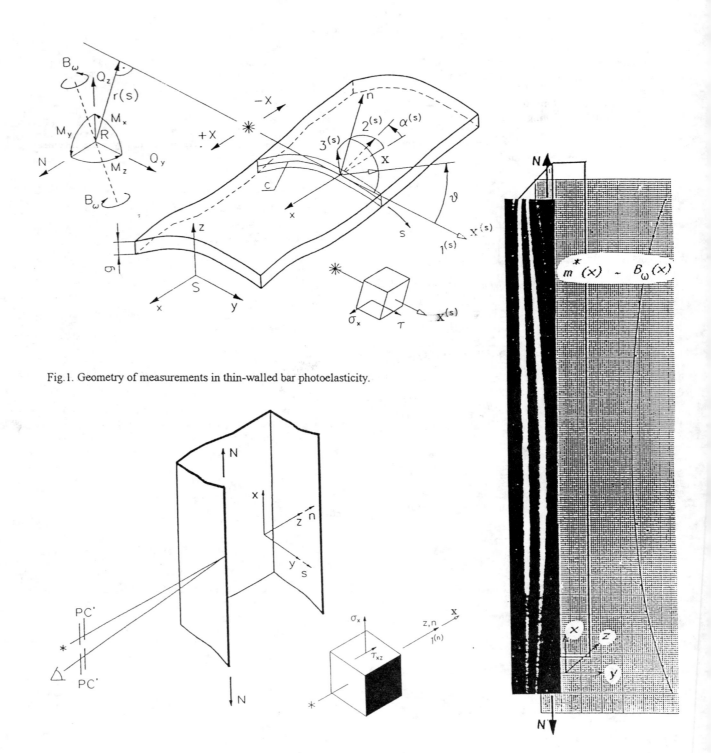

Fig.1. Geometry of measurements in thin-walled bar photoelasticity.

Fig.2. Photoelastic technique in the C-bar measurement.

Fig.3. Results of experiment.

# Color Digital Imaging System for White-Light Isoclinic Analysis

Darrell E.P. Hoy, Wenyuan Zhao
Mechanical Engineering Dept., Box 5014
Tennessee Technological University
Cookeville, TN 38505     E-Mail: DEH8726@tntech.edu

Since 1988, researchers at Tennessee Technological University have been investigating the use of color digital imaging methods in the analysis of photoelastic fringe patterns [1-5]. While most of these efforts have been focused mainly on the analysis of isochromatic fringe patterns, this paper reports on the recent application of color digital imaging to the analysis of isoclinic fringe patterns under white-light illumination [6].

Previous efforts by other researchers in the area of digital isoclinic analysis have employed greyscale imaging systems and monochromatic illumination of the specimens. Of course, in using monochromatic illumination, both the isoclinic and isochromatic fringes appear as "dark bands" superimposed upon each other. Hence, in the analysis of these images, a separation method, such as image division [7], must be employed. In contrast, the use of white-light illumination for isoclinic analysis automatically aids the separation process, since under white-light illumination the isoclinic fringes (and the zero-order isochromatic) appear as dark bands superimposed on the multi-colored isochromatic fringe background. Thus, a color digital imaging system can be employed to readily separate the isoclinic fringes from the isochromatic fringes by means of their color components.

In this paper, Hoy and Zhao report on their recent efforts to apply color imaging methods to white-light isoclinic patterns. The digital imaging system used for this work basically consists of a color imaging camera, a "true-color" imaging board, and associated programming software. The major components of this system are described in more detail in earlier publications [1-3]. Images recorded by this system have a 24-bit color depth, providing for a theoretical color resolution of approximately 16.7 million RGB colors (256 red levels x 256 green levels x 256 blue levels). However, the effective color resolution will usually be less, since it is governed by many factors, including the quality of the imaging camera, digitizing board, and lighting conditions.

After acquisition of the desired color images, pre-processing of the images through the use of digital filters is employed to remove unwanted "noise" from the image. For this purpose, a "median" filter was first used to remove isolated "spot-noise" from the image; then, an averaging filter was employed to provide for smoothing of the image. The final, but important, pre-processing stage involves the separation of the object of interest from the background of the image. This "segmentation" process can either be accomplished by using an automated approach employing background intensity and edge-gradients as separation criteria, or alternately, through a simple "manual" outlining of the specimen boundaries.

After pre-processing, the images are ready for the actual isoclinic analysis. This consists of first identifying (locating) those pixels which lie on the "centers" of the isoclinic fringes in each of the individual isoclinic images. As indicated previously, this separation is accomplished by invoking criteria regarding the RGB color gradients and intensities of the isoclinic fringes as compared to the remaining isochromatic portions of the specimen. To implement these criteria, several variations of typical "fringe-tracing" procedures were initially tried. Unfortunately, it was found that these fringe-tracing approaches ran into lots of practical difficulties in properly-outlining the isoclinic fringes without getting "lost" in the process. Consequently, a somewhat different approach was eventually used in this study with much more successful results.

The isoclinic analysis approach used in this study consists first of identifying isoclinic points by setting fairly-narrow criterion on color gradient and intensity components for the isoclinic fringes. Thus, although not every isoclinic pixel may be found in this first "screening" process, those that do meet the criteria are more likely to be correctly identified then would occur if broader criterion were employed. Then, by repeating this process for the remaining isoclinic images in a series (say every 5 degrees, for example) a composite image can be formed which includes a disconnected "skeleton" of the identified isoclinic pixels. At this stage, the remaining unidentified points on the composite image can be "filled-in" through an interpolation process to provide full-field isoclinic information. It should be noted that as part of this process, any zero-order isochromatic fringes present in the images will also be detected as part of the isoclinic fringe pattern. However, the isochromatic fringes can be then be identified by the fact that, unlike the isoclinic fringes, the isochromatic fringes always appear in the same location in all images, regardless of the polariscope orientation. Thus, to separate the zero-order isochromatic fringes from the isoclinics, a "repetition factor" is introduced during the assembly of the composite image, thereby indicating how many times each point has been identified as lying on a fringe in each separate isoclinic image. Points with a high repetition factor then are taken to be points associated with zero-order isochromatics.

To serve as an example for the development and testing of this method, a 2-D photoelastic model of a split-ring in compression was carefully machined using a numerically-controlled milling machine. A transmission polariscope and the aforementioned color imaging system were used to capture 19 isoclinic images in increments from 0 to 90 degrees. After pre-processing, as described earlier, threshold criterion were set based on the color gradient and intensities of pixels associated with isoclinic fringes. Note that these thresholds can be automatically set to account for any variation in illumination and camera conditions by averaging the color components of the background pixels, which will be similar in intensity and color to that of the isoclinics. The pixels identified as being on the isoclinics were then stored along with the associated isoclinic parameter. This process was then repeated for the remaining images, and a composite skeleton image of the split-ring was formed. Next. the fringes were thinned to find their "centers", and an interpolation of the identified isoclinic pixels was performed to assign values to the remaining pixels in the image. Final display of the results is aided by a pseudo-coloring scheme to identify both the magnitude of the isoclinic parameters, as well as the magnitude of the repetition factor associated with the zero-order isochromatic fringes (Fig. 1).

Evaluation of the results obtained for the split-ring was accomplished by comparisono both to the original isoclinic fringe patterns, and to a published distribution for a split ring of similar geometer (Fig.2) [8]. Overall agreement in both cases was found to be good; however, some anomalous results occurred primarily in regions near the specimen edges and near the regions of load application. For the most part, these anomalous regions are due to the particular procedures selected for use in processing the images (such as the fringe-thinning procedure), and are thus believed to be correctable problems.

References:

[1]   Hoy, D.E.P., "PC-Based Digital Imaging System for Photoelastic-Coating Analysis (2-D)," Proceedings of the First International Mechanical Systems Design Conference, Nashville, TN, June, 1989, pp. P17.1-7.

[2]   Hoy, D.E.P., "Photoelastic Analysis of a Roller Chain Using a PC-Based Digital Imaging System," Proceedings of the First National Applied Mechanisms and Robotics Conference, Cincinnati, Ohio, November, 1989.

[3]   Jouett, J., "Development of a Digital Imaging System for White-Light Isochromatic Fringe Pattern Analysis," Master's Thesis, Tennessee Technological University, Cookeville, TN, 1990.

[4]   Shen, X., "Fringe-Tracing Method for White-Light Isochromatic Patterns Using a Digital Imaging System," Master's Thesis, Tennessee Technological University, Cookeville, TN, 1993.

[5]   Yu, F., Hoy, D.E.P., "White-light Isochromatic Image Processing in HSB Color Space", 1995 Society of Experimental Mechanics Spring Conference, Student Paper Category, 1995.

[6]   Zhao, W., "Development of the Interpolated-Isoclinic-Image Method for Isoclinic Fringe Pattern Analysis," Master's Thesis, Tennessee Technological University, Cookeville, TN, 1995

[7]   Yao, J., "Digital Image Processing and Isoclinics," Experimental Mechanics, Vol. 30, No. 3, Sept, 1990, pp. 264-269.

[8]   Frocht, M.M., "Photoelasticity," John Wiley & Sons, Inc., New York, 1948.

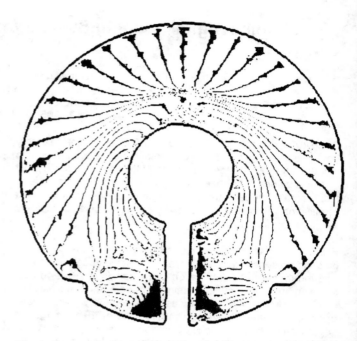

Fig. 1 Composite image of a split-ring in compression showing digital isoclinic data obtained by Hoy and Zhao's method (for clarity, only fringe center lines are shown from the full-field isoclinic data obtained for the ring)

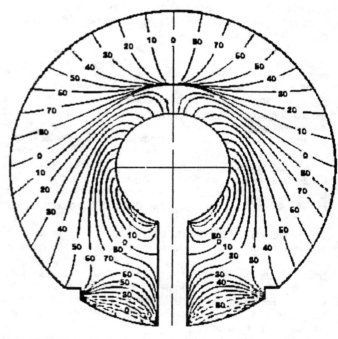

Fig. 2 Published isoclinic data for a similar split ring from Ref [8]

# Monitoring of the Alamillo Cable-stayed Bridge during Construction

Juan R. Casas and Angel C. Aparicio
School of Civil Engineering, Technical University of Catalunya
Gran Capitán s/n. Módulo C1
08034 Barcelona, Spain

The Alamillo cable-stayed bridge, built in Sevilla (Spain) for the EXPO 92 Universal Exhibition over the Guadalquivir river, is a singular and unique structure in the world because of its structural configuration (see Figure 1). In fact, the inclined tower does not present back-stays. Therefore, the loads in the deck (200 m span) should be transmitted to the foundation via the cable-stays and the weight and inclination (32°) of the pylon almost 140 m high. This original configuration, which tries to balance the internal forces in the foundation because of the deck loads with those coming from the pylon weight, derives in the necessity of a very accurate monitoring of the internal forces, both during construction and after completion of the bridge, to achieve a real balance and a correct structural performance. The last is due to the high sensitivity of those internal forces to small changes in the weigh of the elements forming the tower or the deck and in the forces of the stays as well. In fact, in the completed bridge, an error of 10 % in the final weight of pylon or deck respect to design (which is feasible in a non monitored and ill-controled bridge), derives in changes of the internal forces (bending moments) up to 70 %. Because of the unconventional structural design, the construction scheme was also quite different from the standard construction methods used in cable-stayed bridges, where, normally, the first step is the construction of the tower. After that, and by means of the support in the tower provided by the stays, the deck is constructed segmentally. In this case, the construction sequence was as follows:

1) construction of the foundation and backfill of the river dock temporarily.
2) construction of temporary piers to support the deck elements
3) construction of the deck over temporary supports
4) construction of the lower part of the pylon
5) from this point, the following steps were repeated:
   5.1 Erection of the steel segment of the pylon and welding to the previous segment
   5.2 Placement and tensioning of a couple of cables
   5.3 Placement of reinforcing steel and concrete filling of segment

Thus, during the segmental construction of the bridge it was necessary to check that the actions in the different sections will never reach the maximum allowable values adopted in the design. Moreover it should be checked that, in the finished bridge, the differences of weight due to construction errors will be within the tolerance bandwidht adopted. This bandwidht is defined in order to get a sufficient safe and reliable structure during the service life-time. To this end a set of experimental techniques were adopted. The monitoring of the most important variables during construction was accomplished by using a huge amount of instrumentation with different objectives (Figure 1):

1) Straing gages and extensometers in several positions and cross-sections of the steel and concrete parts of the deck to derive the evolution of the internal forces
2) Reinforcing calibrated bars and pressure transducers embbeded in the concrete at several pylon heights to obtain the evolution of internal forces in the reinforced concrete pylon

3) Load cells in the temporary bearings used during the sequential construction of the deck to measure the real weight of the different elements placed in the deck as well as to decide the moment when the those temporary bearings should be removed
4) Clinometers to monitor the rotation at the foundation and the inclination of the tower during its segmental construction
5) Strain gages and pressure transducers to monitor the actual forces in the cables
6) Thermocouples to monitor the thermal gradient and expansion
7) Displacement transducers and accelerometers during the static and dynamic test loading after completion of the bridge [1] and to check the final forces in the cables [2]

The overall instrumentation did perform nicely during the construction period. Only two minor problems were identified. Our previous experience of using strain gages directly attached over the strand wires to measure cable stresses was very satisfactory. However, the epoxy-coated strands used in the cables of the Alamillo bridge did not permit to use this technique. The alternative was to place the strain gages in the anchorage blocks. The intention was to correlate strain in this zone with the cable forces by means of a finite element model. However, the extremely complex stress field of the anchorage zone, and the high sensitivity of the results to the boundary conditions assumed in the mesh, rendered results of limited reliability. Also the pressure transducers (pressiometers) embbeded in the concrete did not work correctly. The basis of the transducer is a flat jack filled with mercury and connected to a pressure transducer.

A total of 294 channels of instrumentation were continuously monitored and automatically recorded on the computer hard disk every hour.

The experience acquised during the monitoring of this bridge shows how only with the help of such important amount of instrumentation it was possible to build the bridge with enough accuracy and safety. The data coming from the instrumentation during the different stages of the construction made it possible to decide in a quick and reliable way about the best sequence of operations and targeted values of the different variables in each construction stage. The differences obtained in a construction stage between the experimental and the theoretical data was passed to the contractor and used to decide the optimum values for the next stage.

References:

[1] Casas, J.R., "Full-scale dynamic testing of the Alamillo cable-stayed bridge in Sevilla (Spain)". Earthquake Engineering and Structural Dynamics, vol. 24, 35-51, 1995.
[2] Casas, J.R., " A combined method for measuring cable forces: the cable-stayed Alamillo bridge, Spain ". Structural Engineering International, Vol. 4, N. 4, 235-240, 1994.

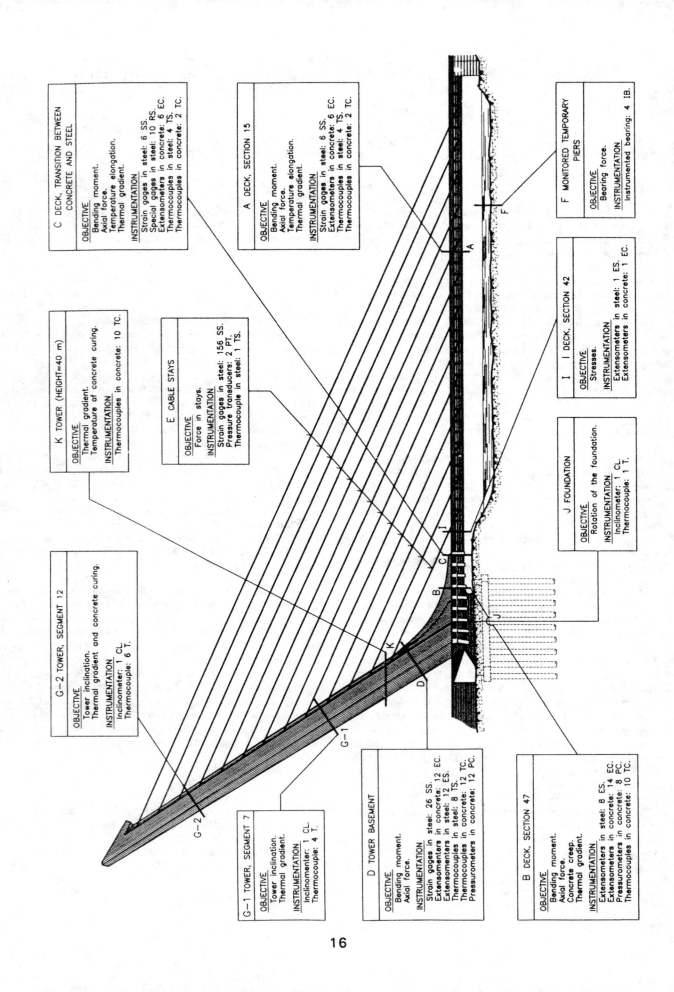

**C DECK, TRANSITION BETWEEN CONCRETE AND STEEL**

OBJECTIVE
Bending moment.
Axial force.
Temperature elongation.
Thermal gradient.

INSTRUMENTATION
Strain gages in steel: 6 SS.
Special gages in steel: 10 RS.
Extensometers in concrete: 6 EC.
Thermocouples in steel: 4 TS.
Thermocouples in concrete: 2 TC.

**A DECK, SECTION 15**

OBJECTIVE
Bending moment.
Axial force.
Temperature elongation.
Thermal gradient.

INSTRUMENTATION
Strain gages in steel: 6 SS.
Extensometers in concrete: 6 EC.
Thermocouples in steel: 4 TS.
Thermocouples in concrete: 2 TC.

**F MONITORED TEMPORARY PIERS**

OBJECTIVE
Bearing force.

INSTRUMENTATION
Instrumented bearing: 4 IB.

**K TOWER (HEIGHT=40 m)**

OBJECTIVE
Thermal gradient.
Temperature of concrete curing.

INSTRUMENTATION
Thermocouples in concrete: 10 TC.

**E CABLE STAYS**

OBJECTIVE
Force in stays.

INSTRUMENTATION
Strain gages in steel: 156 SS.
Pressure transducers: 2 PT.
Thermocouple in steel: 1 TS.

**I DECK, SECTION 42**

OBJECTIVE
Stresses.

INSTRUMENTATION
Extensometers in steel: 1 ES.
Extensometers in concrete: 1 EC.

**J FOUNDATION**

OBJECTIVE
Rotation of the foundation.

INSTRUMENTATION
Inclinometer: 1 CL.
Thermocouple: 1 T.

**G-2 TOWER, SEGMENT 12**

OBJECTIVE
Tower inclination.
Thermal gradient and concrete curing.

INSTRUMENTATION
Inclinometer: 1 CL.
Thermocouple: 6 T.

**G-1 TOWER, SEGMENT 7**

OBJECTIVE
Tower inclination.
Thermal gradient.

INSTRUMENTATION
Inclinomenter: 1 CL.
Thermocouple: 4 T.

**D TOWER BASEMENT**

OBJECTIVE
Bending moment.
Axial force.

INSTRUMENTATION
Strain gages in steel: 26 SS.
Extensomenters in concrete: 12 EC.
Extensomenters in steel: 12 ES.
Thermocouples in steel: 8 TS.
Thermocouples in concrete: 12 TC.
Pressurometers in concrete: 12 PC.

**B DECK, SECTION 47**

OBJECTIVE
Bending moment.
Axial force.
Concrete creep.
Thermal gradient.

INSTRUMENTATION
Extensometers in steel: 8 ES.
Extensometers in concrete: 14 EC.
Pressurometers in concrete: 8 PC.
Thermocouples in concrete: 10 TC.

# Further Improvement in the Manufacture of Sheet Metal Parts

S. Ali Saeedy, Eric J. Obermeyer, S. Abdi Majlessi
Mechanical Engineering—Engineering Mechanics Department
Michigan Technological University
Houghton, MI 49931

The predominant failure modes of sheet metal parts formed by die stamping are either wrinkling (compressive instability) or tearing (tensile instability). Wrinkling, which may occur in the flange as well as in the unsupported areas of the drawn part, is generated by excessive compressive stresses that cause local buckling of the sheet metal. Fracture occurs in a part due to large tensile stresses in the radial direction. The normal compressive force necessary to suppress buckling is provided by a blank-holder or binder. For a given part design and blank geometry, the major factor affecting the occurrence of defects in sheet metal parts is the blank-holder force (BHF). This variable can be controlled to delay or completely eliminate wrinkling and fracture.

A new hydraulic apparatus is designed and constructed by adding a die and punch set, a special blank-holder plate, and a hydraulic binder force system to the frame of an existing hydraulic press, as shown in Figures 1 and 2. The necessary binder force (BHF) is applied at proper locations over the periphery of the blank-holder as a function of time or press stroke. The BHF is delivered by eight single-action hydraulic cylinders stationed around the die cavity. Since the apparatus has been designed for the drawing of square-shaped parts, four of these cylinders are located above the sides of the blank-holder plate, while the remaining four apply pressure to the corners. The hydraulic binder force system (as shown schematically in Figure 3) is capable of sustaining or varying the pressures in the corner cylinders independent of those in the center cylinders. The adjustment of the BHF is performed by employing a number of sensors, hydraulic servo valve actuators, and a microprocessor. The system is capable of controlling the binder force in either an open or closed-loop manner.

The detection of wrinkling is made possible by the use of sensors. Previous work by Pereira and Zheng found the fiber optic displacement sensor to be a viable candidate for this application and for incorporation into a closed-loop controlled BHF system [1]. Two other types of less complex sensors can also be used. The first type, employed by the present apparatus, is an inductive switch which closes an electronic circuit when the formation of wrinkles increases the separation between the blank-holder plate and the die to a preset distance. The second sensor is a LVDT (linear variable differential transducer) which continuously measures the gap between the blank-holder plate and the die. The resolution which can be achieved with these sensors is, however, inferior to that of the fiber optic sensor. The ability to successfully incorporate data regarding the onset of wrinkling into a closed-loop control strategy is dependent upon the sensitivity and location of the sensors. Preliminary results indicate that there may be some limitations to the effectiveness of wrinkle suppression which can be presently achieved by closed-loop control, given the sensitivity which has been observed in these particular sensors.

Incipient tearing in sheet metal parts is not detectable directly with the existing sensors on the market but can be predicted by monitoring the punch force trajectory. A pressure transducer measures the pressure in the punch hydraulic cylinder, and the computer then uses this data to monitor the punch force. During the forming process, the punch force is plotted against the punch displacement, which is detected using the LVDT. The comparison of such a trajectory with prescribed "acceptable" trajectories is done by the microprocessor, and a flag is set if significant discrepancies are detected.

In the closed-loop control strategy, manipulation of the data is done in real-time. The results are used to activate the actuators and adjust the blank-holder force accordingly. In the case of the open-loop control scheme, the pressure in the blank-holder system follows a prescribed trajectory, which is determined off-line. Although such patterns can be developed from experimental data, finite-element analysis allows for specific, systematic solutions using a computer simulation of the process. Wang and Majlessi have employed this method to gain further insight into the effects of time and location-varying BHF and its impact on strain paths within drawn parts [2]. A commercially available three-dimensional finite-element analysis package, LS-DYNA3D, is used for such simulations.

This hydraulic apparatus has been used successfully to examine the overall effect of variable BHF and its local effects on sheet metal part quality, as well as to suggest a method for systematically controlling the BHF as a function of punch travel during the forming process. At the same time, the apparatus is used to classify the formability of different materials by determining their respective limits of drawing without failure under identical forming conditions. Preliminary results indicate that the formability of a given material is greatly enhanced by adjusting the binder pressure with respect to time. Formability is further improved through the local control of binder forces. These advances have become possible due to the use servo valves with micro-second response times and have the potential for further improvement with advances in the adaptation of sensors which can accurately measure small displacements between two rigid surfaces.

References:

[1] Pereira, P. and Zheng, Y.F., "Sensing Strategy to Detect Wrinkles in Components," *IEEE Transactions on Instrumentation and Measurement* 43 (3), June 1994, pp. 442-448.

[2] Wang, Y. and Majlessi, S.A., "The Design of an Optimum Binder Force System for Improving Sheet Metal Formability," *Proceedings of the 18th Biennial Congress of the IDDRG*, International Deep Drawing Research Group, Lisbon, Portugal, May 1994, pp. 491-502.

Figure 2  Photograph of the hydraulic apparatus

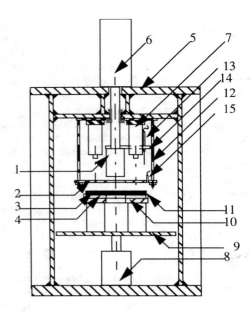

Figure 1  Schematic cross section of the hydraulic apparatus

| | | | |
|---|---|---|---|
| 1) | Punch | 8) | Bolster Hydraulic Cylinder |
| 2) | Blank-Holder Plate | 9) | Bolster |
| 3) | Blank | 10) | Die Support |
| 4) | Die | 11) | Die Guides |
| 5) | Frame (Tinius-Olson) | 12) | Hanging Bars |
| 6) | Punch Hydraulic Cylinder | 13) | LVDT |
| 7) | Blank-Holder Hydraulic Cylinders | 14) | Aluminum Bracket for LVDT |
| | | 15) | Inductive Switch |

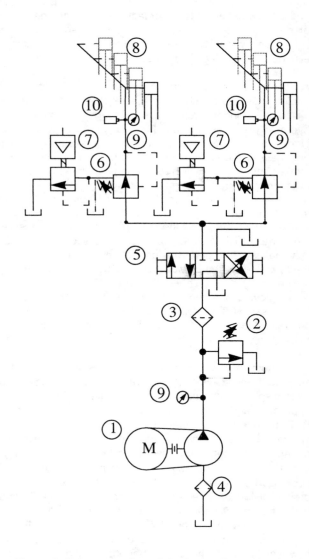

Figure 3:

| | | | |
|---|---|---|---|
| 1) | Hydraulic Power Supply Unit | 6) | Reducing Valves |
| 2) | Pressure Relief Valve | 7) | Proportional Pressure Relief Valves |
| 3) | High Pressure Filter | 8) | Single-Action Cylinders |
| 4) | Low Pressure Filter | 9) | Gauges |
| 5) | 4-Way Valve | 10) | Pressure Transducers |

Figure 3  Schematic view of the hydraulic system for supplying the blank-holder force

18

# STRUCTURAL EVALUATION AND REINFORCEMENT DESIGN
## OF A LARGE STEEL BRIDGE SPAN

**J.L.F. Freire, J.T.P. Castro**
Catholic University of Rio de Janeiro
&
**R.D. Vieira**
CEFET and Strainlab Stress Analysis

The present paper reports an integrity evaluation study and reinforcement design of a large bridge span. The bridge connects two cities separated by a bay and has a daily traffic density of 100 thousand vehicles in both ways. The bridge has 14 km of length, 800 m of which are composed of a steel orthotropic beam section weighing 13 thousand metric tons. Under the steel beam is located the navigation channel, corresponding to a free span of 300 m. The transversal section of the beam is composed of two box sections connected by a steel deck.

The bridge has been in service for 20 years. Periodic non-destructive inspections showed the existence of nucleating and propagating cracks. This fact, allied to the need of increasing the traffic load and the change of ownership, generated a study to evaluate the bridge structural integrity. This structural evaluation work carried out was divided in three phases: Preliminary, Complementary, and Reinforcement Design.

The Preliminary Evaluation started with the analysis of the overall behavior of the bridge. The analysis did not show any structural major problem. There were not complains, indications, or recorded observations of column settlements, local warping, local buckling, excessive stresses or displacements caused by static or dynamic loading. The analysis of routine inspection reports showed that many small cracks nucleated and propagated in certain regions of the box sections. A detailed study was carried out and leaded to the conclusion that these cracks initiated in field- welded joints. These welds were made to connect 15 m length box- section beams. Most of the cracks initiated in the longitudinal welds and propagated along them. Also, a high percentage of these cracks were located in regions where the thickness of the superior deck and stiffeners were respectively 10 and 8 mm.

Fratographic studies revealed that the cracks initiated in hard spots of the field-welded joints. A stress analysis based on the design calculations showed that secondary-transversal stresses caused by the localized and heavy vehicle traffic would induce ranges of $\Delta\sigma$=130 or 140 MPa. For smooth steel sheets this stress level can be accepted but it is known that that the joint details present in the orthotropic upper deck could lead to fatigue-range strengths as low as 70 to 100 MPa. The existence of nucleating and propagating cracks and its confirmation by a simple design stress-

calculation model, indicated the need for a more precise prediction model so that it could predict more accurately the secondary stresses and also give rapid means of comparing alternative solutions (such as reinforcements) in order to decrease the operating stresses. This analysis phase was called Complementary Evaluation and consisted of the development of a finite element model and of the instrumentation with strain gages of one region of the box-section.

The finite element analysis was based in three models. The first model considered the metallic span as long beam and helped to determine the basic effort diagrams and to calculate the primary stresses. The second model was much more localized which was used as an intermediate step toward a very precise sub-model which took into consideration geometric details of the upper deck and stiffeners. The relevant load case for the last two models was the action of the rear wheels of a heavy truck.

Experimental stress analysis was employed with the objectives of getting actual strain data, collect information to build a rain flow histogram for fatigue analysis, and to validate the finite element results. Uniaxial and three element rosettes were employed in the instrumentation. The satisfactory agreement between the experimental results, the finite element models, and the design predictions, made possible the use of very few sensors. Figure 1 highlights the instrumentation of one section by an uniaxial strain gage, U, located in the bottom of a stiffener, and a rosette, R, located over a longitudinal weld which joins the upper deck and one of the section stiffeners. Strains measured by these gages due to the traffic load were recorded. The collection of this type of strain-history data allowed the fatigue-life analysis which employed the rain-flow technique associated to Miner's Rule. The predicted life using this model agreed very well with the crack detection recordings which revealed early-initial cracks after 5 years of bridge operation.

Considering the results reported above it was decided to design a reinforcement of the structure of the upper box-section. It was proposed the insertion of transversal elements as presented in Figure 2. It was found by the finite element calculations that this solution decreases the maximum stresses of more than 40%. This reduction is more than enough to avoid the crack nucleation and also is the easiest one to implement due to operational difficulties. The increase of weight is less than 10% of the original.

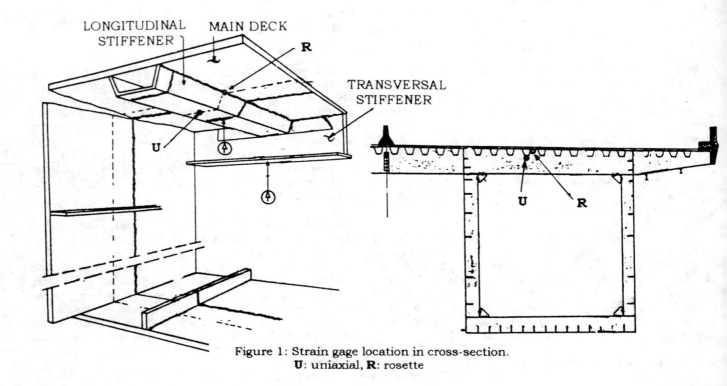

Figure 1: Strain gage location in cross-section.
**U**: uniaxial, **R**: rosette

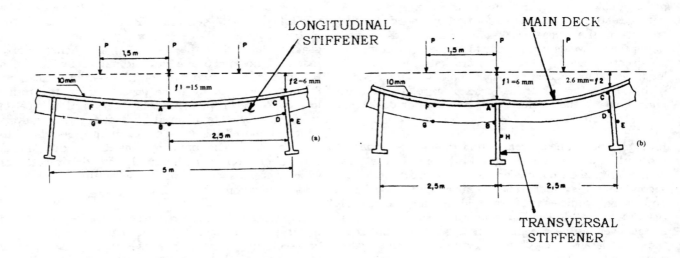

Figure 2: Transversal member to reinforce local main- deck bridge-span.

# An Investigation of Automobile Handling Characteristics with ADAMS

B. K. Cho,    S. J. Song,    G. H. Ryu,    S. W. Cho
Seoul National University
Shilim, Kwanak, Seoul, Korea

Ride and handling of a vehicle are the most important aspects for suspension system but they are contrary to each other. To improve driving performance we must predict the total driving performances for the various design parameters of suspension system at the initial design stage. So the analysis of automobile driving performance must be accomplished with basic raw data in early design stage. With ADAMS[1] we modeled a vehicle suspension including bushing for compliance effect and simulated handling for step steering input for J-turn and pulse input for lane change simulation. We modeled it like Fig.1. We used 33 bodies, 33 joints, 18 force elements and 32 bushings for compliance effect so that it has 114 degrees of freedom. We used the data of spring, damper and bushing from suspension designer and those of tire from manufacturer.

Simulation results for J-turn[2] and lane change[3] were compared with vehicle test results. In vehicle tests, yaw rate, lateral acceleration and roll angle were measured on the point of mass center using gyrometer. The test device diagram is shown in Fig.2. Simulations were performed on the same conditions of tests. For steering input, step function was used for J-turn and pulse function for lane change. According to ISO/DP 7401, for a driving vehicle at 80km/h step and pulse steering input were given as Fig.3. Vehicle test results and simulation results are in Fig.4. They are in good agreement.

We have chosen four evaluation parameters from the J-turn analysis and test. They are steering sensitivity, understeer gradient, roll gain and lateral acceleration response time[4].

① Steering sensitivity describes the change of acceleration per unit change in steer angle at 0.15 g lateral acceleration where lateral acceleration and steer angle is linear. The units are g/100 degrees. This can be written as

$$SS = 100 \frac{da_y}{d\delta_{sw}} \qquad (1)$$

where, SS = steering sensitivity

$a_y$ = lateral acceleration

$\delta_{sw}$ = steering wheel angle

② Understeer gradient means steer response and written as :

$$\delta = \frac{180}{\pi} \frac{l}{R} + K a_y \qquad (2)$$

where, δ = steer angle at the front wheels

$\ell$ = wheel base

R = radius of turn

K = understeer gradient

Using overall steering gear ratio and centrifugal forces, equation (2) can be expressed as :

$$K = \frac{1}{G} \frac{d\delta_{sw}}{da_y} - \frac{lg}{V^2} \qquad (3)$$

where, G = overall steering gear ratio

V = vehicle speed

Understeer gradient is usually derived at 0.15 g lateral acceleration.

③ Roll gain is the amount of roll angle experienced by the vehicle during a turn. Again this is expressed at 0.15 g lateral acceleration.

④ Lateral acceleration response time is a measure of the speed of directional response of vehicles. This is defined as the time required for the lateral acceleration to reach 90% of the ultimate steady state level from the steer input. If a vehicle is designed for better handling performance this value decreases and for better riding performance this value increases.

The derived parameters are listed in Table 1. From this we found that the model vehicle has the characteristics that the handling response is not fast but riding and stability is good.

We can find the transient response characteristics and the frequency response characteristics from the lane change analyses and tests. And those characteristics are evaluated by the 4 parameter method[5]. In 4 parameter method, the yaw rate and the lateral acceleration of the vehicle with pulse input are recorded in time domain and those data transformed into frequency domain. And we extract 4 parameters to understand the handling stability characteristics.

① Steady state gain of yaw rate response( $a_1$ ) denotes "heading easiness" and the greater, the better. It is the yaw rate response gain at 0 Hz.

② Frequency of yaw rate response( $f_n$ ) denotes "heading response" and the greater, the better. It is the frequency of maximal phase change between 0 Hz and maximal frequency of yaw rate response gain.

③ Damping ratio of yaw rate(ζ) denotes "directional damping" as the transient response characteristics in time domain.

④ Phase delay of lateral acceleration response(φ) denotes "following controllability" and the smaller, the better. It is the phase difference of lateral acceleration response at 1 Hz.

Four parameters are depicted in a rhombus as Fig.5. The area of the rhombus denotes vehicle handling performance and the distortion denotes handling tendency. Following the same procedure, 4 parameters are evaluated for the vehicle speed of 100km/h and 120km/h. And all the three rhombuses for 80km/h, 100km/h and 120km/h are plotted in Fig.6. It denotes the variation of handling characteristics with respect to the vehicle speed. From the above, it is found that the designer can predict the steerability of vehicle and can use the 4 parameter method in suspension design.

Vehicle handling characteristic parameters which are very useful for the design of suspension systems are evaluated from our analyses.

References

[1] ADAMS/SOLVER Reference Manual, Mechanical Dynamics Inc., 1994
[2] Milliken, Race Car Vehicle Dynamics, SAE, 1995
[3] Heydinger, et al, "Pulse Testing Techniques Applied to Vehicle Handling Dynamics", SAE paper 930828, 1993
[4] Riede, et al, "Typical Vehicle Parameters for Dynamics Studies Revised for the 1980's", SAE paper 840561, 1984
[5] Mimuro, et al, "Four Parameter Evaluation Method of Lateral Transient Response", SAE paper 901734, 1990

Table 1    Response Parameters

| Parameter | US Products | | | Test Vehicle |
|---|---|---|---|---|
| | Min | Avg | Max | |
| Steering Sensitive (g's / 100 deg SWA) | 0.57 | 1.01 | 2.15 | 0.62 |
| Understeer Gradient (deg/g) | 0.7 | 4.4 | 8.2 | 6.9 |
| Roll Gain (deg/g) | 3.0 | 6.4 | 11.0 | 3.64 |
| Lateral Acceleration Response Time (sec) | 0.28 | 0.41 | 0.77 | 0.48 |

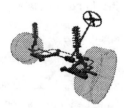

(a) Front Suspension

(b) Rear Suspension

Fig.1 Suspension Modeling

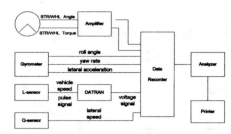

Fig.2 Test Device Diagram

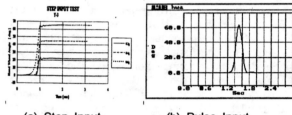

(a) Step Input                    (b) Pulse Input

Fig.3 Steering Input

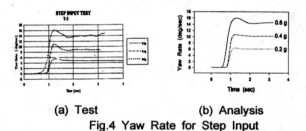

(a) Test                    (b) Analysis

Fig.4 Yaw Rate for Step Input

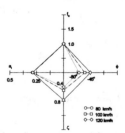

Fig.5 4 Parameter Rhombus

Fig.6 Patern Change for Vehicle Speed

# Strain Gage Application on Wire Ropes

Roberto STEINDLER
Dipartimento di Meccanica e Aeronautica - Università di Roma "La Sapienza"
Via Eudossiana 18 - 00184 ROMA, Italia

**Introduction.-** The rotary bending fatigue test machine of the Department of Mechanics and Aeronautics of the Rome University "La Sapienza" [1] obliges, by means of apposite brackets, rope specimens 1.5 m long to assume a curvilinear configuration (fig. 1): each wire is periodically stressed from compression to tension during the rotations round the rope curvilinear axis. This machine is considerable for its relatively high rotation frequency and its limited weight, but it doesn't simulate any real load condition; so its performances must be compared with those of the conventional machines [2], [3].

Unfortunately, the wire rope stresses are not always well known; in the case of a curvilinear configuration, a frequent hypothesis is that the stersses are pretty near to the complete sliding among the wires values [4]; so, to know exactly the stress values, the best thing to do is to measure the wire strains by means of electric strain gages. As very few authors have applied strain gages to wire ropes because of the small dimensions of the wires [5], a proper technology has been choosen to this aim.

**Experimental set up.-** The strain gages have been applied to three different rope patterns previously assembled on the Department machine: a *wire rope*, construction A+6(1+6+12+18), wire diameter 0.5÷0.6 mm, equivalent diameter 12 mm, crossed winding; a *Seale-Warrington rope*, construction 1[1(1+6)+6(1+6)]+6[1+7+7/7+14], external wire diameter 1 mm, equivalent diameter 18 mm, crossed winding; a *strand*, construction 1+6+12, wire diameter 2.5 mm, equivalent diameter 12.5 mm. In the first two cases a two phase adhesive (powder plus liquid solvent) has been used; the grid gage dimensions have been choiced the same or a little larger than the wire diameters and the gages have been applied on at most two wires (fig. 2). In the third case, the strain gages have been applied on a single wire by means of a liquid adhesive; as now the gage outputs are surely reliable, this case can be considered as a reference for the previous ones.

To verify the strain gage application reliability, their sinusoidal output during the rope rotation has been primarily checked: the rope specimens have been first manually rotated, and the outputs have been measured, at regular angular steps, by a static strain meter; second, during the fatigue tests, the outputs have been measured by a strain conditioner connected to a digital oscilloscope. Afterwards, the experimental peack to peack strains, $\varepsilon$p-p(sp), have been compared with the theoretical ones, $\varepsilon$p-p(th), calculated in the case of complete sliding among the wires $(2\delta\cos^2 (\alpha \pm \beta)/(D+d)$, where $\delta$ is the wire diameter, d is the rope diameter, D is the diameter of the curved configuration of the rope and $\alpha$ and $\beta$ are the helic angles wire-strand and strand-rope [4]): the strain gage application is considerd reliable, if the ratio $\varepsilon$p-p(sp)/$\varepsilon$p-p(th) is near constant along the rope, and if its mean value does not vary for ropes of the same pattern. To measure the curvature radius R=D/2 along the rope assembled on the machine, its trend has been copied on a

rigid cardboard, the coordinates of many points have been measured, the curvature radii have been calculated by means of a cubic polynomial interpolation.

**Test results.-** Five wire rope specimens, each one in a particular configuration, have been assembled on the machine; six strain gages (grid dimensions: 0.6 x 0.6 mm$^2$) have been applied on each specimen and the ropes have been manually rotated. The regular sinusoidal trend of a gage output is shown in fig.3. The whole gage outputs are resumed in Tab. I: the mean values $\varepsilon$p-p(sp)/$\varepsilon$p-p(th) are not very different from rope to rope, they are indipendent from the curvature radii, and the deviations are contained.

Six Seale-Warrington rope specimens have been assembled on the machine; four strain gages (grid dimensions 1.5 x 1.5 mm$^2$) have been applied on each specimen and the ropes have been rotated first manually and after at 5 or 10 Hz frequencies. In fig. 4 there are the gage outputs during a fatigue test: also in the dynamic conditions the outputs are regular sinusoids. Tab. II shows that the mean values $\varepsilon$p-p(sp)/$\varepsilon$p-p(th) are very close to each other, and that the deviations are very small. For this rope the experimental strains are nearer to the complete sliding value among the wires than for the previous rope.

Six strand specimens have been assembled at last on the machine; four strain gages (grid dimensions: 0.6x 0.6 mm$^2$) have been applied on each specimen and the strands have been rotated in both the ways. The gage outputs, regular sinusoids as for the wire ropes, are resumed in Tab. III. For the strands the experimental strains are even nearer to the complete sliding value among the wires.

An interpretation of the different values of the ratios $\varepsilon$p-p(sp)/$\varepsilon$p-p(th) in the three examind ropes is the following: as the wire dimensions increase, the wire sliding increases too, because the friction among the wires decreases.

**Conclusions.-** The strain gage outputs coming from the related tests are reliable; this means that the gages can be applied on wire ropes even on more than a single a wire; so they can be used to study the rope performances, particullary if fatigue loaded.

## References

[1] BRANCA F.P., CAPPA P., STEINDLER R. "Accelerated fatigue tests of wire ropes" Wire Industry pp 654-658 1990.
[2] FEYRER K, HEMMINGER R. "New rope bending fatigue machines constructed in the traditional way" OIPEEC Bulletin No. 45, 1983.
[3] HOBBS R., SMITH B:W: "Fatigue performances of socketed terminations to structural strands" Proc.Inst.Civ.Engr. Part 2. pp 35-48, 1983.
[4] THAON M. "Analysis of ropes fatigue test and use of its results" OIPEEC Round Table, Luxembourg, 1977.
[5] WIEK L. " Strain gage at multi-strand nonspinning ropes" OIPEEC Bulletin n. 37. 1980.

Fig.1 - The rotary bending fatigue test machine

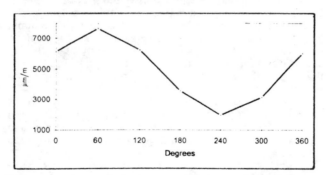

Fig.2 - A strain gage applied on a wire rope

Fig.3 - The static output of a strain gage applied on the wire rope

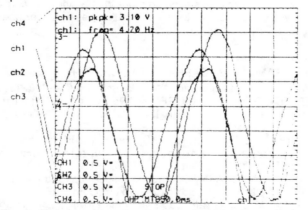

Fig. 4 - The dynamic outputs of the strain gages applied on the Seale Warrington rope

Tab. I - Wire rope: A + 6 (1 + 6 + 12 + 18)
Comparison of the experimental peack to peack strain values, εp-p(sp), with the theoretical ones, εp-p(th), in the case of complete sliding along the wires.

| Rope | Applied strain gages | εp-p(sp)/εp-p(th) | Minimum curvature radius (mm) |
|---|---|---|---|
| 1 | 6 | 1.35 ± 0.18 | 290 |
| 2 | 6 | 1.35 ± 0.20 | 130 |
| 3 | 6 | 1.45 ± 0.14 | 125 |
| 4 | 6 | 1.45 ± 0.12 | 145 |
| 5 | 6 | 1.50 ± 0.10 | 170 |

Tab. II - Seale Warrington rope:
1[1(1+6)+6(1+6)]+6[1+7+7/7+14]
Comparison of the experimental peack to peack strain values, εp-p(sp), with the theoretical ones, εp-p(th), in the case of complete sliding along the wires.

| Rope | Applied strain gages | εp-p(sp)/εp-p(th) | Minimum curvature radius (mm) |
|---|---|---|---|
| 1 | 4 | 1.06 ± 0.03 | 200 |
| 2 | 4 | 1.10 ± 0.03 | 165 |
| 3 | 4 | 1.12 ± 0.05 | 160 |
| 4 | 4 | 1.10 ± 0.06 | 230 |
| 5 | 4 | 1.05 ± 0.05 | 95 |
| 6 | 4 | 1.12 ± 0.06 | 200 |

Tab. III - Strand: 1 + 6 + 12
Comparison of the experimental peack to peack strain values, εp-p(sp), with the theoretical ones, εp-p(th), in the case of complete sliding along the wires.

| Rope | Applied strain gages | εp-p(sp)/εp-p(th) | Minimum curvature radius (mm) |
|---|---|---|---|
| 1 | 4 | 1.02 ± 0.01 | 550 |
| 2 | 4 | 1.07 ± 0.03 | 480 |
| 3 | 4 | 1.05 ± 0.03 | 350 |
| 4 | 4 | 1.04 ± 0.01 | 680 |
| 5 | 4 | 1.01 ± 0.02 | 560 |
| 6 | 4 | 1.06 ± 0.04 | 540 |

# Whole-field Nondestructive Residual Stress Evaluation of the Rails by Twyman/Green Interferometry

B. S. Wang & F. P. Chiang
Department of Mechanical Engineering
State University of New York, Stony Brook, NY 11794

## Abstract

A novel whole-field nondestructive residual stress measurement technology is introduced by using Twyman/Green interferometry. Residual stress relief is achieved by high temperature thermal annealing and the out-of-plane deformation generated by the residual stress relaxation is obtained. One of the advantages of this technique is that the high residual stress gradient can be directly observed. In this paper, the experimental techniques and procedures are described. Its application to residual stress measurement in rails is given.

## Introduction

The significance of residual stresses to the performance of the structures has been well recognized. Quantitative measurement or evaluation of the residual stress is of great interest in engineering applications. The available techniques can be virtually categorized as two approaches: destructive and nondestructive. In the destructive approach, surface stress relaxation procedures, such as hole-drilling, coring or layer removal, are incorporated with deformation or strain measurement schemes, like strain gage method and optical techniques [1],[2],[3],[4], e.g., including holographic interferometry, moire interferometry, laser speckle correlation and shearography. These measurements are pointwise and not quite suitable for whole-field measurement. The most commonly used nondestructive measurement techniques are X-ray and neutron diffraction[5], which determine the interatomic spacing change generated by the residual stress. Residual stress can be extracted by the recorded position of Bragg diffraction at a variety of tilt angles. The disadvantage of X-ray diffraction is its limited penetration ability and the neutron diffraction needs an intense source of thermal neutron whose accessibility is usually limited.

This paper describes a new whole-field, nondestructive residual stress evaluation approach. The whole-field residual stress relief is realized by thermal annealing. Compared with the conventional residual stress relaxation procedure and residual stress measurement approach, this technique is simple, accurate, and especially suitable for the measurement of the residual stress with high gradient.

## Experimental techniques and procedures

The schematic description of the Twyman/Green interferometry is shown in Fig. 1. It consists of a plane mirror and a flat specimen oriented perpendicular to each other and a beamsplitter bisecting the angle between the mirror and the specimen. A carefully adjusted plane wave incident from the right is divided into two waves by the beamsplitter. The incident beams travel separate paths -- one to the plane mirror and the other to the specimen. These two waves are then recombined at the output of the interferometer. In the recorded plane, the complex amplitude of waves from the specimen and the mirror are denoted by $U_1(x,y)$ and $U_2(x,y)$ respectively, which can be written as

$$U_1(x,y) = a(x,y) \bullet e^{-1\,\phi 1\,(x,y)}$$

$$U_2(x,y) = a(x,y) \bullet e^{-1\,\phi 2\,(x,y)} \qquad (1)$$

With proper reparation of both the mirror and the specimen surfaces and proper tuning of the optical setup, zero initial phase difference between the two waves can be achieved. When deformation occurs to the specimen, it leads to the phase change of the object beam, which is denoted by $\phi(x,y)$. The light intensity at the recorded plane will be proportional to

$$I(x,y) = |\,U_1(x,y) + U_2(x,y)\,|^2$$

$$= 4a^2(x,y)\cos^2[\phi(x,y)/2] \qquad (2)$$

The phase $\phi(x,y)$ may be related to the out-of-plane displacement w. The quantitative interpretation of the out-of-plane deformation from the fringe patterns is given by the following equations.

$$w = \frac{n_z \lambda}{2} \qquad (3)$$

where $n_z$ is the fringe orders of the out-of-plane deformation, which equal $0, \pm1, \pm2,...$ and $\lambda$ is the wavelength of the laser, which is 488nm.

To relieve the residual stress by high temperature thermal annealing, the specimen surface is coated with the high temperature resistant and anti-oxidizing metal by vacuum evaporation. Then, the specimen is slowly heated to the annealing temperature and soaked for adequate time to allow sufficient relaxation of the residual stress before it is slowly cooled down to ambient temperature. After the thermal annealing, the residual stress is relieved by softening - a spontaneous decrease of the yield stress. Under the microstructure, the residual stress is associated with the dislocations. In the annealing process, the dislocations are eliminated by climb and cross slip, thus residual stress relaxation is attained through plastic deformation.

## Application to rail residual stress measurement

In the railroad, one scheme to control the wear and shelling on heavy haul freight lines is two-point contact grinding in which the profile of the rail head is regrounded after certain heavy load. The shakedown residual stress is established after the load is withdrawn because of the plastic deformation due to the heavy cold-working. This experimental technique is applied to the whole-field stress measurement of the rail transverse slices. The residual stress is relieved at $900\,^{\circ}$K for eight hours. The out-of-plane plastic deformation produced by the residual stress relaxation is obtained. The fringe pattern is shown in Fig. 2. High gradient residual stress is observed in the crown area of the rail, which is subjected to the heavy contact load.

## Conclusions

A new whole-field, nondestructive residual stress measurement technique is successfully developed by using Twyman/Green interferometry with high temperature annealing for the residual stress relief. Its application to the residual stress measurement in rails is also given. It can also be used for real-time monitoring of the residual stress relaxation by thermal annealing, which is of great interest in engineering applications. This method is a reliable, accurate, practical approach for residual stress measurement approach. It is virtually applicable to the 3-D residual stress measurement of various solids including composites that are accessible to heat treatment.

## Acknowledgment

The support from the Department of Transportation is greatly acknowledged.

## References

1. Makino, A. & Nelson, D. *Exp. Mech.*, 34, (1), 66-78, 1994
2. Nicoletto, G., *Exp. Mech.*, 31, (3), 252-256, 1991
3. Pechersky, M. J., Miller, R. F. and Vikram, C. S., *Optical Engineering*, 34, (10), 2964-2971
4. R. Czarnek, J. Lee, S. Y. Lin, *Residual Stress in rails*, 1, 153-167, Klawer Academic Pub. 1992
5. M. Bourke & A. Needleman etc., *Fundamentals of Metal Matrix Composites* (edited by S. Suresh, A Mortensen and A. Needleman), 61-80, Butterworth-Heinemann, 1993
6. Y. Y. Wang & F. P. Chiang, *Final Report To US DOT*, DOT/FRA/ORD-94/02, DOT/VNTSC- FRA-93-24, 1993

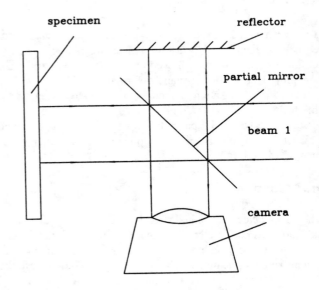

Fig. 1 a sketch of Twyman/Green interferometry setup

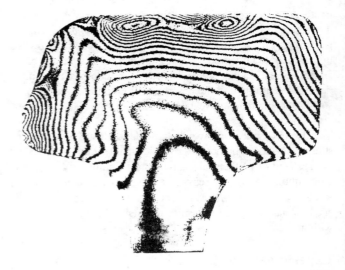

Fig. 2 w-field fringes by Twyman/Green interferometry with annealing

# "Residual Stresses Measurement Using a Radial Interferometer - a Preliminary Analysis"

Armando Albertazzi Gonçalves Jr.
Cesar Kanda
Juliano Boettger
Universidade Federal de Santa Catarina
Caixa Postal 5053
88040-970     Florianopolis - SC
Brazil
e-mail: aag@certi.ufsc.br

Marcos Roberto Rodacoski
Laboratorio Central de Pesquisa e Desenvolvimento
LAC -COPEL/UFPR
Caixa Postal 318
80001-970     Curitiba -PR
Brazil

## ABSTRACT

This paper concerns on the evaluation of a new concept of interferometer, developed to measure residual stresses combining the radial displacement field measured by electronic holography (ESPI) and the hole-drilling method. A preliminary evaluation of the convenience of such approach is presented here. A complete experimental evaluation will be reported in a future paper.

## 1  INTRODUCTION

Residual stresses are present in almost all structures or mechanical components. They may be introduced by the manufacturing or assembling processes or may occur during the life of the structures.

In many cases residual stresses are a decisive factor in the failure of structures, particularly if subjected to alternating loading services or under corrosive environment.

The hole-drilling method is the most accepted among the stress relief techniques. In general, it consists on measurement of strain around a hole using electric strain gages.

## 2  RADIAL INTERFEROMETER

The developed interferometer is composed by a set of conical mirrors to generate double illumination with radial sensitivity in a circular measurement region. With this interferometer only the radial component of the displacement field is measured, although other components (undesirable or not) can be present.

The measurement system is composed by a drilling device, a coherent light source, optical and electronic devices to illuminate and acquire images of the measurement region.

Radial displacements up to 2 μm can be  measured with uncertainties better than ± 0,04 μm.

## 3  HOLE-DRILLING METHOD

A hole is drilled in the studied specimen creating a new surface that relieves the residual stresses in the area surrounding the hole. It is very important that the procedure of drilling the hole no introduces new stresses.[1],[2]

The relieved stresses originate a strain field that is associated with a displacement field.  Measuring this displacement field provides sufficient information to calculate the principal stresses and their orientation.[3]

The displacement field around a hole passing through the thickness of an infinite plate subjected to uniform residual stresses can be described by the following equation:

$$U_r(r,\theta) = -\frac{1+\nu}{2 \cdot E} \cdot r \cdot \left\{ \left[ \left(\frac{R_0}{r}\right)^4 - \frac{4}{1+\nu}\left(\frac{R_0}{r}\right)^2 \right] \cdot (\sigma_1 - \sigma_2) \cdot \cos(2\theta - 2\beta) \right.$$

$$\left. -(\sigma_1 + \sigma_2)\left(\frac{R_0}{r}\right)^2 \right\} \qquad (1)$$

where:

$U_r(r,\theta)$ is the radial displacement [μm]

$r$ and $\theta$ are the polar coordinates [mm] and [rad]

$\nu$ is the Poisson's ratio

E is the Young's modulus [MPa]

$R_0$  is  the radius of the drilled hole [mm]

$\sigma_1$ and $\sigma_2$ are the principal stresses [MPa]

$\beta$ is the angle of the principal directions [rad]

## 4  HARMONIC APPROACH

The principal stresses and their principal directions can be quantified  by a harmonic analysis. The data are sampled from a closed circular ring, formed by a certain number of points of same radius and uniform angular increment.[3]

The radial displacements measured along this ring define a periodic function.  By analyzing equation (1), if the radius is kept constant, $U_r(r,\theta)$ has a constant term and a term in $\cos(2\theta+2\beta)$, a second harmonic, i.e., two periods in $2\pi$. To make it clear, equation (1) can be rewritten as:

$$U_r(r,\theta) = A(r)(\sigma_1 - \sigma_2)\cos(2\theta - 2\beta) + B(r)(\sigma_1 + \sigma_2) \quad (2)$$

where:

$$A(r) = -\frac{1+\nu}{2E}r\left[ \left(\frac{R_0}{r}\right)^4 - \frac{4}{1+\nu}\left(\frac{R_0}{r}\right)^2 \right]$$

$$B(r) = \frac{1+\nu}{2E}r\left(\frac{R_0}{r}\right)^2$$

The Fourier series coefficients computed from the measured displacements along the sampling ring can be used to determine $\sigma 1$, $\sigma 2$ and $\beta$ by:

$$\begin{cases} \sigma_1 = \dfrac{1}{2}\left( \dfrac{S_0}{B(r_i)} + \dfrac{S_{2\theta}}{A(r_i)} \right) \\ \sigma_2 = \dfrac{1}{2}\left( \dfrac{S_0}{B(r_i)} - \dfrac{S_{2\theta}}{A(r_i)} \right) \end{cases} \quad (3)$$

Where:

$S_o$ is the constant term (dc)

$S_{2\theta}$ is the Fourier coefficient of $2\theta$ frequency

$r_1$ is the radius of the measurement ring

The $\beta$ angle is determined by analyzing the sine and cosine terms of the second harmonic of Fourier series.

## 5 LEAST SQUARE APPROACH

There are practical situations where is not possible to sample the displacements around a whole ring, for example, if a region of the fringe map is damaged or a shadow acts on a portion of the image. In these cases is not possible to determine the residual stresses by the harmonic analysis. The least square method can be used to overcome these difficulties. In this way, a set of radial displacements experimentally measured is confronted with equation (1). The values of $\sigma_1$, $\sigma_2$ and $\beta$ are fitted in order to minimize the quadratic error between the experimentally measured displacements and those obtained by equation (1). As a result, $\sigma_1$, $\sigma_2$ and $\beta$ are determined by means of a great quantity of experimental data, reducing the influence of random errors. To simplify mathematical notation, let the stress difference and stress sum be defined as:

$$\sigma_D = \sigma_1 - \sigma_2 \qquad \sigma_S = \sigma_1 + \sigma_2 \qquad (4)$$

The Quadratic Error (QE) is calculated by:

$$QE = \sum_{i=1}^{n} \left\{ U_r^{\bullet}(r_i, \theta_i) - A(r_i)\sigma_D \cos(2\theta_i - 2\beta) - B(r_i)\sigma_s \right\}^2 \quad (5)$$

where:

QE is the quadratic error

n is the number of experimentally measured points

$U_r^{\bullet}(r_i, \theta_i)$ represents the radial displacement experimentally measured for each point

One looks for the values of $\sigma_1$, $\sigma_2$ and $\beta$ that minimize equation (5), what can be done by differentiating QE with respect to each parameter above and solving the nonlinear system that results.

## 6 NUMERICAL SIMULATION

To analyze the influence of some errors associated with the measurement technique and identify the most critical situations and parameters, numerical simulation was used.

A software was developed and implemented to simulate the measurement principle of the radial interferometer proposed here.

In order to simulate different operational condition, the software allows the user to specify several parameters:

- $\sigma_1$, $\sigma_2$ level and direction ($\beta$);
- material properties: Young's modulus and Poisson's ratio;
- hole radius;
- sampling ring position;
- center of sampling ring (centered with the hole or centered with the optical axis of the interferometer).

Several errors can be artificially introduced:

- rigid body motions in directions x and y;
- concentricity errors of the hole with respect to the optical axis of the interferometer
- errors in Young's modulus and Poisson's ratio
- errors in the hole radius
- random errors on the measured displacements.

This software can analyze data through the harmonic algorithm and/or least square approach.

## 7 CONCLUSIONS

Data obtained from simulation allow to conclude that:

- the hole diameter and the Young's Module should be very well known;

- in presence of rigid body motion any misalignment between the hole and optical axis of the interferometer is critical when the sampling ring is centered with the hole. In practice is very difficult to assure that the hole is always centered, so is recommended that the sampling ring be centered with the optical axis of the interferometer.

Typical random errors ( ±40 nm) in the measurement of radial displacement do not introduce prejudicial effects on residual stresses determination when the number of points considered is greater than 50.

Other error sources, inherent to Kirsch formulation were not evaluated. However, this is not a restriction imposed by the radial interferometer, and it affects equally the other methods based in the execution of a hole.

The results of this preliminary analysis are very positive. Presently, we are working to improve fringe quality, to perform automatic fringe analysis and to experimentally validate this interferometer. That will be reported in a future paper.

## 8 REFERENCES

[1] Rendler, N. J. and Vigness, I., "Hole-Drilling Strain-Gage Method of Measuring Residual Stresses", Experimental Mechanics, 12 (6), 1966.
[2] ASTM, Determining Residual Stresses by the Hole-Drilling Method, Standards E837/92. Philadelphia, 1992.
[3] Rodacoski, M. R., "Medição de Tensões Residuais Localizadas Através do Método do Furo Cego e Holografia Eletrônica (ESPI)". Exame de Qualificação de Doutorado, UFSC, Florianópolis, 1995.
[4] Albertazzi, G. J. ,A. et al, "Adequação de um Interferômetro Radial para Medição de Tensões Residuais por Meio da Holografia Eletrônica", III Simpósio de Análise Experimental de Tensões, p.p. 19-26, ABCM, Rio de Janeiro, 1995.

# Accurate Measurement of Residual Stress in Glass Rod by Photoelastic Experiment

Tae Hyun Baek[*1], Jae Choon Lee[*2], Dong Hyun Kim[*3]

[*1]Department of Mechanical Engineering, Kunsan National University, Kunsan, Cheonbuk, 573-701
[*2]Department of Inorganic Materials Engineering, Myung Ji University, Kyung Gi Do, 449-728
[*3]Department of Mechanical Engineering, Won Kwang University, Iksan City, Cheonbuk, 570-749
The Republic of Korea

Photoelastic method based on the stress-optic law is used to measure residual stresses in glass rods which have been heat-treated at different temperatures ranging from 560℃ to 665℃. This research is performed to analyze the variation of residual stresses with respect to heat-treated temperatures of glass rods. In order to measure the stress accurately, both fringe sharpening[1] and multiplication[2] techniques are applied to the determination of photoelastic fringe orders. The experimental results are compared with the calculated values expected by Instant Freezing Model[3].

Each sample is prepared from a commercial sodium borocilicate glass rod which is 60 cm in length and 9.5 cm in diameter. The physical properties, i.e., strain point, Young's modulus, Poisson's ratio, thermal expansion coefficient, and stress-optic coefficient, of the glass rods are 520℃, 70GPa, 0.25, $58 \times 10^{-7}$℃$^{-1}$ and $3.5 \times 10^{-12}$ m$^2$/N(or Brewster), respectively. The glass rods are kept for a certain time in the oven setting at a constant temperature, and they are taken out and cooled at a room temperature. After cooling, each sample is cut with a diamond saw into a cylinder from 20mm to 40mm long.

Each sample is viewed through a circular polariscope equipped with a digital image processing system. Original isochromatic fringe patterns of a sample heat-treated at 650℃ is shown in Fig. 1(a). Fringe multiplication and sharpening techniques are applied to this isochromatic fringe patterns to determine accurate fractional fringe orders. The lower halves of Fig.'s 1 (b) and (c) show two times fringe multiplied pattern and fringe-sharpened lines extracted from the fringe multiplied pattern of Fig.1 (b), respectively. Filon's separation method[4] with the stress-optic law is used to resolve hoop and radial stress components from isochromatic fringes which are the same as in-plane maximum shearing stresses. Fig. 2 shows the experimental results which are analysed from the sample of Fig. 1(c). Numerical values

calculated from Bartenev's Instant Freezing Model[3] can be compared with the experimental results as shown in Fig. 2. The fictitious, i.e., hypothetical instant frozen temperature and thermal expansion coefficient employed in the Instant Freezing Model are varied simultaneously so that the estimated residual stress profiles can be agreed with the experimental results.

Fig. 3 shows distributions of hoop stress components, which are measured from the fringe patterns of the samples heat-treated at different temperatures, i.e., 560℃, 600℃, 650℃, and 665℃, versus dimensionless radius, $R_m/R_o$, where $R_m$ is any measured radius and $R_o$ outer radius. The sample indicated as "AS-RE" in Fig. 3 is cut from a commercial glass rod without heat-treatment. As shown in Fig. 3, all the hoop stress components are changed from tensile stresses to compressive ones at approximate $R_m/R_o=0.6$. In Fig. 4, variation of hoop stress component versus heat-treated temperature is shown. This analysis shows that residual stresses of the glass rods approach zero if a rod is heat-treated near the strain point. According to the photoelastic measurements, residual stress is increased as the heat-treated temperature of a glass rod is raised from 560℃ to 665℃.

References:

[1] Baek, T. H. and Burger, C. P., "Accuracy Improvement Technique for Measuring Stress Intensity Factors in Photoelastic Experiment," KSME Journal, Vol. 5, No. 1, The Korean Society of Mechanical Engineers, 1991, pp 22-27.
[2] Han, B. and Wang, L., "Isochromatic Fringe Sharpening and Multiplication," Experimental Techniques, Vol. 18, No. 6, 1994, pp 11-13.
[3] Bartenev, G. M.,The Structure and Mechanical Properties of Inorganic Glasses, Groningen: Walters-Noordhoff Publishing Company, 1970.
[4] Dally, J. W. and Riley, W. F., Experimental Stress Analysis, 2nd Ed., McGraw-Hill Book Company, 1978.

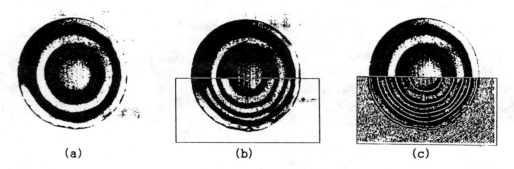

(a)           (b)           (c)

Fig. 1.  Isochromatic fringe patterns of a glass rod heat-treated at 650℃ and cooled to an ambient temperature in natural convective condition.
  (a). Original isochromatic fringe patterns.
  (b). Original isochromatics(upper half) and two times fringe-multiplied patterns(lower half)
  (c). Fringe sharpened lines extracted from the fringe-multiplied patterns.

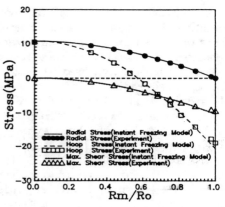

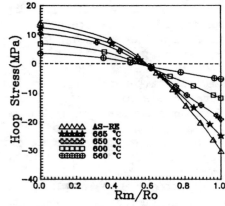

Fig. 2.  Comparison of experimental residual stresses and calculated ones for a glass rod heat-treated at 650℃.

Fig. 3.  Distributions of hoop stress components versus dimensionless radius measured from the glass rods heat-treated at different temperatures.

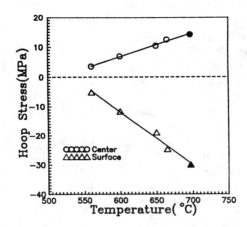

Fig. 4.  Variations of hoop stress component versus heat-treated temperature.

# Residual Stress Interference by Two Micro-Vickers Indentation

Ouk S. Lee
Mechanical Engineering Department
Inha University
Inchon, 402-751 Korea

An electron beam moiré method was employed to measure residual strain produced by the Vickers indenter in a WC-4.7wt.% Co and an aluminum specimens. Line gratings, 57$\mu$m wide by 45 $\mu$m high, with a pitch of 87nm were written by electron beam lithography. Two interior regions of the grating were loaded by the Vickers indenter with 9.8N for 30s. The residual stress interference phenomena caused by two impressions of the Vickers indenter were estimated by using the displacement fringes recorded with the aid of the electron beam moiré(EBM) technique[1].

The estimated residual strains were fitted to the theoretical values estimated by two available models such as Yoffe model[2] and CME(Chiang-Marshall-Evans) model[3].

The pertinent equations for tangential surface residual strain(TSRS) were derived based on the residual stress fields given by the Yoffe and CME models, respectively, as the following :

$$TSRS_{Yoffe} = \frac{B(1+7\nu)}{Er^3} \qquad (1)$$

$$TSRS_{CME} = \frac{H(1-\nu)(1-2\nu)}{E(1-m)\Omega^2}$$

$$\times [\frac{1}{1+3\ln\beta}\left(3\beta\ln\beta - \frac{1}{2}\beta + \frac{3}{2} - \frac{\beta^3}{4\Omega^2}\right)$$

$$-(\beta-1)-(1-m_r)(\frac{1}{\Omega^2}-1)] \qquad (2)$$

where B = a constant representing the strength of the field; r = radial distance from the center of ball indentation; E = elastic modulus; and $\nu$ = Poisson's ratio; H = hardness; m = free surface correction factor for peak load; $m_r$ = free surface correction factor for residual stress; $\Omega$ = normalized radial distance from the center of ball indentation (= r/a); $\beta$ = normalized plastic zone size (= b/a); and b = plastic zone size around indenting impression.

a = radius of ball indentation
  = $\bar{a} \times (\cot (\phi)/4.44)^{1/3}$ \qquad (3)

$\bar{a}$ = half diagonal of the Vickers impression; and $\phi$ = half included angle between opposite faces of the indenter pyramid (= 68°).

In the EBM method, the scan pattern of the SEM acts as a reference grating to produce EBM fringes associated with specimen line gratings written of the thin PMMA resist. The reference pitch can be varied by adjusting either the magnification of SEM or the number of scan lines in the image. Fig. 1 shows a small grating ares of 57$\mu$m wide by 46$\mu$m high covered with EBM fringe pattern in the WC4.7Co specimen. The EBM fringes shown in Fig. 1 were generated by the mismatch in pitches between specimen line gratings $P_s$ = 87nm and scanning lines of EB $P_r$ = 76 nm.

The surface residual deformations produced by Vickers indentation were recorded by using the EBM method. In the EBM method, we could modulate the sensitivity of measurement by adjusting the pitches of specimen line gratings and/or reference gratings. Very fine specimen line gratings as shown in Fig. 2 were needed since the actual surface residual deformation produced by the Vickers indentation was very small.

Fig. 3 shows EBM fringe patterns at magnification of 1100$\times$ on SEM, appeared around two Vickers indenting impression after removing the indenter. The indenting load and time were 9.8 N and 30 s, respectively. The change in EBM fringe pattern (comparing to the EBM linear mismatch fringes) at the near vicinity of the Vickers impression is clearly visible in Fig. 3

The displacement (= N $\times$ p where N = fringe order number by residual displacement and linear mismatch EBM fringes; and p = pitch of reference gratings) along each of the vertical lines were fitted to polynomials of six degrees. The residual strains along vertical lines were estimated from the displacement values as:

$$\varepsilon_{yyres} = p\frac{dN}{dy} - constant \qquad (3)$$

where constant = p $\times$ dN'/dy; and N' = fringe order number of linear mismatch EBM fringe patterns.

The TSRS field produced by two Vickers indentations were derived by using eqs.(1) and (2) with proper coordinate transformation. Fig. 4 shows the location of maximum residual strains which were caused by the two micro-Vickers indentations in a WC4.7Co specimen. The two-indentations were located at a distance 18$\mu$m in both $x$ and $y$ directions. The predictions by the model were found to be agreed well with the experimental results.

An EBM method has been successfully applied to measure very small residual deformation of the order of a few nm in a WC4.7Co and an aluminum specimens. It was found that the Yoffe and CME models successfully predicted the TSRS field interfered by two Vickers indentations after full unloading.

ACKNOWLEDGMENT

The author acknowledges the support of the Korea Ministry of Education (for the mechanical engineering division) during this investigation.

REFERENCES

[1] Lee, O.S. & D.T.Read., Electron beam moiré measurement of elastic-plastic strain transition, at the tip of a sharp notch: will appear, 1995.

[2] Yoffe, E.H., Elastic stress fields caused by indenting brittle materials: Philosophical Magazine A 46, 1882, pp. 617-628.

[3] Chiang, S.S., D.B.Marshall & A.G.Evans., The response of solids to elastic/plastic indentation, 1. Stresses and residual stresses: J. Appl. Phys. 53, 1982, pp. 298-311.

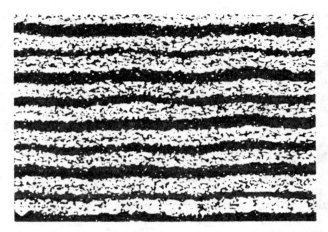

Fig. 2 A typical image of line gratings in a 2000× pattern at a magnification of 60000× on SEM.

Fig. 3 EBM fringe patterns by the linear mismatch and residual deformation at 1100× on SEM

Fig. 1 Linear mismatch EBM fringes by specimen line gratings (pitch = 87nm) and scanning lines of EB (pitch = 76nm) (grating area = 57$\mu$m wide by 45$\mu$m high).

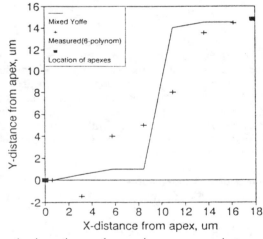

Fig. 4 Location of maximum $\varepsilon_{yy}$ between two indenters in a WC4.7Co specimen.

# Residual Thermal Strain Measurements Inside Pb/Sn Solder Joints

Dai Fulong*, Shi Ling*, Huang Le**, Tang Xiangyun**
* Department of Engineering Mechanics, Tsinghua University
**Department of Material Science, Tsinghua University
Beijing, 100084, P.R. China

One of the most commonly observed problems in the reliability of solder joints is the fatigue failure during thermal cycling. Due to the advent of integrated circuit technology and the requirements of high density for high speed circuitry, powers dissipated from the chips and the temperature regime from power-on to power-off are highly increased. The thermal stresses and strains in solder joints resulting from the mismatch of thermal coefficients of expansion (CTE) between the chip material and the substrate during thermal cycling are the primary cause to fatigue failure of solder joints.

The nonuniformly distributed thermal stresses in the solder joints caused by the voidings & inclusions existed in the solder joints and the complex interactions of creep/plastic deformations will result in the initiation and slow propagation of the fatigue cracks. The development of the residual strains in the solder joints reveals the procession of the damage accumulation till failure. Therefore, understanding the associated stress/strain distributions in the solder joints is very important. to make clear the mechanism of the fatigue failure of solder joints. In this paper, the residual strains of the soft solder alloy of 93.5% wt Pb/ 5% wt Sn / 1.5% wt Ag which has the melting point of 300 ℃ for the first-level package is measured during thermal cycling and the experimental results are compared with the observations from the thermal fatigue test.

Among many advanced optical techniques for in-situ thermal deformation and strain measurement, moir interferometry has been chosen as one of the most powerful tools because of its high displacement measurement sensitivity and high spatial resolution. It is a sensitive whole-field deformation measuring technique based on the formation of fringes by the coexistence of lightwave fronts diffracted from a specimen grating of high frequency (1200lines/mm in this study). A virtual grating created by optical interference is used as the reference grating (Fig.1). Owing to optical interference, a fringe pattern representing the contour lines of the resulting in-plane displacement. Since strains are the derivatives of displacements, they can be easily obtained from the displacement fields.

In this paper, a solder joint specimen is designed to determine the strain accumulation effect inside the area of the solder joint during temperature cycling. The specimen consists of a Cu beam and a Kovar beam bonded together at the ends with 93.5% wt Pb/ 5% wt Sn / 1.5% wt Ag solder alloy. The dimension of the solder joints is 2 mm in length and 0.15 mm in thickness . A crossed-line diffraction grating of 1200 lines/mm is replicated on the lateral surface of the specimen. Fig.2 shows the specimen. The sample is subjected to temperature cycling from -55 ℃ to 125 ℃ till fatigue with a cyclic period of 21 minutes (30 sec. ramp and 10 min. hold period). After thermal cycles of 297 times, the residual U displacement field of the area around the solder joint which is framed in dashed lines shown in Fig.2 is illustrated in Fig.3. It can be seen that the fringes inside the solder joint are much denser than those in the Cu and Kovar beams. The residual shear strain distributions inside the area of the solder joint is acquired and illustrated in Fig.4. We can see that not only the maximum residual strain accumulation occurs at the two outer corners of the solder joint, but several local high strain areas exist in the interior of the solder joint. The macrocrack and failure will first take place in these areas. It can also be seen that there is a drastic variation of strains located at the interface of the solder alloy and the metal substrate, the cracks will extend across this thin area easily. This result is consist with the observation of the crack extension direction obtained by thermal fatigue test.

References

[1] Yi-Hsin Pao, Ratan Govila, Scott Badgley, Edward Jih, " An Experimental and Finite Element Study Of Thermal Fatigue Fracture of PbSn Solder Joints ," Journal of Electronic Packaging, Vol. 115 , March 1993, pp1-8

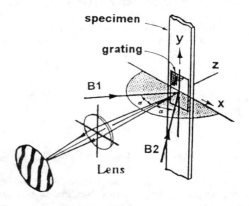

Fig. 1 Moire interferometry

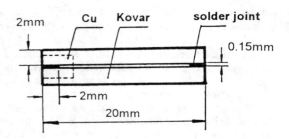

Fig. 2 Dimensions of specimen

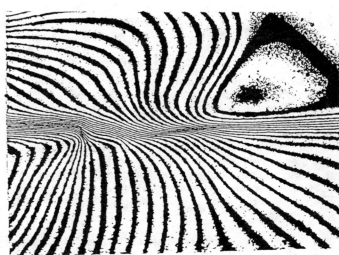

Fig. 3 U displacement field in solder joint
after thermal cycles of 297 times

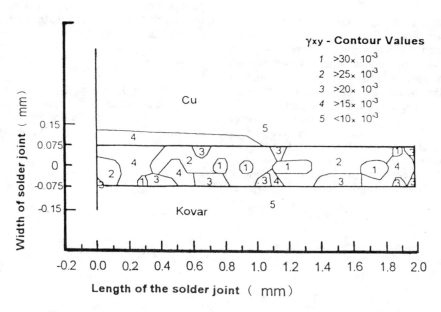

$\gamma_{xy}$ - Contour Values

*1* >30× $10^{-3}$
*2* >25× $10^{-3}$
*3* >20× $10^{-3}$
*4* >15× $10^{-3}$
*5* <10× $10^{-3}$

Fig. 4 Residual shear strain distributions inside the solder joint

# Applications of Infrared Thermography in Non-Destructive Testing of Materials

Miroslaw Jonasz
M. Jonasz Consultants
217 Cadillac Street
Beaconsfield, Quebec H9W 2W7, Canada

## INTRODUCTION

Infrared thermography (IRT) permits rapid, non-contact, and safe inspection of large areas of materials for sub-surface defects. IRT relies on infrared (IR) radiation emitted by an object to measure temperature distribution on the surface of that object. This temperature distribution depends on thermal history of the object and on the presence in the object of defects with thermal properties different from those of bulk object. By optimizing thermal history of an object, the influence of defects on the surface temperature distribution can be maximized, allowing convenient non-destructive testing (NDT) of materials.

IR thermography has been used in diverse NDT applications: finding mines buried under a shallow layer of soil, detecting micrometer-sized cracks in lightly rusted steel surface [1], detecting and evaluating delamination in composite structures [2], as well as detecting delamination of thin-film ceramic coating on jet engine turbine blades [3]. This paper outlines the basics of IRT and applications of IRT in non-destructive testing of materials.

## INFRARED THERMOGRAPHY (IRT)

IRT has several advantages when compared to contact thermometry methods, such as those based on resistance and thermochromic liquid crystals. These advantages are:

- **high speed**: the temperature measurements with the IRT may be as quick as 1 μs ($10^{-6}$ s). The response of other methods is generally slower by several orders of magnitude.
- **high areal and temporal measurement densities**: a typical 256x256-pixel IR imaging device can routinely measure temperature at 65,536 points 30 times per second
- **high spatial resolution**: temperature of a spot as small as several μm in diameter can be measured.

### Thermal radiation and temperature measurements

Every object emits electromagnetic radiation whose spectrum and intensity is highly dependent on the object's temperature. The power of radiation, $M$ [W·m$^{-2}$] emitted by a unit area of the surface of an object at an absolute temperature of $T$ [°K] = $T$ [°C] + 273 is expressed using the following equation:

$$M = \varepsilon \sigma T^4 \tag{1}$$

where $\varepsilon$ [non-dimensional], which varies between 0 and 1, is a material- and temperature-dependent emissivity of the surface, and $\sigma = 5.67 \cdot 10^{-8}$ [W·m$^{-2}$ K$^{-4}$] is the Stefan-Boltzmann constant.

The power of radiation emitted by an object is thus a sensitive indicator of the absolute temperature of the object. The accuracy and precision with which this temperature can be determined depends strongly on the object's emissivity [4]. If emissivity varies slowly with temperature, then (from Eq. 1) the minimum temperature difference, d$T$, resolvable with an IRT device which can resolve a radiation power change of d$M$ equals

$$dT \approx dM / (4 \varepsilon \sigma T^3). \tag{2}$$

For example, given an IRT device, the temperature resolution for a polished aluminum surface ($\varepsilon \approx 0.05$) is about 20 times worse than that for a surface coated with flat black paint ($\varepsilon \approx 0.95$) at the same temperature.

Measurement precision of temperature depends also on the temperature itself and on the wavelength range of an IR imaging device [5]. This latter dependency stems from the relation between the temperature of the surface and the shape of the wavelength spectrum of radiation emitted by the surface. Thermal radiation spectrum, ranging in wavelength from 0 to ∞, peaks at a wavelength, $\lambda_{max}$ [μm], defined by the Wien displacement law:

$$\lambda_{max} = 2898/T \tag{3}$$

where $T$ [°K] is the absolute temperature of the object. Generally, long-wave IR imagers (for example, those sensitive to radiation in a 8-12 μm range) have a temperature resolution greater than that of short-wave imagers (for example, 3-5 μm) at low temperatures (< 30°C for the wavelength ranges mentioned). Such low-temperature range is typical of NDT applications of IRT.

## CHARACTERIZATION OF MATERIALS USING IRT

Non-destructive testing methods which use IRT are based on well established principles of heat transfer in solids [6]. When an object is heated, thermal energy propagates throughout the object via heat diffusion (in the solid) or radiation (in voids). Defects (voids or thermally processed regions) whose thermal properties are different than those of bulk material can significantly alter the rate of heat propagation, and thus influence the volume and surface temperature distributions. An important thermal property in this respect is the thermal diffusivity, $\alpha$ [m$^2$s$^{-1}$], defined as follows:

$$\alpha = K /(c \rho) \tag{4}$$

where $c$ is the specific heat and $\rho$ is the density of the material. Representative values [7] of thermal diffusivity are $110 \cdot 10^{-6}$ $m^2s^{-1}$ (copper), $7 \cdot 10^{-6}$ $m^2s^{-1}$ (stainless steel), and $0.5 \cdot 10^{-6}$ $m^2s^{-1}$ (concrete).

The rate of heat diffusion is characterized with the heat diffusion time, $t$ [s], defined as follows:

$$t = L^2 / a \qquad (5)$$

where $L$ [m] is the thickness of the object which a thermal front is to penetrate and $\alpha$ is the thermal diffusivity of the object's material [6]. Heat diffusion times through 1-mm-thick plates of materials mentioned in the previous paragraph are 0.009 s (copper), 0.14 s (stainless steel), and 1 s (concrete).

Time evolution of the surface temperature of an object is usually induced by a heater whose output is controlled by a trigger or modulator. IR image of the surface temperature distribution is synchronously obtained from an IR camera and can be viewed on-line with a TV monitor. These images are digitized by a frame grabber and stored for analysis. An intermediate image storage device (such as a VCR) can be employed to store long sequences of analog IR images.

If the temperature distribution is observed on the side of the object exposed to the heat flux and if the defect has a low thermal diffusivity, then a "hot" spot develops on the observation side of the object in front of the defect. If the heat source and the IR camera/scanner are on the opposite sides of the object, a "cold" spot develops on the object's surface in the "shadow" of a low-thermal-diffusivity defect.

Temperature differences between various points on the object surface, called the thermal contrast, determine the visibility of a defect with a given IR imaging device. Thermal contrast increases with the difference between thermal diffusivity of a defect and that of the bulk material of the object. Thermal contrast also increases with the ratio of the defect's "diameter" (in a plane parallel to the object's surface) to thickness, $L$, of the object. Defects near the viewed surface of the object produce greater thermal contrast than those buried deep inside the object..

In some cases it is sufficient to passively observe the surface temperature distribution of an object in order to detect a defect. Usually, however, the object must be differentially heated or cooled to induce significant heat transfer inside it. Thanks to a high temperature resolution of IRT (typically 0.05 °C at ambient temperatures) moderate heating on the order of several °C above ambient temperature is usually sufficient. Thus, the effect of temperature dependence of emissivity is minimized. However, uneven heating/cooling of the object and the distribution of emissivity on the object's surface may obscure the influence of the defect on the IR image and reduce thermal contrast. Some of the methods developed to compensate for the detrimental effects of uneven heating and/or low or non-uniform emissivity are:

**Thermal image transfer** [8]. Thermal image which develops on the object surface is transferred via thermal contact to a uniform high-emissivity surface. The thermal image on that surface is then captured with an IR imager.

**Pulse heating** [9]. A pulse of heat is applied to the viewed side of the object and the time evolution of the surface temperature distribution is observed. The average temperature of the object decays exponentially, with a slope of about -1/2 vs. time. At times greater than the heat diffusion time to the defect, a deviation from that slope is observed. Since time evolution of temperature distribution is considered rather than the temperature distribution itself, the effects of uneven heating and of the surface distribution of emissivity are minimized.

**Thermal wave** [10]. Time-modulated heating generates a critically damped thermal wave traveling across the object. The "scattering" of this wave by the defect causes the surface distributions of the wave's amplitude and phase to change as compared with those in an object without the defect. The phase of the wave is much less affected than is the amplitude by uneven heating of the object and by the distribution of emissivity.

## References

[1] Kaufman, I. et al. 1987. Photothermal radiometric detection and imaging of surface cracks. *Journal of Nondestructive Evaluation*, **6**: 87-100.

[2] Cielo, P., Lewak, R., and Balegas, D. L. 1986. Thermal sensing for industrial quality control. *Proceedings of SPIE*, **581**: 47-54.

[3] Tulloch, M. H. 1994. $CO_2$ laser monitors jet-engine quality. *Photonics Spectra, March 1994*, 18-20.

[4] Corwin, R. R. and Rodenburgh, A. II. 1994. Temperature error in radiation thermometry caused by emissivity and reflectance measurement error. *Applied Optics*, **33**: 1950-1957.

[5] Chrzanowski, K. 1995. Comparison of shortwave and longwave measuring thermal imaging systems. *Applied Optics*, **34**: 2888-2897.

[6] Carslaw, H. S. and Jaeger, T. L. 1959. *Conduction of heat in solids*, Oxford University Press, Oxford.

[7] Tossel, D. A. 1987. Numerical analysis of heat input effects in thermography. *Journal of Nondestructive Evaluation*, **6**: 101-107.

[8] Maldague, X., Krapez, J.-C., and Cielo, P. 1991. Subsurface flaw detection in reflective materials by thermal transfer imaging. *Optical Engineering*, **30**: 117-125.

[9] Connoly, M. P. 1991. A review of factors influencing defect detection in infrared thermography: Applications to coated materials. *Journal of Nondestructive Evaluation*, **10**: 89-96.

[10] Busse, G. et al. 1992. Thermal wave imaging with phase sensitive modulated thermography. *Journal of Applied Physics*, **71**: 3962-3965.

# Thermoelastic Stress Analysis of the Interfacial Conditions in Pin-Loaded Lugs

J M Dulieu-Smith, M C Fulton
University of Liverpool
Department of Mechanical Engineering
Liverpool, L69 3BX, UK

## Introduction

Thermoelastic stress analysis (TSA) is a well established experimental technique. The theory, application range, and descriptions and evaluations of the measurement system are reported extensively in the literature. The measurement system used in the work described in this paper is the SPATE equipment which provides high resolution full-field stress information directly from actual components.

Essentially a lug is a protrusion from a larger body, used to facilitate loading, coupling and connecting. The lug contains a circular hole into which a pin is inserted, so that the load is transmitted through the pin into the lug. An area of contact is developed between the pin and the lug (the contact arc) that is dependent on the pin-fit and the pin and lug material. Many studies using either photoelastic or numerical methods have been carried out on pin-loaded lugs/plates (e.g. [1], [2]). Only one previous thermoelastic evaluation has been done which concentrated on the effects of the lug geometry and pin-fit [3]. The present paper investigates the effects of varying the interfacial conditions at the pin-lug contact arc.

## Test Programme and Results

Throughout the tests the geometry of the lugs remained constant; they were 75 mm in width (w) by 12.5 mm thick. The lugs contained a circular hole of diameter (d) 37.5 mm positioned on the longitudinal axis of the lug and 37.5 mm away from the end of the lug (s) (see Fig 1) giving a w/d ratio of 2 and a w/s ratio of 1. In all cases the lugs had square ends. The lug material was either aluminium alloy or mild steel. The pins were silver steel and were manufactured to give either a snug fit or a 0.13 mm clearance fit with the lug-hole. The pins had either a turned finish ($R_A$ = 1.32 $\mu$m) or a ground finish ($R_A$ = 0.40 $\mu$m) and one set of ground pins were hardened to a level of 66 on the Rockwell "C" scale. All of the lug configurations were loaded in a carefully designed jig that ensured symmetrical loading, elimination of bending and enabled the area of interest to be viewed by the SPATE equipment. The load level in the steel lugs was 30 $\pm$ 25 kN and 20 $\pm$ 15 kN in the aluminium lugs; the loading frequency was 10 Hz. One set of tests was carried out using unlubricated pins and another with a thin film of molybdenum disulphate grease applied to the pins. A summary of the lug loading configurations is given in Table 1. In all cases the surface of lug/pin assembly was coated with two passes of RS matt black paint prior to the SPATE tests.

SPATE area scans were taken of the entire lug-end within the influence of the pin. The data was normalised using values taken from the lug as indicated in Fig 1 in a position away from the influence of the pin loading allowing the data to be presented in the form of "stress factors". Using a polar grid with its origin at the centre of the pin stress factor values were obtained in 10° increments from around the hole and the edge of the lug. Five clear stress factor maxima were identified $K_A$, $K_B$, $K_C$, $K_D$ and $K_E$ for each lug configuration as shown in Fig 1. The SPATE output is proportional to the sum of the principal stresses in an isotropic material so away from the pin-lug contact arc and around the edge of the lug the stress factor values are stress concentration factors (SCFs) (i.e. $K_A$, $K_D$ and $K_E$). In all lug configurations $K_A$ was the maximum SCF and this paper deals only with $K_A$.

Values of $K_A$ for each configuration are given in Table 1. The maximum $K_A$ value is given by the unlubricated clearance hardened pin in the steel lug. The minimum $K_A$ value is given by the unlubricated hardened snug-fit pin in the aluminium lug. The unlubricated turned and ground snug-fit pins gave $K_A$ values of 4.39 and 4.66 respectively in the aluminium lug. In the steel lugs $K_A$ was greater than in the aluminium lugs for the unlubricated turned and ground snug-fit pins, but both pin types provided similar $K_A$ values of 5.80 and 5.55. A similar trend is observed for the turned and ground clearance pins; only slightly higher values were obtained from the steel lug but 25% greater $K_A$ values were obtained from the aluminium lug. The hardened snug-fit pins gave the lowest $K_A$ values in the unlubricated configurations. The hardened clearance pins gave up to 30% higher $K_A$ values than the other unlubricated cases. Lubricating the pins had a significant effect on the SCFs in the aluminium lug by reducing the $K_A$ values for the clearance fits to similar levels to those given by the snug-fit ground and hardened configurations. In the case of the steel lugs the lubrication had no overall effect. However both the turned pins gave much higher SCFs than the hardened pins.

## Concluding Remarks

This short paper has only given a snapshot of the results of work carried out during this test programme. It has shown that TSA is particularly useful when examining variations in contact conditions such as changes in material and surface finish. One important practical feature has been highlighted. In most applications the pins in pin jointed connections will be hardened in order to reduce wear and will also have clearance fits to facilitate assembly. This work has shown that for this case the addition of lubrication can reduce the maximum SCF and therefore increase the life of the component.

Other issues that have been investigated in this study and will be reported elsewhere are (i) the position of the maximum SCF, (ii) the extent of the pin/lug contact arc, (iii) the asymmetry of the stress distribution around the pin, (iv) the importance of the contact stresses and (v) separating the SPATE data at the contact arc to give individual component stresses.

### Acknowledgements

The work described in this paper was supported by the EPSRC and J C Banfords Ltd.

### References

1.  Frocht M M and Hill H N, "Stress concentration factors around a central circular hole in a plate loaded through a pin in the hole", J App Mech, 1940, 7, 5-9.

2.  Grant R J, Smart J and Stanley P, "A parametric study of the elastic stress distribution in pin-loaded lugs", J Strain Analysis, 1994, 29, 299-307.

3.  Stanley P and Dulieu-Smith J M, "A thermoelastic study of the stresses in pin loaded lugs", Proc 6th Nat Symp for Exp Mech, 1992, Craiova, 160-169.

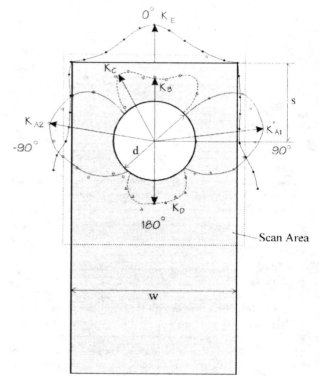

**Fig 1. Lug Nomenclature**

| Table 1 : $K_A$ For Each Lug Configuration | | | | |
|---|---|---|---|---|
| Lug Material | Pin-Fit | Pin Finish | $K_A$ | |
| | | | Unlubricated | Lubricated |
| Aluminium Alloy | snug | turned | 4.39 | 4.75 |
| | | ground | 4.66 | 5.40 |
| | | hardened | 3.68 | 4.48 |
| | clearance | turned | 6.61 | 6.05 |
| | | ground | 6.08 | 5.28 |
| | | hardened | 8.04 | 4.75 |
| Mild Steel | snug | turned | 5.80 | 7.65 |
| | | ground | 5.55 | 4.73 |
| | | hardened | 4.57 | 4.36 |
| | clearance | turned | 6.30 | 8.21 |
| | | ground | 6.20 | 6.27 |
| | | hardened | 8.71 | 6.20 |

# Reproducibility and Reliability of the Response From Four Independent SPATE Systems

J M Dulieu-Smith
University of Liverpool
Department of Mechanical Engineering
Liverpool, L69 3BX, UK

P Stanley
University of Manchester
School of Engineering
Manchester, M13 9PL, UK

## Introduction

The SPATE (Stress Pattern Analysis by Thermal Emissions) system is currently the standard equipment for thermoelastic stress analysis (TSA). The underlying theory for TSA, descriptions of the system and the technique's application range have been well documented in the literature. For quantitative TSA it is essential that the equipment is accurately calibrated [1]. Two calibration studies [2, 3] have been carried out by the UK SPATE Users Group. The results from both showed variations in response of up to 20% from system to system. The present paper describes a third study been carried out by four experienced UK SPATE Users (Users 1, 2, 3 and 4) and coordinated by the UK Users Group. The aim of the study was to assess the long-term reproducibility, reliability and stability of the response from each system and to compare the behaviour of the four systems.

## Test Specimen and Procedure

A specially designed test specimen (see Fig 1) was tested by each participant several times over an eight month period. The specimen was a mild steel cylindrical tube of the dimensions shown in Fig 1. End-caps were welded to each end of the tube and central location pips were machined in the end-caps to ensure pure axial loading. The thermoelastic constant, K, of the material was evaluated independently as $2.96 \times 10^{-6}$ (MPa)$^{-1}$ using experimentally derived values of the relevant properties. The purpose of using a single specimen was to eliminate any differences in material and to minimise any differences in loading. Three pairs of orthogonally aligned strain gauges were mounted on the specimen to provide an independent measure of the applied stress level in the specimen. A thermocouple was also attached to the test specimen so that the surface temperature could be accurately monitored during the tests. The specimen was tested nominally once a month by each participant; the monthly circulation of the specimen was termed a "round". The specimen was coated with two passes of RS matt black paint at the beginning of each round by User 1; the emissivity, e, of the paint was taken to be 0.92 [1].

Each participant's SPATE system was radiometrically calibrated by the manufacturer at the beginning of the programme and at the end. The two values of each detector responsivity, $D_{manf}$, are tabulated below.

An identical test procedure was followed by each participant. The specimen was loaded, as shown in Fig 1, to a level 30 ± 21 kN at a frequency of 10 Hz. (This gave a nominal stress range of 49 MPa and an approximate temperature change of 42 mK in the specimen.) The SPATE detector was set at a working distance of 750 mm from the surface of the cylinder giving a scan spot size of 1 mm; the spatial resolution of the spots was also 1 mm. The sample time and time constant were set to 1 second and 0.1 second respectively. The SPATE sensitivity setting, G, was set so that the signal gave approximately a ¼ full-scale deflection on channel 1 of the correlator. Two line scans were obtained by each participant, one from point 1 to point 2 (see Fig 1), the other from point 2 to point 1 after one specimen had been rotated in the heat machine. Each participant reported: (i) the actual applied load range as read from the test machine, P, (ii) the strain range from each gauge, (iii) the temperature reading from the thermocouple, T, (iv) G and (v) the average SPATE signal from each test, S.

## Analysis and Results

A knowledge of the previously mentioned parameters allows an independent value of the detector responsivity, $D_{calc}$, to be derived for each system as follows

$$D_{calc} = \left[\frac{Ke}{RA}\right]\left[\frac{2048}{G}\right]\left[\frac{PT}{S}\right] \qquad (1)$$

where R is the surface temperature correction factor [1] and A is the cross-sectional area of the test specimen. The first term on the right handside of equation (1) includes parameters that may introduce systematic errors throughout the tests (i.e. the same for each participant). The second term can only be an error as a result of deficiencies in the SPATE correlator or the associated components. The third term will give an error contribution attributable to any inaccuracies in the SPATE signal, the surface temperature measurement and/or the loading system. Errors in the first and second terms will remain constant throughout the tests, the third term provides the only source of random error. The applied stress was independently measured using the strain gauges and from this it is estimated that the possible error in P is ± 5%. The error in T is estimated as ± 0.5%. The error in S for a temperature change of 42 mK and a minimum resolvable temperature change of 1 mK for each system (quoted as standard by the SPATE manufacturers) is ± 2.4%. The total random error in $D_{calc}$ is therefore ± 5.6%. Fig 2 shows values of $D_{calc}/D_{manf}$ derived from the two line scans taken by each organisation at each round. The 3/1 values are for a combination of User 3's detector and User 1's system. The second values for User 1 are with the final value for $D_{manf}$ instead of the initial. The ± 5.6% error band is indicated in the figure; most of the results fall well within this band. The single value at round 4 and for User 2 shows a departure to 1.27, immediately after this measurement their equipment failed. All of User 3's values are well outside the error bands. Interestingly when User 3's detector is used with User 1's system, i.e. 3/1, the difference is corrected indicating that User 3's correlator is at fault. From round 4 onwards User 1's response seems to be decreasing. Using the final value of the detector response from the manufacturer corrects the departure and is indicated in Fig 2 by the second set of values for User 1.

## Conclusions and Recommendations

1. A systematic comparative appraisal of the long-term response of four SPATE systems has been completed.
2. Accepting the manufacturer's specification of 1 mK on the resolution of the 4 detectors, possible random errors in $D_{calc}$ due to errors in the applied load, surface temperature and signal are of the order of $\pm 5\%$.
3. There is clear evidence that faults in the correlator and associated signal processing devices can occur and will result in significant systematic errors.
4. It is evident that the detector responsivity $D_{manf}$ can change significantly with time, e.g., the 8% change for User 1. Where this is so, frequent calibration is essential for reliable quantitative data. It is recommended that further investigation is directed to establishing the source of this drift.

| User | $D_{manf}$ (K/V) | |
|---|---|---|
| | Initial | Final |
| 1 | 11.2 | 12.1 |
| 2 | 3.4 | 3.4 |
| 3 | 4.7 | 4.9 |
| 4 | 9.5 | 9.6 |

## Acknowledgements

The authors wish to thank K. Brown (Defence Research Agency), C. Garroch (Manchester University), M. Fulton (Liverpool University), G. Calvert and K. Allin (Rover Group) and Ometron Ltd.

## References

1. Dulieu-Smith J M, "Alternative calibration techniques for quantitative TSA", Strain, 1995, 31, 9-16.
2. Brown K, "Calibration studies : collaborative report by the UK SPATE Users Group", Proc 2nd Int Conf on Stress Analysis by Thermoelastic Techniques, 1987, London, 205-211.
3. Brown K and Dulieu-Smith J M, "A comparative study of the response of eleven SPATE systems", BSSM Annual Conf, 1995, Sheffield, 34-36.

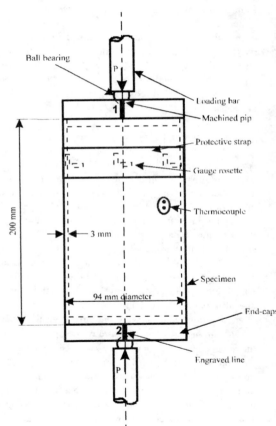

Fig.1 Test specimen and loading configuration

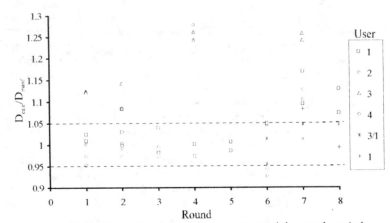

Fig. 2 $D_{calc}/D_{manf}$ for all participants over an eight month period

# Preliminary Studies of Three Dimensional Effects on Artificial Cracks at Simulated Rocket Motor Liners by the Frozen Stress Method

C. W. Smith[a], E. F. Finlayson[a] and C. T. Liu[b]

[a] Department of Engineering Science and Mechanics, Virginia Polytechnic Institute and State University, Blacksburg, VA 24061; [b] OL/AC/PL/RKS, 4 Draco Drive, Edwards Air Force Base, CA 93524-7160

When a crack is located at the interface between two materials, near tip stress analysis is complicated by the fact that the mode 1 and mode 2 stress intensity factors (SIF) cannot be decoupled [1]. However, if the materials are incompressible, and plane strain exists, the near tip interface equations reduce to the more familiar form for isotropic and homogeneous elastic solids [2].

When cracks occur between a solid rocket motor and its rubber liner, the above conditions are approximately realized and occur at a rather low modulus ratio between the two materials. The first author and his colleagues have had considerable success in measuring three dimensional effects in cracked isotropic and homogeneous bodies using a refined frozen stress method [3]. In order to explore the feasibility of such an approach in measuring three dimensional effects in such cracks as described above, a series of experiments were conducted on thick plates in tension containing bondline cracks between two different incompressible materials. Two specimen types were investigated:

Type A - Two commercially available photoelastic materials with the crack along the bondline created by maintaining material separation with a strip of teflon which was later removed. The specimen geometry is specified in Fig. 1 and pertinent material properties are given in Table I where $f_r$ is the material fringe value.

### Table I

| Material | $T_{\text{critical}}$ | $E_{\text{Hot}}$ | $f_r$ |
|---|---|---|---|
| PSM-9 | 160°F | 19.31 MPa | 325.7 Pa-m |
| PLM-4B | 140°F | 7.65 MPa | 262.7 Pa-m |

The thermal coefficients of the two materials were given as $39 \times 10^{-6}$ at room temperature $(T_R)$ and $90 \times 10^{-6}$ at critical temperature $(T_c)$. The bonding agent is PLM-9, which is an epoxy glue chemically similar to PSM-9.

Type B - Pure araldite on one side of the bondline and araldite with 25% by weight of aluminum powder on the other side of the bondline to increase the elastic modulus. After bonding, a machined notch was inserted along the bondline. The pertinent material properties are given in Table II.

### Table II

| Material | $T_{\text{critical}}$ | $E_{\text{Hot}}$ | $f_r$ |
|---|---|---|---|
| Araldite | 280°F | 9.44 MPa | 266.2 Pa-m |
| Aral-Alum | 280°F | 20.06 MPa | ____ |

PLM-9 epoxy was used as the bonding agent. A machined notch was used to simulate the crack. Its dimensions and those of the test specimens are given in Fig. 1.

Both types of specimens exhibited a live residual stress field due to shrinkage of the glue which could not be annealed out because of the constraining effects and in Type A, $T_c$ mismatch also contributed a frozen stress part. Fringe patterns from A and B after stress freezing before and after slicing were used for analysis. A Mode I algorithm [3] for homogeneous material was used to convert the optical data into stress intensity factor (SIF) data. The basic relation used is:

$$\frac{K_{AP}}{q(\pi a)^{\frac{1}{2}}} = \frac{K_1}{q(\pi a)^{\frac{1}{2}}} + \frac{F(\sigma_o)}{q}\left(\frac{r}{a}\right)^{\frac{1}{2}} \qquad (1)$$

$K_{AP}$ = apparent (SIF)  
$q$ = remote stress normal to bond line  
$a$ = crack length  
$r$ = distance from crack tip  

$K_1$ = Mode I SIF  
$\sigma_o$ = Local non-singular normal stress parallel to bond line  

From Eq. (1) $\dfrac{K_{AP}}{q(\pi a)^{\frac{1}{2}}}$ vs. $\left(\dfrac{r}{a}\right)^{\frac{1}{2}}$ is linear.

Type A Results - This type of specimen exhibited a residual fringe field mainly due to the mis-match in $T_c$ values but also partially due to shrinkage of the glue. This field, which was retained throughout the stress freezing process, was not symmetrical with respect to the bond line and yielded different values of $K_1$ on the two sides of the crack. However, when averaged, both the through thickness and slices $L$, $C$ and $R$ agreed closely with the theoretical value of $K_1$ [4], as shown in Table III. Unfortunately, however, the teflon strip did not produce a straight crack front free of near tip distortions which caused some data to be erroneous producing large scatter in $K_{AP}$ vs. $\sqrt{r/a}$ graphs locally. All slices were of the order of 0.889 mm thick.

### Table III($K_1$ in MPa$\sqrt{\text{m}} \times 10^3$)

| Material | $Th^a$ | $TT^b$ | Slice $L$ | Slice $C$ | Slice $R$ |
|---|---|---|---|---|---|
| PLM-4B | 15.17 | 14.95 | 13.18 | 13.05 | 13.75 |
| PSM-9 | 15.17 | 15.17 | 15.96 | 15.44 | 16.53 |
| AVG | 15.17 | 15.06 | 14.56 | 14.24 | 15.14 |

[a] $Th$ = Theoretical result [4]; [b] $TT$ = Through thickness; [c] Estimated from values of $L$

In Table III, the difference between the $TT$ result and $Th$ may be attributed to thicknesswise variations in the SIF which appear to be quite small. Differences in SIF values on the two sides of the crack in the slices may be attributed to the stress frozen field produced by the $T_c$ mismatch which is apparently complex but seems to be averaged out across the bond line. The $TT$ value of $15.06 \times 10^{-3}$ compares favorably with the $L\text{-}C\text{-}R$ average of $14.65 \times 10^{-3}$. Although these results were not unreasonable, scatter in $K_{AP}$ vs. $\sqrt{r/a}$ data and variations in bond thickness together with crack tip irregularities disturbed repeatability. Because of these problems, Type A specimens were replaced by Type B specimens.

Type B Results - Since bonding of the Type B specimen also resulted in a residual stress field it was decided to run two other tests in order to isolate the various effects. Test B-1 was a homogeneous araldite specimen with a Type B vee notch crack and Test B-2 was an araldite specimen with the same crack as B-1 but including a bondline. Table IV compares the differences between the experimental results from tests B-1, B-2, and B with the theoretical result for the homogeneous case.

### Table IV

| Specimen | Percent Difference |
|---|---|
| B-1-TT | -3.43 |
| B-1 Slice Avg. | 4.81 |
| B-2-TT | -2.78 |
| B-2 Slice Avg. | 10.06 |
| B-TT | -7.81 |
| B- Slice Avg. | 16.01 |

The data from which these results were obtained were quite regular and repeatable. From these results, we may conclude the following:

i) From B-1 results, we see that slicing releases live machining stresses trapped near the crack tip which increases the average SIF by 8.24% and the accuracy of the experimental method is of the order of ±3.43%. The maximum differences in $K_1$ values across the specimen thickness was 4.2% (i.e. the order of the experimental error).

ii) From the $B$-2 results, slicing releases live stresses trapped along the bond line which increases the average SIF by 12.84% with an accuracy of ±2.78%. The maximum difference in $K_1$ values across the specimen thickness was 7.3%.

iii) From the $B$ results, slicing releases live stresses trapped along the bond line which increases the average SIF by 23.82%. The maximum difference in $K_1$ values across the thickness was 9.3%.

The SIF distributions for $B$ are given in Table V.

### Table V ($K_1$ in MPa - $\sqrt{m} \times 10^3$)

| Specimen | $L$ | $C$ | $R$ |
|---|---|---|---|
| B | 14.25 | 14.53 | 13.22 |

Based on average slice results, the bond line stresses increased the SIF in the homogeneous specimen by 5.3% and in the bi-material specimen the increase in the SIF was 11.2%. None of the fringe patterns in the above tests revealed any shear mode effects near the crack tip.

Detailed results from the Type B tests will be included in the full paper. The results to date from these three experiments suggest that the Type B specimens can be used in the frozen stress method to measure SIF distributions along the border of a bond line crack provided the SIF variations are significant. These studies are continuing.

Acknowledgement

Support of these studies by Phillips Laboratory under Contract No. NAG-1-1622 with NASA Langley is gratefully acknowledged.

References

[1] Rice, J.R., "Fracture Mechanics Concepts for Interfacial Cracks," *J. Ap. Mech.*, V. 55, March 1988, pp. 98–103.

[2] Hutchinson, J.W. and Suo, A., "Mixed Mode Cracking in Layered Materials," *Advances in Applied Mechanics*, V. 29, Academic Press, 1992, pp. 63–191.

[3] Smith, C.W. and Kobayashi, A.S., "Experimental Fracture Mechanics," Ch. 20 of *Handbook on Experimental Mechanics*, 2nd Revised Ed., VCH Publishers, 1993, pp. 905–968.

[4] Gross, B. and Mendelson, A., "Plane Elastostatic Analysis of V-notched Plates," *Int. J. of Fracture Mechanics*, V. 8, N. 3, September 1972, pp.267–276.

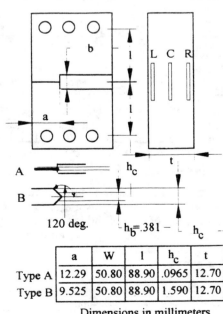

| | a | W | l | $h_c$ | t |
|---|---|---|---|---|---|
| Type A | 12.29 | 50.80 | 88.90 | .0965 | 12.70 |
| Type B | 9.525 | 50.80 | 88.90 | 1.590 | 12.70 |

Dimensions in millimeters
Test specimens
Fig. 1

# ROLE OF MODE-MIXITY ON 3-D INTERFACIAL CRACK TIP STRESSES

Jaydeep K. Sinha and Hareesh V. Tippur†
Department of Mechanical Engineering, 202 Ross Hall
Auburn University, Alabama 36849-5341

## Abstract

The elasto-optic effect is mapped as $(\sigma_x + \sigma_y)$ contours near interface cracks in polymer-metal bimaterials using Mach-Zehnder Interferometry (MZI). The stress fields are investigated when the crack plane is subjected to dominant tensile stresses and pure shear stresses. The optical measurements are examined in conjunction with companion plane stress finite element simulations for estimating the zones of dominant three dimensional (3-D) deformations. Results suggest that in the domain $(x, y > 0)$ the size of the region of 3-D deformations is significantly small for the case of pure shear (both positive and negative shears) when compared to the tensile stress dominated case. The optical data analyzed by incorporating these observations have provided accurate measurement of the crack tip parameters.

## Introduction

The issue of 3-D deformations near interface cracks has drawn attention in recent years [1-3]. Due to the material property mismatch along an interface, 3-D effects may be significantly different near the crack tip when compared to the homogeneous counterparts. Moreover, an interfacial crack inherently undergoes mixed-mode deformations and interfacial failure characterization involves the determination of fracture toughness for a wide range of mode-mixities [4]. Hence, understanding the influence of mode-mixity on interfacial crack tip three dimensionality is important for determining fracture toughness-mixity relationships.

## Optical Mapping and FE Simulations

The test specimens are made from two equal thickness ($B = 6$ mm) PMMA and aluminum sheets joined (elastic mismatch parameter $\epsilon$=0.098) by MMA monomer and a polymerizing agent. A thin Teflon tape insert ($25 - 50\mu m$ thick) was used to produce a sharp edge discontinuity of length 25 mm ($a/W$=0.33; $a$ and $W$ denote the crack length and the specimen height, respectively).

A Mach-Zehnder interferometer was used for mapping stress fields representing contours of $(\sigma_x + \sigma_y)$ (thickness average values) in a 50 mm semicircular region surrounding interface cracks in $y > 0$ domain. Optical interference is related to stress field as, $\delta S = cB(\sigma_x + \sigma_y) = \mathcal{N}\lambda$, $\mathcal{N} = 0, \pm1, \pm2, ...$, where $\delta S$ is the optical path length change due to a combination of refractive index changes and thickness changes, $\mathcal{N}$ denotes fringe orders, and $c$ the elasto-optic constant (for PMMA, $c = -0.92 \times 10^{-10}$ m$^2$/N).

Crack plane subjected to tensile stress: First, near tip $(\sigma_x + \sigma_y)$ field is mapped using MZI in three-point-bend bimaterial beams to simulate dominant tensile stresses on the crack plane. A typical interference patterns is shown in Fig.1(a). Each fringe increment corresponds to an optical path length change of $633 \times 10^{-9}$ m or a change of 1.15 MPa. To obtain an estimate of the size of the dominant 3-D deformations near the crack tip, a complementary linear elastic, plane stress, fi-

---

⁰†Graduate Student and Associate Professor, respectively.

nite element analysis was carried out using ANSYS software package. The finite element model consisted of 2712 eight node plane stress elements and 8405 nodes. The crack tip region was discretized using a fine mesh with 1056 crack tip elements within 0.55B radius. The inner most ring of elements were as small as 0.001a. The model was subjected to three-point loading as was done during the experiments. The $(\sigma_x + \sigma_y)$ contours with levels corresponding to the optical fringe orders were generated from the numerical results. A direct superposition of the optical patterns and finite element contours (dotted lines) around the crack tip is shown in Fig.1(a). Evidently, the match between the two results are good in certain regions around the crack tip while significant departures are observed along the interface, ahead and behind the crack tip. The agreement between the two results suggests that in those regions optical data adequately represent the plane stress behavior. On the other hand, disagreement between the two implies potential influence of 3-D variations in the stresss. The agreement is very good in the region $r/B > 0.25$ and $75° < \phi < 135°$, where $(r, \phi)$ represent the crack tip polar coordinates. In fact, agreement between the fringes and the numerical contours is good even at distances $0.15B$ along $120°$ and $90°$. Such observations have also been reported in Ref.[3] through 2-D and 3-D FE analyses. These observations are quantified by defining error $E_r$ as, $E_r = \left(\sigma_{\alpha\alpha}^{exp} - \sigma_{\alpha\alpha}^{FEA}\right)/\sigma_{\alpha\alpha}^{exp}$, $(\alpha = x, y)$, and $\sigma_{\alpha\alpha}^{exp}$ and $\sigma_{\alpha\alpha}^{FEA}$ are experimental and and finite element values of stresses at a generic point in the field. From the error plots a region of dominant 3-D effects was estimated as shown in Fig.1(b). The shaded region is where the error between the measurements and numerical simulations are within $\pm10\%$ while in the unshaded region 25-30% errors are observed. *It should be emphasized that plane stress assumptions represent the measurements in the shaded region well but $K$-dominant assumptions may still be not valid in this region.*

Crack plane subjected to pure shear: The bimaterial specimens were loaded in asymmetric four-point-bending configuration [4] to simulate pure shear conditions on the crack plane. Since, the crack tip deformations and the fracture toughness and mixity are distinctly different for the cases when the crack plane is subjected to 'negative' and 'positive' pure shears [4], experiments were conducted for both cases. The optical maps of $(\sigma_x + \sigma_y)$ were obtained in the crack tip vicinity and the one for negative shear is shown in Fig.2(a). Synthetic fringes of the same field quantity were obtained from FE computations as done in the previous case. The two contour maps are shown superposed in Fig.2(a). Evidently, the agreement between the two results are excellent in a much larger region when compared to tensile stress dominant case. The agreement between the two results implies validity of plane stress assumptions in those regions while disagreement suggests significant 3-D stress variations. In the region $r/B > 0.25$ and $30° > \phi > 150°$ good agreement between the experimental results and computations in $(x, y > 0)$. Along most of the radial directions outside $r/B > 0.25$ and

$\phi = 30 - 120^o$ fall within $\pm 10\%$ error band. Similar observations were also made regarding positive shear case. This suggests a much smaller zone of 3-D deformations in case of pure shear. Based on these, a schematic of the region of potential 3-D effects is shown in Fig.2(b) (unshaded region). The shaded region corresponds to locations where plane stress assumptions are satisfactory.

The fringe patterns in Fig.1(a) and 2(a) were digitized in the shaded region. The fracture parameters were extracted using over-deterministic least-squares analyses. *The analysis suggested that the data in the shaded region is not K-dominant* and hence higher order terms (typically coefficients of $r^{-1/2}$, $r^o$, and $r^{1/2}$) in the asymptotic field were incorporated to account for possible non-singular contributions to the field. The extracted values of stress intensity factors are tabulated in Table-1 for the three cases reported here. In each case the values of stress intensity factors agree well with computed results. The agreement in shear dominated cases are excellent since the data set for the analysis arrive from a relatively large region surrounding the crack tip. In tensile stress dominated case, however, $Re(Ka^{i\epsilon})$ (the dominant one) agrees well with the computed result while $Im(Ka^{i\epsilon})$ estimates need improvement. This could possibly due to the limited data available for least-squares analysis.

### Conclusions

A complementary optical-finite element investigation of an interface crack in a large elastic mismatch bimaterial system suggests that mode-mixity affects the size of the region of three dimensional effects. The extreme cases of applied load mixities, predominantly tensile stress and pure shear stress (positive and negative), acting on the crack plane suggest that there is a significant reduction in the size of region of 3-D effects in the latter when compared to the former (in $y > 0$ region). This is interesting from the view point of experimental investigation of crack tip stress intensity factors and mode-mixity using near tip measurements. Regions where plane stress assumptions are adequate have been suggested. By incorporating the observations into the optical data analysis, very accurate measurement of near tip parameters has been achieved.

### Acknowledgments

The research is supported by grant NSF-CMS-9313153.

### References

1. Nakamura, T., (1991), Three dimensional stress fields of elastic interface cracks, J. Appl. Mech., 58, 1411-1416.

2. Barsoum R.S. and Chen, T.(1991). Three-dimensional surface singularity of an interface crack. Int. J. Fract., 50, 221-237.

3. Lee, Y.J. and Rosakis, A.J.(1993). Interfacial Cracks in Plates: A Three-Dimensional Numerical Investigation. Int. J. Solids Struc.. 30(22), 3139-3158.

4. Xu, L., and Tippur, H.V., (1993), Fracture parameters for interfacial cracks: Experimental-FE study of crack tip fields and crack initiation toughness, to appear in Int. J. Fract., 1995.

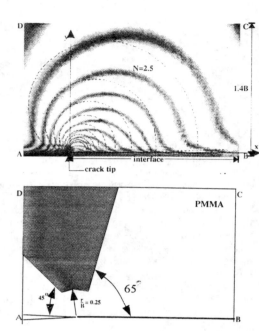

Figure-1: Dominant tensile stress on the interface plane; (a) Comparison of optical and FE contours of $(\sigma_x + \sigma_y)$, (b) Regions of significant 3-D stress variations (unshaded) and plane stress (shaded).

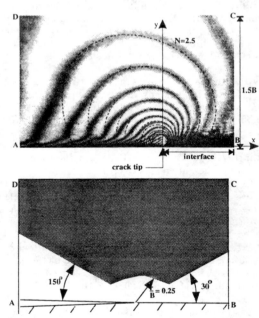

Figure-2: Pure shear stress on the interface plane; (a) Comparison of optical and FE contours of $(\sigma_x + \sigma_y)$, (b) Regions of significant 3-D stress variations (unshaded) and plane stress (shaded).

| Loading | $Re(Ka^{i\epsilon})^{exp}$ | $Im(Ka^{i\epsilon})^{exp}$ | $Re(Ka^{i\epsilon})^{FE}$ | $Im(Ka^{i\epsilon})^{FE}$ |
|---|---|---|---|---|
| Pure shear (+) | -0.08 | 0.42 | -0.10 | 0.38 |
| Pure shear (-) | 0.30 | -0.71 | 0.29 | 0.69 |
| Tensile | 0.58 | 0.18 | 0.56 | 0.06 |

# Experimental Micromechanics Study on Polymer Interface Reinforced with Copolymers

Qing Wang and Fu-Pen Chiang
Department of Mechanical Engineering
State University of New York at Stony Brook
Stony Brook, NY11794-2300

The interface between two immiscible polymers, for example polystyrene (PS) and polymethyl methacrylate (PMMA), is usually very weak. However, when a properly chosen block copolymer is added as an adhesive between them, the interface bond strength is greatly improved. The improvement can be larger than one order of magnitude.

Adhesion is a sufficiently complex and broad area that there are a range of approaches to its understanding. Glassy polymers gain their strength and toughness from the entanglement between the chains. Interfaces between chemically different polymers are normally narrow with respect to the distance between entanglements. Thus without much cross-interface entanglement the adhesion between different polymer phases is normally low. Obviously, any technique that increases the number of chains entangled on both sides of the interface can increase the adhesion. If a copolymer is chose such that each of its blocks is miscible with one or the other of the homopolymers, segregation will tend to occur at the interface for thermodynamics reasons. This causes both the decrease of the interfacial tension and the increase of the adhesion between the homopolymers.

The concept of interface fracture toughness has been used to quantify interface adhesion. An interface is tough if a large amount of energy is dissipated on propagating a crack along it. Typically the energy is dissipated in plastic processes very near a crack tip. However, the amount of energy dissipation is controlled by not only the molecular-scale coupling at the polymer interface but also the bulk properties of the polymers. In glassy polymers, the energy is mainly dissipated in the formation and growth of a crack-tip craze. A craze is a type of planar, cracklike, deformation zone where the two surfaces are joined by fine fibrils of highly drawn and strain-hardened material. Energy is dissipated by drawing the fibrils from bulk material. Changing the properties of the bulk material without changing the propertis of the interface can profoundly change the adhesion.

In this work, a series of specimens of PS-PMMA with interface reinforced by copolymers are tested. Toughness curves are determined for different interfaces with different amount of copolymer added. Fracture behavior during crack propagation is observed in a real time manner by using the environmental function of the scanning electron microscope. At the same time, near field phenomenon at crack tip is quantitatively determined by an experimental micromechanics technique, SIEM (Speckle Interferometry with Electron Microscopy). An attempt is made to relate the mechanics of crack propagation and the atomic-scale processes that occur at a crack tip.

# PHOTOELASTIC DETERMINATION OF STRESS INTENSITY FACTORS FOR INTERFACIAL CRACKS

Carl R. Vilmann and Ibrahim Miskioglu
Mechanical Engineering-Engineering Mechanics Department
Michigan Technological University
Houghton, Michigan 49931-1295

In previous work Baek [1] determined that a 4 term series expansion for the stresses near a crack's tip was necessary if the stress intensity factors were to be accurately extracted from photoelastic data. Baek's work focused on cracks occurring in homogeneous media. The work described here focuses on determining the stress intensity factors for cracks located at the interface between two dissimilar media.

Before attempting to determine the stress intensity factors for crack lying along bimaterial interfaces, a series expansion for the stress field of an interfacial crack was necessary. In 1987 Symington [2] developed this series expansion. Following Williams' [3] work, Symington proposed the function

$$\phi = Re\{r^{\lambda+1}F(\theta,\lambda)\} \tag{1}$$

with
$$F(\theta,\lambda) = a_i\sin(\lambda_i+1)\theta + b_i\cos(\lambda_i+1)\theta$$
$$+ c_i\sin(\lambda_i-1)\theta + d_i\cos(\lambda_i-1)\theta \tag{2}$$

Imposing stress free crack faces and continuity of traction and displacement ahead of the crack tip, Symington found that a complex $\lambda$, $\lambda = \lambda_r + i\varepsilon$, of

$$\lambda_r = N + \frac{1}{2} \qquad N = 0, 1, 2, ...$$

$$\varepsilon = \frac{1}{2\pi}\left(\frac{\mu_2\kappa_1 + \mu_1}{\mu_1\kappa_2 + \mu_2}\right)$$

and
$$\lambda_r = N + 1 \qquad N = 0, 1, 2, ...$$

$$\varepsilon = 0$$

with $\mu_k$ being the shear modulus and $\kappa_k$ determined from

$$\kappa_k = \frac{3 - \nu_k}{1 + \nu_k} \qquad \nu_k = \text{Poisson's Ratio and } k = 1, 2$$

With values for $\lambda_r$ and $\varepsilon$, Symington also found that the constants $a_i ... d_i$ could be related to one complex constant for each $(\lambda_r, \varepsilon)$ pair.

Using Symington's results, a $N$ term series representation for the stress field surrounding an interfacial crack tip can be written in terms of $N$ complex constants. In order to determine these constants from photoelastic data, Symington's series must be fit to experimentally obtained data. Note that the complex constant multiplying the $\lambda_r = 1/2$ term represents the stress intensity factors.

The fitting of Symington's series to photoelastic data using a non-linear least squares approach. Photoelastic data yields the maximum shear stress $\tau_{exp}$ at $M$ data locations. The Maximum shear stress $\tau_{anal}$ can be obtained using the series representation

$$\tau_{anal} = \left[\left(\frac{\sigma_{rr} - \sigma_{\theta\theta}}{2}\right)^2 + \sigma_{r\theta}^2\right]^{1/2} \tag{3}$$

where now $\tau_{anal}$ is a function of the undetermined complex constants using a Taylor's series expansion for $\tau$

$$\tau_{exp\ j} = \tau_{anal_j} + \sum_{i=1}^{n}\left(\frac{\partial\tau_{anal}}{\partial C_i}\right)_j \Delta C_i \qquad j = 1, 2, ..., M$$

with an initial assumption for $C_i$ the least squares approach can be used to refine the coefficients $C_i$

$$[Z^T]\{\tau_{exp} - \tau_{anal}\} = [Z^T][Z]\{\Delta C_i\} \tag{4}$$

where each element of $[Z]$ can be determined using

$$Z_{ij} = \left(\frac{\partial\tau_{anal}}{\partial C_j}\right)_i \qquad i = 1, 2, ..., M \tag{5}$$

and each row of $\{\tau_{exp} - \tau_{anal}\}$ is evaluated at each data point $i$. In equations (4) and (5), the coefficients are all real representing the real and imaginary parts of Symington's coefficients. Equation (4) is unlikely to converge for randomly chosen initial estimates of the coefficients. Convergence was successfully attained when the series was built up slowly. That is, first a 1 term $\left(r^{-1/2}\right)$, 2 coefficients series was fit to the data. Then a 2 term $\left(r^{-1/2}, r^0\right)$, 3 coefficient series was fit with initial estimates for the first term coefficients coming the from the 1 term fit. It should be noted that only one coefficient is necessary to specify the $r^0$ term. The complex portion of the constant multiplying $r^0$ produces no stress.

## EXPERIMENTAL PROCEDURE

The bimaterial beams for the photoelastic tests were prepared by casting PL-8 [4] liquid plastic onto a Homalite-100 precast sheet. A calibration disk was also cast at the same time to obtain the material fringe value $f_\sigma$, of PL-8. A short teflon tape was placed along the interface before casting to obtain a simulated interfacial crack. The beam and the disk were machined smooth on both surfaces and polished. Care was taken not to introduce any residual stresses during this operation. The resulting beam was then loaded in four point bending. The material properties of the beam are given in Table 1, its pertinent dimensions and the loading points are depicted in Fig.1.

Figure 2 shows a typical dark field isochromatic fringe pattern around the crack tip for a load of P = 234 N. Data were collected from both materials ahead of the crack tip, the radial distance for data collection ranged from 0.6 mm to 2.6 mm. A total of 100 data points were collected with 50 data points from each material.

RESULTS AND DISCUSSION

Using an incremental approach, convergence was readily attained through a 3 term $\left( r^{-1/2}, r^0, r^{1/2} \right)$, 5 coefficient series. When more terms are added to the series convergence was impossible. Since that data used to fit the coefficients were sampled very close to the crack's tip, the higher order terms had little effect on the stresses predicted at these sampling points. Thus the $\left[ Z^T \right] [Z]$ matrices in the least squares approach neared singularity and convergence became impossible.

Figure 3 shows a plot of variation of the coefficients $C_1$ and $C_2$ with the number of coefficients used in the least squares approach. Results indicate that as the number of coefficients is increased the agreement between the experimental and predicted values is improved considerably.

REFERENCES:

1.    Baek, T. H., "Study of Mixed Mode Stress Intensity Factors by Two- and Three - Dimensional Photoelasticity," Ph.D. Dissertation, Iowa State University, 1986.
2.    Symington, M. F., "Eigenvalues for Interface Cracks in Linear Elasticity," Journal of Applied Mechanics, Vol. 54, 1987, pp. 973-974.
3.    Williams, M. L., "The Stresses Around a Fault or Crack in Dissimilar Media," Bulletin of the Seismological Society of America, Vol. 49, 1957, pp. 199-204.
4.    Measurements Group, Raleigh, North Carolina

**Table 1: Material Properties**

|  | PL-8 | Homalite |
|---|---|---|
| E (GN/m$^2$) | 2.9 | 4.04 |
| $\nu$ | 0.36 | 0.38 |
| $f_\sigma$ (kN/m) | 9.98 | 24.68 |

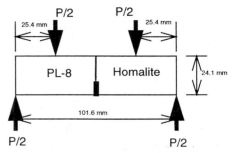

Figure 1.Test Specimen

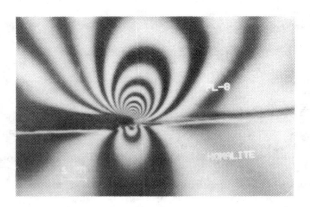

Figure 2. Dark Field Isochromatic Fringe Pattern

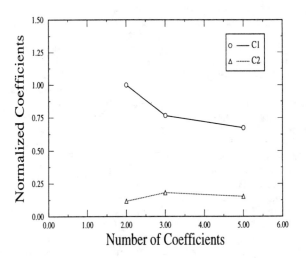

Figure 3. Variation of $C_1$ and $C_2$ with the number of coefficients.

47

# Stress Singularity Field of a Mixed-mode Three-dimensional Crack by an Embedded Speckle Photography

Kenji Machida
Science University of Tokyo
2641 Yamazaki, Noda-shi
Chiba 278, Japan

It is very important to investigate the stress singularity field around the crack front of a three-dimensional crack. In optical techniques, photoelasticity, interferometry, moire technique, holography, caustics and speckle photography are commonly used to detect the stress-strain field. The stress-frozen photoelasticity has made major contribution in the study of 3-D elastic fracture mechanics. Recently, Chiang et al.[1] devised an embedded random speckle method to investigate the interior elastic-plastic deformation of an edge-cracked specimen under bending. The pointwise filtering method is employed to evaluate the displacement from the resulting specklegram. However, it is not easy to determine the fringe spacing and orientation because Young's fringes patterns are generally not clear and low contrast. To determine the resulting displacements from the Young's fringes requires much time and effort. Recently, with the advent of engineering workstation the 2-D fast Fourier transform can be conducted on the large 2-D matrix in a short time. Consequently, we developed the image-processing system based on the 2-D fast Fourier transform using only one Young's fringes pattern of 256x256 pixels[2]. This system does not need the average of diffraction halos measured on many different points. The processed image with a uniform image amplitude is obtained according to the theoretical background.

An experiment was conducted on a compact normal and shear specimen made of Plexiglas. Two plates of different thickness were glued together using the methylene chloride blended with about 10% fine glass beads by weight. The diameter of glass beads was 10-40microns. To measure the displacement at the free surface, a speckle pattern was created by spraying white paint onto the black-painted surface. The loading device proposed by Richard et al. [3] was employed for the mixed-mode loading. This device enables us to carry out the experiment under various mixed-mode loading. The displacement around the crack tip in the plane of different depth was measured on these specimens under the mixed-mode loading using a speckle photography. The 50mW He-Ne gas laser was used as a light source. The specklegram is mounted on the X-Y stage driven by stepping motors controlled by the microcomputer. The Young's fringes pattern is created by pointwise filtering the specklegram using a thin laser beam. A CCD camera takes the Young's fringes patterns, and the image data are stored in the frame memory. The image data are transferred to the engineering workstation. For the determination of the $K_I$ and $K_{II}$ values, the displacement must be measured on many different points around the crack tip. The image-processing system developed in our laboratory was applied to the displacement measurement so that time for the analysis was reduced remarkably.

To obtain the $K_I$ and $K_{II}$ values by using the displacement method, the apparent stress-intensity factors $K_I^*$ and $K_{II}^*$ at $\theta = \pm \pi$ are expressed as the following equations from the linear elastic fracture mechanics:

$$K_I^* = \frac{\left[ v(\pi) - v(-\pi) \right]}{\sqrt{r}} \frac{\sqrt{2\pi}}{\kappa+1} G \quad (1)$$

$$K_{II}^* = \frac{\left[ u(\pi) - u(-\pi) \right]}{\sqrt{r}} \frac{\sqrt{2\pi}}{\kappa+1} G \quad (2)$$

$$\kappa = \begin{cases} 3-4\nu & \text{(plane strain)} \\ (3-\nu)/(1+\nu) & \text{(plane stress)} \end{cases}$$

where u and v are the displacement components along $x_1$ and $x_2$ directions, G is the modulus of rigidity, $\nu$ is the Poisson's ratio and r is the distance from the crack tip. The valid $K_I$ and $K_{II}$ values at r = 0mm can be estimated by the least squares method from $K_I^*$ and $K_{II}^*$ values in the K-controlled field.

Figure 1 shows the 2-D mesh pattern and loading condition of the compact normal and shear specimen. Here, $l_1$ and $l_2$ are 36 and 72mm, respectively. The 3-D mesh pattern was generated by developing the 2-D mesh pattern to the thickness direction. The 3-D finite element analysis was carried out on a half portion of the specimen due to the symmetry with respect to the midsection of the specimen. Two kinds of models were employed. The layer division ratios of two models are 1:1:1 and 1:2:3 from the free surface, respectively. The numbers of elements and joints are 1440 and 7801, respectively.

An example of Young's fringes patterns before and after image-processing is shown in Fig.2. The original images are not so clear that it is not easy to determine the fringe spacing and orientation by the human work. In the normalized image, the solid lines obtained with the image-processing system accurately trace out the centers of each fringe. Thus, the validity and effectiveness of our image-processing system are demonstrated. Although the Young's fringes patterns have low contrast and high noise, the displacement components can be evaluated with accuracy higher than 0.3microns by our image-processing system. Figure 3 shows the variation in $K_I^*$ and $K_{II}^*$ with distance from the crack tip at the free surface of the specimen ($\alpha$=30deg.). $K_I$ and $K_{II}$ values obtained with the experiment are 9.8 kN/m$^{3/2}$ lower and 13.3 kN/m$^{3/2}$ higher than those obtained with the finite element analysis, respectively. In this study, as the data scatters largely near the crack tip, all stress-intensity factors are estimated by the least squares method from $K_I^*$ and $K_{II}^*$ values in the range r=3 to 10mm. Figure 4 shows the variation in stress-intensity factors at the free surface with a load application angle $\alpha$. The stress-intensity factors are estimated assuming the plane stress condition. As $\alpha$ increases, the mode I component of the stress-intensity factors

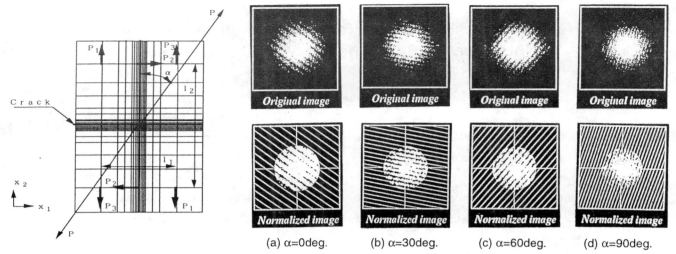

Fig.1 Mesh pattern and loading condition.

(a) α=0deg.    (b) α=30deg.    (c) α=60deg.    (d) α=90deg.

Fig.2 An example of Young's fringes patterns before and after image-processing.

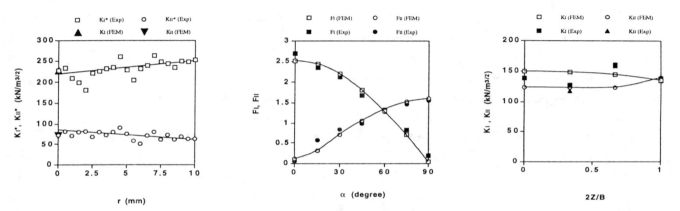

Fig.3 Variation in $K_I^*$ and $K_{II}^*$ at the free surface with distance from the crack tip. (α=30deg. )

Fig.4 Variation in stress intensity factors at the free surface with a load application angle α.

Fig.5 Distribution of stress intensity factors along the crack front. (α=60deg.)

decreases and the mode II component increases. The similar tendency is shown in both stress-intensity factors obtained with the speckle photography and finite element analysis. The difference between both stress-intensity factors is slightly large at α=0 and 15 degrees, but the stress-intensity factors obtained with the speckle photography agree well with those obtained with the finite element analysis at the other part. Figure 5 shows the distribution of stress-intensity factors along the crack front at α=60deg. Here, Z is the distance from the center of the specimen and B is the thickness. In this case, the stress-intensity factors are estimated assuming the plane strain condition. The $K_I$ value obtained with the finite element analysis is maximum at the center of the specimen. It decreases gradually near the free surface and becomes minimum at the free surface. The distribution of $K_I$ value obtained with the speckle photography is similar to that obtained with the finite element analysis. On the other hand, the $K_{II}$ value is minimum at the center of the specimen and increases gradually near the free surface. The similar tendency can be seen in all cases of mixed-mode loading. The stress-intensity factors obtained with the speckle photography agree well with those obtained with the finite element analysis within 4% error at the free surface.

However, the difference between both at the other parts is 5 to 28%. The stress-intensity factors vary in the region from the free surface to 3mm depth, while there is almost no recognizable difference in those values at the inner part of the specimen. The stress-intensity factors at 3mm depth would be recognized as the stress-intensity factors of 3-D crack under the mixed-mode loading. Therefore, it is necessary to estimate the stress-intensity factors at 3mm depth from the free surface.

References:

[1]Chiang, F. P. & Lu, H., "Interior Crack-Tip Elastic-Plastic Field Measurement by an Embedded Random Speckle Method," ASME AMD-91, 1988, pp 205-213.
[2]Machida, K., Kikichi, M., Sawa, Y. & Chiang, F. P., "Young's Fringes Analysis with a Computer Image-Processing System," Optics and Lasers in Engineering, 21(1994), pp 151-164.
[3]Richard, H. A. & Benitz, K., "A Loading Device for the Creation of Mixed Mode in Fracture Mechanics," Int. J. Fract., 22(1983), pp R55-R58.

# A Mechanical Analysis for A Crack Perpendicular to Interface of Bimaterial by Moire Interferometry

Yilan Kang*  Hua Lu **  Youquan Jia*  Yu Qiu*

*Department of Mechanics, Tianjin University, P. R. of China, 300072

**Department of Mechanical Engineering, Ryerson Polytechnic University, Canada, M5B 2k3

The problem of a bimaterial structure with a crack normal and terminating at the interface are received more attention for some investigators. The results of some theoretical investigations are that the stress and displacement field under opening mode (mode 1) loading are found as the following form:

$$\sigma_{ij} = K\, r^{\lambda-1} f_{ij}(\theta) \qquad (1)$$

$$U_{ij} = K\, r^{\lambda} g_{ij}(\theta) \qquad (2)$$

The primary purpose of this paper is to investigate this problem by moir interferometry method. The displacement fields of experiment are analysis and are compared with some theoretical results.

The specimen is made of two kinds of epoxy resin, as shown in Fig.1, and the mechanical properties of the materials are listed in table 1. The specimen is glued with epoxy adhesive that has similar properties with the material 2 in specimen. The thickness of the glue layer is about 0.01-0.02mm. The specimen is under bending moment, $M = 1.62$ NM. In the moire interferometey method, frequency of the specimen grating is $f = 600$ L/mm and second order diffracted of specimen grating is used, so the experimental sensitivity is 0.417 μm. Enlarged moire fringe pattern in crack tip region is shown in Fig.2.

From the displacement field obtained through experiment, it is possible to investigate that whether or not exist singularity nature and how much the power of singularity will be. If the singularity relationship exists as described by equation (2), it should be the linear relationship between log U and log r and slope of straight line being related the power of the singularity $\lambda$. Logarithm for displacement $U_y$ and coordinate r at some point in crack tip region is shown in Fig. 3 and $\lambda_e = 0.435$ is obtained from slope of the straight line by using least square fiting. According to the theoretical research in [1-4], the power of singularity $\lambda$ can be calculated by solving the following equation, which is the smallest real root in range of $0 < \lambda < 1$:

$$2\lambda^2(\alpha-\beta)(\beta+1)-\alpha+\beta^2+(1-\beta^2)\cos(\pi\lambda) = 0 \qquad (3)$$

Where, $\alpha$  $\beta$ are dundurs bimaterial parameters respectively. In this paper the singularity power of the theoretical result is $\lambda = 0.413$. Comparing the two results, the experimental result is slightly larger while the stress singularity $\lambda$-1 is smaller. It is shown that the value of the singularity power has been influenced by effect of interface layer at the crack tip.

$U_y(\theta)/U_y(0)$, along a circular with same radius r in crack tip region, represent the displacement $U_y$ distribution versus angler $\theta$. In Fig. 4, the points are given by experimental value of $U_y(\theta)/U_y(0)$ along the circular in $r = 1$mm and the curve line is drawn by $g_y(\theta)/g_y(0)$ that is function of angler displacement in referent paper [5]. The results of the experiment are agreed with results of the theoretical investigation.

In the equation (2), bringing the power of singularity $\lambda = 0.435$ by the experiment and extracted the experimental displacement values $U_y$ in region near crack tip, the stress intensity factor (SIF) $K = 0.75$ (Mpa $M^{0.565}$) can be obtained.

## Acknowledgements

This work was supported by National Natural Science Foundation of China

## References

[1] Zak A.R. and Williams M.L., J. Appl. Mech., 30, 1963, p142-143

[2] Bogy D.B., J. Appl. Mech., 38, 1971 ,p911-918

[3] Lu M.C. and Erdogain F., Eng.Fracture Mech., 18, 1983, p491-528

[4] Ahmad J., J. Appl. Mech., 58, 1991, p964-972

[5] Chen D.H., Eng.Fracture Mech., 49, 1994, p517-532

Fig.1  Dimension of bimaterial specimen

Table 1, Material Properties

|  | E (Gpa) | $\upsilon$ |
|---|---|---|
| Material 1 | 4 | 0.37 |
| Material 2 | 1.8 | 0.4 |

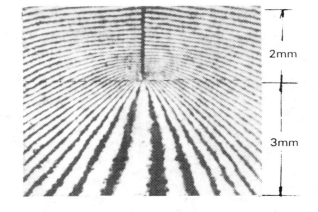

Fig. 2  The moire fringe pattern ($U_y$ field)

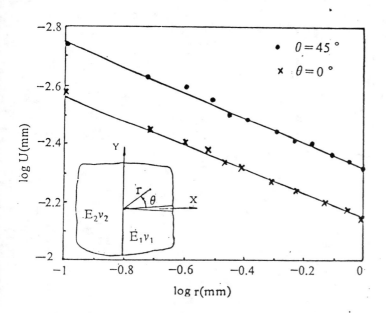

Fig. 3  Log $U_y$ versus log r along $\theta = 0$ and $\theta = 45$

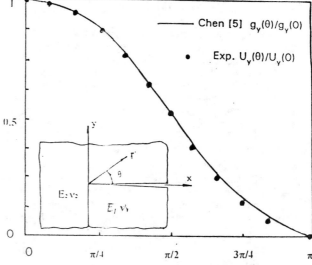

Fig.4  Displacement $U_y$ distribution along the $\theta$

51

# Elastic-Plastic Mixed-Mode (I/II) Fracture in Aluminum Sheet Alloys

Farzad Zafari, M. Ramulu, Albert S. Kobayashi
Mechanical Engineering
University of Washington
Seattle, WA 98195

Considerable effort has been expended in development of ductile fracture characterization of engineering materials for mode I loading, but under mixed-mode condition the crack tip nonlinear behavior is not well understood. Considering that in the real structures loading conditions of the components are rarely uniaxial and considering the use of ductile material in all aircraft structures, a need to understand mixed mode elastic-plastic fracture of ductile material can not be overemphasized.

The elastic-plastic fracture behavior of stable crack initiation, growth, and direction for 2024-T3 and 2XXX aluminum sheet alloys under influence of mixed-mode I/II loading has been experimentally and numerically investigated. The study also includes the thickness effect and 2a/W ratio effect.

The experimental investigation was done using a 100 mm wide tensile dogbone type specimens with a centrally located crack slanted at an angle, see figure 1. The specimens were machined from larger panels which were fatigue tested under constant cyclic loading to provide sharpen crack tips. Fracture testing was performed under crack opening displacement (COD) control loading.

The influence of the ration of mode I/II has been studied by testing specimens with the angle $\beta = 90$ (mode I), 60, 45, 30, and 15 degree, with respect to loading direction. The influence of specimen thickness was studied by testing specimens with thickness of 1.0 mm, 1.6 mm, and 2.54 mm with crack at $\beta = 45$ degree. The influence of 2a/W was studied by testing 1.6 mm thick specimens with 2a/W ratio of 0.3, 0.5, and 0.6 with crack at $\beta = 45$ degree.

Geometric Moiré' method and close-up video taping were employed on all testing. With Geometric Moiré' method full field deformation and displacement information around crack tip were obtained. Figure 2 shows a typical Moiré' fringes, $\beta = 45$, for u and v displacements. With close-up video taping the crack tip opening displacement (CTOD), crack tip opening angle (CTOA), and crack turning angles were captured during the crack initiation and the extension. Numerical analysis, using the non-linear elastic-plastic finite element by ABAQUS program is carried out for two types of models containing a slanted center crack. First type of model is to study the crack growth initiation. This model completely represents the tested specimen with slanted center crack. The second type of model is to study the stable crack growth. This model represents small area around the crack and the crack growth path in detail. The applied boundary values for this model are from the Geometric Moiré' fringes, representing u and v displacements.

Preliminary experimental results, shown in figure 3, indicates that for large amount of crack extension a $\geq 6$ mm, the value of CTOA, based on CTOD measurement at 1 mm behind the crack tip, appears to approach the constant value of 6° for all different crack angles and 2a/w ratios.

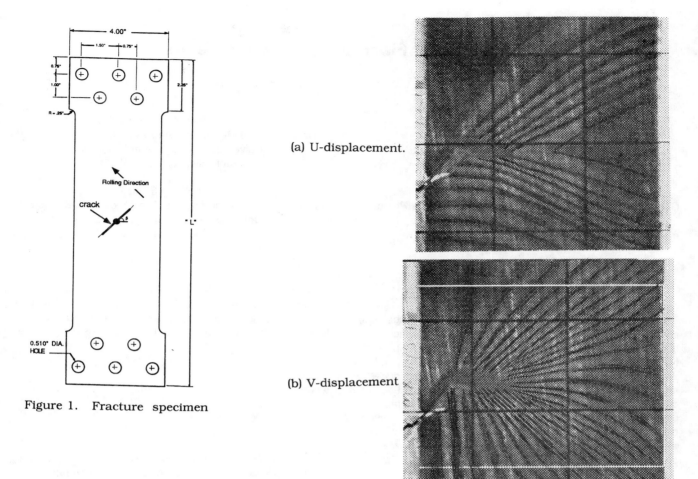

Figure 1. Fracture specimen

(a) U-displacement.

(b) V-displacement

Figure 2. Geometric Moiré' Fringes

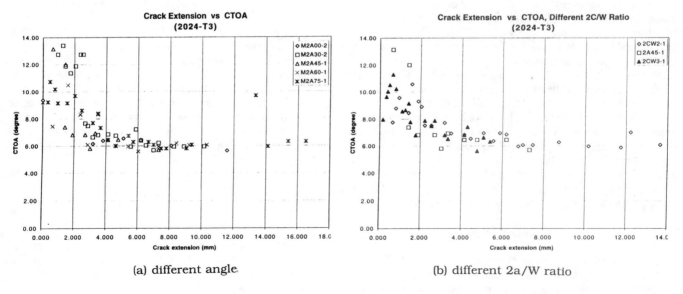

(a) different angle

(b) different 2a/W ratio

Figure 3. Crack extension Vs CTOA,

# Photoelastic Fiber-Optic Accelerometers

Wei Su
MRL Inc.
5653 Stoneridge Drive, Suite 102
Pleasanton, California 94588

Mark D. Morrissey
Consortium for Holography, Applied Mechanics & Photonics
University of Alabama in Huntsville
Huntsville, Alabama 35899

John A. Gilbert
Department of Mechanical and Aerospace Engineering
University of Alabama in Huntsville
Huntsville, Alabama 35899

Yuehong Song
Consortium for Holography, Applied Mechanics & Photonics
University of Alabama in Huntsville
Huntsville, Alabama 35899

## Abstract

This paper introduces a completely new class of fiber-optic accelerometers based on the principles of photoelasticity. The accelerometers rely on a unique photoelastic fiber-optic transducer originally developed as the sensing element for a photoelastic fiber-optic strain gage. The transducer is modified and incorporated into designs developed for two different types of accelerometers. Experimental tests conducted using prototypes built from these designs demonstrate that the units are both cost effective and efficient, making them competitive and comparable to their electrical counterparts.

## Introduction

Many fiber-optic accelerometers have been developed to measure the acceleration of a moving object. In general, these units are very sensitive, weigh less than their electrical counterparts, and have a relatively high signal-to-noise ratio. The optical fibers also have the advantage that they are inert and immune to electromagnetic fields. The majority of the work performed in this area, however, has either focused on a specific application or been directed toward validation of a basic operating principle. Thus, fiber-optic accelerometers lack the sophistication, reliability and cost effectiveness enjoyed by their electrical counterparts. These obstacles currently limit the commercial production of fiber-optic accelerometers and the widespread use of a potentially superior technology. The solution to this problem lies in the development of cost effective and reliable units designed to meet a variety of different engineering applications.

## Transducer Design

The shape and arrangement of the parts contained within an accelerometer may be complicated, however, it is often possible to model the essential components by a relatively simple single-degree-of-freedom system consisting of a mass, a spring and a damper. The acceleration is determined by either measuring the displacement of the mass relative to the base of the accelerometer or by measuring the resultant force, $F_r$, in the spring. When the dimensionless frequency ratio is less than 0.2 and the dimensionless damping factor is zero,

$$F_r = - m a_0 \sin \omega t \qquad (1)$$

where

$$a_0 = - \omega^2 X_0 . \qquad (2)$$

In Eqns. (1) and (2), m is the mass, $\omega$ is the frequency and $X_0$ is the amplitude of vibration of the base. The equations show that the force is directly proportional to the acceleration; $F_r$ can be measured using a photoelastic fiber-optic force transducer.

### Photoelastic Fiber-Optic Force Transducer

Figure 1 shows a schematic diagram of a photoelastic fiber-optic force transducer recently reported by Su et al [1]. It consists of a photoelastic cube, two crossed polarizers and two optical fibers. A stress concentration is produced by the applied load and the quadrature condition is achieved by preloading the transducer. Figure 2 shows the fringe pattern produced when a load P is applied to the sensing element. The stress optic law and the theory of elasticity can be combined to show that for points located directly beneath the load,

$$\frac{\Delta I / I_0}{\Delta P} = \frac{2}{f_\sigma R} . \qquad (3)$$

where $\Delta I$ is the light intensity modulation for a given load increment $\Delta P$, $f_\sigma$ is the material fringe value and R is the radial distance measured from the free surface to the point in question.

Figure 3 shows the force transducer incorporated into an accelerometer. The unit is sealed in an aluminum case having outside dimensions of 41 mm x 35 mm x 20 mm. Optical access to the transducer is provided through two, 200 µm-diameter multimode optical fibers. Fiber-optic ferrules, used to hold the fibers in place, simplify the alignment procedure. A 0.5 pitch GRIN lens is used to collimate the light and increase the optical coupling efficiency.

A prototype was tested using the setup shown in Fig. 4. The accelerometer has a sensitivity of 2 V/g over a frequency range extending from 0 to 600 Hz and a linear amplitude range of 0 to 5-$g$'s. Since the noise level is approximately 5 mV, the resolution is 2.5 m$g$. The transverse sensitivity is less than 1%; the accelerometer is basically lead in/out insensitive provided that the fibers are not subjected to extremely large vibration amplitudes. An average value for the temperature sensitivity is 0.0224 $g$/$^0$C. The noise level is approximately 5 mV, making the resolution 2.5 m$g$.

An alternate design was tested which utilizes a GRIN lens as the sensing element. This unit has a natural frequency of 22.3 kHz and linear amplitude range of ±2000 g's; the accelerometer can accurately measure a shock pulse with a duration greater than 0.224 ms. The unit is housed in a stainless steel case having outside dimensions of 35 mm x 15 mm x 14 mm. The force transducer employs a 1.0 mm-diameter, 0.25 pitch GRIN lens as its sensing element; the lens also acts as a coupler for the optical fibers. The element is placed between two crossed linear polarizers and loaded using a 2 gram seismic mass. The accelerometer employs the same light source, fibers, signal conditioner and display devices shown in Fig. 4.

## Reference

1. Su, W., Gilbert, J.A., Katsinis, C., "A photoelastic fiber optical strain gage," *J. Experimental Mechanics*, **35**(1): 71-76 (1995).

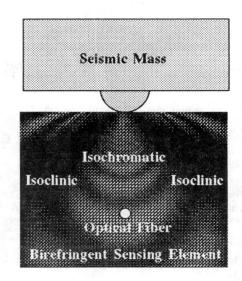

**Figure 2**. Fringe pattern in the birefringent sensing element.

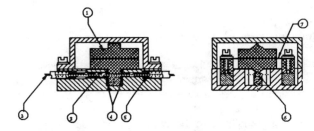

**Figure 3**. General purpose photoelastic fiber-optic accelerometer; 1. seismic mass, 2. optical fiber, 3. GRIN lens, 4. linear polarizer, 5. fiber-optic ferrule, 6. photoelastic sensing element, and 7. support element.

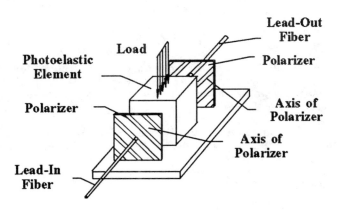

**Figure 1**. A photoelastic fiber-optic force transducer.

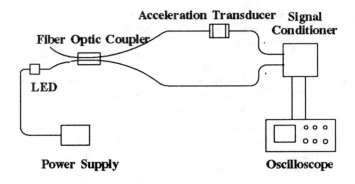

**Figure 4**. The complete acceleration measurement system.

# Multiaxial Transducer Utilizing Bulk Birefringence Based Sensors

J.J. DITRI, A.S. REDNER
Strainoptic Technologies, Inc
North Wales, Pennsylvania
Email: aredner@voicenet.com

K. ZYSK
Arnold Air Force Base
Arnold AFB, Tennessee

## ABSTRACT

The concept of a multiaxial force/moment sensor based on the use of bulk birefringence, as opposed to point strain measurements is introduced. A prototype, two force, bulk birefringence balance was designed, manufactured and tested. Results are given for the static and dynamic response of the balance to various external loads.

## INTRODUCTION

The problem of measuring forces and moments applied to a structure or object arises in many engineering disciplines, with one prominent example being the evaluation of model-aircraft flight dynamics in wind tunnel experiments. Some general requirements of such a force/moment balance are:

- A high speed of response, to enable recording of oscillatory or transient dynamic events,
- High natural vibration frequencies to avoid externally induced resonances,
- High sensitivity to the externally applied forces/moments,
- Application-specific size and load requirements,
- Low cost.

Most force/moment balances incorporate a number of individual strain gages mounted to an intricately designed and machined frame. External forces and moments applied to the balance through an attached object induce strains in the balance. The individual forces are calculated by inverting the information output by the strategically located strain gages. These types of transducers are very expensive and typically have low resonant frequencies in the 5 Hz range. Increasing the resonant frequencies can be achieved by "bulking up" the design (i.e., using a thicker or stiffer frame), but this comes at the cost of greatly decreased sensitivity since the balance will then naturally undergo less strain for a given load.

## BULK BIREFRINGENCE BASED (B³) SENSOR:

To overcome the limitations of current balances, the concept of a "bulk birefringence based" (or B³ ) balance was recently introduced as part of a Phase I SBIR contract between Strainoptic Technologies, Inc., and Arnold Air Force Base. In the new design, optical sensors replace strain gages, and it is the *retardation* induced in a polarized incident light beam passing through the balance which is measured as opposed to direct measurement of the strain. The concept is depicted in Fig. 1. The polarized light beam continually acquires a relative retardation while passing through the balance, and the total retardation upon exiting the balance is given by [1],

$$\delta = \int_A^B C\Delta\sigma(\xi)d\xi \qquad (1)$$

where C represents the local stress-optic constant and $\Delta\sigma$ represents the difference in secondary principal stresses along the path joining end points A and B.

Two major advantages of the B³ balance over more conventional strain gage balances are (a) higher achievable natural frequencies and (b) lower cost. The increase in natural frequency is again achieved by bulking up the balance. However, because the output of B³ sensor is an integrated effect, increasing the dimensions of the structure increases the light path length, and hence, increases the induced retardation as well. In essence, the output of the B³ sensor scales with the dimension of the balance. The lower cost is due to less stringent machining and gage mounting requirements.

A multiaxial B³ balance requires multiple light beams, arranged strategically so as to be optimally sensitive to individual applied loads. The output of each "channel" or beam is a retardation which is dependent upon each of the externally applied forces or moments. Denoting by {δ} a vector of measured retardations, and by {F} a vector of the externally applied forces and moments, the relationship between the two can be written,

$$\{\delta\} = [G]\{F\} \qquad (2)$$

Where [G] is a "sensitivity" matrix which is dependent upon the locations on the balance where sensing takes place as well as its physical characteristics such as size and material.

Provided the determinant [G] does not vanish, Eq. (2) can be inverted to yield the forces as functions of the measured retardations,

$$\{F\} = [G]^{-1}\{\delta\} \qquad (3)$$

## PROTOTYPE B³ BALANCE

A prototype, two channel B³ balance was constructed to asses the operating characteristics such as speed of response, natural vibration frequency and sensitivity. The balance was made of a square cross section PMMA beam with roughly 39 mm sides and a length of 300 mm. Polarized light was passed through the balance both vertically and horizontally. The transmission and reception of light was accomplished via independent fiber optic bundles in two send/receive pairs. Each pair had linear polarizers cemented to their ends, forming miniature plane polariscopes. The orientations of the polarizer/analyzer axes on each sender/receiver pair was chosen to increase or decrease the sensitivity of the individual channels to specific forces. With the chosen orientations, one channel was designed to be predominantly sensitive to axial forces while the other was designed to be predominantly sensitive to flexural forces. The light intensity emanating from either of the receiving channels was therefore of the form,

$$I_i = I_{0i} Sin^2(\pi \delta_i / \lambda) Sin(2\beta_i) + I_{Bi} \qquad (4)$$

where $\delta_i$ was the bulk birefringence acquired along the propagation path of channel "$i$" and $\beta_i$ is the angle between channel i's polarizer/analyzer axes and the (constant) secondary principal stress directions. $I_{Bi}$ represents a background intensity due to ambient light, polarizer inefficiency, etc... The light signal was fed directly to a photodiode which converted the optical signal to a voltage, and the voltage was finally input to a 300MHz digital storage oscilloscope for display and analysis.

The setup of the balance is shown in Fig. 2. Two independent forces could be applied to the balance; one axial and one transverse. The balance itself was supported in a cantilever fashion in a rigid weldment which was attached to a table.

## SAMPLE RESULTS AND CONCLUSIONS

An example of the output of the prototype balance is shown in Fig. 3. Shown there is the output of the Axial channel sensor (the vertically acting channel in Fig. 2) to both axial and transverse applied loads. As can be seen, there is some "cross-talk" of the transverse load into the axial channel, but even in this prototype design the axial channel responds primarily to axial loads. Similar results were obtained for the transverse channel. The resonant frequencies of the prototype balance were estimated by other (dynamic) experiments to start at roughly 500 Hz, well beyond current strain gage based balance capabilities.

## ACKNOWLEDGEMENTS

This work was sponsored by Arnold AFB as part of an SBIR phase I project. The input of Arnold technical personnel is greatly appreciated.

## REFERENCES
[1] ABEN, H., "Integrated Photoelasticity", McGraw-Hill, New York, NY, (1979).

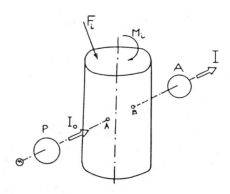

**Figure 1.** Bulk Birefringence Concept.

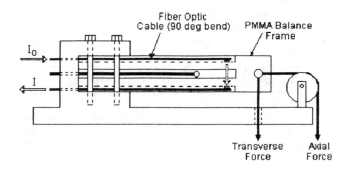

**Figure 2.** Schematic of prototype B³ balance. Light is routed through the balance via sending to receiving fiber optic cables acting as minature polariscopes.

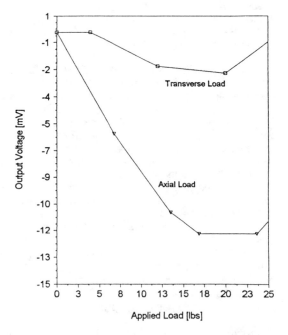

**Figure 3.** Sample response of Axial channel of prototype balance to both axial and transverse forces.

# Damage Evaluation of Fatigue Using Laser Speckle Sensor

## Akira KATO and Koji ITO

Department of Mechanical Engineering,
Chubu University,
1200 Matsumoto-cho, Kasugai, Aichi 487, Japan

## INTRODUCTION

This paper presents a method to evaluate fatigue damage non-contactly using laser speckle sensor.Result of our previous work for static tensile test showed that light intensity distribution of the speckle pattern relates closely to the frequency distribution of the surface profile [1] - [4]. The intensity distribution of the laser speckle broadens with the increase of plastic strain. This is caused by that density of slip bands increases with the increase of the plastic strain and thus ratio of high frequency component in surface profile diagram increases.

When steel specimens are subjected to cyclic loading, slipbands are produced on the specimen surface by fatigue. Density of the slip bands increases with progress of fatigue and then initial cracks are generated in the persistent slipbands. This means that ratio of high frequency component in surface profile will increase corresponding to increase of loading cycles and thus the light intensity distribution of the laser speckle pattern will expand with the progress of fatigue damage. It is presumed that fatigue damage can be evaluated using the laser speckle method.

In this study, we investigated the relation between intensity distribution of the laser speckle pattern and surface properties for specimens subjected to cyclic tensile loading using steel specimens. Intensity distribution of the laser speckle was observed with the increase of number of loading cycles under a constant stress amplitude and change of light intensity distribution of the speckle pattern with the progress of fatigue damage was observed. The possibility of evaluating fatigue damage by the laser speckle was investigated.

## EXPERIMENTAL PROCEDURE

Material used in this experiment is SS330 (JIS) steel. The specimen is a strip with circular notches with large radius at both sides shown in Fig. 1. Stress concentration factor of the specimen is close to 1 and stress distribution at the center of the specimen is considered to be uniform. The specimens were loaded by uni-axial cyclic tension with the minimum load of 0 N. Then the laser speckle was observed at the center of the specimen as shown in Fig. 1. Figure 2 shows layout of the experimental system. He-Ne laser is illuminated on the specimen surface. Diameter of the laser beam is about 1mm. Laser speckle pattern is formed on the ground glass placed in front of the specimen as a screen. Image of the speckle pattern is input into the image-processing system through a CCD camera. Resolution of the image used is $512 \times 512$ pixels and a pixel is expressed with 256 gray levels. The laser speckle pattern can be analyzed automatically and quantitatively using this image-processing system.

## CHANGE OF THE LASER SPECKLE PATTERN UNDER FATIGUE

Figure 3 shows a surface micrograph of the specimen after fatigue. This specimen has been loaded by fatigue stress of $\sigma_a = 150$ MPa(stress amplitude) and

$N = 8 \times 10^4$ (cycles). It is found that slipbands are generated on the surface and the slipband density increases with the increase of fatigue cycles.

Figure 4 shows speckle patterns for different stress cycles under $\sigma_a = 150$ MPa. It is found that speckle pattern expands with increase of the number of stress cycles. Speckle pattern changes corresponding to slipband density

Fatigue tests were made under constant stress amplitudes of $\sigma_a = 140$, 150 and 160 MPa and laser speckle was observed at each number of stress cycles stopping the testing machine. Figure 5 shows relationship between the parameter $B_s$ and stress cycles $N$. This parameter expresses width of light intensity distribution of the speckle pattern. This parameter is defined in our previous papers [1] - [4]. The figure shows that the value of $B_s$ is larger for larger stress amplitude. When stress amplitude is large, slip bands are generated densely. In this case, rate of high frequency component in surface profile diagram increases and then laser speckle expands corresponding to this. The increase rate of $B_s$ to the increase of stress cycles is larger for larger stress amplitude. The value of $B_s$ and the increase rate are different for different stress amplitudes, but tendency of the change of parameter $B_s$ corresponding to stress cycles $N$ is similar for different stress amplitudes. Increase rate of $B_s$ is high in the earlier stage of fatigue and then it becomes lower. And $B_s$ increases markedly again before the final fracture. This seems to be because of increase of slipband density by crack growing.

It was found that there is a linear relationship between $\log(B_s)$ and $\log(N/N_f)$. Here $N_f$ is fatigue life for each stress amplitude. This relation is expressed with the following equation.

$$\log(B_s) = S' + T\log\left(N/N_f\right) \qquad (1)$$

And thus

$$B_s = S\left(N/N_f\right)^T \qquad (2)$$

where $S = 10^{S'}$.

Coefficients $S$ and $T$ were obtained from the experimental results and they are shown in Fig. 6 (a) and (b). Difference of the coefficient $T$ is small for different stress amplitudes. We assume that $T$ is constant for different stress amplitudes and take the average value ($T$=0.286). Then if we take $B_{0.5}$ that is the value of $B_s$ when $N/N_f = 0.5$. Rate of $\left(B_s/B_{0.5}\right)$ is expressed with the following equation.

$$\left(B_s/B_{0.5}\right) = \frac{S\left(N/N_f\right)^{0.286}}{S\left(0.5\right)^{0.286}} = 1.219\left(N/N_f\right)^{0.286} \qquad (3)$$

It is found that the relationship between $\left(B_s/B_{0.5}\right)$ and $N/N_f$ is expressed with one equation and does not depend on stress amplitude. Equation (3) is compared with the experimental data in Fig. 7. The experimental data almost agree with Eq. (3). As fatigue life $N_f$ is unknown before fatigue test, the value of $B_{0.5}$ can not be obtained in advance. But there is a possibility to evaluate fatigue damage using such a relationship that does not depend on stress amplitude.

## REFERENCES

(1) Kato, A., Dai, Y. Z. and Chiang, F. P., JSME Int. J., **34**-3, (1991), 374-380.

(2) Kato, A. and Kawamura, M., Proc. of Asia Pacific Conference on Fracture and Strength 93, (1993), 379-383.

(3) Kato, A. and Kawamura, M., J. of the Society of Materials Science Japan (in Japanese), **43**-489, (1993), 696-702.

(4) Kato, A., Kawamura, M. and Nakaya, I., JSME Int. J., **38**-2, (1995), 249-257.

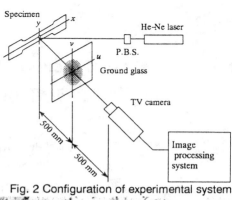

Fig. 2 Configuration of experimental system

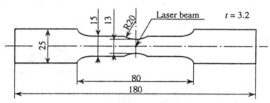

Fig. 1 Test specimen (cyclic tension)

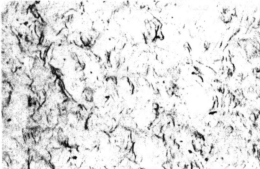

Fig. 3 Specimen surface
($\sigma_a$ = 150 MPa, $N = 8 \times 10^4$)

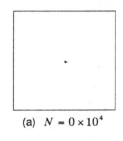

(a) $N = 0 \times 10^4$

(b) $N = 2 \times 10^4$

(c) $N = 8 \times 10^4$

Fig. 4 Speckle patterns ($\sigma_a$ = 150 MPa)

Fig. 5 Relationship between light intensity distribution $B_s$ and stress cycles $N$

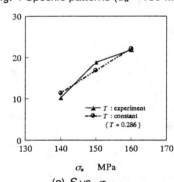

(a) $S$ vs. $\sigma_a$

(b) $T$ vs. $\sigma_a$

Fig. 6 Coefficients $S$ and $T$

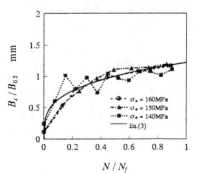

Fig. 7 Relationship between $B_s/B_{0.5}$ and $N/N_f$

# Characterization of Frequency Response of Laser Displacement Meter Using Laser Interferometry and Davies Bar

Akira Umeda and Kazunaga Ueda

National Research Laboratory of Metrology, AIST MITI

1-4 Umezono 1-Chome Tsukuba Ibaraki 305 Japan

Laser interferometry is one of the important optical measurement techniques in the experimental mechanics. The optical equipment such as laser vibrometers or displacement meters uses the optical interference and the Doppler shift as the main working physical principles. Though there has been no method of evaluating the frequency response characteristics of these instruments, it has been widely believed that the equipment has wide enough frequency bandwidth and high response characteristics with almost no delay. The importance of the laser displacement meters and laser vibrometers have increased by the current technology development toward the miniaturization and the expansion of MEMS technology. This paper proposes the novel method of deriving the frequency response characteristics of an optical displacement meter experimentally by showing the experimental results.

The principle of the technique is the comparison between the two measurement of the high speed motion surface in the frequency domain, one using the standard interferometer and the other using the instrument to be tested. Very fast impulse motion of an end surface of a metal bar is measured simultaneouly by a laser displacement meter to be tested and the newly developed laser interferometer (Fig. 1). The bar, Davies' bar, is named after R. M. Davies [1]. The elastic pulse propagating in the bar is generated by the impingement of a projectile to the other end surface of the bar. The projectile is accelerated by the pressurized air. The Laser displacement meter used in the experiment is HS-1100 manufactured by Hoshin Electronics Co., Ltd in Japan, where heterodyne real time fringe counting technique is used. On the other hand, the reference interferometer utilizes the technique of analyzing the phase of the fringe signals after the reflection of the elastic pulse finishes. Fig. 2 shows the block diagram of the laser interferometer with wide frequency bandwidth developed at National Research Laboratory of Metrology (NRLM interferometer). The light source is argon-ion laser with etaron for f requency stabilization. The power is usually 100 mW. The direction of motion is judged by checking the phase change between P-polarized light and S-polirized light. There is 90 degree phase lag between them. The frerquency bandwidth of the photo detector used is approximately 80 MHz. The sampling frequency of the P-polarized and S-polarized light is 100 MHz by Tektronics RTD710 with 10 bit word length. The block diagram of the equipment is shown in Fig. 3. The displacement meter transmitts the digitized measurement results to a personal computer which processes the signals from the two interferometers by Fast Fourier Transform.

Fig. 3 shows the block diagram of the total experimental setup. The record lenght of NRLM interferometer is 32 kword. HS-

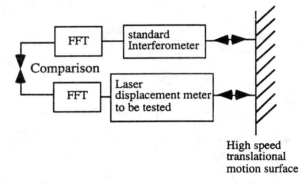

Fig. 1 The principle of the laser displacement meter frequency Characterization.

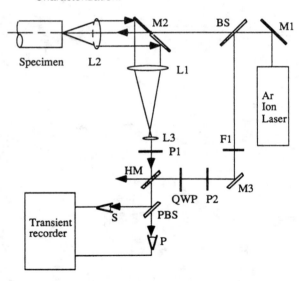

Fig. 2 The Block diagram of the newly developed interferometer

1100 samples the surface displacement at 500 kHz and one record length is 4096 word.

Fig. 4 shows the spectrum of the dynamic displacement measured by NRLM interfermeter and HS-1100, when the tracking is fine. We can recognize the good agreement up to 10 kHz. Fig. 5 shows the time domain signal of the dynaimic displacement when the tracking is not good. This data was taken in the range where the velocity of the end surface motion is a little higher than the specification of HS-1100 in terms of velocity. Fig. 6 shows the time domain signal of the dynamic displacement when the tracking is good. This data was taken in the

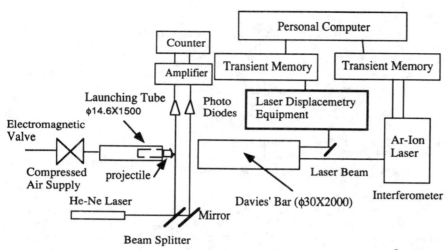

Fig. 3 Set-up of the experimental equipment

range where the velocity of the end surface motion is within the specification of HS-1100 in terms of velocity.

Fig. 7 shows the gain characteristics and the phase characteristics of HS-1100 when the tracking is good. It turned out that the frequency bandwidth of HS-1100 is only up to 20 kHz, though the design value is 100 kHz. The bandwidth of an elastic pulse is the function of the longitudinal wave velocity and the diameter of the bar. The maximum bandwidth by this technique might be up to 500 kHz. The different technique for translational motion generation is required in the frequency range higher than 500 kHz.

Reference

[1] R.M. Davies, A critical studfy of the Hopkinson pressure bar, Phil. Trans., A-240, p375-457(1948).

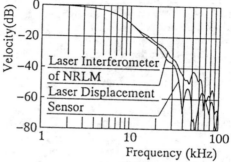

Fig. 4 The power spectrum of the detected velocity of the bar end surface when the tracking is good. The measurement was done using NRLM interferometer and HS-1100.

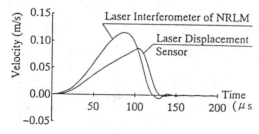

Fig. 5 The example of the experimental data showing that the tracking of HS-1100 to the motion of the end surface is insufficient.

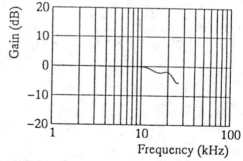

Fig. 7(a) Gain characteristics of HS-1100 when good tracking is shown. The result was derived from the time domain signal shown in Fig. 6.

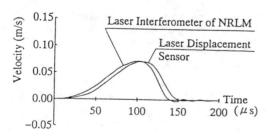

Fig. 6 The example of the experimental data showing that the tracking of HS-1100 to the motion of the end surface is sufficient.

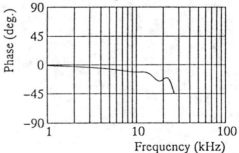

Fig. 7(b) Phase characteristics of HS-1100 when good tracking is shown. The result was derived from the time domain signal shown in Fig. 6.

# Morphological Characteristics of Flying Insects

Seiichi Sudo, Kohji Tsuyuki
Iwaki Meisei University
Iino 5-5-1, Chuohdai, Iwaki 970, Japan

Hiroyuki Hashimoto, Fukuo Ohta, Kazunari Katagiri
Tohoku University
Katahira 2-1-1, Aoba-ku, Sendai 980, Japan

This paper is concerned with the morphological characteristics and the aerodynamic characteristics of flying insects. Some morphological parameters were measured for a variety of insects. The experiments on the aerodynamic characteristics of flying insects were conducted in a small low-turbulence wind tunnel. The flapping frequency was measured with an optical displacement detector. The wings of the dragonfly were observed microscopically making use of the scanning electron microscope. The relationship between total mass and flapping frequency was investigated theoretically and experimentally.

The experiments on the aeroelastic characteristics of flying insects and the measurements of velocity fluctuation around the insect were conducted in a small low-turbulence wind tunnel [1]. A block diagram of the wind tunnel and measuring devices is shown in Fig.1. In the experiments on the measurements of velocity fluctuation, the live insects were stuck on the wooden needle with the adhesive, and mounted in the test section of the wind tunnel. A hot-wire anemometer was used to measure the velocity field. The time-dependent amplitudes of wing flapping were measured with an optical displacement detector. The right forewing and hindwing of the dragonfly were observed microscopically making use of the scanning electron microscope. In addition, some morphological parameters were measured for a variety of insects.

Flow characteristics around a dragonfly were investigated. In the experiment, the live dragonfly *Sympetrum infuscatum* was set in the uniform smooth wind stream. For a suitable air velocity, the dragonfly installed in the wind tunnel flaps with perceiving air flow. Fig.2 (a) shows the output signal from the optical displacement detector. The signal corresponds to flapping of the forewing of the dragonfly. Fig.2 (b) shows the velocity fluctuation generated by the flapping motion, and Fig.2 (c) shows the orbit between the signals (a) and (b). It can be seen that both the displacement of forewing and the velocity generated by the flapping motion are periodic. The predominant peak in the power spectra of the time series signal in Fig.2 (a) corresponds to the flapping frequency of the dragonfly, $f_i$, that is, $f_i$=30.5Hz. In Fig.2 (b), the output signal is at $x/L$=0.636, $y/L$=0.597 and $z/L = -0.075$. The body length of dragonfly is $L$=46.89mm, the length of right forewing is $l$=37.59mm, and the length of right hindwing is $l$=36.06mm.

Microscopic observations on the dragonfly wing were examined with a scanning electron microscope. Fig.3 shows the magnifying photograph of a wing trichiation on the 1st radius of the right hindwing. Dragonfly wings are clothed in microrichia or minute hairs measuring less than 1/10mm in height. Various different forces act on the wing as it moves through the air. Briefly these are the weight of the air, the viscous drag of the air and the weight of the wing itself. Almost all the friction occurs within the very narrow zone of air nearest the wing surface. In flying insects, friction forces within the boundary layer promote smooth or laminar airflow over the surface of the wing. The microtrichiation of the wing surface which increases air resistance within the boundary layer will promote laminar flow and prevent the formation of turbulent eddies.

The usual aerodynamic treatment of insect flight is based on the blade element theory in the study of propellers. It was tentatively applied to insect flight by Osborne, and then with more success by Weis-Fogh [2]. The aerodynamic force $F$ on a wing can be resolved into a component normal to the flow velocity, called the lift, and a component parallel to the flow, called the drag. The lift $F_L$ and drag $F_D$ are

$$F_L = \frac{1}{T} \int_0^T \int_0^l \frac{1}{2}\rho c U^2 C_L \, dx_w \, dt \qquad (1)$$

$$F_D = \frac{1}{T} \int_0^T \int_0^l \frac{1}{2}\rho c U^2 C_D \, dx_w \, dt \qquad (2)$$

where $T$ is the flapping period, $l$ is the wingspan, $\rho$ is the density of air, $c$ is the wing chord, $U$ is the relative velocity, and $x_w$ is the one-dimensional coordinate along the wing. $C_L$ and $C_D$ are lift and drag coefficient. Making the dimensional analysis based on Eqs.(1) and (2), the relation between flapping frequency $f_i$ and the dragonfly mass $m$ found as follows

$$f_i = \alpha m^{-\frac{1}{6}} \qquad (3)$$

where $\alpha$ is the proportionality constant. Fig.4 shows the flapping frequency plotted against the dragonfly mass. It can be seen from Fig.4 that the constant $\alpha$ is $\alpha$=9.332.

References :

[1] Sudo,S., Hashimoto,H., Ohta,F., "Aeroelastic characteristics of dragonfly wings," Proceedings 10th International Conference on Experimental Mechanics, Lisbon, 1994, pp 1397-1402.
[2] Weis-Fogh,T., "Quick estimates of flight fitness in hovering animals, including novel mechanisms for lift production," J.Exp.Biol., Vol.59, 1973, pp 169-230.

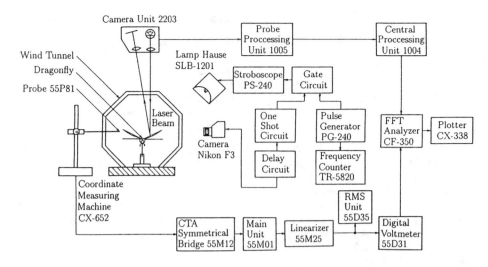

Fig. 1  Block diagram of experimental apparatus

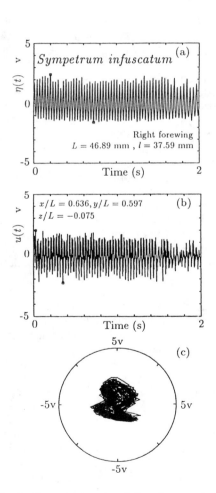

Fig. 2  Output signals of flapping motion

Fig. 3  Expanded photograph of a wing trichiation
(magnifying power: ×2000)

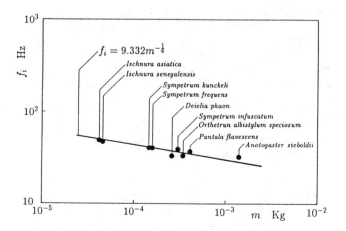

Fig. 4  Relation between flapping frequency
and mass for dragonflies

# Dynamic Strain Measurement
# using Diffraction Grating Strain Sensor

**Anand Asundi**
**Department of Mechanical Engineering**
**The University of Hong Kong, Hong Kong**

The use of diffraction gratings in experimental stress analysis is becoming more widespread. On the one hand moire interferometry utilizes these high frequency gratings to monitor in-plane deformations with sub-micron sensitivity and on a wholefield basis. On the other hand, these same diffraction gratings printed on the specimen can be used for pointwise strain measurement. The principles for both these approaches were proposed some decades ago. However only recently with developments in optics and electronics have the methods achieved practicality. Indeed the diffraction strain gauge has reached a stage where it could be considered as a strong candidate to rival the traditional electrical resistance strain gauge. Sensitivity and range are comparable to the strain gauge, with the added advantage of variable gauge length (area). The only drawback currently is the availability of small diffraction gratings which can readily mounted on the specimen at the desired location akin to strain gauge mounting. In this paper, the characteristic of the diffraction strain sensor for dynamic strain measurement will be investigated.

The basis of the diffraction grating sensor has been well documented and is governed by classical diffraction equation which can written as:

$$\sin \alpha = \sin \beta + m\lambda f$$

where $\alpha$ is the angle of incidence, $\beta$ is the diffraction angle of the $m$ th diffracted beam, $\lambda$ is the wavelength of the incident light and $f$ is the frequency of the diffraction grating. The angles are measured with respect to the normal to the grating plane. For high frequency gratings as used in this system, only the first diffraction orders were visible.

If the diffraction grating is firmly attached to the specimen, such that the grating deforms as the underlying specimen, then the frequency of the grating changes as the specimen is strained or rotated. This would result in a proportionate change in the diffraction angle. However, in addition to strain induced change in diffraction angle, $\beta$ also changes if the specimen undergoes rigid body out-of-plane tilt or in-plane rotation. In general, normal strain and rigid body tilt about one axis cause the diffracted beam to shift in one direction while the in-plane rotation, shear and tilt about the second direction in the grating plane cause the beam to shift in a perpendicular direction. To compensate for the tilt, both the symmetric diffraction orders are utilized. Since rigid body tilt causes both diffraction orders to move in the same direction, while due to strain ( or rotation), the diffraction orders move in opposite directions, it is straightforward to

eliminate the contribution from the out-of-plane tilt. Thus the final schematic of the set-up is as in fig. 1. The shift in diffraction order due to changes in the specimen grating are measured using two Position Sensing Detectors (PSD) with a sensitivity of 0.01 mm. Thus when used with a 1200 lines/mm diffraction grating, strain sensitivities of less than 10 $\mu\varepsilon$ is readily achievable.

For dynamic applications the system schematic is much the same except that the data from the PSDs need to be sampled at a much faster rate ( 1MHz or better). This was done using a digital oscilloscope and/or using a A/D sampling card installed in the PC. The specimen used for this demonstration was a bimaterial with an interface inclusion. Results were previously obtained using Dynamic Photoelasticity. Although this gave whole field information, the exact time for the stress wave to reach the interface was far from accurate. Towards increasing the resolution, it was decided to use the diffraction strain sensor to achieve better resolution. A 1200 lines/mm grating was bonded around the interface using the same process as for moire interferometry. Indeed due to the size of the grating, moire interferometry could also be performed for whole-field analysis, but lack of appropriate hardware for dynamic visualization, did not permit the whole-field analysis. Instead, pointwise analysis was done at different points on either side of the interface. The specimen was impacted using a pendulum type impact mechanism as shown in fig. 2. A typical trace of the output from the two detectors at a representative point near the interface is shown in fig. 3(a). The difference in these two readings appropriately scaled provides the strain distribution as shown in fig. 3(b). From the data, it was observed that for the strain to reach about 10 $\mu\varepsilon$, at the interface it took 46 $\mu$s, while a similar experiment done using photoelasticity was found to give a time of around 70 $\mu$s, providing confirmation of the result. Infact the data obtained from other points did indicate a difference in the stress wave reaching the interface at different positions along the interface as observed using photoelasticity.

Advances in opto-electronics have made the diffraction based strain gauge as feasible alternative to the conventional strain gauges both for static and as shown in this article for dynamic applications. All characteristics of this strain gauge compare favorably with some added advantages as well.

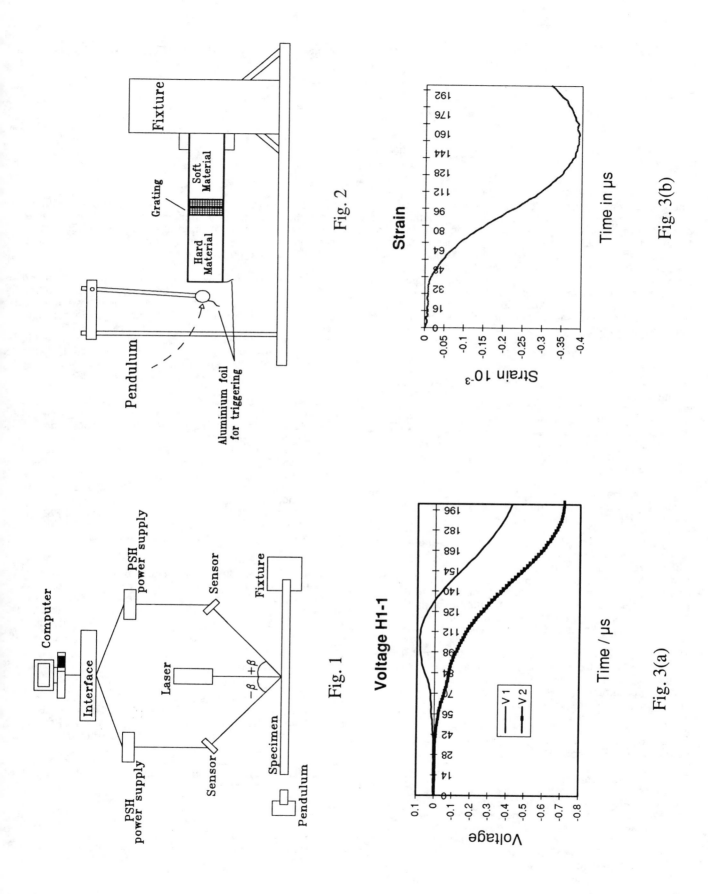

Fig. 2

Fig. 3(b)

Fig. 1

**Voltage H1-1**

Fig. 3(a)

65

# The Relationship Between the Structure Dynamic and Cutting Process Model Parameters

Slavko Dolnišek, Janez Kopač
University of Ljubljana
Faculty of Mechanical Engineering
Aškerčeva 6, 61000 Ljubljanja, Slovenia

The use of sensor systems for tool condition monitoring or to control the process in different machining operations, is one of the most interesting research fields in manufacturing technologies. To control a process it is necessary to use a model-based solutions, a most common classical model in the research of cutting is that from Merchant's theory [1]. He proposed the expression for the input energy (required for the implementation of the process) as a sum of the transformation energy ( used to transform the undeformed material to the chip ) and output energy ( necessary for the chip flow out of the process ) :

$$U_i = U_t + U_o$$

However as a time series solution, Peklenik's proposal for input/output energy relationship was considered [2,3]. The expression for input and output energies in the case of orthogonal cutting is illustrated in Fig. 1. Dynamic structure of a cutting process can be in this way determined by on-line estimation of the parameters in energy equations and finally the transfer function of the cutting process could be estimated [4].

For the verification of the above model, it is necessary to build up a proper machining and measuring system. The sensing system for measuring the parameters in energy equations consists of a force sensor, cutting edge acceleration ( velocity displacement ) sensors and a cutting speed sensor. With its characteristics, they do not interfere within the studied frequency range of the cutting process and enable sensing of all parameters in real time. The greatest problem exists in measuring the speed of the chip flow. On-line possibilities have so far not been materialized so that the speeds had to be defined from interrelations between chip thickness and cutting speeds.

The machining system (machine tool and tool holder) should ensure well-known and unchangeable characteristics throughout a whole range of applied, realistically selected cutting parameters. Suitable static and dynamic characteristics of the machine tool need not be defined since for the verification of the cutting model on the macro level it is enough if the process is observed only in the cutting point and all the necessary characteristics are defined in accordance with this point.

For a clear explanation and presentation of the structure dynamics of the cutting tip, the dynamic characteristics of the particular parts in the cutting assembly (tool holder/dynamometer/machine tool) were first defined using widely known model testing methods [5,6]. An example of determining the frequency response for the tool holder (PTGNL 3225 P22, Sandvik Coromant) is shown in Figure 2. The measured resonant frequencies in the direction of the action of process forces are 4,5 kHz (input direction) and 4,22 kHz (output direction). An important additional element in the measuring chain was also the dynamometer (Kistler, type 9239), its resonant frequency was 6,75 kHz for the response in the direction of the input force and 5,73 kHz for the output force.

By combining the individual elements into a cutting assembly and by measuring the frequency responses of the entire assembly (tool/dynamometer/machine), we defined the peak resonant frequency of the cutting tip in the input direction (3.68 kHz) and in the output direction (2,25 kHz). When the dynamometer is a combined part of the cutting assembly its resonant frequencies lower (to 5,0 kHz in the cutting and 4,28 kHz in the feeding direction) however they are still a have the expected frequency range of the process.

The knowledge about the frequency responses of the cutting tip is necessary for the study of dynamic character of parameters in the input/output energy equations. A comparison between the frequency responses of the structure with the frequency analysis of the measured parameters of the process ( power spectrum of the cutting force and displacement speed ) is shown in figure 3. We can see that the power spectra of the force and speed of relative motions of the tool cutting tip are distributed in agreement with resonant frequency of the cutting assembly. Similar findings can be established for the input and output direction as well as for the changed cutting parameters or different tool wear.

From the above study we can conclude that the energy of the cutting process is in the case of real turning process mainly distributed in the range of the natural frequencies of the cutting assembly which can in this way by its positive damping produce good effects on the dynamic characteristics of the process.

References:

[1]   Merchant, M.E., "Mechanics of the Metal Cutting Process" Intern. Journal of Appl. Physics, Vol 16, 1945, pp. 267 - 275.
[2]   Peklenik, J., Mosedale, T., "A Statistical Analysis of the Cutting System Based on an Energy Principle," Proc. of the 8th Intern. MTDR Conference, Manchester, 1967, pp.209-231.
[3]   Peklenik, J., Jerele, A., "Some Basic Relationship for Identification of the Machining Process," Annals of the CIRP, Vol. 41, 1992, pp. 129 -136.
[4]   Dolinšek, S., "On-line Cutting Process Identification on Macro Level," Ph.D.thesis, University of Ljubljana, 1995.
[5]   Ewins, D., J., "Modal Testing, Theory and Practice," John Wiley & Sons, England 1984.
[6]   Bendat, J., Piersol, A., "Engineering Applications of Correlation and   Spectral Analysis," John Willey and Sons Ltd, New York 1980.

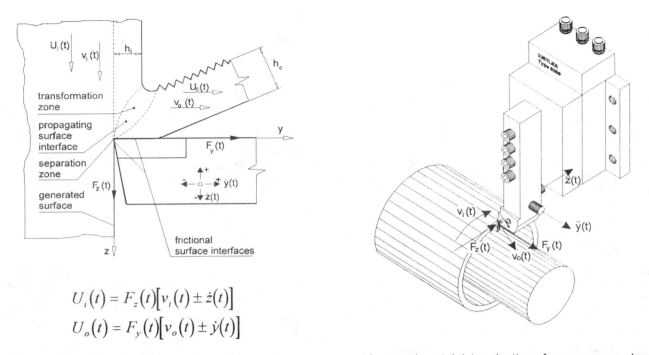

$$U_i(t) = F_z(t)\left[v_i(t) \pm \dot{z}(t)\right]$$

$$U_o(t) = F_y(t)\left[v_o(t) \pm \dot{y}(t)\right]$$

Fig 1: Definition of input output energies and measuring arrangement for experimental determination of energy parameters

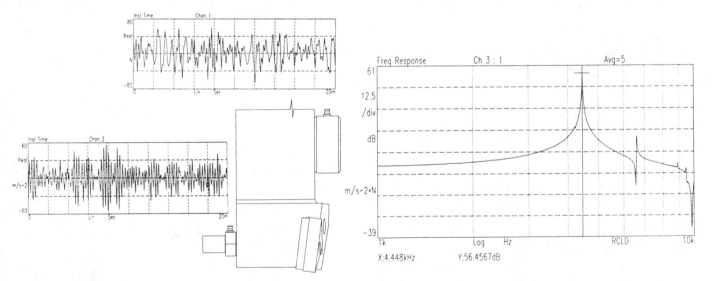

Fig 2: Frequency response of the tool holder in form of inertance

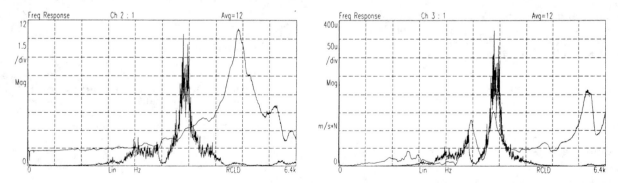

Fig 3: Comparison of the dynamometer and cutting tool frequency responses with measured force and displacement velocity

# VIBRATION BEHAVIOR OF A PARTIAL-BULKHEAD STIFFENED CYLINDER

**N.H.Zhu**, Research Assistant
**F.P.Chiang**, Professor
Laboratory for Experimental Mechanics Research
Department of Mechanical Engineering
State University of New York at Stony Brook
Stony Brook, NY 11794-2300

One of the means of reducing the vibration levels and possibly the noise generation of cylindrical shells is the addition of stiffeners. The stiffeners used are usually either ring stiffeners or longitudinal stiffeners (stringers). The dynamic characteristics of these complex structures are of much interest to the designers. The effect of the ring or stringer stiffeners upon the vibration behavior of cylindrical shells is known to be significant [1-6] most of the earlier work has been reviewed by Leissa [7] in his classic monograph. The considerable interest has also been shown in the application of the finite element method for the prediction of natural frequencies and mode shapes of both stiffened and unstiffened cylinders [8-10]. The natural frequencies obtained by the "exact" theoretical solution or the numerical analysis such as the finite element method usually can agree very closely with the experimental measurement. However it is usually not the case for the comparison of mode shapes. Furthermore, the effect of bulkhead on the vibration behavior of cylindrical shell seems to be still not very clear.

Recently the hull vibration caused by nuclear engine in the new generation of submarine calls some attention to the designers. The vibration characteristics of bulkhead-stiffened cylindrical shells seem still not to be very clear. Currently a comprehensive finite element model of performing the vibration analysis of stiffened cylinder has been built in General Dynamics Electric Boat Division. This finite element based method was initially developed by Accorsi and Bennett [8-9]. The method was general and allowed for detailed modelling of the shell and stiffeners. Wave propagation techniques were applied to determine propagation constants. Obviously this numerical model needs to be verified before its further application of prediction.

The analytical methods usually assume that the stiffeners are uniformly (periodically) distributed along the main structure and the stiffeners themselves are either symmetric or axisymmetric to their central axis. Unfortunately, we know that most of time this is not the case simply due to the tolerance of manufacture and assembly.

The presence of irregularities in nominally periodic structures may localize the modes of free vibration and inhibit the propagation of vibration within the structure. This phenomenon, referred to as normal mode localization, was first predicted by Anderson [11] in a milestone paper and has excited tremendous interest in solid-state physics. His theory basically says that if the state vectors or eigenmodes of the Schrödinger wave equation governing the motion of electrons in a solid should become localized, metallic conduction would become impossible. Thus, an "ordered" solid (i.e., one with a regular crystal lattice) may change abruptly from a metallic conductor to a semiconductor once this order is destroyed by imperfections or impurities, or when the solid becomes amorphous. The importance of this discovery can be gauged by noting that Anderson and Mott shared the 1977 Nobel Prize in physics for their work in this area.

Over the past decade, there has been ever-increasing interest in the phenomenon of mode localization in engineering structures, whereby a particular vibration mode may be confined to a limited region of the structures. Hodges was the first to predict the possibility of this effect, and his milestone paper [12] establishes the connection between engineering structures and previous discovery by Anderson in solid state physics. Later research studies in the field of structural dynamics have shown ([13-18], just name a few) that some nearly periodic structures are highly sensitive to irregularities and may exhibit localized modes of vibration. When localization occurs, the modal amplitude of a global mode becomes confined to a local region of the structure. The regular features of the mode such as the regular spacing of nodal points and lines, and the sinusoidal amplitude modulations are destroyed. All those studies have confirmed that mode localization can occur in realistic structures, and moreover that this effect can be caused by relatively minor structural irregularities. This raises the possibility of significant differences between the predicted behavior of a structure, based on perfect structural properties, and the real behavior of a structure that contains manufacturing imperfections.

As aforementioned the presence of irregularities in nominally periodic structures may inhibit the propagation of vibrations within the structure. The irregularities may localize the vibration modes and confine the vibrational energy to a small region. The consequences of localization can be either damaging, as localized vibrations lead to larger amplitudes, or beneficial, as a means of passive control of vibration propagation. The irregular nature of bulkhead may also localize the vibration modes and cause the vibration energy to be trapped within certain parts of the structure. Hence, the bulkhead may behave as a mechanical filter which permits vibration to propagate only in certain frequency spectrum, and do not allow vibration propagation in other frequencies. Obviously those hypotheses need to be verified by carefully controlled experiment and be analyses by strictly modelled theory.

This paper presents an experimental study of vibration of thin cylindrical shell reinforced by a stiffening partial-bulkhead. For this analysis the optical method of time-average laser speckle photography was used to identify the vibration mode shapes in terms of the slopes of out-of-plane displacement. Experimental measurements of natural frequencies and mode shapes of partial-bulkhead stiffened cylinder were reported and analyzed. The finite element model was verified. Generally the comparisons were good. However, the experimental data also showed the mode localization phenomenon on this complex structure. Due to its nature of non-axisymmetric characteristic the partial-bulkhead had significant local effect on the thin cylindrical shell. At some particular frequencies the bulkhead seemed to behave unexpectedly as an amplifier of the stress wave. This phenomenon obviously deserves further investigation.

In addition it has been successfully demonstrated that the time-average laser speckle photography is an another attractive alternative for the vibration measurement of large structure. It not only cherishes many merits of optical methods, but also it has simple, rugged characteristic. It does not have a stringent vibration-free requirement on the testing environment. The optical components required for performing the test are very simple. It is these unique features that make it a very practical tool for the vibration testing.

# References

[1] Raj, D. M., Narayanan, R. and Khadakkar, A. G., "Effect of Ring Stiffeners on Vibration of Cylinderical and Conical Shell Models", *J. Sound and Vib.*, Vol.179, No.3, pp413-426, 1995.

[2] Bardell, N. S. and Mead, D. J., "Free Vibration of an Orthogonally Stiffened Cylindrical Shell, Part II: Discrete General Stiffeners", *J. Sound and Vib.*, Vol.134, No.1, pp55-72, 1989.

[3] Mustafa, B. A. J. and Ali, R., "Prediction of Natural Frequency of Vibration of Stiffened Cylindrical Shells and Orthogonally Stiffened Curved Panels", *J. Sound and Vib.*, Vol.113, No.2, pp.317-327, 1987.

[4] Mead, D. J. and Bardell, N. S., "Free Vibration of a Thin Cylindrical Shell With Periodic Circumferential Stiffeners", *J. Sound and Vib.*, Vol.115, No.3, pp.499-520, 1987.

[5] Mead, D. J. and Bardell, N. S., "Free Vibration of a Thin Cylindrical Shell With Discrete Axial Stiffeners", *J. Sound and Vib.*, Vol.111, No.2, pp.229-250, 1986.

[6] Beskos, D. E. and Oates, J. B., "Dynamic Analysis of Ring-Stiffened Circular Cylindrical Shells", *J. Sound and Vib.*, 75(1), 1-15, 1981.

[7] Leissa, A. W., *Vibration of Shells*, NASA SP-288, 1973.

[8] Bennett, M. S. and Accorsi, M. L., "Free Wave Propagation in Periodically Ring Stiffened Cylindrical Shells", *J. Sound and Vib.*, Vol.171, No.1, pp.49-66, 1994.

[9] Accorsi, M. L. and Bennett, M. S., "A Finite Element Based Method for the Analysis of Free Wave Propagation in Stiffened Cylinders", *J. Sound and Vib.*, Vol.148, No.2, pp.279-292, 1991.

[10] Orris, R. M. and Petyt, M., "A Finite Element Study of Harmonic Wave Propagation in Periodic Structures", *J. Sound and Vib.*, Vol.33, No.2, pp223-236, 1974.

[11] Anderson, P. W., "Absence of Diffusion in Certain Random Lattices", *Physical Review*, Vol.109, No.5, pp1492-1505, 1958.

[12] Hodges, C. H., "Confinement of Vibration by Structural Irregularity", *J. Sound and Vib.*, 82(3), 411-424, 1982.

[13] Hodges, C. H., and Woodhouse, J., "Confinement of Vibration by One-Dimensional Disorder, I: Theory of Ensemble Averaging" *J. Sound and Vib.*, Vol.130, No.2, pp237-251, 1989.

[14] Hodges, C. H., and Woodhouse, J., "Confinement of Vibration by One-Dimensional Disorder, II: A Numerical Experiment on Different Ensemble Averages" *J. Sound and Vib.*, Vol.130, No.2, pp253-268, 1989.

[15] Pierre, C., "Weak and Strong Vibration Localization in Disordered Structures: A Statistical Investigation" *J. Sound and Vib.*, Vol.139, No.1, pp111-132, 1990.

[16] Bendiksen, O. O., "Mode Localization Phenomena in Large Space Structures" *AIAA Journal*, Vol.25, No.9, pp.1241-1248, 1987.

[17] Langley, R.S., "Mode Localization Up To High Frequencies in Coupled One-Dimensional Subsystems", *J. Sound and Vib.*, Vol.185, No.1, pp79-91, 1995.

[18] Luongo, A., "Mode Localization by Structural Imperfections in One-Dimensional Continuous Systems", *J. Sound and Vib.*, Vol.155, No.2, pp249-271, 1992.

# Modal analysis of Railway Track Components

J. Sadeghi and R. Kohoutek
Department of Civil & Mining Engineering
University of Wollongong
Wollongong, 2522
Australia

There has been considerable development in understanding dynamic behaviour of the track components and the track system during recent decades [1], [2], [3], [4], [5], [6]. Because of today's need for a faster and safer as well as more economical system of transportation in the world, it seems necessary for railway track engineers to improve and develop the track system for a heavier axle load and increased operating speeds [7]. This goal can be achieved by providing better understanding of dynamic behaviour of the track system [5].

Modal analysis is an efficient tool in determining dynamic characteristics of structural systems including railway track system. It is a good means for modelling dynamic behaviour of the track components as well as track system. Modal testing is also a good means of evaluating the suitability of mathematical and finite element models [8]. It provides natural frequency, damping, and mode shapes of track components.

Modal tests have been carried out for isolated timber and isolated concrete sleepers in a laboratory. The same tests have been conducted on a track test bed which consist of subgrade, ballast, sleepers, pads, and rail. The results of these tests including natural frequencies, damping and mode shapes have been presented in this paper. Mode shapes of rail, sleepers and corresponding frequencies obtained from the track test bed are discussed and compared with results of similar tests on the isolated sleepers, leading to a useful conclusion on effective methods of modal testing of track components.

Natural frequencies and mode shapes obtained from tests on an isolated concrete sleeper and on an isolated timber sleeper are compared. It shows that the first, the second and the third natural frequencies of timber sleepers are higher than those of concrete sleepers. However, for frequencies higher than 200Hz, natural frequencies of concrete sleepers are significantly higher than those of timber sleepers. Comparison between mode shapes of concrete and timber sleepers shows some similarities among them while mode shapes obtained from timber sleepers are more smooth and include more torsional modes.

Natural frequencies and mode shapes were obtained for timber sleepers with and without consideration of railpads. The results indicate that natural frequencies of sleepers without considering railpads change significantly specially for higher frequencies. Mode shapes obtained from sleepers without railpads seems to be more smooth due to the stiffer support. Similar tests were carried out on two types of timber sleepers; an old timber sleeper (with considerable wear) and a new one. Modal analysis results obtained from these two tests indicate that timber sleepers' deterioration causes reduction in natural frequencies of the sleepers (for frequencies lower than 200 Hz). However, mode shapes obtained from the old timber are not smooth which leading to concentration stresses in cracked parts.

To investigate effects of ballast and subgrade, limitations in dimensions of track test beds, and importance of boundaries at the end parts of the subgrade, three types of tests were carried out.

First, an isolated concrete sleeper was tested for natural frequencies and mode shapes.

Second, the same test was carried out on a concrete sleepers in the track test bed in the laboratory.

Third, modal analysis was carried out on a concrete sleepers in a field.

Results obtained from the above three tests indicate that ballast and subgrade reduce natural frequencies of sleepers. Mode shapes obtained from sleepers in the track test bed are more complicated than those obtained from the isolated sleepers in the lab. The results also show that discontinuity of rail at the end and fix boundaries considered at boundaries of subgrade in the track test bed cause considerable changes in natural frequencies. This can be due to hinge support considered at the end of the rail and reflection of waves radiation from the fix boundaries of subgrade in the track test bed. Another reason for differences in natural frequencies obtained from the field and the lab is not having minimum number of sleepers in the track test bed as suggested in [10].

In order to obtain natural frequencies and mode shapes of whole track system, modal analysis test was carried out on track test bed in the lab and on sites. Tests on sites were carried out for rail with concrete sleepers and rail with timber sleepers. The results lead to the following conclusion:

1) ballast and subgrade reduce considerably natural frequencies of sleepers and the track system;

2) creation of radiation dampers at the boundaries of ballast and subgrade in railway track test bed is necessary (as suggested in [9]) otherwise it causes unreal increases in natural frequencies of the track system;

3) a proper boundaries at the end of the rail in a track test bed are essential;

4) minimum 20 sleepers in longitudinal section of the laboratory track test bed is essential for reliable model as suggested in [10] and [11].

Comparison between results of modal analysis test on the track system (timber sleepers and concrete sleepers) shows that track system with timber sleepers has relatively lower natural frequencies but more complicated mode shapes than those of track with concrete sleepers.

REFERENCES

[1] Clark. R. A, and Lowndes, V.p., (1979), "Discrete Support Track Dynamics Model, Theory and Program Guide," *British Railways Board Research and Development Division Technical Report TM.TS.95.*
[2] Ono, K., and Yamada, M., (1989), "Study on Vibration Induced in Railway Track and Road Bed," *Trans. of JSCE, Vol. 15,* pp 465-467.

[3] Schwab, C. A., and Mauer, L., (1989), "An interactive Track/Train Dynamics Model for Investigating System Limits in High speed Track," *The Dynamics of Vehicles on Roads and on Tracks, Anderson,* R., (ed.), Proc. 11th IAVSD Symposium, Kingston, Ont., Canada, pp 502-514.

[4] Kohoutek, R., and Campbell, K. D, (1989), "Analysis of Spot Replacement Sleepers," *The 4th International Heavy Haul Railway Conference,* Brisbane, pp 316-321.

[5] Grassie, S. L., (1984), "Dynamic modeling of Railway Track and Wheelsets," *Proc. of 2nd Int. Conf. on recent Advances in Structural Dynamics,* Petyt, M., and Wolfe, H.f. (ends.), ISVR, University of Southampton, pp 681-698.

[6] Dahlberg T. and Nielsen, (1991), "Dynamic behaviour of free-free and insitu concrete railway sleepers," *Solid Mechanics Report F138,* Chalmbers University of Technology, Gothenberg, Sweden, 15 pp.

[7] Cai, Z., (1992), "Theoretical Model for Dynamic Wheel/Rail and Track Interaction," *International Wheelset Congress, Sydney,* pp 127-131.

[8] Ewings D. J., (1984), *Modal Testing: Theory and Practice,* Research Studies Press, England, pp 1-10.

[9] Sadeghi J. and Kohoutek R., (1995), " The complex Response Function of the Support System For Railway Track System," *!4th Australian Conference on the Mechanics and materials,* Tasmania, Australia, 1995, pp 552-557.

[10] Sadeghi J. and Kohoutek R., (1996), "Finite Element Method in Railway track Modelling," *First Australian Congress on Applied Mechanics,* Melbourne, Australia, 1996, pp 465-471.

[11] Sadeghi J. and Kohoutek R., (1995, "Analytical Modelling of Railway Track System," *Australian Journal of Railway Track System,* Sysney, Australia, 1995, pp 12-19.

# The Torsional Vibration of a Damped Continuous Bar.

Sonya Derry*, Simon Drew+, Brian Stone+
*The Orbital Engine Company, Western Australia
+Department of Mechanical and Materials Engineering,
The University of Western Australia, NEDLANDS,
Western Australia 6907. bjs@shiralee.mech.uwa.edu.au

When modelling the vibration of parallel shafts undamped models are typically used. This is because the level of damping in commonly used metals is low and hence the damping contributed from parallel shafts is small compared to the damping of a complete structure. This has been well substantiated for transverse vibration of shafts. However, when the torsional vibration of rotating systems is considered, the levels of damping may be very low even for the complete system. Small sources of damping become significant when the overall level of damping is low. The authors have been modelling torsional vibration using the receptance method and have found it necessary to include the damping in parallel shafts. It is for this reason that the receptances of damped parallel shafts have been derived and are reviewed in this paper. It is of interest to note that several authors have reported simply taking the undamped receptances of shafts and replacing the elastic and/or shear modulus by a complex quantity such as $G(1 + i\eta)$.

Thus the torsional receptance for a free/free bar excited at the end x=L is given by,

$$\alpha_{xL} = \frac{\cos \lambda x}{G(1 + i\eta)J\lambda \sin \lambda L}$$

This does not give the correct receptance for a damped shaft but simply multiplies the undamped receptance by a constant complex number $1/(1 + i\eta)$. The receptance thus clearly still has an infinite value at each of the undamped natural frequencies. It is necessary to return to the basic equations and solve them with a complex modulus. This has been done [1] and the correct receptance is given by,

$$\alpha_{xL} = \frac{2\begin{bmatrix}(a\cosh\lambda Sx \cos\lambda Rx - b\sinh\lambda Sx \sin\lambda Rx) \\ -i(a\sinh\lambda Sx \sin\lambda Rx + b\cosh\lambda Sx \cos\lambda Rx)\end{bmatrix}}{(a^2 + b^2)} \quad .. (1)$$

where,

$$\lambda^2 = \rho\omega^2 / G,$$

$$S = -\frac{\left[(1 + \eta^2)^{1/2} - 1\right]^{1/2}}{\sqrt{2}(1 + \eta^2)^{1/2}} \text{ and } R = \frac{\left[(1 + \eta^2)^{1/2} + 1\right]^{1/2}}{\sqrt{2}(1 + \eta^2)^{1/2}},$$

$$a = 2GJ\lambda\begin{bmatrix}(S + \eta R)\cos(R\lambda L)\sinh(S\lambda L) \\ +(\eta S - R)\sin(R\lambda L)\cosh(S\lambda L)\end{bmatrix},$$

$$b = 2GJ\lambda\begin{bmatrix}(\eta S - R)\cos(R\lambda L)\sinh(S\lambda L) \\ -(S + \eta R)\sin(R\lambda L)\cosh(S\lambda L)\end{bmatrix}.$$

These receptances have been confirmed by using them in standard receptance addition routines. Thus, if a single continuous bar is divided in to several parts and the response found by using the addition routines, the results obtained are the same as for the original bar.

In practice the main unknown is the value of damping to be used and also whether the damping is viscous or hysteretic. For the theoretical results given above the damping has be assumed to be hysteretic so that $\eta$ is a constant. If the damping is viscous then $\omega\xi$ should be substituted for $\eta$. It is one of the aims of this paper to investigate whether hysteretic or viscous is the more appropriate model for damping.

The experimental work was conducted on a steel bar of length 4.51 m and diameter 0.039 m. Impact excitation was employed using a hammer incorporating a load cell and impacting on a small pin attached to the circumference at one end of the bar. A torsional accelerometer was mounted at the end of the bar where the impact was applied. The bar was mounted along its length on relatively soft foam. The experimental result obtained is shown in Figure 1. The magnitude of the torsional acceleration response divided by the applied torque was obtained. Accurate calibration was not employed as the major objective was to attempt to determine the type of damping.

Theoretical responses were obtained for both hysteretic and viscous damping. The value of $G/\rho$ was adjusted to give a correct value for the first non-zero torsional mode. Also the level of hysteretic damping (defined by $\eta$) was adjusted to give a good fit to the first mode. The Q factor obtained from the experimental results for the first mode was 153. For the viscous damping case the value of $\xi$ was chosen so that $\omega\xi$ was the same as $\eta$ at the first mode frequency. The predictions are shown in figures 2 and 3. It is immediately apparent that the viscous model significantly over predicts the damping for the higher modes. The hysteretic model gives modal damping for each of the modes which is closer to the measured values. However, the theoretical results predict that the responses at resonance should be very similar for each of the modes. It is clear that the first non-zero mode has a significantly lower response at resonance than the higher modes. The reason for this is the subject of further investigation.

A comparison of both theoretical predictions with the experimental results indicates that transverse modes were both excited and measured during the experiment, as would be expected for the experimental techniques used. In order to excite the torsional modes alone a torsional exciter is required. Such an exciter is available [2] and it is proposed to use this in further investigations of the response. For a pure torque it will also be easier to obtain calibrated results rather than the qualitative ones presented in this paper.

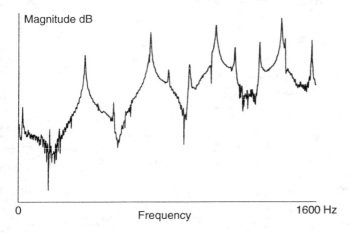

Figure 1  Measured frequency response function

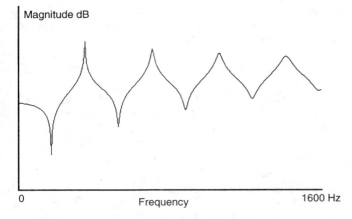

Figure 2  Theoretical frequency response function - hysteretic damping

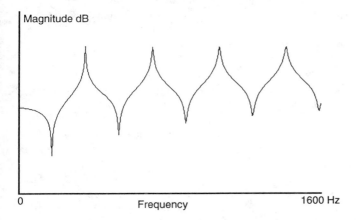

Figure 3  Theoretical frequency response function - viscous damping

The levels of damping found for the steel bar are in the range that is expected. The question is whether these damping levels would be significant in a real system. The authors have found that rolling element bearings contribute very little damping to torsional vibration. However, if flexible couplings are employed these may produce significant levels of damping, at least for the lower frequency modes.

Finally it is of interest to examine the mode shapes of a heavily damped bar as there is some interest in complex modes. It needs to be stressed that the receptance approach used in this paper does not immediately produce modal characteristics. Rather the response including the contributions of all modes is obtained. As the bar is modelled as a continuous bar with distributed mass, stiffness and damping this means that the whole infinite series of modes is included.

Figure 4 shows the set of deflected shapes of a uniform bar excited at one end. The bar has a hysteretic damping ratio $\eta$ = 0.5. This would be a possible value for a rubber/plastic bar. There is no node and there is a significant phase difference in the motion at each end. Also, the amplitude at the non-excited end is reduced.

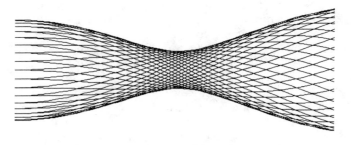

Figure 4  Vibration at first non zero mode for a heavily damped bar - excitation at right hand end.

The torsional receptances of damped continuous beams have been presented in this paper. They have been reported as producing consistent results when used on bars subdivided into several sub-sections. Initial experimental results have shown that a hysteretic model of damping is more realistic than a viscous model (with a constant damping ratio). An interesting result has been obtained, which indicates that if a hysteretic damping model is used, a frequency dependent hysteretic damping coefficient is required. Further experimental work is planned to investigate this in more detail.

Finally the receptances are likely to be of great value in modelling bars with relatively high levels of damping. This would be the case for many non-metallic materials.

References:

[1]    Derry, S. and Stone, B. J., "The torsional receptances in closed form of continuous bars with distributed damping", in preparation.

[2]    Drew S. J. and Stone, B. J., 'Excitation of Torsional Vibration For Rotating Machinery Using a 1.7 Kw Ac Servo-Drive', Second International Conference on gearbox Noise, Vibration and Diagnostics, London, 16-17 November 1995, IMechE Conference Transaction 1995-5, pp171-181.

# Spectral analysis for non stationary signals from mechanical measurements: parametric vs non parametric methods.

Tommaso D'Alessio

Dip. Meccanica ed Automatica III Università di Roma
Via Segre 60, 00146 Roma

## Introduction

The analysis of non stationary signals is of interest in many fields of mechanical measurements: sound, vibration, acceleration studies are only some of possible applications. In recent years, this interest is also meant by the presence on the market of some SW packages which can implement the so-called time-frequency analysis.

Time-frequency analysis can give a global view of the behaviour of non stationary signals by means of the spectrogram, P(f,t), which represents the evolution of the signal spectrum in time. The main problem in this analysis is that of achieving a good trade-off between observation time and accuracy, while computational complexity can also be important when real time or on the field measurements have to be made.

The approach normally followed is based on the hypothesis that the process has a slowly varying spectrum. In this case, the Discrete Fourier Transform (DFT) is applied to successive epochs of the signal, leading to the Short Time Fourier Transform (STFT). The FFT is computationally efficient but has the drawback of averaging non stationarities over the record length.

Some methods have recently been proposed for highly non stationary signals, among which we mention the Wigner-Ville (WV) and the Choi-Williams (CW) distributions that are extensively used. The WV and CW methods can be described with reference to the so called Cohen distribution, that is [1]:

$$P(t,\omega) \propto \iiint \exp[-j(\theta t + \omega\tau - \vartheta u)]\Theta(\vartheta,\tau)x^*(u - \tau/2)x(u + \tau/2)du\,d\tau\,d\vartheta$$

With different choices of the "kernel" $\Theta(\theta,\tau)$, different distributions can be obtained. For instance, with $\Theta(\theta,\tau) = 1$, we obtain the WVD, while if $\Theta(\theta,\tau) = \exp(-\theta^2\tau^2/\sigma)$, we obtain the CWD.

These methods do not require the short - term hypothesis on the stationarity of the signal. However, they show cross terms (artefacts) in the spectrum which mask the true spectrum of the signal, have been mainly applied to simulated signals and perform well only for some classes of signals, so that a careful choice must be made according to the problem at hand. Parametric methods, most often based on Autoregressive (AR) modelling, have also been used, but mainly for stationary signal analysis, or for the case of slowly varying spectra. In the literature, little attention has been up to now devoted to the evaluation of the performance of these methods when applied to the analysis of non stationary mechanical phenomena, so that more extensive studies are needed. Moreover the performance of parametric methods have not been compared with those of non parametric methods.

In this paper, we therefore present an innovative parametric method for spectral analysis of non stationary signals, and compare it with WV and CW methods. This method, based on AR modelling, has the advantage of being adaptive with respect to the variations of the signal spectrum so that it is suitable for the analysis of highly non stationary spectra.

## Materials and methods

The new method is based on the modelling of the discrete-time signal s(nTc) as an AutoRegressive (AR) process of constant order but with time varying coefficient, that is:

$$s(nTc) = - \sum_i a_{pi}(nTc)\, s(nTc - kTc) + n(nTc)$$

where: p is the order of the model, $a_{pi}(t)$ is the time varying coefficient, {n(t)} refers to a white noise process. The method is adaptive because each $a_{pi}(t)$ is represented by a time series where the number of terms of the series is varied (according to an optimality criterium) in order to fit the time varying spectral characteristics of the signals. In this way the method can follow rapidly varying spectra because it has an inherently non stationary structure.

The WV and CW methods have been implemented according to standard algorithms.

## Discussion of the Results

The adaptive AR method has been applied to simulated time-varying processes and to experimentally acquired vibration signals and its results compared with those of the WV and CW transforms. In order to improve the dynamic range, the results of the AR method have been subjected to a log transformation, even if at the expense of the capability of detecting amplitude modulations.

The simulated signals are both non stationary band-pass random processes and combinations of chirp signals, that is frequency modulated signals. In those trials, as it was expected WV (and CW but in a lesser extent) showed the presence of cross terms. As an example, in fig. 1 a) and b) we report the results obtained when analysing chirp signals, respectively with the WV and the AR method. The simulated signal was a sum of three chirps, with initial frequencies respectively of 100, 140 and 180 Hz, with added noise (Signal to Noise Ratio SNR = 20 dB). From fig. 1 a) it is evident that WV method introduces spurious

This test shows that the AR method (with log transformation) gives a better global view of the harmonics of the signal, even if with a more limited resolution.

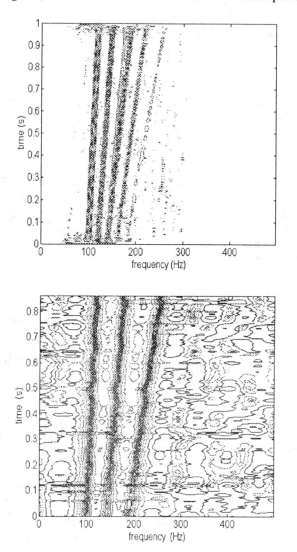

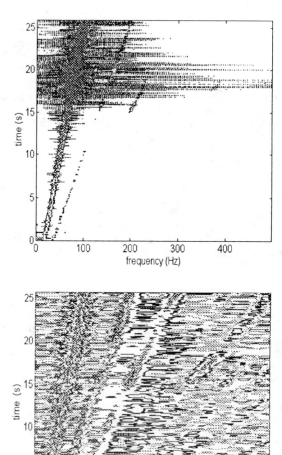

Fig. 1. Performance of the WV method (a) and of the AR one (b) when applied to three simulated chirp signals. The WV method shows some spurious terms which detrimentally affect the interpretation of the spectrum.

terms, which are allocated in between the three chirps, which originate problems in interpreting the spectra.

Finally, the three methods have been applied to experimentally acquired signals from vibration measurements on a rotor, when its rotation speed is increased. In this case, some resonances show up, and the signal can then be represented as a sum of chirp signals with amplitude modulation.

In fig. 2 a) and b) we show the results obtained respectively with the CW method and the AR method.

Fig. 2. Time-frequency contours of the spectra of the vibration signal from a motor obtained with the CW method (a) and the AR method (b). The overall pattern of harmonics of the signal are more clearly readable with the new method.

In conclusion, this comparison of the performance of the three methods shows that no method can be considered as superior in all cases and with respect to all quality indexes. However, it emerged that the new AR method has the advantage of the absence of cross terms, thus leading to more clearly readable spectrograms.

References
[1] Cohen L., Time frequency distibution - A review, Proc. IEEE, vol. 36, 1989, pp. 941 - 981.

# Investigation of Unsteady Fluid Force Acting on Array of Cylinders in Cross Flow

Zhongsen YAN, Hiroki TANAKA, Kazuhiro TANAKA
Mechanical System of Engineering
Kyushu Institute of Technology
680-4, Kawazu Iizuka, 820 Japan

Acoustic vibration occurs in boiler and heat exchanger in some fluid velocity. It can be considered that source of the vibration is fluid dynamic forces acting on tube bundle which is generated by vortex shedding from the tube bundles. Acoustic vibration takes with fluid particle vibration and the vibration changes a state of flow around tubes. Change of the flow also changes the fluid dynamic forces, so that it seems that acoustic vibration has a kind of feed back circuit like a self excited vibration. Tanaka etc. [1] have studied unsteady fluid dynamic force on tube bundle in oscillating flow but many of unsolved problems still remain. Objective of the study is to investigate the effects of acoustic vibration on unsteady fluid dynamic force acting on cylinder arrays in duct.

If velocity of air flow is very small as compared with sonic velocity, influence of compressibility is very small. Then, water flow and air flow are same, if there is no free water surface. From the reason, water flow was used in this study because density of water is greater than air and then greater fluid dynamic force is obtained.

In a case of acoustic vibration, fluid particles vibrate with acoustic vibration and it is necessary to know fluid dynamic force on cylinder arrays in vibrating flow. However, on dynamical point of view, flow state around cylinders in vibrating flow is perfectly same as flow state around vibrating cylinders in steady flow. So that, experiment was conducted with forcedly vibrated models in steady flow.

Fluid dynamic forces change with St number which consists of frequency, velocity and diameter of cylinder. Usual meaning of St number is defined by frequency of vortex shedding but in this case, frequency of forced vibration is important. So that, we induce a St number based on frequency of cylinder vibration and call it mechanical St number to distinguish them. Fluid dynamic forces acting on forcedly vibrating cylinders are studied on various mechanical St numbers.

Experimental apparatus is shown diagrammatically in fig. 1. It consists of water tunnel, oscillator and model cylinders. Size of test section is 320mm in width, 300mm in height and 700mm in length. Oscillator is composed of motor, eccentric wheel, linear slide and connecting rod. Motor is controlled by inverter and the revolution is changed to reciprocating motion by eccentric wheel. The reciprocating motion is transmitted to connecting rod which is guided by linear slide and the rod can oscillate linearly in sinusoidal motion. A support bar is fixed to the connecting rod and model cylinders are settled on the other end of the support bar. Cylinders are made of aluminum rods of 30mm in diameter and 200mm in length.

Strain gauges are put on the support bar to measure fluid force and acceleration meter is also put on the connecting

rod to measure oscillation of cylinder model. Frequency of oscillation is controlled by regulating input volt of motor. Flow velocity is changed by changing revolution of pump in the duct. Data of fluid force and displacement are gathered through sensors and stored to memory of computer.

Two types of cylinder arrays used in this experiment are shown in figure 2. Figure 2(a) shows cylinders in square array of pitch to diameter ratio of 2.6 and figure 2(b) shows cylinders in staggered array of which ratio is P/D of 2.9 and T/D of 2.47. Frequencies of forced vibration of model are varied from 0.5 Hz to 5 Hz. Amplitude of vibration (A/D) is 1/6 and main flow velocity is 0.26m/s.

Figure 3 shows lift force on oscillating cylinders in square array. Abscissa is mechanical St number. Cylinder numbers 1 and 3 are in up stream and 2 and 4 are in rear stream. It is natural that the lift coefficients of cylinder 1 and 3 are almost same because the cylinders are in same geometrical conditions. Lift forces on no.2 and no.4 cylinders are also same. All lift forces start to increase when the St number reaches about 0.1 and become maximum at St number of about 0.2. They decrease above the St number but have small local peaks at about 0.4 and 0.6. It is interesting that, at St number of about 0.2, lift forces on rear cylinders are greater than those on front cylinders though static forces are usually smaller than those on rear cylinders. The fact seems to show that vortices shed from front cylinders make lift force great on rear cylinders. However it is necessary to clarify the the cause in future.

Phase difference of oscillations between lift force and displacement of oscillating cylinder is shown in figure 4. Phase angle of zero to 180 degrees means that lift force goes ahead of displacement and the other degrees, lift force goes behind.The former case is called positive phase difference and the rear case is called negative. Phase difference of cylinder 1 and 3 have the same characteristics because geometrical positions are the same. The phase of cylinder 2,4 are also the same. Lift forces go behind the displacement in very small St number region but they go ahead on St number between 0.1 to 0.2. Phase differences are mostly negative on St number above 0.2 except at St number of about 0.4 and 0.6.

When phase difference is positive , fluid dynamic forces push cylinders to moving direction so that the fluid forces amplify the vibration. On the other hand, if phase is negative, fluid force restrain the vibration. According to the above judgement, vibration occurs on St number between 0.1 to 0.2 and at St number of near 0.4 and 0.6.

Lift coefficient of cylinders in staggered array are shown in figure 5. The lift forces have peak values at St number of about 0.22. Force on front cylinder is also less than those on rear cylinders but lift force on mid cylinder is greatest. It seems that there are strong influences of flow among cylinders.

Phase difference of lift force on cylinders of staggered array are shown in figure 6. The phase varies rapidly with St number so that it is difficult to find out the region of positive phase difference exactly. However, roughly speaking, phase angle of cylinder 1 is positive on St number of about 0.15 and 0.44, those on cylinder 2 is positive on St about 0.1, 0.3, 0.44 and those on cylinder 3 is on St of 0.1 and 0.2. Positive phase angle means that fluid force amplify vibration.

Unsteady fluid dynamic forces acting on oscillating cylinders in a square array and a staggared array were studied experimentally as mentioned above and the test results lead to following conclusion.
(1) All of the lift forces become maximum at St number of about 0.2 from the fact, it is thinkable that, even though cylinder array, fluid force is strongly influenced by karman vortices which may be shed from individual cylinder.
(2) Fluid dynamic force on front cylinder is smaller than those on rear cylinder cylinder or mid cylinder. It is thinkable that vortices shed from front cylinder help a generation of vortics from rear cylinders.
(3) Most of phase angle is positive on St number about 0.2, which is the same St number as St of vortex shedding from single cylinder. It means that most of the cylinder is unstable near St number of 0.2. Phase angle of square cylinder array also has positive value at St number of about 0.4 and 0.6. These unstable points may be double and triple harmony of base St of 0.2.

References
[1] H.Tanaka, "Acoustic Resonant Vibration and Its Exciting Force by Tube Bundle", The American Society of Mechanical Engineers, PVP - Vol. 154, Flow-induced Vibration, Book No. H00469 - 1989

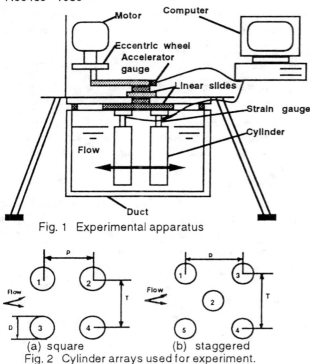

Fig. 1 Experimental apparatus

Fig. 2 Cylinder arrays used for experiment.

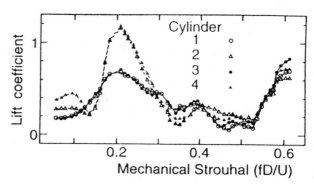

Fig. 3 Lift coefficients on square array cylinders versus mechanical Stl number.

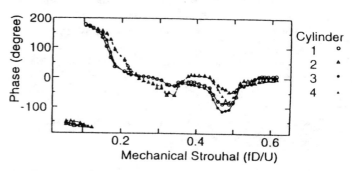

Fig. 4 Phase difference between lift force and cylinder displacement versus mechanical St number.(square array)

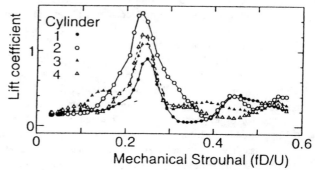

Fig. 5 Lift coefficients on staggered array cylinders versus mechanical St number.

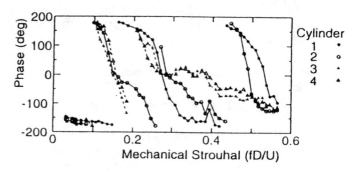

Fig. 6 Phase difference between lift force and cylinder displacement versus St number. (staggered array)

# Finite Element Analysis of Elasto-Dynamic Behavior under Impact Load in Three-Dimensional Model

## G.-W. Hwang and K.-Z. Cho

Department of Mechanical Engineering
Chonnam National University
300 Yongbongdong, Kwangju, 500-757
Republic of Korea

**ABSTRACT** : Stress wave propagation is studied in three-dimensional solid through application of finite element method. A finite element program for elastic stress wave propagation is developed in order to investigate the shape of stress field at time increment. Initial stress wave is generated by unit step function. The reliability and accuracy of the three-dimensional finite element analysis were compared with the analytic solution. The shape of stress wave propagation and, in addition, the stress wave intensity are discussed.

## I. Introduction

The mode convection and transverse waves are generated in the process of stress wave propagation. Response of three-dimensional structures influenced by shock or impact loads is very attractive problems to be solved, because automobiles, aircrafts and all that sort of things, into which an obstacles are crashed, have to be designed with well knowledge about these effects to solid structures.

In rather early time, the theory of stress wave propagation is proposed in an elastic medium by Kolsky [1]. Recently, a large number of investigators have studied stress wave propagation using a boundary element method [2], Dirichlet-to-Neumann(DtN) Method[3,4] and spectrum analysis. The finite element method has been used for structural dynamics[5-7]. The finite element result is convinced of discretization of solution domain. The difficulty lies not in the finite element formulation, but in the calculation necessary to get convergence and accuracy.

In this paper, a finite element program is developed for three-dimensional elastic stress wave propagation in order to investigate the aspect of stress field and the magnitude of stress wave intensity at time increment.

## II. Finite Element Formulation
### 1. Governing Equation

A three-dimensional solid is modelled as a homogeneous, isotropic and elastic hexahedron. Using Newton's law of motion and Hooke's law, the governing differential equation of the stress wave propagation of three-dimensional elastic solid is derived as

$$\rho \ddot{u}_i = (\lambda + \mu)u_{m,mi} + \mu u_{i,mm} \tag{1}$$

where $\rho$, $\lambda$ and $\mu$ are, respectively, the density, the Lamé's constant and the rigidity modulus of the medium. The displacement $U(r, t)$ is a functional relation with propagated radius of stress from impact point. The displacement is assumed as

$$U(r, t) = \frac{1}{r}\{f_1(r-ct) + f_2(r+ct)\} \tag{2}$$

where $r$ is a radius from impact point( $r^2 = x^2 + y^2 + z^2$).

## 2. Finite Element Formulation

For the three-dimensional problem, the time-dependent transient stress wave equation can be obtained by the following differential equation:

$$\rho \frac{\partial^2 u}{\partial t^2} = (\lambda + 2\mu)\nabla(\nabla \cdot u) - \mu \nabla \times \nabla \times u \tag{3}$$

The finite element approximation to the governing equation is based on the eight-node isoparametric element and the shape function satisfies the requirements of $C^0$ continuity condition. The finite element formulation leads to

$$[K_{tt}]\{\ddot{u}\} + [K]\{u\} + [K_{s_2}]\{u\} + \{R_t(t)\} = \{0\} \tag{4}$$

In this equation $[K_{tt}]$, $[K]$ and $[K_{s_2}]$ are, respectively, the inertia matrix, stiffness matrix and boundary matrix, $\{R_t(t)\}$ is the external load vector, u is the unknown nodal displacement vector.

A direct integration methods are at our disposal to solve equation (4), time differential problem, numerically. Using direct implicit method, equation (4) becomes

$$[K^*]\{u\}_{t+\triangle t} = \{F^*\}_{t+\triangle t} \tag{5}$$

where $[K^*]$ is the effective stiffness matrix and $\{F^*\}_{t+\triangle t}$ is the effective load vector.

The nodal displacements from equation (5) are used to evaluate the node point stresses at time.

## 3. Finite Element Model and Materials

The geometric profile of finite element model is shown in Fig.1 and parameters are listed in Table 1. Elements with dimensions of 2.5 mm cube are used.

**Table 1 Material properties of the finite element model**

| Parameter | Description | Value |
|---|---|---|
| E | Young's Modulus | $6.2 \times 10^4 MPa$ |
| G | Shear Modulus | $2.5 \times 10^4 MPa$ |
| $\rho$ | Density | $2300 \, kg/m^3$ |
| $\nu$ | Poisson's Ratio | 0.24 |
| V | Stress Wave Speed | $5600 \, m/sec$ |

A total of 4,800 elements and 6,724 nodes is used in the finite element discretization and total number of degree of freedom is become 20,121.

To study stress waves in the context of this model, we make the following assumption: (1) the finite element model is subjected to a point load of 10 kg, as illustrated in Fig. 1; (2) an initial displacement, velocity and acceleration are taken to zero; and (3) stress wave may be reflected perfectly at the fixed boundary and may be transmitted perfectly at the free boundary.

### III. Results and Discussion

All computations were carried on an CRAY C94A/264 computer in double precision. Convergence and accuracy of direct implicit scheme are limited in time step size, which is $2 \mu$ sec for this problem. The results of finite element analysis are presented in Fig. 2-3. In Fig. 2, the x-directional normal stresses($\sigma_x$) are presented along the thickness of the solution domain. Fig. 3 shows the time response of shear stress($\tau_{zx}$) wave propagation along the thickness of the solution domain. The y-directional stress components have the same magnitudes as that of x components and this direction of stress wave propagation is rotated at an angle of 90 degrees according to the z-axis.

### V. Conclusions

This paper deal with a finite element method and direct integration method for measuring an aspect of stress wave propagation subjected to an impulsive force. The results obtained in this investigation may be summarized as follows.

(1) The variations of stress vs. time were analyzed at several locations. The numerical results are shown to agree well with the theoretical predictions based on the elastic stress wave propagation. Following the order of middle, upper and lower part, the magnitudes of normal stress components are become larger. Because of the repetition of tensile and compression at the impact point, the applied point of impact load has been acting as the source of stress wave.

(2) The shear stress component are become larger in order of upper part, middle part and lower part and consequently the failure of structure would be started at the opposite side of impact point.

### References

1. Kolsky, H., "Stress Waves in Solids," New York Dover Pub. Inc., 1963, pp.4-45.
2. Manolis, G.D., "A Comparative Study on Three Boundary Element Method Approaches to Problems in Elastodynamics," Int. J. Num. Mech. Engineering, Vol. 19, 1983, pp. 73-91.
3. Mansur, W.J., and Brebbia, C.A., "Formulation of the Boundary Element Method for Transient Problems Governed by the Scalar Wave Equation," Applied Mathematics Modelling, Vol. 6, 1982, pp. 307-311.
4. Dohner, J.L., Shoureshi, R., and Bernhard, R.J., "Transient Analysis of Three-Dimensional Wave Propagation Using Boundary Element Method," Int. J.of Num. Methods Eng., Vol. 24, 1987, pp. 621-634.
5. T.E. Simkins, "Finite Elements for Initial Value Problems in Dynamics," AIAA J. Vol. 19, 1982, pp. 1357-1362.
6. R. Riff and M. Brauch, "Time Finite Element Discretization of Hamilton's Law of Varying Action," AIAA J. Vol. 22, 1984, pp. 1310-1338.
7. Z. Kaczkowski, "The Method of Finite Space-Time Elements in Dynamics of Structures," J. of Tech. Physics, Vol. 18, pp. 1982, 467-474.

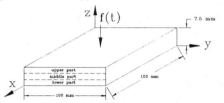

Fig. 1 Schematic diagram of solution domain

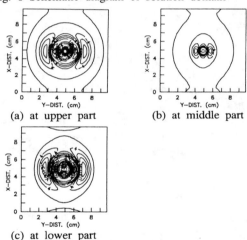

(a) at upper part     (b) at middle part

(c) at lower part

Fig. 2 Iso-line of x-directional normal stress component
(time = $10 \mu$ sec)

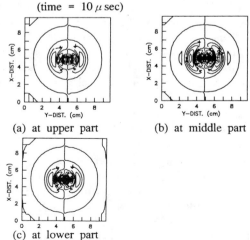

(a) at upper part     (b) at middle part

(c) at lower part

Fig. 3 Iso-line of x-directional shear stress component
(time = $10 \mu$ sec)

# Wave Propagation Past Structural Joints and other Local Non-Uniformities

Lance E. Kannal and James F. Doyle
School of Aeronautics & Astronautics
Purdue University
West Lafayette, Indiana 47907

The analysis of the propagation of stress waves through structures is complicated by the presence of joints and local non-uniformities. These discontinuities act as filters and sources of new waves. For example, an incident flexural wave can generate new flexural as well as longitudinal and torsional waves. It is because of the presence of the myriad of waves (after multiple reflections) that the spectral element method evolved; this is a frequency domain matrix methodology for treating structures as a system of connected waveguides. The goal of the present paper is to extend the established spectral element method to handle wave propagation in arbitrary segments and verify the results experimentally.

In two early papers by Doyle and Kamle [1, 2], an experimental study of wave propagation through joints was performed. The significant aspect of these papers was the frequency domain (or spectral) characterization of both the waves and the structural connectivities; essentially, the complicated convolution relations of the time domain become simple algebraic relations in the frequency domain. This approach is exploited in the monograph [3] to solve a variety of problems involving structural wave propagation. When it is realized that spectral analysis converts a dynamics problem into a series of pseudo-static ones (with frequency as a parameter), then the development of a spectral element analogous to the finite element is quite natural. There is one significant difference between the two elements, however; the spectral element models the mass distribution exactly and consequently is not limited by length or frequency response. That is, a single element can span from one structural joint to another irrespective of the distance. The spectral analysis approach also makes it convenient to analyze higher order structural models, for example, References [4] give a spectral element for deep (Timoshenko) beams, Reference [5] gives one for a deep (Mindlin-Herrmann) rod. The cited references show the spectral element method to be a powerful and versatile tool for the analysis of wave propagation problems in connected waveguides.

For those waveguides having embedded flaws (such as cracks or holes), there are very high stress gradients near the discontinuity but yet the overall structural dynamics is not greatly affected by the local details — the nature of waveguides are such that detailed local wave behavior tends to get smeared over propagation distance. Hence, our basic strategy is to isolate the behavior near the region of local non-uniformity and perform a *Global/Local* analysis. That is, we perform the global analysis in the usual manner in terms of connected waveguides and the local analysis in terms of a spectral super-element. The phrase 'super-element' is commonly used in substructure analysis to describe the major structural components used in the global analysis. The essence of the approach (as used in this paper) is that the complicated region is modeled using very many conventional finite elements. All of the interior degrees of freedom are then (dynamically) condensed leaving just the connection degrees of freedom. As a final step, these are then reduced further so as to be compatible with the waveguide degrees of freedom. As a result, we will have an element that has the same type of nodal degrees of freedom and loads as the connecting waveguides but yet represent a complicated interior region. The advantage of this element is that it gives a mechanism for modeling almost any type of non-uniformity — in essence, it can be used to model any problem that can be modeled using conventional elements.

Experimental examples are given of waves interacting with joints, holes and cracks. Of particular interest is the ability to recover information at a crack tip, say, even though it was condensed out of the super-element model. At each stage, the results are also verified by comparison with a conventional finite element modeling.

# References

[1] **Doyle, J.F. and Kamle, S.**, "An Experimental Study of the Reflection and Transmission of Flexural Waves at Discontinuities", *Journal of Applied Mechanics*, vol. 52, pp. 669–673, 1985.

[2] **Doyle, J.F. and Kamle, S.**, "An Experimental Study of the Reflection and Transmission of Flexural Waves at an Arbitrary T-Joint", *Journal of Applied Mechanics*, vol. 54, pp. 136–140, 1987.

[3] **Doyle, J.F.**, *Wave Propagation in Structures, 2nd Edn*, Springer-Verlag, New York, 1996.

[4] **Gopalakrishnan, S., Martin, M. and Doyle, J.F.**, "A Matrix Methodology for Spectral Analysis of Wave Propagation in Multiple Connected Timoshenko Beams", *Journal of Sound & Vibration*, pp. 11–24, 1992.

[5] **Martin, M., Gopalakrishnan, S., and Doyle, J.F.**, "Wave Propagation in Multiply Connected Deep Waveguides", *Journal of Sound & Vibration*, vol 174(4), pp. 521–538, 1994.

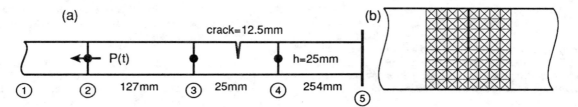

**Figure 1**: Waveguide with a transverse crack. (a) Spectral element model, (b) Super-element mesh.

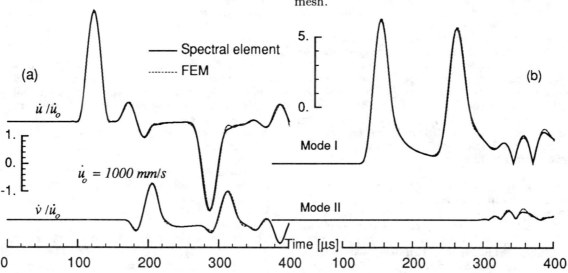

**Figure 2**: Waveguide with a crack. (a) Normalized velocity responses at the impact site, (b) normalized Mode I and Mode II stress intensity factors.

# EXPERIMENTAL MEASUREMENT OF WRINKLING
# IN PLANE ELASTIC SHEETS

C. H. Jenkins, W. H. Spicher, and A. Vedoy
Mechanical Engineering Department
South Dakota School of Mines and Technology
Rapid City, SD 57701

There are many plate and shell type structures that are adequately modeled as membrane structures, that is, structures whose resistance to bending is negligible. Although the real structure has finite bending rigidity, whether large or small, its consideration is not necessary for the desired prediction. Thus classical membrane models formally take plate and shell models and equate the bending rigidity to zero. Since such an activity still admits compressive membrane stress, the classical membrane model is limited in usefulness for modelling no-compression structures, such as pneumatic envelopes like balloons and parachutes. Other examples of important membrane behavior are nonlinear dynamics and contact.

An important point to be made above is that one must be careful to distinguish between structures that can be modeled as membranes, and those structures that are (or are nearly) true membranes. Structures made from very low modulus materials are essentially no-compression structures. Compressive stress (of sufficient magnitude to overcome any tensile prestress) will be mitigated by an out-of-plane deformation or localized buckling called 'wrinkling'. Analysis of wrinkling is important to the understanding and prediction of membrane structural response. Wrinkling, as a local instability, is a precursor to global instability. Other deleterious effects associated with wrinkling focus on snap loading and flutter behavior.

Analysis of wrinkling is largely based upon 'tension field theory' wherein it is assumed that under the action of a specific loading, one of the principal stresses goes to zero while the other remains nonnegative. If the nonnegative principal stress remains greater than zero, a 'tension field' exists. The crests and troughs of 'wrinkle waves' align with the direction of the nonzero principal stress. In tension field analysis, results are only in terms of average strains and displacements, while no detailed information is generated for each wrinkle. A membrane need not be wrinkled over its entire surface, which further complicates the analysis.

Little experimental work exists to verify wrinkle predictions, for at least two reasons. First, being so highly flexible, non-contact methods must be used, else what is to be measured is compromised during the measurement process. Second, the tension field model provides no wrinkle details other than direction and extent, and thus provides little motivation to pursue such data. However, new applications of membrane structures and associated predictive capabilities require greater knowledge of the wrinkle response [1].

In the present work use is made of a capacitance displacement sensor and conductive membrane to provide a three-dimensional mapping of a wrinkled membrane. The sensor is mounted in an x-y-z frame, and automatic data acquisition is incorporated (see Figure 1). Stepper motors provide controlled force application, the magnitude of which is measured by ring-type load cells. A control algorithm is used to provide constant force during data acquisition, for example, in cases where viscoelastic effects are present.

Current capabilities give both wrinkle direction and wavelength; amplitude can be determined if not too large. Figure 2 shows the surface topology of an initially plane membrane subjected to in-plane tension and shear. Future plans include measurement of wrinkle parameters on complex geometries.

Acknowledgements:
The authors wish to thank the National Science Foundation for their support of this research.

References:
[1] Jenkins, C.H., Spicher, W.H., Al-Najdawi, H., and Vedoy, A. (1996). "Wrinkle Prediction and Measurement in Planar Deformation of Elastic Sheets," *Int. J. Solids and Sturctures* (to be submitted).

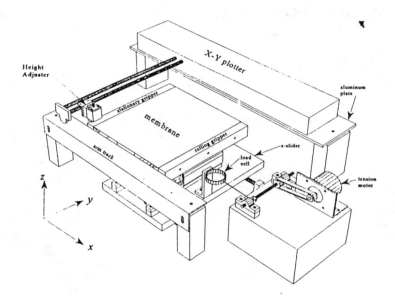

**Figure 1. Test apparatus.**

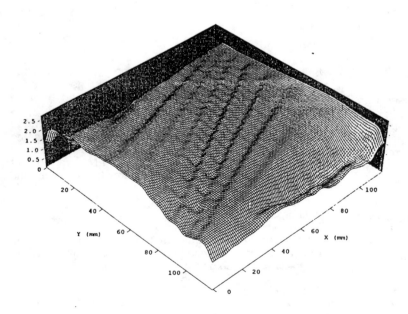

**Figure 2. Surface map of a wrinkled plane elastic sheet.**

83

# Evaluating Disbonds in Lattice/Skin Structures with Electronic Shearography

A. K. Maji* and D. Satpathi
*Air Force Phillips laboratory, Albuquerque, NM 87117-5776

Introduction :

Lattice (ribbed) structures attached to a skin (Figure 1) are being used in a number of space structures (Titan and Delta series) [1]. The future generation of these are being manufactured out of graphite/epoxy composites for a variety of applications such as solar cell substrate, rocket motor casing, payload shroud, etc. The principal mode of initial failure in these structures involve separation between the skin and the ribs, during fabrication or loading. The redundancy of these structures lead to alternate load paths that make it difficult to detect such defects.

Electronic shearography was used to detect disbonds in a rib/skin 'Isogrid' panel. This laser based interferometry technique provides fringe pattern that represents displacement gradients [2]. The ruggedness and portability of the system makes it a prime candidate for in-service inspection of large structures. The observed fringe pattern change dramatically for disbonded ribs and form a basis for detecting disbonds over a large area in one shot. The validity of the technique and the expected fringe pattern were also verified with a finite element analysis of a ribbed shell structure.

Test Set-up :

The ES system used involved a 35mw He-Ne laser, with associated optics. A Shearography camera (model SC4000) and control system (model CCU4000] were used [4]. Digital image processing was performed on a personal computer containing a frame grabber and the 'Imaster' image processing software. The system had a 1/4˚ shearing angle.

Two types of composite isogrid structures (discussed later) were tested : i) an intact square panel 46cm x 46 cm, and ii) a cylindrical structure, 50cm in height and 61cm in diameter. The bottom of the structures were set on a rigid table-top (with c-clamps for the panel and magnetic stands for the cylinder), and out-of-plane point load was applied to interrogate different locations of the structures.

Finite Element Analyses :

FEM Analyses were carried out on a Silicone Graphics workstation at the Air Force Phillips laboratory, NM. A commercially available finite element software, 'IDEAS' (4) ↘ was used because of its ability to incorporate orthotropic material model and its post-processing capabilities. Although a general orthotropic material has 9 independent elastic constants, the number decreases to 5 for transversely isotropic materials such as the graphite/epoxy composites used here. A two dimensional analysis was performed with linear beam elements to model the ribs (dark lines) and three-noded triangular shell elements to model the skin sections. The rib length between the nodes was 9.14 cm, as in the actual panel tested.

Properties of the rib in the fiber direction is different from those in the other two directions. However, for the [0/+60/-60]$_S$ lay-up of the skin, the skin is symmetric and isotropic in its plane while the out-of-plane direction has different properties, dominated by the matrix. Material properties were available from the manufacturer (ICI Fiberite, Tempe, AZ).

The post-processing capabilities of 'I-DEAS' was used to generate contour plots of dw/dx (rotation about the y-axis), since the shearography fringes are sensitive to the same quantity. These contour plots are therefore FEM predictions of shearography fringe pattern. The ribs were 1.27mm thick and 12.7mm high, and the skin was 0.51mm thick, as in the isogrids tested.

Inspection Results :

Figure 2 shows the triangular fringe pattern when the loading is immediately next to an intact rib. The fringes are confined entirely to that triangular pocket. When the load is applied at a disbonded rib, the displacement field spills over into the next triangular segment and the fringe pattern is symmetric about both x and y axes. The same number of fringes can be produced by a load of almost 10% of that of the previous case. The FEM predictions of the fringe pattern can be seen in Figures 3a (intact rib) and 3b (complete disbond).

Acknowledgment :

The shearography equipment was supported by the National Science Foundation Grant no. MSS 9212733. Dr. Maji was supported by the Air Force Phillips Lab.

References :

1. Rhodes M. and Mikulas M.M., "Composite Lattice Structures", NASA Technical Memorandum, TM X-72771, 1975.
2. Hung Y. Y. (1989) "Shearography : A Novel and Practical Approach for Nondestructive Inspection", J. of Nondestructive Evaluation, V 8, No. 2, pp. 55-67.
3. Newman J., "Shearographic Inspection of Aircraft Structure", Materials Evaluation, V49, No.9, 1991.
4. SDRC, "I-DEAS", Structural Dynamics Research Corporation, 2000 Eastman Dr., Milford, OH 45150, 1993.

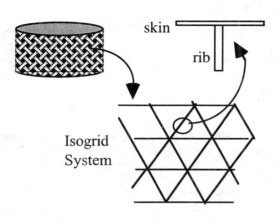

skin

rib

Isogrid
System

Figure 1. Rib-skin Structure (Schematic)

Figure 2. Shearography Fringe Pattern for Intact Rib

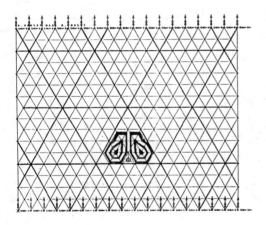

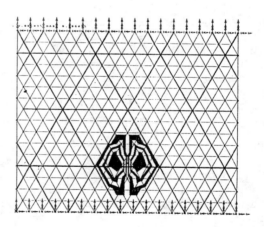

Figure 3a. FEM Predicted Fringe Pattern
(Intact Rib)

Figure 3a. FEM Predicted Fringe Pattern
(Totally Disbonded Rib)

# A Study on the Sound and Vibration Property of Korean Bell

S.H. Kim
Kangwon National University
Chuncheon, Kangwon Do, Korea

J.M.Lee and S.J.Lee
Seoul National University
Sinlim Dong, Kwanak Gu, Seoul, Korea

Vibration and sound property of Korean bell are introduced. Arizona memorial bell of Korean war is shown as the model. The influence of modal prameters and striking condition of the bell are theoretically and experimentally investigated on the simplified model and real bell to identify the vibration response, consequently, sound property. Experimental technique for beat control is proposed , in which the positions of nodal lines are properly shifted by grinding the inside of the bell. Finite element method and modal testing using loud speaker  are used to determine the proper grinding position and the amount. Through the structural modification, the bell comes to generate clear beat in sound.

The Korean bell consists of a main axisymmetric shell with decorative sculptures and carved figures on the surface as shown in Fig.1. Natural frequencies and modes dominate vibration and sound response and are basically determined by the shape and dimension of the main axisymmetric shell and lower thick band. Sculptures, carved figures and casting irregularities introduce slight asymmetry into the bell and beating sounds are generated, which are deemed to be unique and desirable[1]. Clear beat and proper beat frequency are important for the liveliness of the sound, while warble should be eliminated as much as possible in the Western bell[2]. Clear beat is obtained when the optimal striking position is impacted, which can be determined and changed by controling the asymmetry in the mass and stiffness of the shell structure. This property has been theoretically investigated by the authors, in reference[3].

It is difficult to predict vibration and sound property in the design stage. The characteristics of low frequency modes and their beat are analysed and designed by finite element method. Main body is modeled using plate or shell elements and surface carves modeled by increasing thickness or mass density[4]. Fig.2 shows the 1st and 2nd modes, each mode has frequency pair(H,L), which have very close values by slight asymmetry.

After casting, modal testing and grinding are performed to control beat. Table 1 presents natural frequencies and Fig.3 a) shows the 1st (4,0)-mode. Original Dangjwa locates near the antinode of L-mode, which would be strongly excited while H-mode weakly excited, therefore, the position of Dangjwa is not so good for clear beat. Proper position and amount  should be grinded step by step[5], based on the result of the numerical simulation. Grinding goes on until the center of H,L nodal lines moves to the original striking point(Dangjwa), i.e. Dangjwa comes to the optimal striking position for clear beat. Beat frequency is also tuned during the process. Fig.3 b) shows H,L nodal lines after grinding. Impacting Dangjwa will equally excite H,L modes and produce clear beat. Experimental set-up of Fig.4 is used to identify the position of nodal lines of the beat mode. Finally, clear beat is identified by hearing sound and by the measurement  shown in Fig.5.

References :

[1] Y.H.Yum,"A Study on the Korean bells", Research Report84-14, Research Institute of Korean Spirits and Culture,1984.

[2] T.Charnley and R.Perrin,"Studies with an Eccentric Bell", Journal of Sound and Vibration Vol.58(4), 1978, pp 517 -525.

[3] S.H.Kim, W.Soedel and J.M.Lee, "Analysis of the Beating Response of Bell Type Structures", Journal of Sound and Vibration, Vol.173(4), 1994, pp517-536.

[4] S.H.Cheon,J.M.Lee,Y.H.Yum and S.H.Kim,"A Study on the Vibration and Acoustic Characteristics of Korean bell", KSME Journal Vol.13(3),1989, pp397-403.

[5] Y.H.Yum, J.M.Lee, "Arizona Memorial Bell in Korean War",Korean Bell Research Report No.13, 1990, pp143-173.

Table 1 Natural frequency and mode of Arizona Bell.

| mode number | frequency[Hz] | mode |
|:---:|:---:|:---:|
| 1 | 155.0 | (4,0) |
| 2 | 377.5 | (6,0) |
| 3 | 497.5 | |
| 4 | 575.5 | |
| 5 | 742.5 | |
| 6 | 937.5 | |

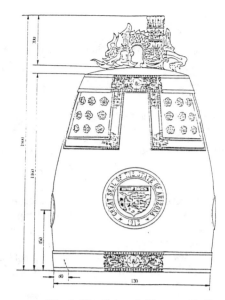

Fig.1 Traditional Korean Bell.

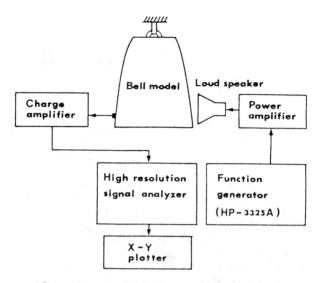

Fig.4 Experimental set-up for modal testing.

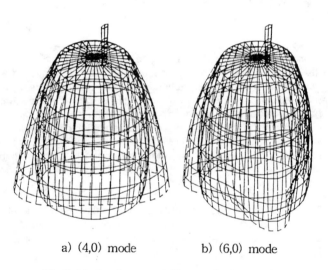

a) (4,0) mode          b) (6,0) mode

Fig.2 Mode shapes of Korean bell by FEM.

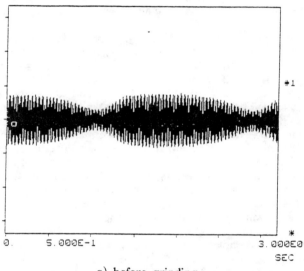

a) before grinding

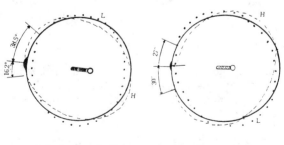

a) before grinding          b) after grinding

Fig.3 H,L mode shapes before and after grinding.

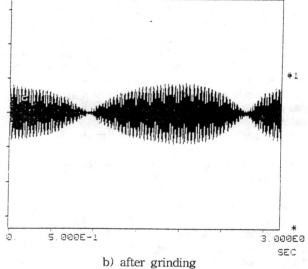

b) after grinding

Fig.5 Beat of (4,0) mode before and after grinding.

# Structural Testing of Externally Prestressed Concrete Beams

Prof. Angel C. Aparicio, Assist. Prof. Gonzalo Ramos and Assoc. Prof. Juan R. Casas
School of Civil Engineering
Technical University of Catalunya (UPC)
C/ Gran Capitan s/n - Modulo C1
08034 Barcelona - SPAIN

External prestressing is widely used in the United States of America and Europe for medium- and long-span bridges. The advantatges of this technique are well-known. However, the ultimate behavior of externally prestressed, monolithic, or segmental beams is not yet fully understood. For that reason, a research program was initiated at the Technical University of Catalunya, Barcelona, Spain (UPC). The program includes numerical studies [1], laboratory model tests, and parametric studies [2]. This paper deals with the laboratory model tests, focusing on the test procedure and the instrumentation used.

The laboratory test program on externally prestressed concrete beams has been developed at the Construction Engineering Laboratory of the UPC. This program includes 9 different box girder beams: 3 monolithic beams spanning 7.20 m, 3 segmental beams spanning 7.20 m and 3 monolithic continuous beams spanning 7.20 + 7.20 m. All these beams were prestressed only with external tendons. The aim of this program was to obtain the increment of stress of the tendons at ultimate and observe the influence of different parameters such as: type of construction (monolithical or segmental), amount of prestressing, slipping of the tendons at the deviators, load scheme and compare the results whit a numerical model of the beams . For the segmental beams, tests on shear capacity of the joints were also performed.

Different variables were measured, mainly forces, displacements and strains. Forces applied on the specimens were measured using load cells and digital pressure transducers. Displacements were measured using LVDTs, taking into account the deformability of the bearings and of the beam supports. The stresses of the tendons were measured with load cells at the anchorages and with strain gages at the strands. The strands were formed by 7 wires, and strain gages were welded at 3 wires at each measure point obtaining very similar values for each wire. Strain gages were also applied for measuring the strain of the concrete in compression and the stress of the reinforcing steel. Slipping of the tendons at the deviators and opening of joints were also obtained by LVDTs. The instrumentation scheme is shown in figure 1.

The instrumentation was connected to a personal computer which was storing all the data at each load step.

In order to improve the reliability of the results, almost every data was measured by two different ways. So, the load was measured through load cells and pression transducers; the prestressing steel stress through load cells and strain gages; and the concrete strain by strain gages on the concrete and on the reinforcing steel bars in compression.

Load cells, LVDTs and strain gages for steel were very reliable. On the other hand, strain gages for concrete (length = 90 mm) gave different results for gages in the same position. The values of concrete strains were sometimes unreasonable and different from the strain measured at reinforcing bars close to the concrete gages. Also some gages were broken due to cracking.

To obtain reliable values of concrete strains, we consider more efficient to measure the strain of reinforcing steel bars in compression. Mechanical devices could also be used, but then the data collection is not automatic, increasing the errors.

Three LVDTs were used to measure the deflection at midspan. From those deflections, it is easy to calculate the curvature of the midspan section by numerical methods. This method is useful when the maximum deflection occurs between the three LVDTs, as happened for the monolithic beams. On the other hand, joint opening was normally non symmetric producing a displacement of the maximun deflection point which sometimes was outside the three LVDTs. Open joints concentrate all the rotations, in failure, in segmental beams and instrumentation should be designed for both states, before and after joint opening.

The results were used to verify a numerical model previously developed for the analysis of monolithic and segmental externally prestressed beams [1]. Very good agreement was found between analysis and tests.

Structural testing is necessary to verify our everyday more sophisticated numerical models. Testing is also useful to identify new problems which cannot be detected with computer models.

## Acknowledgment

This paper is based on research sponsored by the Spanish Ministry of Science and Education (contract PB90 - 0612).

## References:

[1] Ramos, G., Aparicio, A.C., "Ultimate Analysis of Monolithic and Segmental Externally Prestressed Concrete Beams", ASCE Journal of Bridge Engineering, Vol. 1, No. 1, pp 10-18, February 1996.

[2] Aparicio, A.C., Ramos, G., "Flexural Strength of Externally Prestressed Concrete Bridges", accepted for publication in ACI Structural Journal.

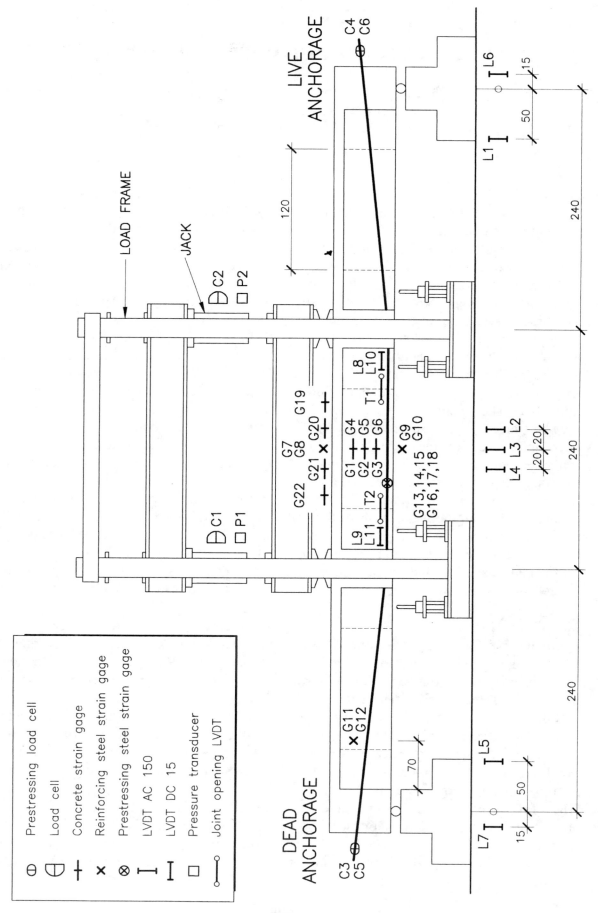

89

# IMPACT RESPONSE OF FOAMED COMPOSITES

Dahsin Liu, Zhenwen Wang, and Xinglai Dang
Dept. of Materials Science and Mechanics
Michigan State University, East Lansing, MI 48824

## INTRODUCTION

Owing to their high energy absorption capability, foamed materials have been widely used in industries for safety related designs. For example, they have been used in the automotive industry in reducing impact damage, improving occupants' safety, and establishing safety parameters. Car bumpers made of foamed materials are believed to be able to absorb impact energy up to a great percentage. Foamed materials have been used in almost every automobile interior component such as instrumentation panel, knee bolster, ceiling, etc. in reducing the peak force introduced to occupants during car collisions. Moreover, they have been used in anthropomorphic dummies such as Hybrid III dummy to resemble human muscles and organs for automotive crashworthiness analysis. The objective of the present study is to investigate the fundamental performance of foamed materials and their composites when subjected to low-velocity impact.

## MATERIALS

In the present study, polystyrene foam, vinyl, and their composites are of primary concerns due to their frequent applications in automotive safety design and analysis. In addition, the foamed composites are constrained around edges and subjected to both dried and wet (saturated with water) conditions to further explore the feasibility of optimizing the energy absorption capability. The following notations are given to individual material combinations: F (2" polystyrene foam), V (0.25" vinyl block), Fv (2" foam bonded with 0.1" vinyl skins on both top and bottom surfaces), F+V (0.25" vinyl block is put above or beneath the foam), Fv+V (combination of Fv and V), CFv (the edges of Fv are enveloped with a piece of tape), FvW (Fv is saturated with water), CFvW (the edges of water saturated Fv are enveloped by a piece of tape).

## IMPACT TESTING

The impact testing is performed with use of a DYNATUP impact testing machine. In order to accommodate specimens with dimensions of 2" by 2" and to characterize material response, an axisymmetrically cylindrical impactor is designed. As shown in Fig. 1, the aluminum impactor has a diameter of 3" and a flat surface. The total weight of the impactor and its holder is 14 lb. In addition, the force transducer is rearranged and placed beneath the specimen holder as shown in the diagram. As a consequence, specimens are required to be carefully aligned with the impacting axis to avoid introducing any bending to the transducer. In this study, three levels of impact velocity are examined. They are around 7 ft/s. 9 ft/s, and 10.3 ft/s. In view of the viscoelastic properties of polystyrene foam and vinyl, a waiting period of at least 24 hours is set for testing same specimen subsequently. The peak force, contact duration, and absorbing energy are of primary concern in this study.

## EXPERIMENTAL RESULTS

Typical experimental results for force-time history and force-deflection relation are shown in Fig. 2 for a Fv+V specimen subjected to a 9 ft/s impact. The energy absorbed by the foamed composites can be calculated by integrating the area enveloped by the force-deflection curve. Experimental results reveal that the higher the impact velocity, the higher the peak force for all types of materials. With the same impact velocity, vinyl introduces much higher peak force but shorter duration time than the foamed material. This result is believed to be attributed to the higher compaction (density) of vinyl when compared to the foamed material. The high peak forces and low duration times in vinyl can be greatly changed, to the levels of foamed materials, by simply placing the vinyl above or below the foamed material. In addition, the peak force in the foam/vinyl composite can be raised slightly by saturating the foam with water. In fact, the initial force-time relation also becomes more rigid.

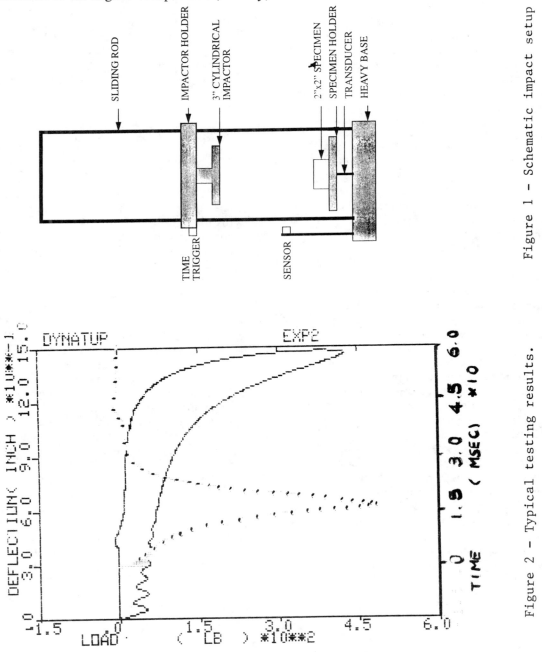

Figure 1 - Schematic impact setup

Figure 2 - Typical testing results.

# The Effects of Hail Damage on the Fatigue Strength of a Graphite/Epoxy Composite Laminate

Richard A. Skordahl (Graduate Student) & Mohammad Mahinfalah (Associate Professor)
Department of Mechanical Engineering And Applied Mechanics
North Dakota State University
Dolve 111
Fargo, ND 58105

Certain fiber reinforced composite structures can be subjected to foreign object impact loading due to hail, tool drops, etc., throughout their service lives. These same structures can be subjected to cyclic loading during portions of their service lives. Therefore, it is imperative that designers be aware of the effects that foreign object impact damage can have on the fatigue performance of fiber reinforced composites.

A number of researchers have documented the post-impact compression behavior of fiber reinforced composites, but very few investigators have looked into post-impact fatigue. Those studies that have looked into post-impact fatigue behavior have limited the impact event to a constant diameter impactor [1-3]. Therefore, an investigation into the effects of different sized impactors on the fatigue strength of a composite laminate has been undertaken at North Dakota State University. Particularly, the effects of hail impact damage on the fatigue strength of a laminate will be investigated.

## MATERIAL SELECTION AND SPECIMEN DESIGN
Since graphite/epoxy is becoming increasingly more popular as an engineering material, a graphite/epoxy material system was chosen for this investigation. The material that will be used for this research is a graphite/epoxy pre-preg donated by Hexcel (Hexcel TSR17/F-515). This material system contains Toray intermediate modulus fibers (E=290 GPa) and Hexcel industrial grade epoxy resin with a 121 °C cure temperature.

The layup chosen for study was a quasi-isotropic stacking sequence given by $[45,0,-45,90]_{2s}$. This layup was chosen because it is the layup most commonly called for in compression-after-impact tests specified by NASA [4].

Although this project involves post-impact fatigue, using this stacking sequence will allow for comparison of the damage imposed by the impact event with the damage that has been documented as part of previous post-impact compression studies.

Each specimen will be impacted with either a 12.7, 25.4, or a 38.1 mm ice-ball to simulate hail impact. The specimen that will be impacted will be rectangular with overall dimensions of 254 mm by 76.2 mm. Although previous work by Husman, Whitney, and Halpin [5] suggests that a ratio of specimen width to projectile diameter of at least 6 may be required to simulate infinite plate conditions, future investigations into the effects of hail-damage will consider the effects of edge conditions and specimen width.

## EXPERIMENTAL
To simulate the hail impact event, a compressed air gun has been designed that will propel ice-balls of the previously mentioned sizes at rigidly clamped specimens. The velocity that will be used for each diameter of ice-ball will be representative of the same diameter hailstone impacting during a hailstorm at ground level. This velocity will include components due to the terminal velocity of the hailstone combined with a 36.6 m/sec component due to wind. Table 1 shows the velocities and resulting kinetic energy at impact that will be used for each diameter of hailstone.

Table 1
Hail Velocities and Impact Energy

| Diameter (mm) | Terminal Vel. (m/s) | Resultant Vel. (m/s) | Impact Energy (J) |
|---|---|---|---|
| 12.7 | 15.88 | 39.95 | .77 |
| 25.4 | 22.47 | 43.00 | 7.13 |
| 38.1 | 27.52 | 45.83 | 27.38 |

After being impacted, some specimens will be non-destructively evaluated to determine the extent of internal damage caused by hailstone impact.

Once the specimen has been impacted, it will be loaded either in tension-tension fatigue using an MTS servo-hydraulic testing machine, or loaded in tension-compression fatigue via a 4-point bending apparatus that has been designed. The tension-tension fatigue tests will be run with a stress amplitude ratio of 10 ($\sigma_{max}/\sigma_{min}=10$) and a frequency of 20 Hz. The stress amplitude ratio and the frequency of test must still be determined for the four-point bending tension-compression test. S-N curves will be generated for each diameter of hailstone to determine if hail impact causes enough damage to decrease the fatigue strength of this particular laminate.

The same compressed air gun will also be used to propel 12.7 mm aluminum spheres at additional coupons. These aluminum projectiles will be propelled at velocities yielding the same kinetic energy possessed by the various sizes of ice-balls. These coupons will also be cyclically loaded and S-N curves generated for each impact energy of the 12.7 mm aluminum projectile. The curves generated from the aluminum impacts will be compared to those generated from ice-ball impact. This will allow for comparison of the reduction in fatigue strength, if any, for the two types of impact events at a given impact energy.

RESULTS

Currently, material characterization testing has been completed, and impact tests with 25.4 mm ice-balls have begun. Impact testing will continue until mid April, and fatigue testing will be completed by the end of May. Complete results will be ready for publication at that time. Any inquiries regarding the results of this investigation can be directed to the authors at the above address.

REFERENCES

1. Avva, V. S., *Fatigue-Impact Studies in Laminated Composites-Final Report, 10 Sep. 1980-31 Dec. 1982.* AFWAL-TR-83-3060, Air Force Wright Aeronautical Labs, Wright Patterson Air Force Base, 1983.

2. Walter, R. W., et al., **"Designing for Integrity in Long-Life Composite Aircraft Structures,"** *Fatigue of Filametary Composite Materials, ASTM STP 636,* K. L. Reifsnider and K. N. Lauraitis, Eds., American Society for Testing and Materials, 1977, pp. 228-247.

3. Cantwell, W., et al., **"Post-Impact Fatigue Performance of Carbon Fibre Laminates with Non-Woven and Mixed-Woven Layers,"** *Composites,* Volume 14, No. 3, July, 1983, pp. 301-305.

4. Cano, Robert J. and Dow, Marvin B., **"Evaluation of the Mechanical Properties and Damage Tolerance of Five New Toughened Matrix Composite Materials."** *Materials Working for You in the 21st Century: 37th International SAMPE Symposium and Exhibition.* Society for the Advancement of Material and Process Engineering, 1992, pp. 1312-1324.

5. Husman, G. E., Whitney, J. M., and Halpin, J. C. **"Residual Strength Characterization of Laminated Composites Subjected to Impact Loading,"** *Foreign Object Impact Damage to Composites, ASTM STP 568,* American Society for Testing and Materials, 1975, pp. 92-113.

# Influence of Notches within Fibre Reinforced Materials under Impact Loads

Prof. Dr.-Ing. Dieter H. Müller, Dipl.-Ing. Thomas Franz, Dr.-Ing. Andreas Tenzler
Bremer Institut für Konstruktionstechnik (BIK), Universität Bremen, FB4
Badgasteiner Straße 1 (FZB)
28359 Bremen, Germany

Because of high specific stiffness and strength the use of FRM can realise a reduction in weight and kinetic energy, especially in high accelerated and/or moved components. But high velocity often leads to a higher danger of impact. The analysis of related impact stresses is complicated by the complexity of the material and the load. Furthermore a related stress increase at critical shape elements like notches or holes causes problems in dimensioning (the stress as regards the strength of the material is called here related stress).

The numerical description of these high dynamic related stresses is restricted by their complexity. Especially at critical profile variations numerical simulation does not lead to accurate results. Therefore at the Bremer Institut für Konstruktionstechnik the photoelastic coating technique as a field measuring method is used for analysing of high dynamic related stresses. A new photo technique combined with digital image processing has been developed. This technique enables the registration of extremely fast related stress variations and the automatic processing of isochromatic images.

For these investigations disc-specimens composed of unidirectional glass-fibre reinforced plastic have been used. The specimens are notched by a hole and bonded with a photoelastic coating. The fibre orientation related to the loading direction varies. Specimens are loaded with an impact at one end into a pneumatic loading device. The impact characteristics impact force, impact duration and impulse can be varied and controlled. This method enables simulation of a wide spectrum of impact situations. The loading device developed for this creates a point impact excitation by a pneumatic driven steel projectile. The specimen is, in mechanical sense fixed free-free, in order to avoid any influence on the wave propagation within specimen.

The photoelastic coating technique (PCT) has proved to be a good field measuring technique by a lot of complex applications [1]. As the PCT is used as single-flash-technique for each impact an image with an exposure time of 0,5 $\mu$s is taken. The delay of the exposure time after the impact loading can be chosen in steps of 1 $\mu$s. The wave propagation within the specimen is depicted by coloured isochromatic fringe images by the use of white light. These images are recorded by a CCD-camera. The image information are direct transferred to a digital image processing [2].

Taking into consideration the stiffening of the specimen by the bonded photoelastic coating, the stress concentration at the notch contour can be calculated from the photoelastic measured isochromatic order with equation (1) [3]:

$$\sigma_1(\theta) = \frac{N \cdot K \cdot K_{xy}}{(1 + \nu_{xy}) \cdot \sqrt{(S'_{11} - S'_{12})^2 + S'^2_{16}(\theta)}} \tag{1}$$

$\sigma_1$ : Principal maximum stress in the notch or hole

N : Fringe order

K : Constant factor of photoelasticity

$S'_{11}, S'_{22}, S'_{66}$: Material characteristics depending on Young's modulus and Shear modulus

$\theta$ : Angle between reinforcement direction and principal max. stress direction

Figure 1 (a) and (b) show the calculated stresses at the notch contour. By a fibre orientation of 0° a symmetrical state of stresses is produced. The influence of the fibres is visible through the asymmetrical state of the stresses by fibre orientation of 45°.

For anisotropic materials the description of the related-stress state in terms of stress is not generally accepted because the relationship between the allowed stress (strength) and related stress valid for isotropic materials does not exist. For FRM stresses are transformed to related stresses by an idealised failure criterion [4]. The related stress $B_\sigma$ can be calculated by equation (2). The material parameters needed for this failure criterion are determined experimentally.

$$\begin{Vmatrix} F_1 \\ F_2 \\ 0 \end{Vmatrix} \cdot \begin{Vmatrix} F_{11} & F_{12} & 0 \\ F_{12} & F_{22} & 0 \\ 0 & 0 & F_{66} \end{Vmatrix} \cdot \begin{Vmatrix} \sigma_L \\ \sigma_T \\ \tau_{LT} \end{Vmatrix} \cdot \begin{Vmatrix} \sigma_L \\ \sigma_T \\ \tau_{LT} \end{Vmatrix} = B_\sigma \tag{2}$$

$$F_1 = \frac{1}{\sigma_{LZ}} + \frac{1}{\sigma_{LD}} \qquad F_{11} = -\frac{1}{\sigma_{LZ} \cdot \sigma_{LD}}$$

$$F_{12} = \frac{2}{\sigma_{45°Z}^2} \cdot \left[ 1 - \frac{\sigma_{45°Z}}{2 \cdot (F_1 + F_2)} - \frac{\sigma_{45°Z}^2}{4 \cdot (F_{11} + F_{22} + F_{66})} \right]$$

$$F_2 = \frac{1}{\sigma_{TZ}} + \frac{1}{\sigma_{TD}} \qquad F_{22} = -\frac{1}{\sigma_{TZ} \cdot \sigma_{TD}}$$

$$F_{66} = \frac{1}{\tau_B^2}$$

$$\sigma_L = \sigma_1(\theta) \cdot \sin^2(\varphi)$$
$$\sigma_T = \sigma_1(\theta) \cdot \cos^2(\varphi)$$
$$\tau_{LT} = \sigma_1(\theta) \cdot \cos^2(\varphi) \cdot \sin^2(\varphi)$$

$B_\sigma$ : related stress

$\sigma_{L,T}$ : stress in/perpendicular to the reinforcement direction

$\tau_{LT}$ : shear stress within the co-ordinates L and T

Figure 1 (c) and (d) show the related stresses calculated from the notch stress. The influence of the fibre direction on the related stress along the notch can be recognised by comparing fig. 1 (a), (b) with fig. 1 (c), (d). Notch stresses in fibre direction lead to a very low related material stress.

For example this can be seen on the specimen with fibre direction 0° at the co-ordinates 90° and 270°. For the existence of maximum related stress dependent on of the fibre directions 0° and 45° a general statement is not possible. At the fibre direction 0° the material is stressed to its maximum by notch stresses in the directions 0° and 180° (perpendicular to the fibre direction). On the specimen with fibre direction 45° the areas perpendicular to the fibre direction are almost stress-free. The maximum related stress exists in the directions 90° and 270° (approximate 45° to the reinforcement direction).

References

[1] Tenzler, A.; Bischof, Th.; Wulf, A.: Interdisziplinäre Kooperation führt zu neuen Erkenntnissen auf dem Gebiet impactbeanspruchter Faserverbundbauteile. VDI-Bericht 1021. Düsseldorf: VDI Verlag, 1993.
[2] Müller, D. H.; Tenzler, A.: Rechnergestütztes Verfahren zur Bestimmung farbiger Isochromatenordnungen in der Spannungsoptik. Vision & Voice Magazine Vol. 7 , No. 1, pp. 34-38, 1993.
[3] Hufenbach, W.; Schäfer, M.; Herrmann, A. S.: Photoelastische Dehnungsmessung und Spannungsverteilung an faserverstärkten Bauteilen. Kunststoffe. München: Carl Hanser Verlag, 1991.
[4] Moser, K.: Faser-Kunststoff-Verbund. Düsseldorf: VDI Verlag, 1992.

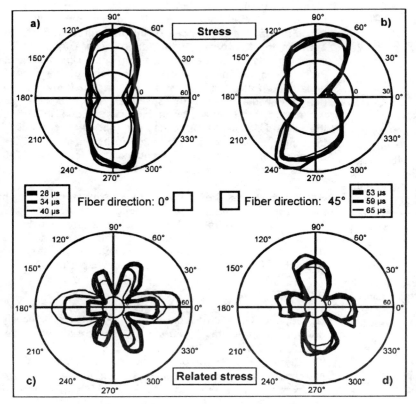

Fig. 1: a, b: Stresses along the hole (values in MPa);

c, d: Related stresses along the hole (values in %)

# Experimental Investigation of the Effect of Flexural-Torsional Coupling on Vibrational Characteristics of Angle-Ply Laminates

Takenori Maeda, Vijayan Baburaj, Tatsuzo Koga
University of Tsukuba
Institute of Engineering Mechanics
Tsukuba, Ibaraki, 305, Japan

This paper mainly presents an experimental study of considering the effect of flexural-torsional coupling stiffnesses on the vibrational characteristics of angle-ply laminates. It consists of a resonance test on a cantilevered laminated plate by using laser holographic interferometry. The accuracy of this experimental study has also been verified by finite element method (FEM) results obtained.

Symmetrically stacked angle-ply laminates, in general, exhibit the flexural-torsional coupling. This coupling effect of the angle-ply laminated composite structures yields undesirable mechanical behaviors. However, according to the classical lamination theory, it can be proved theoretically that both inplane-flexural and flexural-torsional coupling stiffnesses in the constitutive matrix of an angle-ply laminate could be made exactly zero. This requires a special stacking sequence of laminate namely a symmetric-antisymmetric configuration about the middle surface of the plate symbolically expressed as

$$[(A)/(-A)] \tag{1}$$

where

$$(A) = (+\theta/-\theta/-\theta/+\theta) \quad and \quad (-A) = (-\theta/+\theta/+\theta/-\theta)$$

It is consisting of a minimum of eight plies of equal thickness each [1]. On the other hand, if we fabricate a symmetric laminate which has a composition of

$$[(A)/(A)], \tag{2}$$

the out-of-plane flexural-torsional coupling terms, $D_{16}$ and $D_{26}$ remain whereas all other stiffnesses are equal to the values of the special symmetric-antisymmetric angle-ply laminate. Therefore, by comparing the vibrational characteristics of these two types of laminates, we can examine exactly the influence of the flexural-torsional coupling stiffnesses on the laminated plate structures. In addition to that, by examining the fringe patterns of the holography, we can experimentally verify that the [(A)/-(A)] laminate has no coupling terms.

For the [(A)/(A)] laminates, the magnitude of coupling stiffnesses can be changed by the stacking sequence. For example, unidirectional laminates of which fiber orientation are off-axis have the maximum values of flexural-torsional coupling, and this case has been examined by Clary.[2] Whereas the stacking sequence considered here has the minimum values for $D_{16}$ and $D_{26}$ and the laminate is assumed to consist of eight equal thickness plies.

Carbon/epoxy laminated plates having seven different fiber orientations were fabricated and test specimens with a width of 30 mm and an average thickness of 2.09 mm were made out of this. In experiment, the test specimen is clamped firmly between two steel plates and acoustically excited. Since we can observe the transition of the vibrational mode owing to the real-time method of the holography using the thermoplastic plates, when the number of the fringes are maximum, we regard the input frequency of the exciter as the natural frequency of the specimen. Moreover, by adopting the time-average method using the dry plates, which is more sensitive than the thermoplastic plates, the micro-ordered out-of-plane deflection of the plate can be clearly recorded over the whole plate without any contact with the plate model.

The fringe patterns of second flexural mode for the [(A)/(-A)] laminates are shown in Figure 1, in which all fringe patterns are almost symmetrical against the middle chord line. Therefore, it is known visually that the values of the coupling stiffnesses become zero. As shown in Figure 2, the fringe patterns of the [(A)/(A)] laminates are affected by the coupling stiffnesses. It is found that this coupling effects are more significant in the case of symmetric $\theta = 15°$ and $\theta = 30°$ laminates.

In figure 3, the measured frequencies of the first three modes are plotted comparing with the theoretical values. It is found that the differences of the measured frequencies between the two types of the laminates are found to be insignificant so as to the case of theoretical estimation also. Figure 4 shows the variation of the slope of the second nodal line from the chordwise axis against the aspect (length-to-width) ratio of the specimen. For reference, the variation of the frequencies of the first torsional (1-1) and the second flexural (2-0) modes are plotted. The effect of the coupling stiffnesses is expected to be maximum at the degeneration point where the frequencies of the 1-0 and 2-0 modes are equal to each other.

Results show that the effect of the coupling stiffnesses on the resonance frequencies is negligible. However, it is found that the vibrational mode shapes are apparently affected by the torsional coupling stiffnesses, and the degree of this effect is toward to depend on both the fiber orientation and the aspect ratio of the test specimen.

References:

[1] Caprino G. and Visconti I.C., " A note on specially orthotropic laminates," *Journal of Composite Materials*, Vol.16, 1982, pp. 395-399.
[2] Clary R. R., " Vibration characteristics of unidirectional filamentary composite material panels," *Composite Materials: Testing and Design,* ASTM STP 497, American Society for Testing and Materials 1972, pp. 415-438.

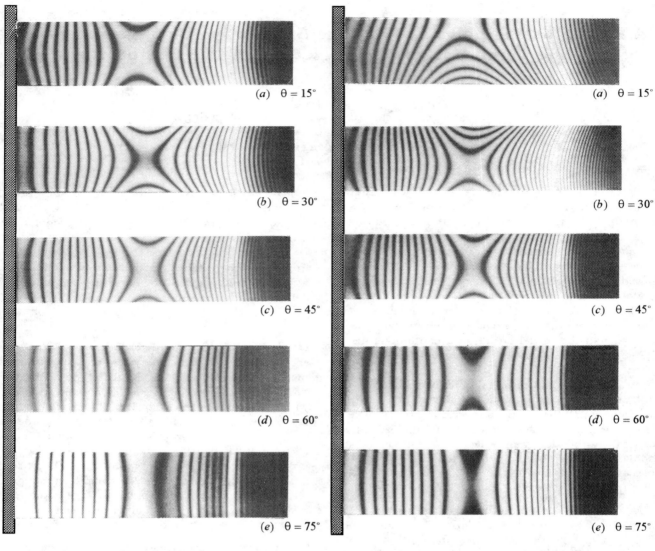

Figure 1 Fringe patterns of second flexural mode for [(A)/(-A)] laminates. (Aspect ratio = 4)

Figure 2 Fringe patterns of second flexural mode for [(A)/(A)] laminates. (Aspect ratio = 4)

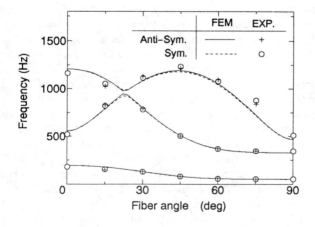

Figure 3 Comparison of frequencies for first three modes. ( Aspect ratio = 4)

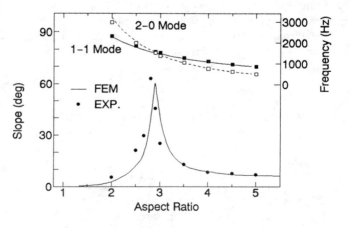

Figure 4 Slope variation of second flexural nodal line. (Symmetric $\theta = 30°$ laminate)

# A Probabilistic Analysis of Fatigue Cumulative Damage and Fatigue Life Using Markov Chain Model in CFRP Composites

Jung-Kyu Kim and Dosik Kim
Department of Mechanical Design and Production Engineering
Hanyang University
17 Haengdang-Dong Sungdong-Ku
Seoul 133-791, Korea

Fatigue of composite materials is a process that is stochastic in nature. An assessment of the safety and reliability of composite structure under fatigue loading therefore requires statistical considerations to account for the variability of damage accumulation process and fatigue life. Bogdanoff et al.[1] have proposed Markov chain(M.C.) model based on the discrete-state and discrete-time Markov process. This model has provided information on entire process of damage accumulation and is computationally easier to use than the model based on a continuous distribution function. However, M.C. model has been applied to investigate the variability of fatigue crack propagation process in metal only. In this study, the fatigue damage accumulation behavior in 8-harness satin woven CFRP composites with a circular hole is examined by changes in residual stiffness under constant amplitude fatigue loading. To describe and analyze the variability of the damage accumulation process and the fatigue life, M.C. model is used and discussed.

Bogdanoff et al. define that the damage state is $j=1,2,...,b$ where state $b$ denotes failure and a duty cycle (DC) is a repetitive period of operation in the life of a component. The state of damage is considered only at the end of each DC. The damage state can only increase by one unit at a time. Such a Markov process is completely described by its probability transition matrix $\mathbf{P}$ $(b \times b)$ and the initial probability distribution of the damage states $\mathbf{p_o}$ $(1 \times b)$. The probability of being in damage state $j$ at time $x$ $(x=0,1,2,....)$ $\mathbf{p_x}$ is then given by Eq.(1).

$$\mathbf{p}_x = \mathbf{p}_o \, \mathbf{P}^x \tag{1}$$

where $\mathbf{P}$ is constructed by the probability of failure $s_j$ and the probability of success $t_j$ in geometric distribution that are calculated from mean and variation of the fatigue life.

The straight-sided specimen(150mm long×20mm wide, 2.2mm thick) with a circular hole($2r$=4mm) of 8-harness satin woven CFRP composites($v_f$=60%) is used. Fatigue tests are performed at a loading frequency of 10Hz, a stress ratio of $R$=0.05 and a ratio of applied stress to ultimate strength $q$ $(\sigma_{max}/(\sigma_{ult.})_{ave.})$ = 0.87 and 0.91. The secant modulus during fatigue life is monitored by extensometer at predetermined number of cycles.

In order to quantitatively estimate the fatigue damage accumulation behavior, the cumulative damage $D^*$ is defined as a function of secant modulus.

$$D^* = (E_o - E_{sn}) / (E_o - E_{sf}) \tag{2}$$

where $E_o$ is elastic modulus at the first cycle, $E_{sn}$ is secant modulus after $n$ cycles and $E_{sf}$ is secant modulus at fatigue failure. Figure 1 shows the variations of cumulative damage $D^*$ calculated from Eq.(2) with number of cycles for $q$=0.87. In this figure, damage curves show considerable intermingling and randomness. Therefore, in this study, the fatigue damage accumulation behavior should be described in a probabilistic manner. Changes of normalized secant modulus with number of cycles are shown in Figure 2 for $q$=0.87 and 0.91. The changes take place in two distinct stages, and the transition between stage I and II occurs between 25 and 30% of fatigue life.

To analyze the probability distribution of the test results, at first the parameters in M.C. model Eq.(1) should be estimated. The transition probability and the state number calculated from the test data are summarized in Table 1. In this Table, the damage state is divided into two stages at each $q$ because of the two-stage nature of stiffness degradation as shown in Figure 2. To examine whether M.C. model is suitable for the analysis of damage accumulation process in composites or not, the predictions of Eq. (1) with parameters in Table 1 are compared with the test data. Figure 3 shows the distribution function of DC at a specified cumulative damage $D^*$. The distribution function of which the cumulative damage $D^*$ in specimen exists in damage state $D_n^*$ after $n$ cycles is shown in Figure 4. In these Figures, a good agreement is found between the predictions of Eq.(1) and the test data. To examine the accuracy in fatigue life prediction of M.C. model, the predictions of Eq.(1) and the 2-parameter Weibull distribution are shown in Figure 5. The predicted distribution of M.C. model is similar to that of 2-parameter Weibull distribution function with Table 1 in predictive accuracy. Also, in CFRP laminates [0/45/90/-45]$_{2s}$ (2), the distribution functions of fatigue life obtained from Eq.(1) and the 2-parameter Weibull distribution function with Table 2 are shown in Figure 6. The predictions both show a good agreement with the test data. Therefore, M.C. model is suitable for the probabilistic analysis of fatigue cumulative damage and fatigue life in material used here and taken from [2].

Acknowledgement

This study was supported by the Korea Science and Engineering Foundation(KOSEF) under Grant No. 941-1000-011-2 , which is gratefully acknowledged.

References :

[1] Bogdanoff, J.L., "A New Cumulative Damage Model, Part 1," Transactions of ASME, Vol. 45, pp. 246-250, 1978.

[2] Shim, B.S., Sung, N.Y., Ong, J.W., "The Analysis of the Fatigue Life Using the Residual Strength Degradation Model in Carbon/Epoxy Composites," Transactions of KSME, Vol. 15, No. 6, pp. 1908-1918, 1991.

Table 1 Parameters in M.C. model and 2-parameter Weibull distribution function

| state no. | q=0.87 | | q=0.91 | |
|---|---|---|---|---|
| | 5 | 7 | 4 | 4 |
| s | 0.9925 | 0.9959 | 0.9584 | 0.9844 |
| t | 0.0075 | 0.0041 | 0.0416 | 0.0156 |
| α (×10²) | 3.41 | | 2.46 | |
| β (×10⁴) | 2483.04 | | 369.09 | |

α : shape parameter
β : scale parameter

Table 2 Parameters in M.C. model and 2-parameter Weibull distribution function in Ref.[3]

| state no. | q=0.6375 | q=0.825 |
|---|---|---|
| | 7 | 6 |
| s | 0.9968 | 0.8361 |
| t | 0.0032 | 0.1639 |
| α (×10²) | 2.46 | 2.17 |
| β (×10⁴) | 2119.25 | 35.02 |

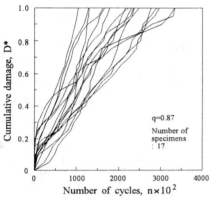

Fig. 1 Changes of cumulative damage with number of cycles

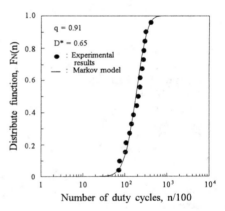

Fig. 2 Changes in secant modulus as a function of normalized life

Fig. 3 The predicted distribution of DC at a specified damage state using M.C. model

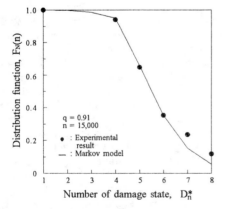

Fig. 4 The predicted distribution of damage state at a specified cycles using M.C. model

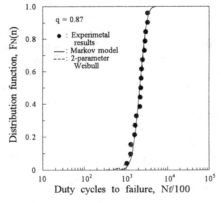

Fig. 5 The predicted distribution of fatigue life using M.C. model and 2-parameter Weibull distribution function

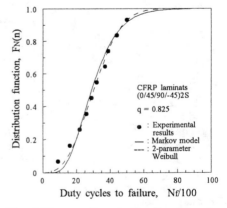

Fig. 6 The predicted distribution of fatigue life using M.C. model and 2-parameter Weibull distribution function [2]

# Net Shape Manufacturing and its Affects on the Impact Response of Fiber Reinforced Plastics

M. Ramulu and D. Arola
Department of Mechanical Engineering, MS 352600
University of Washington
Seattle, WA 98195
USA

The mechanical properties of Fiber Reinforced Plastics (FRP) and the methods employed to obtain net-shape component parts from these materials are important topics. Although considerable effort is placed on optimizing mechanical properties through refined primary processing, the effects of post-mold trimming are often ignored in light of other aspects of material performance. For instance, the impact strength and damage tolerance of FRPs is a critical performance concern. But despite the relevance of surface integrity to the dynamic response of monolithic materials, the affects of manufacturing and surface integrity to the performance of reinforced polymers have not been adequately addressed. Hence, the goal of this investigation was to determine the importance of machining and resulting component edge quality on the impact response of FRPs.

The three most common industrial methods of edge trimming were used in obtaining impact test specimens from a Graphite/Bismaleimide (Gr/Bmi) tape laminate composed of IM-6 fibers and BASF 5240-4 resin matrix. The stacking sequence of the laminate was $[0/45/90/-45]_{6s}$ which resulted in a laminate thickness of roughly 6 mm. An abrasive diamond saw (ADS) with #220 mesh garnet, Polycrystalline Diamond (PCD) orthogonal cutting tools, and the Abrasive Waterjet (AWJ) were utilized in obtaining over 150 specimens from the laminate, 30 each using the ADS and PCD cutters, and 30 each at three individual cutting conditions with the AWJ. The three AWJ parametric combinations AWJ "A", "B" and "C" incorporated the use of garnet with mesh sizes #50, #80, and #150 respectively; each of the three parametric combinations used with AWJ were chosen to provide different degrees of surface quality [1]. The surface roughness and overall integrity of the trimmed edges were evaluated using contact profilometry and scanning electron microscopy (SEM). Impact testing was conducted according to the geometric specifications of ASTM D790-m for three point bend loading with a 16 to 1 span to depth ratio. The impact specimens were oriented such that the trimmed edges were parallel to the plane of the applied load. The impact response of the Gr/Bmi laminate was investigated at 2.25 and 3.75 m/s drop weight impact velocities, both of which were conducted with the minimum energy to failure. To document the characteristics of the impact response, load and load-line displacements were recorded allowing the determination of the peak load, load at failure and energy absorbed throughout the failure process. In addition, high speed photography was also used to locate the initiation of failure and its progression on a ply to ply basis.

From a comparison of the surface roughness and scanning electron microscope analysis of the trimmed edges, it was found that the ADS provided the highest quality machined surface as expected due to the small abrasive garnet (#220). From a microscopic analysis the quality of the PCD trimmed edge was inferior to both the ADS and AWJ machined surfaces. Contrary to the trimmed surface resulting from the other two techniques, the constituents exhibited a low degree of interstitial integrity and significant degrees of matrix debonding along the circumference of the fibers. An example of the microscopic surface features from a -45° ply of the Gr/Bmi laminate trimmed with the PCD is shown in Figure 1. The difference in microscopic features and integrity of the machined surfaces obtained from each technique was not consistent with the surface roughness trends. Although micro features of the ADS and AWJ trimmed surfaces were very similar, the surface roughness of the AWJ specimens was at least an order of magnitude higher; the average roughness of the trimmed surface from each of the sample groups are listed in Table 1. The surface roughness of the PCD trimmed specimens was found to depend on both the ply orientation and measurement direction due to differences in removal mechanisms associated with the fiber orientation [2, 3]. However, the average surface roughness of the PCD specimens was still lower than that obtained from AWJ machining.

The load and load-line displacement records received from impact testing were used to indicate the peak load, fracture load, displacement at fracture and energy absorbed to fracture. An example of the dynamic failure history from an ADS specimen resulting from lower impact velocity (2.25 m/s) is show in Figure 2. The corresponding statistical average of the failure parameters for each trimming process resulting from low and high velocity impact are listed in Tables 1 and 2, respectively. Although the differences in peak load are minimal, the load, displacement and energy at fracture show significant process dependence. The ADS machined specimens exhibited the highest load and energy to fracture which is consistent with the qualitative observations of the surface features. However, the PCD trimmed specimens subjected to low velocity impact failed at a 23% lower impact load and absorbed 18% less energy to fracture than those obtained from the ADS. Furthermore, the presence of the process induced flaws of the PCD trimmed Gr/Bmi is readily apparent from the low standard deviation of the failure parameters. This behavior contrasts the correlation between surface roughness and impact response which is apparent from the other two methods of processing: lower surface roughness implicating higher impact load and energy absorbed to fracture. Similar characteristics are seen from the performance of the Gr/Bmi subjected to high velocity impact although the reduction in impact strength with respect to the ADS specimens is slightly different.

An examination of the failure initiation recorded with the high speed camera did not indicate an obvious trimming dependency. However, the progression of failure was indeed process dependent and appeared to be related to the extension of delamination perpendicular to the line impact load along the laminae. The poor microstructural integrity of the PCD specimens was detrimental to the impact response of the Gr/Bmi laminate. However, the surface roughness of the PCD trimmed edges failed to comply with the inferior impact response. There were no evident changes in interfacial ply/ply or fiber/matrix integrity with the three different AWJ machining conditions; the only difference between the three AWJ groups was the surface roughness. Hence, the reduction in impact strength with surface roughness of the AWJ machined specimens was attributed solely to the machined surface quality and its influence on the stress field near the free edge. Therefore, manufacturing effects are indeed important to the structural response of FRPs under dynamic loading and will be the

topic of our future work.

References:

1.    Ramulu, M. and Arola, D., "The Influence of Abrasive Waterjet Cutting Conditions on the Surface Quality of Graphite/Epoxy Laminates," IJMTM, Vol. 34, (3), pp. 295-313 .

2.    Wang, D. H., M. Ramulu and D. Arola, (1995), "Orthogonal Cutting Mechanisms of Graphite/Epoxy Composite. Part I: Unidirectional Laminate," Int. J. Mach. Tool & Manu., Vol. 35, (12), pp. 1623-1638.

3.    Wang, D. H., M. Ramulu and D. Arola, (1995), "Orthogonal Cutting Mechanisms of Graphite/Epoxy Composite. Part II: Multi-directional Laminate," Int. J. Mach. Tool & Manu., Vol. 35, (12), pp. 1639-1648.

Table 1  Surface Roughness and Impact Response of Gr/Bmi at Low Velocity Impact

| Method of Trimming | Surface Roughness (μm) | Peak Load (N) | Fracture Load (N) | Fracture Displacement (mm) | Energy at Failure (N•mm) |
|---|---|---|---|---|---|
| Abrasive Diamond Saw | 0.23±0.1 | 3062±58 | 2678±261 | 4.85±0.18 | 8101±522 |
| PCD Cutting Tools | 1.4±0.6 | 2892±69 | 2062±168 | 4.49±0.10 | 6672±192 |
| AWJ "A" | 5.43±0.4 | 2981±42 | 2406±223 | 4.57±0.30 | 7170±787 |
| AWJ "B" | 4.73±0.2 | 3020±53 | 2556±219 | 4.65±0.20 | 7493±532 |
| AWJ "C" | 1.8±0.1 | 3008±55 | 2659±161 | 4.81±0.15 | 7771±382 |

Table 2  Impact Response of Gr/Bmi at High Velocity Impact

| Method of Trimming | Peak Load (N) | Fracture Load (N) | Fracture Displacement (mm) | Energy at Failure (N•mm) |
|---|---|---|---|---|
| Abrasive Diamond Saw | 2633±31 | 2906±124 | 6.42±0.34 | 11951±941 |
| PCD Cutting Tools | 2529±42 | 2316±229 | 5.92±0.85 | 10853±563 |
| AWJ "A" | 2401±38 | 2531±185 | 5.40±0.44 | 9158±1032 |
| AWJ "B" | 2376±179 | 2617±160 | 5.28±0.42 | 9138±838 |
| AWJ "C" | 2450±66 | 2770±139 | 5.42±0.29 | 9358±519 |

Figure 1  -45° Ply of the PCD Trimmed Gr/Bmi

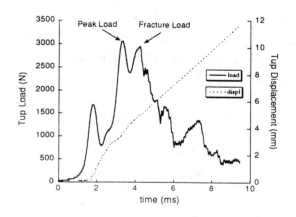

Figure 2  Dynamic Failure of an ADS Specimen

# Accelerated Durability of Continuous Fiber Polymer Composites

**S. E. Groves, S. J. DeTeresa, and M. A. Zocher**
Lawrence Livermore National Laboratory
P.O. Box 808, L-342
Livermore, California 94551
510-422-1331 & 510-422-2438 (fax)

The polymer composites group at the Lawrence Livermore National Laboratory is currently involved with the Boeing Commercial Airplane Group in a five year CRADA (cooperative research and development agreement). The goal of this project is to develop accelerated lifetime characterization methodologies for predicting and enhancing the strength and durability of advanced fiber composites used in high performance structural applications operating at temperatures up to 350°F. This project is part of one of the largest efforts ever to accelerate material characterization of fiber reinforced composites. For polymer composites, aging is accelerated by increasing the normal operational conditions (temperature, environments, loads). Paramount to the success of this effort is the necessity to develop and establish the required techniques to generate, monitor, and verify that our acceleration methods (mechanical, chemical, physical) do not introduce artificial aging mechanisms. From this, one hopes to identify the various chemical and physical response signatures that track the required mechanical response parameters. Once these tracking signatures are identified, an acceleration recipe (Time-Temperature-Load-Environment) could be constructed and implemented on a material system for evaluation of its potential lifetime performance characteristics. Given the ability to experimentally accelerate aging, one would then be able to utilize this data to characterize the necessary parameters in an appropriate mechanical constitutive model (functionally dependent on thermal-viscoelastic-chemical-physical inputs) for predicting residual mechanical properties of the composite material. To accommodate such a material model, a three-dimensional thermo-viscoelastic orthotropic finite element code (ORTHO3D) has been developed with a local volume element homogenization scheme for analyzing and predicting the residual mechanical properties for structural analysis. This technology is generically essential to increasing our "confidence to design, analyze, and build long term primary and secondary composite structures."

# LONG TERM DURABILITY OF POLYESTER THERMOPLASTICS
## BASED ON LABORATORY AND AUTOMOTIVE FIELD STUDIES

A. Golovoy and J. L. Sullivan

Polycarbonate (PC) and polybutylene terephthalate (PBT), as well as blends of PC/PBT, tend to hydrolyze when exposed to high levels of humidity and temperatures. This paper will describe the results of laboratory test procedures for determining the kinetics of hydrolysis, and also compare and discuss the long-term durability of automotive bumpers made of PC/PBT blends, based on field data obtained from various parts of the country. The influence of hydrolysis on mechanical properties is presented and relationships between kinetic results and molecular structure are also presented. Results for both blends and pure PBT are included. Finally, the influence of stabilizers on exposed polymer are also demonstrated.

# Assessment of Durability and Damage of Adhesives in Pure Shear Using a Bonded Beam and Dynamic Mechanical Thermal Analysis

Hal F. Brinson
Department of Mechanical Engineering
and the
Composites Engineering and Applications Center
University of Houston, Houston, TX 77204-4792

Ray A. Dickie and Michael A. DeBolt
Ford Research Laboratory, Ford Motor Company,
Dearborn, MI 48121-2053

A requirement for the proper design of adhesively bonded joints is good information about mechanical properties. While adhesives can usually be tested in bulk like other polymers, it is recognized that adhesive bulk (or neat resin) constitutive properties may not be representative of those in the bonded state. Obviously, the adhesive/adherend interface or interphase has an effect on all bond properties but the effect on failure or rupture is especially significant. For this reason, many prefer to determine the properties of adhesives in the bonded state as results therefrom, of necessity, include information about the condition of the interface. Favorite testing geometry's include single, double or other lap specimen configurations. While such specimen are simple to make and test, stress distributions within the joint are quite complex and include both normal (peel) and shear stresses that vary form point to point. In fact, singular stresses exist at the reentrant corners, making any measure of strength virtually impossible. Discussions of these deficiencies can be found in references [1-3].

Because of multi-axial stress distributions in many standard adhesive test specimens, efforts in recent years have emphasized the development of specimen geometry's in which only a single pure shear stress state exists. Torsion of a two cylindrical tubes joined by a thin adhesive layer (napkin ring, ASTM E229-70) has been used to determine pure shear properties [1,3]. A cone and plate modification of this test which gives a near uniform shear stress in the bond was developed by Grant and Cooper [4]. A beam in four point bending to produce uniform shear forces over a portion of the beam was introduced by Iosipescu [5] and a uniquely shaped specimen to measure shear stress using an axial tension test machine was introduced by Arcan [6]. In these latter two tests the specimens are designed with notches and groves in such a way as to produce uniform shear over the bondline. The only measurements needed for shear modulus and shear strength determination are the applied load, the adhesive thickness and length, and the relative elongation of the adherends along the bondline. However, it is appropriate to note that elaborate fixtures are needed to insure proper loading and very precise notches (Iosipescu) and groves (Arcan) must be machined in the specimens. For this reason, these specimens are more often used for research investigations rather than the routine measurement of properties.

A new easy to make bonded double cantilever beam specimen was introduced by Moussiaux, Cardon and Brinson [7] and was shown to have a pure shear stress in the adhesive layer. One advantage of the specimen is that information on properties can be obtained from a standard three point bend test. Further, as shown by Dickie, et. al.[8,9], the specimen with modified boundary conditions can be used in a dynamic mechanical thermal analysis (DMTA) system to obtain viscoelastic shear properties of adhesive bonds under a variety of conditions of temperature or adhesive adherend/interface conditions.

The purpose of the present effort was to determine if DMTA testing of the bonded beam could give insight to damage resulting from internal flaws, moisture or corrosion. To this end a series of specimens were tested containing different size simulated flaws and various times of moisture or corrosion exposure. Storage modulus, loss modulus, damping ration and glass transition temperature were determined for various exposure conditions as a function of temperature. The results for variation of storage modulus, loss modulus, damping ratio and glass transition temperature with respect to flaw size at 25 º C are shown in Fig. 1. Obviously, the procedure does give information on the effect of flaw size. Other results (not shown) give similar indications for the effect of moisture and corrosion [10].

## References

1.  Anderson, G. P., Bennett, S. J. and DeVries, K. L., *Analysis and Testing of Adhesive Bonds*, Academic Press, NY, 1977.
2.  ASTM Standards, Standard Guide for Adhesive-Bonded Single Lap-Joint Specimen Test Results, *Adhesives*, Vol. 15.06, D 4896 - 89, p.418.
3.  Kinloch, A. J., Adhesion and Adhesives, Chapman and Hall, NY, 1987.
4.  Grant, J. W. and Cooper, J. N., Cone-and-plate shear stress adhesive test, VPI Report CAS/ESM-2, May 1986.
5.  Iosipescu, N., A new adhesive shear test, J. of Materials, 6, 371, 9172.
6.  Weissberg, V. and Arcan, M., "A Uniform Pure Shear Testing Specimen for Adhesive Characterization",

*Adhesively Bonded Joints: Testing Analysis, and Design*, STP 981, ASTM, 1988.

7. Moussiaux, E., Cardon, A. H. and Brinson, H. F., "Bending of a Bonded Beam as a Test Method for Adhesive Properties," *Mechanical Behavior of Adhesive Joints* (A. H. Cardon and G. Verchery, Ed.'s.), Euromech Colloquium 227, Pluralis, Paris, p. 1, August 1987. Also: Moussiaux, E., "Bending of a Bonded Beam as a Test Method for Adhesive Properties," M. S. Thesis Virginia Tech, June 1987.

8. Li, C., Dickie, R. A., and Moreman, K. N., "Dynamic Mechanical Response of Adhesively Bonded Beams: Effect of Environmental Exposure and Inter-facial

Properties", *Polymer Engineering and Science*, Feb. 1990, Vol. 30, No. 4, p. 249.

9. Moreman, K. N., Li, C., Zhang, F., Dickie, R. A., "Determination of the Complex Shear Modulus of Structural Adhesives Using a doubly Clamped Sandwich Beam", *Experimental Mechanics,* June 1992, p. 124.

10. Brinson, H. F., Dickie, R. A. and DeBolt, M. A., "Measurement of Adhesive Bond Properties Including Damage by Dynamic Mechanical Thermal Analysis of a Beam Specimen", J. of Adhesion, Jan. 1996.

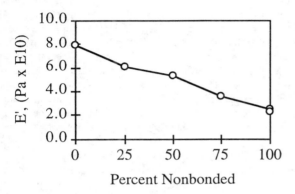

(a)  Storage Modulus, E'

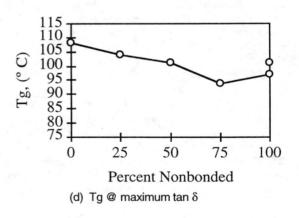

(b)  Loss Modulus, E" @ maximum tan δ

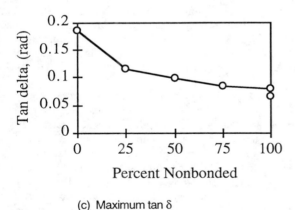

(c)  Maximum tan δ

(d)  Tg @ maximum tan δ

Fig. 1.    Variation of storage modulus, loss modulus, damping ratio and glass transition temperature @ $25\,^{\circ}C$ with simulated flaw size.

# The Durability of Glass-Fiber/Epoxy Composites Evaluated from Single-Fiber Fragmentation Tests and Full-Scale Composites Immersed in Water

Carl R. Schultheisz, Carol L. Schutte, Walter G. McDonough,
Kenneth S. Macturk, Mavyn McAuliffe, and Srikanth Kondagunta
Polymers Division, National Institute of Standards and Technology, Gaithersburg, Maryland, USA 20899

The durability of composite materials exposed to moisture is an important consideration for new uses of composites in automotive, infrastructure or oil production applications [1]. Single-fiber fragmentation tests of E-glass/epoxy model composites have shown degradation of both the strength of the fiber and the strength of the interface after immersion in water at 25 °C and 75 °C [2]. This work has expanded to investigate the durability of full-scale composite materials after immersion in water for comparison with the results from the fragmentation tests. One goal of this research is an assessment of the ability to predict composite structural properties from a small-scale test such as the single-fiber fragmentation test; of particular interest is the possibility that the smaller scale of the test coupled with full immersion and elevated temperatures can provide an accelerated test for composite structures subjected to longer exposure under less severe environmental conditions. Four different composite test methods have been chosen to emphasize different aspects of the problem: tensile tests of unidirectional layups should reflect the degradation of the fiber strength, tests in compression and in Mode I and Mode II delamination fracture should be more indicative of the degradation of the interface.

Specimens have been immersed in water at 25 °C and 75 °C with the thought that elevated temperatures should accelerate the absorption of water and any chemical processes that lead to degradation of fiber and interface. However, the elevated temperatures may affect different processes to different degrees, possibly leading to changes that would not be observed in the life of a structure at the temperature experienced in service. Thus, it is important to correlate results from testing at lower temperatures to results from elevated temperature conditions in order to evaluate the potential application of elevated temperatures for accelerated tests. For example, tests on the matrix indicate that immersion at 25 °C increases the fracture toughness considerably more than immersion at 75 °C [2], reflecting some apparent surface embrittlement at the higher temperature.

In addition to the temperature variation, E-glass fibers having two different coatings were employed: an epoxy-compatible coating (intended to provide a strong interface with the DGEBA/mPDA epoxy matrix [2]) and a vinylester-compatible coating (intended to provide a weaker interface with the epoxy matrix). The different coatings were used in an effort to systematically vary the initial value and rate of change of the interfacial strength. Also, it was expected that the different coatings might provide different levels of protection for the fiber, affecting the rate of fiber degradation.

In the single-fiber fragmentation test [2,3], an epoxy coupon containing a single fiber is loaded in tension, also loading the fiber in tension through shear transfer across the interface. With increasing load, the fiber fractures into smaller fragments until they reach a *critical length* for which the shear transfer across the interface is insufficient to load any of the remaining fragments beyond their tensile strength. The resulting fragment length distribution is then used to calculate the interfacial shear strength from the tensile strength of the fiber [2,3,4]. Water is expected to decrease the interfacial shear strength, resulting in longer fragments. However, water also attacks the glass fibers themselves [5,6], leading to lower tensile strengths, resulting in shorter fragment lengths. Thus, the degradation of the fiber and the interface compete to affect the fiber fragment distribution. A model of Wagner and coworkers [7] was used to determine the strength of both the fiber and the interface from the same test.

Results from the single-fiber fragmentation testing are shown in Figures 1, 2 and 3. The degradation of the E-glass fibers is displayed in Figure 1, which plots the strength at the critical length as a function of the time of immersion. The two fiber coatings lead to similar rates of degradation of the E-glass. The interfacial shear strengths estimated using the model of Kelly and Tyson [4] are shown in Figures 2 and 3 for the two types of fiber coating. The epoxy-compatible coating does provide a slightly better interface, but both coatings result in similar dry interfacial shear strengths of approximately 35 to 40 MPa. The epoxy-compatible coating does show more scatter in the data. The lines in the figures are least squares fits to the data to indicate trends.

The same E-glass/epoxy systems were used to make prepregs in our laboratory, which were then cured into plaques and cut into samples for the tension, compression and fracture tests. The tension samples and end tabs for the tension and compression samples were cut from 6-ply unidirectional plaques, while the Mode I and Mode II fracture samples and the compression specimens themselves were cut from 20-ply unidirectional plaques. For the fracture samples, a polyimide film was inserted at the midplane over part of the layup to provide an initial crack. The Mode I specimens had hinges bonded to the ends to act as grips in a double cantilever beam arrangement [8]; the Mode II samples are end notched flexure specimens loaded in three-point bending [8].

Initial results from the fracture and tension tests [9] on dry samples are shown in Figures 4 and 5. Three plaques were made for each type of fiber coating and for each thickness, and two samples were tested from each plaque. The Mode II delamination data reflects the fragmentation results in that the epoxy-compatible coating shows a slightly stronger interface and more scatter than the vinylester-compatible coating. The Mode I specimens with the vinylester-compatible coating demonstrated more debonded fibers acting to bridge the crack. The tensile strengths are also similar for the two coatings, as expected, since the tensile strength should reflect the fiber strength; the variations follow the fiber volume in each plaque. The lines on the figures are the mean and one standard deviation from the mean for each fiber coating.

[1] C.L. Schutte, <u>Materials Science and Engineering</u>, <u>R13</u>, No. 7, 265, (1994).

[2] C.R. Schultheisz, C.L. Schutte, W.G. McDonough, K.S. Macturk, M. McAuliffe, S. Kondagunta and D.L. Hunston, <u>ASTM STP 1290</u>, American Society for Testing and Materials, Philadelphia, Pa., in press, (1996).

[3] P.J. Herrera-Franco and L.T. Drzal, <u>Composites</u> <u>23</u>, 2 (1992).

[4] A. Kelly and W.R. Tyson, <u>Journal of the Mechanics and Physics of Solids</u>, <u>13</u>, 329 (1965).

[5] R.J. Charles, <u>Journal of Applied Physics</u>, <u>29</u>, 1549 (1958).

[6] A.G. Metcalfe and G.K. Schmitz, <u>Glass Technology</u> <u>13</u>, 5 (1972).

[7] H.D. Wagner, J.R. Wood and G. Marom, <u>Advanced Composites Letters</u> <u>2</u>, 173 (1993).

[8] L.A. Carlsson and R.B. Pipes, <u>Experimental Characterization of Advanced Composite Materials</u>, Prentice-Hall, Inc., Englewood Cliffs, N.J., (1987).

[9] ASTM Standard D3039, Annual Book of ASTM Standards, 15.03, 114 (1995).

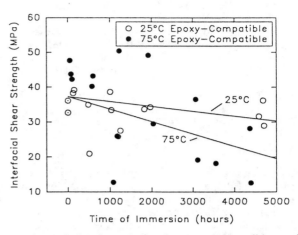

Figure 3. Interfacial strength for the epoxy-compatible coating from the fragmentation tests after immersion at 25 °C and 75 °C.

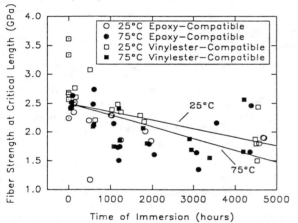

Figure 1. Strength of E-glass fibers with two coatings measured in the fragmentation tests after immersion at 25 °C and 75 °C.

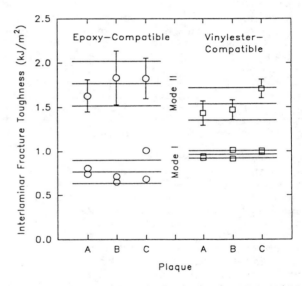

Figure 4. Mode I and Mode II delamination fracture toughness for dry specimens.

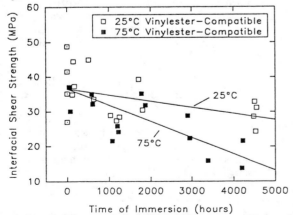

Figure 2. Interfacial strength for the vinylester-compatible coating from the fragmentation tests after immersion at 25 °C and 75 °C.

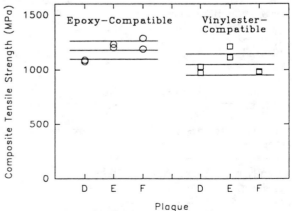

Figure 6. Tensile strengths for the dry specimens.

# Solvent Sensitivity of High Performance Composites

A. Paige Clifton Furrow* , David A. Dillard**
Engineering Science and Mechanics Department
Virginia Tech
Blacksburg, VA 24061-0219

Terry L. St. Clair, and Jeffrey A. Hinkley
Polymeric Materials Branch
NASA-Langley Research Center
Langley, VA 23686

Improved stiffness to weight, strength to weight, and the ability to tailor material properties have all led to the increased utilization of composite materials in primary and secondary structures. The development of improved thermoplastic matrix materials have led to increased utilization of thermoplastic resin systems because of improved toughness, enhanced shelf-life, and processing advantages. The trends towards these high performance polymeric matrix composites have raised new concerns regarding long-term durability issues, including the resistance to environmental stress cracking (ESC) in the presence of certain organic solvents. This paper will report findings on solvent resistance of several high performance polymeric composites which are based on thermoplastic resins or lightly crosslinked resins. Similar results have been reported earlier [1] for a semicrystalline composite resin system and a thermoplastic toughened thermoset system. Environmental stress cracking has been observed in a variety of different polymeric materials over the past 30 years. Our first effort in the area resulted from findings that even brief exposure to certain organic solvents would produce curious spiral cracks and other damage in polyimide adhesive layers bonding titanium or glass substrates [2]. Recognizing that the residual stresses which had lead to the damage in the constrained adhesive layer would also be present within a laminated composite, the paper will discuss a study which extended over several years, involving several sponsors and several polymer/solvent systems. The initial phase of the work was conducted on ICI-Fiberite composites consisting of IM8/954-2 and IM8/ITX[1]. Additional details on this work has been presented in Ref. 2.

The basic problem involves the susceptibility of certain polymers to environmental stress cracking in the presence of certain organic solvents. Although thermosets may exhibit ESC susceptibility, the problem is most widely

---

* currently with Fiber and Sensor Technologies, Blacksburg, VA.
** corresponding author.
[1]954-2 is a thermoplastic toughened cyanate ester and ITX is a semi-crystalline thermoplastic polymer system. Both are produced by ICI-Fiberite.

observed in thermoplastic resins where the lack of chemical crosslinks allows molecules to disentangle without breaking chemical bonds. In semicrystalline polymers, the crystalline regions serve as physical crosslinks which can also enhance resistance to ESC. This paper will suggest that solvents commonly used in conjunction with aircraft structures may induce significant amounts of damage in composite laminates because of the residual stresses present within the plies as well as the reduced toughness of these materials in the presence of certain solvents. Although externally applied stresses may also enhance this process, our work shows that even the residual stresses present in typical thermoplastic composite systems is sufficient to lead to extensive matrix cracking in the presence of some common solvents.

This work focuses on composites produced using IM7 fibers in one of four different high performance resins: LaRC™-IAX[2], LaRC™-IAX2, LaRC™-8515, and LaRC™-PETI-5. The first three are thermoplastic polymides, and the latter is a lightly crosslinked thermoset polyimide; all were developed within the Polymeric Materials Branch at NASA-Langley. The solvents used for the study included common laboratory solvents (MEK, acetone, toluene, diglyme, and TCE 1,1,1) and standard fluids used around aircraft (runway deicer, aircraft deicer, JP5 jet fuel, and Hyjet IV hydraulic fluid). The laboratory solvents listed frequently appear as a component in paint strippers, degreasers, and other fluids used routinely in maintaining aircraft. During the course of the study, it was also found that dye penetrant liquid used for X-radiography also induced significant amounts of matrix cracking in cross-ply laminates.

Specimens used during the testing included unidirectional $[90_4]_s$ coupons used to measure changes in flexural strength with solvent exposure, and $[0, 90, 0_2, 90_2, 0_2, 90_2]_s$ cross-ply laminates which were specially designed to study ESC. This laminate provided 90° groupings containing 1, 2, and 4 adjacent plies to facilitate using a fracture mechanics approach to quantify the ESC phenomenon. All of the groupings would have experienced similar residual stresses, but the available energy release rate should increase linearly with the thickness of the grouping [3]. A classical lamination theory analysis revealed that the residual stresses present in this cross-ply laminate were very comparable to those expected in laminates in common use on aircraft, etc.

The major finding of the study was that composites made of each of the high performance matrix resins showed some susceptibility to environmental stress cracking (ESC). Although most of the resins showed only a mild susceptibility to ESC in the

---

[2] The LaRC trademark is applied to several polymers developed by the Polymeric Materials Branch at NASA-Langley Research Center.

presence of the deicers, jet fuel, and hydraulic fluid, cross-ply composites from all of the resins showed substantial numbers of transverse matrix cracks when subjected to the other solvents. These solvents apparently lowered the critical energy release rate required for fracture; the residual thermal stresses within the plies were then able to induce matrix cracks which, in some cases, approached the saturation crack spacing density which might be observed under mechanical fatigue loading. Figure 1 illustrates the rapid development of matrix cracks in the LaRC™-IAX cross-ply laminate in the presence of the nine different fluids. Some matrix cracking was seen with all of the liquids except aircraft deicer and JP5 jet fuel. LaRC-PETI-5 was designed for enhanced ESC resistance, but continues to show microcracking in some solvents, as shown in Fig. 2.

Three-point bend (transverse flexure) tests were conducted on the unidirectional coupons using one of four different exposure conditions: 1) solvent drop, where a few drops of solvent were placed on the specimen just prior to loading, 2) solvent vapor, in which specimens were tested (above the liquid) in a chamber containing solvent, 3) solvent soak, in which specimens were submerged in the solvent for two weeks prior to testing, and 4) solvent soak-dry, in which specimens soaked for two weeks in solvent were allowed to dry for two weeks at room conditions prior to testing. Figure 3 illustrates the strength retention[3] of the four composite systems in three of the solvents for the "solvent soak" exposure. Significant strength losses can be seen. Interestingly, the strengths observed for the redried specimens returned to the strengths of the control specimens.

In summary, a variety of common solvents can, through ESC, induce significant amounts of matrix cracking in laminated composites. The ESC damage is synergistic, requiring the simultaneous presence of stress and solvent. Thermoplastic composites are believed to be especially susceptible because of the lack of chemical crosslinks to resist ESC, and the high levels of residual stresses present in laminated composites because of the high processing temperatures and glass transition temperatures. Even dye penetrant was observed to induce significant damage in some composites. While the resulting matrix cracking may present certain design problems, it is not clear at this time how seriously such damage may affect strength and durability. Some improvement in solvent resistance can be obtained through proper formulation, although some solvents continue to pose concerns for materials under current consideration.

References

1. H. Parvatareddy, C. Heithoff, P. Clifton, D. A. Dillard and R. Kander, "Environmental Stress Cracking and Solvent Effects in High Performance Polymeric Composites," *ASTM STP* (in press).

2. D. A. Dillard, J. A. Hinkley, W. S. Johnson and T. L. St. Clair, "Spiral Tunneling Cracks Induced by Environmental Stress Cracking in LARC TPI Adhesives," *Journal of Adhesion*, **44**, 1994, 51-67.

3. S. Liu and J. A. Nairn, "The Formation and Propagation of Matrix Microcracks in Cross-ply Laminates during Static Loading", *Journal of Reinforced Plastics and Composites*, **11**, 1992, 158- .

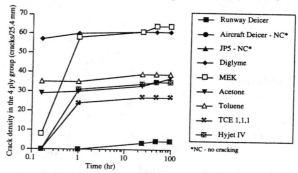

**Figure 1.** **Time dependent matrix microcracking in the center transverse 4-ply group of a [0/90/0₂/90₂/0₂/90₂]ₛ LaRC™-IAX specimen.**

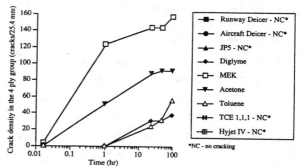

**Figure 2.** **Time dependent matrix microcracking in the center transverse 4-ply group of a [0/90/0₂/90₂/0₂/90₂]ₛ LaRC™-PETI-5 specimen.**

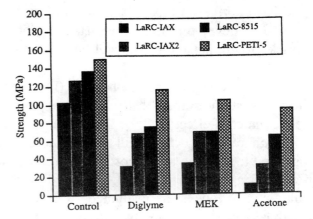

**Figure 3.** **Strength retention of dilgyme, MEK, and acetone LaRC™ solvent soak specimens.**

---

[3] Three point bending strength is based on maximum load at break and the geometry of the test. It does not correct for nonuniformity of the modulus which could result from localized solvent plasticization.

# Effect of Oxygen Embrittlement on Crack Growth in a Nickel-based Superalloy

G. Zhang[1], B.S.-J. Kang[2] and L. Wilson[3]

1  Professor, Beijing Institute of Aeronautics and Astronautics, Beijing 100083, PRC
2,3  Associate Professor and Research Assistant Professor Mechanical and Aerospace
Engineering  Dept.,  West Virginia University, Morgantown, WV 26506

## Abstract

Creep crack growth behavior of metallic and intermetallic alloys can vary widely under various testing environments.  The creep crack growth rates for several nickel-base superalloys have been found to be up to 1000 times of magnitude faster at a given $K_I$ level in air than in an inert gas or in vacuum[1-3].  It has also been reported that the tensile fracture ductility and notch stress rupture lives of several nickel-base superalloys are reduced significantly following exposure to oxygen at high temperatures (T > $627^0C$ )[4,5].  Since the failures occurred intergranularly, and the separated grain boundaries contained oxide wedges, it was suggested that these failures, aided by the applied stress, occurred by the diffusion of oxygen down to grain boundaries to form brittle oxides on grain boundary surfaces.  This serious brittle fracture problem is known as "Stress Accelerated Grain Boundary Oxidation (SAGBO) Embrittlement".  Both stress and oxygen containing environment are necessary for the SAGBO embrittlement to occur.  It has been shown that the diffusion of oxygen into the base metal along grain boundaries leads to the formation of complex oxides (oxides of Nb, Cr, Al, Mo, Ti, etc.) which embrittle the grain boundaries [6,7].  These fine oxide particles may act as the nucleation sites for creep cavity formation, thus increasing the cracking rates.  Also, for nickel-base superalloys containing carbon, gas bubbles may be created along grain boundaries due to the reaction of oxygen with grain boundary carbides to form carbon monoxide or dioxide and thus promote crack initiation and growth.  However, despite investigated extensively, the actual mechanism of creep crack growth subjected to oxidation effect in nickel-base superalloys have not been established yet.  In this research, we aimed to develop a better understanding of the mechanism of SAGBO embrittlement on creep crack growth behavior of nickel-base superalloys.

The commercial Inconel 718 (IN718) superalloy was chosen as a representative material for this study since IN718 is one of the most used superalloys which is also sensitive to environmental effect [3,8,9].  High temperature moire interferometry (HTMI), which is capable of high resolution full-field surface deformation measurement at elevated temperatures, was applied to observe and record, in-situ, crack-tip displacement fields of IN718 specimens under constant applied load at $650^0C$.  Based on the moire fringes, fracture parameters and crack-tip plastic yield zones were evaluated.  We also carried out post-mortem microstructural analyses to correlate the macroscopic fracture behavior with microstructure and chemical transport of the test material subject to SAGBO effect.  Fractographic and metallographic examinations on the fracture surfaces as well as regions away from the crack-tip by using Scanning Electron Microscope (SEM), and the surface elemental analysis by Auger Electron Spectroscopy (AES) were conducted to study the mechanism of the intergranular fracture of IN718 due to SAGBO embrittlement.

A total of six HTMI tests were conducted at 650°C; four tested in air and two tested in pure argon environment. Applied $K_I$ values varied from 0.27 $K_{IC}$ to 0.39 $K_{IC}$, and elastic crack growth was observed for specimens tested in air. Using the near-tip moire fringes, stress intensity factors and crack-tip plastic yield zones were evaluated and compared favorably with the theoretical predictions based on linear elastic fracture mechanics (LEFM). We also conducted microstructural analyses of fractured surfaces and the results showed that creep crack growth in IN 718 at 650°C in air can in general characterized as intergranular fracture and the stress intensity factor ($K_I$) can be used as a governing parameter for the stress-strain field ahead of the crack tip during creep crack growth. Furthermore, the fractured surfaces were polished and examined under SEM. Nb-rich oxide films at grain boundaries near the crack tip region were observed. This indicated that SAGBO embrittlement was caused by oxygen diffusion to grain boundaries in high stress regions and reacting with Nb to form thin brittle $Nb_2O_5$ oxide layers on grain boundary surfaces. Chemical composition of the $Nb_2O_5$ layers was verified using Auger electron spectroscopy (AES). It is suggested that the formation of the brittle $Nb_2O_5$ oxide films resulted in SAGBO embrittlement on Inconel 718 superalloy.

## Acknowledgement

The research work done at West Virginia University is supported by (I) NSF/WVU EPSCoR Computational Materials Research program and (ii) NSF grant no. MSS-9215787.

## References

1.   K. Sadanada and P.Shahinian, "Creep Crack Growth in Alloy 718", Metall. Trans., vol. 8A, pp.439-449, March (1977).

2.   H. F. Merrick and S. Floreen, "The Effects of Microstructure on Elevated Temperature Crack Growth in Nickel-Base Alloys", Metall. Trans., vol. 9A, pp.231-236, (1978).

3.   M. Gao, D. J. Dwyer, and R. P. Wei, "Chemical and Microstructural Aspects of Creep Crack Growth in Inconel 718 Alloy", in Proceedings of International Symposium on Superalloys 718, 625, 706 and Derivatives, TMS, July (1994).

4.   K. R. Bain and R. M. Pelloux, "Effect of Environment on Creep Crack Growth in PM/HIP Rene-95", Metallurgical Trans., Vol.15A, pp.381-388, Feb. (1984).

5.   R. H. Bricknell and D. A. Woodford, "The Embrittlement of Nickel Following High Temperature Air Exposure", Metallurgical Trans., vol.12A, pp.425-433, (1981).

6.   D. A. Woodford, "Environmental Damage of a Cast Nickel-Base Superalloy", Metall. Trans., vol.12A, pp.299-308, (1981).

7.   R. H. Bricknell, R. A. Mulford, and D. A. Woodford, "The Role of Sulfur in the Air Embrittlement of Nickel and Its Alloys", Metallurgical Trans., vol.13A, pp.1223-1232, (1982).

8.   J. F. Radavich, "Superalloy 718-A Look at the First 30 Years", Journal of Metals, pp.35-35, July (1988).

9.   P. Valerio, M. Gao and R.P. Wei, "Environmental Enhancement of Creep Crack Growth in Inconel 718 by Oxygen and Water Vapor", Scripta Metallurgica et Materialia, vol. 30, No.10, pp.1269-1274, (1994).

# Flexural Strength and Fracture Toughness Evaluations of Fine Ceramics at Elevated Temperature

Yasuo Ochi [1] , Kohji Haraguchi [2] , Akira Ishii [1]
1; Dept. of Mechanical and Control Engng.,
Univ. of Electro-Communications,
Chofu, Tokyo, 182, Japan
2; Kohriyama Works, Mitsubishi Electric Co. Ltd.,
Kohriyama, Fukushima, 963, Japan

As fine ceramics has high qualities of strength and brittleness, the strength is controled by the existence of small defects such as pores, inclusions and machining flaws [1] – [3] . Therefore, it is important subjects to make clear the effects of these small defects and the dependence of temperature on the fracture strength and the toughness for certifying the reliability as the advanced structural materials .

In this study, four-point bending tests were conducted on smooth and vicker's indentation-notched specimens of $Al_2O_3$ and $Si_3N_4$ ceramics at room and elevated temperatures ($20 \sim 1200$℃). The detailed observations of fracture surface of smooth specimens by a scanning electron microscope (SEM) was carried out in order to specify the defect morphology as the fracture sites and to study the relation between the defect size and the flexural strength at room and elevated temperatures . The fracture toughness evaluation by the controlled fracture surface (CFS) method was also studied on two kinds of ceramics at room and elevated temperature for vicker's indentation-notched specimens with different load conditions (9.8N and 98N) .

Fig.1 (a), (b) shows the relation between the flexual strength and the test temperature on the smooth and the indentsted-notched specimens. The flexual strength of the smooth specimens decreased with increase in test temperature and the variation of the strength decreased at 800℃ in $Al_2O_3$, and at 1000℃ in $Si_3N_4$, respectively. On the noched specimens, the temperature dependence on the strength decreased on the higher indentation load .

Fracture sites of $Al_2O_3$ were unsintering defects at all temperature conditions , on the other hand , those of $Si_3N_4$ were unsintered defects or pores below the temperature of 800℃, but was solusion defects over the 1000℃. Fig.2 (a), (b) shows the relation between the flexual strength and the size of fracture sites $\sqrt{\phantom{a}}$ area at the room and the elevated temperature. The flexual strength decreased with increase in the size of the fracture site defects, but the dependence of strength on the defect size becames less, and at 1200 ℃ the strength was almost constant with the defect size .

The fracture toughness of the vicker's indentation-notched specimens determined by CFS method decreased with increase in test temperature, but at the indentation load of 98N of $Si_3N_4$ the dependence of the test temperature on the toughness were small. By introducing the assumed equivalent crack length, the relation between the strength and the crack size ( defect size ) in all specimens ( the smooth and the noched-specimens) of $Al_2O_3$ and $Si_3N_4$ ceramics was evaluated in general at room and elevated temperature in this study as shown in Fig. 3 (a) and (b) .

References :

[1] Ochi, Y., Ishii, A., Sasaki, S., Haraguchi, K., " Relation between Bending Strength Distribution and Microstructure of Fracture Sites in Alumina Ceramics, " Proc. of the APCFS' 93, July 1993, pp. 551-556.
[2] Yokobori, T., Sasaki, S., Mori, K., Ochi, Y., Yokobori, A.T.Jr., "The effect of Surface Processing on the Strength of Engineering Ceramics," J. of the Japanese Society for Strength and Fracture of Materials, Vol. 29, No. 3, 1995, pp.72-89 .
[3] Sakaida, Y., Tanaka, K., Suzuki ,K., Kawamoto, H., " Estimation of Gringing Flaw Size of Ground Silicon Nitride Based on Fracture Mechanics, " J. of the Society of Materials Science, Japan, Vol.44, No. 504, 1995, pp.1127-1132 .

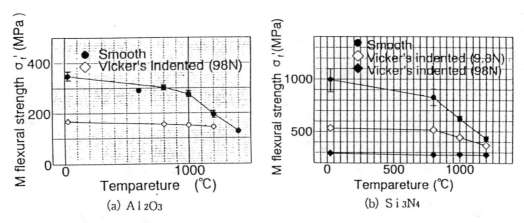

(a) Al₂O₃

(b) Si₃N₄

Fig. 1  Relatiom between flexual strength and test temperature.

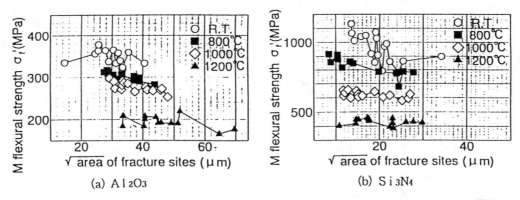

(a) Al₂O₃

(b) Si₃N₄

Fig. 2  Relatiom between flexual strength and size of fracture sites √ area.

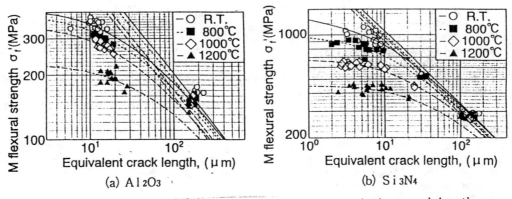

(a) Al₂O₃

(b) Si₃N₄

Fig. 3  Relation between flexural strength and equivalent crack length

# Creep-Fatigue Test on LMFBR Structure with Weldment in Flowing Sodium at Thermal Transient Test Facility

Masayuki Kikuchi, Hisao Umeda

Power Reactor & Nuclear Fuel Development Corporation,Oarai Enjineering Center,
Structure Safety Enjineering Section,
4002 Narita,Oarai-machi,Higashi-Ibaraki-gun,Ibaraki,311-13, Japan

Thermal transient load are one of the mainly load on structural design for Fast Breeder Reactor (FBR). It is difficult to evaluate on effect of various parameters(material, structure,material discontinuities, welding methed and fabrication method) on creep-fatigue failure only by a theory, because of a complicated interaction of each parameters. So the creep-fatigue strength test of structural model is performed under thermal transient loadings to validate and identify a safety margin of structural design criteria of FBR and demonstrate the structural integrity or excellent performance of critical components.

Thermal Transient Test Facility for Structures(TTS) can impose a cyclic severe thermal loading to the structure model in sodium. Fig.1 shows the schematic flow-chart of the sodium loops. TTS have hot and cold sodium loops. Each of these sodium loops is made of a head tank, a dump tank, an electro-magnetic pump and an electrical heater. The cold sodium loop is also provided with a air cooler. A Sodium is circulated by the electro-magnetic pump among the dump tank - the electrical heater (air cooler) - head tank. It also drops only by the gravity in the process of the head tank - test model(bypass line) - dump tank. The cold sodium circulates through the test model, while the hot sodium circulates bypassing the test model. The hot sodium circulates through the test model, while the cold sodium circulates bypassing the test model. And the hot and cold sodium circulate through the test model mutually. And them the test model is loaded by cyclic thermal transients.The TTS offers severe thermal transient load capacity, which is accelerating condition to failure the test model in a short time as compared with the service life of FBR plant. The most severe temperature difference between cold and hot shock condition is 400 ℃ from 650℃ to 250℃ in 10 seconds on inner surface of the test model. The piping diameter of TTS is 6B, the flow rate is 1 ㎥/min normally, and pressure is less than 0.1㎏/㎠G. The sodium flow is controlled automatically by a computer. Test models for TTS are realistic middle size structures of FBR plants.

As comparatively large sodium loops is necessary to perform the thermal transient tests of structural models. These tests performed requires a considerable high cost, and a lot of time. Therefore, we established a experimental technique to obtain a lot of failure data effectively and efficiently of the presentative structure model in only one thermal transient test. One of the experimental technique is to design the structural model, consisting of plural structural elements which were designed to accept suitably different failure damage among the structural elements under the uniform load conditions. In this paper, the authors will introduce an example of acquiring the failure data in the latest test for the purpose of reflecting these data on the development of the creep-fatigue strength evaluation method of welded joints.

Fig.2 shows a profile and dimensions of the test model. Test model is a cocoon-like vessel profiled axisymmetric structure consisting of a main and a internal structure. Main dimensions of the main structure made of austenitic stainless steel SUS304 are 2200 mm in height, 800 mm in inner diameter and 25 mm in thickness. Main dimensions of the internal structure made of SUS304 (a half of the thick-walled cylindrical shell) and 316FR (an other half of the thick-walled cylindrical shell and spherical head) are 1300 mm in height, 456 mm in inner diameter and 20 mm in thickness. The test model was designed to be able to compare the crack initiation at a welded portion and a base metal and to grasp the differences of cracking conditions caused by differences of the welding methods and weldment profiles. The weldment of the main structure were composed of a fillet weld circumferential joints by a shield metal arc-welding(SMAW) and butt-weld longitudinal joints by gas tungsten arc-welding(GTAW) and SMAW. The weldment of the internal structure were composed of fillet weld circumferential joints by SMAW and butt-weld longitudinal joints by GTAW and SMAW. The thermal transient conditions are as specified below. After the high temperature sodium flows in the test model at 600 ℃ for 120 min, the low temperature sodium flows at 250℃ for 60min cyclically.

The design standard for TTS test model(TTS-DS), which is applied to design the structural elements of the test model, is an evaluation method to reasonably shorten the safety allowance of the creep-fatigue strength criteria specified in the high temperature structure design standard[1] for the Japanese Prototype FBR plant. It was already reported by our colleague that the evaluation damage factor:D=1 by TTS-DS meant a crack of about 1mm in depth[2].

After the test, the test model was disassembled to grasp the cracking conditions of each elements. Fig.3 show typical failure mode of the test model. Fig.4 shows the relationship between the creep-fatigue damage factor and the cracking depth of each portions of the test model.

Main results obtained about the failures data of various types of weldment were summarized as follows.

(1) The cracks in depth initiated at longitudinal welded joints of the upper Y-junction, vessel ring and cylindrical shell of the internal structure by GTAW and SMAW ware compared with the cracks in depth of nearly base metals, respectively. As a result, the maximum crack depth at GTAW welded zone was about 5 times of the maximum crack of the base metal, at SMAW welded zone about a little less than 2 times, and at electron beam welding(EBW) welded zone about 2 times. According to these results, the relative relation of the strength at each welded joints is GTAW < EBW < SMAW.

(2) The cracked positions of welded joints were examined about longitudinal welded joints of upper Y-junction and vessel ring, circumferential welded joints at the upper and lower part of Y-junction, and the longitudinal welded joints of the cylindrical shell of the internal structure. As a result, cracks mainly initiated in the weld metal in case of GTAW welded joints, and in the weld metal or heat affect zone(HAZ) in case of SMAW welded joints, while major cracks in HAZ and sub-cracks initiated at the center of weld metal in case of EBW welded joints as crack initiating tendencies.

(3) As a result of the dye penetrant test(PT) of the cylindrical shell of the internal structure, fine cracks occurred over a wide range on the base metal of SUS304. The depth of cracks were max.1.5mm. The depth of cracks of welded joints of 316FR is less than max.0.5mm, which is smaller than the cracks initiated at SUS304 base metal. From these results, the strength of welded joints of 316FR is presumable to be superior to the strength of SUS304 base metal.

References:
[1] Iida,K., et al. Simplified Analysis and Design for Elevated Temperature Components of MONJU, Nuclear Engineering and Design 98, 305-317, 1987
[2]Tanaka,N., et al. Creep-Fatigue Strength Evaluation of a Vessel Model under Cyclic Thermal Transient Loadings, (2)Damage Evaluation by Thermo-elastic Analysis, Conference on Materials and Mechanics, No900-86 40-42, 1990

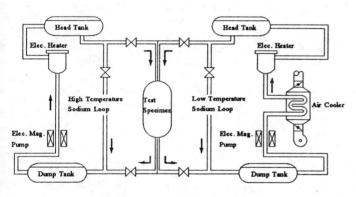

Fig. 1   Sodium Loop Flow of TTS

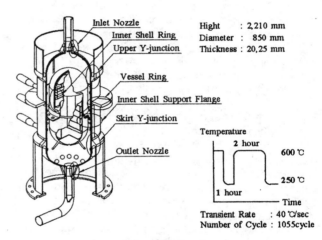

Fig. 2   Model Configuration

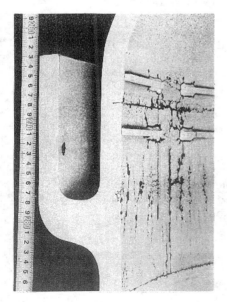

Fig. 3   Damage State at Upper Y-Junction

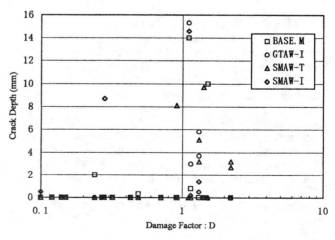

Fig. 4   Damage Factor vs Crack Depth

# AN AUTOMATED SYSTEM FOR TIRE TOPOLOGY MEASUREMENT VIA LASER SCANNING

J. L. Turner*, D. O. Stalnaker*, F. M. Chen*, P. B. Wilson**

\* Advanced Tire Technology, Bridgestone/Firestone, Inc., 1200 Firestone Pkwy, Akron, OH 44317
\*\* LaVergne Technical Center, Bridgestone/Firestone, Inc., I-24 & Waldron Rd., LaVergne, TN 37086

## ABSTRACT

A measurement system for quantifying tire tread surface shape has been developed, tested and placed into field operation. A supplemental software analysis system for tire shape and wear evaluation has also been developed and implemented. This paper overviews and demonstrates the hardware/software system characteristics and performance. The system is called CTWIST, an acronym for Circumferential Tread Wear Imaging System Two.

The tire measurement system consists of a frame for supporting and rotating a mounted tire-wheel assembly, a laser profilometer for measuring the distance to the tire tread surface and a motorized slider to move the laser scanner parallel to the wheel axis (Figure 1). Data acquisition and motion control and measurement is achieved via an IBM compatible PC.

The tire is rotated at approximately one revolution per second while 4096 measurements are made per revolution. Each measurement is accurate to about ± 0.002 inches. The slider is then incremented in the lateral direction and another revolution/measurement cycle is completed. This continues until the tread surface is topologically mapped. Typically, 100 to 150 lateral locations are measured, each consisting of 4096 samples, equally spaced around the tire circumference. The tread map contains about 1/2 million data points and is saved in a computer data file for subsequent analysis. The total data collection process for a tire typically requires less than 5 minutes.

The data files can be interrogated via custom analysis software (DOS and Windows based) which can display circumferential scan lines, lateral tire profiles and colorized maps of tread height. Detailed analyses of the data can be conducted to quantify rib tread wear, lug tread irregular wear (heel-toe wear), tire non-uniformities and more. Several of the analyses are automated to a substantial degree so that required user interaction is kept to a minimum, when desired. Alternatively, sufficient flexibility exists in the software so that the data can be examined in a wide variety of ways, depending upon the needs of the analyst.

Some example applications of the system for wear analysis are illustrated as follows:

Figure 2 shows a gray scale map of tread loss for a tire section. The software normally displays this map in a color format for quick qualitative inspection of wear tendencies. Figure 3 shows a segment of a single circumferential scan line which emphasizes "heel-toe" wear, i.e., a wear gradient occurring in the circumferential direction. The wear analysis software automatically computes the level of heel-toe wear on every tread lug, for each scan line and presents mean and standard deviations tabulated in a wear report. Figure 4 shows the progressive development of heel-toe wear with mileage, as measured with CTWIST.

Another useful wear pictorial is shown in Fig. 5 where new and worn tire profiles of the same tire are compared. The profiles are generated by averaging the radial surface coordinates over 360° for each scan line across the tire. By differencing the profiles, a tread wear profile is produced (Figure 6) in which overall wear levels and relative wear non-uniformities across the tire can be measured. Several wear uniformity indices are computed by the software and summarized in a printed wear report.

Mileage projection analysis software is also available for use with the CTWIST data. By comparing CTWIST tire scans at different miles of testing, projected wear out mileage is computed. Special algorithms have been developed to compensate for tire growth and shape changes that sometimes occur with tire useage.

Published studies showing further applications of the CTWIST system can be found in references [1] and [2]. The system has been patented [3] and is currently in international use by Bridgestone/Firestone Inc..

References:
[1] Stalnaker, D., Turner, J., Parekh, D. Whittle, B. "Indoor Simulation of Tire Wear: Some Case Studies", 14th Annual Conference of the Tire Society, Akron, OH, March, 1995. To appear in **Tire Science and Technology.**
[2] Parekh, D., Whittle, B., Stalnaker, D., Uhlir, E. "Laboratory Tire Wear Simulation Process Using ADAMS Vehicle Model", SAE Paper No. 961001, SAE International Congress, Detroit, MI, Feb., 1996.
[3] Sube, H., Fritchel, L., Siegfried, J., Dory, A., Turner, J., "Method and Apparatus for Measuring Tire Parameters", U.S. Patent No. 5,245,867, Filed: 12-16-91, Date of Patent: 9-21-93.

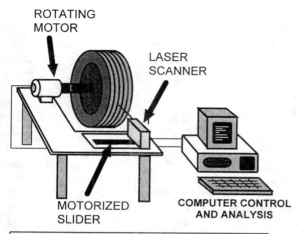

FIGURE 1. CTWIST LASER SCANNER TIRE MEASUREMENT SYSTEM.

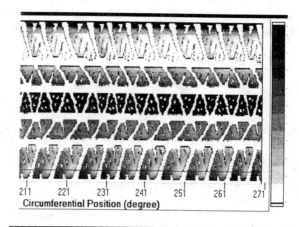

FIGURE 2. TREAD WEAR "INTENSITY" MAP PRODUCED BY CTWIST SOFTWARE.

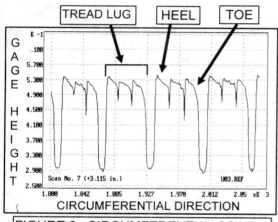

FIGURE 3. CIRCUMFERENTIAL SCAN OF HEEL-TOE WORN LUGS.

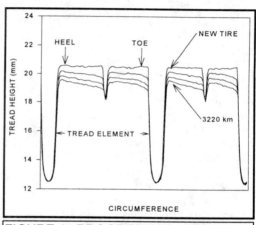

FIGURE 4. PROGRESSION OF HEEL-TOE WEAR WITH MILEAGE.

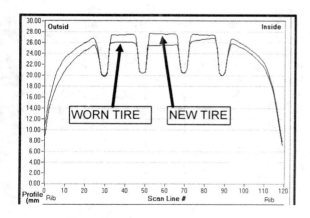

FIGURE 5. COMPARISON OF NEW AND WORN TIRE PROFILES.

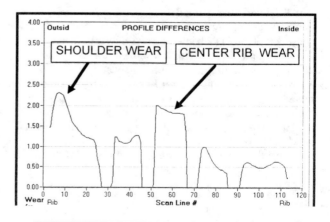

FIGURE 6. TREAD LOSS DISTRIBUTION ACROSS TIRE.

117

# Strain Measurement on An Ultra-thin Metallic Glass Ribbon

Hua Lu

Department of Mechanical Engineering
Ryerson Polytechnic University
350 Victoria Street, Toronto, Ontario, Canada, M5B 2K3

## 1. Introduction

Metallic glasses are a group of new materials which have attracted wide research interests and have had considerable commercial applications. This is so owing to their special magnetic and mechanical properties, such as low coercivity and hysteretic losses, and very high tensile strength at room temperature. Some aluminium-based alloys after detrification can have tensile strength comparable to that of engineering ceramics, yet retain the ductility. In forming metallic glasses from molten metals, crystallization is avoided by rapid cooling. A cooling rate of over $10^5$ K s$^1$ is usually needed. Techniques developed to meet the requirement, such as the melt-spinning and the pulsed laser quenching techniques produce alloys in forms of ultra-thin ribbons or films. Technical challenges arise in fully characterizing the mechanical properties on these thin ribbons. We have adapted a computer vision technique for the purpose. The results shown below shows the unique capability of the technique in the study of metallic glasses.

## 2. Computer vision technique

The technique is developed based on a methodology using image digital correlation for the direct measurement of surface strain, which was proposed by Bruck[1] et al. It obtains kinematic parameters at the centre of a small area of a body by numerically correlating the images of the area under different deformation states. A factor representing the decorrelation between a pair of digitized image subareas is defined and indexed to the displacements and displacement gradients of the centre. The pair of the images is processed to maximize the correlation between them. The measurements are obtained at the end of processing as the factor is belittled to the most. To achieve this, the Newton-Raphson method of successive approximation is employed. This involves a numerical procedure for solving iteratively a system of multi-variable partial differential equations. The procedure has been implemented conveniently on a computer vision system consisting of a CCD (charge-coupled device) video camera with a microscopic zoom lense and a desk top computer installed with a frame grabber, as schematically shown in Figure 1. In a previous paper[2], the author has presented detailed technical measures which have been devised for ensuring reliability of the measurements. These include restricting rigid-body motion, minimizing environmental instability, etc. In particular, a novel scheme has been invented which makes easy to initially estimate deformation parameters at the start of the numerical process. Good estimates for all the variables are vital for the convergence of the iterative process and in turn, for the accuracy of the measurement. The scheme that we developed is an electro-mechanical one which uses a real-time image subtraction in conjunction with a camera repositioning mechanism for compensating for the rigid body motion between two images. Also, two different processing schemes, "average after processing" and "average before processing," are proposed in order to reduce the effect of random error in CCD recorded images. The former average images as many times as pre-specified under same deformation state and then processes a pair of averaged images at two different deformation states. Using a hardware function named "onboard average", the image averaging can be performed almost instantly. Whereas the latter acquire two groups of images and cross-processe the images according to the rule of combination. Thus this scheme generates multiple sets of data. Data obtained under a normal test condition usually show a near-Gaussian distribution. They are then further analysed to yield the mean, the standard deviation and other statistical information. The results may be then expressed as mean $\pm$ maximum possible error with 95% confidence. This scheme usually leads to more reliable results except that, obviously, it requires longer processing time.

## 3. Application to the measurement of E and v

We conducted a test on $Co_{78}Si_9B_{13}$. The sample used in the test is a strip which is 150 mm long, 13.2 mm wide and 0.020 mm thick. The surface of it is spry-painted to create a black speckle pattern on a white background. The sample is then loaded in stages in simple tension on a hydraulic loading apparatus. The images corresponding to different load levels are recorded. The "average before processing" is used in this application.

## 4. Results

The results obtained for longitudinal (y) and transverse (x) strains and the corresponding load and axial stress levels are tabulated in Table1. The same data are used in generating Young's modulus and Poisson's ratio via a linear fitting program. The strains versus stress curves are plotted in Figure 2. Young's modulus is calculated and equal to 132.7 GPa, which matches very well with that obtained using pulse echo method[3]. Poisson's ratio measured is 0.29.

## 4. Discussion and conclusions

Measurements of $E$ for metallic glasses have been made generally by using the "pulse-echo" technique or modified techniques[4]. In these tests, an extensional ultrasonic wave pulse is introduced into a ribbon sample. The velocity, $V_E$, of the wave in the sample is determined by measuring the time duration for a pulse travelling down the sample to complete a round trip. $E$ is then given by $\rho V_E^2$, where $\rho$ is the density of the sample. The measurement of Poisson's ratio, however, needs strain values in both longitudinal and transverse directions of the ribbons. This may be achieved by using special strain gauge with very thin substrate[5]. Typically, however, a ribbon's thickness may be as thin as a few microns. The reliability of the measurements then could be questioned as one considers the reinforcing effect of the gauge. The results from this test trial, however, have proved some superiority of the new technique over the conventional ones. First, the technique is simple and convenient to use. It needs no highly sophisticated electronic equipment, such as an ultrasonic pulse generator and time control device. Secondly, it fully characterizes the elastic constants in a single test. Also, the technique imposes no special requirement on the dimension of the samples.

References:

[1]     Bruck, H.A., Mcneill, S.R., Sutton, M.A., and Peters III, W.H., "Digital Image Correlation using Newton-Raphson Method of Partial Differential Correlation," Experimental Mechanics, pp. 261, Sept. 1989.
[2]     Hua Lu, B. Jue, J. Karpynczyk, 1994, A Computer Vision Technique for Characterization of Surface Deformation in Single Ply Composite Laminates, Proceedings of International Conference on Design and Manufacturing Using Composites, pp.375-384, Montreal, August 1994.
[3]     S.H. Whang, D.E. Polk and B.C. Giessen, "Hardness vs. Young's Modulus of Metallic Glasses," Proceedings of the 4th Conference on Rapid Quenched Metals, pp1365-1368, Sendai, 1981
[4]     A. Kursumovic et al, "Change in The Young's Modulus during Structural Relaxation of A Metallic Glass," Scripta METALLURGICA, VOl. 14, pp1303-1308, 1980.
[5]     C.-P. Chou, L.A. Davis, and R. Hasegawa, "Elastic Constants of Fe(Ni, Co)-B Glasses," J. Of Applied Physics, pp3334-3337, 50(5), May 1979.

Acknowledgement:
The support from Natural Science and Engineering Research Council of Canada to this project is gratefully acknowledged.

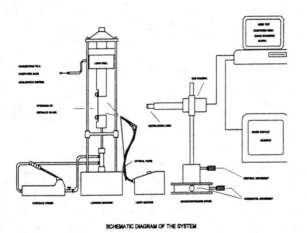

SCHEMATIC DIAGRAM OF THE SYSTEM

**Fig. 1**

**Table 1**

| Load | | Load Difference | Stress | Stress Difference | x Strain Difference | y Strain Difference |
|---|---|---|---|---|---|---|
| P (lb) | P (N) | ΔP (N) | σ (N/mm²) | Δσ (N/mm²) | Δεₓ (με) | Δεᵧ (με) |
| 5.2 | 23.14 | 0 | 87.65 | 0 | 0 | 0 |
| 19.3 | 85.89 | 62.75 | 325.34 | 237.67 | -884.6 | 1706.1 |
| 35 | 155.8 | 132.61 | 589.96 | 502.31 | -1316.3 | 3737.9 |
| 50 | 222.5 | 199.36 | 842.8 | 755.15 | -1979.9 | 5605 |
| 34.9 | 155.3 | 132.16 | 588.26 | 500.61 | -1365 | 3921.2 |
| 19.9 | 88.56 | 65.42 | 335.45 | 247.8 | -1029.4 | 2129.6 |
| 7.8 | 34.71 | 11.57 | 131.48 | 43.83 | -470.8 | 750.6 |

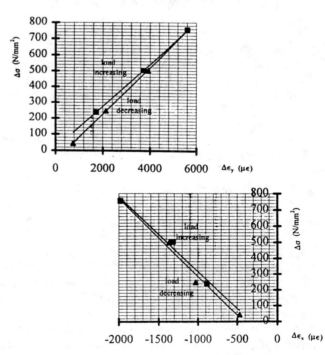

**Fig. 2  Stress vs. Strain Curves**

119

# Moire Interferometry at Cryogenic Temperatures
# for
# Thermal Deformation of Superconducting Composites

Meirong Tu,  Yang Xu,  Peter J. Gielisse, and  Igor Kulisic

Department of Mechanical Engineering
Florida A & M University / Florida State University
College of Engineering
Tallahassee, FL 32310
U.S.A.

The development of large high-field magnets has necessitated the need for the determination and quantification of the effects of stress on the properties of $Nb_3Sn$ superconductors. The thermal contraction characteristics are important aspects in the design and performance of magnets. A mismatch in thermal expansion coefficients of the various components of the superconducting composites creates a residual strain, degrading the superconducting parameters, such as transition temperature, $T_c$, the upper critical field, $H_{c2}$, and the critical current, $I_c$ [1], [2]. In order to accurately evaluate physical performance as a function of temperatures, as well as the thermal strain in active components, a knowledge of the thermal expansion of the superconductor composites is of critical importance.

In this paper we present the thermal strain distribution in superconductor composite cables from liquid nitrogen to room temperature, as determined by a high sensitivity moire interferometry technique. The sample is consists of $Nb_3Sn$ superconductor encapsulated in and reinforced by copper. A cross-section of the sample is shown in Fig. 1. A schematic of the moire interferometry system at cryogenic temperatures for thermal deformation measurement is shown in Fig. 2. It consists of a cryogenic chamber, a set of temperature sensors, a holographic illuminating setup, a receiver assembly and a computer system for task control and fringe processing purposes. The cryogenic system consists of a helium refrigerator, a separate compressor unit and a vacuum chamber. The sample is located inside the cryogenic chamber which is covered with a transparent and optically flat window. Heat can only be removed from the sample by conduction to the two refrigeration stations, the upper and lower flanges. Two E-type thermal couples fixed to the upper and low side of the sample are connected to a Keithley multimeter through a multichannel scanner. The conversion from voltage to temperature is performed in real time. A cross-lined diffraction grating with a frequency of 1200 lines/mm in both directions has been replicated on the sample surface in advance. With the holographic system, a virtual grating with a spatial frequency double that of specimen grating is formed in front of the sample surface. The interference patterns are captured by a CCD camera, which converts optical images into electron images by the photocathode. A sequence of interference fringe patterns is simultaneously captured as the temperature changes. The sample deformation is, therefore, recorded during the entire procedure.

A network program to perform the task sequence has been created. The software package can control all the instruments, reads th0e data and freezes the images taken with the CCD camera. Fringe pattern interpretation and data analysis functions are accomplished by the aid of high resolution frame grabber and image processing boards, with in-house developed softwares.

# References

[1] S.W. Van Sciver, Y.S. Hascicek, and W.D. Markiewcz, "Strain dependence of Bi 2223 tape conductors for application in high field magnets," *US/Japan workshop on high temperature superconductors*, 1993.

[2] G.K. White, R. Driver, and R.B. Roberts, "Thermal expansion of high-$T_c$ superconductors," *International Journal of Thermophysics*, **12(4)**, 1991.

Fig. 1. A cross-section of Nb$_3$Sn superconductor composites cable.

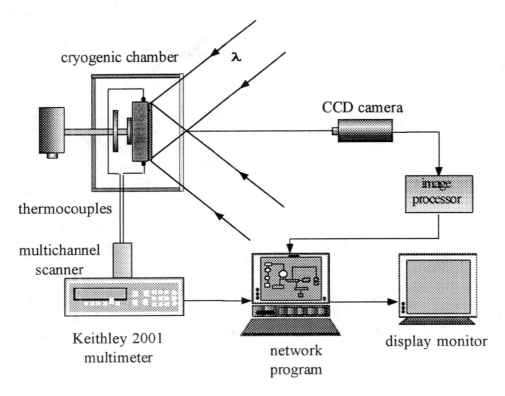

Fig. 2 Schematic of moire interferometry system at cryogenic temperatures for thermal deformation measurement.

# Automated Measurement of Residual Stresses by Phase-Shift Shearography

Y. Y. Hung, K.W. Long *, J.Q. Wang and J.D. Hovanesian
Department of Mechanical Engineering
Oakland University
Rochester Hills, Michigan 48309

The application of shearography for evaluating residual stresses is presented. The approach is based on a combination of a phase-shift shearographic technique and a hole-drilling technique. A rapid process for detection of residual stress using a micro-indentation technique is also presented.

A schematic diagram of the setup is illustrated in Fig. 1. The test object is illuminated with laser light and it is imaged by a video image-shearing camera. A frame grabber installed in a microcomputer is used to digitize and process the acquired images. By digitizing and comparing the two speckle images of the test object before and after deformation, a fringe pattern depicting the displacement derivative distribution is generated by the computer in real-time and it may be instantly displayed on a video monitor. For residual stress measurement, a relatively large shearing is employed. In this case, the technique basically compares the deformation of two different regions on the object surface. In essence, one region acts as a reference for the other as shown in in figure. The fringe pattern produced thus depicts the relative displacement between the two regions. Since the deformation due to stress relief by hole drillng is very localized, the other region is hardly affected and thus it serves as a reference beam. Thus the technique measures the absolute displacements around the neighborhood of the hole. In our setup, only the out-of-plane displacement is measured.

Instead of interpreting fringes, the phase shift shearography is used to automatically deduce the fringe phase distribution around the hole and the residual stresses are thus determined. Phase shift shearography is based on superposing a uniform phase on the original fringe pattern, thus producing a phase shift in the fringe pattern. The phase shift is achieved by simply translating the shearing optics. By digitizing four fringe patterns with a phase shift of 0, $\pi/2$, $\pi$ and $3\pi/2$, the phase value at every pixel can be determined. It should be emphasized that the conventional methods of fringe order determination yields the phase value at only "peak" and "valley" points of the fringe pattern. Fig. 2 shows a typical shearographic fringe pattern depicting the out-of-plane displacement produced by hole-drilling. A plot of the phase distribution along the specified section automatically deduced by the phase-shift technique is also shown in the figure.

For fast detection of residual stresses, we use an indentation method. A micro-indentation is produced on the test object instead of a hole. In the presence of residual stresses, the indentation also causes a stress release. Fig. 3(a) shows a fringe pattern due to an indendation but without residual stresses whereas Fig. 3(b) shows fringe pattern due to indentation and relief of residual stresses. Note that without residual stresses, the fringe pattern is more or less axisymmetrical. The presence of residual stresses will cause the fringe pattern to be deviated from the axisymmetrical form. The principal stress directions are indicated by the two axes of symmetry; the residual stress magnitude is related to the degree of deviation.

The technique presented provides a fast and automated means of determining residual stresses. It can be used in a field/production environment. Besides residual stress measurement, the method is being extended to the measurement of stresses in large structures such as bridges where live, non-removable loads exist.

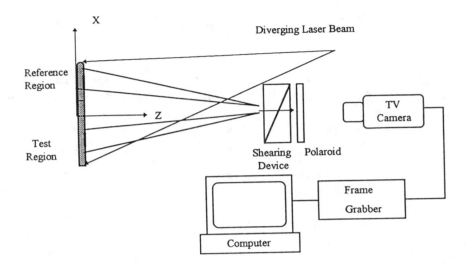

Fig. 1 Schematic Diagram of Shearography for Residual Stress Measurement

Fig. 2 Fringe Pattern Depicting the Out-of-Plane Displacement Around a Drilled Hole

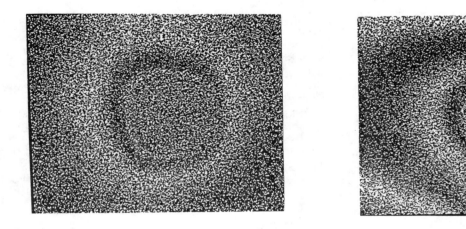

Fig. 3 Fringe Patterns Due to Surface Indentation:
(a) Without Residual Stresses, (b) With Residual Stresses.

123

# Determination of Sub-surface Residual Stress Profiles by a Holographic-Hole Drilling Method

A.Makino   D.V.Nelson [1]

Significant progress has been made to date in the formulation and implementation of a method to measure sub-surface distributions of biaxial residual stresses using the conventional strain rosette hole drilling technique [1-3]. In the last few years, a holographic hole drilling technique has been developed to replace the need for rosettes, and it has produced reliable results for stresses uniform with depth in a fraction of time that is needed in the strain rosette method [4,5]. Additional advantages are: no need for surface preparation and applicability to many regions inaccessible to rosettes. A logical extension is the application of the holographic technique to the determination of sub-surface residual stress profiles. In the incremental holographic technique deformations released by drilling a blind hole in steps into a material are revealed as a series of fringe patterns such as those depicted in Fig.1. In this case, a hole with a 2.4mm diameter was drilled incrementally into a linearly decreasing uniaxial stress field obtained upon unloading from plastic bending a 6061-T6 aluminum beam. The experimental procedure consists of (a) holding the object so that the relative movements between it and the optical setup are minimized, (b) illuminating with laser light the region where the hole is to be drilled, (c) taking a hologram of the object without a hole, (d) drilling the first increment of the hole, (e) viewing the object with the hole through the previously exposed and developed hologram to observe and record the first fringe pattern (this is the implementation of real-time holographic interferometry), (f) drilling the second increment, and so on. The production of fringe patterns in the procedure described above is due to the progressive deformation that changes the path length of the light waves reflected from the object. When the wavefronts emanating from the object, say at step (e) above, are superposed to the reconstructed wavefronts of the object stored in the original hologram taken in step (c), an interference pattern with alternating dark and light fringes is produced at the observation plane. Since a coherent illumination source is used, whenever the path length difference is an integer number of wavelengths there will be either constructive or destructive interference.

The basic piece of information that can be extracted from a fringe pattern is the total surface displacement. Displacements can be expressed as fringe orders or fringe counts, which in turn can be related to the sub-surface stress profile through an iterative mathematical procedure. Since a hole is drilled in a finite number of increments, a continuous stress profile must be approximated by a piecewise continuous profile that is constant over a given drilling increment. With this approach, the total surface displacement field around a hole is considered to be due to the superposition of the effects of the stresses acting individually in their corresponding layers. Approximate formulas for the surface displacements involve influence coefficients which express the proportional contribution of each one the stressed layers. In the case of blind holes, these influence coefficients are obtained by finite element modeling of incremental drilling since no closed form solutions exist. The overall solution for a blind hole drilled in $i$ steps into a residual stress field involves the formulation of a series of $i$ linear systems of equations from which the unknowns, the three components of the stress tensor in each increment $\sigma_{xx}^i$, $\sigma_{yy}^i$, and $\tau_{xy}^i$, can be found.

Figure 2 compares residual stresses determined by the incremental holographic technique with those estimated to exist as a result of plastic bending. These experimental results were calculated with the holograms of Fig.1 plus two additional ones not shown here. Figure 3 shows a more complete series of tests carried out on a similar specimen with a smaller hole diameter, $D=1.6$mm. Agreement between the residual stresses existing in the beams and those calculated by the holographic method is reasonable.

## References

[1] Bijak-Żochowski, M., "A Semidestructive Method of Measuring Residual Stresses," *VDI Berichte*, Vol.313, pp.469-476, VDI-Verlag, Düsseldorf (1978)

[2] Schajer, G.S., "Measurement of Non-Uniform Residual Stresses Using the Hole-Drilling Method. Part I-Stress Calculation Procedures," *J. Eng. Mater. Technol.*, Vol.110, No.4, pp.338-343 (1988)

[3] Schajer, G.S., "Measurement of Non-Uniform Residual Stresses Using the Hole-Drilling Method. Part II- Practical Application of the Integral Method," *J. Eng. Mater. Technol.*, Vol.110, No.4, pp.344-349 (1988)

[4] Makino, A., Nelson, D., "Residual-Stress Determination by Single-Axis Holographic Interferometry and Hole Drilling - Part I: Theory," *Exp. Mech.*, Vol.34, No.1, pp.66-78 (1994)

[5] Nelson, D., Fuchs, E., Makino, A., Williams, D., "Residual-Stress Determination by Single-Axis Holographic Interferometry and Hole Drilling - Part II: Experiments," *Exp. Mech.*, Vol.34, No.1, pp.79-88 (1994)

[1] Postdoctoral Research Affiliate and Associate Professor, Department of Mechanical Engineering, Stanford University, Stanford, CA 94305-4021

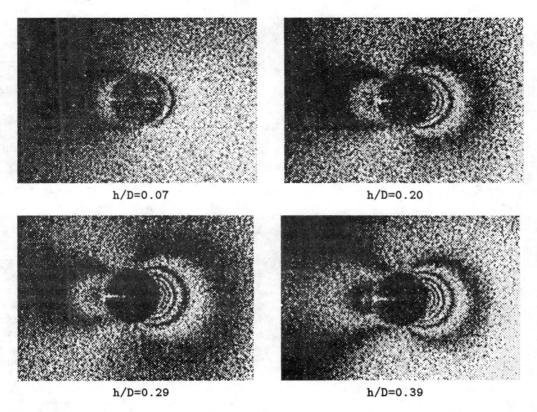

h/D=0.07          h/D=0.20

h/D=0.29          h/D=0.39

Figure 1. Sequence of four fringe patterns obtained by drilling a blind hole into a 6061-T6 aluminum beam that has been bent plastically to generate residual stresses. Illumination from right to left with a 27.5° grazing angle with respect to the object's surface. Hole diameter, $D$=2.4 mm, illumination wavelength, $\lambda$=514 nm (argon-ion laser), maximum sub-surface stress, $\sigma_1$=139 MPa, stress gradient, 140 MPa/mm. Hole depths given as non-dimensional ratios $h/D$, $h$: hole depth.

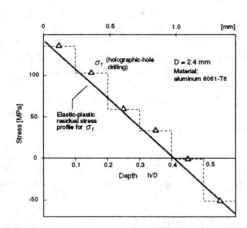

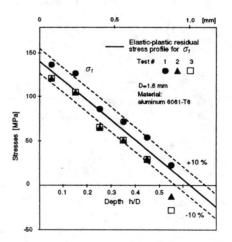

Figure 2. Stress profile for the test shown in Figure 1. $\sigma_1$, maximum principal stress (aligned with the illumination direction).

Figure 3. Stress profile for a plastically bent 6061-T6 aluminum beam probed with 1.6mm diameter holes at three different locations.

125

# Residual Stresses & Holography

by

S.K. Foss[1], D.V. Nelson[2], A. Makino[3]

## Abstract

A new method of determining residual stress magnitudes, including stress variation with depth, has been developed using holography combined with the hole drilling method. The method provides an extremely fast, inexpensive means of stress detection which can be used in the manufacturing environment. To date, this method has been used for quick problem solutions on a variety of products. However, its true worth is perhaps in process control and the reteaching of basic engineering concepts. This paper will discuss several of these "**lessons re-learned**."

## Introduction

Residual stresses exist within everything we surround ourselves with: castings, forgings, machined and welded items to just name a few. Although these stresses are well documented we tend to forget about their existence because of the difficulty of determining their sign and magnitudes in a timely manner. The holographic residual stress[1,2,3] technique provided a way to obtain such information quickly.. Hence, we chose this method for the above reason and because:

- It required NO surface preparation.
- Eliminated the need for installation of strain gages, milling guides, etc..
- Provided information on stresses below the surface.
- Could be used in geometric locations difficult to access by other techniques.

Our investigations were conducted in conjunction with Stanford University and Sandia National Laboratories.

When faced with determining probable cause of failures, some unique yet old lessons had to be re-learned.

**First Problem:** Our first problem concerned about a 50 mm diameter shaft that was "warm" formed to provide a serviceable part. This component exhibited some early fatigue failures that by definition "should not have occurred". The manufacturing history of the part was as follows: The bar was hot drawn with its surface then peeled, normalized and polished to produce a surface 'similar' to a cold drawn bar, leaving the shaft at a 'zero' stress state. The shaft was then induction heated to 570°C, transferred to the forming machine and clamped into two fixtures where the bend was to be made. During this time the shaft cooled to approximately 540°C. This process was then repeated to create as many bends as required. We investigated the shaft at a series of locations, Figure 1, that ran longitudinally along the inner and outer

radius of the bend. The results of this testing are represented in Figure 2 which indicated a **tensile** stress of ½ yield stress residing at the inner radii. These results provided the solution to the fatigue problem, but the real **question** was: "How can a warm forming process generate tensile stresses on the inner surface of the major bend?" **Lesson re-learned:** The subject part cooled too much between the induction heating and the actual forming stages. This left the bar in a condition such that the forming step was actually "cold forming." This generated tensile stresses on the inner radii through material spring-back at the completion of the bend. Key to the solution is the magnitude of the tensile residual stresses, which indicated that yielding had occurred within the part prior to testing for stresses.

**Second Problem:** This problem again revolved around the forming operation of a 50 mm rod. However in this case, electric current passing through the bar would heat it to 1550°F. Those areas that were not to be heated were kept cool through the use of copper chill blocks which shunted the electricity around the undesirable regions. This allows all bends to be made at one time with no temperature loss. The problem occurred when a material deformity, Figure 3, was noted immediately after bending. Concern existed that the "bulging" would generate high tensile stresses and promote early failures.

As in the previous case, we investigated the shaft at a series of longitudinal locations similar to those marked in Figure 1. This time, however, high compressive stresses were detected which indicated that the shaft would not create in-service problems. However, the **question** remained: "What caused the bulging to occur?" **Lesson re-learned:** Chill blocks are used to keep the shaft cool in locations that are not to be hot formed. If this block slips and positions itself too close to the "formed" region a portion of the material directly under this block would be needed to complete the bend. This material, because it could not form around the firmly held dies, "buckled" like a small compression test specimen.

**Third Problem:** This problem is related to a spline shaft and the stresses located on the face of the splines mid-way along the shaft. The final processing of this shaft involves a treatment called "carburizing." This process places the part in an oven that has a carbon rich atmosphere at 1700°F. After a prescribed "soak" period it is then oven cooled with no quenching. This process creates part surfaces which are very rich in carbon and can act as a wear surface. From the temperatures involved, the thermal excursion behaves similar

[1]Senior Engineer, Deere & Company Technical Center, Moline, IL

[2]Assoc. Professor, Stanford University, Stanford CA

[3]Post-Doctoral Research Affiliate, Stanford University, Stanford CA

to a stress relief process. However, our testing of the spline faces revealed rather high tensile residual stresses. This question remains: "What mechanism would allow this to occur?"

**References:**

1. Makino, A., "Residual Stress Measurement Using the Holographic-Hole Drilling Technique." Ph.D. Dis., Stanford University, Stanford, CA (1994).

2. Makino, A. And Nelson, D. V. "Residual Stress Determination by Single-Axis Holographic Interferometry and Hole Drilling, Part I: Theory," EXPERIMENTAL MECHANICS, **34** (1), 66-78 (1994)

3. Nelson, D.V., Fuchs, E.A., Makino, A., and Williams, D.R., "Residual-stress Determination by Single-Axis Holographic Interferometry and Hole Drilling - Part II: Experiments," EXPERIMENTAL MECHANICS, **34** (1), 79-88 (1994)

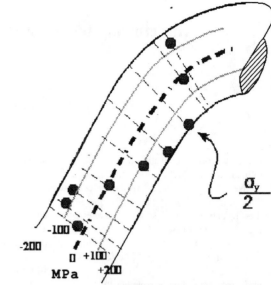

**Figure 2: Longitudinal Stress Test Results**

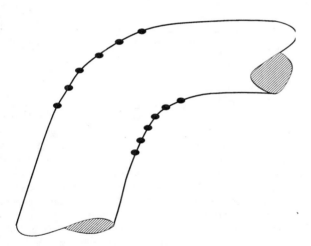

**Figure 1: Formed Rod and Data Location**

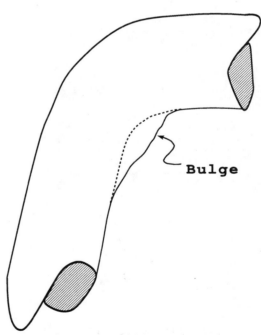

**Figure 3: Bulged Bend**

# Interferometric Strain Rosette for Residual Stress Measurements

Keyu Li
Assistant Professor
Department of Mechanical Engineering
Oakland University
Rochester, Michigan 48309

An interferometric strain/slope rosette technique (ISR) [1] is applied to measure residual stresses in thin-walled structures. The ISR can be used to measure three in-plane strains over a short gage length on the order of 100 $\mu$m. The technique is an important redefinition of the interferometric strain/displacement gage (ISDG) [2]. Its measurement principle is based on interference of laser beams reflected and diffracted from three micro-indentations closely depressed on a specimen. The ISR takes two configurations of 60° and 45°, Fig. 1a and 1b, in which each indentation contains six or eight reflective facets, respectively.

the 60° ISR indentations interfere to create three pairs of interference fringe patterns. The occurrence of strains changes the separating distances among the indentations, and causes the fringes to move. The movement of fringes is measured to determine the change of the indentation separations which is related to strains. A set of ISR indentations contains three pairs of micro-indentations which allow determination of three strain components in the three directions of indentation separations. The governing equations for measuring the three in-plane strain components are as follows,

$$\epsilon_{12} = \frac{\delta m_1 + \delta m_2}{2} \frac{\lambda}{d_{12}\sin\theta} \qquad (1)$$

$$\epsilon_{13} = \frac{\delta m_3 \quad \delta m_4}{2} \frac{\lambda}{d_{13}\sin\theta} \qquad (2)$$

$$\epsilon_{23} = \frac{\delta m_5 + \delta m_6}{2} \frac{\lambda}{d_{23}\sin\theta} \qquad (3)$$

where $d_{12}$, $d_{13}$, and $d_{23}$ are the separations between the three indentations numbered 1, 2 and 3, $\lambda$ is the wavelength of the laser, $\theta$ is the angle between the incident laser beam and the reflected laser beams, and $\delta m_i$ (I=1, 2,...6) is the amount of relative motion of the six interference fringes. For a 60° ISR, the strain components measured are in the directions of 0°, 60°, and 120°. For a 45° ISR, the strain components are in the directions of 0°, 90° and 45° or 135°. Two normal strains and one shear strain component can be determined from the three measured strains using strain transformation equations.

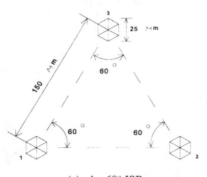

(a) the 60° ISR

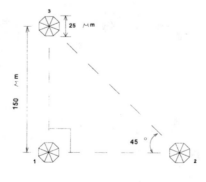

(b) the 45° ISR

Fig. 1: Schematic diagrams of the ISR indentations

When a laser beam normal to the specimen surface impinges on the ISR indentations, diffraction occurs in the reflecting directions from six/eight tiny facets in an indentation. The light rays diffracted from

The ISR has great advantages over resistance strain rosettes because of its extremely short gage length and non-intrusive nature. Its application in residual stress measurements could potentially surpass the resistance strain rosette method. By applying an ISR to a material surface, residual stresses at the location of the ISR may be determined through measuring strains induced by relief of residual stresses due to hole-drilling. Since the gage lengths are extremely short, the ISR accurately measures high gradient strains. For example, the ISR can be applied very close to the hole drilled to measure high gradient strains, the dimension of the drilled hole could be reduced to a considerably smaller scale on the order of 100 $\mu$m. There is no strict requirement for the location of the hole-drilling, as the ISR can be approximated at a point.

Feasibility studies are conducted on a thin-walled tube specimen made of Aluminum 6061-T6. The specimen has been chosen because it fits well into the jaws of a MTS machine. The specimen has an outer diameter of 25.4 mm and a wall thickness of 3.175 mm. The material has a Young's modules of 70 GPa and a Poisson's ratio of 0.33. A 60° ISR is applied to the specimen surface where residual stresses are to be measured. A 25 mW He-Ne laser is used (A 10 mW laser would be sufficient) as the light source. A computer-controlled ISR system was used to process the fringe patterns of the ISR for data acquisition and analysis. The closed loop hydraulic MTS machine is used to apply a constant tensile load of 10 kN to simulate a uniaxial residual stress of 45 MPa in the specimen. The ISR associated with a hole-drilling is used to measure the simulated residual stress. Two steps of measurements are performed. The first step records the interference fringe patterns of the ISR before the hole-drilling. The second step measures the fringe patterns of the ISR after a hole is drilled near the location of the ISR. By comparing the difference between the two measurements, the relieved strains in the specimens are determined, or $\epsilon_{12}$, $\epsilon_{23}$, and $\epsilon_{13}$, in the ISR gage directions are measures. Fig. 2 shows the relative position of the ISR with respect to the hole drilled. The dimensional parameters are measured after the two-step strain measurements.

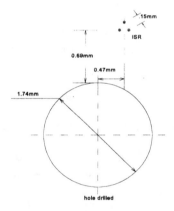

Fig. 2: The position of the hole drilled relatively to the ISR.

Residual stresses can thus be obtained by employing the Kirsch's stress state for an infinite plate when a hole is drilled [3].

$$\epsilon_r = -\frac{\sigma_1+\sigma_2}{E}(1+\nu)\cdot\frac{a^2}{2r^2} + \frac{\sigma_1-\sigma_2}{E}\cdot[-2\frac{a^2}{r^2}+\frac{3}{2}\frac{a^4}{r^4}(1+\nu)]\cos2\theta \quad (4)$$

$$= \frac{\sigma_1 \; \sigma_2}{E}(1+\nu)\cdot\frac{a^2}{2r^2} + \frac{\sigma_1 \; \sigma_2}{E}\cdot[2\frac{a^2}{r^2}-\frac{3}{2}\frac{a^4}{r^4}(1+\nu)]\cos \quad (5)$$

$$\gamma_{r\theta} = \frac{1}{G}\frac{\sigma_1-\sigma_2}{2}\cdot(-2\frac{a^2}{r^2}+3\frac{a^4}{r^4})\sin2\theta \quad (6)$$

where $\epsilon_r$, $\epsilon_\theta$, and $\gamma_{r\theta}$ are the relieved radial, tangential and shear strains measured by the ISR during the hole-drilling, $\sigma_1$ and $\sigma_2$ are the unknown principal residual stresses, $a$ is the radius of the hole, $r$ and $\theta$ are polar coordinates of linear and angular dimensions, E and $\upsilon$ are Young's modulus and Poisson's ratio. As the dimensions $r$ and $a$ are measured using a microscope after the hole-drilling and material constants $E$, $G$, $\nu$ are known, the three unknown $\sigma_1$, $\sigma_2$, and $\theta$ in equations (4-6) can be calculated. In the test, the loading of the MTS machine creates a uniaxial stress state. Thus, of the three equations available (4-6), only one is needed to solve for the unknown principal stress. The results of the residual stress obtained using each of the equations are listed in Table 1.

Table 1: Residual stress computed from equations (4-6) and comparison with the simulated value

| Simulated σ (MPa) | σ from eq (4) (MPa) | σ from eq(5) (MPa) | σ from eq (6) (MPa) |
|---|---|---|---|
| 45 | 30.1 | 53.8 | 75.7 |

The estimated results of residual stresses using equations (4) and (5) are close to the simulated value of 45 MPa. Noting equations (4), (5), and (6) are for an ideal case that a hole is drilled in an infinitely large thin plate, the estimated results are within reason. A better agreement between the simulated stress and those estimated may be possible using finite element analysis. In the experiment, a hand drill was used to perform the hole drilling. The quality of the hole drilled highly depends on the experience of the person who performs the drilling. Errors in the size, dimension and orientation of the hole significantly affect the measurement of the residual strains. Should have a positioned drill be used, the accuracy of the hole-drilling would be increased. The experiment presented demonstrates that the ISR is a technique applicable to residual stress measurements in thin-walled structures. Future research will focus on reducing the size of the hole drilled, blind hole drilling, and measurements in nonuniform residual stress fields.

References

[1]     Li, K., "Interferometric 45° and 60° strain rosettes", Journal of Applied Optics, Vol. 34, No. 28, 1995, pp.6376-6379.
[2]     Sharpe, W. N. Jr., "The interferometric strain gage," Experimental Mechanics, Vol. 8, 1968, pp. 164-170.
[3]     Kabiri, M., "Toward more accurate residual-stress measurement by the hole-drilling method: Analysis of relieved-strain coefficients", Experimental Mechanics, March 1986, pp.14-21.

# Cutting Phenomena of Aramid– Glass Hybrid FRP with Ultrasonic Vibration

**A.K.M. MASUD and Eitoku NAKANISHI: Postgraduate students**
**Jippei SUZUKI: Associate Professor,**
**Kiyoshi ISOGIMI: Professor, Mechanical Engg., Mie University,**
**Kamihama-cho 1515, Tsu, 514, JAPAN**

Cutting of FRP is usually necessary to improve the dimensional accuracy and the surface integrities, but the shortening of tool life by quick wears and damages of the tool edges and the drop of surface integrities by cracking, tearing, peeling and so on of matrix and fibers are invited. It is widely considered that cutting chips are produced ideally by the micro-vibration of tool edge under generally used cutting conditions. Therefore it may be possible to realize an effective cutting by adding ultrasonic vibration to the cutting tool directly with the forced vibrating equipment. In this paper, the aramid-glass hybrid FRP ( laminated plate reinforced with both of hybrid roving cloth of aramid and glass fibers and chopped strand mat of glass fibers ) shown in Fig.1 is chosen as an object. For this hybrid material, the low machinability caused by aramid fibers is especially serious problem. The most important point in adding forced vibration to cutting tool is to detach the tool edge periodically from cutting chips in each cycle. Therefore cutting speed V should be selected so as to be smaller than the retreating speed of tool edge ( critical maximum cutting speed Vc ).

The relative behavior of tool edge to the work is shown typically in Fig. 2. The period of the cutting stage ( contact period with the work ), displacement of the tool edge y and relative cutting speed Vn are considerably changed in each vibrating cycle. Therefore the effects of adding ultrasonic vibration can be expected to be very effective. Non-dimensionalized cutting speeds with parameter (2x $\pi$ xfa) is used to characterize the properties of vibrating cutting in this figure.

The research is performed under the conditions of cutting speeds V = 28.3, 84.8, 169.9 m/min, cutting feed f = 0.05 mm/rev, ultrasonic vibrational frequency f = 20 kHz and half width of amplitude 15 $\mu$ m in two dimentional cutting. The flank wear band width VB, maximum roughness of machined surface Ry are measured and the tool wear configurations, surface integrities and features of reinforced fibers machined are investigated in comparison with normal type cutting.

Figure 3 shows the SEM-photoes of aramid fibers cut with ultrasonic vibration compared with normal cutting.

Fig.4 shows an example of the improvementof surface roughness Ry by adding ultrasonic vibration. We can notice the aramid fibers are cut shortly without long fluffs by ironing with ultrasonic vibration. This may be possibly introduced better surface integrities to be obtained.

Figure 5 shows an example of the development of flank wear width VBmax against cutting distance concerning with or without ultrasonic vibration. These results are derived in cutting aramid-glass hybrid roving cloth under cutting speed V=169.6 m/min. Flank wear VBmax is decreased about 20 $\sim$ 30 % by adding ultrasonic vibration.

Brief summary of conclusions obtained is described as follows.
(1) Concerning to tool wear;
The flank wear band width always decreases without relationships with cutting speeds. This depends on the following facts that the time and distances of actual contact between tool edges and works become very short under the conditions of slower than critical cutting speed and following fractural mechanism of reinforced fibers appears. That is, we can point the continuous change of actual cutting speed by adding ultrasonic vibration and the cutting speed dependence of the fractural strength of aramid fibers. As aramid fibers are not easy to break down and fracture under high cutting speeds, they are elongated by cutting tool edge and rolled into the flank face side. This phenomenon is named "ironing". As a result, very wide rounded wear appears at the cutting edge. The fibers, however, break down and fracture in the successive decreasing period of cutting speed and finally such short intervals of fiber fracture invite narrower and smaller wear on fank face.

(2) Concerning to machined surface integrities;
The following conclusions can be derived in comparison with normal cutting. The slower the cutting speed is, the smaller roughness Ry becomes for slower speed than the critical cutting one. On the other hand Ry hardly changes for higher speed than the critical one.

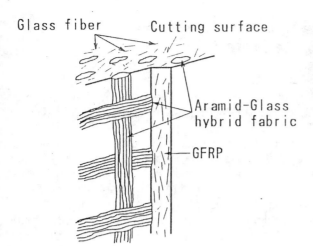

Fig.1  Construction of Aramid-glass FRP.

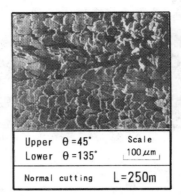 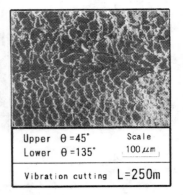

(a)Normal cutting.    (b)With ultrasonic vib.
Cutting speed V=28.3 m/min
Fig.3  Appearance of aramd fibers machined.

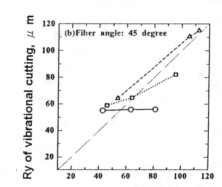

(a) $\theta$ =45°

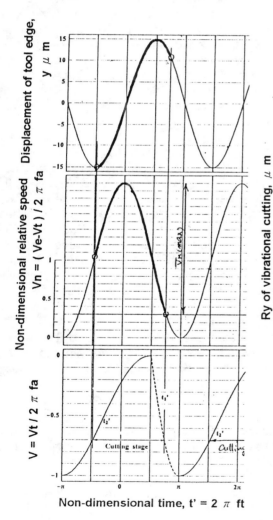

Non-dimensional time, t' = 2 $\pi$ ft

Fig.2  Relative behavior of tool edge to work in
vibrating cutting (Vt=84.82 mm/min ).

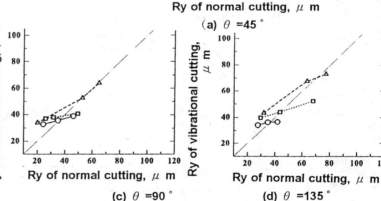

(c) $\theta$ =90°          (d) $\theta$ =135°

$\theta$ :Inclined angle of aramid fibers.
Fig.4  Improvement of surface roughness with
ultrasonic vibration

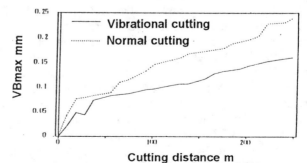

Fig.5  Developement of flank wear width in
aramid fiber cutting( V=169.6m/min ).

131

# Drilling Induced Failure Mechanisms in Carbon Fiber Composite Materials

Zaffar M. Khan*
Department of Aerospace Engineering & Engineering Mechanics, Iowa State University, Ames IA 50011

Ben Mills
School of Engineering & Technology Management Liverpool John Moores University, L3 3AF (UK)

## Introduction:

As advanced composites with tougher resin systems are being developed, optimization of their processing technology is eagerly being sought. One key secondary process is drilling. Drilling constitutes a major secondary operation for joining the structural members of aircraft, automobile, sea vessel etc. The process of drilling of carbon fiber composites has presented numerous problems during the structural assembly. The extremely abrasive nature of carbon fibers quickly dulls sharp tools. Dull drills apply high drilling forces in heat sensitive toughened epoxies which split, tear, pullout and pushdown the fibers and cause delamination. The presence and growth of such flaws on the hole boundaries increases the notch sensitivity which impairs the structural stability, reliability, and durability.

This paper will address the failure modes, pattern, and sequence of drilling induced failure modes in T800/924C high modulus carbon toughened-epoxy laminate having quasi-isotropic ply orientations of $0°$, $-45°$, $+45°$ and $90°$ (fiber volume fraction: 0.65-0.69) in relation to the complexity of drilling dynamics. This particular class of material and ply configuration was used because they led to maximum 'damage tolerance' of aircraft produced by British Aerospace.

## Experiment and Results:

The holes were drilled vertically in the carbon-epoxy laminate by carbide tipped drills using a numerically controlled Wadkin Drill/Mill machine. A computer program was developed to drill the majority of the holes on the left hand side and the test holes on the right hand side of the panel. The test holes were sectioned by a diamond saw as shown in Fig (1). The specimens were vacuum degassed and gold plated for better resolution. The hole boundaries were inspected for fractographic analysis in a Cambridge Scanning Electron Microscope. The surface morphology of damaged fibers were examined microscopically and macroscopically to assess the nature and extent of damage [1]. The microscopic examination of the fractured fibers showed multimode damage development due to the anisotropy of the composite laminate in relation to the drilling thrust and torque. The macroscopic examination of the hole boundaries revealed that the damage scars were spaced apart periodically at an angle of $45°$ (Fig 2). The damaged scars were characterized by a right angle triangular pit containing bundles of fibers that failed due to microbuckling (Fig 3). The post failure diagnoses of the intact $-45°$ fibers in the pit showed a bi-modal fractured surface consisting of tensile and compressive zones separated by neutral axis (Fig 4). The failure modes of the $+45°$ fibers was characterized by a fairly rough outcrop of fibers. Formation of converging fanwise striations on the their fractured surfaces of was attributed to their tensile failure (Fig 5). The $0°$ fibers slid in the matrix socket and formed cusps. The $90°$ fibers were mostly covered by epoxy matrix and partly obliterated by the cutting edge of the drill. Delamination was prominent between the $-45°$ and $90°$ interlayer, close to the drill exit plane.

The presence of drilling induced heat resulted in rapid deterioration of the matrix shear modulus and a marked reduction of compressive strength of the composite laminate leading to fiber instability. The most critical failure mode appeared to be shear crimping of $-45°$ fibers due to microbuckling. The through the thickness drilling forces caused delamination in the resin rich interlayer. The three dimensional stress theory revealed that maximum stress is exerted on the $-45°$ fibers Fig (6) [2]

## Acknowledgements:

I express my thanks to Mr. J. France and R. Gardner, Salford University, UK for assistance with experiment work and gratefully acknowledge the support of British Aerospace.

## References:

[1] Purslow, D.;Fractography of Fiber Reinforced Thermoplastic; Composites; Volume 19, Number 5, p358-366, (1988).
[2] Atlas, E. and Dorogoy, A., Three Dimensional Study of Delamination; Engineering Fracture Mechanics, Volume 33, Number 1, p1-19 (1989).

* Author is a research scholar from National University of Sciences and Technology, Pakistan

**Figures:**

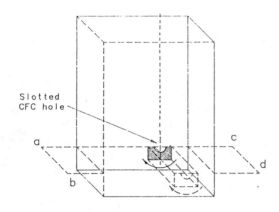

Fig (1): Drawing showing the sequence of sectioning a hole specimen from the composite panel for examination in the scanning electron micrograph.

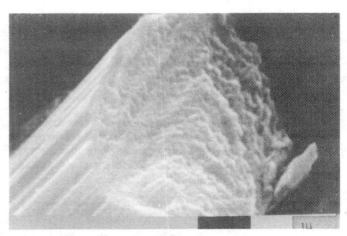

Fig (4): SEM micrograph showing the bi-modal failure of fibers in the damage scar.

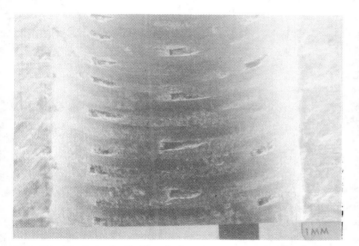

Fig (2): The periodicity of damage scars in the holes.

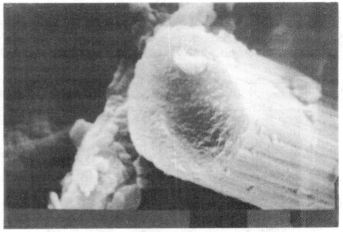

Fig (5): SEM micrograph showing striations on the fractured surface of the pulled out +45° fiber.

Fig (3): SEM micrograph showing the -45° fibers protruding against the 0° fibers in the damage scar.

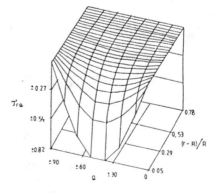

Fig (6): Variation of 3-dimensional interlaminar shear stress around the composite hole with respect to radial distance and angular orientation of fibers [2].

# Crack-Fiber Interactions At Interfaces In Brittle Composites

Michael C. Larson
Department of Mechanical Engineering
Tulane University
New Orleans, LA 70118

This three-dimensional experimental and computational study investigates the influence that interfacial friction, toughness, and roughness have on the progress of a quasi-statically propagating matrix crack. Understanding this localized interaction holds implications for enhancing the global toughness of brittle fibrous composites.

This work uses two sets of experiments to reveal the nature of fracture propagation near interfaces. The first set employs modified double cleavage drilled compression specimens [1] to capture on video the real-time propagation of fractures in the vicinity of frictional interfaces. Some of the specimens contain cylindrical inclusions to represent propagation toward and around fibers in a model brittle composite. Unlike Coyle et. al. [2], who used the DCDC specimen to evaluate the closure force imposed by a bridging fiber, the specimens employed here are formed from a single piece of glass. Hence the crack does not interact with a plane on which diffusion bonding had taken place. The tests permit control over important interfacial parameters. The cases highlighted clearly show the crack retardation near a constrained interface as compared to a monolithic material and a material containing a void.

growth patterns show that the inclusions have a prominent, albeit localized, influence on the shape of the fracture.

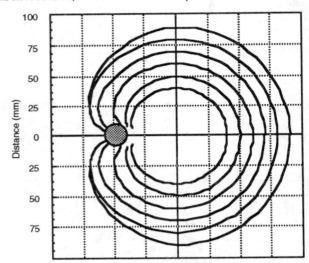

Representative crack growth profiles in the vicinity of a glass inclusion in a cement matrix.

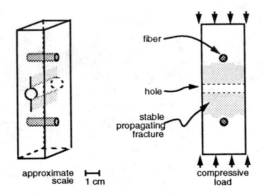

Schematic of the modified dcdc specimen containing model fibers.

The second set of experiments uses glass rods cast in cement as a model brittle-fiber/brittle-matrix composite system. A stable crack is propagated within the specimens by hydraulic pressurization of a fluid. Push-out tests characterize the interface between the glass fiber and cement matrix. A pressure vessel allows independent control of the axial and radial pressures exerted on cylindrical specimens to periodically mark the fracture surface. Characteristic growth history rings are presented for various interface types. The

The experimental findings are guiding two and three dimensional computational simulations which demonstrate the effectiveness of using the surface integral method to represent the matrix cracks and the coupled interfacial sliding zones. This approach offers particular advantages in that only surfaces need to be discretized, and the kernel of the singular integral governing equation is physically meaningful for fracture characterization. An iterative scheme determines the interfacial frictional tractions; embedded crack-tip singularities govern the crack propagation. The explicit modeling of the progress of the matrix crack as it engulfs individual fibers reveals the degree of localized matrix toughening. [3]

References:

[1] Janssen, C., "Specimen for Fracture Mechanics Studies on Glass", Proceedings of the Xth International Congress on Glass, The Ceramic Society of Japan, pp. 23-30, 1974.

[2] Coyle, T.W., Palamides, T.R., Freiman, S.W., Fuller, E.R., and Deshmukh, U.V., "Crack-Fiber Interactions in Ceramic Matrix Composites", Proceedings of the 1987 Northeast Regional Meeting of TMS, May 1989.

[3] Larson, M.C., "Fracture Propagation Near a Frictionally-Constrained Fiber Interface," International Journal of Composites Engineering, [5], pp. 25-36, 1995.

# Effects of the Stress State on the Dynamic Damage Behavior of Particulate Reinforced Titanium Composites

W. Tong and X. Li
Department of Engineering Mechanics &
Center for Materials Research and Analysis
University of Nebraska-Lincoln
Lincoln, Nebraska 68588-0347

Silicon carbide particulate reinforced *titanium* matrix composites (Ti-SiC$p$ composites) with full density and minimum interfacial reaction have been made available due to the recent development in both quasistatic and dynamic high-pressure, warm-temperature consolidation techniques [1,2]. Fig. 1 and Fig. 2 show the experimental schematic of the high-pressure consolidation apparatus. The processed Ti-SiC$p$ composites are shown to have increased stiffness and strength over the unreinforced titanium matrix. The tensile ductility of the composites is strongly affected by the degree of Ti-SiC interfacial reaction during the consolidation and post-consolidation annealing processes [3,4]. The processed composites exhibit also enhanced flow strength and good deformability in compression, as shown in Fig. 3.

Formability and related damage evolution of such materials under *dynamic* loading are regarded to be vital to their secondary rapid forming, machining, cutting, and to the understanding of their wear and erosion properties. Some reinforcement particle damages have been observed during the processing of titanium composites, which can be related to the rapid build-up of very large local high stresses [5,6]. The dynamic damage behavior of the newly developed titanium composites under predominantly compressive loading is the focus of the current investigation.

A Hopkinson bar apparatus with the specimen recovery capability was recently built at the University of Nebraska-Lincoln (UNL) and is utilized in this investigation [7,8]. The apparatus provides a well-controlled stress wave pulse duration and shape. The dynamic stress-strain curves of titanium composites are determined by using straight, short disk specimens for uniaxial compression at strain rates up to $10^4$ per second. Fig. 4 shows the experimental stress-strain relation for a commercial titanium composite [9] under both quasistatic and dynamic compression.

Several specimen designs and test configurations are used to assess the effect of stress states on the dynamic deformation and damage behavior (including *adiabatic shear band formation*) of titanium composites, such as tilt short cylinders for combined shear and compression and dynamic indentation tests. These experiments are carried out on Ti matrix specimens as well. The titanium specimens are made from titanium compacts, which are produced by using the same consolidation and post-consolidation annealing procedures for the titanium composites. Consequently, the effect of variation in matrix materials is minimized and the role of SiC reinforcement particles on the dynamic deformation and damage properties of the composites can be examined exclusively.

Post-mortem scanning and transmission electron microscopy of recovered titanium and tianium composite samples after testing are carried out to study the evolution of microstructural damages with the dynamic loading of various stress states (for example, see Fig. 5). Dynamic finite element simulation are performed to provide a detailed local stress and deformation histories. A rate-dependent viscoplasticity constitutive model with damage criterion is used to correlate the observed deformation and damage of titanium composites with controlled dynamic impact loading. The dynamic indentation process of a titanium composite sample is illustrated in Fig. 6.

This investigation is part of the research effort [10] in providing fundamental understanding and valuable guidance to optimize materials processing for improved performance of the titanium composites and to assess these materials for potential engineering applications.

*Acknowledgments:* This research has been partly supported by grants from the Nebraska Research Initiative (NRI), the Center for Materials Research & Analysis (CMRA) at UNL, and the Layman Faculty Award. The dynamic finite element calculations were carried out on a Cray Supercomputer (model J916), newly installed in the College of Engineering and Technology at UNL. The authors are also grateful to Prof. J. D. Reid of Department of Mechanical Engineering at UNL for helpful discussions.

References

[1] W. Tong, "Full-Density Processing of Advanced Particulate Composites", *Transaction of NAMRI/SME* (in press, May 1996).
[2] W. Tong, G. Ravichandran, T. Christman, and T. Vreeland, Jr., "Processing SiC-Particulate Reinforced Titanium-Based Metal Matrix Composites by Shock Wave Consolidation", *Acta metall. mater.* **43** (1), 235-250 (1995).

[3] W. Tong, G. Ravichandran, T. Christman, and T. Vreeland, Jr.," Effects of Interfacial Reaction on the Mechanical Properties of Ti-SiC Particulate Reinforced Metal Matrix Composites", in: *High Performance Metal and Ceramic Metal Matrix Composites* (Edited by K. Upadhya), The Minerals, Metals & Materials Society (TMS), Warrendale, Pennsylvania, 1994, p.33-47.

[4] W. Tong, G. Ravichandran, T. Christman, and T. Vreeland, Jr., "Processing and Properties of Shock Consolidated SiC-Particulate Reinforced Ti Matrix Composites", *J. de Physique IV*, Colloque **C8**, pp. 331-336 (1994).

[5] W. Tong and G. Ravichandran, "Effective Elastic Moduli and Characterization of a Particulate-Reinforced Metal Matrix Composite with Damaged Particles", *Composite Sci. & Tech.* **52** (2), pp.247-252 (1994).

[6] D. Benson, W. Tong, and G. Ravichandran, "Particle-Level Modeling of Dynamic Consolidation of Ti-SiC Powders", *Modell. Simu. Mater. Sci. Eng.* **3**, 771-796 (1995).

[7] P.S. Follansbee, "The Hopkinson Bar", In: *Metals Handbook*, **8** 9th. ed, ASM, Materials Park, Ohio, pp. 198-203 (1985).

[8] W. Tong and X. Li, UNL Split Hopkinson Bar, Technical Report, University of Nebraska-Lincoln (1996).

[9] S. Abkowitz, P.F. Weihrauch, S.M. Abkowitz, and H.L. Heussi, "The Commercial Application of Low-Cost Titanium Composites", *JOM*, pp. 40-41 (August 1995).

[10] W. Tong and S. Huang, "Application of Digital Image Correlation to Microfracture Testing of Particulate-Reinforced Titanium Composites", 1996 SEM VIII Intl. Congress on Exp. Mech., June 10-13, 1996, Nashville, Tennessee.

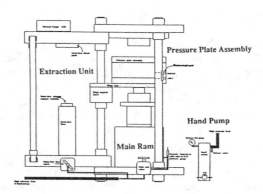

Fig. 1 Schematic of a High-Pressure Materials Processing Piston-Cylinder Apparatus at UNL [1].

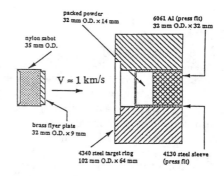

Fig. 2 Schematic of a Dynamic Compactor [2].

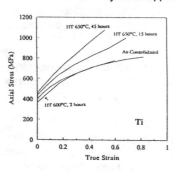

Fig. 3 Quasi-static Compression of Consolidated and Annealed Ti Matrix and Ti-SiCp Composites.

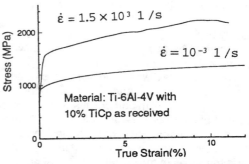

Fig. 4. Rate-Dependence of Flow Stress of Particulate-Reinforced Titanium Composites under Uniaxial Compression.

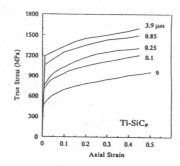

as-received          deformed

Fig. 5 Damage Evolution of a Titanium Composite Subjected to Dynamic Loading.

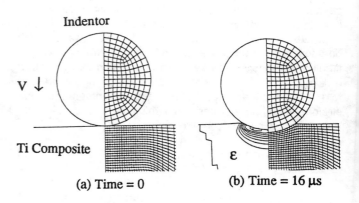

(a) Time = 0          (b) Time = 16 μs

Fig. 6 Large Deformation and Stress Analysis of the Impact Indentation Process of Titanium Composites by Dynamic Finite Element Simulation.

# Cracking Process and Delamination Strength of WC-Co Film Sprayed by High-Speed Flame

Keijiro Nakasa and Masahiko Kato
Faculty of Engineering, Hiroshima University, Higashi-Hiroshima, 739 Japan

Masanobu Kamata and Nobuhiko Hara
Hiroshima Prefectural Industry Center, Kure, Hiroshima, 737 Japan

In order to give higher wear-, heat- and corrosion-resistance to materials, various kinds of coating methods, such as PVD, CVD, spraying, have been developed. However, the coating films can be often delaminated by the application of heat and/or stress cycles, so that it is necessary not only to develop high-performance coating methods but also to construct an appropriate method to evaluate the delamination strength of film. Because the main reason for the delamination in actual structures is the generation of shear stress at interface due to the difference in thermal expansion coefficients and elastic constants between film and substrate, the evaluation method is required which can express the delamination strength under shear stress quantitatively. In the present research, WC(88%)+Co(12%) powder was sprayed on H-11 steel specimen by high-speed flame method, and the cracking and delamination processes were investigated by the tensile test where the load was applied parallel to the film and the delamination of film was caused by shear stress.

During tensile test, the sounds of cracking increases progressively with increase in plastic deformation of substrate, which can correspond to the occurrence of micro cracking in the film and at interface. After the sudden stop of sounds, distinct cracks with almost the same interval appear. This fact means that the division of film occurs repeatedly within relatively narrow load range. The delamination of film occurs after the division has finished.

The interfacial energy between elastic film and elastic-plastic substrate was calculated by expanding the Kendall's equation which had been introduced for the semiinfinitely long film on the substrate in elastic deformation:

$$2 \gamma_{12} = \frac{[P-bB_2 \sigma_{ys}\{1-(E_p/E_e)\}]^2}{2b^2} \cdot \frac{B_1 E_1}{B_2 E_p(B_1 E_1 + B_2 E_p)}$$

Where P is the load at the beginning of delamination, b is the width of specimen, $B_1$ and $B_2$ are the thickness of film and substrate. $E_1$ is the elastic constant of film, $E_2$ and $E_p$ are the elastic and plastic constants of substrate when the stress-strain curve is approximately expressed by that of a linear hardening material, and $\sigma_{ys}$ is the yield strength of substrate.

The crack interval measured after the tensile test are within $\pm 50\%$ larger or smaller than the average value, which means that the division of film occurs not randomly but almost regularly. Fig.1 shows the relation between film thickness and mean value of crack interval. Fig. 2 gives the relation between film thickness and interfacial energy. The interfacial energy slightly decreases with increase in film thickness. When the film with a length L on a substrate receives tensile load, the tensile stress $\sigma_x$ is maximum in the center of film (x=0), and the division occurs when $\sigma_x$ reaches a critical tensile strength of film $\sigma_c$ as long as the delamination does not occur. After continuous division of film, if the shear stress at interface $\tau_{xy}$ reaches a critical shear strength $\tau_c$, the division stops and the delamination occurs. By analytical and experimental considerations, the following relation is obtained:

$$L_m/B_2 = \alpha (\sigma_c/\tau_c)(B_1/B_2)^k$$

where $\alpha$ and k are constants. From the data of Fig.1, $\alpha (\sigma_c/\tau_c) = 0.8$, k=0.6 are obtained.

In order to examine whether the delamination of film occurs just along the interface or not, X-ray beam with 100 $\mu$m diameter was radiated by using a micro area X-ray diffraction apparatus with a curved position sensitive proportional counter. As is shown in Fig.3, peaks from WC are detected on the delamination interface, which means that the film is sheared off leaving parts of film into the concave on substrate formed by sandblasting.

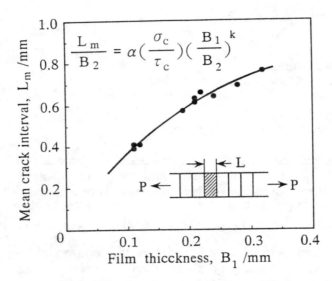

$$\frac{L_m}{B_2} = \alpha\left(\frac{\sigma_c}{\tau_c}\right)\left(\frac{B_1}{B_2}\right)^k$$

Fig.1 Relation between film thickness and mean crack interval.

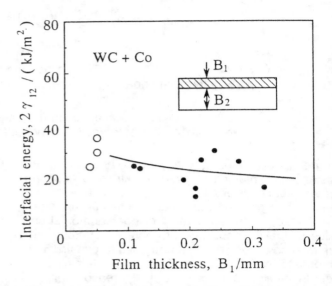

Fig. 2 Relation between film thickness and interfacial energy.

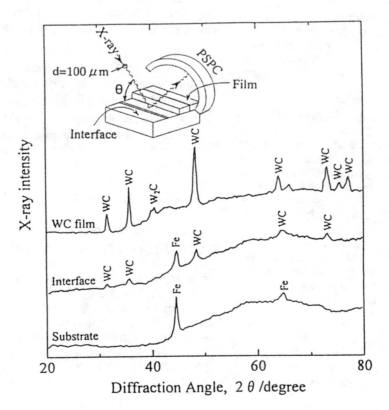

Fig. 3 Micro area X-ray diffraction patterns of delamination surface.

# Experimental Investigation of the Thermal Fatigue Life of Multilayer Thin Film Structures

Xuewei Sun, Sijun He

Department of Engineering Mechanics

Tsinghua University

Beijing 100084, P. R. China

With the development of the electronic industry in recent years, multilayer thin film structure is more and more widely used to diminish the volume of the large scale integrated circuits packaging. It induces many technical problems. Fox example, because of the different thermal expansion coefficient of different layers, thermal stress and strain exist in the structures. During the cycle that devices work and stop working, they are heated and cooled again and again and thermal fatigue problem is resulted. It is emergent for us to research these problems to improve the reliability of the device.

A simple plane model(Fig.1) of multilayer thin film structure simulating to typical structure in electronic packaging is established[1][2]. In the model, some assumption are made as followed: (1) The axial stress in thin film is uniform; (2) The substrate is in pure bending condition; (3) After the deformation, the curvature of the substrate is constant along the length. With the balance equations of the force and the torque of the structure and the relation between stress and strain, t can be used to calculate the plastic strain and then predict the thermal fatigue life of the structures without large scale calculation. The ALGOR Finite Element Analysis System is used to calculate the stress of the multilayer thin film structures under thermal cycle load[3]. Distribution of the displacement and the stress is pictured. The shear stress concentration in the edge of the interface is discussed[4]. The relation between the stress range and the thermal fatigue life of the structure which is similar to Mansion-Coffee equation is built.

To prove the results of the analysis, a thermal fatigue test system is designed to carry on the investigations of the thermal fatigue life of the structures and micro-changes during the cycle. It consists of three parts. The first part is thermal fatigue test machine(Fig.2) which is used to add thermal cycle load without moving the specimens. The temperature ranges between room temperature and 150 ℃. The second part is moire interferometry system which is used to measure the surface stress and displacement. The third part is the long distance microscope system(LDM) (Fig.3) which is used to watch the micro-damage such as micro-crack on the surface. With the system, real-time tests can be realized. Therefore, the change of the micro damage during the thermal cycle can be measured. By using some transparent materials, the interface condition can be watched with the LDM system directly. The relation between crack growth and the thermal fatigue life is determined. An equation to predict the thermal fatigue life of multilayer thin film structure is listed.

Reference:

[1]  King-Ning Tu. "Electronic thin film science," Macmillan Publishing Company, 1992,   pp77~88.
[2]  Cifuents A O.  "A note on the determination of the thermal stresses in multi-metal beams subjected to temperature variations," J. Elect. P., 1991, Vol. 113: pp425~427.
[3]  He Sijun, Sun Xuewei, "Evaluation of thermal stress and strain in electronic packaging multilayered structures," Journal of Tsinghua University, to be published 1996.5.
[4]  Pao Yi-Hsin, Eisele Ellen. "Interfacial shear and peel stresses in multilayered thin stacks subjected to uniform thermal loading,"  J. Elect. P., 1991, Vol. 113: pp164~172.

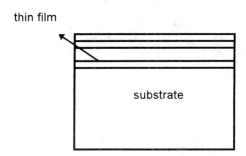

Fig. 1 illustration of the simple plane model of multilayer thin film structure

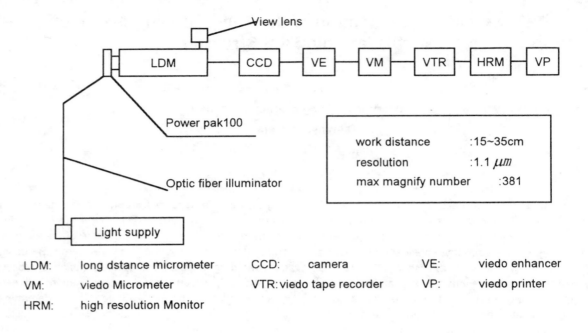

Fig.2 schematic of the LDM system

Within Fig.2:

View lens

LDM — CCD — VE — VM — VTR — HRM — VP

Power pak100

Optic fiber illuminator

Light supply

work distance :15~35cm
resolution :1.1 $\mu m$
max magnify number :381

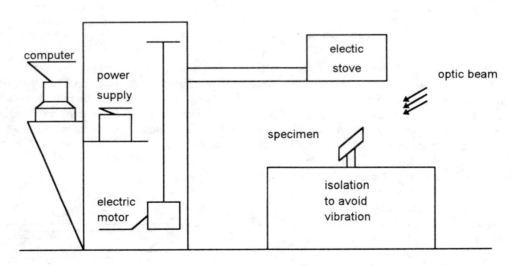

Fig.3 sketch map of the thermal fatigue life test system for thin film stuctures

computer

power supply

electric motor

electic stove

optic beam

specimen

isolation to avoid vibration

# Slow Crack Growth versus Creep Cavity Coalescence: Competing Failure Mechanisms During High-Temperature Deformation of Advanced Ceramics

Michael G. Jenkins and Travis L. Stevens
University of Washington
Mechanical Engineering, Box 352600
Seattle, WA 98195-2600

Advanced ceramics are now at a level of maturity to be alternative materials in certain structural applications. For example, silicon nitride has been identified as possessing the necessary mechanical properties to be exploited for complex-shaped components in advanced gas turbines.

Unfortunately, the widespread use of silicon nitride in such applications is still limited partly by low confidence of design engineers in the long-term reliability of these new materials. This lack of confidence is due primarily to limited data bases on long-term behaviour particularly at elevated temperatures. Failure mechanism maps can be used to address these design concerns. However, many of these fracture mechanism maps have been limited to either static fatigue or fast-fracture strength test results. Use of ceramics in engine components requires mechanical reliability data under a variety of thermal, mechanical, and environmental conditions including cycling.

Isothermal dynamic (monotonically-loaded strength tests) and cyclic fatigue tests are first steps in identifying failure mechanisms (e.g., slow crack growth, SCG) other than those revealed through fast fracture (weakest-link fracture from pre-existing flaws) and static fatigue tests (creep-cavity coalescence). Recently, limited comparisons of flexural static, dynamic, and cyclic fatigue results for silicon nitrides at elevated temperatures have shown the usefulness of an effective time approach for identifying the underlying SCG failure mechanism for all three fatigue modes.

In this study, a commercial, isopressed and HIPed silicon nitride, designated PY6 (GTE Laboratories, Waltham, Mass.) was investigated. PY6 was fabricated using ~6 wt% yttrium oxide as the densification aid resulting in a dense microstructure consisting of 1 to 6 μm long acicular grains surrounded by nominally equiaxed grains 0.1 to 1.0 μm in diameter. Continuous, thin layers of an amorphous yttrium disilicate with crystalline yttrium disilicate at the grain junction triple points separated the $\beta$-Si$_3$N$_4$ grains.

Button-head, tensile specimens with 6.35-mm diameter X 35-mm long gage sections were machined by diamond-grit grinding from as-processed rods 160-mm long and 20-mm in diameter. Tests were conducted on closed-loop, electro-mechanical test machines under electronic load control. Higher frequency (10 Hz) cyclic fatigue tests were performed on a closed-loop servo-hydraulic test machine. Load-time profiles were controlled by trapezoidal or sinusoidal wave-form function generators. Bending was minimized by either self-contained, hydraulic couplers attached to water-cooled grips or water-cooled adjustable, fixed-grips. Compact two-zone resistance-heated furnaces with maximum temperature capabilities of 1650°C were used to heat the specimens in ambient air environments (20-25°C, 30-65 %RH). Strains in the specimen gage sections were measured over 25-mm gage lengths with direct-contact extensometers (~0.5 μm resolution) employing remote capacitance sensors. Static, dynamic, and cyclic fatigue tests were performed at 1150, 1260, and 1370°C.

Static, dynamic, and cyclic fatigue results were compared directly using an effective time to failure approach assuming a common SCG failure mechanism for all three test modes. Combined stress rupture results are presented as log-log plots of maximum stress vs. effective time to failure for static, dynamic, and cyclic fatigue tests at 1150, 1260, and 1370°C. Although this is a common graphical representation of stress rupture results, the usual power law relation between maximum stress, $\sigma_{max}$, and effective time to failure, $t_{eff}$, takes the form:

$$t_{eff} = D\sigma_{max}^{-N} \qquad (1)$$

where D is a constant.

All test results for 1150°C are described by a single curve (N≈64) implying that all failures originated from a similar SCG mechanism previously identified for PY6 at this temperature. For the 1260°C tests, the results fall into two distributions: i) a nearly horizontal line (N≈57) similar in slope to that for the 1150°C results and fitting all dynamic and cyclic test results and ii) a line of sharply decreasing slope (N≈8) fitting the static test results. All results for the 1370°C tests are again represented by a single curve (N≈11) indicating a similar failure mechanism for all the tests although not the assumed SCG mechanism.

Figure 1 shows a schematic representation of qualitative analyses conducted on the fracture surfaces resulting from the static, dynamic, and cyclic fatigue tests. Stress rupture and fracture surface analysis results for 1150°C are consistent with a SCG failure mechanism. For the 1260°C results, static fatigue appears to be more detrimental to the fatigue life than dynamic and cyclic fatigue. The creep damage zone observed in the static tests (Fig. 1b) was not observed for the longer-lived dynamic and cyclic fatigue tests (Fig. 1a). The loading rates of dynamic and cyclic fatigue tests interrupt creep/environmental damage nucleation and accumulation processes. Failures then originate from inherent defects rather than from the accumulation of the creep/environmental damage. However, the stress rupture results for 1370°C do not show similar differences in fatigue behaviour as might be expected based on the results at 1260°C. Identification of the majority of failure origins as creep/environmental damage originating from the surface (Fig. 1c) suggests that rapid oxidation

damage of PY6 at this temperature masks differences in fatigue resistance.

Fatigue and strength results were used to develop the fracture mechanism map shown in Fig. 2 for PY6. A unique feature of Fig. 2 is the obvious difference of the cyclic fatigue results compared to the creep (static fatigue) results. It could be concluded that a conservative test scenario for this material would be to evaluate the static fatigue behaviour using the results as an upper bound for design regardless of the loading scenario for the design. Note that the normalizing temperature in Fig. 2 is 1850°C which was used as an approximation of the dissociation temperature for silicon nitride.

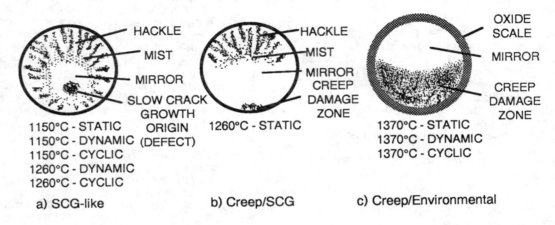

a) SCG-like      b) Creep/SCG      c) Creep/Environmental

Figure 1 Fracture surface features for static, dynamic and cyclic fatigue.

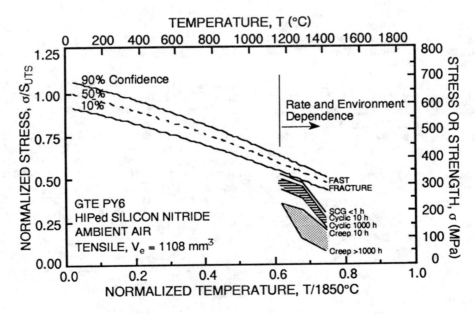

Figure 2 Fracture mechanism map for PY6 in tension.

# High Temperature Fatigue Crack Growth Behavior
# of $\gamma$-Base TiAl Intermetallics

T. Hannson, Y.Mutoh, S.Kurai,
Nagaoka University of Technology, Nagaoka-shi 940-21, Japan
Y.Mizuhara,
Nippon Steel Corp., Nakahara-ku, Kawasaki-shi 211, Japan

Gamma based titanium aluminides with light weight and attractive mechanical properties are most suitable for applications in aerospace structures and automobile components. Their fatigue and fracture characteristics must be understood for materials development as well as structural designing. Recent investigations reveal clearly the mechanisms of fatigue crack growth and fatigue properties at room temperature. However, the characteristics at high temperature have not been well understood. Objectives of the present study are to reveal high temperature fatigue crack growth properties of $\gamma$-base TiAl and to understand their fatigue crack growth mechanisms at high temperature.

Cast and heat treated binary gamma base titanium aluminides, Ti-50at%Al and Ti-46at%Al (hereafter Ti-50Al and Ti-46Al, respectively) and ternary chromium alloyed Ti-47at%Al-3at%Cr (hereafter TiAlCr) were used. The final microstructures were fully equiaxed with average grain diameter of $200\,\mu$m for Ti-50Al and fully lamellar with average grain size of $40\,\mu$m for Ti-46Al. TiAlCr had dominant equiaxed grains with few lamellar grains, average diameter of which was $200\,\mu$m. Few $\beta$-phase particles were also observed in TiAlCr.

Fatigue crack growth experiments were carried out using tensile plate specimens of 1mm thickness, 5mm width and 20mm guage length. An electro-discharge machine center notch of 1mm length and 0.15 width was introduced at the center of specimen as a starter for fatigue crack growth. A fatigue precrack was introduced using the K-decreasing technique up to 0.5mm to avoid the mechanical effect of the notch. Fatigue crack growth tests both at room temperature and 750℃ were carried out inside the scanning electron microscope chamber using a sine wave of 10Hz and stress ratio R of 0.1 and crack growth processes were monitored using the scanning electron microscope. Crack length was measured using scanning electron micrographs taken at magnifications of 1500-2000×.

Figures 1 (a) - (c) indicate relationships between crack growth rate da/dN and stress intensity factor range $\Delta$K for Ti-50Al, Ti-46Al and TiAlCr, respectively. Large scatter of crack growth rates was observed in lamellar microstructure Ti-46Al, in which orientation of lamellar grain affects crack growth resistance [1]. The fatigue crack growth rates at elevated temperature were higher than those at room temperature in all materials tested. At room temperature fatigue crack growth resistance of lamellar Ti-46Al was higher than those of equiaxed Ti-50Al and duplex TiAlCr, in which fraction of lamellar grains were very low and equiaxed grains were dominant. This high crack growth resistance of lamellar microstructure compared to the other microstructures has been reported [2]. At elevated temperature TiAlCr showed higher fatigue crack resistance. From the fatigue crack path observations, a fatigue crack often arrested in ductile $\beta$-phase particles. Therefore, the ductile $\beta$-phase may contribute to crack growth resistance.

Figure 2 shows the in-situ observations of fatigue crack growth process in Ti-46Al at elevated temperature. From these observations, a basic fatigue crack growth mechanism of TiAl can be proposed as follows. During cyclic deformation, microcracks are initiated near crack tip region and grow to coalesce to a main crack. As the results, bridging elements are formed on the crack wake, which will contribute crack growth resistance. This mechanism was basically common in all materials tested and at all temperatures tested. No blunting and resharpening mechanism, which is considered to be the main mechanism of fatigue crack growth in metallic materials, was observed.

Figures 3(a) - (c) show relationships between crack growth rate da/dN and stress intensity factor range normalized by Young's modulus $\Delta$K/E. The crack growth curves at room and elevated temperatures coincided for all materials tested. Therefore, since the basic mechanism of crack growth is common at room and 750℃, the difference of crack growth resistance between room and elevated temperatures mainly results from the difference of Young's modulus.

References:

[1] Gnanamoorthy,R.,Mutoh,Y.,Hayashi,K., Mizuhara,Y., "Influence of Lamellar Lath orientation on the Fatigue Crack Growth Behavior of Gamma Base Titanium Aluminides," Scripta Metallurgica et Materialia, 33-6, pp.907-912, 1995.
[2] Gnanamoorthy,R., Mutoh,Y., Mizuhara,Y., "Fatigue Crack Growth Behavior of Equiaxed, Duplex amd Lamellar Microstructure $\gamma$-Base Titanium Aluminides," Materials Science and Engineering A, in press.

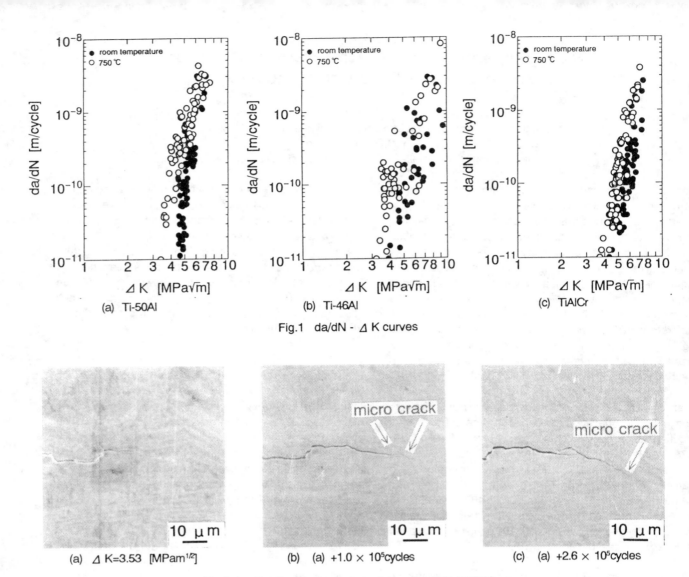

(a) Ti-50Al     (b) Ti-46Al     (c) TiAlCr

Fig.1   da/dN - $\Delta$K curves

(a) $\Delta$K=3.53 [MPam$^{1/2}$]     (b) (a) +1.0 × 10$^5$cycles     (c) (a) +2.6 × 10$^5$cycles

Fig.2 In-situ observations of crack tip   (Ti-46Al, 750℃)

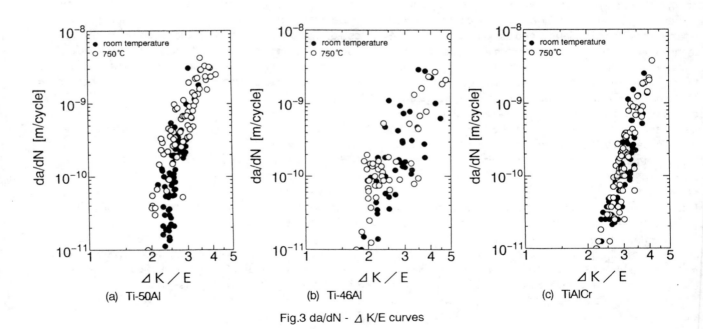

(a) Ti-50Al     (b) Ti-46Al     (c) TiAlCr

Fig.3 da/dN - $\Delta$K/E curves

# Tensile Stress-Strain Response and Creep Properties of Si$_3$N$_4$ Ceramics at Elevated Temperatures

Kenji.Hatanaka, Kenichi Oshita
Department of Mechanical Engineering, Faculty of Engineering,
Yamaguchi University
2557 Tokiwadai, Ube City, 755 Japan
and

Hirohisa Shiota
Department of Mechanical Engineering, Faculty of Engineering,
Gifu University
1-1 Yanagido, Gifu City, 501-11 Japan

The tensile displacement $\delta$ of test specimen with four projections, which was newly designed by the authors, was measured by means of the laser-beam-type extensometer at elevated temperatures. The tensile strain was obtained from dividing the displacement by the initial distance between the two projections. The solid line in Fig.1 shows the relationship between tensile stress and strain of sintered silicon nitride ceramics measured at test temperature T=1300℃ and displacement rate $\dot{\delta}$ =0.06mm/min. The load P-displacement $\delta$ response was calculated through elastic-plastic finite element method, using this stress-strain curve. Subsequently, the new tensile stress-strain curve was determined so that the calculated P-$\delta$ curve might agree with the measured one, referring to the difference between the calculated and measured p-$\delta$ responses. The tensile stress-strain curve estimated in this way is presented by the dashed line together with the measured one in Fig.1. According to the figure, the measured tensile strain is about 10 to 15 percent larger than the corrected strain at a given stress. Thus, correct tensile

stress-strain response can be determined from combining the measurement of the displacement between the two projections and the elastic-plastic finite element method at elevated temperatures.

Creep test was performed using the tensile test specimen mentioned above, and creep displacement was measured by means of the laser-beam-type extensometer. Then the equation expressing the relationship between minimum creep strain rate $\dot{\varepsilon}_c$ and applied stress $\sigma$,

$$\dot{\varepsilon}_c = 1.37 \times 10^{-15} \sigma^{4.09} (\text{sec}^{-1}) \qquad (1)$$

was determined.

Nonelastic finite element analysis was made for the tensile test specimen: First the tensile stress-strain response was calculated by elastic-plastic finite element analysis using the corrected stress-strain response presented in Fig.1. Then this was followed by the steady state creep finite element analysis in which eq.(1) was employed as a constitutive equation.
In the steady state creep analysis, the calculations

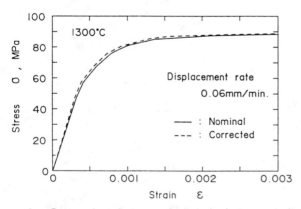

**Figure 1.** Comparison between the nominal stress-strain relationship obtained from the measured P-$\delta$ relationship and the stress-strain relationship corrected using the elastic-plastic F.E.M., under the test condition of the test temperature, 1300 ℃ and the displacement rate, 0.06mm/min.

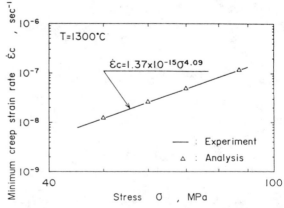

**Figure 2.** Comparison of the constitutive equation (1) determined from experiment and the relationship between minimum creep strain rate and stress calculated through the F.E.M. using the equation.

through non-steady state creep analysis were repeated until the creep deformation reached the steady state as follows; the load increment induced by creep strain was calculated at the respective mesh nodes for every time increment predetermined, and then the equilibrium equations were constructed for these load increments at the respective nodes.

The steady state creep F.E.M. analysis was performed for the specimen with four projections at applied stresses of 50, 60, 70 and 87MPa, using the constitutive equation (1). The relationship between $\dot{\varepsilon}_c$ and $\sigma$ obtained from the calculation is compared with eq.(1) in Fig.2. The open triangles exactly fall on the solid line in the figure. This suggests that the measured minimum creep strain rate is hardly influenced by stress/strain concentration occurring at the root of the projections.

Figure 3 shows the enlarged root area of the projection. The open circles denote the locations of mesh-nodes at time t=0, and they are connected with dashed line. The axial minimum creep strain rates at the mesh-nodes were calculated at $\sigma$ =60MPa and t=14.4hours. The minimum creep strain rate at the parallel part of the specimen was subtracted from them. This quantity was plotted by the solid square marks in Fig.2. According to this figure, the axial creep strain rate in the edge region around the projection-root is slightly larger than the one at the parallel part of the specimen. Meanwhile, it should be noted that the inner edge of the projection has almost the same steady creep strain rate as the one at the central part of the specimen. The good agreement between eq.(1) and the minimum creep strain rate-stress curve calculated through F.E.M. is understood well by such a estimation.

The minimum creep strain rate calculated as an average creep strain rate between the two projections and the one estimated from the creep constitutive equation used for the F.E.M. calculation were compared. Then optimum design of tensile creep specimen with four projections, which was shown in Fig.4, was

performed, so that the difference between the two might be minimized. This includes how to determine width B, thickness t, length of the projection L and radius at the root of the projection R in Fig.4. Figure 5 shows its procedures. First, we determine $R_{B=3,L=5}$ so that $(\dot{\varepsilon}_c - \bar{\dot{\varepsilon}}_c)/\dot{\varepsilon}_c$ may be zero, giving an appropriate value of n in the creep constitutive equation $\dot{\varepsilon}_c = K\sigma^n$, where $R_{B=3,L=5}$ represents radius at root of the projection in the specimen with B=3mm and L=5mm, and $\dot{\varepsilon}_c$ and $\bar{\dot{\varepsilon}}_c$ denote the minimum creep strain rates calculated from the displacement between the two projections through inelastic F.E.M. analysis and determined directly from the creep constitutive equation for a given stress. Then width B, thickness t and radius at root of the projection R are fixed in the ranges of $3.0 \leq B \leq 6.0$, $0.2 \leq t \leq B$ and $0.5 \leq R \leq 0.9$ in mm. Finally, length of the projection L is calculated as a function of $R_{B=3,L=5}$, B and R. It is recommended that the values of B and t are preferentially determined, considering the capacity of testing machine.

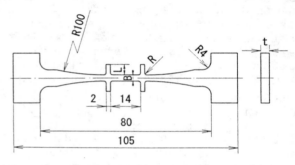

**Figure 4.** Shape and dimensions of test specimen

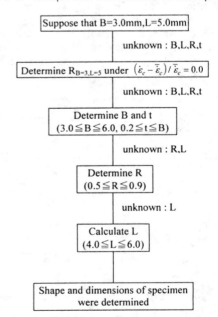

**Figure 5.** Flow chart for determining optimum configuration of projection-accompanied tensile creep specimen

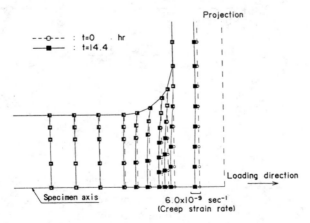

**Figure 3.** Distribution of steady state-axial creep strain rate at mesh-node calculated through the F.E.M.. (T=1300℃, $\sigma$ =60MPa)

# The History of Photoelastic Coatings at Boeing

Ron Slaminko
Experimental Mechanics Laboratory
The Boeing Co.
P.O. Box 3707, MailStop 47-02
Seattle, WA 98124

Photoelastic coatings were first used at Boeing in 1958. Over the last 37 years, this technology has made significant contributions to the development of nearly every major Boeing product from commercial and military airplanes to helicopters and space vehicles.

The Golden Age of photoelastic coatings at Boeing lasted through the sixties and into the seventies, as the company at one time had as many as six photoelasticity laboratories operating simultaneously. Significant research was conducted in all aspects of the technology, from basic coating materials and installation techniques, to the development of custom instruments. The early 60s also saw the development of the epoxy structural models, a technique which greatly expanded the use of photoelastic coatings.

Increased sophistication of finite element methods, as well as development of alternative measurement technologies has led to a decline in the use of photoelastic coatings. Today, only one laboratory remains in operation at Boeing and photoelasticity accounts for only about one third of its activities. Nevertheless, there continue to exist certain design challenges for which photoelastic coating remains the best, and often only, viable method.

The challenge for a photoelastician today is to continually strive to reduce the costs and increase the quality of the technique. Recent advancements in automated analysis and in rapid prototyping are important steps along this road.

This talk will trace the important milestones in the history of Boeing's use of photoelastic coatings, discuss how the tools and processes of the technique have changed and matured over the years, and describe some future challenges.

# Photoelastic Coating and Strain Gage Analysis of Aluminum-Lithium Welded Joints

S. C. Gambrell, Jr., Satish Kumar
Department of Engineering Science and Mechanics
University of Alabama
Tuscaloosa, AL  35487

Because of inherent problems experienced with welding Al-Li alloy, a major research effort is being made to increase reliability of the approximately 36,000 inches of weld in the proposed new Al-Li external fuel tanks of the shuttle. As part of this effort, a photoelastic coating and strain gage analysis of the Al-Li welded joint was made to determine yielding and other characteristics of the joint. Panels of 2195 aluminum alloy were joined with 4030 filler wire at the National Aeronautics and Space Administration-Marshall Space Flight Center having welds with (a) no filler wire in the first pass, and (b) filler wire in the first pass. Tensile tests were conducted on standard dogbone specimens 1.50 inches wide and 0.20 inches thick that were machined from the welded panels (see Figure 1). Results are presented in the form of a fifth order polynomial through the photo-elastic coating and strain gage data. Comparisons were made between the behavior of the two types of weld.

Measurements of the depth (parallel to load direction) of the crown side and root side welds on specimens etched with Keller's etching fluid indicated that, on average, the crown side weld measured 0.34 inches and the root side weld measured 0.24 inches. Referring to Fig. 1, it may be seen that on the root side, the lower fusion boundary lay almost exactly at point 1 and that on the crown side, the lower fusion boundary was between points 1 and 2 approximately 0.045 inches below point 1. Panels (and specimens) had no post-weld heat treatment and were therefore in an "as-welded" condition. Specimens were instrumented on both crown and root sides with PS-1 photoelastic coatings 0.010 inches thick and with CEA-13-032WT-120 strain gages. The photoelastic coating covered the center four inches of the specimen and strain gages were placed on the centerline of the weld and at a location 0.25 inches below the centerline (points 0 and 2, Fig. 1).

Figures 2 and 3 show typical examples of behavior of the specimens. Comparisons of stress-strain and contraction ratio behavior of joints with an without filler wire in the penetration pass are given in Figures 2 and 3, respectively. Data in Figure 2 indicate that at the centerline welds having filler wire in the penetration pass are more ductile than welds having no filler wire. Similar curves were obtained at points 1 and 2 (see Figure 1). Figure 3 indicates that at the centerline strain in the axial direction is disproportionately larger than strain in the transverse direction. Similar curves were obtained at point 2. However, since point 2 is outside the fusion boundaries and in the base material, the contraction ratios were greater than Poisson's ratio for all values of applied stress

In summary, test results indicate that (1) photoelastic coatings provide an exceptionally efficient whole field method to analyze behavior of welded joints and provide an understanding of complex material behavior which cannot be obtained with strain gages, (2) Al-Li welded joints normally have one fusion boundary which is preferred for yielding over the other fusion boundary, (3) Al-Li welded joints exhibit discontinuous yielding as the applied stress increases above the range of 28,000 to 30,000 psi, (4) contraction ratios in Al-Li welded joints differ greatly from Poisson's ratio as the applied stress increases, and (5) because of insertion of the more ductile filler material, Al-Li joints as-welded with filler wire in the first pass are more ductile at the centerline of the weld and at the preferred fusion boundary for yielding than are as-welded joints having no filler wire in the first pass.

The authors wish to thank the National Aeronautics and Space Administration at the Marshall Space Flight Center in Huntsville, Alabama for providing the welded Al-Li panels used for this work.

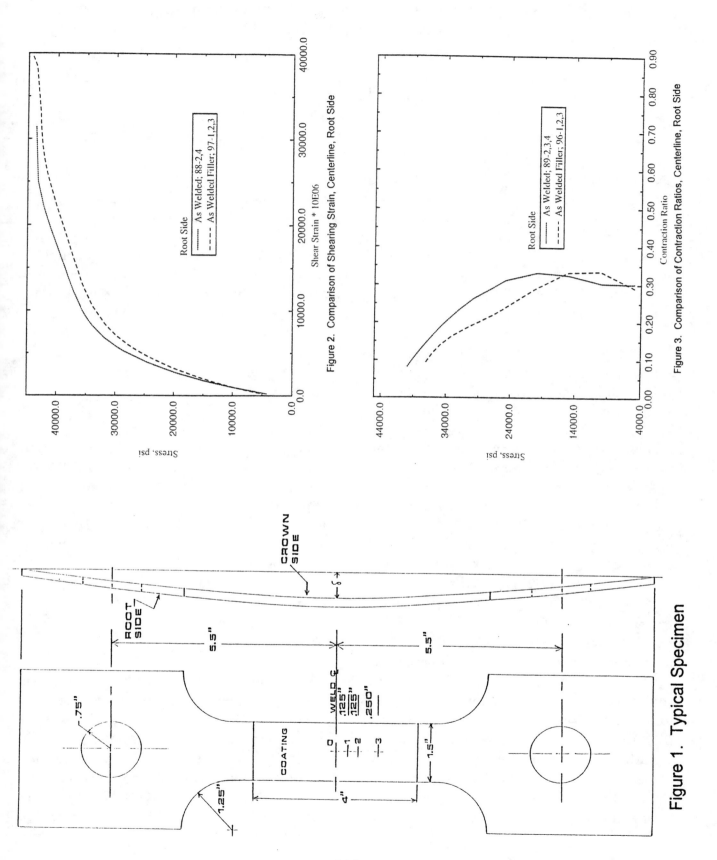

Figure 2. Comparison of Shearing Strain, Centerline, Root Side

Figure 3. Comparison of Contraction Ratios, Centerline, Root Side

Figure 1. Typical Specimen

149

# Industrial Experience in the use of Full-Field Automated Reflection Polariscopy for Airbus Experimental Stress Analysis.

E.W.O'Brien, I.J.Jones
British Aerospace Airbus Ltd.
Filton, Bristol.U K.

Photoelastic stress analysis is used within the Aerospace industry both as a primary stressing technique and as an experimental tool to validate classical and Finite Element structural analyses. It is also used in the design optimisation of aircraft components for weight, cost and structural reliability as well as problem solving and general stress issues.

Currently reflection photoelastic analyses are carried out by highly skilled Engineers performing manual analyses on components and structures, yielding maximum shear values (isochromatics) and principal stress directions (isoclinics) with principal stresses at free edges. In the majority of instances this information is sufficient to define the state of stress in a component, since stress concentrations always occur at free edges.

Increasingly the Experimental Stress Analysis Group at British Aerospace Airbus are being required to determine full field stress distributions for validation of components. The method selected involves employing additional techniques in conjunction with Photoelastic coatings to enable stress separation at numerous points of interest indicated from the Isochromatic fringe pattern. This type of structural survey is somewhat time consuming in both data acquisition and in the post-processing to reduce the information into the required format. There is also an increasing requirement to perform this type of analysis within a very limited time window, when an aircraft is in for a service or a fatigue test is off-line for a routine inspection etc.

When all the above criteria are taken into consideration it becomes apparent that the time has now come to turn to modern technology to enhance the traditional Photoelastic methods to enable them to to cope with the increasing economic pressures that now mean that very short windows of opportunity are available for analysis .

In pursuit of a solution to this problem, BAe Airbus is supporting an international consortium in the development of a full field automated polariscope. This is required to instantaneously collect strain data then process it into a separated principal stress and principal angle format that is easier for the conventionaly trained engineer to handle.

It is therefore clear that modern high-tech methods are required to supplement traditional photelastic techniques that have now been available for 40 years.

Several automated photoelastic analysis systems have been developed over the past 20 or so years, however these systems have concentrated on solving stress analysis on a point by point basis [1,2,3]. The consortium polariscope been developed under the leadership of Sheffield University U.K. is based upon the contemporaneous Phase Stepping Technique and uses CCD cameras, frame grabbing hardware and a Personal Computer to acquire the data. This data is subsequently processed via specifically written software to output Isocromatic and Isoclinic information for each pixel of the CCD image. With a small amount of user input, the individual principal stress magnitudes $\sigma_1$, $\sigma_2$ and $\theta$ are obtained. NB. This is the minimum data required to define the total stress state at a point in a planar structure.

The Phase stepping concept has been simply described[4] as changing the absolute phase of the reference wave in equal steps and measuring the local light intensity after each step. The system that has been developed has in practice achieved this by optical methods.

A general form of the light intensity emerging from the analyser when viewed using circularly polarised light, is given by :-

$$i(x,y) = i_m + i_v(\sin2(\beta-\varphi)\cos\alpha - \sin2(\theta-\varphi)\cos2(\beta-\varphi)\sin\alpha)$$

where $i_v$ is the light intensity emerging from the analyser when all axes of the polariscope and specimen are parallel and the term $i_m$ takes account of stray light. The angles $\beta$, $\varphi$ and $\theta$ are angles between a reference axis and the slow axis of the analyser, output quarter wave plate and specimen respectively. The relative phase $\alpha$ of the two rays formed when light is transmitted through a specimen is directly related to the isochromatic fringe order N by :-

$$\alpha = 2pN = (\sigma_1 - \sigma_2) f.t$$

where $\sigma_1$ and $\sigma_2$ are the maximum and minimum principal stresses respectively, 'f' is the material fringe constant and 't' is the specimen thickness.

By utilising the above relationships, solving for the unknown quantities of '$\theta$', the isoclinic parameter, $\alpha$, the relative phase and the intensities $i_m$ and $i_v$ it is possible by the method of wrapping, to produce a contour map of the isochromatic and isoclinic parameters. By further seeding the resulting $(\sigma_1 - \sigma_2)$ data with a single point value of a principal stress at a free edge or by using an isopachic result at a point internal to the specimen, it is a straight forward calculation, using Frocht's[5] method of shear difference, to determine the separation of the principal stresses over the full field of view.

The main experience so far in the industrial use has demonstrated significant time savings in detailed full field analyses.
For areas of high stress concentration care must be taken to acquire a close up view of the area of interest so that the pixel size allows adequate resolution of the peaks.
The system is at least an order more sensitive than manual polariscopes and research is being conducted in the analysis of stereolithography models and spray on epoxy coatings.

### References.

[1] Allison.IM and Nurse.P. *Automatic photoelastic data.* Proc JBCSA Conference on the Recording and Interpretation of Engineering Measurements. IME London (1972) 203-207
[2] Redner.S *A new automatic polariscope system.* Experimental Mechanics (1974) 486-491
[3] Fessler. H, Marston.RE, Ollerton.E. *A micropolariscope for automatic stress analysis.* Journal of Strain Analysis . 22 ( 1987 ) 25-35.
[4] Hecker.F, Morche. B, *Computer aided measurement of relative retardations in plane photoelastic test data. in Experimental Stress Analysis* . (ed) Wieringa.H, M Nijhoff Publishers. Dordrecht. Netherlands (1986) 535-542.
[5] Frocht. MM. *Photoelasticity Vol 1* . Wiley (1941) 252-286.

# Photoelastic Coating in Jet Motor Engine Design

M. TARONI - SNECMA (France)[1]
D. PARASKEVAS - PK-LAB (France)[2]

## Abstract:

*SNECMA is widely using photoelastic coating in stress analysis for both design and certification tests, together with Finite Element Calculation (FEC) and strain gages. Many examples can be shown, especially in some cases where numeric calculus cannot give accurate results.*

*Three optical devices are used by SNECMA for photoelasticity by reflection:*

- *The polariscopes 030 and 040, furnished by Measurement Group, for standard cases. Large field can be observed and the measurements are made using Babinet compensator or TARDY interpolation method.*
- *The new PK-LAB integrated camera micro-polariscope: its small size allows for use inside a complex structure. Automatic measurements are obtained using the Friedel interpolation method.*

*The link between photoelastic coating, strain gages and FEC methods is illustrated with many actual cases. The authors will show how the combination of these different tools and methods decreases the design time and test costs.*

## Introduction:

The most sollicited parts in jet engines are, at SNECMA, the object of thorough studies aimed at ensuring the reliability of these components while in use, in view of the catastrophic consequences a failure of these parts could generate for the aircraft. The rotating parts (discs and blades, shafts), being the most critical, are thus being characterized at the design and development stages, in a complete manner, taking into account the material used as well as the mechanical stress in these parts.

This last point is being treated by SNECMA using two complementary approaches:

- Fine description of the state of stresses and deformations in the studied parts using FEC.
- Experimental correlation with partial testings of single components or complete assembly, with measurements of local stresses and deformations.

This second phase is necessary in many cases, as, despite the progress in recent years, uncertainties remain with regards to the boundaries conditions.

The techniques used today at SNECMA are based upon the theories of photoelasticity, allowing to correlate the mechanical and optical tensors.

- 3D photoelasticity, by stress-freezing method on epoxy models while loaded, applied mostly to structural parts sollicited in static loads or centrifugal load.

- 2D photoelasticity in situ, by measuring stresses on photoelastic coatings, applied mostly to static loads (ie, pressure on tanks, frame, ...) and high frequency dynamic loads (fan blade).

The access to experimental values of stresses/deformations in critical parts is thus essential to manufacturers for whom the validation of life cycle potentials obtained through calculation is imperative.

## Photoelasticity by reflection at SNECMA:

This method has been developped at SNECMA by F. ZANDMAN, in 1953, under the name Photostress [1] [2].

This technique was used, in some cases as an approach method and sometimes as the only possible method of analysis of the stress concentrations in some accidents of the structure.

This technique, after being temporarily abandonned at SNECMA, was nevertheless used in the group by MESSIER-BUGATTI (landing gear) and by HISPANO-SUIZA (jet engine frame). However, for the past ten years, the technique has been considerably developped at SNECMA for the characterization of composite materials and then for the dynamic characterization of compressor blades (for the characterization of main modes of vibration).(Fig. 3)

## Example of application: Low pressure turbine shaft.

This study was started after problems occured while in use on an empty shaft of an engine's BP turbine. The excessive tightening of the grip supporting the vent tube located inside the shaft was probably at the origin of the problem. The study was centered around finding, through Photostress, the state of stresses on the surface of the shaft connected to the tightening grip as well as the quantification of their values at the most sollicited points. The objective was to optimize the boundaries conditions at the intersection of the shaft's internal coating and the rim put in place by expansion.

A first Finite Elements Calculation (see fig. 1 and table 1) located the hierarchy of stresses at the level of the mating (section BB').

The photoelastic study showed two isotropic points in BB' and two zones of maximum stresses in AA', but the values of the stresses $(\sigma_1 - \sigma_2)$ were greatly different from the first calculation.

According to the precise indications of the Photostress (localisation and direction) strain gages were glued and a second FEC was done with optimized boundaries conditions and a refined size mesh.

The results presented in the following table show a better correlation with the second calculation:

---

[1] Head of Photoelastic and Stereolithography Lab (SNECMA) Société Nationale d'Etude et de Construction de Moteurs d'Aviation - BP 81 - 91003 EVRY Cedex - France.
[2] General Manager - PK LAB - BP 180- 60306 SENLIS Cedex- France.

TABLE 1

| Points | FEC * before test (in MPa) | Photo-stress (In MPa) | Strain Gages (In MPa) | FEC after test (In MPa) |
|---|---|---|---|---|
| AA' | $\sigma_1 - \sigma_2 = 190$ | $\sigma_1 - \sigma_2 = 260$ | $\sigma_1 = 210$ $\sigma_2 = 30$ $\sigma_1 - \sigma_2 = 240$ | $\sigma_1 - \sigma_2 = 250$ |
| BB' | $\sigma_1 - \sigma_2 \cong 300$ | $\sigma_1 - \sigma_2 \cong 0$ | $\sigma_1 = 260$ $\sigma_2 = 240$ $\sigma_1 - \sigma_2 = 20$ | $\sigma_1 - \sigma_2 = 20$ |

* boundaries conditions and size mesh non optimized

### Description of the micropolariscope:

If the surface to be studied is inside a structure, the new PK-LAB micropolariscope[3] is used (see picture 2). It is contained within a box of approximate dimensions 12x5x6 cm, which holds all the typical elements of a polariscope, as well as a color CCD camera and the motors necessary to the movements of the polarizing filters. The light is insured by optical fibers connected to an external source. The system's piloting is done through an electronic box, and the analysis is made from a video image on a monitor. The micropolariscope gives the direction of $\sigma_1$ (greatest stress) and the fraction part, in hundreth of fringe; precision 0,01 fringe.

### Conclusion:

Like photoelasticity on stress-frozen models, photoelastcity by reflexion is an indispensable tool for the conception of jet engines, in order to determine stresses in the concentration zones as well as verify methods of numeric calculations.
Photostress also allows for the localisation and the optimisation of the number of gages to instrument in order to validate the experimental results.
Thus this methodology is a powerful tool that increases reliability and confidence while saving both money and time.

### References:

[1] FLEURY R., and ZANDMAN F, Jauges d'efforts photoélastiques, Compte-rendus, Paris 238,1559 (1954).

[2] ZANDMAN F., REDNER S., DALLY J., Photoelastic coatings, Society for Experimental Stress Analysis, Monograph # 3.

[3] PARASKEVAS D. Micropolariscope par réflexion MPR01, Notice technique, PK-LAB (1996).

[4] BRAILLY P., TARONI M., Analyse expérimentale des contraintes en photoélasticimétrie par réflexion sur arbre de turbine BP, Rapport interne SNECMA, October 1995.

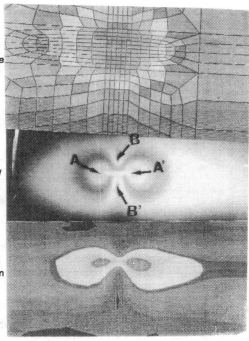

a) 1st FEC coarse mesh size and boundaries conditions not optimized

b) Photoelasticity isochromatics at the outside skin

c) 2nd FEC Refine calculation in critical points

Fig 1: low pressure turbine shaft.
Comparison between photostress and FEC

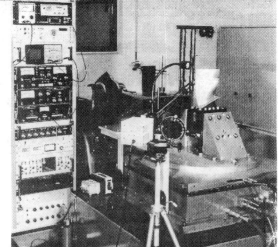

Fig 3: Blades vibration and polariscope by reflection

153

# Long Term Durability of Polymeric Composites
# for Application to
# Supersonic Commercial Aircraft Development

Thomas S. Gates
NASA Langley Research Center
Hampton, VA 23681

## Abstract

High Speed Research (HSR) is the NASA/industry program for development of the technology necessary to design and build a supersonic commercial transport. This program includes many major elements relating to airframe integration and test. One of these major elements, materials durability, exists under the broad materials and structures task. One aspect of the durability program is the development of technology to assess durability of advanced polymer matrix composites (PMC's).

The NASA/industry work on durability of PMC's is a multidiscipline, integrated effort with specific program elements and major identifiable deliverables. Research staff supporting the program include professional engineers, scientists, and technicians with extensive background and experience in engineering mechanics, polymer chemistry, and physics of materials. Both analytical and experimental studies are structured to address the three main program elements: a materials data base including real-time flight simulation, accelerated test methods, and life prediction methodology. Materials used in the studies include graphite/thermoplastic polyimides, graphite/thermoplastics, and graphite/bismalimides.

The first element, materials data base, is an experimental study which addresses long term aging characterization and the generation of a partial data base to describe the behavior due to the interaction of stress, temperature, moisture, and partial pressure. Test are performed over a range of temperatures and include conditions such as isothermal unloaded, isothermal loaded, thermally cycled, isothermal fatigue, in-phase TMF, and flight profiles. For this latter test type, the load/temperature flight profile test is conducted on large tension and compression panels which will accumulate up to 60,000 hours of real time exposure. These panels, removed from test at specific intervals, will be tested for changes in chemical/physical characteristics as well as changes in residual mechanical strength and stiffness. The residual mechanical tests include: open hole tension, open hole compression, unnoticed tension, and unnoticed compression. Separate tests will be performed on panels subjected to a combined temperature/altitude profile as well as materials subjected to moisture absorption to saturation.

The second element, accelerated test methods, addresses the need for relatively short term test methods which can provide information on long term behavior. These methods will be used to screen and rank candidate materials as well as provide predictive tools necessary for design. The methods being developed range from purely empirical to a viscoelastic based constitutive model which can predict the effects of elevated temperature and stress on the long term stiffness of a composite laminate. Verification of the accelerated test methods are made by comparison to test data such as tensile and compressive creep, static stiffness, and residual strength. The effects of physical and chemical aging on long term behavior will be documented. Superposition concepts will be utilized to develop accelerating conditions for both tension and compression.

The third major element, life prediction methodology, will develop the initial data required for the laminate based analysis of damage initiation and growth of unnoticed and notched, unidirectional, cross-ply, angle-ply, and quasi-isotropic laminates under monotonic tensile loading. The testing will account for the effects of aging, elevated temperature and stress states. The analytical models and associated measurement techniques will be developed to assess the relationships between changes in material properties due to aging and varying stress/temperature states. These measurements will also rely upon the long term data base developed in other parts of the program. Stiffness changes and strength degradation due to damage development and aging will be addressed.

# The Role of Interphase in the Long-Term Performance of Polymeric Composites Under Fatigue and Creep Loading

**S. Subramanian, C. T. Liu[1] and K. L. Reifsnider[2]**
**Research Scientist**
**AdTech Systems Research**
**1342, N. Fairfield Road, Beavercreek, OH : 45432**

A systematic study was conducted to examine the influence of fiber surface treatment and sizing on the formation of fiber-matrix interphase and its effects on the mechanical properties of composite laminates. Three material systems having the same Apollo graphite fibers and HC 9106-3 toughened epoxy matrix, but with different fiber surface treatments and sizings were used in this study. The fibers used in the 810 A and 820 A systems received 100 % and 200 % industry standard surface treatments respectively and were sized with Bisphenol-A unreacted epoxy material. The 810 O system was manufactured with 100 % surface treated fiber that was sized with pvp (polyvinylpyrrolidone), a thermoplastic material.

Permanganic etching and scanning electron microscopy results indicate that the interphase is discontinuous and made from linear chain polymeric material in the 810 A system. The interphase in the 810 O system has a gradient morphology while the 820 A system does not possess a well defined interphase. Single fiber fragmentation test results indicate that the 820 A system has the highest interfacial shear strength and the 810 O system, the lowest.

Mechanical test results indicate that the 810 O system possessed a significantly greater longitudinal tensile strength and failure strain compared to the 810 A system. The 810 A and 820 A systems have similar longitudinal tensile properties. The $(0,90_3)_s$ cross-ply laminates from the three material systems exhibit different damage modes and failure mechanisms under monotonic tensile loading.

Fatigue test on cross-ply laminates indicate that the 810 O laminates have longer lives at higher load levels and lower lives at lower load levels compared to the 810 A laminates. The 820 A laminates have longer fatigue lives compared to the other two laminates at all load levels (Figure 1). The 810 O material exhibits greater damage and stiffness reduction than the other two materials (Figure 2). The 810 A and 820 A systems exhibit a brittle stress concentration controlled failure, while the 810 O laminates exhibit global stain controlled failures. Nondestructive evaluation through x-ray radiography indicate greater amounts of interfacial debonds in the 0° ply and local delaminations at the 0/90 interface of the 810 O cross-ply. In contrast, there is very little of these damage modes observed in the 810 A and 820 A laminates [1].

The creep response of these three materials are also significantly different. The 810 A and 820 A laminates exhibit less damage in the form of matrix cracks and interfacial debonding, and undergo less compliance increase. In contrast, the 810 O laminates show more damage and compliance increases.

Based on the experimental results from this study, it may be concluded that the damage mechanisms, failure modes and long-term performance of cross-ply laminates with altered interfacial bonding are vastly different.

### Reference

1. S. Subramanian, J. S. Elmore, W. W. Stinchcomb, and K. L. Reifsnider, "Influence of fiber-matrix interphase on the long-term behavior of graphite/epoxy composites," Presented at the **12th Symposium on COMPOSITE MATERIALS : Testing and Design, ASTM,** May 16-17, Montreal, Quebec, Canada.

---

[1] Philips Laboratory, Edwards Airforce Base, CA : 93524
[2] Alexander Giacco Professor, ESM Department, Virginia Tech., VA : 24061

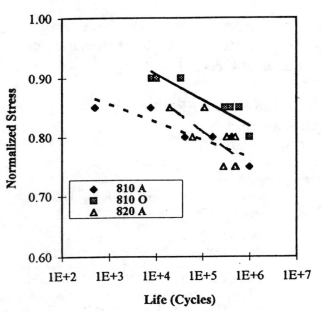

Fig.1 Fatigue lives of 810 A, 810 O and 820 A cross-ply laminates at various load levels.

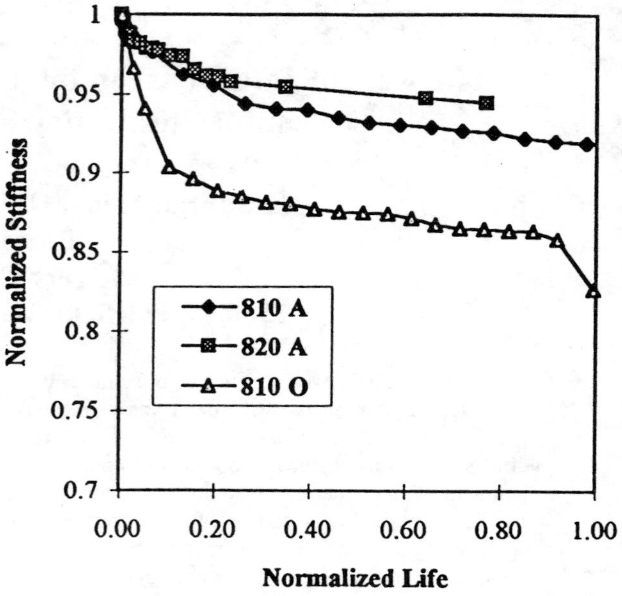

Fig.2 Stiffness reduction in 810 A, 810 O and 820 A cross-ply laminates at 85% applied load level.

# Post Impact Tension/Compression Fatigue of Graphite/PEEK Laminates

P. McAuliffe, S. C. Max Yen, and K. T. Teh
Department of Civil Engineering
Southern Illinois University at Carbondale
Carbondale, Illinois 62901

## SUMMARY

Impact damage whether it be a tool accidentally dropped on an airplanes composite wing or a rock hitting a composite swingarm on a mountain bike may have an effect on the life of that component. Even though this damage may or may not be visible, the strength and fatigue life of the component is frequently reduced. Damage has been shown to reduce the static strengths and fatigue life under tension-tension and compression-compression fatigue of certain composite laminates. For this reason, the designer must consider the possibility and consequences of damage developed during the design lifetime of a composite structure.

In this paper, the fatigue life of post impact Graphite/PEEK composite laminates is presented. The primary objective of this research was to investigate the domination of impact damage toward tension and/or compressive buckling fatigue life of composite laminates. It is known that, upon impact, damages in the form of fiber breakage, fiber matrix disbond, matrix cracks, and delamination are presented in a composite laminate. The susceptibility of propagation of a damage varies from one mode of loading to another. Likewise, the fatigue life of a damage laminate is sensitive to the modes of applied load. For example, the tension fatigue life of a laminate may be reduced due to the existence of transverse matrix cracks. On the other hand, the development of delamination does not directly affect the tension fatigue life of a composite laminate. However, when under the compressive load, the role of damage that affects the fatigue life is likely to reverse. As a result, the tension-compression fatigue characteristics of an impact damaged laminate is very complex and warrants a careful study.

Three Graphite/PEEK composite laminates were used in this study. They were $[0/+15/-15/90]_{3s}$, $[0/+45/-45/90]_{3s}$, and $[0/+75/-75/90]_{3s}$ laminates. Each specimen was 101.6 mm long, 76.2 mm wide, and 4.06 mm thick. With a gage section of 50.8 mm long, the composite specimen is more susceptible to buckling than in-plane compression. To impact the samples, a drop weight impactor was used. Each specimen was impacted with a 44.5 N steel ball free fall from a height of 127 mm. To evaluate the degree of damage, each specimen was subjected to the ultrasonic C-scan inspection before and after the impact. The ultrasonic C-scan signals reflected from the specimen as well as the coordinates of the transducer were collected through a data acquisition system and fed into a personal computer. It should be pointed out that the ultrasonic C-scan is only capable of determining the delamination damage. The typical ultrasonic C-scan images before and after the impact are illustrated in Figure 1. The gray levels shown in Figure 1 represent the strengths of the reflective ultrasonic wave of the composite laminate. It is believed that the strength of the reflective wave may be correlated to the actual material state of the composite. However, such an argument must be quantified by a careful investigation. At present, the shade of gray shown in the images of Figure 1 is used to interpret the degree of delamination damage. The darker shade of gray in Figure 1 represents a stronger reflective wave, therefore, the less damage. It is clear that Figures 1(a) and 1(b) show a great deal of similarity except in the center portion where the impact was taken place. The area of delamination region shown in Figure 1(b) was determined using an image analysis system. In this research the size of the delamination region was considered as an parameter to analyze the fatigue data.

The mechanical tests of this project have included the baseline tension and buckling tests and the tension/buckling fatigue tests at 1 Hz of virgin and damaged laminates. All the mechanical tests were conducted using a MTS machine controlled through a PC equipped with a data acquisition system. The strength data obtained from the baseline tests were used to determine the loads to be used in the fatigue tests. A stress level up to 90% of the tensile strength was used in the fatigue tests. However, a ratio of -1.36 between tensile and buckling stresses was maintained at all times. During the fatigue test, a thermal couple was mounted on the specimen to record the variation of surface temperature with time.

The Table 1 shows a summary of the ultimate strengths of the virgin and damaged laminates used in this study. Clearly, the impact damage has reduced the load carrying capability in tension. On the other hand, the buckling behavior of the composite laminates was slightly affected by the impact damage. The tension and buckling stress limits of the fatigue test were determined based on the values shown in Table 1.

The fatigue life data of virgin and damaged laminates are given in Figure 2. In this figure, the stress are normalized to the corresponding static ultimate strengths of virgin and damaged laminates. Each fatigue life data is plotted against the tensile stress and buckling stress. Based on the data obtained thus far, it appears that the stress to fatigue life relation (i.e. the S-N curve) appear to be different between virgin and damaged laminates. In fact, the fatigue life of the damaged laminates appears to be higher than that of the virgin laminates at the same stress-to-strength ratio. This suggests that the impact damage has changed the material and load transferring characteristics from the virgin material. In other words, a damaged laminate may be viewed as a different material from its virgin state. To investigate this further, it is necessary to completely characterize the types and distributions of impact damage. Another way to analyze the fatigue life data is presented in Figure 3. In this figure, the actual applied stresses are plotted against the fatigue life data. This type of plot together with Figure 2 may be used to separate the stress intensity effect and the material degradation effect due to an impact damage. With the absence of the material property degradation, the fatigue life curve of an impact damaged laminate will be shifted downward to that of the virgin laminates with the slope unchanged. Any material degradation effect will be reflected through the change of slope in the fatigue life curve. From Figure 3, it is suggested that the delamination damage did not affect the compressive fatigue life. However, the impact damage has caused a reduction in fatigue life in actual applied stress. Both the stress intensity effect and the material degradation effect are introduced to the tensile fatigue response of the laminates tested.

Table1. Comparison of ultimate strengths between virgin and damaged laminates.

| | Tension (MPa) | | Buckling (MPa) | |
|---|---|---|---|---|
| Lam | Virgin | Impact | Virgin | Impact |
| ±45 | 634 | 500 | 182 | 168 |
| ±75 | 426 | 302 | 142 | 134 |
| ±15 | 1168 | 865 | 255 | 249 |

(a) Prior to impact

(b) After impact

Figure 1. The ultrasonic C-scan images before and after impact.

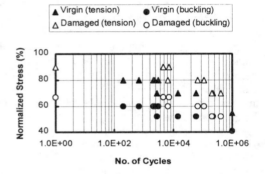

Figure 2. Normalized fatigue life of virgin and damaged laminates $[0/+75/-75/90]_{3s}$.

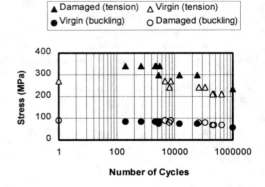

Figure 3. Normalized fatigue life of virgin and damaged laminates $[0/+75/-75/90]_{3s}$.

# MEASUREMENT OF HIGH-STRAIN-RATE PROPERTIES OF POLYMER COMPOSITES BY HOPKINSON BAR TECHNIQUE

Piyush K. Dutta and Barry Coutermarsh
U.S. Army Cold Regions Research and Engineering Laboratory,
Hanover, NH  03755-1290

## Abstract

Experiments were performed to make a preliminary study on the high-strain-rate compression behavior of graphite/epoxy laminates under impact loading by split Hopkinson pressure bar (SHPB).  Short 0.4 inch diameter cylindrical specimens of AS-4/3501-6 graphite-epoxy composite were prepared from 128-ply quasi-isotropic lay-up $[0°/90°/+45°/-95°]_{16s}$ panels in four batches with twelve specimens in each batch.  SHPB's normally generate strain rates in the range of $10^2$ to $10^3$ strains$^{-s}$.  This was to be accomplished primarily by sizing the specimens, and then reducing the incident stress level to a magnitude high enough to cause the specimens to fail.  The lay-up directions to the applied stress play a crucial role in the failure mechanism.  To investigate the size effects, two of the four batches of specimens ($A_1$ and $A_2$), were prepared with the core axis aligned to the panel in-plane (0°) direction, but of different lengths ($A_1$, 0.5 and $A_2$, 1.0 inch).  The core axes of the other two batches were 90° (B specimens) and 45° (C specimens).

Comparison tests were performed at quasi-static rate ($\cong 10^{-3}$ strains$^{-s}$).  As expected, longer ($A_2$) specimens developed lower strain rate than the shorter ($A_1$) specimens. Examination of the failed 0° ($A_1$ and $A_2$) specimens revealed that because of their anisotropic structure they were subjected to severe frictional end effects causing failure by longitudinal splitting probably at stress levels well below the true compressive failure strength of the material.  The 90° (B) specimens were extremely strong.  Under quasi-static load they failed in brittle manner in combination of partial through-the-thickness shear and interlaminar delamination at a stress level much higher than the maximum obtained in SHPB.  The SHPB test stress-strain profiles did not give any clear clue of the mechanism of the failure.  The 45° (C) specimens failed clearly by interlaminar shear in its 45° plane, almost at the same stress levels under both quasi-static and dynamic loads.  Before the failure the quasi-isotropic specimens showed a significant elasto-plastic response.  The failure under dynamic load was primarily elastic and brittle.

The dynamic strain rates were higher than the 50 strains$^{-s}$ desired for all tests.  The target strain rate was only approached using the 1.0 inch $A_2$ specimens where the strain rate was in 68-88 strains$^{-s}$ range.  Future specimens will therefore have to be lengthened or specimen thickness reduced to achieve the desired strain rate.

# Prediction and Measurement of Press-Fit Forces and Stresses in Fiber Reinforced Composite Flywheel Rotors

Charles E. Bakis, Ryan P. Emerson, and Christopher W. Gabrys
Dept. of Engineering Science & Mechanics
227 Hammond Building
The Pennsylvania State University
University Park, PA 16802

Advanced composite flywheel energy storage systems offer the potential of high energy density, power density, and overall efficiency in battery replacement applications. These are particularly important attributes for situations where weight is important, such as in so-called "zero emission" automotive vehicles or where high power delivery is important, as in uninterruptable power supplies. In comparison with other attractive candidate materials, fiber reinforced composite materials are attractive for not only their energy strorage capability but also their potentially less catastrophic failure mode.

Composite flywheel rotors made by filament winding result in high energy density capability if the deleterious effects of tensile radial stresses which develop during rotation are minimized by proper design. Press-fitting multiple rotors onto each other so that each has a beneficial radial compressive stress field superposed onto the operational stress field results in an increased speed capability. Another benefit of press-fitting multiple rings is that stiffer, stronger, lighter rings such as carbon fiber composite can be placed outside less stiff, denser composite, such as glass, so that the outer ring contains the expansion of the inner ring or disk while the inner composite can possibly serve as a low cost hub attachment point. The objective of this research is to measure and model the forces required for pressing composite rings together and the stresses resulting from press-fitting. For press force modeling, the emphasis will be on a simple, accurate, mechanical model, although the finite element method will also be used for comparison purposes. The availability of such models will make it easier to predict the potentially large forces needed to assemble a multi-ring flywheel rotor. These forces are a concern not only from the fabricability standpoint, but also from the design standpoint since achievable press fits and subsequent rotor sped capability depends on the ability to reach the intended state of prestress.

The approach taken in the investigation was to fabricate a series of glass/epoxy and carbon/epoxy composite rings with precisely machined tapers and interferences which allowed a parametric investigation of the effects of ring geometry on press-fit forces and stresses. Ring diameters ranged from 10 to 20 cm, and axial lengths ranged from 1 to 75 cm. All the rings were wet filament wound in-house by an in-situ gellation method which allows for rapid deposition of low cost, thermosetting resin composite [1].

Fibers were hoop wound, meaning that the orientation of the fibers was nearly perpendicular to the spin axis. Interference distances and angles were adjusted for a 50% axial overlap of the ring pairs in the unstressed state. Pressing was done by coating the mating surfaces with room temperature curable epoxy and forcing the rings together with a laminating press. Applied force and strains in the rings were monitored during the pressing operation (Fig. 1).

Ring stresses based on the measured strains were compared to predictions based on anisotropic elasticity theory [2] and a finite element model. Axial press forces were compared to predictions from a simple mechanical model as well as a finite element model (Fig. 2). Friction between the rings was shown to be a major parameter in the prediction of press forces and relatively unimportant in the final state of stress in the rings. The amount of press force was observed to be nonlinearly related to the amount of platen movement — a complicated phenomenon predicted by the simple model. In addition, the model was shown to be capable of predicting the reverse slip of recently pressed rings (before the interfacial epoxy cured). Therefore, it is concluded that the stress analysis tools proposed in this investigation are valuable for designing multiple-ring, press-fit flywheel rotors for high performance as well as fabricability.

References:

1. Gabrys, C. W. and Bakis, C. E., "Fabrication of Thick Filament Wound Carbon/Epoxy Rings Using in-situ Curing: Manufacturing and Quality," *Proc. American Society for Composites,* 9th Technical Conference, Technomic, Lancaster, PA, 1994, pp. 1090-1097.

2. Lekhnitskii, S. G., Anisotropic Plates, Gordon and Breach Science Publishers, New York, 1968.

3. Emerson, R. P. "A Model for Press-Force Prediction of Multi-Ring Composite Flywheels," B. S. Thesis, Dept. of Engineering Science & Mechanics, The Pennsylvania State University, University Park, PA, Dec. 1995.

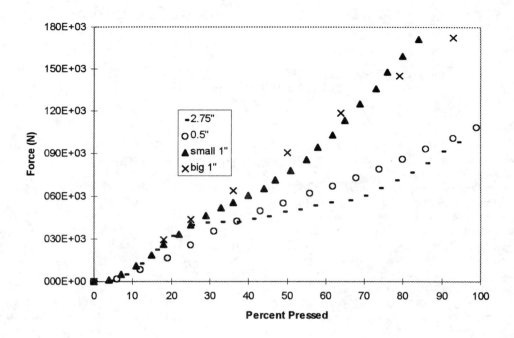

Figure 1.  Experimentally measured force versus displacement.

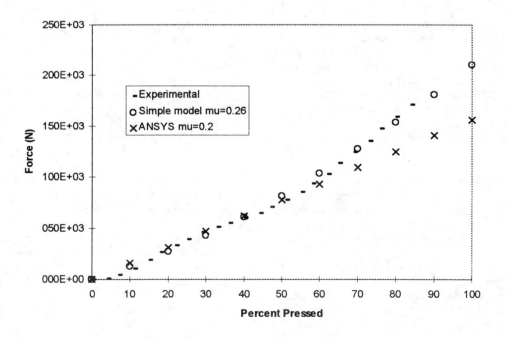

Figure 2.  Experimental, simple model, and finite element results overlaid.

# Fourier Detection and Analysis of Fringe Patterns

C.A. Sciammarella, B. Trentadue, F.M. Sciammarella
Illinois Institute of Technology
Chicago,Illinois 60616

The measurement of displacements by means of optical techniques based on the moiré principle requires two separate steps. The first step is to introduce a carrier to sample the displacement field, the second step is to retrieve the displacement information from the modulated carrier. This paper deals with some aspects of this second operation The carrier can be an actual grating or an optically generated carrier. The displacement information is encoded in a carrier and has to be decoded from the modulated carrier, [1]. The decoding is accomplished by sampling the image with a CCD camera. The sampling array can be mathematically modeled by a sampling vector with characteristic distances $s_x$ and $s_y$ in the x and y directions. The array is characterized by two numbers, $N_x$ and $N_y$, the total number of sampling units. In the frequency plane the sampling vector has a corresponding vector, with characteristic distances $f_x$ and $f_y$, with the relationships, $f_x = 1/s_x$ and $f_y = 1/s_y$. The highest frequencies that can be resolved are given by the Nyquist's limits $N_x/EL$ and $N_y/2L$, where L is a characteristic length, for example the length of the observed field in the x-direction. For the array used in this example the corresponding quantities are, 512x484 pixels. If one normalizes the frequencies by making L=1 the highest frequencies that can be detected are 256 in the x-direction and 242 in the y-direction. The FFT is performed by using hardware associated with the imaging system. The results are displayed as power and phase spectra of the analyzed image.

To get displacement information two states are compared, the initial or reference state and the final or loaded state. The initial state may contain unwanted information and the final state may also contain unwanted information, consequently a filtering operation is required. The filtering operation is an interactive operation and requires judgment from the operator. The program used has pre-designed filters that take advantage of previous knowledge concerning the signal power spectrum. In this particular case the cross-sectional shape of the filter is an ellipse with the major axis in the direction perpendicular to the carrier. By visual inspection the operator selects the position of the ellipse to retrieve the modulated carrier by enclosing the spectrum with a rectangle that provides both the maximum and the minimum axis of the ellipse. The inverse FFT is applied and a fringe

pattern is obtained. Next, the wrapped phase is computed. The operation is applied to both the initial and the final states. The phases of the two states are subtracted and the final wrapped phase is obtained. The derivative of the phase is obtained by differentiating the wrapped phase[2].Two unpleasant aspects of the FFT are frequency leakages and ringing effects at discontinuities. To solve these problem fringes are extended beyond the boundaries of the specimen [3].

The above described procedure can be applied to a number of different techniques, moiré, holographic- moiré, speckle.

## Examples of application

The residual stresses present in a silicon wafer containing memory chips after manufacturing, are studied using a reflection moiré technique. The front surface is reflective in the areas that contains chips. The fringes that contain the slope information are discontinuous Fig. 1, and the Fourier spectrum contains a large number of diffraction spots caused by these discontinuities and by diffracting elements engraved in the chips. Fig. 2 shows the fringe pattern after filtering and fringe extension. Fig. 3 shows the phase field. Since lenses are used to obtain the slope fringes, the distortion caused by the lenses is removed by obtaining a carrier field from reflection in a flat mirror Fig. 4. The final field is obtained by subtraction of these two phase fields, Fig. 5. The operation is repeated by observing fringes in the perpendicular direction. Finally from the analyzed patterns the stress distribution shown in Fig. 6 is obtained. This is but one example of the application of the described procedure. The same process works even if the whole field contains only a fraction of a fringe and no fringe pattern is visible in the recorded image.

References:

[1] Sciammarella, C.A., "Limits to the Accuracy in the Experimental Determination of Displacement Functions," Fringe 93, W. Jupner, W. Osten editors, Akademie Verlag, 1993, pp 347-360.
[2] Sciammarella, C. A., Narayanan, R., "The Determination of the Components of the Strain Tensor in Holographic Interferometry," Experimental Mechanics 24,(4), 1984, pp 257-264.

[3] Sciammarella C.A., Bhat G., "Two Dimensional Fourier Transform Methods for Fringe Pattern Analysis, Proc. of the VII International Congress in Experimental Mechanics, SEM June 1992, pp1530-1538.

a) Vertical Slope Fringe Pattern

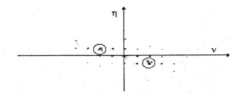

b) Fringe Pattern Fourier Spectrum

Fig.1  Finished  Wafer

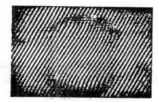

Fig.2  Extrapolated Fringe Pattern

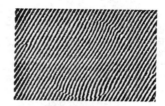

Fig.3  Phase Field with Carrier

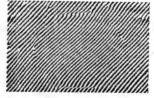

Fig.4  Flat Surface Carrier Reference Field

Fig.5  Pattern Phase after Reference Carrier Field Removal

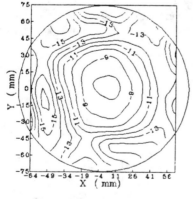

a) Two Dimensional Wiew

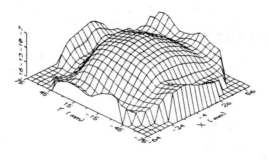

b) Three Dimensional Wiew

Fig.6  Finished Wafer Maximal Principal Stress (MPa)

# Continuous Observation of the Whole Process of Deformation by Digital Speckle Pattern Interferometry

Satoru Toyooka and Xinglong Gong

Graduate School of Science and Engineering, Saitama University

255 Shimo-okubo, Urawa, Saitama, JAPAN

Speckle pattern interferometry (SPI) has some advantages to measure whole deformation field of a rough surface object without any processing or contact on the surface of the object.    A digital processing system which consists of a CCD camera and a microcomputer is easily constructed.      A real-time fringe observation of deformation or vibration of an object can also be done by comparing a current speckle pattern of the object under moving state and a reference speckle pattern of the same object under stationary state.    But when the deformation becomes too larger  to exceed some limited value, correlation between a reference speckle pattern and a current speckle pattern is rapidly decreased and fringe structure disappears.    Then the conventional SPI has been limited to measure only small deformation of the order of the several wavelengths of light, that is usually in the elastic state of deformation.

But at the viewpoint of strength physics and evaluation, investigations of plastic deformation and fracture are more interesting and important.    Recently V.E.Panin and his colleagues proposed "meso-mechanics" in which wavelike propagation of plastic deformation through nonuniform structural elements in an object is introduced[1].    To observe these phenomena, spatio-temporal observation of deformation is required.

We proposed a new system of SPI  to implement dynamic observation of whole process of deformation continuously from the beginning of elastic deformation to the final stage of the plastic deformation until fracture[2].  In the system, a big memory of a computer is utilized to store a lot of frames of speckle patterns.  We call the method as digital speckle pattern interferometry (DSPI).     In this paper interesting propagation of plastic deformation field observed in the new system will be shown.

The experimental setup of the proposed system to observe temporal variation of two components of deformation is shown in Fig.1.  A specimen is set up on tensile equipment which is placed on an optical bench together with optical components.    The $xy$-coordinate system is attached on the object surface.  Two mirrors are placed on the bench perpendicularly to the specimen in the $yz$-plane and $xz$-plane. A laser beam from an Ar-laser is split into two beams by a beam splatter (BS).    Two electro-magnetic shutters are opened and shut alternately and speckle patterns sensitive to the $x$- and $y$-components of in-plane deformation are taken by the CCD camera and fed to the microcomputer through different channels of a color image board (CIB).     These sequences are repeated from the start of the tensile experiment until fracture of the object.     Subtraction of adjacent data of each component generates contour fringes deformation.

In the following experiment, the specimen to be tested was  an aluminum plate having the effective size of 64.0 mm length, 7.9 mm width and 1.7 mm thickness.    The specimen was stretched  by the constant tensile velocity of

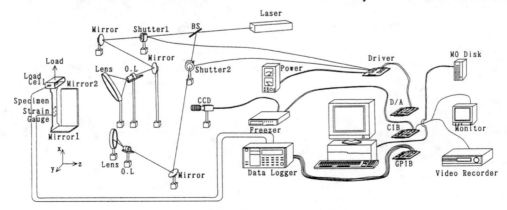

Fig.1 experimental setup of DSPI

0.75 μm/s. The time interval of the two shutters passing the two component beams was 30 ms and the sequences were repeated in every 9 sec from the start of the tensile test until the fracture of the specimen. Over 2000 frames of speckle interference fringes were successively recorded.

Figure 2 is the loading curve monitored by the load cell on the equipment. Ten sets of fringe patterns are picked up and shown in Fig.3. Fringe patterns in the upper side and lower side are *x*- and *y*-component fringes in which the amounts of deformation per fringe spacing are 0.51 μm and 0.43 μm, respectively. Alphabetical marks on Fig.2 and Fig.3 are corresponding. In the process of elastic deformation, uniform and smooth variation of fringes were observed in the pattern *a* and *b*. On the other hand if the deformation state enters in the plastic phase, a lot of interesting variations of fringes were found out. In the *x*-component fringe pattern of *c*, there are three domains with different fringe modes: parallel and right-downward fringes in upper part, parallel and nearly vertical fringes in the middle part and parallel and right-upward fringes in the lower part. Correspondingly in the *y*-component fringe pattern, fringe spacing is different in each domain. In every domain, fringes are almost parallel and equidistant. At the boundaries of domains, anomalous fringes are found. In the fringe pattern of *f*, four domains are recognized. In the x-component fringes, we find fine vertical fringes in the upper part, course vertical fringes in the secondary upper part fringes, only two horizontal fringe in the middle lower part, and one vertical fringes in the bottom part. Correspondingly in the *y*-component fringes, horizontal fringes with different fringe spacing are found. Vertical fringes in the *x*-component and horizontal fringes in the *y*-component observed in the upper two domains mean that each domain is totally rotated with little strain field in the domain. At the boundary of the two upper domains, fringe can not be found. It means that the strain field at the boundary is too much

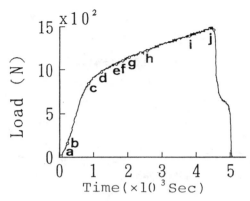

Fig.2 Loading curve

concentrated to keep the speckle correlation. Then fringes disappear. In the lower part of the specimen there are two domains having very little strain fields. In the fringe patterns from *c* to *i*, very complicated and rapid movement of domains and boundaries are found. Correspondingly zigzag variations are found in the loading curve in Fig.2. In the fringe patterns of *j*, the specimen is divided into two domains. The specimen was finally fractured at the boundary of the two domains. Such a final stage that the specimen was finally fractured at the boundary was always found in every experiment.

The experimental results obtained suggest a physical model of plastic deformation. Plastic deformation propagates in a solid object through rotation of domains. There are some kinds of defects at the boundaries of domains or anomaly locations which suffer from severe stress concentration and relaxation move rapidly around the object. When the anomalous bands move from one defect to another, domains are sometimes divided or combined. Finally one anomalous band become stationary and the specimen is fractured. A dynamic process presented here has hardly observed before our experiments. It seems difficult to interpret the physical model by conventional theory. The physical model seems to be interpreted qualitatively by the wave theory of plastic deformation[1].

References
1) V.E.Panin, Yu.V.Grinyaev, V.E. Ergorshkin, I.L. Buchbinder and S.N. Kul'kov,: "Spectrum of Excited States and the Rotational Mechanical Field in a Deformed Crystal", Ixv.VUZ Fiz. 1, 34 (1987).
2) S.Toyooka and X.L. Gong : "Digital Speckle Pattern Interferometry for observing the Entire Process of Plastic Deformation of a Solid Object", Jpn.J.Appl.Phys. 34, pp.L1666-L1668, (1995).

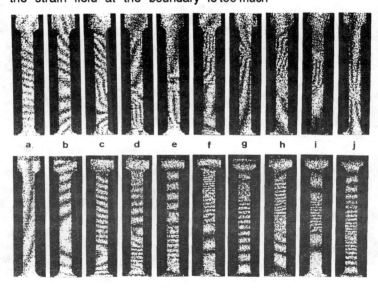

Fig.3 Experimental results

# Modal Testing Of A Turbopump Liner Using Time-Average Panoramic Holo-Interferometry

Jeffrey L. Lindner
Structures and Dynamics Laboratory
George C. Marshall Space Flight Center
Marshall Space Flight Center, Alabama 35812

John A. Gilbert
Department of Mechanical and Aerospace Engineering
University of Alabama in Huntsville
Huntsville, Alabama 35899

## Abstract

This paper describes the first practical application of a relatively new approach to modal analysis in which time-average holograms are recorded through a panoramic system. When inserted into a cylindrical structure, the system allows a relatively large portion of the surroundings to be illuminated and observed. The approach is applied to study the modal response of a turbopump liner designed for use in the Space Shuttle Main Engine.

## Introduction

The time-average holographic recording technique, developed by Stetson and Powell [1], can be used to reveal contours of constant amplitude on the surface of a vibrating object. In this technique, a holo-interferogram is produced by generating a hologram and exposing the recording medium for a period of time during which the test object executes many cycles of steady vibration. In this case, the intensity of the reconstructed image is

$$I \propto J_o^2 \left[ \frac{2\pi}{\lambda} (\boldsymbol{g} \cdot \boldsymbol{d}) \right] \qquad (1)$$

where $\lambda$ is the wavelength of the coherent light used to record and reconstruct the hologram, $\boldsymbol{d}$ is the displacement vector of the surface point under consideration, and $J_o$ is the zero order Bessel function. The sensitivity vector $\boldsymbol{g}$ is defined by $(\hat{e}_2 - \hat{e}_1)$ where $\hat{e}_1$ and $\hat{e}_2$ are unit vectors in the directions of illumination and observation, respectively.

Most attempts to record holograms over extended areas in confined spaces have met with limited success, mainly because current holographic systems provide only spot views within the region of interest. This problem can be eased somewhat by employing time-average panoramic holo-interferometry [2].

## Time-Average Panoramic Holo-Interferometry

Time average panoramic holo-interferometry relies on the standard time-average holographic method but utilizes two Panoramic Annular Lenses (PALs); one to illuminate and the other to view the inner wall of a cavity.

As shown in Fig. 1, the PAL is a single element imaging block comprised of three spherical optical surfaces, and one flat optical surface. Two of the spherical surfaces are mirrored while the third spherical surface and the flat surface are not. Rays are refracted when they contact the first spherical surface, and they are reflecedt off the rear mirrored spherical surface. They travel forward in the lens and strike the front mirrored spherical surface. Reflected back, the rays are refracted at the rear flat optical surface and diverge as they exit the lens. The divergent rays leaving the flat optical surface at the back of the PAL can be "back traced" to form a virtual image. The virtual image is captured by a transfer lens to form a flat annular image. Thus, the continuous field of view surrounding the PAL is mapped via a constant aspect ratio polar mapping [3]. The resolution of the PAL varies from the forward viewing edge to the back viewing edge with an average angular resolution of 6 millirads. Even though the PAL is not strictly afocal, objects appear to be in focus from the lens surface to infinity.

The Cartesian $(x',y')$ and polar $(r',\theta')$ coordinate systems used to define the annular image are shown superimposed on Fig 1. Figure 2, on the other hand, defines the Cartesian $(x,y,z)$ and cylindrical $(r,\theta,z)$ coordinate systems used to describe object space.

Referring to Fig. 2, it is assumed that two opposing collinear PALs are aligned with their optical axes along the z-direction. Coherent light is projected by one PAL from the source point S to a point P located on the wall of a cavity, depicted in the figure as a ring. The image of P is observed by the second PAL at point O. For analysis purposes, unit vectors $\hat{e}_1$ and $\hat{e}_2$ are shown in the direction of illumination and in the direction of observation, respectively. The sensitivity vector, $\boldsymbol{g}$, described in Eq. (1), lies along the angle bisector of $\hat{e}_1$ and $\hat{e}_2$. Figure 3 shows a typical experimental setup for recording panoramic holo-interferograms.

In the center of the illuminated band, $\boldsymbol{g}$ is perpendicular to the optical axis of the system and only radial displacements are measured. Toward the edges of the band, however, $\boldsymbol{g}$ becomes inclined. Assuming that the displacement is purely radial, an error is introduced which depends on the spacing between the lenses and the width of the band. For a more complex situation, the displacement component parallel to the optical axis influences the holographic fringe pattern in areas where the sensitivity vector is inclined; whereas, the circumferential displacement component does not effect the fringe pattern.

## Experimental

The method of time-average panoramic holo-interferometry was used to study the modal response of a turbopump liner designed for use in the Space Shuttle Main Engine. The inlet liner was supported by four foam blocks and 27 elastic cords providing a free-free boundary condition. An accelerometer was radially oriented and bonded to the outer surface of the test article. A signal analyzer was used to run a series of acoustically driven 200 Hz band width sine sweep measurements that roughly identified mode frequencies. High resolution 20 Hz zoom band measurements were then acquired to discretely resolve the mode frequencies.

The experimental setup shown in Fig. 3 was used to acquire the mode shape information for each mode identified during the sine sweep tests. Figure 4 shows a typical modal response recorded at 959.1 Hz. The fringes are related to the peak-to-peak radial displacement of the inner surface of the inlet liner. The magnitude of the displacement can be discretely calculated by applying Eq. (1).

## References

1. Stetson, K.A., Powell, R.L., "Interferometric hologram evaluation and real time vibration analysis of diffuse objects," *J. Opt. Soc. of Am.*, 55, (1965), pp. 1694-1695.

2. Lindner, J.L., Gilbert, J.A., "Modal analysis using time-average panoramic holo-interferometry," to be published in the *International Journal of Analytical and Experimental Modal Analysis*.

3 Lehner, D.L., Richter, A.G., Matthys, D.R., Gilbert, J.A., "Characterization of the panoramic annular lens," to be published in *Experimental Mechanics*.

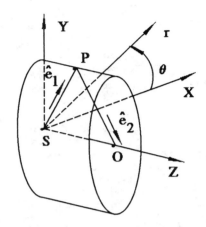

**Figure 2**. Cartesian and cylindrical systems used to describe object space.

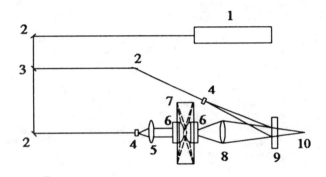

**Figure 3**. Experimental setup; 1. laser, 2, mirror, 3. beam splitter, 4. spatial filter, 5. collimating lens, 6. PAL, 7. inlet liner, 8. transfer lens, 9. thermoplastic plate, 10. image plane on CCD camera.

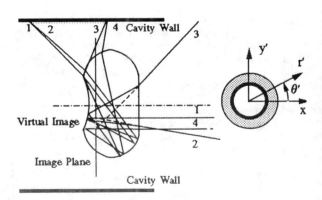

**Figure 1**. Ray diagram and coordinate systems for the image plane.

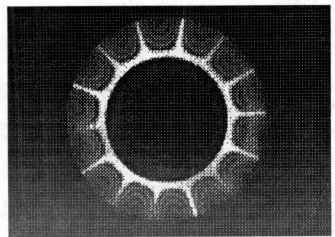

**Figure 4**. A time-average panoramic holo-interferogram recorded at 959.1 Hz on the inside wall of an inlet liner designed for use in the Space Shuttle Main Engine.

# A novel, optical nondestructive deformation analyzer based on electronic speckle-pattern interferometry and a new plastic deformation theory

S. Yoshida, Suprapedi, R. Widiastuti, Marincan, Septriyanti, Julinda, A. Faisal and A. Kusnowo
Research and Development Center for Applied Physics, Indonesian Institute of Sciences
P3FT-LIPI, PUSPIPTEK, Serpong, Tangerang 15310, Indonesia

We apply electronic speckle pattern interferometry (ESPI) to study on deformation and fracture of solid state materials. Our particular interest is to establish a non-contact, non-destructive technique capable of diagnosing the mechanical state of an object as the final prefracture stage, and of predicting the location of the fracture at a certain point sufficiently long before the fracture actually occurs. Theoretical basis of our approach is grounded on a recently developed deformation theory called mezomechanics [1]. The advantage of mezomechanics is that it describes deformation of any stage and related phenomena including material fracture in purely physical terms without relying on any empirical formula. Mezomechanics is applicable to any solid-state material having internal structure universally.

Recently, we have discovered in a tensile experiment that the mezo-scale slip band, called mezoband in mezomechanics, can be visualized by an in-plane sensitive, dual-beam ESPI setup [2]. The mezoband is repeatedly observed on the surface of an aluminum object as a conspicuous bright band structure in fringe patterns generated in the subtraction mode. As this band structure looks whiter than the bright peak of usual subtraction fringes on our white-and black TV monitor, we call it the white band (WB). According to mezomechanics, the plastic deformation is defined as the loss of shear stability. From this viewpoint, it can be said that the WB essentially represents plastic deformation of the object. The most intriguing thing about the WB is that its spatial and temporal behavior provides us information that enables us to infer the evolution of the plastic deformation. Especially, such information obtained in a late stage of plastic deformation can be used to locate the fracture that will eventually occur in the object. In some cases, the time historical trace of the WB indicates the location of fracture at about 70% of its life [2].

Fig.1 shows the experimental arrangement we use to observe the WB. The optical setup consists of two identical in-plane sensitive, dual-beam interferometers [3] sensitive to horizontal and vertical displacements of the object, respectively. Two 25 mW He/Ne lasers are used for the respective interferometers. The aluminum object is attached to a universal tensile machine for a tensile load with a cross head speed of 0.35 mm/min. The two interferometers are switched alternatively by an electronically controlled optical shutters so that interferograms corresponding to horizontal and vertical components of deformation may be obtained independently at each time step. The switching time from the horizontal to the vertical arrangement is set to be negligibly small so that the horizontal and vertical interferograms may effectively correspond to deformation occurring at the same time. The data acquisition interval ranges from 0.5 - 9 s, corresponding to the total deformation of $3 \times 10^{-5}$ - $5 \times 10^{-4}$.

The WB starts appearing in either a horizontal or vertical subtraction fringe pattern at a certain stage of the plastic deformation. As the deformation progresses, it changes in the angle to the tensile axis, the number of the bands observed simultaneously, and the motion. These features of the WB are strongly related to various factors of the material such as the thickness, the grain size and the existence of residual strain. What we have found in a series of tensile experiments include:

(1) If the object is thicker, the WB is likely to move more vigorously on the object surface.
(2) If the object contains a residual strain, the WB stays at the location of the strain till the object fractures there.
(3) In some cases, the WB appears as soon as the object enters the plastic region, it moves vigorously over the object surface till it stays at some location a certain point. In this case, the object fractures where the WB gets stationary.
(4) Normally more WBs are observed simultaneously in an earlier stage of deformation, and as the deformation progresses, the number decreases.
(5) If the WB starts appearing in an earlier stage of plastic deformation, the plastic region (the flat part of the stress-strain curve) is longer and the maximum stress is lower.
(6) The WB usually runs in the direction of the maximum shear stress in an early stage unless a residual strain exists. When the material fractures, the WB always runs along the fracture line.

Fig.2 shows typical WB observed under various conditions. (Note that the object shown in Fig.2 (c) has a hole through which two WBs are running.) Fig.3 shows the time historical trace of the WB observed in a 2 mm thick aluminum object categorized as case (3) mentioned above. The object fractured exactly at the location where the curve converges.

In conclusion, we have discovered that the mezo-scale slip band can be visualized by an in-plane sensitive, dual-beam ESPI setup and that the observation of the slip band provides important information characterizing deformation and fracture. Presently we focus our effort on finding more features of WB that represent prefracture phenomena.

References:
[1] Physical Mechanics of Heterogeneous Media and Materials Computer-Aided Design, Edited by V. E. Panin, Cambridge Interscience Publishing (1996)
[2] S. Yoshida, Suprapedi, R. Widiastuti, Marincan, Septriyanti, Julinda, A. Faisal and A. Kusnowo, "A New Optical Interferometric Technique for Deformation Analyses", presented at 4th International Conference on Computer Aided Design of Advanced Materials and Technologies, Tomsk, Russia, September 1995
[3] Speckle Methodology, edited by R. S. Sirohi, Marcel Dekkr, Inc. New York, Basel, Hong Kong, p.69 (1993)

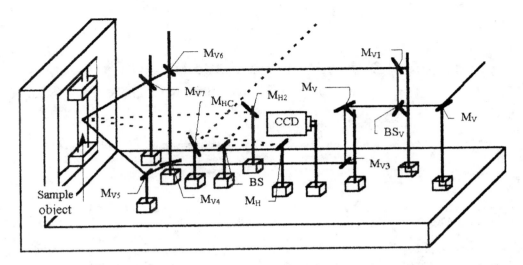

Fig . 1  Experimental arrangement.  M=mirror, B.S.=beam splitter, h=horizontal, v=vertical

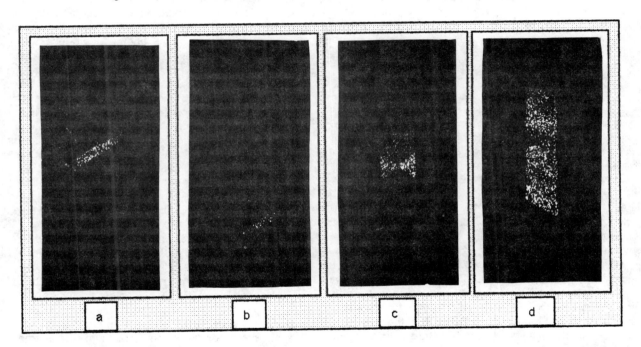

Fig. 2  Typical WB  : (a - b) moving WB; (c) WB developing from a hole; (d) multiple WB's observed simultaneously.

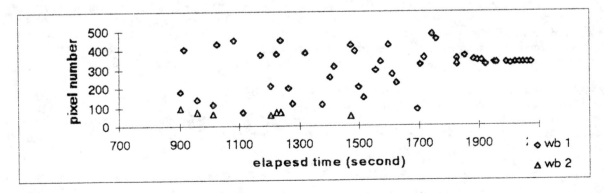

Fig . 3  Time historical trace of WB location

# Application of Dynamic Holographic-Electronic Speckle Pattern Interferometry to Study Full-Field Dynamic Deformations in Solids

Mansour A. Ahmadshahi, Sridhar Krishnaswamy, S. Nemat-Nasser
C. E. Niehoff & Co.
2021 Lee Street
Evanston, IL 60202

Speckle pattern interferometry, be it holographic or photographic, has until now been limited to the study of static deformations, or at most, periodic deformations when an object is under steady-state vibrations. In the latter case, temporal modulation of the amplitude and/or phase of the illuminating lightwave [1,2] has made full-field quantitative measurements of displacement and strain of vibrating bodies possible. However, in view of many technical problems, it has been stated as recently as 1989 that "dynamic speckle-pattern interferometry is not possible," [3].

In this paper, we present the application of dynamic holographic-electronic speckle pattern interferometry to analyze the deformations of diffusely reflecting bodies under transient loads. The out-of-plane deformations of a vibrating plate in resonance has been investigated and the evolution of the fringe pattern during 1/2 cycle of deformation corresponding to 160 ms is presented.

The principle of the DHESPI (Dynamic Holographic-Electronic Speckle Pattern Interferometry) technique is based on recording a sequence of holographic speckle patterns on a photographic emulsion medium using a high-speed camera, and subsequently digitizing the negatives by means of a CCD camera and an image processing system. The digitized speckle patterns are then registered utilizing image correlation techniques. A reference speckle pattern corresponding to the undeformed (or a suitable preceding deformed) state of the object is subtracted from the remaining speckle patterns which are obtained during subsequent deformation. Figure 1 illustrates the dynamic recording of time-varying speckle patterns using a high-speed camera (Cordin model 330A) and an image processing system. The scattered waves due to double illumination of the object are recorded by the high-speed camera as a sequence of snapshots on T-Max P3200 Kodak film.

The evolution of the displacement of a vibrating cantilever beam at resonance is studied. The aluminum cantilever beam is 15.2 cm long, 5 cm wide, and 0.4 cm thick, Fig.2. An argon-ion cw laser is used as the light source which delivers 1.2 W/cm$^2$ power. Laser intensity limitations restrict the field of analysis to a rectangular region inscribed in a circular region 2.4 cm in diameter, as shown in Fig. 2. The cantilever beam is excited by an electro-magnetic shaker.

At a frequency of 3125 Hz, a plate-mode resonance is detected. The optical setup is shown in Fig. 3. The laser beam is passed through a Bragg-Cell, which provides a flash of light equal to 3.2 ms. This period is long enough to expose 80 frames of the high-speed camera which was set to operate at 25,000 frames per second. This corresponds to exposure and interframe times of 20 ms each. The beam is then passed through a pinhole and two well-corrected lenses of 175 mm focal length, to produce a collimated beam 2.4 cm in diameter. This beam is passed through a 50/50 partial mirror, providing two equal intensity collimated beams, one of which illuminates the cantilever beam at an angle of 20 deg with the normal, and the other at an angle of 55 deg with the normal, Fig. 3. The region is imaged onto the film track of the high-speed camera by its internal lens system and three well-corrected lenses of 381 mm, 381 mm, and 175 mm focal lengths, as shown in Fig. 3. The recording medium, T-Max P3200 Kodak film, is reported by the manufacturer to have a resolution of 40 l/mm. The high-speed Cordin camera used in this experiment is capable of at least the same resolving power since its resolution is reported to be 40 l/mm at speed of 2,000,000 frame per second. Therefore, it is expected that at lower speeds, specifically 25,000 frames per second used in this experiment, the resolution of the camera is considerably higher than the film, and consequently, it is the film that determines the spatial resolution of the system.

Figure 4 shows the time-frozen fringes of the vibrating beam corresponding to the maximum displacement, using ESPI and strobing technique. Figure 5 shows the composite image of the evolution of the fringe pattern during 160 ms. The figure represents the subtracted speckle patterns obtained at t = 40 ms, t = 80 ms, t = 120 ms, and t = 160 ms, from the reference speckle pattern obtained at t = 0 ms. The top row represents the subtracted speckle patterns before image processing, and the bottom row shows the results after image processing.

References:

[1] M. A. Ahmadshahi, "Computer Based Techniques for Holographic Fringe Pattern Information Detection, " Ph.D. Thesis, Illinois Institute of Technology, 1988.

[2] C. C. Aleksoff, "Temporally Modulated Holography, " Appl. Opt., 1971, Vol. 10, No. 6, pp. 1329-1341.

[3]  R. Jones, and C. Wykes, Holographic and Speckle Interferometry, Cambridge University Press, Cambridge, U.K., 1989.

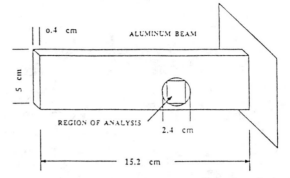

Fig. 2  Cantilever beam and the region of analysis

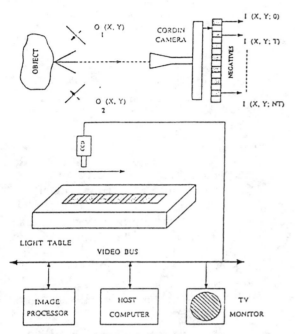

Fig. 1  Schematic representation of dynamic recording of time-varying speckle patterns, and the image processing system

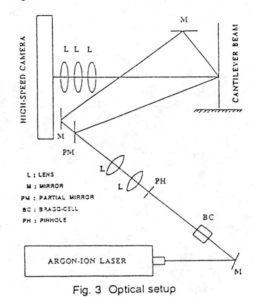

Fig. 3  Optical setup

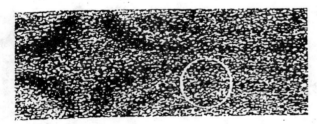

Fig. 4  Time-frozen fringes corresponding to the maximum displacement using electronic speckle-pattern interferometry and strobing technique; the evolution of fringe pattern in the rectangular subregion is studied by dynamic holographic-electronic speckle-pattern interferometry

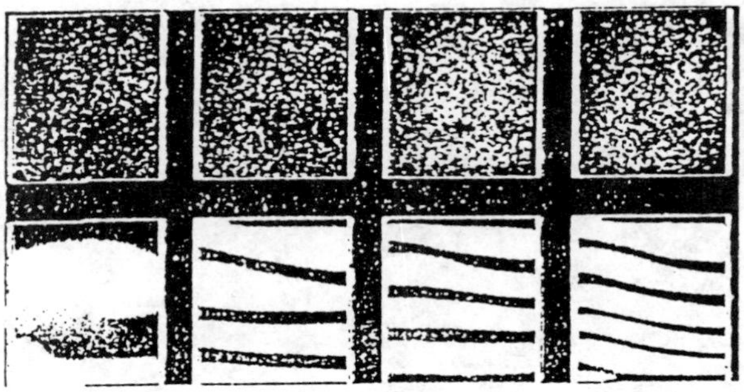

Fig. 5  Evolution of displacement in a rectangular subregion of a cantilever beam during 1/2 cycle of vibration obtained at t = 40 μs, t = 80 μs, t = 120 μs, and t = 160 μs, from the reference obtained at t = 0 μs

# A Novel 3-D Computer Vision Technique for Deformation Measurement and Nondestructive Testing

Y.Y. Hung, B.G. Park and L. Lin
Department of Mechanical Engineering
Oakland University
Rochester Hills, Michigan 48309

A reflective computer vision technique for full-field and noncontact measurement of structural deformation and nondestructive testing is presented. The technique is based on the marriage of a reflective fringe technique and computer image processing algorithms.

The optical arrangement of the technique is shown in Fig.1. The surface of the test object must be specularly reflective so that it acts like as a mirror.. In the case of semi specularly reflective object, a coating of oil is applied to make the surface specularly reflective. A computer generated sinusoidal grating is displayed on the monitor. The fringe pattern is reflected off the object surface, thus forming a virtual image received by the video camera. If the object surface is perfectly flat, a perfect fringe pattern in the form of linear and parallel fringes of equal spacing will be observed. Otherwise, the fringe lines will be distorted due to the variation of the surface slope. Thus the fringe phase distribution carries the information about the surface slope. To extract the fringe phase distribution, the technique employs a phase shift technique which requires sequential digitization of four fringe patterns with a phase shift of $0$, $\pi/2$, $\pi$ and $3\pi/2$. The phase distribution is then translated into surface slope distribution. The measured slope are digitally differentiated to obtain curvature , and integrated to yield surface depth . Taking the difference of the phase distributions before and after deformation allows the object deformation to be measured. In the application to nondestructive testing, the technique detects structural defects by looking for defect-induced strain anomalies. The technique is simple, fast and having a high potential of being developed into a practical tool for deformation measurement and nondestructive testing.

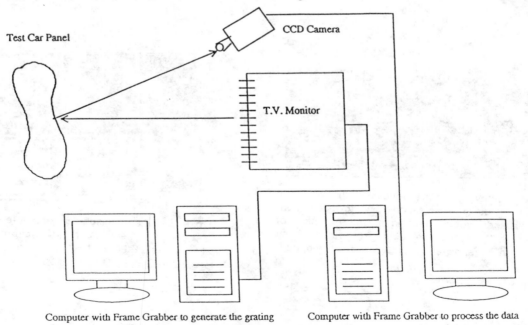

Fig. 1 Schematic diagram of the technique.

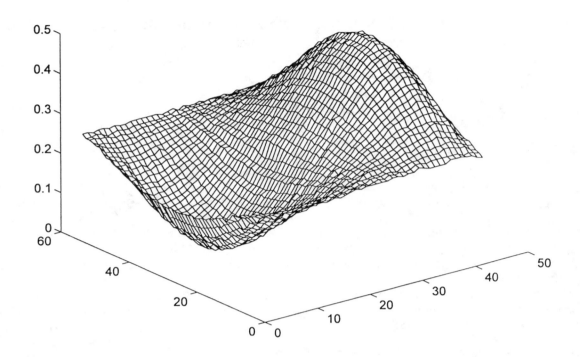

Fig. 2 shows a 3-D plot of the measured deflection of a plate clamped along its boundaries and subject to uniform load.

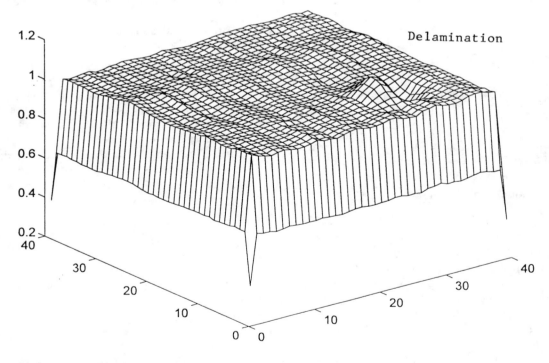

Fig. 3 shows a 3-D plot of the surface deformation revealing a delamination in a composite laminate.

# Hybrid Evaluation of Repair Efficiency of Composite Patching

Wei-Chung Wang and Chiang-Han Day
Department of Power Mechanical Engineering
National Tsing Hua University
Hsinchu, Taiwan 30043
Republic of China

## Abstract

In this paper, the hybrid method which combines electronic speckle pattern interferometry (ESPI) and finite element method (FEM) was used to investigate the repair efficiency of patching by using composite material on composite material plates containing a circular hole. The effect of various fiber orientations and stacking sequences of the specimen and patching was discussed. The data from the interferometric fringe patterns were used as the boundary conditions to FEM to evaluate the repair efficiency.

## Experimental Background

If two laser beams which lie on the horizontal xz plane and formed an equal and opposite angles, $\phi$, with z-axis incident to the test specimen, the in-plane displacement parallel to x- direction, $u$, can be expressed as

$$u = \frac{N\lambda}{2\sin\phi} \tag{1}$$

where $\lambda$ is the wavelength of the laser beam and $N$ is the fringe order.

The geometrical configuration of the specimen is shown in Fig. 1. The test specimen and patching were made from TORAYCA 3051F-15 CFRP. Four different stacking sequences, i.e. $(\pm 45°)_{2s}$, $(0°/+45°/0°/-45°)_s$, $(0°/+45°/90°/-45°)_s$, and $(0°/+45°/-45°)_s$ were used for the specimen and patching. The size of the specimen and patching are 170 mm $\times$ 70 mm and 70 mm $\times$ 70 mm, respectively. The thicknesses are 0.90 mm for 6 ply and 1.20 mm for 8 ply laminates, respectively. Each specimen contains a central circular hole of diameter 30 mm. The patching was achieved by bonding the carbon fiber reinforced plastic (CFRP) laminate onto the CFRP plate by the appropriate adhesives. In all experiments and analyses, specimens are single-sided patched.

## Numerical Scheme

In this paper, a commercial available FEM software, ANSYS, was used in the FEM and hybrid analysis. Due to the symmetry of the problem, only half of the specimen was considered. Three dimensional layered structural solid element (SOLID46) was used to model the composite material. The displacements and stress fields of FEM analysis can be obtained by applying the same force condition as in the experiments. In addition, to implement the hybrid method, the displacement data read from the experimental fringe at locations corresponding to nodal points used in the FEM was employed as the boundary conditions. The "improved" displacements and stress fields can then be obtained. By analyzing the results between the unpatched and patched specimens, the repair efficiency of composite patching can then be evaluated.

## Results and Discussions

A typical ESPI experimental result for patched specimen on patched side is shown in Fig. 2. The displacement field, $u$, for patched specimen on patched side obtained from FEM analysis is shown in Fig. 3. Comparing Fig. 2 with Fig. 3, the displacement field obtained from FEM analysis is not quite the same as that of the experiment. For this reason, hybrid method was employed to "correct" the displacements on the patched side of the FEM model. The stress field can then be obtained from the better FEM model. The repair efficiency is defined as

$$Repair\ efficiency = \frac{(K)_{unpatched} - (K)_{patched}}{(K)_{unpatched}} \tag{2}$$

where $K$ is the stress concentration factor.

From Eq. (2), the repair efficiency obtained from FEM and hybrid method analyses are 29.09% and 16.45%, respectively. Consequently, without using the hybrid method, the repair efficiency obtained by the FEM alone may be overestimated.

**ACKNOWLEDGMENTS**

This research was supported in part by the National Science Council (Grant Nos. NSC83-0404-D007-005 and CS84-0210-D007-002) of the Republic of China.

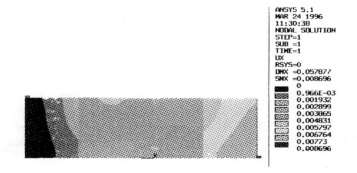

FIG. 3 THE DISPLACEMENT FIELD $u$ OF PATCHED SPECIMEN ON PATCHED SIDE OBTAINED BY FEM [SPECIMEN : $(0°/+45°/0°/-45°)_s$ PATCHING : $(\pm45°)_{2s}$]

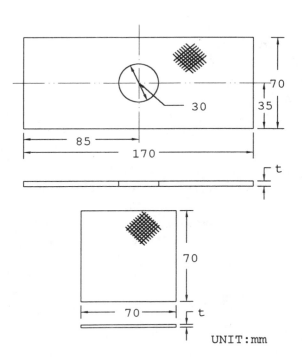

UNIT : mm

FIG. 1 GEOMETRIC OF THE TEST SPECIMEN AND PATCHING

FIG. 2 THE ESPI FRINGE PATTERN OF PATCHED SPECIMEN ON PATCHED SIDE [SPECIMEN : $(0°/+45°/0°/-45°)_s$ PATCHING : $(\pm45°)_{2s}$]

# Can the Fracture Toughness Be Used for Fracture Assessment of Structures ?

Yuh J. Chao
Department of Mechanical Engineering
University of South Carolina
Columbia, SC 29208
Tel:(803)777-5869, Fax:(803)777-0106, E-mail: chao-yuh@sc.edu

Structural integrity assessment is normally performed using methodologies based on fracture mechanics theory. After a mechanics analysis is studied for a flawed structure or a structure with a postulated flaw, material properties, such as fracture toughness, J-R curve are then used to assess the stability/instability of the structure for potential stable or unstable crack propagation.

Plane-strain fracture toughness, $K_{IC}$, has been used widely as a material property to evaluate possible brittle fracture of metallic materials. The fracture assessment procedure can be outlined as (a) determining the critical stress intensity factor $K_{IC}$ following the ASTM standard test method, ASTM E399-83, for the particular material of interest, (b) calculating the stress intensity factor K for a given crack geometry in a structural component under specified loads, and (c) comparing K to $K_{IC}$, to evaluate any possible failure. The common practice of (c) is that the crack would not propagate, i.e. the structure is safe, if $K<K_{IC}$ and otherwise if $K>K_{IC}$. Here, for brittle materials, "not safe" implies a catastrophic failure of the structure due to rapid unstable crack propagation. Although the ASTM standards do not outline the procedures of how to use the $K_{IC}$ determined by the test method, it specifically states "*A $K_{IC}$ value is believed to represent a lower limiting value of fracture toughness*". Thus, the common practice used by industry following the procedure (c) is generally considered conservative.

This paper cites physical evidence (test data from various sources) and theoretical basis ( mathematical mechanics analysis) to demonstrate that the common practice, such as the step (c), is incorrect and often leads to non-conservatism. The paper goes further to recommend a proper procedure in the structural integrity assessment based on detailed mechanics solutions. The presentation is composed of :

- a collection of test data that shows a broad variation of the critical stress intensity factor $K_c$;
- theoretical development in mechanics for the interpretation of the variation of $K_c$ , often known as the constraint effect in fracture;
- why the common practice of using $K_{IC}$ is not conservative in many cases;

- recommendations for proper use of the $K_{IC}$ and procedures for structural integrity evaluation.

The presentation is further extended to demonstrate that other fracture "properties" of engineering materials, such as J-R curve, Jc determined following the ASTM standards, are also *not* material properties and represent a subset of the complete material failure locus. Thus, these values should not be *directly* applied to the assessment of structural integrity. The relations between these material "properties" determined from ASTM standard testing procedures and the general structural geometry are presented.

The test data presented in this paper can be found in many open literature, e.g. [1-3]. The theoretical bases of the constraint effect presented in this paper are primarily from [4-6]. The references are provided for those readers who are interested in this subject.

References :

[1] Sinclair, G.B. and Chambers, A.E., "Strength size effects and fracture mechanics: what does the physical evidence say ?," Engineering Fracture Mechanics, 26(2), 1987, pp.279-310.

[2] Richardson, D.E. and Goree, J.G., "Experimental Verification of a New Two-Parameter Fracture Model," Fracture Mechanics: Twenty-third Symposium, ASTM STP-1189, R. Chona, Ed. American Society for Testing and Materials, Philadelphia, 738-750, 1993.

[3] Smith, J.A. and Rolfe, S. T., "The Effect of Crack Depth (a) and Crack Depth to Width Ratio (a/w) on the Fracture Toughness of A533B Steel," ASME Journal of Pressure Vessel and Technology, 116, 115-121, 1994.

[4] Chao, Y.J., Yang, S., and Sutton, M.A., "On the Fracture of Solids Characterized by One or Two Parameters: Theory and Practice," Journal of the Mechanics and Physics of Solids, 42(4), 629-647, 1994.

[5] Chao, Y.J. and Zhang, X., "Constraint Effect in Brittle Fracture," 27th National Symposium on Fatigue and Fracture, ASTM STP-1296, P.S. Piascik, J.C. Newman, Jr., and D.E. Dowling, Eds., American Society for Testing and Materials, Philadelphia, to appear.

[6] Chao, Y.J. and Lam, P.S., "Effects of Crack Depth, Specimen Size, and Out-of-Plane Stress on the Fracture Toughness of Reactor Vessel Steels," to appear in ASME Journal of Pressure Vessel Technology.

# An Improved Method for Whole-Field Automatic Measurement of Principal Stress Directions

T.Y. Chen and C.H. Lin
Department of Mechanical Engineering
National Cheng Kung University
Tainan, Taiwan, Rep. of China

Conventionally the directions of the principal stresses in a photoelastic model are measured manually by rotating the polarizer and analyzer at the same time. This process can be very tedious and requires skill. Recently various methods have been developed to measure the whole-field principal stress directions using computers and digital image processing [1-3]. In those studies the measurement was made on relatively simple two-dimensional shape and only Mawatari showed the whole-field distribution of the principal stress directions. In this paper an improved method for whole-field automatic measurement of principal stress directions is reported. This method uses only three light-field isoclinic images. Relevant photoelastic theory is derived. Test of this method on a disc under diametrical compression and a frozen-stressed photoelastic slice is demonstrated.

In a plane polariscope setup, a normalized dark-field intensity I of a loaded model can be calculated from the following equation:

$$I(\phi) = 1 - I_L / I_U = \sin^2 2(\phi) \sin^2(N\pi)$$

For three isoclinic images, $I_1$, $I_2$ and $I_3$ acquired at angles of 0, $\pi/8$ and $\pi/4$, the following equations can be derived.

$$\cos 4(\phi) = (I_3 - I_1)/(I_1 + I_3) = Vc$$
$$\sin 4(\phi) = (I_1 + I_3 - 2I_2)/(I_1 + I_3) = Vs$$
$$\phi = \theta + 0.25 \tan^{-1}[(I_1 + I_3 - 2I_2)/(I_3 - I_1)].$$

Then the angle $\phi$ can be determined into the range of $\pi/2$ using the following six conditions.

$$\phi = \theta + 0.25 \tan^{-1}(Vs/Vc) \quad \text{if } Vs \geq 0;\ Vc > 0$$
$$\phi = \theta + 0.25 \tan^{-1}(Vs/Vc) + \pi/4;\ \text{if } Vs \geq 0;\ Vc < 0$$
$$\phi = \theta + 0.25 \tan^{-1}(Vs/Vc) + \pi/4;\ \text{if } Vs \leq 0;\ Vc < 0$$
$$\phi = \theta + 0.25 \tan^{-1}(Vs/Vc) + \pi/2;\ \text{if } Vs \leq 0;\ Vc > 0$$
$$\phi = \theta + \pi/8;\ \qquad\qquad \text{if } Vs > 0;\ Vc = 0$$
$$\phi = \theta + 3\pi/8;\ \qquad\qquad \text{if } Vs < 0;\ Vc = 0$$

The system used consists of a standard diffused-light plane polariscope; a narrow-band filter; a PC-based image processing system. It is carefully calibrated before the acquisition of image data. The specimen used is a circular disk subjected to a concentrated diametrical load, and a frozen-stressed photoelastic slice obtained from a full-scale model of a variable pitch lead screw. Figure 1 shows the dark-field isoclinic images of the two specimens.

A grey-level representation of the determined principal stress directions of the circular disc is shown in Fig. 2 and that for the photoelastic slice is chown in Fig. 3. A comparison of the digitally determined principal stress directions along a horizontal line across the half-height point of the upper-half disc to those determined from the theory and the Tardy compensation method is shown in Fig. 4. It can be observed that the agreement among them is good. The difference between them is less than 2.8 degrees except at regions near the isochromatic fringes. A comparison of the digitally determined principal stress directions of the slice to the results obtained from the Mawatari method and the Tardy method is plotted in Fig. 5. It can be observed that both results are in close agreement with the values obtained by the Tardy method except at several points where the values are overshot due to isochromatic fringes. However the processing time required is about 25% less than that use of four frames.

In conclusion, an improved method for whole-field determination of the principal stress directions is presented. Relevant theory is derived. Test of this method on a two-dimensional disc and a three-dimensional photoelastic slice shows its usefulness. The results agree well to the values obtained from the Tardy method and the theory, or the Mawatari method. An accuracy of 2.8 degrees is achievable by using the developed method.

Reference
1 Yao, J.Y.,"Digital Image Processing and Isoclinics," Expl. Mech., 30(3), 264-269, 1990.
2. Brown, G.M. and Sullivan, J.L.,"The Computer-aided Holophotoelastic Method," Expl. Mech., Vol. 30(2), pp. 135-144, 1990.
3. Mawatari, S., Takashi, M., Toyoda, Y., and Kunio, T., "A Single-valued Representative Function for Determination of Principal Stress Direction in Photoelastic Analysis," Proc. 9th Intl. Conf. on Expl. Mech., Vol. 5, pp. 2069-2078, 1990.

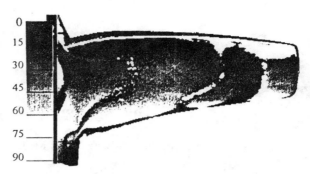

Fig. 3 Gray-level representation of the principal stress directions of a photoelastic slice

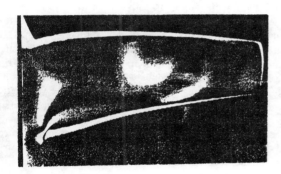

Fig. 1 Dark-field isoclinic images of a disc and a photoelastic slice.

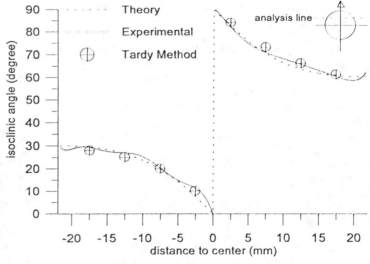

Fig. 4 Comparisons of the results of a disc from experimental, theoretical, and the Tardy method.

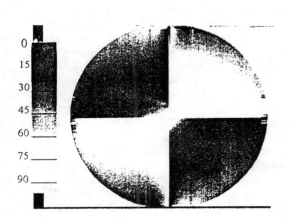

Fig. 2 Gray-level representation of principal stress directions of a disc.

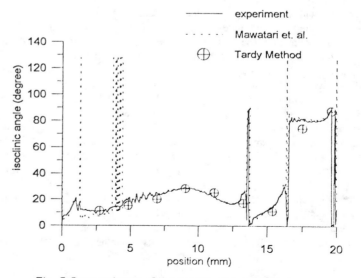

Fig. 5 Comparisons of the results of a slice from experimental, Mawarari, and the Tardy method.

179

# Experimental Evidence and Modeling of the Differing Time Scales of Structural Recovery and Mechanical Relaxation Observed During Aging of Glassy Polymers

Carl R. Schultheisz, Dina M. Colucci and Gregory B. McKenna

Polymers Division, National Institute of Standards and Technology, Gaithersburg, Maryland, USA 20899

Following a rapid change in temperature (T-jump) below the glass transition temperature ($T_g$), amorphous polymers show an evolution in both glassy structure (e.g., volume or enthalpy) [1,2,3] and mechanical properties [1,4]. The volume evolution has come to be known as structural recovery [2,3,5] and the evolution of mechanical properties, which is generally attributed to the structural recovery, was labeled physical aging by Struik [1]. Struik studied the physical aging of a number of polymers following quenches from above $T_g$ to below, and found that, to first order, the behavior could be explained using a time/aging time equivalence similar to the time/temperature equivalence used to model the temperature response of the viscoelastic behavior of polymers. The time/aging time equivalence leads to an aging time shift factor $a_{t_e}$, where $t_e$ is the aging time. The rate of aging is often evaluated through the shift rate $\mu = d\log(a_{t_e})/d\log(t_e)$. For many polymers, $\mu$ is found to be constant and near to unity for isothermal tests after quenches well below $T_g$ (in a regime where the material has achieved a constant temperature but is still far from equilibrium) [1].

Because the volume recovery is expected to be the thermodynamic parameter that determines the viscoelastic response, it has generally been assumed that both the volume recovery and the mechanical properties will evolve at the same rate. Struik [1] employed this assumption in a derivation indicating that $\mu \leq 1$. However, some research has indicated that different properties of glasses can evolve at different rates. Scherer [5] cites results of experiment with inorganic glasses that indicate different rates of evolution in the refractive index, electrical resistivity and thermal expansion coefficient. Roe and Millman [6] studied polystyrene and found differences between the evolution of the creep compliance and the enthalpy relaxation. Also, experiments with a model epoxy (DGEBA/polypropylene oxide, $T_g = 42.4\ °C$ from DSC at 20 °C/min [7]) tested using the NIST torsional dilatometer [8,9,10], in which the volume and torsional response can be measured simultaneously, have indicated differences in the rates of change of the volume and the mechanical properties after upward and downward temperature jumps. These differences depend both on the direction of the jump and the temperature.

The results from the torsional dilatometer have been investigated in two ways. The first method employed a phenomenological approach in which the volume and mechanical response are assumed to be controlled by separate clocks, and the different behaviors are investigated separately. The equations describing the volume recovery employ derivations developed by Narayanaswamy [11], Moynihan, et al. [12], Tool [13] and Kovacs, et al. [14] (or KAHR). Experiments have shown that the volume recovery cannot be modeled using a single exponential function [2]; the spectrum of recovery times is captured using a sum of exponentials or a stretched exponential function. The latter formulation has been used in this study, as it requires fewer parameters. In addition, it has been assumed that the evolution of the volume and the mechanical response are controlled by two separate clocks; the NMTKAHR phenomenological model of the volume recovery employs an internal time that is related to the experimental time through a shift factor that depends explicitly on the temperature and the relative deviation from the equilibrium volume (denoted by $\delta = (V - V_\infty)/V_\infty$ where $V_\infty$ is the equilibrium volume at infinite time). The total shift factor is thus given by $a_\delta a_T$, and the dependence of these terms on the volume and temperature is that suggested by KAHR [14]: $a_\delta$ is an exponential function of $\delta$, while $a_T$ is an exponential function of the difference between the actual temperature and a reference temperature. The results of this modeling have been shown previously [15] in a comparison of the shift factors (plotting $\log(a_{t_e})$ versus $\log(a_\delta)$). Since the volumetric shift factor is an exponential function of $\delta$, a plot of $\log(a_{t_e})$ versus $\log(a_\delta)$ is identical in form to a plot of $\log(a_{t_e})$ versus $\delta$. However, the results from experiments performed at different temperatures indicated that the coupling between temperature and volume may be somewhat more complicated than assumed for the model. In addition, while the asymmetry of approach from above or below a given temperature is captured by this model, Kovacs, et al. [14] indicate that this form of the shift factor is not capable of reproducing the expansion gap phenomenon [2].

The second investigation of the results from the torsional dilatometer has been through a simulation employing a thermoviscoelastic constitutive model developed by Caruthers and coworkers [16] within the framework of rational thermodynamics [17,18]. The model has shown considerable promise for describing structural recovery [19] and nonlinear viscoelasticity [20]. This model employs a single internal time controlled by the configurational entropy; however, the model appears to capture the differences in time scales for the evolution of the volume and the mechanical properties, and can reproduce both the asymmetry of approach and the expansion gap. This model does require data on a number of material properties, and a complete set of these properties is as yet only available for poly(vinyl acetate) (PVAc). The simulations were therefore carried out using the data for PVAc, with the temperature jumps performed between the same points relative to the glass transition of the material [21]. Thus, the comparison between the experiments and the model is still somewhat qualitative. However, the results from the modeling are quite encouraging, showing some remarkable quantitative agreement considering the different properties of the materials.

Figure 1 contrasts the evolution of the volume and the mechanical properties of the epoxy measured in the NIST torsional dilatometer. The data was taken in T-jumps to a final temperature of 32.8 °C; the magnitude of the jump is indicated in the figure. The volume recovery is plotted in the form of the volumetric shift factor $a_\delta$, while the mechanical response is shown in the form of the aging time shift factor $a_{te}$. It can be seen that for down-jumps, the volume and mechanical response achieve equilibrium at the same time, while for up-jumps the mechanical response reaches equilibrium before the volume. (For down-jumps to 35.5 °C, the mechanical properties achieved equilibrium before the volume, but for up-jumps to 35.5 °C, the volume equilibrated first.) It can also be seen that the shift factors have different magnitudes; the aging time shift factor is about 4 times the volumetric shift factor.

Figure 2 contains the same experimental data from the epoxy, now plotted as $\log a_{te}$ versus $\delta$ directly ($\delta = (V - V_\infty)/V_\infty$). Also shown are results of the thermoviscoelastic simulations using material properties for PVAc. It can be seen that there is fairly good quantitative agreement, and similar agreement was found for the T-jumps to 35.5 °C. This result is quite interesting since the PVAc required approximately two orders of magnitude longer times to achieve equilibrium. The thermoviscoelastic model employs a single internal time, but these results indicate that a single clock coupled with differences in the relative magnitude in the terms that appear in the equations can lead to different rates of evolution of various phenomena.

[1] L.C.E. Struik, Physical Aging in Amorphous Polymers and Other Materials, Elsevier, Amsterdam, 1978.

[2] G.B. McKenna, Comprehensive Polymer Science, Vol. 2: Polymer Properties, C. Booth and C. Price, ed., Pergamon Press, Oxford, p. 311-362, 1989.

[3] A.J. Kovacs, Fortschr. Hochpolym.-Forsch., 3, p. 394. 1964.

[4] A.J. Kovacs, R.A. Stratton and J.D. Ferry, J. Phys. Chem., 67, p. 152, 1963.

[5] G.W. Scherer, Relaxation in Glass and Composites, Wiley, New York, 1986.

[6] R.-J. Roe and G. M. Millman, Polymer Eng. Sci., 23, p. 318, 1983.

[7] A. Lee and G.B. McKenna, Polymer, 31, p. 423, 1990.

[8] R.S. Duran and G.B. McKenna, J. Rheology, 34, p. 813, 1990.

[9] M.M. Santore, R.S. Duran, G.B. McKenna, Polymer, 32, p. 2377, 1991.

[10] G.B. McKenna, Y. Leterrier, C.R. Schultheisz, Polymer Eng. Sci., 35, p. 403, 1995.

[11] O.S. Narayanaswamy, J. Am. Ceram. Soc., 54, p. 491, 1971.

[12] C.T. Moynihan, P.B. Macedo, C.J. Montrose, P.K. Gupta, M.A. DeBolt, J.F. Dill, B.E. Dom, P.W. Drake, A.J. Esteal, P.B. Elterman, R.P. Moeller, H. Sasabe and J.A. Wilder, Ann. N.Y. Acad. Sci., 279, p. 15, 1976.

[13] A.Q. Tool, J.Res. NBS, 37, p. 73, 1946; also J. Am. Ceram. Soc., 29, p. 240, 1946.

[14] A.J. Kovacs, J.J. Aklonis, J.M. Hutchinson, A.R. Ramos, J. Polymer Sci. Polym. Phys. Ed., 17, p. 1097, 1979.

[15] C.R. Schultheisz, G.B. McKenna, Y. Leterrier and E. Stefanis Proc. Soc. Exp. Mech., p. 329, 1995.

[16] R.M. Shay Jr. and J.M. Caruthers, Proc. North American Thermal Anal. Soc., 1988; also "Mechanics of Plastics and Composites," ASME AMD-Vol 104, 1989.

[17] B.D. Coleman and W. Noll, Rev. Mod. Phys., 33, p. 239, 1961.

[18] B.D. Coleman, Arch. Rat. Mech. Anal., 17, p. 1, 1964; also Arch. Rat. Mech. Anal., 17, p. 230, 1964.

[19] D.S. McWilliams and J.M. Caruthers, Soc. Rheology Ann. Mtg., 1993.

[20] D.M. Colucci, Ph.D. Thesis, Purdue University, West Lafayette, IN, 1995.

[21] C.R. Schultheisz, D.M. Colucci, G.B. McKenna and J.M. Caruthers, "Mechanics of Plastics and Plastic Composites," ASME AMD-Vol. 215, p. 251, 1995.

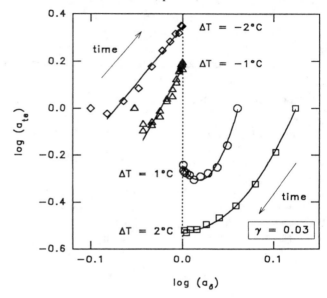

Figure 1. Comparison of the evolution of $\log(a_{te})$ and $\log(a_\delta)$ for temperature jumps to $T_0 = 32.8$ °C, twists applied with $\gamma = 0.03$.

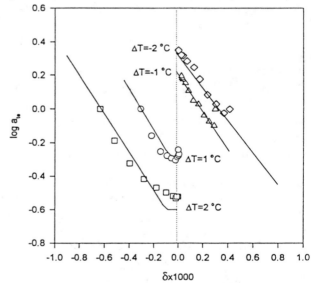

Figure 2. Comparison of the evolution of $\log(a_{te})$ and $\delta$. Symbols represent jump experiments with model epoxy to $T_0 = 32.8$ °C, with applied strain of $\gamma = 0.03$. Lines are thermoviscoelastic simulation results for PVAc at $T_0 = 27.4$ °C.

# Nonlinear Polymer Response Under Biaxial Stress States

H.B. Lu and W.G. Knauss
Graduate Aeronautical Laboratories
California Institute of Technology
Pasadena, CA91125

**Introduction** The nonlinear thermo-mechanical behavior of PMMA under combined axial and torsional loadings at temperatures between room temperature and $120°C$ is investigated. Tubular specimens are used in the experiment to achieve relatively uniform stress and strain fields. The surface deformations of the specimen are measured by the digital image correlation technique [1] that is capable to provide non-contact deformation characterization on curved specimen surface. In this abstract only results on the uniaxial and multiaxial creep at temperatures $80°C$ and $110°C$ are reported.

**Experimental** Tubular PMMA specimens (glass transition $T_g = 110°C$) are used in order to separate the effects of volumetric and shear deformations. A Russell's environmental chamber provides an environment of constant humidity and constant temperature. Loading is applied through an MTS system with the dual capacity of $15000\ N$ axial load and $168\ Nm$ torque. A random black speckle pattern formed on the specimen surface is traced through the digital image correlation method to determine the local surface deformation in the center of the test section.

As demonstrated by Knauss and Kenner [2], the moisture content in amorphous polymers has a significant effect on the viscoelastic behavior. The effect of volumetric dilatation due to moisture content on the creep behavior is the same as that due to the temperature. In the following measurements, the effect of the moisture content is not to be investigated. Thus the specimens are stored and tests are conducted at the same relative humidity (6%) at all times except during the time when the specimen is taken out from the container and placed inside the environmental chamber.

At each temperature the same specimen is used repeatedly. A used specimen is then annealed for $4\ hr$ at $115°C$ in a hydraulic oil bath and cooled down at $5°C/hr$ to room temperature. This specimen is then used for the next test under different loadings after it has been stored in the humidity-controlling belljar for at least 3 days. Preliminary results indicate that there is no difference in the torsional creep compliance measured from a specimen stored for 15 and for the same specimen annealed and stored for 3 days. Specimens treated in this way do not appear to be subject to physical aging.

**Results and Discussion** We present first the torsional creep compliance at different stress levels at $80°C$ (Fig. 1). The torsional creep compliance is defined as the ratio of the local surface shear strain to the surface shear stress.

The surface shear stress equals $TR/I$ with $T$ denoting the applied constant torque, $R$ the outer radius, $I$ the polar moment of inertia. The hollow circle symbols represent the results from a cylindrical specimen having an outer diameter of $22.23\ mm$ and a wall thickness of $1.59\ mm$ and the solid square symbols represent the results from a specimen having an outer diameter of $25.15\ mm$ and possessing a wall thickness of $3.18\ mm$. In both cases the torsional creep rate increases as the applied shear stress increases; in this sense the applied shear stress controls the torsional creep rate. However, the creep compliances at shear stresses of $1.2\ MPa$ and $1.5\ MPa$ tend to be coincident at the beginning but deviate as time increases. This is probably so because in the initial stage the shear strains are small ($< 1\%$) such that the linearity range has not been exceeded and the material behaves as a linear viscoelastic solid, but as the shear strain increases the nonlinearity effect becomes apparent so that the torsional creep compliance deviates. In this sense the nonlinearity is controlled by the magnitude of the shear strain . We therefore expect that the deformation rate is controlled by both stress and strain in the nonlinear viscoelastic range. We also observe that the torsional creep rate for a thicker walled specimen is slower than that for the thin walled specimen (cf. curves at $\tau = 1.2PMa$). This phenomenon should not occur in linear viscoelasticity because the material behavior is strain (or stress) independent. As the strain varies over the wall thickness, the stress is no longer a linear function of the radial coordinate if any of the material exceeds the linear range. Nonlinearity makes the material "softer". For thicker specimen, the nonlinearity is less pronounced and therefore the creep rate measured from the surface shear deformation is slower.

We turn next to results from combined axial and torsional loading. We observe from Fig. 2 that a superposition of either an axial tensile or compressive stress on a pure torsion increases the creep rate. However, a superposed tensile stress increases the rate definitely more than that of a compressive stress. In both cases (superposed tension or compression) the maximum shear stress is the same but the hydrostatic stresses are different. If one thinks of the response to a stress state with a maximum shear stress and zero hydrostatic stress as an intrinsic shear response one expects that as the intrinsic shear stress and the corresponding shear strain increase the creep rate increases. For the pure torsion with superposed tensile or compressive stress, the intrinsic shear is the same, and in this case the role of volumetric deformation emerges. For the superposed tensile stress case, the hydrostatic stress and the volumetric deformation (free volume variation) are positive, and the shear creep rate is accelerated over the intrinsic shear response. On the other hand, for the superposed compressive stress case, the volumetric deformation (free volume variation) is negative, which slows down the creep rate with respect to the intrinsic shear case.

We consider next the torsional creep compliances for multiaxial creep and torsional creep for a specimen having an outer diameter of 25.15 $mm$ and a wall thickness of 3.18 $mm$ at $110°C$ (Fig. 3). It is apparent that the torsional creep rate is increased when a tensile stress is superposed on pure torsion ($\sigma = 1.5\ MPa$, $\tau = 0.9\ MPa$). The creep rate is increased so much that the specimen soon buckled and broke. However, contrary to the behavior observed at $80°C$, it is now found that a superposed compressive stress slows down the torsional creep rate. This observation indicates that there exists a competition in the "total" creep rate between the intrinsic shear and (negative) volumetric deformation. As long as the effect of the intrinsic shear is more dominant than the (negative) volumetric deformation, the creep rate is accelerated with respect to pure torsion (under zero axial load) (Fig. 2). However, if the (negative) volumetric deformation is more dominant, the creep rate is slowed down despite an increase in shear rate due to the intrinsic shear stress. This phenomenon is clearly dependent on the closeness of the glass transition.

**Conclusions:** Experimental results to date indicate that well below the glass transition temperature either a superposed tensile stress or a compressive stress increases the torsional creep rate, with a tensile stress providing distinctly more creep acceleration than a compressive stress. However, in the vicinity of the glass transition, a superposed compressive stress decreases the torsional creep rate while a tensile stress increases it. These observations reveal that both volumetric deformation (free volume) and deviatoric deformation contribute to the nonlinear viscoelastic behavior of polymers. However, the effect relative contribution of any volumetric vis-a-vis shear deformation in controlling deformation rates is probably a continuous function of the temperature with a possibly pronounced sensitivity in the vicinity of the glass transition temperature.

**References**

[1] Lu, H.B., Vendroux, G. and Knauss, W.G., Surface Deformation Measurements Via Digital Image Correlation. GALCIT SM Report 96-1, California Institute of Technology, 1996
[2] Knauss, W.G. and Kenner, V.H., On the Hygrothermomechanical Characterization of Polyvinyl Acetate, J. Appl. Phys., **51**(10), pp. 5131-5134, 1980

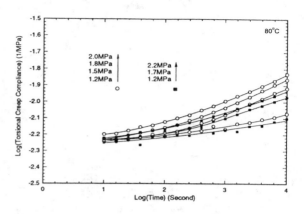

Figure 1: Torsional Creep Compliance at $80°C$

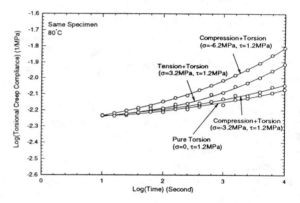

Figure 2: Torsional Creep Compliance at $80°C$

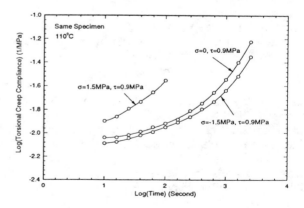

Figure 3: Torsional Creep Compliance at $110°C$

# Viscoelastic Responses and Physical Aging in Rubber-Toughened Epoxy Glasses

Andre Lee
Michigan State University
Department of Materials Science and Mechanics
E. Lansing, MI. 48824

Rubber-toughened epoxy is the basis for many structural applications involving brittle neat epoxy resins. This is because of the two phase morphology produces great improvements in fracture resistance with a minimal reduction in its other physical and mechanical properties. However the viscoelastic responses for two phase materials are complex, but understanding these time-dependent properties is important in many structural applications of these materials. In many applications, long term performance is a great importance. It is well known that for any glass-forming materials including thermoset polymers exhibit a slow but significant evolution in the physical and mechanical properties after quenched from above the glass transition, $T_g$ to below it and then aged isothermally in the glassy state.

In many of our previous works [1-3] involving isothermal physical aging study of the model epoxy glasses, the classical time - aging time superposition principle was observed in both linear viscoelastic and non-linear viscoelastic regions after a sudden quenched from above $T_g$ to below $T_g$. The classical time - temperature superposition was also observed in both small-strain stress relaxation and large deformation creep experiments.

The present work, we focused on the influence of physical aging in the epoxy matrix phase to the overall linear viscoelastic responses of rubber-toughened epoxy glasses. Isothermal small-deformation creep compliance and small-strain relaxation experiments were performed at different times after a quenched from above $T_g$ of the epoxy phase. All experiments were performed in the uniaxial manner in both tension and compression. Samples toughened with different weight fraction of rubber and different sizes of rubber domain were also investigated. The results of creep compliance curve and relaxation modulus curves obtained at different elapsed times (aging time) are to be presented and discussed in terms of time - aging time superposition principle.

The epoxy resin used in this study was a epoxide terminated diglycidyl ether of bisphenol A (DGEBA) and cured with a diamine terminated polypropylene oxide to form network. The epoxide to amine was that of stoichiometric ratio. The elastomer used to toughened the epoxy network glasses were carboxyl-terminated random copolymer of butadiene acrylonitrile (CTBN) of different molecular weight. The size of the rubber-reinforced domain can be control by using different molecular weight of CTBN or varying thermal curing schedule. Both methods of controlling size were used.

The mechanical tests were performed using a computer-controlled servo-hydraulic testing machine, equipped with an over for temperature control. The temperature was controlled with an ATS 3-zone temperature controller. Measurements of the temperature between the top and bottom of the sample showed that the gradient was less than 0.2 $^{\circ}$C. Oven stability was better than $\pm$ 0.1 $^{\circ}$C during each physical aging experiment.

The mechanical tests were carried out in uniaxial extension and compression under both stress relaxation and creep conditions. Deformations or loads were applied periodically at aging time, $t_e$, that doubled with each test, i.e., $t_e$ = 30 min., 60 min., 120 min., etc.. The duration time of the deformation/load to aging time was 0.025. The stress relaxation modulus $E(t)$ and the creep compliance $D(t)$ were calculated with usual manner. Each stress relaxation and creep compliance curves was analyzed by using the Kohlrausch-Williams-Watts [4,5] stretch exponential function with three fitting parameters. The parameters are related to the zero-time properties, characteristic relaxation/retardation time and the shape parameter of the curve of interest.

If the stress relaxation or creep compliance curves obtained at different aging time are said to be obeying time - aging time superposition principle with horizontal shift along the time axis, values of zero-time parameter and the shape parameters must be the same at different aging time. If we have time - aging time superposition, the aging time shift rate can be obtained using the ratio of characteristic time with respect to a characteristic time of a given reference aging time.

Initial results of this study have shown that the classical time - aging time superposition was observed for rubber-toughened epoxy under the small-load creep experiment, while under the similar isothermal aging condition the superposition of time and aging time was not longer valid for small-strain stress relaxation. These results suggest that when the epoxy matrix phase undergo physical aging, the interphase between rubber and epoxy change with aging time. Further, it is possible there exist a lag between the stress field and strain field in the presence of this interphase. This experimental observation is somewhat unexpected. More experimental results and analytical analysis are needed to better understanding the viscoelastic responses of multiphase polymeric materials.

## References

1.      Lee, A., and McKenna, G. B., Polymer **29**, 1812 (1988).

2.      Lee, A., and McKenna, G. B., Polymer **31**, 423 (1990).

3.      Lee, A, Santore, M. M., Duran, R. S., and McKenna, G. B., J. Non-Crystalline Solids **131-133**, 497 (1991).

4.      Kolrausch, F., Pogg. Ann. Phys., **12**, 393 (1847).

5.      William, G., and Watts, D. C., Trans. Faraday Soc., **66**, 80 (1970).

# Transient Phenomena in Torsional Creep Measurements

Igor Emri, Robert Cvelbar
University of Ljubljana, Center for Experimental Mechanics
Cesta na Brdo 49, 1000 Ljubljana, Slovenia

Anatoly Nikonov
Faculty of Math. and Mech., Saratov State University
Astrakhanskaya 83, Saratov 410071, Russia

## INTRODUCTION

Within the realm of linear viscoelasticity, mechanical properties of polymers (in time domain) are given as material functions, elicited from the response to a constant load. In theory this load has the form of a step function of time, meaning that it has to be applied instantaneously. In the case of a shear these functions are the creep compliance, $J(t)$, obtained in response to a constant stress, and the relaxation modulus, $G(t)$, when material is loaded with constant strain. To obtain a complete relaxation and/or creep curve (master curve), experiments are usually performed at different constant temperatures within a certain time interval, commonly called the *Experimental Window* [1,2]. For practical reasons, the upper boundary of this window is restricted to about $10^4$ seconds (this is roughly three hours). To obtain an additional decade of data one would need to prolong the experiment to about thirty hours. This is not only time consuming, and therefore expensive, but also technically a demanding task. Creep and relaxation experiments require a very accurate temperature control, for some materials within $0.01°$ C, which is for long experiments not easily accomplished [2].

In reality it is impossible to apply an instantaneous load; the step function is thus replaced by a ramp function, with the rise time $t_0$, as it is schematically shown on Fig. 1. As a result the acceptable measurements can begin only after a certain time $t_1$, when the response to the ramp excitation comes sufficiently close to the corresponding step response. This is displayed in the right part of Fig. 1. Most experimentalists take $t_1$ as a "rule-of-thumb" to be one decade of time after the loading, i.e., $t_1/t_0 = 10$.

The shifting of the segments of creep or relaxation curve along the logarithmic time scale, according to the time-temperature superposition principle, is more accurate the wider the experimental window is [2]. We have therefore investigated the possibilities of broadening the experimental window in the direction of the lower boundary, rather than extending the measuring time over $10^4$ seconds, as schematically shown with dotted line and question mark in Fig. 2. This can be achieved by decreasing the rise time of the ramp function, and starting with measurements as soon as possible. In theory, if one could apply an instantaneous load, this boundary could be extended, on the logarithmic time scale, to minus infinity. These examinations gave interesting results indicating that the "rule-of-thumb" might fail when more accurate results are required. We discuss here our findings related to that problem.

## NUMERICAL EXPERIMENTS AND CONCLUSION

We have used the Cole-Cole function [1] for modeling the *true* creep compliance,

$$J(t) = J_g + \frac{J_e - J_g}{1 + \sqrt{(\tau / t)}},$$  (1)

using: $J_g = 10^{-9}$ mm$^2$/N, $J_e = 1.001 \times 10^{-5}$ mm$^2$/N, and $\tau = 1$ second. Here $J_g$ and $J_e$ represent the glassy and the equilibrium compliance, respectively. The *true* creep compliance is shown in Fig. 1 as a solid line, and is indicated as a ramp function with the rise time $t_0 = 0$. Next we have calculated the response to the ramp loading,

$$\sigma(t) = \sigma_0 \frac{t}{t_0}, \quad 0 < t \leq t_0,$$
$$\sigma(t) = \sigma_0, \quad , \quad t > t_0,$$  (2)

using the stress-strain relation

$$\varepsilon(t) = \int_0^t J(t - \xi) \dot{\sigma}(\xi) d\xi$$  (3)

where $\sigma(\xi)$ is given with Eq. 2. The *measured* creep compliance, $J_{ramp}(t)$, was then obtained from the relation,

$$J_{ramp}(t) = \frac{\varepsilon(t)}{\sigma_0},$$  (4)

as it is commonly done in evaluation of experimental data. *Measured* $J_{ramp}(t)$ are for five different rise times, $t_0 = 0.001, 0.01, 0.1, 1$ and $10$ seconds shown in Fig. 1. Finally, the discrepancy between the *true*, $J(t)$, and *measured*, $J_{ramp}(t)$, creep compliance was defined as

$$Error = \frac{J(t) - J_{ramp}(t)}{J(t)} \cdot 100 \ [\%].$$  (5)

From Fig. 2 it appears that the differences between the *true* and *measured* creep compliance become negligible within one decade after the loading. This is particularly true for short rise times. However when deviations are displayed in relative terms, using Eq. 5, the conclusion is quite different. Results are shown in Fig. 3, from which it can be clearly seen that the difference between the two curves effectively vanishes only after more than two decades, except for the loadings with the rise time $t_0 = 1$ and $10$ seconds. These two, however, are not acceptable, as they significantly narrow the experimental window. These observations, of course, depend on the error that is accepted in the first measurement after the loading. This evaluation error must be added to the overall experimental error, therefore it seems reasonable to require that the first should not exceed 0.1%. Figures 4 and 5 show the results of these analysis.

Figure 4 displays the rise time, $t_0$, as function of the $t_1$, which indicates the beginning of measurements. The vertical dashed line defines the beginning of the four decades wide *Experimental Window*. From this it can clearly be seen that the specimen must be loaded faster than in 0.01 seconds in order to start measurements at 1 second.

Figure 5 presents the ratio $t_1/t_0$ as a function of the rise time, $t_0$, and therefore is a counterpart to the information presented in Fig. 4. In real experimental situations the exact rise time, $t_0$, is usually measured and then the necessary "waiting time" should be determined accordingly. This can be readily picked from this diagram.

Summarizing we may conclude:
1. The common "rule-of-thumb", to start the measurements one decade after the loading, fails if more accurate results are required.
2. It is relatively easy to fulfill the conditions required for the *Experimental Window* with the width of four decades.
3. Widening *Experimental Window* for an additional decade, becomes a very demanding task. It requires loading times that are shorter then one millisecond.

When approaching such short loading times we are faced with another problem, related to the resonance ringing of the measuring apparatus. This problem has been addressed elsewhere [3], however, it will be discussed in oral presentation.

## REFERENCES

[1] N.W. Tschoegl, "The Phenomenological Theory of Linear Viscoelastic Behavior", Springer Verlag, Berlin, 1989.
[2] J.J. Aklonis, W.J. MacKnight, "Introduction to Polymer Viscoelasticity", 2nd ed., John Wiley and Sons, New York, 1983.
[3] R. Cvelbar, I. Emri, N.W. Tschoegl, "Analysis of Transient Phenomena in Creep Compliance Measurements of Viscoelastic Materials", SEM 1994 Spring Conference, Baltimore, 1994, pp 663-668.

## FIGURES

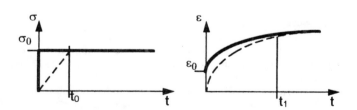

Fig. 1. Step and ramp loading and corresponding time dependent (creep) responses

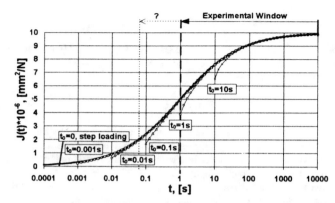

Fig. 2. Creep compliance as a response to a step and ramp loadings.

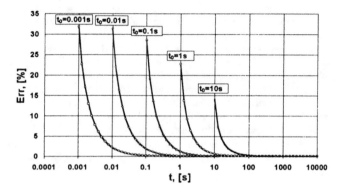

Fig. 3. Measurements error after the loading.

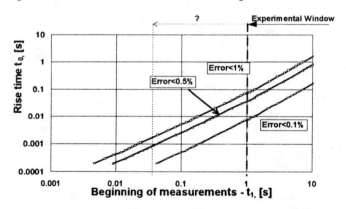

Fig. 4: Required rise time for a given beginning of measurements.

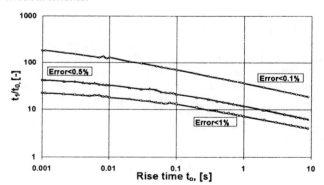

Fig. 5: Ratio $t_1/t_0$ as function of rise time.

# Extension of Zandman Coatings -
# Isodyne Coatings and Permanent Strain Coatings

Jerzy T. Pindera

Department of Civil Engineering, University of Waterloo, Waterloo, Ontario, Canada N2L 3G1

**Overwiew.** Procedures of birefringent coating proposed by Mesnager in 1930, followed by Oppel in 1937 and others and developed analytically and technically by Zandman with coworkers [16-19] are well presented in bibliography [5, 6, 2, 3, 1]. Recent developments in nondestructive isodyne stress analysis and better understanding of the actual mechanisms of the mechanical and optical creep and relaxation processes in polymeric materials opened new perspectives in application of the birefringent coatings. As result, the established term "photoelastic coatings' does not seem any longer commensurate with the extend of applications of those coatings in engineering mechanics and design. Evidence presented below appears to justify introduction of a more general term "Zandman coatings"which would encompass a more general class of physical interactions and evaluation procedures. To reliably evaluate the recorded data it is necessary to know the pertinent material functions, such as: mechanical and optical creep and creep recovery compliance functions; the analogous relaxation function; the linear limit stress function; and the spectral dependence of birefringence [8-10, 12, 14]. Such set of data represents an essential component of the evaluation procedures. Figs. 1 and 2 illustrates the issue: e. g. the optical relaxation modulus is constant for a large class of polymers; and the linear limit stresses depend on other physical parameter and on time.

**Isodyne coatings**. It is demonstrated that the method of isodyne coatings yields data on the normal and shear stress components acting at the surface of metallic and composite objects [11, 12]. It is known that the experimentally determined isodyne surfaces carry information on the normal and shear force intensities which are acting on cross-sections parallel , or normal, to the direction of differentiation. Thus, the slopes of the force intensities, ( the slopes of the isodyne functions), are proportional to the normal and shear stress components[12]. A set of isodyne surfaces related to 4 or 5 measurement planes within the thickness of a plate allows to obtain a good insight into the values and actual variation of stress components with the thickness coordinate. When a birefringent plate is attached to the surface of an object the induced isodyne fields are related to the strain state at the object surface, provided that a set of theoretical requirements is satisfied [15, 12].

Reliability of evaluation of the stress/strain state at the object surface depends of two known main factors: reinforcing effect of the coating and the transfer function relating the stress states in isodyne coating amd in object.

The reinforcing effect of the isodyne coating depends roughly on the ratio of elastic moduli, which is noticeably influenced by time. For a 5 mm thick isodyne coating made of a polyester resin, which is attached to a steel object, the reinforcing effect is equivalent to an thickness alteration of the object of about 0.1 mm - this is usually within the manufacturing tolerances. In addition, the apparent elasticity modulus of the coating decreases rapidly because of the mechanical creep [8, 9]. To facilitate the stress evaluation, the transfer function mentioned above and given in a general form

$$\sigma_{xxs} = \sigma_{xxs}(\sigma_{xxc}, \sigma_{yyc}, \nu_c, \nu_s, E_c/E_s)$$

can be conveniently presented in a graphical form [11, 12].

Measurements are performed in a constant deformation mode, which allows elimination of the optical creep, whereas the stresses in a coating are continuously relaxing, Fig. 1 [9, 10]. To increase magnitude of the optical effect it is advantageous to use the technique of the spacial frequency modulation [11, 12]. An example of an isodyne coatings measurement is given in Fig. 2, which is self-explanatory.

**Permanent strain coatings.** Permanent strain occurs in particular regions of metallic structures or components, loaded beyond the two-dimensional value of yield stress. Evidently, within such regions the strain and stress states consist of superposed permanent and elastic components., which are not simply additive. In metallic materials such as steel the permanent - or plastic - strain is characterized by the presence of the effects of dislocations, called Lüders lines. Three pieces of information are needed to describe strain/stress field in the presence of local plastic deformations: boundary of a plastically deformed region; data on the total strain in the elastically and plastically deformed regions; data on the permanent strain in the plastically deformed regions. The convencional photoelastic coatings procedures supply rather qualitative information on local plastic deformation because of the lack of a sufficiently reliable theoretical basis - Their theoretical foundations are often speculative, based on assumed but not tested physical and mathematical models [13, 3].

It is shown that it is possible to develop procedures yielding quantitative data on the regions and magnitude of intertwined local plastic and elastic deformations by integrating three measurement procedures: brittle coatings [4] for determination of boundaries of plastic deformation [7] , Fig. 4; birefringent coatings for determination of the principal strain differences in the elastic and plastic regions [7], Fig. 5; isodyne coatings for determination of all three parameters of a plane stress field [12]. This procedure requires that a specific set of definitions and conditions is satisfied, such as: the density of Lüders lines is taken as a measure for plastic deformation,; coating is deformed within the linear limit strain; and the testable assumption that the resulting elastic stresses within the plastic region are not larger that the equivalent yield stress (Huber-Mises-Hencky hypothesis).

It should be noted that linear limit strain of a typical birefringent coating is roughly 100 times higher than the yield stress of a low carbon steel and that after a plastic deformation the birefringent coating is subjected to a constant deformation mode with an imposed deformation field.

## References

[1] Aribert, J. M. and Lachal, A., "Elasto-plastic stress analysis by birefringent coatings", Journal de Mécanique Appliquée, **1** (4) 1977, pp 377-401.

[2] Dantu, M. P., "Étude des Contraintes dans les Milieux Hétérogène, Application au Beton", Annales de l''Institut Technique du Bâtiment et des Travaux Publique, (121), 1958, pp 55-77.

[3] Gerberich, W., Stress Distribution About a Slowly Growing Crack

Determined by the Photoelastic Coating Method", Technical Report No. 32-208, Jet Propulsion Laboratory, Pasadena, California, 1962.

[4] Kohn, S., Karwoitsky, Tacguet, "Les émaux et vernis craquelant," Recherche Aéronautique, **13**, 1950.

[5] Mesnager, A., "Sur la determination optique des tensions intérieures dans les solides à trois dimensions", Comptes Rendus Acad. Sc. Paris, **190**, 1930, p 1249-1250.

[6] Oppel, G., "Das Polarisationsoptische Schichtverfahren zur Messung der Oberflachenspannungen am beanspruchten Bauteil ohne Model", Zeitschrift des VDI, **81**,1937, pp 603-804.

[7] Pindera, J. T., " On Application of Brittle Coatings for Determination of Regions of Plastic Deformations", Rozprawy Inżynierskie (Engineering Transactions), **V** (1),1957, pp 33-47.

[8] Pindera, J. T., "Contemporary Methods of Photoelasticity", Państwowe Wydawnictwa Techniczne PWT, Warszawa, 1960.

[9] Pindera, J. T., "Rheological Responses of Model Materials", Wydawnictwa Naukowo-Techniczne, Warszawa, 1962.

[10] Pindera, J. T. and Straka, P., "On Physical Measures of Rheological Responses of Some Materials in Wide Ranges of Temperature and Spectral Frequency", Rheologica Acta, **13**, 1974, pp 338-351.

[11] Pindera, J. T., Issa, S. S. and Krasnowski, B. R., "Isodyne Coatings in Stress Analysis". In: Proceedings of the 1981 Spring Meeting. Society for Experimental Stress Analysis, Brookfield Center, CT, 1981, pp 111-117.

[12] Pindera, J. T. and Pindera, M.-J., "Isodyne Stress Analysis", Kluwer Academic Publishers, Dordrecht, 1989.

[13] Pindera, J. T., "Comments on modeling plastic deformation of low carbon steel". In: A. S. Krausz et al (Eds), Constitutive Laws of Plastic Deformation and Fracture, Kluwer Academic Publishers, Dordrecht, 1990, pp 279-284.

[14] Pindera, J. T., "On the Physical Basis of Characterization of Time-dependend Polymeric Materials", Proceedings of 1993 SEM Conference on Experimental Mechanics, SEM, Bethel, CT, 1993, pp 813-822.

[15] Pindera, J. T., "Problems of Contemporary Photomechanics", Proceedings 1995 SEM Conference, SEM,Bethel, CT, 1995, pp 191-198.

[16] Zandman, F., "Analyse des Contraintes par Vernis Photoélastique", Groupement pour l'Avancement des Méthodes d'Analyse des Contraintes, **2** (6), 1955, pp 1-12.

[17] Zandman, F., "Mesures photoélastiques de déformations élastiques et plastiques et des fragmentations cristallines dans les métaux", Rev. Métall., **53**, 1956.

[18] Zandman, F., Redner, S. S. and Riegner, E. I., "Reinforcing Effect of Birefringent Coatings", Experimental Mechanics, **2** (2), 1962, pp 55-64.

[19] Zandman, F., Redner, S. S. and Dally, J. W., "Photoelastic Coatings", The Iowa University Press and Society for Experimental Stress Analysis, Brookfield Center, CT, 1977.

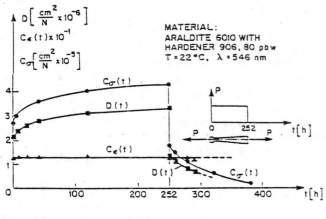

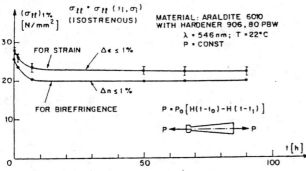

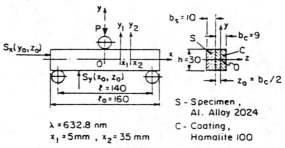

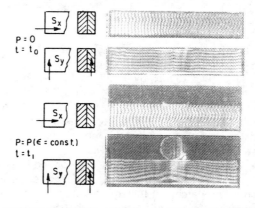

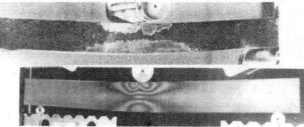

Fig. 1 (top left) Mechanical and optical creep and creep recovery of an isodyne coating.

Fig. 2 ( bottom left) Linear limit stress of an isodyne coating.

Fig. 3 (top right) Isodyne coating in stress analysis of a steel beam.

Fig. 4 ( middle right) Limits of plastic deformation in a steel beam indicated by brittle coating.

Fig.5 (bottom right) Total elastic-plastic effect in birefringent coating on a steel beam.

# A Photoelastic Study of the Effectiveness of Bonded Repairs on Aging Aircraft

R. L. Hastie, R. Fredell, and J. W. Dally
Department of Engineering Mechanics
2354 Fairchild Drive, Suite 6H2
U.S. Air Force Academy, CO 80840-6240

As we enter the 21st century, with curtailed acquisition budgets, the procurement of new aircraft systems for the Department of Defense will be limited. For this reason, the development of repair systems for extending the life of existing aircraft, while maintaining the safety of crews and the systems, will become more critical. In 1993 approximately 51% of the USAF aircraft were over 15 years old, and 44% were over 20 years old. The development of improved and integrated repair methods are essential if we are to maintain the airworthiness, safety and economical operation of the aircraft serving the nation in the next decade.

Our research has focused on the repair of pressurized fuselages, where relatively high stresses are imposed on thin skin in each high altitude flight. Damage in the form of fatigue cracks occurs with time at highly stressed rivet holes. Timely thorough inspections and repairs are required to avoid catastrophic failures similar to the Aloha Airlines incident. The method of repair [1] investigated in this paper involves hot bonding patches over the cracks from the outside of the aircraft as illustrated in Fig. 1. The patch reinforces the cracked region and carries the load over the crack with a corresponding decrease in the stresses and in the stress intensity factor in the damaged region. The critical stress regions in the patch, skin, and adhesive are shown in Fig 1.

This abstract describes a photoelastic investigation of an aluminum 2024 T3 center cracked tension panel 150 mm wide by 1.5 mm thick (6 inch by 0.062 inch) that has been repaired on one side by cold bonding an elliptical shaped patch over the 25 mm (1 inch) crack. GLARE 2 a 1.5 mm (0.062 inch) thick layered composite consisting of four thin sheets of aluminum and three layers of unidirectional Glass Fiber Reinforced Plastic (GFRP) was employed for the patch. Birefringent coatings [2] were bonded to both sides of the specimen to determine: (1) The stress distribution in the patch, (2) the redistribution of stresses in the tension panel under the patch, and (3) the reduction in the stress intensity factor due to the patch.

We have conducted three experiments with the same tension panel. In the first, the panel was not repaired and we collected isochromatic data to establish a reference base for the shear distribution in the damaged region and for determining the stress intensity factor $K_I$. Since a theoretical solution is available for the center cracked tension panel, we were able to demonstrate the accuracy of the experimental approach and the data analysis method.

The experimental approach for the first experiment consisted of bonding two rectangular pieces of photoelastic coating adjacent to the crack. One piece of coating is oriented with a free edge along the x axis to give a relation for $K_I$ and $\sigma_{ox}$ in terms of the coating strain $\varepsilon_x$. The second piece of coating, with a free edge oriented along the y axis, gives a second independent relation for the two unknown parameters in terms of coating strain $\varepsilon_y$. We have derived a linear equation giving $K_I$ in terms of data ($N_x$, $r_x$, $N_y$ and $r_y$) taken from the edges of the coating.

In the second experiment, we cold bonded a 50 mm (2 inch) by 100 mm (4 inch) elliptical patch over the 25 mm (1 inch) crack and used the same photoelastic coatings to determine the effectiveness of the repair. We have used the isochromatic data presented in Figs. 2 and 3 to quantify the redistribution of the shear stresses in the damaged region and to determine the reduction in the stress intensity factor due to the repair.

In the third experiment we bonded an elliptical piece of birefringent coating over the patch. The fringe pattern permitted us to determine the regions of high stress in the patch above and below the crack line, and to determine the shear transfer length at four different regions of the patch. The fringe patterns also provided insight for the design of an improved patch geometry.

## ACKNOWLEDGMENTS

We would like to thank Col. Cary Fisher for his encouragement in pursuing this research area, and to Lt. Col. McGillen and the Air Force Office of Scientific Research for providing the seed funding to develop experimental methods to study bonded aircraft repairs.

## REFERENCES

[1] Baker, A. A. and R. Jones, Bonded Repair of Aircraft Structures, Martinus Nijhoff Publishers, Boston, MA 1988.

[2] Zandman, F. S. Redner and J. W. Dally, Photoelastic Coatings, Iowa State Press, Ames, IA 1977.

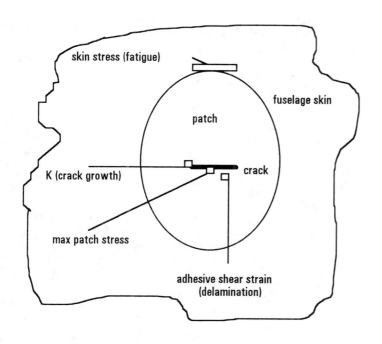

skin stress (fatigue)

fuselage skin

patch

K (crack growth)

crack

max patch stress

adhesive shear strain
(delamination)

Fig 1  Elliptical Patch Showing Regions of
Critical Stresses and Stress Intensities

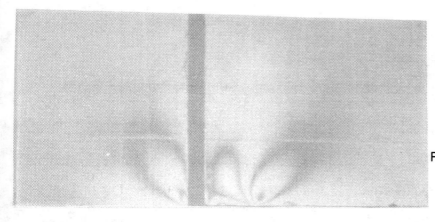

Fig 2  Isochromatic Fringes from Unpatched
Center-Cracked Tension Panel

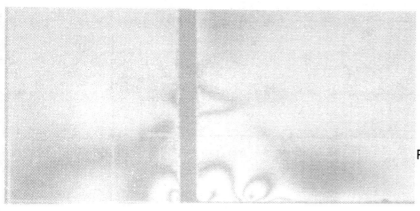

Fig 3  Isochromatic Fringes from Patched
Center-Cracked Tension Panel

# Photoelastic Coating - 40 Years Evolution of Measuring Techniques

Alex S. Redner
President
Strainoptic Technologies, Inc.
108 W. Montgomery Avenue
North Wales, PA  19454

The first publication by Mesnager [1] on the principle of Photoelastic Coatings, appeared in 1930.  But it was not until the publication by Zandman in 1956 [2] that the concept was recognized by the engineering community as a revolutionary tool that, unlike model technology, was capable of solving practical design and structural stress problems.

It is remarkable that the fundamental concept remained essentially unchanged over a period of 40 years, and unmatched by numerous full-field techniques that were developed over this long period of time.  What makes photoelastic coatings a choice design and "fast prototyping" tool, is its ability to solve problems that cannot be tackled by FEA, in particular:

- Resolution of stress field on a "zero" gage length.
- Measuring stresses due to assembly operations.
- Ability to identify regions of yielding, without assuming material properties.
- Measurements results not affected by load-distribution assumptions in vicinity of the force-application areas.

Also, low cost and speed of execution, makes photoelastic coating an ideal "rapid proto-typing" method.

The evolution of measuring techniques used for data acquisition followed closely the trends in instrumentation technology.  From the beginning, the classical "fringe counting" concept was abandoned, since within the range of elastic strains in structures seldom more than 2 fringes, and in many applications less than one fringe were observed.

The measuring method in early devices (Figure 1) relied mostly on the Tardy and Babinet compensators [3].  It took little time to acknowledge that the structural lab technicians could not master these visual techniques, and in 1962, reflection polariscopes incorporated an easy to use Babinet-Soleil (double-wedge) uniform field compensator, providing a numerical readout of the measured fringe order. (Figure 2)

While easier than the Tardy and Senarmont analyzer rotation method, these compensators had similar limitations:  direction of principal stresses needed to be measured before fringe order could be measured, and the resolution remained limited to $\pm$ 0.02 fringes.  Moreover, to obtain quantitative results, relatively thick coatings were needed, generating sizable incertitude related to correction factors [3][4].

These correction factors remained for years a major limitation, restricting the use of coatings to qualitative rather than quantitative results.

"Spinning Analyzer" automatic polariscopes developed in the seventies [5] were not suitable for use in reflection, since these devices were heavy, used moving parts, and required servos for 1/4 wave plate positioning.

It was not until 1985 that the Spectral Contents Analysis, or SCA measuring technique was developed [6] permitting a 10-fold increase in sensitivity, and eliminating visual judgmental factor from the readout.

The SCA technique is based on the use of a spectrophotometer for measuring the transmitted light intensity (see Figure 3) at several wavelengths $\lambda_i$, and then solving the system of equations (1) to extract the retardation $\delta$ and fringe order N.

$$\left(I/_{Io}\right)_i = \sin^2 \; \pi\delta/_{\lambda_i} = \sin^2 \pi \, N_i \quad (1)$$

This PC-based data acquisition method made it possible for laboratory technicians to accurately acquire and plot the results of testing and moved the photoelastic coating to the present-day technology.

Over a period of the last 10 years, numerous advances were incorporated by researchers, equation (1) above, adding capabilities of sign recognition, dispersion correction and self-calibration feature that is essential to assure certifiable results.

As the PC-based data acquisition system became the hub of all measuring and laboratory tool, the 'SCA method permitted use of this simple and economical tool for logging the Photoelastic Coating results, yielding readily data files, graphs, tables, etc....

Presently, the technique offers resolution of 0.002 fringes, permitting use of photoelastic films 0.5mm thick or less, and the strain measuring sensitivity of 5 microstrain. The speed of data acquisition is limited by A/D converter and number of wavelengths included for analysis. Speeds in excess of 5KHz are routinely handled by this method.

Full field techniques using SCA based multiwavelength-multi-image solutions are certainly possible, and their future introduction will further enhance the techniques of photoelastic coating.

The SCA method places the photoelastic coating back where it belongs; e.g. a full-field technique, that permits not only the appreciation of the nature of the stress field, but providing also, accurate quantitative results.

References:

[1] Mesnager, M., "Sur la Determination Optique des Tensions Interieures dans les Solides a Trois Dimensions," Comptes Rendus, Paris, 190, 1249, 1930.

[2] Zandman, F. & Wood, M.R., "Photo Stress, A New Technique for Photoelastic Stress Analysis," Product Engineering, McGraw-Hill, pp 167-178, September, 1956.

[3] Zandman, Redner & Dally, "Photoelastic Coatings," SESA Monograph #3, Iowa University Press, 1977.

[4] Reese, R.T. & Kawahara, W.A., "Handbook of Structural Testing," The Fairmont Press, pp 226-236,1993,

[5] Redner, A.S., "New Automatic Polariscope System," Experimental Mechanics 14 (12), 486-491, 1974.

[6] Redner, A.S., "Photoelastic Measurements by Means of Computer-Assisted Spectral Contents Analysis," Experimental Mechanics, 25 (2), pp 148-153, 1985.

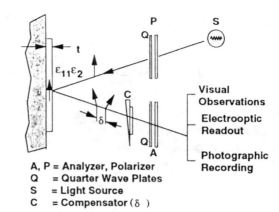

A, P = Analyzer, Polarizer
Q    = Quarter Wave Plates
S    = Light Source
C    = Compensator ($\delta$)

Fig. 1: Measuring Method in Early Devices

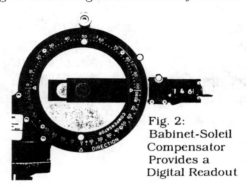

Fig. 2: Babinet-Soleil Compensator Provides a Digital Readout

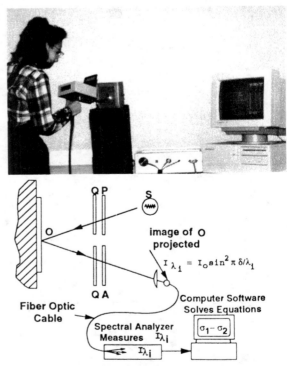

$$I_{\lambda_i} = I_o \sin^2 \pi \delta / \lambda_i$$

Fig. 3: Reflection Polariscope using PC-Based SCA Readout

# CORNEAL BIREFRINGENCE THIRTY YEARS LATER

Joseph D. Hovanesian, Ph.D. and
Professor of Mechanical Engineering
Oakland University

John A. Hovanesian, M.D.
Chief Resident of Ophthalmology
Henry Ford Hospital

In 1996 the first investigations were made of using stress birefringence in human corneal tissue as a means of measuring intraocular pressure. Others have since studied corneal birefringence changes in traumatic and surgical wounds. Recently, with the evolution of corneal refractive surgeries such as radial keratotomy (RK) and photorefractive keratectomy (PRK), a renewed interest has arisen in investigating the biomechanics of cornea through birefringence. We review previous work in this field and the potential for future applications.

# An investigation of yield in normalised mild steel using a photoelastic coating.

Ian M. Allison,
University of Warwick,
Coventry, Warwickshire, CV4, 7AL, UK.

## Introduction

The characteristic profile of the load-displacement curve for stress relieved mild steel loaded in uniaxial tension is well known. Figure 1 shows an idealisation of the observed behaviour which assumes an initial phase of linear-elastic extension, followed by non recoverable deformation at constant stress. This provides the basis for plastic analysis of structures and is almost universally accepted in current design codes. The existence of upper and lower yield points, and the development of slip bands or Luder's lines during post yield deformation is described in many materials science texts. [1][2][3].

The availability of thin photoelastic coatings bonded to mild steel test pieces by adhesives which are capable of sustaining substantial plastic strain provides an ideal opportunity for monitoring the progress of yield in a tension piece as the overall uniaxial displacement is increased. Details of the test apparatus are shown in figure 2. The test piece, in the form of a shouldered strip, is illuminated by monochromatic polarised light in a special reflection polariscope incorporating a half silvered mirror which allows the optical pattern to be observed and photographed at normal incidence. To ensure yield initiates at a known location a slightly smaller fillet radius was machined at one end of the test piece. The coating was extended well past the shoulder fillets at both ends of the testpiece, so that the onset of yield was not influenced by end effects associated with the termination of the coating. The coating sensitivity is chosen so that the yield strength of the steel corresponds to about one fringe. This makes it easy to monitor the onset of yield, and to identify the location of the yield front.

## Experimental studies.

Careful tests show that slip initiates in the fillet radius at the end of the gauge length, at a mean stress well below the yield strength of the material, as indicated by location 1 in figure 3. This is not unexpected since the geometric stress concentration in the fillet radius makes the local fillet stress greater than the mean tension based on the applied load and the area of the cross section. The upper yield stress, $\sigma_u$, is only reached at location 2, when the slip plane progresses completely across the test piece section and the mean tension falls suddenly to a lower value, $\sigma_o$. This whole process is triggered by a very small crosshead movement, and great care was needed to halt the deformation process in sufficient time to photograph the yield front during its initial passage across the testpiece.

The plane on which yield occurs is inclined to the axis of the test piece. If the extension is continued at a sufficiently high strain rate to maintain a load equivalent to the upper yield stress, as indicated by location 4, the advancing yield front is inclined at $45^o$ to the uniaxial load, and it appears that slip is occurring on the plane subjected to the maximum shear stress. However if the cross head movement ceases, the axial tension falls to the lower yield stress $\sigma_o$, indicated

by location 5, and further local yielding rotates the plane of the yield front to an angle of $65^o$ as shown in figure 4(a). During subsequent tests it was found that this result could be repeated at successive sections as the yield front progressed along the gauge length.

Further straining of the test piece at an intermediate rate produces the yield front with two inclined sections which are illustrated in figure 4(b). Continued steady extension causes the yield front to progress along the full gauge length to location 6 whilst the applied load remains constant. It is apparent that this extension at constant load is a function of the test piece geometry rather than a characteristic material property. Once the gauge length is fully yielded, work hardening of the material begins and the applied load increases progressively to the maximum value.

In undertaking these studies some difficulty was encountered in obtaining reproducible results from different batches of nominally identical strip. Residual stresses associated with the rolling process used in the preparation of the as received material prevented formation of a clear shear front. It was necessary to undertake a carefully controlled annealing process in order to bring the stock material to a satisfactory condition. Once the annealing process has been introduced it was possible to manufacture a series of testpieces which exhibited consistent behaviour. Nowadays most structural steel is supplied in the form of rolled sections which incorporate substantial residual stresses. Although material in this condition has the advantage of an enhanced elastic range and increased yield strength, it seems unlikely that such sections will ever exhibit the traditional yield behaviour.

## Conclusions.

1. A photoelastic coating has been used to study details of the yielding process in normalised mild steel.

2. Observations made during these tests provide an explanation of the upper and lower yield points, and shows that the plastic extension which occurs at a constant load is associated with propagation of a yield front along the test piece gauge length.

## References

1. Strength of Materials and Structures (2nd Ed) J Case and A H Chilver. Edward Arnold 1971.

2. Mechanical Metallurgy G E Dieter. McGraw Hill Kogakusha Ltd. 1976.

3. Advanced Mechanics of Materials H Ford and J M Alexander. Longman 1962.

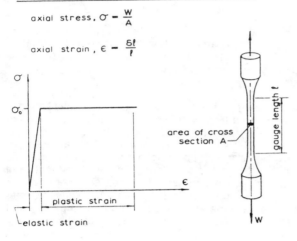

IDEAL STRESS-STRAIN CURVE FOR MILD STEEL

axial stress, $\sigma = \dfrac{W}{A}$

axial strain, $\epsilon = \dfrac{\delta \ell}{\ell}$

**Figure 1.** Idealised stress-strain plot for tensile loading of mild steel.

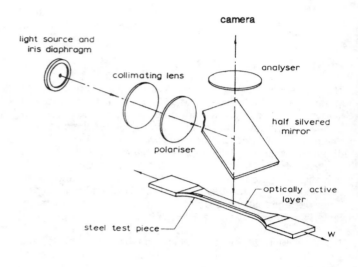

**Figure 2.** Reflection polariscope for observing yield propagation in mild steel strip.

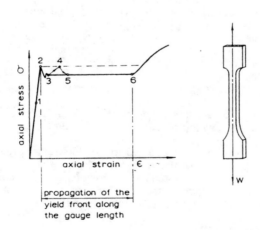

**Figure 3.** Post yield behaviour of stress relieved mild steel.

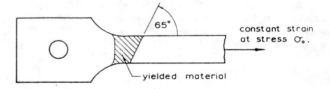

**Figure 4(a)** Stationary yield front at fixed deformation.

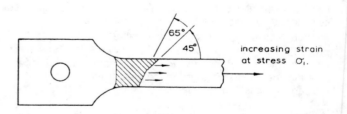

**Figure 4(b)** Propagating yield front under increasing deformation.

196

# Measured Effects of Long-term Exposure to Elevated Temperatures and Loads on Composite Materials

**Kirk R. Lupkes, Research Assistant**
**Mark E. Tuttle, Professor**

**Dept. Mechanical Engineering**
**MS 352600**
**University of Washington**
**Seattle, WA 98195-2600**
**USA**

## ABSTRACT

Advanced fiber-reinforced composites are currently being used in many structural applications in the aerospace, automotive, and other industries. Due to the polymeric matrix the mechanical properties of composites are time dependent and are sensitive to environmental conditions such as temperature or humidity levels. Therefore the long term durability of composite structures is of concern.

In an on-going research project at the University of Washington, the long term mechanical performance of composite material systems of interest to the aerospace industry is being studied. Thus far the behavior of a graphite/ bismaleimide composite system (IM7/5260) has been studied most extensively, including measurement and prediction of the creep response of IM7/5260 laminates exposed to cyclic loading and temperatures [1,2], as well as the measurement of mass loss and residual stiffness and strength following long-term exposure to constant elevated temperatures and loads [3].

The topic of the present paper is the mass loss and residual stiffness and strength exhibited by three different composite systems following long-term exposure to elevated temperatures and tensile loading. Specifically, composite laminates fabricated using the Dupont K3B/IM7, Dupont R1-16/IM7, or NASA PETI-5/IM7 systems are being exposed to a constant temperature of 177°C (350°F) and constant tensile loading sufficient to cause axial strains of either 0.2% or 0.4% for times up to 4000 hrs.

The test procedures and protocols are similar to those described in [3]. Briefly, tensile specimens with nominal in-plane dimensions of 25 x 300 mm (1.0 x 12 in) are mounted in spring-loaded lever-arm test frames. The test frames were designed and built at UW, and were sized such that 48 frames can be placed within a single laboratory test oven. Hence, 48 tensile specimens can be exposed to constant elevated temperatures and loading simultaneously. Specimens with the following layup are tested for each of the three composite material systems under investigation: $[0]_8$, $[90]_{16}$, and $[45/0/-45/90]_{3s}$.

Specimens are removed from the test oven and evaluated every 1000 hrs (roughly 42 days) of exposure. The following properties are measured following each 1000-hr increment:

- specimen weight

- axial tensile stiffness of all specimens

- open-hole compression strength of the $[45/0/-45/90]_{3s}$ specimens, using an "open-hole compression test fixture" developed at Northrop Corp.

- unnotched tensile strength of the $[0]_8$ and $[90]_{16}$ specimens, and

- shear stiffness and strength, using $[90]_{16}$ specimens and an Iosipescu test fixture

The presentation will include a description of the testing fixtures being used, a more detailed discussion of test protocols, and a summary of results obtained to date.

## ACKNOWLEDGMENTS

This work was sponsored by a grant from the Boeing Commercial Airplane Co. This financial support as well as the many helpful discussions with Robert Shaffnit of the Boeing Co. is gratefully acknowledged.

## REFERENCES

1. Tuttle, M.E., Pasricha, A., and Emery, A.F., "The Nonlinear Viscoelastic-Viscoplastic Behavior of IM7/5260 Composites Subjected to Cyclic Loading", JRNL OF COMPOSITE MATERIALS, Vol 29, No. 15 (1995).

2. Tuttle, M.E., Pasricha, A., and Emery, A.F., "Time-Dependent Behavior of IM7/5260 Composites Subjected to Cyclic Loads and Temperatures," PROCEEDINGS, SES/ASME/ASCE Conference on Composite Materials - Nonlinear Effects, Charlottesville, VA, June 6-9, 1993.

3. Tuttle, M., Delaney, A., and Emery, A., "Mass Loss and Residual Stiffness and Strength of IM7/5260 Composites Subjected to Elevated Loads and Temperatures," PROCEEDINGS, 1995 SEM Spring Conference, Grand Rapids, MI, pp 499-506

# Measurement of Residual Stress in Laminated Composites

P. G. Ifju, B. C. Kilday, S. Liu, and X. Niu
Department of Aerospace Engineering, Mechanics & Engineering Science
University of Florida
Gainesville, FL 32611-6250

A novel method of measuring residual stress in laminated composite materials is being developed at the University of Florida. This method involves the use of moiré interferometry [1] and the replication of moiré gratings onto composite laminates during the curing process. The deformation of the grating due to residual stresses can then be referenced to the original unstressed state. As a result, the absolute value for the thermal induced residual strain can be determined. Additionally, the strains induced by mechanical and hygrothermal stress, as well as machining processes can be reference back to the unstressed state of the laminate.

With the ever increasing use of composite materials in the aerospace industry, comes the need to accurately predict mechanical properties, including the tensile, compressive and shearing strengths. Residual stresses induced during cure can severely degrade these properties. This residual stress is evidenced on two levels of the laminate: the fiber level, and ply level. On both scales, residual stresses develop due to the relative mismatch in the Coefficient of Thermal Expansion (CTE) of the fiber and the matrix, as well as the shrinkage of the matrix during cure. This paper will address the residual stresses at the ply level due to both CTE mismatch and shrinkage effects.

In order to measure residual stresses in composites, one must be able to refer back to the stress-free state of the material, that is, the state just before the onset of matrix cure. At the stress free state, the matrix material is fluid and thus can not transmit stress. When the matrix material solidifies, a bond between the fiber and matrix is formed, initiating the potential for stresses to arise. Initially, matrix shrinkage due to polymer cross-linking contributes to the residual stress. After full cure, further residual stress develops as a result of the CTE mismatch between the fiber and matrix, as the panel is brought to room temperature.

There has been a great deal of experimental work conducted to determine the residual stress in laminated composite materials. This work can be grouped into three categories: cutting and drilling methods, imbedded sensor methods, and deformation measurements on nonsymmetric lay-ups. Cutting and hole drilling techniques [2-5] have been used to create a free edge in composite laminates relieving residual stress. In these methods, the relieved stresses near the free edge cause deformation, which when recorded by strain gages or full-field optical methods, can be used to determine the residual stress. These methods can give accurate data; however the specimen is destroyed by the procedure, and time dependent information cannot be extracted from the same sample. By imbedding a sensor in a laminate, destruction of the specimen is not required, but these methods require cumbersome temperature compensation. Additionally, when the sensor is disconnected, the reference is lost; therefore, testing over a long period of time is not practical. The use of nonsymmetric lay-ups to produce warped panels has been implemented to measure residual stress [6]. Cross-ply panels of $[0_n/90_n]_T$, when cured, warp during the cooling process. The warpage can be related to the residual stress. This method is simple to implement but is specifically tailored to cross-ply type configurations.

In this study, strains due to residual thermal stress were determined using moiré interferometry. A method of replicating a diffraction grating on the surface of composite panels during the curing process was developed. A reference grating mold of 1200 lines/mm was replicated on a special tool made of Astrositall, which is an ultra low expansion material (Fig. 1). Over the curing temperature range the deformation of the tool was shown to be negligible. The grating layer was thin (typically about 25 micrometers); therefore, thermal expansion of the grating itself is negligible. This grating acts as a permanent reference to the point at which residual stresses were first induced. AS4/3501-6 prepreg material was placed on the grating mold with subsequent layers of bleeder and breather plies. The assembly was then placed into a sealed vacuum bag and was put into an autoclave where the prepreg manufacturer's suggested temperature, pressure and vacuum profiles were applied. The temperature was ramped from ambient, to 107°C, where it was held for one hour at 10 psi. following the first cure cycle, a second ramp to 177°C and 100 psi was applied, then held for four hours. During the first autoclave cycle, a constant vacuum was maintained inside the vacuum bag. After cure was complete, the consolidated panels were quickly separated from the tool. Once the tool and the panels were cooled, moiré interferometry was performed at room temperature. The deformation of the panel was measured using a moiré interferometer that was tuned with the grating mold on the tool [7]. Since the tool experienced no significant deformation due to the temperature change and pressure, the strain due to residual stress was recorded on the composite panel. The reference grating on the tool acts as a datum to which the deformation of the panel can be compared. This

198

method relies on the assumption that the stresses are "locked" into the composite at the time the grating is formed.

The procedure described above was used to measure the thermal strains on unidirectional panels and multi-directional panels. The unidirectional information was used to determine the free thermal expansion of an unconstrained layer. This information was then used along with the strains measured on the multi-directional panels to determine the residual stresses. As a first step in the analysis of the residual stresses, laminate theory was incorporated.

References

1. D. Post, B. Han and P. G. Ifju, "High Sensitivity Moiré: Experimental Analysis for Mechanics and Materials," Mechanical Engineering Series, Springer-Verlag, New York, NY, 1994.

2. H. E. Gascoigne, "Residual Surface Stresses in Laminated Cross-Ply Fiber-Epoxy Composite Materials," *Proceedings of the VII International Congress on Experimental Mechanics*, Las Vegas, NV, pp. 1077-1084, June 1992.

3. D. Joh, K. Y. Byun, J. Ha, "Thermal Residual Stresses in Thick Graphite/Epoxy Composite Laminates-Uniaxial Approach," *Experimental Mechanics*, Volume 33, No. 1, pp. 70-76, March 1993.

4. J. Lee and R. Czarnek, "Measuring Residual Strains in Composite Panels Using Moiré Interferometry," *Proceedings of 1991 SEM Spring Conference on Experimental Mechanics*, Milwaukee, WI, 405-415 (1991)

5. Residual-Stress Measurement in Orthotropic Materials Using the Hole-Drilling Method," Experimental Mechanics, Vol. 34, No. 4, Dec 1994, pp. 324-333.

6. M.S. Wilenski, E. Shin, R. J. Morgan and L. T. Drzal, "Cure Effects on Microcracking in IM7 Fiber/Matrimid 5292 BMI Composites" Proceedings of the American Society for Composites, Santa Monica, CA, October 18-20, 1995, pp. 271-280.

7. D. Post and J. D. Wood, "Determination of thermal strains by Moiré Interferometry," *Experimental mechanics*, Vol. 29, No. 3, pp. 318-322, (1989).

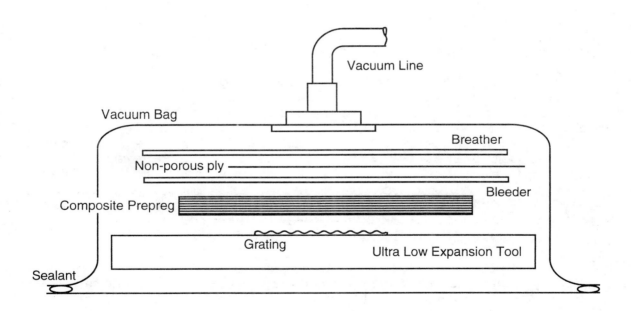

Fig.1 Moire grating replication during laminate fabrication.

# APPLICATION OF CARBON FIBER COMPOSITE FOR BRIDGE COLUMNS

M.G. Abdallah[1] and R.J. Nusimer[2] F. Seible[3], and R. Burgueno[3]

## ABSTRACT

The outstanding mechanical and chemical characteristics of carbon fiber composites contribute to their wide use in the aerospace industry. The success of using advanced composites in the aerospace and defense industries has been of great interest to civil engineering applications. The high costs of these materials and their manufacturing processes have kept these materials in the aerospace and defense industries. The applications of advanced composite materials for civil engineering structural components and complete systems have been demonstrated in several applications around the world.

The "tailoring" characteristics of advanced composite materials in comparison with conventional steel and concrete structural materials proposes their suitability for civil engineering applications. Carbon fiber composites satisfy the need for new and more durable materials for new civil engineering structures, the rehabilitation and renewal of existing structures (buildings and bridges). Carbon fiber composites in combination with their high strength, chemical and fatigue resistance, and vibration damping characteristics can be cost-affectively employed, particularly in the seismic retrofitting of building and bridge structures.

The aging and deterioration of the US bridge infrastructure systems and their affects on the nation's economical growth have been discussed and reported in trade journals, magazines, and in the media. The ARPA (Advanced Research Projects Agency) TRP (Technology Reinvestment Project) funded a research program; "Advanced Composites for Bridge Infrastructure Renewal." Program objectives are to investigate and to assess technical and economical feasibility of using advanced composite materials for rehabilitation and for new bridge systems. As part of this ARPA-BIR Program, carbon composite shell systems for concrete columns subject to seismic loads are being developed.

As a result of this research program, concepts were developed to combine conventional civil structure materials (concrete) and a carbon fiber composite shell in concrete filled shell systems. The concrete takes the compression load. The carbon fiber shell system functions are: (1). Formwork for the concrete, (2). Confinement of the concrete, and (3). Tension force transfer in both longitudinal bending and shear. The advantage of this system compared to concrete filled steel tube systems are: (1). Light weight, (2). Tailorable fiber orientation for load directions, and

(3). Durability for fatigue, seismic loads, and chemical resistance. This development include large scale fabrication and testing of pilot columns, and the assessment of both conventional and composite materials used in the design of bridge columns.

Two design concepts are being developed. The first design concept uses a carbon fiber composite shell lapped with steel anchorage bars. The steel reinforcement is confined to the plastic hinge region only and the carbon shell is terminated above the foundation. The second design concept uses a carbon shell jacketed into the foundation. In the second design concept, there is no steel reinforcement in the columns.

The carbon/epoxy shells were fabricated by a wet filament winding process. The carbon fiber shell manufacturing techniques, column concrete casting, and instrumentation are reviewed. The two column design concepts testing equipment and test results are presented.

The conclusion of this development research proves the feasibility of using carbon fiber composite materials for bridge columns. Based on performance and service life assessment, advanced composite materials can be competitive to conventional materials in the infrastructure for bridge rehabilitation and renewal.

------------------------------------------------------------------

1.  Senior Research Scientist, Hercules Inc. CPD, SLC, UT 84118-0748
2.  Program Manager, Alliant Techsystems, Magna, UT 84044-0098
3.  Division of Structural Engineering, University of California, San Diego, La Jolla, California 92093-0085

# LOAD TRANSFER ACROSS SEAMS
# IN A FLEXIBLE COMPOSITE

C. H. Jenkins, R. Skalleberg, and S. Wen
Mechanical Engineering Department
South Dakota School of Mines and Technology
Rapid City, SD 57701

Considerable effort has gone into understanding the behavior of bonded joints in classical composites. In such composites, the adherends are orders of magnitude stiffer and thicker than the adhesives. New applications of flexible composites are emerging, for example in pneumatic structures such as high-altitude scientific balloons. In these flexible composites, the differences in stiffness and thickness between adherend and adhesive are much reduced.

These materials can be classified as highly-flexible polymer fiber/polymer matrix composites. Two types of fiber reinforcements are under consideration: continuous or scrim-type, and non-woven or random. Since these materials are substantially different from classical composites, their response under service conditions is unknown, especially with regards to the inevitable seams which must occur to construct large structures such as balloons from numerous smaller panels or gores. For example, questions arise about load transfer from gore to gore across the seam, and what role the seam parameters, such as fiber spacing and orientation, will play.

The research described here used a large and detailed three-dimensional finite element model to analyze the load transfer in a bonded seam within a unidirectional scrim-type composite material (see Figure 1). In particular, the effects of changes in fiber spacing and the relative stiffness between fiber and matrix, were investigated. Over the range of values examined, it was found that the load transfer is highly sensitive to modulus differences between fiber and matrix, but relative unaffected by changes in fiber spacing. Figures 2 and 3 show the effects of modulus ratio on load transfer. We compare various values of $E_{fiber}$ to $E_{matrix}$ ($E_f/E_m$). The upper curves correspond to the lower adherend fiber, while the lower curves correspond to the upper adherend fiber. Note that for the homogeneous case ($E_f/E_m = 1$), stresses between the fibers match rapidly just after the joint discontinuity, while for $E_f/E_m = 100$, and the same overlap length, the stresses just match at the model boundary. Other important aspects such as fiber orientation and realistic material behavior are discussed [1].

Experimental verification of analytical predictions provides additional challenges. Because of the extreme flexibility of the material, classical methods such as strain gages, cannot be used. A discussion is presented on a seam test options, including novel methods for experimental strain analysis.

Acknowledgement:
The authors wish to thank the NASA for their support of this research.

References:
[1]     Jenkins, C.H., Skalleberg, R., and Wen, S. (1996). "Load Transfer in Scrim-Type Composite Adhesive Joints," *Composites Part B Engineering* (to be submitted).

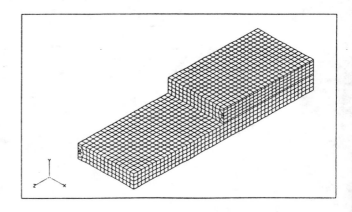

Figure 1. FEM joint model.

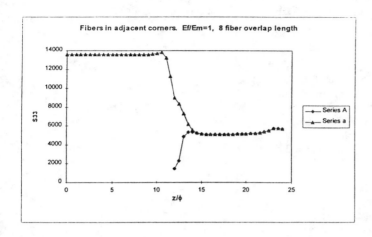

**Figure 2. Axial stress along "fibers" for the homogenous case.**

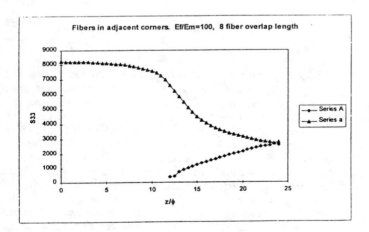

**Figure 3. Axial stress along fibers, fibers 100 times as stiff as matrix.**

203

# Automatic Whole–Field Measurement of Photoelastic Fringe Orders Using Generalized Phase–Shift Method

Eisaku Umezaki and Hiroshi Watanabe
Nippon Institute of Technology
4–1 Gakuendai, Miyashiro, Saitama 345, Japan
and
Akira Shimamoto
Saitama Institute of Technology
1690 Fusaiji, Okabe, Saitama 369–02, Japan

The phase–shift method, which can be used to obtain the relative fringe orders from a combination of several images taken by the rotation of optical components, is promising for the determination of fringe orders in the whole field. This method assumes that the time–series light intensity at any point obtained by the rotation of optical components lies exactly on a sinusoidal curve. Actually the light intensity does not lie exactly on such a curve because of noise caused by the variation in the intensity of a light source and by dust on optical components. Such noise has an adverse effect on the results obtained by the phase–shift method.

In this study, a generalized phase–shift method is developed for suppressing such adverse effects and for automatically measuring photoelastic fringe orders in the whole field as follows. When the polarizer and analyzer in the dark– and light–field plane polariscopes with the monochromatic light source are simultaneously rotated by $\theta$ from a selected reference, $R$, the light intensities, $I_d$, $I_l$, at any point emerging from the dark– and light–field are

$$I_d = I_0 \sin^2 2(\phi - \theta) + B \tag{1}$$

$$I_l = -I_0 \sin^2 2(\phi - \theta) + a^2 + B \tag{2}$$

where $I_0 = a^2 \sin^2 \pi N$, $a$ is the amplitude of polarized light transmitted through the polarizer, $N$ is the fringe order, $\phi$ is the direction of principal stress, $\sigma_1$, to $R$ and $B$ is the background light intensity.

$I_0$ and $B$ in eqs(1) and (2) can be calculated by applying the Fourier–series expansion to the time–series intensity data, $I_{dk}$ $(k=0,1,2,...,n)$, obtained according to the rotation of the polaroids at every angle, $\Delta\theta(=\theta/n)$, from $\theta=0$ to $\theta=\pi/2$ in a dark–field plane polariscope at each point as

$$I_0 = 2\sqrt{a_1^2 + b_1^2} \tag{3}$$

$$B = -\frac{I_0}{2} + a_0 \tag{4}$$

where

$$a_0 = \frac{1}{n} \sum_{m=0}^{n-1} I_{dm} \tag{5}$$

$$a_1 = \frac{2}{n} \sum_{m=0}^{n-1} I_{dm} \cos\left(m\frac{2\pi}{n}\right) \tag{6}$$

$$b_1 = \frac{2}{n} \sum_{m=0}^{n-1} I_{dm} \sin\left(m\frac{2\pi}{n}\right) \tag{7}$$

$a^2$ can be separated from $I_0$ by applying the Fourier–series expansion to the time–series intensity data, $I_{lk}$ $(k=0,1,2,...,n)$, obtained according to the rotation of polaroids at every angle, $\Delta\theta(=\theta/n)$, from $\theta=0$ to $\theta=\pi/2$ in a light–field plane polariscope at each point as

$$a^2 = a_0' + \frac{I_0}{2} - B \tag{8}$$

where

$$a_0' = \frac{1}{n} \sum_{m=0}^{n-1} I_{lm} \tag{9}$$

Hence the relative fringe orders, $N$ is obtained as

$$N = \frac{1}{2\pi} \cos^{-1}\left(1 - \frac{2I_0}{a^2}\right) \tag{10}$$

The accuracy of the method depends on the amount of noise and the noise distribution in the data, the number of points constituting the data, and the fringe order and direction of principal stress at a measure point. In order to investigate the effects of these factors on the accuracy, a computer simulation is used for the time–series intensity data with noise. The amount of noise, $\Delta I$, is determined by random numbers in the range of $\pm1\%$, $\pm3\%$, $\pm5\%$, $\pm10\%$, $\pm15\%$ and $\pm20\%$ of the light intensity at each point on the time–series intensity data with reference to an actual intensity data in a circular disk subjected to a diametrically compressive load. An amplitude, $a^2$, of 160 and background intensity, $B$, of 40 are used, which are commonly encountered. Numbers of points constituting the data, $n$, of 3,10,50,100 and 120 are used.

Figure 1 is the effects of the number of points constituting the data, $n$, and the fringe order at a measured point, $N$, on the error of the fringe orders, $|\Delta N|$, obtained for $\Delta I=\pm15\%$ and $\phi=0$deg. The errors increase near $N=0$ and 0.5 except those for $n=3$, and decrease with increase of $n$. $n$ above 100 gives almost constant error for the fringe order at each measured point. The average of the error for $n=100$ shown in Fig.1 is $\pm0.004$ fringe.

Furthermore, the proposed method is applied to experimental

images obtained from a circular disk subjected to a diametrically compressive load. This model is made of an epoxy resin plate. The time–series intensity data at each pixel are obtained from 129 images, which are taken between $\theta=0$ to 90deg using an automatic polariscope system as shown in Fig.2.

Figures 3 and 4 show the relative fringe orders, $N$, obtained by the proposed method and theory, respectively. In these figures, the black regions are assigned the value of $N=0$, and the white ones $N=0.5$. The regions change from black to white as the value of $N$ increases from 0 to 0.5. Figure 5 shows the fringe orders obtained along horizontal lines of $y/a=0$ with $a$ radius. The proposed method gives a large fringe order at the left edge, at which the theoretical value is zero. This results from initial stress called edge stress, which is due to causes, for example, oxidation, and moisture absorption of epoxy, other than the load given to the disk. The results obtained by the proposed method are in good agreement with those obtained by the theory except for the above–mentioned region.

Consequently, a computer simulation shows that the proposed method accurately measure the fringe orders for the time–series intensity data which are composed of almost 100 light intensity values, and is almost independent of the amount of noise. The error of the measurement of the photoelastic fringe orders is ±0.004 fringe. Furthermore, an application of the method to the experimental images obtained from a circular disk subjected to a diametrically compressive load shows that the result is in good agreement with the theory.

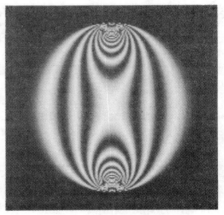

Fig.3 Fringe orders measured by proposed method

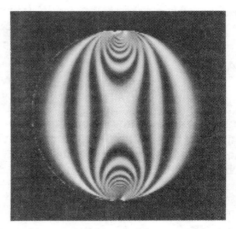

Fig.4 Theoretical fringe orders

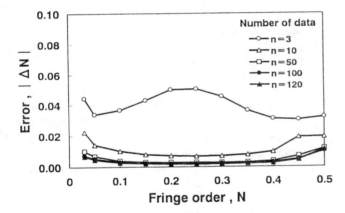

Fig.1 Effects of fringe order at measured points, $N$, and number of points constituting time–series intensity data, $n$, on error of fringe orders, $|\Delta N|$, for $\Delta I=\pm15\%$ and $\phi=0$deg

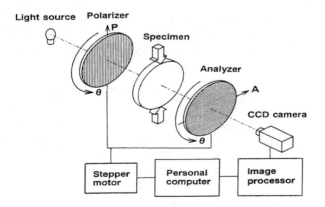

Fig.2 Experiemntal setup for automatically measuring fringe orders in the whole field

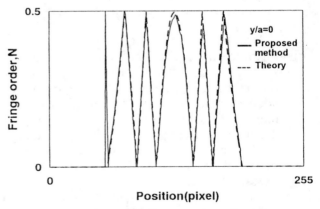

Fig.5 Distributions of fringe orders along horizontal line through the center of circular disk

# High Speed Shearography
## for Measuring Transient Deformation and Vibration

Y.Y. Hung, C.T. Griffen and F. Chen
Department of Mechanical Engineering
Oakland University
Rochester Hills, Michigan 48309
Tel: (810) 370-2238

This paper presents a high speed recording technique which adds a time the conventional shearography. With a large shear, it allows time-dependent displacement of an object to be studied using a high speed image acquisition system. This new technique is particularly useful for measuring transient deformation and complex vibrational modes.

Three techniques of shearography have been used for vibration measurement. These are: the time-averaged technique, the stroboscopic technique and the double-pulsed technique. The first two techniques are only applicable to measurement of the mode shapes of steady state vibrating structures. In the case of double-pulsed shearography, the surface displacement gradient of a transiently vibrating structure at only two discrete times can be compared. Therefore the traditional shearography recording techniques generally do not have the time dimension. In this paper, shearography is extended to allow time-dependent displacement in an object to be studied by continuously digitizing the speckle images of a deforming object using a high speed digital image acquisition system.

A schematic diagram of the set-up is illustrated in Fig. 1. The object to be studied is illuminated with a point source of coherent light and it is imaged by an image-shearing video camera. The camera allow brings the images of the test object and the reference object to overlap and interfere, producing a speckle pattern. The key to the video recording in this scheme is the shearing crystal which has a large shear. The shearing crystal brings two nonparallel beams scattered from test object surface and from the reference object to become collinear or nearly collinear. As a result, the spatial frequency of the speckle pattern is very low, and thus it is resolvable by video image sensors such as a CCD sensor. In the study of time-dependent deformation of a test object, the speckle patterns received by the image-shearing video camera are continuously digitized at a predetermined rate using a high speed image acquisition system and stored in the memory of the system. The image acquisition system used in the experiment is a Kodah EktaPro Model 4540 High Speed Motion Analyzer, which has a maximum frame rate of 40,500 frames/sec. After recording, the images are downloaded to a video tape and can be played back at the normal video rate of 30 frames per second. A fringe pattern can be produced by computing the difference of any two speckle images. These images are then digitized by a microcomputer such as a 486-computer through a frame grabber. The displacement versus time for any point of interest can be extracted by plotting the phase change of the speckle pattern at the point versus time from the computer memory. The total phase change can be obtained by integrating the phase curve. Fig. 2 shows the phase variation versus time of a point on an object vibrating at 600 Hz acquired at a speed of 4,500 frames per second.

In essence, the technique is equivalent to many massless and noncontact displacement sensors for measuring dynamic displacement. For example, a typical image digitization of 256x256 is equivalent to 65,536 sensors. Moreover, the technique does not influence the real behavior of the structure under study.

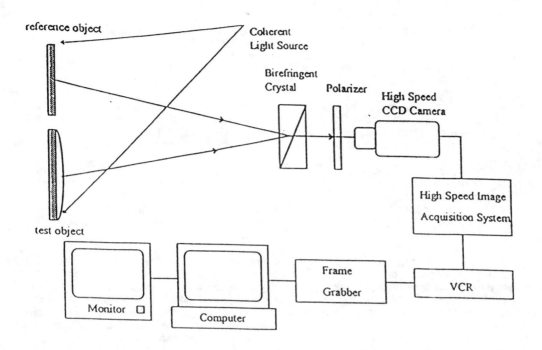

Fig. 1  Schematic Diagram of the High-Speed Shearographic System

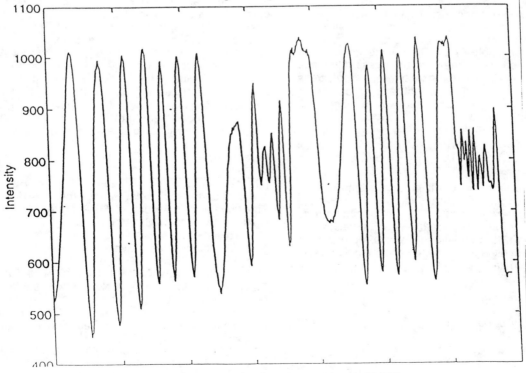

Fig. 2  Fringe Phase Versus Time of an Object Vibrating at 600 Hz.

# Photoelastic Analysis Using a Linearly Polarized RGB White Light

Jin'ichiro GOTOH, Satoru YONEYAMA, Shizuo MAWATARI, Masahisa TAKASHI
Laboratory of Experimental Solid Mechanics, Aoyama Gakuin University
6-16-1 Chitosedai, Setagaya-ku, Tokyo 157, JAPAN

Phase shifting methods with various types of image processing technique, such as Fourier transform[1] and/or Diagonal Summation Theorem[2], have often been proposed in two dimensional photoelastic analysis particularly for the separation of isochromatics from isoclinics using a set of images through a plane polariscope. In spite of several advantages in these methods, however, difficulties have remained in case of dynamic problems, such as impact, moving crack and photoviscoelastic analysis, because a set of multiple data, at least two, at a single instant is required for complete analysis. Several methods[3] utilizing circular polarized white light suffer from similar problems in the analysis of dynamic phenomena.

In an image data obtained with a multi-wavelength polarized light under a dark field condition, only isoclinics and zero-order isochromatics make the darkest (black) fringes and their location do not vary. On the other hand, the location of isochromatic fringes depend on the wavelength of incident light. Thus, if we can produce a mixed RGB incident light having several wavelengths, principal stress difference and principal stress direction are easily separated from a single plane polarized image data through a plane polariscope.

The authors would like to discuss a new method for RGB white light photoelasticity and to show firstly the effectiveness of the method with an example of computer simulation using a photoelastic RGB white image data constructed theoretically. The principal stress difference (isochromatics) is easily separated from the principal stress direction (isoclinics). The brightness intensity of photoelastic image through analyzed with a white light involving a set of RGB light is,

$$I(x,y,\lambda) = a_\lambda^2 \sin^2\left[2\{\varphi(x,y) - \theta\}\right] \cdot \sin^2\left\{\frac{C_\lambda}{\lambda}\delta(x,y)\right\} + R(x,y) \cdots (1)$$

where, $\lambda$ is wave length of the light, $a_\lambda$ the amplitude of each light, $\varphi(x, y)$ principal stress direction, $\theta$ polarized angle, $\delta(x, y)$ retardation, $C_\lambda$ Brewster's constant, $d$ thickness of the specimen and $R(x, y)$ noise distribution function. Thus we have equation (2) which represent the relationship between the birefringence and the gray level of each RGB image data.

$$\{I(x,y,\lambda_G) - I(x,y,\lambda_B)\}a_{\lambda_R}^2 \sin^2\{C_{\lambda_R}\delta(x,y)/\lambda_R\}$$

$$+ \{I(x,y,\lambda_B) - I(x,y,\lambda_R)\}a_{\lambda_G}^2 \sin^2\{C_{\lambda_G}\delta(x,y)/\lambda_G\} \quad \cdots\cdots (2)$$

$$+ \{I(x,y,\lambda_R) - I(x,y,\lambda_G)\}a_{\lambda_B}^2 \sin^2\{C_{\lambda_B}\delta(x,y)/\lambda_B\} = 0$$

The method proposed in this study is briefly summarized as follows;

1] to obtain a plane polarized image data with a RGB white light using a color CCD camera and to separate each RGB data from only one image data.
2] to determine fringe order at only one point for initial value.
3] to solve a non-linear equation (2) numerically under the condition that gray level of brightness data with one, at least, of wavelengths is not zero.
4] to evaluate the distribution of principal stress difference and principal stress direction over the whole field.

It should be pointed out that the calculation in this method could be highly accurate over the whole field excepting points at which a few exceptional conditions has to be considered, because of the adequacy of the initial value. The values of fringe order and birefringence direction on points affected by the exceptional condition, at which the gray level of images with each wavelength is coincide and zero, could be easily interpolated from those around the point.

Fig. 1 shows an example set of plane polarized RGB image data from contact stress of McEwen's study[4]. The wave length of Fig. 1(a) is 620 nm(Red), (b) is 540 nm(Green) and (c) is 440 nm(Blue). The ratio $a^2$ of these light intensities is R:G:B=2.5:2.0:1.5. The gray levels on the y=300 line of the image data are shown in Fig. 2. The accurate principal stress difference and principal stress direction are successfully calculated from the RGB plane polarized image data previously as shown in the Fig. 3 and Fig. 4. It is confirmed that this method will be applicable not only to dynamic but to time dependent phenomena.

References:

[1] Morimoto, Y., Morimoto, Y. Jr., Hayashi, T., "Separation of Isochromatics and Isoclinics Using Fourier Transform and Its Accuracy," SEM 50th Anniversary Spring Conference, 1149-1158, 1993.
[2] Takashi, M., Mawatari, S., Toyoda, Y., Kunio, T., A New Computer Aided System for Photoelastic Stress Analysis with Structure-Driven Type Image Processing," Applied Stress Analysis, Ed. Hyde, T.H. & Ollerton, E., Elsevier Appl. Sci., London & New York, 516-525, 1994.
[3] Voloshin, A. S., Redner, A. S., "Automated Measurement of Birefringence: Development and Experimental Evaluation of the Techniques," Experimental Mechanics, 29-3, 252-257, 1989.
[4] McEwen, E., "Stresses in Elastic Cylinders in Contact along a Generatrix," Philosophical Magazine, 40, 454, 1949.

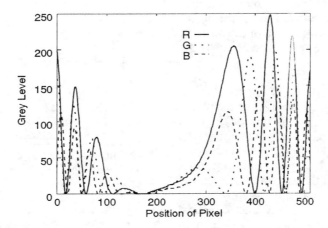

(a)                                (b)                                (c)

Fig. 1    Plane polarized image data - polarized angle $\theta$=15 deg. -

(a) Red: $\lambda_R$=620 nm, (b) Green: $\lambda_G$=540 nm, (c) Blue: $\lambda_B$=440 nm

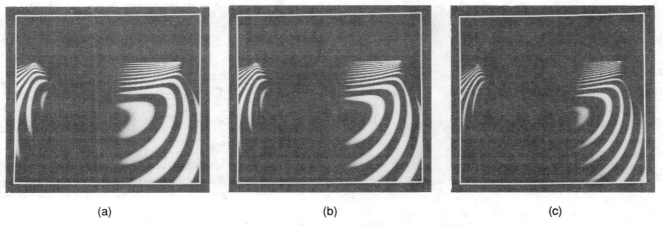

Fig. 2    Gray levels on y=300 line of the plane polarized RGB image data.

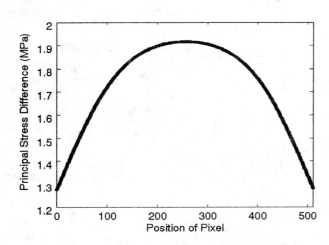

Fig. 3    Principal stress difference calculated

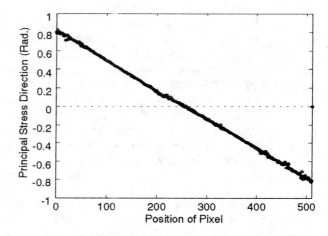

Fig. 4    Principal stress direction calculated

# ELECTRONIC SPECKLE PATTERN SHEARING INTERFEROMETER USING TWO HOLOGRAPHIC GRATING

C. Joenathan and L. Buerkle
Department of Physics and Applied Optics
Rose Hulman Institute of Technology
5500 Wabash Avenue
Terre Haute, IN 47803

Electronic Speckle Pattern Shearing Interferometer (ESPSI) is an alternate method for measuring displacement of objects with variable sensitivity [1-6]. Shearing interferometers provide derivatives of displacements whereas conventional interferometers reveal information about object displacement. A common approach is to illuminate the object that scatters light and a Michelson interferometric arrangement is used to generate two images of the object sheared on the CCD camera by tilting one of the mirrors. Most of the commercial ESPSI systems use the Michelson type arrangement.

The method we are proposing is a new technique of obtaining shear between the two images of the object which provides greater flexibility and simplicity in the experimental arrangement. Two holographic gratings are fabricated and upon proper angle of illumination only two beams are generated. The first holographic grating splits the incident beam equally into the zero order and one of the first orders. The second holographic grating is then used to remove the tilt between the two diffracted beams. The sheared beams are then imaged by a camera lens onto the photosensor placed at the image plane. Phase stepping routines can be easily accomplished with this interferometer by translating one of the grating.

The holographic gratings were fabricated using two collimated beams incident on a photographic plate. These gratings are recorded on Agfa-Gaevert 8E75 plates, which have an emulsion thickness of 7 μm and resolution of 3000 lines/mm. Holographic gratings were made for two different beam angles $\theta_1 = 21.5°$ and $\theta_2 = 50°$, giving fringe spacing of 500 lines/mm and 1340 lines/mm respectively. The plates were processed and bleached in bromine vapor under a fume hood to increase their diffraction efficiency. The measured diffraction efficiencies of the two gratings were 31% (21.5°) and 57% (50°). To determine the range at which the two sheared wavefronts have the same intensity, data points of the intensities of the zero and the two first diffraction orders were taken for angles of incident in the range between 0° and 40°.

In this system as shown in Fig. 1, the laser beam is expanded filtered by a spatial filter assembly. An achromat images the illuminated object onto the

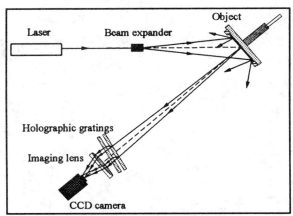

Fig. 1: Experimental arrangement of the ESPSI arrangement using two holographic gratings

photosensor of the CCD camera. Two holographic gratings placed in front of imaging lens splits the incoming beam into two orders of almost equal

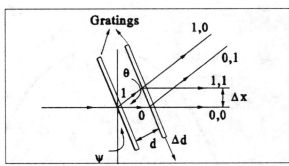

Fig. 2: Schematic of diffraction and generation of the two sheared wavefronts from the two volume holographic grating

magnitude. This results in two sheared images of the object on the photosensor. This method provides a large flexibility in shear and greatly simplifying the experimental arrangement. The two holographic gratings can also be placed in front of the photosensor of the camera. However, care must be taken to avoid the other orders from reaching the photosensor. It should be noted that thin-hologram generates higher diffraction orders that result in multiple beam interference.

A holographic grating is located in front of another identical holographic grating as shown in Fig. 2. The shear $\Delta x$ between the two images is

$$\Delta x = d \left| \frac{\sin(\theta - \psi)}{\cos(\psi)} \right| \qquad (1)$$

where $d$ denotes the distance between the two holographic grating, $\psi$ is the angle the light is incident onto the grating, and $\theta$ gives the direction in which the first order is diffracted. Both angles are measured from the surface normal of the grating. The speckle size to be resolved by the CCC camera can be adjusted by the aperture in the imaging lens. The two holographic gratings are mounted on a rotating stage which is rotated until the two sheared waves are of equal intensities on the CCD camera. An optimum tilt angle can be found by focussing the laser beam to a small spot on the object until the two sheared images of the spot do not overlap.

Various factors cause lower visibility fringes to be obtained with this interferometer. Differences in the intensities of the two sheared bemas can reduce visibility. Speckle decorrelation that occurs due to the finite aperture size of the camera lens can result in low visibility. With thin holograms influence from the higher order causes additional decorrelation. In this ESPSI system a grating with 590 lines/mm with a Q parameter of 6.4 (refractive index is assumed to be approximately 1.5) and the emulsion thickness is 7 µm was used.

In the present method discrete phase steps are introduced between the two sheared images by translating the grating with a piezoelectric transducer. The grating is mounted on a translation stage that can be moved by applying an appropriate voltage. Translation of the grating by a distance $\Delta d$ results in a phase shift between the zero and the first diffraction order. The PZT was calibrated by observing a certain number of fringes move on the TV monitor as the voltage to the PZT was increased. The voltage required to introduce a $\pi/2$ phase step was then calculated. The displacement of the PZT to introduce a $\pi/2$ phase step in the grating method is relatively large compared with the modified Michelson interferometric setup. Therefore this system is less prone to miscalibration error, the major source of error in phase measuring interferometry [7].

A 10-mW He-Ne laser was used in the experiment. Measurements were made on a circular diaphragm clamped along the edges and loaded at the center. A speckle pattern resulting of the object in its initial state is recorded and stored in the frame grabber board. When the object is deformed, the corresponding speckle pattern is subtracted from the image stored in the frame grabber and a fringe pattern depicting the derivative of displacement of the object deformation is displayed on the TV monitor. For phase stepping analysis a sequence of four patterns each of them separated by a phase step of $\pi/2$ is stored. A low pass filter and subsequent averaging with a 9 x 9 window removed the speckle noise in the fringes.

Because of the limited power of the laser, it was not possible to make measurements on the entire object but only on a small portion of the object. The fringes obtained with the system had a visibility of about 60%. The main reason for this low contrast is the amount of decorrelation introduced in the system. Decorrelation is introduced by the defocus of the sheared images and due to the mismatch of the intensities of the two sheared images.

We have demonstrated the concept and working of an electronic speckle shearing pattern shearing interferometer with two holographic gratings which provides great simplicity in the experimental arrangement. We also propped another simple ESPSI system using a holographic grating and a ground glass screen [8]. However, the present interferometer has been found to have greater flexibility and simplicity.

## REFERENCES

1. J. A. Leendertz and J. N. Butters, An image-shearing speckle pattern interferometer for measuring bending moments, J. of Physics E: Scientific Instruments, 6, 1107-1110 (1973)
2. Y. Y. Hung and C. E. Taylor, Measurement of slopes of structural deflections by speckle shearing interferometry, Experimental Mechanics, 14, 281-285 (1974)
3. R. Krishna Murthy and R. S. Sirohi, Speckle shearing interferometry: a new method, Applied Optics, 21, 2865-2867 (1982)
4. Y. Y. Hung and C. Y. Liang, Image shearing camera for direct measurement of surface strains, Applied Optics, 18, 1046-1051 (1979)
5. P. Hariharan, Speckle shearing interferometry: A simple optical system, Applied Optics, 14, 2563-2564 (1975)
6. C. Joenathan and R. Torroba, Simple electronic speckle shearing pattern interferometer, Optics Letters, 15, 1159-1161 (1990)
7. C. Joenathan, Phase measuring interferometry: new methods and error analysis, Applied Optics, 33, 4147 - 4155 (1994)
8. L. Buerkle and C. Joenathan, Electronic speckle pattern shearing interferometer using a holographic grating, Proc. SPIE, 2662, 509-514 (1995)

# Shape Measurement by Grid Projection Method without Influence of Aberration of Lenses

Motoharu FUJIGAKI and Yoshiharu MORIMOTO

Department of Opto-Mechatronics, Faculty of Systems Engineering,
Wakayama University.
Sakaedani, Wakayama 640, Japan.

Grid projection methods have been often used for non-contacting shape measurement. Conventional analysis methods are not accurate because the center positions of the grids are calculated with a pixel unit. Recently phase analysis methods which provides accurate positions of grids are proposed[1]. We have been also proposing some phase analysis methods for grid projection methods, such as the Fourier transform grid method[2], the Gabor transform grid method[3], the wavelet transform grid method[4], the phase shifting method using extraction of characteristics[5], and the phase shifting method using Fourier transform[6].

In usual grid projection methods, lens center positions and directions of a camera and a projector are used as geometric parameters for shape calculation(Fig. 1). The three-dimensional coordinates of a point on the surface of the specimen are calculated as an intersection between two lines, $L_c$ and $L_p$; the line $L_c$ passes through the center of the camera lens from a pixel point on the image plane, the other line $L_p$ passes through the center of the projector lens from a pixel point on the grid slide film.

The accuracy becomes high by analyzing the phases of projected grids on the object. Then the influence of aberrations of lenses becomes conspicuously. Figure 2 shows a scheme of a kind of aberration of lens. Fig. 2(a) is original grids. Figure 2(b) is the image of (b). In practice, the lens center is not a point because of the aberration of the lens. This is the main reason of the error.

In this paper, therefore, we propose a new method to determine the above two lines($L_c$ and $L_p$ in Fig. 1) by not using the positions of the lens centers. We call it the two-reference plane method using Fourier transform (TRPM/FT) with which a shape can be calculated without influence of aberrations of lenses completely. A reference plane drawn a two-dimensional grid is moved along the normal direction of the plane by a known distance to determine three-dimensional coordinates in the space between the reference planes before and after moving.

A scheme of the two-reference plane method is shown in Fig. 3. Both a point $C_\alpha$ on the reference plane $\alpha$ and a point $C_\beta$ on the reference plane $\beta$ are recorded at a point C on the image plane. The three-dimensional coordinates of $C_\alpha$ and $C_\beta$ are obtained accurately by calculating the two-dimensional phases of the grids using the Fourier transform grid method. As a specimen point S recorded at the point C exists on the line $C_\alpha C_\beta$, the three-dimensional coordinates of $C_\alpha$ and $C_\beta$ provide the geometric parameter on the point C. Like this, the three-dimensional coordinates of $C_{i\alpha}$ and $C_{i\beta}$ can be obtained for each pixel point of $C_i$ on the image plane. The set of the three-dimensional coordinates of $C_{i\alpha}$ and $C_{i\beta}$ on every pixel point $C_i$ is recorded as the camera geometric parameter without influence of the aberration of the camera lens. Similarly, about a projector, the phase data of the grids projected onto the two reference planes are recorded as a projector parameter without influence of the aberration of the projector lens. From the projector parameter, the three-dimensional coordinates of points $P_\alpha$ and $P_\beta$ which have the same phase of the projected grid as the phase at the point S of the specimen can be found out. Then, the point S can be calculated as the intersection between the imaging line $C_\alpha C_\beta$ and the projecting line $P_\alpha P_\beta$.

The application of the TRPM/FT combined with the phase shifting method using Fourier transform is shown in Fig. 4. Figure 4(a) is the specimen. Figure 4(b) is the measured shape of the specimen. Figure 4(c) is the cross section of the measured shape of the specimen. This result shows that this method is useful for a shape measurement without influence of aberrations of lenses.

References:
[1] M. Takeda, K. Mutoh, "Fourier transform profilometry for the automatic measurement of 3-D object shapes," Applied Optics, 22-24, 3977-3982, (1983).
[2] Morimoto, Y. Seguchi, Y. and Higashi, T., "Two-dimensional Moire Method and Grid Method Using Fourier Transform," Experimental Mechanics, 29, 4, 399-404, (1989).
[3] Fujigaki, M., Inoue, H., and Morimoto, Y., "Application of Gabor Transform to 3-D Shape Analysis Using Grating Pattern Projection Method," Proceedings of International Symposium on Advanced Technology in Experimental Mechanics at Tokyo, JSME, 67-72 (1995)
[4] Morimoto, Y., and Imamoto, Y., "Application of Wavelet Transform to Displacement and Strain Measurement by Grid Method," Proceedings of the 1995 SEM Spring Conference on Experimental Mechanics at Grand Rapids, 898-903(1995)
[5] Morimoto, Y., and Fujisawa, M., "Fringe Pattern Analysis by Extraction of Characteristics Using Image Processing," Proceedings of the 1993 SEM 50th Aniversary Spring Conference on Experimental Mechanics at Dearborn, 36-44(1993)
[6] Morimoto, Y., and Fujisawa, M., "Fringe Pattern Analysis by a Phase-shifting Method using Fourier Transform, Optical Engineering, 33, 11, 3709-3714(1994)

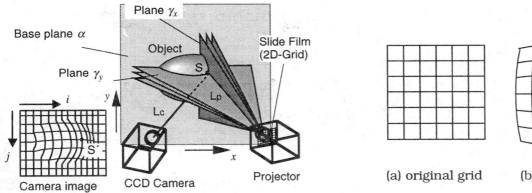

Fig. 1 Shape measurement by grid projection method

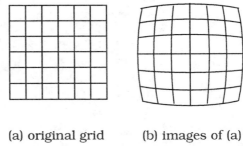

(a) original grid     (b) images of (a)

Fig. 2 Scheme of aberration of lens

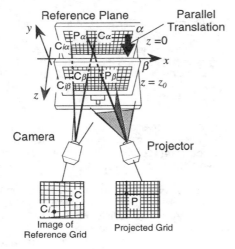

(a) images of reference plane

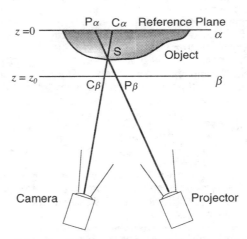

(b) calculating method of 3-dimensional coordination of object

Fig. 3 Principle of Shape measurement without aberration of lenses

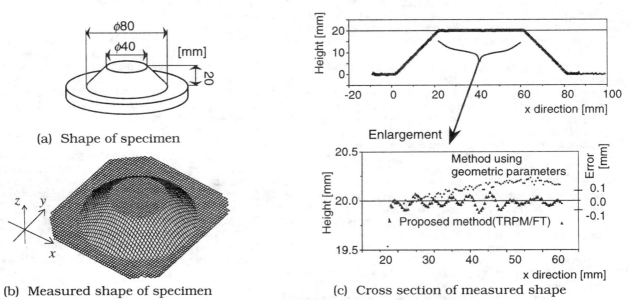

(a) Shape of specimen

(b) Measured shape of specimen

(c) Cross section of measured shape

Fig. 4 Application of TRPM/FT

# Fatigue Evaluation of the Holston River Bridge

J. Harold Deatherage, David W. Goodpasture, Edwin G. Burdette
Department of Civil Engineering
University of Tennessee
Knoxville, Tn. 37996-2010

In January 1992, the Holston River Bridge in East Knox County suffered a full height fatigue failure of the east bound fascia girder. The crack propagated through the bottom flange of the girder and tore through the web to within a few inches of the top flange. The Tennessee Department of Transportation began construction immediately to repair the bridge and retrofit the area where the failure initiated to assure that the problem would not reoccurr. The retrofit repairs were concentrated in the areas of the bridge were the cross frrames, lateral bracing, and the cantilevered outriggers tie into the main girders. Figure 1 is a cross section of the bridge at the failed location. Fugure 2 is an elevation view of the bridge.

In January 1993 the Department of Transportation entered into a contract with the University of Tennessee to evaluate the efffectiveness of the repairs. The objectives of the research were as follows:
   A. To determine the effectiveness of the repairs in reducing the stress ranges in the web gap where the cross frame, lateral bracing, and the cantilevered outrigger frame into the main fascia girder.
   B. To estimate the portion of the fatigue life of critical details on the bridge which had been expended at the time of failure.
   C. To estimate the remaining fatigue life of critical details based on current and estimated future usage.
   D. To evaluate the effects of removing lateral bracing on critical sections in the second span of the bridge.
   E. To evaluate the effects of impact on critical sections in the second span of the bridge.

The bridge was instrumented at approximately 150 locations with strain gages to monitor the response of the bridge to normal traffic, controled loads, and restricted loading conditions that commonly occur during maintaince operations. Early in the study , it was determined that several locations on the bridge were particularly sensitive to fatigue damage. Those locations were as follows:
   A. The web gap in the fascia girder where the cross frame and the lateral bracing frame into the fascia girder.
   B. The area at the end of the stiffener which was part of the retrofit repair to stiffen the web gap area. The retrofit repair had transferred the out-of-plane distortions from the web gap to the area adjacent to the stiffener creating a new fatigue prone area.
   C. The web of the floor beams adjacent to the termination of the flange.
   D. The web gap where the floor beam ties into the main girders.
   E. The main girder web area at the end of the lateral bracing gusset plates tabs.

The strain gage data also provided information which addressed concerns regarding high stresses in the folowing:
   A. The flanges of the main girders.
   B. The cantilevered outriggers.

The Optim MEGADAC 5017A series data acquisition system was used to capture dynamic analog data from the strain gages in real time. The MEGADAC converts the analog data into digital data and sends it to a host computer (PC) for storage. Optim's Test Control Software (TCS) management package was used to interface between the MEGADAC and the PC.

The strain gage data obtained for normal traffic conditions and restricted traffic conditons was analyzed using the rainflow data reduction technique to determine the root mean cube (RMC) stresses for all the instrumented locations.

Controled load tests, using a single vehicle with a known weight, were performed to determine the following:
   A. The ability of the bridge to distribute loads lateraly across the bridge.
   B. Factors that influence impact on fatigue prone details.
   C. Deflection of the main girders of the bridge under known loads. These measured deflections were then compared to calculated deflections using various analysis techniques.

It can be concluded that the repairs made as a result of the 1992 failure indeed reduced the stress ranges in the web gap at the cross frame conection. There is, however, the potential that future cracks may develop at the ends of the added stiffener plate. Additonal repairs are planed for 1996 which will provde enough redundancy so that if a crack does develop, the bridge will maintain integrity and insure the safety of the public.

Additionally, it can be concluded that the presence of lateral bracing does decrease the deflections of the bridge during normal traffic conditions and does enhance the ability of the bridge to distribute loads laterally to adjacent girders.

The work reported here was sponsored by the Tennessee Department of Transportation (TNDOT) and The Federal Highway Administration (FHWA). The conclusions presented here are not necessarily those of TNDOT or FHWA

214

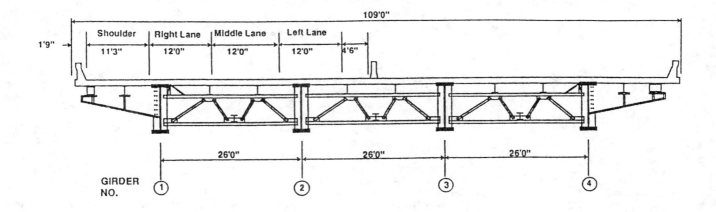

**Figure 1: Cross Section of Bridge at Cross Frame**

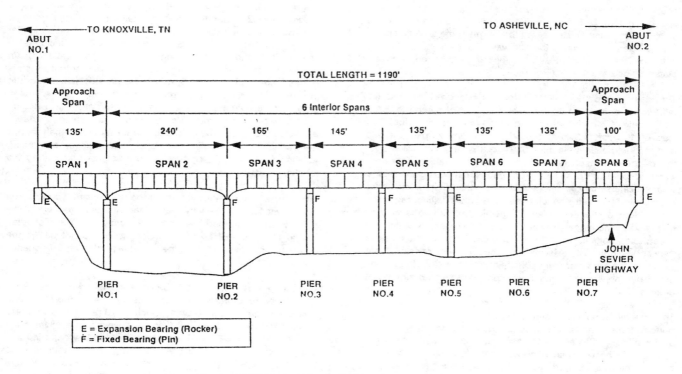

**Figure 2: Elevation View of Bridge**

# Evaluation and Repair of the North Avenue Pedestrian Bridge

Anatol Longinow and Gary J. Klein
Wiss, Janney, Elstner Associates, Inc.
330 Pfingsten Road
Northbrook, Illinois 60062


Kassim Tarhini
Civil Engineering Department
Valparaiso University
Valparaiso, Indiana 46383

The North Avenue pedestrian bridge is a three-hinge, steel arch bridge which supports a reinforced concrete walkway. The bridge span is 189 ft (57.6m) over Lake Shore Drive, on the near north side in Chicago, Illinois. The horizontal center to center distance between the ribs is 12 ft 10 in. (3.9m). The north elevation of the bridge is shown in Figure 1. The vertical distance from the top of steel at the center of the arch to its lowest portion just below the lower hinge is 25 ft 4 inches (7.72m). The cross section of the arch ribs is built up (welded) from plates and structural angles. This cross section tapers up in size from a minimum of 16 in. (40.6cm) at the center of the span to 27.5 in. (70cm) near the lower hinges. The walkway consists of 4 in. (10.2cm) deep, concrete-filled steel grid over a corrugated steel deck. The walkway is supported by inverted T-sections which are welded along its sides. The walkway has three expansion joints and is connected to the arches with T-shaped hangers and double-angle spandrel columns. These vertical support members are bolted to steel gusset plates located along the length of the arch rib and to the T-section beams along the walkway. The arch ribs are braced in the horizontal direction by T-sections and are bolted to gusset plates welded to the ribs (Fig. 1).

The steel arch portion of the bridge is supported on massive reinforced concrete abutments which consist of spread footings and pedestals. The bridge was designed for dead load plus a live load of 100 psf (4.8 kPa) placed on the entire span. It was designed and built in the mid 1940's as a WPA project. Recently, this bridge was inspected and structurally evaluated. This work was prompted by complaints from pedestrians using the bridge who indicated that the bridge vibrated perceptibly, even under normal wind and traffic conditions. There was a distinct sag in the center hinge of the arch. Visual inspection of the bridge showed no cracks in the hinges, minor damage to expansion joints, and few missing bolts in the west lateral bracing member just above the center hinge. The existing local corrosion was not significant to reduce the load-carrying capacity of the structure. In general, the visual inspection of the main span revealed no significant defects.

The general purpose computer program SUPERSAP was used to perform three-dimensional static and dynamic structural analysis of the bridge. The arch was modeled using straightline beam elements. The concrete deck was modeled using rectangular plate elements supported by beam elements along its sides. The deck was supported from the arch by means of truss elements. Figure 2 shows an isometric line drawing of the bridge model generated by the computer program. Various live loading combinations were considered in the static analysis. A split loading distributed over a half-span proved to be the critical loading. Based on this, it was determined that the allowable stresses in the main arch members were exceeded by as much as 70% with respect to current design specifications. The same structural model was used to perform a frequency analysis of the bridge. It was determined that several frequencies were below 1 Hz and many frequencies were below 6 Hz.

An experimental program was undertaken to measure the bridge frequencies. Experimental data were collected using a Sprengnether Type VS-1200 seismograph which was located at the fourth vertical member west of the central hinge of the south rib. This instrument was permanently located at this position during the vibration measuring effort. Data were also acquired using a three-component accelerometer via a Scientific Atlanta Model SD 380Z 4-channel spectrum analyzer. The accelerometer was moved to a number of positions on the deck of the bridge for data acquisition. The Sprengnether system includes a seismometer and a combination signal conditioning-light beam galvanometer recorder. It provides an electrical output which is proportional to the velocity and includes an electrical network to provide a recording output proportional to either displacement, velocity or acceleration. The seismometer has three vibration transducers which measure vibrations in three mutually perpendicular axes. The Scientific Atlanta spectrum analyzer has the capability of sampling the data, automatically computing (displacement, velocity or acceleration) spectra and storing the results.

The people who complained about the bridge were correct. The bridge was found to be very lively. Many frequencies were below 6 Hz which confirmed the computer analysis. The Canadian bridge code as well as other foreign codes do not permit the construction of pedestrian bridges with the fundamental frequency below 6 Hz.

The bridge was determined to be under-designed with respect to current code requirements. Allowable stresses in the main arch members were exceeded by as much as 70 percent. It was also determined that at least the first ten lowest frequencies of the bridge were below 6 Hz. Because of this and low damping, the bridge could be easily excited by joggers and runners who frequently cross the bridge. Economical retrofits were developed and implemented to bring the bridge up to required capacity.

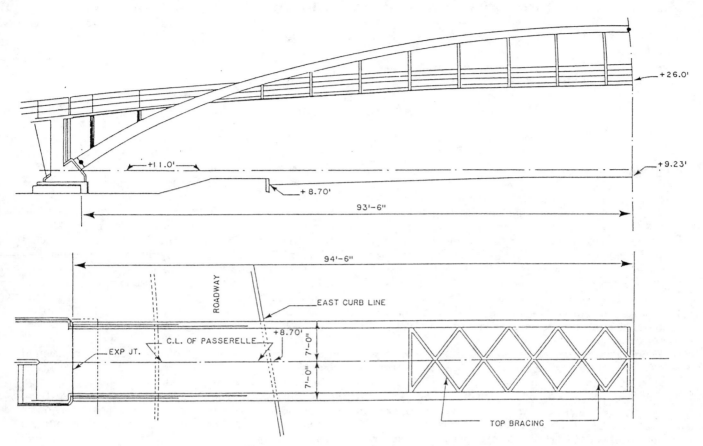

Fig. 1  Half vertical elevation, southwest portion

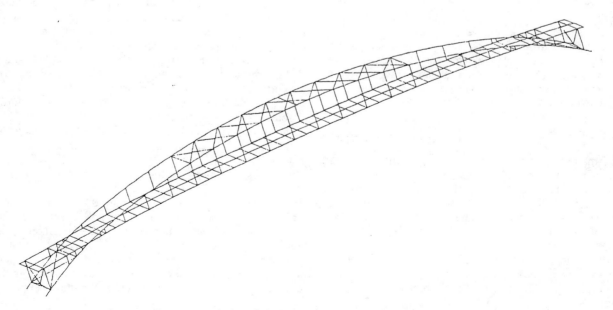

Fig. 2  Analytic model of bridge, isometric view

217

# Experimental Study of a Segmental Bridge Structure

M. Zoghi, Ph.D.
The University of Dayton
T.J. Beach, P.E.
CON/SPAN Bridge Systems
Dayton, Ohio

## Introduction

As part of bridge replacement program, a deteriorated 10 m (33 ft) long existing steel bridge with timber deck structure on concrete abutments was replaced recently with a 11 m (36 ft) span precast concrete modular buried bridge structure. The new 12.8 m (42 ft) long bridge, designed for an AASHTO HS-25 Truck Loading, consisted of seven arch box modular units. Each segment was backfilled with granular material according to ODOT's 304 Grading requirements and was compacted at relative compaction rate of 95% per Standard Proctor Test.

Following the bridge installation, a full-scale load test was conducted on the middle unit. Vertical and horizontal deflections and crack widths were continuously monitored while 44.5 kN (10-kip) load increments were applied on the segment by means of a hydraulic jack. Maximum measured deflection was less than 38 mm (one and one-half inches) at 900 kN (200 kips) applied load which was the hydraulic jack capacity. This final load was equivalent to seven and one-half times the design load [1].

In addition to the field data from measured live-load deflections, coupons of reinforcing bars and core samples of concrete were tested in the laboratory to obtain the tensile strength of reinforcing steel and compressive strength of concrete at the time of load-test. The experimental data and load-deformation characteristics of the reference precast concrete arch segment will be presented herein.

## Experimental Program

A schematic diagram of the test unit along with the instrumentation is exhibited in Figure 1. It should be noted that the test plan drawing shown herein, is different than the actual test set-up for clarity. The Dywidag® bars and jacking beam were installed 90 degrees from the plan view of the reference drawing.

Following the backfilling process, two high strength Dywidag® rods were embedded and grouted into rock below the bridge. The proximity of bedrock at the bridge site enabled the installation and anchoring of these rods possible. The rods pierced through the arch top of the center unit of the bridge and protruded above the soil cover. They were then coupled to a jacking system that was comprised of a yoke, jacking beam and a 900 kN (100-ton) hydraulic jack. The hydraulic jack reacted between a beam tied to the rods and a beam centered on the structure that distributed the load to two 1.22 m (4 ft) long steel tubes. The tubes were supported at each end on top of the precast unit. This resulted in a loading pattern of approximately 1.22 m by 1.22 m (4 ft by 4 ft).

A deflection test frame was affixed to the under side of structure prior to load application. Locations of seven of the sixteen dial indicators, used for deflection measurement, are exhibited in the accompanying figure. The remainder of dial gauges (not shown) were installed to the adjacent bridge segments to furnish independent measurement of deflection for the test unit relative to the adjacent ones.

After the dial indicators were zeroed, the first load was applied up to 44.5 kN (10 kips). Enough time elapsed for the load to stabilize. The dial indicators were recorded at this time. In time periods of approximately 3 to 4 minutes, the load was increased to the next increment (i.e., 89 kN, 133.5 kN, ...) and deflections were recorded accordingly. Cracking was monitored throughout the test program. Following the final loading of 900 kN (200 kips), the jacking system and deflection frame were dismantled and the test unit was replaced by a newly manufactured precast segment. When unloaded, the test unit exhibited no visual signs of distress and could have remained in place.

## Observations Following the Field Experiment

The structure rebounded to 6.35 mm (0.25 in.) permanent deflection when the load was removed. Crack widths at center closed to widths prior to test. Examination of the test unit, after the fill soil was uncovered, indicated that no cracking had occurred on the outside surface in neither the legs nor the top. Also, inside cracks had closed to the degree that they could not be seen on the edge of unit.

After the experiment was complete, actual material properties of the test unit were determined. Accordingly, coupons of the welded wire fabric representative of the steel used in the reference bridge structure as well as core samples of concrete were submitted to the Ohio Department of Transportation (ODOT) Bureau of Testing for laboratory testing. A tensile strength of $f_y$ = 577 MPa (83,700 psi) for steel and a compressive strength of $f_c$ = 49.5 Mpa (7,175 psi) for concrete were reported.

## Test Results

The center line displacement recorded during the load test and the corresponding load increments were compared with the results of Finite Element Analysis (FEA). The results revealed that both FEA and field data followed essentially the same trend up to 266 kN (60 kips) load, beyond which there appeared to be a minor deviation between them [2].

The deflection at AASHTO's full service load for both FEA and field measurement was 1.5 mm (one-sixteenth inch). This was only 12% of the L/800 per allowed AASHTO Specifications. The deflection corresponding to the minimum required ultimate strength was about 4.5 mm (0.18 inch) based on FEA during the field load test. The maximum deflection at center line of the structure was less than 38 mm (one and one-half inches) at 900 kN (200 kips) applied load as measured. This compared with 44.5 mm (one and three-quarter inches) calculated by FEA.

## Conclusions

Data from measured live-load deflections were compared with finite element computer analysis. The results of the load test revealed a good correlation between the computer model and the bridge structure's field performance.

The center unit of the installed bridge performed satisfactorily under extreme loading conditions. It carried a load greater than seven and one-half times AASHTO's heaviest design service load (HS-25) which was the maximum hydraulic jack capacity of 900 kN (200 kips), and the unit did not fail. The experimental data from this comprehensive full-scale test validates the structural integrity of the reference bridge structure.

## References

[1]    Zoghi, M., "Predicting Performance of A Long-Span Precast Concrete Arch Culvert," Final Report Submitted to the Ohio Department of Transportation, January 1994, 23p.

[2]    Katona, M.J., Smith, J.M., Odello, R.S., and Allgood, J.R., "CANDE - A Modern Approach for the Structural Design and Analysis of Buried Culverts," FHWA Report RD 77-5, October 1976.

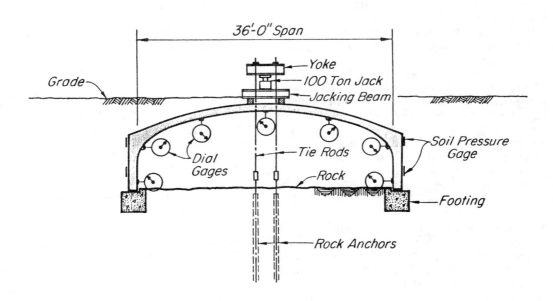

Figure 1

219

# X-Ray Stress Measurements on Large Structures

Beth Pardue
TEC
10737 Lexington Drive
Knoxville, TN 37932

Tremendous technology advances have been made in recent years in x-ray stress analysis. Now measurements can be made quickly and precisely on a variety of materials ranging in size from electronic components to multi-ton size structures. Whereas the smaller components can be measured conveniently in a laboratory environment, large structures often require field measurements.

Stress measurements have been made on large steel and aluminum aerospace structures and nickel-based corrosion resistant structures with portable x-ray equipment. These measurements were made in situ to check the integrity of the component or validate correct processing. Thus the portable x-ray stress technique can be applied successfully to large structures to monitor their current condition, monitor changes with time, or evaluate repairs. Residual stresses, which are the stresses that remain in a part after all loading stresses are removed, affect the expected lifetime of a structure. Failures due to increased loading, fatigue, or stress corrosion cracking are often related to unfavorable (usually tensile) residual stresses.[1] Monitoring of the residual stress state allows timely repair or replacement of a component.

The portable x-ray technique can be used on a wide variety of materials and material conditions. The material must exhibit long-range crystallinity and should be fine-grained with random grain orientation. Weldments, heat-affected zones, base materials, castings, extrusions, and wrought materials are all potential candidates for the x-ray stress technique. Keep in mind, however, this technique is not a flaw detection method.

The following examples illustrate the versatility of the x-ray stress technique on large structures. The first case involved a high-strength steel. Measurements were made at the edge of a fastener hole that connected the structure to a mating structure. Measurements were made at 0°, 45°, 90°, and 135° directions at each location. Measurement validity was checked using the identity

$$\sigma_0 + \sigma_{90} = \sigma_{45} + \sigma_{135}.$$

Subsurface measurements were also made after electrochemically removing small layers of material. These measurements were made to monitor the stresses in a structure that had been in service and determine if the structure could continue in service.

The second example was stress measurements made on an aluminum structure to validate a proprietary forming process. This structure required low (<35 MPa) stresses on the outer surfaces for optimum service life. The proprietary process combined thermal treatment with forming to produce the final structure, thus eliminating several processing steps. The desired residual stress state was also obtained without further processing.

The final example was stress measurements on a nickel-based structure used in a corrosive environment. The objective of these measurements was to check for proper heat treatment. Measurements were made from the weld through the heat-affected zone into the parent material. These stresses were used to evaluate the structure for its usefulness in a corrosive environment.

This paper discusses the logistics and results of these unique measurements. The success of the measurement technique in these cases indicates its usefulness in monitoring large structures.

References:

[1]   Noyan and Cohen, Residual Stress Measurement by Diffraction and Interpretation, Springer-Verlag, 1987.

# The Stiffness Decoupler - A New Approach to Base Isolation of Structures

K.K. Hu, P.G. Kirmser, S.E. Swartz
Department of Civil Engineering
Kansas State University
Manhattan, KS 66506-2905

A new base isolation system has recently been patented [1]. The basic philosophy behind the design shown in Fig. 1 is to provide the bearing strength which is needed to support a structure, and at the same time, enough flexibility to reduce the response of the structure to the horizontal accelerations of the ground which occur during earthquakes. The structural response at all levels above the base should be that of lateral, rigid body motions at substantially reduced accelerations. The device is also designed to resist vertical motion.

As seen in Figs. 1 and 2, the major components used in the stiffness decoupler are steel pipes filled with concrete to provide flexible supports, sliding plates to provide mobility, and a caisson-like exterior support to carry the bearing load. Other backup systems, such as loose cables and gapped bearing walls, may be provided as additional safety measures for important structures.

## Major Functions of Components
Pipes:
- Control the dynamic response of the structure
- Provide self-centering
- Provide damping
- Reduce the contact forces to the bearing plates
- Provide resistance to overturning
- Allow for sufficient lateral movement

Sliding plates:
- Provide freedom of relative movement between the structure and the caisson
- Provide the appropriate amount of friction to resist windshear
- Serve as a friction damper to help dissipate earthquake energy

Caisson:
- Provide the major support for the structure
- Provide appropriate stiffness of the structure to service loads

## Design of the Pipe
The pipe sizes are selected to allow large lateral deformations with maximum strain levels up to four times the yield strain. For the mild steel used, ($f_y$ = 60 ksi or 410 MPa), the yield plateau extends to about ten times the yield strain before the onset of strain hardening. For an ultimate stress of 80 ksi (550 MPa) test data in the literature give a lower limit of about 9,000 cycles before an elastic-plastic fatigue failure. For 16 cycles per earthquake (60 seconds duration) the number of large earthquake events would be 560.

## Numerical Modeling
In order to demonstrate the effectiveness of this system a four story, three bay building was analyzed when subjected to the following earthquakes: El Centro, Pacoima, Mexico City, Taft and Loma Prieta [2]. The results are presented in Table 1.

Table 1.  Effects of Different Earthquakes.

|  | El Centro (0.348g) | Pacoima (1.17g) | Mexico (0.17g) | Taft (0.18g) | Loma Prieta (0.485g) |
|---|---|---|---|---|---|
| Max Acc at Story 1 (ft/s²) | 2.22 (0.069g) | 2.55 0.079g) | 1.75 (0.054g) | 2.59 (0.080g) | 3.23 (0.100g) |
| Max Acc at Top Story (ft/s²) | 1.35 (0.042g) | 1.53 (0.048g) | 1.81 (0.056g) | 0.85 (0.026g) | 1.15 (0.036g) |
| Max Disp    (ft) | 0.559 | 0.564 | 0.472 | 0.460 | 0.985 |
| Max Rel Disp    (ft) | 0.476 | 0.414 | 0.700 | 0.177 | 0.267 |
| Max Interstory Drift (ft) | 0.0045 (0.0004h) | 0.0044 (0.0004h) | 0.0060 (0.0005h) | 0.0025 (0.0002h) | 0.0034 (0.0003h) |
| Max Base Shear (k) | 162 (0.057W) | 155 (0.055W) | 215 (0.076W) | 46 (0.016W) | 121 (0.043W) |

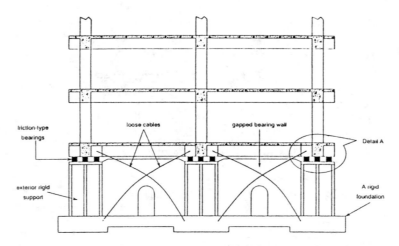

Fig. 1. A Structure Supported on the Stiffness Decoupler.

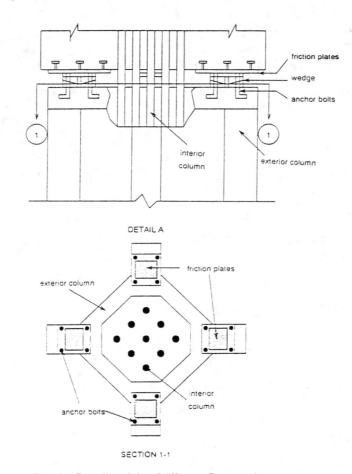

Fig. 2. Details of the Stiffness Decoupler.

## References

[1]     Hu, Kuo-Kuang, Kirmser, Philip G. and Swartz, Stuart E., **Stiffness Decoupler for Base Isolation of Structures**, U.S. Patent No. 5,386,671, Feb. 7, 1995.

[2]     Gattani, S., **Structural Optimization to Mitigate Natural Hazards Using Stiffness Decoupler**, PhD dissertation, Kansas State University, Manhattan, Kansas, 1993.

222

# MONITORING OF STRUCTURAL INTEGRITY USING EXPERIMENTAL TECHNIQUES

**J.L.Freire, J.T.P.Castro**

Catholic University of Rio de Janeiro

&

**R.D.Vieira**

CEFET-RJ and Strainlab Stress Analysis

Civil structures such as bridges, buildings, theaters, coliseums, and stadiums must last for long times due to their large construction costs, important social functions, and slow and difficult recuperation and rebuilding. The extended life of these structures and their maintenance for safe and reliable use depend on the rapid identification of structural damage mechanisms and the monitoring of the structural response under test and operational loads.

The planned monitoring of the response of the structures allows the knowledge and understanding of the relationship between service loads and response parameters such as stresses and displacements. The response analysis allows the confrontation between the actual and predicted ( modeled ) structural behavior.

Several simple or complex experimental techniques can be used in the monitoring of structures. The present paper will dedicate special focus to discuss case studies where conventional strain gages, displacement transducers and analysis equipment where used to investigate and to monitor the structural response of medium to large structures under in-lab tests or service operation.

Proof-tests help to certify the strength response of a structure, to identify the components that control its behavior, and also to determine its response under specified and controlled load conditions. Several proof-tests in bridges showed that their strengths are generally larger than the expected values, but in some cases, they can be under design predicted values due to some weak and very localized section or point of the structure. Therefore, the search for any extra or even the exact strength of a structure should be related to results acquired from monitored proof-tests. An example of this comes from the in-lab test of a composed reinforced concrete slab supported by a steel trussed beam. The structure failed catastrophically in the proof test before reaching the expected maximum load. The reason for that was the brittle unstable propagation of a welding defect which was located in the middle section of the main tensile beam of the steel truss. Figure 1 shows the sketch of the 20m long slab, and plots of applied test loads in function of displacements and strains measured by sensors, located in a section nearby the initial fracture site. The strain gage SGC, located in the concrete

(compression) side presented a small non-linear response after the load P reached 50 kN. The strain gage SGA, located in the external side of the steel beam, presented an abrupt change in its response after the 50 kN load and indicated clearly that something was becoming unstable. The non-linear behavior of the load-displacement curve is, in this case, more difficult to interpret due to its smooth first derivative change, although the lack of rigidity after the 50 kN load may be considered serious. The structure failure occurred at 60 kN and could be avoided if all three sensor responses were taken into consideration while load were being increased.

The monitoring of induced loads generated during the structure construction may be important when there is need to update the calculation models or to extend or re-direction its range of applications. Figure 2 shows strains measured by one of several strain gages installed in the longitudinal and transversal beams of a large theater roof located in a mall. The roof was designed to support new stores. Due to its large span (50×50m²), all beams had heavy sections and were prestressed. The strain- history showed in Figure 2 starts with initial (60%) prestressing of beam II and follows recording the effects caused by the prestressing of the transversal beams. The recording ends with the registration of the final residual strain after the unloading of the roof which supported a final proof- test. The proof -load was gradually induced to the roof by pumping 400 thousand liters of water to fill 10 specially built water-tanks on the roof. The total monitoring time of this test took around 30 days and used only 24 concrete strain gages at a total cost very low when compared to the cost of the roof.

The prediction of the dynamic response of large structures, such as a stadium, through mathematical modeling generally needs experimental confirmation. The same difficulty appears when the forcing (public) function, amplitude and frequency, need to be known. For example, how these functions differ in two cases: people jumping with some rhythm; and people jumping in disorder after a goal in a soccer game? Another question to be answered is: what happens to a soccer stadium when it is used as a music hall for pop-music shows? Figure 3 shows the dynamic response of an stadium designed and built in the late 40's for a public of 200 thousands. In the early 90's steel-column stiffeners were introduced between the upper and lower galleries to increase the natural frequency and lower the stadium displacement amplitudes under service load. The monitoring of this stadium has being made since then with the help of displacement transducers, to measure the gallery deflection, and strain gages installed in complete Wheatstone bridges, to determine the static and dynamic axial loads actuating in the steel columns.

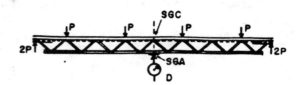

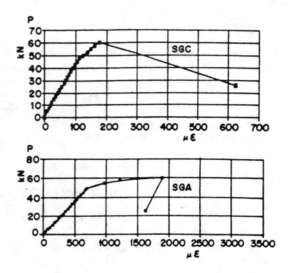

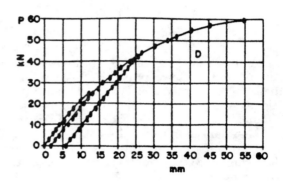

Figure 1: Strain and displacement response of composed slab loaded to rupture.

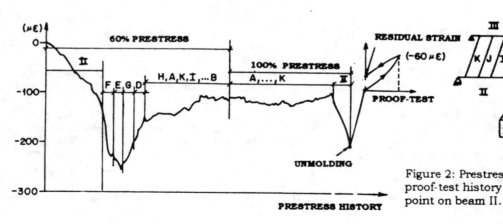

Figure 2: Prestress, unmolding and proof-test history of strain-monitored point on beam II.

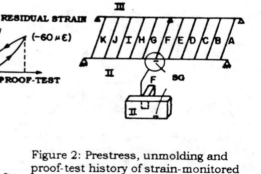

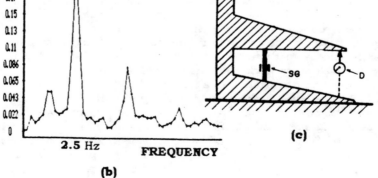

Figure 3: Dynamic response of stadium column. **a)** strain×time, **b)** spectrum, **c)** stadium sketch

2.5 Hz    **FREQUENCY**

**(b)**

# Static and Dynamic Tests of Driven Piles in Loess Soil

Edwin G. Burdette, J. Harold Deatherage, David W. Goodpasture
Dept. Of Civil Engineering
The University of Tennessee
Knoxville, TN 37996-2010

State bridge engineers in Tennessee are currently analyzing the state's bridges for seismic loading, a particularly important consideration for the western portion of the state in the region close to the New Madrid fault. The soils in West Tennessee consist of a wind-deposited soil known as loess. In the analysis of these bridges, modeling of the soil-pier interface where friction piles are used in loess presents a challenge. Because realistic values of stiffness are not available, this interface is currently modeled as fixed, a condition that cannot be perfectly achieved. A desire to obtain a more accurate model led to a research project directed toward the determination of realistic values of spring stiffnesses to represent the resistance of the soil to lateral movement of the friction piles.

A decision was made to perform quick-release ("pluck") tests on single piles to determine the desired values of stiffness. First, a prestressed concrete pile, 356 x 356 mm (14-in.), was driven to a "typical" depth (4.6 m - 7.6 m) in loess soil. Then a 44.5 kN (10,000 lb.) weight consisting of steel plates with holes in the center allowing them to slide over the pile were affixed to the portion of pile above ground. A reaction frame was built, and a horizontal load was applied to the pile. A load sufficient to produce a predetermined lateral displacement was applied. Then a quick-release mechanism was tripped, removing the load on the pile almost instantaneously.

Before the pile was loaded and released, instrumentation was applied to the pile and to the steel mass on top of the pile. Three types of instrumentation were used: LVDT's, accelerometers, and velocity meters. The data from the velocity meters in the early tests proved to be virtually useless; so these were omitted from later tests. The applied load was measured with a 111 kN (25 kip) load cell. When the load was released, the pile mass oscillated in free vibration. The data from the load cell, LVDT's, and accelerometers were monitored with time via digital computer using a data acquisition board Model DT2836 manufactured by Data Translation.

Several instrumentation problems, in addition to those already mentioned regarding the velocity meters, occurred in the early tests. The accelerometers used in the first tests had a range of ± 1.0 g, based on results from other reported tests which indicated low accelerations. The data obtained were essentially meaningless because the early accelerations were in fact greater than 1.0 g's. In later tests accelerometers with ranges of ± 10 g's were used, and the data were realistic and consistent with the LVDT data. Problems with the load cell signal also occurred in the early tests; in one set of tests the noise was approximately as large as the output signal. To reduce the noise level, a capacitor was introduced into the system with the result that, although the noise level was almost eliminated, the signal became time dependent. The cure was worse than the ill. Finally, a wiring system as devised to eliminate most of the noise without introducing a time dependency.

The LVDT data providing displacement versus time proved to be the most reliable and useful as reasonably clean sinusoidal plots were obtained. From these traces of decaying displacement versus time, values of frequency, damping, and stiffness were obtained. These values were found to vary with the displacement of the pile mass at release.

Values of damped frequency varied from as low as 3.5 Hz at displacements approaching 25 mm (1.0 in.) to as high as 6.5 Hz at small displacements on the order of 1.0 mm (0.04 in.). The damping ratios also varied widely from as low as 4 percent to as high as 13 percent of critical damping, but the values could not be correlated to displacement level. Stiffness values, the primary focus of the work, were found to diminish with an increase in displacement of the pile mass. For the last set of tests -- performed after the instrumentation problems had been solved -- the stiffness varied from 7.5 kN/mm (42.7 k/in.) at a displacement of 0.46 mm (0.018 in.) to 3.08 kN/mm (17.6 k/in.) at a displacement of 31.5 mm (1.24 in.).

While the focus of the research was on dynamic testing, a static test was performed each time a dynamic test was performed. A static "secant" stiffness was obtained by simply dividing the static load by the deflection. Interestingly, the secant stiffnesses thus obtained were very close to the dynamic stiffnesses. In the last, most reliable, set of tests, the ratio of dynamic stiffness to static stiffness varied from 0.87 to 1.27 with an average of 1.03. These results lead to the conclusion that static tests, which can be conducted much easier and less expensively than dynamic tests, are adequate to determine stiffness values of piles for purposes of structural modeling.

The work reported here was sponsored by the Tennessee Department of Transportation (TNDOT) and the Federal Highway Administration (FHWA). The conclusions presented are those of the authors and are not necessarily those of TNDOT or FHWA.

# An Apparatus for Measuring a Time-Dependent Poisson Ratio

Tanja Skitek, Igor Emri
University of Ljubljana
SLO-1000 Ljubljana, Slovenia

N.W. Tschoegl
California Institute of Technology
Pasadena, CA 91125, U.S.A.

## INTRODUCTION

Polymeric and composite materials are gaining importance in different engineering fields. When used as structural materials they can be exposed to a combination of mechanical and thermal loading, as well as to extreme environmental conditions. In order to predict the stress-strain state of such material, say in the linear viscoelastic domain, one needs at least two time-dependent material functions. For the octahedral form of constitutive equations these two material functions are shear, $G(t)$, and bulk, $K(t)$, moduli. It is relatively easy to measure the shear relaxation modulus, $G(t)$, however, it is quite difficult, if not impossible, to determine accurately the bulk modulus, $K(t)$. In our experience, the most important obstacle is the fact that the two material functions cannot be measured on the same specimen simultaneously. This requirement becomes apparent in interconversion of material functions, which will, in most cases, produce instabilities [1].

The easiest way to determine two material functions simultaneously is to perform experiments in uniaxial tension, measuring the relaxation modulus, $E(t)$, and the corresponding time-dependent Poisson ratio, $\nu(t)$. $G(t)$ and $K(t)$ can then be evaluated, using the correspondence principle, in Laplace space [1]:

$$\overline{G}(s) = \frac{\overline{E}(s)}{2(1 + s\overline{\nu}(s))}, \text{ and} \tag{1}$$

$$\overline{K}(s) = \frac{\overline{E}(s)}{3(1 - 2s\overline{\nu}(s))}. \tag{2}$$

Here $\overline{E}(s)$ and $\overline{\nu}(s)$ are the Laplace transforms of $E(t)$ and $\nu(t)$. Expressing $E(t)$ and $\nu(t)$ in terms of relaxation spectra $H^E(\tau)$ and $H^\nu(\tau)$ [2],

$$E(t) = E_e + E_d \sum_{i=1}^{n} H_i^E \exp\left(-\frac{t}{\tau_i^E}\right), \text{ and} \tag{3}$$

$$\nu(t) = \nu_e - \nu_d \sum_{i=1}^{n} H_i^\nu \exp\left(-\frac{t}{\tau_i^\nu}\right), \tag{4}$$

Eq's (1) and (2) can be inverted in closed form.

Hence,

$$K(t) = \sum_{i=1}^{n} \left\{ \begin{array}{l} \left[ K_e + \left[ \frac{E_e + E_d H_i^E n}{3(1 - 2\nu_e + 2n\nu_d H_i^\nu)} - K_e \right] \exp\left(-\frac{t\alpha_i}{\tau_i^\nu}\right) \right] \\ + \frac{E_d H_i^E n}{3(1 - 2\nu_e + 2n\nu_d H_i^\nu)} \left( \frac{\tau_i^E - \tau_i^\nu}{\alpha_i \tau_i^E - \tau_i^\nu} \right) \bullet \\ \bullet \left[ \exp\left(-\frac{t}{\tau_i^E}\right) - \exp\left(-\frac{t\alpha_i}{\tau_i^\nu}\right) \right] \end{array} \right\}, \tag{5}$$

$$G(t) = \sum_{i=1}^{n} \left\{ \begin{array}{l} \left[ G_e + \left[ \frac{E_e + E_d H_i^E n}{2(1 + \nu_e - \nu_d nH_i^\nu)} - G_e \right] \exp\left(-\frac{t\beta_i}{\tau_i^\nu}\right) \right] \\ + \frac{E_d H_i^E n}{2(1 + \nu_e - \nu_d nH_i^\nu)} \left( \frac{\tau_i^E - \tau_i^\nu}{\beta_i \tau_i^E - \tau_i^\nu} \right) \bullet \\ \bullet \left[ \exp\left(-\frac{t}{\tau_i^E}\right) - \exp\left(-\frac{t\beta_i}{\tau_i^\nu}\right) \right] \end{array} \right\}, \tag{6}$$

where

$$\alpha_i = [1 - 2\nu_e] \Big/ [1 - 2\nu_e + 2n\nu_d H_i^\nu], \tag{7}$$

$$\beta_i = [1 + \nu_e] \Big/ [1 + \nu_e - \nu_d nH_i^\nu], \tag{8}$$

$$E_d = E_g - E_e, \text{ and} \tag{9}$$

$$\nu_d = \nu_e - \nu_g, \tag{10}$$

and $E_g$, $\nu_g$, $E_e$ and $\nu_e$ are respectively glassy and equilibrium moduli of uniaxial relaxation and Poisson ratio.

In this paper we present an apparatus that allows simultaneous measurements of the relaxation modulus, $E(t)$, and the corresponding time-dependent Poisson ratio, $\nu(t)$.

## THE APPARATUS AND PRELIMINARY RESULTS

The apparatus is schematically shown in Fig. 1. The specimen is deformed symmetrically from both ends, as shown in Fig. 2, assuring that the middle of the specimen does not move. At this point we are measuring transverse strain as function of time. The time-dependent Poisson ratio is than obtained from:

$$v(t) = \frac{\varepsilon_t(t)}{\varepsilon_{l,0}} = \frac{-\Delta h(t) / h_0}{\Delta l / l}. \qquad (11)$$

Simultaneously we also measure the force to obtain the uniaxial relaxation modulus,

$$E(t) = \frac{\sigma(t)}{\varepsilon_{l,0}} = \frac{F(t) / h_0 b_0}{\Delta l / l_0}. \qquad (12)$$

Here $h_0$, $b_0$ and $l_0$ are dimensions of the specimen, and $\Delta l$ its deformation, as shown in Fig. 2.

Preliminary measurements, using the setup displayed in Fig. 3, were performed at room temperature on a soft polyurethane. One of the results is presented in Fig. 4, showing the excessive noise in measuring the Poisson ratio. This is by and large due to the insufficient temperature control and contact measurements of lateral contraction.

We are in the stage of rebuilding of the environmental chamber and introducing an optical method for lateral contraction measurements.

## REFERENCES:

[1] N.W. Tschoegl, "The Phenomenological Theory of Linear Viscoelastic Behavior", Springer Verlag, Berlin, 1989.
[2] I. Emri and N.W. Tschoegl, Rheol. Acta, **33**: 60-70, (1994).

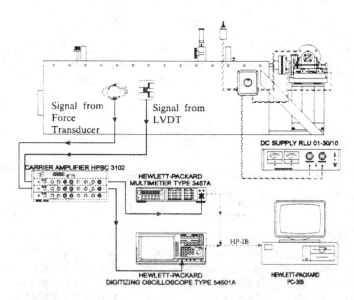

Figure 3: Experimental setup

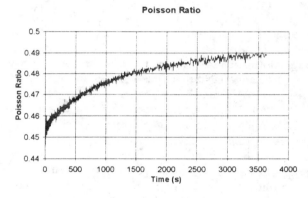

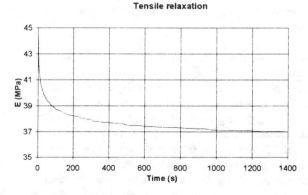

Figure 4: Preliminary results on soft polyurethane

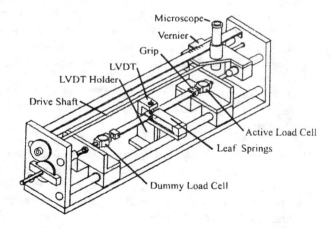

Figure 1: Schematic of the measuring apparatus

Figure 2: Schematic of the specimen, deformed symmetrically from both ends

# Experimental Investigation of the Nonlinear Viscoelastic Response and Subsequent Volume Changes of Two Engineering Polymers in Tension and Compression

Dina M. Colucci, Paul A. O'Connell, and Gregory B. McKenna

Polymers Division, Structure and Mechanics Group, National Institute of Standards and Technology
Gaithersburg, MD 20899

The investigation of the large deformation sub-yield behavior of amorphous polymer glasses is important in developing efficient methods for the determination of material parameters that are relevant to nonlinear viscoelastic constitutive descriptions of these materials. While there has been a significant amount of work to characterize the stress-strain response in uniaxial deformations of polymer glasses, much of this work has focused on experiments in constant rate of deformation conditions and with emphasis on yielding behavior [1-3]. In addition, only a few studies have dealt with volume changes during deformation [4-5]. Using dilatometry, Whitney and Andrews determined the volume changes incurred during constant rate of compression for polystyrene, poly(methyl methacrylate) PMMA, polycarbonate PC and poly(vinyl formal) samples at room temperature. In their work, Whitney and Andrews observed a volume contraction until yield when the volume became approximately constant. Others have also examined changes with deformation in the "free volume" using positron annihilation lifetime spectroscopy as a probe [5-7]. The results of these studies are somewhat controversial and we only signal them to the reader who is interested.

Here we describe investigations using single step stress relaxation experiments on glassy PC and PMMA in both tension and compression. The results reported here include both the stress relaxation response and the changes in lateral dimension during the relaxation experiment. The commercial grade PC and PMMA used in this study were quenched from above their glass transition temperature to room temperature then tested in a MTS 810 tensile testing machine*, modified in our laboratory for computer control. The tests were conducted under uniaxial deformation with a lateral extensometer attached to the sample center, used to monitor the lateral dimensional changes, while an axial extensometer was used to control the applied strain.

Due to space considerations, only the data for the quenched PC are presented; however, the features of the results presented here are followed by the PMMA experiments.

The experimental results are shown in terms of the stress relaxation modulus in Figures 1 and 2 for the tension and compression results, respectively. In both cases the relaxation modulus is found to decrease as the absolute magnitude of the applied axial strain $\epsilon_a$ increases. The lateral strain $\epsilon_l$ measurements are analyzed in terms of volume changes due to deformation by the ratio of $V/V_o$ where V is the current volume and $V_o$ is the initial undeformed volume. In the case of uniaxial tension, the results are not surprising. The initial volume is found to increase with increasing applied axial strain, and at a constant strain to decrease, relaxing with time as shown in Figure 3. The slopes of the curves in Figure 3 indicate that the rate of relaxation increases as $\epsilon_a$ increases. For the compressive case shown in Figure 4, the initial volume is found to decrease with increasing deformation as expected. However, it is very suprising that the volume decreases with time as relaxation occurs, since one would expect that after the initial volume decrease, the volume would attempt to return to the original deformation free state. The rate of volume change increases slightly with increasing deformation, but the results are not as pronounced as in the tension case.

In summary, single step nonlinear stress relaxation studies were performed under tension and compression while simultaneously monitoring the volume. The results show the time dependent change of the relaxation modulus and volume for PC even at temperatures 100 °C below $T_g$. The rate of volume change was found to increase in both tension and compression as the absolute magnitude of applied strain increased. In the compression results, further densification was observed after an initial volume decrease even though one would expect the volume to increase with time in an attempt to return to the deformation free state as was observed in the tension results. The cause of this counter-intuitive behavior and its extension to other materials is still under investigation.

*Certain commercial materials and equipment are identified in this paper to specify adequately the experimental procedure. In no case does such identification imply recommendation or endorsement by the National Institute of Standards and Technology, nor does it imply necessarily that the product is the best available for the purpose

[1] Bauwens-Crowet, C., Bauwens, J.-C., and Homes, G., J. Polym. Sci., 1969, A-2, 735

[2] Fung Y.C., *Foundations of Solid Mechanics*, Prentice Hall International Series in Dynamics, Prentice-Hall, Inc., Englewood Cliffs, New Jersey, 1965, pp 128-131.

[3] Yee, A.F. and Detorres, P.B., Polymer Eng. Sci., 1974, 14, 691.

[4] Whitney, W. and Andrews, R.D., J. Poly. Sci. : Part B, 1967 No. 16 2981

[5] Yee, A.F., J. Poly. Sci. : Part B Polymer Physics, 1995, 33 77

[6] Hasan, O.A., Boyce, M.C., Li, X.S., and Berko, S., J. Polym. Sci.: Part B, Physics, 1993, 31, 185.

[7] Ruan, M.Y., Moaddel, H., Jamieson, A.M., Simha, R. and McGervey, J.D., Macromolecules, 1992, 25, 2407.

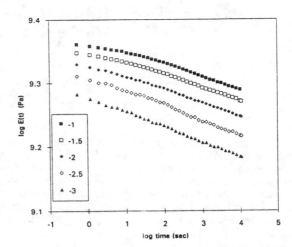

Figure 2: Stress relaxation modulus as a function of axial strain in compression. Numbers in the legend refer to the applied axial strain level, in percent.

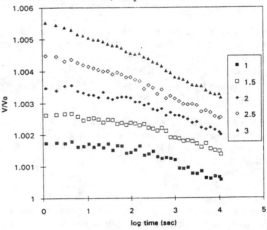

Figure 3: Time dependent volume changes as a function of axial strain in tension. Numbers in the legend refer to the applied axial strain level, in percent.

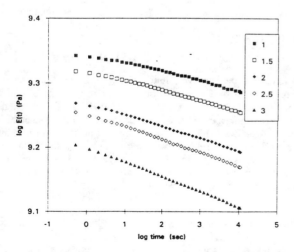

Figure 1: Stress relaxation modulus as a function of axial strain in tension. Numbers in the legend refer to the applied axial strain level, in percent.

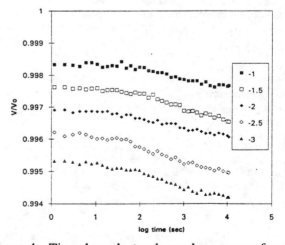

Figure 4: Time dependent volume changes as a function of axial strain in compression. Numbers in the legend refer to the applied axial strain level, in percent.

# To What Extent Can the Numerics Give Support to the Experimental Evaluations

Boris Štok, Pino Koc
Faculty of Mechanical Engineering - University of Ljubljana
Aškerčeva 6, 1000 Ljubljana
S L O V E N I A

In order to retrieve from an experiment the information that an experimentalist is looking for several conditions have to be fulfilled. Any departure from this fulfilment can give rise to possible serious consequences, thus losing the demanded reliability of the experiment and leading to erroneous conclusions. Being aware of these facts it is desirable that the experimentalist when designing his experiment takes also, apart from the usual experimental experience, full advantage of the available computational potential.

Numerical evaluation of the experimentally achieved data is inevitable part of postprocessing. But here, apart from this common way of using numerics, we want to address some further aspects which can be considered before all by advanced numerical means. The achieved reliability of computer simulations based on advanced computational techniques enables analyses that can be efficiently utilized in the preprocessing as well as in the postprocessing part of the experiment, thus offering a possibility for considerable implementation of the basic laboratory experiment. From the solution point of view the related tasks can be treated on one hand as direct boundary problems, and as indirect, i.e. inverse, problems on the other hand.

When referring specifically to the characterization of materials the mathematical structure of a relationship governing the considered phenomenology is assumed known while parameters specifying the relationship are to be identified. Often, due to complex material behaviour different specific experiments, limited usually to simple loading cases and specimen geometries, are needed for a proper parameter estimation. Not always, however, the complete characterization is achieved. In contrast to this experimental experience, any computer based approach that is aiming at release of the severity of conditions imposed in the experiment, leading consequently to possible simplification of the experimental set-up itself and to reduction of individual experiments needed for a more complete material characterization, is most welcome. By introducing computer simulations to resimulate a real complex experiment, a powerful means of material characterization is established. At least two aspects can be considered. First, when performing a computer simulation under the same conditions that specify a real experiment it is possible, by imposing the equivalence of the computed and measured responses, to carry out the correspondent estimation of material properties in a rather effective way. Second, by proper validation of simulated responses and the correspondent sensitivity analysis it is possible to address the problem of parameter identifiability on one side, and the problem of optimal design of experiment on the other side.

In the problem of material characterization a solution of the inverse problem is actually following solution strategies used in extremum problems [1]. In identification/estimation problems the responses of two systems are considered. The first is related to the real physical model and second is related to the mathematical model, which is supposed to represent the behaviour of the physical model equivalently. The objective of any such problem is to enforce the response of the mathematical model to be as close as possible to the physical one. Of course, this is achieved only by a proper adjustment of material parameters, which finally yields the sought material characterization. In the sequel, when referring to the considered two systems, the associated quantities will be addressed as "experimental" or "numerical".

Let denote the difference between the correspondent "experimental" and "numerical" quantities assembled in vectors $Y$ and $U(p)$ by $E(p)$

$$E(p) = Y - U(p) \qquad (1)$$

The scalar objective function $S(p)$ which is to be minimized is written in a matrix form as a sum

$$S(p) = E(p)^T W E(p) + \alpha (Hp)^T Hp \qquad (2)$$

where the superscript $T$ indicates the matrix transpose. The role of weighting matrix $W$ is to introduce unequal weights to physically different quantities while the regularization matrix $H$, weighted respectively by a scalar coefficient $\alpha$, is included in order to attenuate large changes of parameters in the first steps of iteration procedure. The computed response $U(p)$, which is usually obtained by the Finite Element Method analysis, is a function of material parameters vector $p$, assumed in the computational analysis. The necessary condition for $S(p)$ to be stationary is that the matrix derivative of $S(p)$ with respect to $p$ be equal to zero

$$X^T(p)\, W E(p) - \alpha H^T Hp = 0 \qquad (3)$$

Here, the matrix $X(p)$, called also the sensitivity matrix, is defined as

$$X^T(p) = \nabla_p U^T(p) \qquad (4)$$

Vector $p$, minimizing the considered objective function in accordance with (3), is obtained iteratively. With $v$ being the iteration counter the relationship relating the responses $U(p^v)$ and $U(p^{v+1})$ in two subsequent iteration computations can be approximated by the linearized Taylor series expansion of $U$ in the parameter space

$$U(p^{v+1}) = U(p^v) + X(p^v)[p^{v+1} - p^v] \qquad (5)$$

The substitution of this relationship in (3) yields a set of equations

$$\left(X^T(p^v)\, W X(p^v) + \alpha H^T H\right) p^{v+1} = \\ X^T(p^v)\, W\left(X(p^v)p^v + E(p^v)\right) \qquad (6)$$

which is used as the iterative solution algorithm for obtaining a new estimate of vector $p$. The search for the extremum of the objective function $S(p)$ is relying on the sensitivity analysis of each single parameter in vector $p$, establishing thus its influence on the calculated primary variables. Due to high implicit dependence and non-linearity the solution is obtained iteratively. The sensitivity coefficients are calculated using finite differences, requiring thus in an n-parameter problem (n+1) direct problem analyses for each iteration. The finite difference approach of the sensitivity analysis being very time consuming it should be replaced with other methods, whenever possible.

In an iteration solution procedure the Gauss method [2] gives both, the direction and the magnitude of variation in the parameters estimate. Small parameter variations usually decrease the objective function. Occasionally however, the variation indicated by the method is so large that the successive estimates oscillate or the procedure becomes unstable. This can result either from a near-linear dependence of the sensitivity coefficients or from a very bad initial parameter estimation. One of solutions to overcome this trouble, but not the best one, is to decrease the number of parameters that are being estimated. Another problem arises when large variations in the estimated parameter set are obtained in the iteration, and the solution of the direct problem fails. In such case some constraints on the parameters range must be introduced, though because of the diversity of the material properties involved in the identification, it is difficult to find suitable constraints for them. By introducing a scaling algorithm considering the imposed limits the solution of the direct problem is reachieved.

In our investigations we are particularly interested in the estimation of temperature and time dependence of thermo-mechanical properties of materials. In the sequel two study cases are considered. In the first case the temperature dependence of thermal parameters governing the heat conduction in a solid is to be estimated (Fig. 1) while in the second case the viscoelastic properties of a hyperfoam (Fig. 2) are sought. For this purpose the correspondent numerical models as shown in Figures 1 and 2 are used as experimental substitutes.

In the first case the measurement of the thermal evolution due to the internal heat source is provided by sensors located at points A, B, C, D. Sensors C and D are used to detect the departure from the boundary conditions as assumed in the numerical model. Based on the described inverse computational technique the thermal dependence of heat capacity and heat conductivity is estimated. A piecewise linear dependence is assumed. In Fig. 3 the estimated dependences (white marks) are plotted against the theoretical ones (black marks) used in the analysis of the direct problem that served as the substitute for the real experiment.

In the second case the indentation of an elastomeric foam specimen subjected to indentation by a hemispherical rigid punch is considered [3]. In order to attain the system response information to be used later in the material characterization the resulting indentation force $F_z$ and displacements of several surface points are registered. Viscoelastic characterization when the exponential representation in terms of the Prony series is adopted consists of the determination of the series coefficients $G_\infty$, $K_\infty$, $G_b$, $K_b$, and the correspondent relaxation times $\tau_i^G$ and $\tau_i^K$. According to the assumed relationship the degree of fitting to the experimental data is adjustable by the number of terms included in the series. The results of the identification [4] with different numbers of Prony series terms are displayed in Fig. 4, and compared with the "experimental" normalized relaxation curve (marked 1). The considered combinations $G_i$-$\tau_i^G$ (1-1, 2-2, 2-0, 5-0) are marked from 2 two 5.

REFERENCES

[1] Beck J.V., Arnold K.J., Parameter Estimation in Engineering and Science. John Wiley & Sons Inc.,1977.

[2] Arora, J.S., Introduction to Optimum Design. McGraw-Hill Book Company, 1989.

[3] Hibbit, Karlsson & Sorensen, Inc. ABAQUS/Standard 5.4, Example Problems Manual., 1994.

[4] Koc P., Štok B., "Material Characterization Through a Numerical Solution of Inverse Boundary-Value Problem", 1st Int. Conf. On Mechanics of Time Dependent Materials, Ljubljana, September 1995, pp 79-84.

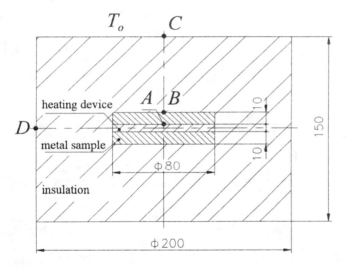

Fig. 1: Experimental arrangement

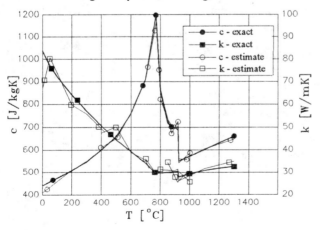

Fig. 3: Identified thermal properties

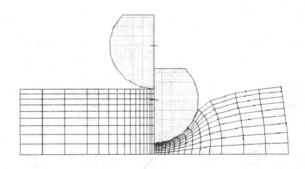

Fig. 2: FEM model of foam indentation (undeformed - deformed)

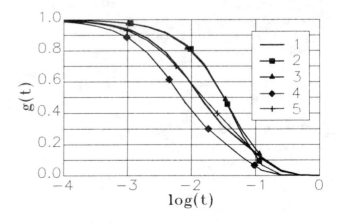

Fig. 4: "True" and identified relaxation curves

# Nondestuctive Strength Evaluation of Ceramic-Metal Joints by Ultrasonic Technique

Yoshio ARAI, Eiichiro TSUCHIDA and Motoki YOSHINO
Saitama University, 255 Shimo-Ohkubo, Urawa, Saitama 338, JAPAN

The introduction of ceramic-metal joining is important to apply the ceramics to the structural components. It could make the best use of the merit and make up for the demerit. The fracture strength of the ceramic-metal joints is, however, influenced by the thermal loading history and the defect around the joint part. The defect is induced by the residual stresses and the stress concentration(the singular stress field) caused by the difference of the thermal expansion coefficients and the elastic moduli [1] [2] [3] [4] [5].

In this study, strength of ceramic, $Si_3N_4$, and stainless steel,SUS304, joints is evaluated by ultrasonic technique nondestructively. Material properties and conditions of joining are listed in Tables 1 and 2, respectively. The configuration and dimensions of specimens are shown in Fig. 1. The specimens are subjected to a thermal cycle of which the maximum temperatures are $773 \sim 1073$ K. Four point bending tests after thermal cycle were conducted. The defect or damage on the interface is detected by the relative height of ultrasonic wave reflected on ceramic-metal interface. The ultrasonic echo voltage reflected on the ceramic-metal interface were measured before and after the thermal cycle. Illustration of the ultrasonic measurement system is shown in Fig. 2. The central frequency of the ultrasonic pulse were 20 MHz and the focus type transducer was used. The incident angle is 30° in water.

The relations between the ultrasonic echo voltage, $V_m$, reflected on the interface and the time are shown in Fig. 3. Fig. 3(a) shows the reflected wave from smooth specimen without thermal cycle. Fig. 3(b) shows the reflected wave from specimen subjected thermal cycle with maximum temperature 773K. The second wave with arrow mark increase corresponding to the damage due to the thermal cycle. From this result, the relative intensity between the top $\pi/2$ phase and the next $\pi/2$ phase can be used to evaluate the damage due to the thermal cycle. Relation between strength, $\sigma_b$, and reflected wave intensity, $\bar{V}_m$, is shown in Fig. 4. The bending strength of the ceramic-metal joints decrease with increasing the maximum temperature of the thermal cycle. The bending strength can be estimated from the dimension of the ultrasonic echo voltage.

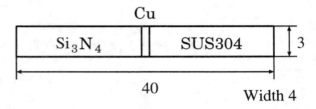

Fig. 1 Specimen configuration(unit:mm).

Table 1 Mechanical properties

|  | $Si_3N_4$ | Cu | S45C |
|---|---|---|---|
| E(GPa) | 304 | 108 | 206 |
| $\nu$ | 0.27 | 0.33 | 0.30 |
| $\alpha(\times 10^{-6})$ | 3.0 | 17.7 | 12.0 |

Table 2 Condition of joining

| Brazing filler | : | Ti-Ag-Cu |
|---|---|---|
| Temperature | : | $1073 \sim 1123K$ |
| Atmosphere | : | Vacuum. $1 \times 10^{-5}$ torr |
| Interlayer | : | Cu (thickness 0.2mm) |

# References

[1] Dalgleish, B. J., Lu, M. C. and Evans, A. G., Acta Metall., 36-8 (1988), 2029.

[2] Cao, H. C., Thouless M. D. and Evans, A. G., Acta Metall., 36-8 (1988), 2037.

[3] Evans, Lu M. C., Schmauder S. and Ruhle, M., Acta Metall., 34-8 (1986), 1643.

[4] Evans, A. G., Dalgleish, B. J., He, M. Y. and Hutchinson, J. W., Acta Metall., 37-12 (1989), 3249.

[5] Kobayashi, H., Arai, Y., Nakamura, H. and Sato, T., Mater. Sci. and Engng, A143, (1992), 91.

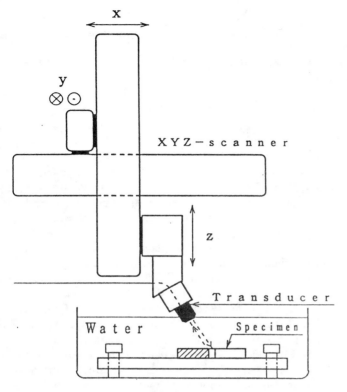

Fig. 2 Illustration of ultrasonic measurement.

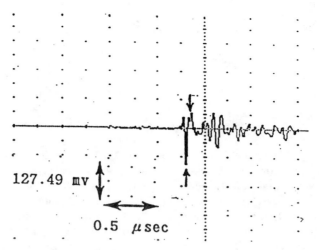

(b) Reflected wave from specimen with thermal cycle.
Fig. 3 Reflected wave configuration(cont.).

127.49 mv

0.5 μsec

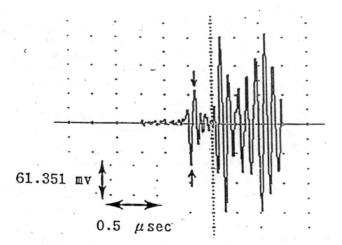

61.351 mv

0.5 μsec

(a) Reflected wave from smooth specimen.
Fig. 3 Reflected wave configuration.

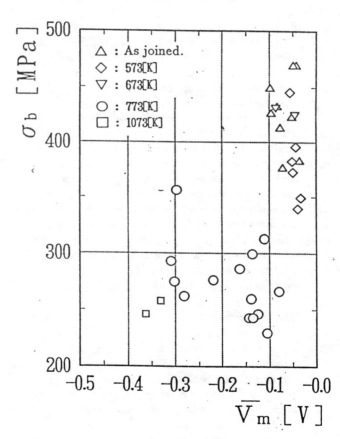

△ : As joined.
◇ : 573[K]
▽ : 673[K]
○ : 773[K]
□ : 1073[K]

Fig. 4 Relation between strength, $\sigma_b$, and reflected wave intensity, $\bar{V}_m$.

# Composite Structure NDE with Laser Doppler Vibrometer

F. P. Sun,  F. Lalande and  C. A. Rogers
Center for Intelligent Material Systems and Structures
Virginia Polytechnic Institute and State University
Blacksburg,  Virginia  24061-0261

Delamination and debond are typical defects in fiber reinforced composite structures. The occurrence of these defects reduces the integrity as well as the load carrying capability of structure significantly.  The detection of this type failure is difficult due to the fact that they are typically invisible from the structure surface and that the material is nonmagnetic and nonconductive, making most of the conventional NDE techniques ineffective.

A new NDE technique is developed to detect delamination and debond of composite structures. It exploits the local membrane vibration effect of the defective area of panel structures and the noncontact and fast scanning features of laser Doppler vibrometer. The basic principle of the technique is to actuate the structure with a wide frequency band. The selection of the band is such that the low order flexural vibration modes of the defective area of the structure will be excited, resulting in a relative higher vibration response in the debond area than in the well-bonded area. The surface flexural vibration is sensed by  a laser Doppler vibrometer in a non-contact fashion.  As the laser scans through the entire surface, a 3D image of flexural vibration intensity of the composite structure is formed,  and the defective area will be visualized by its prominently higher vibration response.

The technique uses non-intrusive excitation and the measurement of structure vibration. The structures are excited by either a thin piezoceramic patch bonded to the surface of the structure or an acoustic radiator placed behind  the structure. This results in a spatial uniform actuation of the structure which helps a reliable identification of damage location. To gain a better signal-to-noise ratio in response, a fast sweep sine excitation, known as  "chirp sine" is adopted which has a higher spectral power density than conventional band random.  The modal response of the structure, picked up by a laser Doppler vibrometer, is then processed into a single DC value equal to the RMS of the vibration velocity. This simplifies the analysis and enhances the response image, which makes  the  interpretation of the response for the structural defects more straightforward.

The technique has been tested on two engineering applications. First, the retrofit of concrete structure such as bridge columns with fiber reinforced composite in the form of wrapping is becoming a prevalent technique and feasible solution for aging infrastructures. This new repair scheme requires a matching NDE technique to verify the quality of the bond between composite and concrete. A cement concrete beam with composite patches  bonded on it is tested.  The system setup is given in Figure 1. Both the center debond and the edge debond are detected and the reliable visualization of debonds and its dependency on excitation frequency band are investigated.  The  modal response image for the edge debond  is shown in Figure 2. The dashed line indicates the debond area. Another application is the delamination detection of composite twisting box of helicopter blade.  In this case, the composite box, which has an induced delamination in the center, is uniformly excited by a set of tweeters on one side while the laser senses the response on the other side of the wall of the box. The modal response is given in Figure 3. In both applications, the defects are clearly visualized by their high local vibration level. The frequency band of excitation is primarily determined by trial and error with some guidance from the local membrane vibration theory, which will also be introduced in the paper.

The work demonstrates a high potential for this technique to be implemented in composite NDE engineering practice such as in-situ damage detection of composite repair to concrete civil infrastructure, aircraft metallic structure, and general quality control of composite product during manufacturing. However, the challenge of this technique in  is the selection of appropriate excitation frequency band when dealing with complex structures and unknown  debonds and delaminations.

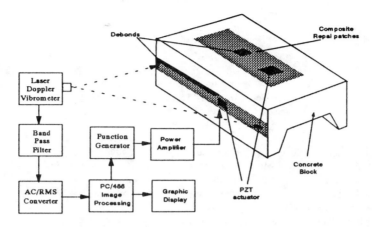

Figure 1 Experimental setup of the NDE system using PZT patch for actuation
and laser Doppler vibrometer for response detection

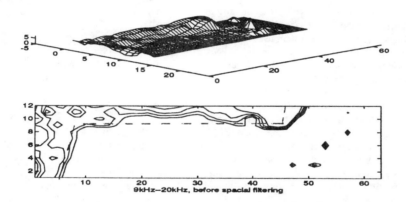

9kHz—20kHz, before spacial filtering

Figure 2 The vibration response of a composite patch bonded to concrete beam with edge disbond.
The dashed line indicates the debond border and the solid lines are the contour of the vibration level.

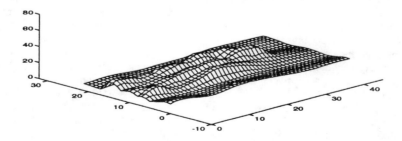

Figure 3 The vibration response of a composite twisting box with center delamination.
The rectangular plateau in the center is the image of the delamination.

235

# Time-averaged Digital Specklegraphy (TADS) for NDE of Crevice Corrosion and Composite Debond

Feng Jin and Fu-pen Chiang
Department of Mechanical Engineering
State University of New York at Stony Brook
Stony Brook, NY 11794-2300

Corrosion is one of the major factors that affects the structure integrity of aging aircraft. It often leads to catastrophic structure failures. The commonly found types of corrosion in aircraft structures are [1]: surface corrosion; pitting; intergranular corrosion; exfoliation; crevice corrosion; stress-corrosion cracking; microbial corrosion and filiform corrosion. Being a hidden defect, crevice corrosion is insidious in that the thinning of the metal is not detected until the structure integrity of the aircraft has been compromised.

There are several optical NDT methods applied to detection of structural defects and surface corrosion. Doyle et al. [2] proposed a laser-based profilometer to locate and measure corrosion fatigue cracking in boiler tube. Similar principle of laser light scattering was used in the work of Buerkle et al. [3] The system uses laser light scattering to count defect features rather than image them. It has been used successfully in a laboratory environment on both polished and unpolished metal samples containing scratches, fatigue cracks, and holes. Shearography has shown promise in inspecting aircraft structures.[4] It has been used to inspect the strain field in riveted lap joints under tensile loads as well as for the NDT of composite and honeycomb repairs. An enhanced visual technique for surface inspection called D sight [5][6][7] has been applied to detecting cold-worked holes, corrosion, and fatigue cracks associated with high stress-intensity factors. It is a simple process that provides a visual method to enhance small amplitude surface undulations on flat and moderately curved surfaces. Another technique that has been proposed to evaluate impact and fabrication damages in composite is a digital image correlation technique [8].

A novel optical system integrates high resolution CCD, fiber optics and image processing was developed to address the problems of NDE of crevice corrosion and composite debonds raised by aerospace industry. When an optically rough surface is illuminated by laser light, a random interferometric pattern called speckle is generated in front of the surface covered by the reflected wavelets. If the surface is under motion these speckles also move accordingly. By recording the speckles contained in a plane in front of the surface as a time-average the resulting specklegram will yield a variety of information concerning the displacement of the surface. The motion of the speckle is sensitive to the first order derivative of the out-of-plane displacement of the surface. Upon applying thermal or vacuum loading to the specimen, any local slope changes on the surface will cause drastic varying of the corresponding speckles. Such kind of anomalies usually indicate the weakened regions of the structure.

In this system the laser light was introduced to specimens by single mode optical fibers (Fig.1). The live speckle patterns were recorded by a high resolution CCD camera (2029 × 2048 pixels) and imported to a computer via a image interface board. Several frames of speckle pattern were averaged and the resultant patterns were displayed on the monitor in a real time fashion (Fig.2). Further image processing was applied to enhance the visual effect (Fig.3). Several crevice corrosion samples and a composite panel of honeycomb structure with an artificial delamination were used to demonstrate the validation of the technique. It was shown the resolution of this system is as high as $10^{-4}$ grad in slope changes. However its low requirement on environmental conditions makes it a promising NDE tool for field tests.

## Acknowledgement

The authors gratefully acknowledge the financial support by AFOSR through contract No. F49620931021.

## References

1. D. J. Hagemaier, A. H. Wendelbo, Jr., and Y. Bar-Cohen, "Aircraft Corrosion and Detection Methods", Materials Evaluation, 43( March, 1985), pp426-437.
2. James L. Doyle, G. R. Wood and Phillip D. Bondurant, " Using laser-based profilometry to locate and measure corrosion fatigue cracking in boiler tubes", Materials Evaluation, 51(May, 1993), pp556-60.
3. J. Buerkle, D. Dunn-Rankin, K. Bowo, and J. C. Earthman, "Rapid Defect Detection by Laser Light Scattering", Materials Evaluation, 50(June 1992), pp670-77.
4. John W. Newman, "Shearographic Inspection of Aircraft Structure", Materials Evaluation, 49(September, 1991), pp1106-1109.
5. J. P. Komorowski, D. L. Simpson, and R. W. Gould, " Enhanced Visual Technique for Rapid Inspection of Aircraft Structures", Materials Evaluation, 49( December, 1991), pp1486-90.
6. Omer L. Hageniers, "DiffractoSight - a new form of surface analysis", SPIE 814(1987), pp193-99.
7. Rodger L. Reynolds and Omer L. Hageniers, " Optical Enhancement of Surface Contour Variations for Sheet Metal and Plastic Panel Inspection", SPIE 954(1988), pp208-16.
8. S. S. Russell, M. A. Sutton, and H. S. Chen, " Image Correlation Quantitative Nondestructive Evaluation of Impact and Fabrication Damage in A Glass Fiber-Reinforced Composite System", Materials Evaluation, 47(May, 1989), pp550-57.

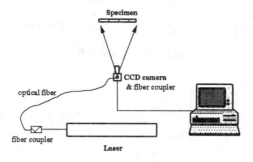

Fig. 1 System setup of TADS

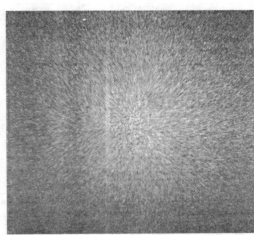

a. Debond in composite panel      b. Crevice corrosion in aluminum assembly

**Fig.2 Speckle patterns of TADS showing hidden defects**

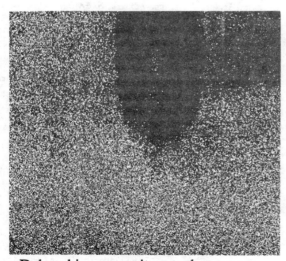

a. Debond in composite panel      b. Crevice corrosion in aluminum assembly

**Fig.3 Speckle patterns of TADS after digital image processing**

# Application of Digital Image Correlation to Microfracture Testing of Particulate-Reinforced Titanium Composites

W. Tong and S. Huang
Department of Engineering Mechanics &
Center for materials Research and Analysis
University of Nebraska-Lincoln
Lincoln, Nebraska 68588-0347

The initiation and growth of damages at macro to micro scales in titanium composites are the focus of this investigation. Particulate reinforced titanium matrix composites are relatively a new class of metal matrix composites, which are superior to aluminum matrix composites in some high temperature (up to 650°C) and corrosive conditions [1-7]. Typical microstructures of such a two-phase composite is shown in Fig.1. Particulate-reinforced titanium composites are shown to have increased stiffness and strength; but their tensile ductility is strongly affected by the degree of metal-ceramic interfacial reaction during the consolidation and post-consolidation annealing processes (e.g., see Fig. 2).

A compact tensile substage apparatus with a computer-integrated digital image acquisition system is used for fracture testing of titanium composites under both optical and electron scanning microscopes. Fig. 3 shows the schematic of the experimental set-up and related data acquisition and processing flow chart. The compact tensile substage (approximately 100 mm x 125 mm x 100 mm in size), shown in Fig.4, is designed specifically to fit the JEOL JSM-840A SEM at the University of Nebraska-Lincoln (UNL). The jaws on the tensile substage move in opposite directions to minimize movement of area of interest. The load is quasi-statically imposed via an operating handle assembled onto a SEM cover port. The displacement resolution is 7.05 μm per revolution of the input shaft.

Digital image correlation techniques [8,9] are applied to deduce the deformation field at the damage processing zone around the macroscopic damage region. Such deformation fields are resolved at several different length scales (ranging from the order of 1 mm to 1 μm) by conducting the tests at different magnifications. Fig. 5 shows a calibration tensile test of a perforated sample. The corresponding full field displacements are given in Fig. 6. The field of view of Fig. 6 is about 3.5 mm by 2.5 mm.

Different degrees of severity of deformation fields at the macroscopic level are controlled by using perforated, bluntly-notched and sharply notched tensile testing specimens. Preferred sites of damage initiation are also introduced by selected indentation marks on the matrix, particle, and the matrix-particle interface region. The growth of the macroscopic crack and the development of the microdamages in the composites are evaluated from the measured deformation fields at both continuum and reinforcement particle levels.

This investigation is part of the research effort [1,10] in providing fundamental understanding and valuable guidance to optimize materials processing for improved performance of the titanium composites and to assess these materials for potential engineering applications.

*Acknowledgments:* The research reported here has been partly supported by the Layman Faculty Award and grants from the Research Council and the Center for Materials Research & Analysis (CMRA) at UNL. The authors are also grateful to Prof. Brian W. Robertson of CMRA Central Facility for Electron Microscopy at UNL for helpful discussions.

## References

[1] W. Tong, "Full-Density Processing of Advanced Particulate Composites", *Transaction of NAMRI/SME* (in press, May 1996).

[2] W. Tong, G. Ravichandran, T. Christman, and T. Vreeland, Jr., "Processing SiC-Particulate Reinforced Titanium-Based Metal Matrix Composites by Shock Wave Consolidation", *Acta metall. mater.* **43** (1), 235-250 (1995).

[3] W. Tong, G. Ravichandran, T. Christman, and T. Vreeland, Jr.,"Effects of Interfacial Reaction on the Mechanical Properties of Ti-SiC Particulate Reinforced Metal Matrix Composites", in: *High Performance Metal and Ceramic Metal Matrix Composites* (Edited by K. Upadhya), The Minerals, Metals & Materials Society (TMS), Warrendale, Pennsylvania, 1994, p.33-47.

[4] W. Tong, G. Ravichandran, T. Christman, and T. Vreeland, Jr., "Processing and Properties of Shock Consolidated SiC-Particulate Reinforced Ti Matrix Composites", *J. de Physique IV*, Colloque **C8**, pp. 331-336 (1994).

[5] W. Tong and G. Ravichandran, "Effective Elastic Moduli and Characterization of a Particulate-Reinforced Metal Matrix Composite with Damaged Particles", *Composite Sci. & Tech.* **52** (2), pp.247-252 (1994).

[6] D. Benson, W. Tong, and G. Ravichandran, "Particle-Level Modeling of Dynamic Consolidation of Ti-SiC Powders", *Modell. Simu. Mater. Sci. Eng.* **3**, 771-796 (1995).

[7] S. Abkowitz, P.F. Weihrauch, S.M. Abkowitz, and H.L. Heussi, "The Commercial Application of Low-Cost Titanium Composites", *JOM*, pp. 40-41 (August 1995).

[8] T.C. Chu, W.F. Ranson, M.A. Sutton and W.H. Peters, "Applications of Digital-Image-Correlation Techniques to Experimental Mechanics", *Exp. Mech.* 25 (3), 232-244 (1985).

[9] G. Vendroux and W. G. Knauss, "Deformation Measurements at the Sub-Micron Size Scale: II. Refinements in the Algorithm for Digital Image Correlation", GALCIT SM Report 94-5, California Institute of Technology (1994).

[10] W. Tong and X. Li, "Effects of the Stress State on the Dynamical Damage Behavior of Particulate-Reinforced Titanium Composites", 1996 SEM VIII Intl. Congress on Exp. Mech., June 10-13, 1996, Nashville, Tennessee.

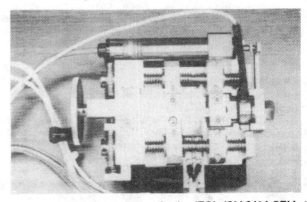

Fig. 2 Tensile Ductility of Ti-SiC*p* Composites with Different Degrees of Interfacial Reaction [3,4].

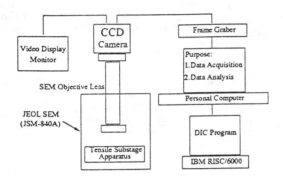

Fig. 1 Micrograph of a Particulate-Reinforced Titanium Composite.

Fig. 3 Schematic of the Experimental Set-Up.

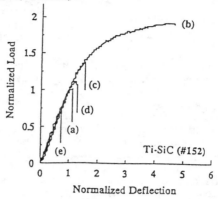

Fig. 4 Compact Tensile Substage for the JEOL JSM-840A SEM at the University of Nebraska-Lincoln.

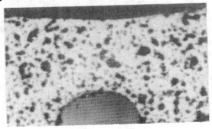

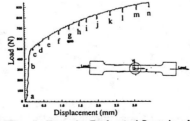

Fig. 5 Calibrating Tensile Test of a Perforated Sample. A Digital Image was Taken at the Load Level Each Letter Indicates. Some Relaxation of the Load was Observed.

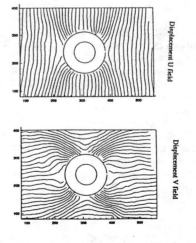

Fig. 6 The Full-Field Displacements Computed by Digital Image Correlation for Load Level G.

# Phase-stepped deflectometry applied to shape measurement of bent composite plates

Nicolas Fournier, Michel Grédiac, Pierre-Alain Paris, Yves Surrel
Centre Sciences des Matériaux et des structures
Département Mécanique et Matériaux
Ecole des Mines de Saint-Etienne - 158, Cours Fauriel
42023 SAINT-ETIENNE CEDEX 2, FRANCE

The experimental characterization of the mechanical properties of composite materials and structures presents specific difficulties due to their anisotropy . First, many more independent parameters are to be determined than for isotropic materials. As an example, the bending properties of a symmetric laminated plate are described by six independent parameters, instead of two parameters for an homogeneous plate. Second, the basic assumption of uniform states of strain within the specimens may be far from reality because of end-constraint effects, e.g. in shear tests. As a result, identification procedures based on the processing of whole displacement fields on composite plates have been proposed, [1] for instance.

This paper presents an optical method for the measurement of such fields. The experimental procedure is based on deflectometry, a technique which permits to measure the slopes field of the bent specimen. Only ray-optics are involved in this technique.

The experimental setup described in figure 1 is a conventional basic telescopic deflectometer [2][3] with a sinusoidal spatial filter at the focal plane of the field lens. A collimated laser beam is reflected by the surface of the test object and focused on the filter. The image of the object is projected onto a screen by the imaging lens.

The geometry of the focalised reflected beam on the filter depends of the local slopes of the tested surface : a variation of the local slope at a given point changes the direction of propagation of the reflected ray. This corresponds to a lateral displacement at the focal plane. If the surface is flat, rays are all focused at the same point which moves with a tilt of the object. If the surface is not flat, the point becomes a spot. If a slit is placed in the focal plane, a family of neighbouring ray directions, associated to object points having neighbouring slopes, is selected. In other words, a contour of slope isovalue is observed on the imaging screen. In order to have more information at once, this single slit can be replaced by a set of parallel slits, that is a grid. Then, a whole set of slope contours can be observed on the imaging screen, looking much like an interferometry fringe pattern.

The intensity profile observed on the screen at that stage is binary, with step variations of light from one 'fringe' to the other (also, the sharp edges of the lines introduce diffraction). It is better to have a spatial filter that approximates a sinusoidal transmittency, so that the transmitted intensity be a sine function of the displacement of the spot in the focal plane. The intensity observed at a given point of the image plane is then a sine function of the slope at the corresponding object point. To get the value of the slope at a point, it is necessary to measure the phase of the intensity function at that point. This is exactly the same problem as in interferometry (e.g. Fizeau interferometry), where the intensity is a sine function of the deflection. The quasi-sinusoidal filter is obtained by taking a picture out of focus of a pattern of parallel lines. The spatial period is 1.89 mm. So, a phase variation of $2\pi$ corresponds to a slope variation of $9.5.10^{-4}$ rad (with the focal length of the field lens = 1 m).

It is very simple to introduce a phase-stepping procedure in our setup. The filter is placed on a translation stage, and many pictures are acquired, with a motion of the filter in between. The set of acquired images is processed with the software 'Frangyne'[4][5] which has been developed in the laboratory, in order to get a phase field.

To measure the variation of slopes due to the bending load, a phase field is measured at the initial state, and another one when the plate is bent. The difference between these fields yields a phase field proportional to the slope field due to bending.

The slope is measured along two directions, $x$ and $y$. A rotation of the filter through an angle of 90° allows the measurement of slope fields. An example obtained with an unidirectional glass/epoxy plate is given in figure 2. That slope field is compared to the corresponding one computed with a finite element program. As may be seen, both patterns are very similar.

Full-field techniques are of invaluable interest in mechanical engineering. In this domain, phase-stepped deflectometry offers many advantages comparatively to interferometry :
• The technique is based on the measurement of the direction of propagation of light, and not of optical thickness, so:
    -it is basically insensitive to vibrations: the specimen to be tested and the setup can be located on different structures;
    -temporally incoherent light can be used;
    -the sensitivity can be adjusted within a large range, by varying the spatial frequency of the filter.
These properties constitute dramatic improvements on interferometry for the on-site industrial engineering use.
• A tilt of the tested object does not disturb the experimental results;
• Results are very precise : it has been checked that the phase can be determined with an accuracy of 1/200 of the spatial period of the grid. With a period of 1.89 mm, the sensitivity is about $5.10^{-6}$ rad ;
• Only one numerical derivation is required to obtain the curvatures, which are the most important data for the study of bending properties ;
• Dynamic studies can be performed with a chopper located between the source and the tested specimen : this setup will be used for the characterisation of vibrating composite plates by modal analysis [6]

References :
[1] M. Grédiac, A. Vautrin, "A new method for determination of bending rigidities of thin anisotropic plates", ASME, Journal of Applied Mechanics/Vol. 57, 1990, pp. 964-968.
[2] E. Liasi, W. North, "Retroreflective moiré using a telescope" ,Optical Engineering / November 1994 /Vol. 33 No. 11 / pp. 3723-3726.
[3] O. Kafri, K. Kreske, "Comparison and combined operation of a moiré deflectometer, Fizeau interferometer,

and schlieren device" ,Applied optics/ December 1988 / Vol. 27 No. 23 / pp 4941-4946.

[4]   Y. Surrel, B. Zhao, "Phase-stepping : application to high-resolution moiré", Spie Vol. 2003 Interferometry VI (1993) / pp 159-170.

[5]   Y. Surrel, B. Zhao, "Moiré and grid methods : a 'signal processing' approach", Spie 1994.

[6]   M.Grediac, P.A. Paris, "Direct identification of elastic constants of anisotropic plates by modal analysis : theoretical and numerical aspects", Journal of Sound and Vibration, accepted for publication, 1996.

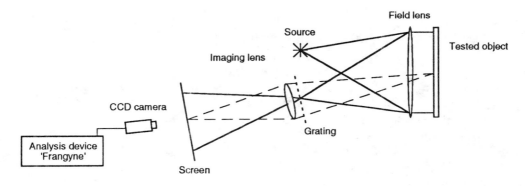

Fig. 1 : Experimental setup

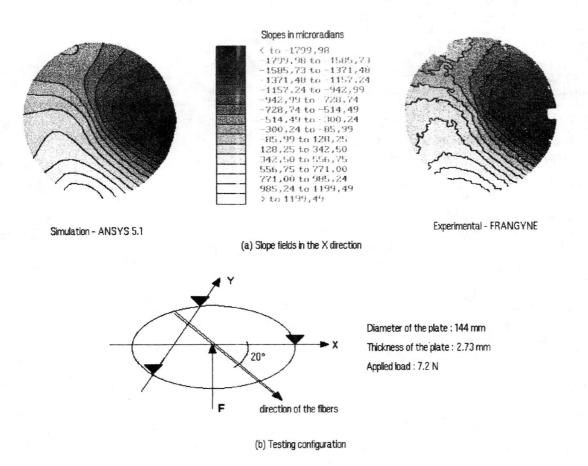

Slopes in microradians

| < to -1799,98 |
| -1799,98 to -1585,73 |
| -1585,73 to -1371,48 |
| -1371,48 to -1157,24 |
| -1157,24 to -942,99 |
| -942,99 to -728,74 |
| -728,74 to -514,49 |
| -514,49 to -300,24 |
| -300,24 to -85,99 |
| -85,99 to 128,25 |
| 128,25 to 342,50 |
| 342,50 to 556,75 |
| 556,75 to 771,00 |
| 771,00 to 985,24 |
| 985,24 to 1199,49 |
| > to 1199,49 |

Simulation - ANSYS 5.1

Experimental - FRANGYNE

(a) Slope fields in the X direction

Diameter of the plate : 144 mm

Thickness of the plate : 2.73 mm

Applied load : 7.2 N

(b) Testing configuration

Fig.2 : Example of slope contour map obtained with an unidirectional glass/epoxy plate

241

# Discrete Wavelet Analysis of Acoustic Emissions – Identification of CFR Composite Failure Modes

Gang Qi[1], Alan Barhorst[2], Javad Hashemi[2]

Department of Mechanical Engineering
Texas Tech University
Lubbock, TX 79409-1021

Presented is a study of the application of discrete wavelet analysis to acoustic emissions (AE) used in non-destructive material evaluation. The discrete wavelet based analysis is a relatively new mathematical method which has been shown to be a powerful tool in the analysis of transient signals (Daubechies, 1988; Newland, 1993). It provides a way to transform one dimensional signals in the time domain into the two dimensional time-frequency domain. The method developed in this work is based on Daubechies' wavelets and the method reveals a potential for the application of discrete wavelets in the AE area.

A series of tensile tests were performed on 12-layer laminate carbon fiber reinforced composite (CFRC) material specimen. The specimen were loaded monotonically under quasi-static conditions. The first group of tests utilized unidirectional specimen $[0^0]_{12}$, the second group utilized cross-ply laminates $[0^0/90^0]_{6s}$. A typical waveform collected is shown in Figure 1. In order to eliminate the effects of sensor and preamplifier dynamics, these effects were deconvolved from the detected AE signals. The real AE source is then decomposed into different wavelet levels (eleven in all) using the wavelet-based AE analysis algrithm developed by the authors. The decomposed AE signals in level 7, 8, and 9 are shown in Figure 2. Visually, the waveforms in these three levels can be identified to be distinct according to the duration and amplitude. Each level may be examined for its specific frequency range, energy change rate, and percentage of total energy it occupies. The information carried by different levels are arranged to indicate the AE source in various frequency channels. Then the energy in each level is calculated and compared to the total energy carried by the AE signals.

A general trend is observed by investigating the en-

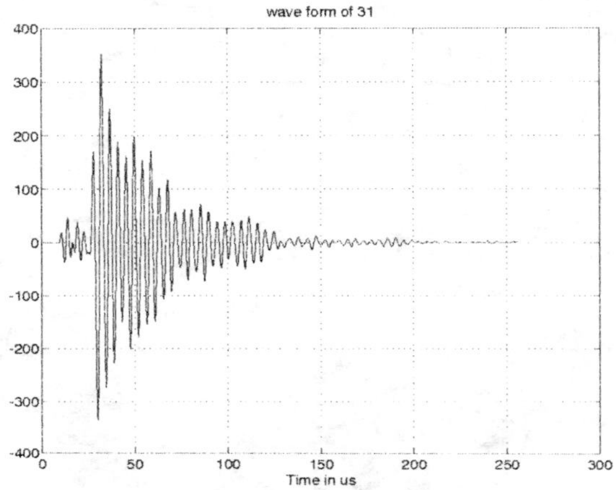

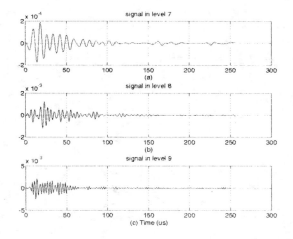

Figure 1: AE waveform

Figure 2: AE waveform in different wavelet levels

---

[1] PhD student
[2] Assistant professors

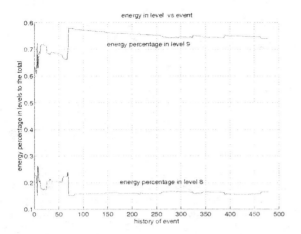

Figure 3: Energy percentage of 3 mm notched cross-ply of of second test of level 8 and 9

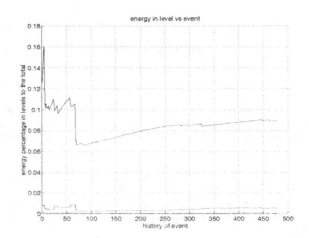

Figure 4: Energy percentage of 3 mm notched cross-ply of of second test of level 7

ergy distribution of decomposed AE signals. This trend indicates that the energy in the AE signals are essentially concentrated in three levels (levels seven, eight, and nine) representing frequency rages of 50-150 kHz, 150-250 kHz, and 250-310 kHz respectively. Furthermore, the energy percentages in levels seven, eight, and nine are found to be 8%, 15%, and 75% respectively as shown in Figure 3 and Figure 4. The analysis indicates that the information in the three dominant wavelet levels may be related to different failure modes associated with the fracture of CFR composites.

The conclusion drawn from the preliminary results can be stated as follows. Wavelets provides a unique way to analyze the AE signal by decomposing the signal into different wavelet levels. Each level represents the component of decomposed AE signal within a certain frequency range and it captures any local disturbance and displays the disturbance in its dominant level. Therefore, the investigation of internal defects in a material is more readily facilitated. The energy carried by the AE signal takes into consideration the entire waveform instead of only partial information like total counts or event counts from traditional AE analysis. The wavelet level energy of the decomposed AE signal provides a deeper inspection of the AE source. The wavelet-based techniques may also be used to predict an empirical relationship of wavelet level energy and the parameters of fracture mechanics such as stress or stress intensity factors. This work is in progress.

More extensive research on different materials, different loading sequences, and loading methods is also in progress.

## Acknowledgement

The authors wish to thank the Wind Engineering Research Center at Texas Tech University for funding this project.

## References

Daubechies, I. (1988). Orthonormal bases of compactly supported wavelets. *communication on Pure and Applied Mathematics*, XLI:906–996.

Newland, D. E. (1993). *Random Vibrations, Spectral and Wavelet Analysis*. Longman Scientific & Technical, Essex, England.

# Instrumentations and Experimental Techniques for Evaluating Long-term Engineering Performance of Wood-based Composites

R. C. Tang
Professor and
School of Forestry
Auburn University, AL 36849

J. H. Pu
Research Technologist
J. M. Huber Corp.
Commerce, GA 30529

J. N. Lee
Graduate Research Assistant
School of Forestry
Auburn University, AL 36849

A major concern in the development of wood composite products, and the selection of such products as building construction materials, and/or as components in structural systems, is their serviceability or lifetime engineering performance. The acceptance of wood composite products in structural applications would be enhanced if satisfactory and reliable long-term engineering performance of those wood composite products or structural members under actual or simulated in-service environments could be shown and evaluated. The creep and creep-rupture (duration of load: DOL) experiments are considered the primary methods for the evaluation of long-term engineering performance of wood composite structural members/systems subjected to changing environments. In this paper, the designs of computer-monitored testing facilities for creep/DOL testing of structural size wood composite beams and small size wood composite panel products are addressed. The experimental design, testing procedures and environmental conditions are discussed.

## Instrumentations

To collect reliable data on the long-term engineering performance of wood composite structures exposed to changing environments, multi-space testing frames interfaced with computer-controlled data acquisition systems must be constructed. These facilities must be placed inside a computer-controlled environment room in order to collect the data for the conditions that simulated the in-service environments or in an open shed for testing under real in-service environments. In both cases, large room is needed to house the multi-space testing frames. Therefore, the costs for conducting creep/DOL experiments are very high and the testing works are very time-consuming. Due to the limitation of paper length, only the instrumentations and experimental techniques/procedures developed at Auburn University for the creep/DOL tests of solid and composite beams and wood composite panel products under bending are presented.

## I. For Full Size Structural Members

**A. Loading Apparatus:** A 14-space creep/DOL testing frame was designed and constructed for testing solid wood beams and composite beams, up to the size of 35.56 cm (14 in.) deep and 6.4 m (21 ft) long in bending under two-point load by using a lever-cable system [1]. A single loading mechanism with a lever mounted overhead in the frame is shown in Fig. 1. The support and load apparatus were fabricated basically following the specifications as given in ASTM Standard D 198-76 (Now designated as D 198-84). Lateral supports were provided for each beam at an interval of 122 cm (4 ft) for preventing the possible development of torsional creep. The beam deflections were measured by using a yoke mounted rotary potentiometer with a precision sprocket. A plastic chain attached to the beam was passed along the edge of this sprocket so the changes of vertical displacement of the beam could be converted to voltage output.

**B. Testing Environments:** To control the testing environments, a humidity control system was installed atop the creep/DOL loading frame and enclosed by heavy-duty plastic sheets. The dimension of this enclosure is 4.88 m (16 ft) high, 6.10 m (20 ft) wide, and 7.32 m (24 ft) long and it is housed in a large room installed with an electric heating system which controls the temperature in this large room and the enclosure.

## II. For Small-Medium Size Structural Members

**A. Loading Apparatus:** Seven loading frames, each capable of testing 4 pieces of structural wood composite members up to the size of 6.35 cm (2.5 in.) thick x 11.43 cm (4.5 in.) deep x 243.84 cm (96 in.) long, were constructed for the long-term engineering performance tests. The loading mechanism is similar to that designed for testing full-size structural members. The loads applied to each testing specimen were provided by using an adjustable length cantilever and a cable/pulley system (4 in each frame). A load cell was attached to each cable individually to calibrate the load applied to the system. To minimize the localized crushing in the tested members, bearing pads were placed at each load-and support-point. The mid-span deflection measuring system for each testing members and the data acquisition system were identical to those used for the testing of full-size structural members and the elapsed time-to-failure was recorded.

**B. Testing Environments:** A walk-in environmental manufactured by Parameter Generation and Control, Inc., was used to house all the seven testing frames. All the environmental conditions chosen for the creep/DOL tests can be controlled and maintained by this conditioner through a dedicated wall-mounted micro processor-based programmer.

**C. Moisture Content (MC) Measurement:** Multi-channel Triton 2100 moisture meters with various length electronic probes were used to measure the MC at different depth of loaded members and unload dummy specimen during the test for collecting the data of MC gradients and contours.

## III. For Composite Panel Specimens

**A. Loading Apparatus:** Seven double-deck loading frames, capable of testing 24 specimens simultaneously in each frame, were constructed for the creep/DOL tests of wood composite panel specimens up to the size of 2.54 cm (1 in.) thick x 8.89 cm (3.5 in.) wide x 60.96 cm (24 in.) long (Fig. 2). A RDP DCT-1000 transducer was used to measure the creep deflection of each specimen by moving the transducer along a pair of parallel sliding bars on the top of each deck.

**B. Testing Environments:** One walk-in environmental room with a microprocess-2000 controller, one uncontrolled environment room and one open shed, were used for the long-term engineering performance test of wood composite panels exposed to different environmental conditions.

### Experimental Techniques and Procedures

At present, no standards are available for creep/DOL tests of wood composite structures. Following experimental techniques and procedures are based on the experiences collected at Auburn University during the last 15 years.

**I. Test specimens:** Variables considered should include the number, direction, size and pre-conditioning and these variables may vary with the processing parameters. Also, the method of sample selection shall be dependent on the purpose of test under consideration and sufficient number of specimens shall be tested to permit the performance of statistical analysis of the test data.

**II. Test Procedures:**

(a) Span, supports and methods of loading shall be similar to those used in the static testings and the time for total load applied to the specimen shall be less than 10 seconds.
(b) The load level and duration shall be dependent on the purpose of the test. For creep test, low level load shall be used whereas high level load shall be considered in the DOL tests. Load histories such as the constant loads, repeating constant loads and cyclic constant loads may be considered.
(c) Continuous monitoring the displacement in the specimens is essential for collecting reliable time-dependent data and first measurement shall be conducted within 10 seconds after load was applied.
(d) Wood composites are hygrothermal materials and hence the changes of MC and thickness swelling shall be monitored.
(e) The engineering properties of wood composites are greatly influenced by the mechanical and environmental loading histories and thus the residual properties shall be evaluated.

**III. Test Environments:** Constant environmental conditions (RH and T), simulated in-service environmental conditions (controlled) and actual in-service environments (open shed) shall be considered in long-term engineering performance tests.

**Model Development:** Predicting models with the consideration of material/processing variables, mechanical loading and environmental loading histories shall be developed.

### Remarks

Standards for long-term engineering performance tests of wood composites should be developed. Since long-term engineering tests are high cost and time-consuming, academic, governmental and industrial cooperation at national or international level is highly recommended.

### References

[1] Leichti, R. J. and R. C. Tang. Predicting the load capacity of wood composite I-beams and sawn lumber. Wood and Fiber Science, 21(2):142-154. 1989.

[2] Fridley, K. J., R. C. Tang and L. A. Soltis. Thermal effect on the DOL of solid lumber. Wood and Fiber Science, 21(4): 420-431. 1989.

[3] Pu, J. H., R. C. Tang and C. Y. Hse. Creep behavior of sweetgum OSB: Effect of load level and relative humidity. Forest Products Journal, 44(11/12):45-50. 1994.

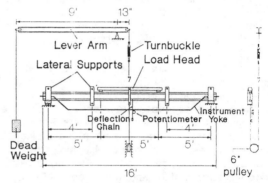

Fig. 1.    Sketch of a single loading mechanism for the long-term loading frame.

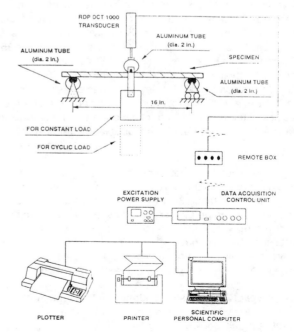

Fig. 2.    Loading protocal and data acquisition system.

245

# Measurement of Mechanical Properties of Knots in Lumber

Lei Luo
John Z. Wang
Graduate Student
Assistant Professor
Institute of Wood Research
Michigan Technological University
Houghton, MI 49931

A fundamental understanding of the effects of knots on the mechanical properties of lumber is essential for the efficient utilization of wood as a natural resource. To evaluate the effects of knots on the mechanical behavior of wood with elasticity theory, knots could be regarded as elastic inclusions in wood matrix with different mechanical properties, Eshelby's theory of an ellipsoidal inclusion [1] may be used to obtain the stress and displacement field at every location of the lumber boards. In order to conduct the theoretical analysis with this inclusion method, the mechanical properties of the knots have to be known in advance. Thus it is indispensable that experiments be carried out to determine the elastic properties of knot itself, including moduli of elasticity and Poisson's ratio.

In the experiments in this paper, knots were separated from the original lumber boards of Eastern White Pine (*Pinus Strobus L.* ), and were machined into circular disks. The moisture contents of the specimens were at about 10~12%. Ten knot specimens of circular disks with diameters around 25 mm (1 inch) and thicknesses around 5~7 mm(0.2~0.28 inches) were tested. A compressive load was applied along the diameter of the disk. A strain gage rosette (CEA-06-062UR-120) was bonded to the center of the knot with M-bond AE-10, as shown in Fig.1. After 12 hours of curing at room temperature (24°C) , leadwires were attached to the strain gages with M-line solder 361A (63-37) tin-lead solder. The resistance of each strain gage is 120.0±0.4% at room temperature. The gage factor is 2.080±0.5% and the transverse sensitivity is 0.9~1.3%. The strain gage rosette was connected to a strain indicator(P-3500) via a switch-and-balance unit (SB-10). Diametral compression load was applied on a SATEC testing machine. The locations of the three strain gages on every specimen are shown in Fig.1. At about every 22 N (5 lbs) load increment, the strain gage readings of the three strain gages were recorded respectively. The specimens had linear behavior at loads below 660 N (150 lbs).

The distance from the location of each strain gage to the center of the disk was measured. Assuming that the stress field of an anisotropic circular knot disk subjected to diametral compression can be approximated as that in an isotropic disk [2], the stresses at the location of each strain gage can be calculated . The experimental data (strain gage readings) were analyzed with linear regression method to determine the strain at the location of each strain gage, as shown in Table 1.

If the center of the knot is coincident with the center of the disk, which is the case of specimen #5, then the disk is cylindrically orthotropic, as shown in Fig.1(a) . For strain gage #1 in

Fig.1(a), $\sigma_R = \sigma_{y1}$, $\sigma_T = \sigma_{x1}$, $\epsilon_R = \epsilon_1$ . For gage #3, $\sigma_R = \sigma_{x3}$, $\sigma_T = \sigma_{y3}$ , $\epsilon_R = \epsilon_3$ . For strain gage #2 , $\sigma_R = \sigma_{-45}$ , $\sigma_T = \sigma_{45}$ , $\epsilon_R = \epsilon_2$ . For cylindrically orthotropic disk in the state of plane stress, $E_R$ and $\nu_{RT}$ can be solved as :

$$E_R = \frac{\sigma_{y1}\sigma_{y3} - \sigma_{x3}\sigma_{x1}}{\epsilon_1\sigma_{y3} - \epsilon_3\sigma_{x1}} \tag{1}$$

$$\nu_{RT} = \frac{\epsilon_3\sigma_{y1} - \epsilon_1\sigma_{x3}}{\epsilon_3\sigma_{x1} - \epsilon_1\sigma_{y3}} \tag{2}$$

For specimen #5 , $E_R$ = 1.4517 GPa (2.108 × 10$^5$ psi), $\nu_{RT}$ = 0.42. Practically, it is difficult to obtain specimens with the center of the knot exactly located at the geometric center of the disk. In this case, the strain gage rosette is bonded so that at least two of the gages were along the tangential direction of the knot, as in Fig. 1(b). $E_T$ and $\nu_{TR}$ can be solved similarly. For specimen #3, $E_T$ = 0.9324 GPa (1.354 × 10$^5$ psi), $\nu_{TR}$ = 0.25. In practice, it may be impossible to bond a strain gage rosette in such a way that at least two of the three gages were aligned along the radial or tangential directions. As in the test, except for specimen#3 and specimen #5, each of the other eight specimens has only one strain gage aligned along the radial direction. In this case, the relationship between $E_R$ and $\nu_{RT}$ can be obtained.

$$E_R\epsilon_R + \nu_{RT}\sigma_T = \sigma_R \tag{3}$$

Since the Poisson's ratio and the ratio $E_R/E_T$ in wood are relatively constant[3], the values of $\nu_{RT}$ and $E_R/E_T$ from specimen #5 & #3, together with the theoretical stresses and measured strains along the radial direction, were used to calculate the values of moduli of elasticity of the other specimens. The results are listed in Table 2.

## References

[1] Eshelby, J.D., The determination of the elastic field of an ellipsoidal inclusion, and related problems , Proceedings of Royal Society, London, Series A. 241 , pp 376-396, 1957.
[2] Frocht, M.M., Photoelasticity, Vol. II, John Wiley & Sons, Inc., pp 121-129, 1948.
[3] Bodig, J. & Goodman, J.R., Prediction of elastic parameters for wood, Wood Sci., 5(4) : 249-264,1973.

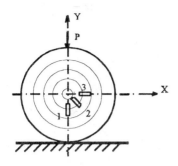

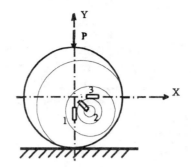

(a) material center coincident with
geometric center

(b) material center not coincident with
geometric center

Fig .1 Specimen configuration to determine elastic properties of knotwood materials

Table 1    Experimental  Strains / Applied  Load  ( με / N )

| Knot  # | 1 | 2 | 3 | 4 | 5 | 6 | 7 | 8 | 9 | 10 |
|---|---|---|---|---|---|---|---|---|---|---|
| Gage 1 | -8.96 | -6.52 | -11.6 | -15.5 | -10.4 | -11.1 | -10.5 | -8.80 | -8.53 | -11.0 |
| Gage 2 | -1.90 | 1.00 | -2.14 | 9.47 | -9.39 | 6.66 | 4.44 | 3.42 | 5.09 | -0.94 |
| Gage 3 | 2.40 | 14.9 | 3.12 | 8.79 | 5.31 | 16.5 | 11.4 | 7.63 | 9.07 | 2.84 |

Table 2 Moduli of Elasticity $E_R$ & $E_T$ Obtained from Experiments ( GPa )

| Knot # | 1 | 2 | 3 | 6 | 7 | 8 | 9 | 10 | Average |
|---|---|---|---|---|---|---|---|---|---|
| Radial Gage # | 3 | 1 | 3 | 1 | 1 | 1 | 1 | 3 | |
| $E_R$ | 2.778 | 1.885 | 1.956 | 1.358 | 1.501 | 2.005 | 2.001 | 3.068 | 2.069 |
| $E_T$ | 1.781 | 1.208 | 1.254 | 0.870 | 0.962 | 1.285 | 1.283 | 1.967 | 1.326 |

Note : $\nu_{RT} = 0.42$, $E_R/E_T = 1.56$

# Strain Measurement on Wood

Joseph R. Loferski, Associate Professor
Virginia Polytechnic Institute and State University
Department of Wood Science & Forest Products
Brooks Center - 1650 Ramble Road
Blacksburg, VA 24061-0503

Laboratory and field experiments in wood engineering often rely on transducers to measure strain. Each type of device has certain limitations and considerations which generally dictate its applicability to wood. This paper discusses some of the issues related to using traditional strain measurement devices on wood and wood-based materials, including electrical resistant strain gauges, clip gauges, and extensometers.

The objective of the paper is to identify the techniques that have been developed for measuring strain, especially on wood materials. To produce quality strain measurements on wood and wood-based materials, attention to many details is required. Because wood is non-homogeneous, hygroscopic, and isotropic, and has anatomical variability, attention to details is required which is often not necessary on isotropic, homogeneous materials. Furthermore, since wood is an electrical- and thermo-insulator, attention must be directed to heat dissipation when using some strain measurement devices. A variety of strain measuring systems are available to researchers in wood mechanics and wood engineering for application to wood and wood-based materials. The devices are extensometers, clip gauges, bonded electrical strain gauges, tell-tale gauges and full-field strain measuring systems. This paper describes the first four methods of measuring strain on wood. Other papers in these proceedings provide techniques for producing full-field strain measurements.

A novel technique for measuring micro- and macromechanical properties of individual wood fibers

Stephen M. Shaler, Laurence Mott, and Leslie H. Groom

One of the most common components in structural composites are wood fibers, with the mechanical properties of these composites dictated by the physical and mechanical properties of these natural fibers. Traditional single fiber testing and preparation protocols led to understanding of the relationships between wood cell wall microstructure and fundamental gross mechanical properties. However, single wood fiber mechanical testing has remained both a slow and frequently tedious exercise. Characterizing and quantifying the micromechanical properties of single fibers such as fracture mode has also been limited due to the nature of inherent problems in these procedures.

Rapid uniaxial fiber testing techniques have been developed by our research team and used to obtain representative pulp properties. This paper presents single fiber macromechanical properties of the most commercially important specie, loblolly pine (*Pinus taeda* L.). The tensile strength and modulus of elasticity of virgin fibers taken from positions throughout the entire tree are compared to data gathered for various recycled wood fiber types (old corrugated cardboard, old newsprint, mixed office waste, and tissue). Mechanical testing was conducted using a micromechanical testing apparatus and a miniature load cell. A unique fiber gripping assembly was developed which allowed the fiber ends to rotate freely during testing. Post-failure fiber cross-sections were obtained with the aid of a confocal laser scanning microscope. The cross-sectional areas allow us to convert the load-elongation curves obtained during tensile testing to stress-strain curves and thus obtain strength and modulus values. This procedure is shown in Figure 1.

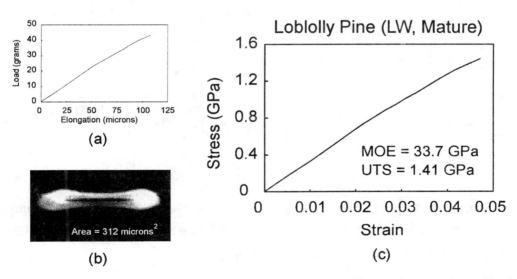

Figure 1. Sequence of data collection for determination of mechanical properties of individual wood fibers include: (a) acquisition of load-elongation data from tensile testing, (b) determination of the fiber cross-section adjacent to the failure site with a confocal laser scanning microscope, and (c) converting the load-elongation curve to a stress-strain curve.

Micromechanical properties of the wood fiber cell wall will also be reported. The availability of the environmental scanning electron microscope (ESEM) has made quantitative investigations of this type feasible. Successive, high magnification, digitally-acquired images of individual fibers under uniaxial tension in the ESEM were subject to a full-field digital image correlation algorithm. The resulting data were used to create strain maps of highly localized regions of the cell wall, such as in Figure 2 which shows longitudinal and transverse strain maps of a 'defect-free' fiber. This strain mapping technique should also prove to be quite useful in determining strain concentrations in fibers containing natural and gross processing-induced defects. The strain maps are supplemented with high resolution dynamic video tape footage of fracture behavior characteristics to specific fiber types. The use of the ESEM in conjunction with a digital-image based analysis furthers understanding of the stress/strain distribution within the cell wall.

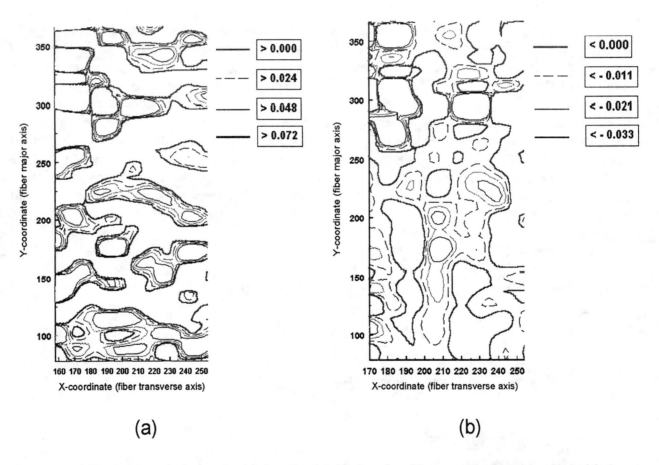

(a)                                    (b)

Figure 2. Full-field strain map of a 'defect free' loblolly pine fiber as calculated by digital image correlation. The fiber is under an applied tensile strain of 0.5%, with the corresponding strain maps referring to components (a) $\varepsilon_{yy}$, and (b) $\varepsilon_{xx}$.

# Density Determination of a Wood Particle Mat During Consolidation Using Nuclear Technology

Paul M. Winistorfer, Associate Professor
William W. Moschler, Research Associate
Wei Xu, Post-Doctoral Research Associate
Department of Forestry
B.L. Bledsoe, Professor
Department of Agricultural Engineering
The University of Tennessee, P.O. Box 1071, Knoxville, Tennessee 37901-1071

The densification of a wood composite mat during pressing ultimately influences the performance of the panel in-service. As the mat is compacted during the press cycle, a density distribution results through the thickness of the panel. This density distribution is commonly referred to as the vertical density profile. The vertical density profile is quantitatively related to important end-use properties of the panel such as bending strength, thickness swell, water absorption, and edge machining characteristics. We have quantified the role of the density profile as related to thickness swell, internal bond and water absorption characteristics of wood-based panel products (see citations below). This characterization however, is a post-press evaluation of this important phenomena. There is a growing interest in measuring this and other internal mat properties in situ, or in real-time during pressing.

We have developed a radiation-based system for monitoring the densification of wood-based mats during consolidation in a laboratory hot-press. This on-going work has been sponsored by several groups, including the National Particleboard Association, the USDA National Research Initiative Competitive Grants program (grant no. 92-37103-8082), and the Tennessee Agricultural Experiment Station.

A radiation system was developed for attachment to a 2' x 2' laboratory hot-press. The press is a single-cylinder, up-acting device that has been retrofitted with a programmable digital logic controller for control of press position, press closure rate, and press cycle parameters (velocity, acceleration). A computer is interfaced to the both the radiation-based monitoring system and the press controller for extraction of radiation counts (transmitted radiation at the detectors) and press cycle parameters (time and position).

The radiation-based monitoring system is a mechanical positioning device that translates three radioactive sources (cesium[137]) and electronic detection equipment in horizontal alignment with the up-acting bottom platen of the hydraulic press. The mechanical translation system is composed of three yokes that span the press opening distance (over the top of the press), each yoke holding a radioactive source and detector, coupled to three gear-driven transmissions that control the rate of travel of the yoke-devices relative to the initial set positions of 25%, 50% and 75% of the press opening distance at any time. We are monitoring density in three horizontal planes of the mat, at these three positions, at all times during press closure and throughout the remainder of the press cycle.

The densification of the mat is influenced by mat moisture content, press closure rate, press temperature, the nature of the furnish material and interactions of these parameters and other variables. Studying the densification of the mat during pressing is providing valuable insight into the densification mechanism and resulting influence on the panel properties. Density measurements will be presented for various laboratory studies that have examined a number of different processing parameters.

References:

Winistorfer, P.M., T.M. Young, and E. Walker. 1996. Predicting and comparing density profiles using nonparametric regression. Wood and Fiber Science 28(1):133-141.

Winistorfer, P.M. and W. Xu. 1996. Layer water absorption of medium density fiberboard and oriented strandboard. Forest Products Journal 48(6): IN PRESS.

Xu, W. and P.M. Winistorfer. 1996. A procedure to determine water absorption in wood composites. Wood and Fiber Science 27(2):119-125.

Xu, W. and P.M. Winistorfer. 1996. Fitting an equation to vertical density profile data using Fourier analysis. Holz als Roh- und Werkstoff 54(1996):57-59.

Winistorfer, P.M., W. Xu, and R. Wimmer. 1995. Application of a drill resistance technique for density profile measurement in wood composite panels. Forest Products Journal 45(6):90-93.

Xu, W. and P.M. Winistorfer. 1995. A procedure to determine thickness swell distribution in wood composite panels. Wood and Fiber Science 27(2):119-125.

Xu, W. and P.M. Winistorfer. 1995. Layer thickness swell and layer internal bond of medium density fiberboard and oriented strandboard. Forest Products Journal 45(10):67-71.

# Dynamic Model for Analysis of Periodic Circular Wood Cutting Process Stability

B. Bučar, M. Houška

University of Ljubljana, Biotechnical Faculty, Department of Wood Science and Technology,
Rožna dolina, c. VIII/34, SLO-1000 Ljubljana, Slovenia

Shown is a dynamic model of periodic circular cutting of oriented wood tissue in which both the properties of the material and the dynamic properties of the machining system have been considered. The specificity of periodic orthogonal circular cutting of wood tissue, which can be treated with a still acceptable approximation as a natural orthotropic cellular composite, is in that the load on the knife is not merely a consequence of the instantaneous material flux, but depends also on the instantaneous orientation of the wood tissue and its mechanical properties. The cutting or exciting force is the result of internal and external modulation. The internal modulation is the result of the effect of the properties of the machined material which are given by specific cutting pressure $k_S$, while the external modulation is the consequence of the varying material flux which is affected by relative displacements between the workpiece and the tool. Relative displacements, which are the consequence of the manner of excitation and dynamic properties of the machining system, are also the cause of self-excitation occurrence. As in the process of cutting, the cutting or self-exciting force depends on relative displacements between the tool and the workpiece, the dynamic model developed is non-linear. Variability of the cross-sectional area of the chip that is being formed means variable material flux at an unchanged cutting speed, and hence also a variable load on the knife or tool.

From the aspect of the manner of excitation and response of the structure of the machining system, the process of periodic circular cutting of wood tissue consists of specific periodic forced and natural oscillations which interact mutually, that is modulate the cutting force and determine the initial conditions $(x_0, \dot{x}_0, y_0, \dot{y}_0)$ of each subsequent cut and hence also the stability or instability of the cutting process. The requirements for the stationary state of the cutting process are met only in the case of time-invariable initial and final energy states of the tool between successive cuts.

Although a mechanical machining system is a distinctly dynamic system, it is sufficient for the dynamic analysis of the cutting process if we know the dynamic behaviour of the structure at the contact point between the knife and the workpiece [1]. The setting up of the dynamic model of discontinuous periodic circular cutting, which is shown in Figure 1, is based on the acceptance of the assumption that due to a sufficiently large rigidity of the workpiece clamping system we can take into account only the displacements of the structure of the tool-machining system which reflect in relative movement between the tool and the workpiece (Fig. 2). Modulation of the chip thickness $Z(\varphi)$ in the deformation area of the knife, which depends on the rotation angle $\varphi$ and on the oscillation of the tool in the X and Y directions, can be expressed in the following form

$$Z(\varphi) = X \cdot \sin(\varphi) - Y \cdot \cos(\varphi)$$

The occurrence of nonlinearity in the process of cutting is conditioned by geometric parameters of the knife and the limit kinematic conditions of cutting. By limit kinematic conditions are meant the cutting speed $v$ and the speed of oscillation of the knife $\dot{z}(t)$, which uniformly determine the direction and magnitude of instantaneous speed in the process of cutting. In the case

$$\alpha = arctg\left(\frac{\dot{z}(t)}{v}\right)$$

where $\alpha$ is tooth clearance angle, the process of cutting is non-linear [2]. Namely, there occurs additional force which is the result of the immersion of the knife into the workpiece in the normal direction with respect to the direction of cutting. In this way, the push-off or radial component of the cutting force increases independently of the cross-sectional area of the chip.

For a system with known dynamic properties $G(\omega)$ we can thus represent in-plane relative oscillatory movement between the structure of the machining system and the workpiece at the condition

$$k \cdot 2\pi + \varphi_v \le \varphi_i \le k \cdot 2\pi + \vartheta;\ k = 0, 1, 2\ldots$$

by the following two differential equations [3]

$$m_x \cdot \ddot{x} + c_x \cdot \dot{x} + k_x \cdot x = k_s\left(\varphi, h_\varphi\right) \cdot b \cdot$$

$$\cdot \left[ \frac{e_z}{2} \cdot \sin(2\varphi) - \frac{x(\varphi)}{2} \cdot \sin(2\varphi) + \right.$$

$$\left. + y(\varphi) \cdot \cos^2(\varphi) + z_{i-1}(\varphi) \right]$$

$$m_y \cdot \ddot{y} + c_y \cdot \dot{y} + k_y \cdot y = k_s\left(\varphi, h_\varphi\right) \cdot b \cdot$$

$$\cdot \left[ e_z \cdot \sin^2(\varphi) - x(\varphi) \cdot \sin^2(\varphi) + \right.$$

$$\left. + \frac{y(\varphi)}{2} \cdot \sin(2\varphi) + z_{i-1}(\varphi) \right]$$

where m, $\omega_0$, $\zeta$ are the modal mass, angular natural frequency and damping ratio, respectively.

In the case when the condition $F_R = 0$ (b = 0) is met there is no excitation and the structure of the machining system oscillates freely in the both directions. Free vibration of the structure of the machining system can essentially be described with two homogenous differential equation with constant coefficients with different initial conditions of oscillation $\left(x_0, \dot{x}_0, y_0, \dot{y}_0\right)$. The initial conditions of free vibration are conditioned by time variability of the components of the cutting force, which components differ in periodic circular cutting in most cases.

Irrespective of the anisotropy and variability of mechanical and physical properties of wood tissue, the theoretical predictions of stability estimated by running the computer simulation of the proposed dynamic model were found to be in good agreement with the measurements obtained from actual cutting tests under various technological parameters. By simulation of the represented dynamic model it is possible to analyse the process of cutting wood tissue in its entirety and it can thus serve for optimisation of the selection of tools and technological parameters of machining.

References:

[1] Minis, I.E.; Magrab, E.B.; Pandelidis, I.O. 1990: Improved methods for the prediction of chatter in turning. Part 1: Determination of structural response parameters. J. Eng. Ind. 112(2):12-20

[2] Bučar, B.; Kopač, J. 1996. Dynamic model for the determination of instability of periodic circular cutting of wood tissue. Holz Roh-Werkstoff 54 (1996) 19-25

[3] Bučar, B. 1996: Cutting force modulation in periodic circular cutting of wood tissue as self-exited system. Dissertation thesis. University of Ljubljana, Faculty for mechanical engineering, 137 pp.

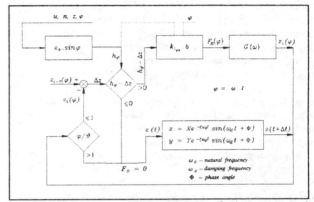

Fig. 1: Schematic representation of the assumed dynamic model of periodic discontinuous orthogonal circular cutting of wood tissue; u - feed speed (m/min), n - rotational speed (min$^{-1}$), z - number of teeth on tool, $\vartheta$ - angle at maximal radial immersion

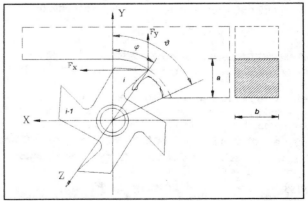

Fig. 2: Direction of oscillations of the mechanical structure of a machining system with two degrees of freedom $X$, $Y$, and modulation of the chip thickness $Z(\varphi)$

# Elastic Transverse Impact On Fixed End Beam

**DULAL GOLDAR**

Professor of Structural Engg., Department of Civil Engineering,
Delhi College of Engineering, Delhi- 110 006, INDIA.

The author [1] studied three different cases of Simply supported (s.s) beam with equal over- hang (size: 253 x 24.3 x 12.5 mm thick, urethane rubber, PSM-4) of variable spans 90, 120 and 150 mm  for central impact by a freely falling striker using dynamic photoelasticity. The beam striker mass ratio (2.675) was kept constant. The following observations were recorded: (i) Irrespective of span of the beam used, 'pressure bulb' like fringes developed during the early stage of  impact which typically occurs when a 'semi-infinite' plate is subjected to a point load normal to the boundary, and therefore, during the period when pressure bulb like fringes appeared, a 'semi-infinite' plate behaviour has been attributed to beam model. (ii) The occurrence of 'zero- order' fringe at the top boundary of the beam model is attributed to an 'elastically supported' beam behaviour. (iii) For a s.s beam with over-hang, the initial transient was generally short- lived and then followed by a quasi- static situation for the rest of the duration of impact, unlike what generally happens in exactly s.s beams without over-hangs.

An 'elastically supported' beam behaviour from the above study on s.s beam gave further impetus to study fixed end beam. Central transverse impact on a fixed end beam was analysed on the basis of beam vibrations and the mathematical solution is obtained using differential equations of vibrations and suitable boundary conditions. The present analysis is confined to impact situations where plastic flow extends only to the vicinity of the contact point and does not penetrate throughout the entire cross section. Hertz law of contact is used to take into account local indentation. The analysis does not consider rotatory inertia, internal damping and viscoelasticity.

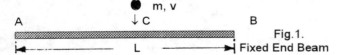

Fig.1.

Fixed End Beam

As shown in Fig.1 a fixed end beam AB of length L was impacted by a freely falling mass m with a contact velocity v at the point C. At fixed support boundary conditions were taken as (a) slope is zero i.e. $\partial w / \partial x = 0$ at x = 0 and (b) deflection is zero i.e $w = 0$ at x = 0. The equation of forced vibration [2] is given by

$$EI \partial^4 w / \partial x^4 + \rho A \partial^2 w / \partial t^2 = F(c,t).$$ The trans.-verse deflection w can be represented by,

$$w = \sum_{t=1}^{\infty} X_i < x > q_i < t >,$$ where $X_i < x >$ is one of an infinite number of terms representing the normal harmonics of the free beam vibrations, whose form is governed by the boundary conditions and quantity $q_i < t >$ is determined by substituting in the Lagrangian equation the value of kinetic energy and potential energy of the beam. The generalised expression of the deflection is given by

$$w < x,t > = \sum_{i=1}^{\infty} X_i \left[ q_o \cos \omega_i t + (\dot{q}_o / \omega) \sin \omega_i t \right] +$$

$$\frac{X_i < c >}{\rho A \omega_i \int_o^l X_i^2 \, dx} \int_0^{\bar{t}} F < \bar{\tau} > \sin \omega_i (t - \bar{\tau}) \, d\bar{\tau}$$

Since contact force pattern is not known an analytical contact force is assumed in the form: $F = B \sin \xi t$, in which B and $\xi$ are constant and are given by

$$\xi^5 = \frac{V_o k_2^2}{\ddot{A} m^2 M^2} \left[ \frac{\{M + X_1 < c >\} \xi^2 - M \omega_1^2}{\xi^2 - \omega_1^2} \right]$$

and

B = $\dfrac{V_o m M \xi (\xi^2 - \omega_1^2)}{\left[ (M + X_1 < c >^2) \xi - M \omega_1^2 \right]}$ from there

expressions for deflection and stress can be determined. In the present analysis low velocity impact (less than 2 m/s) was generated by assuming a freely falling mass at the centre of the beam.  A computer program in Turbo C++ was written for analytical study.

For comparison data was taken from reference [3] and [4] and contact force histories for fixed end beam of size 860 x 50.14 x 25.35 mm thick impacted by a mild steel striker of  30 mm diameter is shown in Fig.2. It was found that maximum contact force obtained theoretically for simply supported beam in reference [4] and that obtained in the present analysis are of the same order. There was some difference in magnitude of  contact force for contact velocity more than 2 m/s (Fig.3). From the above comparison it was observed that maximum contact force is the same irrespective of support conditions.

Using the same program contact force histories were obtained for a fixed end beam of different materials like mild steel, aluminium and PMMA of size 270 x 25 x 12.5 mm thick impacted at centre by a striker of mass 41.5 gm and diameter of 13.5 mm. A composite plot of contact forces for the above beams are shown in Fig.4 which indicates that different materials exhibits different magnitudes of maximum contact forces and its duration of contact. The author conducted experiments using a contact force transducer fabricated by him [1, 5, 6] on a simply supported beam of span 120 mm with equal over-hang (total length of the beam = 270 mm) and using striker of mass 41.5 gm and diameter 13.5 mm. The maximum contact force generated in the experiments for Aluminium and PMMA were 501.7 N and 299.3 N respectively. This indicates that for slender beam the present formulation may be satisfactory but for short beam or deep beam more rigorous analysis is required.

Using the same program deflection and stress histories were obtained at central point for a fixed end beam (860 x 50.74 x 25.35 mm) impacted at the centre by a striker of 30 mm diameter and mass 885 gm. The results obtained were comparable with the results of reference [3], and maximum deflection was 0.158 mm at time 0.629 ms and the maximum stress was 1.94 N/mm$^2$ at time 0.629 ms. The time of occurrence of maximum deflection and stress remained almost same for different striker velocities. The stress histories for the fixed end beams made of different materials like mild steel, aluminium and PMMA (size: 270 x 25 x 12.5 mm) impacted by a striker of mass 41.5 gm and diameter 13.5 mm were calculated and are shown in Fig.5. It indicates that mild steel beam exhibited maximum stress, PMMA beam developed minimum stress whereas aluminium beam indicated intermediate value. The time of occurrence of maximum stress was also different for different materials.

## ACKNOWLEDGEMENT

The author acknowledges the work done by Pawan Kumar Dewari ( graduate student of structural Engineering) in the present analytical study under the guidance of the author and grateful to the authority of Delhi College of Engineering for providing all necessary help.

## REFERENCES
1. Goldar, D., "Photoelastic Studies of Transverse Impacted Simply Supported Beams", Ph.D thesis, Panjab Unv.,Chandigarh, India, August 1981.
2. Goldsmith, Warner, "Impact" Edward Arnold Publishing Ltd. 1960.
3.Schwieger, H., "Central Deflection of a Transversely Struck Beam" J. E/M, 166- 169, April 1970.
4. Schwieger, H., "A Simple Calculation of Transverse Impact on Beams and Its Experimental Verification", J. E/M, 378- 394 November 1965.
5. Goldar, D. et al., "Development and Calibration of a Dynamic- Contact- Force Transducer" J. E/M , 187- 190, September 1984.
6. Goldar, D., "Mathematical Modelling for 'Dynamic Amplification Factor': Central Impact on Beams", 13- 19 Proc. VI Intl. Cong. on E/M, Portland, June 6- 10, 1988.

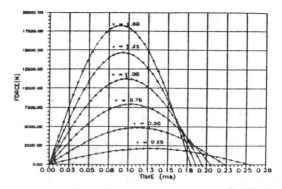

Fig.2. Contact Force Histories for Fixed End Beam for Different Striker Velocity

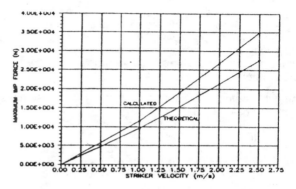

Fig.3. A Comparison between the Calculated Maximum Impact Force and Maximum Impact Force Obtained in Ref.[4]

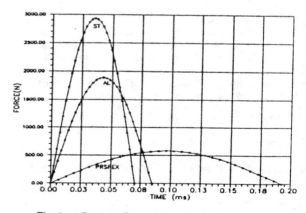

Fig.4. Contact Force Histories for Fixed End Beams of Different Materials (Size: 270x25x12.5 mm)

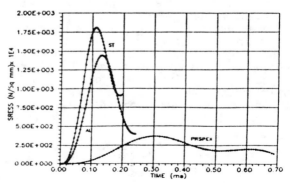

Fig.5. Central Stress Histories for Fixed End Beam of Different Materials (Size: 270x25x12.5 mm)

255

# A Self-Teach Laboratory for Multi-DOF Vibration.

Timothy Barrett-Leonard, Nathan Scott & Brian Stone
Department of Mechanical and Materials Engineering,
The University of Western Australia, NEDLANDS,
Western Australia 6907. bjs@shiralee.mech.uwa.edu.au

Work at the University of Western Australia in developing interactive learning environments for engineering related subjects has led to the development of HyperCard™ stacks for thermodynamics and dynamics. These computer packages have proven successful in areas where understanding dynamic systems is of critical concern.

As student numbers in Universities grow faster than the facilities can cope, it is clear that the impracticalities of creating real-life physical models to demonstrate motion, may be overcome by using computer simulations. Animations incorporated into HyperCard stacks seem to provide a good substitute for real-life physical situations. However, if a student *only* uses computer simulations, he or she may fail to see the imperfection of the theory and the true complexity of the real-life system.

On the subject of student laboratories Lyons[1] makes some very important observations:
- Students learn best when all their senses are involved, and laboratories use the most senses.
- Removal from the real world is dangerous for engineering students, who must know the limits of theory.
- There is no substitute for hands-on experience of real engineering objects.

As Cawley[2] shows, current student laboratory technique fails to recognise many of these criteria. This is mainly due to limited teaching-staff time. Cawley states "..the major achievements of traditional laboratory teaching are the illustration of lecture material and/or the teaching of 'technician level' experimental method such as familiarisation with standard measuring equipment and the systematic recording of observations and results." Cawley goes on to suggest that a "...major revision" of Engineering Laboratory programs is required to justify the "...very expensive, contact time between staff and small groups of students".

The short-comings of traditional laboratory teaching, the improvements in computer technology and the recognition of the importance of hands-on experience have led to the creation of the current project. The need in engineering is for laboratories that require limited student supervision but still allow interaction with real-life physical models.

This paper describes an investigation of a possible compromise solution to the need for laboratories and the limitations of staff time. If a laboratory can be so designed that it does not require an instructor but is self-contained and the student is in control then the problem of laboratories requiring too much staff time is removed. Such a student controlled laboratory would require that all the instructional material be available and readily comprehensible. The experimental rig would also have to be inherently safe and fairly easy to operate. It is possible to aim at the above objectives by using a computer to present the instructional materials and also control the experiment(s). This is then not completely "hands on" but a real experiment is conducted, the hard-ware is visible and the student does have control over some rig parameters. This paper describes the development of such a computer controlled laboratory for the teaching of multi-DOF vibration.

The rig is an adaptation of the rig used by Lyons[1] for a "Multi-purpose Vibration Teaching Laboratory." The rig consists of a 12mm thick aluminium plate mounted on 4 springs located near the corners of the plate. Three transducers triangularly placed under the plate act as both dampers and as a means of measuring the vibration. The excitation force is provided by two out-of-balance masses mounted on connecting gears and driven by an electric motor. The motor speed and transducer data are fed to a computer. For this project the exciter is set to produce a force in the vertical direction only.

The motor console can be placed in three different positions on the rig as shown in figure 1. These allow for investigation of one, two and three degree of freedom systems. Other positions are available on the plate for the motor console but are temporarily blocked for this project to stop students misplacing the motor console.

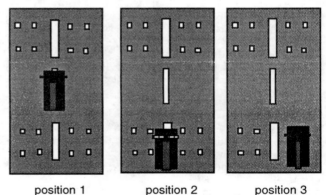

position 1        position 2        position 3

Figure 1  Three positions of the motor console.

When placing the motor console off-centre the plate "tilts" due to the weight of the motor and gear arrangement. A screw arrangement allows the user to compensate for this static deflection by adjusting the rest position of each of the position transducers. This is essential since the transducers can only measure over a range of about 10 mm, which can easily be exceeded by static deflections only.

Measurement of the bounce, pitch and roll of the plate has been achieved with use of the data from three transducers which measure vertical displacement only. To measure bounce, an average of the displacement of the three transducers was taken; to measure the pitch and roll the difference in displacement between the transducers and the physical distance between the transducers are used to get an estimate for the angular displacement. Although the rig is only excited by vertical forces, it is observed that the plate vibrates in the other primary directions as well, due to imperfect alignment of the springs and dampers. In order to measure these horizontal vibrations (slip, skid and yaw), transducers were added around the rig in the horizontal plane. Again, adjustment is needed to centre the transducers.

When the rig is excited near a natural frequency, there is a possibility that the transducers could be damaged. To prevent damage the vertical transducers are protected by alloy stoppers and the horizontal transducers by rubber stoppers.

The supervising computer is also programmed with a numerical model of the hardware, and can not only measure the performance of the actual equipment, but also a theoretical prediction based on the model. The model used is that of a rigid mass supported by 4 springs and three viscous dampers (the displacement transducers). The harmonic excitation force comes from the rotation of the out of balance masses. In practice this model can be used to represent many real life situations. Figure 2 shows the model on which the theory is based.

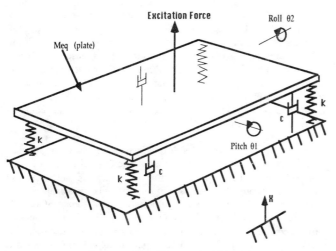

Figure 2  The Theoretical Model

Viscous damping was assumed in the theoretical model even though the damping is probably due to *friction*. This was done deliberately so that there would be some error in the predictions of the theoretical model, so that the student is alerted to the subtleties of modelling a 'real' vibrating system.

The student interacts with the rig using a computer program that runs on the supervising computer. This program allows the user to enter a desired motor-speed history graphically (see figure 3). The graph is used by the software to drive a D-to-A converter which controls the speed of the exciter motor on the rig. The *actual* speed of the motor during the experiment is measured using a high-resolution M15 encoder. A theoretical prediction of the motion can be superimposed on the measured response. The software also has another mode which allows the student to predict the natural frequencies and compare these to measured values. The experience of driving a rig and acquiring 'real' data is valuable for an early-year engineering student; the challenge of explaining why the actual response of the rig deviates from the theoretical prediction is also educational.

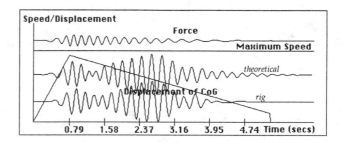

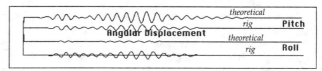

Figure 3    The appearance of the screen of the supervising computer for the two-degree-of-freedom case, showing the motor-speed history, theoretical and actual responses.

It is possible to only show a sample output, figure 3. However similar results can be obtained for both one DOF and three DOF set up. It is also possible to provide steady state excitation and also observe the transient decay when the motor is stopped. As intended the theoretical results produced by the software did not produce an ideal match with the results from the rig. This is due to assumptions in the theoretical model which did not take into account the uneven stiffness of the rig or the inherent stiffness of the transducers. The results however do demonstrate the effect of varying the physical parameters and allow identification of some of the possible errors of the theoretical model. The results also provide an insight into the modelling of multi-DOF vibration for the student engineer and ensures they are critical of the assumptions used in modelling.

In summary, the rig is designed for student use. The rig has properties built in, as with any real vibrating system, that make it difficult to model. The result is a rig that provides a method for predicting and measuring multi-DOF vibration and demonstrates the fundamental difficulties in fully predicting the behaviour of such a system. The rig may also be used for more complex vibration modelling. For example, if one of the rotating masses is removed the exciting force is a rotating force rather than in the vertical direction alone. The rig then would have to be modelled by more than three DOF.

Finally it is clear that the use of a friendly front end to a laboratory is a possible means of making the exercise far more efficient in staff time.

References:

[1]  Lyons, M., Li, X., Scott, N. and Stone, B. J., 'A Student Controlled Vibration Laboratory', Australasian Association for Engineering Education Conference, Sydney 1994. 385-388.

[2]  Cawley, P., *"Is Laboratory Teaching Effective?"*, International Journal of Mechanical Engineering Education Vol 17, No 1. 1987

# Cross-roads of Engineering Experimental Mechanics

Jerzy T. Pindera

Solid Mechanics Division, Department of Civil Engineering, University of Waterloo
Waterloo, Ontario, Canada N2L 3G1

A strange situation exists in contemporary experimental mechanics. The development of new experimental methods and techniques of stress/strain/motion analysis is impressive, [9]. The development in the general measurement science is fantastic - for example, we can reliably measure time periods in the range of femtoseconds, or the forces in the range of picoNewtons to measure the stretch of a DNA molecule. Measurement problems ceased to exist - pertinent modern theories and techniques allow performing measurements with an error less that one part in a million or in a billion. Thus, we can easily observe atoms and we do not need to speculate what happens during inelastic deformation.

However, the very carefully conducted experiments were not able to predict such catastrophic structural failures as the collapse of the Tacoma Narrows Bridge or the problems with the space shuttle. In both cases the needed theory was well known but disregarded; e. g. the theory of the aeroelastic interaction which caused the bridge collapse was an integral part of the courses on airplane design for about 10 years before the bridge was designed. Such a disregard of available knowledge is not isolated. For instance, it is known for about 60 years that stresses in notches in plates are three-dimensional [26]; that the difference between the surface stresses and the internal stresses can reach 30%; and that the thickness stresses at the crack tip are not negligible [15, 16, 22]. However, - contrary to the available analytical and experimental evidence, [6, 12, 18, 19] - the typical measurements, including the photoelastic measurements, are conducted as if no local effects existed and if the stress states in plates or beams were plane regardless of the magnitude of the gradients of the in-plane stresses. This results in significant evaluation errors. It is also well documented that the mechanical and optical responses of polymers in function of time and spectral frequency, including the ranges of the linear viscoelastic behaviour, are not simply coupled [14, 20], but this fact is also ignored. The known dependence of the path of the energy flow on the density gradients, which is extensively used in scientific research, is ignored in theories of engineering experimentation despite the fact that if may contribute up to 40% of the total observed effect [4, 7, 20, 21]. In all analytical models of the elastic-plastic deformations it is customary to neglect the inherently coupled thermodynamic responses within the elastic and plastic ranges; this results in errors of unknown magnitude, [14, 17, 20, 27]. It is still customary to neglect the influence of the measurement systems on the experimentally determined quantities, so the response of the system "machine-specimen" is often understood as the actual response of the tested material; this results in misunderstanding of the obtained data and in introduction of such artifacts as the "elastic hysteresis" as legitimate physical quantities [2, 16]. A strange belief exists that an analytical solution could be rigorous with respect to the physical problem under consideration, or that an experiments yields always correct results, so the theoretical framework of an experiment is neither discussed nor given. Such facts appear to justify the statement that "half or more of the numerical data published by (engineering) scientists in their journal articles are unusable because there is no evidence that the researcher actually measured what he thought he was measuring, and no evidence that the possible sources of errors were eliminated or accounted for", [3]. Evidently, influence of the prevailing paradigm is strong in engineering mechanics, including the traditional format of engineering research, [11].

On the other hand, the rapid expansion of the goals, scope and depth of modern engineering and the interaction with scientists and mathematicians has also altered the field of engineering experimental mechanics, EM. This process leads to an understanding of the developing EM as inherently intertwined with analytical and numerical mechanics, with physics, materials science, information theory, electronic data processing and evaluation, etc [13,14]. As one of the consequences, the traditional distinction between scientists who produce knowledge and engineers who apply this knowledge to solve technological tasks is becoming blurred. Thus, a typical theoretical task such as search for the mechanism of observed phenomena -, e.g., "Why gases dissolve in liquids" - is becoming also engineering tasks when the answer for a typical engineering question "How gases dissolve in liquids" is insufficient for a rational optimization of a design. Evidently, the goal is to make quantitative predictions of solubility of real systems from first principles ( thermodynamics, statistical mechanics, molecular first principles, etc.). Thus, a new trend has developed which could be called Advanced Experimental Mechanics or AEM.

Summarizing, two distinct trends emerged in the EM during the last decades. The first one is the continuation of the conventional engineering approach based on a set of rather intuitively accepted and not necessarily compatible physical or mathematical models, [25]. The second one, AEM, follows the patterns of development of reliable scientific theories, so succinctly presented in the form "Guess - compute consequences - compare with experiment. If it disagrees with experiment, it is wrong," [5]. With regard to applied mechanics this definition supports the known statement that the "Experimental and analytical mechanics depend on each other and the one discipline cannot exist without the other. Therefore, the often encountered competition and conflict between them is only destructive" [13].

The above mentioned notions of "guess" and "experiments" are differently understood in the traditional EM and in the developing AEM, because of the different prevailing paradigms [11]. The differences at the theoretical level and the practical consequences are serious. In the traditional, phenomenological , or intuitive, approach the basic relations are often accepted intuitively, as a separate entity, and the physical and mathematical simplifications are not justified; in this approach the measured and evaluated results of an experiment are always correct when the accuracy of measurements is satisfactory. As a results, the basic theoretical relations may violate some scientific principles, as the equilibrum principle or the principle of energy conserrvation, and the values of modulus of elasticity may depend on the loading conditions. In the physical approach the demarcation line between a metaphysical theory and a physical theory is testability, [23]. The physical-scientific approach is based on the notions of physical models of selected aspects of reality which are rationally simplified to mathematical models and finanaly represented by manageable analytical relations; the reality is understood as perceived reality represented by a system of not refuted physical and mathematical models, [1, 8, 14, 16, 17, 20]. Thus, in the development of a theory the term "guess" is understood as a partly speculative activity within the constraints imposed by the principle of correspondence, [10]. In the physical-scientific approach a theory can never be empirically verified, but can be empiricall refuted or falsified, [23]. In this framework a development of a theory is a rational deductive process which does not allow any violation of the basic, nonrefuted theories, and which results in development of analytical solutions, or models, which are physically admissible, [23]; e.g., the energy and power must be finite. Also the term "experiment" is clearly defined within the physical approach. Specifically, the results of an experiment are meaningless when no information is given on the theory of the experiment and no proof is given that the technique of experiment satisfied theoretical requirements. Shortly: " no theory - no experiment".

Summarizing, the physical-theoretical approach is not only elegant and intellectually pleasing approach, but it is also very practical. It is needed by the the modern engineering to efficiently solve the interrelated technological - societal-economic tasks, such as the new concept of the product realization process, where a product's design, development and manufacture are dictated by its life cycle; such tasks require that the responses of materials in given conditions are known, that the residual and load-induced stresses are reliably determined, that the local effects are considered, that the stress redistributions during the service life are reliably predicted, etc.

Consequently, it could be accepted as an axiom, that in modern engineering design - which must be reliable, safe and cost-effective - nothing is more practical than a reliable theory based on reliable and pertinent physical model, provided that the efficacy and limitations of the constructed model and subsequently constructed theory are well understood and properly tested. In this formulation the notion of a "theory" denotes a physical theory which is compatible with all not refuted theories; and the notion of "testing" denotes the actual physical experiment performed according to requirements of the pertinent physical theory of experiment. Thus, the major task of Advanced Experimental Mechanics is to test the reliability and acceptable ranges of applicability of analytical and numerical procedures used in engineering design. The criterion for a rational choice of direction at the present cross-roads of the phenomenological and physical trends in engineering research is: " If it disagrees with an experiment which is based on a theoretically correct physical model it is wrong." Incidentally, this is also a solution to the problem how to deal with the huge number of the presently published papers - the demarcation line is the theoretical reliability of the underlying physical models. However, a departure from the traditional oversimplifications and acceptance of the physical reality as represented by a system of tested and not refuted analytical relations, together with a proper understanding of the contemporary trends of societal development, requires suitable essential changes in engineering curricula , [24]. Experience shows that the more demanding engineering curricula, both intellectually and scientifically, would assure that the new generations of engineers would develop the needed attitude of open minded, dedicated and efficient modern Renaissance men [16].

References

[1] Brillouin, L., Scientific Uncertainty and Information, Academic Press, New York, 1964.

[2] Dean, R. C., "Truth in Publication", Trans. of the ASME, Journal of Fluid Engineering 99 (2), 1977, p.270.

[3] Doeblin, E. O., Measurement Systems. Application and Design. McGraw-Hill Book Co., New York, 1983.

[4] Faris, G. W. and Byer, R. L., "Quantitative Three-dimensional Optical Tomographic Imaging of Supersonic Flow", Science 238, 1987 pp 1700-1702.

[5] Feynman, R., The Character of Physical Law, The MIT Press, Cambridge, Massachusetts, 1993.

[6] Gerberich, W.," Stress Distribution About a Slowly Growing Crack Determined by the Photoelastic Coating Method", Technical Report No. 32-208, Jet Propulsion Laboratory, CIT, Pasadena, 1962, pp 1-24.

[7] Hecker, F. W., Pindera, J. T. and Wen ,B.., "Actual Light Deflections in Regions of Crack Tips and Their Influence on Measurements in Photomechanics", Optics and Lasers in Engineering, 22, 1995, pp 325-345.

[8] Kac, Mark, "Some Mathematical Models in Science", Science 166, 1969, pp 469-474.

[9] Kobayashi, A. S. (Ed), Handbook on Experimental Mechanics, Second Revised Edition, Society for Experimental Mechanics and VCH Publishers, New York, 1993.

[10] Krajewski, W., Correspondence Principle and Growth of Science, D. Reidel Publishing Company, Dordrecht, 1977.

[11] Kuhn, T. S., The Structure of Scientific Revolution, University of Chicago Press, Chicago, 1962, 1970.

[12] Ladevèse, P. (Ed), Local Effects in the Analysis of Structure, Elsevier, New York, 1985.

[13] Leipholz, H. H. E., "On the Role of Analysis in Mechanics", Trans. of the CSME, 7 (1) 1983, pp. 3-7.

[14] Pindera, T. T., "Foundations of Experimental Mechanics: Principles of Modelling, Observation and Experimentation", In: J. T. Pindera (Ed), New Physical Trends in Experimental Mechanics, International. Centre for Mechanical Sciences, Springer-Verlag, Wien, 1981, pp 188-236.

[15] Pindera, J. T. and Krasnowski, B. R., "Determination of Stress Intensity Factors in Thin and Thick Plates using Isodyne Photoelasticity" in: L. A. Simpson (Ed), Fracture Problems and Solutions in the Energy Industry, Pergamon Press, 1982, pp 147-156.

[16] Pindera, J. T., "Advanced Experimental Mechanics in Modern Engineering Science and Technology", Transactions of the CSME, 11 (3), 1987, pp 125-138.

[17] Pindera, J. T., "Advanced Experimental Mechanics and its Components: Theoretical, Physical, Analytical and Social Aspects", in: A. P. S. Selvadurai (Ed), Developments in Engineering Mechanics, Elsevier, Amsterdam-New York, 1987, pp 367-414.

[18] Pindera, M.-J., Pindera, J. T. and Ji, X., "Three-dimensional Effects in Beams - Isodyne Assessment of a Plane Solution, Experimental Mechanics, 29 (1), 1989, pp 23-31.

[19] Pindera, J. T., "Local Effects and Defect Criticality in Homogeneous and Laminated Structures", Trans. ASME, J. Pressure Vessel Technology, 111, 1989, pp 136-150.

[20] Pindera, J. T. and Pindera, M.-J., Isodyne Stress Analysis, Kluwer Academic Publishers, Dordrecht, 1989.

[21] Pindera, J. T., Hecker, F. W. and Wen, B., "Testing theoretical bases of caustic methods in fracture mechanics and stress analysis", Theoretical and Applied Fracture Mechanics, 15, 1991, pp 11-33.

[22] Pindera, J. T. And Liu, X., "On the Actual Three-dimensional Stresses in Notches and Cracks", Composites Engineering 1 (1) 1992, pp 281-301.

[23] Popper, K. R., The Logic of Scientific Discovery, Harper and Row, New York, 1968.

[24] Sherbourne, A. N., "Basic Sciences in Civil Engineering", Presented at the 1992 Annual Conf. of the CSCE, May, 1992.

[25] Sokolnikoff, I. S., Mathematical Theory of Elasticity, McGraw-Hill, New York, 1956.

[26] Thum, A. et all, "Verformung, Spannung und Kerbwirkung (Deformation, Stress and Notch Action), VDI-Verlag, Düsseldorf, 1960.

[27] Zehnder, A. T., "On the temperature distribution at the vicinity of dynamically propagating cracks in 4340 Steel", J. Mech. Phys. Solids, 39, 1991, pp 385-415.

# Numerical Phase Shifting Technique for Fringe Pattern Analysis in Real Time Investigation

Fabrice Brémand
Université de Poitiers
Laboratoire de Mécanique des Solides
Boulevard 3,  Téléport 2,  B.P. 179
86960 Futuroscope CEDEX

Phase shifting method for numerical fringe pattern analysis is a powerful tool in the photomechanical field. Usually the phase, containing the mechanical information, is determined from several shifted images of the same state. These phase shifts can be performed by several ways depending on the method, for example by moving a mirror as in interferometry, by translating a grating as in projection moiré. Consequently, practical real time applications are not allowed. We propose a way to numerically shift the phase from the recording of only one image of the fringe pattern. Finally, a moiré application is presented.

Let us remind the classical phase shifting technique. At least three images of the same fringe pattern should be recorded with a C.C.D. camera with a known phase shift. Then the mechanical parameter of interest is given by the phase $\phi$ of the image [1] :

$$\tan\phi = \frac{(I_3 - I_2) + (I_1 - I_3)\cos\phi_{21} + (I_2 - I_1)\cos\phi_{31}}{(I_2 - I_3)\sin\phi_{21} + (I_2 - I_1)\sin\phi_{31}} \tag{1}$$

where $I_i$ (i=1,2,3) are the gray level in a point (x,y) of the image i and $\phi_{21}$, $\phi_{31}$ are the known phase shifts between the three images.

The relation (1) has the big advantage to be insensitive to the local noise of the images. Let us consider, in a first time, a one dimension signal $I_1(x)$ of the form (it is often the case in the photomechanical field) :

$$I_1(x) = e(x)(a + b\cos(\phi(x))) \tag{2}$$

Where e(x) is the incident light intensity, a is the average and b is the amplitude of the cosine signal. To solve the problem, we need to know e(x), and we assume a and b are independent of the point; then it is possible to determine $\phi(x)$ by an inverse cosine function. This leads to a wrapped phase which is not very easy to unwrapped. Our solution consists to numerically shift the fringes to get three signals leading to the use of equation (1). This can be achieved by a derivative operation.

But a quadrature filtering on equation (2) does not give a good phase shifting due to the presence of e(x). The solution consists in dividing (2) by e(x) to get a new initial signal $i_1(x)$ such as :

$$i_1(x) = I_1(x)/e(x) = a + b\cos(\phi(x)) \tag{3}$$

Now a and b can be evaluated by statistical data given from an histogram. The light intensity e(x) should be recorded when there is no fringe and is used to define the shape of the object. The first derivative of $i_1(x)$ gives

$$I_2(x) = b\phi'(x)\sin(\phi(x)) = b\phi'(x)\cos(\phi(x) - \pi/2) \tag{4}$$

$$I_3(x) = -I_2(x) \tag{5}$$

Let us assume that $\phi'(x)$ is close to a constant, then one can obtain two new signals $i_2(x)$ and $i_3(x)$ by adding the average a and by transforming the contrast b in using the standard deviation. Finally we get three phase shift signals $i_1(x)$ and $i_2(x)$, $i_3(x)$ given by :

$$i_2(x) = a + b\cos(\phi(x) - \pi/2) \tag{6}$$

$$i_3(x) = a + b\cos(\phi(x) + \pi/2) \tag{7}$$

Numerically, the quadrature filtering operation is made by a local convolution with two filters (Fig. 1), but in two dimensions the problem is more complicated because we should shift fringes normally to their direction. The choice of both filters can be automatically made prior each analysis by a FFT on each image.

| Fringe direction | filter (+$\pi$/2) | filter (-$\pi$/2) |
|---|---|---|
|  | -1  0  1<br>0  0  0<br>-1  0  1 | 1  0  -1<br>0  0  0<br>1  0  -1 |
| | -1  0  -1<br>0  0  0<br>1  0  1 | 1  0  1<br>0  0  0<br>-1  0  -1 |
|  | 0  -1  0<br>-1  0  1<br>0  1  0 | 0  1  0<br>1  0  -1<br>0  -1  0 |
|  | 0  1  0<br>-1  0  1<br>0  -1  0 | 0  -1  0<br>1  0  -1<br>0  -1  0 |

Fig. 1 : The different two dimension quadrature filters

We have assumed $\phi'(x)$ is closed to a constant, this means that the fringe order should be strictly increasing or decreasing. Consequently the fringes should almost have the same direction with the same pitch. A complete study on the variation of $\phi'(x)$ can be found in [2].

Nevertheless, several experimental techniques are concerned : moiré, fringe projection... The example shown on figure 2 represents the horizontal component determination of the displacement field for a disk submitted to a diametrical compression in a classical moiré analysis (reference line frequency : 40 lines/mm).

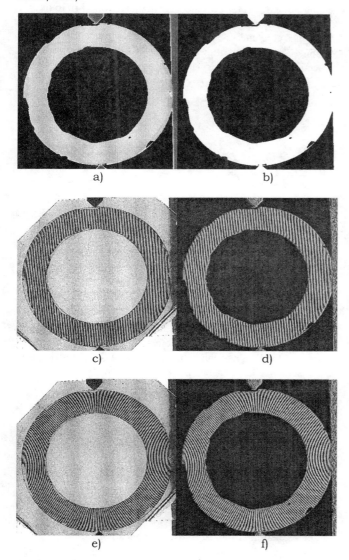

Fig. 2 : Classical moiré fringe for the horizontal displacement component of a disk under diametrical compression. : a) initial light intensity e(x), b) mask of the object, c) non deformed fringe pattern $I_1(x)$, d) numerical phase shift $i_2(x)$ of fig. 2c, e) deformed fringe pattern, f) numerical phase shift ($-\pi/2$) of fig. 2e,

On figure 2e, one can remark that the fringe spacing is not constant, therefore the filtering operation gives us a sufficiently good phase shift allowing the use of equation (1). Then a phase unwrapping algorithm is used to restore the continuity of the phase [3] By comparing the two phase fields given by the initial and the loaded states, one can obtain the displacement values (Fig. 3).

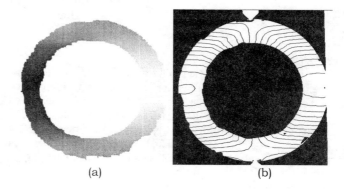

(a)                                    (b)

Fig. 3 : Horizontal components of the displacement field (a) is a representation in gray level : white is 0.633 mm and black is -0.611 mm, (b) is a representation in level line (0.05 mm between lines).

On this example, the phase is obtained with 20° of errors, corresponding to an accuracy on the displacement equal to 0.002 mm.

In conclusion we have shown the possibility to numerically analyze a fringe pattern from only one image. This technique can be only used if the fringe order is strictly increasing for example as in classical interferometry or in moiré technique. Because of no physical phase shift is required, it is now possible to store the images of the fringe pattern in real time during the test. The numerical analysis can be made later. The phase shifting procedure is made by convolution with a special filtering operation using the first derivative of the image. For that the local fringe orientation is needed and is given by the FFT of the image.

REFERENCES :

[1] Dandliker R., Thalmann R. "Heterodyne and quasi-heterodyne holographic interferometry" Opt. Eng., Vol. 24, n°5, pp 824-831, 1985.

[2] Chevallier E. "Contribution au quasi-hétérodynage à une image dans l'analyse de réseaux de franges pour des applications temps réel" DEA de Mécanique, University of Poitiers. 1995.

[3] Brémand F. "A phase unwrapping technique for object relief determination" Optics and lasers in engineering, vol.21, n°1, pp 49-60, 1994.

# Planar Surface Reconstruction using Soliton Wavelet and Structured Light

**William F. Ranson, III  and David N. Rocheleau**
Department of Mechanical Engineering
University of South Carolina
Columbia, SC

## ABSTRACT

A method is presented for finding the spatial position and orientation of a planar surface using structured light. The purpose of the work is to provide the foundation for mapping regular and irregular surfaces for use in spatial surface reconstruction. The results of this work will lead to applications in the evaluation of pre- and post-surface deformation, and the reconstruction and representation of higher ordered surfaces. The latter having application as an alternative approach for capturing surfaces in direct geometric terms as opposed to the copious data discretization methods employed in surface reconstruction today.

## APPROACH

The approach proceeds in three steps. First, structured light conditioned in the form of circular rings is projected onto a planar surface inclined in space. The circles undergo a deformation following the rules of projective space geometry, resulting in the image of ellipses on the inclined plane. Next, the edge of a single ellipse is captured using a two-dimensional edge detection technique using the soliton wavelet.

The final step is completed as follows. Knowing the size and position of the original circle and using the edge detected ellipse, a triangulation technique is used to identify the space coordinates of the major and minor axes of the ellipse. Using this information, the space coordinates of the plane are determined. The equation of the plane leads directly to the roll, pitch, and depth translation of the inclined plane.

## PROJECTION OF STRUCTURED LIGHT

A laser light source projects a structured light pattern in the form of circular rings. Each circular ring is a central projection of a cone of laser light. When a plane intersects the cone of light the projected image on the plane is a conic section. The projected conic sections are restricted to a circle or an ellipse for this work, as opposed to a hyperbola or parabola. Figure 1 shows the top view of the central projection of the laser light source.

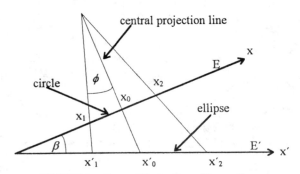

FIGURE 1 - Central Projection of Laser Source

The fan half-angle of the light is $\phi$. The E-plane intersects the cone normal to the central projection line forming a circle conic section. Plane E' intersects the cone at an angle $90°-\beta$ to form an ellipse conic section. The central projection line intersects the two planes at $x_0$ and $x_0'$, with the side intersections denoted by $x_1$, $x_2$, and $x_1'$, $x_2'$. Accounting for the fan $\phi$ half-angle in the central projection the coordinate transformations are:

$$x_1' = \frac{x_1}{\cos\beta + \tan\phi\,\sin\beta} \tag{1a}$$

$$x_0' = \frac{x_0}{\cos\beta} \tag{1b}$$

$$x_2' = \frac{x_2}{\cos\beta - \tan\phi\,\sin\beta} \tag{1c}$$

The angle $\beta$ can be found using (1a-c) and the difference equations for the E-plane coordinates; i.e., $(x_0-x_1) = (x_2-x_0)$.

$$\beta = \tan^{-1}\left[\frac{\left(x_2' - x_0'\right) - \left(x_0' - x_1'\right)}{\left(x_2' - x_1'\right)\tan\phi}\right] \tag{2}$$

It is interesting to note the (2) is independent of the circle conic section coordinates $x_0$, $x_1$, $x_2$; therefore, as long as $\phi$ is known, the angle $\beta$ of the E'-plane can be found. If the E'-plane undergoes a D-translation, the translation can be found by knowing the original $(x_0-x_1)$ distance and the angle $\beta$ found in (2).

$$D = \frac{\left(x_0' - x_1'\right) + \left(x_0 - x_1\right)\left[\sin\beta\tan(\phi-\beta) - \cos\beta\right]}{\cos\beta\tan(\phi-\beta) + \sin\beta} \tag{3}$$

## EDGE DETECTION USING SOLITON WAVELET

In previous work [1,2] the analytical wavelet function, based on the soliton phenomenon as applied to edge detection, has been shown to be an optimal wavelet for detecting a step edge; and therefore, performs very well in this application.

The wavelet function $g^j(x,y)$ used for edge detection is given in reference [2] where j denotes the different resolutions of the wavelet. The steps for the two-dimensional edge detection are as follows:

1. Get the profile of $g^j(x,y)$.
2. Convolve the digital image with the discrete function of $g^j(x,y)$—first in the x-direction, then in the y-direction.

3. Search for zero crossings in the two convolutions performed in step 2. The location of zero crossings indicate edges in the original signal.

Often when the plane is rotated the edges of the projected image as viewed by the camera become blurred. The wavelet operator even in the presence of this slight blurring identifies the midsection of the circle or ellipse boundary quite nicely.

## TRIANGULATION OF PROJECTION

A general geometric model for triangulation [3] is used in this work. A calibration plane is used to determine the central length projection of the laser, L and its fan half-angle, $\phi$ ; the camera distance, C and its focal length, F; and the angle between the laser source and the camera detector, $\theta$. Calibration is performed using the central point of the projection as a known reference point to the plane, $z_{ref}$. Its corresponding point on the image plane is $x_{ref\_i}$. ($y_{ref\_i} = 0$ because $y_s = 0$). Looking at another central image point, $x_{0i}$ compared to $x_{ref\_i}$, and denoting $\Delta x_{0i} = x_{0i} - x_{ref\_i}$, its coordinates in the camera coordinate system are:

$$z_0 = \frac{z_{ref}}{1 + \frac{\Delta x_{0i} z_{ref}}{F(x_s + z_s \tan\theta)}} \tag{4}$$

$$x_0 = x_s - (z_0 - z_s)\tan\theta \tag{5}$$

Knowing the $\phi$ fan half-angle of the laser, the coordinates of a point to the left $(x_1, z_1)$ and to the right $(x_2, z_2)$ of $(x_0, z_0)$ can be found. The left $(x_1, z_1)$ coordinates have a $\tan(\theta - \phi)$ term; the right $(x_2, z_2)$, a $\tan(\theta + \phi)$.

$$z_1 = \frac{z_{ref}\left(x_s + z_s \tan(\theta - \phi)\right)}{\left(x_s + z_s \tan\theta\right) + z_{ref}\left(\frac{\Delta x_{1i}}{F} - \tan\theta + \tan(\theta - \phi)\right)} \tag{6}$$

$$x_1 = x_s - (z_1 - z_s)\tan(\theta - \phi) \tag{7}$$

For the y-direction the projection of the laser length is used to determine the y-coordinates of points above and below the central projection, where $\tan\phi_{proj} = \tan\phi/\cos\theta$. Coordinates $(y_3, z_3)$ are above the x-axis, and $(y_4, z_4)$ are below.

$$z_3 = \frac{F z_s \tan\phi_{proj}}{F \tan\phi_{proj} - y_{3i}} \qquad y_3 = z_3 \frac{y_{3i}}{F} \tag{8,9}$$

## ORIENTATION OF PLANE

Triangulation is used to determine the camera coordinates of the x- and y-diametral axes of the ellipse. Equation (2) can be used to determine $\beta$ with the minor axis of the ellipse as the axis of rotation. Another approach is to use Plücker [4] line coordinates of the diametral axes to determine the plane in camera coordinates. If the Plücker line coordinates for these axes are ($\underline{S}_1 ; \underline{S}_{01}$) and ($\underline{S}_2 ; \underline{S}_{02}$) the plane equation is

$$\underline{r} \cdot \underline{S}_1 \times \underline{S}_2 = \underline{S}_{01} \cdot \underline{S}_2 = -\underline{S}_{02} \cdot \underline{S}_1 \tag{10}$$

The plane normal $\underline{S}_1 \times \underline{S}_2$ can be rotated into the original z-axis of the plane using a quaternion rotation [5]. The quaternion q = {d, [a, b, c]} = d + a $\underline{i}$ + b $\underline{j}$ + c $\underline{k}$ can be converted to respective rotations about the x, y, and z axes to determine the orientation of the plane.

## EXPERIMENTAL RESULTS

Experiments testing the theory put forth in this paper were performed. The experimental apparatus consisted of a laser light projected at a plane and a camera capturing the image of the laser light on the plane. The laser was mounted on a translation table in order to determine its original distance, L to the plane and also to determine the $\phi$ fan half-angles of the rings of projected light. The camera was mounted to a translation table to determine its original distance, C to the plane and its focal length, F. The camera-laser orientation angle, $\theta$ was measured as accurately as possible. Nine tests were run and are reported below.

| | X-rotation | | Y-rotation | | Z-rotation | |
|---|---|---|---|---|---|---|
| | Actual | Calc | Actual | Calc | Actual | Calc |
| 1 | 0 | **0** | 63° | **61.8°** | 0 | **0** |
| 2 | 0 | **0** | 50° | **47.9°** | 0 | **0** |
| 3 | 0 | **0** | 40° | **38.3°** | 0 | **0** |
| 4 | 45.5° | **45.8°** | 0 | **0** | 0 | **0** |
| 5 | 55° | **52.4°** | 0 | **0** | 0 | **0** |
| 6 | 65° | **60.4°** | 0 | **0** | 0 | **0** |
| 7 | 25° | **25.4°** | 11° | **9.9°** | 0 | **2.2°** |
| 8 | 15° | **16.1°** | 21° | **20.2°** | 0 | **2.9°** |
| 9 | 25° | **25.3°** | -9° | **-8.1°** | 0 | **-1.8°** |

In tests 1-6 pure rotations about a single axis were performed and equation (2) was used to calculate the single rotation angle. In tests 7-9 a quaternion rotation approach using equation (10) was used to back out the three rotation angles.

## CONCLUSION

This work establishes the basis of further work in the field of surface reconstruction where progressively more and more complex surfaces will be reconstructed using structured light and edge detection with the $\Psi$-transform. Good results are expected based on the accuracy, obtained at multi-resolutions if necessary, of the soliton wavelet edge detection technique; and, the invariant nature of how any algebraic manifold—defined by a single or several equations—is transformed to a like manifold under a projective transformation. This last statement leads us to believe that the work will have direct transitional application to the evaluation of surfaces of higher order.

## REFERENCES

[1] Ranson, W.F. and Vachon, R.I., "Wavelet Based Strain Measurement Applications in Optical Stress Analysis," Proceedings of SEM Conference on Experimental Mechanics, pp 894-897, Spring 1995.

[2] Chen, R., "Two Dimensional Edge Detection of Images Using Wavelet Analysis," Masters Thesis, University of South Carolina, May 1996.

[3] Jalkio, J.A., Kim, R.C., and Case, S.K., "Three dimensional inspection using multistripe structured light," Optical Engineering, Vol. 24 No. 6, pp 966-974, Nov/Dec 1985.

[4] Hunt, K.H., Kinematic Geometry of Mechanisms, Oxford University Press, Oxford, UK, 1978.

[5] Rocheleau, D.N., "Assembly Modeling of Spatial Mechanisms using Geometric Constraints," Ph.D. Dissertation, University of Florida, May 1992.

# Investigation on Displacements due to Normal and Tangential Loads on a Finite Width Bar

**M. Ciavarella, G. Demelio, W.M. Sun, B. Trentadue**
Dipartimento di Progettazione e Produzione Industriale
Politecnico di Bari  - Viale Japigia, 182 - 70126  BARI - ITALY

## INTRODUCTION

Contact problems are encountered in many different engineering applications. An important way to access the contact resistance of materials is the fretting-fatigue test [1], recently applied to ceramic materials [2]. A schematic view of the typical configuration of this test is shown in Fig. 1A. In general the thickness of the bar is assumed to be much greater than the contact semi-width, so that each body can be approximated as a half-plane. Analytical solutions for the half-plane loaded by line contact forces are available [3]. Recently Nowell and Hills [1] provided numerical extensions of these solutions if a bulk tension acts on the half-plane. Other studies [4,5,6] discuss the effect of finite thickness of the bar on the traction due to normal or combined loads applied by a punch of the same material. The above studies do not solve completely the problem of the fretting fatigue tests, where the stress field on the bar depends on how the equilibrium is achieved. Because of significant frictional stresses the problem assumes an incremental character, even in the normal load case. Numerical solution of this type of problems is wrought with a certain degree of uncertainty in defining geometrical constraints and convergence of the procedure.

## EXPERIMENTAL

Amongst the experimental techniques, the classical moirè interferometry [7] is chosen in order to determine displacement fields resulting from a localized contact. This well known technique gives a direct measure of the in-plane displacement field, with a high sensitivity ($1/2f_s$ if $f_s$ is the frequency of the grating) and an excellent contrast. Using an application of it, the super-moirè method [8], frictional contact problems have been already approached by the authors in [9,10].

The problem of a bar clamped between two cylinders and pulled from one extremity is studied. The normal load is 350 N (contact area of ~10 mm), the tangential load 60 N in order to be near to the sliding limit ($\mu$=0.2). Tab.1 shows the dimensions of the specimens (see symbols in Fig. 1B). Gratings with sensitivity 0.5$\mu$m (=$1/2f_s$) are replicated on the specimens. Real time images are taken by a CCD camera and treated with a PC image processing system, as discussed in a previous study [10].

## RESULTS

The displacement fields due to the normal load were firstly analyzed. For the "half-plane" specimen, the Ux(N) field on the surface (Fig. 2A) agrees well with the analytical solution, whereas for the specimens "1" and "2" (Fig. 2B and 2C) a tensile area (i.e. $\varepsilon_x$ >0) is found at the end of the contact (Fig. 3A).
The displacement fields due to tangential load and the extent of the adhesive contact area is then obtained by means of digital image processing [13]. Some results are shown in Fig. 3B.

## CONCLUSIONS

The fretting-fatigue line contact test introduces unexpected tensile stresses in thin specimens eventually responsible, for brittle materials, of a crack propagation different from the one reported in [2]. The experimental technique has shown to be suitable for the study of this kind of problems.

## REFERENCES

[1] Nowell D, Hills DA, "Mechanics of fretting fatigue testing", *Int. J. Mech. Sci.*,vol.29, No.5, 1987.
[2] Okane M, Satoh T, Mutoh Y, Suzuki S, "Effect of relative slip amplitude on fretting fatigue behaviour of silicon nitride", JSME, A, 39, 1, 1996.
[3] Smith J O, Liu C K, "Stress due to tangential and normal loads on an elastic solid", *Trans ASME, Series E, J. Appl. Mech.*, vol 20, 1953.
[4] Bentall RH, Johnson KL, "An elastic strip in plane rolling contact, *Int. J. Mech. Sci.*, 1968, vol.10.
[5] Keer LM, Farris TN, "Effect of finite thickness and tangential loading on development of zones of microslip in fretting", *ASLE Transaction*, vol.30, 2, 1987,.
[6] Nowell D, Hills DA, "Contact problems incorporating elastic layers", *Int. J. Solids and Struct.*, 1988, V. 1.
[7] Post D, "Moirè Interferometry: Advances and Application", *Experimental Mechanics*, 31(3), 199.
[8] Demelio G, Pappalettere C, Sun WM, Trentadue B, "Experimental stress analysys for contact problems with friction by means of Moirè-interferometry"; Photomécanique 95, Cachan, Paris 14-15-16 Mars 1995.
[9] Ciavarella M, Demelio G, Trentadue B, Sun WH, "Studio sperimentale delle tensioni in problemi di contatto con attrito per mezzo della moirè-interferometria", XXIII Convegno AIAS , 1994.
[10] Trentadue B, Sun WM, Pappalettere C, "Study of a super-moirè interferometry by means of an image processing program", ÖIAZ Journal, Sept. 1995.

| specimen | h [mm] | l [mm] | s [mm] | R [mm] |
|---|---|---|---|---|
| 1 | 20 | 170 | 10 | - |
| 2 | 10 | 170 | 10 | - |
| half-plane | 250 | 280 | 10 | - |
| disk | - | - | 10 | 135 |

Tab. 1 - Main specimen dimensions (see Fig.1B).

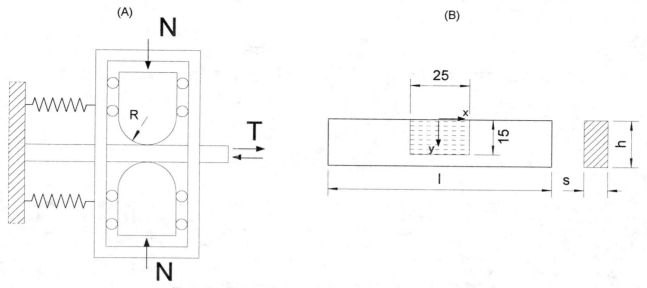

Fig.1- Contact configuration (A) and specimens (B).

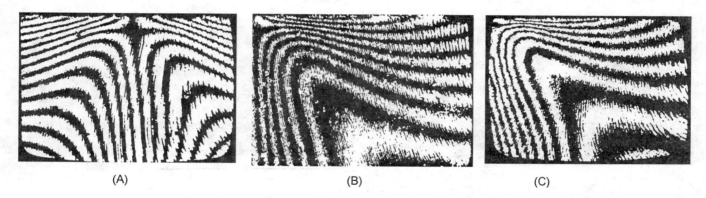

Fig.2- Ux(N) field: (A) half-plane, (B,C) specimen 1,2

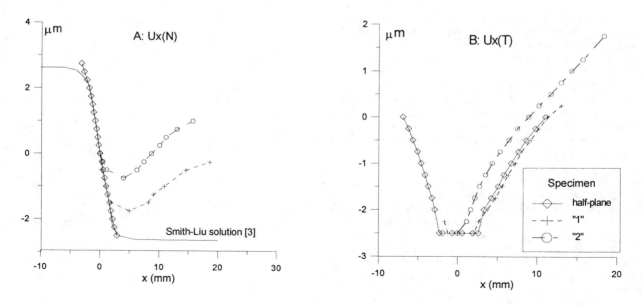

Fig.3- Ux(N) (A) and Ux(T) (B) fields

# Optimizing Load Cell Design Using an Experimental/Numerical Method

Zhikai Guo and Bryan R. Oakes
SI Technologies, Inc.
4611 South 134th Place
Seattle, WA 98168, USA

A strain gage based bending beam load cell was designed for on-board weighing systems for the trucking industry. Because it is used in an on-board application, this load cell should be designed to be rugged, low profile and fatigue resistant. The output of the load cell is also required to be adequate to achieve high accuracy and a good signal to noise ratio. Therefore, a hybrid experimental/numerical method was utilized to optimize the load cell design and to determine the output of the load cell.

Figure 1 shows the dimensions of a bending beam load cell and the loading fixtures. The load cell is 330 mm long, 72 mm wide, 24 mm high and made of AISI 4340 alloy steel heat-treated to RC42. It is bolted on the T-1 steel bearing plate. The test load is applied through the loading plate.

A moiré interferometry technique [1] was used to study the displacement fields of the load cell. A 600 lines/mm specimen grating was transferred to the load cell surface. A difference of one fringe order in the moiré fringe corresponded to a displacement of 1/1200 mm or 0.833 µm. This provided enough resolution to study the displacement fields. The load was applied incrementally. Both u- and v-displacement fields were recorded simultaneously [2] with the applied load.

The applied loading condition was then used to drive a 2-dimensional, linear elastic finite element model with the experimentally-determined boundary conditions. The displacement fields were computed and output from the FEA program. The computed displacements were within 5% compared to the measured displacements. This validated the accuracy of the finite element model. The strain fields were also computed to optimize the strain gage locations on the load cell. The stress output was used to verify the strength, fatigue life and to calculate the safety factor of the load cell.

Strain gages were then installed on the locations determined from the finite element analysis. The strain gage data was recorded along with the applied loads. The experimental data was compared to the FEA data. It was found that the computed strains at the strain gage locations were very accurate. Finally, the strain data was used to estimate the output of the load cell at the maximum capacity. Since the load cell used a Wheatstone bridge circuit, the output of the load cell depended on the strain gage outputs in each arm [3,4]

In conclusion, optimizing the design of a rugged, low profile load cell for on-board application can be achieved by using a hybrid experimental and numerical method. The experimental results showed that the 2-dimensional finite element model can accurately simulate the load cell under the loading conditions. The output of the load cell can be estimated using finite element analysis.

*Reference:*

[1] Post, D., "Moiré Interferometry", Handbook on Experimental Mechanics, ed. A. S. Kobayashi, Prentice-Hall, 314-387 (1987).
[2] Guo, Z. K. and Kobayashi, A. S., "Simultaneously measurement of u- and v-displacement fields by moiré interferometry", Experimental Techniques, Vol.17, No. 5. September/October, 21-23 (1993).
[3] Dally, J. W. and Riley, W. F., "Experimental Stress Analysis", 2nd ed., McGraw-Hill (1978).
[4] Hannah, R. L. and Reed, S. E., "Strain Gage User's Handbook", Elsevier Applied Science (1992).

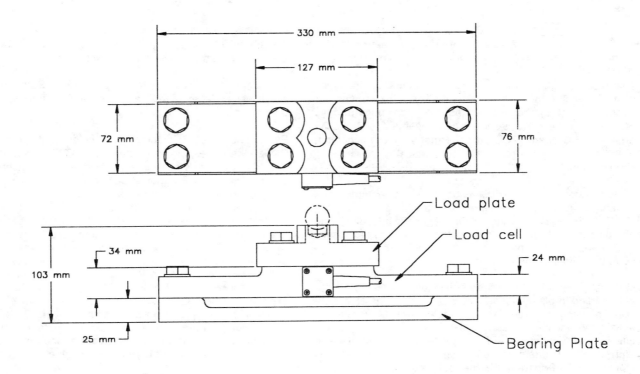

Figure 1.   Load Cell and Testing Fixtures

# Thermal Deformation Measurement in SMT Assembly by Moire and Holographic Interferometry

Dai Fulong*   Wang Weining**   Shi Ling*   K.M.Leung**   Zou Daqing*
*Department of Engineering Mechanics, Tsinghua University, Beijing, P.R. China
**Department of Physics and Materials Science, City University of Hong Kong, Hong Kong

The rapid progress made in surface mount technologies (SMT) has led to the higher reliability requirements for surface mount assemblies. As the only mechanical means of attaching the surface mount components (SMC) to the printed circuit board (PCB), the thermal fatigue mechanism of the solder joint is one of the most critical issues in SMT development.

In this paper, the three-dimensional thermal deformations observed in a surface mounted plastic-quad-flat-pack (PQFP) assembly during power cycling by using the combination of moire interferometry and holographic interferometry are presented. The two techniques are complementary in the experiment.

Moire interferometry is a whole-field optical technique for determining in-plane displacements U and V. It is an optical method using coherent light and featuring subwavelength sensitivity and high spatial resolution. The holographic interferometry used in the study for taking the out-of-plane thermal displacement measurements is a classical off-axis type capable of operating in the real time, double exposure or time average modes. The double exposure mode is adopted in the test.

The experiment is run on a 95mm by 75mm FR-4 epoxy/glass circuit board module with a single centrally mounted PQFP, which has 100 gull wing shape leads. The gull wing leads are soldered to the surface of PCB at their bottom ends and their top ends are fixed to the edges of PQFP. Two leads of the PQFP are connected to a DC voltage. When power is applied , IC inside the PQFP dissipated electric power, and the assembly deforms. Temperatures are measured with copper-constantan thermcouples taped to the upper surfaces of both PQFP and PCB. In the in-plane displacements experiment using moire interferometry, three pieces of diffraction gratings are replicated on the surface of PQFP, the upper and lower surfaces of the PCB, respectively, as shown in Fig.1. Suppose the displacements along the thickness of PQFP are identical, then the displacements of the top ends of leads have the same values as those along the edges of PQFP. On the other hand, the displacements of the bottom ends of the leads equal to those points on the upper surface of PCB. The PCB is clamped elastically along its two longer edges,

very similar to what it is in the actual service. Both the upper and lower surfaces of PCB are measured by turning around the specimen.

Fig. 2 shows the U displacement fields of the surface of PQFP, the upper and lower surfaces of PCB, respectively. The fringe patterns are taken at the thermal equilibrium of the module after 15 minutes' power on at 1.09 Watt. The x direction shear displacements of the top and bottom ends of the leads and their distributions along edge AB are illustrated in Fig.3. Fig.4 shows the V field fringe patterns of the surface of PQFP, upper and lower surfaces of PCB, respectively.For top ends of each lead along edge AB, Vt is calculated from Fig.4 as 3.96um. The fringe order of the bottom ends of the leads is determined as 6 through real-time observation, so Vb=2.5 um. Fig.5 shows the double exposure holographic interferograms of the front and back sides of the sample at power level 1.09 Watt. By applying the "building bridge" technique, the absolute out-of-plane deformations of both the top and bottom ends of leads can be determined. Fringe patterns in Fig.5 have the bridge on.

It can be concluded that the mismatch of CTEs between the chip carrier and the substrate will cause three-dimensional displacements in the leads and solder joints. The deformation patterns are regular and symmetric. The maximun shear deformations of the leads occur at the four corners of PQFP. Therefore, the solder joints at these positions run the highest risk of thermal fatigue failure.

References:

[1]   Y.F.Guo, C.G. Woychik, "Thermal Strain Measurements of Solder Joints in Second Level Interconnections Using Moire Interferometry ", Journal of Electronic Packaging, Vol. 114, March 1992, pp.88-92.

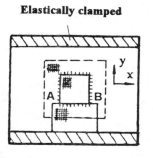

Fig. 1　Arrangement of specimen gratings

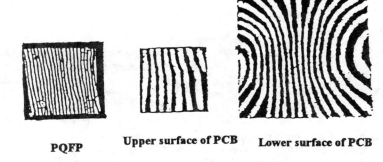

**PQFP**　　**Upper surface of PCB**　　**Lower surface of PCB**

Fig. 2　U displacement fields of the module

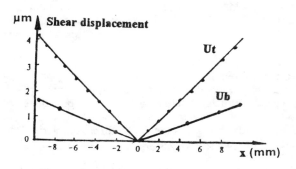

Fig. 3　x direction shear displacements
of the leads along edge AB

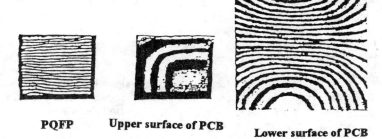

**PQFP**　　**Upper surface of PCB**　　**Lower surface of PCB**

Fig. 4　V displacement fields of the module

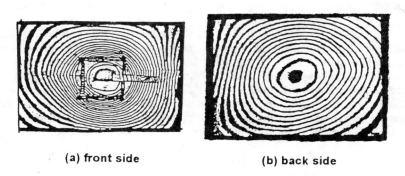

(a) front side　　　　(b) back side

Fig. 5　Holographic interferograms of the module

# Integration of Microscopic Material Level and Macroscopic NDE of Aged Steel Structures

Daniel N. Farhey,  A. Emin Aktan,  Aniruddha M. Thakur,  Relva C. Buchanan,  Narayanan Jayaraman
Dept. of Civil & Env. Eng.  and  Dept. of Materials, Sc., & Eng.
University of Cincinnati
Cincinnati, OH 45221

Aged pre-A7 steel bridges still continue to serve the public. Some of these historic landmark bridges are monumental and a source of pride for the community. Based on visual inspection and over-simplified analytical modeling, some of these bridges are being under-rated. Hence considered to pose public safety risk, some bridges are being removed without reliable evidence. Idealized analysis and reduction of effective cross-sectional areas which exhibit signs of corrosion, compounded by increasing live-load and traffic, typically lead to posting. Accurate evaluation may render cost-effective preservation.

In previous studies, the impact of microscopic material deterioration on bridge capacity has been approached. However, there is no rational conceptualization for accurately identifying and incorporating the effects of material aging and deterioration on bridge reliability.

Aktan et al. [1, 2] tested to failure two decommissioned pre-A7-steel truss bridges, constructed in 1914 with built-up members and rigidly riveted connections (Fig. 1). The bridges were subjected to nondestructive and then to destructive field tests. The experimental study indicated that widespread corrosion with especially deep rust-pits, distributed within some of the critical members and connections, did not adversely affect structural performance. The findings of this research and truss members salvaged from the two test bridges were used in the actual study to develop a rational approach on the effects of material aging and deterioration. This study integrates microscopic material level analysis, meso-level mechanical tests on coupon specimens, with macroscopic nondestructive evaluation

A detailed three-dimensional FE analysis, accounting for stress concentration (Fig. 2), was used to predict the critical regions of the built-up structural-steel members. These critical stressed regions were then sampled to perform rigorous mechanical coupon tests and microstructural tests. In addition, different less-stressed regions were also sampled for comparison of stress influence.

The coupon samples used to study the mechanical properties, simulate different levels of high stress, and provide artificially-stressed specimens for further microstructural analysis. Global 18-in.-long (457 mm) and local 6-in.-long (152 mm) coupon specimens were sampled (Figs. 3a and 3b, respectively). The coupon specimens were tested with full computer-automated real-time control and monitoring of the different loading stages. The loading rates were:  (1) Up to yield–stress rate of 18.2 kN/min. (4000 lbf/min.); (2) yield plateau–strain rate of 3%/min.; and, (3) after yield plateau–strain rate of 5%/min. To measure the strain, the specimens were instrumented with DCDT's, attached by blade-type sharp contact avoiding slippage.

The micro-samples were used to study the microstructural evolution under known environmental and loading conditions. The 1-in. (25.4 mm) diameter micro-samples were core-drilled from different locations of the structural members and the previously-tested coupon specimens. These samples were examined using Scanning Electron Microscope (SEM) at 25 kV for their morphological differences. Contemporary structural steel was also micro-sampled and examined to compare the effect of aging on the structural steel members of the test bridges.

The microstructure of historic steel revealed large quantities of MnS inclusions of various shapes and sizes, as compared with contemporary structural steel with small quantities of spherodized MnS inclusions. Thus, aging alone cannot be attributed to causing the changes in the microstructure of the aged steel members of a bridge.

Morphological differences in the grain and inclusion structure were observed in the unstressed and stressed regions of the member. Major observations were made on the microstructure of a naturally stressed region: Segregation of pearlite and MnS inclusions, and flow of grains. Segregation of inclusions was more influenced by the tensile stress than the compressive stress. Hence, the flow pattern along with the microcracking has a serious impact on the life expectancy of the member, eventually leading to mechanical fracture.

Stress-assisted aging seems to affect the microstructure, which may eventually lead to undesirable failure modes of the structure. The local stress-concentration should be addressed in the design process of built-up and riveted members by relevant local analysis, appropriately accounting for long-term aging effects. Furthermore, periodical condition assessment and rating procedures could encompass micro and meso levels of correlation in addition to practical visual inspection techniques for estimating the actual extent of deterioration.

References:

[1] Aktan, A.E., Lee, K.L., Naghavi, R., Hebbar, K., "Destructive Testing of Two 80-Year-Old Truss Bridges," *Transportation Research Record*, 1460, TRB, 62-72, 1994.
[2] Aktan, A.E., Naghavi, R., Farhey, D.N., Lee, K.L., Aksel, T., Hebbar, K., "Nondestructive/Destructive Tests and Associated Studies on Two Decommissioned Steel Truss Bridges," *FHWA/OH-95/013*, Cincinnati Infrastr. Inst., 1994.

Fig. 1. Alkire Road Test Bridges

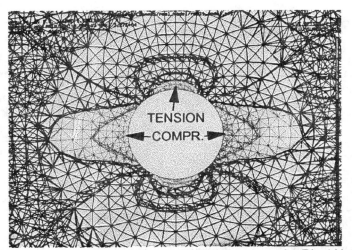

TENSION

COMPR.

Fig. 2. FE Modeling and Stress Distribution around a Rivet Hole

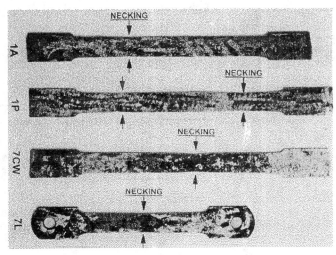

Fig. 3a. Global Coupon Specimens

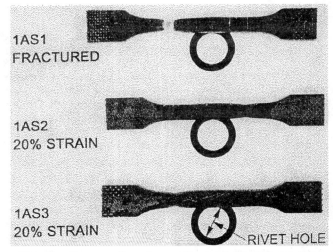

1AS1
FRACTURED

1AS2
20% STRAIN

1AS3
20% STRAIN

RIVET HOLE

Fig. 3b. Coupon Specimens from Rivet Hole Vicinity

# Steel Bridge Rating Using the Falling Weight Deflectometer Technique

Hani G. Melhem, Suresh Kumar Iyer, and Kuo-Kuang Hu
Department of Civil Engineering
Kansas State University
Manhattan, KS 66506

The goal of this research is to develop a computer program which would yield structural capacity information on bridge decks and bridge superstructures from the data recorded by the Falling Weight Deflectometer (FWD). FWD's are the fastest and simplest NDT devices used for structural evaluation of existing pavements. Due to their ability to apply heavy loads, produce multi-point deflection basins, and simulate actual wheel loads, they have become quite popular and are presently used on a regular basis by several highway departments in the U.S.

Data obtained by FWD on bridges can only be qualitative and --to some extent-- quantitative but mainly indicative of the condition of the reinforcing steel and concrete in the deck and superstructure. Following discussions with the sponsoring agency, it was found appropriate to include in this study other measuring devices to calibrate the FWD data and to acquire additional information not readily obtainable from the FWD. Such information will include the natural frequency of the structure, which can be related to the stiffness and consequently to the deflections of the bridge and to its response to impact.

In order to reach this objective, several tasks are first carried to identify the correlation between the bridge dynamic response to impact and the structural properties of the bridge (i.e. stiffness and rigidity of connections) and the structural behavior of the bridge (such as static load deflection). These include the development of a methodology for measuring the actual natural frequency of a bridge and its structural elements, and the identification of the hardware and software configurations necessary to generate a pulse load and record the dynamic response of the test specimens. The same techniques should then be applicable to actual structures.

The research approach utilized is closer to that used by Samman and Biswas [1,2]. A set of frequency-response function is used as signatures. The signatures are typically obtained by controlled vibration tests. Based on techniques of digital signal processing and pattern recognition, the bridge signatures are examined and analyzed. Recognition of signatures is done by preprocessing (noise elimination and signal smoothing), processing, and interpretation. A similar approach was used by Mazurek [3].

A special computer program is implemented to calculate the natural frequency and mode shape functions of bridges. The input will be the basic information on the bridge (type, span length, number of spans, cross section, etc.). KDOT will select up to three bridge types that the program should be able to analyze. Results from the program (computed response) will be compared to the actual response (response measured with techniques and instruments developed in the experimental program to establish relationships and obtain correction factors. Program results will also be compared to known theoretical solutions. Several bridges are being considered. KDOT will provide input on the program performance and scope.

Other approaches being investigated in this research include studying of the seismic response of the bridge superstructure (response to lateral, i.e. horizontal, loads), identifying the correlation between the natural frequency of the structure and the deflection (elastic behavior), and investigating other methods of damage assessment such as acoustic emission.

The methods and programs developed in the course of this project could be used on new bridges to compare the actual and theoretical stiffness of the structure and structural components, and to monitor the rate of deterioration of exiting as well as new bridges (as they get older) between consecutive evaluations. If used on a regular basis over the years, this can become an indication of the quality of construction of new bridges and a means of quality assurance.

## ACKNOWLEDGMENT

This reserach is supported by KTRAN Project Number KSU-96-1, "Bridge Rating Using the KDOT-FWD and Other Methodologies," funded by the Kansas Department of Transportation. The assistance of Mr. Gary Chan, the KDOT project monitor, is much appreciated. The effort of Khalid Niazi, and Vijayanath Bhuvanagiri, Ph.D. students at KSU, is acknowledged.

References:

[1] Samman, M.M., and Biswas, M., "Vibration Testing for Nondestructive Evaluation of Bridges - I" Journal of Structural Engineering, Vol. 120, No. 1, Jan. 1994, pp. 269-289.

[2] Samman, M.M., and Biswas, M., "Vibration Testing for Nondestructive Evaluation of Bridges - II," Journal of Structural Engineering, Vol. 120, No. 1, Jan. 1994, pp. 290-306.

[3] Mazurek, D.F., "Monitoring Structural Integrity of Girder Bridges through Vibration Measurment", Ph.D., Dissertation, The University of Connecticut, 1989.

# Acoustic Emission Tester for Aircraft Fire Extinguisher Bottles

Alan G. Beattie
Department 9711
Sandia National Laboratories
Albuquerque NM 87185-0615

The Aircraft Industry employs spherical bottles containing pressurized Halon 1301 ($CF_3Br$) to extinguish engine and cargo hold fires. Current Department of Transportation, (DOT) regulations require periodic testing of these bottles. The only test method allowed by DOT regulations at this time is hydrostatic testing for inelastic expansion of the bottles. This test requires that the sealed bottles be opened, emptied, pressurized with water in a water bath, refilled with Halon 1301 and then resealed.

The production of Halon 1301 throughout the world was stopped in January 1994 because of its Ozone depleting properties. The Airline industry has an exemption to continue using Halon fire extinguishing agents through the year 2000. At this time no totally satisfactory substitute exists. Halon from the bottles undergoing the hydrostatic test must be recovered, refined and reused. A test of the bottle integrity which did not require removal of the Halon would save much time and expense for the Airlines.

The FAA and the Air Transport Association (ATA) has sponsored the development of an acoustic emission test for Halon bottles. The necessary over pressure to conduct an acoustic emission test is applied by heating the sealed bottles to a temperature of 145 F. This takes the pressure to at least 30% above the estimated maximum pressure seen. As the bottle is heated, it is monitored by a six channel acoustic emission system. The spherical bottle is held in a special fixture where six spring loaded sensors are positioned on the bottle in a fixed geometry. The sensors are mounted on the end of rods which extend along radii of the sphere. Adjusting the distance of the sensors from the center allows the fixture to accommodate spheres from 5 to 16 inches in diameter. This covers a large majority of the Halon bottles in use in the current air fleet. The fixture is mounted in an industrial oven with sheathed and surface temperature controlled heaters. The bottle temperature is monitored by the computer with a thermocouple applied to on the bottle's surface

The acoustic emission system is based upon the Physical Acoustics Corporation (PAC) AEDSP-32/16 digital acoustic emission board. Three boards are mounted in a 66 MHz 486 computer. These boards contain a digital processor with a 16 bit word and a maximum digitization frequency of 8 MHz. The large dynamic range allows triggering at a very low signal level with out losing high amplitude data. The system is triggered at a 25 dB level (17 microvolt out of the sensor). PAC nanno 30 sensors are used. These have a response peak between 300 and 350 KHz. The board frequency band pass is set at 250 to 1200 KHz. This restriction to high frequencies is necessary to ignore the low frequency sound waves traveling through the Halon inside the bottle.

The bottle wall thicknesses are about .07 inches. Unfortunately the bottles are not smooth spheres. Mounting lugs and ports are welded onto the bottle. These cause distortions of the acoustic waves traveling along the bottle wall. At the low signal amplitudes seen in these spheres, the distorted wave can produce triggering on either the extensional or the flexural portion of the wave. To achieve reasonable accurate location on detected signals, an over-determined data set is taken (a wave which excites 4 or more sensors). A non-linear least squares program is used to calculate the most probable location of the event on the sphere. The fit first tries the extensional velocity and if that fails, the flexural velocity. The computer ignores the waves if it can not locate the wave with relatively high probability with one of these two wave velocities. Approximately 80% of the events are located.

To estimate the significance of the events a clustering algorithm is used. A cluster is defined as all events which fall within a circle with a 15 degree radius which lies on the surface of the sphere. The center of the circle is the average coordinates of all the included locations. In addition, an average value of an acoustic emission parameter (currently, the ringdown count) is calculated.

A prototype of this tester has been installed in the Walter Kidde testing facility in Wilson N.C. where it is running AE tests on bottles returned for repair or testing, before they are hydro tested. Two hundred bottles will be tested and the tester will then be shipped to Pacific Scientific Co. in California where another two hundred bottles will be tested. These are the two major manufacturers of aircraft Halon Bottles in this country.

At this date, one hundred and one bottles have been tested. Seventy seven had three or less located events. Of the rest, twenty-one had between 4 and 16 located events. Only three had more than 30 located events and these three were the only bottles with ten or more events in a single cluster. Two of these bottles had cluster locations at doubler plates, applied to the surface with fillet welds. These plates hold positioning fixtures for mounting the bottles. One of these had a poorly formed fillet weld and evidence of high heat on the inside of the bottle and the other had a tungsten inclusion in the filet weld. The third bottle had been repaired at a much earlier date with the replacement of two complete ports. It was impossible to examine the inside of the bottle near these welded ports. The curve of acoustic emission count as a function of temperature for the major cluster in this bottle suggested flaking of corrosion or weld flux rather than the crack growth indicated by these curves for the other two bottles. While these three bottles were definitely selected by the tester as being much worse than the other bottles, all bottles passed the hydrostatic test.

If enough bad bottles are not found to allow the establishment of a rejection criteria for the acoustic emission test, an alternative procedure will be to reject any bottle which is not better than the three questionable bottles which have already been found at Walter Kidde. Only bottles which failed this test would be required to under go a hydrostatic test. While this procedure would not eliminate hydrostatic tests, according to the above statistics, the number of such tests could be reduced by 97 percent.

If the future tests bear out the present results, a request for an exemption will be submitted to the DOT around October this year to allow members of the ATA to use the acoustic emission test as an adjunct to or in place of the hydrostatic test.

# Whirling of Sun Gear Shaft in Planetary Gear Train Affected by Torque

Masanobu Yoshino
Lecturer
Nagaoka College of Technology
888 Nishi-katakai Nagaoka
Niigata 940 Japan

Shigeo Yanabe
Professor, Dr.
Nagaoka University of Technology
1603-1 Kamitomioka Nagaoka
Niigata 940-21 Japan

Concerning rotating machines including gear trains with backlash, characteristic of lateral or bending vibration of the machines are often influenced by a transmitted torque. However, Effects of the torque on the vibration have not been clarified yet. The present paper shows one example of this kind of vibration, which was observed in a sun gear shaft of planetary gear train, and investigates its vibrational characteristics and mechanism.

Figure 1 shows an outline of the experimental apparatus used here. It is composed of a variable speed motor, one stage star-type planetary gear increaser (speed ratio of 9.83) and dynamometer. The sun gear shaft has no bearings and is supported by three planet gears and a spline. Gears used here are spur gear with 1.5 mm module and 20° pressure angle.

Lateral vibration responses of sun gear shaft under various load torque conditions are shown in Fig.2. These responses show that the lateral vibration amplitude becomes suddenly larger at a certain rotational speed and an onset speed of this unusual vibration becomes higher with increase in torque. Figure 3 shows a variation of the lateral vibration amplitude during torque loading and unloading torque. This figure shows that the amplitude varies with load torque and the response shows a hysteresis nature. FFT analysis shows that the value of main frequency of the vibration is three times of an internal gear speed. In order to investigate characteristics of the unusual vibration, an additional large mass was attached to the sun gear shaft (see Fig.1) and the same experiments were carried out. However, the onset speed of the abnormal vibration did not change. Next, a torsional stiffness of a shaft coupling which connects the motor shaft and the internal gear shaft was changed (see Fig.1). The results are shown in Fig.4. The figures show that the onset speed of the vibration becomes lower with decrease in coupling torsional stiffness and the vibration disappears when a rubber coupling is used. Response curves of torsional vibration of internal gear and the lateral vibration of sun gear shaft are measured simultaneously and the results are shown in Fig. 5 (a) and (b). Figure 5 shows that both response curves are in good accordance. It means that the unusual lateral vibration of sun gear shaft occurs in a resonance of the torsional vibration of the system. Effects of the load torque(LT) on the torsional vibration response are shown in Fig. 6. Solid curves denote measured vibration responses, dashed lines denote imaginary response curves which are not observed and dot-dash curves show assumed back bone curves of nonlinear system[1]. The figure shows that the nonlinear resonance curve approaches a linear resonance curves with increase in the load torque, and according to this the onset speed of the unusual vibration becomes higher (from P1 to P3) as the load torque increases. These results suggest that the unusual lateral vibration of the sun gear shaft appears in the following process. When a gear train comes into a nonlinear torsional resonance, engaging gear teeth often separate. During the teeth separation, the sun gear shaft loses its support and goes down due to gravity, because the shaft has no bearings. For the teeth engagement, the shaft is loaded and goes back to a self-centering position.

Conclusions are summarized as follows.
(1) The lateral vibration response shows the hysteresis nature against the rotational speed and load torque.
(2) The onset speed of the unusual lateral vibration becomes higher with increase in load torque and coupling torsional stiffness.
(3) The vibration is strongly connected with the nonlinear torsional vibration response of the system associated with the gear backlash and load torque.

References:

[1] BOGORYUBOV,N.N., and MITROPOLISKII,Yu.A. : Problems of the asymptotic theory of nonstationary vibration, Kyouritsu syuppan, 1965,p219-229.(translated by Masuko,M. in Japanese)

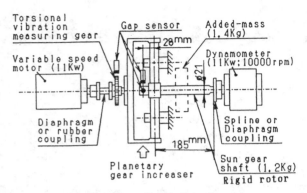

Fig. 1 Experimental apparatus

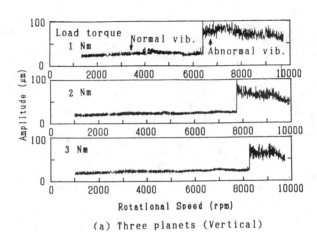

(a) Three planets (Vertical)

Fig. 2 Variation of lateral vibration response of sun gear shaft due to load torque

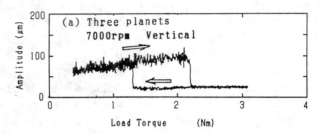

Fig. 3 Variation of the lateral vibration amplitude during torque loading and unloading

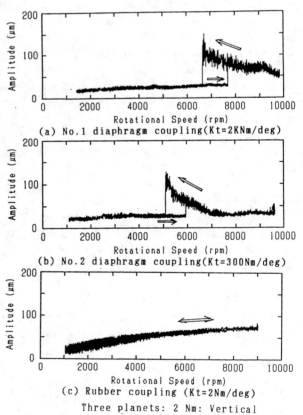

(a) No.1 diaphragm coupling(Kt=2KNm/deg)

(b) No.2 diaphragm coupling(Kt=300Nm/deg)

(c) Rubber coupling (Kt=2Nm/deg)

Three planets: 2 Nm: Vertical

fig. 4 Effects of coupling torsional stiffness on the lateral vibration response

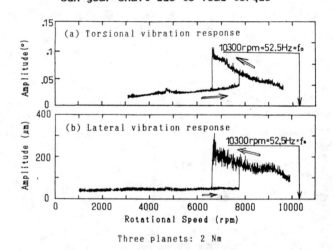

Three planets: 2 Nm

Fig. 5 Response of torsional and lateral vibration of sun gear shaft

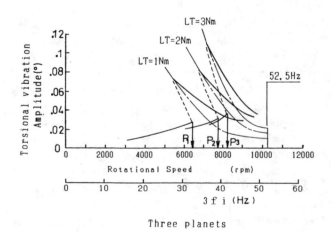

Three planets

Fig. 6 Variation of torsional vibration response due to load torque

276

# Time-dependent Structural Behavior of Wood Composite Panels: Effect of Environmental Conditions

R. C. Tang, J. N. Lee
Professor and Graduate Research Assistant
School of Forestry
Auburn University, AL 36849

J. H. Pu
Research Technologist
J. M. Huber Corp.
Commerce, GA 30529

Wood composite panel products are known to be hygrothermo-viscoelastic materials. Therefore, relative humidity (moisture), temperature, load and time factors must be considered collectively and dependently when assessing the serviceability or durability of these products in structural applications under long-term exposure of changing environments. In this paper, the environmental effects on the time-dependent structural behaviors, creep and creep-rupture (duration of load:DOL), of flakeboards and oriented strandboards (OSB) are presented. Environmental factors considered are controlled environmental conditions of constant relative humidities (RH) at constant temperatures, cyclic RH at a constant temperature and uncontrolled environmental conditions. Specimens, 1.27-1.91 cm (0.5-0.75 in.) thick x 7.62 cm (3 in.) wide x 45.72 cm (18 in.) long, were concentratedly loaded in bending on a 40.64 cm (16-in.) simple-supported span for 3 months under the environmental conditions designated and then unloaded for a one-month recovery. Load level of each group was based their ultimate static bending strength (MOR: Modulus of Rupture). Daily changes of deflections were measured by a LVDT connected to a computer-interfaced data acquisition system.

The long-term engineering performance (durability and serviceability) of wood composites is known to be influenced by processing variables, such as wood species, flake/particle configuration and alignment, adhesive type and content, mat moisture content, press types and press conditions and by in-service environmental conditions [1]. It is recognized that experiments of creep and DOL, the time-dependent behavior of materials under load, are the primary methods for the evaluation of their long-term engineering performance exposed to different environmental conditions. Due to the limitation of paper length, only limited cases of key processing variables, and mechanical and environmental loading histories are discussed.

In general, constant medium RH (65%) or low RH (< 65%) at a temperature of 23.9°C (75°F) will not have a great influence on the creep performance of wood composite panels when they are loaded in bending at a stress level (equal to or less than 40% of MOR [1]. However, significant decrease of creep resistance may occur when the panels are exposed to constant high RH (i.e. ≥ 90%) at same temperature. It seems that the effect of cyclical RH of 65% ↔ 95% on a 96-hour frequency at that temperature (23.9°C) is between those two constant RHs (65% and 95%) but such effect will be enhanced if the load level was increased (Fig. 1 and 2) [2]. Studies of flakeboards indicated that their flexural creep behavior is also very sensitive to high RH, especially when

imposed in a cyclic fashion and fast changes in cyclic RH of 65% ↔ 95% yielded an acceleration in creep over those subjected to a slowly changed rate (Fig. 3).

At elevated temperature (i.e. T ≥ 32.2°C (90°F)), creep rate of wood composite panels will be accelerated especially under the humid environments (e.g. RH ≥ 90%) [3]. The tertiary creep was observed in the commercial OSBs, which are commonly used for the roofing or flooring, when they are exposed to an environment of 35°C (95°F) and 95% RH (Fig. 4). In addition, significant weakening effect on the creep resistance of commercial OSB products under cyclic RH (65% ↔ 95%) was observed when the temperature was elevated from 23.9°C (75°F) to 35°C (95°F) as shown in Fig. 5 and 6.

The effect of stress levels (40%, 60% and 80% MOR) on the creep and DOL behavior of PF-bonded southern pine OSB exposed to the uncontrolled indoor environments was studied and significant effect due to the fluctuation of RH and T on the creep/DOL of OSBs tested was not observed. The creep deflections for the 40% MOR stress level group tested under uncontrolled indoor environment are relatively lower than those subjected to identical loads but exposed to a controlled cyclic 65% ↔ 95% RH at a constant temperature of 23.9°C. However, OSB exposed to uncontrolled outdoor environment (open-shed) crept more than those exposed to the controlled cyclic 65% ↔ 95% RH. This suggests that the creep/DOL behavior of wood composite panels will be greatly influenced by the rate and duration of the hygrothermal sorption.

## Remarks

Wood composite panels are hygrothermal materials and their engineering performance will be greatly influenced by the mechanical and environmental loading histories. To better understand wood composite panels' long-term engineering performance for the improvement of existing structural designs as well as for the development of new structural applications for these products, systematic and collaborative investigations should be launched by the joint efforts of industrial, governmental, and academic communities.

## References

[1] Tang, R. C. and E. W. Price. Parameters that may affect creep and duration of load behavior of wood composite panel products. Proceedings of 1994 IUFRO S5.02 Timber Engineering Conference held in Sydney, Australia on July 5-7, 1994.

[2] Pu, J. H., R. C. Tang and C. Y. Hse. Creep behavior of sweetgum OSB: Effect of load level and relative humidity. Forest Products Journal, 44(11/12):45-50. 1994.

[3] PU, J. H., R. C. Tang and E. W. Price. Effect of hot and humid environmental conditions on the creep behavior of commercial OSB. For. Prod. J., 42(11/12):9-14. 1992.

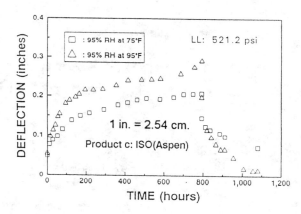

Fig. 4.  Effect of temperature on creep of commercial ISO-bonded OSB.

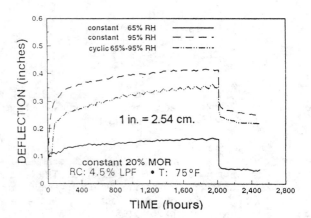

Fig. 1.  Effect of RH on creep of sweetgum OSB under low constant load (20% MOR)

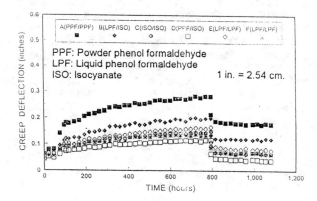

Fig. 5.  Creep of six commercial OSB (A - F: (face adhesive)/core adhesive)) under cyclic 65% -- 95% RH at 23.9°C (75°F)

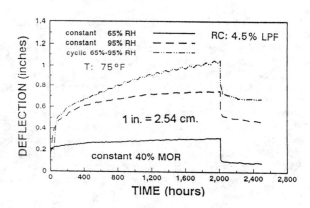

Fig. 2  Effect of RH on creep of sweetgum OSB under high constant load (40% MOR)

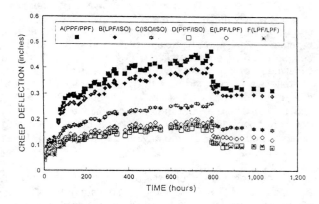

Fig. 6.  Creep of six commercial OSB (A - F: (face adhesive)/core adhesive)) under cyclic 65% -- 95% RH at 35°C (95°F)

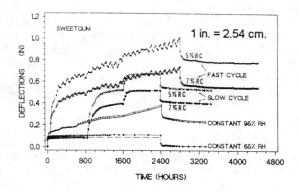

Fig. 3.  Creep of flakeboards under constant 65% and 95% RH, slow and fast cyclic 65% -- 95% RH at 23.9°C

278

# Development of Tension and Compression Creep Models for Wood Using the Time-Temperature Super-Position Principle

Joseph R. Loferski, Associate Professor, Dept. of Wood Science & Forest Products
Brian H. Bond, Graduate Student, Dept. of Wood Science & Forest Products
Jacem Tissauoi, Graduate Student, Dept. of Civil Engineering
Siegfried M. Holzer, Professor, Dept. of Civil Engineering
Virginia Polytechnic Institute and State University
Blacksburg, VA 24061-0503

In order to design for creep in wood structures, a long-term creep law is needed. To date, there are no long-term creep models or practical methods to investigate the effect of creep on the safety or serviceability of wood structures and structural wood-composites. In this project, long-term creep models were developed for wood in tension and compression using the time-temperature superposition principle (TTSP). The principle states that the long-term response of a polymer at a lower temperature is equivalent to the short-term response at a higher temperature. The objective of this paper is to discuss the experimental techniques used to develop data for the application of the TTSP principle to wood.

Accelerated creep tests were conducted in tension and compression using small clear specimens of Douglas-fir, southern pine, yellow-poplar, and wood composites. The specimens were tested at moisture contents of 6, 9, and 12 percent, and at temperatures between 20°C and 80°C. The strain was measured using bonded electrical resistance strain gauges.

The individual creep compliance for each temperature was shifted along the log-time axis to obtain a "master" curve that describes the creep response of the specimens. The shift factors followed the Arrhenius formulation that describes the shift factor relation for polymers in the glassy region.

Master curves were successfully developed for all the specimens tested in the environmental conditions tested. Power law models were developed using a non-linear regression analysis technique to represent the master curves. The success of the project hinged on developing and refining the experimental techniques to measure very small changes in strain on the specimens. This required accurate alignment of strain gauges, specimens, load, and the load frame and accurate control of relative humidity and temperature to achieve success in these experiments.

To verify the creep laws which are obtained from short term testing using the TTSP principle, long term creep tests under constant environment are being conducted. The presentation will highlight problems and techniques associated with conducting these sensitive experiments.

# Time-Dependent Strength of Wood Subjected to Several Loading Conditions

Jen Y. Liu, Robert J. Ross, Erwin L. Schaffer
USDA Forest Service, Forest Products Laboratory
One Gifford Pinchot Drive
Madison, Wisconsin 53705–2398

This paper presents resulting equations of an analysis of time-dependent strength of polymeric materials under constant, ramp, or sinusoidal loading [1,2]. The analysis is based on the Reiner–Weissenberg strength theory in conjunction with Eyring's three-element mechanical model. This theory states that failure depends on a maximum value of the intrinsic free energy that can be stored elastically in a volume element of the material. The mechanical model, which consists of a linear spring in series with a parallel array of another linear spring and an Eyring dashpot, provides a good description of rheological material properties. The strength model has the peculiar features of predicting (1) the upper stress limit at which the material ruptures immediately upon application of load and (2) the lower stress limit at which the material can sustain the applied load indefinitely. Additional clarifications of the resulting equations, where necessary, are made in this work.

## Rupture Under Constant Loading [1]

The expression for the time at failure $t_c$ is

$$t_c = \frac{1}{\beta_c E_a K_1} \ln\left[\frac{\tanh(\beta_c \overline{\sigma}_c / 2)}{\tanh(\beta_c \overline{\sigma}_{ef,c} / 2)}\right] \qquad (1)$$

where $\beta_c$ is stress coefficient, $E_a$ is anelastic modulus, $K_1$ is a function of the activation energy, $\overline{\sigma}_c$ is the applied stress at rupture, and the effective stress $\overline{\sigma}_{ef,c}$ is

$$\overline{\sigma}_{ef,c} = \overline{\sigma}_c - \left[2E_a\left(R_1 - \overline{\sigma}_c^2 / E_e\right)\right]^{1/2} \qquad (2)$$

where $R_1$ is material resilience and $E_e$ is elastic modulus.

From Eqs. (1) and (2), we obtain the upper stress limit at $t_c = 0$ with $\overline{\sigma}_c = \overline{\sigma}_{ef,c}$ as

$$\overline{\sigma}_c = (E_e R_1)^{1/2} \qquad (3)$$

and the lower stress limit at $t_c = \infty$ with $\overline{\sigma}_{ef,c} = 0$ as

$$\overline{\sigma}_c = [2E_a E_e R_1 / (2E_a + E_e)]^{1/2} \qquad (4)$$

## Rupture Under Ramp Loading [1]

Ramp loading is expressed by $\sigma_r = \alpha\, t_r$, where $\alpha$ is a constant denoting the rate of loading. When $\sigma_r$ reaches $\overline{\sigma}_r$ at rupture, $t_r$ has two values that were not properly stated in Ref. [1]. One of the two values is $\infty$, which should be discarded; the other is

$$t_r = \overline{\sigma}_r / [E_a K_1 \sinh(\beta_r \overline{\sigma}_{ef,r})] \qquad (5)$$

in which

$$\overline{\sigma}_{ef,r} = \overline{\sigma}_r - \left[2E_a(R_1 - \overline{\sigma}_r^2 / 2E_e)\right]^{1/2} \qquad (6)$$

Equation (5) is in a more precise form than that in Ref. [1]. When $\overline{\sigma}_r = \overline{\sigma}_{ef,r}$, then $t_r = 0$; we obtain from Eq. (6)

$$\overline{\sigma}_r = (2E_e R_1)^{1/2} \qquad (7)$$

When $\overline{\sigma}_{ef,r} = 0$, then $t_r = \infty$; we obtain

$$\overline{\sigma}_r = [2E_a E_e R_1 / (E_a + E_e)]^{1/2} \qquad (8)$$

## Rupture Under Sinusoidal Loading [2]

Consider a sinusoidal stress

$$\sigma_f = \sigma_c + \sigma_0 \sin(\omega t_f + \phi) \qquad (9)$$

where $\sigma_c$ is constant mean stress, $\sigma_0$ is amplitude of cyclic stress, $\omega$ is circular frequency, $t_f$ is time, and $\phi$ is phase angle. Fatigue failure time is

$$t_f = \left(\frac{1}{E_a K_1 \beta_c}\right) \ln\left[\tanh\left(\frac{\beta_c \overline{\sigma}_c}{2}\right) \middle/ \tanh\left(\frac{\beta_c \overline{\sigma}_{ef,c}}{2}\right)\right] \qquad (10)$$

in which

$$\overline{\sigma}_{ef,c} = \overline{\sigma}_c - E_a \overline{\varepsilon}_{a,c} \qquad (11)$$

with

$$\overline{\varepsilon}_{a,c} = \left[ \frac{2}{E_a}\left( R_1 - \frac{\overline{\sigma}_c^2}{E_e} - \frac{\overline{\sigma}_c \overline{\sigma}_0}{E_e}\sin\phi \right) \right]^{1/2} \qquad (12)$$

When $\sigma_c = \overline{\sigma}_{ef,c}$, then $t_f = 0$ and

$$\overline{\sigma}_c = -\frac{\overline{\sigma}_0}{2}\sin\phi + \frac{1}{2}(\overline{\sigma}_0^2 \sin^2\phi + 4E_e R_1)^{1/2} \qquad (13)$$

and when $\overline{\sigma}_{ef,c} = 0$, $t_f = \infty$ and

$$\overline{\sigma}_c = -\frac{E_a \overline{\sigma}_0 \sin\phi}{E_e + 2E_a} + \left[ \left( \frac{E_a \overline{\sigma}_0 \sin\phi}{E_e + 2E_a} \right)^2 + \frac{2E_a E_e R_1}{E_e + 2E_a} \right]^{1/2} \qquad (14)$$

For structural members of wood, the phase angle $\phi$ stays at $\pi/2$ [2].

We note when $\sigma_0 = 0$ in Eq. (9), the case of sinusoidal loading reduces to that of constant loading; when $\sigma_c = 0$, the analysis breaks down, as can be seen from Eqs. (13) and (14). This is because the analysis in Ref. [2] considers whole cyclic loading only and the elastic strain energy stored in a whole cycle is 0. If the material is to fail, failure should occur in less than one cycle when the stored strain energy reaches $R_1$, which was not clearly stated in Ref. [2].

Some numerical results reported in Ref. [1] for Douglas-fir beams were in close agreement with existing test data [3,4] (Fig. 1). They were obtained with the following input: $E_e = 11,200$ MPa, $E_a = 150$ MPa, $R_1 = 0.34$ MJm$^{-3}$, $\beta_c = 0.5984$ MPa$^{-1}$, $K_1 = 8.8779E-17$ s$^{-1}$, and $\beta_r = 0.6540$ MPa$^{-1}$.

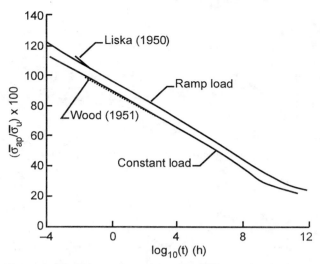

Figure 1—Variations of stress level at failure with logarithm of time for constant and ramp loading ($\overline{\sigma}_{ap}$ is applied stress at failure; $\overline{\sigma}_u = 53.1$ MPa)

References:

[1] Liu, J.Y., Schaffer, E.L., "Energy Criterion for Load Duration Problem in Wood," In: Sture, S., (ed.), Proceedings of 10th Engineering Mechanics Conference, American Society of Civil Engineers, Vol. 2, pp 1323–1327, 1995.

[2] Liu, J.Y., Ross, R.J., "Energy Criterion for Fatigue Strength of Wood Structural Members," Journal of Engineering Materials and Technology, American Society of Mechanical Engineers, (in press), 1996.

[3] Liska, J.A., "Effect of Rapid Loading on the Compressive and Flexural Strength of Wood," Report No. 1767, Forest Products Laboratory, USDA Forest Service, Madison, WI, 1950.

[4] Wood, L.W., "Relation of Strength of Wood to Duration of Load," Report No. 1916, Forest Products Laboratory, USDA Forest Service, Madison, WI, 1951.

# Development and Assessment of Soybean-Based Adhesive/Wood and Agrofiber Composites

Daniel Adams, Monlin Kuo, Deland Myers, Daniel Curry, and Howard Heemstra
Iowa State University
Ames, IA 50011

## INTRODUCTION

There is currently much interest in the use of non-traditional adhesives and fibers in wood-composite products. The adhesive considered in this investigation is derived from soy protein. In addition to wood, the fibers under consideration are cornstalks and switchgrass, commonly available in the midwestern U. S. The objectives of this inter-disciplinary research included determining proper soybean-based adhesive formulations, determining proper blends of wood and agricultural fibers, determining optimum processing conditions, and manufacturing and testing soybean-based adhesive wood and agrofiber composites.

Results from three sets of experiments are presented. First, strength and durability tests were performed to determine the feasibility of using soybean proteins as adhesive for wood fiber hardboards. Tests were conducted on boards produced with no adhesive, with phenol-formaldehyde adhesive, and with different percentages of soybean protein adhesive. A second set of experiments was performed to evaluate various soy proteins for use as adhesives. These evaluations were based on both strength and durability test results. Finally, tests were conducted to evaluate switchgrass and cornstalk fiber, both as a replacement and in a mixture with wood fibers.

For both adhesives, the mixtures of agrofiber to wood fiber considered were 100/0, 75/25, 50/50, 25/75, and 0/100. The fiber to be used (air-dried ponderosa pine, corn stalk, and switchgrass) was weighed and mixed with water and 1% by mass crystallized aluminum sulfate. Soybean protein adhesive was added and the mixture was adjusted to a pH of 4.0 with sulfuric acid. After mixing, the fiber suspension was drained, cold pressed to remove excess water, then hot pressed at 350 °F, forming the finished hardboard. Two hardboard densities were fabricated: low density (0.85 g/cc) and high density (1.0 g/cc).

The hardboards were tested for durability and strength. Durability testing consisted of measuring the amount of thickness swell and water absorption in samples that were either boiled for two hours or soaked in cold water for 24 hours. Internal bond tests were conducted to determine the strength of the adhesive bonding. Three-point bending tests were used to determine the modulus of elasticity and modulus of rupture.

## RESULTS AND DISCUSSION

Durability and strength tests were performed to determine the optimum percentage of soy protein to be used as an adhesive. The soy protein considered was Arpro 2100, a purified soy protein with a 90% protein content. Ponderosa pine wood fibers were used in constructing the hardboards. Soy adhesive percentages considered were 0%, 2%, 3%, and 4%. Additionally, 2% phenol-formaldehyde adhesive was included for comparison, the same percentage used in commercial hardboards. In general, strength and stiffness were found to increase as the percentage of protein increases. Hardboards produced with soy protein adhesive performed nearly as well as those produced with 2% phenol-formaldehyde adhesive. Internal bond tests indicated that hardboards bonded with soy protein adhesive compare favorably to those bonded with 2% phenol-formaldehyde adhesive when tested under dry conditions.

The percentage of soy protein adhesive present in the hardboards affected the amount of water absorption and thickness swell for both high and low densities. As the percentage of adhesive increased, the amount of thickness swell and water absorption decreased. Low density boards bonded with 2% phenol-formaldehyde showed better durability than the boards bonded with soy protein adhesive.

A second set of durability and strength tests were performed to evaluate several soy protein products for use as an adhesive. The soy products tested in this experiment were Honey Mead 90 (HM90, Honey Mead Products, Co.), Arcon VR (Arcon, ADM Products, Inc.), and Arpro 2100 (Arpro, ADM Products, Inc.). These products contain 50%, 60% to 70%, and 90% protein, respectively. Soy adhesives based on these products were used at 2% by weight based on dry fibers. Boards bonded with 2% phenol-formaldehyde (PF) adhesive and bonded without any adhesive also were prepared for comparison. Results of three-point bend testing indicate that boards bonded with 2% Arpro 2100 had the highest modulus of rupture, modulus of elasticity, and internal bond strength, followed by 2% Arcon VR and 2% HM90. Similar results were obtained for the internal bond strength. Boards bonded with Arpro 2100 demonstrated superior internal bonding compared to boards bonded with Arcon VR and HM90. It is evident that differences in adhesive strength of these three soy products are related to their protein content. Results of durability testing were not as conclusive as those from strength testing. In the 2-hour boiling test, all three adhesives performed about the same in the high-density boards.

However, Arcon 2100 performed much better in low density boards

A third set of durability and strength testing was performed to evaluate hardboards produced with varying percentages of wood and agricultural fibers. The mixtures of agrofiber to wood fiber considered were 100%/0%, 75%/25%, 50%/50%, 25%/75%, and 0%/100%. Two types of agrofibers were considered: switchgrass and corn stalks. Both agrofibers were fiberized using a Sprout-Bauer machine. Arpro 2100 soy protein as well as PF adhesive were evaluated. Although the 100% wood fiber hardboards produced the highest strengths, mixtures of wood and agrofibers showed promising results. As the percentage of the agrofiber increased, the modulus of rupture, modulus of elasticity, internal bond strength, and tensile strength decreased. At the same mixture ratio with wood fibers, corn stalk fibers produced higher strength properties than switchgrass fibers.

## ACKNOWLEDGEMENTS

This research was supported by the Iowa Soybean Promotion Board.

# Issues in Workforce Composition Analysis

D. C. Koeck and J. D. Rogers
Sandia Naitonal Laboratories
Albuquerque, NM  87185

## Introduction

An issue of paramount interest to United States industry is the supply and quality of human resources available for this country's scientific and technological activities. Science and engineering personnel are vital in meeting national challenges in the areas of scientific research, education, technological competitiveness and national security. The changing composition of the workforce, and the attendant responsibilities that an organization has to assure equal opportunity, give rise to various issues. This paper discusses some of the issues associated with the scientific and technical workforce. Specifically, it explores some of the questions pertaining to workforce composition and the measures of workforce composition. It is hoped that this paper will be useful to those responsible for developing and implementing personnel policies for the scientific and technical workforce.

## Demographics

A clear and factual picture of the current situation and recent trends in workforce demographics is very important to rational and effective policy formulation. Workforce 2000, a Labor Department study produced by the Hudson Institute in 1987, predicted dramatic changes in the American workforce by the year 2000. The paper stated that "only 15% of the new entrants to the labor force over the next 13 years will be native white males, compared to 47% in that category today." These projections, widely disseminated and extremely influential, were simply a mistake. The paper was actually referring to a new measure, "Net New Worker", that was developed in that paper. The Net New Worker measure can be thought of in the following manner. Consider the total pool of new entrants into the workforce - new graduates, immigrants, etc. That group defines the New Workers. Now, make replacements from these New Workers to account for exits from the workforce - retirements, deaths, etc., but do so with direct gender/ethnic replacements. That is, for each white male that exits the workforce, replace him with a white male from the New Workers group. After all exits from the total workforce have been replaced in this manner, the people remaining in the New Workers group are the Net New Workers - the group that is only 15% white male. Thus, the Net New Worker measure can be thought of as a sort of "first (or perhaps second) derivative" of the workforce composition.

## Workforce Analysis

Measurement of the characteristics of the current workforce is required by the Department of Labor (DOL) for many employers. To detect possible bias in hiring or promotion practices, the DOL expects companies to monitor the percentages of women and minorities in a given job classification (on-roll percentages or utilization) and in hires and promotions, and compare those values to reference values called availabilities. Availability is calculated from recent hiring and promotion data and from external data such as census data for the specific job classification. This process is illustrated in Figure 1. It shows the 70 - 30 mix of internal movements to external hires with the indicated percentages of women. This mix and set of pool compositions leads to the 18.5 % reference value for the group of interest.

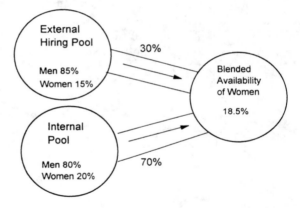

**Figure 1.  Calculation of availability**

Workforce compositions can be thought of in terms of process flow with "pools" representing job classifications and "pipes" representing hiring and promotion. To understand the dynamics of the processes that determine workforce composition, it is useful to visualize internal personnel movements in terms of "flows". By using these flow analogies, insights can be gained with respect to hiring and promotion of women and minorities within job classifications. A flow diagram illustrating this concept is shown in Figure 2.

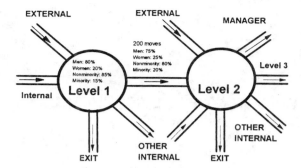

**Figure 2. Pools and Pipes Illustration**

The "pipes" and "pools" indicate sources, pathways, and destinations for entries to and exits from these populations. The synergy between the two job classifications is clearly illustrated in this manner. Changes in the utilization (on-roll percentage) of a targeted group in one "pool" can affect the availability in job classifications that are fed by that "pool" as illustrated in the availability calculation described in Figure 1. For example, aggressive hiring of women into an entry level position may result in the appearance of bias against women in the next higher level since the calculated availability of women for the higher level would suddenly increase but it would take time for the new-hire women to attain the required experience to be considered for advancement.

If the goal is for utilization to equal availability, there can be a problem. In a static situation, the percentages of a targeted group (women or minorities) among new graduates and the on-roll population, in the absence of bias in the organization, are equal and unchanging. That is, the two expected compositions, hiring and on-roll, would be the same. If, however, the hiring availability changes rapidly and there is a low turn-over of the on-roll population, the two compositions can differ substantially just due to the inertia of the system. This needs to be recognized when a company performs its workforce analysis.

The Hypothetical Corporation
There are a number of things that can disturb the balance between utilization and availability, but most of these are related to changing availabilities. Rapidly rising availabilities will result in rising utilization, but at a much slower rate, especially if people remain in the same job classification for a long time. Most technical people are hired into a job classification and expect to retire from that same job classification since only about 10% are typically promoted into supervisory ranks. In comparison to this rather static job classification, women are being awarded advanced degrees in the physical sciences and engineering in rapidly increasing numbers. In the physical sciences 18.8% of the PhDs awarded in 1992 went to women, whereas they made up only 15.2% of the PhDs in 1989. In engineering, the numbers went from 5.9% to 8.8% over the same period.

A simple model was constructed to get an idea of just how much the utilization of women would lag their availability (measured in new graduates) in the absence of any preference. No experienced hires were considered since they were assumed to be balanced by attrition. In this manner a Hypothetical Corporation was established in the year 1960 consisting of 2000 scientists and engineers ranging in age from 25 to 59 with 1.5% being women. Attrition, above that needed to balance experienced hires, was assumed to be 2.5% in all age groups, and everyone was assumed to retire at age 60. It is necessary to hire 85 new staff, 25 year olds, each year to keep the Hypothetical Corporation in steady state. The availability was assumed to be the PhD graduation rate for women in the physical sciences and engineering weighted in the ratio of one third to two thirds, respectively. The availability, thus calculated and projected to the year 2000, is shown as the upper curve in Figure 3. The lower curve shows the resulting utilization of women in the Hypothetical Corporation. Clearly, even in the absence of any bias, utilization cannot match availability for cases where the availability is changing rapidly. In order for the utilization to match the availability, in this example, women would have to be hired at twice their availability rate.

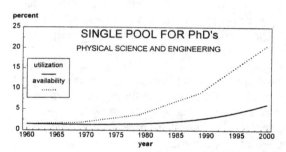

**Figure 3. The Hypothetical Corporation**

Summary
The field of human resources presents many challenges to corporate management. Studies in the field can be misinterpreted, leading to errant policy decisions. Careful analysis is called for in interpreting the data and formulating personnel policy. In particular, care is needed in cases where the population demographics are rapidly changing. If a targeted group is increasing in availability in the hiring pool, but there is low turnover, it is almost certain that the on-roll utilization of that group will show a shortfall. It needs to be recognized that this is a result of system dynamics, not bias in hiring or promotion.

# FROM INVENTION TO INNOVATION: CREATION OF VALUE THROUGH INTELLECTUAL PROPERTY DEVELOPMENT

Kristin B. Zimmerman, PhD
Thomas E. Anderson, PhD
General Motors R&D Center
Warren, MI 48090

## ABSTRACT

Invention, or the creation of new knowledge, is an important first step, but only the first step, on the path to innovation and commercial opportunity. Once an invention has been made (and presumably protected through patent or copyright), the work of innovation begins. This presentation will define the issues involved in moving from an idea or invention through the technical hurdles of implementation to commercial reality. In parallel with the technical development a definition of the market opportunity is required, including delineation of competitive advantages offered by the new technology. Edison's invention may have been the light bulb, but the innovation of an infrastructure to supply electricity was the key to successful commercialization of the technology.

# ENVIRONMENTAL ASSESSMENT OF VEHICLES

Dr. J. L. Sullivan
Ford Research

The automobile manufactures are increasingly expected to improve the environmental performance of their products, namely vehicles. However, methods need to be developed which permit a reliable environmental assessment of such a product. Otherwise, measures taken to improve the environmental performance at one stage of its life cycle may in fact lead to a greater reduction in environmental performance at another stage. Life Cycle Analysis (LCA) is a new methodology which can provide such assessments. The Life Cycle Design (LCD) methodology is subsequent approach which then combines the LCA derived environmental metrics with cost and performance metrics, which are so important in today's competitive market. This presentation focuses on the state of development of LCA and LCD and their use in the auto industry.

# Technical Challenges in Operating an Aging Commercial and Military Transport Aircraft Fleet Provide Impetus for New R&D Initiatives

Dr. Charles E. Harris
Assistant chief, Materials Division
Mail Stop 188M
NASA Langley Research Center
Hampton, VA 23681

In April 1988, an Aloha Airlines Boeing 737-200 experienced an in-flight structural failure in which a large section of the upper fuselage ripped open and separated from the aircraft. The failure resulted from multiple site damage (MSD) and corrosion. MSD is the link-up of small fatigue cracks extending from adjacent rivet holes in a fuselage longitudinal lap joint. The accident focused international attention on the problems of operating an aging commercial fleet. In 1990, approximately 46% of the U.S. commercial air transport fleet was over 15 years old, and 26% was over 20 years old. If current usage and replacement trends continue, the number of aircraft over 20 years old will double by the year 2000 [1].

Commercial transport aircraft enter service with a "design economic life goal" consisting of a specified number of landings, number of flight hours, and years of service. With proper maintenance, corrosion protection and control, inspection, and repair programs, the airframe is viewed as having an "infinite" fatigue life. Therefore, the continued operation of high time aircraft is an economics issue. When is it more cost-effective to replace an old aircraft rather than continuing to pay high supportability costs? A "high time" airplane is one that exceeds one or more of the three parts of the original design economic life goal. For example, provided below are recent data on the DC-9 commercial transport fleet [2]:

    Initial delivery data: 1965
    Number of aircraft produced: 976
    Number of aircraft still active: 881
    Design life goal*:  # of landings: 40,000
                        # of flight hours: 30,000
                        # of years: 20
    Average age of active fleet: 27.67 years
    Number of "high time" aircraft: 840

*McDonnell-Douglas has conducted full-scale fatigue tests well beyond the original design life goal. The current test-supported life of the DC-9 is 102,400 landings and 78,000 flight hours.

In the early 1990's time frame, the commercial industry standard practice was to inspect the airframe visually for damage. Various levels of inspections were performed ranging from daily walk-around inspections to detailed tear down inspections. Instrumented NDE methods such as eddy current probes were only used to inspect those local regions of the structure where previous cracking problems had occurred. While these methods were labor intensive and highly subjective, they were acceptable because the airframe was designed to survive a two-bay skin crack with a severed frame or stiffener. This design criterion represents a crack that is so large that it can be detected in obvious ways and the operator does not have to search for small fatigue cracks to insure the structural integrity of the airframe. This philosophy overlooked the possibility of the large crack developing in an aging structure with fatigue damage where the residual strength would be lower than in the new airplane. Therefore, advanced technology is necessary to allow the industry to economically assess the durability of high time airplanes and to maintain the airframe so that adequate residual strength is available for all conceivable damage scenarios. This advanced technology includes better fracture mechanics based analysis methods to predict fatigue crack growth and residual strength. These methods supplement the full scale fatigue tests conducted by the manufacturers. Using tests and analytical results, the hot spots are identified, critical crack sizes are specified, and inspection intervals are determined.

The military transport aircraft fleet is also aging [3]. There are several important fundamental differences between the service history of the military transport fleet and the typical commercial airline fleet. One significant difference is that the military transport airplanes may be much older in years but may not have nearly as many flights as a commercial transport aircraft. Also, the typical down time between flights for a commercial aircraft may be a fraction of the down time for an Air Force transport aircraft. This is reflected in a fundamental difference in the service environment within which the aircrafts are maintained, inspected, and repaired. These differences between the commercial and military environments may result in some differences in the technology requirements.

An interesting example comparing military and commercial transport aircraft service history is the Boeing 707 and the USAF KC-135A Tanker. Both of these Boeing manufactured aircraft share many common design features and were placed in service in the mid-1950's. A partial comparison of the commercial and military fleet service history is given below:

    Number of 707 delivered:  728
    Number of KC-135A delivered:  732
    Median flight hours:  707 fleet:  48,065
                          KC-135 fleet:  13,404
    Median number of flights:  707 fleet:  18,632
                               KC-135:  2,982

Most of the B-707 commercial transport aircraft have been retired. However, the USAF is still operating most of the original aircraft in the KC-135 Tanker fleet and would like to extend the fleet life for another 25 years or more. Because of the very long life of these aircraft, airframe life extension is receiving considerable attention by the Air Force Materiel Command.

The desire to extend the life of the KC-135 Tanker fleet another 20-30 years raises several important technical questions. In particular, are there long-term time-dependent materials degradation processes occurring which may become synergistic with cyclic loading-dependent fatigue crack initiation and growth? The USAF is practicing aggressive corrosion protection and control programs which will prevent unacceptable levels of corrosion from occurring. However, protective coatings will not prevent the exposure of the newly created fracture surfaces of fatigue cracks to a corrosive environment. Will the effects of the environment accelerate fatigue crack growth in a manner that cannot be predicted by our current fracture mechanics based damage tolerance methodologies? Research is required to better understand the effects of environment of fatigue crack

initiation and residual strength. Analytical methods need to be developed that properly account for the synergy between the environment, time, and spectrum loading effects.

Perhaps the technical area requiring the most technology development is nondestructive inspection (NDI). More reliable and economical inspection methods are needed to find smaller cracks in riveted and mechanically fastened structure, to detect disbonds in bonded structure, and to detect and map the degree of severity of corrosion. The detection of cracks and corrosion in second layer and hidden structure is particularly challenging. The objective of the technology development should be to find smaller damage and simultaneously improve the probability of detection capability of the inspection systems. Cost effectiveness is also a consideration. An obvious way to reduce cost is to lower the time required to perform the inspection. Broad area rapid scanning techniques and a greater reliance on robotics is one possible way to lower inspection costs.

The FAA, NASA, and the USAF have developed a cooperative research effort aimed at providing a technological basis for ensuring the continued safe operation of the U.S. commercial airplane fleet and the military transport fleet. These government sponsored R&D Programs are closely coordinated with complementary activities being conducted by industry. For example, the full-scale fatigue tests conducted by the manufacturers provide essential data necessary to verify the advanced methodologies being developed in the R&D programs. Furthermore, the test articles provide a test bed for determining the capability of new NDI techniques under development.

## References

1. 1991 International Conference on Aging Aircraft and Structural Airworthiness, proceedings edited by Charles E. Harris, NASA CP-3160, National Aeronautics and Space Administration, Washington, D.C., 1992.

2. Proceedings of the FAA/NASA 6th International Conference on Continued Airworthiness of Aircraft Structure, edited by Catherine A. Bigelow, DOT/FAA/AR-95/86, Federal Aviation Administration, Washington, D.C., 1995.

3. Second USAF Aging Aircraft Conference, proceedings edited by C. I. Chang, AFOSR-TR-94-0756, Bolling Air Force Base, Washington, D.C., 1994.

# Aging Aircraft Life Extension - Composite Repairs of Primary Metallic Structure

J. B. Cochran, R. P. Bell and H. R. Michael
Lockheed Martin Aeronautical Systems
Department 73-25, Zone 0160
86 South Cobb Drive
Marietta, GA  30063

## Introduction

It is, and has been for many years, common practice to repair aircraft structures using repair doublers of like material, and attach to the structure with metal fasteners. This approach has the advantage of compatibility of materials and simplicity of analysis. In cases where the repair member thickness is restricted, however, a material with strength and modulus of elasticity greater than the damaged material should be used. Also, when a repair doubler is installed with fasteners, additional fatigue crack sites are created at the fastener holes, where eventual cracks may result. Repairs of metal structures using bonded doublers made from composite materials offer the potential of increased time between inspections, reduced repair time and provide the advantage of thinner repair members and elimination of repair fasteners.

Lockheed began studying the concept of using composite materials for the repair of C-141 airframe components in 1984. During 1987, WR-ALC awarded Lockheed Martin Aeronautical Systems a contract to study this concept for use on the C-141B weapon system. This paper will cover the selection of candidate locations, selection of configuration and materials for repairs, and the analytical evaluation of the repairs for structural adequacy and durability on the C-141B.

- The areas selected for repair are actual C-141 potential problem areas.

- The repair is to be bonded to the structure and fasteners are not to be used for its attachment to structure.

- The structure to be repaired is to be disturbed as little as possible. This is done to eliminate the possibility of damage due to removal and installation of fasteners.

- Maximum advantage is to be taken of the use of available materials, fabrication and installation methods, test data and service experience.

- In keeping with the goal of minimum development testing, detailed Finite Element Models (FEM) are used extensively to predict the stress distribution in the original structure.

- The repair is sized such that it reduces the stress level in the repair/prevent area by a minimum of fifteen (15) percent. This reduced stress level will result in significant retardation in crack growth rate as well as reduced inspection burden, down time and costs.

## Design Studies for Repair Locations

The design of composite repairs for primary structural areas of the C-141B aircraft is based on two primary criteria. First, the general repair technology is based on work that significantly reduces cost, time, and risk. Second, a research and development phase was undertaken to make the optimum use of this technology for the selected structural areas on the C-141 aircraft. These composite repairs form the basis from which future repairs or preventive maintenance actions can be implemented on in service aircraft.

A feasibility study resulted in selection of five (5) locations on the C-141B aircraft for study of repair/reinforcement with composite materials. The locations are identified as:

- Inner Wing to Outer Wing Lower Surface Rear Beam Joint - WS 405

- Wing Lower Surface Panel Riser Weep Holes and Rib Clip Attachment Holes - Typical on Inner Wing

- WS 77 Inner Wing Aft Corner Fitting to Beam Cap

- Vertical Stabilizer/Dorsal Longeron Intersection at Vertical Stabilizer Front Beam

- FS 998 Fuselage/Main Landing Gear Frame

These five areas were chosen on the basis of need and not necessarily for ease of application of composite repairs. The areas chosen provide a good cross section of problems facing the composite repairs. These repair locations are in Figure 1.

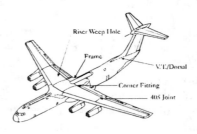

*Figure 1. Repair Study Locations*

## Materials and Processes

After several investigations of different adhesives, FM73M, a structural film adhesive system from American Cyanamid, curable at 80°C (176°F) with negligible performance penalty, was selected as the primary adhesive system. FM73M adhesive has an improved shelf life and moisture resistance compared to other adhesives and provides excellent durability with simple surface preparation.

Boron Fiber Reinforced Plastics (BFRP) was the choice over Carbon Fiber Reinforced Plastics (CFRP) as a general repair material. Boron fiber offers superior stiffness, fatigue strength and its coefficient of thermal expansion is closer to aluminum than that of carbon fibers. Low electrical conductivity of boron fiber systems allows eddy current inspection equipment to detect minor cracks under repair patches. In addition, boron fiber composite patch forms barrier to further corrosion.

When selecting a boron fiber composite material the basic selection is between two systems supplied by Textron. For repair work the Textron 5521/4 material is preferred because of its lower cure temperature. This also results in lower inducted thermal stresses for on-site cured patches and reduced thermal input required to the repair area. The slight penalty in reduced physical properties at lower temperatures has not been a limiting factor in current repair applications.

Surface preparation is perhaps the most important aspect of composite repair of metallic structure. Studies revealed that a silane adhesive promoter with alumina grit-blasting or grit-blasting with a phosphoric acid paste etch served as a simple treatment and provided high bond durability without aggravating a stress-corrosion condition.

## Structural Analysis

The main goal of composite repair of metal structures is to reduce stress levels and consequently retard crack initiation and/or crack growth that results in enhanced durability. Preliminary sizing of repairs are made and the sizes finalized using detailed Finite Element Models (FEM). The FEMs are used to determine stress distributions in the structure with and without repairs. The anistropic properties of composite laminates are calculated by using a Lockheed developed computer program. The bond in each FEM is modeled using linear elastic elements to determine bond shear stresses. The adhesive bond is modeled as linear CFAST elements, and their stiffness is calculated separately. Model results show that the composite doubler reduces stress in the substructure at the end of the composite doubler which is acceptable as long as the area does not contain a stress riser such as a fastener hole or radii. Applying these stress reductions to the damage tolerance analysis of the repaired area shows a magnitude of increased fatigue life as demonstrated in Figure 2.

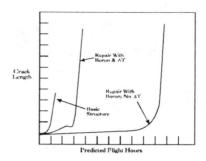

*Figure 2. Fatigue Life Enhancement*

## Repair Installation

Two methods of doubler installation to the structure were examined. In the first method a precured patch is bonded in position, and in the second method, a patch is entirely cured in place. Each method has its advantages and disadvantages. A precured patch develops the optimum properties of a laminate since it can be cured under controlled temperature and pressure. The subsequent bonding of the precured patch to the structure is governed by the structure's configuration. This method of repair installation is best suited for the Boron/Epoxy system where its relatively large stiffness prevents a good fit to complex contours or structure with small radii. A cured in-place patch has the advantage of being molded to the contour and shape of the repair area. This attribute is the most important factor in considering this type of repair. However, less than ideal curing conditions mean that the optimum properties of the material are not realized. Due to the different temperature expansion rates between boron and aluminum and graphite and aluminum, it is essential to cure at the lowest possible temperature, consistent with strength and other requirements, to keep built-in stresses in the repair area to a minimum. In addition, the local heat sink developed in a heavy aluminum structure often prevents the attainment of higher temperatures. Lockheed currently uses a "forced hot air" impingement process contained in a special customized chamber to apply evenly distributed heat to the repair area.

Several different ways of applying pressure during cure to the repair area were considered. The accessibility to the repair area and the environmental conditions dictate that no single method is suitable for all cases. The normal methods of applying pressure to the bond line such as autoclave or press are not possible. Other means such as direct mechanical pressure, local vacuum bagging or inflatable bladders can be used. Each one of these methods has limitations so the particular selection will depend upon the location, shape, extent of repair and accessibility.

## Verification

A test program to provide design and application verification was accomplished to substantiate the analytical process already conducted. The test program demonstrated realistic analytical correlation in both static strength and crack growth retardation. These tests, combined with in-service aircraft experience, have strengthened confidence in composite repair usage and lead to a full realization of this technology.

# The Effect of Elevated Temperature Exposure on the Damage Tolerant Properties of Aluminum Alloys Intended for Elevated Temperature Application

Anthony P. Reynolds
University of South Carolina
Department of Mechanical Engineering
Columbia, South Carolina 29208

Because of their ease of fabricability, durability, and good specific properties, precipitation hardened Aluminum alloys have been the materials of choice for fuselage and wing skins on subsonic aircraft for over 50 years. At the present time, precipitation hardening alloys are being evaluated for use in elevated temperature applications such as supersonic transport aircraft. These applications require stability of mechanical properties, implying stable microstrucutures. Precipitation hardened aluminum alloys present special problems with regard to elevated temperature service. Generally, the microstructure of such alloys are not stable for long times at elevated temperature. Previous studies have shown that tensile strength and ductility are not adequate indicators of microstructural stability. While tensile properties remain nearly constant, fracture toughness may show significant degradation after elevated temperature exposure. The use of these alloys for elevated temperature applications will therefore require better understanding of the related mechanisms of microstructural evolution and property degradation. In the work reported below, the feasibility of using short term elevated temperature exposure data to predict the effects of long term exposure at some lower temperature was evaluated.

Three developmental, high strength, precipitation hardened aluminum alloys were evaluated. The alloys had the following nominal compositions: Al-5.4Cu-0.5Mg-0.5Ag-0.12Zr-0.3Mn (alloy 1), Al-3.5Cu-0.96Li-0.4Mg-0.42Ag-0.12Zr-0.3Mn (alloy 2) and Al-3.4Cu-0.8Li-0.4Mg-0.5Ag-0.14 Zr (alloy 3). Alloys 1 and 2 were recrystallized. Alloy 1 has a random texture while alloy 2 exhibited a strong GOSS, recrystallization texture. Alloy 3 was predominantly unrecrystallized and showed a strong deformation texture and grains which were highly elongated in the rolling direction. Each of the alloys was provided in the T8 condition in 2.3 mm thick sheet. The alloys were subjected to elevated temperature exposures of duration from 100 to 9000 hours depending on the exposure temperature. The exposure temperatures were 93°C, 107°C, and 135°C.

R-curve behavior and relative strength of the alloys were determined before and after elevated temperature exposures. J-R curves were produced according to ASTM E-1152 using 50.8 mm wide, compact tension specimens and unloading compliance to measure crack length. J-integral values were converted to K (elastic stress intensity). Rockwell A scale hardness was used to determine the relative strength of the alloys as a function of exposure. Changes in fracture surface morphology resulting from elevated temperature exposure were examined with the scanning electron microscope (SEM).

The evolution of hardness as a function of exposure time is similar in alloys all of the alloys. Alloys 1 and 2 exhibit increased hardness with exposure time at 93°C and 107°C for times to 3000 hours. Exposure at 135°C results in steady or initially increasing hardness followed by declining hardness at longer times for all three of the alloys. Alloy 3 exhibits increasing hardness for up to 7000 hours at 107°C. This is followed by decreasing hardness between 7000 and 9000 hours. The observed changes in hardness are not large in any of the alloys: ranging between 1 and 3 points on the Rockwell A scale. The observed increases in hardness resulting from the elevated temperature exposures may be explained thusly: the precipitation aging temperature for each of the alloys investigated is higher than the exposure temperatures, therefore, at the exposure temperatures there will be solute available for additional precipitation. At long exposure times, the additional solute will be consumed and precipitate coarsening will occur. The lower the temperature of exposure, the longer the time required for the onset of precipitate coarsening and reduced strength/hardness.

Figure 1 illustrates the effect of exposure on the fracture resistance of alloys 1 and 2. In all cases the fracture resistance is represented by the R-curve value at a physical crack extension of 2mm. At constant time of exposure, for both alloys, increasing exposure temperature results in decreased fracture resistance. This reduction in fracture resistance is accompanied by an increase in the area fraction of intergranular fracture.

Figure 2 illustrates the fracture resistance of alloy 3 as a function of time and temperature of exposure. Depending on the conditions of elevated temperature exposure, alloy 3 exhibited three distinctly different types of R-curve. The first type of R-curve is characterized by stable crack growth at toughness levels similar to or slightly higher than alloys 1 and 2; this type of R-curve is representative of the behavior of T8 material and material which had been exposed for 9000 hours at 107°C (open circles in figure 2). The second type of R-curve is characterized by initial crack extension (up to about 0.5 mm) similar to that in T8 material followed by unstable crack growth or pop-in at a low, constant, stress intensity level. The initial pop-in event typically results in crack extension of greater than two millimeters. This type of R-curve behavior was observed in material which had been exposed at 107°C for times between 1500 and 7000 hours (solid circles in figure 2). The third type of R-curve behavior observed is stable tearing at toughness levels below that observed for T8 material. This type of behavior is typical of material which has been exposed at 135 °C (open squares in figure 2).

Each of the types of R-curve produced by testing of alloy 3 results in a characteristic fracture surface morphology. T8 material and that exposed for 9000 hours at 107°C exhibit predominantly transgranular microvoid coalescence. Alloy 3 exposed at 135°C fails by dimpled intergranular fracture. After exposure at 107°C for times between 1500 and 7000 hours, failure occurs by a mixture of dimpled intergranular and brittle appearing, smooth intergranular fracture. Interestingly, the unstable crack growth (pop-in behavior) and brittle intergranular fracture occur after exposure times and temperatures which correspond to increased strength in alloy 3.

The mechanical property and fracture morphology evolution experienced by alloys 1 and 2 as a result of elevated temperature exposure is readily explained by the nucleation and growth of grain boundary precipitates. This phenomenon, although undesirable, is expected and may be accounted for when predicting the mechanical properties of an alloy in the long term. The behavior of alloy 3 after exposure at 107°C is unexpected and would confound most attempts to determine long term properties by accelerated testing via exposure at temperatures above the anticipated service temperatures. This difficulty illustrates the danger of so-called "accelerated tests" which may not result in valid conclusions due to the possibility of introducing degradation mechanisms which do not relate to service conditions or, more alarming, fail to characterize degradation mechanisms which do correspond to service conditions.

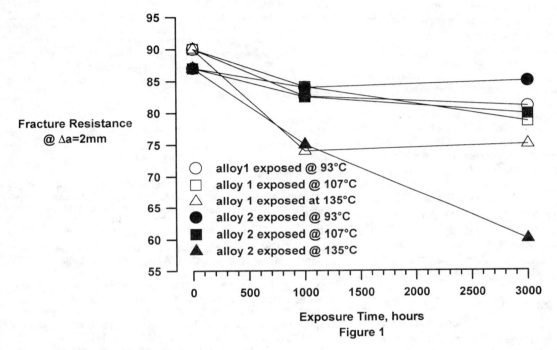

Fracture Resistance @ Δa=2mm

○ alloy1 exposed @ 93°C
□ alloy 1 exposed @ 107°C
△ alloy 1 exposed at 135°C
● alloy 2 exposed @ 93°C
■ alloy 2 exposed @ 107°C
▲ alloy 2 exposed @ 135°C

Exposure Time, hours
Figure 1

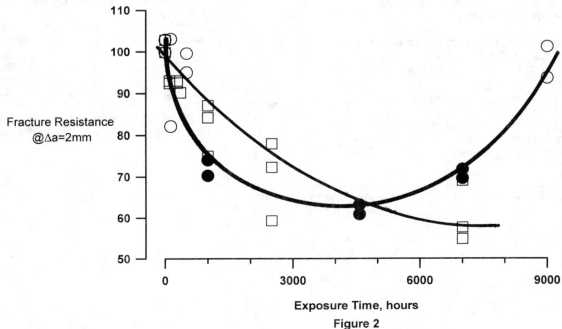

Fracture Resistance @Δa=2mm

Exposure Time, hours
Figure 2

293

# Dynamic response of strain gages up to 300kHz

Kazunaga Ueda, Akira Umeda
National Research Laboratory of Metrology
1-1-4, Umezono, Tsukuba, Ibaraki, 305, Japan

Although strain gages are widely used for dynamic measurement, their dynamic characteristics have not been thoroughly investigated. There are only a few data concerning the extent to which the strain gages can be applicable to dynamic measurement. Recently, we developed a novel method for evaluating dynamic characteristics of strain gages up to 200$\mu\varepsilon$ in strain and up to 200kHz in frequency using elastic waves and the laser interferometer[1],[2]. In this report, the ranges of the method are extended to about 2000$\mu\varepsilon$ in strain and to 300kHz in frequency. This report also mentions self-generated voltages[3],[4].

Figure 1 shows the apparatus. A cylindrical projectile is driven by compressed air and strikes one end of a cylindrical bar, to which test strain gages are glued. A longitudinal elastic wave pulse, whose frequency band reaches to 300 kHz, is generated by the strike and propagates down the bar, imparting an impulsive input to the gages. The one-dimensional elastic wave theory relates the input strain $\varepsilon_i(t)$ to the velocity $v_{LI}(t)$ of the other end of the bar as follows:

$$\varepsilon_i(t) = v_{LI}(t+l_g/C) / 2C \qquad (1)$$

where $C$ is the wave velocity in the bar and $l_g$ is the distance from the gages to the bar end. The velocity of the bar end is measured accurately by the laser interferometer[5]. Comparing the gages output $\varepsilon_o(t)$ with the input in the frequency domain, the transfer function $G(j\omega)$, the gain $g(\omega)$ and the phase $\phi(\omega)$ characteristics are determined with the following equations[1]:

$$G(j\omega) = L[\varepsilon_o(t)] / \{L[\varepsilon_i(t)] G_c(j\omega)\} \qquad (2)$$

$$g(\omega) = |G(j\omega)| \qquad (3), \qquad \phi(\omega) = \arg\{G(j\omega)\} \qquad (4)$$

where $\omega$ is the angular frequency. The term $G_c(j\omega)$ in Eq.(2) is needed to compensate for the dispersion of elastic waves, and is calculated using Skalak's analytical solution[6],[1].

Figure 2 shows the gain and phase characteristics of strain gages of different gage lengths(3,10,20mm). Figure 3 gives the characteristics of the 10mm gages at different strain levels(360,750,1720$\mu\varepsilon$). Static gage factors are taken for the references of the gain in these figures. From the figures, it can be seen that the gage length is one of the major factors which constitutes the dynamic response of strain gages, and that the static gage factor is applicable to the dynamic measurement in ordinary engineering situations. Table 1 compares some values of cut-off frequency, above which the gain is less than -3dB. The cut-off frequencies experimentally determined by this method are consistent with the estimates by other authors[7],[8],[9].

Self-generated voltage was a serious problem for wire gages[4],[10]. In the case of foil gages tested here, this phenomenon is also observed with repeatability. The self-generated voltage increases as the strain rate increases, but its timewise change is not always proportional to the strain rate (Fig.4), in contrast with Vigness's model[10]. The self-generated voltage may not be so serious a problem for the foil gages as it was for the wire gages, as long as they are used in the elastic regime, because it is only about 1% of the real output signal (Fig.5).

References:
[1] Umeda, A., Ueda, K., "Characterization of strain gage dynamic response using Davies' bar and laser interferometer", Proc. VII Int. Cong. on Exp. Mech., Las Vegas, June 1992, pp.837-842.
[2] Umeda, A., Ueda, K., "Measurement of the strain gage dynamic transverse and longitudinal sensitivity using pulse elastic waves and laser interferometry", Proc. 10th Int. Conf. on Exp. Mech., Lisbon, July 1994, pp.319-324.
[3] Stein, P.K., Private Communication, June 1992.
[4] Nisbet, J.S., et al., "High-frequency strain gauge and accelerometer calibration", J. Acoust. Soc. Am., 32-1, pp.71-75, 1960.
[5] Ueda, K., Umeda, A., "Characterization of shock accelerometers using Davies bar and laser interferometer", Exp. Mech., 35-3, pp.216-223, 1995.
[6] Skalak, R., "Longitudinal impact of a semi-infinite circular elastic bar", J. Appl. Mech., 24, pp.59-64, 1957.
[7] Oi, K., "Transient response of bonded strain gages", Exp. Mech., 6-9, pp.463-469, 1966.
[8] Bagaria W.J., Sharpe,Jr., W.N., "Temperature and rise-time effects on dynamic strain measurement", Exp. Mech., 20-6, pp.205-210, 1980.
[9] D'Acquisto, L., Tschinke, M.F., "A digital system to consider noise and dynamic conditions in strain gauge measurement", Proc. XIII IMEKO World Cong., Torino, Sept. 1994, pp.1887-1892.
[10] Vigness, I., "Megnetostrictive electricity in strain gauges", Rev. Sci. Instrum., 27-12, pp.1012-1014, 1956.

Table 1 Comparison of cut-off frequencies

| Gage length | Experiment by the authors | | | Analysis by D'Acquisto & Tschinke | Estimate by Oi | Revised estimate by Bagaria & Sharpe,Jr. |
|---|---|---|---|---|---|---|
| | 359-370$\mu\varepsilon$ 97-104s$^{-1}$ | 745$\mu\varepsilon$ 294s$^{-1}$ | 1709-1734$\mu\varepsilon$ 718-751s$^{-1}$ | | | |
| 3mm | >288kHz | | >293kHz | 737kHz | >360kHz | >660kHz |
| 10mm | 239kHz | 244kHz | 215kHz | 221kHz | >170kHz | >210kHz |
| 20mm | 117kHz | | 132kHz | 110kHz | > 95kHz | >108kHz |

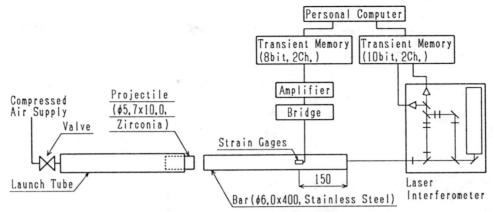

Fig.1 Block diagram of the experimental apparatus

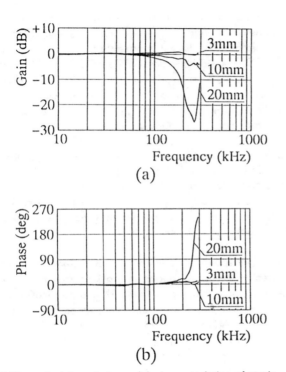

Fig.2 The gain (a) and phase (b) characteristics of strain gages of 3,10,20mm at 1720~1750με

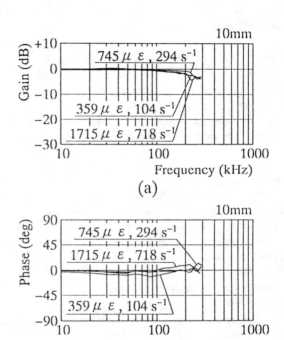

Fig.3 The gain (a) and phase (b) characteristics of the 10mm strain gages at 360,750,1720με

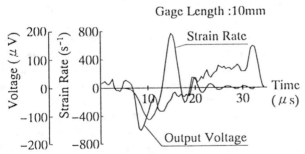

Fig.4 Comparison of the self-generated voltage with the strain rate determined by the interferomery

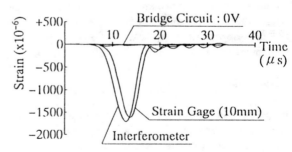

Fig.5 Comparison of the self-generated voltage with the real output signal and with the input strain determined by the interferometry

# Non Contact and Whole Field Strain Analysis with a Laseroptical Strain Sensor

Dr. Andreas Ettemeyer

Dr. Ettemeyer GmbH & Co.

Memminger Str. 72/207

D-89231 Neu-Ulm

Germany

The requirements of components and elements in automotive and aircraft industries, in apparatus engineering and terotechnology have been steadily increasing during the last decades. Therefore better knowledge about materials is necessary and new approaches have to be gone in material testing .

Nowadays in mechanical material testing strains are measured only between two distinctive points on the sample with probes or by optical analysis of two marked positions on the surface of the sample. Informations about eventual inhomogeneous strain distribution between these two points can not be obtained by these methods.

With a new laseroptical strain sensor many questions in material testing can be answered, which conventional methods did not solve. The laseroptical strain sensor was designed for whole field analysis of deformation- and strain-fields on the surface of the sample. It requires no marking on the sample and is measuring without contact on nearly any surface.

The laseroptical strain sensor uses the principle of laser-speckle-interferometry [1] and can substitute simultaneously a great number of conventional strain gauges. Therefore defects in the sample can be detected far beyond damage. Inhomogenities inside the structure are made visible, strain fields and stress concentrations, crack propagation, shear bands etc. can be seen.

The sample is illuminated with infrared laser light and observed with a high resolution video camera. Laser illumination and camera are integrated into a small casing (160mm x 80mm x 100mm), fig. 1. The measuring field of the sensor is approx. 30mm x 40mm, the working distance 240mm from the surface of the sample. Then deformations as small as 0.1μm resp. strains of 0.001% can be measured [2].

While the sample is loaded the deformation of the surface of the sample produces socalled interference fringes. These are displayed online on a video monitor and show the deformation field of the investigated object. The evaluation software ISTRA for windows enables fast and automatic analysis of the interference fringes and their quantitative transformation into deformation and strain fields. Of course the results can be displayed graphically and postprocessed afterwards.

According to the high sensitivity of the system investigations can already be carried out at very little load and little strains. Therefore it is possible to see inhomogenities and defects inside the material non destructively. Using an automatic serial measurement technique large deformation and strain values can be measured as well. Events like yielding of material, crack growth and inhomogeneous deformations during loading can be analysed.

For example fig. 2 shows the measurement of a flat steel sample during tensile test. The test was carried out in 10 measuring steps and the elongation and strain fields were measured at each step. In the figure the strain field at certain load levels is displayed showing clearly the shear bands at higher loading levels.

The high spatial resolution of the system is especially interesting for applications in fracture mechanics where crack opening, crack growth etc. should be measured. Fig. 3 shows the strain distribution of a notched sample in tensile test. At the bottom of the notch a crack is producing a local strain concentration which is made visible by the laseroptical strain sensor.

As the laseroptical strain sensor can be applied to any non reflective surface, investigations of difficult materials like rubber-metall-composites, bondings, ceramics, fibre reinforced plastics, textiles and many others are possible.

In summary this new laseroptical strain sensor gives much more informations about the behaviour of materials than could be achieved with conventional techniques. Additional no marking is required on the sample and it provides full field information within the whole measuring field. The measuring information is directly corresponding to numerical results from e.g. FEM calculations which can be compared with the experimental results. Therefore this new sensor will be very interesting for the development of new materials and connection techniques, especially for non isotropic materials like reinforced plastics, composite materials, etc..

References:

[1]   R. Jones and C. Wykes, Holographic and speckle interferometry, 2nd edition, Cambridge University Press, Cambridge 1989

[2]   A. Ettemeyer, Miniaturisierte Speckle-Sensoren für die Qualitätsprüfung, Laser 95 Conference, Juni 1995

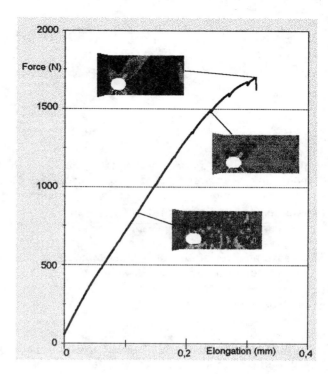

Fig. 2:   Tensile test on a steel sample. The graphic is presenting the strain distribution at different load levels.

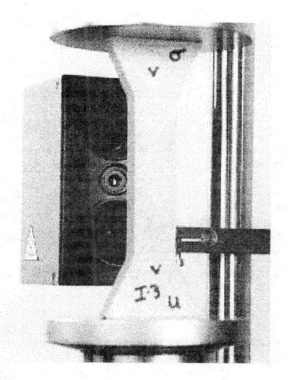

Fig. 1:   Laseroptical strain sensor in tensile testing machine

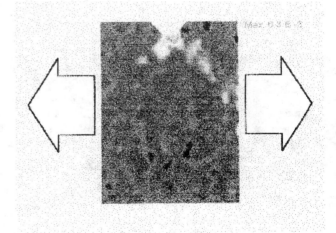

Fig. 3:   Fracture mechanics probe: a crack at the bottom of the notch produces increased strains.

# HIGH TEMPERATURE STRAIN GAGES WITH APPLICATION OF NEW ORGANOSILICATE ADHESIVES

by E. J. Nekhendzy, V. A. Kratikov,Y.I. Khodobin, R.A. Tarasov
NPO CKTI

194031, Polytechnicheskaya, 24, St. Petersburg, RUSSIA

S.P. Wnuk, V.P. Wnuk
Hitec Products, Inc.
P.O. Box 790, Ayer, MA 01432, USA

High temperature strain gages (HTSG), based on the organosilicate adhesives of OS-82-01 (B-58) and other types have been previously developed in USSR.  Material is applied as a precoat and then as adhesive, bonding the sensitive grid to the sublayer, by a simple painting technique, followed by polymerization (hardening) through heat treatment at 300°C.  These HTSG were suitable for long-term service to 550°C and have been used extensively for power and other equipment testing under operating conditions. The subject of this report is the development of HTSG based on a new generation of improved organosilicate adhesive materials which increase heat resistance and upper temperature limit of HTSG while maintaining low cost and simplicity of painting technology.  The new adhesive material OS-92-18 has improved bonding properties over OS-82-01.  The polymerization mode is the same,  heating at a rate of 1 to 2°C/min up to 300°C, and holding at 300°C for one hour.

Four lots of HTSG made with adhesive OS-92-18 in quantities of $n = 10$; 7; 6; 5, were tested without loading for heat resistance, adhesion, and cohesion by a series of temperature cycles to 550, 600, 650, 700, 750°C with a one hour isothermal duration at maximum temperature, and cooling to 20°C after each cycle.  One lot of HTSG, n-11 was installed (welded) on a pure bending beam of a NPO CKTI high temperature test rig and tested by loading to strains of 1000 to 1350 mkm/m at temperatures of 20, 375, 20, 405, 605, 20, 700, 20°C. The strain sensitive element was a grid of nichrome wire 0.02mm dia., 10.3 mm long with 5 loops, and a nominal resistance of 400 Ohm.  Strain sensitivity (K-Factor), creep (relaxation) and resistance to ground per OIML Recommendation No. 62 [2] and State Russian Standard GOST 21616-91 [3] were measured.  Strain sensitivity and creep characterize strain transfer from the beam to microwire and are extremely sensitive to elastic-viscous properties of adhesive and adhesion to the beam.

Figure 1 shows resistance to ground vs temperature for all tests.  According to [3] only the minimum values are plotted.  Figure 2 presents the gage factor K determined at testing temperatures.  Gage factor changes slightly with temperature in the 20 to 375°C.  In the range of 375 to 685°C the sensitivity decreases with temperature $-3.77 \times 10^{-4}$/ °C.  At 700°C gage factor somewhat increases again, probably because the adhesive congeals, and its elastic modulus increases.  The relative r.m.s. deviation within sampling is less than 2.1%.  A constant gage factor value at 20°C after temperature cycles to 605°C and 700°C confirms that adhesion is fully retained. This is the significant positive result of the development.  The creep of HTSG is the result of stress relaxation within adhesive layer at a given constant strain of the test beam.   There is no creep within OS-92-18 adhesive in the temperature range of 20 to 375°C.  Creep at 605°C and 700°C are shown in Figure 3.  The creep measurement was possible due to a proposed procedure excluding drift and intrinsic creep of the beam from the output signal of the strain gage.  The hourly creep value is certified as a systematic error.

**Conclusions:**  The operating temperature of HTSG based on organosilicate adhesives is increased to the 700 to 750°C range for isothermal conditions and temperature cycling.  The manufacture and bonding of HTSG is still performed by an economical and simple paint application technology.  Small lots of HTSG made with OS-92-18 adhesive are currently being manufactured.

## REFERENCES

1.  Nekhendzy, E.Ju., "Kharitonov N.P., "Strain Gages For Static Strain Measurements at Elevated Temperatures," Leningrad, "Znaniye," 1962, 59pp.
2.  OIML, International Recommendation No. 62., "Performance Characteristics of Metallic Resistance Strain Gauges."
3.  State Russian Standard GOST 21616-91., "Strain Gages General  Specifications."

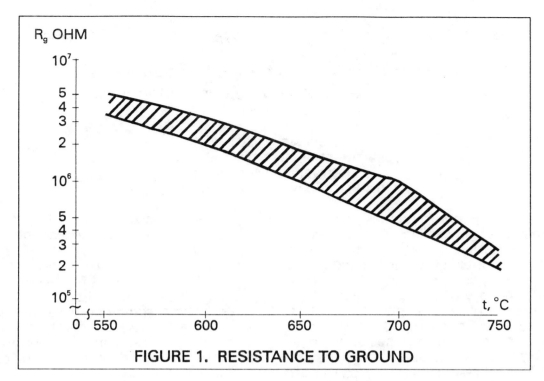

**FIGURE 1. RESISTANCE TO GROUND**

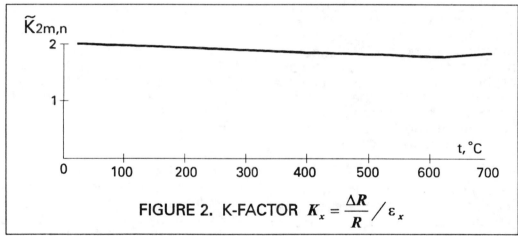

**FIGURE 2. K-FACTOR** $K_x = \dfrac{\Delta R}{R} \Big/ \varepsilon_x$

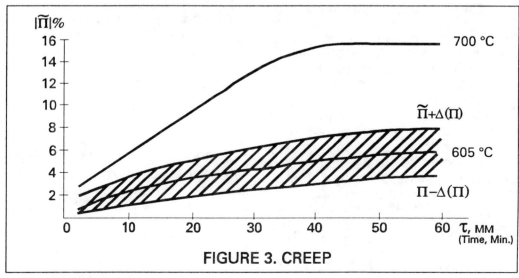

**FIGURE 3. CREEP**

# An Innovative Method for the Measurement of Post-Penetration Residual Velocity

Shi-Wei Ricky Lee
Department of Mechanical Engineering
The Hong Kong University of Science and Technology
Clear Water Bay, Kowloon, Hong Kong

In impact testing, photo diodes are widely used to measure the velocity of the projectile. The velocity is obtained from the time interval to sweep two points in the path of the projectile. For pre-impact velocity measurement, since the trajectory of the projectile is deterministic, only two pairs of photo diodes are needed. However, once the projectile penetrates the target, the post-penetration trajectory becomes unpredictable. Therefore, the measurement of residual velocity of the projectile after penetration is rather difficult. A conventional way to measure the post-penetration residual velocity is to use two arrays of photo diode pairs. This technique requires relatively sophisticated electric circuits. Besides, the photo diodes are easy to be false-triggered by the debris from the target. Another approach is to use the high speed camera. However, this method is very costly so that not every experimentalist can afford it.

A simple and low cost technique is introduced in this paper for the measurement of post-penetration residual velocity. Since the path of the projectile is unpredictable after penetrating through the target, the measuring device must be able to cover a certain area. Another requirement is that the device should not be false-triggered by the debris from the target. Therefore, instead of parallel arrays of photo diode pairs, two pieces of thin glass plates are used. The main reason for selecting glass is its brittleness which will lead to an instant signal on breakage. In addition, the glass plate is relatively strong for the debris but can be easily smashed by the projectile. A W-shaped conductive silver print is painted on one side of each glass plate as demonstrated in Figure 1. The two glass plates are clamp-mounted behind the target (see Figure 2). By breaking the glass plates consecutively, a signal as shown in

Figure 3 is recorded from which the residual velocity of the projectile can be calculated. One may question the effect of energy consumption in breaking the glass plate. This factor can be corrected as follows. The projectile is dropped as a free-fall object onto the glass plate. The threshold energy to break the glass ($E_g$) can be found from the height of the impactor. Therefore, from the energy consideration, the corrected residual velocity ($V_{rc}$) can be calculated as

$$V_{rc} = \sqrt{V_{rm}^2 + \frac{2}{M} E_g} \qquad (1)$$

where $V_{rm}$ and M are the measured residual velocity and the mass of the projectile, respectively. It should be noted that the aforementioned residual velocity is obtained by assuming a trajectory normal to the glass plates. If the post-penetration path of the projectile greatly deviates from the assumed path as shown in Figure 4(a), the resulting data may not be reliable. An elementary analysis can be performed to estimate the error as follows. As presented in Figure 4(a), the worst case in measurement is that the projectile hits the corner of the second glass plate. Beyond this limit, the test must be void. Since the effective area of the glass plate is a square, the largest possible deviation of trajectory can be estimated as

$$\phi_{max} = \tan^{-1}\left(\frac{d}{\sqrt{2}L}\right) \qquad (2)$$

where all the symbols are shown in Figure 4(a). Consequently, referring to Figure 4(b), the largest possible error $(\varepsilon_r)_{max}$ in residual velocity measurement would be

$$(\varepsilon_r)_{max} = \frac{V_{rm} - V_r}{V_r} = \cos(\phi_{max}) - 1 \qquad (3)$$

By specifying the geometry in Figure 4(a), the maximum allowable error in residual velocity measurement can be estimated. Therefore, the present approach provides a simple and low cost method with controllable error for the measurement of post-penetration residual velocity.

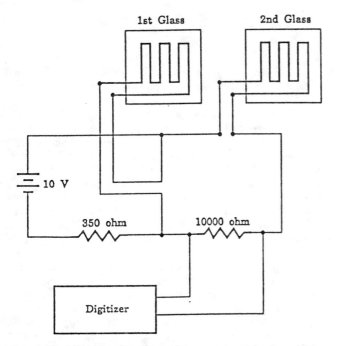

Fig. 1 Residual velocity measurement circuit

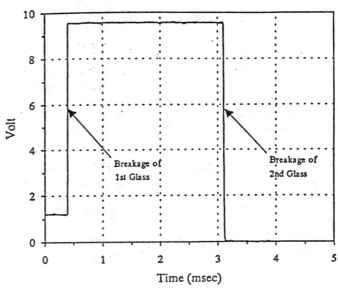

Fig. 3 Signal output from measurement circuit

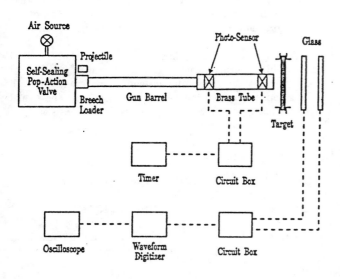

Fig. 2 Schematic diagram for impact facility.

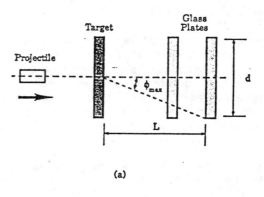

(a)

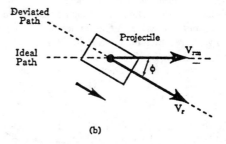

(b)

Fig. 4 Error analysis for velocity measurement: (a) deviation of trajectory after penetration; (b) vector diagram of residual velocity.

# Interlaminar Shear Testing of Composites

Sastry Chimalakonda
Graduate Student
Department of Mechanical Engineering
Northern Illinois University
DeKalb, IL 60115

Scott R. Short
Assistant Professor
Department of Mechanical Engineering
Northern Illinois University
DeKalb, IL 60115

Interlaminar shear failure (delamination) is a prominent failure mode for polymer-matrix composite materials. Interlaminar shear stresses are routinely generated in composite structures as a result of free edges, ply drop-offs, three-dimensional stress fields, etc. Accurate characterization of interlaminar shear failure is a prerequisite to maximum utilization of these important engineering materials.

A number of experimental methods have been proposed to characterize the shear behavior of composite materials. Although the torsion test of a tube theoretically provides a uniform shear stress state in the gage section of the test specimen, torsion tests are expensive to conduct. Although most other shear tests use inexpensive coupon-type specimens, they are beset with problems related to the nonuniform stress state produced during testing.

A variation of the industry standard interlaminar shear test, the short-beam shear test, has been proposed by Short [1]. This test method involves subjecting a sandwich beam, referred to as the SCS (steel/composite/steel) test sample, to four-point (quarters) flexure (Fig. 1). The SCS test sample consists of a coupon of composite material bonded between two strips of heat-treated steel. The steel face strips help to dissipate the local stress concentrations which have been shown to initiate failure near the loading region in the short-beam shear test [2]. Thus, the complicated failure modes, i.e., shear/compression, resulting from the crushing and buckling of the specimen near the loading region in the standard short-beam shear test are not observed in the SCS shear test. By avoiding these complicated failure modes, a much more representative characterization of Mode II failures, i.e., interlaminar shear, can be obtained.

Camping and Short [3] used a novel crack-detection device to further show that a shear failure produced in the SCS test method initiates along the midthickness plane of the composite coupon approximately halfway between the load and support points in the region of maximum interlaminar shear stress. Upon reaching a critical size, the shear failure propagates away from the site of initiation in both directions along the length of the specimen. The crack always reaches the specimen end closest to the crack initiation site before being driven back into the specimen, past midspan, onto the site of crack termination near the load point farthest from the failed end. This failure process is illustrated in Fig. 2.

Stress analysis complications introduced by the layered structure of the SCS test sample prompted Short to address the role of the through-thickness normal stress, $\sigma_z$, in a qualitative manner only. It was reasoned that the magnitude of $\sigma_z$ in the region between the load and supports damps out to such a degree that it can be considered to be fairly negligible on the failure plane (midplane).

In light of this qualitative approach with regard to the magnitude of the through-thickness normal stress, $\sigma_z$, and in order to bring closure to the previous research, a more accurate analysis of the magnitude of the through-thickness normal stress, $\sigma_z$, existing within the SCS test sample is desirable. The specific objective of this research was to more thoroughly investigate the role that the through-thickness normal stress, $\sigma_z$, plays in interlaminar shear failure in the SCS test method. The finite element software program Ansys™ was used to model the SCS test sample and predict the magnitude and distribution of $\sigma_z$.

A finite element model capable of simulating the experimental behavior of the layered SCS test sample was constructed. Four-node plane stress elements were used. The model incorporated resin-rich layers, referred to as "lumped epoxy," near the midthickness region of the beam. These regions allowed the finite element model to simulate the nonlinear shear behavior of the graphite-epoxy material. This model resulted in close agreement with the midspan deflection and the midspan strain experimental results. Varying the distribution of the lumped epoxy within the graphite-epoxy coupon did not significantly affect the kinematic results. Results of a contact stress analysis using the same model indicated that the maximum level of the through-thickness normal stress, $\sigma_z$, acting on the failure plane (midplane) of the SCS test sample between a load and support is approximately 5 % of the maximum interlaminar shear stress acting on the failure plane.

By confirming that the magnitude of the through-thickness normal stress is relatively insignificant as compared to the magnitude of the interlaminar shear stress at the instant of failure, the proposed SCS interlaminar shear test method can be considered to be a valid tool for characterizing the Mode II delamination resistance of fiber-reinforced composite materials.

References:

[1] Short, S.R., *Characterization of Interlaminar Shear Failures of Graphite-Epoxy Composite Materials*, Ph.D. Dissertation, The University of Dayton, Dayton, OH, 1990, pp. 16-20.

[2] Whitney, J.M., Browning, C.E., "On Short-Beam Shear Tests for Composite Materials," *Experimental Mechanics*, Vol. 25, No. 3, 1985, pp. 294-296.

[3] Camping, J.D., Short, S.R., "Crack-Detection Device for Brittle-Matrix Composite Materials," *Experimental Techniques*, Vol. 19, No. 6, 1995, pp. 15-18.

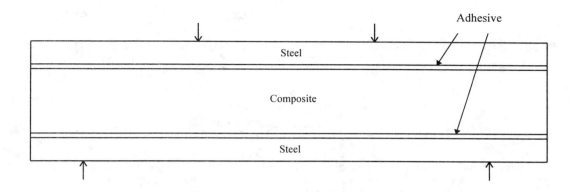

Fig. 1 SCS test sample.

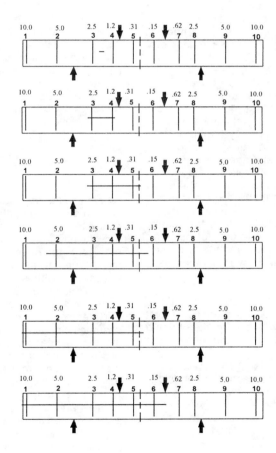

Fig. 2. Propagation of shear failure in an SCS test sample. (Integers correspond to sensor number; decimal numbers correspond to voltage drop of sensor used to monitor crack propagation.)

# Analyses of Double Cantilever Beam Adhesion Test Specimens

K. L. DeVries  and P. R. Borgmeier
University of Utah
College of Engineering
Salt Lake City, Utah 84112

Engineering design typically requires the joining of component parts. An ever increasingly common method of doing this is with adhesives. The calculation to predict the strength of an adhesive joint is no mean task. Predicting the strength of welded or pinned joints also is not easy. The parameters required to predict strength are generally determined from experiments. It is not easy to define the strength of an adhesive even though a large number of adhesive joint tests have been standardized by ASTM or other agencies. The "apparent strength" of an adhesive depends on the test method used to measure this entity. In fact, in comparing the "strength" of adhesives, an adhesive that appears superior in one test may actually appear inferior when tested by another method. For a given test method, what may appear to be relatively minor changes in geometry can have dramatic effects on test results. For example, one of the most common test methods is the "lap joint." Test results are typically reported as shear force per unit area (load at failure divided by the bonded area). Adhesive handbooks are available that list this "average shear strength" for literally thousands of commercial adhesives [1]. Such listings might be reviewed as implying that in "design" one can calculate the required bonded area for a joint by dividing the design load by these average stress values. Such is, in general, not the case. Differences in adhesive thickness, adherend thicknesses, and/or amount of overlap for a given set of adhesive and adherend materials can dramatically affect lap joint strength. This also is true for most other adhesive joint geometries. In fact, the results from almost all adhesive strength tests do no lend themselves in simple straightforward ways to the prediction of strength of other joints that differ in even subtle details from the test configuration.

In the 1960's and 1970's, researchers began exploring the use of the concepts of fracture mechanics in adhesive joint analysis [2-6]. These methods have the potential of using the results from a test joint to predict the strength of other joints with different geometries.

In a common fracture mechanics approach, the conditions for failure are calculated by equating the energy lost from the strain field as a "crack" grows to the energy consumed in creating the new crack surface. This energy per unit area, $G_c$, determined from standard tests is called, by various names including the specific fracture energy, the fracture toughness or the energy release rate.

In 1975, ASTM Committee D-14 adapted a test configuration and testing method with fracture mechanics ramifications based on pioneering efforts of Mostovy and Ripling [4, 7]. The method is described in ASTM D 3433. Figure 1 shows the shape and dimensions for one specimen type

recommended for use in this standard. The specimen is composed of two "beams" adhesively bonded over much of their length as shown in Figure 1. Testing is accomplished by pulling the specimen apart by means of pins passing through the holes shown near the samples left end. This mode sample configuration and loading to failure gives rise to the sample's nickname, "split cantilever beam." The other recommended geometry in ASTM D 3433 has the adherends tapered. While the analysis to be presented here is confined to the first geometry, this general insight into behavior and conclusion would also apply to the tapered sample.

The authors view the adaptation of standard ASTM D 3433 as a major advancement. It will be demonstrated, however, that one must be very judicious and careful in preparing specimens, conducting the tests, analyzing the results, and utilizing them for comparing adhesives for use in mechanical design.

ASTM D 3433 in Section 11 lists the following equation for the calculation of $G_c$:

$$G_c = \frac{\left[4L^2(\max)\right]\left[3a^2 + h^2\right]}{Eb^2h^3}$$

Where L is the applied load at failure, a is the length from the loading pins to the adhesive crack front, E is the modulus of elasticity of the material in the adherend and the other terms are obvious from Figure 1. The first term in this equation represents the energy associated with bending stresses and the second term is intended to account for the energy associated with shear stresses. This latter term is not unique, its value depending on method calculation and details of the assumed boundary conditions [see page 43-46 of Reference 8]. Furthermore, the derivation of the equation assumes standard "ideal" cantilever boundary conditions, i.e. the cantilever assumed end is rigidly fixed with no rotation of or stress in the beams beyond this point. It is also assumed that during deformation energy is stored only in the beams; any energy stored in the adhesive is neglected. The validity of these assumptions is dependent on the ratio of a/h, the relative adhesive thickness and the relative moduli of the adherend and adhesive.

In order to explore the validity of such assumptions and the importance of including the various terms in fracture mechanics analyses, a thorough, careful finite element analysis (FEA) of constant depth double cantilever beam adhesive specimens was undertaken using an ANSYS FEA code. Samples were constructed, tested, and the experimental results compared with the predictions of the finite element analysis. This comparison reveals that there are many practical situations where neglecting the above factors result in large differences and/or scatter in the experimentally determined values of $G_C$ and/or predicted strengths in design analyses. As a case in point, refer to Figure 2. This figure compares the G value versus a/h calculated using the equation from ASTM D 3433, with that obtained in this study using FEA. These FEA values agree quite well with analytical analysis to account for shear and end rotation [9-10]. Referring to Figure 2, it can be seen that with the recommended specimen, a/h would typically vary from as small as 2 to as much as 20 before one would anticipate the end effects near the right end should become significant. This is an a/h region where these non bending and simple shear effects are large, resulting in G values calculated by the recommended equation, differing significantly from the "correct" value. Furthermore, if advantage is taken of the full working length of the specimen, G values, calculated from the test results, differ significantly as the adhesive crack grows resulting in large scatter in the data. It is also important to note that Figure 2 includes only the energy associated with shear and non-ideal end conditions but ignores any energy in the adhesive (i.e. assumes zero adhesive thickness). For thick and/or compliant adhesives this latter aspect not only makes a significant contribution but its inclusion in the analysis provides important information and additional insights into behavior. Examples of these are the effect of adhesive thickness on strength and as demonstrated by the authors in a recent paper [11] facilitates prediction of the exact locus of the fracture path through the adhesive. In addition, when FEA was used for the fracture mechanics analysis (which included the above factors) the agreements with experiments was typically better than 5% (in one worst case, 10%) while it differed by as much as 50% when the simpler equation was used.

Acknowledgment: The authors appreciate the support of the National Science Foundation (DMR-9014565 and CMS-9522743) of this research.

References:

[1]    *Adhesives - International Plastics Selector*, Edition 6, D.A.T.A. Publishing, San Diego, California (1991).
[2]    Irwin, G.R., Fracture mechanics applied to adhesive systems, in *Treatise on Adhesion and Adhesives Volume I Theory* (Edited by R.L. Patrick), pp. 233-267, Marcel Dekker, Inc., New York (1967).
[3]    Williams, M.L., The continuum interpretation for fracture and adhesion, *Journal of Applied Polymer Science* **13**, 29-40 (1967).
[4]    Ripling, E.J., Mostovoy, S. and Patrick, R.L., Application of fracture mechanics to adhesive joints. *Adhesion*, ASTM STP **360**, 5-16 (1964).
[5]    Gent A.N., Fracture mechanics of adhesive bonds, *Rubber Chemistry and Technology* **47**(1), 202-212 (1974).
[6]    Anderson, G.P., Bennett, S.J., DeVries, K.L., *Analysis and Testing of Adhesive Bonds*, pp. 135-150, Academic Press, New York, NY (1977).
[7]    Mostovoy, S. and Ripling, E.J., *Journal of Applied Polymer Science* **15**, pp. 641-659 (1971).
[8]    Timoshenko, S.P. and Goodier, J.N., *Theory of Elasticity* 3rd Edition, McGraw Hill, New York, NY (1970).
[9]    Raasch, J., *International Journal of Fracture* 7, 289-300 (1971).
[10]    Kanninen, M.F., *International Journal of Fracture* 9, 83-92 (1973).
[11]    DeVries, K.L. and Borgmeier, P.R., Prediction of failure in polymeric adhesives, *1st International Congress in Adhesion Science and Technology,* Amsterdam, The Netherlands, October 16-20 (1995).

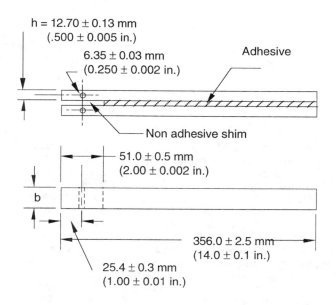

Figure 1. Flat adherend specimen from ASTM D 3433

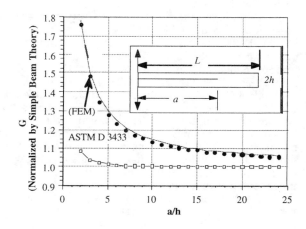

Figure 2. Comparison of normalized G values versus a/h for the suggested geometry given in ASTM D 3433 using the ASTM equation and FEA

# Deformation and Stress Analyses of Double-lap Adhesive Joints with Laminated Composite Adherends

M. Y. Tsai
Department of Engineering Science and Mechanics
Virginia Polytechnic Institute and State University
Blacksburg VA 24061-0219

J. Morton
Structural Materials Center, DRA
Farnborough, Hampshire, GU14 6TD, UK

and D. W. Oplinger
Federal Aviation Administration Technical Center
Atlantic City International Airport, NJ 08405

Adhesively bonded joints have potential to replace conventional fastener and rivet joints, especially in the application to the laminated composite structures. The adhesive bonding has merits, over other jointing methods, of the avoidance of drilling holes and reduction of stress concentrations. Double-lap adhesive joint, due to its simple configuration and lower peel stress characteristics, is often used in determining the adhesive properties for stress analyses and material quality assurance, and in the structure joining application. However, the mechanics of the laminated composite double-lap joints is not well understood. Therefore, understanding the mechanics of double-lap joint is crucial in the application of this joint on laminated composite structures.

The double-lap joints with unidirectional ($[0]_{16}$) and quasi-isotropic ($[0/90/-45/45]_{2s}$) composite adherends, under tensile loading, are investigated experimentally using a moiré interferometry and numerically using a finite element method. The geometry of the test specimens shown in Figure 1 is in accordance with ASTM D-3528 standard, which is adopted for determining adhesive shear strength for joints with isotropic adherends. In the experimental study, back-to-back strain gages (G1/G2 and G3/G4 in Figure 1) in the far field of the joint are used to monitor the loading conditions. The strain gage responses indicate the specimens were properly loaded without any load eccentricity occurring. Under these perfect loading conditions, the full-field moiré interferometry was employed to measure the surface in-plane deformations of the joint overlaps. The moiré displacement fields for these composite double-lap joints were determined within the load level in which the adhesive still remains linear and elastic. In the numerical analyses, a linear-elastic two-dimensional finite element model was performed to simulate the deformations and stress distributions of these composite double-lap joints.

Experimental and numerical results are presented in Figures 2 and 3 for longitudinal displacement fields and adhesive shear stress (strain) distributions, respectively. Moiré fringe patterns indicate that, unlike the unidirectional joint, the quasi-isotropic joint not only has relatively dense fringes due to relatively low longitudinal stiffness, but also shows, in the -/+ 45° laminae, the local fringe waviness which results from interlaminar shear stresses near (and on) the free surface in the off-axis plies due to the free edge effects. It is shown that the displacement fields from the moiré and numerical analyses are in a good agreement, respectively, for both of the joints, except for the fringe waviness, due to the three-dimensional free-edge phenomenon, shown in quasi-isotropic joints. Note that for the clarity of presentation numerical results only show the fringes with twice increment as moiré fringes. For normalized adhesive shear strain (stress) distributions, it is shown in Figure 3 that the distributions from the experimental and numerical analyses for both joints are not uniform. The non-uniformity of adhesive shear for the quasi-isotropic joint is higher than that for the unidirectional joint. That is, the quasi-isotropic joint has higher maximum adhesive shear strain (stress) than the unidirectional joint. This non-uniformity of the adhesive strain (stress) distributions is well predicted by the finite element analysis. It is also found that the difference of the adhesive shear non-uniformity between unidirectional and quasi-isotropic joints is mainly attributed to the different longitudinal stiffness.

The deformations and mechanics of the joints, from the experimental observation and numerical simulation, are illustrated in Figure 4. Figure 4(a) shows the deformation of a quarter of the double-lap joint. It is observed that there are transverse normal stresses ($\sigma_y$) in the mid-plane of the adherend and the strap moment, $M_u$, in the mid-plane of the strap, besides the longitudinal force, T/2. This force and moment equilibrium system results in the compressive deformations in the transverse direction near the extremity of the adherend and the tensile deformations near the extremity of the strap. The resulting adhesive stress system is shown in the free-body diagram in Figure 4(b). One-dimensional shear-lag closed-form solutions are examined and compared with the moiré and finite element analyses. It is shown that one-dimensional solutions, which neglect the bending and shear deformations of adherends, gave a reasonable prediction of the general trends of adhesive shear stress (strain) distributions, but not the maximum values of adhesive shear stress (strain) which is about 33% higher than the experimental and numerical solutions.

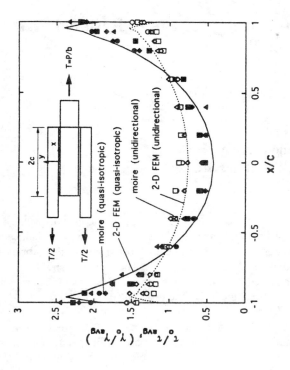

Figure 3. Adhesive shear stress (strain) distributions from FEM and moiré experiment.

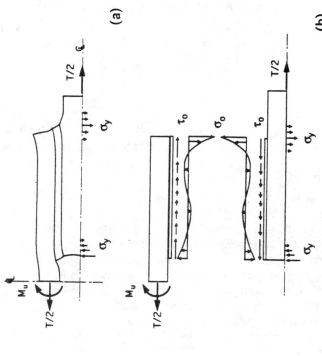

Figure 4. (a)Deformation of a quarter of double lap joint, (b) free-body diagram.

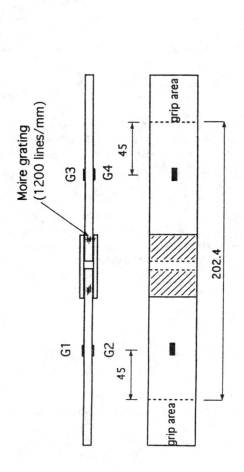

Figure 1. Configuration of specimen, strain gage and moiré grating instrumentation.

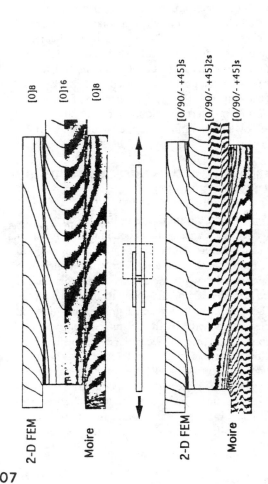

Figure 2. Horizontal displacement fields from FEM and moiré experiment.

307

# Stress Field of Reinforced Matrix with Imperfect Interface Under Residual Stress and Transverse Loading

B. S. Wang, F. P. Chiang & S. Y. Wu

Lab. for Experimental Mechanics Research
Department of Mechanical Engineering
State University of New York at Stony Brook
Stony Brook, NY 11794-2300

## INTRODUCTION

Interface in composite material plays a significant role in both overall and local properties of the composites. It is known that imperfect conditions exist in the matrix reinforcement interface because of the coating, diffusion or chemical reaction between the constituents and preliminary damage in the interface. The existence of the imperfect interface and residual stresses greatly affects the stress distribution and damage mechanism of the composites. Hostile stress distribution leads to the damage of the composites, especially brittle reinforced matrix composites which are susceptible to the interfacial debonding and the propagation of the debond crack. Several analytical works [1], [2], [3] have been done to mechanically model the imperfect interface and to study the effect of the imperfect interface to the mechanical behavior and failure mechanism of the composites. The current work is to experimentally evaluate the damage mechanism of reinforced matrix with different interfacial bonding conditions and the residual stress by incorporating with the available analytical results.

## EXPERIMENTAL AND ANALYTICAL STUDY OF INTERFACIAL STRESS FIELD

In order to understand the influence of the presence of the imperfect interface on the interfacial debonding, the growth of the crack and the failure of the composites, the maximum shear stress fields of the reinforced polymer matrix are obtained experimentally by photoelasticity. The experimental specimens are made by casting the epoxy resin sheet with the inclusions. The specimens with residual stresses and different bonding properties are made. By the normal casting, perfectly interfacial bond is generated between the epoxy resin (or the matrix) and the inclusion (or the reinforcement). The weak interfacial bond is achieved by application of the debond agent along the interface. In the perfect interface, both displacements and tractions are continuous across the matrix/reinforcement interface. Whereas for the imperfect bond case (or weak bond in the experimental specimen ), the tractions are still continuous because of equilibrium but the displacements can be discontinuous across the interface and the tangential traction can be completely lost for ideally lubricated matrix/reinforcement contact. The residual stress state is controlled by the curing process. Usually, the shorter the curing time, the larger the residual stress.

The above mentioned specimens with different interfacial bonding and residual stresses are loaded by remote single tension. By examining the specimens in the polariscope, the isochromatic fringes, which represent the average maximum shear stress $\tau_{max}$ through the thickness, are attained. Fig. 1 is a typical dark field isochromatic fringe pattern of a specimen with weakly bonded interface. The quantitative interpretation of the maximum shear stress from the fringes are obtained by the following equation.

$$\tau_{max} = nf / 2d$$

where n is the fringe order which is equal to 0, 1, 2..., f is the optical material fringe coefficient and d is the thickness of the specimen. The experimental results are compared with analytical solutions of the perfectly bonded circular elastic inclusion in an infinite elastic matrix subjected to remote single tension which was carried out by Goodier[4]. The comparisons are shown in Fig. 2. The analytical results of the normalized maximum shear stress $\tau_{max}/\sigma_{\infty}$ along the perfect interface with three typical $\mu_m/\mu_i$ ratios are given. The experimental results of the maximum shear stress of the reinforced matrix specimens with perfect and weak interface conditions are also shown in the plot.

## CONCLUSIONS

For the perfectly bonded interface, both experimental and analytical results show that for matrix with rigid inclusion, the maximum value of the maximum shear stress is approximately 60% higher than that of the homogeneous material. Both its quantitative value and location of the maximum value are dependent on the Poisson's ratio ν of the matrix material. With the increase of the ν, the quantitative value decreases.

For the weakly bonded specimen, the distribution of the maximum shear stress along the interface is similar to that of the perfectly interfacial bond, but its quantitative value increases. The maximum increase can be more than 100%. Therefore, the local debond or crack initiation is easier to occur in weakly bonded interface. The initial debond or crack starts along the interface, especially around the top or bottom side of the inclusion along the loading direction.

The existence of the residual stresses can be beneficial as well as detrimental to the composites depending on both the interfacial properties and the loading state.

## ACKNOWLEDGMENT

The financial support from the Air Force Office of the Scientific Research with grant No. F496209310219 is gratefully acknowledged.

## REFERENCES

[1] Hashin, Z (1991), *J. Appl. Mech.*, *(58)*, p444
[2] Pagano, N. J. & Tandon, G. P. (1990), *Mech. Mater.* *(9)*, p49
[3] Achenbach, J. D. & Zhu, H. (1989), *J. Mech. Phys. Solids*, *(37)*, p381
[4] Goodier, J. N. (1933), *J. Appl. Mech.* *(1)*, p39
[5] Wang, B. & Chiang, F. P. (1995), *Proc. of the SEM Spring Conference*, Michigan, p199

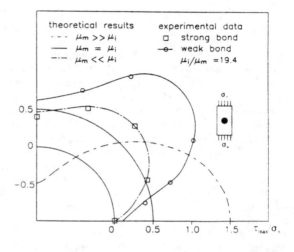

Fig. 2 $\tau_{max}/\sigma_\infty$ of experimental and analytical results along the perfectly or weakly bonded interface

Fig. 1 dark field isochromatic fringe pattern with weak interface

# Drop Weight Testing of Concrete Beams Externally Reinforced with Carbon Fiber Reinforced Plastic (CFRP) Strips

D.M. Jerome
Senior Research Engineer
Wright Laboratory
101 West Eglin Parkway, Suite 326
Eglin Air Force Base, Florida 32542-6810

C.A. Ross
Professor Emeritus
University of Florida
Graduate Engineering and Research Center
1350 North Poquito Road
Shalimar, Florida 32579

Laboratory size 7.62 x 7.62 x 76.2 cm plain lightweight concrete beams were externally reinforced with variable thickness CFRP strips and tested both statically in a load frame, and dynamically in a drop weight impact machine. The one, two, and three ply CFRP strips were applied to the tensile side of the concrete beams using a two-part epoxy adhesive and a vacuum fixture technique. Some three ply panels were also applied to the sides of several of the beams in addition to the three ply bottom tensile strips. A total of seventy-two beams in six different configurations were tested. All testing was conducted in three (center) point bending mode (Fig. 1), and the beams were simply supported. The dynamic tests were conducted at various drop heights to vary the loading rate, hence the strain rate in the beam test samples. The weight of the impact hammer and tup was 43.7 kg. The tup was instrumented with strain gages and calibrated statically in a compression load frame. Comparison of the measured load duration to the beam fundamental period showed the loading to be purely impulsive. All beams were instrumented using electrical resistance strain gages and a non-contact displacement gage which recorded displacement versus time. Strains and strain rates were then determined at up to three locations in the midspan cross section of each beam. Loads, displacements, impact velocities, accelerations, strains and high speed film data were all recorded, and detailed analyses were subsequently conducted. Beam midspan accelerations were obtained by double differentiation of the midspan displacement versus time data, and in turn, the beam's inertial loads were determined using the beam's effective mass. Beam bending loads were determined from the difference between the load versus time and the inertial load versus time data. Beam bending loads versus displacements were then determined. Various measures of merit were used to compare and contrast the six different beam types; peak tup, inertial, and bending loads, peak displacement, and fracture energies were calculated for all beams. The use of such thin, external CFRP reinforcement on beams is a new technique [1], and has been shown to provide modest flexural strength increases [2].

**Characterization of the Concrete** In order to characterize the concrete used in the beam test specimens, a series of static and dynamic compression and splitting tension tests were conducted. The static tests were conducted on a load frame, and the dynamic tests were conducted on a 5.08 cm diameter Split Hopkinson Pressure Bar (SHPB). Test results for the lightweight concrete used in the beam samples were then compared to normal weight concrete of varying unconfined compressive strength.

The results from all of the quasistatic and SHPB direct compression tests indicate that in compression, the lightweight concrete behaves identically, at least within the scatter of the data, to its normal weight counterpart, when loaded either quasistatically or dynamically. In compression, lightweight concrete shows moderate strain rate sensitivity, similar to its normal weight counterpart, with increases in strength up to 2.3 times the static value at strain rates from 100 to 300/sec.

In tension, the lightweight concrete does not appear to fall within the scatter of the data when compared to five different strength normal weight concrete mixes. In fact, the data show that the lightweight concrete is less strain rate sensitive than its normal weight counterpart, being shifted about a half-decade in strain rate for a constant dynamic tensile strength. In other words, lightweight concrete must be loaded about 3 times faster in order to achieve the same dynamic tensile strength as normal weight concrete. In either case, the normal and lightweight concrete have a higher strain rate sensitivity in tension than in compression.

**Static Beam Bending Experiments** Results from the static three (center) point bending experiments show that beams with three ply CFRP on the sides as well as the bottom are clearly able to take the most load prior to failure, and have the largest energy absorption or fracture energy capacity of all six different beam types tested.

Beams with two ply CFRP on the bottom only have the next highest energy absorption or fracture energy capacity, due to their high ductility and relatively high load carrying capability. Conversely, the experimental evidence indicates little to no benefit is realized using nylon fibers in the concrete mix as a potential technique to increase load, displacement, or fracture energy capacity, when compared to similarly reinforced beams without the nylon fibers added to the mix. It was thought that the nylon fibers should provide some additional energy absorption capacity by providing "bridges" across cracks thereby attenuating cracking.

There are still tremendous gains over the plain concrete beams in terms of load and displacement capacity, even with the bottom only one, two, and three ply CFRP reinforced beams. Increases of

2 to 4 in load and 11 to 17 in displacement are quite easily achieved with the addition of the CFRP. Consequently, increases in energy absorption or fracture energy from 30 to 80 are also achieved, when compared to the baseline plain concrete beams.

**Dynamic Beam Bending Experiments** Results from drop weight impact testing show that the measured peak amplitude of the tup load increases with an increase in drop height, along with corresponding increases in the calculated peak inertial load and peak bending load. This is consistent with other results [3]. Most of the load recorded by the tup is inertial in nature, therefore it is not surprising to see the tup load increase with drop height. The increase in peak bending load with increasing drop height implies an increase in beam "impact strength" with an increase in the load or stress rate, hence strain rate. Data from strain gages located on the bottom or tension side of the beams indicated an increase in strain rate with drop height. The peak bending load increase was highest for the "less reinforced" or less stiff beams, gradually declining in value as beam stiffness increased.

For the plain concrete beams, the maximum displacement (at failure) decreases with an increase in drop height. However, for those beams reinforced with CFRP, the displacement at failure increases with an increase in drop height.

Fracture energy consistently increases with an increase in drop height, which is in consonance with nonlinear fracture mechanics theory. This theory purports that immediately ahead of a moving crack is a zone of microcracking called the process zone. Since the size of the process zone is dependent upon crack velocity, a faster crack has a larger process zone. Higher stress rates propagate cracks more quickly, thereby creating a larger process zone. This zone of increased microcracking may explain the increasing fracture energies recorded at increasing drop heights.

The tup load pulse also foreshortens with increasing drop height. This would seem to indicate that the failure is occurring more quickly as the drop height is increased. Since the tup measures the total resistance the beam offers to include both bending and inertial forces, a foreshortening of the bending load versus time curve would also indicate a foreshortening in the time to failure.

**Static versus Dynamic Beam Bending Experiments** The average static peak bending load was always less than the dynamic peak bending load, even at the lowest drop heights. The increase in peak bending load with drop height is attributed to strain rate effects in the concrete.

The dynamic fracture energy is larger than the static fracture energy for the plain concrete beams. However, for the remainder of the beams all reinforced with external CFRP, the dynamic fracture energies were all consistently less than the static fracture energies. The addition of external CFRP to the beam significantly stiffens the beam, thereby enhancing the beam's brittle behavior when loaded dynamically. This implies that a high strength plain concrete beam is "dynamically equivalent" or has the same energy absorption capacity, as a normal strength concrete beam which has been externally reinforced with CFRP.

The peak displacements were always less under dynamic loading when compared to the quasistatic loading case. Except for the plain concrete beams, the dynamic fracture energies were always less than the static values, even though the peak dynamic bending loads were typically 2 - 3 times higher than the peak static bending loads. This would seem to indicate that displacement is the limiting parameter in determining dynamic fracture energy. This implies that for a given drop height, i.e. strain rate, a beam has a fixed capacity to absorb energy, dictated by the concrete's "impact strength" and limited by displacement, emphasizing the brittle nature of concrete.

The mechanism by which the beams failed dynamically did not change appreciably from the static loading case; failure of all beams with only tensile CFRP reinforcement was one of shear failure in the concrete at approximately one quarter span from beam midpoint, followed by delamination and peeling of the CFRP. Failure of beams with CFRP on the sides as well as the bottom was concrete shear failure followed by CFRP side panel splitting and buckling along the major shear crack in the concrete. Failure of the plain concrete beams was one of flexure, with a single flexural crack at beam midpoint merely breaking the beam into two pieces, creating two new fracture surfaces.

**Acknowledgments** This research was supported by the Wright Laboratory Air Base Technology Branch at Tyndall Air Force Base, Florida. Use of the load frames and drop weight impact machine owned by this organization is also gratefully acknowledged.

**References**
1. Kaiser, H., "Strengthening of Reinforced Concrete with Epoxy-Bonded Carbon Fiber Plastics," Doctoral Dissertation , ETH, 1989, (in German).

2. Ross, C.A., Jerome, D.M., and Hughes, M.L., "Hardening and Rehabilitation of Concrete Structures Using Carbon Fiber Reinforced Plastics (CFRP)," WL-TR-94-7100, Air Force Wright Laboratory, Eglin Air Force Base, Florida 32542-6810, December 1994.

3. Banthia, N., Mindess, S., Bentur, A., and Pigeon, M., "Impact Testing of Concrete Using a Drop-weight Impact Machine," Experimental Mechanics, Volume 29, Number 1, March 1989, pages 63-69.

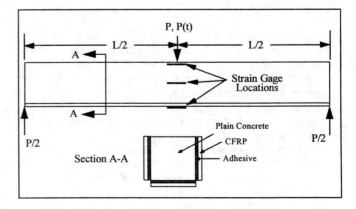

**Figure 1. Mode of Loading for Static and Dynamic Beam Bending Experiments**

# A Method of Pulsed Holographic Microscopy to Photograph Fast Propagating Cracks with Higher Spatial Resolution

Shinichi SUZUKI
Department of Energy Engineering
Hibarigaoka 1-1, Tempaku-cho, Toyohashi, 441 Japan

When brittle materials fracture, there appear fast propagating cracks whose speed is at several hundred m/s or more. In order to understand the rapid fracture phenomena, it is important to develop experimental techniques to take microscopic photographs of the fast propagating crack tips, because the fracture of the materials occurs in the very vicinity of the crack tip. The present paper describes a method of pulsed holographic microscopy (PHM) which is developed for microscopic photographing of fast propagating cracks and has the spatial resolution above 400 lines/mm. The resolution is about three times as high as that of PHM which has so far been used in the study of dynamic fracture.

Figure 1 shows the schema of the holographic recording of a fast propagating crack[1]. When the crack is propagating in the specimen, collimated laser beam from a pulsed ruby laser impinges on the specimen surface perpendicularly. The reflected light beam from the specimen surface is half reflected by the beam splitter, passes through the imaging lens and, falls onto the holographic plate. This is the object beam. The imaging lens makes the real image 1 of the specimen in front of the holographic plate. On the real image 1 there appear aberrations due to the imaging lens. The reference beam simultaneously falls onto the holographic plate obliquely, then, the object beam is recorded as a hologram.

After development, we illuminate the hologram with the reconstruction beam from a c.w.He-Ne laser. The reconstruction beam is the conjugate beam of the reference beam, therefore, the hologram reconstructs the conjugate beam of the object one. The conjugate of object beam follows the same optical path as the object beam in the opposite direction. The conjugate object beam makes the real image 2 at the position where the specimen existed at the holographic recording. The real image 2 has little aberration of the imaging lens, because the conjugate beam passes through the imaging lens along the optical path same as the object beam in the opposite direction. This method makes it possible to achieve high spatial resolution without designing and constructing a special lens[2], and, allows us to use a camera lens of high numerical aperture on the market. The spatial resolution of the optical system is more than 400 lines/mm (OTF) in the present study.

Figure 3 shows an example of the microscopic photographs of fast propagating cracks in PMMA plate specimen. The dark in the photograph is the crack, which is of the opening mode. Crack speed was at 267m/s.

The schematic diagram of a crack tip in PMMA is shown in Fig.4. There is the craze layer at the crack tip. In the craze layer two crack surfaces are already open, but the fibrils which are bundles of chain molecules bridge the two crack surfaces and apply pulling force (craze stress) on them.

The illumination light which falls on the specimen surface at the recording is not reflected at the craze layer, because the two crack surfaces are open there. It can accordingly be said that the tip of the crack shown in Fig.3 is the craze tip, and the point A in the photograph is probably the crack tip. The length of the craze layer is about 60 μm. The craze layers shown in [3] are longer than that in Fig.3. The difference is due to the difference of molecular weight of PMMA. We can measure not only crack opening displacement but also craze opening displacement, which are both called COD. The measurement result is shown in Fig.5. This figure shows that the high resolution PHM can measure COD which is smaller than 10 μm and which was difficult to be measured up to now. From the photograph in Fig.3, we measure the CODs up to 7mm from the craze tip along the crack. In the region where the distance r from the craze tip is greater than 200 μm, the CODs are proportional to √r, which result is in agreement with the theoretical result of linear elastic fracture mechanics. On the other hand, in the region of r<100 μm, the CODs are smaller than the line of √r which is determined from the COD data in the region of r greater than 2mm by the least square method. This is due to the craze stress.

In conclusion, we can say the followings. (1) The method of lens assisted holography with the correction of aberrations of the imaging lens can take high resolution photographs of rapidly propagating cracks, that is more than 400 lines/mm. (2) The method can measure CODs which is smaller than 10 μm and was difficult to be measured up to now.

## References

[1] Suzuki,S., Homma,H. and Kusaka,R., "Pulsed Holographic Microscopy as a Measurement Method of Dynamic Fracture Toughness for Fast Propagating Cracks", J. Mech. Phys. Solids, 36-6, 1988, pp.631-653.
[2] Briones,R.A., Heflinger,L.O. and Wuerker,R.F., "Holographic Microscopy", Appl. Opt., 17-6, 1978, pp.944-950.
[3] Suzuki,S., Measurement of Crack and Craze Opening Displacement of Rapidly Propagating Cracks by Means of Pulsed Holographic Microscopy", Proc. 9th Int. Conf. Exp. Mech., Copenhagen Denmark, August 1990, pp.1833-1842.

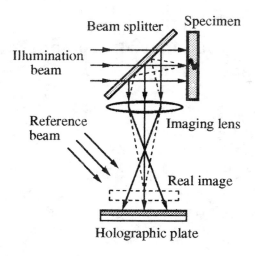

Fig.1 Holographic recording of
a propagating crack.

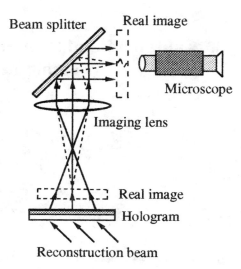

Fig.2 Reconstruction of the real image
of the crack.

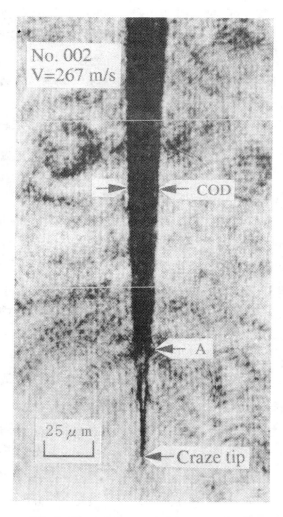

Fig.3 The microscopic photograph of
a fast propagating crack.

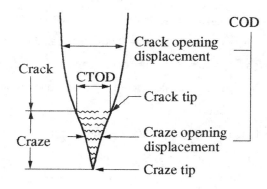

Fig.4 The Schema of the crack tip in PMMA.

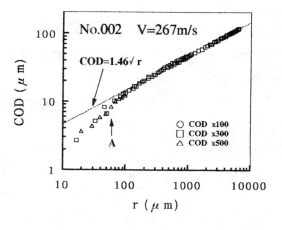

Fig.5 COD versus r

313

# Measurements of Interlaminar Fracture Toughness in Composite Laminates under Impact Loading

Y.Yamauchi, M.Nakano, K.Kishida

Department of Precision Science and Technology,

Faculty of Engineering, Osaka University

2-1 Yamada-Oka Suita Osaka 565, Japan

In composite structures, small interlaminar delaminations are occasionally introduced during manufacturing or working processes. Starting from these defects, unexpected fractures can occur under impact loading. In these cases, stress waves induced by the impact loading impinge obliquely to such defects and produce combined mode stress states around the crack tips. Therefore, it is very important to estimate accurately the dynamic interlaminar fracture toughness and to make the fracture initiation criterion clear for composite laminates under combined mode loading. The dynamic fracture toughness values can be defined as the critical dynamic energy release rates at the fracture initiation. The accurate estimation of the dynamic energy release rate and the precise detection of the fracture initiation time are necessary in an impact fracture test.

In the present study, we try to develop a new fracture test for composite laminates using center-cracked disk specimens. The dynamic fracture toughness can be estimated by combining experiments with numerical stress analyses. Figure 1 shows the one-point impact test apparatus used for the experiments. The impact load is measured with the strain gage on the input bar. The strain gages are set on the two crack tips to detect the onset of the fracture. The dynamic energy release rates are evaluated from the superposition integrals of the step response functions for the cracked disk. The step response functions are numerically calculated with the dynamic finite element analyses [1].

Using this method, the dynamic interlaminar fracture toughness values for unidirectional CF(carbon fiber)/epoxy composite laminates were estimated. The characteristic of this testing method is that, by selecting the angle of the center crack relative to the direction of the loading, arbitrary combined mode I/II stress states can be easily obtained. Evidently, a pure mode I loading test can be conducted when the angle is 0 degrees. As a result of the finite element analyses, it was found that a static pure mode II test can be performed when the angle is 11.2 degrees. Therefore, we selected 0, 5.8 and 11.2 degrees for the angle of the center crack.

The results of the experiments are as follows. Figure 2 shows the interlaminar fracture toughness under pure mode I and combined mode I/II loading in the impact tests. The dotted line in the figure is $G_{If} + G_{IIf} = G_{Ic}$, where $G_{Ic}$ is the pure mode I interlaminar fracture toughness under the impact loading. Since the combined mode interlaminar fracture toughness values were above the dotted line, the fracture criterion based on the energy was not suitable for the interlaminar fracture toughness in the composite laminates. In the impact tests, however, even if the angle of the center crack was 11.2 degrees, the mode I component

314

existed about 10%. It is difficult to perform the pure mode II test under the impact loading. Using the linear extrapolation, we evaluated the pure mode II interlaminar fracture toughness under the impact loading from these results. Figure 3 shows the loading rate effects on the interlaminar fracture toughness under pure mode I and mode II loading. The value extrapolated above is used as the dynamic pure mode II fracture toughness. It was found that the interlaminar fracture toughness in the composite laminates subjected to the impact loading was about 30% lower than that measured by the quasi-static loading tests in mode II as well as mode I.

Reference:

[1] Nakano, M., Kishida, K., "Numerical Computation of Dynamic Stress Intensity Factor for Impact Fracture Toughness Test," Engineering Fracture Mechanics, Vol.36, No.3, pp.515-522, 1990.

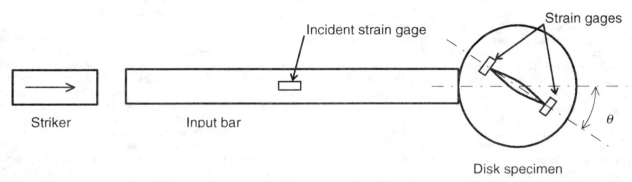

Fig.1   Impact apparatus for combined mode fracture using center-cracked disk specimen

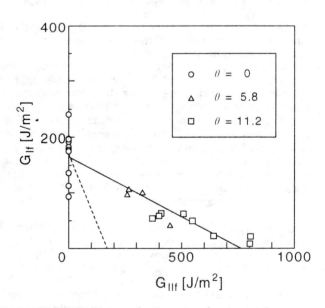

Fig.2   The interlaminar fracture toughness under pure mode I and combined mode I/II loading in the impact tests

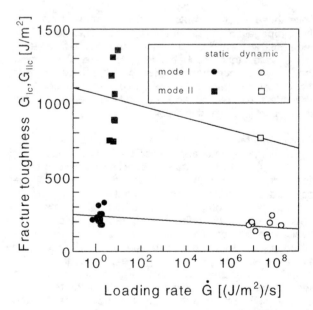

Fig.3   Loading rate effects on the interlaminar fracture toughness under pure mode I and mode II loading in the composite laminates

# Mechanics of Dynamic Crack Propagation along Bimaterial Interfaces: The Intersonic Regime

Raman P. Singh and Arun Shukla
Dynamic Photomechanics Laboratory
Department of Mechanical Engineering and Applied Mechanics
University of Rhode Island
Kingston, RI 02881

An experimental study was conducted to investigate intersonic crack propagation along bimaterial interfaces subjected to impact loading. The bimaterial specimens were impacted with a projectile fired from a gas gun, which caused a crack to initiate and subsequently grow along the interface. The crack propagation phenomenon was observed using dynamic photoelasticity in conjunction with high-speed photography.

In homogeneous materials, the observation of crack speeds greater than the shear wave velocity, $v > c_s$, or the plane velocity, $v > c_l$, is limited to cases when the loading is applied directly to the crack tip or under some other extreme condition. For remotely loaded cracks energy considerations make it impossible for the crack tip velocity to exceed the Rayleigh wave velocity of the parent material [1, 2]. On the other hand, it has been recently demonstrated that intersonic crack propagation along bimaterial interfaces is possible even under remote loading conditions [3, 4, 5]. If there exists a significant mismatch in the wave speeds across the bimaterial interface then the crack can propagate intersonically with respect to the more compliant material while it is still subsonic with respect to the stiffer material. Under such conditions only a finite amount of energy has to be supplied to the crack tip to maintain extension as the propagational velocity approaches the lower of the two Rayleigh wave velocities [6].

Despite these initial attempts, the phenomenon of intersonic crack propagation is still more or less unexplored. The experimental evidence is very limited and there still does not exist a valid theoretical solution for the intersonically propagating interface crack. In view of this, the current study presents recent experimental observations on interface failure in the intersonic regime and interprets these observations based on currently available theory.

The experimental setup used to investigate crack propagation along a bimaterial interface subjected to impact loading is shown in figure 1. The bimaterial specimen is placed on the optical bench of a high speed Cranz-Schardin spark-gap camera and impacted by a projectile fired from a gas gun. This impact results in a compressive wave that traverses the width of the specimen and reflects as a tensile wave from the opposite free surface. The reflected wave loads the crack tip resulting in crack initiation and subsequent crack growth. The dynamic stress field produced by the propagating crack is observed using dynamic photoelasticity in conjunction with high speed photography. This is made possible by the transparent and photoelastic nature of the compliant half of the bimaterial specimen. The photographic images provided by the high speed camera represent the full field isochromatic fringe patterns for the stress field surrounding the propagating interface crack.

A schematic of the bimaterial specimen itself is shown in figure 2. The specimen consists of a compliant half bonded directly to the stiff half. The compliant half was chosen to be a transparent and photoelastic polyester resin (Homalite-100), while aluminum was chosen as the other half. This combination provides a significant mismatch in the mechanical properties of the two materials comprising the bimaterial interface.

This specimen was impacted with a steel projectile (12.5 mm diameter and 100 mm long) fired at a velocity of 30 m/s, which resulted in dynamic crack propagation along the bimaterial interface. The history of the crack tip velocity was determined from the crack tip location as a function of time and is plotted in figure 3. After initiation the crack rapidly accelerated to the shear wave velocity of the more compliant material, $c_s^{HOMALITE}$. Thereafter, the crack tip velocity continued to increase beyond the shear wave velocity until it reached about 120% of the shear wave velocity. Subsequently, the crack tip velocity stabilized and remained at 120% of $c_s^{HOMALITE}$ for the rest of the interface fracture process. The terminal crack tip velocity observed in this series of experiments was around 120% of the shear wave velocity, but less than the dilatational wave velocity of the more compliant material ($c_s^{HOMALITE} < v_{TERMINAL} < c_l^{HOMALITE}$). Thus, this phenomenon is termed as *intersonic crack propagation*.

A direct consequence of intersonic crack propagation is the formation of a mach wave (or line-of-discontinuity) in the stress field surrounding the moving crack tip. The propagating crack tip acts as a source of shear and plane waves which radiate out into the material and establish the stress field that surrounds the crack tip. If this source (the crack tip) propagates faster than the shear wave velocity then the spreading out of the shear waves is limited and a mach wave (or line-of-discontinuity) forms. Experimental evidence of the mach wave is shown in figure 4 in the form of discontinuous isochromatic fringe contours. The line originates at the crack tip and radiates out into the material. To the best of the author's knowledge this is first direct observation of mach wave formation resulting from intersonic crack propagation along a bimaterial interface.

A *secondary* mach wave was observed in addition to the previously discussed mach wave (the *primary* mach wave). This secondary mach wave was separated from the primary mach wave by a "zone" characterized by a set of isochromatic fringes parallel to the bimaterial interface. This zone represents large scale contact (2-3 mm) which occurs behind the crack tip. The contact of the crack surfaces was a dynamic process and the contact zone propagated along the bimaterial interface along with the crack tip. The trailing edge of the contact zone,

316

as characterized by the secondary mach wave, also propagated at the same velocity as the crack tip. Thus, the size of the contact zone remained relatively constant at around 2-3 mm.

At the present there is only one theoretical study in print [7] which investigates intersonic crack propagation along an elastic-rigid interface. This analysis shows considerable qualitative agreement with the experimental observations discussed earlier. Nevertheless, there are differences and shortcomings which warrant further investigation. These aspects will be presented in greater detail at the meeting.

## REFERENCES

[1]   Broberg, K. B., "The propagation of a Griffith crack, *Archiv fur Fysik*, Vol. 18, 1960, pp. 159-192.

[2]   Freund, L. B., "Dynamic fracture mechanics", <u>Cambridge Monographs on Mechanics and Applied Mathematics</u>, Cambridge University Press, 1990.

[3]   Liu, C., Lambros, J., and Rosakis, A. J., "Highly transient elastodynamic crack growth in a bimaterial interface: Higher order asymptotic analysis and optical experiments," *Journal of the Mechanics and Physics of Solids*, Vol. 41, 2, 1993, pp. 1887-1954.

[4]   Lambros, J. and Rosakis, A. J., "Dynamic decohesion of bimaterials: Experimental observations and failure criteria", *International Journal of Solids and Structures*, Vol. 32, No. 17/18, 1995, pp. 2677-2702.

[5]   Singh, R. P., and Shukla, A., "Subsonic and intersonic crack growth along a bimaterial interface", To appear in the *Journal of Applied Mechanics*, 1996.

[6]   Yang, W., Suo, Z., and Shih, C. F., "Mechanics of dynamic debonding," *Proceedings of the Royal Society of London*, Vol. A433, 1991, pp. 679-697.

[7]   Liu, C., Huang, Y. and Rosakis, A. J., "Shear dominated transonic interfacial crack growth in a bimaterial-II. Asymptotic fields and favorable velocity regimes," *Journal of the Mechanics and Physics of Solids*, Vol. 43. No. 2, 1995, pp. 189-206.

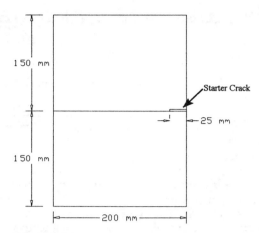

Figure 2. Schematic of the bimaterial interface specimen used to investigate intersonic crack propagation.

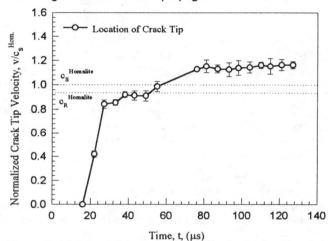

Figure 3. History of the crack tip velocity for intersonic crack propagation along a Homalite-100 / aluminum bimaterial interface.

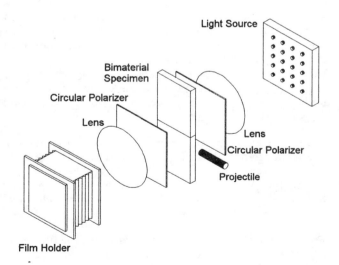

Figure 1. Experimental setup for investigating the fracture of a bimaterial interface subjected to impact loading by a projectile fired from a gas gun.

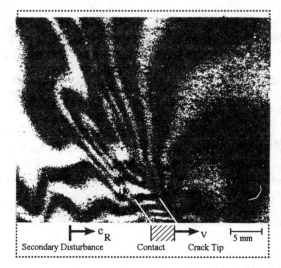

Figure 4. Details of the isochromatic fringe patterns around the intersonically propagating crack tip showing the *primary* and *secondary* mach waves, the dynamic moving contact zone and the secondary disturbance.

317

# Grating interrogation using oblique diffraction for dynamic local strain determination

Valéry Valle, Mario Cottron, Alexis Lagarde
Université de Poitiers
Laboratoire de Mécanique des Solides
Boulevard 3, Téléport 2, B.P. 179
86960 Futuroscope CEDEX

The measurement of mechanical quantities without contact, without destruction of the specimen or in hostile environment can be achieved by the optical investigations. The grid method [1], one of these, allows to determine the magnitude and the orientation of the principal strain as well as the rigid body rotation [2]. This is achieved by the comparison between the geometry of a deformed crossed grating (pitch and orientation of each direction of grating) with the geometry of the same grating in the initial state. The analysis of the grating is obtained by an optical Fourier transform or a numerical one [3][4]. This method is performed for the measurement of small and large strains in static regime with a strain sensitivity comparable of the one obtained by strain gauge [5]. We present an extension of this optical method adapted to the local measurement of strains during a dynamic loading.

In order to separate on a same photographic film the different spots of each step of the dynamic event, we change the orientation of the incident laser beam. We have so to take account of the diffraction phenomenon in oblique incidence [6]. In our case, we store on the photographic film the 0 order and the +1 and -1 orders associated with each grating direction. At each step of the recording we have to solve a non-linear system of 15 equations with 14 unknowns. The comparison of these 14 parameters with the quantities at the initial state gives the components of the strain tensor, of the rigid body rotation and of the rigid body displacement.

We presente briefly an optical device developed for dynamic investigations. For this raison, we have made a new camera with elements adapted to work in this regime. Technically, we have preferred the solution without rotating elements (mirror, turbine, ...) and chosen the acousto-optic components which have been recently employed for many optical devices. The variation of the orientation of the incident laser beam and the obtention of sequential informations during the dynamic event are respectively achieved by an acousto-optic deflector and an acousto-optic shutter[7]. So we can also define the complete optical device on figure 1 which utilizes the different elements previously described.

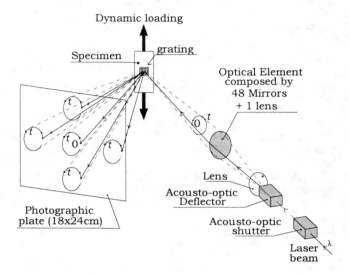

Fig. 1 Experimental device

A study of the optical efficiency of our experimental device shows that the use of a recording film of 400 ASA sensitivity with a 50 mW laser power gives a minimum exposure time equal to 0.5 µs. In these conditions, the developed device can be applied for a strain measurement during a dynamic loading of a minimal duration equal to 50 µs. To determine the position of the 120 spots (5 orders of diffraction x 24 states of loading) recorded on the photographic film, we use a digital image processing coupling with a CCD camera. With an adapted analysis device [8] (using a spot by spot analysis) we can obtain a strain sensitivity equal to $10^{-4}$.

For all the experimental investigations, the diameter of the measurement base is of about 1 mm. The density of the crossed grating is equal to 200 lines per millimeter. We have compared the strain optically measured and those obtained by a classical extensometry using a strain gauge.

First we have made two static tests in uniaxial tension and we show on the same figure (Fig. 2) the good agreement between these two sensors.

We can see on figure 2 that this method responds very correctly on a range of strain of few $10^{-4}$ to few $10^{-2}$. There is no limitation for the measurement of the large strain while the grating doesn't unglue from the specimen.

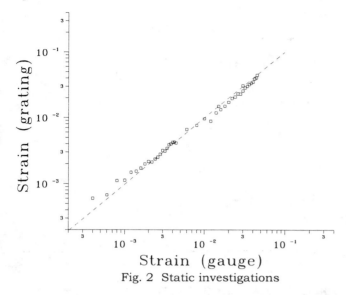

Fig. 2  Static investigations

In a second time (Fig.3), we have made a dynamic test using the impact of a mass on the mobile grip of the specimen. For this compression test we have chosen the frame rate equal to 35 kHz and an exposure time of 2.8 µs.

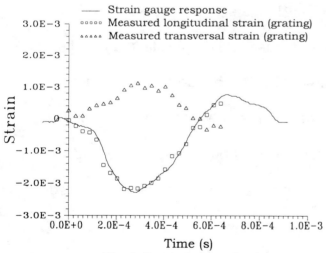

Fig. 3  Dynamic investigation

The tests given in this paper are only examples of the possibility of this method. In fact, the frame rate and the exposure time can be adapted to faster dynamic test limited by a maximum of 500 kHz.

In conclusion, this measurement method performed by an interrogation of the grating using the optical diffraction with an oblique incidence allows to determine not only the strain tensor given by the optical diffraction in normal incidence but also the six

rigid motion of a measurement base of 1 mm. The use of acousto-optic components allows to separate easily the information during a dynamic or a static loading and to record 24 states of the specimen at up to 500,000 frames per second. The acquisition of this information by specific device composed by a digital image processing using a CCD camera gives a quasi-automatic analysis. The direct determination of strains without any contact is well adapted to the analysis of impact loadings with the measurement directly obtained from the specimen, to the study of  behavior laws in static and dynamic loading or to the control of structures under vibratory regimes.

REFERENCES:

[1] Sevenhuijsen P.J., "Grid method : a new future", Proceeding of SEM Spring Conference, 1989.

[2] Brémand F., Lagarde A., "Analyse spectrale bidimensionnelle d'un réseau de traits croisés. Application à la mesure des grandes et petites déformations", C.R. Académie des Sciences, t. 307, serie II, p 683-688, 1988.

[3] Brémand F., Dupré J.C., Lagarde A., "Non-contact and non disturbing local strain measurement methods. I - Principle", European Journal of Mechanics, A/Solids, vol 11, n°3, p349-366, 1992.

[4] Cardenas-Garcia J.F., Wu M.S., "Further development of the video optical diffractometer for strain measurement", Proceeding of the SEM Spring Conference 1989.

[5] Dupré J.C., Cottron M., Lagarde A., "Phase shifting technique for local measurements of small strains by grid method", Proceedings 10th International Conference on Experimental Mechnics, 1994.

[6] Valle V., Cottron M., Lagarde A., "Utilisation du phénomène de diffraction sous incidence oblique d'un faisceau laser par un réseau croisé pour la mesure locale en statique et dynamique des déformations et des mouvements de solide", Mechanics Research Communications, Vol 22, n°2/95, p. 103-107, 1995.

[7] Brillouin L., Ann. de Phys. 17, 103, 1921.

[8] Valle V., Cottron M., Lagarde A., "Dynamic optical method for local strain measurement: principle and characteristics", proceeding of the Euro DYMAT 94, C8, p. 59-64, 1994.

# THE ROLE OF NONDESTRUCTIVE EVALUATION

# IN OUR INFRASTRUCTURE

Charles J. Hellier

Hellier Associates, Inc.
Niantic, Connecticut 06357

## ABSTRACT

There is no doubt that our aging or inadequate infrastructure is in trouble! Since engineers believe that we're dealing with "a series of accidents just waiting to happen," significant failures in the past support this theory. The Hartford Civic Center, the Kansas City Hyatt Regency, and the Mianus River Bridge are just a few examples of past failures that were all unexpected. These and other catastrophic failures confirm the problems that exist in our infrastructure due to poor design, deterioration, lack of inspection, overloading, inadequate maintenance and the "low bid" syndrome. Finding and correcting all the problems may be an impossible task but through the use of current nondestructive evaluation methodology, the risks of failure can be minimized.


Keywords: failure, inspection, disaster, testing, prevention, structures, qualifications

# Instrumentation, Testing and Monitoring of
# The Construction and Service of a Steel-Stringer Bridge

V.J. Hunt, A. Levi, R. Barrish, K. Grimmelsman, A.E. Aktan, A.J. Helmicki
Infrastructure Institute, University of Cincinnati
Cincinnati, Ohio 45221-0071

In view of our significant current and future investment in steel stringer bridges, we see great benefits in having a clear and complete understanding of their behavior. Further, the events or processes in each stage of their lifetime which significantly degrade or damage a bridge must be cataloged and integrated within this context. This can be accomplished only by a properly designed field instrumentation and monitoring program conducted in the context of a structural-identification study. For example, the impacts of initial cracking, shrinkage, and creep of the concrete slab and its interaction with the steel grid system, in conjunction with the pavement-soil-and-substructure, can only be fully appreciated by instrumenting and monitoring the actual field strains that accumulate at the critical locations and boundaries over the long term.

During the first 2 phases of the research, "Instrumentation, Testing and Monitoring of RC Deck-on Steel Girder Bridges", researchers performed basic laboratory studies and field rehearsals to develop techniques for successful instrumented monitoring applications.

The first objective for the third phase of the project is to understand and document the actual absolute state-of-stress in a typical jointless continuous composite reinforced concrete deck-on-steel stringer bridge, together with the corresponding causative effects that lead to force and distortion. This objective will be accomplished by collecting a complete set of strain, distortion, inclination, displacement and temperature response data for a typical test specimen: the three-span, 170 foot Cross-County Highway over Hamilton Avenue bridge (HAM-126-0881) (Fig. 1). The data will be collected by instrumentation of the concrete substructure, driven steel piles (Fig. 2), girders and cross-braces, and concrete deck at each critical step in the fabrication and construction process including cambering (Fig. 3), transportation (Fig. 4), erection and subsequent phases (Fig 5). Traffic loading and environmental impact will also be monitored via an automatic weigh-in-motion scale and a rugged weather station. The stresses will be evaluated starting from construction and through the initial year of service. Diagnostic tests such as impact modal testing and controlled truck-loading will be conducted on the bridge immediately following construction, so that the baseline mechanical characteristics of the bridge can be established and an accurate finite-element model can be calibrated. Data acquired through instrumentation will be used to conceptualize less-understood or unknown phenomena that influence bridge performance and to verify design assumptions and rating models. Since complex time-dependent self-equilibrating effects such as thermal gradients, creep and shrinkage are involved, extensive cause-effect analysis efforts and nonlinear finite-element expertise are required.

The second objective is the continued exploration and advancement of the state-of-knowledge in bridge instrumentation and the further evaluation of the feasibility and reliability of other commercially available bridge monitoring and nondestructive evaluation technologies. Guidelines are needed for interpreting bridge response data and relating this to health. In conjunction with this, a systematic and rigorous study for establishing the most reliable and feasible sensors, data-acquisition systems and data processing techniques that will optimally serve for long-term bridge health monitoring are needed. While a rigorous study and implementation of sensors has been carried out in prior research, other emerging technologies, such as: radio telemetry or wireless communication between the bridge-mounted transducers and the central data-acquisition system, strain sensors manufactured with superalloy materials such as Iconel to withstand the extremely high temperatures found in pre-construction cambering or welding of steel members, sensors manufactured with "memory alloy" materials which change their magnetic characteristics permanently in direct proportion to the maximum applied strain or deformation, sensors built on the high speed, precision, and stability of fiber optics, instrumented elastomeric bearings and fixtures, and many others will be evaluated for this project.

Currently the substructure construction and instrumentation is completed and continuous data for over 6 months is been collected from drilled pier shafts, pier columns and abutment piles. In addition to that critical data has been compiled from cambering, transportation and erection of the girders. Long term behavior of the structure is being continuously monitored with 108 substructure and 46 superstructure strain gages with built in thermistors At the ultimate state the bridge will be instrumented with 115 substructure and 234 superstructure transducers continuously monitoring the bridge for both long term environmental and traffic related stresses. An intelligent monitoring system which is going to be able to discern critical events at the serviceability and damageability limit states and will be able to make decisions pertaining to system settings will be developed. Information which is deemed relevant by the monitor will be processed into visual graphics, which would be quickly conceptualized and checked for reliability by a bridge engineer.

# LEFT BRIDGE HAMILTON 126-0881

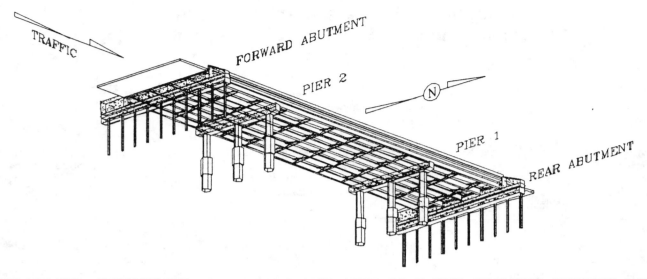

TRAFFIC

FORWARD ABUTMENT

PIER 2

N

PIER 1

REAR ABUTMENT

PROPOSED STRUCTURE: CONTINUOUS ROLLED STEEL BEAM WITH COMPOSITE CONCRETE DECK, INTEGRAL ABUTMENTS AND CAPS AND COLUMN PIERS.

SPAN LENGTHS: EAST SPAN 40'-2 1/4"; CENTER SPAN 88'-5 5/8"; WEST SPAN 40'-3 3/8"

**Fig. 1: Test Bridge**

**Fig. 2: Driven Abutment Piles & Instrumentation**　　**Fig. 3: Cambering of Girders & Instrumentation**

**Fig. 4: Transportation of Girders**　　**Fig. 5: Instrumentation After Erection of Girders**

# Bridge-Type-Specific Management of Steel-Stringer Bridges in Ohio

M. Lenett, F.N. Catbas, V.J. Hunt, A.E. Aktan, A.J. Helmicki, S.J. Shelley
Infrastructure Institute, University of Cincinnati
Cincinnati, Ohio 45221-0071

The long-term global objective of this research is to develop and demonstrate the concepts and tools for bridge management in the next century. We need to accomplish the following for rational and optimum bridge management: (1) objective global condition assessment; (2) rating and evaluation of performance; (3) evaluation of future performance and reliability; (4) evaluation of maintenance and renewal options; (5) planning and decision making. Instrumented monitoring and modal analysis are being considered as an evaluation tool for the bridge-type-specific management of steel-stringer bridges in Ohio. Bridge-Type-Specific management is based upon a primary set of condition assessment, rating and maintenance operations tailored for a family of bridges possessing similar behavior characteristics by rigorously testing and analyzing a representative statistical population.

Both of these evaluation tools may be applied at several levels of sophistication and rigor, naturally leading to different levels of comprehensiveness and reliability in the results. The writers have established the proper use-modes for both tools, and demonstrated their applicability for objective bridge condition assessment by taking advantage of several destructive tests on decommissioned bridges. The current objective is to rigorously demonstrate and verify that these two tools are effective for the non-destructive evaluation of steel-stringer bridges which may be possibly affected by any level of hidden deterioration or damage. In particular, these tools have to be demonstrated to the satisfaction of ODOT engineers and officials so that they may be legally used for supporting decision-making by ODOT in any of their current and future operations. Since both of the experimental technologies may be applied independently, or in combination and in accordance with a multitude of use-modes, the main product of the research will be establishing a matrix of experimental options provided by the two technologies of modal testing and instrumentation versus the types and levels of deterioration and damage which may be affecting and accurately diagnosed for steel-stringer bridges.

The objective of the research will be accomplished by utilizing a "typical" steel-stringer bridge, scheduled for renewal, as a test specimen (Fig. 1). This bridge will be instrumented and subjected to modal tests in the first month of the project to establish its baseline. A customized "drop hammer" will be utilized to provide a consistent, repeatable impact with sufficient mass to excite the bridge modes at many nodes about the deck (Figs. 2 and 3). Swept-sine forced excitation will also be conducted with an electrodynamic actuator. Our instrumentation-based monitoring strategy will include accelerometers, vibrating wire strain gages, resistance foil strain gages, pendulous tiltmeters, and LVDT displacement transducers (Fig. 4). Static loading and crawl-speed truck tests will be conducted for corroboration with the modal test results and to simulate traffic conditions. Daily and long-term environmental effects will be tracked via regular baseline testing and boundary condition monitoring.

Over the course of the first year, the bridge will be subjected to a series of deliberately induced damage, simulating typical deterioration and damage scenarios which may affect steel-stringer bridges. The researchers will verify and demonstrate the success of the two experimental tools to diagnose the induced damage after the application of each scenario. Thirty-five damage scenarios will include long-term deterioration effects such as due to the loosening and/or breaking of connections, fatigue-fracture, dislocated bearing, corrosion and reduction of effective area and inertia of steel members and connections, loss of chemical bond providing composite action, cracking and delamination of deck concrete. Retrofit in terms of stiffening and strengthening of certain connections and members will be simulated. At the end of the first year, the bridge will be demolished. Streamlined procedures and algorithms will be developed in the second year for the detection of these and other damage-types.

Successful simulation of the deterioration, damage and retrofit scenarios will be accomplished through the guidance of an expert panel of ODOT, FHWA and private consulting engineers. This panel will design each type of induced-damage to correspond to a realistic natural deterioration and damage scenario. The damage described by the panel will be induced by a contractor, who will be under the direct supervision of the researchers. Due to the required research effort and the limited timeframe of the project, the exact location and severity of the damage will be controlled by the research team. Following each damage-induction, researchers will conduct their experiments (modal and truck-load tests) and evaluate the results together with the expert panel. It is important that the test results will be made available to the general bridge research community and the researchers will use the experimental results not only to test their proposed damage indicators based on bridge flexibility, but also other promising damage indicators (e.g. critical member strain, strain energy, neutral axis location, modal frequencies, modal damping, modal assurance, and modal curvature) that have been proposed by other researchers. The research and the test-specimen will therefore serve as a national test-bed for bridge global non-destructive evaluation.

**Fig. 1: Steel-Stringer Test Bridge**

**Fig. 2: Impact Modal Testing**

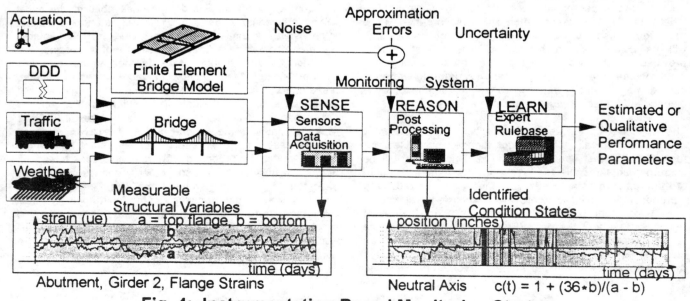

DECK
CROSSFRAME
CUT LINE

DROP or SLEDGE HAMMER

DAMPER

FORCE SENSOR HAMMER TIP

ICP POWER SUPPLY

INPUT MODULE

PCB 393C ACCEL.

HP3566A SIGNAL ANALYZER

GP-IB

PC

HP 715 WStation

**Structural Identification & Analytical Damage Indices**
Mass, Stiffness, Damping

**Experimental Damage Indices**
Deflection & Curvature of the Uniform Load Surface

**Modal Parameters**
Modal Flexibility
Mode Frequencies
Mode Shapes
Response Amplitude
Response Phase

**Fig. 3: Modal Impact Test System Configuration for Detection of Induced Damage**

Actuation

DDD

Traffic

Weather

Finite Element Bridge Model

Bridge

Noise

Approximation Errors

Uncertainty

Monitoring System

SENSE
Sensors
Data Acquisition

REASON
Post Processing

LEARN
Expert Rulebase

Estimated or Qualitative Performance Parameters

Measurable Structural Variables

Identified Condition States

strain (ue)    a = top flange, b = bottom
b
a
time (days)

Abutment, Girder 2, Flange Strains

position (inches)

time (days)

Neutral Axis    $c(t) = 1 + (36 \ast b)/(a - b)$

**Fig. 4: Instrumentation-Based Monitoring Strategy**

# A Simple Intensity Based Fiber Optic Sensor for Health Monitoring of Structures Using Displacement Measurements

Frank Sienkiewicz, Arun Shukla and Jason Gomez
Dynamic Photomechanics Laboratory
Department of Mechanical Engineering and Applied Mechanics
University of Rhode Island
Kingston, RI  02881

## ABSTRACT

A fiber optic sensor has been developed and tested for static and dynamic strain and displacement measurements. The sensor incorporates an extremely simple design, light source, and detector. Testing was done using quasi-static extension, a simple oscillating cantilever beam, and a small shaker capable of frequencies up to 10 kHz. The sensor shows response over a wide range with linear response for a displacement range of approximately 20 mm. For small displacements, the sensor shows excellent frequency response over the range tested (~0-10 kHz).

## SENSOR DESIGN

The sensor presented in this paper utilizes a continuous piece of multimode optical fiber 'tied' into the shape of a figure of eight. A photograph of a sensor is shown in figure 1. The geometry allows the natural stiffness of the fiber to act as a restoring force which holds the shape of the sensor during extension and compression. Put simply, the fiber will attempt to 'unwrap' itself and return to a straight line were it not for the constraint imposed by the knot geometry. The sensor functions as an intensity based optical fiber strain or displacement sensor when it is bonded to a body at two points, one on each side of the loops. Since multimode fiber is used in the construction, a simple LED/PIN diode can be used for the light source and detector.

As the two fixed points are displaced with respect to each other, the radii of curvature of the sensor bends changes. A tensile strain would result in a shrinking of the sensor loops and drop in light intensity measured at the detector. Conversely, a compressive strain would result in an expansion of the loops and an intensity increase at the detector.

The light source was a Motorola MFOE1200 diode coupled to a simple driver circuit utilizing a 10v DC supply. The detector was a Motorola MFOD1100 (matching component for the diode) with an 18v DC bias, which was coupled to a simple twenty times amplifier and a variable DC offset. The amplifier was powered with a ±12v DC supply.

## EXPERIMENTS, RESULTS, AND DISCUSSION

To investigate the range of the sensor an experiment was performed on an Instron testing machine using a sensor with an initial dimension (x in figure 1) of approximately 150 mm. The cross head on the testing machine was then extended at a slow speed while the sensor output was captured on a digital storage oscilloscope. Extension was continued until the sensor failed in fracture. The data shown in figure 2 is the sensitivity plot derived

from this experiment. The plot shows the sensitivity, defined as the change in output per unit input (5 mm extension), as a function of sensor dimension. This figure illustrates the various sensitivity regions and the fact that the sensitivity is directly related to the size of the sensor. As the sensor size decreases, the loop radii decreases and consequently, more light is lost per unit input.

The sensor design was then tested for repeatability in construction. Four sensors were tied and bonded between a linear translation stage and a fixed reference point. The sensors were connected one at a time to the light source/detector combination and displaced 3 mm. Output was recorded and compared. Figure 3 shows the resulting plot for the sensors. The figure shows that a fairly good degree of repeatability is possible. It should be noted that the technique used to construct these sensors utilized no special equipment. A jig and consequently more control is currently under investigation which, given the decent results shown, should provide identical sensors each and every time.

A sensor was then bonded to a cantilever beam opposite an electrical resistance strain gage. The beam was displaced and allowed to vibrate freely while both the strain gage output and the optical fiber sensor output were captured on an oscilloscope. The fiber sensor output was zero shifted and linearly scaled to fit the strain gage data. The fiber optic sensor matched the electrical resistance strain gage quite well and showed no hysterisis. This experiment also served as a low frequency response test (approximately 25 Hz) for the sensor. Additionally, the sensor was bonded to a fixed point and a Wilcoxon Research electromagnetic/piezoelectric shaker system. The shaker was driven by a Hewlett Packard spectrum analyzer which also acquired and fast Fourier transformed data from both the sensor and an accelerometer built into the shaker. In all cases, the fiber optic sensor showed perfect agreement with the accelerometer in the frequency domain.

## CLOSURE

A fiber optic sensor which is capable of low frequency displacement has been demonstrated. The sensor showed excellent agreement with conventional sensor technology in the quasi-static regime. However, unlike conventional sensors, the fiber optic sensor provides virtually no reinforcing effects which may bias test results. The simple components and construction make it ideal for many applications where cost and ease of use may be factors. Low frequency displacements with a linear range of 20 mm have been shown. Further experiments utilizing the sensor on a model bridge structure (figure 4), where the structure will contain undamaged and damaged members, are currently under way. The viability of utilizing the sensor for supplying data to use in modal analysis of the structure will be explored, and this data will be presented at the conference.

## ACKNOWLEDGEMENT

The authors would like to acknowledge the Air Force Office of Scientific Research for their support under grant numbers F49620-93-1-0290 and F49620-93-1-0475.

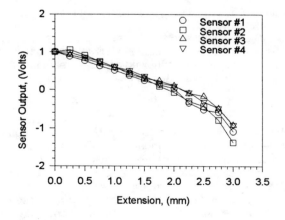

Figure 1. Photograph of the fiber sensor configuration.

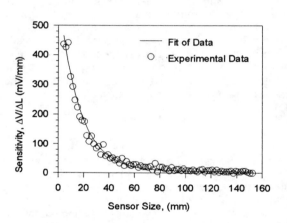

Figure 2. Plot sensitivity versus sensor size for the fiber optic sensor.

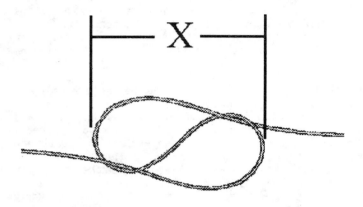

Figure 3 Plot of sensor output versus extension for four different sensors to determine the repeatability of construction.

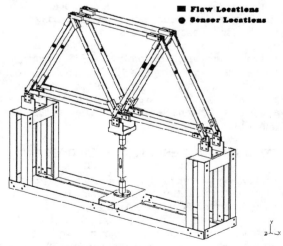

Figure 4. Model bridge structure with fiber optic sensors to provide data for modal analysis.

# Vibration Measurement of Composite Plates Containing a Circular Defect by ESPI

Wei-Chung Wang[*] , Shu-Yu Lin#, Chi Hung Hwang#
Department of Power Mechanical Engineering
National Tsing Hua University
Hsinchu, Taiwan 30043
Republic of China

## Abstract
In this paper, by using the image signal subtraction electronic speckle pattern interferometry(ESPI) method, the displacement of modal mode of composite plates with different diameter cutouts were measured. According to those recorded fringe patterns, the change of vibration characteristics were discussed.

## Introduction
In practice, cutouts may be needed to meet the design requirement. Occasionally, defect can also be easily caused by an impact on composite structures. Dynamic characteristics of composite structures would then be changed. The ESPI is a convenient, powerful and whole-field technique to investigate the dynamic characteristics.

## Theory
In this paper, the video signal subtraction ESPI method was adopted for vibration measurement. Theoretical investigation shows that the interferometric brightness B should be related as

$$B \propto J_o(\kappa \zeta a) - 1 \qquad (1)$$

where $\kappa = 2\pi/\lambda$, $\zeta = 1 + \cos\theta$, $\lambda$ is the wavelength of the light source, a is the vibration amplitude and $\theta$ is the illumination angle of object-light beam. And the associated vibration amplitude can be expressed as

$$a = \lambda \zeta_i / [2\pi(1 + \cos\theta)] \qquad (2)$$

and $\zeta_i$ is the value of $\zeta$ to minimize eq. (1).

## Experimental Background
As shown in Fig. 1, the test specimen was made in 16-ply unidirectional CFRP laminate. The thickness-through defect is located at center of the specimen. Four different diameters of the cutout, d=0 mm, 15 mm, 30 mm and 45 mm were adopted in this paper.
A vibration system was used to provide the driving force and control the vibration frequency. The driving force was monitored and recorded by a spectrum analyzer by an attached force sensor.

Boundary conditions are three edges free and one edge clamped. And first three fundamental modal shapes were obtained.

## Results and Discussions
Typical first three mode fringe patterns of $[0]_{16}$ defect free and defect of diameter 45 mm are shown in Figs. 2 - 4, respectively.
In Fig. 2, the first modal shapes are caused by bending displacement. The bending rigidity should be reduced because of the cutout, however, no significant difference can be observed except the case of d = 45 mm. For the case of d = 45 mm, the fringes are no longer straight across the cutout. The typical fringe patterns of second modal mode are shown in Fig. 3. This modal mode can be recognized as twist mode. Since the circular cutout is located at the center of each specimen, the anti-twist capability would change little. Therefore, the fashion of fringe patterns remains the same as the defect-free one. The fringe patterns of the third modal mode are shown in Fig. 4. Note that in this modal mode, it happens to be that the cutout is located at the place where the maximum displacement occurs. The fashion of the fringe patterns only changes very slightly from the case d = 0 mm to d = 45 mm.

## Acknowledgments
This research was supported in part by the National Science Council (Grant Nos. 82-0401-E007-299, NSC-82-0618-E007-323, NSC 83-0401-E007-007 and NSC 84-2212-E007-062) of the Republic of China.

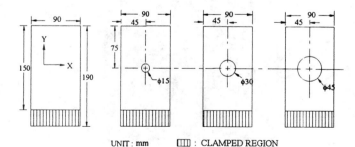

UNIT : mm     IIII : CLAMPED REGION

Fig. 1 Test specimens

* Professor
# Graduate Student

(a) Defect free                    (b) d =45 mm

Fig. 2 First mode ESPI fringe patterns of $[0]_{16}$ composite plates

(a) Defect free                    (b) d =45 mm

Fig. 3 Second mode ESPI fringe patterns of $[0]_{16}$ composite plates

(a) Defect free                    (b) d =45 mm

Fig. 4 Third mode ESPI fringe patterns of $[0]_{16}$ composite plates

# Vibration Measurement of Composite Plates Containing Defect at Different Depths by Amplitude Fluctuation ESPI Method

Wei-Chung Wang[*], Chi-Hung Hwang[#], Shu-Yu Lin[#]
Department of Power Mechanical Engineering
National Tsing Hua University
Hsinchu, Taiwan 30043
Republic of China

## Abstract

Defect can be easily caused by an impact on composite structures. In this paper, by employing the amplitude fluctuation electronic speckle pattern interferometry(ESPI) method, the displacement of modal modes of composite plates with different depths of circular defects were measured. According to the recorded fringe patterns, the change of vibration characteristics and difference between amplitude fluctuation ESPI method and image signal subtraction ESPI method were discussed.

## Theory

The brightness distribution $B_{IM}$ of image signal subtraction ESPI method(ISSEM) can be related as

$$B_{IM} \propto |J_o(k) - 1| \qquad (1)$$

where $k = 2A\pi(1 + \cos\theta)/\lambda$, A = vibration amplitude, $\theta$= incident angel of object beam, $\lambda$ = wave length of the light source. As for amplitude fluctuation ESPI method(AFEM), the brightness distribution can be expressed as

$$B_{IM} \propto |J_1(k)| \qquad (2)$$

and the associated vibration amplitude can be related as

$$A = \frac{\lambda \zeta_i}{2\pi(1 + \cos\theta)} \qquad (3)$$

with $k = \zeta_i$, eq. (2) will be nulled.

## Experimental Background

As shown in Fig. 1, the test specimen was made from 16-ply unidirectional CFRP laminate. Two types of defects were studied, i.e., thickness-through defect and defect at different depths. The shape of the defect is circular with a diameter of 45 mm. Four different depths were adopted for the non-thickness-through defect, i.e., defect was located at the 4th layer or 8th layer or 12th layer. Boundary conditions for composite plates studied in this paper are three edges free and one edge clamped.

A shaker was used to provide the driving force and a function generator with power amplifier was used to supply fixed vibration frequency to the composite plates. With help of a force sensor attached on the specimen, the driving force was monitored and recorded by a spectrum analyzer.

---

[*] : Professor
[#]: Graduated student

## Results and Discussions

Typical fringe patterns of thickness-through and defect at 4th-layer are shown in Figs. 2 and 3, respectively. Images of through-thickness defect shown in Fig. 2 were obtained by ISSEM. As for Fig. 3, the fringe patterns of the defect located at the 4th layer were obtained by AFEM. Comparing those images, the images obtained by AFEM are finer and clearer than those obtained by ISSEM. The main reason is that the fringe order of ISSEM is around local minimum of the brightness while in the AFEM the fringe order is located where the brightness is totally vanished.

Two special phenomenons can be observed in Figs. 2 and 3. First, fringe pattern of first modal mode shows a little bend around the defect and the fringes are wider. Since the location of neutral axis is changed due to the cutout, therefore, the displacement around defect is non-symmetric. Moreover, the bending rigidity of the specimen should be reduced owing to the cutout. Therefore, the out-of-plane displacement will be enlarged around the defect and the fringe patterns will be bent. Secondly, the fringe patterns of third mode will concentrate around the defect as the depth of defect increases. The major reason is that the moment rigidity will decay as the depth of defects increases and finally the defect region will behave as a membrane and some local behavior around the defect would occur.

## Acknowledgments

This research was supported in part by the National Science Council (Grant Nos. 82-0401-E007-299, NSC-82-0618-E007-323, NSC 83-0401-E007-007 and NSC 84-2212-E007-062) of the Republic of China.

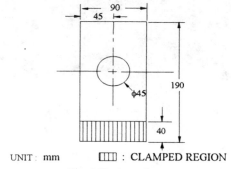

UNIT : mm          [IIII] : CLAMPED REGION

Fig. 1 Test specimens

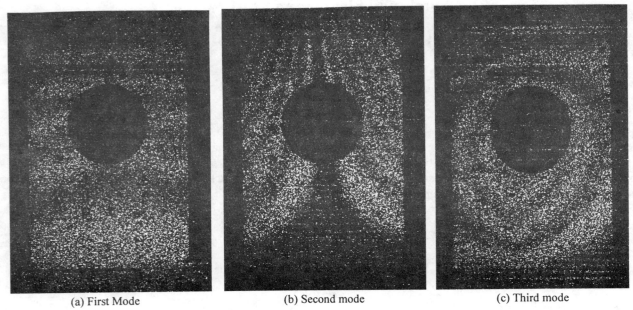

(a) First Mode            (b) Second mode            (c) Third mode

Fig. 2 The fringe patterns of thickness-through circular defect of $[0]_{16}$ composite plate by image signal subtraction ESPI method

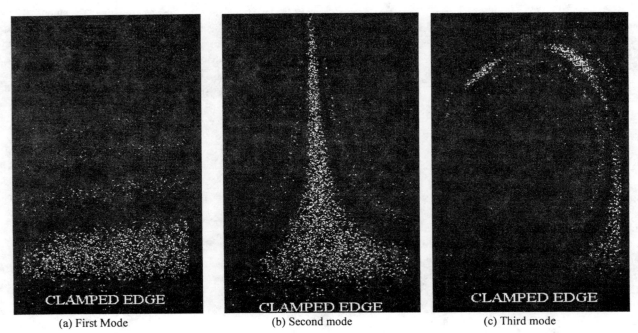

(a) First Mode            (b) Second mode            (c) Third mode

Fig. 3 The fringe patterns of the 4-layer circular defect of $[0]_{16}$ composite plate by amplitude fluctuation ESPI method

# The Experimental Analysis of Kinematics and Contact Stresses of Double-Dwell Cams

Ming-Jong Wang
Associate Professor
Department of Mechanical Engineering
Ming Hsin Institute of Technology and Commerce
Hsinfong, Hsinchu County, Taiwan 304
Republic of China

Wei-Chung Wang
Professor

Yeu-Ming Chen
Graduate Assistant

Department of Power Mechanical Engineering
National Tsing Hua University
Hsinchu, Taiwan 30043
Republic of China

Cam-follower systems can be classified by type of motion program. The double-dwell(RDFD) cam is one of the typical motion programs often used in industries. For the design of a double-dwell cam, just like other kinds of cam, the kinematics is first considered. Since the first, second and third derivatives of its displacement function are its velocity, acceleration and jerk functions respectively, the kinematic characteristics of every cam depend on its displacement function. The choice of cam's displacement function must meet the following constraints: (a) The cam's displacement function must be continuous through the first and second derivatives of displacement across the entire interval(360 degrees). (b) The jerk function must be finite across the entire interval.

Based on the kinematics of cams, a wide variety of mathematical expressions can be used to define a double-dwell cam's motion program. Four different plate cams respectively defined by simple harmonic, cycloidal, 3-4-5 polynomial and modified trapezoidal functions were investigated in this paper. Simple harmonic and cycloidal curves belonging to basic curves[1] were used because of their simplicity of construction and ease of analysis. Kinematically speaking, cycloidal curve is suitable for a double-dwell cam while simple harmonic curve is not due to the discontinuity of its acceleration curve. The purpose to choose simple harmonic curve is trying to investigate the effect of the acceleration discontinuity on the contact stresses of a rotating cam. For many machine requirements, basic curves may require modifications in the characteristic curves of displacement, velocity, and acceleration. There are four ways, i.e., (1) combining portions of basic curves, (2) polynomial equations, (3) the method of finite differences, and (4) fourth derivative curve[1], to consider the problem of special curve shapes. Among them, the first and second ways are more often used. That's why one typical curve of the first and second ways was chosen as test specimens. The modified trapezoidal curve, a combination of the cubics and the parabolic curves, represent the first group. The 3-4-5 polynomial cam represent the polynomial group. For a proper cam design, accurate analysis and control of the velocity and acceleration

curves are required. This is especially true of the acceleration curve which is the determining factor of the dynamic load and vibrations of a cam follower system. The acceleration curve can affect the contact stresses of a rotating cam vitally. So, the acceleration curve plays an extremely important role on both kinematics and contact stresses of a rotating cam. The cam mechanism of a valve tappet was studied. The schematic of the cam mechanism is shown in Fig. 1. In order to make sure the kinematics of this cam mechanism conforms to the theoretical results, a LVT (linear velocity transducer) and spectrum analyzer were used to measure cam's velocity curve and differentiate the velocity curve to obtain each cam's acceleration curve.

In addition to the consideration of kinematics, the contact stresses of a cam should be considered to get good wear-resistant performance. As cam's surface wear is mainly caused by the maximum contact shear stress(MCSS), it is essential for further research of cam's contact stresses problem to determine the MCSS and its location. There is little literature concerning about the cam's contact stresses of a rotating cam. Some books referring to the cam's contact stresses by Chen[2] and Rothbart[1] are still based on the Hertz theory[3] which can not fully describe the contact problem of rotating cams pointed out by authors' previous researches[4,5]. For a complex engineering problem such as the contact stresses problem of rotating cams, a lot of experimental works should be done before an analytical solution is reached. The traditional digital photoelastic method would be an excellent experimental method at static state to find cam's MCSS directly. It is very difficult to measure the MCSS of a rotating cam unless the digital photoelastic system with added functions of synchronous trigger and continuous image taking is used. This new system has been developed by authors[4,5] as shown in Fig. 2. The MCSS and its location of each rotating plate cam during its rise at different rotation speeds and static state were found respectively. The influence of cam's rotation speeds and cam's profile for the behavior of each cam's MCSS was investigated and compared to each other. Finally, different viewpoints among contact mechanics, kinematics and cam's profile would be discussed and compared.

The results can offer cam's designer a new consideration to make compromise among contact mechanics, kinematics and cam's profile.

Acknowledgements:

This research was supported in part by the National Science Council (Grant Nos. NSC-82-0115-C-159-507-E, NSC-83-0117-C-159-010 and NSC-84-2212-E007-078) of the Republic of China.

References:

[1] Rothbart, H. A., 1956, *Cams - Design, Dynamics and Accuracy*, John Wiley, N. Y., pp. 270-275.

[2] Chen, F. Y., 1982, *Mechanics and Design of Cam Mechanisms*, Pergamon Press Inc., New York, USA,

[3] Hertz, H., Uberdie Beruhrung fester elastischer korper (On the contact of elastic solids) *J. reine und angewandte Mathematik*, 92, 156-1.(For English translation see Miscellaneous Papers by H. Hertz, Eds. Jones and Schott, London: Macmillan, 1896.)

[4] Wang, M. J., Wang, W. C., "Investigation of Contact Stresses of a Rotating Cam by a Digital Photoelastic Method", *Strain*, Vol. 31, No. 1, pp17-24, 1995.

[5] Wang, M. J., Wang, W. C., "Photoelastic Investigation of Contact Stresses of Rotating Cams," Proceedings of the International Symposium on Advanced Technology in Experimental Mechanics, Tokyo, Japan, Nov. 9-10, 1995, pp. 43-48.

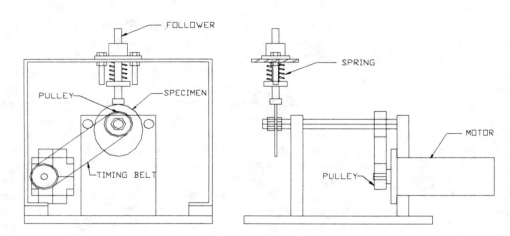

Fig. 1 Schematic of the cam mechanism[4,5]

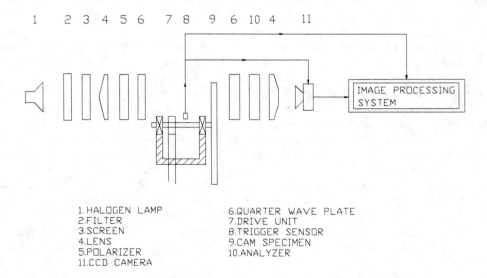

1.HALOGEN LAMP
2.FILTER
3.SCREEN
4.LENS
5.POLARIZER
11.CCD CAMERA

6.QUARTER WAVE PLATE
7.DRIVE UNIT
8.TRIGGER SENSOR
9.CAM SPECIMEN
10.ANALYZER

Fig. 2 Digital photoelastic system with added functions of synchronous trigger and continuous image taking[4,5]

# Analysis of Growing Crack Tip Deformation Using Both In-plane Deformation and Caustics Obtained from Out-of-plane Displacement

P.F. Luo*, J.S. Wang*, Y.J. Chao** , and M.A. Sutton**

*Department of Mechanical Engineering
Chung Hua Polytechnic Institute
Hsin Chu, Taiwan, 30067

**Department of Mechanical Engineering
University of South Carolina
Columbia, SC 29208

The stereo vision is used to study the fracture behavior in the compact tension (CT) specimen (Fig. 1) made from 304L stainless steel, which is a ductile material. During crack tip blunting, initiation, and growth in the CT specimen, both in-plane and out-of-plane displacement fields near the crack tip are measured by the stereo vision.

Based on the plane stress assumption and the deformation theory of plasticity, the J integral is evaluated along several rectangular paths surrounding the crack tip by using the measured in-plane displacement field. Prior to crack growth, the J integral is path independent. For crack extension up to $\Delta a \approx 3$ mm, the near field J integral values are 6% to 10% lower than far field J integral values. For the crack extension of $\Delta a \approx 4$ mm, the J integral lost path independence. The far field J integral values are in good agreement with results obtained from Merkle-Corten's formula, which used the load versus load-line displacement curve for the CT specimen to compute the J integral values.

The experimental strain field is obtained by smoothing the measured in-plane displacement field, and is close to the HRR strain field for crack extension up to 0.773 mm, and gradually deviates from the HRR field under the crack growth of 1 mm to 4 mm. Both J-$\Delta a$ and CTOA-$\Delta a$ are obtained by computing the J integral value and crack tip opening angle (CTOA) at each $\Delta a$. Results indicate that CTOA reached a nearly constant value at a crack extension of $\Delta a = 3$ mm with a leveled resistance curve thereafter.

The out-of-plane displacement $w(x,y)$ is obtained by stereo vision. It is noted that points $(x,y)$ form a rectangular array around the crack tip. The measured out-of-plane displacement was smoothed by one-dimensional cubic spline smoothing and the rectangular array was mapped point by point through the mapping equation [1]

$$X_i = x_i - 2z_0 \frac{\partial f}{\partial x_i} \qquad (1)$$

to the virtual screen (Fig. 2). $z_0$ is the distance between the specimen surface and the virtual screen. The reflected optical fields for different values of z0 are generated (Figs. 3 to 5). The central parts of these reflected fields contain no rays, and these parts are shadow spots.

By measuring the maximum transverse diameter D of the generated shadow spot(width of caustic in the direction perpendicular to the crack line), the J integral can be determined by [2]

$$K_I = \frac{ED^{5/2}}{10.7z_0 \nu h} \qquad (2)$$

where E is the elastic modulus, $\nu$ is the poisson's ratio, h is the specimen thickness, and $K_I$ is the mode I stress intensity factor.

If the plane stress HRR field dominates, the J integral can be evaluated by [2]

$$J = S_n \frac{\alpha \sigma_0^2}{E} \left[ \frac{E}{\alpha \sigma_0 z_0 h} \right]^{\frac{n+1}{n}} D^{\frac{3n+2}{n}} \qquad (3)$$

where $\sigma_0$ is the yield stress, $\alpha$ is the strain hardening coefficient, n is the strain hardening exponent, and $S_n$ is a numerical factor dependent on n.

As shown in Fig. 6, it is indicated that for the crack extension up to $\Delta a = 0.25$ mm, the J integral value evaluated by using the diameter D of the shadow spot is in good agreement with both the far field J integral value evaluated from the out-of-plane displacement field and the results obtained form Merkle-Corten formula. It is also noted that beyond the crack growth of $\Delta a = 0.25$ mm, the J integral value evaluated by using the shadow spot gradually deviates from the other two results as the crack growth increases.

Acknowledgment:

The authors wish to thank the National Science Council in Taiwan for the support of the project through grants NSC 83-0401-E-216-001, and NSC 84-2212-E-216-005.

References:

[1]. Rosakis, A.J. and Zhender, A.T., "On the Method of Caustics: an Exact Analysis Based on Geometric Optics," Caltech Report, SM84-1.

[2]. Zehnder, A.T. and Rosakis, A.J., "A Note on the Measurement of K and J under small Scale Yielding Conditions Using the Method of Caustics," *International Journal of Fracture*, Vol.30, R43-R48, 1986.

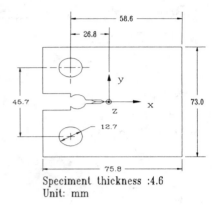

Specimen thickness :4.6
Unit: mm

Figure 1 : Specimen configurations and dimensions for 304L SS CT specimen

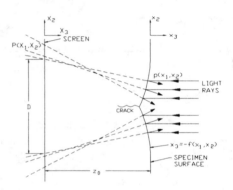

Figure 2 : Formation of caustic upon reflection

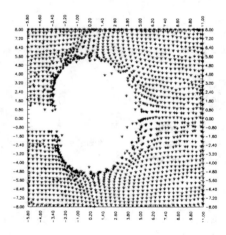

Figure 3 : Shadow spot ($Z_0$=40 mm) for 304L SS CT specimen with 12400 N ( $\Delta a$=0.025 mm)

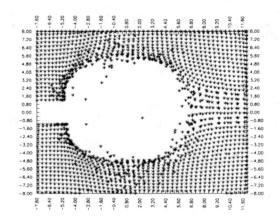

Figure 4 : Shadow spot ($Z_0$=12 mm) for 304L SS CT specimen with 13900 N ( $\Delta a$=2.067 mm)

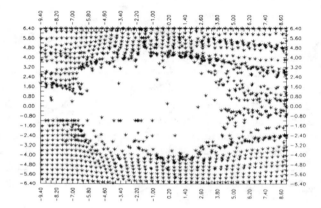

Figure 5 : Shadow spot ($Z_0$=7 mm) for 304L SS CT specimen with 12800 N ( $\Delta a$=3.956 mm)

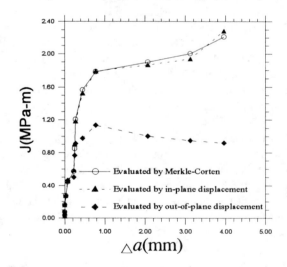

Figure 6 : comparison of J integral value

334

# The Determination of Fiber-Bridging Tractions in Fiber-Reinforced Composites

*Chao-Hsun Chen and Ren-Roe Chang*

**Institute of Applied Mechanics National Taiwan University, Taipei, Taiwan, R.O.C.**

## *EXTENDED ABSTRACT*

A formulation is systematically derived for a fully or partially bridged straight crack in anisotropic materials such as fiber-reinforced composites. The dislocation density distribution corresponding to the measured COD of the bridged crack in composite specimen is obtained by the method of electronic-speckle-pattern interferometry (ESPI). With the dislocation density distribution as input in the equilibrium equations along crack surfaces , the fiber-bridging tractions exerted on the crack surfaces by intact bridging fibers can be determined. The tractions can be expressed either as a function of the position along the crack or a function of the crack opening displacement.

## *Formulation of Partially Bridged Crack*

When the bridged area of the crack is much larger than the diameter and spacing of bridging fibers , the fiber-bridging force can be modeled by continuously distributed tractions exerted on the crack surfaces.

Figure 1a shows schematically a bridged straight crack along the $\hat{x}_1$ axis which makes an angle $(\frac{\pi}{2} - \theta)$ with the direction of fibers. In Fig. 1a the farfield loading is denoted by $\hat{T}_{2i}$ and the bridging-force is denoted by $\hat{p}_i$. The problem shown in Fig. 1a is solved by superposing the two problems shown in Fig. 1b and Fig. 1c and the only condition to be satisfied is the boundary condition on crack surfaces , as shown below:

On the $\hat{x}_1$ axis from (-c , 0) to (c , 0) , which corresponds to the location of the bridged crack , the stress components in Fig. 1b are

$$\hat{\sigma}_{2i}(\hat{x}_1) = \hat{T} \tag{1}$$

the stress components in Fig. 1c are

$$\hat{\sigma}_{2i}(\hat{x}_1) = \frac{\hat{L}_{ik}}{2\pi} \int_{-c}^{c} \frac{d\xi}{\hat{x}_1 - \xi} \hat{b}_k(\xi) \tag{2}$$

then , the boundary condition at crack faces becomes

$$\hat{T}_{2i} + \frac{L_{ik}}{2\pi} \int_{-c}^{c} \frac{d\xi}{\hat{x}_1 - \xi} \hat{b}_k(\xi) = \hat{p}_i(\hat{x}_1) , \quad -c < \hat{x}_1 \tag{3}$$

With the dislocation density distribution as input in the equilibrium equations along crack surfaces , the fiber-bridging tractions exerted on the crack surfaces by intact bridging fibers can be determined.

## Specimen Preparation and Experimental Set up

Epoxy (resin : Gy 260 , hardner : B206 , EPOCONE CHEMICAL CO. TAIWAN ) and glass fibers (HEXCEL KNYTEX Weft D155 ) are made into our composite specimens by RTM (resin transfer molding) method . Thus the specimens with intact fiber- bridgeing and fiber-bridgingless central crack were ready for test as shown in Fig. 2a & 2b . A laser interferometry technique named ESPI (Electronic Speckle Pattern Interferometry ) is used to measure the COD of the specimen. The experimental set up for ESPI is shown in Fig. 3 .To avoid rigid body motion , which may exceed 20 microns , of the specimen during stretching . The specimen is stretched by a micromechanical test machine (shown as Fig. 4) which has two clamps that move simultaneously in opposite directions to keep the center of the specimen ,

## Result and Analysis

Figure 5a,b show the ESPI fringe pattern of the fiber-bridged matrix crack under far-field tensile force 7.5kg. Figure 6a, 6b, 6c and 6d plot the measured COD of the fiber bridged crack. Using our proposed model to analyze the datas. The results show that we only need two Chebyshev polynomial terms to approximate the crack opening profile, (the solid-line curves shown in the figures represent our Chebyshev polynomial solutions ). Figure 7a and figure 7b plot the bridging-traction distribution corresponding to the crack opening profile shown in figure 6a,b and figure 6c,d, respectively. Since the COD decays to zero from middle to both tips of the crack, the bridging traction distribution falls off from the crack center to the tips.

Figure 8 plots another COD result of the fiber bridged crack. We attempt using the bridging-traction-distribution analysis to handle the experimental result. The solid lines in Figure 8 represent the COD under three different far-field loadings with interfacial properties $\mu = 0.27, \sigma_c = 0.18 MPa, \sigma_d = 3.0 MPa$ substituted into the theory of Chen et.al, [1995]. We can see from the figure that in general the COD measured under three sets of different tensile loadings can be approximated by one set of material interfacial properties. This result can be seen as a justification to our theoretical model.

From the above results we have demostrated that the artifical fiber-bridged crack can be made by laser cutting process, and the distribution of bridging traction distribution can be calculated through the COD field measured by ESPI technique .

## References:

Chen, Chao-Hsun, Chang, Ren-Roe and Pao-Hwa Jeng, (1995),"On the Fiber-Bridging of Cracks in Fiber-Reinforced Composites," Mechanics of Materials 20, pp.165-181.

## Acknowledgements:

This work is supported by the National Science Council of R.O.C., NSC-81-0405-E002-01.

# A Tomographic Technique for Determining Contact Stress

Matthew W. Witte with Joseph Hovanesian and John Hovanesian
Product Engineer, Chrysler Corporation
800 Chrysler Dr. East
Auburn Hills, MI 48326

A new method to experimentally measure reactive and interactive forces between contacting objects is presented. This new method of determining contact stress by projections is relatively easy to apply and has a very broad measurement range with the potential for very good resolution. It is easy to understand and is inexpensive to apply. While the technique is in its infancy, it may become a viable tool for measuring contact stress in many applications.

The proposed method relies on the theory of tomography. Tomography is best known from the medical application called Computerized Axial Tomography, or CAT, where cross sectional views of objects are reconstructed from x-ray projections. In the proposed method, a finite dimensional approximation of the actual distribution of contact stress is reconstructed from projection data. This projection data consists of friction force readings taken from an array of thin strips placed within the contact interface. Conceptually, the method is much like finding the tight spots in the distribution by locating which strips are held the tightest. By taking many measurements in many directions, a quantitative estimate of the distribution of contact stress can be recovered.

## The Apparatus

The apparatus is shown schematically in Fig. 1. [3] An array of weighted bins representing a known distribution of normal stress is placed on the platform. The bins sit on an array of strips that are isolated from the bins by thin sheets of teflon. The strips are "reeled-in" by a motorized pulley which hangs on a free-swinging pendulum. The friction reaction force is measured by a transducer which reacts the friction force of each strip. Finally, the platform is rotated so strips can be pulled over several directions.

While this configuration is useful to demonstrate the technique, it is quite labor intensive. Further development may lead to an automated system which will facilitate data acquisition, but the fundamentals of the technique should remain the same.

## Formulation Of The Problem

The objective of the tomographic analysis is a *finite dimensional estimate* of the stress distribution. This estimate will be calculated from the series of friction measurements, or projections, taken at several angles, $\theta$. (See Figure 2.) Assuming Coulomb friction, the friction force, or projection, on a given strip will be

$$f_{\theta_m \, i} = \mu \sum_{j=1}^{n} u_{m_{ij}} a_j \qquad (1)$$

where n is the number of pixels contacted by strip i at angle $\theta_m$, $u_{m_{ij}}$ is the area of contact between strip i and pixel j, and $a_j$ is the average pressure over pixel j. The pressures $a_j$ represent the desired solution and will be designated as a column vector $A(1 \times j)$.

Several friction measurements are taken at each angle. We will take k total measurements and store the friction data in an array $W$ of dimension (kx1). Let $U$ be the (k x $n^2$) matrix of contact areas between a strip and pixel. Then

$$U A = W \qquad (2)$$

is the matrix equation which represents the friction projections, the contact areas, and the contact stresses. $U$ is called the *influence or observation matrix*, analogous to the stiffness matrix of finite element analysis. It is easily determined by the projection angles and the dimension of the reconstruction space. We have selected a set of projection angles which makes the formulation very straight forward for our 3x3 example. [2]

With this formulation, the entire problem of reconstruction by projections is reduced to solving the system (2) for the vector $A$. Note however, that (2) may be an overdetermined problem. In the presence of noisy data, some method is required for determining a solution. Gauss's method of least squares is suggested. It entails solving the so-called normal equation

$$U^T U A = U^T W . \qquad (3)$$

Output error approximately equal to the input error is typical with a least squares reconstruction. While this is a reasonable expectation, the output error is generally quite high due to uncertainty in the friction measurements. A better inversion technique is sought to improve the final result. The method of weighted least squares allows such an improvement, but requires multiple measurements at each projection point. This method entails solving the system

$$U^T G^{-1} U A = U^T G^{-1} W \qquad (4)$$

where $G$ is the diagonal matrix with the variances of the multiple readings as entries. The experimental results show a two fold improvement in output accuracy over least squares alone. Furthermore, this computation is not much more complicated than the solution for system (3).

## Experimental Results

The tomographic reconstruction of contact stress was experimentally verified on a 3x3 grid of 2.5 inch square-base bins. Data was collected at eight projection angles: $0^\circ$, $18.4^\circ$, $26.6^\circ$, $45^\circ$, $63.4^\circ$, $71.6^\circ$, $90^\circ$, and $135^\circ$. Reconstruction by least squares agrees with the known value to within 20% at each point (see Fig. 3). The actual pressure resolution was remarkably high. A minimum threshold of 1.2 KPa (0.18 psi) with pressure resolution of 0.4 KPa (0.05 psi) was obtained.

Reconstruction by Weighted Least squares was accomplished by repeating the data collection for a total of five trials and solving equation (4) as described. The maximum variation at any cell was reduced to 10% in this case. In light of the difficulties inherent in precisely measuring friction, this is a very encouraging result.

## Summary

A tomographic technique for determining the distribution of stresses between contacting objects has been presented. By simply measuring the friction force required to move strips within the contact interface, an approximation of the contact stress distribution can be made. The current investigation assumes that a Coulomb friction law applies. A result within 20% is demonstrated for tomographic reconstruction by least squares and within 10% for reconstruction by weighted least squares. These results pertain to a 3x3 array of known weighted bins that have a base size of 2.5 inches. This is admittedly coarse for most practical applications, but the technique shows great promise.

As the technique is developed, we should find it simple to improve spatial resolution by decreasing the size of the reconstruction pixels. This will by accomplished by reducing the width of the strips used for the friction measurement. Also, the method may allow recovering a continuous contact function. The correlation between a finite dimensional reconstruction and a continuous distribution is already well established [1]. Finally, a better physical understanding of the friction process with improved mathematical description could improve the accuracy of this method significantly.

## References

[1] Katz, M. B. 1978. *Questions of uniqueness and resolution in reconstruction from projections*. Lecture notes in biomathematics, ed. S. Levin, vol. 26. New York: Springer-Verlag.

[2] Witte, M. W. 1993. *The determination of contact stress by projections*. Ph. D. Dissertation, Oakland University. Rochester, MI.

[3] Witte, M.W., Hovanesian, J.D. and Hovanesian, J. A., A Tomographic Technique for Determining Contact Stress. *Experimental Techniques*. Vol 19, No. 4, July/Aug 1995. pp 9 - 12.

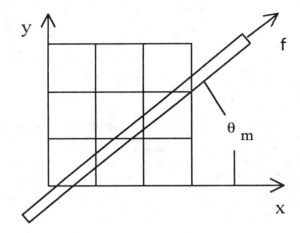

**Figure** 2. A Projection at angle $\theta m$

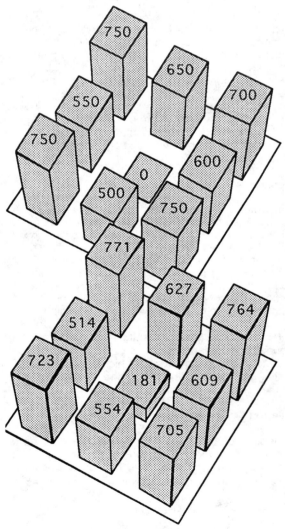

**Figure 3.** A Distribution and Reconstruction by Least Squares

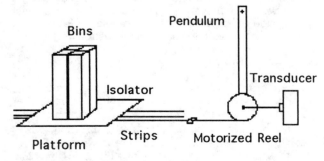

**Figure 1.** Friction Dynamometer

# Stresses in Rigid Pavement Due to Environmental Factors

J.J. Von Handorf, S.M. Sargand, G.A. Hazen
Center for Geotechnical and Environmental Research
Ohio University
Athens, OH  45701

Stresses in rigid pavement result from a number of complex environmental and load factors. It is important to fully understand these factors since rigid pavements are used in a large portion of the highways in the United States. When the current AASHTO design procedures were developed, the effects of environmental factors were not fully recognized. Today, with the use of more precise electronic instruments, it is possible to accurately measure the effects of environmental factors. These measurements can be compared to a mechanistic design model to verify its accuracy. As part of a national effort to improve pavement design, a test road was constructed in Delaware County, Ohio. In the months of October, 1995 through January, 1996, the first nondestructive field test was conducted on three sections of this pavement to determine the magnitude of variations of stress in rigid pavement caused by temperature and moisture changes.

It is well known that environmental factors are very important to pavement design for several reasons. First, changes in temperature and moisture in a slab cause expansion and contraction. As this movement is resisted by the surrounding slabs, dowel bars, base material and the weight of the slab; stresses develop within the slab. Over time, the cycle of rising and falling temperatures, and therefore stresses, leads to fatigue problems in the pavement. Second, large temperature and moisture gradients between the top and bottom surfaces of the slab cause curling and warping. Temperature curling and moisture warping result in constantly changing deflections and stresses. In some cases, relatively small areas of the slab are in contact with the base. These effects accelerate fatigue failure. Other environmental considerations that lead to increased stress include pumping and deformations of the subgrade. Accurate determination of stresses induced by environmental factors is very important to better understand pavement performance.

The strain gauge monitored in this experiment is one that has been used successfully in the past at Ohio University. It is a 350Ω full Wheatstone bridge configuration embedded transducer specifically designed to measure changes in strain and temperature in concrete. The operating temperature is -20°C to +80°C, and the strain limit is plus or minus 0.5% strain. The gauge consists of a rubber coated sleeve measuring 10.0 cm long and 1.7 cm in diameter, with a steel flange on both ends measuring 2.0 cm in diameter (Figure 1). Change in strain is measured using a four-wire system. Change in temperature is measured independent of strain using a three-wire system. Six of these strain gauges are placed in each section, at 0.686, 1.524, and 2.286 meters from the approach side joint along the longitudinal centerline of the slab. One gauge is placed 2.54 cm from the top and another is placed 2.54 cm from the bottom surface of the PCC.

Installation of these gauges during the construction period is a difficult process. The gauges must first be positioned correctly in the slab. As the paver and spreader pass, the gauge cannot be rotated, displaced, overstrained, or destroyed. To accomplish this, a procedure was adopted based on past experience in other projects. Shortly before the paver reaches the section, plastic ties are used to tie the gauges to small steel chairs, holding them at the correct elevation and position in the slab. Next, a four-sided steel box fabricated from 22-gauge sheet metal measuring 30.5 x 15.2 x 19.0 or 26.7 cm high (depending on concrete thickness) is placed around the gauges and chairs (Figure 2). The box is stabilized on each corner by steel pins which are pushed into the base material to prevent movement as the paver and spreader pass. Concrete is then placed by hand and vibrated inside the boxes. After the paver and spreader pass, the boxes are carefully removed and the position of the top gauge is checked. Concrete is added to replace the volume of the box, and the area surrounding the gauges is vibrated to eliminate any discontinuities. Finally, the paving crews smooth this area and the remaining wet concrete to ensure a flat driving surface. Throughout the construction process, this procedure was extremely effective.

Three sections of the test pavement were monitored. Data acquisition systems were used to take five temperature and five strain readings from each gauge at the end of every half hour. Readings were averaged, and this value was stored in ASCII text format in the data acquisition systems. After four days, the data was downloaded to a laptop computer for analysis. A "C" program then converted the raw data to changes in temperature, strain, and stress using a series of response equations. Although the strain gauges are capable of measuring temperature and strain as the concrete cures, construction procedure did not allow

339

this. Therefore, absolute strain cannot be determined. For each four-day period, the initial temperature and strain condition was assumed to be zero. Changes in stress and temperature were calculated for each time period.

Data from this experiment gives an accurate picture of the magnitude of the change in stress that develops in rigid pavement as a result of temperature and moisture changes. Results from three sections were compared to a finite element model. These sections are subjected to the same environmental conditions, but differ in lane width, base materials, concrete thickness, and drainage conditions. Data show substantial variations with sections for stress as a function of temperature.

References:

[1]    Yu, H.T., Smith, K.D., Darter, M.I., "Field and Analytical Evaluation of the Effects of Tied PCC Shoulder and Widened Slabs on Performance of JPCP," Colorado Department of Transportation, October, 1995, pp 4-10.

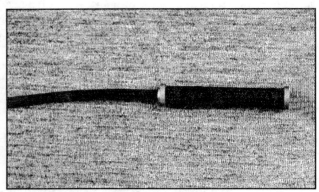

**Figure 1** Typical Strain Gauge Used

**Figure 2** Strain Gauge Field Installation

# Monitoring Dynamic Response of Pavement by Strain Gauges

A.A. Sharkins, S.M. Sargand, I.S. Khoury
Center for Geotechnical and Environmental Research
Ohio University
Athens, Ohio 45701

Mechanistic procedures are becoming the method of choice for future pavement design. The stresses due to dynamic loading are one of the key parameters in Portland Cement Concrete (PCC) pavement design. Currently, stresses are determined using numerical methods such as finite element and closed form solutions. These models do not account for all the factors which influence pavement performance. Limited amounts of field data is available in literature to verify the predicted stresses. Strains within a PCC pavement structure can be measured with the use of embedment strain gauges. The dynamic strains are due to non-destructive tests, such as the Falling Weight Deflectometer (FWD) or vehicle loading.

The Ohio Strategic Highway Research Program (SHRP) Specific Pavement Studies (SPS) Test Road is located on U.S. 23 between the city of Delaware, Ohio and the Marion County line. The DEL-23-17.48 project incorporates 18 SPS-2 (Strategic Study of Structural Factors for Rigid Pavements) experiments. SPS-2 sections are fully instrumented to monitor dynamic responses. Since the basic plan proposed by SHRP was limited, the Ohio Department of Transportation (ODOT) and the Ohio University Center for Geotechnical and Environmental Research (CGER) opted to develop a more comprehensive instrumentation plan for DEL-23-17.48. Instrumentation proposed under the Long Term Pavement Performance (LTPP) program includes using the H-type embedment strain gauge for monitoring strains. The H-type gauge is used to measure strain at the top and the bottom of the PCC along the outside wheel path. Another embedment strain gauge type selected by ODOT and CGER was the full bridge embedment transducer. This transducer is temperature compensated and is used to measure strain on the top and on the bottom of the PCC in the centerline. All strain gauges were chosen based upon service life, accuracy, durability, and strain magnitude capabilities.

During construction of the Ohio Test Road, a new type of embedment strain gauge became available. ODOT and CGER evaluated the benefits of utilizing this new embedment strain gauge, and the gauge was incorporated as part of the response parameters instrumentation in selected SPS-2 experiments. The Ohio Test Road is the first test road to utilize its performance capabilities. The gauge is constructed of a sensing grid encased in a corrosion resistant material. The sensing grid is fabricated of modified Karma foil on a polyimide backing. The grid has an active gauge length of 100 mm. (4 in.), a grid resistance of 120 ohms ± 0.8%, and a gauge factor of 2.05 ± 1.0%. Corrosion protection is provided by a 130×17×10 mm. (5×0.7×0.4 in.) nominal outer body constructed of a polymer/concrete composite. The sensing grid compensates for thermal effects over a wide range of temperatures. The recommended operating temperature range is -5°C to +50°C, with an extended range of -30°C to +65°C.

Following SHRP instrumentation plans for strain gauges, gauges are mounted longitudinally at specified transverse locations of the outer wheel path (see Figure 1). Strain is measured at the top and the bottom of the PCC slab. One gauge is embedded 2.54 cm. (1 inch) below the PCC surface and a second gauge is embedded 2.54 cm. (1 inch) above the base. This positioning provides for complete embedment of the gauges in the concrete and locates the gauges equally distant from the neutral axis of the PCC slab. To guarantee that the gauge is properly located in the PCC slab, a unique installation procedure is practiced. This procedure utilizes a specially designed pattern, steel stands, and sheet metal boxes for locating and protecting the gauges prior to and during the paving process. A steel pattern with specific distances marked off is used to pinpoint the position for the center of the gauge. Independent steel chairs, specially designed for the gauge by CGER personnel, support a pair of embedment gauges at the correct elevations. The chairs are set apart at a distance, which allows some overhang of the gauges for proper anchoring in the PCC, and fastened to the base at the proper transverse positions in the slab. Embedment gauges are secured to the stands with plastic cable ties creating a gauge unit (see Figure 2). During the paving process the gauge unit experiences forces which can affect its location. These forces are primarily due to flowing forces created by the head of concrete riding in front of the spreader and paver and settling forces created by the vibrators. The location of the gauge unit is protected by a sheet metal box which anchors to the base as a rigid shield, yet the shield can be disassembled into four components for easy removal. Before the paver passes the instrumented section, the lead wires of the gauges are pulled across the base to the edge of the PCC slab and the boxes are filled with concrete by hand. The concrete is compacted with a portable vibrator to assure that the gauges are thoroughly encapsulated and that all voids are eliminated. Then more concrete is piled on top and around the box to further protect the positioning. Every gauge is continuously monitored during the paving process to make sure that the gauge does not break or experience strain beyond its limitations. Once the spreader and paver have passed the instrumented slab, the protective boxes are removed and the positions of the gauges are verified. A small amount of concrete is added to the area above the gauges to fill the void created by removing the box. The area is then compacted with the vibrator and the PCC surface is finished. The lead wires of the gauges are pulled from the edge of the PCC slab, under the asphalt shoulder, and directly into a pull-box situated next to the instrumented section where the wires can be stored or connected to the data acquisition system for monitoring and collecting test data.

Falling Weight Deflectometer testing is the non-destructive technique applied to determine the dynamic strains induced in the PCC slab subjugated to different loads. An impulse load is applied to the PCC surface through a circular foot print placed directly over the gauge locations by the FWD. The FWD is equipped with seven geophones to measure the deflection of the pavement for each drop. Strains induced from the impulse loads are measured and recorded with a high speed data acquisition system. Recently developed, the data acquisition unit is a 16 bit system with 4 megabytes of acquisition and storage memory. A test is initiated and concluded with a keyboard trigger. Data is collected at 2000 points per second and filtered at 100 hertz. Gains are adjusted for optimal signal acquisition. An IEEE-488 interface is used in conjunction with a 486-66DX portable computer to operate the software for the data acquisition system and store test data. The test data is down-loaded for further analysis. The data is evaluated and the results of the embedment strain gauges are correlated with the responses of other embedment strain gauges installed in the same positions in other slabs. The findings of the FWD tests will be reported and the performance of strain gauges will be discussed.

References:

[1]    Cable, J.K., Rohde, J.R., Lee, D.Y., Klaiber, F.W., "Pavement Instrumentation Experimental Project No. 621," Iowa State University Civil Engineering Department, March 1988, pp 1-10.

[2]    Van Deusen, D.A., Newcomb, D.E., Labuz, J.F., "A Review of Instrumentation Technology for the Minnesota Road Research Project," University of Minnesota Department of Civil and Mineral Engineering, April 1992, pp 1-24.

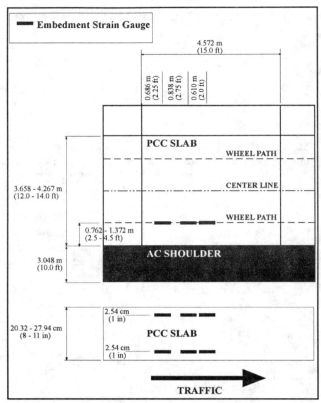

**Figure 1**   Instrumentation Layout

**Figure 2**   Field Installation of Gauge

342

# AN EXPERIMENTAL STUDY ON MECHANICAL BEHAVIOR OF GILDED AND PAINTED LEATHER OF THE XVIII CENTURY

F.BONETTI, P.CAPPA (SEM member)
University of Rome "La Sapienza"
Department of Mechanics and Aeronautics
Via Eudossiana, 18
00184 Rome - Italy

According to a well established cooperation [1,2] between the Italian Central Restoration Institute (ICRI), that is a branch of the Italian Ministry for Cultural Properties, and the Department of Mechanics and Aeronautics of the University of Rome "La Sapienza", a joint research project has recently begun on the study on antique (XVII-XVIII Century) gilded and painted leather. This leather artifacts (notably certain types of decoration such as wall hangings, altar frontals or paintings), require supporting and tensioning structures for proper conservation. These structures must be able to follow the artifact's changes in size automatically, keeping it flat without subjecting it to major increases or reductions in tension. The study of structures for controlled tensioning has been part of the research program of the ICRI since the early I950s, with the design and construction of frames for canvas paintings; these are based on elastic tensioning systems fitted with helical springs that act through tension or compression [3-7]. In almost half a century, these frames have proved to keep the works flat and, through their constant action, even to correct previous deformations. In leather conservation practice, this need has only recently been felt [8].The "Leather Section" of the ICRI decided to adapt this tensioning technique to certain types of decorations in gilded and painted leather that, generally, suffered the following damages as: deformations, widespread damage to the grain layer and partial detachment along the glued joins of the skins. These damages are due to fixed wooden frame on which the paintings were usually mounted by perimetral nailing; in fact, the thermohygrometric excursions caused the leather to be damaged due to lack of compliance by the frame.

The aim of the joint research project was to identify the optimum tensioning values for antique gilded and painted leather and to develop both a support structure with an elastic tensioning system. To provide proper tensioning for antique works in gilded and painted leather, it is essential to determine the mechanical characteristics of such artifacts, but it is usually very difficult to find appropriate test samples (i.e. antique decorated leather). Studies on the mechanical behavior of new leather cannot provide data applicable to old material owing to differing workmanship and histories of mechanical stress.

Tensioning tests both for elasticity and for break-point were carried out on three sets of samples of antique gilded and painted leather (XVII-XVIII Century). Of the source skins, designated $\alpha$, $\beta$, $\gamma$ one was heavily punched, with the tooling patterns moving in straight lines; one was embossed with circular motifs; and the third was only gilded and painted.

Forty samples were obtained, according to international standard I.U.P./6 [9] (width of section =10 mm, free length between clamps =50 mm), taken from adjacent zones of the skin along three directions at 45° to each other (these directions will be later appointed as A, B and C) in order to assess the material's anisotropy.

The experimental setup used for the tension tests (See Fig.1) consists of: (a) manual tensioning device currently used in tests of photoelasticity; (b) bending type load cell for measuring tension force (full scale = 245.60N, accuracy 60*10-3N); (c) strain gauge DC conditioning system (accuracy 0.025%); (d) linear variable differential transformer (LVDT) for displacement measurements of the free end of the sample (full scale =25 mm, accuracy 0.06mm); (e) power supply and AC conditioning unit for LVDT; (f) platinum thermometer (PT100, accuracy 0.1°C); (g) relative humidity transducer with plastic layer (full scale =100%, accuracy 1%); (h) power supply and conditioning unit for tem-

perature and relative humidity transducer; (i) acquisition and A/D converter (16 bit, up to 100,000 readings/s), (j) control unit for data gathering and custom software for data post-processing; (k) leather sample.

Tensile tests results are given as ultimate stress $\sigma_{br}$ (load at break/cross sectional area before loading) and strain $\varepsilon_{br}$ (elongation at break/length before loading), but these values should be considered as global values, i.e. ignoring variations in thickness occurring in each sample with respect to the mean value and the reduction in the cross sectional area due to tooling. Similar provisos apply to stress tests in the elastic field with regard to Young's modulus (E) and the elastic limit ($\sigma_{el}$).

The value of the Young's modulus (stress/strain) of the antique decorated leather, even with limits deriving from the material's typical anisotropy and non-homogeneity and from the variability in thickness and workmanship, can be a useful, concise parameter for characterizing mechanical properties.

Before testing, all samples were conditioned for 48 hours in the laboratory. Tests were conducted at a much lower rate than the I.U.P./6 specifications of 100 mm/minute, to minimize the visco-elastic behavior of the leather.

Table I summarizes the parameters identifying the sample types, the mean value of the ultimate stress and strain and the relative maximum dispersion percentage ($\Delta\sigma/\sigma$ and $\Delta\varepsilon/\varepsilon$). The dispersion of the results is due in part to the nature of leather, and in part to the diverse working and histories of mechanical and chemical stress of the individual source skins. For comparison, a new skin with vegetable tanning can show ultimate stress and strain as a function of the direction of the cut and of the body area in the range of 15-37MPa and 30-70%. The effect of weakening on the old leather is thus evident when one compares these values with those for skin $\beta$ (4-7.6MPa, 7-22%), which was least affected by workmanship.

Table II gives the parameters identifying the type of sample, Young's modulus and the elastic limit. Note that Young's modulus was calculated as the slope of the line interpolating the $\sigma-\varepsilon$ curve in a limited range of strain ($\varepsilon$ between 0.01 and 0.025). This choice derives from the fibrous structure of the leather which requires a pre-load so that the fibers collaborate fairly uniformly in bearing the load. As to the elastic limit, it is difficult to assess it precisely because of leather's intrinsically non-linear nature. Nevertheless it was decided to estimate this limit as the value at which the $\sigma-\varepsilon$ curve and the interpolating line differ by 10%. The authors, however, are aware of the limits of the criterion proposed. The observations made for rupture tests also apply here.

A novel elastic system was designed and applied on a XVIII century altar frontal; the elastic system is based on aluminum tubes on ball bearings in order to minimize friction in the direction of tension and can be easily adjusted as a function of the preload imposed so as to guarantee, thanks to a much higher compliance with respect to the artifact, a limited maximum variation of force in view of predicted thermohygrometric variations. The data gathered through experimental tests on the mechanical behavior of antique decorated leather samples helped the choice of the level of tensioning to apply to the actual artifact.

## REFERENCES

1. G.Accardo, D.Amodio, A.Bennici, P.Cappa, G.Santucci, M.Torre "Strain fields on the statue of Marcus Aurelius", Experimental Mechanics, December, pp 380-385, 1990.

2. Accardo G., Amodio D., Bennici A., Cappa P., Santucci G., Torre M. "Stuctural Analysis of the equestrian monument to Marcus Aurelius", Software for Engineering Workstation, v6,n2, pp 58-61, 1990.

3. R. Carita, "Considerazioni sui telai per affreschi trasportati su tela" ("Considerations on frame for convas paintings"), Bollettino dell'Istituto Centrale del Restauro, 19-20 (1954), pp. 131-154. In Italian.

4. R. Carita, "Sul restauro dei dipinti Caravaggeschi della Cattedrale di Malta" ("On the restauration of Caravaggio's paintings at the Malta cathedral"), Bollettino dell'Istituto Centrale del Restauro", 29-30 (1957), pp. 41-82. In Italian.

5. G. Urbani, "Il restauro delle tele del Caravaggio in San Luigi dei Francesi a Roma" ("On the restauration of Caravaggio's paintings at the San Luigi dei Francesi in Rome"), Bollettino dell'Istituto Centrale del Restauro, 1966, pp. 35-77. In Italian.

6. G. Accardo, A. Bennici, M. Torre, Tensionamento controllato della tela ("Controlled tensioning system of paintings"), in G. Basile, ed.,Il San Girolamo di Caravaggio a Malta: dal furto al restauro, ICR, Roma l991,pp 31-36. In Italian.

7. G. Accardo, A. Bennici, M. Torre, "Sistema elastico di tensionamento" ("Elastic tensioning system"), in G. Basile, ed.,Il San Girolamo di Caravaggio a Malta: dalfurto al restauro, ICR, Roma 1991, pp. 39-44. In Italian.

8. Schultze A., "First experiences with a tight metal-stretching-frame system for leather tapestries in climatically instable rooms" ICOM-CC Working Group on Leather Interim Symposium The Treatment of and Research into Leather, Amsterdam 5-7 April 1995.

9. U. Fiore, ed., Metodi internazionali per l'analisi fisica dei cuoi (I.U.P.) "Methods internationally used to analyse leathers") Stazione Sperimentale per l'Industria delle Pelli e delle Materie Concianti, Napoli, s.d. In Italian.

Table I Results of tensile rupture tests.

| Identification of skin sample / Sample orientation / Number of samples examined | $\sigma_{br}$ (MPa) $\Delta\sigma_{br}/\sigma_{br}$ (%) | $\varepsilon_{br}$(mm/mm) $\Delta\varepsilon_{br}/\varepsilon_{br}$ |
|---|---|---|
| α / A / 3 | 3.5 ± 50% | 0.31 ± 20% |
| α / B / 4 | 6.8 ± 15% | 0.17 ± 25% |
| α / C / 2 | 2.4 ± 30% | 0.07 ± 4.5% |
| β / A / 3 | 7.6 ± 30% | 0.07 ± 20% |
| β / B / 3 | 4.0 ± 15% | 0.22 ± 13% |
| β / C /3 | 6.3 ± 35% | 0.07 ± 7% |
| γ / A / 3 | 7.1 ± 15% | 0.07 ± 35% |
| γ / B / 3 | 4.1 ± 54% | 0.03 ± 60% |

Table II Results of tensile tests in the elastic fields.

| Identification of skin sample / Sample orientation / Number of samples examined | $\sigma_{el}$ (MPa) $\Delta\sigma_{el}/\sigma_{el}$ (%) | E (MPa) $\Delta E/E$ (%) |
|---|---|---|
| α / A / 6 | 1.5 ± 50% | 31 ± 60% |
| α / B / 7 | 1.7 ± 15% | 48 ± 15% |
| α / C / 4 | 1.5 ± 30% | 69 ± 45% |
| β / A / 6 | 3.5 ± 30% | 186 ± 30% |
| β / B / 7 | 3.0 ± 40% | 65 ± 18% |
| β / C / 3 | 4.4 ± 25% | 174 ± 22% |
| γ / A / 3 | 5.8 ± 35% | 167 ± 18% |
| γ / B / 6 | 3.0 ± 80% | 120 ± 88% |

Fig.1- Schetch of the experimental test set-up.

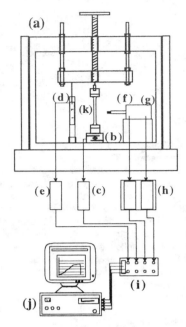

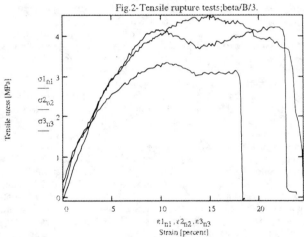

Fig.2- Tensile rupture tests;beta/B/3.

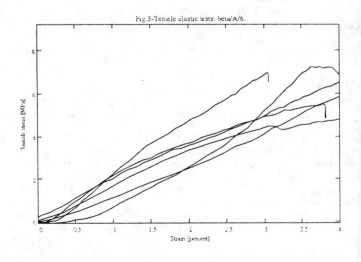

Fig.3-Tensile elastic tests: beta/A/6.

# Performance Evaluation of Endoscopic Optical Systems by means of Digital Fourier Analysis

F.P. Branca, T. D'Alessio*, Z. Del Prete, F. Marinozzi, E. Pichini

Department of Mechanics and Aeronautics, Rome's University "La Sapienza"
v. Eudossiana 18, 00184 ROMA

* Department of Mechanics and Automatics, III Rome's University
v. C. Segre 60, 00146 ROMA

We propose the application of image analysis to the quality and efficiency control of optical systems in clinical endoscopes (Fig.1). This allows an objective evaluation of their functionality, providing adequate servicing and resulting in a less expensive maintainance.

Concerning the optical system, clinical endoscopes are composed of [1]:

- one or more bundles of "non-coherent" optical fibres, consisting of coated fibres arranged at random (Fig.2a), for the trasmission of white light from the light source to the operatory field in order to simply lighten it;

- a "coherent" bundle in which the optical fibres are arranged at both ends so that they bear the same relationship to each other as at the other end. In this way a clear image can be trasmitted from the operatory field to an eyepiece in order to be seen by the doctor (directly or on a monitor). Furthermore, the ends of the bundle are cut and polished with particular accuracy (Fig.3a).

- a wide-angle lens at the entrance of the coherent bundle in order to enlarge the optical field, even though with distorsion;

- an objective of low-magnifing power microscope type at the exit of the endoscope, in order to collect the image and carry it directly to the operator or to a vision system (camera or telecamera).

The performance of the endoscopic optical system becomes worse if, owing to a wrong mantainance, infiltrations occur somewhere in the instrument or if some fibres break off for prolonged operation or bites of the patients. Infiltrations leave dirt deposits on the optical surfaces, or give rise to unstickings between the surfaces in contact. The break off of the fibres brings to a decrease in the capacity of carrying the light (either the white light for the lightening or that one corresponding to the image brightness).

Regarding to the characterization and the quality control of the non-coherent fibres bundle, we carried out measurements of light transmission through the endoscope from its standard light source to a photodiode: the ratio between the energy at the optical output and the one supplied gives the transmittance of the endoscope; differences of this ratio from a standard can be related to the transmittance efficiency.

Regarding to the characterization and the quality control of the coherent system (the coherent fibre bundle and all the components for the image transmission) we applied image analysis methods (pattern recognition) and the bidimensional Fourier transformations [2]: if the endoscope frames a uniform lightened field, a CCD vision system looking through the endoscope sees an image or the regular pattern of the fibres in the coherent bundle (the "honeycomb" in Fig.3a). By means of the digital processing of the acquired frame it is possible to gather information about the regularity of the pattern of the coherent fibres (Fig.3b), the presence of defects or of broken up fibres.

Therefore, for the characterization of the optical system we simply carried out acquisitions of images: first of all, with a CCD camera we looked through the endoscope at a white screen to obtain a uniform field. The analysis of the coherent fibres pattern allows the determination of some quality control parameters: the visibility of the fibres as an average along a diameter or on the complete field is related to the presence of dirt deposits on the optical surfaces; the signal to noise ratio on all the field of view depends on the general wear of the endoscope; the brightness of the optical system in standard conditions is an index of the capability of the system to transmit light. Furthermore, it is possible to establish the fibres spatial frequency (Fig.3c) or enhance irregularities due to breakups of one or more fibres in the fibre bundle or to defects (pits) on the optical surfaces.

Using a chart-gage as the image to look at through the endoscope, it is possible to determine other parameters typical for optical systems: the resolution of the endoscope, its aberration, the distorsions that the endoscope introduces on the image at the center and on the border zone, and so on.

## REFERENCES:

[1] *Fibre-optic endoscopy* - P.R.Salmon - Pitman Medical Publishing Company (1974)

[2] *The Fourier transform and its applications* - R.N. Bracewell - M$^c$ Graw Hill (1986)

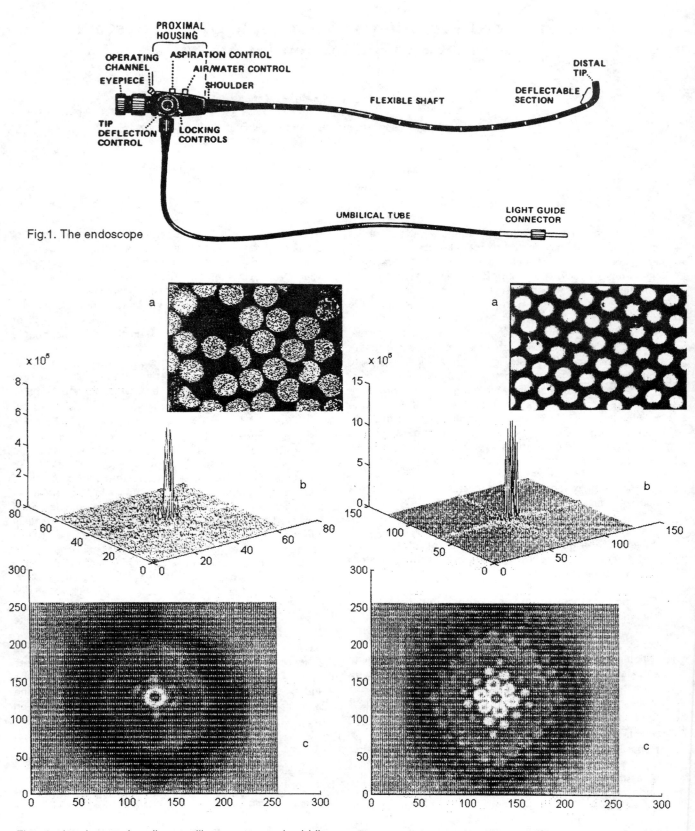

Fig.1. The endoscope

Fig. 2. Incoherent bundle: a, fibres pattern; b, bidimensional Fourier transform; c, correlation transform

Fig. 3. Coherent bundle: a, fibres pattern; b, bidimensional Fourier transform; c, correlation transform

# A New Device for Evaluation of the Batteries State of Charge

**P.Cappa (SEM Member) - L.Fedele (SEM Student Member) - V.Naso**
**University of Rome "La Sapienza"**
**Department of Mechanics and Aeronautics**
**Via Eudossiana, 18 - 00184 - ROMA**
**Tel.:(+39.6) 44585271**
**Fax:(+39.6) 4881759**

The real time evaluation of the charge level and of the efficiency of lead-acid batteries is of big importance for mechanical applications. Today, some of them find their own limits in the efficiency of the electrochemical accumulators [1]: *hybrid and electrical means of transportation, hybrid and electrical submarines, bio-medical* systems. However, *the state of charge of the electrochemical accumulators is function of a large number of variables*, not easily controllable. Moreover *chemical and electric phenomena occur not easy to be forecast* [2].

Traditionally such measurements are based on the evaluation of the **density** and/or of the **voltage** of the battery. Both present expressive limits [1]; in fact:

* the measurement has to be performed many hours after the last charge/discharge cycle
* the measurement of density presents working troubles, especially for packages with an elevated number of batteries and jelly type batteries
* the required statistic elaboration of the data, adds a further uncertainty.

Moreover, innovative state of charge evaluation methods are proposed, even if not commonly employed yet [3, 4].
The uncertainties in the state of charge measures based on the voltage of the battery cell are of the order of the 20%; in case of the measure of the density, they are slightly inferior.

A new experimental device for more precise measurements, based on thermal considerations, has been undertaken at the University "La Sapienza" in Rome.

The charge evaluator for lead-acid batteries, that has been projected and built in Rome, substantially consists of an adiabatic calorimeter, which allows the execution of an energy balance of one lead-acid battery element [5, 6]. The measurement of the electric energy in and out is made by means of the evaluation of the voltage and the current. Thanks to the thermocouple arranged in correspondence of the cell, it is possible to appreciate the heat dissipated from the battery, during the charging and discharging cycles. The digital data are acquired and elaborated by a personal computer, that allows the execution of the energetic balance:

$$E_b = E_1 - E_2 - E_t \qquad (1)$$

where:

$E_b$, is the energy accumulated in the battery, to be evaluated

$E_1$, is the electric energy addressed to the battery (charge)

$E_2$, is the electric energy withdrawn from the battery (discharge)

$E_t$, is the thermal energy dissipated from the battery

The precision of the energetic balance and the quickness of the charge measurement is possible thank to the calorimeter, made adiabatic due to a water jacket thermoregulated with respect to the cell temperature.

The reliability of the proposed technique and the comparison with the traditional remembered methods have been demonstrated experimentally. The positive result of the tests induces us to propose an *innovative charge index* of the batteries, useful on the mechanics systems that employ electrochemical accumulators [6]. In this way, long term tests are still in progress and thus no results are available at the moment.

Acknowledgements:

This work is supported by the Italian Company FAAM S.p.A. from Monterubbiano (Ascoli Piceno).
The authors wish to thank Mr. Francesco Rapanotti for the skilful help given in assembling the experimental layout.

References:

[1] Bode H., *"Lead acid batteries"*, John Wiley & Sons, New York, 1977.
[2] Armenta-Deu C., Donaire T., *"Statistical analysis of the error function in the determination of the state-of-charge in lead/acid batteries"*, Journal of Power Sources, 39 (1992), 95-105.
[3] Barton R.T., Mitchell P.J., *"Estimation of the residual capacity of maintenance-free lead-acid batteries"*, Journal of Power Sources, 27 (1989), 287-295.
[4] Armenta C., *"Determination of the state-of-charge in lead-acid batteries by means of a reference cell"*, Journal of Power Sources, 27 (1989), 297-310.
[5] Bernardi D., Pawlikowsky E., Newman J., *"A general energy balance for battery systems"*, Journal of

Electrochemical Society: Electrochemical Science and Technology, Vol. 132, No. 1, January 1985.

[6] O'Brien B., *"A battery management system for electric buses"*, Proc. of the Ninth Annual Battery Conference on Applications and Advances, Long Beach (CA), 11-13/1/94.

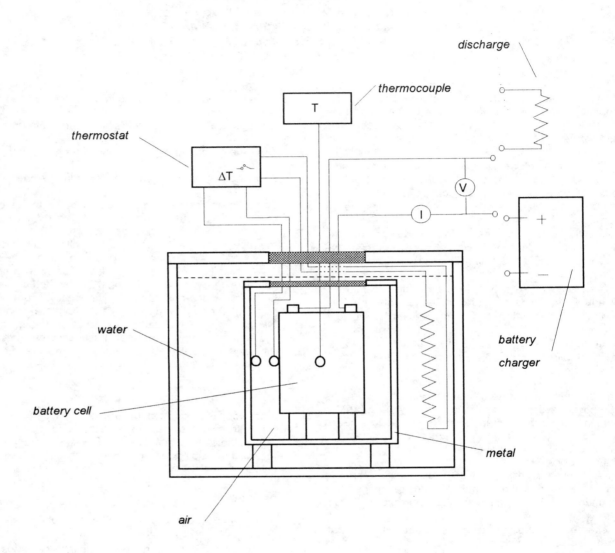

**Fig. 1 - Outline of the thermal evaluator for batteries state of charge**

# Dynamic Fracture Behavior of Brittle Polymers Under Biaxial Loading

K. ARAKAWA, D. NAGOH and K. TAKAHASHI
Research Institute for Applied Mechanics,
Kyushu University
Kasuga 816, Fukuoka, Japan

Many experimental studies have been made on the relation between dynamic stress intensity factor $K_{ID}$ and crack velocity $\dot{a}$. However, different experiments derived significantly different types of $K_{ID}$-$\dot{a}$ relationships. The authors also studied this problem using the method of caustics and measured $K_{ID}$ values during crack propagation which included both acceleration and deceleration in one fracture event [1, 2]. Among the interesting determinations made were: First, the relation between $K_{ID}$ and $\dot{a}$ was not unique. Second, $K_{ID}$ was an increasing function of $\dot{a}$ but also dependent on crack acceleration $\ddot{a}$. Finally, $K_{ID}$ for a constant velocity $\dot{a}$ was larger when the crack was decelerated than when it was accelerated.

The purpose of the present work was to study this problem in more detail using a modified Cranz-Schardin type high-speed camera which permitted simultaneous records of caustic patterns and corresponding specimen-focussed images [3]. Single-edge-cracked tensile specimens of PMMA and epoxy were biaxially pin-loaded so that cracks could experience acceleration, deceleration and re-acceleration stages in a single fracture process. $K_{ID}$-$\dot{a}$ diagram was determined for the three stages of acceleration, deceleration and re-acceleration. Attention was focussed particularly on the effects of $\dot{a}$ and $\ddot{a}$ on $K_{ID}$.

Experiments were performed on the specimens of 5mm-thick PMMA and epoxy plates. The specimen geometry is shown in Fig. 1. The dimensions were 120 mm in length and 170 mm in width. A sharp precrack was generated by momentum-controlled chisel-impact into a pre-machined saw-cut on the specimen edge. Load introduction was achieved through the use of steel pins and V-shaped fixtures as shown in Fig. 1. All specimens were tested under a displacement controlled condition using a tensile testing machine. Tests were performed at room temperature and at a constant crosshead rate of 1 mm/min.

Figure 2 shows high-speed photographs of the crack propagation in an epoxy specimen, where series (a) represents the specimen-focussed images, and (b) the corresponding caustic patterns. As seen, size of the caustic at a crack tip increased in an early stage of crack propagation, then decreased in the middle stage, and increased again in the final stage. This was typical fracture behavior in the specimen geometry and loading method employed.

Figure 3 shows variations of $K_{ID}$ and crack length $a$ versus time $t$. There existed three stages of noticeable $K_{ID}$ increasing, decreasing and re-increasing regions. Slight changes are seen in the slope of $a(t)$ curve. To minimize data scattering in evaluating fracture parameters, the authors employed a data-fitting

procedure [1]; obtained values of $K_{ID}$ and $a$ were expressed as ninth order polynomials of $t$ based on the least square method so that they fitted observed values most closely. Crack velocity $\dot{a}$ and acceleration $\ddot{a}$ were obtained from the first and second time derivatives of $a(t)$, respectively.

Figure 4 shows values of $K_{ID}$, $\dot{a}$ and $\ddot{a}$ as a function of $a$. As readily seen, the change in $\ddot{a}$ was qualitatively in accord with the one in $K_{ID}$. However, it is worth noting that $\dot{a}$ gave rise earlier than $K_{ID}$ associated with $a$; $K_{ID}$ corresponding to crack velocity was larger when the crack was decelerated than when it was accelerated (see points A' and B'). Similar results were obtained by the authors for specimens which were uniaxially pin-loaded [1, 2].

Figure 5 shows the values of $K_{ID}$ expressed as a function of $\dot{a}$, i.e. the $K_{ID}$-$\dot{a}$ diagram, where arrows indicate the progressing direction of fracture. Three stages of distinct crack acceleration, deceleration and re-acceleration can be seen in one fracture process. Although $K_{ID}$ is shown to increase with $\dot{a}$, it should be noted that their relation was not unique. For a constant $\dot{a}$, the decelerating crack had a larger value of $K_{ID}$ than the accelerating or re-accelerating one. Such was also the case with other specimens tested, and this situation was qualitatively in accord with that obtained for uniaxially pin-loaded specimens [1, 2].

The authors have determined $K_{ID}$-$\dot{a}$ relationships for PMMA, epoxy and Homalite-100 specimens [1, 2]. Their results have suggested that $K_{ID}$ was expressed as two parametric functions of $\dot{a}$ and $\ddot{a}$, i.e. $K_{ID}(\dot{a}, \ddot{a})$, thus that $K_{ID}(\dot{a}, \ddot{a}=\text{constant})$ was uniquely related to $\dot{a}$. The value of $\ddot{a}$ should then be inversely determined if both the $K_{ID}$ and $\dot{a}$ are known. This was examined using the results in Figs. 4 and 5.

In Fig. 5, the intersection of the $K_{ID}$-$\dot{a}$ diagram is indicated by the open circle, where each value of $K_{ID}$ and $\dot{a}$ was identical in the two stages of crack acceleration and re-acceleration. Corresponding values of $\ddot{a}$ are indicated in Fig. 4 (see points A'' and C''). It should be emphasized that the two values of $\ddot{a}$ were nearly equal for the accelerating and re-accelerating crack which were determined at different time $t$ and crack length $a$. This clearly appears to indicate that $K_{ID}$ was strongly dependent on both $\dot{a}$ and $\ddot{a}$, and that neither $t$ nor $a$ influenced the $K_{ID}$ values.

References:

1. K. Takahashi and K. Arakawa, *Exp. Mech.* 27 (1987) 195-200.
2. K. Arakawa and K. Takahashi, *Int. J. Frac.* 48 (1991) 103-114.
3. K. Arakawa and K. Takahashi, *Int. J. Frac.* 48 (1991) 245-259.

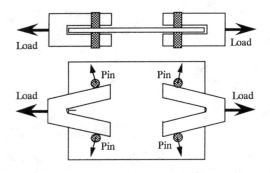

Fig. 1. Specimen geometry and loading method.

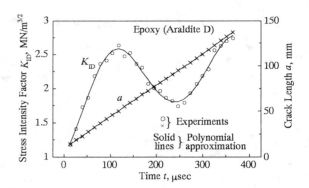

Fig. 3. Stress intensity factor $K_{ID}$ and crack length $a$ for an epoxy specimen as a function of time $t$.

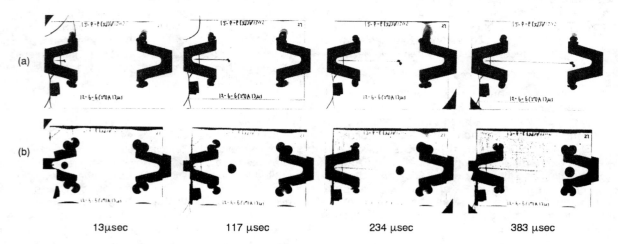

| 13μsec | 117 μsec | 234 μsec | 383 μsec |

Fig. 2. Example of dynamic crack propagation in an epoxy specimen under biaxial loading condition.
(a) specimen-focussed images, (b) caustic patterns

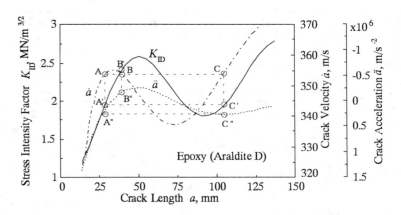

Fig. 4. Stress intensity factor $K_{ID}$, crack velocity $\dot{a}$ and acceleration $\ddot{a}$ for an epoxy specimen as a function of crack length $a$.

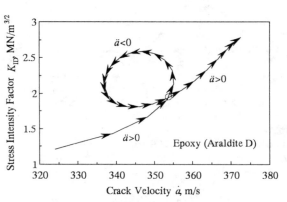

Fig. 5. Relation between stress intensity factor $K_{ID}$ and crack velocity $\dot{a}$ for an epoxy specimen.

# Dynamic Fracture of Brittle Materials

K. Ravi-Chandar and B. Yang
Department of Mechanical Engineering
University of Houston
Houston, TX 77204-4792

The dynamic fracture behavior of brittle materials is explored using experiments and simulation. The morphology of the fracture surface is examined in great detail in four polymers: two thermoplastics - polymethylmethacrylate and polycarbonate, a lightly crosslinked elastomer - Solithane 113, and a thermoset polyester - Homalite-100. The fracture surface markings are examined to determine the micromechanisms of brittle dynamic fracture. This examination reveals clearly that the operating micromechanism that governs dynamic fracture in brittle materials is the nucleation, growth and coalescence of microcracks.

After this qualitative examination and interpretation of the fracture surface markings, the specific feature of conic markings on the fracture surface are quantified. These conic markings are interpreted as the result of an encounter between two microcrack fronts. Their size, distribution and spacing are examined to indicate that as the crack grows, more microcracks are nucleated farther ahead of the approaching crack front; thus we refer to this as stress induced nucleation of microcrack nuclei. Following this quantification, a very simple nucleation and growth model of dynamic fracture is developed. Imposing a nucleation and growth criterion based on experimental observations, a numerical simulation is performed which recreates the experimental observations, not only of the microscopic surface features, but also of the macroscopic behavior such as the constancy of the crack speed. Thus, the simulation provides the link between the micromechanical modeling and the macroscopic fields that are developed and points a way towards a predictive model for dynamic fracture, including simultaneous nucleation and growth of flaws.

In order to explore this connection a little more, a cohesive zone model of dynamic fracture was developed; the present implementation is only for mode III fracture, but this clearly illustrates the influence of the crack tip process zone in dynamic fracture. In this analysis, the crack is confined to grow along a thin weak layer ahead of the initial crack. The boundary initial value problem for anti-plane shear is solved together with the force separation law for the layer material using a finite difference computational scheme; a separate crack growth criterion is not required in this simulation. The development and growth of a process zone near the crack tip are tracked completely in the numerical solution to this problem. The results of the simulation indicate that the dissipation rate at the crack tip in the evolving process zone depends both on the rate of applied loading and on the size of the process zone. This result is used in suggesting that the velocity of brittle cracks is limited not by the Rayleigh wave speed, but by the growth of the process zone near the crack tip.

# Proposed Mixed-mode Dynamic Fracture Toughness Testing Method Using a New Specimen

H. Wada and A. Hinoshita

Department of Mechanical Engineering, Daido Institute of Technology,
2-21 Daido-cho Minami-ku, Nagoya 457, Japan

C. A. Calder and T. C. Kennedy

Department of Mechanical Engineering, Oregon State University,
Corvallis, Oregon 97331, U.S.A.

The use of linear-elastic fracture mechanics is indispensable for evaluating the strength of machines and structures, since the maximum principal stress failure law does not apply for fracture of brittle materials with internal flaws. Although the dynamic fracture toughness has been measured with several experimental techniques[1,2,3], most of these measurements were for mode I loading. However, not all cracks in a structure are under mode I deformation. Accordingly, it is important to measure the mixed-mode dynamic fracture toughness for structural materials since cracks are usually subjected to mixed-mode deformation. A simple, accurate testing method is desired for determining the mixed-mode dynamic fracture toughness over a wide range of opening and sliding modes. In this study, we apply a combination technique[4] that makes use of a strain gage experimental technique and a dynamic finite element method (FEM) to determine the mixed-mode dynamic fracture toughness. To calculate the dynamic stress intensity factors (SIF) precisely, simple stress wave propagation in the specimen is desired. Hence, several new specimens were studied for simulation of dynamic stress and SIF.

Figures 1, 2 and 3 illustrate a rectangular plate specimen (RPS), a quarter ring plate specimen (QRPS) and an elbow plate specimen (EPS) respectively, which were examined in this study. The material for all specimens was commercially available PMMA. The ratio of the opening mode to the sliding mode deformation can be changed by adjusting the crack position or the hitting point.

Figure 4 illustrates the measuring and recording devices associated with an impact fracture apparatus using an air gun. The load history was obtained from a strain history measured with strain gages mounted of a point 70 mm from the impact end of the PMMA striker bar. The impact fracture test was conducted to assess the mixed-mode dynamic fracture toughness testing method under single-point bending for several specimens of PMMA. To measure the dynamic SIF $K_I(t)$ and crack initiation time, a single axis strain gage[5] was mounted in the vicinity of the crack tip. However, one can not determine a dynamic SIF $K_{II}(t)$ from the signal of a single axis strain gage. To measure both SIF's, three strain components near crack tip are required. The technique combining experiment and numerical calculation appears valid for eliminating the additional strain gage measurements. The isoparametric quadrilateral element was employed for the simulation of stress wave propagation with dynamic FEM. The quarter-point displacement technique (QPDT)[6] was applied to calculate the SIF's $K_I(t)$ and $K_{II}(t)$. Nine-point Gauss integration was employed for the quarter-point element and all other elements. Several specimen configurations were chosen to assess the accuracy of the stress simulation for the dynamic stress wave propagation problem.

Figure 5 depicts a typical example of the comparison between the numerical and measured results for the dynamic opening mode SIF $K_I(t)$ and the procedure for determining dynamic fracture toughness by the combination technique. A crack is located at $\theta_c = 45°$ in the specimen, and the crack length is 20 mm as shown in Fig.2. The specimen was loaded by hitting it with the striker at the point r=80 mm and $\theta_P = 11.25°$. As would be expected, the time histories of both results for the dynamic SIF $K_I(t)$ were found to be in excellent agreement until the crack initiation point. The experimental results in Fig.5 show that the gage signal undergoes a sudden increase with crack initiation. The dynamic fracture toughness $K_{Id}$ and $K_{IId}$ can be determined from the SIF $K_I(t)$ and $K_{II}(t)$ in the FEM results at the crack initiation point. Figure 6 depicts a relation between $K_{IId}/K_{Id}$ and S/L for RPS. We can see in this figure that it is possible for $K_{IId}/K_{Id}$ to give mixed mode dynamic fracture toughness within from 0.0 to 1.0. Figure 7 depicts also a relation between $K_{IId}/K_{Id}$ and $\theta_p/\theta_c$. We can see in this figure that it is possible for $K_{IId}/K_{Id}$ to give the mixed mode dynamic fracture toughness within from 0.0 to 1.8, wide by comparison to that for RPS.

Consequently, the following conclusions may be drawn: The QRPS is easy to machine by using a lathe. The QRPS allows the crack location and the loading point to be moved without a modification of specimen configuration. The FEM mesh for QRPS is easy to generate although it has a curved boundary. The different ratios of $K_{Id}$ and $K_{IId}$ can be obtained by changing the crack position $\theta_c$ and the loading point.

References:
[1] Yokoyama, T. and Kishida, K., Exp. Mech., 29-2, (1989), 188.
[2] Kalthoff, J. F., Int. J. of Fract., 27(1985), 277.
[3] Wada, H., et al., Eng. Fract. Mech., Vol.46, 4(1993), 715.
[4] Nakano, M., et al., Proc. of the International Symposium on Impact Engineering Vol. II, Sendai, Japan, November 2-4, (1992), 581.
[5] Kurosaki, et al., JSME, 56-524, A(1990), 195.
[6] Lim, I. L., et al., Eng. Fract. Mech., Vol.44, 3(1993), 363.

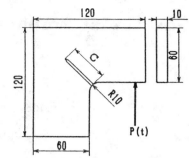

Fig.3 Elbow plate specimen(EPS)

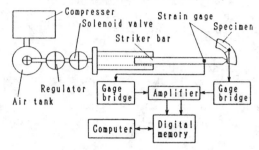

Fig.4 Impact fracture apparatus using air gun

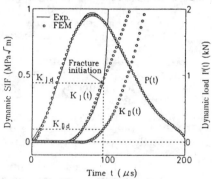

Fig.5 Determination of fracture toughness(QRPS)

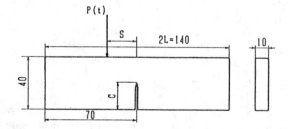

Fig.1 Rectangular plate specimen(RPS)

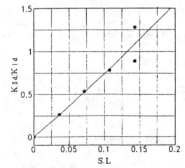

Fig.6 Relation between $K_{IId}/K_{Id}$ and S/L

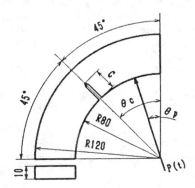

Fig.2 Quarter ring plate specimen(QRPS)

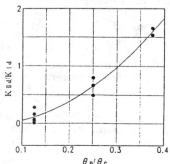

Fig.7 Relation between $K_{IId}/K_{Id}$ and $\theta_p/\theta_c$

# Short Pulse Impact in Graphite Epoxy Composites

H.A. Bruck
J.S. Epstein

Idaho National Engineering Laboratory
P.O. Box 1625
Idaho Falls, Idaho, 83415-2218

There is a great deal of interest in characterizing the dynamic mechanical behavior of laminated graphite epoxy composites for military and aerospace applications. Current research efforts have been directed at measuring the strength lost because of accumulated damage. Very little work has been done to determine how this damage is accumulated during dynamic mechanical loading. Of particular interest is the effect of short duration (< 1 µs), high intensity stress pulses on mechanical behavior such as delamination.

In this work, a magnetic flyer plate apparatus is presented for generating a short duration stress pulse in a unidirectional graphite epoxy laminated composite [1]. The magnetic flyer plate consisted of a 0.254 mm thick, 6.25 mm wide strip of aluminum. A current was passed through the strip in one direction, then passed behind it in the opposite direction to generate the opposing magnetic fields that accelerated the plate. The current was dumped from an 18 µF storage capacitor at 10 kV using a spark gap. To determine the velocity of the flyer plate, shorting pins were placed at several locations along the flight path of the flyer plate and the time to impact was measured. These velocity measurements were compared with theoretical predictions (Figure 1). It was determined that the deviations between theoretical and experimental velocitites were consistent with the observations of Snowden [2].

To image the short duration stress pulse generated by the magnetic flyer plate, a dynamic moiré interferometer was used [3]. The interferometer measured the full-field displacements on the surface of a specimen in the direction that the stress wave propagated. A pulse ruby laser was used in the interferometer capable of generating high-intensity pulses lasting for approximately 20 nanoseconds. Moiré fringe patterns were captured on high-speed Polaroid film.

Gratings were placed on the front and back surfaces of specimens. A special 1200 line/mm dual frequency grating was used on the front of the specimen so that a helium-neon laser could be used to align the interferometer. On the back, a regular 300 line/mm grating was used for a diffraction gage. The diffraction gage consisted of a 2 mm diameter He-Ne laser beam with a fiber optic sensor placed approximately 1 meter from the specimen and aligned along the first diffraction order of the grating. By placing the sensor at an appropriate distance from the specimen, the diffraction gage was able to detect the exact time that a stress wave passed a given location along the length of the specimen from the deflection of the laser beam. These data could then be used to determine the proper trigger time for the ruby laser.

A short duration stress pulse was characterized for a 0° unidirectional graphite epoxy specimen (see Figure 2). The specimen was 4.5 mm thick, 11.7 mm wide, and 150 mm long. The end of the specimen was placed 7 mm from the flyer plate, which resulted in an impact velocity of approximately 200 m/sec. The moiré interferometer covered 42 mm of the specimen, starting at a location 35 mm from the impacted end of the specimen. The diffraction gage was positioned at the edge of the grating closest to the impacted specimen end.

The stress pulse captured in the experiment appears to have indiscernible fringes (see Figure 2). In fact, as the fringe density increases the contrast of the fringes appears to decrease to the level of noise in the interferogram. This contrast effect was explained by analyzing the dynamic effects on the acquisition of high density fringe fields. From this analysis it was determined that the fringe contrast for a Gaussian light source was determined by *the dynamic fringe contrast factor*, $\exp\left(\dfrac{-\Phi_d}{4\ln 2}\right)$, where $\Phi_d = \omega_f c t_e / 2$ is the *dynamic fringe phase-shift factor*, $\omega_f$ is the angular fringe frequency, c is the wave speed in the material, and $t_e$ is the exposure time. The variation of the dynamic fringe contrast factor with the dynamic fringe phase-shift factor can be seen in Figure 3. The parameters in the dynamic fringe phase-shift factor can be chosen so as to optimize the fringe contrast in order to discern the fringe data.

## References

[1] Jacobson, R.S., "Magnetic Acceleration of Flyer Plates for Shock Wave Testing of Materials", Sandia Corp., Livermore, CA, Sept. 1967.

[2] Snowden, W.E., "Crack Growth in Glass Subjected to Controlled Impacts", Ph.D. Thesis,

Lawerence Berkeley Laboratory, University of California-Berkeley, Nov. 1976.

[3] Epstein, J.S., Deason, V.A., and Abdallah, M.G., "Impact Wave Propagation in a Thick Composite Plate Using Dynamic Moiré Interferometry", <u>Optics and Lasers in Engineering</u>, vol. 17, pp. 35-46, 1992.

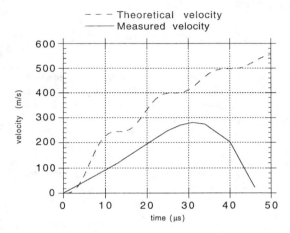

Figure 1. Plot of theoretical versus measured velocity for magnetic flyer plate .

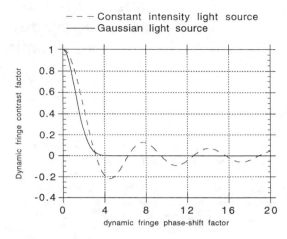

Figure 3. Plot of dynamic fringe contrast factor.

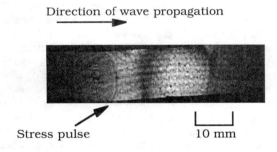

Figure 2. Stress pulse captured in graphite epoxy composite

# Visualization of Stress Waves in Blasting Processes by a Laser-shadowgraph Method and its Applications to Dynamic Fracture Control

Yuichi Nakamura

Yatsushiro National College of Technology

2627 Hirayama-shinmachi, Yatsushiro City, Kumamoto 866, Japan

Dynamic fracture control in blasting is very important in underground excavation and demolition of concrete structures. As pointed out by Fourney et al[1], ideal fracture control implies specification of the number of fracture planes, the initiation sites, the direction of fracture propagation and the stress field driving the fracture front. For the purpose, the smooth blasting methods, for example, the cushion blasting, are commonly employed. However, the conventional smooth blasting methods are not sufficient to control the number of fracture planes and the direction of fracture propagation. These requirements in fracture control are especially important in partial demolition of concrete structures. The conversion and the transmission of explosive energy to the surroudings constitute a very complicated process. Therefore, it is necessary to examine the dynamic mechanism of stress waves, gases and cracks in the blasting process for achieving high degree of fracture control.

In this paper, experimental results on visualization of the stress wave in blasting by a laser-shadowgraph method are presented and a new method for fracture controlled blasting is suggested.
The shadowgraph system using a ruby laser as a light source is set up. To synchronize the emissions of the laser beam with the blasting phenomena, a pokels cell Q switch with 20nsec exposure time, two delay time generators, and a firing circuit to initiate the electric detonator are used. These enable us to get a giant pulse beam at a desired time and to obtain the high spatial and time resolved instantaneous visualization photographs. The optical arrangement is shown in Fig. 1. This system consists of a set of concave schlieren mirrors of $150$ mm in diameter and $1500$ mm in focal length. The mirrors are used in an off-set arrangement. The shadowgraph image near the test section is recorded on the film by using the camera lens with long focal length. A filter with high transmittance at the desired wave lengths ($693.5$ nm, band width $12$ nm) is placed in the front of the camera lens to prevent the optical noise arised from explosion of explosives.

Experiments are made on stress waves interacting with a circular hole. The interaction phenomena are of importance in blasting operations for achieving fracture control. Model experiments are carried out with the PMMA plate of $20$ mm in thickness as a transparent material and the electric detonator. The detonator contains $0.4$ g of PETN (pentaerythritoltetranitrate). The PMMA plate are $200 \times 200$ mm. The longitudinal elastic wave velocity of the PMMA plate is $2.62$ km/sec. This value is obtained by the ultrasonic pulse method. The piezoelectric gauge for detecting the pressure pulses of stress waves is attached to the free surface of the plate at a distance of $150$ mm from the center of the charge hole. The gauge consists of a PZT disk and an electrical capacitance. The disk is $6$ mm in diameter and $2$ mm in thickness. The capacitance is placed across the output terminals of the disk. The double pin ionization gauge is plugged on the base of the charge hole to define the initiation time of the detonator. A phototransistor is used to detect the

pulsed laser beam. These signals are led to two digital storage-type osilloscopes.

To obtain a complete understanding of the dynamic behaviour of cracks in a blasting process for the development of fracture plane control methods, a high-speed video camera system of the digital storage- type is used. Framing rates of the camera can be varied from 30 to 40500 frames per second. The system is capable of recording 49152 frames of a dynamic event and the motion analysis of the digital images is practicable by the programmable operations. Figure 2 shows the experimental setup using a video camera system. The mortar specimen is also used to demonstrate the effectiveness of the presented fracture control method. The size of the mortar specimen is $300 \times 300 \times 100$ mm.

Examples of the shadowgraphs obtained are shown in Fig. 3. Several incident stress waves are visible. The data from shadowgraphs of stress waves in the PMMA plate without a circular hole is analyzed to obtain the positions of the stress waves with time.
The first incident stress wave emanating from the charge hole arrives the piezoelectric gauge after about $50$ $\mu$ sec. The velocity of the stress wave near the free surface placed at a distance of $150$ mm from the charge hole is about $2.7$ km/sec and nearly equal to the longitudinal elastic wave velocity of the PMMA plate. Figure 3 (a) shows the behaviour of incident stress waves interacting a circular hole of $15$ mm diameter in the PMMA plate. The shadowgraphs show the behaviour of reflected waves, deformations of the circular hole and the generation of converging shock waves in the hole by interaction of incident waves with the hole. Figure 3(b) is in the case that the hole has two notches along the propagation direction of the incident waves. It can be seen that the well-known shadow spots are produced in the vicinity of the notches. These are caused by the tensile deformation of the material near the notches. From the fact, it might be expected that utilization of the circular hole with notches is effective as the guide hole technique for achieving high degree of fracture control. Figure 4 shows the recorded images of the high speed video camera sysytem. It is shown from Fig. 4(a) that two cracks, which originated from the apexes of the noches, propagate in the direction opposite to each other and controlled fracture planes are produced. In Fig. 4(b), the mortar specimen is used as a model material. After the formation of controlled cracks, the explosion gases start to expand and penetrate into the cracks. These results show that the presented method is feasible means in controlling the orientation of the fracture planes and in driving the controlled cracks to greater distances.

References:

[1]Fourney, W. L., Dally, J. W., Holloway, D. C., "Controlled Blasting with Ligamented Charge Holders," Int. J. Rock Mech. Min. Sci. & Geomech. Abstr., Vol. 15, 1978, pp. 121-129.

M-1 Concave Mirror
M-2 Mirror
C Camera

R-L  H-L

M-2  L

M-1

C   M-2   M-1

Explosion
Chamber

H-L He-Ne Laser
R-L Ruby Laser
L Concave Lens

Fig. 1 Optical arrangement for shadowgraphy.

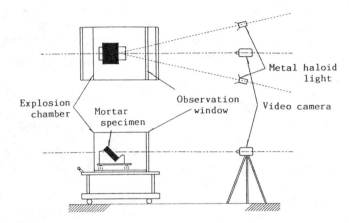

Metal haloid
light

Explosion
chamber    Observation
window

Mortar
specimen    Video camera

Fig. 2 Experimental setup using a video camera.

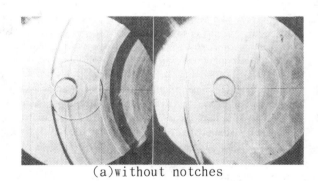

(a)without notches

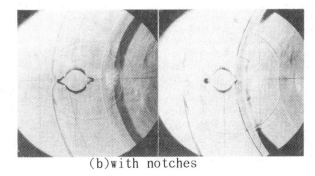

(b)with notches

Fig. 3 Shadowgraphs of stress waves interacting
with a circular hole.

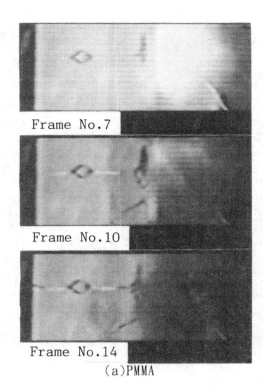

Frame No.7

Frame No.10

Frame No.14

(a)PMMA

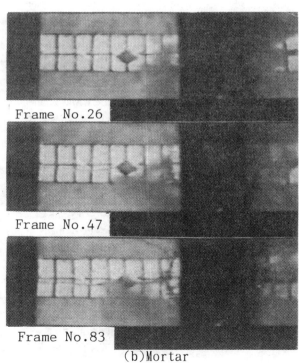

Frame No.26

Frame No.47

Frame No.83

(b)Mortar

Fig. 4 Crack propagation in blasting recorded by the high-
speed video camera with the framing rate, 18000 frames
per second.

# Aging Petrochemical Plants

Robert M. Kay
Exxon Chemical Company
Baton Rouge Chemical Plant
4999 Scenic Hwy.
Baton Rouge, LA. 70821

While most of today's petrochemical plants were built in the period from 1950 to 1980, a number of units were in operation prior to this time period. These earliest units were often an integral part of oil refineries built at the turn of the century and played a key role in supporting the Allied effort during World War II. Petrochemical plants, like small cities, have an extensive infrastructure consisting of sewers, underground piping, buildings and utility systems that were originally built for a design life of 15 to 30 years. Unlike our cities, however, they contain hundreds to thousands of miles of above ground piping, and hundreds of pressure containing vessels concentrated into an area typically measured in acres.

The safe containment of chemicals produced by the Petrochemical industry has received heightened public attention in recent years by a few high profile incidents which resulted in numerous fatalities. This led to a joint effort by the Chemical Manufacturer's Association (CMA) and the Occupational Safety and Health Administration (OSHA) to develop a comprehensive set of performance standards designed to reduce the accidental release of any chemical. The outcome has been documented in CMA's Process Safety Management (PSM) and OSHA regulation 29 CFR Part 1910, "Process Safety Management of Highly Hazardous Chemicals; Explosives and Blasting Agents". These two documents, in conjunction with site specific management systems written to meet these performance standards have had the largest single impact on the industry in recent years.

An integral part of an operating petrochemical plant is its inspection program. The heightened attention for the safe containment of chemicals coupled with the age of many plants has elevated the importance being given to the inspection of plant equipment and facilities. This is also reflected in the number of relatively new and revised American Petroleum Institute (API) codes governing the inspection of pressure vessels, piping and atmospheric tanks[1]. Most CMA member plants have adopted the principles of these inspection codes as "recognized and generally accepted good engineering practices"[2]. The net effect of implementing these codes is the systematic inspection of all the major containment facilities within a plant. Several states are currently considering legislation that would incorporate these codes into state laws regulating the operation of petrochemical plants. The major challenge facing domestic petrochemical plants is implementing inspection programs which comply with these codes in the most cost effective manner.

Similar in coverage, these API codes each address inspection intervals based on a maximum time period or remaining "corrosion rate life"[3]. All three prescribe periodic external inspections while API-510 and API-653 additionally require internal inspections intervals. The API-570 "Piping Inspection Code" provides for wall thickness inspection intervals for three classes of process streams, each grouped by their severity should a leak occur. This consequence-based classification is expected to be incorporated into all these codes in the form of a risk-based inspection (RBI) methodology.

Petrochemical facilities are normally constructed of carbon steel and, therefore, subject to environmental corrosion. Corrosion of underground piping, structural supports and tank bottoms (underside) are just of few examples of inspection concerns that increase with the age of a plant. Corrosion through insulation (CTI), most common of which is corrosion under insulation (CUI), is one of the most prevalent and insidious problems in the industry. Besides difficult to detect, CUI can be extremely aggressive and localized at sites prone to trapping water (see figures 1 and 2 for typical CUI locations). Conventional inspection methods used to detect CTI include physical removal of the insulation to allow visual or ultrasonic pulse-echo inspection, and x-ray or gamma ray transmission radiography/radioscopy. These conventional methods, however, are expensive, time consuming and may not detect a problem unless 100% inspection is performed.

A joint effort by the Materials Technology Institute of the Chemical Process Industry, Inc. (MTI) and its member petrochemical companies is currently underway to assess existing and emerging state-of-the-art nondestructive evaluation (NDE) technologies which may be applied to CTI inspection. In a preliminary report, MTI has identified several NDE methods in various levels of development from being studied in idealized laboratory environments to completion of

---

1.  API-510, API-570 and API-653 govern the inspection of pressure vessels, piping and atmospheric storage tanks respectively.

2.  From OSHA 1910.119(j)(4)(ii), "Inspection and testing procedures shall follow recognized and generally accepted good engineering practices."

3.  Corrosion rate life (yrs.) =
    $$\frac{\text{remaining corrosion allowance (mm)}}{\text{corrosion rate (mm./yr.)}}$$

field trials which include acoustic emission, deep penetrating eddy current, electromagnetic pulse decay, microwave, and ultrasonic guided waves.

A brief description of each these methods is as follows:

Acoustic Emission Testing (AET) involves the detection of ultrasonic noise energy that is spontaneously released by defects in materials when they undergo deformation, typically generated by pressure testing or thermal changes. This method is capable of detecting and characterizing corrosion and cracking in piping and pressure vessels but does not quantify the extent of the defect. Computerized time-of-arrival techniques can be utilized to help locate the general area of a defect for visual inspection.

Deep Penetrating Eddy Current methods rely on the principles of electromagnetic inspection. Current loops, or eddy currents, are induced in a conducting material by an applied varying magnetic field using an energized coil. Defects such as cracks and corrosion alter the eddy currents in the material causing a corresponding change in the magnetic field within and near the component. These changes can then be detected and quantified by measuring these fields. This method is limited in its ability to characterize some types of defects.

Electromagnetic Pulse Decay is a relatively new variation on electromagnetic inspection involving pulsed eddy currents. As the pulsing coil generates an eddy current, the receiving coil monitors its decay in time. When the currents have fully diffused through the wall, their signature changes dramatically. The time required to reach full diffusion through the wall is then correlated to the wall thickness.

Microwave techniques function in a way similar to those of radiography using a beam of microwave energy to strike the surface of a dielectric component. Flaws and defects are found through the differential absorption and/or scattering of this energy. This is a developing technology that has just emerged from the laboratory.

Ultrasonic Guided Waves make use of high frequency mechanical vibrations which are launched at one position in a component under inspection. These waves travel along the component for up to several meters. Defects cause some ultrasonic energy to be reflected back where they can be received and detected. With proper wave parameter selection, nearly 100% of the entire cross-section of the component can be inspected.

The primary goal of these and other emerging inspection techniques is to provide global inspection methods that are cost effective, portable and functional in a petrochemical facility. Combined with RBI methodologies, they should enable an aging petrochemical industry to meet an ever increasing level of safety while maintaining their global competitiveness.

Figure 1

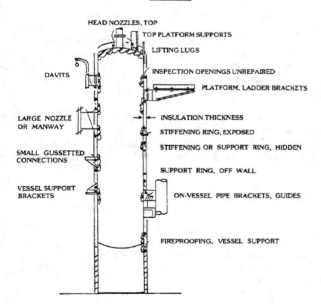

Figure 2

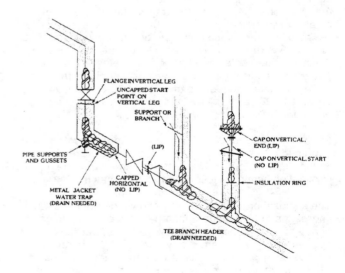

TRAPPED WATER
WATER ENTRY POINT
IMPEDIMENT TO DRAINAGE
POTENTIAL WICK ACTION
PROBABLE CORROSION ZONE

# CONTAINMENT STRATEGY FOR THE SAFE DISPOSAL OF NUCLEAR WASTE

Willis L. Clarke
Lawrence Livermore National Laboratory
7000 East Avenue, L-204
Livermore, CA 94550

Thomas W. Doering
Framatome Cogema Fuel
(formerly B&W Fuel Company)
Las Vegas, NV 89109

## ABSTRACT

More than 20,000 metric tons of spent fuel from commercial nuclear power plants are located in temporary storage at 109 reactors across the U.S. By the year 2010, about 63,000 metric tons of spent fuel from nuclear power plants and 8,000 metric tons of solidified nuclear waste from defense programs will require permanent disposal.
Most plants store the spent fuel in pools of water, which acts as a radiation shield and coolant. A few plants store spent fuel above ground in special concrete or steel casks. Both types of storage are temporary, and the storage pools at some plants are almost full. The U.S. is not the only country facing the disposal issue. Around the globe, virtually all nations that use nuclear power are exploring approaches to safely dispose of radioactive waste.

Regardless of what site is eventually approved, a permanent repository for nuclear waste must comply with many federal, health, and safety regulations as well as extensive technical requirements. A key criterion is for essentially complete containment of nuclear waste for 300 to 1,000 years after permanent closure of the repository. Following that containment period, the release per year of any radionuclide (specific nuclear species) from the system cannot exceed 1 part in 100,000 of the inventory present 1,000 years following closure. This rate cannot be exceeded for at least 10,000 years.

Such rigid expectations for a man-made system are unprecedented in history. For perspective, 10,000 years is the interval since the last Ice Age, and the great pyramid of Cheops is less than half as old as that.

The disposal problem is urgent, and we do not have much knowledge of how modern materials placed in a geological site and subjected to initially high temperatures will behave during thousands of years. Scientists obviously do not have a hundred centuries to validate a system. Thus, much of our development work at Livermore is based on predictive models and accelerated-age testing of materials and systems intended to delay the effects of water and other processes. Our overall task is essentially one of risk assessment.

Our current responsibility is focused on the engineered barrier system for an underground repository. This system includes the containers that will hold the waste and a complex series of interactions of the waste form and man-made waste package with the immediate or near-field environment.

The system of man-made and geological barriers that will isolate nuclear waste include:

- A robust waste package consisting of multiple containment barriers, each with a different purpose. We are studying various metal and alloy disposal containers that will surround either canisters or uncanistered designs.

- An engineered system of diffusion barriers, which may include packing materials around the waste package and backfill around the packing.

- The near-field environment, which can extend several hundred meters into the surrounding rock. Natural barriers, such as zeolitic rocks with high sorption capacity, can slow the migration of radionuclides.

- The far-field environment or ambient natural system, which can slow the migration of radionuclides in the geosphere. An arid climate with low precipitation, high evaporation, and no ground saturation will minimize the transport of radionuclides by water.

Our tasks can be broken down into four major areas: characterizing the waste itself, evaluating materials for the waste package, defining the near-field environment, and analyzing the long-term performance of barrier systems.

## ACKNOWLEDGMENTS:

This work was supported by the Yucca Mountain Site Characterization Project. Work performed under the auspices of the U.S. Department of Energy by Lawrence Livermore National Laboratory under contract W-7405-ENG-48.

# Fatigue Crack Growth Behavior of Creep Damaged Specimens of Type 304 Stainless Steel

S.B.Lee, B.S.Park, and J.Y.Kim

Korea Advanced Institute of Science and Technology
373-1 Kusong dong, Yousung-gu, Taejon 305-701, Korea

The high temperature structures suffer from rapid varying fatigue loads as well as static loads at high temperatures. Since creep damage such as voids or microcracks are produced by static loads at high temperatures, when a crack extends by the rapid loads, the interaction by prior creep damage occurs. Although, recently, more attention is focused on the crack growth behavior under the condition of creep damage, it is still difficult to define the amount of creep damage quantitatively and to study the influence of the crack growth rates. In the present study, the influence on the fatigue crack growth behavior is investigated with prior creep-damaged Type 304 stainless steel whose chemical composition is shown in Table 1.

At first, various amount of creep damage are induced to smooth specimens under a constant tensile load around $600^{\circ}C$ with different loading times.(Table 2). The amount of damage is calculated by equation (1).

$$D = 1 - \frac{E^e}{E} \qquad (1)$$

where $E^e$ is young's modulus of the damaged specimen and E is young's modulus of the undamaged specimen[1] . Rockwell hardness of damaged material was also measured. The scanning electron microscope is used to observe the microcracks or microcavities caused by creep damage. From the damaged smooth specimen, compact tensile specimens (width=50mm, thickness=3mm) are made. Finally, with the CT-specimens the fatigue crack growth tests are performed with a closed-loop servohydraulic fatigue test machine under constant amplitude loading conditions. To consider the crack closure effect, block loadings which first have load ratio of 0.1 and then 0.3 were used(Fig.2), Crack opening load is determined from the results of strain gage signals which are attached to the crack tip region. To measure the crack length, crack propagation gauge was used. Crack growth rate is calculated according to ASTM E647[2]. Stress intensity factor is calculated by equation(2)

$$\Delta K = \frac{\Delta P}{B\sqrt{W}} \frac{(2+\alpha)}{(1-\alpha)^{3/2}} F(\alpha) \qquad (2)$$

Fatigue load with the load ratio of 0.1 is used to propagate the crack to a certain amount of crack length and then load with load ratio of 0.3 is used.

From the tensile test, the amount of creep damage curve defined by equation (1) is obtained against total creep strain that has been produced during creep test. The amount of creep damage is increased exponentially in accordance with the amount of total creep strain. Rockwell hardness of damaged material increases as creep damage increases. It is shown that the fatigue crack growth rate of damaged specimen increases significantly even though crack opening load increases(Fig.5,6). For this reason, the change of failure mode is considered. Conventionally, fatigue crack growth rate is dominated by the crack tip plastic region, and the plastic deformation near the crack tip can produce compressive residual stress field, so it has beneficial effect of raising crack opening load . But in case of damaged specimen crack opening load has no effect on the crack growth rate. Instead, from SEM observation it is found that the failure mode is intergranular type which are different from conventional transgranular type of fatigue failure (Fig,7). In figure 7, it is found that there are many small cracks near the crack tip region and the crack propagation path is not straight. So, it can be considered that the increase of fatigue crack growth is due to the crack growth mode changes from a transgranular type to an intergranular type when the crack encounters microcavities or microcracks that are evidences of creep damage. The raising effect of crack opening load  is due to the surface roughness cause by intergranular failure

References :

[1] L.M.Kachanov,"Introduction to continuum damage mechanics",Martinus Nijhoff Publ.,1986.
[2] "Standard Test Method for Measurement of Fatigue Crack Growth Rates," in Annual Book of ASTM Standards E647-88,pp679-706,1993.

Table 1. Chemical composition of 304 stainless steel.

| C | Mn | Si | Cr | Ni | P | S |
|---|---|---|---|---|---|---|
| 0.08 | 2.0 | 1.0-2.0 | 10.5-18.0 | 8.0 | 0.045 | 0.03 |

Table 2. Creep test conditions and creep damage.

| Smooth Spec. | Temp. (°C) | Load (kN) | Time (hr) | Total Strain | Damage (D) | Fatigue Spec. |
|---|---|---|---|---|---|---|
| SP-1 | 583 | 24 | 267 | 0.022 | 0.03 | CT-1 |
| SP-2 | 583 | 30 | 45.7 | 0.034 | 0.0315 | CT-2 |
| SP-3 | 602-605 | 31.4-31.5 | 45.8 | 0.055 | 0.035 | CT-3 |
| SP-4 | 583-606 | 30-34.5 | 414.3 | 0.09 | 0.052 | CT-4 |

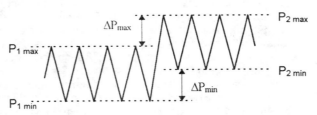

Fig.1 Load shape for fatigue crack growth test.
($P_{1\,max}$ =2.5kN, $P_{2\,max}$ =2.75kN, $R_1$ =0.1, $R_2$ =0.3)

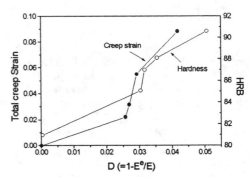

Fig.2 Damage vs. total creep strain and Rockwell hardness number

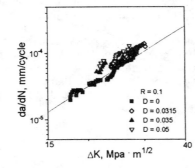

Fig.3 Fatigue crack growth rate vs. ΔK (R=0.1)

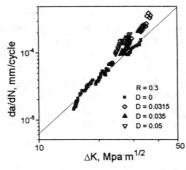

Fig.4 Fatigue crack growth rate vs. ΔK (R=0.3)

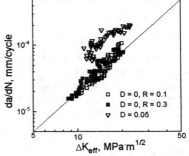

Fig.5 Fatigue crack growth rate vs. $\Delta K_{eff}$ (R=0.3)

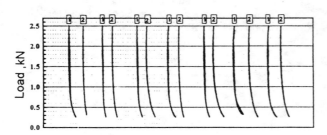

Fig.6 Reduced strain-load graph.
(1: undamaged, 2: damaged)

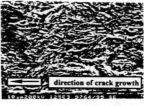

(a) Undamaged  (b) Damaged(D=0.0315)

(c) Side view

Fig.7 Photographs of the fatigue cracked surface

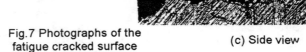

# Strain Distribution Induced by Implanted Tibial Component With Various Stem Geometries

Abraham Salehi
Mike Cooper
Smith & Nephew Orthopaedics
1450 E. Brooks Road
Memphis, Tennessee 38116

Abstract:

This study was performed to evaluate differences in tibial strain after implantation of the tibial trays with different stem geometries using the photoelastic coating method. The implants are made of titanium alloy and were press fit in synthetic tibias. The tibias were then coated with the photoelastic plastic of a uniform thickness. The load was applied on the medial condyle by a uni-femoral component and differences in principal strains and their directions along the medial and lateral planes of the tibias were measured. The results indicated that the stem stiffens the tibia, thus decreasing its surface strain as compared to the strain recorded for the intact tibia (without the implant). A slot (tong) in the distal region of the stem reduces the added stiffness caused by the stem and allows the bone to deform easier, which in turn causes the tibia's surface strain in the slot region to come closer to that of the intact tibia.

Introduction:

In knee arthroplasty, often the stems are used in order to provide greater stability for tibial base plates. Stems are connected to the trays by means of a Morse taper mechanism. These stems are approximately 100-150 mm long and 8-12 mm in diameter. The stems fill the diaphyseal shaft, thus stiffening the tibias and making the tibias structurally more stable. It is hypothesized that a rigid diaphyseal stem may make a point contact with the lateral cortex of the tibia, resulting in "end of stem" (tip) pain. A possible cause of tip pain could be the stiffness mismatch between the bone and the metal stems. In order to reduce the stiffness of the distal end of the stem, slots are created at the distal end. These slots reduce distal bending stiffness in the sagittal plane, thus the rigidity of the stem becomes more compliant with that of the surrounding bone, which in turn may reduce possible incidence of tip pain. The clinical findings showed the use of a stem with a flexible distal end resulted in fewer tip pain complaints [1,2]. A similar concern, stress-shielding and the associated mid-thigh pain, is well recognized in total hip arthroplasty [3].

The objective of this study is to illustrate and quantify the effect of solid and slotted stems on the load transfer to the tibia, in general, and near the distal tip, in particular, utilizing the photoelastic coating technique. This technique provides full-field strain information which is accurately readable at any point for both direction and magnitude.

Materials And Methods:

Two trays, as shown in Figure 1, are used in this study. The tray with medial and lateral fins includes a 125 mm solid stem and a 132 mm stem having a 65 mm distal slot (tong). The

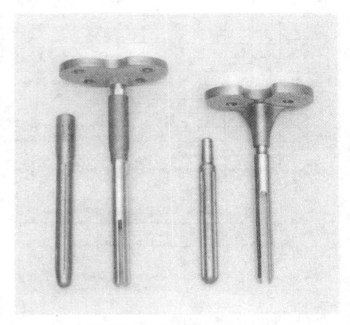

**Figure 1. Tibial Trays With Solid and Slotted Stems**

tray without the fins includes a 150 mm solid stem and a 150 mm stem with a 40 mm distal slot. Five synthetic tibias were selected. These tibias are similar to natural tibias in length and cortical diameter. Standard surgical procedure and instrumentation was used to implant the tibial prostheses. The tibias were coated with a photoelastic coating (PL-8, Measurement Group / Raleigh, NC) of uniform thickness. They were then sectioned distally and placed in a metal fixture and potted in FastCast. The medial condyle was subjected to 2003 N by a MTS machine. Upon loading of the coated tibias, they were viewed under polarized light and fringe patterns were photographed for qualitative observation. The differences in principal strains were then measured at each premarked point along the medial and lateral planes of the tibia.

Results And Discussions:

*On the medial aspect of the tibia:*

The 150 mm slotted stem transferred approximately 11% more strain to the tibia than the corresponding solid stem. The 132 mm slotted stem transferred approximately 21% more strain than the corresponding solid stem. The 132 mm slotted stem is nearly 2.5 times more flexible than the 150 mm slotted stem at the distal tip. The surface strain of the

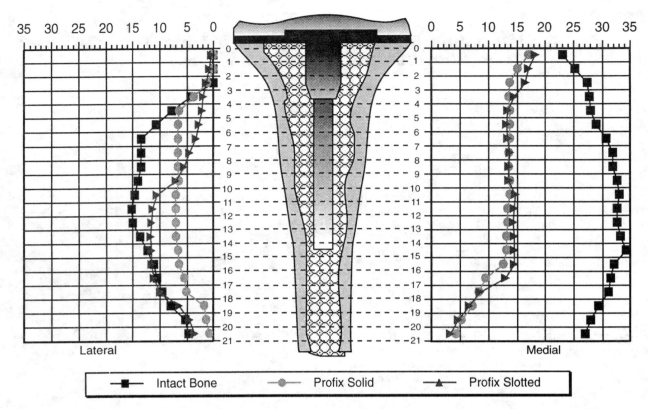

**Figure 2. Distribution of Normalized Strain on the Medial and Lateral Plains of the Tibia**

tibia having a 132 mm slotted stem is approximately 44% higher than the tibia having the 150 mm slotted stem. Figure 2 illustrates the normalized difference in principal strain values along the medial and the lateral aspects of the tibias. A more flexible stem allows the tibia to deform similar to the intact tibia, which causes the osteotomized tibia to have a surface strain closer to that of the intact tibia. For added tibial stability, sometimes it is necessary to use a longer and more rigid stem. However, the distal stiffness of a stem could be tailored to provide a more compliant implant with the surrounding bone. The difference in strain between the tibias having solid and slotted stems begins where the slot starts. In general, the strain in the intact tibia is higher than the strain in osteotomized tibias (tibias with implants).

*On the lateral aspect of the tibia:*
The surface strain for the intact tibia is higher than those osteotomized tibias having either solid or slotted stems. The left side of Figure 2 illustrates the distribution of the difference in principal strain along the lateral plane of the tibias. The magnitudes of the surface strains for the tibias having slotted stems suddenly rise to a higher level at 70 mm and 110 mm below the tibial plateau. These locations correspond to the starting point of the slot in different stems. The surface strain for the tibia having a 125 mm solid stem is nearly 19% higher than that of the tibia having a 150 mm solid stem. The longer the stem, the lower the surface strain. This condition induces greater stability by increasing the tibia's overall stiffness. The resulting tibia's surface strain, however, deviates by a greater amount from the strain seen in an intact tibia.

Conclusions:
The surface strain of a tibia decreased upon implantation of the tibial tray with a stem (solid or slotted, short or long).

A longer stem caused a greater decrease in the tibia's surface strain than did a shorter stem.

Slots reduced distal bending stiffness, thus it became more compliant with that of the surrounding bone.

Surface strain near the distal end of a tibia having a slotted stem was closer to that of the intact bone than was the surface strain for a tibia with a solid stem.

References:
[1] Cameron, H.U., "End of Stem Pain in the Tibial Component Following Noncemented Stem Tibial Component Insertion", The Am. J. of Knee Surgery, Summer 1993, Vol. 6, No. 3, pp. 112-114.

[2] Cameron, H.U., "Clinical and Radiologic Effects of Diaphyeal Stem Extension in Noncemented Total Knee Replacement", CJS, Vol.38, No. 1, February 1995, pp. 45-50.

[3] Bobyn, J.D., Mortimer, E.S., Glassman, A.H., Engh, C.A. Miller, J.E. and Brooks, C.E., "Producing and Avoiding Stress Shielding: Laboratory and Clinical Arthroplasty", CORR, N274, pp. 79-96, January 1992.

# Fuzzy Logic Approach for Analysis of White-Light Isochromatic Fringes

Darrell E.P. Hoy,   Fan Yu
Mechanical Engineering Dept., Box 5014
Tennessee Technological University
Cookeville, TN 38505      E-Mail: DEH8726@tntech.edu

Since 1988, researchers at Tennessee Technological University have been investigating the use of color digital imaging methods in the analysis of photoelastic fringe patterns [1-5]. Most of these efforts have been focused on various approaches to the analysis of isochromatic fringe patterns, with some work in the area of isoclinic analysis. In this paper, the authors report on the recent application of color digital imaging to the analysis of white-light isochromatic fringe patterns using a fuzzy logic approach.

Previous efforts by other researchers in the area of digital isochromatic analysis have employed greyscale imaging systems with monochromatic illumination of the specimens. The use of monochromatic illumination presents the problem of identifying the whole-order fringe numbers, since each isochromatic fringe appears as a similar "dark band" in the image. Thus, manual identification of the whole order fringes is usually required. In contrast, the use of white-light illumination for isochromatic analysis automatically provides for whole-order fringe identification, since under white-light illumination the fringes form a unique multi-color sequence. By taking advantage of this fact, a color digital imaging system can beused to determine the complete fringe number at any desired point ina white-light image.

At Tennessee Tech, Hoy and co-workers have been investigating several different approaches to effectively implement color digital imaging for white-light isochromatic analysis. Among the earlier efforts in this area were: (1) direct RGB (red-green-blue) color matching along a line of interest [1], (2) direct HIS (hue-intensity-saturation) color identification [2-3], and (3) isochromatic fringe-tracing [4]. Overall, these early approaches showed the promise of the color digital imaging approach to isochromatic analysis; however, their reliability was not as high as desired..

Hence, recent efforts by Hoy and Yu have focused on applying more "intelligence" to the fringe identification process through various probabilistic and fuzzy logic techniques. In these newer approaches, it is recognized that in practice, the proper identification of the fringe number at a point is not always a straightforward determininistic matter of matching each poin'ts spectral (color) components to a calibration specimen, since various factors such as illumination quality, camera/digitizing board response, high fringe gradients, etc. provide a range of color values that are associated with a given fringe number. In addition, other factors such as fringe continuity and fringe color-sequence requirements also influence the assignment of a particular fringe number to any given point-of-interest in the image. With this in mind, it is felt to be most suitable to take a "confidence level " approach to fringe number determination in which each fringe number assignment is associated with a confidence factor expressing the probability of the correctness of that assignment. After the initial assignment, this confidence factor is iteratively improved through the application of the color

sequence and continuity requirements mentioned earlier. The actual implementation of this methodology can take various forms; in this particular paper, Hoy and Yu report only on their most recent effort in this direction, that is, the application of fuzzy logic methods to the identification of white-light isochromatic fringes.

In this work, fuzzy set theory and fuzzy logic were introduced as the basis for the fringe number decision process. The spectral components of the pixels of interest are treated as elements of fuzzy sets. These spectral components, represented in HSB (hue, saturation, brightness) color space are derived from the basic broad-band RGB (red, green, blue) spectral components sensed by the digital imaging system. It should be noted that the use of HSB color components, instead of RGB components, is beneficial in that it helps to distinguish between the attributes associated with the color of the image (hue and saturation) from that associated with the intensity of the image (brightness) [5].

The fuzzy inference rules and subsets established for fringe pattern identification are formulated based on weighted inputs from a calibration specimen (a beam in pure bending was used in this study). The fringe numbers obtained from this fuzzy inference system are associated with confidence factors based on their "grades-of-membership" in the corresponding fuzzy sets. Thus, considering hue, saturation, and brightness as basic inputs, with the fringe number N and its confidence factor CF as the output, the task at hand is to construct a set of fuzzy rules R which can be used to determine a mapping from the inputs to the output,i.e., $(H,S,B) \to N$. In determining this mapping, a weighting system is used which reflects the relative importance of the H, S, and B parameters for different fringe number regions. For example, for fringe numbers near zero, the fringes are basically devoid of color and therefore the intensity parameter dominates; in the remaining regions the hue and saturation are of greater importance.

In this work, the domains of the input parameters were defined as follows: hue $[0°, 360°]$; saturation $[0.0, 1.0]$; and brightness $[0.0, 1.0]$. The corresponding ranges for the outputs are: fringe number $[0.0, 4.0]$, and confidence factor $[0.0, 1.0]$. Note that the range of the fringe number N was defined to be from 0.0 to 4.0, since under white light, fringes of a number higher than this tend to be visually indistinct and thus difficult to identify accurately. In forming the fuzzy subsets, the domains of H, S, and B were divided into twenty- five, eleven, and eleven intervals, respectively (see Fig. 1 for an illustration of the S and B intervals). The domain of N was divided into thirty-three intervals. These particular divisions of intervals were based on "experience", and can be readily adjusted as desired.

In this study, the membership functions selected for the fuzzy subsets were simple triangular functions, although other kinds of functions can be used. Using these membership functions, a "crisp" numerical value is transformed into a corresponding fuzzy variable, which is referred to as "fuzzification". Calibration values of H, S, B, and N are used to formulate the rules which make up the "fuzzy rule-base" R, as follows:

Let $h_i$, $s_i$, and $b_i$ be the "ith" fuzzy subsets of the variables H, S, and B; then from the calibration data, the "ith" fuzzy rule can be established as:

Rule $R_i$: If the hue H is $h_i$, and if the saturation S is $s_i$, and if the brightness B is $b_i$, then the fringe number N is $z_i$, for i=1,2,... m rules.

Now, given the "crisp" values h', s', b' for an "unknown" point-of-interest:

Premise: If H is h', S is s', B is b'

Inference: N is $z_i'$, where $z_i'$ is a fuzzy subset of N.

Note that as a consequence of the overlapping of the fuzzy subset intervals (Figs. 1), the fringe number of the point-of-interest will have a nonzero degree of membership in two adjacent fuzzy subsets $z_i$. Thus, the fringe number of the point will be given by a new fuzzy subset Z', which is the union of the two adjacent subsets $z_i'$. As a last step, the final output fringe number is desired to be a crisp value; hence, "defuzzification" of Z' is required. This defuzzification is accomplished using the gravity-center-of-area method to produce a final fringe number value $Z_c'$, with an associated confidence factor CF derived from the grade of membership of the fringe number.

Using the methodolgy described above, photoelastic models of a split-ring in compression and a beam in pure bending were used as test cases for this method. After capturing the images using the color digital image processing system, they were processed with the aid of a computer program developed to implement the previously-described fuzzy logic methodology. The results obtained from these two test cases is shown in Figures 2 and 3. As can be seen from the figures, the obtained results show good agreement with both a calculated solution (in the case of the beam), and a manually-measured set of data (for the split ring). Further development and testing of this method on additional examples is planned.

## References

[1] Hoy, D.E.P., "PC-Based Digital Imaging System for Photoelastic-Coating Analysis (2-D)," Proceedings of the First International Mechanical Systems Design Conference, Nashville, TN, June, 1989, pp. P17.1-7.

[2] Hoy, D.E.P., "Photoelastic Analysis of a Roller Chain Using a PC-Based Digital Imaging System," Proceedings of the First National Applied Mechanisms and Robotics Conference, Cincinnati, Ohio, November, 1989.

[3] Jouett, J., "Development of a Digital Imaging System for White-Light Isochromatic Fringe Pattern Analysis," Master's Thesis, Tennessee Technological University, Cookeville, TN, 1990.

[4] Shen, X., "Fringe-Tracing Method for White-Light Isochromatic Patterns Using a Digital Imaging System," Master's Thesis, Tennessee Technological University, Cookeville, TN, 1993.

[5] Yu, F., Hoy, D.E.P., "White-light Isochromatic Image Processing in HSB Color Space", 1995 Society of Experimental Mechanics Spring Conference, Student Paper Category, 1995.

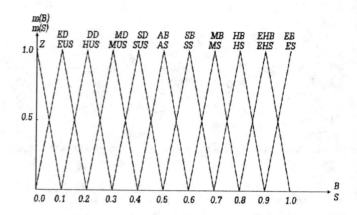

Fig. 1 Division of the saturation and brightness domains into fuzzy regions with the corresponding fuzzy membership functions.

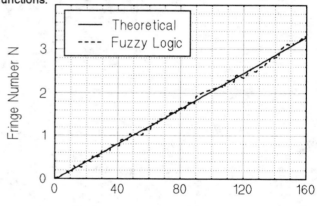

Fig. 2 Fringe number distributions for theoretical and fuzzy logic methods along a selected line in a beam in pure bending.

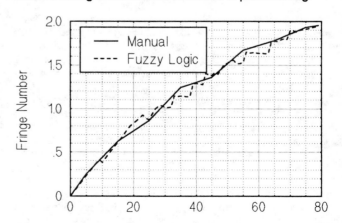

Fig 3. Fringe number distributions for manual and fuzzy logic methods along a selected line in a split-ring under compression.

# Assembly Stresses Effects on Multiple Holes

N. T. Younis       S. J. Baker
Associate Professor     Research Assistant
Department of Engineering
Purdue University at Fort Wayne
Fort Wayne, IN 46805-1499

The problem of determining and reducing stress concentrations around holes in plates occurs in many design situations. Extensive literature is available on the study of stress concentrations around holes [1-5]. All these studies deal with a central hole or central hole and auxiliary holes in a region where the stress is uniform without the holes.

In many design situations or practical repairs the circular holes are not central nor drilled in places where the stress distribution is uniform. In a previous study, the photostress method (birefringent coatings) was used to study the interaction between the stresses around a circular hole, nonuniform assembly stresses and contact stresses [6]. It was concluded that the combined effect of the assembly and contact stresses generally causes an increase the stresses in the vicinity of the hole.

In this study, the photostress method is used to:
1. Determine Stress concentration factors around a circular hole with two defense holes.
2. Identify and measure assembly stresses.
3. Study the interaction among the three holes, nonuniform assembly stresses and contact stresses.

Five different aluminum plates that are 20.32 cm long, 7.30 cm wide and 0.32 cm thick are considered. Three holes are drilled through each plate at different locations. The research program consisted of three stages. First, the plates are loaded and the fringe patterns are studied to identify the effects of the assembly stresses near the fixtures. In the second stage, one hole is drilled through each plate and the stress concentration factors are determined using the normal incidence method [7, 8]. The first plate has a central hole and the second to the fifth plates have holes located at 1d, 2d, 2.5d and 3d below the center line where d is the diameter of the hole. In the third stage of the study, the two defense holes are drilled and the stress concentration factors at each hole are determined. Each specimen was subjected to three different loads and each experiment was repeated three times.

The effects of the size and location of the holes are investigated. The size of the middle hole is kept constant while the size of the two auxiliary holes varied. It can be seen from the experimental results that the defense holes tend to decrease stress concentrations around the middle hole when the holes are drilled near the center of the plates. However, different results are obtained when the holes approach the non linear stress field close to the fixture. In fact, in the vicinity of the non linear assembly stresses the stresses around the upper and lower holes are different.

References:

[1] Kirsch, G., "Die Theorie der Elasticitat und die Bedurfnisse der Festigkeitlehre," Z. Ver. Deut. Ing., Vol. 2, 797-807, 1898.

[2] Heywood, R. B., Designing by Photoelasticity, Chapman & Hall, Ltd., London, 296-298, 1952.

[3] Peterson, R. E., Stress Concentration Factors, John Wiely & Sons, Inc., New York, 1974.

[4] Erickson, P. E. and Riely, W. F., "Minimizing Stress Concentrations Around Circular Holes in Uniaxially Loaded Plates," Experimental Mechanics, Vol. 18, 97-100, 1978.

[5] Greenwood, J. A.,"Exact Formulae for Stresses Around Circular Holes and Inclusions," Int. J.Mech. Sci., Vol. 31, 219-227, 1989.

[6] Younis, N. T. and Bredemeyer, D. M., "Assembly Stresses Effects on Stresses Around Circular Holes," Proceedings of the 1995 SEM Spring Conference, 882-888.

[7] Dally, J. W. and Riley, W. F., Experimental Stress Analysis, 3rd Ed., McGraw Hill, New York, 1991.

[8] Introduction to Stress Analysis by the PhotoStress Method, Tech Note TN-702, Measurements Group, Inc., Raleigh, NC.

# Photoelastic Property of Silicon Single Crystal

Yasushi Niitsu and Kenji Gomi

Department of Mechanical Engineering, Tokyo Denki Univ.,
Kanda-Nishikicho 2-2, Chiyodaku, Tokyo, 101 JAPAN

We have developed the optical birefringence measurement by using the photoelastic modulator and the polarized laser. The equipment adopts the He-Ne infrared laser as a light source to measure the stress in semiconductor wafers. The magnitude of birefringence and its directions are obtained simultaneously and quantitatively by our developed equipment[1]. In this article, the authors present the photoelastic property of silicon single crystal[2-4]. The photoelastic properties of Si wafers are investigated. The photoelastic coefficients are obtained for several directions in {111}, {110} and {100} crystal planes. From the experimental results, the photoelastic constant depend on the crystalline orientation and the birefringence direction doesn't coincide with the principal stress direction. By the stress strain analysis of silicon single crystal, it is found that the birefringence direction coincides with the principal strain direction and the relation between the principal strain difference and the retardation is independent of crystalline orientation. Brewster's law is described by the linear relation between the optical retardation and principal stress difference. But our results show that the photoelastic coefficient of linear relation between the retardation and principal strain difference is more essential than Brewster's constant. Based on our experimental and theoretical results, the optical birefringence is correspond to principal strain difference essentially.

Recently, the production technology of small precision devices, for example, VLSIs and sensor devices, has been significantly advanced. Therefore, to achieve the production of higher grade and advanced micro devices, the improvement of the quality of Si wafer and the stress evaluation method of silicon substrate are required[5][6]. In this study, we developed the equipment which had ability of stress measurement in silicon substrate by using infrared laser as a light source. The photoelastic properties of Si single crystal should be investigated to measure the stress in silicon substrate.

Figure 1 shows the construction of the birefringence measuring system[2-4]. This equipment adopts an 8mW He-Ne infrared laser ($\lambda$=1150nm) as a light source. The PEM converts linearly polarized light into oscillating elliptic light at its 42kHz($=\omega/2\pi$) resonant frequency. The detected light intensity of alternative components of resonant frequency $I_{AC1}$ and its double frequency $I_{AC2}$ are measured by two lock-in amplifiers, the direct component $I_{DC}$ are measured by voltmeter. These values are written as follows,

$$I = I_{DC} + I_{AC1} \sin\omega t + I_{AC2} \cos 2\omega t + \cdots \tag{1}$$

where

$$I_{DC} = \frac{\alpha I_0}{4} \left\{ 1 + J_0(\delta_0) \cdot \sin\gamma \cdot \sin 2\theta \right\} \tag{2}$$

$$I_{AC1} = A \frac{-\alpha I_0}{2} J_1(\delta_0) \cdot \sin\gamma \cdot \cos 2\theta \tag{3}$$

$$I_{AC2} = B \frac{\alpha I_0}{2} J_2(\delta_0) \cdot \sin\gamma \cdot \sin 2\theta \tag{4}$$

where, I is the light intensity transmitted by the analyzer, $I_0$ the light intensity before transmitting by polarizer, $\alpha$ is the transparency of the Si wafer, $\gamma$ is the retardation of the specimen, $\theta$ is the angle of the birefringence of the specimen, $\delta_0$ is the amplitude of the modulator retardation which is proportional to the applied oscillating PEM voltage, $J_0(\delta_0) \sim J_2(\delta_0)$ are Bessel functions. The retardation $\gamma$ and the birefringence direction $\theta$ of sample are determined simultaneously with measured values of $I_{AC1}$, $I_{AC2}$ and $I_{DC}$ without rotating the sample[2].

To investigate the influence of the crystalline orientation on photoelastic properties, we prepared 12 rectangular samples as shown in Fig. 2. The figures show the tensile specimen, crystal systems and commercial Si wafers that were used in the experiments. The size of the rectangular samples were $0.5\sim0.6\times5.0\times50$mm. The rectangular samples were reinforced at both ends with PMMA plates. Tensile load was applied to longitudinal direction with the screw type loading equipment. The measurements of $I_{AC1}$, $I_{AC2}$ and $I_{DC}$ for each specimen was obtained for $0\sim4.90$MPa tensile stress levels. Figure 3 shows the linear relations between retardation and principal stress for 12 specimens. The retardation of Si single crystal is proportional to the applied stress and the photoelastic constant depends on crystal orientation.

Optical birefringence is due to the anisotropy of dielectric constant. Suppose that the deviation of dielectric tensor

$e_{ij}'$ is proportional to the deviatoric strain tensor $\varepsilon_{ij}'$, because the strain tensor corresponds to the anisotropy of density. By the way, the stress-strain relation of Si crystal is written by,

$$\begin{bmatrix} \sigma_{11} \\ \sigma_{22} \\ \sigma_{33} \\ \tau_{12} \end{bmatrix} = \begin{bmatrix} C_{11} & C_{12} & C_{12} & 0 \\ C_{12} & C_{11} & C_{12} & 0 \\ C_{12} & C_{12} & C_{11} & 0 \\ 0 & 0 & 0 & C_{44} \end{bmatrix} \begin{bmatrix} \varepsilon_{11} \\ \varepsilon_{22} \\ \varepsilon_{33} \\ \gamma_{12} \end{bmatrix} \quad (5)$$

$C_{11} = 165.7$ GPa, $C_{12} = 63.9$ GPa, $C_{44} = 79.6$ GPa

where $\sigma_{ij}$ and $\varepsilon_{ij}$ show the stress and strain tensor, and $C_{ij}$ is material constants. The results of Fig. 3 are calculated into strain base using Eq.(5). Figure 4 shows a relation between retardation and principal strain difference for 12 specimens. The retardation of Si single crystal is proportional to the strain difference, and the strain-retardation coefficient independent of crystal orientation.

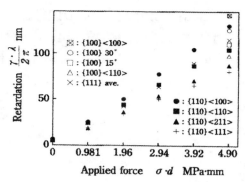

Fig. 3   Relation between retardation and applied force

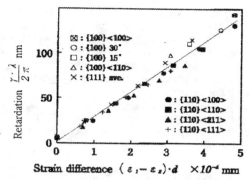

Fig. 4   Relation between retardation and strain difference

Conclusions:

(1)  Based on our experimental and theoretical results, the optical retardation of Si single crystal is proportional to principal strain difference essentially.

(2)  The strain-retardation coefficient of Si single crystal is independent of crystal orientation.

References:

[1] Niitsu, Y., Ichinose, K., Ikegami, K., "Stress Measurement of Transparent Materials by Polarized Laser", JSME Int. J., Vol. 38, No.1, pp.68-72, 1995.

[2] Niitsu, Y., Gomi, K., "Stress Measurement in Si wafer using Polarized Infrared Laser Photoelasticity", Proc. of Mechanics and Materials for Electronic Packaging ASME, AMD-Vol.187, Volume2, pp.37-40, 1994.

[3] Niitsu, Y., Gomi, K., "Influence of Crystal Orientation on Photoelastic Property of Silicon Single Crystal", Proc. of Advanced in Electronic Packaging ASME, EEP-Vol.10-2, pp.1239-1245, 1995.

[4] Niitsu, Y., Gomi, K., Ono, T., "Investigation of Photoelastic Property of Semiconductor Wafers", Proc. of Applications of Experimental Mechanics to Electronic Packaging ASME, EEP-Vol.13/AMD-Vol.214, pp.103-108, 1995.

[5] Date, K., "Stress Measurement with High Sensitivity in Wafer Using Infrared Photoelasticity", Proc. Advances in Elec. Pack. ASME, Vol.2, pp.985-989, 1992.

[6] Iwaki,T., "A Method of Analyzing a Photoelastic Image", Trans. JSME (Jpn.), Vol.57-539A, pp.190-194, 1991.

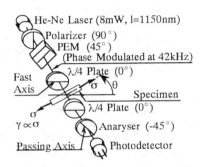

Fig. 1   Schematic figure of the birefringence measuring system

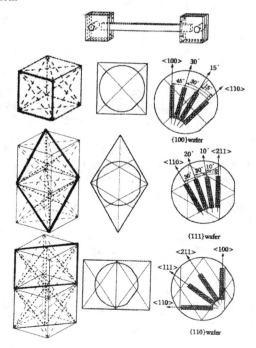

Fig. 2   Tensile specimen, crystal systems and wafers

# Examples of Industrial Analysis Using a 3D Fully Automated Photoelasticimeter (3D CAPE) - Technical and Economical Aspects. Link with the Finite Elements Calculus.

D. PARASKEVAS - PK LAB (France)[1]

## Abstract

*The new PK-LAB's device for the study of tridimensionnal stress-frozen photoelastic models, the 3D CAPE, allows to greatly reduce the number of studied slices. It also eliminates the preliminary research of main planes, by reconstituting the tridimensionnal state of the stresses, regardless of the slice's orientation.*

*Finally, the measurement and the calculation being fully automated with the help of a PC, this device's industrial use is very simple and allows for an easy link with the FEC.*

## Link between 3D photoelasticity and the FEC

It is a well known fact that the comparison of the results obtained by both methods is very delicate, as soon as one focuses on zones of complex stresses (gradiants, holes and openings, connection between thin and thick parts,...).

The use of electric gages is not always possible, and isn't possible at all during the design stage.

The difficulty is worsened by the fact that 3D photoelasticity only gives partial informations, especially in the industrial world.

Of course, it is possible to obtain elementary « cubes » on a few points and solve entirely the tridimensionnal problem. However, this solution, described [1] [2] and sporadically used for over 50 years, is unthinkable in our industrial context: an average study, such as the examples we will show, corresponds to the study of 2000 to 4000 different points. The cost and the necessary delays associated with a complete study, according to the classical means, is completely prohibitive.

## The 3D-CAPE (Computer Aided PhotoElasticimeter)

The prototype of this device was first presented at the « 1995 SEM Spring conference and exhibit » in Grand Rapids, Michigan, on June 12th 1995.

Based on a principle of double oblique incidence, which is known [3], one uses 3 new technologies for the realization of these measures:

- Gratings with a parabolic profile for sharing informations in parallel.
- Optical fibers.
- Silicium based photodetectors with an integrated operational amplifier and a fast frequency response (50 kHz).

The basic diagram (fig 1) shows the general arrangement of the device.

The image of the studied slices, observed in the POLARISCOPE zone by a CCD camera, is memorized by the PC, then the slices are automatically transferred and studied point by point in the PONCTUAL MEASURE zone.

We use the classical technique with two wave lengths ( simplification of the spectral analysis), to eliminate any ambiguity.

The complete measure, fully automated, takes about 2 ms. One can directly program, from the screen, the exploration paths (lines, circles, ellipses). One can also ask for a cartesian scan of a zone and obtain directly an « image » in stresses.

The results can be expressed in principal stresses, shear stresses, Von Mises, etc...

For each point, one has all the elements of the stress-tensor deviator.

## Main results

We show the results of industrial studies using this new device, focusing particularly on three aspects:

- The quantity of information obtained.
- The link with FEC.
- The economic balance (time and delays).

As an illustration, one can consider the analysis of the segment ab between two holes of a part in torsion. (Fig. 2)

For a segment of an approximate length of 20 mm, one must cut:

- Classical way:
  - 20 slices between ab, at + 45°
  - 20 slices between a' and b', at - 45°.
  Hence a total of 40 slices.

One can note that the ending slices must be tangent to the holes, and that the values of $\pm$ 45 are approximative.

[1] Dimitri PARASKEVAS - PK LAB - General Manager - BP 180 - 60306 SENLIS CEDEX - FRANCE
Associate Professor - Université Technologique de Troyes - FRANCE

• With the 3D-CAPE. One takes only *one slice*, in the plane perpendicular to the diagram, and containing a and b.

No hypothesis is formulated on the main directions.

## Conclusion

The main conclusion is that stress frozen photoelasticity, through the use of two new techniques:

- Stereolithography
- 3D CAPE.

becomes again an industrial tool of great importance to help the FEC:

- Validate results.
- indispensable complement in zones where the FEC is not pertinent.

## Acknowledgements

The conception of this device has benefited from the support of:

ANVAR : Agence Nationale pour la VAlorisation de la Recherche (France).

CRP: Conseil Régional de Picardie (France)

The first device was acquired by SNECMA.

## References

[1] FROTCH M, Photoelasticity, Volume 1, pp. 252-285, John Wiley & sons Inc, 1941.

[2] DALLY J.W., and RILEY W.F., The stress freezing method, *Experimental stress analysis*, 2nd ed. pp 490-497, McGraw-Hill, 1985.

[3] PARASKEVAS D., Etude théorique et expérimentale de la photoélasticimétrie tridimensionnelle, CETIM, Rapport n° 15 G 151 (77 pages), January 1982.

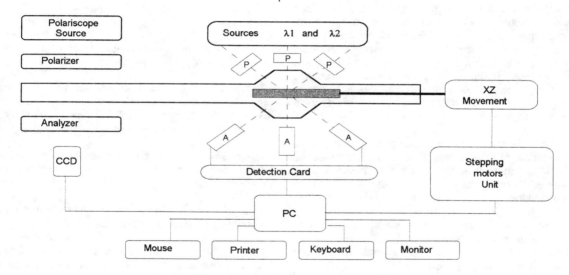

Figure 1: Basic diagram of the 3D-CAPE

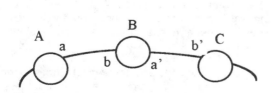

Figure 2: Illustration of results

Figure 3: Turbine Mock-up(Courtesy of SNECMA)

# A study on Stress-Strain Behaviors of Dual Phase Steels caused by the change in various Microstructural Factors

Yong-Seok Yu, Myung-Jin Choi, Taek-Yul Oh
Kyung Hee Univ. Department Of Mechanical Engineering
Kyungido 170-73 Koera

Dual Phase Steel, which consists of ferrite of high ductility and martensite raising the hardness of steels, has been developed from the need of high strength and ductility.

It attracted the attention in the technical aspect that Dual Phase Steel shows a higher workability than the Standard High Strength Low Alloy (HSLA) under the same tensile strength. The mechanical properties of Dual Phase Steels are up to the factors like martensite volume fraction, grain size, phase morphology, hardness ratio and added element, etc.

Accordingly, using the finite element method, this study aims at MVF, grain size, strength ratio of the dual phase steels and the estimation of the strain-stress deformation behavior of dual phase steels attendant on two phase morphologies, with which the experimental curve is compared. At the same time, the observation of the formation process of void by the steels' ductility fracture, its comparison with the calculated value of stress distribution in the structure and its review has been made using finite element method.

After the measurement of deformation rate of each phase among the whole phases ranging from the estimated area of the void growth to the fracture, the information have been obtained by using the optical microscope and image analyzer at the longitudinal cross-section of the specimen.

Typical mesh of two dimensions was used to this study to get the theoretical stress-strain curve, where the node J is thought to be a fixed point, and unmovable toward the both directions of x and y as shown in Fig. 1.

On the other hand, all the nodes on AB line have been assumed to move only to the x direction. In the case of all modes on CD line, it is possible that the nodes move toward the direction x and y only under the restriction that the displacement of y direction should be same.

The rest meshes correspond to the half section of experiment specimen while AB correspond to the diameter of specimen.

Piecewise linear analysis is used to analyze the problems in the plasticity of the materials.

The stiffness matrix to each increment depends on the current stress status of the finite elements and the final non-linear result is obtained by the accumulation of the increments of displacement and stress. Its result depends on the selection of users, since algorithm is assumed to be linear among the consequence loads.

Here, each table of plastic material is used to make the input easier, which is stress-strain deformation function to each non-linear materials.

The distribution of stress-strain within structure conforms to the result of this study also in the case of the application of FEM. in fig. 2 and fig. 3, the stress and strain obtained between the node point of 180 and 196 along G-G section in fig. 1 is shown.

It is estimated through the application of the numerical analyses using FEM that the tendency of the deformation reaches the highest at the ferrite and the lowest at the martensite. The reason that the deformation reaches the lowest is ferrite has high pre-deformation.

The largest deformation of Martensite takes place at the interface of the ferrite in order to keep the compatibility with the ferrite and that of the ferrite takes place at the center from the restrained point of martensite.

As shown on the figure, the stress at the martensite is higher than at the ferrite and the maximum stress takes place when the deformation of martensite is the largest.

This distribution of the internal stress flow represents the possibility of void growth at the interface, the inconsistent area of stress-strain. The fracture of crystallization takes place at the center of martensite, where the deformation is the smallest and the stress is the largest, which is thought to be the origin of the void growth.

The following results are obtained through the comparison and study of the curve using the specimen, having changed the MVF, which is the microstructural factors of dual phase steels, grain size, phase morphology and hardness ratio.

1. The theoretical curve used the FEM confirms very well to the experimental one in general and it was proved that this could be good means for the stress-strain study of two phase alloy.

2. The difference between theoretical and experimental curves is likely to be smaller as the hardness ratio becomes lower, which could be explained by the connection with the effect modulus of plastic constraint.

Namely, the experimental and theoretical curves are thought to come closer since the effect of plastic constraint decreases and fraction ductility increases as the hardness ratio and internal stress decreases.

3. It was made clear through the 3 steps adjustment of grain size of dual phase steels that the calculated value curve conforms to the experimental curve as the grain size decreases.

4. By changing two phase morphology into connected and unconnected series, the mechanical property is compared on the spot. Two phase morphology of connected type showed a high stress flow.

5. The void growth, which is made mainly at the martensite concentrated place, starts at the plastic strain area exceeding the capitulation point and is observed at the Martensite Particle and Martensite-Ferrite interface.

6. The distribution of the internal stress was maximum at the $\alpha$ phase and minimum at the $\gamma$ phase. The strain of $\gamma$ phase exists at the interface of $\alpha$-$\gamma$ phase and the maximum stress of $\gamma$ phase takes place when the strain of $\gamma$ is the maximum.

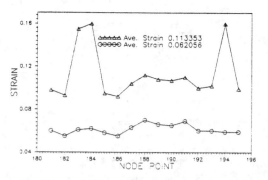

Fig. 2 Longitudinal Strain Distribution along G-G of Fig.1

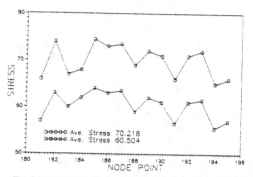

Fig. 3 Longitudinal Stress Distribution along G-G of Fig.1

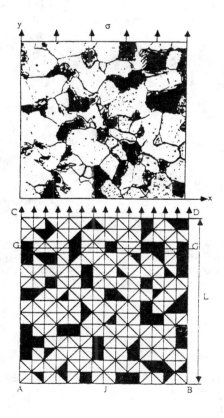

Fig. 1 Ilustration of F.E.M Modeling

# Vibration Control of a Moving Structure by Neural Network

Sin-Young Lee,  Heon-Sul Jeong

Kunsan National University

Kunsan, Chonbuk 573-701 KOREA

In moving structures such as robots and feeders of production lines, vibrations while moving may not be ignored. Recently it becomes a big problem to control the vibration in a motion because moving structures are in more high-speed, large-sized and light weighed. In this study a nonlinear system is modelled by using neural networks and the vibration in motions is controlled actively by using neural network controller.

A neural network is composed of unit cells so called neuron which has multi inputs and single output. An internal state of each neuron $U_i^n$ ( $i$th unit of $n$th layer) and output $O_j^{n-1}$ ( $j$th unit of $n-1$th layer) are expressed as follows by using weighting coefficients $W$ and thresholds $\theta$.

$$U_i^n = \sum_{j=1}^{k} W_{j,i}^{n-1,n} O_j^{n-1} + \theta_i^n \tag{1}$$

$$O_i^n = f(U_i^n) \tag{2}$$

Error back propagation algorithm is a learning method proposed by Rumelhart[1] for a multi-layer type neural network system. The sum of error squares in the last layer is used as an estimation function as follows.

$$J = \sum_{i=1}^{m} (T_i - O_i^N)^2 / 2 \tag{3}$$

Where $T_i$'s are ideal outputs for inputs. The optimal network is the state where the estimation function becomes minimum, and learning of weighting coefficients between layers and that of thresholds of each layer was done by the deepest gradient method. Each values are adjusted by a partial differential multiplied by a negative number which is called as a learning rate[2].

Hidden layers are adjusted by the error back propagation from next layer as eq. (4).

$$\delta_j^n = \left( \sum_{k=1} \delta_k^{n+1} W_{i,k}^{n,n+1} \right) f'(U_i^n) \tag{4}$$

For fast converging, moments of the previous adjustment values were used. A 4 layer neural network is used as system network which represents the physical characteristics of an structure. The inputs of the first layer are state values and control values. The second layer is a typical hidden layer and the outputs of the third layer are the changes of state values during a given time step. The internal state of each unit of the fourth layer is the sum of the output of the unit of the first layer an the outputs of the corresponding unit of the third layer[3].

The optimal control sets up an estimation function for a purpose of a control object  and determines control inputs which minimizes the estimation function. In order to induce a control system by using neural network, the motion of a given structure should be obtained in a system network. Next, a neural network controller which minimizes the estimation function is made by learning. In this study a system network and a neural network controller were arranged as a cascade shape. The neural network controller is composed of 3 layers. Its inputs are state variables at a given time and outputs are control inputs at next time. The sum of estimation functions for state variables and for control inputs is considered as a total estimation function. If the initial conditions are given, state variables at each time are given by the system network and control inputs by the neural network controller. The weighting coefficients and thresholds are adjusted by back propagation of error signals. The values of adjustment are the sum of those of each unit circuit which are given from the partial derivatives of the total estimation function with respect to each weighting coefficients or thresholds. The calculation of an error signal starts from one time step to the previous time step. In each unit circuit the error signal is back propagated in the direction from output layer to input layer.

To investigate validity of this method, an experimental apparatus was made and tested(Fig. 1). The model is composed of a DC servomotor, carrier and a flexible plate. Its motion were measured by a gap sensor and an encoder. A trapezoidal, cycloid and trapecloid type trajectories were used in this experiment(Fig. 2). Computer simulations and experiments were done for each trajectory. The computer simulation showed good control results(Fig. 3), but the experimental results(Fig. 4) were not so good with respect to those of simulation. The reasons may be due to the phase lag of gap conversion from the real gap between the flexible plate and carrier to neural network controller via media such as A/D converter, a programmed filter and system neural network.

References:

[1]   Rumelhart, D.E., Hinton, G.E., Williams, R.J. "Learning Representations by Back- propagation Errors", Nature, 1986, Vol. 323, pp533-536.

[2]   Asou, H. "Neural Network Information Processing", Tokyo, Industrial Book Co., 1988, pp.39-54.

[3]   Shiotsuka, T., Ohta, K., Yoshida, K., Nagamatsu, A., "Identification and Control of Four Wheel Steering Car by Neural Network", Trans. of JSME, 1993, Vol. 59(C), pp. 708-713.

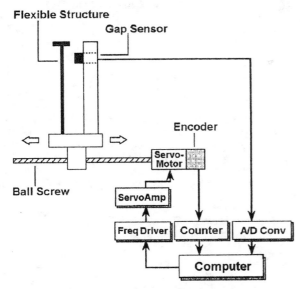

Fig. 1 Layout of Experimental apparatus

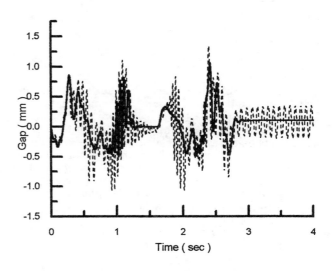

Fig. 3 Result of computer simulation

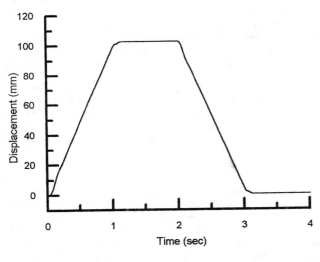

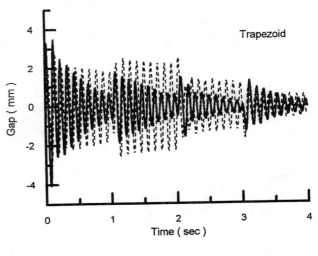

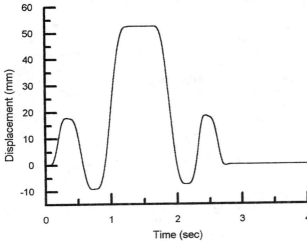

Fig. 2 Sample trajectories

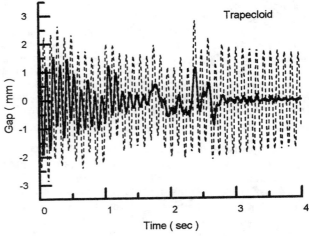

Fig. 4 Results of control experiments

# Oblique Impact Of A Rotating Elastic Solid On A Deformable Surface

S. J. Haake
Department of Mechanical and Process Engineering
The University of Sheffield, Mappin Street, Sheffield, S1 3JD, England.

Dynamic impacts of objects on surfaces are very important in the world of sport. In some sports elastic deformation occurs in the ball (if there is one) while in others elastic/plastic deformation occurs in the surface. A golf shot begins with an elastic impact between the ball and the club followed by flight through the air and a complex impact involving slip and rotation in which the turf is permanently deformed. This paper researches the factors involved in the ball/turf impact using both experimental and numerical techniques.

Golf ball impacts were carried out on natural turf using a ball firing device. Stroboscopic photographs of the impacts were taken and the results analysed to determine velocity, spin and angle before and after impact. The velocity was varied between 17 and 27 ms$^{-1}$ while the backspin of the ball was varied between 0 and 800 rad s$^{-1}$. In some cases the angle of impact was varied between 35 and 55°. Not surprisingly, it was found that, in general, the angle of impact equalled the angle of rebound and that an increase in the velocity of the ball resulted in the ball rebounding faster.

In many of the impacts backspin was removed from the ball and it rebounded with topspin. In some of the impacts the ball clearly slipped throughout and rebounded with backspin or with less topspin than that required for it to roll off the surface. A convenient way to determine whether the ball slipped at the end of the impact is to compare the ball's linear velocity $v_{linear}$ with the rotational velocity of its surface relative to its centre ($\omega r$). This is given by,

$$\Delta V = v_{linear} - \omega r \qquad (1)$$

If $\Delta V$ is zero then the ball is rolling and if $\Delta V$ is high and positive then the ball is slipping with relative backspin. Figure 1 shows this relative velocity versus backspin for three greens with increasing resilience factor. The resilience factor gives an indication of the "hardness" of the green and is calculated using an impact hardness tester and a traction apparatus [1]. A resilience factor of 1 gives an average green, while resilience factors less than 1 and greater than 1 indicate a softer and harder than average green respectively. The impact velocities varied between 17 and 27 m s$^{-1}$ and the angle of impact was fixed at 45°.

In Fig 1 (a) for a relatively "soft" green with a resilience factor of 0.6, $\Delta V$ is approximately zero regardless of the initial backspin of the ball. As the resilience factor increases (Fig. 1 (b)) the impacts with initial backspins of around 700 rad s$^{-1}$ the high values of $\Delta V$ show that the ball was slipping at the end of impact. For a resilience factor of 1.4 (Fig 1 (c)) many of the impacts with backspins over 400 rad s$^{-1}$ show evidence of slipping. Thus, the more resilient the green, the higher the chance of backspin being retained after the ball has rebounded and the lower the initial amount of backspin required to do so.

Figure 2 shows $\Delta V$ for impact angles of 35 and 45° for a green with a resilience factor of 1 and with a similar range of velocities to those in Fig. 1. It can be seen that in many of the impacts the ball slipped as it left the surface and that the shallower the impact angle the lower the initial backspin required before some is retained after the impact.

Figure 2 displays clearly the problem of analysing tests on natural turf which inherently has a large amount of scatter in it. More tests clearly have to be carried out before good statistical accuracy is found.

A finite element study of the problem was carried out. The sphere was modelled with a central core and an outer shell and consisted of 2304 elements. The surface was considered to be multi-layered and consisted of three layers with a total of 5200 elements. Simple vertical and oblique impacts were used to verify the model by dropping the sphere on a constrained steel block. Good correlation was found between the experimental results and the FE model.

The model was used to predict the velocities and spin for a non-spinning oblique impact on a three layered artificial turf system. The material characteristics of the turf and the ball were determined from static compression tests. It was found that the impact time correlated well with that found on natural turf [2].

Using the model it was found that, as impact progressed, the rotation of the sphere increased until it began to roll across the surface up the inclined face of the pitchmark. The velocity of the surface of the ball in contact with the turf and the absolute velocity of the ball is shown in Fig 3 (a). This is used to calculate $\Delta V$ in Figure 4.

The topspin of the ball increase quite rapidly and the velocity of the surface of the ball increases accordingly. At the same time the linear velocity decreases to a minimum before increasing to the value at which it leaves the turf. It is interesting to note that in region B the ball is actually spinning faster than the rolling spin and the forces acting on the ball are trying to reduce the topspin rather than increase it. This is an effect similar to that found by Gobush [3] with golf ball impacts on club heads.

At the end of impact the rotational velocity and the linear velocity are almost matched and the ball rebounds with topspin roughly equal to the rolling spin. This impact corresponds to one of those in Fig. 1 (a) where the initial spin was set at zero. The work will move on to modelling impacts with backspin on artificial turf. Once this has been verified then the work will consider the ultimate objective of modelling rotating oblique impacts on natural turf.

References:

1. S. J. Haake, "The impact of golf balls on natural turf. I. Apparatus and test methods", *J. Sports Turf Res. Inst.*, **67** 128-134 (1991).

2. S. J. Haake, "Apparatus and test methods for measuring the impact of golf balls on turf and their application in the field", PhD thesis, The University of Aston in Birmingham, UK, pp 203 (1989).

3. W. Gobush, "Spin and the inner workings of a golf ball" in *Golf - The Scientific Way* A. J. Cochran, Ed. (Aston Publishing Group, Hemel Hempstead, UK, 1995) pp. 141-145.

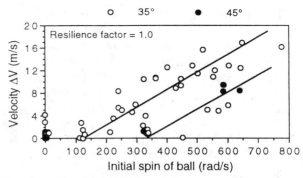

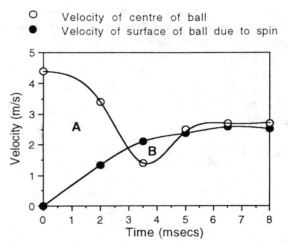

Figure 2. Graph of $\Delta V = v_{linear} - \omega r$ (velocity of the surface of the ball relative to the turf) versus initial backspin of the ball for impacts between 17 and 27 ms$^{-1}$ at impact angles of 35 and 45°.

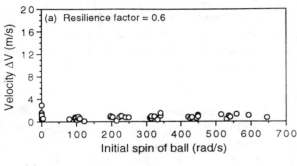

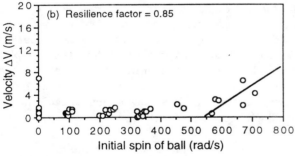

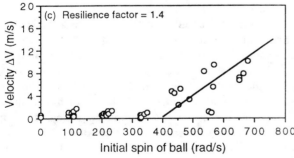

Figure 1. Graphs of $\Delta V = v_{linear} - \omega r$ (velocity of the surface of the ball relative to the turf) versus initial backspin for golf ball impacts between 17 and 27 ms$^{-1}$ on greens with resilience factors of (a) 0.6, (b) 0.85 and (c) 1.4.

Figure 3. Rotational velocity of the surface of the ball and linear velocity of the ball versus time after initial impact calculated using finite element analysis.

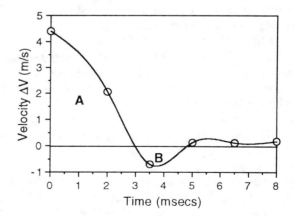

Figure 4. Graph of $\Delta V = v_{linear} - \omega r$ (velocity of the surface of the ball relative to the turf) versus time after initial impact calculated using finite element analysis.

377

# Application of Caustic Method to Dynamic Phenomena
## (Characteristics of Caustics Created in Two Dimensional Cutting)

Jianding WANG: Guest Researcher, Virginia Polytech. Inst. State Univ., USA
Jippei SUZUKI: Associate Professor, Mie University,
Kiyoshi ISOGIMI; Professor, Mechanical Engg., Mie University,
Kamihama-cho 1515, Tsu, 514, JAPAN

It is very important to expand the applicability of caustic experimental method to dynamic problems, which has been mainly used for only static analysis in the two dimensional contact problems. In this paper, authors tried to apply this method to one example of dynamic problems and to clarify the cutting forces and internal stresses induced actually inside and at the boundaries of the cutting tools and works in cutting operations, which are necessary for improvement of cutting performance of tools and development of the techniques of fine and highly integrated machining of various new materials such as composites and so on. In the first step of this research, two dimensional simple cutting is adapted as an object. It is most important purpose to establish the conviction for the possibility to analyse by applying thismethod.

The caustic patterns created by the reflected light rays from the front surface of the work neighbour of the contact region with cutting tool edge are observed and investigated about the characteristics in detail.The cutting type employed is plunge type two dimensional cutting with constant feed rate. The cutting conditions are shown in Table 1.

Figure 1 shows the shematic experimental feature. The experiment is performed for rake angle $\alpha$ =-15 $\sim$ +15 ° and relief angle $\gamma$ =1 $\sim$ 15 ° under constant conditon sof cutting speed and cutting width. The reflecting typ eof caustic experiment is adopted by coating Al thin fil m on one side of specimen ( work).

The most important factor which affects strongly on the caustic patterns created in cutting operation is cutting forces ( main force F1 and back force F2 ). Table 2 shows these forces values measured under the various conditions listed in table 1. These values change by angles $\alpha$ , $\gamma$ and cutting stages ( transient or stable).

Figure 2 shows a typical caustic pattern created. The configuration of caustics observed in two dimensional cutting looks like that created under concentrated load, but somewhat different. The caustics are deformed in the direction of top and bottom.

We can evaluate the characteristics of caustics with the longitudinal and traversal dimensions. Figure 3 shows an example of the relationships between the legth of caustic and cutting feed rate in comparison with caustic patterns obtained in experiment and calculated curves. The dimensions of caustics increase clearly with the incriment of feed rate. Moreover the practical patterns have good agreement with calculated curves.

The change of configurations of caustics patterns are investigated at each stage of cutting situations during cutting operation, that is, starting instance, transient stage, stational stage and after finishing. Detail consideration, however, can not been described here. It will be presented in Conference.

The caustics calculated should be derived by the analysis under dynamic loading in this case such a cutting operation. This condition can be simulated to the problem which load acting along the plate edge travels with the appropriate speeds. A typical one of calculated caustic curve derived is shown in Fig. 4 under cutting speed of 100 m/sec. Caustic curves created under static load is also shown in this figure. The speed employed here is tremendously faster than that of actual cutting experiment 12.6 m/min ( that equals 0.2 m/sec ). It is clarified the caustic is somewhat influenced only if the travelling speed is very fast.

Overcoming many difficult problems, the following brief results are obtained.
(1) The dynamic caustic patterns obtained for two dimensional cutting are somewhat different in their characteristics from those for static concentrated loadings.
(2) Caustic patterns created depend on the deformations of the work induced in direction of the thickness.
(3) The changes of caustic configurations can be characterized clearly for each cutting condition.
(4) By the simulation of caustic curves for travelling loads along the boundary line of half plane, caustics created in very high cutting speed condition are definitely distinguished from the statical one, but the differences are very slight under the conditions employed in this experiment. Therefore we can conclude caustics created in statical loading can be simulated approximately with enough accuracy for all cases of the cutting conditions employed in this research.

Table 1 Parameters of cutting.

| Cutting speed V mm/min | 12.6 |
| Feed rate   f mm/rev. | 0.10,0.20,0.31,0.41,0.51 |
| Nominal dimensions of | Diameter D=100 mm |
| works | Thickness t=5 mm |

Table 2 Cutting forces.

| Feed rate mm/rev. | Main force MPa | Back force MPa | Resultant force MPa |
|---|---|---|---|
| 0.10 | 13.0 ~ 17.2 | 3.86 ~ 7.20 | 13.7 ~ 18.0 |
| 0.20 | 25.4 ~ 28.9 | 3.19 ~ 11.6 | 22.9 ~ 31.2 |
| 0.31 | 30.7 ~ 43.0 | 2.15 ~ 16.7 | 32.9 ~ 46.1 |
| 0.41 | 39.5 ~ 55.7 | 1.31 ~ 21.0 | 42.4 ~ 59.5 |
| 0.51 | 47.1 ~ 71.3 | 0.24 ~ 24.1 | 47.1 ~ 72.7 |

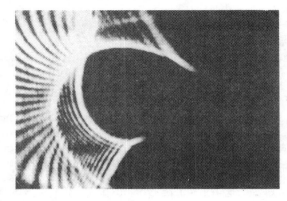

Fig.2 Example of caustic pattern obtained practically.

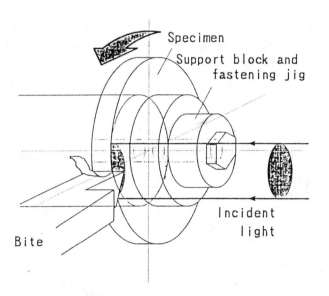

Fig.1 Shematic feature of experiment.

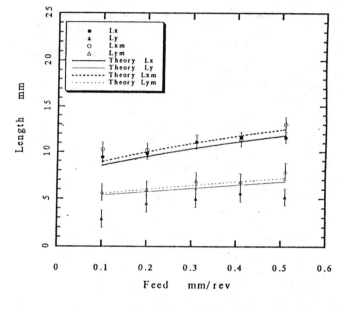

Fig. 3 Relationship between feed and caustic dimensions.

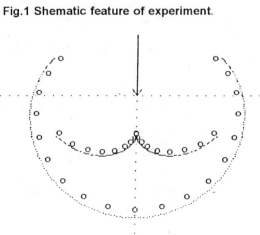

----- Dynamic(U=100m/sec), ○ Static
Fig.4 Dynamic and static caustics.

379

# Stress Intensity Factor for Plates of Discontinuous Cross Section with Corner Cracks under Out-of-plane Bending

E. Matsumoto, H. Fujiwara, A. Saito and K. Kushiki
Kinki University
Higashiosaka, Osaka 577
JAPAN

Plates with discontinuous cross section are often used as structural elements of aerospace and civil engineerings. These elements would experience large stress concentration at the inner corner and it is afraid to grow cracks according to increment of load. The stress intensity factor will be solved using the experimental stress analysis by a reflective photoelasticity for the plates with discontinuous cross section under transverse bending load[1],[2].

PSM-1, which is a specially annealed polycarbonate plastic, is ideally suited for the double layered reflective photoelasticity for this experimental work. Extreme care was paid to cut the plate by sawing. To obtain the clear image of isochromatic pattern, a mirror-like reflecting surface of thin silver layer is evapolated in vacuum on one surface of the model plate. Two plates were adhered by epoxy resin to make the model sandwiched the silver layer as shown in Fig. 1. The artificial corner cracks in this figure were milled using the diamond disc saw of 0.2mm thick and 100mm in diameter. The 90 degree sharp tip configuration of saw was given and enough lubricating oil was poured to prevent the residual stress. The crack angle and depth as shown in Fig. 1 are varied according to Table 1. The crack angle is milled keeping a specified angle using a jig.

General setup of the reflective photoelasticity is shown in Fig. 2. The polarized light, which will illuminate the loaded model M ,comes back at the reflecting surface in the model and are changed the light path 45 degree through a half mirror H. The isochromatic images of the loaded model would be collected on the CCD camera C. The model will be loaded by out-of-plane bending as shown in Fig. 3. The stress fringe value $f$ of the used material was measured from the test of the similar four point bending and

$$f = \frac{I\ N}{T^2\ M} \qquad (1)$$

where the stress fringe value $f$ of the material for models was measured by pure bending and Is 7.0Kn/m.

The model plate was put in the loading setup to give out-of-plane bending and the isochromatic fringes were observed at several increments of load. The isochromatic fringes were collected using the CCD camera and zoomlens in Fig. 2. The fringe around the crack tip was enlarged and the lens system was controlled so that a clear image was appeared in Fig. 4. A lots of those images were stored in the magneto-optical disk unit and used for the analysis of the stress intensity factors, which has already shown in [1],[3].

The non-dimensional stress intensity factors of $K_i$ and $K_{ii}$ are denoted by the following expression:

$$\overline{K_i} = \frac{K_i}{\sigma \sqrt{A}} \quad , \quad \overline{K_{ii}} = \frac{K_{ii}}{\sigma \sqrt{A}} \qquad (2)$$

The effective stress intensity factor is defined as follows[4]:

$$\overline{K_{eff}} = \sqrt{(\overline{K_i})^2 + (\overline{K_{ii}})^2} \qquad (3)$$

The stress intensity factors obtained in this experimental work is summarized in Figs. 5 for crack depth and 6 for crack angle. After decreasing monotonically for deeper crack, Fig. 5 shows almost constant value of $\overline{K_i}$ for $A/B$ greater than 0.2,. For various crack depth, $\overline{K_i}$ 'S are maximum at $\phi = 0°$ and decrease monotonic for larger crack angle. $\overline{K_{ii}}$ 's also decrease and show almost same value in Fig. 6. In Fig. 7, the effective stress intensity factor is given and show the similar tendency to $\overline{K_i}$.

## References

[1] Matsumoto,E.,Fujiwara,H., Saito,A. and Ui,Y. "Stress intensity factors of finite strip with edge cracks under out-of-plane bending", Recent Advance In Experimental Mechanics,July 1994,Pp.171-175.

[2] Fujiwara,H., Matsumoto,E. and Saito,A."Stress intensity factors for stepped plates with corner cracks under in-plane bending load," ATEM '95,JSME-MMD, November 1995,pp.95-100.

[3] Sanford,R.J. and Dally,J.W."A general method for determining mixed-mode stress intensity factors from isochromatic fringe patterns,"Engineering Fracture Mechanics 11, 1979,pp.621-633.

[4] Zhang,P. and Burger,C.P."Transient thermal stress-intensity factors for short edge cracks with equal depth of crack tip,"Engineering Fracture Mechanics 24,4, 1986,pp.589-599.

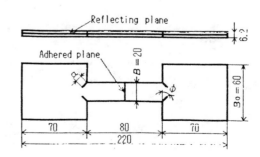

Fig. 1  Configuration of models

## Table 1  Parameters of model

| $\phi$ | 0°, | 15°, | 30°, | 45°, | 60° |
|---|---|---|---|---|---|
| $a/B$ | 0.05, | 0.10, | 0.15, | 0.20, | 0.25 |

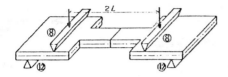

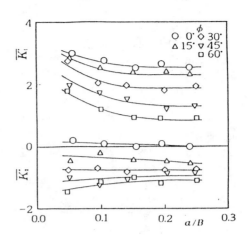

Fig. 5  Variation of stress intensity factors for $a/B$

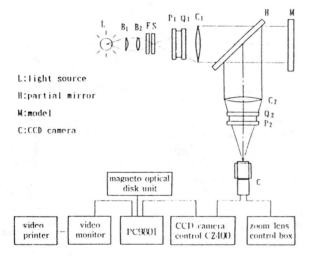

Fig. 2  Out-of-plane four points bending

L:light source
H:partial mirror
M:model
C:CCD camera

Fig. 3  Experimental setup and image storage system

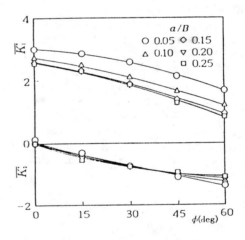

Fig. 6  Variation of effective stress intensity factor for $\phi$

Fig. 4  Isochromatic fringe pattern printed by video printer

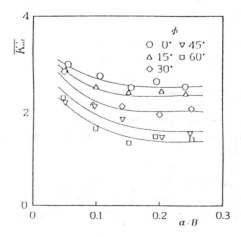

Fig. 7  Variation of effective stress intensity factor versus $a/B$

# Photoelastic Analysis of Panel-Stiffened Plates with Cracks

A.D. Nurse
Department of Mechanical Engineering
Loughborough University of Technology
LE11 3TU, U.K.

R.L. Burguete, E.A. Patterson
Department of Mechanical & Process Engineering
University of Sheffield, Mappin Street
S1 3JD, U.K.

Current techniques used to determine stress intensity factors (SIFs) of cracks in stiffened plates include analytical methods, the finite-element method, and photoelasticity [1-3]. To model stiffened plates involving some degree of complexity either experimentally or numerically appears to be a more straight-forward task than using analytical methods. In this paper, the use of transmission photoelasticity is demonstrated for the determination of stress intensity factors for a series of panel-stiffened plates in tension for cracks developed at a central hole.

All the experiments were performed on epoxy resin plates of thickness 3mm (Fig.1). The models comprise a centrally-panelled plate (Fig.1a), and an edge-panelled plate (Fig.1b). The stiffening members, made from the same sheet of epoxy resin of thickness 3mm, were attached to the both sides of the plates using epoxy-based adhesive. This is intended to model the attachment of stiffener panels by either bonding or by integral machining. The bonding does not obstruct the normal process of extracting the fringe order using the polariscope. An example of the isochromatic fringe pattern from a bonded section of the edge-panelled plate is shown in Fig.2. To load the specimens a metal clamp was bolted to each end of the plate to apply a tensile stress in the parent plate only. No load was applied directly to the stiffeners.

The cracks were produced artificially by introducing a short 'starter' crack at the hole and then incrementally extending the crack in a straight line to beyond the edge of the stiffener panels. At each increment the Mode I stress intensity factor $KI$ was determined for various values of the crack length $a$ using a procedure developed by the authors [3,4].

The validity of the photoelastic data is brought into question when the crack tip approaches the edge of a stiffener panel because it enters a region influenced by three-dimensional stress effects. However, an approach similar to that used in reflection photoelasticity in which birefringent coatings are attached to components, can be adopted to obtain suitable data. It is assumed that the stiffener panel behaves in a manner analogous to the coating in reflection photoelasticity. A region running parallel to the edge of the stiffener will be in a state of three-dimensional stress and must be ignored in the data collection process. The extent of this region being from the edge of the stiffener to a distance of about three times the thickness of the panels from the same edge. Data can still be collected, however, in the vicinity of the crack tip from either the unstiffened or stiffened section of the plate outside of this region.

As the panelled plates consist of two dissimilar thicknesses there are two possible values of the model fringe constant. The material fringe constant was determined using a tensile specimen made from the original epoxy resin sheet. To determine the two possible model constants for the panelled plates the material constant was divided by the parent plate thickness (~3mm) and the combined panel and plate thickness (~9mm) respectively. For the different sections of the panelled plates the fringe order can be determined using conventional approaches, however, the appropriate model fringe constant must be used.

To enable the effect of the stiffeners on the stress intensity factors to be assessed a comparison was made with a solution for the unstiffened hole-in-the-plate problem given by Ball [5]. The nominal applied stress $\sigma$ is assumed to be the applied load divided by the nominal area of the parent plate only. The results of normalised $KI/Ko$ (where $Ko = \sigma(\pi a)^{0.5}$) from the photoelastic analysis are plotted against normalised crack length $a/w$ (where $w$ is the total plate width) in Fig.3. For the centre-panelled plate the reduction in SIF is as much as two-thirds for a crack up to the edge of the panel. As the crack advances into the thinner plate section the SIF increases to be close to the solution of Ball. The reverse trend occurs for the edge-panelled plate.

In conclusion, the results of the normalised SIF for the panel-stiffened plate show a marked reduction in comparison with the unstiffened plate as expected. For the cases investigated it has been shown that this reduction is also affected by the position of the stiffening panels.

Acknowledgement

The authors are grateful to Mr. John Driver at the University of Sheffield for his careful and accurate preparation of the models used.

References

[1]     ROOKE, D.P., and D.J. CARTWRIGHT, Compendium of stress intensity factors, Ministry of Defence, HMSO, London, 1976.

[2]     RAMESH CHANDRA and K. GURUPRASAD, "Numerical estimation of stress intensity factors in patched cracked plates", *Engng. Fract. Mechs.*, **27**, pp559-569, 1987.

[3]     NURSE, A.D., S. GÜNGÖR and E.A. PATTERSON, "Experimental determination of stress intensity factors for cracks in thin plates with stiffeners", *J. Strain Analysis Engng. Design*, **13**(3), pp235-240, 1995.

[4]     NURSE, A.D., and E.A. PATTERSON, "Determination of predominantly Mode II stress intensity factors from isochromatic data", *Fatigue Fract. Engng. Mater. Struct.* **16**(12) pp1339-1354, 1993.

[5]     BALL, D.L., "The development of Mode I linear-elastic stress intensity factor solutions for cracks in mechanically fastened joints", *Engng. Fract. Mechs.* **27**(6), pp653-681, 1987.

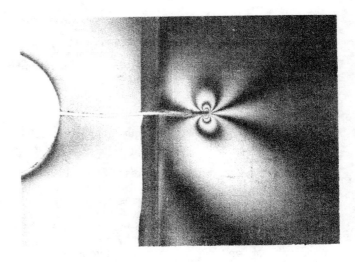

Figure 2:  Isochromatic fringe pattern around a crack tip in the panel-stiffened plate.

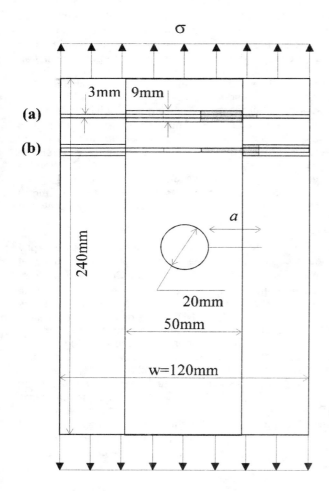

Figure 1: Geometry of panel-stiffened plates.

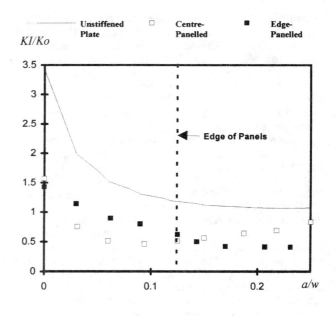

Figure 3:  Plot of normalised stress intensity factor (*KI/Ko*) versus normalised crack length (*a/w*).

# Digital Shearography for NDT of Reinforced Concrete

W. Steinchen,  L.X. Yang,  G. Kupfer
University of Kassel
Dept. of Mechanical Engineering
Laboratory of Photoelasticity, Holography and Shearography (SHS)
Mönchebergstr. 7,  34109 Kassel,  Germany

Nondestructive testing and strain analysis of reinforced concrete are vital parts in civil engineering. Shearography, as a tool of noncontacting whole-field strain analysis, has been used as a method of NDT in mechanical engineering during the last few years. This paper presents the digital shearography as well as its applications for NDT and strain measurement of reinforced concrete.

Shearography is an optical technique which permits full-field, noncontacting measurement of displacement derivatives [1]. Strains are functions of the displacement derivatives, thus shearography measures directly the strain informations and it is suited well for either NDT or strain analysis. Because shearography uses the so called "self-referencing" optical system, the requirement of the experimental environment is not strict and the vibration isolation used for holography is not required. The applications of phase shifting and digital techniques for shearography allows this optical measurement with [a] no vibration isolation, [b] filmless and real time observation and [c] automatic and quantitative evaluation of the testing results. Thus, the digital shearography permits the measuring and testing in the workshop and can generally meet the conditions of reinforced concrete used in construction sites.

*Real-time observation of the testing results:* The experimental setup of digital shearography for NDT is shown in Fig. 1. The tested object is illuminated by an expanded laser beam from the upper part of the measuring device (the laser beam on the lower part is adjusted additionally for the purpose to measure strain and for this case the shutter 6 is closed). The light reflected from the object surface is focussed on the image plane of an image shearing CCD-camera in which a Michelson interferometer is implemented in front of its lens so that a pair of laterally sheared images of the object is generated on the image plane of the CCD-camera by rotating the mirror 1 for a very small angle from the normal position. The two sheared images interfere with each other producing a speckle pattern. The intensity distribution of the speckle pattern is detected by the camera and is stored in one frame; we call it the reference frame. When the object is deformed, the intensity distribution of the speckle pattern is slightly altered and recorded by the camera again. A commercially available image processing board (IM-640/A/1/2/N from Matrox Company) allows to subtract the arriving image from this one in the reference frame in real time. The result of the subtraction operation between the two digitized images yields a fringe pattern, i.e. so called "digital shearogram", and it is therefore displayed on the monitor in real-time (at video rate). Fig. 2 shows the real-time observation of microcrack using digital shearography for a reinforced concrete beam loaded in the middle. The

microcracks were not observed when the preload is less than 5.5 kN (left). However, the first microcrack can be seen by a loading from 5.5 to 7.5 kN (middle). The cracks became more and more and grew bigger and bigger by increasing the load. It is obvious that the demonstration of microcracks by digital shearography is very simple and direct.

*Quantitative evaluation of the testing results:* The quantitative evaluation of the shearogram requires to determine the phase distribution of the speckle patterns before and after deformation. Thus, the phase shifting technique is used in this experimental setup. In general, three unknowns are existing in an interferogram; they are the average intensity $I_0$, the modulation of the interference term $\gamma$ and the phase distribution $\phi$. In order to calculate the phase distribution $\phi$, it is necessary to record three or four intensity distributions. For each recorded intensity an additional 90° phase (four measurements) for only one beam in the Michelson interferometer is shifted. The piezoelectric transducer actuated mirror 2 is used in Fig. 1 just for this purpose. Digitizing four intensity patterns provides four equations. Thus, the phase distribution $\phi$ can be calculated from the these recorded intensities [2]. By iterative processing, the phase distribution $\phi'$ after the deformation can be calculated analogously. Once these data are taken, the phase ditribution of the shearogram can be determined simply by subtracting $\phi$ from $\phi'$. Fig. 3 shows the 3D demonstration of the shearogram shown in Fig. 2 (right).

*Pure in-plane strain measurement:* Shearography measures directly strain information, but usually it includes both the in-plane strain, e.g. $\partial u/\partial x$, and the out-of-plane component, e.g. $\partial w/\partial x$. Therefore, the single beam shearographic interferometer is usually applied as an industrial tool only for NDT. For measuring the strains, the same but two mutual illuminating beams, i.e. the illuminating beams from mirrors 3 and 4 in Fig.1 resp., are introduced in this measuring device. The shearograms for each illumination direction are evaluated by applying the phase shifting technique. The result by subtracting the phase maps of the two shearograms yields a new fringe pattern depicting the pure in-plane strain [3]. Fig. 4 shows the shearographic measurement of local strain $\varepsilon_{xx}$ in a gravel position (in the middle) of a concrete lump and its quantitative evaluation in the x-direction.

As an industrial tool for NDT and strain measurement, digital shearography is rapidly gaining acceptance by industry. It is expected that a wide range of applications using this technique will be seen in the near future.

*Acknowledgement:* The authors gratefully acknowledge the support by DFG, Deutsche Forschungsgemeinschaft, FRG, project no. Ste 248/15-1.

*References:*

[1] *Hung, Y. Y.:* Shearography: A new optical Method for Strain Measurement and Nondestructive Testing. Opt. Eng. 21 (1982), pp. 391 - 395.

[2] Steinchen, W., Yang, L., Schuth, M., Kupfer, G.: Dehnungsmessung mit digitaler Shearografie. **tm** - Technisches Messen 62 (1995) 9, pp. 337 - 341.

[3] Yang, L., Steinchen, W., Schuth, M., Kupfer, G.: Precision measurement and nondestructive testing by means of digital phase shifting speckle pattern and speckle pattern shearing interferometry. Measurement 16 (1995), pp. 149-160.

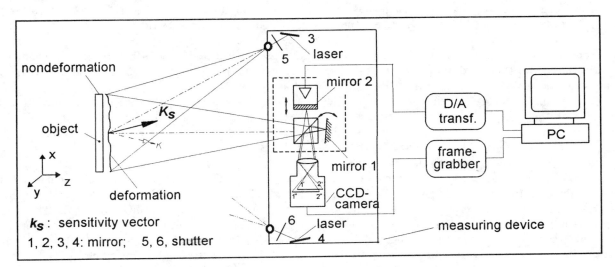

Fig. 1. Experimental setup of digital shearography for NDT and strain measurement

Fig. 2. Real-time observation of microcrack using digital shearography for a reinforced concrete beam loaded from 4 to 5.5 kN, from 5.5 to 7.5 kN and from 14 to 18 kN resp. (from left to right)

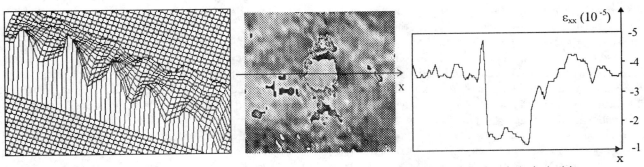

Fig. 3. Three-dimensional demonstration of the shearogram shown in Fig. 2 (right).

Fig. 4. Shearographic investigation of the local strain ($\varepsilon_{xx}$) in a gravel position of a compressive concrete lump; phase map of shearogram depicting the strain $\varepsilon_{xx}$ (left) and its quantitative evaluation in the x-direction (right)

# Experimental Investigation on the Dynamic Characteristics of Helical Gears

Chan Il Park
Dept. of Precision Mechanical Eng.
Kangnung National University
Kangnung, Korea, 210-702

Jang Moo Lee
Dept. of Mechanical Design and Production Eng.
Seoul National University
Seoul, Korea, 151-742

In the helical gears, the contact line changes as the meshing progresses and compliance along the contact line is not uniform. So the dynamic tooth load changes along the tooth trace. Non-ideal gear meshing due to compliance variation and tooth error results in the coupled torsional and bending vibration of gear system. The mesh force caused by vibration is transmitted to the housing through bearings and shafting. And the noise is propagated to the air by housing panel vibration. Therefore it is very informative to investigate the dynamic characteristics of helical gears with tooth error. Many researchers presented the results of study concerning each of dynamic tooth force, gear vibration and gear noise[1]. But experimental evaluation dealing with all the gear vibration and noise transmission procedure together was not published. This paper deals with the experimental investigation of dynamic tooth load, gear vibration, gear noise and bearing vibration caused by gear vibration.

For this experiment, a power absorbing test rig is specially designed. For gear noise measurement, the test rig is installed in a semi-anechoic chamber to reduce unwanted noise. The rig is powered by DC motor and the power is transmitted to a test gear through the toothed belt and pulley. The test gear is connected with the dynamometer through output shaft. DC dynamometer loads the test gear and output shaft. For lubrication, special lubrication setup is designed and oil is forced to feed during the test. The test rig layout is shown in Fig.1.

The test gear is machined by the grinding machine and is casehardened by carburizing. To check the effect of tooth lead error, we use the test gears with three kinds of tooth error-(1) driving gear with linear tip relief and driven gear with linear tip relief and linearly increasing lead error, (2) the above driving gear and driven gear with linear tip relief and linearly decreasing lead error, (3) the above driving gear and driven gear with linear tip relief and no lead error. The experiment is performed by varying rpm from 500 to 1400 and input torque from 19.6 N·m to 98 N·m. Operating tooth root strain, gear vibration, gear noise and bearing vibration are measured in this experiment.

The dynamic tooth load could be obtained by measuring the tooth root strain distribution. For tooth root strain measurement, a strain gage per tooth is attached to 5 teeth selected in the rotational direction by changing the position along the tooth trace and strain gages are attached near to the fillet of back face of meshing surface to avoid the interference between teeth. In this test we used the strain gage of $120\Omega$, gage length 0.3 mm. Strain gage location along the tooth trace is shown in Fig.2.

For gear vibration measurement, two aluminium blocks are attached to the driven gear and an accelerometer is bolted on the block as shown in Fig.3. The line of accelerometer is connected with a slip ring through the hole of shaft machined intentionally. The accelerometer signal is amplified in the pre-amplifier and noise of signal is removed in the low pass filter. The signal is combined with rotational component and radial component of gear vibration. Pure rotational vibration and radial vibration is calculated by the addition and subtraction of the signals and the signal is stored in the tape recorder. Also, an accelerometer is mounted on the outer ring of bearing supporting the test gear in order to measure the bearing vibration and the signal is recored in the tape recorder. And power spectrum of the signals is obtained by 2 channel FFT analyser.

For gear noise measurement, 12 mm microphone is mounted at a distance of 0.3 m above the test gear and sound pressure level is measured at each operating condition. And the narrowband signal analysis is performed by 2 channel signal analyser.

Through this study, root strain distribution is investigated under varying rpm and torque. A relation between gear vibration and bearing vibration is discussed and the characteristics of rotational gear vibration and radial gear vibration are discussed in frequency domain. Also, a relation between gear vibration and sound pressure level is discussed.

References:
1. Townsend, D.T., Ed., Dudley's Gear Handbook, 2nd ed., McGraw-Hill, New York, 1992.

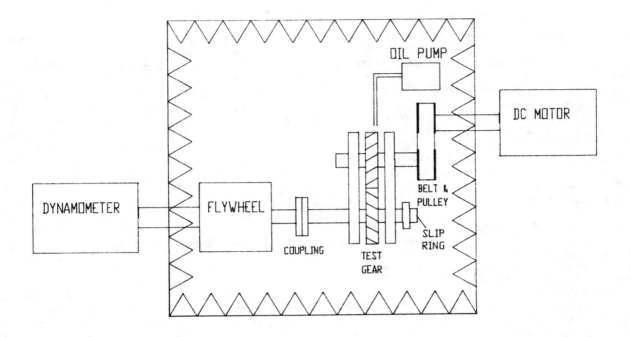

Fig.1 Test rig layout

| | mm |
|---|---|
| NO 1 | 1 5 |
| NO 2 | 5 25 |
| NO 3 | 9 |
| NO 4 | 12 75 |
| NO 5 | 16 5 |

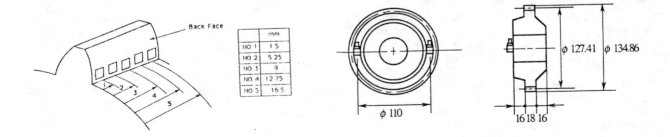

Fig.2 Strain gage location

Fig.3 Accelerometer location

# Piezoelectric Accelerometers Application on Sandwich Glasses

Giacomo KAJON (*) - Lucilla MONTELEONE (**) - Roberto STEINDLER (**)

(*)    Experimental Institute of Italian Railways; Piazza Ippolito Nievo 46; 00153 ROMA; Italia
(**)   Department of Mechanics and Aeronautics - Rome University  "La Sapienza"
       Via Eudossiana 18; 00184 ROMA; Italia

Windshield locomotive glasses have a sandwich structure: they are made by two tempered glass sheets with a policarbonate plate between them, and two layers of polyvinyl butyral (PVB) join the policarbonate plate to the glass sheets. The windshield glasses are continuosly stressed in various ambiental and termomechanic conditions: a stone or a bird that hit a locomotive running at a speed of about 300km/h can cause serious damages to the glasses (cracks, failures). Furthermore these accidents may happen at a temperature lower than 0°C and higer than 30-35°C. Because of their heavy work conditions, the glasses must be severely tested in dynamic conditions before being accepted [1].

The application of piezoelectric accelerometers to the sandwich glasses during their dynamic acceptance tests, particularly when impulsive loads are applied to them, has been considered in this paper. Also the strain gage application has been studied in previous papers [2], [3] and important static and dynamic informations on the glasses behaviour (stress and strains of the sandwich structure and of its components) have come out from this application. The aim is now to measure displacements of some sandwich glasses and sandwich component samples; for this reason the piezoelectric accelerometers have been applied to these samples. The displacement values come from acceleration signals and they give further informations about the glass vibrations due to a shock, and about the vibration propagation and the vibration frequencies. Moreover, using the piezoelectric accelerometer, it is possible to determine also the beginning of failures in the examined glasses.

The applicability of the piezoelectric accelerometers to the sandwich glasses and to their components (tempered glasses and policarbonate plates) has been tested. The accelerometers have been applied to the above mentioned materials simply by means of apposite wax. To verify the agreement of the accelerometer outputs with the behaviour of the materials, first of all, accelerometers have been applied to tempered glasses and to policarbonate plates: these plates have been hit by a hammer with a piezoelectric transducer on, and the accelerometers have measured the delay with respect to the hit, i.e. they have made it possible to calculate the sound speed in the materials. So it has been possible to calculate also the Young modulus of the materials and to compare the values coming from bending tests and from the bibliography. The comparison has been satisfactory and a positive judgement about the piezoelectric accelerometer application to the sandwich glasses has come out.

Afterwards the dynamic tests have been made on a sandwich glass plate having dimentions of 300x300mm$^2$ and 20mm thickness (two 4mm thick temprate glass sheets and a 12mm thick policarbonate plate inside) and on plates of its components of the same size. During these tests the plates have been borne by a brass structure with two opposite edges clamped and the other two opposite edges free (fig.1). A rubbery gasket has been placed between the plate and the bearing structure, to avoid the direct contact among these two materials and to damp the eventual external vibrations. The impulsive load has been reproduced throwing a 50g steel ball against the plates in different points and from different heights. The piezoelectric accelerometer, with frequency response 50kHz (-3dB), has been placed at the center of the plate in all the tests, and it has been connected to a charge amplifier. The signal coming from the charge amplifier has been shown by a digital oscilloscope and then has been transferred to a personal computer.

The acceleration signal had to be transferred to the PC because the displacement signal has been obtained by the acceleration signal by means of a double numeric integration. The displacement signal given by the analogic integration of the charge amplifier was not considered reliable because the double analogic integration of the charge amplifier caused resonance problems in our frequency range [4].

Beginning with the sandwich glass plate, the displacement has been obtained from the acceleration signal, converting this signal from the time domain (fig.2) to its power spectrum in the frequency domain using the fast Fourier transform (fig.3). In the frequency domain it is also easier to study the glasses behaviour. As shown in fig.3 a continue component in the acceleration signal is immediatly recognized. This component is not due to a physic phenomenum, so it has been eliminated applying a numeric high pass filter to the acceleration signal in the frequency domain. After this filtering the numeric integration has been made directly in the frequency domain (fig.4). The inverse fast Fourier transform applied to the displacement power spectrum in the frequency domain, has given the displacement signal in the time domain as wanted (fig.5).

The displacement trend, given by the double digital integration, has been confirmed comparing it with the output coming from an LVDT transducer (carrier frequency: 10kHz). So again a positive judgement about the piezoelectric accelerometer application has come out.

The displacement signals coming out from the piezoelectric accelerometers applied to the tempered glass plate show a trend similar to the trend of the sandwich glass plate even if the damping is lower (fig.6), while the policarbonate plate displacement trend shows a different trend as it takes a longer time to extinguish the vibrations (fig.7). Furthmore the displacement values of the sandwich glass are greater than those of the tempered glass and lower than those of the policarbonate glass, according to the fact that the sandwich glass is a composit material, and it has an intermediate behaviour between its components.

The conclusion is that the piezoelectric accelerometers are appliable to the sandwich glasses during their acceptance tests; so it is possible to obtain interesting informations about the accelerations and displacements of the sandwich glasses and of its components.

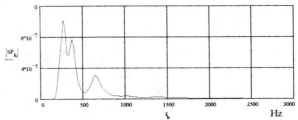

fig. 4 - Displacement power spectrum from fig. 3

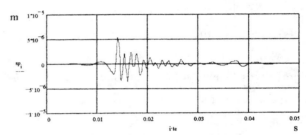

fig. 5 - Displacement trend of the sandwich glass obtained by Inverse Fast Fourier Transform (from fig. 4)

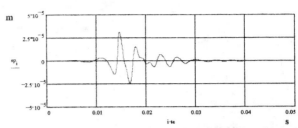

fig. 6 - Displacement trend of the tempered glass.
Throw height: 200mm
Impulsive load at the center of the plate

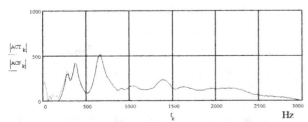

fig. 1 - The glass plate bearing structure with the sandwich glass and the piezoelectric accelerometer.

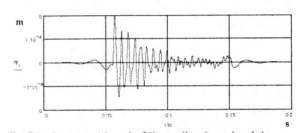

fig. 7 - Displacement trend of the policarbonate plate.
Throw height: 200mm
Impulsive load at the center of the plate

fig. 2 - Acceleration trend of the sandwich glass.
Throw height: 200mm
Impulsive load at the center of the plate

### References

[1] Specifica tecnica per la fornitura di vetri di sicurezza per rotabili ferroviari. Specifica tecnica F.S. S. MB/A. 03/ST 115.1 1988

[2] Kajon G., Steindler R.: "Strain gage behavior on sandwich glasses", VII International Congress on Experimental Mechanics - Las Vegas (U.S.A.) 8-11 June 1992, pp. 686-691.

[3] Kajon G., Steindler R.: "Strain gage behavior on sandwich glasses. Second part.",SEM Spring Conference, Dearborn (U.S.A.) 7-9 June 1993, pp. 72-80.

[4] Bruel & Kjaer: "Piezoelectric Accelerometers and Vibration Preampilfier" 1987.

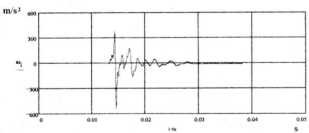

fig. 3 - Acceleration power spectrum (with and without filter) from fig. 2

# Material Damage Research Using

# FEM Modal Analysis and Experiment Data

Lin Lichuan   Chen Changsong
Central South University of Technology
Changsha Hunan 410083 P. R. C.

**Abstract**

Using analytical and experimental modal analysis and adopting statistical treatment method such as NPE. COD. and NSP, in this paper, the damage Location of steel plate is studied. The steel plate is divided a mesh of $4 \times 12$. To make the analytical modal analysis data suit with modal test data, the influence of mass of sensor, hole of plate and un-even of thickness are all considered. A defect of 1 mm hole may be identifed. Some significant conclusion are obtained.

## 1  Introduction

Recently, much attention has been focused on the problem of detecting, locating and quantifying damage in structure. Presently, there are some methods based on different theories.

Firstly, The method only use modal testing and Frequency-Response Function to locate and estimate damage, such as FRF [1] and mode shapes [2]. Secondly, methods adopt FEM model updating and error maxtrice to locate damage site and size [3~5]. Thirdly, methods adopt analytical model analysis, modal test and statistical treatment to locate damage, such as NPE. COD. and NSP [6] Pattern identification is used to deal with modal data, such as neural network [7].

In this paper, the analytical modal analysis and modal test are carried out. At the same time, methods of NPE. COD. and NSD are adopted to comprehensively deal with modal parameters. A real steel plate, which is sixty centimeters long, ten centimeters wide and its thickness is six millimeters. To get its analytical modal parameters, it is divided into a mesh of $12 \times 4$, and its shape is showed by Figure 1. To make the analytical data identify experiment data, The influence of mass of sensor, hole of plate and the uneven of thickness are considered. Some significant conclusions are derived. This method can locate 1 mm hole.

## 2  FEM Model analysis

In order to verify the application of the method based on NPE. COD and NSD [6] in material damage dection, the free-free steel plate serves as the basical model, (Figure 1).

To model the damage of material, some holes with different diameters are made. Which cause the decrease of mass and stiffness. Different diameters represent the degree of damage, and the locations of holes indicate the damage place. In this method, modal para meter only is Natural frequencies. After anlalyzed, the first seven natural frequencies are obtained. Three different diameters case are think about, which are 1. 0 mm, 2. 0mm, 2. 5mm. The damage Locations are presumed in four places, which are directed by their coordinates (1,1), (2,2), (5, 1), (6,2). Altogether, twelve case are thinked about. The analytical data are written in Table 1, whose model modes are showed in Figure 2.

## 3  Modal Test

A actual steel free-free plate is taken as the testing object. The holes are made in the element of (5,1) Firstly, a hole with the diameter of 1. 0mm is tested. Modal test adopted pulse excitation. Then the modal test of holes with diameters of 2. 0mm and 2. 5mm are carried out, on the other hand, a crack is modeled. Those data are showed in Table 2, whose mode shapes are showed in Figure 3.

## 4  Damage Detection and Evaluation

In order to Using above analytical natural frequencies to dectect the damage in element (5,1), a method based upon NPE. COD. and NSD. is developed. Its principle is if the modeling case is highly relative with the actual damage both in Location and in damage degree, their relation coefficient is every large (the maximum is 100). After inputing both analytical and experimental natural frequencies, every case's indexes are obtained by the method. These indexes'values are showed in table 3.

## 5  Corclusions

From above, some conclusions are obtained:
Firstly, using analytical modal analysis and modal test and adopting NPE. COD and NSD statistical methods can locate and quantify material damage. Presently, a defect of 1 mm hole can be identified. More little damage need study later, but this method

is in prospect.

Secordly, the effect of this method is confined by many factors, the main are analytical analysis and experiment accuracy and the choice of identifiable parameters. To improve the precision of damage identification, some improvement must be adopted. The first path is improving FEM technigne precision. The second one is to enhance the precision of the experiment equipments. The third one is to select parameter which is more sensitive to damage, such as dynamic stress, modal shapes and others. The fourth one is to adopt more suitable method of statistical treatment and patten identification

## References

[1]  Springer W. T. , Lawrence K. L. and Lawley T. J. "Damage Assessent Based on the structural Frequency-Response Function" Exp. Mech. Vol. 28 No. 1,1−15(MARCH 1988).

[2]  Idichandy V. G. and Ganapathy "Modal Parameters for structural Integrity Monitoring of Fixed Offshore Platforms" Exp. Mech. Vol. 30 No. 4,382−391 (DEC. 1990).

[3]  Jimin He "Sensitivity Analysis and Error Matrix Method Using Measured Frequecy Response Function (FRF) Data" Proceedings of the 11th IMAC 1079−1082(FEB. 1993).

[4]  Docbling S. W. , Hemey F. M. , Barlow, Petarson L. D. , Farat "Damage Detection in a Suspened Scale Model Truss Via Model Update" Proceedings of the 11th IMAC 1083−1094 (FEB. 1993).

[5]  Hemey F. M. and C. Farhat "Structura Damage Detection Via a Finite Element Model Updating Methodology" Modal Aualysis Vol. 10, No. 3 152−166 (July 1995).

[6]  Friswall M. I. , Penny J. E. T. and Wilson D. A. L. "Using Vibration Data and Statistical Measures to Locate Damage In Structures" Modal Analysis Vol. 9 No. 4 227 − 238 (Oct. 1994).

[7]  Ceravolo R. and Stefano De "Damage Location in Structures Through a Connectivistic Use of FEM Modal Analysis" Modal Analysis Vol. 10, No. 3 178−186 (July 1995).

# Static and Dynamic Testing of Tubular Sections in Bending Collapse: Experimental Method

J. Francois Corbeil, P.Eng., M.A.Sc.; Jean Arteau, P.Eng., Ph.D.; André Lan, P.Eng., M.Eng.
Safety Engineering Program
Institut de recherche en santé et en sécurité du travail du Québec (IRSST)
(Quebec Occupational Health and Safety Research Institute)
505 de Maisonneuve Blvd. West
Montreal, Quebec, Canada H3A 3C2

Ironworkers frequently use a fall protection system called a horizontal lifeline so that they can be arrested if an accidental fall from heights occurs. This type of device consists of two anchor posts that are secured to a structural steel beam, with a steel wire rope between them (see Figure 1a). Since this protective device has always been designed according to the principles of statics, the result has therefore been anchor posts that are rigid and very heavy [1].

The generalization of this protective technique requires a reduction in the weight of the anchor posts, among other things. Hence, a study was conducted to develop new anchors whose characteristics are: lightness, user-friendliness and safety for the worker. To obtain these characteristics, the anchor post capacity to absorb the energy of the worker's fall through plastic deformations was considered [2]. As a result, the anchor posts are now used not only to position the horizontal lifeline, but as an energy absorber as well (see Figure 1).

Since the force on an anchor post is similar to a bending load with a shear force, the energy of the fall is absorbed by a local plastic collapse mechanism forming near the embedded base of the post. To maximize this energy absorption while minimizing the weight of the anchors, steel or aluminum tubular sections were considered. To select these sections, the properties of a large number of tubular sections were needed in terms of behaviour, performance and reliability in absorbing the energy in large-displacement bending collapse loading. Unfortunately, such data are not available in the literature.

To get around this difficulty, a two-part experimental program was developed [2]. The first part consisted of quasi-static large-displacement bending tests on tubular sections. The second part dealt with full-scale dynamic tests on the protective device equipped with different tubular sections acting as deformable anchor posts. The experimental procedures developed in this study, despite being inspired by similar testing programs described in the literature [3 and 4 among others], are unique in that they have led to original results.

The purpose of the quasi-static large-displacement bending tests was to obtain the energy absorption properties of tubular sections, such as the maximum moment and the energy absorbed for a given bending rotation of the section. A quasi-static bending test is in fact a simplified but representative version of the forces acting on an anchor post of a horizontal lifeline, except for the loading rate. The test is performed as follows: with one section end embedded, a force is exerted at constant velocity on the other end until the sample has bent approximately 45° with respect to its initial position (see Figure 2). During this time, a data acquisition system measures the force and displacement. To do this, a load cell is placed in series with the chain of the electric hoist and a cable potentiometric position transducer records the lateral deflection of the section by sliding on a rail, with only the vertical component being measured. The measurements are then analyzed with a calculation procedure using MATLAB software to obtain, in the form of a graph, the bending moment and the energy absorbed in relation to the bending of the sections. The test is therefore simple and rather inexpensive to perform, considering the quality of the resulting information.

This type of test also evaluates the consequences of the following critical factors on the performance and reliability of the sections undergoing bending collapse: the loading temperature may cause brittle fractures at low temperature; the orientation of the load on the section; the variation in the material's mechanical properties; and the presence of residual stresses caused by a longitudinal weld in the steel sections.

In total, 462 tests were carried out on samples from 47 types of tubular sections of eight grades of commercially available steel and aluminum. The energy absorption properties obtained were used to determine the most interesting sections for the potential anchor posts of a horizontal lifeline.

Although very useful, these tests cannot represent loading similar in all respects to that found in the dynamic loading of a horizontal lifeline. Therefore, in the second part of the experimental program, dynamic tests on horizontal lifelines (see Figure 3) were performed, by using the most promising sections as deformable anchor posts and applying forces on them under conditions that are representative of those prevailing on construction sites. The two posts were anchored rigidly in the bases and a steel rope was stretched between them. Then, a drop mass attached by means of a lanyard to the device was raised a certain height before being released. Of the variables studied in this research, emphasis was on the following: testing temperature (-40 and +25°C); free fall height (1.2 and 2.4 m); and drop mass (100 and 200 kg).

The instrumentation in these tests consisted of many sensors: up to 10 position transducers, D1 to D10 (to evaluate the displacement of the top of the posts and the drop mass), as well as 2 load cells, FA and FM (to determine the forces generated on the mass and on the anchors). With a data acquisition system paired with an automated calculation procedure, not only can the energy absorption properties of the section undergoing dynamic loading be obtained, but also an energy assessment of the device (energy to be dissipated vs energy absorbed by deformation). As a result, this energy balance validated the experimental procedure as well as the concept of deformable anchors. Furthermore, to evaluate the loads and the magnitude of the deformations that can appear when a load is applied to the sections, tests were performed with large-deformation strain gages bonded to the sections.

In total, 146 dynamic tests were carried out on 24 types of tubular sections to check the resistance and structural integrity of the posts. Next, 3 of these sections were selected and 43 tests were carried out on them to establish the performance and reliability of these deformable anchors. At the end of this experimental process, two sections (one of aluminum, the other of steel) were chosen to act as energy absorbing anchor posts because they meet the performance, user-friendliness and reliability criteria desired.

In summary, the experimental program which was developed has produced results that are both exceptional and original, while meeting the goals of the research. In fact, not only did they lead to the development of two typical anchors for horizontal lifelines, but they also contributed to a better understanding of the large-deformation and bending collapse phenomena. Furthermore, with these tests, both standard sections and materials (whose uses had never included major plastic deformations and collapse) were characterized.

References:

[1] Arteau, J., Lan, A., Corbeil, J.F. "Use of Horizontal Lifelines in Structural Steel Erection", 1994 International Fall Protection Symposium, San Diego, 32 p., 1994.

[2] Corbeil, J.F. Deformable Anchors for a Horizontal Lifeline, thesis submitted in partial fulfilment of the requirements for the degree of M.A.Sc., Department of Mechanical Engineering, Ecole Polytechnique, Université de Montréal, Montreal, 341 p., 1995 (in French).

[3] Kecman, D. Bending Collapse of Rectangular Section Tubes in Relation to the Bus Roll Over Problem, thesis submitted in partial fulfilment of the requirements for the degree of Ph.D., School of Automotive Studies, Cranfield Institute of Technology, England, 235 p., 1979.

[4] Sulowski, A.C., Miura, N. Horizontal Lifelines, report 83-294-H, Ontario Hydro, 99 p., 1983.

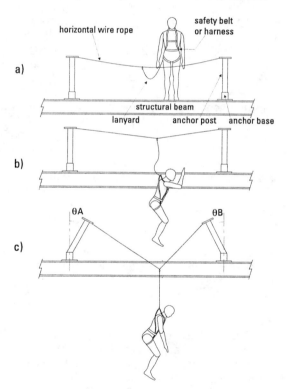

Figure 1: Components and operation of a horizontal lifeline protective device.
a) Device in the initial fall position.
b) Device at the instant when it starts to operate.
c) Device with deformed anchor posts once the fall has been arrested.

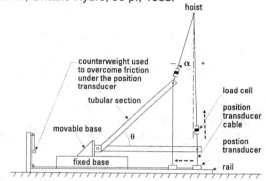

Figure 2: Test bench for quasi-static bending of tubular sections.

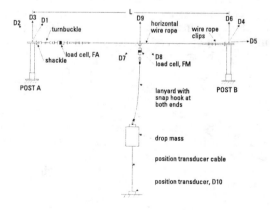

Figure 3: Test bench for a dynamically loaded horizontal lifeline equipped with deformable posts.

# Time dependent plasticity of refractory metals near room temperature

**B. Weiss and *R. Stickler
**Inst.of Solid State Physics and *Inst. of Physical Chemistry-Material Science
University of Vienna, Waehringerstr.42,1090 Vienna ,Austria

It is well known that bcc refractory metals and alloys exhibit a characteristic deformation behaviour at temperatures below 0.2 $T_m$. This includes a strong temperature and strain rate dependence of the flow stress and a strong impurity/dislocation interaction which is attributed to intrinsic properties of screw dislocations (1,2).

Most investigations were performed with single crystals at stresses near the macroscopic flow stress , only few investigations were carried out at stress levels below this flow stress. In this paper a short review on literature information, mainly determined for Fe, is given. We shall focus on the study of deformation processes of high melting point transition metals (Mo, Ta) in the stress regime between the elastic limit and the macroscopic flow stress and in the temperature range below 0.15 $T_m$.

Several test procedures (3) have been applied in this investigation: loading-unloading experiments to reveal minor changes in the stress-strain hysteresis loops, short-time creep tests (temperature step tests and stress step tests) to reveal critical strain values. All tests were carried out at temperatures between 15° C to 180° C. In addition, compression tests were performed to obtain information on stress relaxation. To collect data on the long-time behaviour at constant stress standard creep tests up to 150 h were carried out in the same stress and temperature range. Microstructural changes were followed up by a special SEM channeling contrast method.

A summary of results for recrystallized Mo is shown in Fig.1. In the stress-temperature diagram typical limits can be identified which separate areas of elastic and anelastic deformation , microplastic deformation and macroscopic flow. It could be shown that the macroscopic flow stress for a constant temperature is sensitively depending on the strain rate. This investigation revealed the existence of an intrinsic flow stress, corresponding to strain rates near $\varepsilon_{pl} < 10^{-7}$/sec. The microplastic behaviour, associated with a decreasing creep rate may be related to the mobility of edge dislocations. Above the intrinsic flow stress we observed typical creep curves with increasing creep rates. It may be speculated that in this stress range the plasticity is governed by an increasing contribution of the movement of screw dislocations.

The results show that for Mo the intrinsic flow stress falls considerably below the flow stress determined by conventional testing. This implies that macroscopic deformation near room temperature occurs below the conventionally determined yield stress, with strain values of several percent given a sufficient loading time.

References:

1. J.W. Christian, Some surprising features of the plastic deformation of body centred cubic metals and alloys, Met.Trans., Vol 14a, (1983), 1273
2. A. Seeger, Temperature and strain rate dependent plasticity of bcc metals, Zeitsch. f. Metallkunde, 72, (1981), 369
3. M. Fischer, D.L. Chen, B. Weiss and R. Stickler, Time and strain rate dependent plasticity of recrystallized Mo near room temperature, Proc. of the 1. Int. Conf. on Mechanics of Time Dependent Materials, Ljubljana, Ed. E. Emri and W.G. Knaus (1995), 108

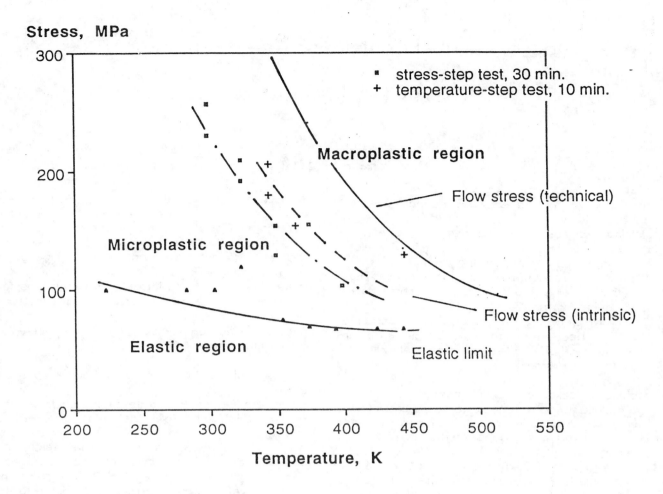

Fig.1   Compilation of test results for recrystallized Mo in a stress-temperature diagram.
Regions of microplasticity and macroscopic flow stress are indicated.

# Effect of the Fiber Contents on Creep Behavior of FRTP

S. Somiya, K.Igarashi, N. Iwamoto

KEIO University

3-14-1 Hiyoshi Kohoku

Yokohama 223 JAPAN

ABSTRACT ;

The fiber volume fraction dependence of creep behaviors have been studied on carbon fiber and stainless steel fiber reinforced thermoplastic resin with bending creep test. It is well known that the viscoelastic behavior of composites of the resin matrix mainly depends on viscoelasticity of the matrix resin [1-2]. But the effect of composed fibers on creep behavior of FRP have been discussed a little. In this report, the relationship between fiber volume fraction and creep behavior been researched and discussed the estimation method of creep compliance of material of arbitrary fiber volume fraction.

## Materials and Experimental method ;

The materials used were short carbon fiber reinforced thermoplastic polyimide resin(CFRTP) and short steel fiber reinforced a blend polymer of Polyphenylene ether and Polystyrene(MFRTP). The fiber volume fraction (weight fraction) of CFRTP are 0(0), 3.7(5), 6.7(10) and 15.6(20)% and for MFRTP they are 0.7(5), 1.5(10) and 2.4(15)%. The creep compliance value has been measured with three point bending test method in hot air oven.

## Master curves of creep compliance on CFRTP Polyimide of each fiber volume fraction's material

The creep compliance curve of CFRTP was calculated by the creep curves under some temperature conditions. After shifting these curves to the horizontal direction, a master curve was obtained from curves on each fiber volume fraction's material. Because these data showed a straight line on the graph for the relationship between shiftfactor and 1 / test temperature, it is recognized that the creep behavior depends on an Arrhenius type molecule movement. Fig. 1 shows the four master curves of 4 kinds of materials. The shape of four master curves look like the same pattern even though the value of creep compliance and the position on physical time axis are different.

## Master curves of creep compliance of MFRTP of PPE resin

Fig.2 shows the mater curves of creep behaviors of MFRTP on each fiber volume. This master curve of creep compliance was obtained by shifting creep compliance curves under some test temperature conditions. Fig.3 shows 3 master curves of specimens. The used shift factors to draw each master curve showed a straight line on an arrhenius type graph. From this result, MFRTP of each fiber content shows a linear viscoelastic behavior as an arrhenius type too. The shape of three master curves look like the same pattern even though the value of creep compliance and the position on physical time axis are different as same as the case of CFRTP.

## Discussion of effect of fiber volume fraction on master curve

From these two results of materials, it is confirmed that FRTP as CFRTP of Polyimide resin and MFRTP of Polyphenylene show an Arrhenius type as the same as the matrix resins. To discuss the relationship between some master curves of material of each fiber volume fractions of each FRTP, using two shift factors, which were modules shift factor to the horizontal direction and time shift factor to the vertical direction, we tried to make one total master curve for all materials even though the different fiber contents. After shifting all master curves to the standard curve, Fig.4 shows the total master curve of CFRTP and Fig.5 shows the total master curve of MFRTP.

## Conclusions;

The means of the shift factor for the vertical direction depends on the change of the Young's Modules which is directly depended on the amount of fibers and the means of the shift factor for the horizontal direction depends on the effect of the interception of the movement of molecule by the contained fibers.

## Reference;

[1] Somiya, S.,Iwamoto, N., "Effect of fiber content on creep behavior of CFRTP of thermoplastics polyimide resin," Proc. of second International Conf. Composite Engineering, 1995, pp.112-114.

[2] Somiya, S., ,"Creep behavior of a Carbon fiber reinforced thermoplastic polyimide resin" J. of Thermoplastic composite materials, Vol. 7 1994, pp.91-99.

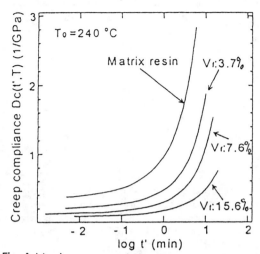

Fig. 1 Master curves of creep compliamce on polyimide resin and it's CFRTPs

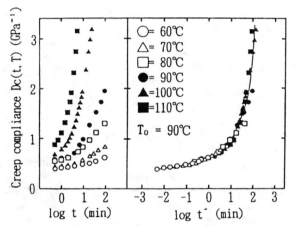

Fig. 2 Compliance curves and master curve on steel fiber reinforced Polyphenylene Ether resin(MFRTP) for the material of 5 % on weight parents.

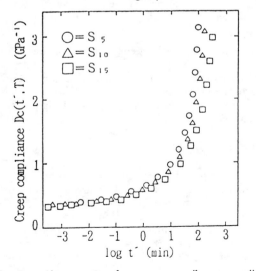

Fig. 3 master curves of creep compliance on three kinds of fiber volume fraction'smaterails of MFRTP

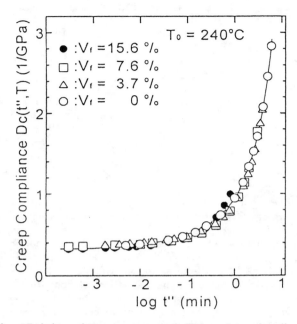

Fig. 4 Total master curve on each fiber volume fraction's material of CFRTP of Polyimide resin

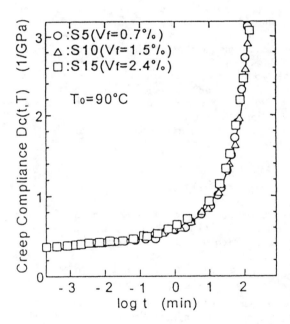

Fig. 5 Total master curve on each fiber volume fraction's material of steel fiber reinforced PPE resin

# Theoretical and Experimental Studies in the Mechanical Behavior of Solid Polymer Foams

Herbert Weber

Institut für Mechanische Verfahrenstechnik und Mechanik
University of Karlsruhe
D–76131 Karlsruhe
Germany

Solid polymer foams are extensively used in many fields of techniques. Examples are cushions in transportation of sensitive goods, bumpers of cars for shock absorption and sandwich structures. The analysis of the static and dynamic behavior of structures which consist completely or partially of solid polymer foam requires the knowledge of the multiaxial material behavior. The derivation of constitutive relations for this behavior starting from a microstructural model which considers the structure of the cells is extremely difficult. Most investigations of this kind are restricted to small deformations and only yield equations for the dependence of the Young's modulus of the foam on that of the matrix material and on microstructural parameters like cell geometry and volume fraction [1]. From uniaxial relaxation tests with closed and open cell foams in a large range of deformations it turns out that the phenomenological behavior of foams is nonlinear viscoelastic, compressible and in most cases homogeneous and isotropic. Therefore at least closed cell foams may be regarded as "simple materials" for which Cauchy's stress tensor $\mathbf{T}$ depends on the history of the deformation gradient $\mathbf{F}$ only, i.e. $\mathbf{T}$ is a functional of $\mathbf{F}$. A restriction on the form of this functional arises from the principle of objectivity. It can be shown that in the following form

$$\mathbf{T}(t) = \mathbf{R}(t)\,\mathbf{f}[\mathbf{G}(s)]_{s=-\infty}^{t}\,\mathbf{R}^{T}(t) \qquad (1)$$

the constitutive equation is objective for arbitrary functionals $\mathbf{f}$. In equation (1) $\mathbf{G}$ is Green's strain tensor, $\mathbf{R}$ represents the rotation tensor and $s$ characterizes times previous to the actual time $t$. The subscript $T$ denotes transposition. The dependence of $\mathbf{T}$, $\mathbf{G}$ and $\mathbf{R}$ from the spatial point $\boldsymbol{X}$ has been omitted for brevity.

For $\mathbf{f}$ we may choose the most general single–integral relation of the theory of nonlinear viscoelasticity with which eqn. (1) yields

$$\mathbf{T}(t) = \mathbf{R}(t) \int_{-\infty}^{t} [\phi_0 \mathbf{I} + \phi_1 \mathbf{G} + \phi_2 \mathbf{G}^2]\,ds\;\mathbf{R}^{T}(t). \qquad (2)$$

$\phi_i$, $i = 0, 1, 2$, are material functions which depend on the invariants of $\mathbf{G}$ and on $t - s$. By series expansion of the $\phi_i$ with respect to the invariants of $\mathbf{G}$ we can derive constitutive equations of arbitrary order of nonlinearity.

In an important field of applications the loading of foamed structures consists of a static preload which in many cases produces large deformations to which vibrations with small amplitudes are superimposed. The relevant loading history can be expressed by

$$\mathbf{G}(t) = \mathbf{G}_m + H(t)\bar{\mathbf{G}}_0 e^{i\omega t} \qquad (3)$$

$$\mathbf{R}(t) = \mathbf{R}_m + H(t)\bar{\mathbf{R}}_0 e^{i\omega t}. \qquad (4)$$

$\mathbf{G}_m$ and $\mathbf{R}_m$ are the time independent strain and rotation tensor in the totally relaxed static equilibrium state due to the preloading and $\bar{\mathbf{G}}_0$ and $\bar{\mathbf{R}}_0$ are complex amplitude tensors of the superimposed harmonic vibrational deformation. $H$ is the Heaviside step function and $\omega$ represents the circular frequency of the excitation. The additive decomposition of $\mathbf{G}$ and $\mathbf{R}$ according to (3) and (4) into a static and a dynamic part, respectively, implies that $\bar{\mathbf{G}}_0$ and $\bar{\mathbf{R}}_0$ are not independent from $\mathbf{G}_m$ and $\mathbf{R}_m$. Introduction of eqns. (3) and (4) into (2) results in an additive decomposition of $\mathbf{T}$ into a static part $\mathbf{T}_m$, a dynamic part $\bar{\mathbf{T}}_0 e^{i\omega t}$ and in additional terms which represent the effect of dynamic rigid body rotation. The complex stress amplitude tensor $\bar{\mathbf{T}}_0$ which is the quantity of interest in problems with harmonic excitation of a statically predeformed foam structure depends linearly on the strain amplitude tensor $\bar{\mathbf{G}}_0$ and on the prestrain $\mathbf{G}_m$. If we start from a second order representation of (2) the relation between $\bar{\mathbf{T}}_0$ and $\bar{\mathbf{G}}_0$ contains six complex dynamic moduli which can be determined in vibration tests [3].

In order to characterize the general material behavior of solid polymer foams we first perform a series of relaxation tests in tension and compression and construct from the results isochroneous stress–strain curves. With a closed cell PE–foam a good fit to these curves (Fig. 1) is performed by the equation

$$\sigma(t) = E_1^*(t)\epsilon_m + E_2^*(t)\epsilon_m^2 + E_3^*(t)\epsilon_m^3 \qquad (5)$$

where $\epsilon_m$ represents the applied constant linear or engineering strain and $E_i^*(t)$, $i = 1, 2, 3$, are quasi–relaxation moduli in tension/compression. This means that they are derived from a non perfect relaxation experiment in which the loading to the constant strain $\epsilon_m$ is not a step function but needs some time $t_b$. If we assume that the relaxation moduli $E_i(t)$, $i = 1, 2, 3$, for ideal relaxation tests may be represented by a Prony–series expansion

$$E_i(t) = a_{i0} + \sum_{j=1}^{n} a_{ij} e^{\lambda_{ij} t} \qquad (6)$$

then the quasi–moduli $E_i^*(t)$, $i = 1, 2, 3$, can also be represented by Prony–series analogous to (6) with coefficients $a_{ij}^*$ and exponents $\lambda_{ij}^*$. Between the coefficients and exponents of (6) and (7) the following relations excist [4]

$$a_{i0} = a_{i0}^* \quad \text{and} \quad \lambda_{ij} = \lambda_{ij}^* \qquad (7)$$

$$a_{ij} = a_{ij}^* \frac{\lambda_{ij}^i t_b^i}{i} \left\{ e^{\lambda_{ij} t_b} \left[ (\lambda_{ij} t_b)^{i-1} - (i-1)(\lambda_{ij} t_b)^{i-2} + - \cdots \right. \right.$$
$$\left. \left. + (-1)^{i-1}(i-1)! \right] + (-1)^i (i-1)! \right\}^{-1} \qquad (8)$$

With (8) and (9) the correct moduli $E_i$ follow from (6) (Fig. 2) and eqn. (5) can be written with $E_i$ instead of $E_i^*$. The nonlinear approximation problem is solved by a procedure which is described in [4]. A theory to the third order in linear strain $\epsilon_m$ requires the expansion of (2) to the third order in **G** by series expansion of the functions $\phi_i$. Such a constitutive equation contains 12 material functions which must be determined by suitable experiments. The relaxation tests in uniaxial tension or compression are not sufficient to determine all material functions. An additional type of test is relaxation in simple shear which can be realized by torsion of cylindrical specimens. The measured torque $M_t(t)$ and axial force $F_a(t)$ follow from the component equations of the constituitive equation by integration over the specimen's cross section. They depend on the rotation angle $\Phi_m$ by

$$M_t(t) = G_{p1}^*(t)\Phi_m + G_{p2}^*(t)\Phi_m^3 \qquad (9)$$
$$F_a(t) = A_p^*(t)\Phi_m^2 \qquad (10)$$

Here $G_{p1}^*$, $G_{p2}^*$ are relaxation functions which depend on the shear relaxation moduli and the geometry of the specimens. $A_p^*(t)$ is a relaxation function which is also geometry dependent. Both, $G_{p1}^*$, $G_{p2}^*$ and $A_p^*$ must be corrected for exact relaxation and then can be approximated by Prony series in a procedure similar to that described for the moduli $E_i$ (Fig. 3). Though the described experiments are very simple from the theoretical point of view their correct realization and evaluation pose some problems. The specimens are bonded to end plates at their faces which prevents lateral deformation in these parts of the specimens. Therefore in tension/compression the longitudinal strain is not constant. We also need information on the Poisson's ratio of the material under investigation. With an optical 3-D displacement measuring system consisting of a fringe projection method for the out of plane components and a digital white light speckle correlation method for the in-plane components [5] all data for correct evaluation of these experiments are provided. In the torsion experiments much emphasis must be given to the simultaneous measurement of torque and of the one order of magnitude smaller axial force. A special transducer has been developed which yield results of sufficient accuracy [4].

The moduli $E_1$, $E_2$, $E_3$, $G_{p1}$, $G_{p2}$ and $A_p$ which follow from experiment and depend on the material functions together with additional relations between these functions exclusively from theory are not sufficient for complete material characterization in the case of a third order theory. Therefore we performed pure bulk tests in addition to the previously explained experiments.

**References:** [1] Hilyard, N. C. (ed.), "Mechanics of Cellular Plastics", Macmillan, New York 1982; [2] Lockett, F. J., "Nonlinear Viscoelastic Solids", Academic Press, London 1972; [3] Weber, H., "Characterization of Nonlinear Viscoelastic Materials for a Special Class of Loading Histories", in Zyczkowksi, M. (ed.), "Creep in Structures", IUTAM Symposium Cracow/ Poland 1990, Springer–Verlag, Berlin 1991, 203 — 208; [4] Thole, J., "Investigation of the Relaxation Behavior of Soft Polymer Foams (in German)", Diplomarbeit, Institut für Mechanische Verfahrenstechnik und Mechanik, University of Karlsruhe 1995; [5] Wolf, Th., Gutmann, B., Weber, H., "Fuzzy Logic Controlled Optical Measurement of Large Polymer Foam Deformations", in: Emri, I., Knauss, W. (eds.), "Mechanics of Time Dependent Materials", Proc. 1st. Int. Conf., Ljubljana 1995, SEM 1995, 224 — 229

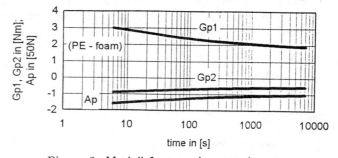

Figure 1: Stress–strain dependence

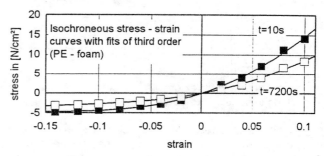

Figure 2: Moduli from tension/compression experiments

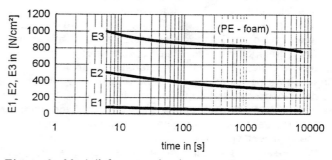

Figure 3: Moduli from torsion experiments

# Transient Behavior from Stable-to-Unstable Crack Growth in a Viscoelastic Wide Strip

Kazuo OGAWA*, Akihiro MISAWA** and Masahisa TAKASHI*
*Dept. of Mech. Eng., Aoyama Gakuin University
6-16-1, Chitosedai, Setagaya-ku, Tokyo, 157 JAPAN
**Dept. of Mech. Eng., Kanagawa Institute of Technology
1030,Shimoogino, Atugi-shi, Kanagawa, 243-02 JAPAN

The crack growth behavior as well as the mechanical properties of polymer such as epoxy resin shows, in general, remarkable dependence on time and temperature. In previous papers[1] by the authors, slow and stable crack growth behavior was carefully observed using a wide strip specimen with a long (semi-infinite) crack parallel to top and bottom grips, under a constant rate of displacement and several temperatures above the glassy temperature Tg of the material. As the results, the possiblity of time and temperature independent crack growth resistance was already discussed standing on precise and reproducible crack growth curves and an extended J-integral[2][3] for a linearly viscoelastic.

In this study, the authors will discuss on crack growth behavior below the glassy temperature Tg in a viscoelastic epoxy strip. Below the glassy temperature Tg, not only stable but unstable crack growth of a single main crack and branching to multicracks occur.

Fig.1 shows fracture surface obtained by different temperature conditions. Above the glassy temperature Tg, fracture surface is covered as a whole with fine stream line mark depending on experimental conditions of strain rate and temperature. The characteristic mark is observed, however, as shown in Fig.1 at lower temperature than glassy temperature Tg. This type of characteristic mark appears when crack changes its speed of extension from stable to unstable (rapid). The characteristic parabolic mark, on which we pay attention to, shows remarkable temperature dependence in spite of the condition below the glassy temperature Tg. The shape and location of the parabolic mark on fracture surface gives us important information on the transient behavior of crack growth. The features of fracture surface were investigated measuring several items as shown in Fig.2. In the figure, I is the very smooth initial crack made carefully, and II the stable and III the unstable crack growth region. L1 and L2 are the lengths of stable and unstable crack length, respectively. L1 decreases with decrease of temperature, while L2 increases. Also, it will be noteworthy that the feature of this parabolic mark are remarkably dependent on temperature.

Several aspects of transient behaviors changing from stable to unstable and/or braching crack growth revealed the evidences as follows;
1] Temperature and time dependent transient process exists at the stage from stable to unstable crack growth.
2] Crack length increment during stable growth becomes shorter with decrease of temperature and increase of strain rate.
3] On the other hand, the increment during transient process increases with decrease of temperature and increase of strain rate.
4] Length of unstable single crack growth varies with temperature and strain rate to a branching of crack.

On the other hand, careful observation of fracture surface produced in the transient process from stable to unstable crack growth gives several important clues for better understanding of fracture mechanism of the type of material. The micro-structure of amorphous polymer like epoxy resin consists of 3D crosslinks and entanglements of long molecular chain. The fracture surface configuration shows remarkable dependence on time and temperature. Quantitative evaluation of the characteristics feature was performed by use of a laser microscope and a computer-aided configuration analysis based on the image processing technique.

Then, some possibly and clue for the clarification of fracture mechanism in this kind of material are suggested discussing the relationship between crack growth behavior and the configuration of the characteristic feature on fracture surface.

## ACKNOWLEDGEMENTS

The authors appreciate a partial financial supports of the Center for Science and Engineering Research, Research Institute of Aoyama Gakuin University.

## REFERENCES

[1] Ogawa, K., A. Misawa, M. Takashi and T. Kunio. "Evaluation of crack growth resistance and fracture surface characteristics in several in epoxy resins" Proc. 6th Int. cof. Vol. 4 pp105-110, 1991.
[2] Rice, J. R. "A path independent integral and the approximate analysis of strain concentration by notches and cracks" J. App. Mech., 35, pp379-386, 1968.
[3] Ogawa, K. and M. Takashi. "The quantitative evaluation of fracture surface roughness and crack propagation resistance in epoxy resin" Trans. JSME. Ser. A, 56, pp1133-1139, 1990.

**(a) T = 393K**

**(b) T = 363K**

**Fig.1 A Typical Examples of Fracture Surface**

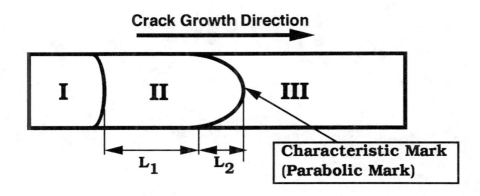

**Crack Growth Direction**

I     **Initial Crack**    II    **Stable Crack Growth**
III    **Unstable Crack Growth**

**Fig.2 Schematic Diagram of Fracture Surface**

# Effects of Fluids on Polymeric Composites
## A Review

Y. J. Weitsman

The University of Tennessee
and Oak Ridge National Laboratory

ABSTRACT

The presentation will focus on sorption processes of fluids by polymeric composites. These processes exhibit various kinds of departures from classical Fickian predictions. Some of these departures can be attributed to the time-dependent behavior of the polymer and are not necessarily associated with irreversible damage. Other departures are much more pronounced and are correlated with permanent loss of material integrity.

Effects of fluids on the mechanical performance of polymeric composites will be reviewed, considering aspects of deformation, strength and fatigue life.

# Development and Characterization of Brittle-Matrix Model Composites

Roger D. Cordes
Research Assistant

Isaac M. Daniel
Professor

Robert R. McCormick School of Engineering and Applied Science
Northwestern University
Evanston, IL 60208

The study of brittle matrix composites is of interest because it includes the group of ceramic matrix composites. These composites are promising for high temperature applications due to their superior stiffness, strength, and fracture toughness over conventional glasses and ceramics. The behavior of these composite materials is intimately related to the deformation and failure mechanisms, such as matrix cracking and fiber debonding. The properties of the constituents, i.e., matrix, fiber and interface or interphase, are related to these mechanisms and dictate their exact sequence, interactions, and magnitudes. The micro-mechanics of the stress transfer and fracture of brittle matrix composites have been studied experimentally and analytically by many investigators [1-3]. While the identification of the various failure mechanisms has been advanced along with the creation of numerous models, accurate prediction of the overall macroscopic behavior of the composites from the constituent and interfacial properties has not been achieved. The various analytical models proposed to date are deficient, incomplete, or lack experimental substantiation. Ultimately, it is desired to develop a realistic analytical model with a range of applicability verified by testing model materials. Model materials are advantageous because commercial brittle or ceramic materials are expensive and are not amenable to control and variation of constituent properties or geometric parameters such as fiber spacing.

The objective of this investigation was to study the effects of constituent properties and geometric parameters on the overall behavior of brittle matrix composites by developing and testing model composites. The model composite materials studied included a silicon carbide fiber/barium borosilicate glass system, a polyvinyl-alcohol fiber/epoxy system, and two fiber optic/epoxy systems. Single fiber tests were used to characterize the interfacial bonding and sliding characteristics for each system. The use of a transparent matrix allowed clear observation of the failure mechanisms, i.e., matrix cracking, fiber debonding, and fiber fractures, under longitudinal tensile loading.

The first system was fabricated by embedding silicon carbide fibers in a barium-borosilicate glass. The single and multiple fiber specimens were fabricated by sandwiching the fibers between pieces of glass. The sandwich was heated under slight pressure to the softening point of the glass for 75 minutes. The multiple fiber specimens that were tested under longitudinal tension displayed similar fracture processes as the common, commercial ceramic matrix composites. Elastic loading up to the proportional or elastic limit was followed by transverse matrix cracking developing and increasing up to a saturation level causing a pronounced softening or plateau in the stress-strain curve. Debonding was observable and progressive during the plateau region and upon further loading. The transverse strain, which was initially negative due to Poisson's effect, reversed during the formation of matrix cracks and the accompanying debonding.

The second system consisted of polyvinyl-alcohol fibers embedded in a brittle epoxy resin. It was found that interfacial properties and overall stress-strain behavior were sensitive to postcuring of the specimens using heat treatment, which increases the ultimate strain of the epoxy. In the as-cured specimens, the epoxy matrix was very brittle and high density matrix cracking followed by instant debonding was observed. In the postcured specimens, the matrix ultimate strain was higher and the resulting crack density in the composite decreased. Debonding initiation and growth were clearly observed for varying degrees of heat treatment and varying volume fractions from 10 percent to 48 percent.

The last two systems investigated consisted of glass fibers (optical fibers) coated with acrylate and polyimide coatings and embedded the same brittle epoxy matrix used for the polyvinyl-alcohol fibers. The polyimide coating produced a high interfacial strength resulting in high matrix crack density (see Figs. 1 and 2). The acrylate coating, with a lower interfacial strength, produced fewer cracks given similar volume fractions. For the high matrix crack density, the matrix cracking was rapid and total debonding accompanied it. For lower volume fractions, progressive debonding was observable. All experimental results, i.e., crack density, debonding, stress-strain behavior, were compared with analytical model predictions.

## References

[1] Lee, J.-W., and Daniel, I.M., "Deformation and Failure of Longitudinally Loaded Brittle-Matrix Composites," Composite Materials: Testing and Design (Tenth Volume), ASTM STP1120, 1992, pp. 204-221.
[2] Pryce, A.W., and Smith, P.A., "Behaviour of Unidirectional and Crossply Ceramic Matrix Composites under Quasi-Static Tensile Loading," J. of Mat. Sci., Vol. 27, 1992, pp. 2695-2704.
[3] Barsoum, M.W., Kangutkar, P., and Wang, A.S.D., "Matrix Crack Initiation in Ceramic Matrix Composites, Parts I and II," Comp. Sci. and Tech., Vol. 44, 1992, pp. 257-282.

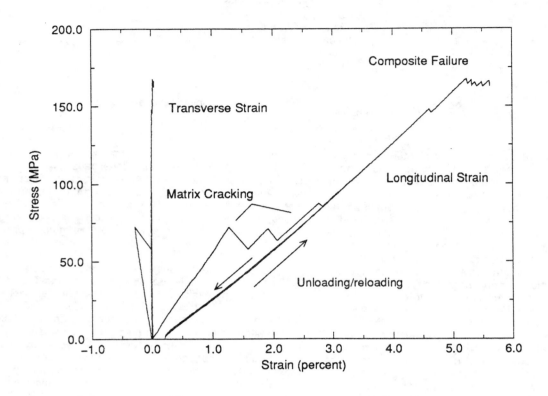

Fig. 1 The stress vs. strain response of a polyimide–coated
fiber optic fiber/epoxy composite (volume fraction=5.3%).

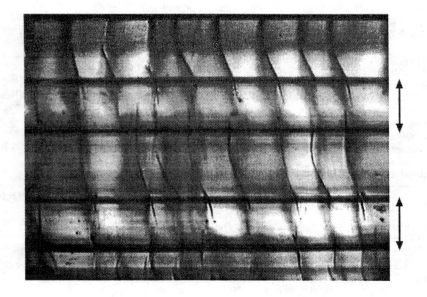

Fig. 2 Cracking in polyimide-coated fiber optic fiber/epoxy composite.
Arrows indicate location of fibers (fiber diameter is 245 microns).

# Whole-field investigation of end-constraint effects in off-axis tests of composites

Ezéchiel Alloba, Fabrice Pierron, Yves Surrel, Alain Vautrin
Centre Sciences des Matériaux et des Structures
Département Mécanique et Matériaux
École des Mines de Saint-Étienne
158, cours Fauriel
42023 SAINT-ÉTIENNE Cedex 2, FRANCE

Many shear test methods have been developed for composites among which the unidirectional off-axis tensile test has a particular place. This test is a classical one used to determine shear properties of unidirectional composites. However, end-constraint effects due to the clamping of the sample in the grips have prevented this test to be widely used. Indeed, though it is possible to correct shear modulus data [1], the shear strength cannot be obtained because of the stress concentrations near the tabs. A recent paper [2] has shown that the use of oblique tabs can lead to a homogeneous stress state, but only partial experimental validation was provided, using strain gauges. The above is also supported by recent results on the shear strength obtained from 10° off-axis tests on carbon/epoxy composites [3]. The purpose of the present paper is to take advantage of an optical whole-field strain measurement technique to investigate stress concentrations near the tabs in a 10° off-axis test on a carbon/epoxy unidirectional composite, when different types of end conditions are used.

The principle of the 10° off-axis tensile test [4] consists in applying uniaxial tension to a coupon of unidirectional composite such that the fibres make an angle with the specimen, as described in Fig.1. The use of oblique tabs enables displacements to be imposed on a theoretical line of iso- longitudinal displacements. According to [2], the angle $\phi$ between the isodisplacement line and the specimen axis is given by :

$$\text{Cotg } \phi = -\frac{S_{16}}{S_{11}} \qquad (1)$$

where $S_{ij}$ are the components of the stiffness tensor in the axes of the specimen. For our material, this angle was 24.2°.

The optical method used in this study is a grid method, where a pattern of crossed or unidirectional parallel black and white lines is marked onto the sample surface. This pattern acts as a spatial carrier. In-plane displacements modulate locally the phase of this pattern. It is possible with a CCD camera to evaluate precisely the phase of the pattern of lines. The zoom magnification is chosen so that the test grid is sampled at a frequency of three pixels by grid period. If two images are processed, one in an 'initial' state and the other in a 'final' state, the subtraction of the corresponding phase fields gives a phase proportional to the in-plane displacements occurring during the test, where a phase variation of $2\pi$ corresponds to a displacement equal to the grid pitch. With a unidirectional grid, the component of the displacement perpendicular to the grid lines is obtained. The use of a crossed network gives the two components of the in-plane displacement, and, by differentiation, the three components of strains and the local rotations. In this study, only unidirectional grids will be used.
A temporal phase shifting method is used that enables the measurement the local phases with an accuracy better than $2\pi/200$. This means that the displacement field is obtained

with an accuracy of 1/200 of the pitch. Temporal phase shifting is obtained by motion of the camera.

This technique has been used to investigate the end-constraint effects during off-axis testing of composite materials. The whole surface of a unidirectional T300/914 [10°]$_{16}$ carbon/epoxy sample has been covered with a 2 lines/mm unidirectional grid, providing measurement of the longitudinal displacements over a length between grips of 115 mm. The specimens were about 15 mm wide. The tests have been performed using a specially designed tensile testing fixture which enables better control of the boundary conditions as a guiding rail prevents the rotation of the grips. In order to view the area near the grips for oblique boundary conditions, oblique grips have been machined.
Different end conditions have been used in this study: straight grips with no end-tabs (type 1), straight grips with composite end-tabs (type 2) and oblique grips with no end-tabs (type 3).
Experiments have been done at very low strains. A first image is taken in the initial state, then a load of P= 1000 N (30 MPa) is applied. A final image is taken, and the differences between initial and final phase fields provide the displacement data. Strains are obtained by numerical differentiation of the displacements.

The displacement field obtained from specimen type (1) (Fig. 2a) shows isodisplacement lines which are vertical at the ends of the specimen and which progressively bend to become parallel at the centre. These conditions are the closest to the theoretical conditions of full clamping. It can easily be seen from this figure that the longitudinal strain will not be uniform. Indeed, if the longitudinal strain field obtained from this specimen is compared to that of a finite element model using full clamping boundary conditions (Figs. 3), then the strain concentrations near the gripping area clearly appear. Premature failure is to be expected there, as checked experimentally [3].

Now, for type (2) specimens, which are usually modelled as full clamped specimens, the longitudinal displacement field (Fig. 2b) is characterised by isodisplacement lines that are oblique in the whole field, more spaced at the specimen ends than in the centre. This result shows that some rotation of the specimen occurs in the grips. This is due both to the shear deformation of the composite tabs and to the shearing of the glue. The amount of rotation is quite important and explains why composite tabbing is better than aluminium tabbing, which will be closer to the full-clamped conditions. This has also been checked experimentally where composite tabbed specimens failed at higher stresses than aluminium tabbed ones [3].

As expected, the use of oblique boundary conditions results in a uniform longitudinal displacement field (Fig. 2c), with parallel and equidistant isodisplacement lines with an angle with respect to the longitudinal axis of the specimen equal to the tabs inclination. The resulting longitudinal strain field is then uniform and failure will occur at much higher stresses, as showed in [3]

In conclusion, it can be said that the optical method used in this paper is easy enough to set up (bonding of a grid onto the specimen and processing of two images), and very sensitive. A whole-field measurement provides a great amount of information and enables a systematic control of the testing conditions otherwise difficult to achieve.

It clearly appears from the results presented in this paper that the use of oblique end-tabs results in a uniform longitudinal displacement field, hence a uniform longitudinal strain field. This result has been claimed for a while within the composite community, but had up to now never been fully checked experimentally. Moreover, it was shown that the use of composite tabs results in quite an important amount of rotation of the specimen in the grips, thus reducing the strain and stress concentrations. Again, this result had been suspected by researchers but the present results settle that point.

References:

[1] Pindera, M.-J., Herakovich, C.T., "Shear Characterization of Unidirectional Composites with the Off-axis Tension Test", Experimental Mechanics, vol. 26, pp.103-112, 1986.
[2] Sun, C.T. and Chung I., "An Oblique End-tab Design for Testing Off-axis Composite Specimens", Composites, vol. 24, pp. 619-623, 1993.
[3] Pierron, F., Vautrin, A., "The 10° Off-axis Tensile Test: A Critical Approach", Accepted and to appear in Composites Science and Technology, 1996
[4] Chamis, C.C., Sinclair, J.H., "Ten-deg Off-axis Test for Shear Properties in Fiber Composites", Experimental Mechanics, vol. 17, pp. 339-346, 1977.
[5] Surrel, Y., Zhao, B., "Simultaneous u-v Displacement Field Measurement with a Phase Shifting Grid Method", Interferometry '94, 16-20 May 1994, Warsaw (Proceedings to appear in SPIE).

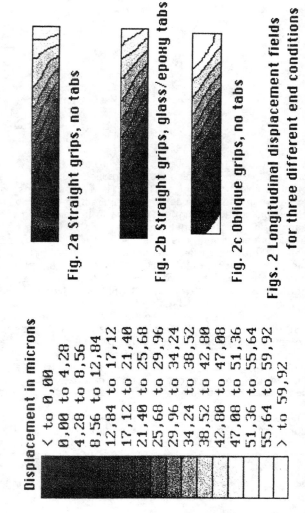

Fig. 2a Straight grips, no tabs

Fig. 2b Straight grips, glass/epoxy tabs

Fig. 2c Oblique grips, no tabs

Figs. 2 Longitudinal displacement fields for three different end conditions

**Displacement in microns**

| | |
|---|---|
| < to 0,00 | |
| 0,00 to 4,28 | |
| 4,28 to 8,56 | |
| 8,56 to 12,84 | |
| 12,84 to 17,12 | |
| 17,12 to 21,40 | |
| 21,40 to 25,68 | |
| 25,68 to 29,96 | |
| 29,96 to 34,24 | |
| 34,24 to 38,52 | |
| 38,52 to 42,80 | |
| 42,80 to 47,08 | |
| 47,08 to 51,36 | |
| 51,36 to 55,64 | |
| 55,64 to 59,92 | |
| > to 59,92 | |

Fig. 1 Schematic view of the off-axis tensile test

Fibres
U isodisplacement lines
φ
θ
P  P

**Strain in microstrains**

| | |
|---|---|
| < to 411 | |
| 411 to 468 | |
| 468 to 525 | |
| 525 to 582 | |
| 582 to 639 | |
| 639 to 696 | |
| 696 to 752 | |
| 752 to 809 | |
| 809 to 866 | |
| 866 to 923 | |
| 923 to 980 | |
| 980 to 1036 | |
| 1036 to 1093 | |
| 1093 to 1150 | |
| 1150 to 1207 | |
| > to 1207 | |

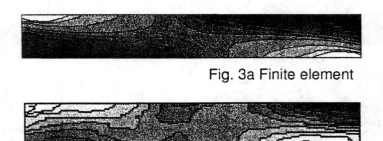

Fig. 3a Finite element

Fig. 3b Experimental

Figs. 3 Longitudinal strain obtained by finite element and experiment (grid method)

# The Effects of Residual Stress on the Physical Aging
# of a Thermoplastic Composite

David R. Veazie
Assistant Professor, Department of Engineering
Clark Atlanta University
Atlanta, GA  30314

## Introduction

Long term durability is an important issue in the selection and design of high temperature polymer matrix composites (PMC's) for structural applications in the next generation commercial aircraft. This high speed civilian transport for the post-2000 marketplace is expected to be a supersonic aircraft capable of Mach 2+ cruise while carrying 300 passengers. This sustained cruise will result in skin temperatures near 200°C, a high temperature environment for polymeric composites that are expected to exhibit time dependent, viscoelastic properties. In order to screen materials for selection in long term tests, accelerated test methods and associated analytical models must be developed which provide the means for characterizing the time dependent properties and predicting the long term behavior from short term test data. Due to the explicit time dependence of viscoelasticity, creep and creep recovery tests are a natural choice for studying the time dependent aging process.

When a polymer matrix is cooled to below its glass transition temperature, $T_g$, the material does not achieve instantaneous thermodynamic equilibrium. Instead the free volume, enthalpy and entropy evolve over time toward their hypothetical equilibrium values. Physical aging is the change in the mechanical and physical properties of the material during this time. Physical aging occurs when a polymer is subjected to a temperature bounded by $T_g$ above, and the temperature of the highest secondary transition below. Struik [1] showed that it was possible to isolate the physical aging process in polymers from other behaviors by performing isothermal creep compliance tests and using superposition techniques to establish the aging related material constants. Several experimental studies have illustrated that the matrix dominated composite properties of continuous fiber reinforced PMC's, namely the shear and transverse response, are affected by physical aging in a manner similar to pure polymers [2,3,4].

The thermoreversibility of the physical aging process allows the material to be rejuvenated by heating it 10°C to 40°C above $T_g$ and holding it there until a state of equilibrium free volume is reached. This rejuvenation process followed by quenching is required in short term testing to erase any prior physical aging history and ensure that all specimens start the test sequence in the same unaged condition.

Internal (residual) stresses, caused by the mismatch in the coefficients of thermal expansion between the fibers and the matrix with the large temperature differential, arise in certain PMC's following cool down from this stress-free rejuvenation temperature. It is suggested that the changes in the mechanical and physical properties (i.e., creep compliances) of PMC's over time, may not be totally attributed to the physical aging phenomenon. The relaxation of these thermal residual stresses may, at least in part, influence the viscoelastic properties found in short term tests. Very little information is available on this reduction in residual stress and its effects on the physical aging of high temperature PMC's.

This study is undertaken to qualitatively assess the importance of thermal residual stress relaxation on the short term (momentary) creep compliances used in predicting the long term behavior of the IM7/K3B high temperature composite. Experimental results from neat K3B resin, along with micromechanical analyses and the finite element method, is used to compare the transverse creep compliances ($S_{22}$) from momentary tests.

## Experimental Procedures and Equipment

The material system chosen for this study was a continuous carbon fiber reinforced thermoplastic polyimide fabricated by DuPont and designated IM7/K3B. The unaged $T_g$ in the composite as measured by Dynamic Mechanical Analyzer (DMA) $G''$ peak was 240°C. Change in the $T_g$ from the unaged condition over extended aging times was measured by industrial studies and found to remain within 3°C over 10,000 hours of isothermal aging at 170°C [3]. For this study, it was therefore assumed that chemical aging of the composite would not occur and the $T_g$ would remain constant over the duration of the tests.

Rectangular test specimens similar to those described in ASTM Specification D3039-76 measuring 20.32 cm. by 2.54 cm., and consisting of 12 plys of approximately 0.0135 cm. thickness, were cut from laminated panels. All of the creep tests were performed in convection ovens equipped with digital controllers. Thermal apparent strain was corrected for by using the compensating gage technique. A uniaxial constant load was applied through a dead-weight cantilever arm tester that reacted at a point outside the test chamber. Strain in the gage section was measured with two back-to-back high temperature foil strain gages applied in the center of the specimen. Creep strain was converted to compliance and measured as a function of test time and aging time. Specific procedures and techniques relating to testing and data reduction may be found in Veazie and Gates [4].

## Micromechanical Modeling of the Composite

In this study, a unidirectional composite was modeled and a square array packing of circular cross-section fibers was assumed. A schematic of the cross-section of the unidirectional fiber reinforced composite is shown Fig. 1a, and for a normal load applied in the $x_2$-direction, the composite is subjected to plane strain deformation. Furthermore, due to symmetry and the periodicity of fiber spacing, the state of stress and deformation in the composite can be completely defined by the stresses and strains in a quarter region of a unit cell as shown in Fig. 1b.

It can be easily verified that the proper boundary conditions on the quarter unit cell shown in Fig. 1b are given by

$$u_2(x_1,0)=0 \ , \quad \tau_{12}(x_1,0)=0 \ , \quad \text{for } 0 \le x_1 \le b \qquad (1.1a,b)$$

$$u_2(x_1,b)=d_2 \ , \quad \tau_{12}(x_1,b)=0 \ , \quad \text{for } 0 \le x_1 \le b \qquad (1.2a,b)$$

$$u_1(0,x_2)=0 \ , \quad \tau_{12}(0,x_2)=0 \ , \quad \text{for } 0 \le x_2 \le b \qquad (1.3a,b)$$

$$u_1(b,x_2)=d_1 \ , \quad \tau_{12}(b,x_2)=0 \ , \quad \text{for } 0 \le x_2 \le b \qquad (1.4a,b)$$

where $d_1$ and $d_2$ are constants that need to be determined from the solution procedure. Of course, the stresses and displacements in the quarter unit cell must satisfy the equilibrium, compatibility and the constitutive equations. The fibers are modeled as isotropic, linear elastic solids with properties of IM7, and a perfect fiber/matrix interface is assumed. Experimental data from momentary creep tests of neat K3B was used as the input for modeling the matrix. The creep compliance of the viscoelastic, physically aging matrix, $S(t)$, is described with a three parameter fit model,

$$S(t)=S_o e^{(t/\tau)^\beta} \qquad (2)$$

where $S_o$ is the initial compliance, $\beta$ is a curve shape parameter, $t$ is time, and $\tau$ is the relaxation time [4]. Through the use of the finite element method, the creep compliance of the composite is found in the absence of the thermal residual stresses.

## Results and Discussion

The quarter unit cell was subjected to uniform traction applied in the $x_2$-direction of $\sigma_o = 2.68$ MPa. Linear viscoelastic behavior was assumed at this applied stress level and at the 225°C aging temperature because of the sufficient testing performed to confirm the validity of Boltzman's superposition principle and proportionality [4]. The duration of each loaded (creep) segment was 1/10th the duration of the prior total aging time, in this case 2, 4, 10, 24, 48, 72, and 96 hours, and the finite element method was used to determine $S_{22}$. The resulting transverse creep compliance curves from the momentary tests are plotted (log-log) in Figure 2 along with the numerically determined compliance curves from the finite element analysis (no thermal residual stresses) for the different aging times. It is customary to employ small vertical (compliance) shifts (as compared to the horizontal shifts in terms of double-log scale plots) to reduce and present the data [3,4].

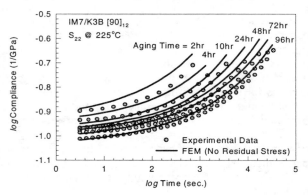

Figure 2. Log $S_{22}$ as a function of log time from momentary tests and the finite element method for the different aging times.

## Concluding Remarks

In the analysis presented here, the IM7/K3B composite shows evidence of a small, non-aging, stress relaxation. Attributing this phenomenon to thermal residual stresses might not be conclusive here, however assessing this effect on the time dependent properties and prediction of the long term behavior of PMC's may prove useful.

## Acknowledgments

The author gratefully acknowledges Dr. Thomas S. Gates of the NASA Langley Research Center for providing the materials used in this study.

## References

[1] Struik, L. C. E., Physical Aging in Amorphous Polymers and Other Materials, Elsevier Inc., New York, NY, (1978).

[2] Sullivan, J. L., "Creep and Physical Aging of Composites," Composite Science and Technology, 39, 207-232, (1990).

[3] Gates, T. S. and Feldman, M. "Time-Dependent Behavior of a Graphite/Thermoplastic Composite and the Effects of Stress and Physical Aging," Journal of Composites Technology & Research, 17, (1), 33-42, (1995).

[4] Veazie, D. R. and Gates, T. S., "Physical Aging Effects on the Compressive Linear Viscoelastic Creep of IM7/K3B Composite," NASA-TM 110224, December (1995).

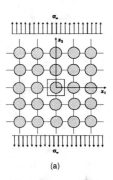
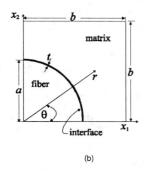

(a)                (b)

Figure 1. (a) Transverse cross-section of the composite and (b) the quarter unit cell.

# Parametric Study on the Sensing Region of a Driven PZT Actuator-Sensor

Jaime Esteban, Frederic Lalande, and Craig A. Rogers
Center for Intelligent Material Systems and Structures
Virginia Polytechnic Institute and State University
Blacksburg, Virginia 24061-0261

A health monitoring technique, which uses integrated piezoceramic (PZT) actuator-sensors to track the high frequency point impedance of a structure to identify damage, has been studied at the Center for Intelligent Material Systems and Structures [1-3]. It has been shown that the sensing area of the PZT actuator-sensor is localized to its near vicinity, and therefore making this technique very reliable to detect damage within a given region, without being affected by the loading or the boundary conditions. An extensive modeling effort has been carried out to understand this localization phenomena, which has been attributed to the high frequency content of the technique and the energy dissipation mechanisms contributing to the attenuation of the propagating wave induced by the PZT. These dissipation mechanisms are the inherited internal friction of the material and structural joint discontinuities.

A methodology has been derived for one dimensional structures with the use of a wave propagation approach based on continuum mechanics to model the high frequency vibrations of the structure; a complex modulus approach to approximate material damping and a nonlinear joint model for the structural joint dissipation. Analytical and experimental procedures has been jointly implemented in order to obtain the necessary parameters needed to model the attenuation of the vibration energy. In this paper, qualitative assessments on the PZT's low-power induced wave and its interaction with the structure and the various dissipative mechanisms will be addressed.

Therefore, the purpose of this paper is to apply the one dimensional model previously developed [4-7] to the study of the factors to consider when attaching the integrated PZT actuator-sensor to a real structure for health monitoring purposes. Factors that will be consider in this parametric study are related to the material of the structure (thickness, stiffness, density, internal damping), to the loading effect, to jointed connections (bolt mass, stiffness, number of joint discontinuities), and to the location of the PZT actuator-sensor on the structure. The effect of these factors on the interaction of the PZT actuator-sensor with the structure will be reproduced through measurements of the electrical impedance of the system and the electrical gain across structural discontinuities. The parametric study will help in the understanding of the induced wave propagation behavior in the structure and the range of its sensing region.

The motivation of this parametric study is to have a better understanding on "how to go about" when attaching PZT patches to a structure for health monitoring with the use of the impedance based NDE technique. Various real life scenarios have been reproduced and investigated to have a feeling of the PZT's induced wave interaction with critical areas to account for in a structure. Some of the results will be outlined in the following paragraphs; graphical plots of these results will be presented in the conference proceedings.

It has been found that impedance measurements would shift to the right and would have an increase in amplitude for stiffer materials, while most damped materials would tend to give more shallow signals. These factors should be taken into account when attaching PZT close to areas of different materials. For this reason, further investigation of material effect on the propagating wave was done with the use of interlayered structures, and it was observed that for interlayers softer than the transmitted material, the sandwiched area acts as an energy absorbent, bringing the amplitude of the response down, while the opposite effect is observed when a harder material is encrusted into the sandwiched region. An interesting conclusion was drawn from the analysis of cross-sectional discontinuities; it has been found that such discontinuities are a major source of reflections and that even for relatively small cross-sectional differences, the wave transmitted across the discontinuity is attenuated. Another blocking effect of the propagating wave was observed when attaching a concentrated mass in the structure. First, an analysis of end-mass loading showed that mass addition has a down shifting effect on the impedance measurements. Then, a concentrated mass was attached in order to block the propagation of the induced wave; a large attenuation of the propagating wave was observed, due to multiple reflections at the point of attachment.

An extensive analysis of multi-member junction followed: It has been observed that junctions at right angles tend to transmit more poorly the PZT's induced wave. Moreover, acute angle orientation of members with respect to the propagating wave tends to increase the amplitude of the impedance signal, while the opposite effect was observed for obtuse angles. Other interesting conclusions were drawn when attaching three or four members into a junction. A more realistic scenario was reproduced by introducing nonconservative bolted junctions. A nonlinear approximation of the dynamics of such joints was implemented to reproduced the wave interaction with dissipative members of the structure, other than the inherited material damping, an extensive analytical derivation of the nonlinear joint modeling is given in reference [4]. At a first glance, it was observed that the size of the bolt plays a great role in the attenuation of the propagating wave, while the bolt material was less crucial. On the other hand surface finishing and clamping force at the matting section are the most important factors to consider when evaluating the energy dissipated at the bolted joint. Triangular and square bolted configurations were treated to observe the attenuation in close-bolted structures. It was observed that, besides the wave reflections suffered at the angled junctions, great energy losses are sustained at the bolted connections. Moreover, the sensing range of the PZT's induced wave is greatly localized after one bolted joint, regardless of its size. These findings were corroborated with a multi-member bolted structure, in which a crack was simulated to observe impedance measurements for various bolted arrangements. It was concluded that the sensing region of the induced wave was mostly concentrated before the first strong bolted connection, and that no changes in impedance measurements are observe after a second strong bolted connection. Numerically, the amplitude of the response after the bolted joint is one order of magnitude less than before the bolt, and therefore localizing the induced wave to the proximity of the source. The effect of using a weaker bolt at the joint sensibly ameliorates these results, but still the energy concentration is reduced to the first bolted junction.

With the guidelines here presented, a more precise manner to go about when attaching PZT patches to structures for health monitoring implementation is made possible. Due to the qualitative information obtained about incipient damage with the use of the impedance based NDE technique, this study only pretend to give a feeling about the wave interaction with the monitored structure, other than real quantification of the energy dissipation and exact sensing range. Moreover, these sort of exact measurements become an impossible task due to the high frequency range of operation of this NDE technique (30-150 kHz), and very little additional information would be gain. Also, wave attenuation due to damping in the structure coming from energy dissipative mechanisms, are highly frequency dependent, and thereby the difficulty to track the impedance signal behavior.

Acknowledgment:

The authors would like to acknowledge the support of the National Science Foundation.

References:

[1]     Sun, F.P., Chaudhry, Z., Liang, C., and Rogers, C. A., "Truss Structure Integrity Identification Using PZT Actuator-Sensor," Proceedings ICIM'94, International Conference on Intelligent Materials, 5-8 June, 1994, Williamsburg, VA, pp. 1210-1222.

[2]     Rogers, C. A., and Lalande, F., "Solid-State Active Sensing for In-situ Health Monitoring," Society for Machinery Failure Prevention Technology Showcase, Mobile, AL, April 22-26, 1996; in press.

[3]     Chaudhry, Z., Joseph, T., Sun, F., and Rogers, C. A., "Local Health Monitoring of Aircraft via Piezoelectric Actuator/Sensor Patches," Paper N0. 2443-29 SPIE 1995 North American Conference on Smart Structures and Materials, San Diego, CA, 26 Feb.-3 Mar., 1995, in press.

[4]     Esteban, J., Lalande, F., Chaudhry, Z., and Rogers, C. A., "Modeling of Wave Propagation and Energy Dissipation in Joints," Proceedings 37th AIAA/ASME/ASCE/AHS/ASC Structures, Structural Dynamics, and Materials Conference, April 15-17, 1996, in press.

[5]     Esteban, J., Lalande, F., Chaudhry, Z., and Rogers, C. A., "Supporting Results on the Modeling of Wave Propagation and Energy Dissipation in Joints," to be published.

[6]     Esteban, J., Lalande, F., and Rogers C. A., "Theoretical Study of Wave Localization Due to Material Damping," SPIE's 1996 Symposium on Smart Structures and Materials, Feb. 26-29 1996, San Diego, CA, in press.

[7]     Esteban, J., Lalande, F., and Rogers C. A., "Study of Wave Localization Due to Material Damping: Results," to be published.

# A photoelastic study of contact between a cylinder and a half-plane

R L Burguete and E A Patterson
Department of Mechanical and Process Engineering
The University of Sheffield
Mappin Street
Sheffield S1 3JD
England

## Introduction

Photoelasticity was employed to study a cylinder in contact with a half-plane. Both bodies were modelled in epoxy resin. Three loading cases were examined, namely (i) a cylinder standing on its end and subject to a normal compressive load, i.e. as a circular punch; (ii) a cylinder lying on its side subject to a load normal to the plane; and (iii) a cylinder on its side subject to both normal and tangential loads. The cylinders and half-plane were stress-frozen with a known coefficient of friction. An automated system based on phase-stepping was used for the analyses. Stress separation was performed using the shear difference method.

In these tests the coefficient of static friction in epoxy resin during the stress freezing process was controlled by using a powder lubricant. This has enabled the authors to perform contact studies in which the effect of friction on the sub-surface stress field can be observed. In these experiments the coefficient of friction was set at two different values, namely 0.2 and 0.9.

For the cylinder on its side a complete solution of the stress distributions in the half plane is defined by equations 1 to 4 which are from Hills et al [1].

$$\frac{\sigma_x}{p_0} = y\left[2 - \frac{s}{\left(1+s^2\right)^{\frac{1}{2}}} - \frac{\left(1+s^2\right)^{\frac{1}{2}}}{s} - \frac{x^2 s^3}{\left(1+s^2\right)^{\frac{3}{2}}\left(s^4+y^2\right)}\right]$$
$$+ f\left\{\frac{xy^2 s}{\left(1+s^2\right)^{\frac{1}{2}}\left(s^4+y^2\right)} - 2x\left[1 - \frac{s}{\left(1+s^2\right)^{\frac{1}{2}}}\right]\right\} \quad\ldots\ldots\ldots(1)$$

$$\frac{\sigma_y}{p_0} = -\frac{y^3\left(1+s^2\right)^{\frac{1}{2}}}{s\left(s^4+y^2\right)} - f\left[\frac{xy^2 s}{\left(1+s^2\right)^{\frac{1}{2}}\left(s^4+y^2\right)}\right] \quad\ldots\ldots\ldots\ldots(2)$$

$$\frac{\tau_{xy}}{p_0} = \frac{-xy^2 s}{\left(1+s^2\right)^{\frac{1}{2}}\left(s^4+y^2\right)}$$
$$+ f\left\{y\left[2 - \frac{s}{\left(1+s^2\right)^{\frac{1}{2}}} - \frac{\left(1+s^2\right)^{\frac{1}{2}}}{s} - \frac{x^2 s^3}{\left(1+s^2\right)^{\frac{3}{2}}\left(s^4+y^2\right)}\right]\right\} \quad\ldots(3)$$

$$s^2 = \frac{1}{2}\left\{-\left(1-x^2-y^2\right) + \left[\left(1-x^2-y^2\right)^2 + 4y^2\right]^{\frac{1}{2}}\right\} \quad\ldots\ldots\ldots\ldots(4)$$

where x is defined here as x/a (where a is the semi-contact width), y is y/a and $p_0$ is the peak compressive stress on the elliptical contact stress distribution. The coefficient of friction is denoted by f and is set to zero for normal load only.

The analysis of an elastic punch on elastic half space will be compared to the only other available data for this type of contact which comes from a study by Olukoko et al [2] which was performed using both the Finite Element and the Boundary element methods.

## Methodology and Results

The work was carried out by modelling the components using an epoxy resin (MY750) for which the material properties are described in [3]. These were loaded as shown schematically in Fig. 1 using a system of weights. They were subjected to a thermal cycle which locked in the stresses for later analysis.

In these tests the loads applied were such as to induce very small strains in the models to ensure that the stress field remained elastic and also that the analysis was easier to perform by having low fringe gradients. After stress freezing a slice was cut from the models in a plane as shown in Fig. 1. The slices were placed in a monochromatic light (sodium light λ = 589.3 mm) dark field circular polariscope. Data was collected using an automated system as described by Carazo-Alvarez et al [4]. The method of phase stepping provides isochromatic fringe values and isoclinic angle data for the whole field analysed which then allows stress separation to be performed giving the cartesian stress components.

The results of the experiments are shown in Figs. 2(a) to 2(c). The stress distributions obtained show a close agreement with the theoretical data in all cases. There are some minor discrepancies away from the contact region which are due to errors arising from damage to the slices, and these are manifested as spurious peaks. In the cases where the stress distribution does not match the theoretical line away from the contact region, there is a discrepancy between the experimental model and the theory due to the fact that the theory assumes an infinite half plane which is clearly not the case for the models tested.

## Conclusions

Stress distributions for the tests were obtained and these confirm the theoretical stress distributions which were obtained by others. Controlled friction at the interface was also achieved and this was verified in these tests. These results represent the first quantitative data to be obtained from such an experiment in terms of cartesian components of stress. They also provide confirmation of the theories that had been verified previously using finite element analysis. The study demonstrates the enhanced potential of photoelasticity when it is used with modern image and signal processing techniques. The automated system was shown to work well with the complex stress fields which arise due to contact.

### References
[1]Hills D A, Nowell D and Sackfield A, Mechanics of elastic contacts, Butterworth-Heinemann, 1993
[2]Olukoko O A, Becker A A and Fenner R T, Three benchmark examples for frictional contact modelling using finite element and boundary element methods, J Strain Analysis, 28(4), pp. 293-301,1993
[3]Burguete R L and Patterson E A, Photo-mechanical properties of some birefringent polymers around their glass transition temperatures, Exptl Mech, in press, 1996
[4]Carazo-Alvarez J, Haake S J and Patterson E A, Completely automated photoelastic fringe analysis, Optics and Lasers in Engineering, 21, pp. 133-149, 1994

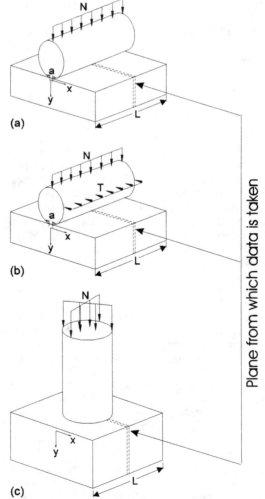

Fig. 1: Schematic diagram of model geometries and loading arrangement

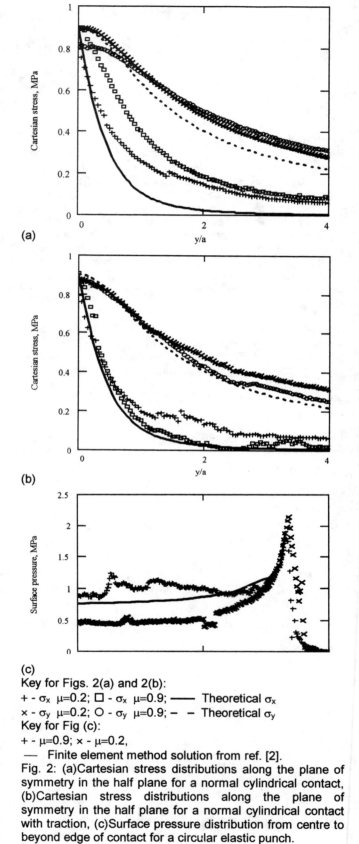

Key for Figs. 2(a) and 2(b):
+ - $\sigma_x$ $\mu=0.2$; □ - $\sigma_x$ $\mu=0.9$; —— Theoretical $\sigma_x$
× - $\sigma_y$ $\mu=0.2$; O - $\sigma_y$ $\mu=0.9$; – – Theoretical $\sigma_y$
Key for Fig (c):
+ - $\mu=0.9$; × - $\mu=0.2$,
—— Finite element method solution from ref. [2].
Fig. 2: (a)Cartesian stress distributions along the plane of symmetry in the half plane for a normal cylindrical contact, (b)Cartesian stress distributions along the plane of symmetry in the half plane for a normal cylindrical contact with traction, (c)Surface pressure distribution from centre to beyond edge of contact for a circular elastic punch.

# A Combined Method with Transmitted and Scattered Light for 3-D Photoelastic Stress Analysis

Koji EZAKI, Atsuki IKEDA, Shizuo MAWATARI, Masahisa TAKASHI

Dept. of Mech. Eng., Aoyama Gakuin University

6-16-1 Chitosedai, Setagaya-ku, Tokyo 157, JAPAN

Photoelasticity is, as well known, a basic and useful method for stress analysis in transparent model, with which the magnitude and the directions of secondary principal stresses in planes perpendicular to light path can be measured. These quantities could be evaluated by two different methods using transmitted or scattered light photoelastic technique. In the former method, however, 3-D photoelastic model has to be mechanically sliced successively to evaluate the rotation of principal birefringent axis along the light path. In the latter method, the scattered light do not have sufficient intensity of light to make good contrast enough to analyze the secondary principal stresses accurately. This paper aims to develop a nondestructive method for 3-D photoelastic stress analysis by combining experimental data from transmitted and scattered light photoelasticity.

According to the equivalence theorem[1][2] in photoelasticity, a Jones matrix of 3-D model can be expressed by the product of matrices of an equivalent retarder and an equivalent rotator. Thus, the intensity $I_t$ of the transmitted of light through a plane polariscope in which the angles of principal axes of polarizer and analyzer are $\alpha$ and $\beta$ to the $Ox$ axis, respectively, is expressed as follows.

$$I_t = \frac{A^2}{2}[1 + \cos 2(\alpha - \varphi)\cos 2\{\beta - (\varphi + \theta)\} + \sin 2(\alpha - \varphi)\sin 2\{\beta - (\varphi + \theta)\}\cos \delta] \qquad (1)$$

where $A$ is the amplitude of monochromatic incident light, $\varphi$ is the azimuth of the fast axis of the equivalent retarder, $\delta$ is the retardation of the equivalent retarder, $\theta$ is the characteristic angle of the equivalent rotator.
On the other hand, intensity of the scattered light through a 3-D model is given as follows, when the azimuth of the axis of an incident light is denoted as $\alpha$ and the observing direction to the $Ox$ axis is $\psi$, respectively,

$$I_s = kA^2[1 - \sin 2(\alpha - \varphi)\sin 2\{\psi - (\varphi + \theta)\} - \cos 2(\alpha - \varphi)\cos 2\{\psi - (\varphi + \theta)\}] \qquad (2)$$

where, $k$ is the light scattering coefficient.

The intensities $I_{t1}$ and $I_{t2}$ through a plane polariscope in the case that two sets of the angles of principal axes of polarizer and analyzer are given as $(\alpha_1, \beta_1)$ and $(\alpha_2, \beta_2)$, are obtained from eq(1). When taking $\alpha_2 = \alpha_1 + \pi/4$ and $\beta_2 = \beta_1 + \pi/4$ and selecting a particular combination of the angles between polarizer and analyzer, i.e., $\alpha_1 - \beta_1 = \pi/2$, $\alpha_1 - \beta_1 = \pi/4$, we have the following expression as,

$$\theta = Cos^{-1}\left(\pm\sqrt{\frac{1}{2}\left[1 + \frac{A^2 - (I_{t1} + I_{t2})}{\sqrt{\{A^2 - (I_{t1} + I_{t2})\}^2 + \{A^2 - (I'_{t1} + I'_{t2})\}^2}}\right]}\right) \qquad (3)$$

$$\delta = Cos^{-1}\left(1 - \frac{2}{A^2}\sqrt{(I_{t1} - I_{t2})^2 + (I'_{t1} - I'_{t2})^2}\right) + 2N\pi \quad (N = 1, 2, ...) \qquad (4)$$

$$\varphi = \frac{1}{2}\left[2\beta_1 - \theta + Cos^{-1}\left\{\pm\sqrt{\frac{1}{2}\left(1 - \frac{I_{t1} - I_{t2}}{\sqrt{(I_{t1} - I_{t2})^2 + (I'_{t1} - I'_{t2})^2}}\right)}\right\}\right] \qquad (5)$$

where, $I_{t1}, I_{t2}$ and $I'_{t1}, I'_{t2}$ are the intensity of the transmitted light in the case that $\alpha_1 - \beta_1 = \pi/2$ and $\alpha_1 - \beta_1 = \pi/4$, respectively. Here, eq.(3) gives us the fact that the characteristic angle $\theta$ of the equivalent rotator can be separated from the intensity of transmitted light through the 3-D block model in a plane polariscope. Eq.(4) represents the retardation of the equivalent retarder. Also, eq.(5) shows that the fast axis of the equivalent retarder can be separated. Thus, it follows that both the characteristic parameters of an equivalent retarder and an equivalent rotator can be determined only by use of the intensity data of transmitted light through the 3-D photoelastic model in a plane polariscope when adopting appropriate combinations of polarization angles.

Taking the variation of thickness of the model into account as shown in Fig.1, let us denote three Jone's matrices of 3-D blocks before and after grinding thin layer off, and of a ground-off layer itself as $J_{t+\Delta t}, J_t, J_{\Delta t}$, respectively. Here, since $J_{t+\Delta t}$ has to be equal to the product of $J_t$ and $J_{\Delta t}$, the characteristic parameters of the ground-off layer are obtained as follows.

$$\delta_{\Delta t} = Cos^{-1}\left(1 - \sqrt{\{Re(J_{\Delta t22}) - Re(J_{\Delta t11})\}^2 + \{Re(J_{\Delta t12}) + Re(J_{\Delta t21})\}^2}\right) + 2N\pi$$

$$(N = 1, 2, 3, ...) \qquad (6)$$

$$\theta_{\Delta t} = Cos^{-1}\left[\frac{Re(J_{\Delta t11}) + Re(J_{\Delta t22})}{2 - \sqrt{\{Re(J_{\Delta t22}) - Re(J_{\Delta t11})\}^2 + \{Re(J_{\Delta t12}) + Re(J_{\Delta t21})\}^2}}\right] \quad (7)$$

$$\varphi_{\Delta t} = \frac{1}{2}\left(Cos^{-1}\left[\frac{Re(J_{\Delta t22}) - Re(J_{\Delta t11})}{\sqrt{\{Re(J_{\Delta t22}) - Re(J_{\Delta t11})\}^2 + \{Re(J_{\Delta t12}) + Re(J_{\Delta t21})\}^2}}\right] - \theta_{\Delta t}\right) \quad (8)$$

Eq.(6) expresses the retardation, also eq.(7) and eq.(8) express the characteristic angles of the rotator and the birefringent axis of the ground-off layer, respectively. By repeating the procedure mentioned above, the magnitude and the direction of secondary principal stress in the ground-off layer perpendicular to the transmitted light direction can be determined.

In the case of the scattered light method, considering particular combinations of the azimuth of the axis of the incident light and the observing direction as $\alpha_2 = \alpha_1 + \pi/2$ and $\psi_2 = \psi_1 - \pi/2$, in addition to certain combinations of the angles between $\alpha_1$ and $\psi_1$, i.e., $\alpha_1 - \psi_1 = 0$ and $\alpha_1 - \psi_1 = \pi/2$, we have,

$$\delta = Cos^{-1}\left(\frac{\sqrt{I_{s3}^2 + I_{s4}^2}}{kA^2} - 1\right) \quad (9)$$

$$\theta = -\frac{1}{2}Tan^{-1}\frac{I_{s4}}{I_{s3}} \quad (10)$$

$$\varphi = \frac{1}{2}\left\{\alpha_1 - \theta - \frac{1}{2}Cos^{-1}\left(\frac{I_{s1} + I_{s2} - 2kA^2}{\sqrt{I_{s3}^2 + I_{s4}^2} - 2kA^2}\right)\right\} \quad (11)$$

As shown in the previous section on the transmitted light method, the three characteristic parameters are expressed in similar forms with the case of transmitted light, respectively.

A 3-D photoelastic block model adopted in this study is made of an araldite B-CT 200 epoxy-resin with a hardener HT903. After removing residual stresses at high temperature, the 3-D model is cut and polished in a 34mm cube. As shown in Fig.2, the model is loaded by a concentrated force 60 N at the center of top surface and supported by three points at the bottom, then stresses are frozen in usual manner in a temperature chamber of 120℃. After stress was frozen in a 3-D block model, scattered light photoelastic data were measured at first. And the three characteristic parameters along two different light paths were calculated by the Jones calculus discussed previously. In next, after grinding-off every 1mm thick thin layer, the stress frozen model was placed at an assigned location in the light path to realize the exact perpendicularly to the incident polarized light. For every step of grinding-off work,

a set of four pieces of fringe pattern through a plane polariscope was taken by a CCD camera as image data with 256 grey levels of brightness[3]. Then, the three characteristic parameters in a ground-off layer are successfully separated with the procedure mentioned before using two sets of four images obtained before and after every step of grinding-off work. Moreover, the secondary principal stresses and their directions are determined by computing the Jones matrices mentioned above.

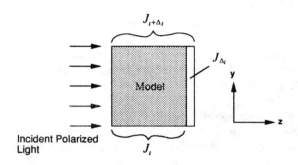

Fig.1 3-D Model before and after Grinding-off Thin Layer

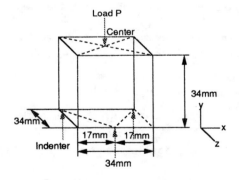

Fig.2 3-D Photoelastic Model and Loading

References:

[1] Theocaris, Gdoutos, Matrix Theory of Photoelasticity, Springer Series in Optical Sciences Volume 11, 1979, pp.132-183
[2] Aben, H.K. : Optical phenomena in photoelastic models by the rotation of principal axes.
Exp. Mech. 6, pp.13-22 (1966)
[3] Masahisa TAKASHI, Shizuo MAWATARI, Yoshiaki TOYODA, A New Computer-Aided System for Photoelastic Stress Analysis with Structure-Driven Type Image Processing, Applied Stress Analysis, pp.516-515 (1990)

# Photoelastic Analysis of Polycarbonate Loaded by Spherical Indentator Using Strain-Freezing Method

Akira Shimamoto[*1], Eisaku Umezaki[*2] and Susumu Takahashi[*3]

[*1] Saitama Institute of Technology
1690 Fusaiji, Okabe, Saitama 369-02, Japan
[*2] Nippon Institute of Technology
4-1 Gakuendai, Miyashiro, Saitama 345, Japan
[*3] Kanto Gakuin University
4834 Mutuura, Kanagawa, Yokohama 221, Japan

Hardness test is one of the basic material testings. There are several theoretical and experimental studies of the relation between the hardness and resistance to deformation because the test does not need a standardized specimen and is simple and speedy comparing with the other tests such as tension test. Polymers, ceramics and composite materials have difficulty in making a standardized specimen because they, which are generally used under severe conditions such as at lower and higher temperature, have too soft, hard or brittle property, or the amount of material necessary to make the specimens is not obtained adequately. Hence the method suitable for evaluating those material properties is not established. The hardness test is estimated to be effective for those materials with such properties or under the conditions judging from characteristics of this test. Furthermore, the test is used not only to evaluate the hardness of materials, but also to measure the fracture toughness of brittle materials such as ceramics, the strength of thin films and residual stresses. Now the test has a wide range of application.

This study investigates strain behavior in polycarbonate loaded by a spherical indentator using the strain-freezing method to establish a method of evaluating the material properties of polymers which have been widely used as machine parts and structural members because of a high elastic modulus and strength.

Square plates (65mm×65mm×3mm and 65mm×65mm×9mm) are cut from a strip of polycarbonate (Lexan 9030) available in the market. One to five plates stacked and fixed by bolts are used as specimens. This technique which uses stacked plates as a specimen is hereafter referred to as a plate-stacked technique. The plates are annealed to remove initial strain before the stacking. After strain freezing, a specimen is separated into plates. Photographs are taken of isochromatic fringes in a photoelastic equipment. The specimens are strain-frozen at $T$=155°C under dead loads of $P$=5,10,15,20 and 25N using a hardness tester as shown in Fig.1 put in a strain-freezing furnace. The total strain, $\varepsilon$, and principal-strain difference, $\varepsilon_1-\varepsilon_2$, are obtained by measuring fringe order, $N$, and the radius of fringe loop on a negative through a magnifying projector of 10-fold magnification. The Meyer hardness, $H_m$, is also obtained by measuring the diameter of a cavity on the negative through the projector. The diameters of a cavity and fringe loop are the average value of two measurements in the directions perpendicularly inspecting each other.

Fig. 2 shows the isochromatic fringes obtained under $P$=10N for specimens which is composed of one-plate 9mm thickness and three-plate 9mm thickness. The diameters of the fringe loops and the cavity obtained from the one-plate specimen almost equal those obtained

from the three-plate one. Fig. 3 shows the effect of the number of plate which composes a specimen on hardness. It is found that specimens of 6mm, 9mm and 12mm thickness are necessary for obtaining reliable hardness under $P$=10N, $P$=15N and 25N, and $P$=25N, respectively. These facts indicate that the plate-stacking technique, which does not need slicing of specimens, can be used to analyze plastic strain in specimens under spherical indentation loadings on the basis of the strain-freezing method.

Fig. 4 and 5 show the isochromatic fringes obtained under $P$=20N and the principal-strain difference, $\varepsilon_1-\varepsilon_2$, measured in square ABCD shown in Fig.5, respectively. Fig. 6 shows the principal-strain difference, $\varepsilon_1-\varepsilon_2$, along line ADE. From Fig.6, $\varepsilon_1-\varepsilon_2$ is maximum at the edge of the cavity made by the spherical indentator and decreases with increase of the length from the edge. Fig. 7 shows the relation between the isochromatic fringe order near the cavity, $N$, and the total strain, $\varepsilon$, and principal-strain difference, $\varepsilon_1-\varepsilon_2$. The relations between $N$ and $\varepsilon$, and $N$ and $\varepsilon_1-\varepsilon_2$ are proportional. The straight line between $N$ and $\varepsilon$ does not coincides with the origin. Fig. 8 shows the relation between hardness, $H_m$, and the total strain, $\varepsilon$, and principal strain, $\varepsilon_1-\varepsilon_2$. The relations between $H_m$ and $\varepsilon$, and $H_m$ and $\varepsilon_1-\varepsilon_2$ are proportional. The straight line between $H_m$ and $\varepsilon_1-\varepsilon_2$ does not coincides with the origin. However hardness $H_m$ is obtained by measuring $\varepsilon_1-\varepsilon_2$.

Conclusions reached are as follows.
(1) A plate-stacking technique simplifies the strain analysis based on the stress-freezing method because there is no necessity for slicing specimens
(2) The whole-field strain distribution under spherical-indentation loadings is obtained by the strain-freezing method.
(3) The proposed method is effective to analyze strain under spherical-indentation loadings.

References:
[1] Tabor, D., "The Hardness of Metals", (1951), Oxford, pp.67.
[2] Takahashi, S., Suetsugu, M. and Shimamoto, A., "A Basic Study of Plastic Strain Freezing by Photo-plastic Experiment", JSME International Jounal (in Japanese), 30-266(1987), pp.1237-1242.
[3] (ed.) Yoshizawa, T., "Hardness test method and its application"(in Japanese),(1967), Syokabo, Tokyo, pp.7-29.
[4] Murakami, Y. and Yuan, P., "Analysis of Brinell Hardness by Finite Element Method (2nd Report, Analysis of Elastic-Linear-Hardening Materials and Correlation of the Results with Actual Materials)", Trans. Japan. Soc. Mech. Eng.(in Japanese), 57-533(A) (1991), pp.162-169.
[5] Ishibashi, T. et al., "The Measuring Method about Flow Stress-

Strain Characteristics of Plastics Using the Indenting Hardness Test by a Spherical Indenter", Trans. Japan. Soc. Mech. Eng.(in Japanese), 54–501(A)(1988),pp.1158–1164.

[6] Shimamoto, A. and Takahashi, S., "Calibration of Materials for Photoelastoplasic Models", Exp. Mech., 30–2(1990),pp.114–119.

[7] Shimamoto, A. and Takahashi, S., "Experimental Studies on the Photo–Plastic Analysis of Indentation in the Plane Strain Field", Trans. Japan Soc. Mech. Eng.(in Japanese),54–498(A)(1988), pp.379–384.

[8] Nakamura, M. and Tozawa, Y.,"On Metal Flow by Indentation of the Indentor under Plane Strain Condition (Research on Hardness from the Viewpoint the Plasticity of Metal Ⅲ), J. Japan Soc. Tech. Plasticity (in Japanese), 17–180(1976), pp.23–30.

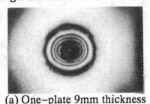

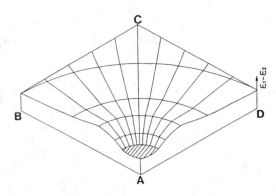

Fig.5 Distribution of principal strain difference ($\varepsilon_1 - \varepsilon_2$) measured in square ABCD

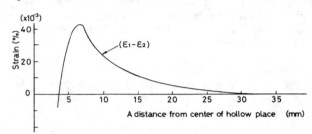

Fig.6 Distribution of principal strain difference ($\varepsilon_1 - \varepsilon_2$) along the ADE line

Fig.1 Hardness tester

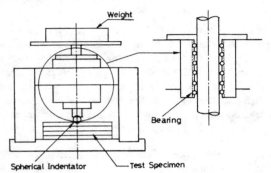

(a) One–plate 9mm thickness  (b) Three–plate 9mm thickness

Fig.2 Isochromatic fringes obtained under $P$=10N

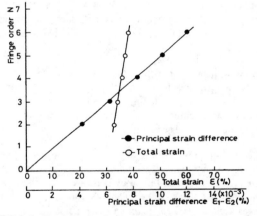

Fig.7 Relation between isochromatic fringe order near cavity ($N$), total strain ($\varepsilon$) and principal strain difference ($\varepsilon_1 - \varepsilon_2$)

Fig.3 Relation between thickness of specimen (t) and hardness ( $H_m$)

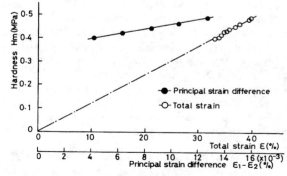

Fig.8 Relation between hardness ( $H_m$), total strain ( $\varepsilon$) and principal strain difference ($\varepsilon_1 - \varepsilon_2$)

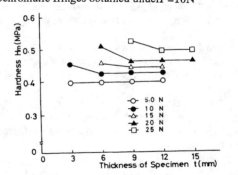

Fig.4 Isochromatic fringes obtained under $P$=20N

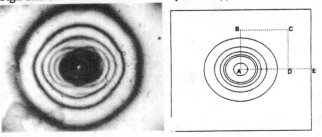

# A Study on the Development of Stress Optic Law of Photoelastic Experiment Considering Residual Stress

Jai-sug Hawong[*], Jae-guk Suh[**], Sun-ho Choi[*]

[*] Department of Mechanical Engineering, Yeungnam University, Gyungsan City,712-749, Korea
[**] Dept. of Industrial Safety Management, Kyungdong Junior College, Gyungsan City,712-900, Korea

Photoelastic experiment has been restricted by two significant problems as following. The first problem is manufacture of model specimen for complicated shape of element and the second problem is residual stresses contained in the photoelastic model materials. In this paper, the stress optic law that can be used in photoelastic model materials with residual stress was developed. It was assured in this paper that the stress optic law developed in this research was useful.

Eq(1) is stress optic law for photoelastic experiment material without residual stress.

$$\frac{f \cdot N}{t} = \sigma_1 - \sigma_2 = \sqrt{(\sigma_x - \sigma_y)^2 + 4\tau_{xy}^2} \qquad (1)$$

where N is the fringe orders, f and t are respectivly stress fringe value and thickness of specimen. If large residual stresses or large residual fringe orders are contained in the photoelastic experemental specimen, good results of the photoelastic experiments can not be obtained from Eq(1). Therefore, we developed Eq(2), which can be usefully applied to the bad photoelastic experimental specimen with residual stress.[1]

$$(\sigma_{x1} - \sigma_{y1})^2 + 4\tau_{xy1}^2 = \frac{N_2^2 + (m-1)N_o^2 - mN_1^2}{m(m-1)a^2t^2} \qquad (2)$$

$N_O$ : residual fringe orders
$N_1$ : fringe orders at load $P_1$
$N_2$ : fringe orders at load $P_2$
m : ratio of loads ($P_2/P_1$)

where $P_1$ and $P_2$ are the same type loads but magnitude of each load is different

The validity of the stress optic law developed in this paper is studied by following experiments, that is, disk under diametral compressive load, plates with hole and plate with central crack(mode I). In the disk under diametral compressive load, Fig.1(a) shows isochromatic fringe pattern obtained from stress freezing method. It is considered as residual isochromatic fringe pattern. Fig.1(b) shows photoelastic fringe pattern superposed fringe pattern of disk under diametral compressive load on the initial residual isochromatic fringe pattern. Experimental data obtained from Eq(2) are almost corresponded with the theoretical values as shown in Fig.2. Fig.3(b) shows isochromatic fringe patterns superposed fringe pattern of plate with hole under uniform tension load on the residual isochromatic fringe pattern[Fig.3(a)]. Fig.5(b) shows isochromatic fringe patterns supperposed isochromatic fringe pattern of cracked plate on the initial residual isochromatic fringe pattern. In the problems of stress concentration facter and stress intensity facter, we could obtain good results such as Fig.4 and Table(1) in bad photoelastic experimentat specimen contained residual stress such as Fig.3(a) and Fig.5(a).

The results obtained by stress optic law considering residual stress for specimen with residual stress agree with experimental data obtained by applying general stress optic law to the disk specimen without residual stress, therefore the validity of the stress optic law considering residual stress introduced in this paper was verified. We can know that the stress optic law developed in this study can be applied to the stress distribution, stress concentraition factor and stress intensity factor etc.. and applied to the photoelastic experimental of bad specimen involved small or large residual stress inevitably resulted from molding and cutting model specimen. It is inferred that the stress optic law can be applied to the photoelastic experiment for the composite materials or bi-materials.

References:

[1] Suh, J.G., "A Study on the Development of Stress Optic Law Consider ing of Residual Stress in Photoelastic Experiment", Ph. D of Yeungnam Univ., 1995.
[2] Howland, R. C. T., 1930, "On the Stresses in the Neighbourhood of a Circular Hole in a Strip under Tension",Phil. Trans. Ray. Soc., Vol. 299, pp. 48-86
[3] Feddersen, C. E., "Discussion", ASTM STP 410, (1967) pp. 77-79

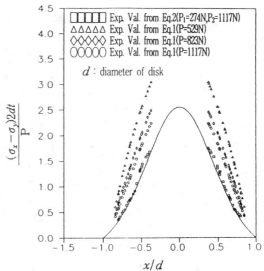

(a) Residual isochromatic fringe pattern (b)Isochromatic fringe pattern with residual isochromatic fringe pattern

Fig 1 Isochromatic fringe patterns of disk under diametral compressive load

Fig.2 The distribution of $(\sigma_x - \sigma_y)2dt/\mathrm{P}$ with $x/d$ when residual stress exists $(y/d=0)$

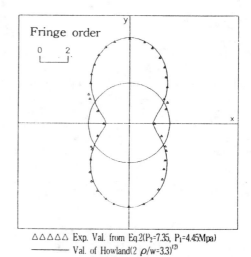

(a) Residual isochromatic fringe pattern (b) Isochromatic fringe pattern with residual isochromatic fringe pattern

Fig.3 Isochromatic fringe patterns of the plate with hole

△△△△△ Exp. Val. from Eq.2(P₂=7.35, P₁=4.45Mpa)
—— Val. of Howland(2 ρ/w=3.3)[2]

Fig.4 Stress distribution($\sigma_\theta/\sigma_0$) around a hole centeted at the center of the plate under uniform tension

(a) Residual isochromatic fringe pattern (b) Isochromatic fringe pattern with residual isochromatic fringe pattern

Fig.5 Isochromatic fringe patterns of the plate with central crack

Table 1 Stress intensity factors with residual stress ( $K_0 = \sigma_0\sqrt{\pi a}$ )

| Parts of specimen | | | $K_I/K_0$ | $K_{II}/K_0$ |
|---|---|---|---|---|
| Eq. (1) | Upper part | 784N | 1.094 | 0.102 |
| | | 470N | 1.035 | 0.154 |
| | | 235N | 0.982 | 0.173 |
| | Lower part | 784N | 0.918 | -0.193 |
| | | 470N | 0.819 | -0.228 |
| | | 235N | 0.794 | -0.242 |
| Eq. (2) | Upper part | | 1.133 | 0.043 |
| | Lower part | | 1.151 | 0.010 |
| Feddersen's results[3] | | | 1.112 | 0 |

# Analysis and Behavior of Bonded Double Containment Joints

Sameh S. Issa, Moudar H. Zgoul
University of Jordan
Faculty of Engineering and Technology
Amman 11942, Jordan

Upgrading the quality of the bonding technique depends, to a great extent, on suggesting a successful theoretical approach for formulating the analysis. The desired algorithm would enhance the prediction of the stresses and strains that are prevailing in bonded joints. The fulfillment of this task, in a satisfactory manner, requires precise experimental data acquired by means of an approach that provides fieldwise observations. The interaction between the adherend and adhesive materials in the bonded joints plays decisive role for the stress/strain analysis.

The photoelastic coating technique was selected for its characteristics in visualizing the course of strains in the surface to which the coating is attached. A reflection polariscope furnished with microscope was used for monitoring the optical changes (Fig. 1).

The finite element approach was implemented in exploring the effect of the different forces acting on the bonded joint. An attempt was made to develop a suitable stress function. Numerous curve fitting trials were carried out with partial success so far.

The adhesive bonding technique has been applied increasingly throughout Civil and Mechanical industrial structures [1,2]. This type of bonding is known for its strength in resisting shear forces, however, it tends to peel when subjected to normal tensile forces. To minimize the detrimental effect of peeling double containment joints are suggested. This explains the great attention paid towards highlighting the nature of the stress and strain distribution around the bond layer of a double containment joint. Issa *et al* [3] explored the state of strain in and around the bond layer by means of the photoelastic coating technique. The experimental results obtained from the latter work are the basis for judging the reliability of the present work.

A section in a gear box casing is considered. It has four corners, where four corner-pieces are used to assemble the walls of the gear box casing. Each corner-piece has two double containment joints. The test specimen consists of an aluminum corner-piece (Fig. 2)of 9x35x45 mm with two slots for guiding the plate beams which are presented here by two wall bars 9x9 mm in section. The slots were coated with a thin layer, 0.8 mm, out of a mixture of the two components of the epoxy resin adhesive, Araldite 2004. For further details regarding the loading frame, photoelastic coating, and the use of strain gages, with short grids to measure the strains, and thus to determine the loads applied on the double containment joints, the reader is referred to Issa [3].

The rotational and translational characteristics of the beam plates within the webs of the containment joint have a decisive effect on the course of strain in the bond layer. The points of the webs that constrain the kinetic freedom of the beam plates are referred to hereafter as the supporting points. The latter points were allocated by means of photoelastic analysis as well as by the finite element approach (Fig. 3). The commercially available computer package ALGOR was implemented in the theoretical analysis where good agreement with the photoelastic one was obtained.

The arrangement of the supporting points and the high ratios of the elastic moduli $E_{st}/E_{pl}$ = 68.7 and $E_{alu}/E_{pl}$ = 23.3 reveals that only very miner shear stresses may exist in the bond layer. Thus, one may assume with acceptable accuracy that only $\sigma_1$ does prevail. The normal stress $\sigma_1$ is at right angle to the bond layer and is given by

$$\sigma_1 = \frac{h}{f_\sigma} N \ldots\ldots\ldots\ldots\ldots\ldots\ldots(1)$$

in which h; is the thickness of the coating material, $f_\sigma$; is the optical stress constant of the coating material, and N; is the isochromatic order along the interface between the bond layer and the adherends (Fig. 4).

The normal stresses are determined along the bond layer, then by means of curve fitting technique a function, $\phi$, that describes the course of stresses is formulated. The so obtained functions represent the stress distributions over the horizontal and the vertical directions, respectively:

$$\sigma_y = \frac{\delta^2 \phi}{\delta x^2} \ldots , \ldots \sigma_x = \frac{\delta^2 \phi}{\delta y^2} \ldots\ldots\ldots(2)$$

The body forces are assumed constant. To reinstate the prevailing stress functions, φ, one needs to integrate twice the functions obtained from the process of curve fitting. As the curve fitting is conducted so to match with experimentally achieved values, the resulting stress functions are considered to satisfy implicitly the equation :

$$\frac{\delta^4 \phi}{\delta x^4} + 2\frac{\delta^4 \phi}{\delta x^2 \delta y^2} + \frac{\delta^4 \phi}{\delta y^4} = 0 \ldots\ldots\ldots(3)$$

The satisfaction of Eq. 3 reveals that the equilibrium as well as the compatibility conditions are fulfilled. A smart selection of the functions utilized in the curve fitting task would require choosing functions that can be handled easily as far as integration and differentiation are concern. There is still plenty of room for improving the output of this task in the present work.

References:

[1] Laermann, K.-H., Schorn, H., and Issa, S. S. "Spannungsoptische Untersuchungen an Verbundproben mit Reaktionsharzmörtel als Verbindungsmittel" J. Materialprüf, 20(7), pp 251-256, 1978.

[2] Sadek, M. M. "Design Philosophy for Fabrication by Bonding" Proc. of CETIM Conference, Le College en Mecanique, Paris, pp 234-248, 1981.

[3] Issa, S. S., Al-Abbas, R., and Sadek, M. M. "Photoelastic Investigation on the Characteristics of Bonded Double Containment Joints" VDI-Berichte, No. 940, pp 547-556, 1992.

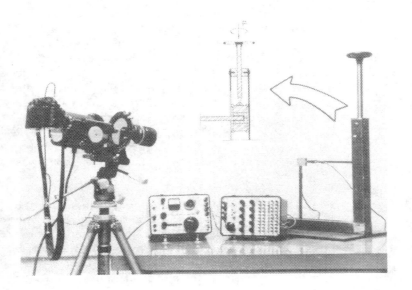

Figure#2 The selected finite mesh of the corner piece when subjected to loads.

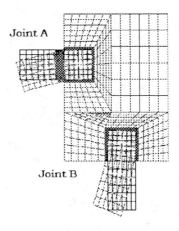

Figure#1 Experimental Setup

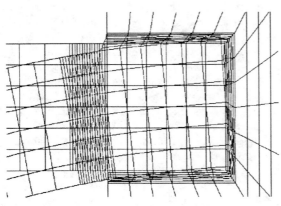

Figure#3 A magnified course of deformation of the bond layer in joint A

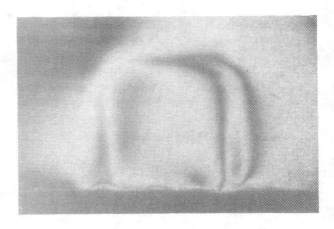

Figure#4 A sample of the isochromatic fringe pattern obtained of joint B.

# Stress Measurement by Infrared Laser Photoelasticity

Yasushi Niitsu and Kenji Gomi

Department of Mechanical Engineering, Tokyo Denki Univ,
Kanda-Nishikicho 2-2, Chiyodaku Tokyo, 101 JAPAN

As infrared ray has strong transmission force, the infrared photoelasticity has bright possibility of stress measurement of several materials; for example, ceramics, engineering plastics, composite materials, bones and bio-tissues. We have been developing the high-precision stress measuring method using a photoelastic modulator and polarized laser[1]-[3]. On the other hand, we researched the basic photoelastic properties of silicon and Ga-As single crystals using the photoelastic modulator and the infrared polarized laser[4]-[6]. The equipment adopts the He-Ne infrared laser, with 1150nm wavelength, as a light source to measure the stress in semiconductor wafers, ceramics, and so on. By using a high frequency modulation method, the magnitude of birefringence and its direction are obtained simultaneously and quantitatively. In the paper, the measuring principle and method are explained.

Figure 1 shows the schematic figure of the birefringence measuring system. This equipment adopts an 8mW He-Ne infrared laser ($\lambda$=1150nm) as a light source. Laser light pass through the polarizer, photoelastic-modulator, two quarter wave plates, birefringent sample and analyzer, and reaches into the photodetector. The PEM converts linearly polarized light into oscillating elliptic light at its 42kHz resonant frequency. The detected light intensity includes the direct component, alternative components of resonant frequency $I_{AC1}$ and its double frequency $I_{AC2}$, and higher frequency components. The measured light intensity is expanded by Fourier's components as follows,

$$I = I_{DC} + I_{AC1} \sin \omega t + I_{AC2} \cos 2\omega t + \cdots \quad (1)$$

where I is the light intensity transmitted by the analyzer. $I_{AC2}$ component is caused by non-linear effect. $I_{DC}$, $I_{AC1}$ and $I_{AC2}$ are written by

$$I_{DC} = \frac{\alpha I_0}{4} \left\{ 1 + J_0(\delta_0) \cdot \sin\gamma \cdot \sin 2\theta \right\} \quad (2)$$

$$I_{AC1} = A \frac{-\alpha I_0}{2} J_1(\delta_0) \cdot \sin\gamma \cdot \cos 2\theta \quad (3)$$

$$I_{AC2} = B \frac{\alpha I_0}{2} J_2(\delta_0) \cdot \sin\gamma \cdot \sin 2\theta \quad (4)$$

where $I_0$ the light intensity before transmitting by polarizer, $\alpha$ is the transparency of the sample, $\delta$ is the retardation of the specimen, $\theta$ is the angle of the birefringence of the specimen, $\delta_0$ is the amplitude of the modulator retardation which is proportional to the applied oscillating PEM voltage, $J_0(\delta_0)$, $J_1(\delta_0)$ and $J_2(\delta_0)$ are Bessel functions. The notations A and B are constants which are independent of both $\delta$ and $\theta$. The second term of Eq. (2) is eliminated by adjusting the PEM retardation amplitude $\delta_0$. The direct component $I_{DC}$ is independent of both the retardation $\delta$ and angle $\theta$ of birefringence of sample.

The detected light intensity of alternative components of resonant frequency $I_{AC1}$ and its double frequency $I_{AC2}$ are measured by two lock-in amplifiers. The direct component $I_{DC}$ are measured by voltmeter.

The retardation $\delta$ and the birefringence direction $\theta$ of sample are determined simultaneously with measured values of $I_{AC1}$, $I_{AC2}$ and $I_{DC}$ without rotating the sample by following relations,

$$\gamma = \sin^{-1} \sqrt{ \left( \frac{I_{AC1}}{I_{DC} \cdot 2 J_1(\delta_0) \cdot A} \right)^2 + \left( \frac{I_{AC2}}{I_{DC} \cdot 2 J_2(\delta_0) \cdot B} \right)^2 } \quad (5)$$

$$\theta = \frac{1}{2} \tan^{-1} \left( \frac{I_{AC2} \cdot J_1(\delta_0) \cdot A}{I_{AC1} \cdot J_2(\delta_0) \cdot B} \right) \quad (6)$$

Photoelastic constants of silicon single crystal of {100} and {111} faces were determined[4],[5]. The photoelastic property depend on crystal face and direction. Figure 2 shows the tensile loaded and bended specimen of {100} surface silicon single crystal, and the measurement result of stress distribution in the specimen. The tension and bending direction is equal to <110> crystal direction.

Dotted lines show the calculated stress distribution by tensile load. The arrows show the measurement results. Measured stress distribution is agree well with the calcu-

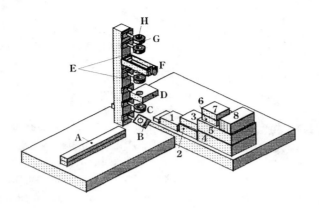

A: Infrared Laser
B: Mirror
C: Polarizer
D: PEM
E: Quarter Wave Plate
F: X-Y Stage
G: Analyzer
H: Photo Detector

1: PEM Controller
2: Laser Power Supply
3: Signal Conditioning
4: 2-Phase Lock-In Amp.
5: 2-Phase Lock-In Amp.
6: Voltmeter
7: Voltmeter
8: Strain Amp.

*Fig. 1 The construction of the birefringence measuring system.*

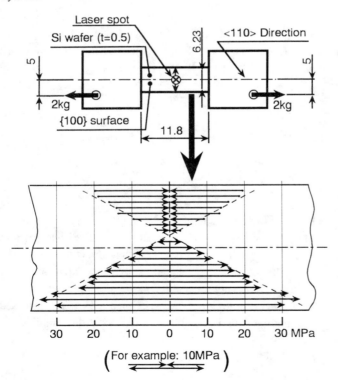

*Fig. 2 Specimen and experimental result of stress distribution measurement. Tensile load is applied on the Si crystal specimen. Bending stress distribution is measured.*

lated result. This result confirms the possibility of stress measurement of silicon with infrared laser photoelasticity. The signal noise is less than 0.6 MPa in the experiment.

References:

[1] Niitsu, Y., Ichinose, K. and Ikegami, K., "Stress Measurement of Transparent Materials by Polarized Laser", JSME Int. J. Series-A,, Vol. 38, No.1, pp.68-72, 1995.
[2] Ichinose, K. and Niitsu, Y., "Scanning Stress Measurement Method by Laser Photoelasticity", JSME Int. J. Series-A, Vol.38, No.4, pp.500-505, 1995.
[3] Niitsu, Y., Ichinose, K., Ikegami, K., "Micro-stress Measurement by Laser Photoelasticity", Mech. and Materials for Electronic Packaging: Vol.2, ASME-AMD-Vol.187, ASME-1994 WAM, pp.29-35, (1994)
[4] Niitsu, Y., Gomi, K., "Stress Measurement in Si wafer using Polarized Infrared Laser Photoelasticity", Proc. of Mechanics and Materials for Electronic Packaging ASME, AMD-Vol.187, Volume2, pp.37-40, 1994.
[5] Niitsu, Y. and Gomi, K., "Influence of Crystal Orientation on Photoelastic Property of Silicon Single Crystal", Proc. of Advanced in Electronic Packaging ASME, EEP-Vol.10-2, pp.1239-1245, 1995.
[6] Niitsu, Y., Gomi, K. and Ono, T., "Investigation of Photo-elastic Property of Semiconductor Wafers", Proc. of Appli-cations of Experimental Mechanics to Electronic Packa-ging ASME, EEP-Vol.13/AMD-Vol.214, pp.103-108, 1995.

# Development of Multi-channel-type Photoelastic Apparatus and Quantitative Characterization of Residual Strain Profiles in Mass-produced GaP Wafers

Yoshitsugu Nishiwaki, Masayuki Fukuzawa, and Masayoshi Yamada
Department of Electronics and Information Science,
Kyoto Institute of Technology,
Matsugasaki, Sakyo-ku,
Kyoto 606, JAPAN

Gallium phosphide (GaP) crystals are grown by the liquid-encapsulated Czochralski (LEC) method, whose (100) wafers are currently used as substrate to fabricate light emitting diode (LED). It is well known that a part of thermal stresses during crystal growth and cooling processes is frozen into a crystalline ingot as residual stresses or strains. When the ingot is sliced to make wafers, the residual stresses or strains may be partially relieved but still remain in the wafers. There is a serious problem that the wafers are often cracked during their handling or processing to fabricate LED. This cracking may be presumed to be due to residual and/or process-induced strains. Therefore, it is strongly demanded to develop a photoelastic apparatus, with which we can make in short time the quantitative characterization of residual strain profiles of mass-produced GaP wafers with standard dimensions.

In conjunction with crystal growth, several investigators[1,2] measured residual stress profiles existing in thick (more than 2 mm) specimens, using conventional plane and/or circular polariscope. Yamada[3,4] has recently established the quantitative photoelastic characterization technique in thin (typically 0.3 mm) wafers mass-produced for LED. However, the apparatus used was a scanning type requiring long time for whole wafer measurement and poor in spatial resolution.

In this paper, we present a new type of photoelastic apparatus (Fig. 1) developed for quantitative characterization of residual strain profiles in mass-produced LEC GaP wafers. The apparatus is not a scanning type but a multi-channel type using a two-dimensional detector array combined with an image grabber board installed in the computer. The optical configuration is similar to the plane polariscope, except that the angular directions: $\phi$ and $\chi$ of the polarizer and analyzer may be controlled by a computer. In this apparatus, we do not observe isoclinics and isochromatics as conventional polariscope observations but measure the transmitted light intensities: $I_\perp$ and $I_\parallel$ while rotating simultaneously the polarizer and analyzer under the two conditions of the crossed ($I_\perp$: $\chi$-$\phi=\pi/2$) and the paralleled ($I_\parallel$: $\chi$-$\phi=0$) polarizer and analyzer as measured in the scanning type[3].

Figure 2 shows a set of two-dimensional maps of transmitted light intensity measured at the three different angles: $\phi$=0, $\pi/4$, and $\pi/2$ under the crossed condition in a standard GaP wafer sliced from the seed side of an crystalline ingot. The measurement was made at 512×512 mesh points by controlling the variable power supply for the lamp with the digital/analog converter shown in Fig. 1, since the dynamic range of multichannel detector was limited and besides the analog/digital converter was only of 8-bits resolution. It was found that multiple fringes were not observed due to a small amount of birefringence and it was therefore difficult to evaluate quantitatively residual strain level with the conventional method using fringe order difference.

In order to deduce the phase retardation $\delta$ and principal direction $\psi$ of the small amout of strain-induced birefringence from $I_\perp(\phi)$ and $I_\parallel(\phi)$ measured as a function of $\phi$, we may make the sine and cosine transformations for $I_r(\phi)$ defined by the following relationship[3,5]:

$$I_r(\phi) \equiv I_\perp(\phi)/(I_\perp(\phi) + I_\parallel(\phi)) = \sin^2 2(\phi - \psi) \sin^2(\delta/2). \quad (1)$$

Once we obtain $\delta$ and $\psi$, we can evaluate the following residual strain components at each mesh points[3,5]:

$$|S_r - S_t| = [(S_{yy} - S_{zz})^2 + (2S_{yz}^2)]^{1/2}, \quad (2)$$

$$|S_{yy} - S_{zz}| = \frac{\lambda\delta}{\pi d n_0^3} \left| \frac{\cos 2\psi}{p_{11} - p_{12}} \right|, \quad (3)$$

$$|2S_{yz}| = \frac{\lambda\delta}{\pi d n_0^3} \left| \frac{\sin 2\psi}{p_{44}} \right|, \quad (4)$$

by using the apropriate values for wavelength $\lambda$, wafer thickness d, refractive index $n_0$, photoelastic constants $p_{ij}$'s.

The upper, middle, and bottom two-dimensional maps shown in Fig. 3 are $|S_r - S_t|$, $|S_{yy} - S_{zz}|$, and $|2S_{yz}|$ components deduced from Fig. 2, respectively. The total measurement time including the data processing time was reduced to several minutes, and also the spatial resolution (512×512) was much improved in comparison with the scanning type (40×40)[3]. The characterization results on various mass-produced GaP (100) wafers will be presented in the congress.

References:

[1] Nygren, S. F., J. Cryst. Growth **19**, 21 (1973).
[2] Kotake, H., Hirahama, K., Watanabe, M., J. Cryst. Growth **50**, 743 (1980).
[3] Yamada, M., J. Appl. Phys. **72**, 3670 (1992).
[4] Yamada, M., J. Appl. Phys. **74**, 6435 (1993).
[5] Yamada, M., Rev. Sci. Instrum. **64**, 1815 (1993).

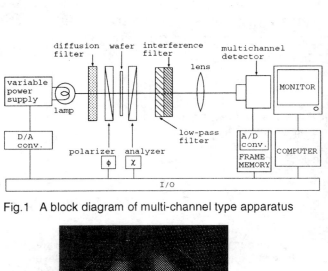

Fig.1 A block diagram of multi-channel type apparatus

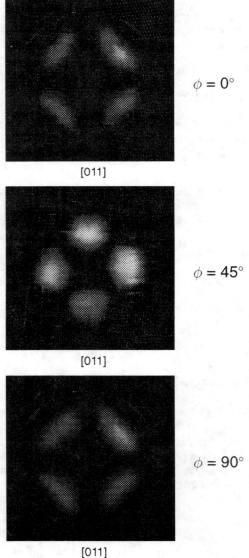

$\phi = 0°$

[011]

$\phi = 45°$

[011]

$\phi = 90°$

[011]

Fig.2 Two-dimensional distribution maps of the transmitted light intensities measured under the cross condition of polarizer and analyzer at $\phi = 0°$, $\phi = 45°$, and $\phi = 90°$

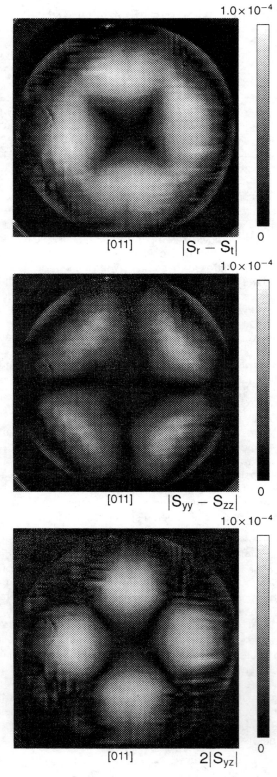

$1.0 \times 10^{-4}$

0

[011]  $|S_r - S_t|$

$1.0 \times 10^{-4}$

0

[011]  $|S_{yy} - S_{zz}|$

$1.0 \times 10^{-4}$

0

[011]  $2|S_{yz}|$

Fig.3 Two-dimensional distribution maps of strain components: $|S_r - S_t|$, $|S_{yy} - S_{zz}|$, and $2|S_{yz}|$, measured in a mass-produced GaP wafer

424

# $T_\varepsilon^*$ Integral Analysis for Aluminum CT Specimen

Y. Omori[1], H. Okada[2], K. Perry, Jr.[3], J.S. Epstein[3], S.N. Atluri[2] and A.S. Kobayashi[1]

[1] University of Washington, Department of Mechanical Engineering, Seattle, WA, USA
[2] Georgia Institute of Technology, Computational Modeling Center, Atlanta, GA, USA
[3] Idaho National Engineering Laboratory, Idaho Falls, ID, USA

## 1. Introduction

The J integral has been used extensively as a fracture parameter to characterize the crack tip field because theoretically it is a path independent integral. The authors and their colleagues, however, have shown experimentally and numerically that the far and near field J integral values differs with stable crack growth [1-3]. On the other hand, Atluri et al [4] have shown through extensive finite element (FE) analysis, that the $T_\varepsilon^*$ integral reached a steady value and is path independent under large scale yielding, loading and unloading and stable crack growth. In this paper, the $T_\varepsilon^*$ integral values associated with a stably propagating crack in both CT (compact) and SEN (single edge notched) specimens of 2024-T3 aluminum alloy are presented.

## 2. T* Integral

The $T_\varepsilon^*$ integral, which is a general path independent integral, is defined as [5],

$$T_\varepsilon^* = \int_{\Gamma_\varepsilon} \left( W n_1 - t_i \frac{\partial u_i}{\partial x_1} \right) d\Gamma_\varepsilon \qquad (1)$$

where $\Gamma_\varepsilon$ is a stationary contour very close to the crack, $W$ is the work density and $t_i$ and $u_i$ are traction and the displacement, respectively.

## 3. Method of Approach

The CT and SEN specimens were fatigue precracked and highly polished prior to laying down a Moiré grating. Coarse crossed grating of 40 lines/mm was transferred onto the specimen surface. A four beam Phase Shifting Moiré interferometer was used to obtain the orthogonal displacement fields, u and v. The specimens were subjected to uniaxial tensile load in a displacement controlled testing machine. The applied displacement was gradually increased and the load, the load-line displacement, the Moiré interferometry fringe patterns, and crack extension were recorded at the end of each incremental increase in applied displacement. The crack extension was measured on the uncoated side of the specimen.

## 4. Results

A total of four of CT and fourteen of SEN specimens were tested. Fig. 1 shows typical Moiré fringe patterns of the u and v displacement fields of CT specimen. 5 and 6 steps of stable crack growth were recorded with maximum crack extension of 5.5 mm and 10.61 mm for CT and SEN specimens, respectively. Fig. 2 shows the CTOA variations with crack extension of CT and SEN specimens. The CTOA is defined as the included angle subtended by the crack opening displacement (COD) 1.0 mm from the current crack tip. CT and SEN CTOA's reached a steady value of about 5.5 degree after a maximum value of about 20 degree. Fig. 3 shows the $T_\varepsilon^*$ integral values evaluated by using the Moiré displacement field and by the FE analysis for a contour $\Gamma_\varepsilon$ of $\varepsilon = 0.5$ mm, which indicate the size of $\Gamma_\varepsilon$ is shown in Fig. 4. The $T_\varepsilon^*$ values scattered though, it reached a steady state value after a crack extension of 4.0 mm. Although the displacement, strain and stress values near the crack tip from the Moiré fringe pattern and the FE analysis is not very accurate, the results for CT and SEN, also experimental and FE results show good agreement with each other.

## 5. Acknowledgments

The experimental analysis at the University of Washington is supported DOE Grant DE-FG06-94ER14490. The numerical analysis at the Georgia Institute of Technology is supported by DOE Grant DE-FG06-94ER14491.

References

[1] Dadkhah, M. S., Kobayashi, A.S., and Morris, W.L., "Crack Tip Displacement Fields and $J_R$ Curves of Four Aluminum Alloys", *Fracture Mechanics: Twenty-Second Symposium*. Vol. 1, eds. S.N. Atluri, J.C. Newman, Jr., I.S. Raju and J.S. Epstein, ASTM STP 1131, 1992, pp. 135-153

[2] Dadkhah, M. S. and Kobayashi, A.S., "Two-Parameter Crack Tip Stress Field, Associated with Stable Crack Growth in a Thin Plate", *Fracture Mechanics Twenty-Fourth Symposium*, ASTM STP1207, eds. J.D. Lmdes, D.E. McCabe and J.A. M. Boulit, 1994, pp. 48-61.

[3] May, G.B. and Kobayashi, A.S., "Plane Stress Stable Crack Growth and J-Integral/HRR Field", *Int. J. Solid and Structures*, Vol. 37, No. 617, 1995, pp. 857-881

[4] Brust, F.W., Nishioka, T., Atluri, S.N. and Nakagaki, M., "Further studies on Elastic-Plastic Stable Fracture Utilizing the T* integral", *Engineering Fracture Mechanics*. Vol. 22, 1985, pp. 1079-1103.

[5] Brust, F.W., McGowan, J.J. and Atluri, S.N "A Combined Numerical/Experimental Study of Ductile Crack Growth after a Large Unloading, Using T*, J and CTOA Criteria, *Engineering Fracture Mechanics*. Vol. 23, 1986, pp. 537-550.

[6] Nikishkov, G.P. and Atluri, S.N., "An Equivalent Domain Integral Method for Computing Crack-Tip Integral Parameters in Non-Elastic, Thermo-Mechanical Fracture", *Engineering Fracture Mechanics*. Vol. 26, 1987, pp. 851-867.

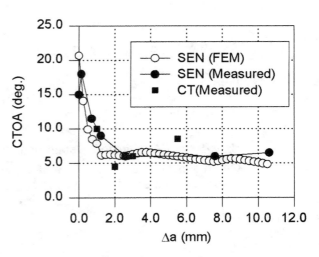

Fig. 2  CTOA during crack extension
for CT and SEN specimen.

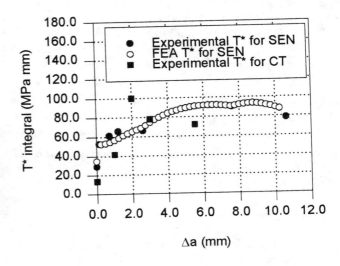

Fig. 3  $T_\varepsilon^*$ integral for G : h = 2.5 mm
and various $\Gamma_\varepsilon$ 's for CT and SEN specimen.

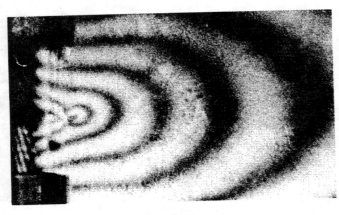

(a) u field

(b) v field

Fig. 1  Moiré fringe pattern for CT specimen.

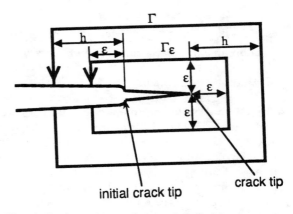

Fig. 4  Path and area integral definitions.

426

# Interaction between Corrosion and Fatigue of Aluminum Alloy

M.L.Du[1], F.P.Chiang[1], S.V.Kagwade[2] and C.R.Clayton[2]
[1]Department of Mechanical Engineering
State University of New York at Stony Brook, Stony Brook, NY 11794-2300
[2]Department of Materials Science and Engineering
State University of New York at Stony Brook, Stony Brook, NY 11794-2275

Many of the aircraft in service today have exceeded their original design life span and economic considerations have driven the industry toward the retention of older aircraft. Corrosion and fatigue are two major factors that contribute to these aging of aircraft. These two factors act synergistically in various ways. The mechanism of synergism is often studied simultaneously [1,2,3]. However, it is likely that corrosion and fatigue processes do not occur at the same time. When aircraft is in flight, cyclic loading is at its maximum, while corrosive processes is minimal. And when the aircraft is on the ground, the corrosive process is at its maximum, and there is little cyclic loading. In this investigation, specimens made of Al2024-T3 are first subjected to fatigue and then to corrosion and then to fatigue again (fatigue-corrosion-fatigue). The sample is designed with continuous radius between ends and it dimensions were shown in Ref. [4].

Both fatigue and corrosion cause damage to metallic materials that manifest themselves macroscopically in the form of surface roughness change. Those damage could be fatigue induced slip lines, intrusion/extrusion, grain rotation and/or corrosion pits, intergranular corrosion etc.[5]. Traditionally surface roughness is measured by a mechanical profilometery, which has some obvious drawbacks. Instead we use the technique of Laser Speckle Sensor [6] to monitor the surface roughness change during the process of fatigue-corrosion-fatigue.

It is observed that corrosion pits is the overwhelm corrosion form in the fatigued aluminum surface. As shown in Fig. 1, fatigue induced damage sites are favorite place to coalesce pits. As a result, the fatigued micro-crack and slip bands are blunted and stopped by corrosion pits. That's why the total fatigue lives of our test are greater than that of fatigue alone test if the initiation loading cycles is larger than half of fatigue alone life. Fig.2 shows the total fatigue life related to the initial fatigue cycle after which samples are immersed in 3.5 wt% of sodium chloride solution. The total life is the sum of the initial fatigue cycle before corrosion and the number of cycles to failure after corrosion. The y-axis in the right of the figure is a scale normalized by 380,000 which is the life of fatigue alone test in the air [4].

As an in-situ monitor, the LSS technique shows that corrosion pits change surface obviously all over the exposure surface, while fatigue process change surface roughness relatively local. Fatigue crack initiates at roughened surface and in return, surface is roughened more due to crack initiation and propagation. This, in terms of cross correlation coefficient change with the loading cycles, is shown in Fig. 3. The correlation coefficient at point 1 is drastically dropped due the crack initiation and propagation. Points 1and 3 are located at the surface near two opposite edge of test sample, respectively. Point 2 is located at the center of the sample surface.

Two concluding remarks are made: (1) Corrosion pits tend to coalesce in the mechanical damage sites, such as micro-crack, extrusion and intrusion and voids. (2) The total fatigue life of fatigue then corrosion and then fatigue again test is longer than that of fatigue test alone due to the crack blunting caused by pitting process.

Acknowledgment-This study is supported by the U.S. Air Force, Office of Scientific Research through the University Research Initiation Propgram grant No. F496209310218.

## References

[1] Duquette, D .J., 1990, ``Chemo-mechanical Interactions in Environmentally Induced Cracking," *Corrosion*, Vol.46, No.6, pp.434-443.

[2] Pao, P. S., Gao, M., and Wei, R. P., 1988, ``Critical Assessment of the Model for Transport-Controlled Fatigue Crack Growth, "*Basic Questions in Fatigue: Volume II, ASTM STP 924* , R.P.Wei, and R.P.Gangloff, Eds., pp.182-195.

[3] Piascik, R.S. and Gangloff, R. P., Aqueous Environment Effects on Intrinsic Corrosion Fatigue Crack Propagation in An Al-Li-Cu Alloy," Environment Induced Cracking of Metals, Eds. R.P. Gangloff and M.B.Ives, National Association of Corrosion Engineers, Houston, pp.233-240.

[4] Du, M. L., Chiang, F. P., Kagwade, S. V. and Clayton, C. R., 1995, ``Effect of Corrosion on the Subsequent Fatigue Properties of Aluminum Alloy Sheet," *1995 SEM's Spring Conference* , Grand Rapids, Michigan, June 12-14.

[5] Lin, T. H., and Ito, Y. M., 1969, "Mechanics of a Fatigue Crack Initiation Mechanism," *Journal of the Mechanics and Physics of. Solids*, Vol.17, pp.511-523

[6] Chiang, F. P., Du, M.L. and Li, S., "Early Stages of Fatigue Damage of Fastener Holes Monitored by Laser Speckle," Structural Integrity of Fasteners, ASTM STP 1236, P.M. Toor, Ed., 1995, pp.143-154.

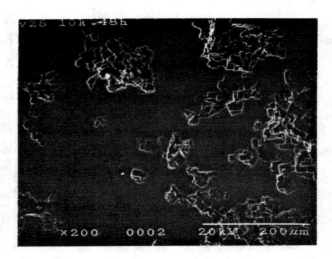

Fig. 1 Corrosion pits coalesce at the sites of mechanical damage due to fatigue process. Pitting blunts the micor-crack should be noted.

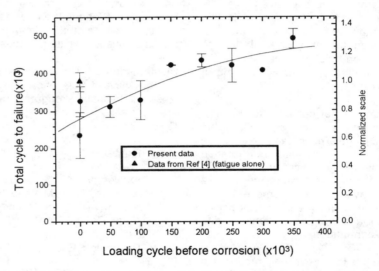

Fig.2. The total life of complete test as a function of the initial loading cycles.

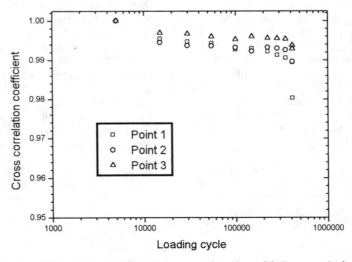

Fig. 3 The cross-correlation coefficient of speckle patterns as a function of fatigue cycle for a typically corroded sample.

# Strength and Fracture Toughness of the Silicon Nitride and Silicon Nitride/Ag-Cu-Ti Joints

Itamar Ferreira
Department of Materials Engineering
College of Mechanical Engineering
State University of Campinas (UNICAMP)
13083-970 - Campinas, SP, Brazil.

One of the most critical problems in structural ceramics and metal/ceramic joints applications is the difficulty in fracture toughness evaluation of these materials by using simple, accurate, reproducible, and economical methods. The fracture toughness evaluation of metal/ceramic joints is a very new and delicate subject, due to the complexity of the stress distribution in the metal, ceramic, and interface, as a result of the thermal and elastic properties mismatch of these materials. Nowadays, the evaluation of the fracture toughness of metal/ceramic joints is impracticable, because it depends on several parameters that are not usually found.

The aim of this paper is to propose a simplified method for fracture toughness evaluation of metal/ceramic joints, and to analyze the results by using the Weibull model. The base of this simplified method is by using little specimens, and the utilization of the linear elastic fracture mechanics philosophy, in order to minimize the residual stress from the mismatch of thermal and elastic properties of the metal, and ceramic. In this situation, the fracture toughness parameter has been designed, in this paper, as apparent fracture toughness - $K_{IC/AP}$.

It was used two ceramic materials: the first one is a sintered silicon nitride (high strength) - HSSN; the other one is a hot pressed silicon nitride (low strength) - LSSN. It was used CUSIL ABA - 27.5%Cu - 2.0%Ti - Ag (balance) as the brazing filler in a thin foil form of 50 $\mu$m thick. The brazing conditions were: 1120K; 10 minutes; vacuum ($10^{-5}$ torr). The modulus of rupture (MOR) and the fracture toughness ($K_{IC}$ for the monolithic ceramics, and $K_{IC/AP}$ for the metal/ceramic joints) has been characterized by using the four point bend test, in monolithic specimens (silicon nitride only), and $Si_3N_4$/Ag-Cu-Ti/$Si_3N_4$ joint specimens. The specimen dimensions were 3x3x30 mm$^3$ for MOR, and 2x4x30 mm$^3$ for fracture toughness tests. The metal/ceramic interface has been positioned in the center of the specimen; the fracture toughness specimen contain a chevron notch on the metal/ceramic interface. The fracture toughness has been calculated by using the equation proposed by Munz [1]. The two-parameter Weibull distribution has been used.

The Fig. 1 shows the MOR results for the monolithic ceramics, in the Weibull probability paper. It is possible to observe that these results agree in a very good way the Weibull model. The LSSN, hot pressed silicon nitride, shows a very low MOR middle value (failure-50%) - 110.6 $MPa$-, and Weibull slope - b=3.5. On the other hand,

the HSSN, sintered silicon nitride, shows high MOR middle value -446.2 $MPa$-, and Weibull slope - b=12.7. The Weibull slope for the LSSN is very low when comparing to the usually values for hot pressed silicon nitride found in the technical, and scientific references, i.e. b=7, and for the HSSN the Weibull slope agree with the values usually found for sintered silicon nitride, i.e. b=13.

The Fig. 2 shows the MOR results for the $Si_3N_4$/Ag-Cu-Ti/$Si_3N_4$ brazed joints. The results from the LSSN joints do not agree the Weibull model; however, if rejecting the lower result it is possible to fit two straight lines to the others points; with respect to the failure probability one of these lines from 13.6% to 40.9%, and the other one from 40.9% to 95.5%. On the other hand, the HSSN joints agree in a very good way the Weibull model; but that can be a result of the few number of points (only five). The MOR middle values are 60.0 $MPa$ for the LSSN, and 230.2 $MPa$ for the HSSN. The joints for both silicon nitrides gave lower MOR, and Weibull slope values when comparing to the monolithic silicon nitrides.

The Fig. 3 shows the $K_{IC}$ results for the monolithic silicon nitrides. This figure presents some important tendencies, in spite of the low number of specimen. Firstly the $K_{IC}$ results agree in a very good way the Weibull model, because the correlation factors are very high; secondly the HSSN presents higher levels of Weibull slope when comparing to the LSSN, following the same tendency of the modulus of rupture. In other words, the Weibull slope associated with the $K_{IC}$ can be used as an indication of the quality of the ceramic material, in the same way is in the case of the modulus of rupture. The $K_{IC}$ middle values are 1.47 $MPa\sqrt{m}$ for the LSSN, and 2.95 $MPa\sqrt{m}$ for the HSSN.

The Fig. 4 shows the $K_{IC}$ results for the $Si_3N_4$/Ag-Cu-Ti/$Si_3N_4$ joints. These results do not agree the Weibull model in a very good way, because the correlation factors are low - 0.93 for the LSSN, and 0.92 for the HSSN. When comparing the joint to the monolithic ceramic, the Weibull slope, associated with the fracture toughness, increased from 5.2 to 9.3 for the LSSN, and decreased from 9.2 to 7.5 for the HSSN. The fracture toughness middle values are 1.04 $MPa\sqrt{m}$ for the LSSN/Ag-Cu-Ti/LSSN joints, and 2.09 $MPa\sqrt{m}$ for the HSSN/Ag-Cu-Ti/HSSN joints. These values decreased, about 30%, when comparing the joints to the monolithic silicon nitrides. These results mean that the "apparent fracture toughness parameter" is conservative.

429

References:

[1]    Munz, D,    Hinsolt, G.,    Eschweiler, J., "Effects of Stable Crack Growth on Fracture Toughness Determination for Hot-pressed Silicon Nitride at Elevated Temperatures," ASTM Special Technical Publication 745, 1981, pp 69-84.

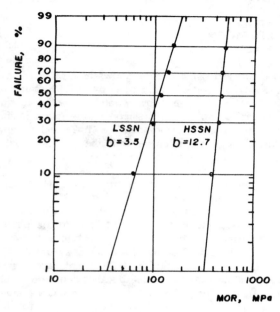

Fig. 1  Modulus of rupture as function of failure
probability / Weibull probability paper, for
the two monolithic silicon nitrides.

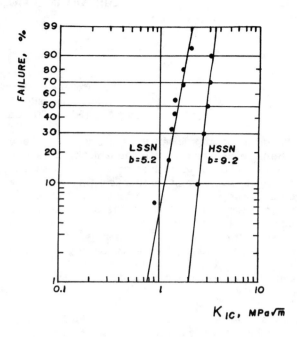

Fig. 3  Fracture toughness as function of failure
probability / Weibull probability paper, for
the two monolithic silicon nitrides.

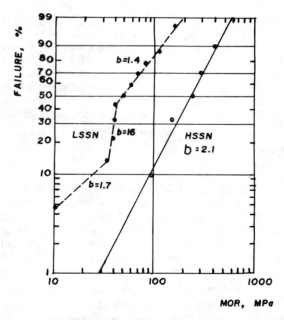

Fig. 2  Modulus of rupture as function of failure
probability / Weibull probability paper, for
the silicon nitride / Ag-Cu-Ti  joints.

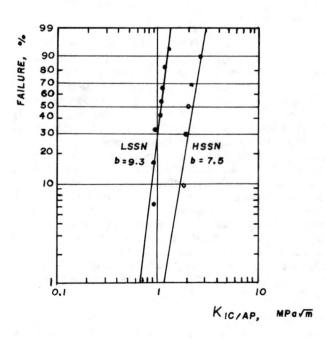

Fig. 4  Fracture toughness as function of failure
probability / Weibull probability paper, for
the silicon nitride / Ag-Cu-Ti  joints.

# Deformation of Explosion Clad Plate with a Crack

Isamu Oda and Kazuhiko Shiraishi
Kumamoto University
Dept.of Mech.Engg.
Kurokami 2-39-1
Kumamoto , 860 , Japan

The bonded dissimillar plates are often used for chemical apparatus and pressure vessels for the purpose of corrosion resistance and heat resistance. The failures of those apparatus and vessels lead to serious accidents. Therefore , it is highly important to examine the deformation and the fracture of the dissimilar plate. The bonded dissimilar plate has the material inhomogeneity , the residual stress and the change of the material characteristics by bonding. There have been few papers which discuss the effects of these factors on the fracture behavior of the bonded dissimilar plate. In the present paper , an explosion clad plate is dealt with as an typical example of the bonded dissimilar plate. The effects of those factors on the deformation behavior of the clad plate with a crack are examined.

The explosion clad plate used in the present study is composed of SUS316 stainless steel for clad metal and SB42 mild steel for base metal. The clad metal , SUS316 steel , has somewhat higher yield strength and higher elongation percentage than those of the base metal , SB42 steel. Tensile tests were carried out by using rectangular plate specimens extracted from the clad plate. Figure 1 shows the shape and dimensions of the central portion of specimens. Four types of specimen are used. They are two homogeneous and two inhomogeneous types. Each specimen has an artificial through-thickness edge crack in its center. The crack plane is perpendicular to the explosive interface. The microhardness test on a vertical section of the clad plate indicates a remarkable hardening in the vicinity of the bonded interface as shown in Fig.2. The in-plane residual stress parallel to the bonded interface was tensile in the bonded region and compressive in the apart region from the interface. A tensile load perpendicular to the crack plane is applied to the specimen. Stress , strain , plastic zone near a crack and the crack opening displacement are examined by the experiment as well as the analysis. In the analysis , the deformation near the tip of a crack in a plane stress field , which is uniaxial tension , is investigated. An elasto-plastic finite element analysis with an incremental theory of plasticity is used. The material is assumed to harden according to a power law relation between stress and strain suggested by Swift. The material inhomogeneity , the residual stress and the metallurgically affected layer by the explosive bonding are considered in the analysis.

Figure 3 shows the relationships between crack opening displacement , $V_g$ measured by means of a clip gauge and applied net stress , $\sigma_n$. The crack opening displacement of the homogeneous stainless steel specimen (Type UH) is lower than that of the homogeneous mild steel specimen (Type BH). It is caused by the difference of mechanical properties of materials. The crack opening displacement $V_g$ of the inhomogeneous specimen (Type UI) is almost the same as that of the homogeneous specimen (Type UH) at a relatively low applied stress level. At a high applied stress level , however , the $V_g$ vale of Type UI is lower than that of Type UH , even if the crack tip material of two specimen types is exactly the same. This phenomenon is caused by the hardened zone ahead of the crack tip in the inhomogeneous specimen. The crack opening displacement is considerably influenced by the plastic deformation near a crack. The hardened zone in the inhomogeneous specimen restrains the plastic deformation , hence the crack opening displacement , at a high applied stress level.

The effects of the material inhomogeneity , the hardened zone and the residual stress on the deformation behavior are revealed. The deformation near a crack tip is mainly dominated by the material at the crack tip and the highest-strength material ahead of the tip. The crack opening displacement increases remarkably after the crack-tip plastic zone passes through the highest-strength area close to the explosive interface.

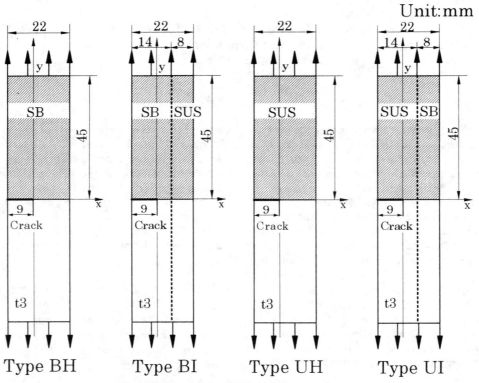

Type BH     Type BI     Type UH     Type UI

**Fig.1 Central portion of specimen**

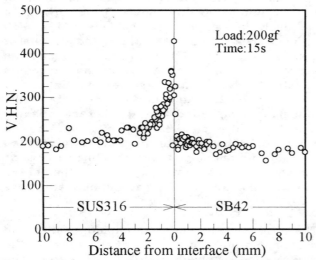

**Fig.2 Microhardness profile on section of clad plate**

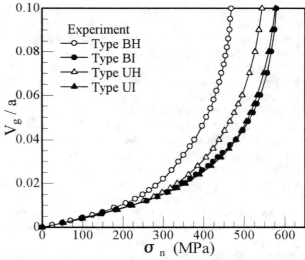

**Fig.3 Relationships between crack opening displacement and applied net stress**

# A New High Velocity Micro-Particle Impact Technique Applied to Abrasive Waterjet Cutting Head Design

Madhusarathi Nanduri, David G. Taggart, Thomas J. Kim
Waterjet Laboratory
Department of Mechanical Engineering and Applied Mechanics
University of Rhode Island
Kingston, RI 02881, USA

## Abstract
A new Micro-Particle Impact Technique (MPIT) has been developed to investigate the abrasive particle distribution within the mixing tube of an Abrasive Water Jet (AWJ) system. MPIT can also be used to investigate the more fundamental aspects of micro-particle impact and damage phenomena. Results show that this new technique is viable and will prove to be a very effective tool in AWJ research as well as in impact wear studies.

## Background
AWJ technology has been growing rapidly in the last decade because of its effectiveness and versatility in material removal applications. It has been used to machine difficult-to-machine materials such as super alloys, advanced ceramics and composites [1], [2]. AWJ technology has recently experienced several advances that have led to a significant increase in the number of industrial applications [3], [4]. However, since the technology is not sufficiently developed for successful use in many high precision machining and finishing applications, further improvements are required.

In a AWJ system, high pressure water is discharged through a sapphire or diamond orifice. The resulting high velocity jet passes through a mixing chamber producing a partial vacuum that entrains the abrasive particles fed from a hopper. Momentum transfer from the jet to the abrasive particles takes place within a narrow mixing tube. The high energy jet thus formed, is a unique cutting tool that has wide-spread applications. The AWJ system in the University of Rhode Island can pressurize water up to 370 MPa. The water velocity at this maximum pressure is about 700 m/s. Abrasive particles (typical size between 100 - 400 microns, hence, micro-particles) can reach up to 70 - 80% of the water velocity.

Improvements in abrasive cutting head design (including the mixing tube) are required for advancing the AWJ technology into high precision arenas [5]. Progress in cutting head design demands a thorough understanding of the complex three phase (water, air and abrasive) mixing process inside the cutting head [6]. Theoretical and experimental investigations on abrasive particle path, distribution and behavior are still ongoing.

## Procedures
MPIT has been developed to investigate the abrasive particle distribution within the mixing tube of an AWJ system. The experimental setup is shown in figure 1. The technique employs a gas gun to fire projectiles through the abrasive entrained waterjet. The projectiles are retrieved without further damage in a simple catcher unit. The gas gun apparatus uses helium pressurized up to 7 MPa (1000 psi) to propel 12.7 mm diameter cylindrical projectiles. Projectile velocities in the range of 20-300 m/s are easily achievable by varying the projectile material and length.

Abrasive particle distribution within the jet is influenced by: 1. AWJ system parameters such as water pressure, abrasive - water flow ratio, abrasive type, size and shape, orifice size and 2. Mixing tube parameters such as diameter, length, inlet angle and mixing tube wear. Using MPIT, particle distribution in the jet is revealed by the different patterns of impacts observable on the projectile.

## Experiments
The first experiment with MPIT was conducted using a hardened 25.4 mm long steel projectile with a velocity of about 45 m/s. It was fired perpendicularly through the jet whose velocity was about 600 m/s. Estimated abrasive particle velocity was about 400 m/s. A straight line of impacts were obtained on the surface of the projectile indicating lack of rotation during its flight.

It is well known in AWJ community that keeping the ratio, R, of orifice diameter to mixing tube diameter around 0.3 - 0.4 (all other process parameters remaining constant) will result in optimum mixing and cutting conditions. As a first step in understanding abrasive particle distribution in the mixing tube under different mixing conditions, a set of three tests were conducted. Three different mixing conditions were generated by varying the orifice / mixing tube diameters as follows. Condition 1: 0.33/1.09 mm (R = 0.3); condition 2: 0.279/1.27 mm (R = 0.22); condition 3: 0.457/1.09 mm (R = 0.42). Constant AWJ and gas gun parameters were: abrasive - Barton Mines Garnet #80; abrasive flow rate - 7.6 g/s; water pressure - 310 MPa; projectile - aluminum T-6061, 12.7 mm diameter, 25.4 mm long; projectile velocity - 70 m/s. The stand-off distance between the jet and the projectile was kept constant at 2.5 mm.

## Observations

The targets (projectiles) tested under the three mixing conditions are shown in figure 2. Damage is visible along the center line of each target surface. Optical micrographs of the individual target surfaces subjected to conditions 1, 2 and 3 are shown in figures 3, 4 and 5 respectively. The micrographs reveal the pattern and density of impacts on the targets. Clearly, condition 2 was the least efficient and condition 3, the most efficient. It was clear that MPIT can differentiate between different particle distributions and thus lead to an understanding of the AWJ mixing process. Detailed work on the effect of each of the AWJ parameters and the development of procedures to quantify the results are underway.

MPIT can also be used to investigate the more fundamental aspects of micro-particle impact and damage phenomena. By varying the velocity of the projectile, water pressure and abrasive flow rate, single micro-particle impacts can be obtained on the target. Single particle impact studies have been conducted extensively [7]. However, high velocity single micro-particle impacts such as those that are obtainable using MPIT have not been hitherto reported to the authors' knowledge. The damage caused by the high velocity abrasive particles entrained in water on the target can be analyzed using optical and scanning electron microscopy to study damage mechanisms and modes. Thus, MPIT can be an invaluable tool in high velocity impact and erosive wear studies.

## References

[1] Hashish, M. "Cutting with Abrasive Waterjets," Mechanical Engineering, March 1984, pp.60-69.

[2] Kim, T.J., Sylvia, J.G. and Posner, L. "Piercing and Cutting of Ceramics by Abrasive Waterjet," Proc. Winter Annual Meeting of the ASME, Production Engineering Division, Miami Beach, Florida, Nov. 1985, pp.19-24.

[3] Ness, E.A., Dubensky, E., Haney, C., Mort, G. and Singh, P.J. "New Developments in ROCTEC Composite Carbides for Use in Abrasive Waterjet Applications," Proc. 12th Inter. Conf. on Jet Cutting Tech., Rouen, France, Oct. 1994, pp.195-211.

[4] Vijay, M.M. "Advances in the Applications of High Speed Fluid Jets," Proc. 4th Pacific Rim Int. Conf. on Water Jet Tech., Shimizu, Japan, April 1995, pp.27-46.

[5] Nanduri, M., Taggart, D.G., Kim, T.J., Ness, E. and Risk, E. "Effect of Offset Bores on the Performance and life of Abrasive Waterjet Mixing Tubes," Proc. 8th American Water Jet Conf., Houston, Texas, Aug. 1995, pp.459-472.

[6] Raissi, K., Basile, G., Cornier, A., and Simonin, O. "Abrasive Air Water Jet Modelization," Proc. 8th American Water Jet Conf., Houston, Texas, Aug. 1995, pp.153-170.

[7] Tilly, G.P., "Erosion Caused by Impact of Solid Particles," Treatise on Mat. Sci. and Tech., vol. 13, Wear, D. Scott, Ed., NY: Academic Press, 1979, pp.287-319.

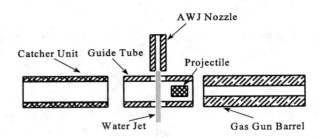

Fig. 1 Schematic of MPIT

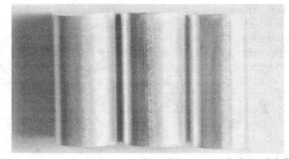

Fig. 2 Impacted targets. Condition 2,1,3 (left to right)

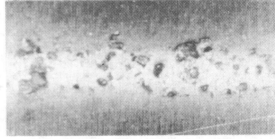

Fig. 3 Optical micrograph of condition 1

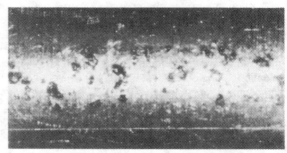

Fig. 4 Optical micrograph of condition 2

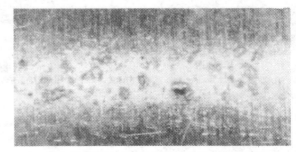

Fig. 5 Optical micrograph of condition 3

# TIME DEPENDENT BEHAVIOR OF MODE I DELAMINATION IN UNIDIRECTIONALLY REINFORCED CF/PEEK UNDER CYCLIC LOADING AT ELEVATED TEMPERATURE

Takayuki KITAMURA*, Ryuich OHTANI* and Yoshihiko UEMATSU**
*    Dept. of Engineering Physics and Mechanics, Kyoto University
Kyoto, 606-01, Japan
**   Dept. of Mechanical Engineering, Osaka University
Osaka, Japan

Characteristics of delamination crack growth in a carbon fiber reinforced plastic (CFRP) is investigated under high temperature fatigue focusing on the time-dependent behavior due to creep of matrix and the stress shielding at the crack tip due to the fiber bridging.

The tests are conducted at 473K using double cantilever beam (DCB) specimens of a unidirectionally reinforced laminate, APC-2, which consists of carbon fibers, AS4, and a thermoplastic polymer, poly-ether-ether-ketone (PEEK). The loading conditions are listed in Tables 1 and 2. Tables 1 and 2 tabulate the conditions in cycle-dependent fatigue and time-dependent one, respectively. Some tests are conducted under constant stress intensity factor (constant $K$ or $\Delta K$) conditions in order to examine the effect of the fiber bridging. Others are carried out under load-controlled ($P$-controlled) conditions.

Figure 1 shows the dependence of crack propagation rate per unit cycle, $da/dN$, on the period of cycle, $1/\upsilon$. The crack propagation behavior is divided in to two regions where $da/dN$ is constant and $da/dN$ is inversely proportional to $1/\upsilon$, respectively. Since $(1/2\upsilon)$ is equal to the loading period in a cycle, the crack propagation rate per unit time, $da/dt$, is constant in the latter region. Thus, the crack propagation in high temperature fatigue is characterized by cycle-dependent type and time-dependent one.

Figure 2 (a) shows the relationship between the crack propagation rate per unit cycle, $da/dN$, and the stress intensity factor range, $\Delta K$. It shows fairly good correlation except early stage of the tests as usually observed on the crack propagation in room temperature fatigue and the relationship is formulated by

$$da / dN = C_f \Delta K^{m_f} \qquad (1)$$

where $C_f$ and $m_f$ are material constants.

In a previous paper, authors reported that in sustained load (static creep) conditions, the crack propagation rate, $da/dt$, is govern by the elastic stress intensity factor, $K$, due to the small scale creep where the creep deformation is confined in the vicinity of the crack tip.   Then,   in the time-dependent

Table 1 Test conditions in fatigue with high frequency of cycle. Cycle-dependent crack propagation (Fig.2(a)).

| | $\Delta K_{apply}$ Constant Tests | | | | | | $\Delta P_{apply}$ Constant Tests | | | | |
|---|---|---|---|---|---|---|---|---|---|---|---|
| Test No. | 1 | 2 | 3 | 4 | 5 | 6 | 7 | 8 | 9 | 10 | 11 |
| Load Waveform | | | | | | | | | | | |
| $R=P_{min}/P_{max}$ | 0.1 | | | | | | 0.1 | | | 0.1 | |
| $\Delta K_{apply}$ (MPa√m) | 1.83 | 2.08 | 2.37 | 2.57 | 2.80 | 3.00 | — | | | — | |
| $\Delta P_{apply}$ (N) | — | | | | | | 171 | 205.2 | 171 | 205.2 | |
| $P_{max}$(N) | — | | | | | | 190 | 228 | 190 | 228 | |
| $1/\upsilon$ (s) | 1 | | | | | | 0.5 | 0.5 | 2 | 2 | 20 |
| Symbol | O | △ | □ | ◇ | ▽ | ▷ | △ | O | □ | ◇ | ◖ |

Table 2 Test conditions with stress hold (low frequency of cycle). Time-dependent crack propagation (Fig.2(b)).

| | $K_{apply}$ Constant Tests | | | | | | $P_{max}$ Constant Tests | | | | | | | | |
|---|---|---|---|---|---|---|---|---|---|---|---|---|---|---|---|
| Test No. | 12 | 13 | 14 | 15 | 16 | 17 | 18 | 19 | 20 | 11 | 21 | 22 | 23 | 24 | 25 |
| Load Waveform | | | | | | | | | | | | Static creep | | | |
| Test Temp. (K) | 473 | | | | | | 473 | | | | | | 473 | 443 | 453 | 483 |
| $R=P_{min}/P_{max}$ | 0.1 | | | | | | 0.1 | | | 0.1 | | — | | — | | |
| $K_{apply}$ (MPa√m) | 2.50 | 2.70 | 2.90 | 3.10 | | 3.25 | — | | | — | | — | | — | | |
| $P_{max}$ (N) | — | | | | | | 228 | 190 | 228 | 228 | | 228 | 249 | 249 | | |
| $\Delta P_{apply}$ (N) | — | | | | | | 205.2 | 171 | 205.2 | 205.2 | | — | | — | | |
| $t_H$ (s) | 360 | | | | | | 3600 | 3600 | 360 | 10 | | — | | — | | |
| $1/\upsilon$ (s) | 380 | | | | | 1752 | 4992 | 4764 | 1752 | 20 | | — | | — | | |
| Symbol | ● | ▲ | ■ | ◆ | ▼ | ▶ | ▲ | ■ | ● | ◖ | | × | + | ✛ | ✧ | ★ |

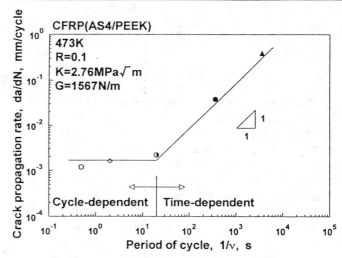

Fig.1 Relationship between crack propagation rate per unit cycle and period of cycle.

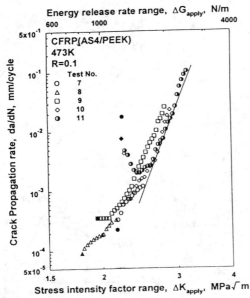

Fig.2(a) Relationship between crack propagation rate per unit cycle and stress intensity factor range.

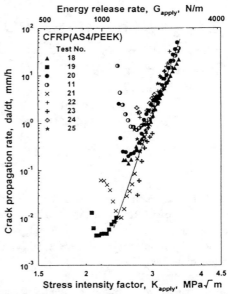

Fig.2(b) Relationship between crack propagation rate per unit time and stress intensity factor.

type under the cyclic loading condition, the crack propagation rate, $da/dt$, is plotted against $K$ as shown in Fig.2(b). It reveals that $da/dt$ is correlated well with $K$ as

$$da / dt = C_c K^{m_c} \qquad (2)$$

where $C_c$ and $m_c$ are material constants. Moreover, the relationship coincides with that in the static creep.

The transition between the time-dependent crack propagation and the cycle-dependent one is given by

$$\int_0^{t_1} C_c K^{m_c} dt = C_f \Delta K^{m_f} \qquad (3)$$

equating the propagation during a cycle due to the each types. Here, $t_1$ is the cycle period.

Figure 3 shows the change in the crack propagation rate under constant $\Delta K$ conditions in the cycle-dependent fatigue. It shows that $da/dN$ decreases and reaches constant rate as the crack propagates. The high $da/dN$ at the early stage is also observed in the load-controlled tests as shown in Fig.2. As the starter crack is introduced by inserting a thin film in the laminates during the fabrication of CF/PEEK composite plate, there is no fiber bridging at the initial stage. The decrease in $da/dN$ under a constant $\Delta K$ could be attributed to the formation of fiber bridging on the cracked faces as the crack propagates. The constant $da/dN$ in Fig.3 suggests that the formation and the break of bridged fibers balance each other and the crack propagates under a steady effect of the shielding. Thus, the initial crack propagation gives the upper bound of $da/dN$ while the saturated propagation rate at the later stage shows the lower bound. Figure 4 show the upper and lower relations between $da/dN$ and $\Delta K$ obtained by the $\Delta K$-controlled tests as well as by the load-controlled tests.

Similar result is obtained for the relationship between $da/dt$ and $K$ in the time-dependent fatigue.

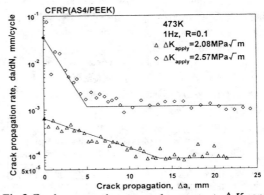

Fig.3 Crack propagation rate under constant $\Delta K$ condition.

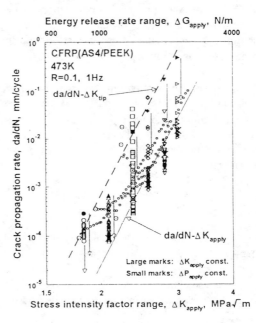

Fig.4 Relationship between crack propagation rate and stress intensity factor range under constant $\Delta K$ condition.

# Time Dependent Failure Mechanisms of Fatigued SMC

Bernd von Bernstorff

Fasertechnik
BASF Aktiengesellschaft, Ludwigshafen
Germany

In order to anticipate long-term fatigue behavior of composites monotonic and reversible loading experiments were conducted and the progress of material destruction was observed. Fatigue damage is related to the micromechanics of deformation and fracture in the material. Experimentally, the general degradation of the microstructure which leads to progressive reduction in mechanical properties and the rate of crack formation and delamination growth was described in terms of static strength, stiffness loss and damping behavior of the investigated SMC material.

In contrast to the formation of a single propagating crack, various failure mechanisms occur in SMC depending on the fracture strain $\varepsilon_B$ and the volume fraction V of the individual components in the composite. For SMC, the strength and volume fraction of the glass fiber bundles is large enough to withstand additional loads transferred from a cracking resin phase. As the load F on the composite increases, the more brittle resin progressively fragments and forms a multiple crack pattern with even spacing between the cracks (Fig. 1 [1]).

As in the tensile case, multiple cracking also occurs in SMC subjected to cyclic loading stresses. Though the fatigue loading stresses are generally much lower than the monotonic tensile fracture stress, again, the fatigued specimen will fail and will show a similar crack pattern with even crack spacings between the cracks as observed under tensile failure (Fig.2). Obviously, a maximum crack density exists for fiber-reinforced composites which is characteristic for the material composition but independent of the loading history. Because the crack density can be correlated directly with the stiffness of the specimen, Reifsnider et al. [2] proposed a stiffness-based failure criterion as the failure limit for composites subjected to cyclic stresses. As damage progresses under cyclic loading, a uniform pattern of cracks is formed in the resin and Mode II fiber/matrix-interfacial failure occurs. The mechanisms involved can be explained and described by calculating the forces transmitted between the fibers and the resin [3]. It was observed that different load amplitudes gave rise to equivalent damage pattern in the material. As a consequence, the same state of damage as that reached after very long fatigue periods can be achieved by superimposing a number of shorter fatigue tests in which the load amplitude is progressively increased. Because the stiffness steadily decreases during fatigue test, the individual stiffness/load amplitude-curves for differently loaded specimens can be shifted along the axis for the number of load cycles. By this means, master curves can be compiled for the stiffness decrease and the damping behavior for fatigued SMC (Fig. 3 [4]).

References:

1. G.A. COOPER, "Fracture and Fatigue", Vo. 5 (Academic Press, New York, London, 1974)

2. K.L. REIFSNIDER, W.W. STINCHCOMB and T. K. O´BRIEN, "Fatigue of Filamentary Composite Materials", ASTM STP 636 (American Society for Testing and Materials, Philadelphia, Pennsylvania, 1977).

3. B. von BERNSTORFF, "Zum Schwingfestigkeitsverhalten glasfaserverstärkter Harzmatten", VDI Fortschrittberichte, Reihe 5, Nr. 174, Düsseldorf 1989

4. B. von BERNSTORFF, G.W. EHRENSTEIN, "Failure mechanism in SMC subjected to alternating stresses", Journal of Materials Science 25 (1990) 4087 - 4097

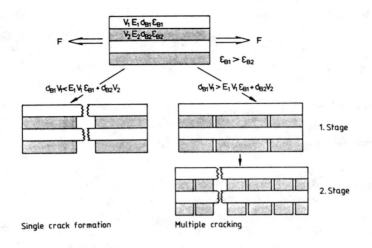

Legend  V        Volume fraction
        E        Modulus
        $\delta_B$   Fracture stress
        $\varepsilon_B$   Fracture strain
        Index number indicates
        number of component

**Figure 1**  Possible fracture modes for composite
materials with different ultimate strains
of the components [1].

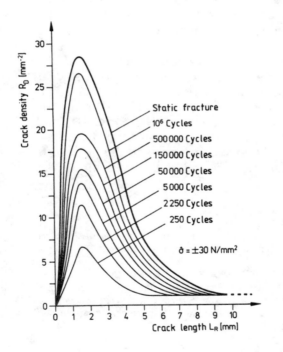

**Figure 2**  Crack length distribution as a function of
fatigue time. For comparison, the crack
length distribution of a monotonic fractures
specimen is also plotted.

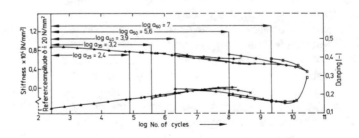

**Figure 3**  Construction of stiffness and damping
master curves for fatigued SMC.

# Time and Temperature Dependence on Flexural Fatigue Behavior of Unidirectional CFRP Laminates Using Pitch-based Carbon Fibers

Yasushi MIYANO*, Kuniaki NAKAMURA**, Masayuki NAKADA* and Michihiro MOHRI***

* : Materials System Research Laboratory, Kanazawa Institute of Technology
  Ohgigaoka Nonoichi Ishikawa 921, Japan
** : Graduate School, Kanazawa Institute of Technology
*** : Central Technical Research Laboratory, Nippon Oil Company, Ltd.
  Chidori-cho Naka-ku Yokohama 231, Japan

The objective of this paper is to establish experimentally the time and temperature dependence on flexural fatigue strength of unidirectional CFRP laminates using pitch-based carbon fibers. A method is also proposed to determine long term fatigue behavior of CFRP laminates based on short term fatigue testing results.

The time and temperature dependence on the flexural static strength of unidirectional CFRP laminates (Granoc XN40/25C, Nippon Graphite Fiber) were determined from testing at various deflection rates and temperatures. The left side of Fig.1 shows the flexural static strength versus time to failure at various temperatures. The flexural static strength remarkably depends on time to failure and temperature. The right side of Fig.1 shows the master curve of flexural static strength versus reduced time to failure at a reference temperature $T_0=25°C$ obtained by shifting horizontally these curves to the left side. Since the flexural static strength at various temperatures can be superimposed so that a smooth curve is created, the time-temperature superposition principle is applicable. The master curve can be divided into three distinct groups of curves in the wide range of reduced time to failure, each corresponding to a different mode of fracture shown in Fig.2, that is tensile fracture in the range of short time and low temperature, compressive fracture in the range of intermediate time and temperature, and microbuckling fracture in the range of long time and high temperature. Fig.3 shows the time-temperature shift factors obtained experimentally for the master curve of flexural static strength. These shift factors almost agree with those for the storage modulus of the matrix resin. It can be considered that the time and temperature dependence of the flexural static strength of CFRP laminates are controlled by the viscoelastic behavior of the matrix resin.

The time and temperature dependence on the flexural fatigue strength of CFRP laminates were determined experimentally from testing performed at various frequencies and temperatures. Fig.4 shows the flexural fatigue strength versus the number of cycles to failure $N_f$ (S-N curve) at a frequency f= 5Hz. The flexural fatigue strength also depends remarkably on temperature as well as $N_f$. The time-temperature superposition principle for the flexural static strength of CFRP laminates is applied to the flexural fatigue strength. The upper side of Fig.5 shows the flexural fatigue strength versus reduced time to failure $t_f'$. Connecting the points of the same $N_f$ on these curves, the master curves of flexural fatigue strength for constant $N_f$ are constructed as shown in the lower side of Fig.5. The master curves can be also divided into three distinct groups of curves in the wide range of reduced time to failure, each corresponding to a different mode of fracture. The master curves of flexural fatigue strength show characteristic curves in each range, that is slight change with $N_f$ as well as time and temperature in the range of short time and low temperature, remarkable change with $N_f$ as well as time and temperature in the range of intermediate time and temperature, and inverse relation with $N_f$ in the range of long time and high temperature. Fig.6 shows the S–N curves at f= 0.05Hz. The solid lines in this figure show the predicted S–N curves obtained from the master curves of flexural fatigue strength as shown in the lower side of Fig.5. Since the predicted and experimental S–N curves agree with each other, the time-temperature superposition principle for the flexural static strength also holds for the flexural fatigue strength. Therefore, the flexural fatigue strength for a given number of cycles to failure at an arbitrary frequency and temperature can be determined by using the master curves shown in Fig.5.

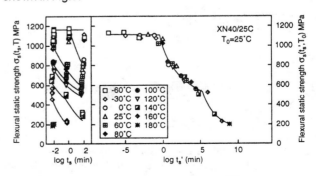

Fig. 1 Master curve of flexural static strength

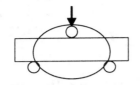

Tensile fracture
T=-60°C, V=200mm/min

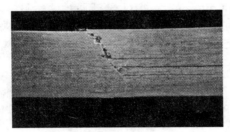

Compressive fracture
T=60°C, V=2mm/min

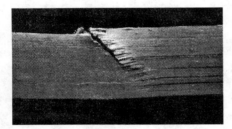

Microbuckling fracture
T=180°C, V=0.02mm/min

1mm

Fig. 2 Fractographs after bending static test

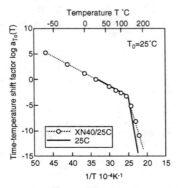

Fig. 3 Time-temperature shift factors for flexural static strength
of CFRP laminates XN40/25C and the storage modulus
for matrix resin 25C

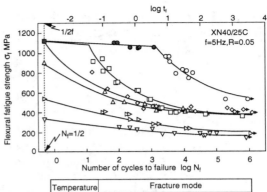

| Temperature °C | Fracture mode | | |
|---|---|---|---|
| | Tensile | Compressive | Microbuckling |
| -30 | ● | ○ | |
| 25 | ▩ | □ | |
| 80 | | ◇ | |
| 120 | | △ | |
| 160 | | | ▷ |
| 170 | | | ▽ |

Fig. 4 S-N curves for frequeny f=5Hz at various temperatures

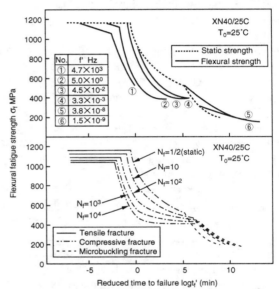

Fig. 5 Master curves of flexural fatigue strength

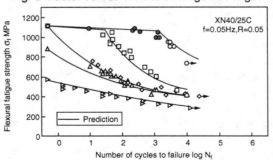

| Temperature °C | Fracture mode | | |
|---|---|---|---|
| | Tensile | Compressive | Microbuckling |
| -60 | ● | ○ | |
| -15 | ▩ | □ | |
| 25 | | ◇ | |
| 60 | | △ | |
| 140 | | | ▷ |

Fig. 6 S-N curves for frequency f=0.05Hz at various
temperatures

# Time Dependent Phenomena on Using Composite Materials for High Temperature Aircraft Applications

A. Horoschenkoff*, K. Schmidtke*, M. Reiprich**
*Daimler-Benz AG, Research and Technology
P.O. Box 80 04 65, 81663 Munich, Germany

**Daimler-Benz Aerospace Airbus
P.O. Box 10 78 45, 28183 Bremen, Germany

An investigation programme was launched to assess the long-term use of composite materials for supersonic civil transport (SCT) systems. The specific material aspects caused by the stringent conditions for SCT systems are discussed. Depending on the maximum speed (Mach 2.0 to 2.4), the structure of SCT systems is heated up to temperatures of about 120 to 150 °C. Regarding the cruising altitude of approx. 20 km, exposure to UV light and aggressive media (ozone) will occur. Life cycles of more than 60,000 hours under these severe conditions must be guaranteed for SCT systems, which considerably exceed military aircraft missions. These stringent requirements affect the properties and performance of composite materials and therefore have to be considered when qualifying these materials for SCT applications. Figure 1 shows some of the main topics to be focused on.

In a first step the physico-chemical and mechanical degradation caused by ageing under constant and cycling thermal loading (-55 to +150 °C) was investigated. The investigation programme was performed on three commercially available composite materials (all carbon-fibre-reinforced) and the corresponding neat resin castings. Each system represents a typical chemical class of resin systems: A Bismaleimide (BMI), having a glass transition temperature of $T_g = 220°$ C, an Epoxy (EP, $T_g = 195°$ C), and Polyetheretherketone (PEEK, $T_g = 145°$ C). Ageing procedures were applied up to 20,000 hours at constant temperatures of up to 230°C. A variety of thermal cycles was investigated to simulate different loading conditions. In agreement with the service temperature expected, the reference test temperature was 150°C for the thermoset materials (for PEEK 120°C). Nondestructive testing (C-Scans, X-Ray, tomography) as well as physico-chemical (DSC, DMA, TGA) and mechanical characterization methods (notched compression, shear tests) were used to analyse material degradations. Accelerated ageing procedures and characterization methods were applied for predicting the long-term behaviour (Arrehenius equation and time-temperature-superposition principle).

The investigations show that the epoxy composite tends to exhibit better long-term performance up to temperatures of about 180° C than the BMI, which is normally assessed as a candidate for high-temperature applications. At higher temperature levels, both materials failed with respect to long-term ageing. Divergent material degradation routes and interaction between physical and chemical (oxidation) ageing processes were identified at the different temperature levels investigated. Consequently, accelerated ageing procedures (i.e. higher temperature levels) have to be applied carefully, at least when used with commercial composite materials which are being modified to fulfill the different requirements. Further examinations, i.e. fatigue behaviour of aged materials, are necessary to verify the use of composite materials as a structural material for high-temperature applications.

Acknolegement:

The authors would like to thank the University of Kaiserslautern (IVW), the University of Munich, the Federal Armed Forces University of Munich, the Federal Institute for Materials Research and Testing in Berlin, the University of Erlangen/Nürnberg and the University of Kassel, ABHTA Consortium (BRITE-EURAM project).

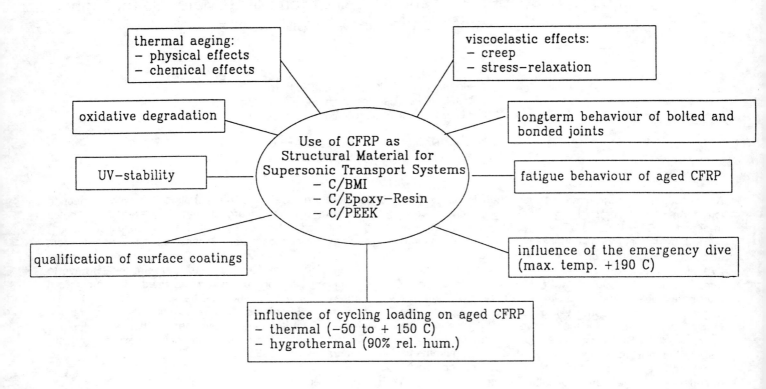

Figure 1: Material aspects concerning the long-term use of composite materials at high temperatures

# VISCOELASTIC ANALYSIS OF RESIDUAL STRESS IN INJECTION MOLDS OWING TO MOLDING CONDITIONS

Minoru Shimbo*, Yasushi Miyano* , Shinniti Nagata**,Masashi Yamabe***, Mamoru Ishijima***
* Professors; SEM Members , ** Graduate Student, Materials System Research Laboratory
Kanazawa Institute of Technology, 7-1 Ohgigaoka, Nonoichi, Ishikawa 921, Japan
*** Nissan Motor Co. Ltd. 560-2 Okatsukoku, Kanagawa, 243-01, Japan

## INTRODUCTION

The residual stress in plastics generated during the molding has direct effects on the strength and deformation of the molded parts. The study of the generation mechanism and a prevention method of residual stresses has recently become a serious subject with the development of new materials and the advancement of processing techniques. It is difficult to determine how residual stress are generated because there many factors that cause residual stresses, e.g. flow of polymer, non-uniformity of temperature distribution during cooling process, molecular orientation, time-temperature dependence of mechanical behavior, etc., and the combination of these factors. Although there are many qualitative studies concerning the generation mechanism of residual stress, the quantitative studies considered theoretically the relationship between the thermoviscoelastic behavior and residual stress are little [1-4].

The purpose of this paper is to clarify experimentally and theoretically the generation mechanism of residual stress in injection molds owing to molding conditions. Polypropylene (PP) resin plates are molded under various molding conditions which changed dwelling, injection speed and molding temperature and these thermoviscoelastic properties which have a direct effect on their residual stresses are carefully measured. The residual stresses in PP resin plates are measured by a layer-removal method and are calculated by using a thermoviscoelastic model[3,4]. By comparing these residual stresses under various molding conditions with the thermoviscoelastic properties mentioned above, the generation mechanism of residual stress in injection molds owing to molding conditions is discussed.

## EXPERIMENTS

Specimens and molding conditions used here are

### Table 1 Molding conditions of specimens

| Case | Molding condition | Dwelling (MPa) | Injection speed (mm / s) | Molding temperature (Core,Cavity ) (°C) |
|------|-------------------|----------------|--------------------------|------------------------------------------|
| Case A | Standard | 25 | Standard 15 | Symmetry (32,33) |
| Case B | Low dwelling | 10 | Standard 15 | Symmetry (32,33) |
| Case C | High dwelling | 40 | Standard 15 | Symmetry (32,33) |
| Case D | High speed injection | 25 | High 29 | Symmetry (32,33) |
| Case E | Asymmetry molding temperature | 25 | Standard 15 | Asymmetry (36,57) |

shown in Table 1. As shown in this table, five kinds of specimens with widths of 300 mm and a thickness of 3 mm which were molded under various molding conditions which changed dwelling, injection speed and molding temperature were prepared.

Fig. 1 shows the preparation of test pieces which measure viscoelastic behavior and residual stress. The storage moduli and thermal expansions which have direct effects upon residual stress were measured carefully for these specimens cut from various parts, directions and layers. The storage modulus was measured by using a viscoelastic analyzer and the expansion and contraction of the gage length of the specimens during heating and cooling were measured.

The residual stress distributions in the specimens was measured by using the layer-removal method. Two strips with a width of 4 mm and a length of 70 mm as shown in figure 1 were cut in the molding and transverse directions from the five kinds of specimens. The lower surfaces of the strips were removed successively with emery paper at room temperature. The changes of curvature of the strips were measured using a microscope. The residual stresses of the specimen were obtained by substituting the measured curvatures into the equation from the layer-removal method [5] .

## RESULTS AND DISCUSSIONS

Fig. 2 shows the temperature dependence of the storage moduli of various specimens in the molding direction on case A which were cut from the vicinity of gate. The storage moduli for various layers agree

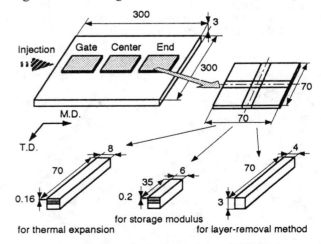

Fig.1 Preparation of test piece of PP plate

fairy well each other, and the difference of storage moduli against thickness is very small. Now the similar results for storage moduli of other specimens were obtained. This indicates that the modulus changes with temperature, but is homogeneous and isotropic over the whole plate.

Fig. 3 shows the thermal expansions versus temperature of various specimens in the molding direction on case A which were cut from the vicinity of gate. The thermal expansions in the outer layer are very different from that of the middle and inner layers, and that of the outer layer are larger than that of the middle and inner layers. The measured results for the thermal expansions of other specimens showed similar tendency and those of transverse direction of specimen were small compared to molding direction generally. It is considered that anisotropy and heterogeneity through the thickness are occurred because of the molecular orientation during injection process.

Fig. 5 shows the residual stress distributions of five kinds of specimens in the molding direction which were molded under various molding conditions which changed dwelling, injection speed and molding temperature. The solid lines indicate the experimental results and doted lines indicate numerical results calculated using thermal and mechanical properties mentioned above based on thermoviscoelastic model [4]. The experimental results agree well with numerical results. The residual stress distribution is tensile in the vicinity of the outer layers, and is compressive in the middle region on all cases. It is found that the residual stresses generated in thermoplastic resins during injection molding due mainly to a combination of heterogeneity and anisotropy of thermal expansion by crystallization and molecular orientation during the injection process, and the residual stresses generated during injection molding is influenced considerably of injection speed (case D) among molding conditions.

REFERENCES
(1) Miyano,Y., Shimbo,M., Sugimori,S., Kunio,T., Pro..SEM Spring Conf., Exp. Mech., (1988),619.
(2) Shimbo,M., Sugimori,S., Miyano,Y., Kunio,T., Pro. KSME/JSME Conf., Exp. Mech., (1990),37.
(3) Miyano,Y., Sugimori,S., Shimbo,M., Kunio,T., Pro. 9th Int Conf.,3, (1990),277.
(4) Miyano,Y., Shimbo,M., Pro.SEM Spring Conf., Exp. Mech., (1993),866.
(5) Schwarzl,F., Staverman,A.J., J.Apl. Phys., vol.23, p.838, 1952.

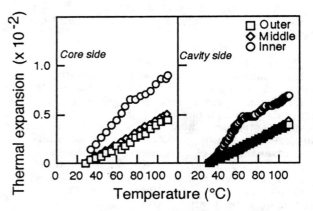

Fig.3  Thermal expansion of various layers (Case A:Gate:M.D.)

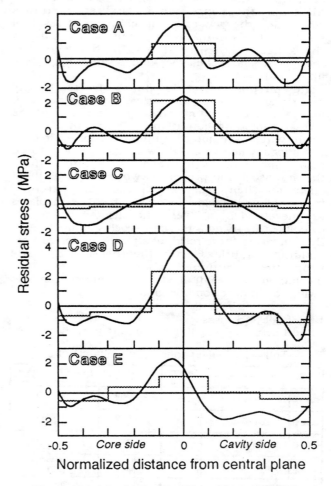

Fig.5  Residual stress with various conditions (Gate:M.D.)
— Exp. result
--- Nume. result ($\xi$ =0.1)

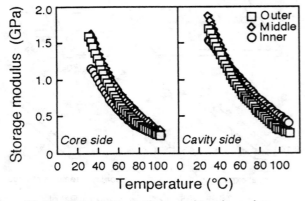

Fig.2  Storage modulus of various layers (Case A:Gate:M.D.)

# DYNAMIC DUCTILE FRACTURE
# AN EXPERIMENTAL-NUMERICAL ANALYSIS

Jonghee Lee, Matthew T. Kokaly and Albert S. Kobayashi
University of Washington
Department of Mechanical Engineering
Seattle, Washington 98195-2600, USA

## METHOD

A new moire interferometry technique [1], which combines the advantages of geometric moire and traditional moire interferometry, was used to measure the large strains in the vicinity of a running crack tip. The method uses a low-spatial frequency, i.e. 40 lines per mm in this study, steep grating on a mirror finished specimen surface to achieve high contrast moire fringes on the specimen surface. Four frames of the moire fringe patterns corresponding to the dominant vertical displacements were recorded by an IMACON 790 camera. Multiple recordings of identically loaded SEN specimens at different delay timing were necessary to capture much of the fracture event which lasted about 1.2 milliseconds.

The finite element (FE) model consisted of a truncated SEN specimen with prescribed vertical displacement data, together with an assumed vanishing tangential surface traction on a horizontal cross section 10 mm from the crack. This truncated SEN specimen consisted of graded finite elements with the smallest element of 0.25 mm square along the crack. A dynamic elasto-plastic FE analysis was conducted by driving the FE model with the measured time-varying displacement boundary conditions and the crack tip location. The FE results were then used to compute the J and $T^*_\varepsilon$ integral values following the procedure developed by Okada and Atluri [2]. The area integrals involving the inertia terms in these contour integrals was less than 3 percent of the total integral value thus reducing the dynamic J and $T^*_\varepsilon$ integrals to their static counterparts. J integral was computed along a square contour, $\Gamma_\varepsilon$ of 4 x 4 mm square, which remained fixed in size and which moved with the crack tip. The $T^*_\varepsilon$ integral was computed along an oblong contour which elongated with the moving crack tip and which was located 2 mm, i.e. $\varepsilon = 2$ mm, from the crack. This use of a near-crack contour in the integration process greatly simplified the $T^*_\varepsilon$ computation where the contour integral behind the propagating crack was ignored.

## RESULTS

Figure 1 shows a typical dynamic moire fringe patterns associated with a propagating crack in 7075-T6 and 2024-T3 SEN specimens. While the crack in the 7075-T6 specimen accelerated from a crack velocity of 35 m/s, it gradually decelerated from an initial high of 5 m/s. and arrested in the 2024-T3 specimen. Figure 2 shows the variations in the crack tip opening angles (CTOA) in the two specimens. The CTOA reached a steady state value after an initial high value similar to that observed by Dawicke et al [3]. The close matches between the computed and measured crack opening profiles validated the FE modeling of the dynamic ductile fracture experiments. The influence of the initial crack tip blunting is maintained throughout the crack extension history. The FE analysis was then used to compute the dynamic J and the $T^*_\varepsilon$ integral values shown in Figure 3. While the near field J continually decreased after reaching a maximum value, the $T^*_\varepsilon$ reached a steady state value with crack propagation.

Both the $T^*_\varepsilon$ integral and CTOA remained constant during the dynamic fracture event. The large and precipitous drop at the CTOA at its initial phase of rapid crack propagation is probably due to the crack tip blunting prior to crack extension.

## ACKNOWLEDGMENT

This study was supported by Office of Naval Research Contract N0001489J1276. The authors acknowledge the patience and encouragement of Dr. Y.D.S. Rajapakse, ONR during the difficult period of the experimental analysis.

## REFERENCES

[1] Wang, F.X., May, G.B. and Kobayashi, A.S., 1994, "Low-Spatial Frequency Steep Geomentric Grating for Use in Moire Interferometry," *Optical Engineering*, Vol. 33, pp. 1125-1131.
[2] Okada, H. and Atluri, S.N., "$T^*_\varepsilon$ integral evaluation from experimental displacement field for a plate with stably propagating crack: Development of calculation procedure and implication of $T^*_\varepsilon$," to be submitted.
[3] Dawicke, D.S., Sutton, M., Newman, J.C. and Bigelow, C.A., 1995, "Measurement and Analysis of Critical CTOA for Thin-Sheet Aluminum Alloy Materials," *Fracture Mechanics, 25th Volume*, ed. F. Erdogan , ASTM STP 1220, pp. 358-379.

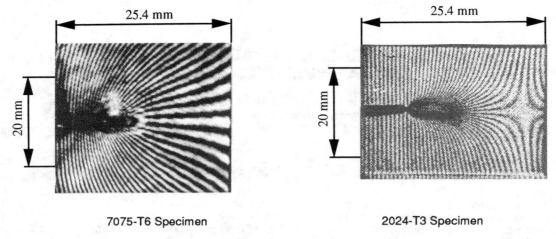

7075-T6 Specimen                                    2024-T3 Specimen

Figure 1.  Dynamic Moire Patterns of Fracturing Aluminum SEN Specimens

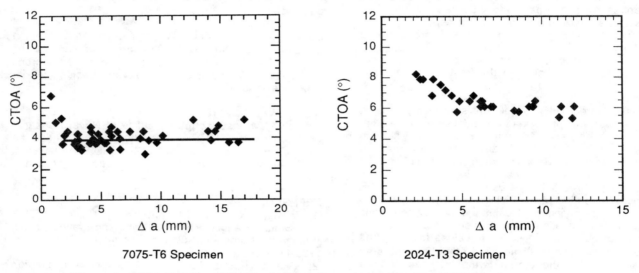

7075-T6 Specimen                                    2024-T3 Specimen

Figure 2.  CTOA Variations With Rapid Crack Extension in Aluminum SEN Specimens

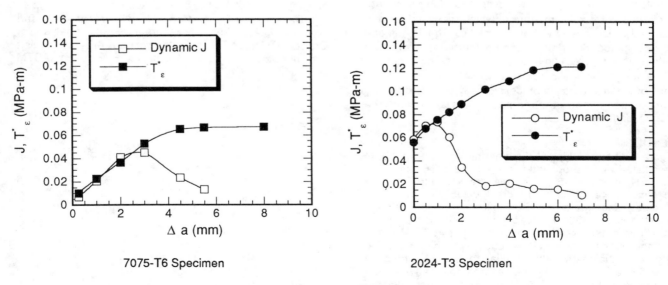

7075-T6 Specimen                                    2024-T3 Specimen

Figure 4. $T^*_\varepsilon$ and J Variations in Aluminum SEN Specimens, $\varepsilon$ = 2 mm.

446

# The Dynamic Fracture Toughness Evaluation of Metal Matrix Composites

M. K. Park, S. M. Bahk
Myongji University, Seoul, Korea
S. K. Choi
Keumkang Lt. Central Research Institute, Kyunggi-Do, Korea

Light weight engine components are under development in Korea using various manufacturing processes to produce aluminum base metal matrix composites(MMC) to meet challenges of future demands for higher fuel efficiencies and lower vehicle emissions. Many fabrication processes are currently available to manufacture reliable metal matrix composites(MMC) and to achieve the goal of making light weight engine components. Also, dynamic properties such as dynamic fracture toughness are known to strongly influence the fabrication processes and nature of reinforcing fibers.

The dynamic fracture toughness values may be numerically same as those of crack arrest fracture toughness. However, it has been postulated that although a fracture may be initiated by static loading, the material at some small microscopic distance ahead of the fracture initiation site will be effectively loaded under dynamic conditions and therefore, dynamic fracture toughness is a better indication of a material resistance to crack propagation than the toughness from static loading.

In this study, the squeeze casting process was selected to produce $Al_2O_3$-$SiO_2$-$ZrO_2$ ceramic fiber reinforced Al matrix composites. The $ZrO_2$ fiber is added as a reinforcing agent to determine extent of mechanical stabilization of the composites, especially at elevated temperatures. The ceramic fiber volume fractions of the preforms for the squeeze casting are 7 and 11% respectively.

Three point bend tests were briefly conducted to establish base line data for static loading conditions and Charpy impact tests were performed to evaluate dynamic fracture toughness of the MMC. Three point bend specimens as well as Charpy impact test specimens were prepared from the squeeze casted MMC containing 7 and 11% fiber volume fractions and also, from unreinforced A356 aluminum casting alloys for comparison purposes.

The Charpy impact test machine was instrumented to obtain dynamic responses from the tests of the MMC specimens at low impact velocities. The block diagram of the computer assisted instrumented Charpy impact test system is described in Fig.1

The result shows that the tensile strength and elastic modulus have been improved 15-20% by adding more than 15% fiber volume fraction which there is a slight improvement on tensile strength and elastic modulus for the addition of less than 15% fiber volume fractions. The dynamic fracture toughness of MMC was reduced to 25% of unreinforced Al alloy by the 11% addition of the reinforcement. Further additions of fiber reinforcement to Al matrix can improve mechanical properties but it can deteriorate the dynamic fracture toughness.

References:

[1] Lim, T., Han, K. S., "Fabrication and Mechanical Properties of Aluminum Matrix Composite Materials," J. Com. Mater., Vol. 26 No. 7, 1992, pp 1062-1086.

[2] Dinwoodie, J., " Automotive Applications for MMC's Based on Short Staple Alumina Fibers," SAE Technical PaperSeries, 1992, No.870437

[3] Suresh, K. V., John, L. D., "Performance Characteristic of Metal Ceramic Composites Made by the Squeeze Casting Process," Ceram. Eng. Sci. Proc., Vol.9, 1988, pp.579-576

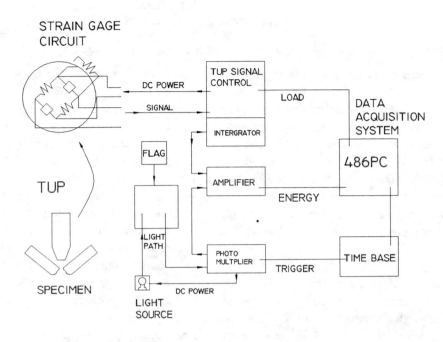

Fig.1 Block diagram of computer assisted instrumented
Charpy impact test system

# INVERSE ANALYSIS FOR EMBEDDED FRACTURES

William D. Keat
Dept of Mechanical and Aeronautical Engineering
Clarkson University
Potsdam, NY   13699

Michael C. Larson
Department of Mechanical Engineering
Tulane University
New Orleans, LA   70118

This work deals with a combined experimental and theoretical effort to develop a crack detection and characterization methodology based on measurements of surface deformations. Such a technique holds significance for monitoring the development of cracks within laboratory test specimens and for providing a basis for new field level nondestructive evaluation techniques. The computational intensiveness of conventional numerical methods as well as a lack of experimental data have precluded the development of such a capability in the past.

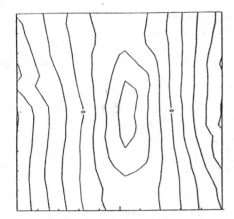

Contours of surface displacement produced by a pressurized crack

At the heart of the computational portion of the new methodology is the three-dimensional Surface Integral and Finite Element method for fracture analysis. Free surfaces are accounted for by coupling a multipole-based surface integral scheme with a finite element analysis approach. The method has proven to be accurate and efficient for solving direct problems of near-interface fractures in multiple-layered and bounded domains. The deformation field induced on a free surface by the presence of a fracture can be determined as the superposition of contributions due to a surface integral model of the fracture and a finite element model of the uncracked bounded domain. The long range goal is the development of a nonlinear inversion scheme which is both robust enough to converge under the expected noise levels and fast enough to be of practical value when monitoring a structure in real time.

Results presented here attest to the feasibility of the proposed strategy. Numerical studies conducted using a nonlinear least-squares algorithm specially tailored for use with the surface integral formulation have defined the applicable range of fracture geometries. Convergence is addressed in light of experimental error, nondimensional depth, and the number of degrees of freedom used to represent the geometry. Measures taken to improve both the resolution and the speed of the inversion process are also discussed.

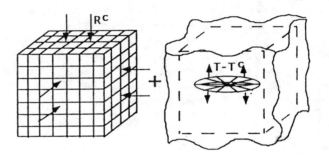

Finite Element representation of a block with no crack

Surface Integral representation of a crack in an infinite medium

The experimental portion of the effort is key to the program. The worth of the above inverse solver as a useful tool is being demonstrated by using actual measurements and comparing the results with known solutions. Quasi-static fracture propagation tests have been designed such that a three-dimensional embedded fracture of known shape, orientation, and loading can grow within a medium while surface displacements are measured. The experimental specimens are fabricated from a transparent brittle material in which hydraulically driven fractures can be visually observed. As the fracture progresses, the evolving displacements induced at the surface of the specimen are measured by laser interferometry.

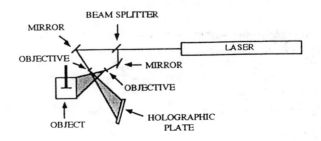

Laser interferometry setup

# Develope a 3-D Contact Pressure & 2-D Slip Displacement Detecting Sensor.

## Sung-hoon Kim, Kyu-zong Cho

Chonnam National Univ.
300 Yongbong-Dong
Kwangju-City, Korea

In this study, 3-dimensional contact pressures & 2-dimensional slip displacements detecting sensor has been developed for analyzing the contact phenomena. The develped sensor is composed of two parts, the upper part measures 3-dimensional contact pressures and the lower part measures 2-dimensional slip displacements. It could measure not only 3-dimensional contact pressures but also 2-dimensional slip displacements at the same time and same point. The calibrated results show of developed sensor that good linearity, sensitivity and repetition, and also it show small interference at each directional components.

So, this miniature sensor will be helpful for analyzing the contact surface problems, as like the contact phenomena analysis of automobile tire which has complicated small tread pattern block.

## Introduction

In study contact phenomena, it is important to know the distribution of contact pressures and slip displacement on the contact surface.

Especially, in tire contact phenomena, which accour between soft material (tire) and hard material (ground), load, it is possible to ignore the deformation of hard material, but the deformation of soft materials must be considered.

When eximinate the deformation of soft materials on wntach surface, it is necessary to measure the distribution of 3-dimensional contact pressure and 2-dimensional slip displacement at the same time and same point.

In this study, 3-dimensional contact pressures and 2-dimensional slip displacements detecting sensor has been developed for evaluating the contact phenomena.

The sensitivity, linearity and repetition the developed sensor will be proven by calibration test.

## Design Sensor

In the tire contact problem, when the tire drivven momally, pressure were introduced that the vertical direction pressure is $0 \sim 0.25$ kg/mm$^2$ and the horizontal direction pressure is $0 \sim 0.1$ kg/mm$^2$. So, measuring range of pressures was determined that the vertical range is $0 \sim$ 0.5 kg/mm$^2$ and the horizontal range is $0 \sim 0.2$ kg/mm$^2$.

In normal driving tire, since the slip displacement of the tread is known that the minimum value is 0.5 mm. the measuring range of slip displacement is decided to $0 \sim 1.0$ mm with minimization of resisting force.

In this study, the attaching straingages method was used, because this method is suitable for measuring dynamic and static load. Force transducer generally employ sensing elements that convert the applied force into a deformation of an elastic element.

The disigned sensor made from the material which have good stiffness and high strength, because a good stiffness make sensor to have a good sensitivity and high strength make a sensor to have a good linearity.

Because the applied force make a complicated deformation, it is important to separate the components in each direction. The shape of pressure sensor was decided that disk type load cell having contact probe for easily separate deformations (strains) in each directions.

The decided shape of sensor was composed of two part, one is to measure pressures and the other is to measure slip displacements. Fig. 1 shows the shape of the pressure detecting element. The shape of the pressure sensor have a disk which is used to measure horizontal pressures and a probe which is used to measure vertical pressure and trnsmit horizontal pressure.

For measuring pressures preciously, the area of the probe is as small as possible. Since there is need to space for measuring slip displacements, it is impossible to decrease the area infinitely. Therefore, the contact probe was designed the tube type.

Fig. 2 is shows the decided shape of measuring slip element. In the slip displacement detecting element, the shape is similar to the shape of the pressure detecting sensor, it have a disk and a pin. The disk is used to measure the slip displacement which is transmitted by the pin. The pin must be sufficiently flexible and have a elastic behaviour, because it move with being driven into the rubber of tire tread.

Each disk have the same size, the outer diameter is $\phi$ 25 mm and the inner diameter is $\phi$ 15mm. The thickness of measuring pressure disk is 1.2 mm and that of measuring slip displacement disk is 0.3 mm.

The shape of pin is tapered for strengthening when it transmit slip displacements from the contact surface to the bottom disk.

## Circuits

For exact measuring, it is necessary to minimize the interference of each direction.
therefore, it is important to determine the location of strain gages.

Fig. 3 shows that the location of gage which was decided to minimize the interference. Gages, which were attached on the disk, are to measure horizontal direction pressures and the others, attached on the tube, are to measure vertical direction pressure. For the minimizing interference, gages compose the circuit and this method have been used.

Wheastone bridge circuit is introduced that it is suitable for reducing the thermal effect and increasing the sensitivity of sensor. In this study, it was used. And then, twelve gages were attached on determined positions of pressure measuring element.

Fig 4 shows that the location of gages, which is similar to the positions of the horizontal pressure measuring element, were attached on the slip displacement measuring element. For the slip measuring element, eight gages were attached on it.

## Calibration test

The calibration test was preformed, for verifying the characteristic of the manufactured sensor. In testing, it is considered that is written below.
- repetition : The same pressure and displacement make a same detecting results with several test.
- linearity : Increase and decrease of pressure or displacement is in proportion to the increase and decrease of detecting results.
- interference : Any direction component should not effect to the others directions.

Fig. 5 shows the schematic diagram that calibrate pressure detecting element.
In Fig 5 (a), the holder and weights was used to load horizontal direction pressure, and the weights was compared to detected results.
The increment of given horizontal pressure is 0.1 kg, during 0 ~ 2 kg. In vertical direction test, Fig. 5(b), the load-cell was used to compress the sensor. And then, the value, which was detected by the designed sensor, were compared to measured results by load cell.
The increment of given vertical load is 10 kg during 0 ~ 80 kg.

Fig. 6 shows the diagram that evaluate the displacement detecting part. In this test, the precious extensiometer calibrator was used to give displacement the displacement detecting part.
The increment of given displacement is 0.1 mm during 0 ~ 1 mm.
Also, each test was performed in the direction of 0° ,30° ,45° ,60° and 90° from x-axis.

## Results

Fig. 8 ~ Fig. 13 show results of horizontal pressure calibration test.
Fig 8. shows that the interference of X-direction pressure are 0.9% in Y-direction and 1.7 % in Z-direction. Fig 9. shows that the interference of Y-direction pressure is 0.2% in X-direction and 5.8 % in Z-direction. Fig. 10 ~ Fig. 12 show results of test which were performed in 0°, 30°, 45° and 60° from X-axis. Fig. 13 shows results of vertical pressure calibration test and that the repetition and linearity of the developed sensor are credible.

These show that the linear constants of sensor are 232 strain/kg (X-direction), 252.13 strain/kg (Y-direction) and 5.04 strain/kg (Z-direction).

Fig. 14 ~ Fig. 18 show results of slip displacement calibration test. Fig. 14 shows that the interference of X-direction slip is 4.35 % in Y-direction and Fig. 15 shows that the interference of Y-direction slip is 4.35 % in X-direction. The linear constant of slip measuring element are 347.5 strain/mm (X-direction) and 537.73 strain/mm (Y-direction).

As results, the developed sensor have a good linearity and repetition and this miniature sensor will be helpful for analyzing the contact surface problems, as like the contact phenomena analysis of automobile tire which has complicated small tread block.

## Reference

1. 한국 종합 특수강 주식회사, 1978, " 특수강 ", PP 343 ~ 347
2. H. O. Fuchs, R. I. Stephens, 1980, " Metal Fatigue In Engineering ", A Wiley-Interscience Publication, PP 69
3. R. E. Peterson, 1974, "STRESS CONCENTRATION FACTORS ", A Wiley-Interscience Publication, pp
4. Stephen P. Timoshenko, 1989. S. Woinowsky-Klieger " Theory of Plates and Shells ", Mc-Grow Hill, PP 51 ~ 78
5. Warren C. Young, 1986, " Roark's Formulars for Stress and Strain " PP 391~4406. James W. Dally, William F. Riley, 1991, " Experimental Stress Analysis ", PP 214~261,
7. Gere, Timoshenko, 1990, " Mechanics of Material ", PP 260~267
8. 김기환, 국윤환, 김관휴, 1981, " 평상용 동력측정장치의 제작에 관한 연구 "
9. 上田次男 外, 1986, " 센서 인터페이싱 "
10. 백수현, 1990, " Sensor Hand Book "
11. S. A. Lippmann and K. L. oblizajek, 1974, " The Distribution of Stress Between the Tread and the Road for Freely Rolling Tires ", Uniroyal , Inc , S. A. E.
12. Marion G. Potinger, 1991, " Apparatus for measuring Tire tread Force and Motion ", The Uniroyal Goodrich Tire Company, United States Patent
13. PRECISION MEASUREMENT Co. , 1991, " Tire - Road Contact Presuure Sensor "

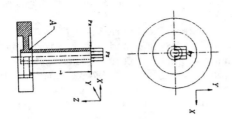

Fig. 1 The Structure of Pressure Measuring Part

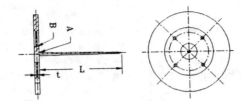

Fig. 2 The Structure of Slip Measuring Part

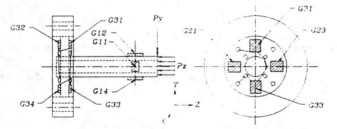

Fig. 3 Positions of Gage for measuring Force

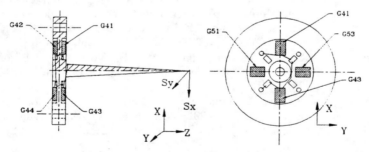

Fig. 4 Positions of Gage for measuring Slip

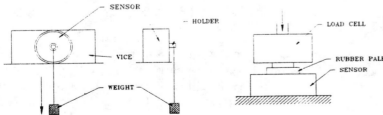

Fig. 5 Schematic Diagram of Force Calibration System.

EXTENSIOMETER CALIBRATOR

Sensor

Fig. 6 Schematic Diagram of Slip Displacement (X,Y) Calibration System.

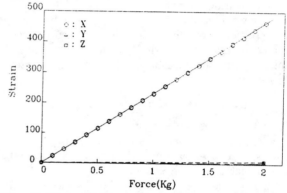

Fig. 7 Force Calibration Results At 0 Degrees from X Axis.

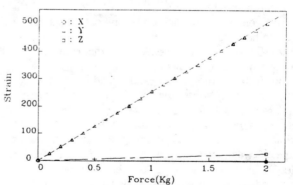

Fig. 8 Force Calibration Results At 90 Degrees from X Axis.

452

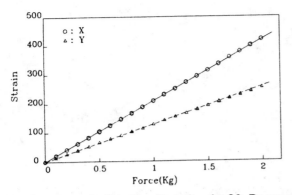

Fig. 9 Force Calibration Results At 30 Degrees from X Axis.

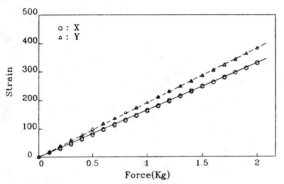

Fig. 10 Force Calibration Results At 45 Degrees from X Axis.

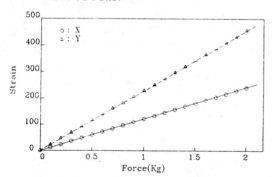

Fig. 11 Force Calibration Results At 60 Degrees from X Axis.

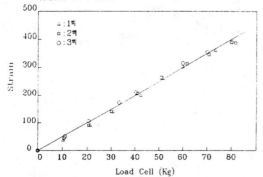

Fig. 12 Force Calibration Results (F-z and Load-Cell)

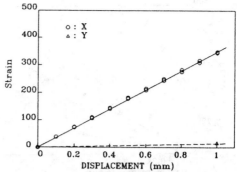

Fig. 13 Displacement Calibration Results At 0 Degrees from X Axis.

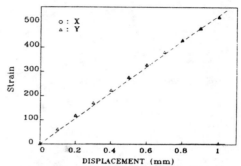

Fig. 14 Displacement Calibration Results At 90 Degrees from X Axis.

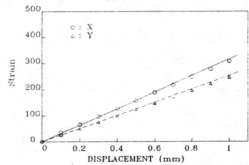

Fig. 15 Displacement Calibration Results At 30 Degrees from X Axis.

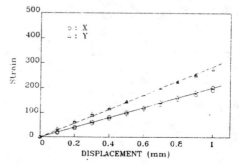

Fig. 16 Displacement Calibration Results At 45 Degrees from X Axis.

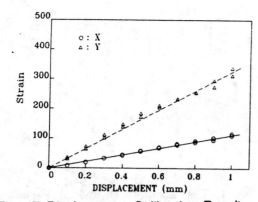

Fig. 17 Displacement Calibration Results
At 60 Degrees from X Axis.

# A New Strain Gage Method For Measuring The Crack Propagation Toughness In Non-isothermal Fields

R.J. Sanford[1], G.S. Sayal[2]
Department of Mechanical Engineering
University of Maryland
College Park, MD 20742

The instantaneous dynamic stress intensity factor associated with a propagating crack can be measured with strain gages properly positioned and oriented relative to the path of the crack. Using a procedure similar to that developed previously for determining the stress intensity factor from a single strain gage [1], Dally and Sanford introduced a method of measuring the propagation toughness, $K_{ID}$ [2]. They used a series of strain gages positioned along a line parallel to the line of crack propagation and recorded a series of strain-time traces as the crack propagated past the gages.

The approach was extended to a third-order theory by Dally, Sanford and Berger [2, 3, 4]. By considering a non-rectangular strain gage rosette with its adjacent arms positioned in a rotated coordinate system relative to the line of propagation of the crack, the expression for the dynamic strain response using a three parameter representation is obtained as :

$$2\mu\epsilon_g = A_0 f_0^{\phi d} + A_1 f_1^{\phi d} + B_0 g_0^{\phi d} \qquad (1)$$

where, $f_0^{\phi d}$, $f_1^{\phi d}$ and $g_0^{\phi d}$ are functions of crack tip velocity, orientation of the arms of the strain gage rosette and the velocity dependent position parameters.

Two basic problems are encountered in measuring $K_{ID}$ using a line of single element strain gages deployed on a gage line positioned at a fixed distance above the crack propagation line. The first problem is to locate the crack-tip as the crack propagates past the gages and to track its movement with time during the entire event. The second problem deals with the quantity of data generated from a line of gages.

Berger, Dally and Sanford [4] solved these problems by developing an algorithm where triangulation was used to locate the crack tip using strain data from two adjacent gages. An iteration scheme was incorporated in the algorithm to determine the value of $\frac{A_1}{A_0}$ providing a solution with three parameter accuracy. As a portion of the crack-tip locating algorithm, the value of $K_{ID}$ was determined. Its inclusion in the program automates the data processing and permits $K_{ID}$ to be measured many times as the crack propagates between two gages, thus, permitting an over-deterministic analysis of the results. Unfortunately, the method is limited to isothermal strain fields and the analysis is time consuming.

The current work is an extension of earlier concepts and uses

pairs of strain gage rosettes to develop a new strain gage technique for determining $K_{ID}$ which overcomes the earlier limitations. The strain gage rosettes are positioned at a predetermined angle so as to get discrete values of $K_{ID}$ at predefined positions relative to the gages. An advantage of this method is that the crack-tip position is known relative to the discrete points automatically without going through any iterative procedure. Unlike all the previous methods, this method does not require us to estimate $A_1$. Besides, this method has an inherent advantage that it is applicable to non-isothermal fields as well by virtue of suitable interconnection of the strain gages comprising the rosettes.

This paper describes the analytical development of this new technique and its experimental verification through tests on 7075-T651 aluminum SEN specimens. The three terms of equation (1) were studied independently to determine ways of eliminating the $B_0$ and $A_1$ terms. It was found that by positioning a rectangular rosette at an angle of 23° relative to the crack line, the $f_1^{\phi d}$ term vanishes at $x = 0$, i.e. at the position of the crack tip. Moreover, the $g_0^{\phi d}$ term being independent of the perpendicular distance from the crack line could be eliminated by subtracting the strain response of one rosette from another vertically displaced rosette. Thus, by using pairs of rectangular rosettes, suitably wired into a 4 arm bridge circuit (Figure 1), both the $f_1^{\phi d}$ and $g_0^{\phi d}$ terms could be eliminated at one discrete location which is directly above the crack tip. The strain response at this discrete location is used to calculate the propagation toughness from the final equation,

$$\frac{2\mu\{\epsilon_g\}}{A_0} = (f_0^{\phi d})_2 - (f_0^{\phi d})_1 \qquad (2)$$

where, $\epsilon_g = \left\{(\epsilon_g)_2 - (\epsilon_g)_1\right\}$, and the subscripts 1 and 2 are used for the two rosettes. For a fixed orientation of the rosette, $f_0^{\phi d}$ is a constant at the discrete location. Therefore the right-hand-side of equation (2) is a constant. A generic curve for specific values of the rosette parameters at a crack velocity of 825 m/s is shown in Figure 2.

Finally, the normalized strain value at the crack tip ($x = 0$) position is used in equation (2) to determine $K_{ID}$ using $K_{ID} = \sqrt{2\pi}A_0$.

This analytical formulation was verified experimentally. Five pairs of rectangular strain gage rosettes were mounted on the specimen and the specimen was loaded until failure occurred by dynamic crack propagation. The strain time traces obtained from the experiment are shown in Figure 3. The av-

[1]Professor, SEM Fellow
[2]Mechanical Engineer, MSME 1995

erage velocity of propagation of the crack was calculated as 825 m/s and the propagation toughness, $K_{ID}$, varied from 49.8 MPa$\sqrt{\text{m}}$ to 54.1 MPa$\sqrt{\text{m}}$. The value of the crack propagation toughness, $K_{ID}$, for 7075-T651 aluminium SEN specimen has been earlier obtained by Sanford [5] using the classical moire optical method. He measured $K_{ID}$ at 675 m/s as 54 MPa$\sqrt{\text{m}}$. Thus, the experimental results are in close agreement with earlier results obtained on the same material.

## References

[1] J. W. Dally and R. J. Sanford. Strain gage methods for measuring the opening-mode stress-intensity factor, $K_I$. *Experimental Mechanics*, 27(4):381–388, 1988.

[2] J. W. Dally and R. J. Sanford. Measuring the stress intensity factor for propagating cracks with strain gages. *ASTM Journal of Testing and Evaluation*, 18(4):240–249, 1990.

[3] J. W. Dally, R. J. Sanford, and J. R. Berger. An improved strain gage method for measuring $K(t)$ for a propagating crack. *Journal of Strain Anal. Eng. Design*, 25(3), 1990.

[4] J. R. Berger, J. W. Dally, and R. J. Sanford. Determining the dynamic stress intensity factor with strain gages using a crack tip locating algorithm. *Engineering Fracture Mechanics*, 36(1):145–156, 1990.

[5] R. J. Sanford. A moire study of dynamic crack propagation in aluminium. In *Proceedings of the 1991 SEM Spring Conference on Experimental Mechanics*, pages 344–349, Milwaukee, WI, June 1991. Society of Experimental Mechanics.

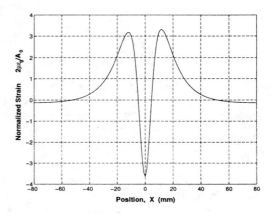

Figure 2: Representative rosette response curve for strain gage pairs at 9 and 20 mm with tilt angle = 23° and crack velocity = 825 m/s.

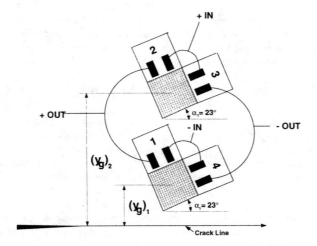

Figure 1: Gage layout and inter-gage wiring

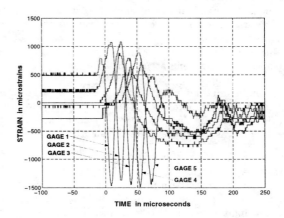

Figure 3: Strain-time traces recorded in the experiment for an aluminium SEN specimen

# Application of a new signal conditioner on long-term strain gage measurements

P.CAPPA (SEM member), Z.DEL PRETE (SEM member), F.MARINOZZI
University of Rome "La Sapienza"
Department of Mechanics and Aeronautics
Via Eudossiana, 18 - 00184 - ROMA
Tel.:(+396) 44585273
Fax.:(+396) 4881759

Among the different strain gage measurement techniques proposed, in 1983 the possibility of getting directly the electrical resistance variation had been analyzed [1]; such a configuration will be appointed as DRM (Direct Resistance Method). Apparently, the DRM comparatively examined with the Wheatstone bridge needs a greater number of connection lead wires (4 for each strain gage) as to remarkably reduce the effects induced by the lead wire themselves and does not allow the compensation of the effects induced on the strain gage by temperature variations. However, it greatly simplifies the measurement equipment in a way that it results easily made of an ohmmeter. Such a configuration has later been experimentally examined [2,3] and the potencies held by the DRM have been confirmed.

The effects induced by a relay switch control unit, not devoted to strain-gage measurements, have been analyzed [4,5]. The results obtained with a computerized acquisition system, able to follow static or quasi-static phenomena, have shown worth considering zero-shift values, in one week tests ($-30$ to $+10$ $\mu m/m$). It has, therefore, been examined the possibility of adopting the DRM even for dynamic measurements, utilizing high-speed digital multimeters ($\leq 100\ 000$ readings/s) [6]. The collected data have shown remarkable uncertainties on the observed values ($\cong 200$ $\mu m/m$). Then, the possibility of improving the metrological performances, by acting on the electrical current direction to reduce the thermoelectrical phenomena effects which occur at the switch control unit contacts, has been evaluated. A comparative examination of the obtained results together with those relative to the measurement equipment based on the DRM [7] have not yet shown significant differences even in two-week tests.

The tests which have been carried out so far by utilizing off the shelf instrumentation have shown the potentialities of the DRM and, the development and realization of a strain-gage channel founded on such a principle has appeared of interest.

A strain-gage signal conditioning scheme, which appeared to be innovative, have been proposed [8] and is appointed as DRM. It is based on a potentiometric circuit with twin constant current suppliers. From the experimental tests carried out on our prototype the following has been highlighted: a satisfying sensitivity ($\cong 1 \mu m/m$), a graduation line which might be considered linear (nonlinearity error less than $1 \mu m/m$), low values of zero-shift ($<1 \mu m/m$) throughout 60 hour test, and, in the end, a global temperature coefficient which can be considered negligible in usual utilization ($0.1 \mu m/m/°C$).

The aim of the present research project is the evaluation of the prototype previously described in long-term strain measurements to point out its effective reliability in field applications such as mechanical structures, bridges and buildings. The experimental analysis is focused on monitoring the metrological performances of the new conditioner in long time continuous utilization (3-5 months) comparatively with a traditional Wheatstone Bridge device. Parameters such as zero-shift, external temperature, housing temperature will be analyzed simultaneously for both systems.

In order to minimize power consumption and to improve the reliability of whole system, the long-term test will be conducted by alternatively switching on and off the circuitry under test and the instrumentation when a set of measurement has to be taken. To establish a correct temporization of the power-up and subsequent data acquisition sequence, some warm-up tests has been carried out. The collected data suggest that DRM-SG has a relatively short warm-up time and an output shift of only about 5 $\mu m/m$ (from $t=t_0$ to $t \rightarrow t_\infty$), both for $120\Omega$ (Fig.1) and $350\Omega$ (Fig.2) strain gages. WB chip exhibits a slower warm-up and a shift of about $50 \mu m/m$. This unequal behaviour is related to the difference between thermal time constants of the examined systems. DRM-SG is composed by separated small chips that exhibit a relatively short thermal transient compared to that of the bigger WB chip. The extremely low temperature coefficient of DRM-SG was already pointed out in a previous article [8]. The use of transducers with higher resistance ($350\Omega$ instead of $120\Omega$) allow a smaller current to be supplied by the circuit and thus a lesser increase of chip temperature. Anyway, a common warm-up interval can be fixed in about 1hour for the WB circuit and 15 minutes for the DRM-SG; after this time length the experimentalist can be quiet sure that measurements are not affected by warm-up induced transients.

Actually the long-term test is in progress and thus no results are yet available.

## REFERENCES

1. Nelson E.J., Sikorra C.D., Howard J.L. "*Measuring strain gages directly without signal conditioning*", **Experimental Techniques**, v7, n9, pp26-28, 1983.
2. Zachary L.W., McConnell K.G., Younis N.T. "*Accounting for lead wire resistance changes and loss of zero in long-term strain measurements*" SEM Spring Conference

on Experimental Mechanics, Albuquerque NM, pp201-204, June 4-6, 1990.

3. Cappa P., McConnell K.G., Zachary L.W. *"Zero-shift values of automatic and inexpensive strain gage instrumentation systems"*, **Experimental Mechanics**, v31, n1, pp88-92, 1991.

4. Cappa P. *"A comparative examination of automatic sequential direct systems for strain-gage data readings based on a low-cost switch-control unit"*, **Experimental Techniques**, pp13-15, September, 1989.

5. Cappa P. *"An experimental analysis of the zero-shift values of automatic and inexpensive strain gage instrumentation systems"*, **Experimental Mechanics**, pp 88-92, March, 1991.

6. Cappa P., Del Prete Z. *"An experimental analysis of accuracy and precision of a high speed strain gage sys-* *tem based on the direct resistance method"*, **Experimental Mechanics**, pp78-82, March, 1992.

7. Cappa P., Del Prete Z., McConnell K.G., Zachary L.W. *"Zero-shift evaluation of automatic strain gage systems based on direct and reverse-current method"*, **Experimental Mechanics**, pp293-299, December, 1993; was presented at VII International Congress on Experimental Mechanics, Las Vegas NV, 8-11 June 1992.

8. Cappa P., Del Prete Z., Marinozzi F. *"Experimental analysis of a new strain-gage conditioner based on a constant current method"*, accepted for publication on **Sensors and Actuators**.

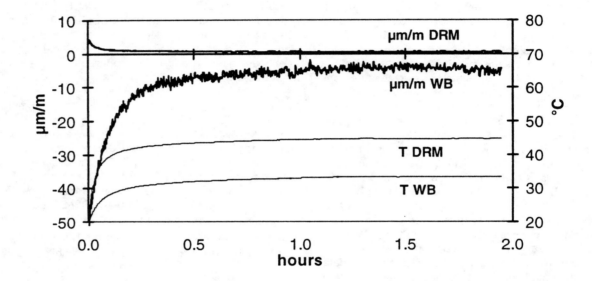

Fig.1 Warm-up test, 120 $\Omega$.

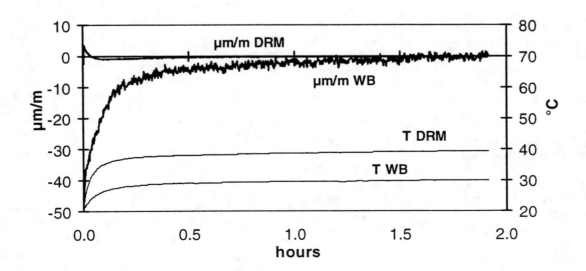

Fig.2. Warm-up test, 350$\Omega$.

# "Wireless strain-measurement using a prestressed sensor"

L. Nilly, N. Nicoletti, M. Renner
Modelling and Identification in Automatics and Mechanics - ESSAIM
12, Rue des Frères Lumière
68093 Mulhouse Cedex
France

The analysis and design of engineering structures usually require strain measurement. But fitting-out a mechanical component with strain gages is laborious in the industrial environment. Moreover, we soon come up against problems such as the non re-use of the sensor, the wired data communication and the cost of implementation. So there is a need for a simple, low cost sensor whose electrical quantity is processed and can be wireless transmitted to a computer if needed.

This sensor is fitted on the structure whose properties have to be defined. In this case, strains are not measured on the structure but on its additional component, according to the position of its locating points. This position is determined by the strain gages bonded on this part. This fitting-out principle has been patented (no 93.01408).

The geometry of the sensor has been designed in order to give the sensing element a mechanical gain, set-up prestressing and a light stress at the locating points [1,2]. It is founded on the bending stress of the elastic member. The set-up process includes prestressing and favors the implementation and the maintenance of the sensor. Thanks to this geometry, strain measuring can be more generally used for measuring stresses such as traction, compression, bending stresses and their combination.

The theoretical properties of the sensor have been defined by the Finite Element Method. Through its prestress, the behavior of the sensor is non-linear. Figure 1 describes the strain of the sensing element according to the relative displacement of the locating points. Part A of the plot describes the set-up prestressing of the sensor. Part B shows the sensor's behavior under compression. A model of the sensing element allows the simulation of the sensor under different stresses and the definition of its dynamic behavior. Using these simulations, sensors can be rapidly adapted to new applications.

A full bridge of gages turns the strains applied on the sensing element into an electrical quantity. A conditioner placed near the gage ensures its excitation, amplification and the output voltage. The sensor only needs to be powered (10-30V) to be ready for use. It delivers an output signal of 0 to 5V. Fgure 2 describes the sensor developed.

This sensor proves useful in civil engineering and weighting. It could be used in non destructive evaluations of bridges. That is why portable stations of data acquisition have been developed. These stations placed near the sensor store the signal delivered and transmit information to a computer by radio transceivers. The user can install several sensors and stations. A wireless local area network is then obtained. A software program on a laptop computer commands the start of acquisition, sampling, the duration of acquisition and the number of sensors used. The information delivered by all the sensors are stored in real time. When data acquisition is completed, the user asks the transmission of information from the stations to the computer via radio transceivers. This method offers real advantages: noises and disturbance due to wired communication are avoided and sensors with their data acquisition system are mobile. The principle of this wireless local area is illustrated in figure 3.

This sensor and its data acquisition and communication station prove versatile. This system is of use in several fields, like the automotive and aircraft industry, civil engineering, weighting....

References:

[1] Perronne J.M. "Mesures et analyse en ligne de déformations de composants mécaniques: application au freinage automobile et généralisation à d'autres systèmes" Thèse au Laboratoire MIAM de l'ESSAIM; Université de Haute Alsace Mulhouse FRANCE

[2] Perronne JM., Renner M., Gissinger GL, "Dynamic aspects of a calliper brake system" AVEC'94 Society of Automotive Engineers of Japan IC. 24-28 October 1994

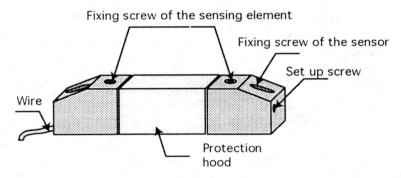

Figure 1: Behaviour simulation of the prestressed sensor

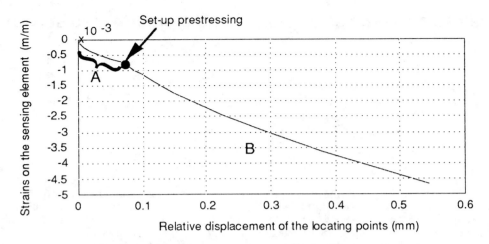

Figure 2: Prestressed sensor developed.

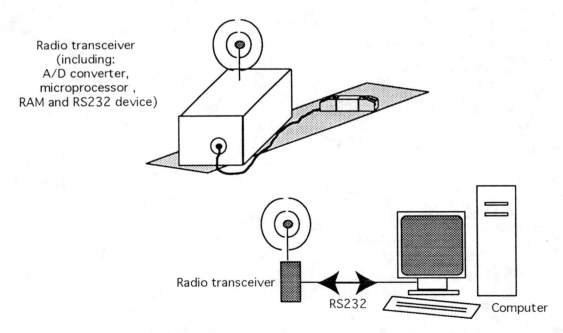

Figure 3: Wireless data acquisition and communication system

# VIBRATION MEASUREMENT BY DIGITAL SPECKLE IMAGE PROCESSING

**N.H.Zhu**, Research Assistant
**F.P.Chiang**, Professor
Laboratory for Experimental Mechanics Research
Department of Mechanical Engineering
State University of New York at Stony Brook
Stony Brook, NY 11794-2300

Mode shape identification in vibration testing has never been an easy task. The schemes of accelerometer array measurement, stroboscopic light freezing, and even the 200-year-old Chladni method are still prevalent in current engineering practices. Obviously, these methods have many limitations and need to be replaced. With the advent of laser technology in the early 1960's, a variety of laser based optical techniques mushroomed in the field of experimental mechanics for vibration measurement. Among those were holographic interferometry, laser speckle interferometry/photography, electronic speckle pattern interferometry, shearography, scanning laser doppler vibrometer and moiré interferometry.

Compared to traditional methods, optical metrology techniques have apparent superiority. Optical methods can readily provide a whole-field measurement of the vibrating object and make the visualization of mode shapes possible. Furthermore, these optical schemes also have advantages such as high sensitivity, non-contact, and (usually) real-time. Ironically, the high sensitivity of these optical approaches limits their introduction to an industrial environment due to the requirement of high mechanical stability on the entire apparatus. Therefore, most optical approaches such as holographic interferometry used with continuous wave lasers have so far been restricted to a laboratory environment. In addition, some techniques such as scanning LDV require specialized equipment, and are therefore not easy to operate. In practical vibration testing one most often only needs to know where nodal (or anti-nodal) lines or points are. Thereafter, one can simply attach the accelerometers to perform exact measurement of acceleration, velocity, etc. Therefore, the qualitative information is most useful and appreciated in mode shape identification. In this paper we developed a novel approach based on the digital speckle image processing to visualize the vibration mode shape qualitatively. A rather detailed description of theory is given in the following paragraphs.

It is well known that speckles are created due to the random interference of light waves bouncing back from an optically rough surface illuminated by a coherent light source such as a laser. These speckles are referred to as *objective speckles* and are formed in the entire space covered by the reflected light. If the surface is viewed either by the eye or via a lens, the speckles vary in size due to the resolution limit of the eye or lens and are referred to as *subjective speckles*. First consider a surface illuminated by coherent light and its imaged subjective speckles formed by a lens. Note that the lens is now focused on the surface. If the surface has an angular tilt, i.e., the surface at the anti-nodal areas is moving in the direction of view, there will be no change in the subjective speckles for speckle photography since the brightness of a speckle is independent of the phase of the objective beam. For speckle interferometry, on the other hand, since a reference beam is added, the sensitivity to this out-of-plane deformation will be achieved. Actually, it is the absence of reference beam that leads to a much less stringent requirement of mechanical stability on the apparatus for speckle photography than for speckle interferometry. Now the lens is deliberately set to focus on a plane in front of the surface, the objective speckles in this plane will have lateral movement because of the angular tilt of the surface at its nodal regions [1]. Therefore, the subjective speckles will also move accordingly due to the lateral motion of the objective speckles in that defocused plane. If the surface has a flexural vibration, i.e., a constant change of angular tilt, the subjective speckles will become blurred or streaked at the nodal regions.

Now we have two approaches to extract the vibration information from this blurred speckle image. From the point of view of image processing the visible texture of this blurred speckle image will be altered and the contrast of those areas will be drastically decreased. In contrast, at the region of anti-nodal line there will be no angular vibration. Therefore, the subjective speckle pattern will remain the same, and that is to say that the high contrast of speckle pattern still remains. If the image containing fuzzy subjective speckle is registered on a CCD camera instead of conventional camera, image edge detection algorithm can be used to filter out the mode shapes. That is due to the fact that edge detection algorithms such as Laplacian operation attenuate the low spatial frequencies of image. The regions of constant intensity become black whereas the regions of rapidly changing intensity values are highlighted. Therefore, a clear picture showing the vibration mode shape can be obtained on a TV monitor after the image processing by the interfaced computer. In this project we have tested many different edge detection techniques such as Sobel, Kirsch, Laplacian, Roberts, Wallis, etc.. They all work very well. In addition, a new algorithm based on local intensity statistics was also developed. For local area of every image there is the estimated standard deviation defined as

$$V(i,j) = \frac{1}{W^2} \sum_{k=i-w}^{i+w} \sum_{l=j-w}^{j+w} [O(k,l) - M(k,l)]^2 \qquad (1)$$

The $V(i,j)$ is computed at each pixel over some $W \times W$ neighborhood where $W = 2w + 1$. The $M(i,j)$ is the estimated mean value of the original image at point $(i,j)$, which is computed as

$$M(i,j) = \frac{1}{W^2} \sum_{k=i-w}^{i+w} \sum_{l=j-w}^{j+w} O(k,l) \qquad (2)$$

We design an algorithm as

$$N(i,j) = M(i,j) + V(i,j)(O(i,j) - M(i,j)) \qquad (3)$$

And $w = 1$, i.e., $3 \times 3$ window size is used. The enhanced image is increased in amplitude with respect to the original at pixels that deviate significantly from their neighbors, and is decreased in relative amplitude elsewhere. Due to intrinsic property of statistics there is no directional bias in detecting edge. Hence, in this respect, local statistical differencing detection is better than any of the algorithms mentioned above. Also, by using digital Fourier spectrum filtering, one can easily filtering out the low spatial frequencies in the frequency domain. And the final processed image can be obtained by performing reverse Fourier transform after highpass filtering in the frequency domain. As a result, we obtain a image of which the regions of constant intensity become black whereas the regions of rapidly changing intensity values are highlighted.

Another approach is using two speckle images which correspond to the initial state without vibration of the object and the final state with vibration of the object, respectively. One can readily find different levels of correlation on different parts of the vibrating surface. In the region of the nodal areas, since the strong angular vibration causes a blurred subjective speckle pattern, the speckle patterns of the two images are decorrelated. On the other hand, in the region of anti-nodal areas, since the subjective speckle pattern remains the same due to the non angular vibration, the speckle patterns of the two images are highly correlated. It is well known that cross-correlation coefficient is a measure of the degree of similarity between two different functions or images. Hence, two images of speckle patterns before and after the vibration of the object are captured and stored in the computer. Each image is then subdivided and the cross-correlation coefficients of corresponding subsets in the two images can be calculated accordingly. For digitized images, and for each subset we have

$$C(i,j) = \frac{\sum_{k=i-w}^{i+w} \sum_{l=j-w}^{j+w} I_1(k,l) I_2(k,l)}{\sqrt{\sum_{k=i-w}^{i+w} \sum_{l=j-w}^{j+w} I_1^2(k,l) I_2^2(k,l)}} \qquad (4)$$

where $I_{1,2}(k,l)$ is the gray level of two images at pixel position $(k,l)$ in each subset. The cross-correlation coefficient $C(i,j)$ is computed at each pixel of entire image over some $W \times W$ neighborhood where $W = 2w + 1$. In this system a $3 \times 3$ subset is adopted, i.e., $w = 1$. The window size can also be $5 \times 5$ or $7 \times 7$, etc. As the window size increases the system has more resistance to local noise. However, the average effect of a large window will also cause detailed information to be lost. As aforementioned, these calculated correlation coefficients represent the similarity between the speckle image with vibration and the speckle image without vibration. Therefore, a Chladni-like pattern should be seen provided that the correlation coefficients can be transformed into an image. Thus, it becomes necessary to perform gray level scaling so as to fit the cross-correlation coefficients into the display range. The algorithm used in this system is just a simple linear stretch function defined as

$$I_f(i,j) = a + b[1 - C(i,j)] \qquad (5)$$

where $I_f(i,j)$ is the final image intensity at $(i,j)$ pixel position and $a$ and $b$ are just scaling constants which can be adjusted until a satisfying image quality is obtained ($a = 50, b = 255$ were used in our program). Finally this coefficient-generated image can be displayed on a TV monitor to show the vibration mode shape. Note that, according to Eq (5), the dark areas in the image should correspond to anti-nodal regions whereas the light areas should correspond to nodal regions.

The entire system is fairly simple. It consists of a He-Ne laser, a beam expander, a $512 \times 512$ CCD camera and a PC with a frame grabber. The algorithm discussed above was implemented in a program written in ANSI C. Obviously, by using laser speckle method, the vibrating objects need not to be in a horizontal position and the testing object can have curved surface. In addition the amplitude range to be detected can be much larger. Overall, this proposed technique not only inherits the merits of conventional optical schemes such as non-contact, non-destruction and whole-field, but also possesses unique features such as noise-resistance, simplicity and user-friendliness. It has been successfully tested in the shipyard of General Dynamic Electric Boat Division. It is authors' believe that this technique should become a new practical engineering tool for in-situ vibration testing.

## References

[1] Chiang, F. P. and Juang, R. M., "Vibration Analysis of Plate and Shell By Laser Speckle Interferometry", *Optica Acta*, Vol.23, No.12, pp.997-1009, 1976.

# Measurement of Three Dimensional Shape and Its Surface Strain by Digital Image Correlation Method

T. Mihara, H. Sumitomo, M. Yoshinari, K. Date
Faculty of Engineering, TOHOKU University
Aramaki, Aoba-ku, 980-77, Sendai, JAPAN

Authors have been developed the measurement system of surface strain and three dimensional shape by using image correlation method. (Fig.1)

In this study, measurement technique of surface strain and three dimensional shape were combined to make non-contact strain measurement of three dimensional shape specimen. Pairs of stereo images each of which consists of 512x512 pixels were stored digitally before and after deformation. In each stereo pair images, the same point on the specimen surface was identified as using image correlation technique. Around each 21x21 pixels on the reference image ( right image before deformation ), standard reference areas consist of 9x9 pixels were defined. Then, similarity of digitized intensity distribution of brightness of the reference area was compared with the one of the comparison area of 9x9 pixels in comparison images successively by using correlation function technique. Identification means that the same point has the most similar intensity distribution around the point in the reference area. In this experiment, then, reference image must be compared with three comparison images, left image before deformation, right and left images after deformation. Using these analytical procedures, three dimensional shapes could be calculated with the estimated parallax between pairs of right and left images by stereoscopy. Comparing with the estimated shapes of the specimen before and after deformation, three dimensional strain could be estimated. Though larger $\theta$ may lead to high accurate shape measurement by stereoscopic theory, also increase the distortion between stereo images and parallax mismatching. In this experiment, stereo angle $\theta$ decided 2.5 degree as the most adequate condition by experimental investigations.

After defining strain expression on three dimensional shape specimen surface with grid method, non-contact two dimensional strain distribution were measured. This paper presents a basic optical setup, algorithm of image correlation and results of strain distribution of three dimensional shape specimen surface. As the sample of large scale deformations, three dimensional shape rubber specimens (one of them were shown in Fig.2) were stretched and pressed. Measurement area of every specimens was 50x50 mm.

As the results, basic procedures of strain distribution measurement of three dimensional shape specimen surface were proposed. Using these procedures, strain distribution of three dimensional shape specimen surface could be measured with the simple optical setup consisted of pair of video cameras and personal computer without any special lighting equipment and surface treatment on specimen.(Fig.3, Fig.4)

## References

1).Peters, W.H, Ranson, W.F., Sutton, M.A. and Chu, T.C., "Application of Digital Image Correlation Method to Rigid Body Mechanics", Opt. Eng.,22(6), (1983)
2).Kahn-Jetter Z.L. and Chu T.C., " Three-dimensional Displacement Measurements Using Digital Image Correlation and Photogrammic Analysis" , Experimental Mechanics , 30(12), 10-16 (1990)

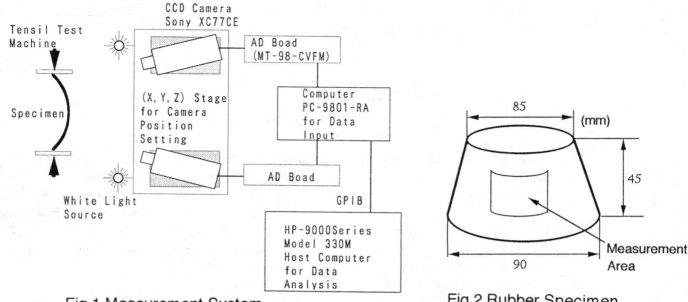

Fig.1 Measurement System

Fig.2 Rubber Specimen

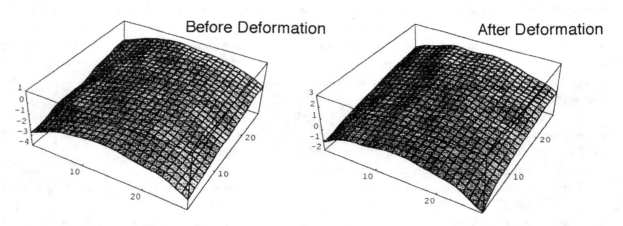

Before Deformation

After Deformation

Fig.3 Three Dimensional Shape Measurement (Compressional Deformation)

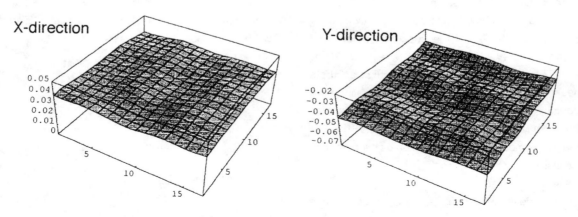

X-direction

Y-direction

Fig.4 Strain on Three Dimensional Specimen Surface

# Improvement of Optical 3-D Deformation Measurement
## by Fuzzy Logic Control

Herbert Weber, Thomas Wolf, Bernd Gutmann
University of Karlsruhe, Institut für Mechanische Verfahrenstechnik und Mechanik
D-76128 Karlsruhe

In the mechanics of materials tensile and compression tests are widely used for material characterization. For simple interpretation of tests, i.e. for the determination of Young's modulus and Poisson's ratio the deformation of the specimens should be exactly homogeneous. Unfortunately specimens of polymeric materials which usually are bonded to endplates at their faces exhibit an inhomogeneous deformation field which cannot be neglected in the evaluation of the tests. Therefore we have to determine the 3-D deformation field of the specimen which is calculated from the 3-D displacement vector field, i. e. from the in-plane and out-of-plane components of the surface displacements. We are mostly interested in the behavior of polymer foams under large deformations, especially in compression. For such test conditions most of the well known measurement techniques like holographic interferometry are not practicable, because they are too sensitive. Grid methods like in-plane moiré fail, because it is impossible to attach a narrow grid on the rough and soft surface of the specimens.

In order to solve the problem of determining the 3-D displacement field of foamed polymers, two different measurement techniques have been combined. With a fringe projection technique the contour of the deformed and undeformed specimen is measured and from these data the out-of-plane component of the 3-D displacement vector field is calculated. The in-plane component is determined by a digital speckle correlation method.

For the evaluation of the phase values from which the specimen contour is determined a phase-shifting technique is used. Due to reflections of the rough surfaces of the foam specimens the images are generally of such poor quality that the phase unwrapping procedure results in numerous errors in the contour data. Provided the filters are adapted to the wavelengths of the projected fringes, 2-D band pass filtering [1] of noisy fringe data can reduce errors. But important details of the contour may be suppressed by this method. Therefore we propose to use a new technique of error reduction in the phase unwrapping process. It consists in the application of a fuzzy controller [2] by which expert knowledge is introduced into the phase unwrapping process. A simple fuzzy controller uses the phase difference between the phase values of two neighboring pixels in the wrapped phase image as a first linguistic input variable. In the case of noisy fringe images a second input variable is required. Because the deformation of the foam specimens do not exhibit pronounced gradients in the contour we expect that the fringe wavelength $\lambda$ on the object does not differ much from that of the reference plane. So we use the distance of the

pixels under observation to the last detected phase jump as a second input data. As an output variable we use singleton 0 when there is no phase jump, and 1 indicating a phase jump. For this three simple fuzzy sets the connecting rules of the input and output variables can be summarized in a matrix. Figures 1 (gray level plot of the specimen's contour without fuzzy) and 2 (gray level plot of the specimen's contour with fuzzy) give an example of the error reducing capability of the developed fuzzy controller. More comfortable controllers with different linguistic variables have also been developed [3]. These sets are more independent from the knowledge about the expected deformation of the specimens.

The digital speckle correlation method for the determination of the two in-plane components of the 3-D displacement vector field of the specimen's surface uses white light speckles instead of laser speckles because they are less sensitive to decorrelation effects caused by strain. The speckle pattern can be created by airbrushing the specimen's surface or by illuminating the rough surface from a high angle to the viewing direction. Correlation of small subsets of the deformed and undeformed state of the digitally recorded speckle patterns results in the correlation function. The surface is divided in subsets with a minimal size of 16 to 16 pixels. The position of the maximum value in the correlation function, i.e. the "correlation peak" yields the desired in-plane displacement vector components of the center point of the subset. A successive scanning of all subsets results in the field of the in-plane components of the surface displacement. Strain leads to decorrelation effects caused by deformation of the speckle pattern or by changes in the illumination. Decorrelation of the pattern produces so called 'false alarms'. These are peak values in the correlation function which are higher than the correlation peak which describes the correct displacement of our subset pattern. As in the unwrapping process, fuzzy logic may also be applied to reduce errors in the digital speckle correlation techniques. The expert knowledge which can be used to create an effective fuzzy controller relies on the fact that the axial displacement of the specimen's surface has an approximately linear dependence from the distance to the fixed endplate of the specimen. So this predisplacements can be introduced to the correlation subset. Now the position of the correlation peak only gives the deviation of the target position from the preestimated position and is expected to be small. The deviation of the correlation peak from the center represents the first linguistic input variable. As a second input variable, we use the 'peak-to-correlation energy, which is a measurement for the signal to noise ratio [4]. The output variable consists of 6 singletons as an indication of the peak quality. Figures 3 (in-plane displacement vector field without fuzzy) and 4 (in-plane displacement vector field with fuzzy) demonstrate the efficiency of the proposed method of error reduction. The fuzzy sets are still in further development. For instance it is possible to introduce the peak shape as an additional input variable in order to take the influence of strain into account.

The described improvements of optical 3-D deformation measurement by utilizing fuzzy logic control make it possible to determine the mechanical relaxation behavior of uniaxially loaded specimens of solid polymer foams, i. g. closed cell PE-foam, in a range of longitudinal strain from -30% to 10% [3]. It turns out that the longitudinal strain between the endplates of the specimen deviates about 10% from the average longitudinal strain which cannot be neglected in the calculation of the relaxation modulus. On the other hand, for PE-foam, the time dependent Poisson's ratio $\nu(t)$ depends on the longitudinal strain in the range between 0,15 for -15% longitudinal strain and 0,35 for 5% longitudinal strain and $t \to \infty$. The limit for an unstrained material is:

$$\nu(\varepsilon = 0, t \to \infty) = 0,28$$

References:
[1] Wolf T., Bilger C., Weber H.: The Combination of Projected Fringe Technique and Digital Speckle Correlation to Measure the 3-D Displacement Vector Field of Foamed Polymers (in German); ÖIAZ, Heft 9, 1995, pp 271-274.
[2] Wolf T., Gutmann B., Weber H.: Fuzzy Logic Controlled Optical Measurements of Large Polymeric Foam Deformations; Proc.,1st Conference on Mechanics of Time Dependent Materials, Ljubljana 1994, SEM, pp 224-229
[3] Wolf, T.: Development of an Optical 3-D Measurement System for Foamed Polymers (in German). PhD Thesis, University of Karlsruhe, Karlsruhe 1996
[4] Wolf T., Gutmann B., Weber H.: A Fuzzy Logic Controlled Optical Measurement System to Detect 3-D Displacements (in German); Mustererkennung 1995, Springer Verlag 1995, pp 334-345

Fig. 2: Error reduction with the use of fuzzy logic

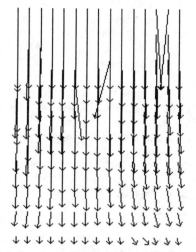

Fig. 3: In-plane field without fuzzy logic

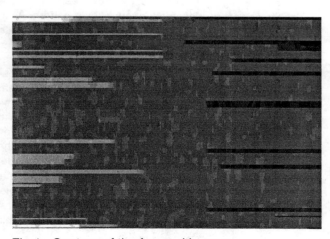

Fig.1: Contour of the foam with errors

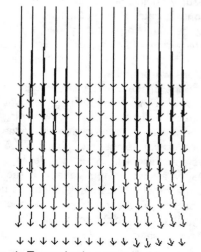

Fig. 4: Fuzzy logic controlled in-plane field

# Optical Surface Roughness Measurement Using Standard Deviations of Two-dimensional Gaussian Function Approximating Scattered Light Intensity Distribution

Masanori Kurita and Zhicong Deng
Dept. of Mech. Engg., Nagaoka University of Technology
Kamitomioka, Nagaoka,940-21 Japan

When a beam of light illuminates the surface of a specimen, a scattered light will broaden as the surface roughness increases. Thus, the surface roughness can be evaluated from the broadness of the scattered light intensity distribution curve. A new optical method was proposed for measuring the surface roughness from the broadness of a scattered light which is evaluated using the two standard deviations (s.d.) of a two-dimensional (2-D) Gaussian function approximating the scattered light intensity distribution.

Figure 1 shows a system for optically measuring surface roughness. The surface of six kinds of ground specimens with the arithmetic mean roughness $Ra$ of ·0.05 to 1.6 $\mu$m were illuminated with a halogen light. The scattered intensity distribution was measured with a CCD camera connected with a personal computer. Figure 2 shows measured intensity distributions of the scatterd light. The scattered intensity distribution was approximated by a 2-D Gaussian function and its broadness was evaluated by using the s.d.'s, $\sigma_x$ and $\sigma_y$, of the function. Figure 3 shows the variation of $\sigma_x$ and $\sigma_y$ as a function of $Ra$. The standard deviation $\sigma_x$ with respect to the direction perpendicular to the grinding direction increased with increasing $Ra$. On the other hand, the s.d. $\sigma_y$ with respect to the grinding direction almost remained unchanged independent of $Ra$.

A three-dimensional surface roughness profile was measured with a stylus type surface roughness tester and the distribution of the facet angle of the roughness profile (the profile angle) $\theta$ was caculated. Figure 4 shows the distribution of the profile angle $\theta$. It was also approximated by a 2-D Gaussian function as shown in Fig.5. The s.d.'s $\sigma_{\theta x}$ and $\sigma_{\theta y}$ of the 2-D Gaussian function were also calculated to evaluate the broadness of the distribution of $\theta$. Figure 6 shows the variation of $\sigma_{\theta x}$ and $\sigma_{\theta y}$ as a function of $Ra$. The variation of $\sigma_{\theta x}$ and $\sigma_{\theta y}$ shown in Fig.6 is similar to that of $\sigma_x$ and $\sigma_y$ shown in Fig.3. Figure 7 shows the variation of $\sigma_x$ of the scattered light as a function of $\sigma_{\theta x}$ of the profile angle. The s.d. $\sigma_x$ increases with increasing $\sigma_{\theta x}$, indicating that the distribution of the scattered light reflects that of the profile angle. The distribution of the profile angle can be used as a more accurate measure of the surface profile than $Ra$ and the maximum height $Ry$ by the stylus method which give only the information of the height of the surface profile.

This opitical method allows rapid and simultaneous measurement of the surface roughnesses in two perpendicular directions. It also permits noncontact and in situ surface roughness measurement and can even measure soft materials without scratching the surface of the specimen.In addition, this technique has a simpler measuring system and it is more insensitive to vibration compared with the optical stylus method.

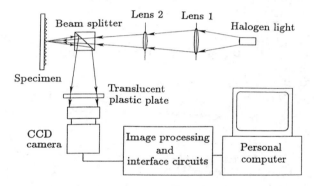

**Fig.1** System for optically measuring surface roughness.

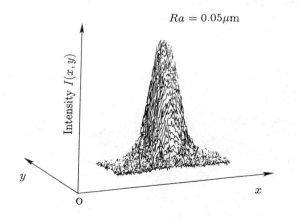

**Fig.2(a)** Measured intensity distribution of scattered light.

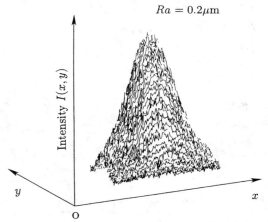

$Ra = 0.2\mu\mathrm{m}$

**Fig.2(b)** Measured intensity distribution of scattered light.

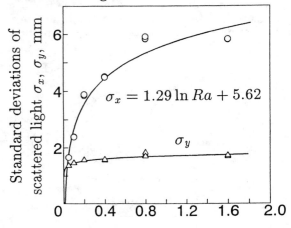

$$\sigma_x = 1.29 \ln Ra + 5.62$$

**Fig.3** Variation of the standard deviations $\sigma_x$ and $\sigma_y$ of intensity distribution of scattered light as a function of $Ra$.

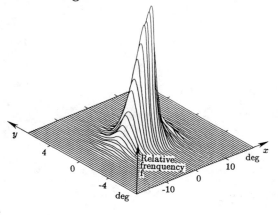

$Ra = 0.2\mu\mathrm{m}$

**Fig.4** Distribution of measured surface profile angle $\theta$ .

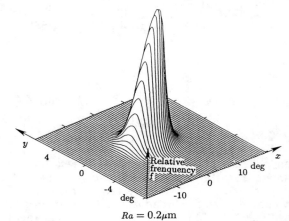

$Ra = 0.2\mu\mathrm{m}$

**Fig.5** 2-D Gaussian function approximating surface profile angle distribution.

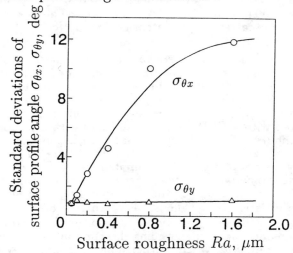

**Fig.6** Variation of standard deviations $\sigma_{\theta x}$ and $\sigma_{\theta y}$ of surface profile angle distribution as a function of $Ra$.

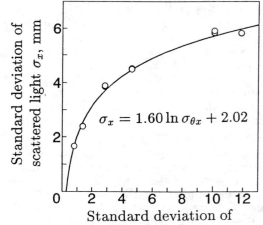

$$\sigma_x = 1.60 \ln \sigma_{\theta x} + 2.02$$

**Fig.7** Variation of standard deviation (s.d.) $\sigma_x$ of intensity distribution of scattered light as a function of s.d. $\sigma_{\theta x}$ of surface profile angle distribution.

# Modified Grid Method for Plastic-Strain-Ratio Measurement in Sheet Metal

S. Y. Lin, R. Czarnek, and P. K. Chaudhury
Concurrent Technologies Corporation
1450 Scalp Avenue
Johnstown, PA 15904

A Modified Grid Method (MGM) has been developed to measure large surface strains (> 1%) on deformed sheet metals. It provides a more precise, global and effective plastic strain ratio (r-value) measurement than the ASTM Standard Test Method (E517-92). The MGM uses an automatic measuring system as Figure 1 shows (including a precision motion stage, an imaging system, and controlling software) and a specialized numerical analyzer for high-precision surface deformation measurement and strain analysis. In addition to higher precision, MGM allows continuous measurement, requires fewer specimens, and lowers overall costs.

The r-value is a widely used parameter in the sheet forming industry that is related to the formability of a sheet metal. The r-value is the ratio of the true strain occurring in the width direction to the true strain in the thickness direction, while a specimen is loaded in tension in the longitudinal direction. In the ASTM Standard Test Method, specimens are either scribed or indented on the gage section and pulled in tension to 10-15% longitudinal strain. Dimensional measurements are made using calipers before and after the test. Therefore, for a single specimen, only one data point is obtained at a given strain level. To increase precision, several specimens are tested.

The MGM test procedure includes specimen preparation, tension testing, picture printing, measurement, and analysis. Figure 2 shows the test setup. Except for tension testing and picture printing, all procedures are automated. Instead of being scribed or indented, a specimen is marked with a matrix of dots with the automatic measuring system. The specimen is then tested in tension while a camera records the specimen deformation at predetermined strain values. This allows dynamic measurement at various strain levels from a single test. The automatic measuring system digitizes the location of dots on printed pictures before and after deformation. The digitized data are then analyzed with a group of computer programs for data smoothing, strain calculation, and r-value calculation.

Table 1 lists the estimated displacement error band of a single specimen under routine operation. The displacement error band of MGM is 5μm in regular resolution mode and 4μm in high-resolution mode, compared to ASTM's 13μm and 25μm in transverse and longitudinal directions, respectively. In the regular resolution mode, measurements are carried out frame-by-frame (a few dots per frame) while in the high resolution mode measurements are made dot-by-dot. In addition to high precision measurement, significant improvement in r-value precision is achieved through over sampling and data smoothing effects with more than 100 data points collected on a single specimen. The resulting error band in r-value from MGM is approximately 10% of that obtained with the ASTM Standard Test Method as Figure 3 shows. This allows precise r-value measurement even at low strain (~5%).

With the higher precision and continuous measurement of MGM, fewer specimens are required to achieve the same or better results than caliper measurement methods. With the automated measuring system and computerized analysis, the time for each test is also reduced. The overall costs, for the same precision level, are lower for MGM than for the ASTM Standard Test Method.

This automatic measuring system is now being used routinely for two-dimensional measurements such as r-values tests. In the meantime, the system is being enhanced to measure the strains in three-dimensional shapes such as a limited-dome-height test specimen.

This work was conducted by the National Center for Excellence in Metalworking Technology, operated by Concurrent Technologies Corporation under contract to the U.S. Navy as part of the U.S. Navy Manufacturing Science and Technology Program

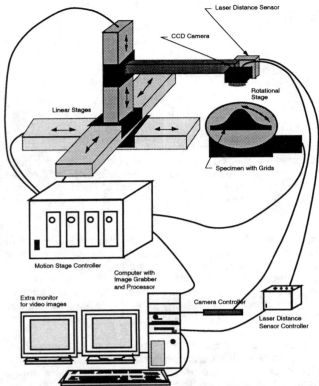

Figure 1    Automatic Non-Contact 3-D Surface Deformation Measuring System

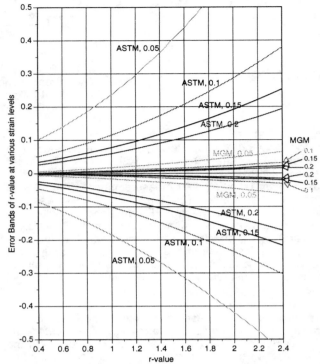

Figure 3    The r-value error bands versus r-value of ASTM Standard Test Method and Modified Grid Method at various strain levels in loading direction; the error bands are based on the worst scenario of a single reduced-size specimen

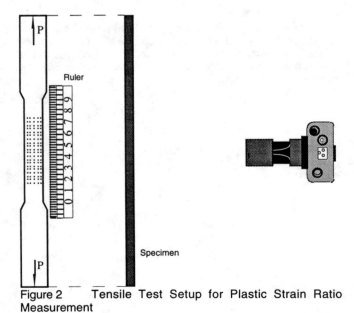

Figure 2    Tensile Test Setup for Plastic Strain Ratio Measurement

Table 1    Estimated Displacement Error Band of a Single Tensile Test Specimen

| METHODS | ERROR BAND |
|---|---|
| ASTM STANDARD TEST METHOD | ±13µm -±25µm |
| MODIFIED GRID METHOD WITH A DIGITIZER (picture magnification factor= 2.6) | ±7µm |
| MODIFIED GRID METHOD WITH AN AUTOMATIC MEASURING SYSTEM (regular resolution mode, picture magnification factor= 2.6) | ±5µm |
| MODIFIED GRID METHOD WITH AN AUTOMATIC MEASURING SYSTEM (high resolution mode, picture magnification factor= 2.6) | ±4µm |

470

# Uitra-high Sensitivity Moiré Interferometry
# by the Aid of Electronic-liquid phase-shifter and Computer

Luo Zhishan   Zhang Heshui   Mu Zongxue   Su Fei

Department of Mechanics and Engineering Measurement

Tianjin University,Tianjin,300072,China

Meirong Tu

Department of Mechanical Engineering

Famu/Fsu College of Engineering

Tallahassee,Florida 32316－2175

This paper presents a new phase-shifter of electric-liquid (Fig. 1),which produces different changes of the phase by adjusting the micro change of voltage to change the velocity of ion movement when the laser beam passes through the liquid; We can prove, the changes of phase $\triangle\varphi_\lambda$ of the laser beam,whose beam wavelength is $\lambda$,are directly proportional to the voltage changes $\triangle U$ of two sides,that is

$$\triangle\varphi_\lambda = K \cdot S \cdot 2\pi \cdot \triangle U /\lambda \qquad (1)$$

where S is the optical distance when the laser beam passes through the liquid,K is a proportional constant.

This paper used an optics-electronic—computer system (Fig. 2). An electric—liquid trough 11,a high accurate power source of direct current and a data voltmeter 12 are installed in the system to realize a meticulous regulation of phase,and set a microscope lens 7 before a TV camera 8,so it can reach partial amplificative observation for the dense fringes.

This shifter not only can be adjusted far from the measured object and testing table,but also is easy to make, and the cost is low. It can reach a stable,high sensitivity and high precise adjustment. It also can reach shifting between two fringes as many as 12 times.

The light intensity of moiré interferometry when using the shifter can be proved by the following equation

$$I = D + C(\alpha,\beta,I_\circ) \cdot \cos[(\varphi_1-\varphi_2)/2+i \cdot \Delta\varphi_\lambda] \qquad (2)$$

where D is a deviation value that shows the influence of background brightness,the second item is the specific property function of reflecting the specimen deformation and difference of phase change; $\varphi_1,\varphi_2$ are phase angles of two interfering beams $S_1$ and $S_2$,i is the number of shift sets,$\triangle\varphi_\lambda$ is the phase change every time a phase shifts,$\alpha$ are the amglitudes of two interfering beams $S_1$ and $S_2$,$\beta$ is the specific property factor of the photoactive object,$I_0$ shows the light strength of interfering beam;that is , the brightness I is adjusted by modulating the phase.

The shifting fringes can be real—time frozen,stored, filtered,sharpened by the computer,at last,it can accomplish addition and subtraction of the shifting fringes. It reaches a sensitivity above 35 nm/fringe when the frequency of the specimen grating is 1200 1/mm and uses a He—Ne laser.

This paper studied the distribution along the radial for elastic modulus of cortical bone (Fig. 3). Here,the author used this micromechanics method,and the variation laws between layers was obtained for the first time. That is , the elastic modulus increased progressively from the inside of the radial to outside,but the elastic modulus of every sticking layer (collagen fibers) between the lamellar bones,arose a low value(Fig. 4).

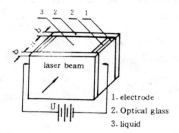

Fig. 1　Electric—liquid trough

1. electrode
2. Optical glass
3. liquid

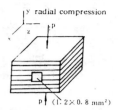

Fig. 3　Specimer

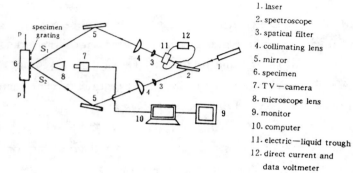

1. laser
2. spectroscope
3. spatical filter
4. collimating lens
5. mirror
6. specimen
7. TV—camera
8. microscope lens
9. monitor
10. computer
11. electric—liquid trough
12. direct current and data voltmeter

Fig. 2　Optics—electronic—computer system

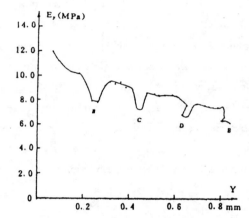

Fig. 4　The distribution along the radial for elastic modulus of cortical bone

# Contribution of experimental mechanics for the integration of residual stress problem in mechanical design and in quality control

J. LU
LASMIS, Université de Technologie de Troyes,
B.P. 2060 - 10010 Troyes cedex
FRANCE

There is an increasing interest in how the state of residual stress affects the mechanical properties of a material and its structure. The failure of a structure or a mechanical component is not only due to external loads. Residual stress is an important parameter in this respect. All manufacturing processes, for example, introduce a new state of residual stress. These stresses can have a positive effect, such as increasing the fatigue limit in the case of compressive surface stress, or they can have a negative effect decreasing the stress corrosion behaviour of a material in the case of tensile residual stresses.

Basic and applied research in the field of residual stress has been accelerated in the last few years. Residual stress in taken into account in advanced design in the aerospace, automotive and nuclear industries. Now event the microelectronic industrie start to take the residual stress for the dimensionnel stability of electronic packaging.

The introduction of advanced materials has also contributed to the development of knowledge in the field of residual stress. In fact, many new materials are multi-materials e.g. metal matrix composites, plasma sprayed coating, PVD and CVD coatings, which contain residual stresses as a result of the thermal and mechanical incompatibilities of the different phases of the material or structure.

Many research efforts have been conducted recently in the field of residual stresses. This presentation is a review of diffferent studies carried out in our laboratory.

The first part of the work [1] deals with the residual stress measurement techniques and the overall necessity to combine destructive (incremental hole drilling method) and non-destructive (x-ray and neutrons diffraction) methods in order to evaluate precisely the residual stresses distribution. A special attention is paid to residual stress induced in advanced materials such as MMCs and monocristal materials. Other examples will be shown concerning the residual stresses induced by different manufacturing processes.

The second part of this work presents the different models to predict the residual stresses induced by the following processes: shot peening, cold rolling, welding, grinding, laser quenching and cutting.

The experimental techniques developed above can contribute to the development of the model of prediction residual stress. Using the results calculated by the modeling, it is more easier to take the residual stress into account during mechanical design.

Two kinds of models can be mentioned: analytical models and numerical models. In our case, the models for the mechanical surface treatment are developed for shot peening [2] and for cold rolling [3]. Concerning the welding, the thermal cutting, the grinding, and the heat treatment (quenching), several finite element codes were used or developed [4]-[5]. The results have shown a good agreement between the model prediction and the experimental results. But we can also see that the 3D calculations are necessary to obtain good results for all the directions. If we use a 2D calcultation, the residual stresses evaluation good agreement for one direction only. So in the future, 3D calculation will take more importance for real case modeling [4].

The third part presents the residual stresses obtained by thermal spraying coating technology which is widely used in the biomedical, automobile, aerospace, textile, and power industries. Different coating systems (Zirconia, $Al_2O_3$, $Cr_2O_3$, WC-Co, NiCrAlY) manufactured by different processes (HVOF, APS, VPS, ATCPS) will be studied. Other parameters such as the size of the sample, the thickness of the coating, the pre- and post heat treatment and the mechanical treatment will be also studied. The effects of the residual stress on the toughness and strength of the coatings are also discussed.

The last part shows the effect of residual stresses on the fatigue behaviour. A model based on the finite element method for the prediction of the relaxation of the residual stresses was developed for the 2D case [6]. This model can predict the effects of the different loading conditions: such as the loading ratio R, the mean stress, the stress amplitude, the material behaviour (cyclic hardening or cyclic softening), and the level of the initial residual stresses. The more important thing is the following prediction: for a cyclic hardening material, the residual stress is stabilised after first cycles of loading, for a cyclic softening material, the residual stress can relax during a very long time. In the future, a 3D model will be developed.

473

With the development of different experimental and numerical techniques, it's now possible to introduce the residual stress in the design office for the integrated design of mechanical components. A new approach of concurrent engineering applied on the design of mechanical components with the residual and applied stresses consideration. Figure 1 shows the different connexion of the residual stress integrated design with other sectors which are active in the concurrent engineering appraoch. A mechanical component designer can simulate dynamical characteristics, material processing, and product life.

## Conclusion

The residual stress consideration is becaming important today for two reasons: the introduction of multimaterials which induces residual stress, the necessity for the designer to reduce safety coefficient to be competitive. Basic research has bought a better understanding of the phenomena relative to residual stress. For industrial applications, future developments are necessary:

(1) Concerning measurement techniques:
(a) Improvement of ultrasonic measurement methods
(b) Optical method for the strain measurement for the destructive techniques; the main objective is to develop integrated quality control tool

(2) Concerning the processing and materials
(a) Development of new prestress processes: ultrasonic shot peening, laser shock
(b)) Optimization of residual stress in advanced materials: functional gradient coating system, MMC, electronic packaging, intermetallic materials.

(3) Concerning modeling
Integrate the modeling method of residual stress in a global life design (3D) and create optimization codes for the design of mechanical components with concurrent engineering approach.

## Reference

[1] Handbook of measurement of residual stresses, SEM (Society for Experimental Mechanics, USA), 1996, Edited by J.Lu, M.James, G.Roy

[2] Lu, J., Peyre, P., Omam Nonga, N., Benamar, A., Flavenot, J.F., "Mechanical surface treatments, current trends, and future prospects", Surface Modification Technologies VIII, TMS, Edited by T.S.Sudarshan and Jeandin, Sept. 1994, pp589-601

[3] Benamar, A., Lu, J., Flavenot, J.F., Barbarin, P., Chalant, G., Inglebert, G., "Modeling residual stresses by cold rolling an austenitic stainless steel," **Residual stress**, Edited by V.Hauk, H.P.Hougardy, E.Macherauch, H.D.Tietz, DGM, Verlag, 1992, pp891-900

[4] Roelens, J.B., Maltrud, F., Lu, J., Determination of residual stresses in submerged arc multi-pass welds by means of numerical simulation and comparison with experimental measurements, **Welding in the wold**, vol.33, N°3, pp152-159, 1994

[5] Proceedings of the national conference on the residual stress and design office, CETIM, SENLIS, 1991

[6] Lu, J., Flavenot, J.F., Turbat, A.,"Prediction of the residual stress relaxation during fatigue", Mechanical relaxation of residual stresses, ASTM, STP993, 1988, pp75-90.

[7] Akrache, R., Lu, J., "Prediction of fatigue life for three-dimensional structures by a finite element method", MAT-TEC 96, Edited by J.LU, IITT International, pp251-259

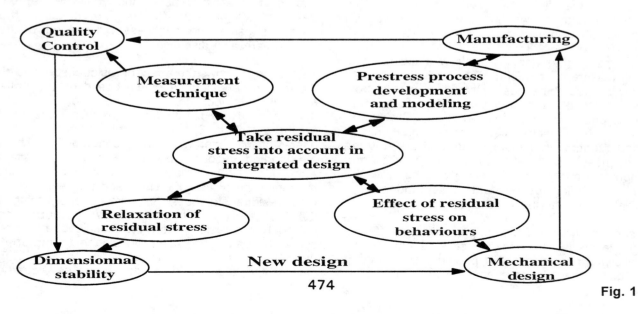

New design

474

**Fig. 1**

# Evaluation of Stress Corrosion Process by X-Ray Diffraction Technique

Hiroshi Kato and Kosuke Nakai

Department of Mechanical Engineering, Faculty of Engineering, Saitama University

255 Shimo-Okubo, Urawa, Saitama 338, Japan

When metallic materials suffer tensile stresses under the corrosive environment, the stress corrosion occurs and many fine cracks appear on the surface of materials. With increasing of the number and the length of the crack, the stress relaxation occurs on the surface. The present work is concerned with measurement of the stress relaxation during the stress corrosion of brass plates under an ammonia gas atmosphere. The x-ray diffraction analysis was used to evaluate stresses on the surface of specimens.

Specimens of 85 mm × 25 mm × 4 mm in size were prepared from brass plates of Cu-38.94 wt% Zn so that a specimen axis was parallel to a rolling direction. The specimens were heated at 483 K for 60 min, then cooled to room temperature in the furnace to remove residual stresses. The surface of the specimen was polished in the direction of the specimen axis with emery papers, then finished by buffing.

A strain gage was mounted on the specimen surface opposite to that for the x-ray diffraction analysis, and was coated by wax. Then, the specimen was fixed to a bending equipment and was bent to a required strain of 900, 1200 and $1500 \times 10^{-6}$ on the surface. The bending equipment with the specimen was set in a container filled with ammonia gas, as shown in Fig. 1. Every 30 min, outputs of the strain gage were measured and the specimen was removed from the bending equipment for observation of the surface through the optical microscope and for the x-ray diffraction analysis. The number of the crack in a length of 2 mm was measured along the specimen axis, and the diffraction angle was measured at the center of the specimen. After measurement, the specimen was fixed again to the bending equipment and was bent to the same strain as that just before removal to suffer the stress corrosion again.

The x-ray diffraction analysis was carried out in air to obtain the x-ray strain constant. The analysis was carried out with the Cr-K$\alpha$ ray diffracted from the (022) plane of the brass in a strain range from 0 to $1500 \times 10^{-6}$ at an interval of $250 \times 10^{-6}$. The tube voltage and current were 40 kV and 30 mA, respectively. From the gradient M (=d(2$\theta$)/d(sin$^2\psi$)) of the curve, the x-ray strain constant (dM/d$\varepsilon$) was obtained to be $-14.0 \times 10^{-6}$/(strain of $10^{-6}$).

Then, the stress change on the specimen surface was analyzed during the stress corrosion process. The analysis was carried out at six diffraction angles (sin$^2\psi$= 0, 0.1, 0.2, 0.3, 0.4 , 0.5). The analysis was done twice for each specimen, and results were averaged.

A typical specimen surface suffered the stress corrosion is shown in Fig. 2. With the increase in the initial strain, the number of the crack increased and the length of the crack decreased. The length of the crack developed with elapsed time. Variation of the number of the crack with time is shown in Fig. 3. In the figure, the ordinate is the number of the crack in the unit length measured in the direction of the specimen axis. In case of the specimen of the initial strain of $900 \times 10^{-6}$, the number of the crack began to increase at 60 min after start of corrosion, and became steady at times more than 200 min after the start of corrosion. In cases of specimens of the initial strain of 1200 and $1500 \times 10^{-6}$, the number of the crack began to increase steeply at 60 min.

Variation of the strain with time was measured on the opposite surface by the strain gage. Although the strain deceased with time from the start of corrosion, the change of the strain was very small and was 12, 45 and 71 ×$10^{-6}$ at 270 min from the start of corrosion for specimens of initial strains of 900, 1200 and $1500 \times 10^{-6}$, respectively. These strains were equivalent to stresses of 0.9, 3.4 and 5.4 MPa by using Young's modulus of 77 GPa.

With the increase in the initial strain, the number of the crack increased on the specimen surface. When the brass plate suffered a tensile stress of about 69 MPa, which was derived from the initial strain of $900 \times 10^{-6}$, cracks appeared and developed on the surface of the specimen in the ammonia gas atmosphere. And, in specimens suffering tensile stresses, the stress relaxation occurs significantly on the specimen surface.

From the x-ray diffraction profile, the peak position was determined with the cross-correlation method and the stress was obtained. Variation of the stress with time is shown in Fig. 4. No clear change of the stress was obtained in the specimen of the initial strain of $900 \times 10^{-6}$. In case of specimens of the initial strains of 1200 and 1500× $10^{-6}$, however, the stress began to decrease at 60 min after the start of corrosion. The time when the stress began to decrease was in good agreement with the time when cracks appeared on the surface of the specimen. The stress decreased to a value of 20 MPa at 180 and 270 min after the start of corrosion then took a constant value.

Although the strain measured by the strain gage on the opposite surface of the specimen showed only a slight change, the surface stress measured by the x-ray diffraction analysis largely changed following appearance of surface cracks. This shows that the stress relaxation occurred only very near the surface following cracking of the surface.

The relation between the number of the crack and the released stress is shown in Fig. 5. Measured data were on a curve for specimens of different initial strains.

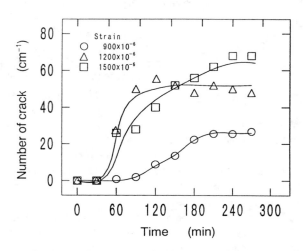

Fig. 3 Variation of number of crack with time

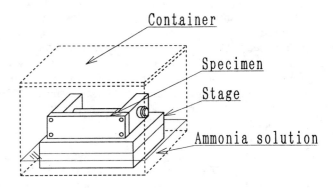

Fig. 1 Setup for stress corrosion experiment

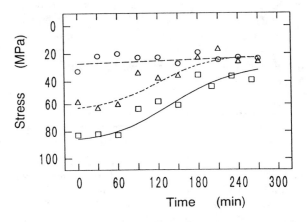

Fig. 4 Variation of stress on surface with time

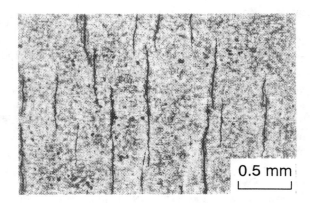

Fig. 2 Typical specimen surface at 270 min after start of corrosion. Initial strain was 900 ×10⁻⁶

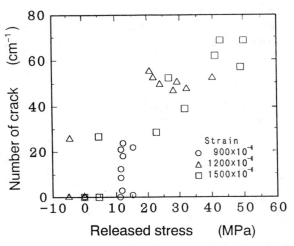

Fig. 5 Relation between number of crack and released stress

476

# Modeling The Residual Strains in a Burnished Annular Plate.

Nathalie Nicoletti, Dominique Fendeleur, Evelyne Aubry, Marc Renner
Modeling and Identification in Automatics and Mechanics
12, rue des Freres Lumiere
68093 Mulhouse cedex
France

The introduction of prestresses is commonly used in mechanics to improve the behaviour and the material properties of structures. Burnishing is one of these particular processes ; it induces residual strains and stresses in a structure by local plastic deformation. It is used to increase the fatigue endurance of the material or to improve the dynamic behaviour of the structure (increase of critical speed, modification of undesirable frequencies...).

The aim is to model these residual strains in annular discs with the finite element method. The disc is divided into three zones : the internal zone (radius between the bore and the rolling path), the rolling path (where plastic deformation occurs), and the external zone (radius between the rolling path and the external diameter).

First, strain gauges or rosettes are used to verify the homogeneity, the shape and the principal directions of the residual strains. Gauges are put on both sides of the plate to avoid flexural effects. Figure 1 describes the measurements obtained for the radial and tangential strains : radial strains are wholly compressive ; tangential strains are compressive in the inside zone and tensile in the external zone, with a large change at the tensioning radius. The results are found homogeneous all over the plate. The measurements agree with the literature [1, 2] except for the principal directions which appear not to be radial and tangential all over the disc as usually admitted, but only in the external zone.

Then burnishing is modeled using the finite element method. A model is proposed which is assumed to be plane, but no constraint about the direction of the strains is assumed. A radial pressure, constant in the disc-thickness, is applied in successive stages in order to model real burnishing, contrary to other modeling processes where the pressure is applied at the same time all over the zone to be burnished. The pressure is applied in stages of 10 degrees ; a greater stage leads to non-homogeneous strains, and a lower stage leads to numerical problems. With 10 degrees, the strains appear to be homogeneous. The shape of the radial and tangential strains agrees with the experimental results (Fig. 1), but two theoretical loadings (P and 1.1 P) are necessary to find the inside and the outside experimental values. The model gives radial and tangential strains in the external zone and additional shear strains in the internal zone (Fig. 2). Figure 3 describes the angle between one principal direction and the radial direction ; it shows that the principal directions are radial and tangential only in the external zone, which correctly predicts our experimental results.

The strains at one point during the burnishing process were also measured and compared with the above modeling process ; the signal delivered by gauges and the calculated signal show the same variations which once again validates our model. Figure 4 describes the calculated signal. It can be decomposed into three periods. The first one occurs before the passage of the rollers near the gauges ; the strains are small and negative. The second one occurs during the passage of the rollers near the gauges ; a large change of amplitude is observed ; the strains become positive in a sudden high peak , they change sign, and then they decrease rapidly to a small and negative value. The last period describes the variation of the strains after the passage of the rollers ; the negative amplitude of the strains increases a little.

References:

[1] Schajer G.S., 1983, "Analysis of roll tensioning and its influence on circular saw stability", Wood Science and Technology, 17(4), pp287-302.

[2] Schajer G.S., Mote C.D.Jr, 1979, "Roll tensioning and residual stress analysis", Proceedings of 6th Wood Machining Seminar, University of California Forest Products Laboratory, Richmond, California, pp295-308.

Figure 1 : comparison between the modeled radial and tangential strains and the measurements (x)

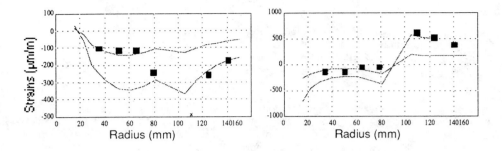

Figure 2 (calculated strains ; a-radial b-tangential c-shearing) and Figure 3 (principal directions)

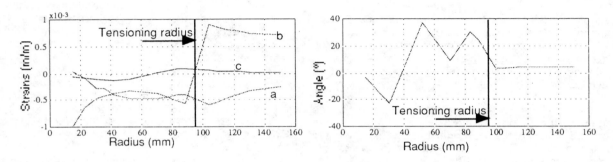

Figure 4 : strains calculated during the burnishing process at one point

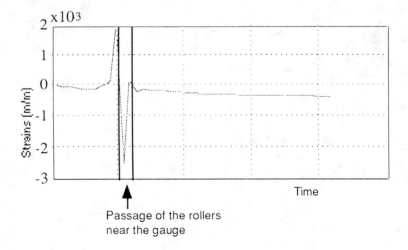

# Measurement of Residual Stress in SSME AT HPFTP 3rd Impeller Pump Side Rub Stop

Gregory R. Swanson
Aerospace Engineer
ED25/ Structural Mechanics Team
NASA, Marshall Space Flight Center
MSFC, AL

A measurement of residual stress in the Space Shuttle Main Engine (SSME) Alternate Turbopump (AT) High Pressure Fuel Turbo Pump (HPFTP) third impeller pump side rub stop is presented. A cross section of the pump shows the location of the third impeller (figure 1). The measurements were made as a response to a failure that occurred very early in the pumps operating life cycle. This rapid aging of the pump to failure had not been analytically predicted.

The Advanced Technology (AT) High Pressure Fuel Turbo Pump (HPFTP) is being developed by Pratt and Whitney (P&W) for NASA, Marshall Space Flight Center. The AT HPFTP will replace the current HPFTP (built by Rocketdyne) on the SSME as part of a block change upgrade with the first flight scheduled for 1997. The HPFTP is a single shaft machine that operates at 37,000 rpm providing the SSME with 68 Kilograms per second (150 pounds per second) of liquid hydrogen at 41.37 MPa (6000 psia). The current pump requires detailed inspections between flights and complete overhaul after only 5000 seconds of operation. The AT HPFTP is designed to provide substantially longer life between overhauls and minimal inspection between flights. The design requirements are 60 flight equivalents (engines are tested for a full duration mission on the ground before acceptance for flight) with an analytical safety factor of 4.

An early development version of the HPFTP experienced a failure in the pump third impeller shroud and splitter, liberating pieces of the titanium impeller that lodged downstream in the flow path. The failure was so early in the pumps life cycle and had such high potential for catastrophic engine failure should it occur again (a fuel pump failure leaves the engine system momentarily operating oxygen rich, the resulting high temperatures and pressures will overspeed the turbopumps to burst and literally burn the metal in the combustion chambers and ductwork within a few seconds) that immediate corrective action was required.

An investigation team was tasked with explaining how the failure initiated, propagated to part liberation, and how to avoid this in production hardware. Due to the sever environment and tight space limitations inside the turbopump, direct measurements of the stresses and strains on the impeller during operation were not possible. It was also not possible to economically duplicate the impeller boundary conditions in a laboratory rig, so only post engine test run hardware was available for examination. The failure initiation sight was determined from physical examination of the hardware to have occurred in the pump side rub stop of the third impeller. The third impeller has rub stops to limit the shaft axial travel during engine start and shutdown transients when the hydrostatic thrust balance system is not pressurized with liquid hydrogen.

Before the failure the impeller had been analytically predicted to meet the 60 mission equivalent requirement, with a safety factor of 4. Reanalysis after the failure included detailed thermal heating from metal on metal rub in a liquid hydrogen environment [1], and nonlinear plastic finite element analysis of the rub stop (figure 2). These analysis predicted mechanical and thermal stresses beyond yield would occur, but the actual strain range was elusive since many assumptions had to be made in the analysis.

Metalagraphic examination confirmed that the rub stop had experienced the high temperatures required for a phase change in the titanium material used for the impeller, partially confirming the thermal analysis. The residual stress measurement by the hole drilling method [2] proved nearly 689.5 MPa (100ksi) residual tensile stress was present at the rub stop surface. This residual stress is sufficient to initiate fatigue cracks during subsequent rub events. This experimental confirmation of the shroud rub stop failure mode allowed redesign of the impeller and thrust balance system to ensure the AT HPFTP will meet its full life requirements.

References:

[1] Goode, Brian K., "3rd Impeller Thermal Analysis", unpublished work.

[2] Measurements Group, Inc., "Measurement of Residual Stresses by the Hole-Drilling Strain Gage Method", Measurements Group Tech Note TN-503-3.

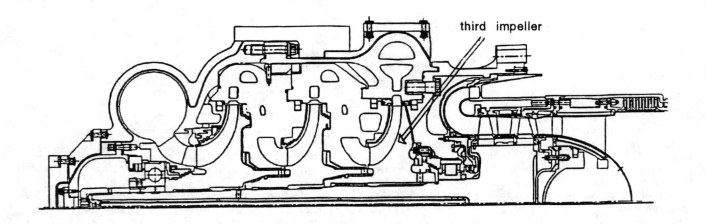

Figure 1.  Cross section of P&W AT/HPFTP

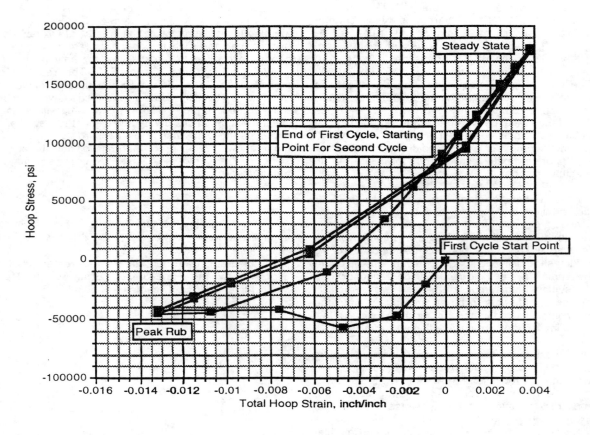

Figure 2.  Results from nonlinear finite element analysis

# The Experimental Investigation on Residual Deformation of Single-shear Sheet Specimen Using Ultrasonic Technology

Xuewei SUN

Dept. of Eng. Mech., Tsinghua University, Beijing 100084, P. R. China

Koichiro KAWASHIMA

Dept. of Mech. Eng., Nagoya Institute of Technology, Nagoya 466, Japan

The single-shear sheet specimen(SSSS, Fig.1) has been used to measure ultimate shear strength of sheet material. In these days this kind of specimen is getting more and more application[1]. Some standard test methods of this kind of specimen have been established, for example, in United States and China etc. In order to analyze in detail the stress distribution of nearby shear path under various load levels, we carried out stress analysis of SSTs by FEM and measured the residual deformation of SSSS[2].

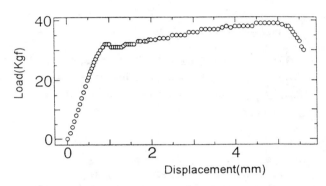

Fig. 2 load vs. displacement of specimen PVC-11

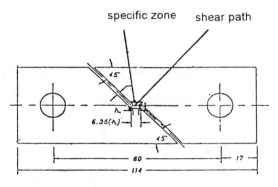

Fig. 1 Single-shear sheet specimen(SSSS)

In this research the single-shear sheet specimen made of PVC plastic was used. Firstly, the specimen was tensed up to variant plastic state using simple specific tensile test equipment. Figure 2 shows the relation between load and displacement of specimen PVC-11. Then specimen was unloaded. The loading and residual displacements between two load pins were recorded. The small block cut off from central zone of unload specimen was polished using polishing machine. The thickness of the block was measured. Finally, we measured the velocity of ultrasonic wave in the specimen using low frequency acoustic microscope Olympus UHP-100 and Panametrics Model 5900 PR 200MHz computer controlled pulser/receiver. The residual deformation in the shear path of specimen was obtained by means of calculation curve which has been established in advance. The velocity of ultrasonic wave in the special zone of specimen was measured using "time-of-flight" method[3]. The special program which was compiled according to the "zero cross" method was used in this experiment. That measure principle and system is showed in Figure 3. Figure 4 shows typical echo signals of ultrasonic wave in the specimen PVC12-1.

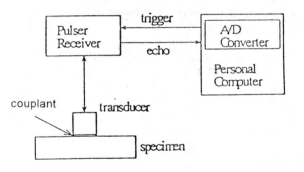

a. System

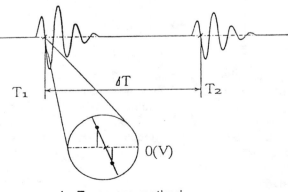

b. Zerocross method

Fig. 3 Measuring of ultrasonic velocity

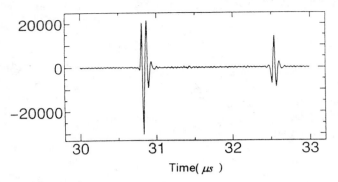

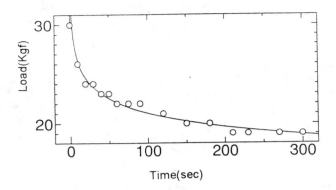

Fig. 4 Typical echo signals of unltrasonic wave(PVC12-1)

Fig. 5 Relaxation of the specimen PVC-11

The velocity of ultrasonic wave can be got according to the formula $V_I = 2\delta / \Delta T$, where $V_I$ is ultrasonic velocity; $\delta$ is the thickness of the block; $\Delta T$ is the time difference between two echo signals.

The main results of this research are following:
1. the curve of relaxation of specimen(Fig. 5).
2. the relation between width of necking zone of specimen and residual displacement(Fig. 6).
3. the relation between ultrasonic velocity and residual displacement(Fig. 7). The experiment shows that ultrasonic velocity decreases with increasing of residual displacement. The maximum decreasement of velocity has reached 15 percent.

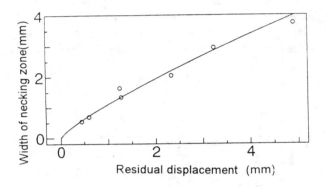

Fig. 6 Width of necking zone vs. residual displacement

This research shows that the strain distribution in shear zone of specimen by measuring is coincided with the analytic result by FEM. This method can be used effectively to measure the residual deformation of various sheet specimens.

Acknowledgment

Thanks are due to Mr. Tanaka, Mr. Yamamoto, Mr. Nishimura and Dr. Okade for help in the experiments.

References:

[1] Breindel, W. W. et al, "Evaluation of a Single-shear Specimen for Sheet Material", Proceedings, the 61st Annual Meeting of ASTM, June. 1958. Vol. 58, pp862-867.
[2] Sun, X. W. et al, "Quantitative Plastic Deformation Analysis by Means of Thermoplastic Effects", Transactions of SMiRT 12, Elsvier Science Publishers B. V., Aug. 1993, Vol. G, pp213-218.
[3] Kawashima, K. et al, "Identification of Anistropic Elastic Constants of Aluminum Composites Reinforced with Short Alumina Fibers by the Double Transmission Ultrasonic Method", Proceeding of 21st QNDE, Aug. 1994, at Snowmass.

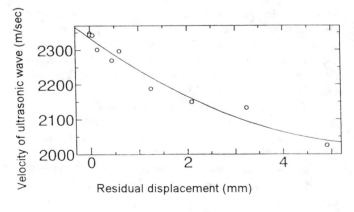

Fig. 7 Ultrasonic velocity vs. residual displacement

# Digital Speckle Metrology: Techniques and Applications

F. Chen, C.T. Griffen, Y.Y. Hung
Dept. of Mechanical Engineering
Oakland University
Rochester Hills, MI, USA

Digital speckle metrology, which includes both speckle interferometry and speckle photography methods, is an extension of conventional speckle metrology by using a video camera as the recording media and a computer system for fringe pattern acquiring/generating, processing and analyzing. What follows briefly describes several practical techniques used in digital speckle metrology and some application examples.

**Techniques:** Speckles location rearranging for tolerating rigid body motion can be achieved by rearranging the registered speckles having four pixels or more the same values. Speckles phase rearranging for speckles cancellation and fringe patterns enhancement can be accomplished by rearranging the registered speckles in such a way that some speckles in a undeformed image are out of phase with those in a deformed image.

Digital Fourier transformation can be used for phase extraction of any carrier like fringe patterns which includes Young's fringe patterns. The speckle noise can be suppressed during filtering process. For digital speckle photography, it can be exploited to generate Young's fringes in a computer.

A piece of glass can be inserted in and taken out of the illumination light path up to 4K Hz to generate a set of dynamic carrier for vibration testing up to 400Hz if 10 times sampling frequency is chosen.

For a transient problem, an alternative way is that fringes can be breaked into several zones which in each zone the fringes are monotonical so that digital Fourier transformation technique can be utilized to extract the phase maps. These phase maps can then be stitched together to form the whole phase map. The methodology is similar to finite element.

Double strobing with strobing phase varying can be employed to measure large vibration using digital speckle interferometry. The displacement between the two strobings can be chosen so that it is still in the measurement range and the strobing phase can be selected to control the gradient of the displacement to optimize strobing light.

The shape of a tested object can be obtained together with vibration information using the same optical setup by two-wavelength method. For digital speckle interferometry or TV holography, it is robust and practical.

The iteration algorithm is designed to reconstruct fringe patterns from the calculated phase map. When combined with a set of computer generated carrier, speckle noise can be eliminated using DFT method. Signal to noise ratio of the fringe pattern can be increased.

A software package has been implemented into PC and workstation computers to optimize usage of the above techniques and some other techniques such as speckle maximizing, etc.

**Applications:** Fig.1 shows the processed fringe patterns for a crack specimen under dynamic loading. Fig.2 demonstrates the deformation of a computer chip. Fig.3 illustrates the computer generated Young's fringe patterns of a cantilever beam subjected to a concentrated load at one end and fixed boundary at the other end using digital white light speckle photography method. Fig.4 presents fringe patterns under same vibration load with different strobing phases using double strobing technique to prove that TV holography can be used to measure large vibration. Fig.5 gives a mode shape pattern of a fluid reservoir model with a half level fluid inside and subjected to a harmonic excitation. We see that there is almost no response in the top half portion. Fig.6 represents the mode shape fringe patterns of a scaled vehicle. We can observe that there are both global modes and local modes. Fig.7 provides a application example of iteration algorithm. The fringe patterns are obtained when the plate with four edges clamped was excited at 850 Hz. Fig.8 stands for the vibration fringe patterns used for unwelded spots detection. Fig.9 depicts an example of obtaining both shape and vibration. In conclusion, digital speckle metrology is a practical tool in engineering field as well in academic community. Some advances have been described, some can be found in other literature and yet some still need to be accomplished. It should be noted that all processed fringe patterns have gray level.

**References:**

[1]. F. Chen, C.T. Griffen, Y.Y. Hung, "Practical Techniques of Processing and Analyzing Speckled Fringe Pattern in Digital Speckle Interferometry", SPIE, Vol.2544, 1995.

[2]. C.T. Griffen, F. Chen, Y.Y. Hung, "Digital Laser Speckle Photography for Vibration and Shape Measurement", to be published

[3].D.J. Chen, F.P. Chiang, "Computer Aided Speckle Interferometry Using Spectra Amplitude", Appl. Opt., Vol.32, No.2, pp225-236, 1993.

[4].C.T. Griffen, F. Chen, Y.Y. Hung, "Measurement of Vibration & Shape Using Defocused Speckle Photography", ISATA, Italy, 1996.

[5]. F. Chen, C.T. Griffen, G. M. Brown, T. E. Allen, "Measurement of Shape and Vibration Using a Single Electronic Speckle Interferometry Configuration", SPIE, Denver, 1996.

[6]. F. Chen, C.T. Griffen, Y.Y. Hung, "Panel Vibration Distribution Analysis Using TV Holography: A Preliminary Study", ISATA, Italy, 1996.

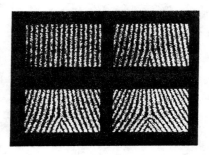

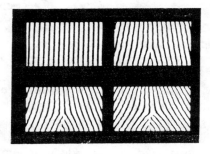

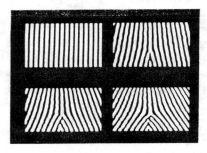

Fig.1

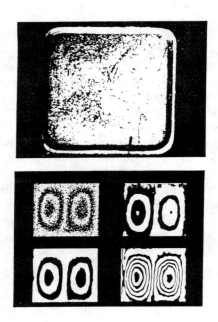

Fig.2

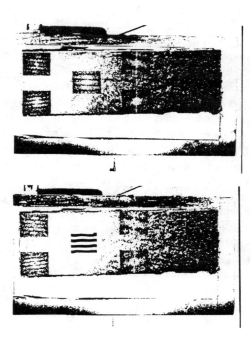

Fig.3

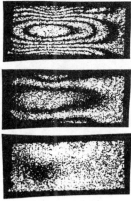

Fig.4

478Hz        956Hz

Fig.5

Fig.6

Fig.7

Fig.8

Fig.9

# Speckle Interferometry with Electron Microscopy and Its Applications

Qing Wang and Fu-Pen Chiang
Department of Mechanical Engineering
State University of New York at Stony Brook
Stony Brook, NY11794-2300

Speckle photography is a well-developed full field technique for measuring displacement and strain. The fundamental limitation of optical speckle methods (laser speckle and white light speckle methods) is the fact that one cannot measure displacement smaller than the size of speckles. However, the smallest speckle that can be created using optics has a dimension of one half of the wavelength of the radiation. The laws of physics dictate that the smallest observable object cannot be smaller than the wavelength of the radiation that is used to form its image. Thus the fundamental limiting factor of any optical speckle method is the wavelength of the radiation that is used to record the speckles. When He-Ne laser is used, the theoretical limit of spatial resolution is approximately $0.3\mu m$ (1/2 of average wavelength of the laser radiation). But the practical limit is about 10 times larger, i.e. $3\mu m$, which is essentially the lower bound of optical speckle methods.

One of the choices to break this fundamental barrier is to use the electron microscope. A novel technique SIEM (Speckle Interferometry with Electron Microscopy) emerges as an experimental micromechanics tool, which combines the speckle photography, digital image processing and electron microscopy. Chiang first introduced the concept of SIEM and demonstrated its feasibility in 1982. Particles with size of only a small fraction of a micron can be created by either a vacuum or physical/chemical vapor deposition processes, or other surface treatment techniques. While they are not visible through an optical microscope, they are easily observable under a scanning electron microscope (SEM) or transmission electron microscope (TEM). Once recorded, specklegram can be processed by either a laser beam probing or whole field Fourier filtering. Obviously such a approach has a much higher sensitivity and spatial resolution than conventional optical speckle methods.

How to create a micro-speckle pattern with controlled speckle size, random distribution and desired density? Will such speckle patterns remain stable during a sequence of mechanical loading? Will large strain influence the measurement accuracy? How to overcome the effect of large rigid body translation and rotation at high magnification? …. Many technical details are not clear until a real test is conducted by SIEM. Several works that have done recently are: characterization of interphase mechanical properties of composites, effect of adhesive thickness on adhesion, near field phenomenon at crack tip, mechanical behavior of a single fiber, micro-buckling of fibrous polymeric composite material, etc. These examples are presented to demonstrate some aspects of the capability of SEIM.

# The Analysis of Shadow Mask Vibration Mode for CDT Through the Use of ESPI

Won-Hyun Kim, Seog-Weon Chang, Sei-Hyun Kim, Dong-Su Ryu
Daewoo Electronics Co., Ltd.
412-2 Chungchon-Dong Pupyong-Ku
Incheon, Korea

Electronic Speckle Pattern Interferometry (ESPI) is a useful opto-electronic testing technology utilized in a wide range of applications. In this study, the natural vibrating mode of the shadow mask for CDT (Cathode Display Tube) has been tested through the use of ESPI.

The shadow mask containing a great number of holes is used to pass electronic beam injected through a curved thin panel so that the electronic beam collides accurately on fluorescent materials having desired colors thus making sure that the colors of the screen are not blurred and maintained in a clean state.

The shadow mask is connected to the several points of a frame surrounding it by mean of spot welding. The frame, used to fix the shadow mask, is mounted on the inner side of CDT through the use of fixing clips.

The objective of this study is to analyze the results of the mode analysis on the microphone phenomenon of the screen, generated when the sound is increased after a speaker is mounted on the monitor of a multimedia PC.

The principle of ESPI is used in order to test a vibration mode type; the natural vibration mode and frequency of the shadow mask for CDT, used to create resonance through the use of speaker instead of the Vibration Exiter have been measured with ESPI and out-of-plane interferometry configuration has been given.

Fig.1 illustrates the cross-section of the shadow mask for CDT. In Fig.2, a real mode shape that is being resonated at 229Hz of the shadow mask measured with ESPI is illustrated.

References :

[1] Gary L. Cloud, "Optical Methods of Engineering Analysis", Cambridge University Press, 1995. pp.453-476

[2] Bernard Grop,"Basic Television and Video Systems", McGraw-Hill Book Co. 1984. pp.89-90.

[3] R.Iones, C.Wykes, "Holographic and Speckle Interferometry", Cambrige University Press, 1989. pp.165-195

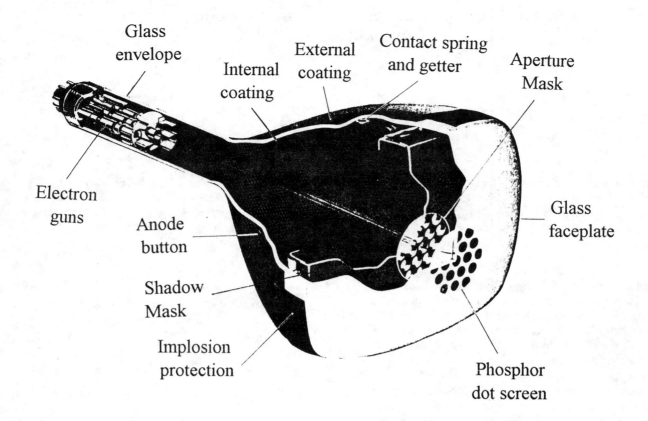

Fig. 1 The cross-section of the shadow mask for CDT

Fig. 2 Real mode shape at 229Hz of the shadow mask measured with ESPI

# Three Dimensional Photoelastic Analysis of Cylindrical Pipe under Internal Pressure Restricted Radially at One End of the Pipe

H. Fujiwara, E. Matsumoto and A. Saito
Kinki University
Higashiosaka, Osaka 577
JAPAN

The round pipe partially prevented from radial displacement will be investigated under pressure load by three dimensional photoelasticity. The three dimensional photoelastic pipe of epoxy resin, which is inserted into a thick plate, is heated up to the critical temperature in the stress-freezing oven and the internal pressure is applied. This state will be maintain during the temperature inside of the oven is controlled down to the room temperature. The stress freezed model was sliced to solve the stress distribution of this problem.

The 3-D pipe models and the thick circular plate were milled from the raw material of epoxy blocks. The combined model in Fig. 1 was assembled inserting the pipe lightly into the hole of the thick plate. The stress distribution of the pipe wall is solved under the constraint of radial displacement of the thick plate.The loading apparatus was specially designed to give only pressure load to the model without unfavorable axial constraint. The model in Fig. 1 was put in the loading apparatus. The configuration factors of the models are shown in Table 1 and d= 50 mm. The relative position of the pipe and the thick circular plate is shown using the longitudinal coordinate in Fig. 1.The stress fringe value of this material was measured using the disc of epoxy.
The stress in the model under pressure load is freezed in the stress-freezing oven[1]. The circular pipe model was set in the oven.The temperature inside the oven rises steadily to 130°C and then keeps for 30 minutes. The pressure load by compressor was applied to the inside of the pipe and then soaked the model for 30 minutes until a uniform temperature throughout the model was obtained. The model was cooled slowly enough for temperature gradient to be minimized until 70°C. The applied pressure was controlled to constant value of 24.5~58.8 kPa.
Fig. 2 shows the sliced position and each slices of the model. Axial slice(a), a quarter circular slice(b) and full circular slices(c) are selected for the follwing analysis. Those are selected and cut each 5 mm interval and filed finely to 3 mm thick. Besides, a quarter circular slices are cut in the state of 2.5 mm offsetted each other for the assembled region shown in Fig. 2(b). The both ends of each slice are polished to the wedge shape(Fig. 4 and 5) to read the fringe number. The isochromatic fringe of the

polished slices were observed through the soaking liquid. The stress fringe value is 29.1~32.2 kN/m at the stress freezing temperature.

## Experimental Results

The circular pipe was cut apart shown in Fig. 2 and after polishing each slice the isochromatic fringe was observed and some examples are shown in Figs. 3 and 4. Using the number of isochromatic fringe, $N$ and slice thickness, $t'$, the circumferential stress on the inner and outer surfaces are denoted in the followings:

$$(\sigma_t)_1 = (N/\alpha t') - p \quad \text{for outer surface} \quad (1)$$

$$(\sigma_t)_2 = (N/\alpha t') \quad \text{for inner surface} \quad (2)$$

Those stresses are summarized in Fig. 5 with parameters of thickness ratio. It can be seen that there are very typical steep variation along the longitudinal position around the combination part of pipe and thick plate. In these distribution, the maximum of circumferential stress is clearly observed and the result is summarized in Fig. 6.

## References

[1] J.W. Dally & W.F. Riley "Experimental Stress Analysis", McGraw-Hill Book Co.,pp.490-531.

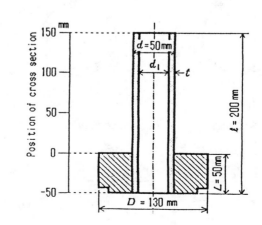

Fig. 1 Configuration of model

Table 1  Form factors of model

| $l/d$ | 4.0 | | | |
|---|---|---|---|---|
| $D/d$ | 2.6 | | | |
| $L/d$ | 1.0 | | | |
| $t/d$ | 0.04 | 0.08 | 0.10 | 0.12 |

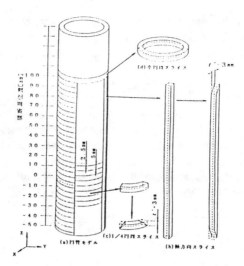

Fig. 2  Slice plan of round pipe model

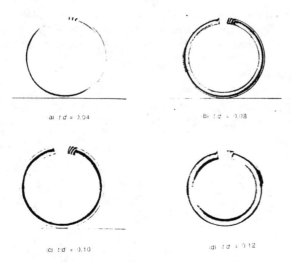

Fig. 3  Isochromatic fringes of circular slices

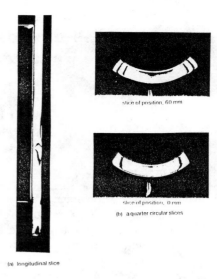

(a) longitudinal slice

slice of position, 60 mm

slice of position, 0 mm

(b) a quarter circular slices

Fig. 4  Isochromatic fringes of a quarter circular and longitudinal slices ($t/d$ =0.10)

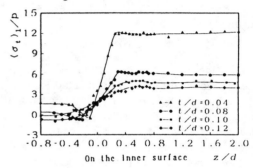

On the inner surface   $z/d$

- ▲—▲ $t/d$ =0.04
- ●—● $t/d$ =0.08
- ◆—◆ $t/d$ =0.10
- ◆—◆ $t/d$ =0.12

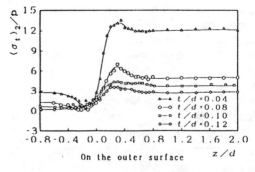

On the outer surface   $z/d$

- ▲—▲ $t/d$ =0.04
- ○—○ $t/d$ =0.08
- □—□ $t/d$ =0.10
- ○—○ $t/d$ =0.12

Fig. 5  Variation of circumferential stresses on inner and outer surfaces to longitudinal position

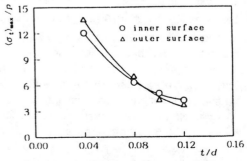

- ○ inner surface
- △ outer surface

Fig. 6  Maximum circumferential stress on the inner and outer surfaces for $t/d$

490

# Automated Deformation Measurement with Incorporation of Electronic Speckle Shearography and Carrier Technique

Baishi Wang

Department of Mechanical Engineering
State University of New York
Stony Brook, NY 11794-2300

Xi Zhang

Shanghai Marine Diesel Engine
Research Institute
Shanghai, P. R. China

## Abstract

Electronic speckle shearography ( ESS ), which combines shearography and computer image processing is a practical and useful method for deformation measurement and nondestructive testing because of its simple optical arrangement, low environmental requirement and filmless operation. But the output of ESS is in the form of fringe pattern which is not appropriate for engineering design. For automatic quantitative determination of the deformation by ESS, the quantitative value of the deformation should be yielded from the fringes. The fringes should be firstly decoded by computer, i.e. the sign and the order of the fringes should be determined without any ambiguity and then fringes are identified. Phase shifting is a feasible method for automatic generation of the deformation field. But it needs special phase shifting apparatus and $2\pi$ ambiguity may exist in unwrapping procedure. Optical carrier modulation technique is another simple approach for identifying of the fringes. Because of the monotonic property of the carrier fringes, the deformation fringe order and sign can be distinctly determined by the distortion amount of the modulated fringes.

In the paper, carrier technique is incorporated with electronic speckle shearography for automated determination of the out-of-plane deformation fringes. The carrier fringes are generated by translating the beam expander or its corresponding lens along the beam direction. Because of the shearing property of the speckle shearography, the derivative of the spherical phase change, or the linear phase change, is recorded by the CCD camera and image processing system. By subtracting the speckle patterns snapped by the CCD camera before and after the translation of the beam expander or its corresponding lens, carrier fringes -- parallel lines with constant spacings, are obtained. The carrier pitch is linearly proportional to the lens translation amount which can be automatically quantified with the using of the stepping motor. If deformation occurs between the two snaps, the deformation fringes will be modulated by the carrier fringes. The parallel carrier fringes are distorted because of the phase change due to the out-of-plane deformation of the specimen. The automated decoding of the deformation is realized by a sequence of the image processing algorithms. First, the fringe pattern is smoothed and filtered and the centers of the light and dark fringes are extracted, traced and coded. Then the distortion amounts of the carrier fringes are computed. Finally, the whole-field deformations are automatically generated by using interpolation scheme such as least mean square etc. All the above operations are performed under software control. This technique is applied to the out-plane deformation measurement of the exhaust valve in the cylinder head of the diesel engine. Its successful application to the automated valve deformation measurement shows that this technique is feasible, reliable, simple and useful for engineering analysis. The new technique can also be used for the development of the in-situ deformation measurement system.

## References

Hung, Y. Y., "Shearography: a new optical method for strain measurement and nondestructive testing," *Optical Engineering*, 21, 1982

Toyooka, S., Nishida, H. & Takezaki, J., "Automatic analysis of holographic and shearographic fringes to measure flexural strains in plates," *Optical Engineering* 28, 1989

Ganesan, A. R., Kothiyal, M. P., & Sirohi, R. S., " Simple image processing techniques for the contrast enhancement of real-time digital speckle pattern interferometry fringes," *Optical Engineering*, 28, 1989

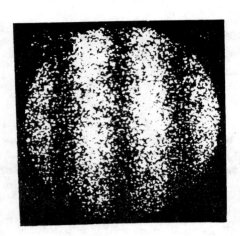

(1) ΔR = 0.14mm

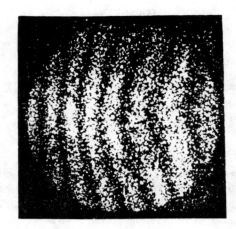

Fig. 2 the deformation fringes modulated by the carrier fringes

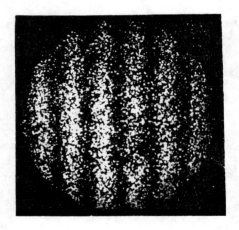

(2) ΔR = 0.25mm

Fig. 1 the carrier fringes with different pitches

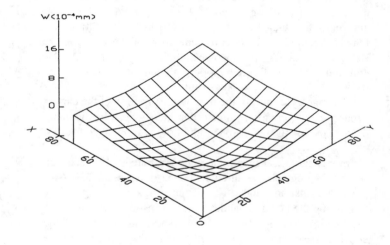

Fig. 3 the plot of the out-of-plane deformation of the exhaust valve

# Digital Shearing Speckle Correlation Fringe Pattern Formed by Using A Linear Correlation Calculating Method

Y.M. He, B.B.Zhang
Dept. of Mechanics
Huazhong University of Science and Technology
Wuhan, Hubei Province 430074
P.R. China

The Digital Speckle Pattern Interferometry ( DSPI )[1,2] or the Electronic Speckle Pattern Interferometry ( ESPI ) not only has the characteristcs which the laser speckle interferometry has , but also has the characteristcs of not requiring holographic plates and restoring and displaying experimental results quickly. So the DSPI is widely used for measuring displacement field. The Digital Shearing Speckle Pattern Interferometry (DSSPI) is a practive measuring technique for the detection of strain field. As a shearing lens is used, it can eliminate most of enviroment disturbance.

Either using DSPI or DSSPI , the algrithms which are used for calculating and forming a correlation fringe pattern in a computer are the same. The subtraction mode and add mode algrithms are generally used. Because the fringe visibility formed by the subtraction mode is higher than that formed by the add mode,the subtraction mode is applied more often. However the fringe pattern can not be easily observed on the monitor screen as its grey values are small and distribute in a narrow range. To improve the quality of a correlation fringe pattern, a linear correlation method is emploied for generating a correlation fringe pattern.

The subtraction mode is widely utilized to generate a correlation fringe pattern because its calculating speed is the fastest and the correlation fringe pattern can be displaied almost on−time. The basic principle of this method is that the two digital composed light intensities are subtracted each other and the absolute value of their remainder is taken as

$$I(x,y) = |I_2(x,y) - I_1(x,y)|$$
$$= 4[i_1(x,y)i_2(x,y)\sin^2(\beta + \Delta\varphi / 2)$$
$$\times \sin^2(\Delta\varphi / 2)]^{1/2} \qquad (1)$$

In the above expression, the last term $\sin^2(\Delta\varphi / 2)$ expresses the low frequncy components of the correlation fringe pattern, and other terms are the high frequncy components which only express the speckle noise and do not include deformation information. By analysing Eq. ( 1 ) several disadvantages can be found below because of using subtraction mode. (1) The correlation fringe pattern is modulated by the speckle pattern $(i_1 i_2)^{1/2}$. If $(i_1 i_2)^{1/2}$ is not even on the object, the light intensity of a digital fringe pattern is also not even. This makes a great difficulty for analysing the fringe pattern. (2) The grey values of a fringe pattern are so small that the fringe pattern is difficultly observed on a monitor screen.

From Eq. (1), if $\Delta\varphi = 2n\pi$, the light intensity before deformation is equal to that after deformation. This means that the correlativity of the two speckle patterns before and after deformation is the best. If $\Delta\varphi = (2n+1)\pi$ , the difference of the light intensities before and after deformation is the greatest , so they have the worse correlativity. Based on the simple principle , within a small range of a digital speckle pattern ( ie. whthin n × n image elements), the correlative coefficient of the two composed speckle patterns can be calculated

$$\gamma(\Delta\varphi) = \, < (I_1 - <I_1>_{n \times n})(I_2 - <I_2>_{n \times n}) >_{n \times n}$$
$$\times [ <(I_1 - <I_1>_{n \times n})^2 >_{n \times n}]^{-1/2}$$
$$\times [ <(I_2 - <I_2>_{n \times n})^2 >_{n \times n}]^{-1/2} \qquad (2)$$

Where $I_1$ and $I_2$ are the light intensities of two composed speckle patterns before and after deformation respectively. The mathematical operator $< \cdot >_{n \times n}$ expresses taking an average within a range of $n \times n$ image elements.

Let

$$<i_1>_{n \times n} = \, <i_2>_{n \times n} = \, <i>_{n \times n}$$

and suppose that the phase change $\Delta\varphi$ is a constant in the range of the $n \times n$ image elements. Some middle results can be obtained [3]

$$<I_1>_{n \times n} = 2<i>_{n \times n}$$
$$<I_2>_{n \times n} = 2<i>_{n \times n}$$
$$<I_1 I_2>_{n \times n} = 6<I>_{n \times n}^2 + 2<i>_{n \times n}^2 \cos\Delta\varphi$$
$$<(I_1 - <I_1>_{n \times n})(I_2 - <I_2>_{n \times n}) >_{n \times n}$$
$$= 2<i>_{n \times n}^2 + 2<i>_{n \times n}^2 \cos\Delta\varphi$$
$$<(I_1 - <I_1>_{n \times n})^2 >_{n \times n} = 4<i>_{n \times n}^2$$
$$<(I_2 - <I_2>_{n \times n})^2 >_{n \times n} = 4<i>_{n \times n}^2$$

Substitute the middle results above into Eq. (2), the relation between linear correlation coefficient with the deformation phase can be expressed

$$\gamma(\Delta\varphi) = \frac{[2<i>_{n \times n}^2 \quad 2<i>_{n \times n}^2 \cos\Delta\varphi]}{4<i>_{n \times n}^2}$$
$$= (\cos\Delta\varphi + 1) / 2 = \cos^2(\Delta\varphi / 2) \qquad (3)$$

So the correlation coefficient varies between zero and one. The result is fitted with that of the gualitative analysis ahead. In the measuring system adopted in this paper, the maximum grey of a digital image is 255, and the minimum grey is 0. In order to compare the linear correlation method with the subtraction mode , the expression below is used to form a digital speckle correlation fringe pattern

$$I(\Delta\varphi) = 255[1 - \gamma(\Delta\varphi)] = 255\sin^2(\Delta\varphi / 2) \qquad (4)$$

Compairing Eq. (4) with Eq. (1), the forms of the digital speckle fringe patterns generated by the two methods respectively are the same, but the linear correlation method has overcome several disadvantages produced by subtraction mode.

Figure 1(a) is a fringe pattern photograph obtained by using the subtraction mode. Because the greies of the pattern are small and distribute in a narrow range, the fringe pattern should be enhanced by using a digital image processing method before taking the photograph. The fringe pattern obtained by using the linear correlation calculating method is shown in figure 1(b). The grey values of this digital fringe pattern are distributed widely in the range of 0~255, and its light intensity is not affected by the background. So it does not need to be enhanced by using any digital image processing techniques, and this avoides the image distortion. The advantage is very important for analysig a speckle correlation fringe pattern.

Analysing the Eq. (4), the light intensity of the fringe pattern obtained by the linear correlation calculating method varies smoothly according to the sinusoidale function. However practically, noise still exists in the fringe pattern because of the effect of electronic noise of the TV camera. As the electronic noises change with the time, so two random noise patterns are mixed with the two speckle patterns taken in different times. This makes the correlation coefficient also affected by the noises. One of the main effctive methods to resolve the problem is to choose a lower noise TV camera.

It is greatly acknowledged for the mechanical Structure Strength and Vibration Laboratory of Xi'an Jiaotong University to give the financial support.

Reference

(1) Butters, J.N., Leedertz, J.A., "Speckle Pattern and Holographic in Engineering Metrology"' Opt. Laser Technol., 1971,3(1), pp26—30.
(2) Jones, R., wykes, C., "Holographic and Speckle Interferometry." Cambridge university press, 1983: Chap.4
(3) Goodman, J.W., "Laser Speckle and related Phenomena", Springer—Verlag:Berlin, 1975: Chap.2

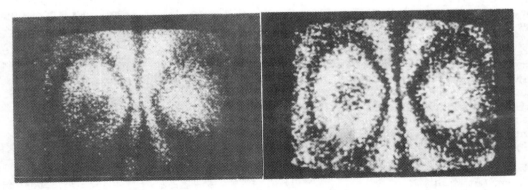

(a) Subtraction mode          (b) Linear correlation method

Fig. 1 Digital shearing speckle correlation fringe patterns

# Study of the mechanical properties of plain concrete under dynamic loading

Carlo Albertini, Ezio Cadoni, Kamel Labibes
European Commission, Joint Research Centre
Institute for System, Informatics and Safety
T.P.480, 21020 Ispra (VA) Italy

The knowledge of the influence of increasing loading rate on the true stress-strain diagram of plain concrete with real size aggregate is of basic importance for assessing the resistance of civil engineering structures against accidental loadings, like those occurring in impacts, explosions and earthquakes.

The Hopkinson bar technique is a widely used technique to determine the mechanical properties of structural materials under high loading rates; while standard Hopkinson bars with a diameter in the range of 10-20 mm are sufficient for dynamic testing of fine-grained materials like steel, much bigger bars are needed to load representative plain concrete specimen with real-size aggregate. Moreover, a special equipment is needed to allow the observation of the instantaneous distribution of stress and strain over the cross-section of large concrete specimens. Such distribution is in fact far from being homogeneous, due to the progressive cracking of the material during the loading process.

For the purpose of studying the dynamic properties of plain concrete, a special Hopkinson bar system has been developed and installed in the Large Dynamic Testing Facility (LDTF) of the Joint Research Centre at Ispra.
As a first operation, in this dynamic test, a hydraulic actuator is pulling 32 cables of high-strength steel (100m long) and the pretension stored in these cables is resisted by one grounded explosive bolt in the blocking device (Fig. 1). The successive operation is the rupture of the explosive bolt which gives rise to a tensile mechanical pulse of rectangular shape, propagating along the Hopkinson bar system.

As shown in Fig. 1, the system actually consists of two bundles of 25 aluminium bars to which the concrete test specimen is glued using an epoxy resin. The bar bundles were constructed using two square aluminium bars of 20 cm side subdivided by electroerosion into 25 pairs of bars. In this way, concrete specimens of 20 cm size are tested and by instrumenting each individual bar in the bundle with strain gauge, measures are obtained of the incident, reflected and transmitted pulses concerning the portion of the concrete specimen cross-section facing each pair of bars in the bundle.

During the fracturing process, each pair of bars in the bundles is in one of the following situations:

1. Facing an uncracked portion of the specimen cross-section, therefore measuring a small relatively reflected pulse and a large transmitted pulse.
2. Facing a partially cracked portion of the specimen cross-section, therefore in a situation intermediate between 1. and 3. below as concerns reflected and trasmitted signals.
3. Facing a cracked portion of the specimen cross-section, therefore measuring a reflected pulse of same amplitude, but of opposite sign to the incident pulse, while the correlated transmitted pulse decrease to zero.

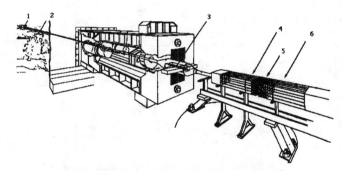

**Figure 1** - Experimental set-up: 1- hydraulic actuator; 2 - cables of pretension; 3- explosive bolt; 4- strain gauges in the incident bar bundle; 5 - specimen; 6 - strain gauges in the trasmission bar bundle.

By means of the Hopkinson's bar bundle it is possible to measure step by step the true resisting cross-section of the test specimen and thereby determine the crack propagation path and also the crack propagation speed can be evaluated. These parameters allow a reconstruction of the true stress-strain diagram of the material up to fracture of the test specimen. The tests show the ability of the Hopkinson bar bundle to measure both the parameters of the uniform deformation phase and the fracturing phase of plain concrete under dynamic loading.
Fig.2 shows the record of the incident, reflected and trasmitted pulses from the non-subdivided part of the Hopkinson bar, while Fig.3 shows the same type of record

obtained from a few bars in the bundle. One notes that the incident pulse is homogeneously distributed between the bars in the bundle. Figs. 4 and 5 illustrate the situations 1, 2, and 3 described above for a few bars of the bundle and, therefore, confirm the possibility of measuring the true resisting cross-section of the test specimen, the load acting on it, the deformation and the crack propagation path and speed.

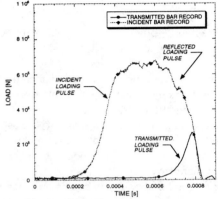

**Figure 2** - Records of incident, reflected and trasmitted pulses from the whole bar

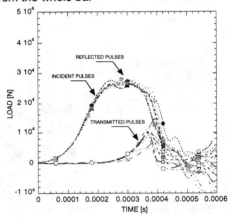

**Figure 3** - Records of incident, reflected and trasmitted pulses from few bars of the bundle

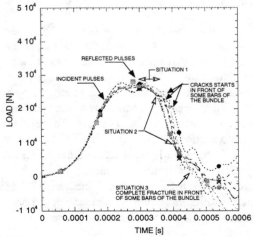

**Figure 4** - Record from imput bars bundle correlation between reflected pulses and deformation - fracture phases

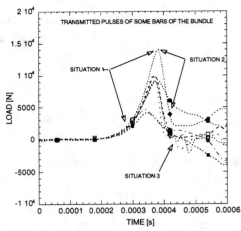

**Figure 5** - Record from output bars bundle; correlation between transmitted pulses and deformation - fracture phases

Through the analysis of reflected pulses it has been possible to represent the crack propagation path, as shown in Fig. 6 (the number point out the time in µs), where is observable the crack position at different times till to failure.

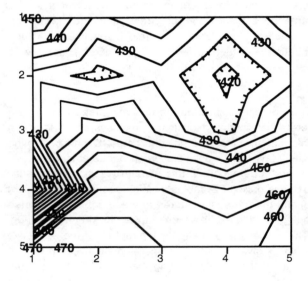

**Figure 6** - Crack propagation path

A detailed analysis of the test results is therefore expected to lead to an accurate determination of the true stress-strain diagram of plain concrete and of the fracture mechanics parameters governing crack propagation and ultimate failure of the material.

As a results the Hopkinson bar bundle technique allows the experimental observation of the instantaneous distribution of stress and strain over the cross-section of large concrete specimens with real size aggregate, subjected to high loading rates. A detailed description of the true stress-strain diagram will be appear in extended paper.

# Finite Element Modeling of Photoplastic Processes
# In the Cold Drawing of Polycarbonate Bars

Jonah H. Lee and Dong J. Choi
Department of Mechanical Engineering
University of Alaska Fairbanks, Fairbanks, AK, 99775-5900

Cold drawing of polycarbonate bars [1] is simulated by the finite element method using rate-dependent viscoplastic constitutive equations with molecular isotropic resistance and rubber-like anisotropic resistance. The rate-dependent viscoplastic constitutive equation for large deformations [2] is implemented in the general-purpose finite element program ABAQUS [3] with the user material routine (UMAT). The (mechanical ) material parameters for the finite element analysis are chosen to close-fit the load-displacement curve from numerical analysis (at one strain rate) to that of the experimental one in the cold drawing process. Stress and fringe contour patterns are obtained and are significantly influenced by unloading and relaxation time. Short unloading and long relaxation time are used to simulate the experimental unloading procedure.

Stretches calculated from the finite element analysis are used to produce equivalent photoplastic fringe patterns by different optical-mechanical relationships. Gaussian or non-Gaussian assumptions with constant or varying random polymer link number are used in various combinations in the optical-mechanical relationships. The fringe patterns obtained using the plastic stretch in the loaded state are significantly different from those after unloading and relaxation. The viscoplastic finite element analysis with the optical-mechanical relationships produces fringe patterns similar to experimental ones. Fringe patterns from finite element analysis, when compared with experimental results, using the non-Gaussian optical-mechanical relationship yield better results than using the Gaussian-optical mechanical relationship.

The frozen-strain-slicing technique in photoplasticity [4] and the photoplastic optical-mechanical relationship are assessed by comparing results of finite element analysis with experimental ones in the cold drawing process under several different strain rates. The numerical results show that high residual stress exists at the neck initiation area after unloading and relaxation steps. This shows that the strain-frozen and sliced sample for photoplastic experiment should be taken reasonably away from the neck initiation zone.

The proposed non-Gaussian optical-mechanical relationship with the present viscoplastic modeling simulates the experimental photoplastic results well. This verifies the usefulness of the present physically-based viscoplastic constitutive equations and the proposed optical-mechanical relationship to realistic polycarbonate deformation process and the photoplastic procedure. The importance of the rubber-elasticity component in the mechanical and optical-mechanical constitutive equations is clearly demonstrated. Also the current study shows the importance of both the residual stress for the photoplastic technique and the unloading and relaxation steps in viscoplastic modeling.

References:

[1] Lee, J.H., Simon, D.F., Choi, D.J., "Photoplastic studies of strain distributions in the cold drawing of polycarbonate cylindrical bars: the rate effect.,", Experimental Mechanics, 35 (1995), 182-191.

[2] Boyce, M.C., Parks, D.M., Argon, A.S., "Large inelastic deformation of glassy polymers. Part I: rate dependent constitutive model," Mechanics of Materials, 15 (1988).

[3] Abaqus Users Manual, Hibbit, Karlsson & Sorensen, Inc.

[4] Burger, C.P., "Nonlinear Photomechanics," Experimental Mechanics, 20 (1980), 381-389.

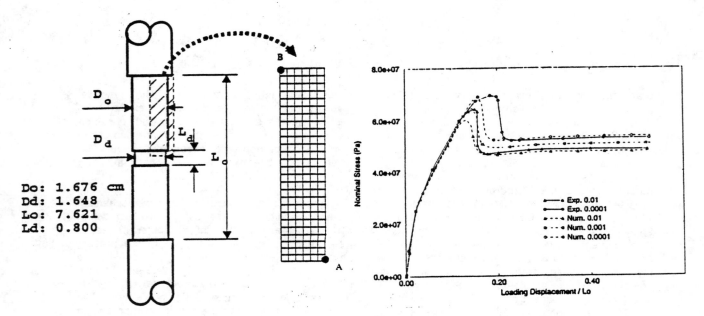

Do: 1.676 cm
Dd: 1.648
Lo: 7.621
Ld: 0.800

Fig. 1 The finite element model.

Fig. 2 Comparison of experimental
and numerical uniaxial stress-strain
curves at different strain rates.

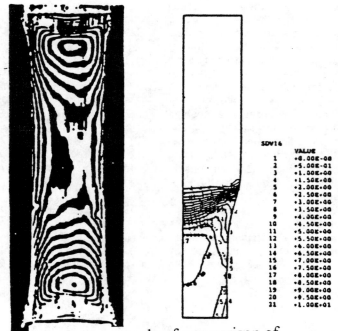

Fig. 3 An example of comparison of
experimental and numerical fringe
patterns.

498

# 600℃ CREEP ANALYSIS OF METAL MATERIAL
# WITH MOIRE INTERFEROMETRY METHOD

Xie Huimin    Dai Fulong
(Tsinghua University, Beijing, China, 100084)
Peter Dietz    Axel Schmidt
(Technical of Clausthal, Clausthal-Zellerfeld, Germany, 38678)

Loaded metal material at high temperature will produce creep deformation. With the increase of the creep time, a lot of minute cracks will be formed in the plastic area of the material, from which the crack will expand. Finally, the structure will be damaged. There are a lot of such examples, as fractures of turbine fans, expansions of main steam pipeline and superheater pipe. With increase of these accidents, the study on fracture mechanism of structures at high temperature is highly valued. At present time, creep deformation is usually measured with the standard tensile creep test method. Its experimental results can only offer the average strain along the given length, and thus cannot reflect the rules of the non uniform strains in the minute crack area of the measured object during its damage procedure. With the development of fracture mechanics on high temperature problems, there is an urgent need for the new measuring methods which offer the full field deformation at high temperature. Moire interferometry method is a new optical measuring technique, which can offer the real time deformation field of the measured object with high sensitvity. Since the 1980s, it has became an effective measuring method on the non-uniform deformation field for the strain analysis[1].

In this paper, a combination of holographic gratings and moire interferometry is used to give an experimental study on the tensile creep deformation of a carbon steel specimen at 600℃. The residual deformation fields of the specimen in the minimum cross section and the changing rules of the strain concentration different creep time were obtained.

A plate type tensile specimen with a centrical hole was manufactured with a sheet of No. 20 carbon steel plate (the thickness is 2mm) as in Fig. 1. A high frequency grating for high temperature was attached on the specimen surface by using two deposited metal layers method[2].

Before the creep test, the specimen grating was placed into the moire interferometry optical system (M. I. O. S.), and the null moire pattern was recorded. After that, the specimen was strored into a high temperature oven of DSS-universal test machine to conduct a creep temperature test. In this test, the temperature T=600℃, tensile load P=490 N. The test lasted 40 hours. At different creep time the specimen was unloaded and placed into the M. I. O. S. for recording the moire fringe patterns of residual creep. The moire patterns of residual creep up to 40 hours were obtained.

The strain cocentration factor $K_t$ is defined as the ratio between the creep strain at point S on the boundary of hole and the creep strain at the far field. With the experimental results, the changing rules of the creep concentration fact are analysed. And it can be concluded the creep strain concentration factor of the tensile specimen (No. 20 steel) takes a direct propotion with the parameter of time during its first creep stage.

References:
[1] Post, D. "Developments in Moire Interferometry", Opt. Eng., 21, (3), pp458—467, (1982).
[2] Xie Huimin, Yuan Jie Dai Fulong, "Production of Holographic Grating for High Temperature", Optical Technology, (3), pp14—16, (1993).

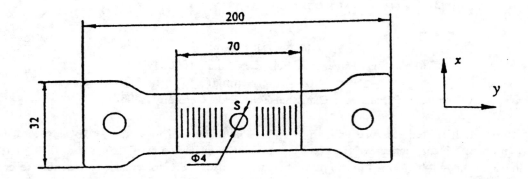

Fig. 1 a schematic diagram of the specimen with a centrical hole

# Determination of the Stress Intensity Factor for Steel Materials and 7075-T6 Aluminum Alloy using the Reflected Caustic Method

Seiji.Tsukagosi*, Akira.Shimamoto**, Susumu.Takahashi*

*Kanto Gakuin Univ

4834 Mutsuura-cho Kanazawa-ku Yokohama 236 Japan

**Saitama Institute of Technology

1690 Fusaiji Okabe-cho Saitama 369-02 Japan

## Introduction

The rapid development of manufacturing in recent years has promoted the making of a variety of larger scale, lighter weight and higher speed mechanical structures, and accompanying this, the steel materials for the various structures involved in ship building, aviation, bridge building, nuclear reactor power generation and petro-chemical plants have come to be used under increasingly severe conditions. In relation to this, there has been active development of all kinds of materials which have high strength and high toughness. When using only conventional material dynamic methods to plan structures and machinery with these materials, fracture breakdowns have occurred in spite of the fact that stress suitably lower than the design stress was involved. However, general mechanical structures are rarely under mono-axial stress, and it is normal for them to be subjected to impact or repeated loads. In particular, the fact that there are clearly problems with impact fracture caused by impact stress is important in view of reliability assurance and countermeasures to prevent breakdowns. Notably, when considering the location of crack tip stress, which is present in the majority of fractures, the stress intensity factor is one of the most important parameters in fracture mechanics, and cracking behavior can be quantitatively discussed by introducing this stress intensity factor. Moreover, in order o evaluate the safety of machines and structures which use impact loads, it is necessary to accurately measure the dynamic fracture toughness $K_{ID}$ of the material used. Numerical analysis such as FEM (finite element method) and experimental analyses such as the instrumented Charpy impact tester have been offered as methods to determine this fracture toughness $K_{ID}$. Among these, the caustics method can easily derive the stress intensity factor, which is one of the parameters necessary for the consideration of stress locations in the vicinity of cracking. In dynamic fracture problems, an analytic method is utilized which combines the caustics method with high speed cameras. In this study, we took a series of dynamic caustics image photographs of a number of test pieces with the same shape using a single flash stroboscope, and we conducted basic research relating to the dynamic fracture behavior of aluminum alloy 7075-T6 which had a V-notch on one side.

## Principles of the Caustic Method

When a test piece to which a load has been added is irradiated with light, changes of plate thickness are being produced by the concentration of stress on the crack tip, and this allows caustics images to be obtained on a screen. The static stress intensity factor $K_I$ and the dynamic stress intensity factor $K_{Id}$ are derived by measuring the diameter D of this caustics image and substituting these values into Equations (1) and (2).

$$K_I = \left(1.671 / z_0 t |c_0|\right) \times \left(1 / \lambda^{3/2}\right) \times \left(D / 3.16\right)^{5/2} \quad \cdot \quad \cdot \quad (1)$$

$$K_{Id} = \frac{1}{\lambda^{3/2}} \frac{2\sqrt{2\pi}F}{3(3.17)^{5/2} z_0 c d_{eff}} D^{5/2} \quad \cdot \quad \cdot \quad \cdot \quad (2)$$

Here, $\lambda$ is the constant which is determined by $(Z_0+Z_i)/Z_i$; $Z_i$ is the distance between the test piece up to the focal point of the convergent light; $Z_0$ is the distance between the test piece and the screen; C is the optical constant; $D_{eff}$ is 1/2 of test piece thickness t; and F is the correction factor which is indicated by the function $V/C_R$, the ratio between the crack development velocity V and the Rayleigh wave speed.

## Experimental Device

In order to measure the static fracture toughness, a Tensilon type universal tester was used to conduct three point bending tests at a cross hed speed of 0.5 mm/min. The fracture load was determined based on the maximum value of the load-time curve obtained by this test, and the static fracture toughness $K_{IC}$ was derived.

The impact bending tester and the measurement system for the purpose of measuring the dynamic stress intensity factor $K_{Id}$ are indicated in Figures 1 . Fracture was caused by applying an impact load to the bending test piece utilizing the free fall of a drop hammer. The distortion pulses transmitted by the drop hammer at this time were read by a semiconductor distortion gauge, and by recording this on a digital storage oscilloscope, the uniform impact load conditions could be determined. Triggered by the contact of the drop hammer and the test piece, a series of dynamic caustics images were taken with an interval type high speed photographic device using a stroboscope delay circuit to

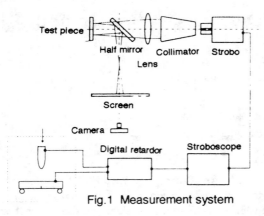

Fig.1 Measurement system

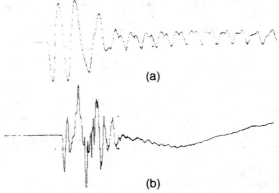

(a)

(b)

Fig.2 Distortion pulse waveform

cause single flashes at 40 $\mu$sec intervals. The crack advancement velocity v was measured with the crack gauge attached near the tip of the test piece. The distortion pulse waveforms measured from the drop hammer are indicated in Figure 2.

Figure 2 indicates a situation in which impact loads were applied to the same kind of test pieces, but (a) is with a continuous distortion pulse waveform, and (b) is with an abnormally applied [distortion pulse waveform]. If these abnormal results were excluded, uniformity of the impact load could be verified.

### Results and Discussion

A series of photographs of dynamic caustics images is indicated in Figure 3. The diameter D of these caustics images were measured, and the changes over time of the dynamic stress intensity factor $K_{Id}$ are indicated in Figure 4. As time passes the dynamic stress intensity factor $K_{Id}$ gradually becomes larger, and at the same moment that cracking develops, this rapidly drops off. The dynamic fracture toughness $K_{ID}$ was determined to be the value immediately prior to the development of this cracking.

The results of the static fracture toughness $K_{IC}$ and the dynamic fracture toughness $K_{ID}$ are indicated in Table 1. Compared to the static fracture toughness $K_{IC}$, the dynamic fracture toughness $K_{ID}$ is a value lower by about 20%. The Kalthoff formula which considers the inertia effect was utilized in the calculation of the dynamic fracture toughness $K_{ID}$, but with the impact bending test, there have been reports that, after floating up and separating from the support point, the bending test piece once again makes contact with the support point. This is thought to be caused by low order bending maneuvers produced by the impact load on the test piece, and it is necessary to conduct further study on the question of how this has an effect on the dynamic stress intensity factor $K_{Id}$.

### References

1 J.F.Kalthoff, International Journal of Fracture 27, (1985).227-298
2 P.S.Theocaris, ACTA MECHANICA, 87, (1991), 133-159
3 S.Takahashi and K.Shimizu ; Machine Reserch 37.4(1985) 485-495

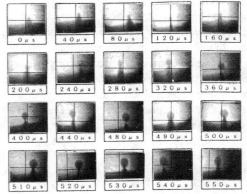

Fig.3 Dynamic caustics images(160mm×35mm a/w=0.1)

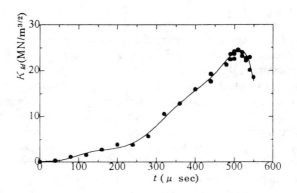

Fig.4 The changes over time of the $K_{Id}$

Table 1. The results of the static fracture toughness $K_{IC}$ and the dynamic fracture toughness $K_{ID}$

| a/w | $K_{IC}$(MN/m$^{3/2}$) | $K_{ID}$ (MN/m$^{3/2}$) |
| --- | --- | --- |
| 0.1 | 31.8 | 24.5 |
| 0.2 | 32.0 | 23.7 |
| 0.3 | 31.8 | 25.4 |
| 0.4 | 29.9 | 23.4 |

# The Effect of Magnetic Field on the Experimental Determination of $K_I$ by Means of ACPD Technique

J. H. Lee, M. Saka and H. Abé
Department of Mechanical Engineering,
Tohoku University, Sendai 980-77, Japan

A method based on alternating current potential drop (ACPD) for the experimental determination of the Mode I stress intensity factor, $K_I$, has been proposed by Saka et al. [1]. Since high frequency A-C current flows on the specimen surface and around the crack due to the skin effect, the potential drop which changes with the load gives significant information about $K_I$. It has recently been found that the change in potential drop due to load depends on the positions of power supply lines and measuring probe lines because of the different amount of the induced electromotive force due to magnetic field. The purpose of the present study was clarifying the effect of the magnetic flux in the air on the change in potential drop due to load for the ferromagnetic and paramagnetic materials. Additionally the effects of the demagnetization and the crack length on the change in potential drop were examined.

The specimens were made of steel(JIS G4103 SNCM439) as an example of ferromagnetic material and aluminum alloy (JIS H4000 A2017) as an example of paramagnetic material. Three kinds of the specimens each with different crack lengths were prepared for respective materials. For the measurement of potential drop, A-C current of 1 A with a frequency 10 kHz was supplied through the power amplifier to the specimen by a function generator. The potential drop was measured by using a lock-in amplifier and digital voltmeter under the static load condition by three point bending.

In order to examine systematically the effect of magnetic flux on the change in potential drop due to load, four kinds of measuring systems designated SYSTEM 1 to SYSTEM 4 were prepared. In SYSTEM 1, the magnetic flux around the specimen was removed by using the characteristic of coaxial transmission line. The amount of induced electromotive force in the other three systems were controlled by adjusting the distance between current supply line and potential measuring line to have different amount of that each other. In SYSTEM 4 as shown in Fig. 1, the induced electromotive force was largely increased by extending the potential measuring lines to the vicinity of the current supply points and winding the potential measuring lines as a coil. The amounts of the induced electromotive force in SYSTEMs 2, 3 and 4 were 1.6, 13.8 and 64.9 mV, respectively.

In order to remove the magnetization caused by residual stress and loading history in ferromagnetic materials, demagnetization has generally been done. Some specimens were demagnetized by slowly decreasing the amplitude of A-C current supplied to an electromagnet from 15 A-20 V to zero.

Four kinds of the experiment designated Case A to Case D were carried out for each measuring system. In Case A and Case B, ACPD was measured by increasing and decreasing the load, respectively, applied to the specimen which was not demagnetized. In Case C and Case D, on the other hand, ACPD was measured by increasing and decreasing the load for the demagnetized specimen. The specimens were demagnetized only at the state that the initial load had been applied to the specimen from which increasing or decreasing the load was started.

The relationship between the change in potential drop and that in $K_I$ was not linear in SYSTEMs 1 and 2 for not demagnetized steel as shown in Fig. 2, where the change in potential drop was denoted by $\Delta E$ and increasing and decreasing the load were denoted by arrow. The change in potential drop obtained in SYSTEMs 1 and 2 for aluminum alloy decreased linearly with increasing $K_I$. The absolute value of the change in potential drop was less than 1 $\mu$V within the examined $K_I$ for respective materials. However the amount of the change in potential drop was largely increased in SYSTEMs 3 and 4 as shown in Fig. 3. Also the relationship between the change in potential drop with that in $K_I$ was linear for respective material. From these results, two facts can be found. First, if the amount of the magnetic flux in the measuring system is increased, a large amount of the change in potential drop can be measured. Second, the relationship between the change in potential drop and that in $K_I$ is linear without any treatment in the case of the measuring system with a large amount of magnetic flux in the air.

The relationship between the change in potential drop and that in $K_I$ was linearized by demagnetization in the case of the measuring system without or with a little amount of magnetic flux in the air for steel as shown in Fig. 4. It was found from the comparison of Fig. 5 with

Fig. 3 that demagnetization had almost no effect on the change in potential drop in the case of the measuring system with a large amount of magnetic flux.

The change in potential drop per unit change in $K_I$ was independent of the respective materials as shown in Fig. 6, where the $K_I - K_{Ii}$ in the abscissa was used for arranging the results obtained from the different values of initial load, which was denoted by $K_{Ii}$ in terms of $K_I$, so that they start from the same point.

The sign of the change in potential drop per unit $K_I$ with increasing the load for the paramagnetic material in the system without magnetic flux in the air is negative, but it is positive for the ferromagnetic material. The amount of the change in potential drop increases largely with increasing the magnetic flux of the measuring system. In the case of the measuring system with a large amount of magnetic flux, the relationship between the change in potential drop and that in $K_I$ is linear without demagne-

tization and demagnetization has almost no effect on the change in potential drop. In all measuring systems, the change in potential drop due to load is independent of the crack length. For the application of ACPD technique to the experimental determination of $K_I$, a measuring system with a large amount of magnetic flux in the air such as SYSTEM 4 is suitable.

Acknowledgment

This work was partly supported by The Ministry of Education, Science, Sports and Culture under Grant-in-Aid for Developmental Scientific Research (B)(2)055555028.

Reference

[1] Saka, M., Nakayama, M., Kaneko, T. and Abé, H., "Measurement of Stress-Intensity Factor by Means of A-C Potential Drop Technique," Experimental Mech., 31 (3), pp 209-212, 1991.

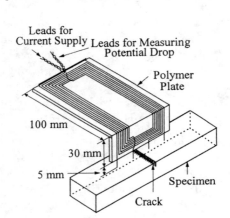

Fig. 1 Diagram showing SYSTEM 4

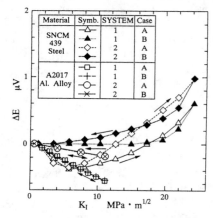

Fig. 2 Change in potential drop with $K_I$ measured by SYSTEMs 1 and 2 for not demagnetized specimen with crack length of 6.1 mm

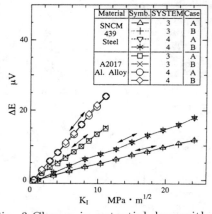

Fig. 3 Change in potential drop with $K_I$ measured by SYSTEMs 3 and 4 for not demagnetized specimen with crack length of 6.1 mm

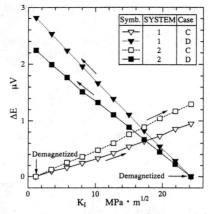

Fig. 4 Change in potential drop with $K_I$ measured by SYSTEMs 1 and 2 for demagnetized steel specimen with crack length of 6.1 mm

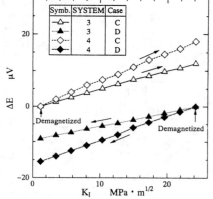

Fig. 5 Change in potential drop with $K_I$ measured by SYSTEMs 3 and 4 for demagnetized steel specimen with crack length of 6.1 mm

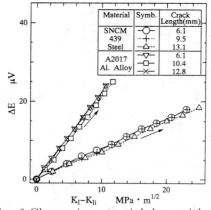

Fig. 6 Change in potential drop with $K_I$ for different values of crack length in SYSTEM 4

# A new procedure for the determination of stress intensity factors from thermoelastic data

R A Kitchin, A D Nurse* and E A Patterson
Department of Mechanical and Process Engineering,
University of Sheffield, Mappin St. Sheffield, S1 3JD, UK,
*Department of Mechanical Engineering,
Loughborough University of Technology, UK

In recent years attempts have made to determine stress intensity factors using thermoelasticity. The expression for the sum of the principal stresses around the crack tip was derived using the Westergaard equations[1]. Although this method appears to be reliable for mode I cracks, the solution has been shown to be less dependable for pure mode II and mixed mode cracks[2]. A similar problem has also been found to exist when using photoelastic solutions[3], where the limit of accuracy is that $K_{II}/K_I$ must be less than 0.7 when using the Westergaard equations. In an attempt to obtain reliable stress intensity factors from photoelastic data[4], the Muskhelishvili complex solution[5] was used and gave accurate values for stress intensity factors, compared with established theory, for predominantly mode II cracks, in addition to mode I and mixed mode cases. This procedure has now been extended for use with thermoelastic data.

The thermoelastic analysis was carried out with the use of a SPATE (Stress Pattern Analysis by Thermal Emission) system, which uses an infra-red detector to measure very small changes in temperature that occur in materials subjected to cyclic load. The frequency of the cyclic loading must be sufficient to achieve adiabatic conditions in the test piece. The area of interest on the surface of the specimen is scanned by the detector to establish a map of data. The signal from the detector, S is proportional to the sum of the principal stresses at the point of interest, i.e.

$$\Delta(\sigma_1 + \sigma_2) = AS \tag{1}$$

where A is a calibration factor.

The stress field equations used in the photoelastic procedure[4] were modified to describe the sum rather than the difference of principal stresses. The generalised stress field surrounding a crack tip is defined using the Muskhelishvili[5] approach in which the in-plane stresses are represented by two analytical functions $\Phi(z)$ and $\Psi(z)$ of the complex variable $z = x + iy$ where x and y are rectangular co-ordinates. The in-plane rectangular components of stress in a stressed body in the absence of body forces can be written as:

$$\sigma_x + \sigma_y = 2\left(\Phi(z) + \overline{\Phi(z)}\right) \tag{2a}$$

$$\frac{\sigma_y - \sigma_x}{2} + i\tau_{xy} = \overline{z}\Phi'(z) + \Psi(z) \tag{2b}$$

where the overbar denotes the complex conjugate and the prime denotes differentiation. To derive an expression for the sum of the principal stresses, only equation (2a) is required and thus only the analytical function, $\Phi(z)$ need be used, unlike photoelasticity where both functions are needed. The stress equations are generated from a Fourier series in complex form where the coefficients of each term are variables that allow different stress states to be described. The mapping and boundary conditions are exactly as those used in the photoelastic procedure[4]. In the same manner, the application of these conditions results in an expression for the complex stress function:

$$\Phi(\zeta) = A_o + \frac{A_o + \overline{A_o} + \overline{B_o}}{(\zeta^2 - 1)}$$
$$+ \sum_{N=1}^{\infty}\left[\left(\frac{2N}{\zeta^{2N}}\right)\left(\frac{\zeta^2 + 1}{\zeta^2 - 1}\right)\overline{A_N} - \frac{\overline{A_N}}{\zeta^{2N}} - \frac{\overline{B_N}}{\zeta^{2N}} + A_N\zeta^{2N}\right] \tag{3}$$

where $\xi$ is a complex variable in the mapping plane (Figure 1); and $A_N$ and $B_N$ are unknown series parameters which are used to describe the generalised state of stress around the crack tip.

A general expression for the sum of the principal stresses can be written for the physical plane, using the co-ordinate system in the mapping plane by substituting equation (3) into equation (2) and observing that the sum of the principal stresses is a stress invariant thus equation (1) becomes:

$$\Delta(\sigma_1 + \sigma_2) = 2\Delta\left(\Phi(\xi) + \overline{\Phi(\xi)}\right) = AS \tag{4}$$

The real parts of $A_N$ and $B_N$ describe a Mode I stress field and the imaginary parts describe a Mode II stress field. The complex stress intensity factor $K_I + iK_{II}$ is calculated using the limiting value of $\Phi(\zeta)$ as $\zeta \to \pm 1$, i.e.

$$\Delta(K_I + K_{II}) = A_o + \overline{A_o} + B_o + 4\sum_{N=1}^{\infty}(A_N) \tag{5}$$

The parameters, $A_N$ and $B_N$ must be determined to solve the problem and thus calculate $\Delta K_I$ and $\Delta K_{II}$.

Expressions for the real and imaginary parts of $A_N$ and $B_N$ were written using equations (3) and (4). These expressions were implemented in the new computer program, which evaluates stress intensity factors from thermoelastic data in the form of $\Delta K_I$ and $\Delta K_{II}$ in MPa√m. Thermoelastic data is collected over a full field area, to produce an array of approximately 100 data points surrounding a crack tip. These points are input to a new computer program, with the thermoelastic calibration factor and the crack length, to solve for the stress intensity factor utilising a Newton-Raphson iteration scheme. Statistical calculations are performed and the mean and variance of the least-squares fit of the solution to the data points are also provided as output. This rapid data processing technique solves for $K_I$ and $K_{II}$ in minutes. Experience with these stress solutions also shows that the technique is robust in the vicinity of other singularities and boundaries[6].

The solution was tested using an aluminium panel containing a central mode I notch. A cyclic load at a frequency of 8 Hz, was applied to the panel. The SPATE pattern was recorded, calibrated and interrogated and the stress intensity factor, $\Delta K$ was determined for increasing notch lengths. The values of $\Delta K_I$ were compared to those determined from theory[7] in Figure 2, and were within 8%. The zones of validity of the data points were investigated and found to be similar to those used in the photoelastic procedure. The thermoelastic technique has the advantage that the data must be collected under cyclic loading thus the crack driving force, $\Delta K$, is determined directly from the data, unlike in photoelasticity where $\Delta K$ is inferred from the maximum and minimum stress intensity factors. The procedure is also non-contacting and consistent results are obtained by spraying the surface with black paint.

It was concluded that the new procedure for determining the stress intensity factor, $\Delta K$, from thermoelastic data surrounding notches or cracks under fatigue loading was more reliable and robust than previous thermoelastic solutions.

1. Stanley, P and Chan, W K, The determination of stress intensity factors and crack-tip velocities from thermoelastic infra-red emissions, Proc. Int. Conf. on Fatigue of Engineering Materials and Structures (IMechE), Sheffield, (1), 105-114, 1986
2. Stanley, P and Dulieu-Smith, J M, Progress in the thermoelastic evaluation of mixed mode stress intensity factors, Proc. SEM Spring Conf. on Experimental Mechanics, 617-623, 1993
3. Nurse, A D and Patterson, E A, Photoelastic determination of stress intensity factors for edge cracks under mixed-mode loading, Proc. 9th Int. Conf. on Experimental Mechanics, Copenhagen, (2): 948-957, 1990
4. Nurse, A D and Patterson, E A, Determination of predominantly Mode II stress intensity factors from isochromatic data, Fatigue Fract. Engng. Mater. Struct., 16 (12), 1339-1254, 1993
5. Muskhelishvili, N I, Some basic problems of the mathematical theory of elasticity, 3rd. edn. Noordhoff, Groningen, 1963

6. Nurse, A D, O'Brien, E W, and Patterson, E A, Stress intensity factors for cracks at fastener holes, Fatigue Fract. Engng. Mater. Struct., 17, (7), 791-799, 1994
7. Edwalds, H L and Wanhill, R J H, Fracture Mechanics, Edward Arnold, 1991

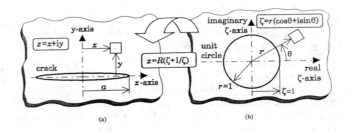

Figure 1. Crack co-ordinate systems in (a) physical and (b) mapping planes [4]

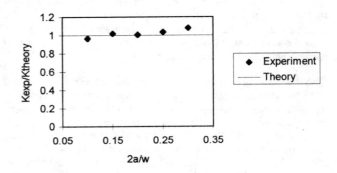

Figure 2. Stress intensity factor, $\Delta K_I$ ,with increasing notch length, where 2a = notch length and w = panel width

# Measurement of Crack Tip Location, Orientation, and Mixed Mode Stress Intensity Factors Using Near Crack Tip Strain Gages

Gregory R. Swanson
Aerospace Engineer
ED25/ Structural Mechanics Team
NASA, Marshall Space Flight Center
MSFC, AL

Professor Loren W. Zachary
Aerospace Engineering and Engineering Mechanics
Black Engineering Building
Iowa State University
Ames, IA

An experimental method for determining crack tip location, orientation, and mixed mode stress intensity factors using near crack tip strain gage data is presented. A set of strain gages are placed on the surface of a test specimen in the relatively near field of a crack tip. From the strain gage data and the relative location of the strain gages to each other the location of the crack tip and its orientation relative to the strain gages is derived along with mixed mode stress intensity factors. The method is based on an iterative multiple linear least squares routine that provides a best fit to generalized Westergaard equations that describe the strain field near a crack tip [1]. The four parameter strain field relative to a cylindrical crack tip coordinate system is shown in equations (1) and (2). Figure 1 shows the local crack tip coordinate system along with the global system used to locate the crack tip.

$$2 \mu \varepsilon_i = A_0 r_i^{-1/2} [ k \cos ( \theta_i / 2 ) - (1/2) \sin \theta_i \sin ( 3\theta_i / 2 ) \cos ( 2 \alpha_i ) + (1/2) \sin \theta_i \cos ( 3\theta_i / 2 ) \sin ( 2 \alpha_i )] + B_0 [ k + \cos ( 2 \alpha_i )] + A_1 r_i^{1/2} \cos ( \theta_i / 2 ) [ k + \sin^2 ( \theta_i / 2 ) \cos ( 2 \alpha_i ) - (1/2) \sin \theta_i \sin ( 2 \alpha_i )] + B_1 r_i [ (k + \cos ( 2 \alpha_i )) \cos \theta_i - 2 \sin \theta_i \sin ( 2 \alpha_i )] \qquad (1)$$

where,

| | | |
|---|---|---|
| $\mu$ | = | Shear Modulus |
| $\varepsilon_i$ | = | Stain Gage Reading |
| $r_i$ | = | Distance to gage |
| $\theta_i$ | = | Angle to gage |
| $\alpha_i$ | = | Gage angle relative to crack tip |
| $A_0$ | = | Constant |
| $B_0$ | = | Constant |
| $A_1$ | = | Constant |
| $B_1$ | = | Constant |
| $k$ | = | $( 1 - \nu / 1 + \nu )$ |

and,

$$KI = \sqrt{2 \Pi a} \ A_0 \qquad (2)$$

From the fit of the Westergaard functions crack tip location and orientation are derived relative to the coordinate system that describes the strain gage locations and orientations and the Mode I or mixed Modes I and II stress intensity factors are also fit.

Numerous residual weighting schemes were developed and a parametric numerical study was run to quantify the methods stability and sensitivity to experimental error. A "perfect fit" strain gage data set was created and then perturbed with a random number generation routine to simulate experimental error and noise. The maximum amount of noise was varied from 1 to 20 micro strain and several data sets with 100 gage reading subsets were generated. Using the sets of noisy data the methods response to different levels of noise was quantified, and the best numerical iteration scheme selected. Figure 2 shows the improvement in fit for various schemes using the 5 micro strain noise case.

The methods ability to located a crack tip allows the monitoring of a crack tip location on the surface of a specimen as the crack propagates. The calculation of the crack orientation shows the direction a crack is growing at the time the strain gage data was collected.

Finally, actual experimental strain data from a compact tension crack specimen and a mixed mode plate specimen are processed by this method and the results compared with the known crack tip location and Modes I and II stress intensity factors.

References:

[1] Dally, J. W. and Sanford, R. J., "Strain-Gage Methods for Measuring the Opening-Mode Stress-Intensity Factor, KI", Experimental Mechanics, Volume 27 Number 4, pages 381-388, 1987.

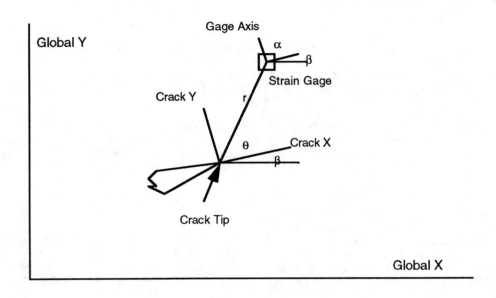

Figure 1. Crack tip and strain gage coordinate system

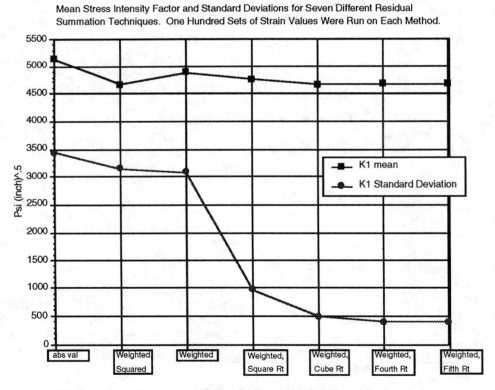

Mean Stress Intensity Factor and Standard Deviations for Seven Different Residual Summation Techniques. One Hundred Sets of Strain Values Were Run on Each Method.

Figure 2. Mean and SD of KI vs Weighting Method

# Crack Initiation and Propagation in Stress Interaction Field

Sam-Hong Song[*], Joon-Soo Bae[**]

* Department of Mechanical Engineering, Korea University, 5-1, Anam-Dong, Sungbuk-Ku, Seoul, Korea
** Graduate School, Korea University, 5-1, Anam-Dong, Sungbuk-Ku, Seoul, Korea

Crack initiation may be associated with defects existing in machine components, and it is important to understand cracking behavior in the vicinity of the defects. When the structural element has several defects, the fatigue life is influenced by the relative locations of the defects so that many studies have been proposed. Song[1] studied the interaction of two hole defects by finite element method. Stress intensity factors of two cracks were obtained [2][3], and the configurations of two cracks were investigated [4]. But there are few studies which deal with the crack initiation when two hole defects are located adjacently and aligned perpendicular to axial loading direction. In practice, the defects and stress concentrations are variously located. Therefore, the coordinates of hole notches are considered as a function of its angular and radial location in the present work(Fig.1). The crack initiation life and propagation behavior were investigated with considering interaction of two hole defects. Two types of loading were used to examine the effect of applied loading.

In the present study, fatigue testing was carried out using Bending and Torsional Testing Machine(TB10, Shimazu, maximum moment amplitude 98N-m, 2000rpm). Bending testing specimen and torsional testing specimen are illustrated in Fig.2 and Fig.3 respectively. The material used in bending testing was Al-5086 recommended in ASTM. The material selected for torsional testing was Cr-Mo steel, SCM 415 recommended by Korea standard specification. Hole notches were machined of 0.5mm depth and located by degree of 0°,30°,45°,60°,and 90° respectively.

First, the crack initiation life under bending applied loading is investigated. Stress concentration factor($K_t$) was computed by finite element method and compared with crack initiation life. The comparison between crack initiation life and $K_t$ under bending applied loading is shown in Fig.4. The results show that $K_t$ is not directly related to crack initiation life. Upon yielding, the local stresses are no longer related to the nominal values by $K_t$. Therefore, the local strain is obtained and compared with crack initiation life. The results obtained at various stress concentrations by varying the location of two hole defects show that the relation between the magnitude of local strain and crack initiation life doesn't have consistent relationship. As this discrepancy is attributed to stress distribution and gradient in the vicinity of hole defects, so the plastic strain area is used for linearizing crack initiation life. New parameter $A_{p\varepsilon}$ which contains local strain magnitude and area terms as follows is proposed.

$$\Lambda_{p\varepsilon} = \varepsilon_l \times (\frac{\Lambda}{\Lambda_1})^3 \qquad (1)$$

$\varepsilon_l$ : local strain
$A$ : area of local plastic strain
$A_1$ : area of local plastic strain at one hole notch

Increasing area of plastic strain increases $A_{p\varepsilon}$ and thereby crack initiation lives are linearized as a line(Fig.5).

The crack initiated at stress concentrations propagates in mixed mode stress field in this work. The propagation rate and direction are affected by relative positions of two hole defects. When the distance of two hole defects is short enough(l=3) the cracks are coalesced into another hole defect at θ=45°, and when the distance is within some bounds(l=5), the cracks propagate toward the other hole defect and come to be arrested gradually. The crack propagates straight when the distance is above a specific bound(l=6).

When the applied loading type is changed, crack initiation life and propagation behavior are changed. To examine this effect, torsional loading was applied at the torsional testing specimen with the same notches as in the case of bending. Crack initiation life in bending reveals a great difference due to a small change of strain concentration factor. However strain concentration factor in the torsional loading changes more than in the case of bending, but there is not so much difference of crack initiation life.

Reference
[1] Sam Hong Song, Jin Bong Kim,"Analysis of Stress Distribution Around Micro Hole by F.E.M.", KSME Journal, Vol.18, No.3, 1994, pp 555-564.
[2] Murakami and S.Nemat-Nasser, "Interaction dissimilar semi-elliptical surface flaws under tension and bending", Engineering Fracture Mechanics, Vol.16,1982,pp 373-386.
[3] C. Mauge, M.Kachanov, "Anisotropic material with interaction arbitrarily oriented cracks. Stress intensity factors and crack-microcrack interactions", International Journal of Fracture 65, 1994, pp 115-139.
[4] W.O.Soboyejo, "On the prediction of the fatigue propagation of semi-elliptical defects", ASTM STP 1122, 1992, pp 435-438

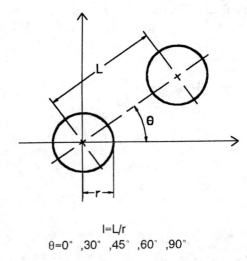

l=L/r
θ=0° ,30° ,45° ,60° ,90°

Fig.1 The positions of two hole notches

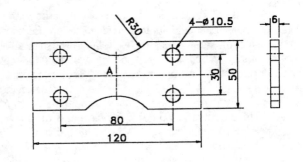

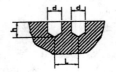

Detailed drawing of A

Fig.2 Geometries of bending testing specimen

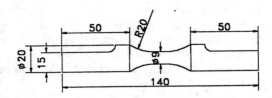

Fig.3 Geometries of torsional testing specimen

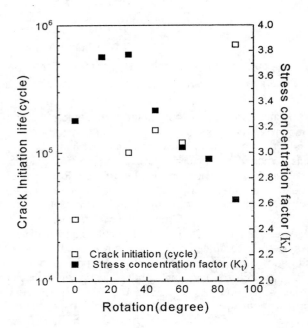

Fig.4 Relation between crack initiation life and stress concentration factor

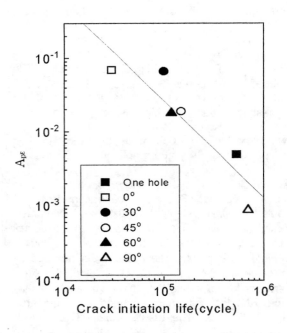

Fig.5 Relation between $A_{p\varepsilon}$ and crack initiation cycle

$$( \ A_{p\varepsilon} = \varepsilon_1 \times \frac{\text{Area of local plastic strain}}{\text{Area of local plastic strain at one hole}} )$$

510

# Evaluation of Fracture Strain from Measurements of Aspect Ratio for Ferrite Grains

Makoto Ohashi

National Res. Inst. of Police Sci.

6,Sanban-cho,Chiyoda-ku,Tokyo 102, Japan

In the failure analysis of mechanical components and assemblies, examination of the fracture surface with a scanning electron microscope is commonly employed standard practice in the determination of the cause or the mechanism of fracture. However, fractographic examination provides little information for failure analysis, if the fine details on the fracture surfaces are mechanically or chemically damaged during and after the fracture. Then, it is desirable to develop a new experimental technique for providing more positive and quantitative information regarding the fracture behavior of a component, even when fractographic examination is difficult to apply. For this purpose, an extensive metallographic study was performed on a commercial structural steel to evaluate the fracture strain of a failed component from the measurements of aspect ratio for the ferrite grains immediately underneath the fracture surface.

The material used in this study was a commercial structural steel with a tensile strength of 470MPa. The geometries of tensile specimens used are shown in Fig.1. In the present paper, preliminary test was performed on the unnotched specimen to obtain the relationship between plastic strain and aspect ratio of the ferrite grains for the calibration procedure. Then, the fracture strains of notched specimens with different notch acuity were evaluated from the measurements of aspect ratio through the calibration curve obtained above, to substantiate the applicability of the proposed method.

The relationship between plastic strain and aspect ratio for the ferrite grains was obtained from the detailed metallographic observations on the longitudinal midsection through the fractured half of the unnotched specimen. The effective plastic strains along the tensile axis of the unnotched specimen were determined at intervals of 0.5 mm in the necked region from the reduction of net area by equation (1) as

$$\varepsilon_p = 2\ln(d_0/d) \tag{1}$$

where $\varepsilon_p$ is the effective plastic strain, $d_0$ is the initial value of diameter and d is the final value of diameter at each section. The value of aspect ratio was measured on micrograph as the ratio of major axis to minor axis for each ferrite grain. The average value of aspect ratio for 10 ferrite grains was determined in correlation with the effective plastic strain at a given field of view. From a series of measurements of aspect ratio on a wide range of plastic strain, it was possible to draw a calibration curve to correlate the plastic strain with aspect ratio. Fig.2 shows these measurements of aspect ratio as a function of plastic strain. The solid line was the best fit relation for each set of data using the least square method. The aspect ratio, determined as the ratio of major axis to minor axis of the ferrite grain, was well expressed as a function of plastic strain over the entire range by equation (2) as

$$y = 1.26 \times 4.09^x \tag{2}$$

where y is the aspect ratio, x is the plastic strain.

In the second, tensile tests were conducted on the notched specimens with notch root radius of 6mm, 3mm, 1mm, 0.5 mm. Then, the fracture strain of each specimen was determined by equation (1), where $d_0$ is the initial value of diameter and d is the final value of diameter at the minimum section. The measured value of fracture strain was found to decrease gradually with increase of notch acuity. Hence, all specimens were sectioned longitudinally at the midsection, polished and etched for metallographic observations to measure the aspect ratio of the ferrite grains immediately underneath the fracture surfaces. In order to perform the analysis with sufficient accuracy , the aspect ratio was measured for 9 views along the fracture surface at intervals of approximately the same distance, including 2 views in the shear-lip zone at the notch tip. Thus, the fracture strain of each specimen was deduced from the average aspect ratio for 9 views through the use of equation (2).

Fig.3 compares the results of the estimated fracture

strains with the measured values ranged from about 0.25 to 0.75. As may be clearly seen, it is obvious that the estimated values were found to be in reasonably good agreement with the measured values within an error of about 1 to 8 pct. Accordingly, it can be said that the technique just described makes it possible to obtain an appropriate estimate of the fracture strain from the detailed metallographic examination with reasonable accuracy, regardless of the amount of plastic strain. In other words, this approach boasts an advantage compared with the previously described methods for evaluating the plastic strain, such as the laser speckle method[1]-[2] and the X-ray diffraction method[3]-[4]. That is to say, the laser speckle method or the X-ray diffraction method can not be applied successfully to the components that failed under a relatively large scale yielding, because the changes of the intensity distribution of the laser speckle, or the X-ray half-value breadth become smaller in the large plastic strain region. On the other hand, the technique proposed here, can be successfully applied for a relatively wide range of plastic strain beyond a plastic strain of about 0.2, because of remarkable dependence of aspect ratio on the plastic strain in that region. As such, the proposed method can be adopted as a useful technique for providing more positive and quantitative information regarding the fracture behavior of a component, even when electron fractography is difficult to apply.

References:

[1]     Kato,A. and Kawamura,M., "Measurement of Plastic Strain in Steel Specimens by Means of Intensity Distribution of Laser Speckle," J.Soc.Mat. Sci.,Japan, 43 (489),pp696-702,1994.
[2]     Dai,Y.Z.,Kato,A. and Chiang,F.P., "Fatigue Monitoring by Laser Speckle," Int. J. Fatigue, 13 (3), pp227-232, 1991.
[3]     Tanaka,K.,Fujiyama,K. and Nakamura, K., " Fracture Toughness and X-ray Diffraction Observation of Fracture Surface of Structural Low-carbon Steel," J.Soc. Mat. Sci., Japan, 29 (316), pp 62 -68,1980.
[4]     Yajima,Z.,Hirose,Y.,Tanaka,K. and Ogawa, H., " X-ray Fractographic Study on Fracture Toughness of Ductile Cast Iron at Low Temperatures," J.Soc. Mat.Sci., Japan,32 (363), pp 1345-1350,1983.

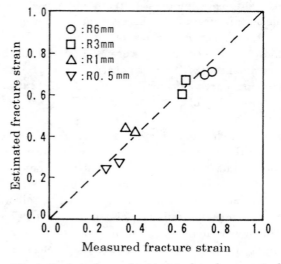

Fig.2 Relation between aspect ratio and effective plastic strain.

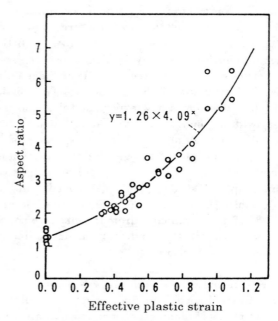

Fig.3 Comparison of estimated and measured fracture strain for notched specimens.

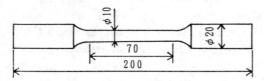

(a)Unnotched round bar tensile specimen.

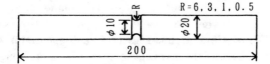

(b)Notched round bar tensile specimen.
Fig.1 Geometries of tensile specimens.
(dimensions in mm)

# A General Form for Calculating Residual Stresses Detected by Using

# Holographic Blind-Hole Method

## S. T. Lin

Mechanical Department of National Taipei Institute of technology

A general form for calculating residual stresses measured by using holographic blind-hole method was introduced in this paper. With the application of this general form, three relative displacements obtained from one interference fringe pattern are sufficient to determine residual stresses. The interpolating calculations, even in the non-phase-shifting holographic interferometer, for determining the fractional fringe orders of the data points can be avoided due to its more flexiable selections of data points. This of course make the holographic blind-hole method easily usable with or without the phase-shifting equipments.

## The Displacement Field Due to a Blind-Hole Drilling

Since the residual stresses on the surface of a body can be seperated into a mean stress $\sigma_m$ and a pure shear stress $\sigma_s$. The principal stresses can then be expressed as

$$\sigma_{max} = \sigma_m + \sigma_s \tag{1a}$$

and

$$\sigma_{min} = \sigma_m - \sigma_s \tag{1b}$$

where $\sigma_{max}$ and $\sigma_{min}$ are maximum and minmum principal stresses, respectively. Let

$$\sigma_m = C_m \cdot E \tag{2a}$$

and

$$\sigma_s = C_s \cdot E \tag{2b}$$

where $E$ is the Young's modulus of an isotropic material. $C_m$ and $C_s$ are two dimensionless coefficients. Once a blind-hole is drilled into the surface of the solid body, the mean stress $\sigma_m$ and shear stress $\sigma_s$ will relieve simultaneously. Referring to Fig.1 and Lin et al[1], the displacement field can be expressed as

$$\vec{d} = [C_m U_m + C_s U_s \cos 2(\theta + \alpha)]\vec{e}_r$$
$$+ C_s V_s \sin 2(\theta + \alpha)\vec{e}_\theta$$
$$+ [C_m W_m + C_s W_s \cos 2(\theta + \alpha)]\vec{k} \tag{3}$$

where $\vec{e}_r$, $\vec{e}_\theta$, and $\vec{k}$ are the unit vectors of the radial, tangential and normal directions, respectively. $\theta$ is the angle measured from the direction of the maximum principal stress to the x-axis. $U_m$, $U_s$, $V_s$, $W_m$, and $W_s$ are displacement constants.

## The General Form

The physical meaning of the interference fringe pattern obtained from the holographic interferometry can be expressed as

$$\vec{K} \cdot (\vec{d}(p_{i1}) - \vec{d}(p_{i2})) = \Delta N_i(p_{i1}, p_{i2})\lambda \tag{4}$$

where $\vec{K}$ is the sensitivity vector, $\lambda$ is the laser wave length, $\vec{d}(p_{i1})$ and $\vec{d}(p_{i2})$ are the dislacement vectors of points $p_{i1}$ and $p_{i2}$, respectively. $\Delta N_i(p_{i1}, p_{i2}) = N(p_{i1}) - N(p_{i2})$ is

513

the difference of fringe orders of points $p_{i1}$ and $p_{i2}$. By substituting eq.(3) into eq.(4) with $i=1$-$3$, we have the following compact equation:

$$[a_{ij}(p_{i1}, p_{i2}, \alpha_i)][c_j] = |\Delta N_i(p_{i1}, p_{i2})|\lambda$$
$$i, \; j=1\text{-}3 \qquad (5)$$

where

$$a_{i1} = (\Delta U_{mi} \vec{e}_r(\alpha_i) + \Delta W_{mi} \vec{k}) \cdot \vec{K}$$

$$a_{i2} = (\Delta U_{si} \cos 2\alpha_i \vec{e}_r(\alpha_i) +$$
$$\Delta V_{si} \sin 2\alpha_i \vec{e}_0(\alpha_i) +$$
$$\Delta W_{si} \cos 2\alpha_i \vec{k}) \cdot \vec{K}$$

$$a_{i3} = (-\Delta U_{si} \sin 2\alpha_i \vec{e}_r(\alpha_i) +$$
$$\Delta V_{si} \cos 2\alpha_i \vec{e}_0(\alpha_i) -$$
$$\Delta W_{si} \sin 2\alpha_i \vec{k}) \cdot \vec{K}$$

$$(6)$$

and

$$c_1 = C_m$$
$$c_2 = C_s \cos 2\theta \qquad (7)$$
$$c_3 = C_s \sin 2\theta$$

and, the relative displacement constants are

$$\Delta U_{mi} = U_m(p_{i1}) - U_m(p_{i2})$$
$$\Delta U_{si} = U_s(p_{i1}) - U_s(p_{i2})$$
$$\Delta V_{si} = V_s(p_{i1}) - V_s(p_{i2}) \qquad (8)$$
$$\Delta W_{mi} = W_m(p_{i1}) - W_m(p_{i2})$$
$$\Delta W_{si} = W_s(p_{i1}) - W_s(p_{i2})$$

Referring to Fig.2, it should be noted that $p_{i1}$ and $p_{i2}$ lie on the same radial line with an angle $\alpha_i$ measured from x-axis, and $p_{i1}$ and $p_{i2}$ lie on the circles with diameters $D_{i1}$ and $D_{i2}$, respectively.

Some experiments were also carried out to demonstrate the applications of this general form.

## Reference

1. Lin, S. T., Hsieh, C.T., and Hu, C. P., "Two Holographic Blind-hole Methods for Measuring Residual Stresses," Experimental Mechanics, 34(2), 141-147 (1994).

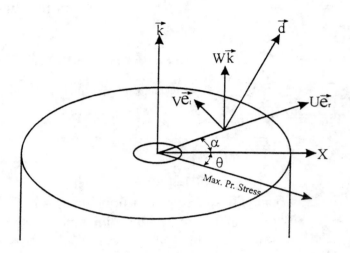

Fig. 1 Coordinats and displacement vector in an axi-symmetric body

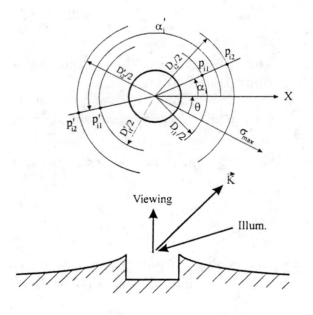

Fig. 2 The sensitivity vector and the points around a blind-hole

# RESIDUAL STRESSES IN HIGH PRESSURE LAMPS

B. E. Buescher, D.A. Anderson, K.E. Perry[2], C.E. Scott[3,] R.L. Williamson
and J.S. Epstein

Idaho National Engineering Laboratory
PO Box 1625
Idaho Falls, ID 83415-2218

2) Nike Air Laboratory
1 Boweman Drive, MJ3,
Beaverton, OR 97005

3) General Electric Lighting Products
Comp 5437, Nela Park
Cleveland, OH 44112

Moire interferometry was used to determine the residual stresses in a series of 250 watt sodium vapor alumina end cap to lamp housing seals. Issues to be discussed will be the experimental procedure developed for the destructive sectioning the end cap from the housing, grating replication, phase shifting moire in light of small displacements and data interpretation in light of a special crimping operation used to seal the tungsten tubes inserts into the end caps. Of particular interest is a periodic variation in the hoop strains due to the shrink fit of the end seal around the tungsten filler tube which itself is ellipsoidal in shape due to it's pinch seal. These results were confirmed using a finite element analysis. This periodic variation in hoop stress is one of the possible causes of cracking observed in the end caps during the braze operation.

# Reliability of a Single Crystal NiAl Alloy for Turbine Blade Applications

J. Salem, R. Noebe, J. Manderscheid
NASA Lewis Research Center
Cleveland, Ohio

and

R. Darolia
General Electric Aircraft Engine Co.
Cincinnati, Ohio

As part of a co-operative agreement with General Electric Aircraft Engines, NASA LeRC is modifying and experimentally validating a reliability code for use in design of components made of brittle NiAl based intermetallic materials.

NiAl single crystal alloys are being actively investigated as a replacement for Ni-based single crystal superalloys in high pressure turbine engine sections. The driving force for the research lies in the numerous property advantages offered by NiAl alloys [1] over their superalloy counterparts. These include higher melting point, greater thermal conductivity, better oxidation resistance, a better response to thermal barrier coatings, and a reduction of density by as much as a third without significantly sacrificing creep strength. The current drawback is their lack of ductility. Consequently, a significant effort is being made to develop testing and design methodologies that will account for the lack of ductility.

The approach is to modify existing test methods and brittle design methodologies, such as those in the Ceramic Analysis and Reliability Evaluation of Structures (CARES) code [2], and to experimentally verify the results.

Validation and component analysis involves the following steps: determination of the statistical nature and source of fracture in a high strength, NiAl single crystal turbine blade material; measurement of the failure strength envelope of the material; coding of statistically based reliability models; verification of the code and models within; and modeling of actual components including dovetail pullout specimens. As the material being considered is very brittle, highly anisotropic (Young's modulus varies 95 to 271 GPa), and made in relatively small billets (25 x 50 x 100 mm) that will be used individually to produce a vane or blade; the statistical nature and source of fracture is being studied via flexural testing of beam specimens [3], statistical, analysis, and fractography [4]. Flexural testing allows many samples to be removed from a given region of a billet, thereby allowing determination of billet-to-billet and within billet consistency, factors that will vary vane reliability. Further, in contrast to tensile testing, flexural testing allows the location of failure to be readily identified because the asymmetry of flexural loading results in a specific fracture pattern.

Flexural strength results to date indicate the material to exhibit a wide dispersion in strength (Fig. 1) that can be characterized via normal or Weibull [5] statistics. Failure origins were determined for most of the specimens tested. In all cases failure occurred from singular, coarse interdendritic precipitates or associated carbide particles.

Other strength tests planned for verification work include flexure (3 and 4-point), pure tension, pure compression, torsion and biaxial flexure. To date, uniaxial and biaxial flexural tests have been conducted, and a torsion specimen is being designed and verified relative to handbook solutions.

References

1. R. Darolia "NiAl For Turbine Airfoil Applications," in

Structural Intermetallics, ed. R. Darolioa et al., TMS Warrendale, PA, pp. 495-504, 1993.

2 . N. Nemeth, J. Manderscheid, J. Gyekenyesi, "CARES Users and Programmers Manual," NASA Technical Paper TP2916, 1990.

3. ASTM C 1161-90 "Standard Test Method for Flexural Strength of Advanced Ceramics at Ambient Temperature," American Society for Testing and Materials Annual Book of Standards, Vol. 15.01, 1990, pp. 333-339.

4. "Fractography and Characterization of Fracture Origins in Advanced Structural Ceramics," MIL-HDBK-790, (July, 1992).

5. W. Weibull, "A Statistical Theory of the Strength of Materials," Ingeniors Vetenskaps Akademien Handlinger, No. 151, 1939.

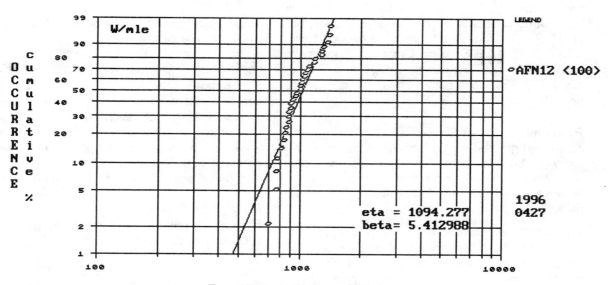

1. Weibull distribution of four-point flexural strength of NiAl alloy, AFN12.

# Thermal Spray Technologies for Infrastructure Repair and Maintenance

C.C.Berndt, M.L.Allan[†], H.Herman, J.Brogan, R.Benary, R.Zatorski and M.Leote[*]
State University of New York at Stony Brook
Materials Science and Engineering
105 Old Engineering
Stony Brook, NY 11794-2275

[†] Brookhaven National Laboratory
Upton, NY 11973

[*] Triborough Bridge and Tunnel Authority
Randall's Island, New York, NY 10035

## Introduction

Thermal spray involves the injection of feedstock materials into a high temperature heat source. The material is melted and propelled towards the substrate where it rapidly cools and forms a coating. Thermal spray has been used extensively by many industries over several decades to form protective and functional coatings. The technology has re-energized over the last 5 year as a viable and economic method of forming barrier and corrosion resistant coatings on infrastructure.

Thermal spray technologies have the ability of on-site repair of infrastructure. Several major demonstrations of these activities have recently been carried out by the Thermal Spray Laboratory (TSL), SUNY-Stony Brook, under the support and auspices of the US Army Corps of Engineers, CERL, and the Triborough Bridge and Tunnel Authority, New York City. These programs are described below.

## Removal of Lead-Base Paint

Traditional grit blasting of hydraulic structures and highway bridges potentially involves the wide distribution of lead contaminate some distance from work sites and inflicting unacceptable health risks.

An alternative means of surface preparation, patented by the US Army Corps of Engineers, is on-site vitrification of hazardous waste. That is, thermal spraying of specially-developed molten glass to encapsulate and chemically stabilize lead-based paint and rust. The encapsulate is then removed by chipping-off relatively large chunks, which are readily removed for disposal.

The objective has been to develop technology and guidance for maintenance where work will involve the removal of a coating material containing lead-based paint or other hazardous waste. Spray techniques and glass deposit chemistries and encapsulation effectiveness are being testing and optimized.

## Automated Thermal Spray Technology

TSL has developed and demonstrated on Interstate 495 an integrated robotic advanced thermal spray coating system for field application to civil works infrastructure. Material feedstock products include, but are not limited to, thermally sprayed metallic corrosion/erosion resistant coatings such as zinc and aluminum-zinc alloys on steel structures, and thermally sprayed polymers (see below).

The demonstration indicated that there was no need to completely contain the grit blasting procedure within the usual shroud since the vacuo-blast system was quite successful. Furthermore, the video observation and quality control system allowed removal of the coating applicator from a potentially hazardous and unsafe procedure; i.e., the operator can be located away from the process. Such automation has the potential of increasing the overall process economics and efficiency of coating application.

## Metal Sprayed Coatings

Experience with thermal spray coatings in the UK and Europe extends back to the 1940's. In the US, metal sprayed coatings are presently being specified and used by Florida DOT, ConnDOT, Caltrans, Oregon DOT, Ohio DOT and others. The conservative life time for a 10 mil thickness of Zn (or Zn-Al alloy) is ~25 years and can be extended a further 15 years by the application of an vinyl paint system. Initial application costs are $10.00 per square foot or ~$0.45 per square foot per year.

Coatings can be applied as either sacrificial systems on metal structures or for impressed current cathodic protection of concrete structures. In the latter case, the sprayed coating acts as an anode which is connected to the rebar frame of the structure. Thus, corrosion and concrete disbondment of the structure can be completely mitigated.

## Thermal Spray of Polymers

Working with industrial partners and local DOTs, TSL has demonstrated the utility of innovative hi-molecular weight and commingled/post consumer recycled polymer blends as low-VOC (volatile organic compounds) compliant coatings for thermal spray applications, with special attention to corrosion control of infrastructure systems.

Material specifications for various polymer coating blends for thermal spray applications are being developed. A number of polymers have recently been combustion sprayed on various sections of the Triborough Bridge. These barrier coatings can be applied throughout the year - thereby extending the maintenance campaigns of infrastructure.

## Outreach Activities

TSL, being an educational and research institution, has trained some 6 students specifically in the area of infrastructural maintenance and repair. The training includes both the fundamental theory and practical application of coatings on bridges of the TBTA and Region 10 of the NYS-DOT.

TSL has representation within several professional societies on the following committees: National Association of Corrosion Engineers T6-H-45, American Welding Society C2, ASM International - Thermal Spray Society, and the Steel Structures Painting Council C.1.2.B.

TSL has inaugurated a homepage on the WWW for infrastructure activities. The address is:
   http://doL1.eng.sunysb.edu/infra/

## References

### Polymer spraying

J.A.Brogan, K.A.Gross, Z.Chen, H.Herman and C.C.Berndt, "Investigation of combustion sprayed hydroxyapatite/polymer composite coatings", pp. 159-164 of "1994 Thermal Spray Industrial Applications", Ed. C.C.Berndt and S.Sampath, Pub. ASM International, Cleveland, OH-US, 1994.

J.A.Brogan, J.Margolies, S.Sampath, H.Herman, C.C.Berndt and S.Drozdz, "Adhesion of Combustion-Sprayed Polymer Coatings", pp. 521-526 of 1995 Advances in Thermal Spray Science and Technology", Ed. C.C.Berndt and S.Sampath, ASM International, Materials Park, OH-USA, 1995.

J.A.Brogan, R.Lampo and C.C.Berndt, "Thermal Spraying of Polymers", Proc. 4th World Congress on Coating Systems for Bridges and Steel Structures, 1-3 February, 1995, St. Louis, MO-USA. pp. 200-212.

### Automated thermal spray system

R.Benary, R.V.Gansert, C.C.Berndt, S.Sampath, H.Herman and V.Hock, "Field Evaluation and Economic Impact of an Automated Thermal Spray System (ATSS) for Infrastructure Rehabilitation", pp. 621-626 of 1995 Advances in Thermal Spray Science and Technology", Ed. C.C.Berndt and S.Sampath, ASM International, Materials Park, OH-USA, 1995.

R.V.Gansert, R.Benary, C.C.Berndt, and H.Herman, "Automated thermal spray system (ATSS) for rehabilitation and maintenance of infrastructure", pp. 445-450 of "1994 Thermal Spray Industrial Applications", Ed. C.C.Berndt and S.Sampath, Pub. ASM International, Cleveland, OH-US, 1994.

### Metal spraying

C.C.Berndt, S.Reddy and M.L.Allan, "Optimization of Thermal Spray Parameters for Cathodic Protection of Reinforcement in Concrete", pp. 51-64 of Innovative Ideas for Controlling the Decaying Infrastructure, Ed. V.Chaker, Pub. NACE International, 1995.

C.C.Berndt, S.Reddy and M.L.Allan, "Thermal Spraying of Zinc onto Concrete", Proc. 4th World Congress on Coating Systems for Bridges and Steel Structures, 1-3 February, 1995, St. Louis, MO-USA. pp. 182.

### Removal of lead-base paint

J.Karthikeyan, J.Chen, G.A.Bancke, H.Herman, C.C.Berndt and V.T.Breslin, "Thermal Spray Vitrification Process for the Removal of Lead Oxide Contained in Organic Paint", pp. 599-604 of 1995 Advances in Thermal Spray Science and Technology", Ed. C.C.Berndt and S.Sampath, ASM International, Materials Park, OH-USA, 1995.

## Acknowledgments

The authors are grateful to Tafa, Inc. (NH), Plastic Flamecoat (TX), the NY Science and Technology Foundation, Region 10 of the NYS-DOT, the TBTA, and US-Army CERL for support in these activities.

# AUTHOR INDEX

| Author Name | Page No. |
|---|---|
| Abdallah, M.G. | 200 |
| Abdi Majlessi, S. | 17 |
| Abe, H. | 503 |
| Adams, D.O. | 282 |
| Ahmadshahi, M.A. | 170 |
| Aktan, A.E. | 270 |
| Aktan, A.E. | 321 |
| Aktan, A.E. | 323 |
| Albertini, C. | 495 |
| Ali Saeedy, S. | 17 |
| Allan, M.L. | 518 |
| Allison, I.M. | 195 |
| Alloba, E. | 405 |
| Anderson, D.A. | 515 |
| Anderson, T.E. | 286 |
| Aparicio, A.C. | 15 |
| Aparicio, A.C. | 88 |
| Arai, Y. | 232 |
| Arakawa, K. | 349 |
| Arola, D. | 100 |
| Arteau, J. | 392 |
| Asundi, A. | 64 |
| Atluri, S.N. | 425 |
| Aubry, E. | 477 |
| Baburaj, V. | 96 |
| Bae, J.S. | 509 |
| Baek, T.H. | 29 |
| Bahk, S.M. | 447 |
| Baker, S.J. | 367 |
| Bakis, C.E. | 160 |
| Barhorst, A. | 242 |
| Barrett-Leonard, T. | 256 |
| Barrish, R. | 321 |
| Beach, T.J. | 218 |
| Beattie, A.G. | 273 |
| Bell, R.P. | 290 |
| Benary, R. | 518 |
| Berndt, C.C. | 518 |
| Bledsoe, B.L. | 251 |
| Boettger, J. | 27 |
| Bond, B.H. | 279 |
| Bonetti, F. | 343 |
| Borgmeier, P.R. | 304 |
| Branca, F.P. | 345 |
| Bremand, F. | 260 |
| Brinson, H.F. | 104 |
| Brogan, J. | 518 |
| Bruck, H.A. | 354 |
| Bucar, B. | 252 |
| Buchanan, R.C. | 270 |
| Buerkle, L. | 210 |
| Buescher, Jr., B.E. | 515 |
| Burdette, E.G. | 214 |
| Burdette, E.G. | 225 |
| Burgueno, R. | 200 |
| Burguete, R.L. | 382 |
| Burguete, R.L. | 411 |
| Cadoni, E. | 495 |
| Calder, C.A. | 352 |
| Cappa, P. | 343 |
| Cappa, P. | 347 |
| Cappa, P. | 457 |
| Casas, J.R. | 15 |
| Casas, J.R. | 88 |
| Castro, J.T.P. | 19 |
| Castro, J.T.P. | 223 |
| Catbas, F.N. | 323 |
| Chang, R.R. | 335 |
| Chang, S.W. | 487 |
| Chao, Y.J. | 176 |
| Chao, Y.J. | 333 |
| Chaudhury, P.K. | 469 |
| Chen, C. | 390 |
| Chen, C.H. | 335 |
| Chen, F. | 206 |
| Chen, F. | 483 |
| Chen, F.M. | 116 |
| Chen, T.Y. | 178 |
| Chen, Y.M. | 331 |
| Chiang, F.P. | 25 |
| Chiang, F.P. | 45 |
| Chiang, F.P. | 68 |
| Chiang, F.P. | 236 |
| Chiang, F.P. | 308 |
| Chiang, F.P. | 427 |
| Chiang, F.P. | 461 |
| Chiang, F.P. | 486 |
| Chimalakonda, S. | 302 |
| Cho, B.K. | 21 |
| Cho, K.Z. | 78 |
| Cho, K.Z. | 450 |
| Cho, S.W. | 21 |
| Choi, D.J. | 497 |
| Choi, M.J. | 372 |
| Choi, S.H. | 417 |
| Choi, S.K. | 447 |
| Ciavarella, M. | 264 |
| Clarke, W.L. | 360 |

Clayton, C.R. .............................. 427
Cochran, J.B. ............................. 290
Colucci, D.M. ............................. 180
Colucci, D.M. ............................. 228
Cooper, M. ................................. 363
Corbeil, J.F. ............................... 392
Cordes, R.D. .............................. 403
Cottron, M. ................................. 318
Coutermarsh, B. ......................... 159
Curry, D. .................................... 282
Cvelbar, R. ................................. 186
Czarnek, R. ................................ 469
D'Alessio, T. .................................74
D'Alessio, T. ............................... 345
Dai, F. .........................................33
Dai, F. ....................................... 268
Dai, F. ....................................... 499
Dally, J.W. ................................. 190
Dang, X. .......................................90
Daniel, I.M. ................................ 403
Darolla, R. .................................. 516
Date, K. ...................................... 463
Day, C.H. ................................... 174
Deatherage, J.H. ........................ 214
Deatherage, J.H. ........................ 225
DeBolt, M.A. ............................... 104
Del Prete, Z. .............................. 345
Del Prete, Z. .............................. 457
Demelio, G. ................................ 264
Deng, Z. .................................... 467
Derry, S. ......................................72
DeTeresa, S.J. ........................... 102
DeVries, K.L. ............................. 304
Dickie, R.A. ................................ 104
Dietz, P. .................................... 499
Dillard, D.A. ............................... 108
Ditri, J.J. .....................................56
Doering, T.W. ............................. 360
Dolinsek, S. .................................66
Doyle, J.F. ...................................80
Drew, S. ......................................72
Du, M.L. ..................................... 427
Dulieu-Smith, J.M. ........................37
Dulieu-Smith, J.M. ........................39
Dupre, J.C. ...................................7
Dutta, P.K. ................................. 159
Emerson, R.P. ............................ 160
Emri, I. ...................................... 186
Emri, I. ...................................... 226
Epstein, J.S. .............................. 354
Epstein, J.S. .............................. 425
Epstein, J.S. .............................. 515
Esteban, J. ................................ 409
Ettemeyer, A. ............................. 296

Ezaki, K. .................................... 413
Faisal, A. ................................... 168
Farhey, D.N. .............................. 270
Fedele, L. .................................. 347
Fendeleur, D. ............................. 477
Ferreira, I. ................................. 429
Finlayson, E.F. .............................41
Foss, S.K. .................................. 126
Fournier, N. ............................... 240
Franz, T. .....................................94
Fredell, R. ................................. 190
Freire, J.L.F. ...............................19
Freire, J.L.F. ............................. 223
Fujigaki, M. ................................ 212
Fujiwara, H. ............................... 380
Fujiwara, H. ............................... 489
Fukuzawa, M. ............................. 423
Fulton, M.C. .................................37
Furrow, A.P.C. ............................ 108
Gabrys, C.W. .............................. 160
Gambrell, Jr., S.C. ...................... 148
Gates, T.S. ................................ 154
Gielisse, P.J. .............................. 120
Gilbert, J.A. .................................54
Gilbert, J.A. ............................... 166
Goldar, D. .................................. 254
Golovoy, A. ................................ 103
Gomez, J. .................................. 325
Gomi, K. ..................................... 368
Gomi, K. ..................................... 421
Goncalves, Jr., A.A. ......................27
Gong, X. .................................... 164
Goodpasture, D.W. ..................... 214
Goodpasture, D.W. ..................... 225
Gotoh, J. .................................... 208
Grediac, M. ................................ 240
Griffen, C.T. ............................... 206
Griffen, C.T. ............................... 483
Grimmelsman, K. ........................ 321
Groom, L.H. ............................... 249
Groves, S.E. ............................... 102
Guo, Z. ...................................... 266
Gutmann, B. ............................... 465
Haake, S.J. ...................................3
Haake, S.J. ................................ 376
Hansson, T. ............................... 143
Hara, N. ..................................... 137
Haraguchi, K. .............................. 112
Harris, C.E. ................................ 288
Hashemi, J. ................................ 242
Hashimoto, H. ..............................62
Hastie, R.L. ................................ 190
Hatanaka, K. ............................... 145
Hawong, J.S. .............................. 417

xl

Hazen, G.A. ................339
He, S. ................139
He, Y.M. ................493
Heemstra, H. ................282
Hellier, C.J. ................320
Helmicki, A.J. ................321
Helmicki, A.J. ................323
Herman, H. ................518
Hinkley, J.A. ................108
Hinoshita, A. ................352
Holzer, S.M. ................279
Horoschenkoff, A. ................441
Houska, M. ................252
Hovanesian, J.A. ................194
Hovanesian, J.A. ................337
Hovanesian, J.D. ................122
Hovanesian, J.D. ................194
Hovanesian, J.D. ................337
Hoy, D.E.P. ................13
Hoy, D.E.P. ................365
Hu, K.K. ................221
Hu, K.K. ................272
Huang, L. ................33
Huang, S. ................238
Hung, Y.Y. ................122
Hung, Y.Y. ................172
Hung, Y.Y. ................206
Hung, Y.Y. ................483
Hunt, V.J. ................321
Hunt, V.J. ................323
Hwang, C.H. ................327
Hwang, C.H. ................329
Hwang, G.W. ................78
Ifju, P.G. ................198
Igarashi, K. ................396
Ikeda, A. ................413
Ishii, A. ................112
Ishijima, M. ................443
Isogimi, K. ................130
Isogimi, K. ................378
Issa, S.S. ................419
Ito, K. ................58
Iwamoto, N. ................396
Iyer, S.K. ................272
Jayaraman, N. ................270
Jenkins, C.H.M. ................82
Jenkins, C.H.M. ................202
Jenkins, M.G. ................141
Jeong, H.S. ................374
Jerome, D.M. ................310
Jia, Y. ................50
Jin, F. ................236
Joenathan, C. ................210
Jonasz, M. ................35

Jones, I.J. ................150
Josepson, J. ................9
Jovanovic, D.B. ................9
Julinda, ................168
Kagwade, S.V. ................427
Kajon, G. ................388
Kamata, M. ................137
Kanda, C. ................27
Kang, B.S.J. ................110
Kang, Y. ................50
Kannal, L.E. ................80
Katagiri, K. ................62
Kato, A. ................58
Kato, H. ................475
Kato, M. ................137
Kawashima, K. ................481
Kay, R.M. ................358
Keat, W.D. ................449
Kennedy, T.C. ................352
Khan, Z.M. ................132
Khodobin, Y.I. ................298
Khoury, I.S. ................341
Kikuchi, M. ................114
Kilday, B.C. ................198
Kim, D. ................98
Kim, D.H. ................29
Kim, J.K. ................98
Kim, J.Y. ................361
Kim, S.H. ................86
Kim, S.H. ................450
Kim, S.H. ................487
Kim, T.J. ................433
Kim, W.H. ................487
Kirmser, P.G. ................221
Kishida, K. ................314
Kitamura, T. ................435
Kitchin, R.A. ................505
Klein, G.J. ................216
Knauss, W.G. ................182
Kobayashi, A.S. ................52
Kobayashi, A.S. ................425
Kobayashi, A.S. ................445
Koc, P. ................230
Koech, D.C. ................284
Koga, T. ................96
Kohoutek, R. ................70
Kokaly, M.T. ................445
Kondagunta, S. ................106
Kopac, J. ................66
Kraikov, V.A. ................298
Kramer, B. ................5
Krishnaswamy, S. ................170
Kulisic, I. ................120
Kumar, S. ................148

Kuo, M. .....................282
Kupfer, G. .....................5
Kupfer, G. .....................384
Kurai, S. .....................143
Kurita, M. .....................467
Kushiki, K. .....................380
Kusnowo, A. .....................168
Labibes, K. .....................495
Lagarde, A. .....................7
Lagarde, A. .....................318
Lalande, F. .....................234
Lalande, F. .....................409
Lan, A. .....................392
Larson, M.C. .....................134
Larson, M.C. .....................449
Lee, A. .....................184
Lee, J.C. .....................29
Lee, J.H. .....................497
Lee, J.H. .....................503
Lee, J.M. .....................86
Lee, J.M. .....................386
Lee, J.N. .....................244
Lee, J.N. .....................277
Lee, O.S. .....................31
Lee, S.B. .....................361
Lee, S.J. .....................86
Lee, S.W.R. .....................300
Lee, S.Y. .....................374
Lee. J. .....................445
Lenett, M. .....................323
Leung, K.M. .....................268
Leote, M. .....................518
Levi, A. .....................321
Li, K. .....................128
Li, X. .....................135
Lin, C.H. .....................178
Lin, L. .....................172
Lin, L. .....................390
Lin, S.T. .....................513
Lin, S.Y. .....................327
Lin, S.Y. .....................329
Lin, S.Y. .....................469
Lindner, J.L. .....................166
Liu, C.T. .....................41
Liu, C.T. .....................155
Liu, D. .....................90
Liu, J.Y. .....................280
Liu, S. .....................198
Loferski, J.R. .....................248
Loferski, J.R. .....................279
Long, K.W. .....................122
Longinow, A. .....................216
Lu, H. .....................50
Lu, H. .....................118

Lu, H.B. .....................182
Lu, J. .....................473
Luo, L. .....................246
Luo, P.F. .....................333
Luo, Z. .....................471
Lupkes, K.R. .....................197
Machida, K. .....................48
Macturk, K.S. .....................106
Maeda, T. .....................96
Mahinfalah, M. .....................92
Maji, A.K. .....................84
Makino, A. .....................124
Makino, A. .....................126
Manderscheid, J. .....................516
Marincan, .....................168
Marinozzi, F. .....................345
Marinozzi, F. .....................457
Masud, A.K.M. .....................130
Matsumoto, E. .....................380
Matsumoto, E. .....................489
Mawatari, S. .....................1
Mawatari, S. .....................208
Mawatari, S. .....................413
McAuliffe, M. .....................106
McAuliffe, P. .....................157
McDonough, W.G. .....................106
McKenna, G.B. .....................180
McKenna, G.B. .....................228
Melhem, H.G. .....................272
Michael, H.R. .....................290
Mihara, T. .....................463
Mills, B. .....................132
Misawa, A. .....................400
Miskioglu, I. .....................46
Miyano, Y. .....................439
Miyano, Y. .....................443
Mizuhara, Y. .....................143
Mohri, M. .....................439
Monteleone, L. .....................388
Morimoto, Y. .....................212
Morrissey, M.D. .....................54
Morton, J. .....................306
Moschler, W.W. .....................251
Mott, L. .....................249
Mu, Z. .....................471
Mueller, D.H. .....................94
Mutoh, Y. .....................143
Myers, D. .....................282
Nagata, S. .....................443
Nagoh, D. .....................349
Nakada, M. .....................439
Nakai, K. .....................475
Nakamura, K. .....................439
Nakamura, Y. .....................356

Nakanishi, E. ............130
Nakano, M. ............314
Nakasa, K. ............137
Nanduri, M. ............433
Naso, V. ............347
Nekhendzy, E.J. ............298
Nelson, D.V. ............124
Nelson, D.V. ............126
Nemat-Nasser, S. ............170
Nicoletti, N. ............459
Nicoletti, N. ............477
Niitsu, Y. ............368
Niitsu, Y. ............421
Nikonov, A. ............186
Nilly, L. ............459
Nishiwaki, Y. ............423
Niu, X. ............198
Noebe, R. ............516
Nurse, A.D. ............382
Nurse, A.D. ............505
Nusimer, R.J. ............200
O'Brien, E.W. ............150
O'Connell, P.A. ............228
Oakes, B.R. ............266
Obermeyer, E.J. ............17
Ochi, Y. ............112
Oda, I. ............431
Ogawa, K. ............400
Oh, T.Y. ............372
Ohashi, M. ............511
Ohta, F. ............62
Ohtani, R. ............435
Okada, H. ............425
Omori, Y. ............1
Omori, Y. ............425
Oplinger, D.W. ............306
Oshita, K. ............145
Paraskevas, D. ............152
Paraskevas, D. ............370
Pardue, B. ............220
Paris, P.A. ............240
Park, B.G. ............172
Park, B.S. ............361
Park, C.I. ............386
Park, M.K. ............447
Patterson, E.A. ............382
Patterson, E.A. ............411
Patterson, E.A. ............505
Perry, K.E. ............515
Perry, Jr., K. ............425
Pichini, E. ............345
Pierron, F. ............405
Pindera, J.T. ............9
Pindera, J.T. ............188

Pindera, J.T. ............258
Plouzennec, N. ............7
Pu, J.H. ............244
Pu, J.H. ............277
Qi, G. ............242
Qiu, Y. ............50
Ramos, G. ............88
Ramulu, M. ............52
Ramulu, M. ............100
Ranson, III, W.F. ............262
Ravi-Chandar, K. ............351
Redner, A.S. ............56
Redner, A.S. ............192
Reifsnider, K.L. ............155
Reiprich, M. ............441
Renner, M. ............459
Renner, M. ............477
Reynolds, A.P. ............292
Rocheleau, D.N. ............262
Rodacoski, M.R. ............27
Rogers, C.A. ............234
Rogers, C.A. ............409
Rogers, J.D. ............284
Ross, C.A. ............310
Ross, R.J. ............280
Ryu, D.S. ............487
Ryu, G.H. ............21
Sadeghi, J. ............70
Saito, A. ............380
Saito, A. ............489
Saka, M. ............503
Salehi, A. ............363
Salem, J.A. ............516
Sanford, R.J. ............455
Sargand, S.M. ............339
Sargand, S.M. ............341
Satpathi, D. ............84
Sayal, G.S. ............455
Schaffer, E.L. ............280
Schmidt, A. ............499
Schmidtke, K. ............441
Schultheisz, C.R. ............106
Schultheisz, C.R. ............180
Schutte, C.L. ............106
Sciammarella, C.A. ............162
Sciammarella, F.M. ............162
Scott, C.E. ............515
Scott, N. ............256
Seible, F. ............200
Septriyanti, ............168
Shaler, S.M. ............249
Sharkins, A.A. ............341
Shelley, S.J. ............323
Shi, L. ............33

| | |
|---|---|
| Shi, L. | 268 |
| Shimamoto, A. | 204 |
| Shimamoto, A. | 415 |
| Shimamoto, A. | 501 |
| Shimbo, M. | 443 |
| Shiota, H. | 145 |
| Shiraishi, K. | 431 |
| Short, S.R. | 302 |
| Shukla, A. | 316 |
| Shukla, A. | 325 |
| Sienkiewicz, F. | 325 |
| Sikon, M. | 11 |
| Singh, R.P. | 316 |
| Sinha, J.K. | 43 |
| Skalleberg, R. | 202 |
| Skitek, T. | 226 |
| Skordahl, R.A. | 92 |
| Slaminko, R. | 147 |
| Smith, C.W. | 41 |
| Somiya, S. | 396 |
| Song, S.H. | 509 |
| Song, S.J. | 21 |
| Song, Y. | 54 |
| Spicher, W.H. | 82 |
| St. Clair, T.L. | 108 |
| Stalnaker, D.O. | 116 |
| Stanley, P. | 39 |
| Steinchen, W. | 5 |
| Steinchen, W. | 384 |
| Steindler, R. | 23 |
| Steindler, R. | 388 |
| Stevens, T.L. | 141 |
| Stickler, R. | 394 |
| Stok, B. | 230 |
| Stone, B. | 72 |
| Stone, B.J. | 256 |
| Su, F. | 471 |
| Su, W. | 54 |
| Subramanian, S. | 155 |
| Sudo, S. | 62 |
| Suh, J.G. | 417 |
| Sullivan, J.L. | 103 |
| Sullivan, J.L. | 287 |
| Sumitomo, H. | 463 |
| Sun, F.P. | 234 |
| Sun, W.M. | 264 |
| Sun, X. | 139 |
| Sun, X. | 481 |
| Suprapedi, | 168 |
| Surrel, Y. | 240 |
| Surrel, Y. | 405 |
| Sutton, M.A. | 333 |
| Suzuki, J. | 130 |
| Suzuki, J. | 378 |
| Suzuki, S. | 312 |
| Swanson, G.R. | 479 |
| Swanson, G.R. | 507 |
| Swartz, S.E. | 221 |
| Taggart, D.G. | 433 |
| Takahashi, K. | 349 |
| Takahashi, S. | 415 |
| Takahashi, S. | 501 |
| Takashi, M. | 1 |
| Takashi, M. | 208 |
| Takashi, M. | 400 |
| Takashi, M. | 413 |
| Tanaka, H. | 76 |
| Tanaka, K. | 76 |
| Tang, R.C. | 244 |
| Tang, R.C. | 277 |
| Tang, X. | 33 |
| Tarasov, R.A. | 298 |
| Tarhini, K.M. | 216 |
| Taroni, M. | 152 |
| Teh, K.T. | 157 |
| Tenzler, A. | 94 |
| Thakur, A.M. | 270 |
| Tippur, H.V. | 43 |
| Tissauoi, J. | 279 |
| Tong, W. | 135 |
| Tong, W. | 238 |
| Toyooka, S. | 164 |
| Trentadue, B. | 162 |
| Trentadue, B. | 264 |
| Tsai, M.Y. | 306 |
| Tschoegl, N.W. | 226 |
| Tsuchida, E. | 232 |
| Tsukagosi, S. | 501 |
| Tsuyuki, K. | 62 |
| Tu, M. | 120 |
| Tu, M. | 471 |
| Turner, J.L. | 116 |
| Tuttle, M.E. | 197 |
| Ueda, K. | 60 |
| Ueda, K. | 294 |
| Uematsu, Y. | 435 |
| Umeda, A. | 60 |
| Umeda, A. | 294 |
| Umeda, H. | 114 |
| Umezaki, E. | 204 |
| Umezaki, E. | 415 |
| Valle, V. | 318 |
| Vautrin, A. | 405 |
| Veazie, D.R. | 407 |
| Vedoy, A. | 82 |
| Vieira, R.D. | 19 |
| Vieira, R.D. | 223 |
| Vilmann, C.R. | 46 |

von Bernstorff, B. ......................437
Von Handorf, J.J. .......................339
Wada, H. ..................................352
Wang, B.S. ..................................25
Wang, B.S. ................................308
Wang, B.S. ................................491
Wang, J. ...................................378
Wang, J.Q. ................................122
Wang, J.S. ................................333
Wang, J.Z. ................................246
Wang, M.J. ................................331
Wang, Q. ....................................45
Wang, Q. ...................................486
Wang, W. ...................................268
Wang, W.C. ................................174
Wang, W.C. ................................327
Wang, W.C. ................................329
Wang, W.C. ................................331
Wang, Z. .....................................90
Watanabe, H. .............................204
Weber, H. ..................................398
Weber, H. ..................................465
Weiss, B. ...................................394
Weitsman, Y.J. ...........................402
Wen, S. .....................................202
Widiastuti, R. .............................168
Williamson, R.L. .........................515
Wilson, L. ..................................110
Wilson, P.B. ...............................116
Winistorfer, P.M. .........................251
Witte, M.W. ...............................337
Wnuk, S.P. ................................298
Wnuk, V.P. ................................298
Wolf, T. ....................................465
Wu, S.Y. ...................................308

Xie, H. ......................................499
Xu, W. ......................................251
Xu, Y. .......................................120
Yamabe, M. ...............................443
Yamada, M. ...............................423
Yamauchi, Y. ..............................314
Yan, Z. .......................................76
Yanabe, S. .................................275
Yang, B. ....................................351
Yang, L.X. .................................384
Yen, S.C. ...................................157
Yoneyama, S. .............................208
Yoshida, S. ................................168
Yoshinari, M. ..............................463
Yoshino, M. ...............................275
Yoshino, M.. ..............................232
Younis, N.T. ...............................367
Yu, F. .......................................365
Yu, Y.S. ....................................372
Zachary, L.W. ............................507
Zafari, F. ....................................52
Zatorski, R. ...............................518
Zgoul, M.H. ...............................419
Zhang, B.B. ...............................493
Zhang, G. ..................................110
Zhang, H. ..................................471
Zhang, X. ..................................491
Zhao, W. .....................................13
Zhu, N.H. ....................................68
Zhu, N.H. ..................................461
Zimmerman, K.B. ........................286
Zocher, M.A. ..............................102
Zoghi, M. ...................................218
Zou, D. .....................................268
Zysk, K. ......................................56